Special Edition

USING 1-2-3® 97

Special Edition

USING 1-2-3® 97

Joyce Nielsen with

Janice Snyder • Elaine Marmel • Brian Underdahl • Shane Devenshire • Sue Plumley • Bruce Lill • Stan Doherty

Special Edition Using 1-2-3 97

Library of Congress Catalog No.: 95-73278

ISBN: 0-7897-0143-x

99 98 97 6 5 4 3 2 1

Interpretation of the printing code: the rightmost double-digit number is the year of the book's printing; the rightmost single-digit number, the number of the book's printing. For example, a printing code of 97-1 shows that the first printing of the book occurred in 1997.

Screen reproductions in this book were created using Collage Plus from Inner Media, Inc., Hollis, NH.

Credits

PRESIDENT
Roland Elgey

PUBLISHING DIRECTOR
David W. Solomon

TITLE MANAGER
Kathie-Jo Arnoff

EDITORIAL SERVICES DIRECTOR
Elizabeth Keaffaber

MANAGING EDITOR
Michael Cunningham

DIRECTOR OF MARKETING
Lynn E. Zingraf

ACQUISITIONS MANAGER
Elizabeth South

ACQUISITIONS EDITOR
Angie Wethington

SENIOR PRODUCT DIRECTOR
Lisa D. Wagner

PRODUCT DIRECTOR
Robin Drake

PRODUCTION EDITOR
Julie A. McNamee

EDITORS
Elizabeth Barrett
Jim Bowie
Nick Critsky
Kate Givens
Lisa M. Gebken
Thomas F. Hayes
Theresa Mathias
Sarah Rudy
Linda Seifert

STRATEGIC MARKETING MANAGER
Barry Pruett

PRODUCT MARKETING MANAGER
Kris Ankney

ASSISTANT PRODUCT MARKETING MANAGERS
Karen Hagan
Christy M. Miller

TECHNICAL EDITORS
Brian Ellison
Lee Mosqueda
Janice Snyder

MEDIA DEVELOPMENT SPECIALIST
David Garratt

TECHNICAL SUPPORT SPECIALIST
Nadeem Muhammed

ACQUISITIONS COORDINATOR
Tracy C. Williams

SOFTWARE RELATIONS COORDINATOR
Susan Gallagher

EDITORIAL ASSISTANT
Virginia Stoller

BOOK DESIGNER
Ruth Harvey

COVER DESIGNER
Dan Armstrong

PRODUCTION TEAM
Michael Beaty
Bryan Flores
DiMonique Ford
Tony McDonald

INDEXER
Tim Tate

Composed in *Century Old Style* and *Franklin Gothic* by Que Corporation.

About the Authors

Joyce J. Nielsen is an independent computer consultant, specializing in writing and developing books based on microcomputer software applications. Prior to her work as a consultant, Joyce was a Senior Product Development Specialist for Que Corporation. She is the author or coauthor of more than 15 computer books, including Que's *Special Edition Using Lotus SmartSuite 97 for Windows 95*, *Special Edition Using Freelance Graphics 96 for Windows 95*, and *Word for Windows 95 Visual Quick Reference*. Nielsen also worked as a research analyst for a shopping mall developer, where she developed and documented computer applications used nationwide. She received a Bachelor of Science degree in Quantitative Business Analysis from Indiana University. You may contact her via CompuServe at **76507,2712** or via the Internet at **jnielsen@iquest.net**.

Janice A. Snyder is an independent consultant, specializing in microcomputer desktop applications and Web page authoring. She has worked with 1-2-3 spreadsheets for 12 years, since the days of Release 1A. She is the revision author of Que's *Easy 1-2-3 Release 5 for Windows* and *1-2-3 Release 5 for Windows Quick Reference*, development editor for *Special Edition Using 1-2-3 Release 5 for Windows* and *I Hate 1-2-3 for Windows*, and technical editor for Que College's *Lotus 1-2-3 SmartStart*. Snyder also has coauthored or edited many other books for Que Corporation, including books on MS Office, Word, Excel, PowerPoint, Access, dBASE, Quicken, Quickbooks, WinFax Pro, WordPerfect, Quattro Pro, and Internet applications.

Elaine Marmel is President of Marmel Enterprises, Inc., an organization which specializes in technical writing and software support and training. Elaine spends most of her time writing and is the author of several books on *Word for Windows, Word for the Mac, Excel, 1-2-3 for Windows, Quicken for Windows,* and *Quicken for DOS*. Elaine also is a contributing editor to *Inside Peachtree for Windows*, a monthly magazine published about the accounting package.

Elaine left her native Chicago for the warmer climes of Florida (by way of Cincinnati, OH; Jerusalem, Israel; Ithaca, NY; and Washington, D.C.) where she basks in the sun with her PC and her cats, Cato and Watson. Elaine also sings in the Toast of Tampa, an International Champion Sweet Adeline barbershop chorus.

Brian Underdahl is an author, independent consultant, and custom application developer based in Reno, Nevada. He's the author or coauthor of over 25 computer books, as well as numerous magazine articles. He has also acted as a product developer and as a technical editor on many other Que books. His e-mail address is **71505,1114** on CompuServe.

Shane Devenshire is an independent consultant specializing in project management, databases, graphics packages, and the scientific and business application of spreadsheets. He is a founding partner of the MAR&SHA Corporation, a computer consulting company providing application development, programming, and training in both the mainframe and personal computer areas. He has written over 260 computer-related articles for 20 journals here and abroad. He has been a guest editor for *PC World* magazine in 1994 and 1995 and has been on the product review board of INFO World. He has 3 years experience in the bio-tech arena, 5 years in business management, and 13 in computer related industries. He coauthored *Managing Data with Excel, Excel Expert Solutions, Using 1-2-3 Release 4 for DOS*, and *Making Microsoft Office Work*.

Sue Plumley has owned and operated her own business for eight years. Humble Opinions provides training, consulting, and network installation, management, and maintenance to banking, education, medical, and industrial facilities. In addition, Sue has authored and coauthored over 50 books for Que Corporation and its sister imprints, including *10-Minute Guide to Lotus Notes 4, Special Edition Using Windows NT Workstation,* and *Easy Windows 95*. You can reach Sue via the Internet at **splumley@citynet.net** or on CompuServe at **76470,2526**.

Bruce Lill has spent the last five years living Lotus Notes. He started working with Notes at Sprint, implementing its first Notes network, and hasn't stopped since. He is currently the manager of Sykes Enterprises, Inc.'s Kansas City office, where he teaches Notes development and administration, he's a CLI/CLP, and develops Notes applications. The applications have run from Sales tracking for the paper industry, to a 1-2-3- and Notes-based expense report, and even the state police's case management.

Stan Doherty is a User Assistance Architect at Lotus Development Corporation. Stan works in the SmartSuite group and writes sample applications, help, and hard copy documentation about LotusScript.

Adam Kornak is a senior consultant with Software Spectrum in Chicago. He has worked with Lotus Notes and the Smartsuite family of products for over four years. His interest in computers goes way back to 5th grade when he got his first Atari system for Christmas. Much of his time in the computer industry has been spent teaching and writing training manuals. Special thanks to his family and future bride Julie for their love and support.

We'd Like to Hear from You!

As part of our continuing effort to produce books of the highest possible quality, Que would like to hear your comments. To stay competitive, we *really* want you, as a computer book reader and user, to let us know what you like or dislike most about this book or other Que products.

You can mail comments, ideas, or suggestions for improving future editions to the address below, or send us a fax at (317) 581-4663. For the online inclined, Macmillan Computer Publishing has a forum on CompuServe (type **GO QUEBOOKS** at any prompt) through which our staff and authors are available for questions and comments. The address of our Internet site is **http://www.quecorp.com** (World Wide Web).

In addition to exploring our forum, please feel free to contact me personally to discuss your opinions of this book: I'm **74404,3307** on CompuServe, and **lwagner@que.mcp.com** on the Internet.

Thanks in advance—your comments will help us to continue publishing the best books available on computer topics in today's market.

Lisa Wagner
Senior Product Director
Que Corporation
201 W. 103rd Street
Indianapolis, Indiana 46290
USA

Contents at a Glance

VI Integrating 1-2-3

VII Customizing 1-2-3

Table of Contents

II Working with Charts and Maps

IV Analyzing the Worksheet

Introduction

When Lotus 1-2-3 was introduced, DOS was the major operating system for personal computers. As the computer industry has grown and matured, however, so have the needs of computer users. More powerful hardware, operating systems, and operating environments—such as Windows 95—are in use today, as are more powerful software packages—such as 1-2-3 97 for Windows 95.

Whether you are relatively new to spreadsheets or are an experienced 1-2-3 user, this book can help you quickly get up to speed with 1-2-3. Following the Que tradition, *Special Edition Using 1-2-3 97* leads you through the basics of everyday spreadsheet tasks and into the intermediate and advanced features of 1-2-3. This book provides the most extensive tutorial and reference coverage available for the new 1-2-3 97 for Windows 95.

Que's unprecedented experience with 1-2-3 and 1-2-3 users has helped produce this high-quality, informative book. But a book such as *Special Edition Using 1-2-3 97* doesn't develop overnight. This book represents long hours of work from a team of expert authors and dedicated editors.

The experts who worked on this book include managers, consultants, trainers, experienced 1-2-3 users, and Lotus product design and documentation professionals. They know firsthand the many ways people use 1-2-3 daily and are familiar with what you expect when turning to *Special Edition Using 1-2-3 97.* They know how to answer your questions about 1-2-3 quickly, clearly, and completely. The authors of this book have used 1-2-3 and have taught others how to use 1-2-3 to build many types of spreadsheets—from accounting and general business applications to scientific applications. This experience, combined with the editorial expertise of the world's leading computer-book publisher, brings you outstanding tutorial and reference information.

The authors of *Special Edition Using 1-2-3 97* wrote new sections and new chapters covering the new features of 1-2-3 97 for Windows 95. If you have used a previous version of 1-2-3, you can easily find and learn what makes 1-2-3 97 so different from earlier versions of 1-2-3. You learn more than what the new features of 1-2-3 97 are; this book explains the exact benefits of the new features to your work. You learn, for example, how to use the Lotus InfoBox to quickly perform "live" editing on your worksheet. You also learn how to use the Team Computing features to effectively collaborate with others.

This introduction provides a road map to using this book. To help you find the information you need, turn to the section, "A Quick Tour of This Book." You can use this introduction as a reference to the organization and conventions of *Special Edition Using 1-2-3 97.* ■

Who Should Read This Book?

Special Edition Using 1-2-3 97 is written and organized to meet the needs of a wide range of readers, from casual 1-2-3 users to accomplished and expert 1-2-3 users who have upgraded to 1-2-3 97 for Windows 95. This book provides the tips and techniques necessary to help you get the most from the program.

If you are relatively new to using 1-2-3, this book helps you learn the basics so that you can quickly begin using 1-2-3 for your needs. In particular, Part I, "Everyday Worksheet Tasks," teaches basic to intermediate-level concepts for understanding 1-2-3, including the commands, special uses of the keyboard and mouse, features of the 1-2-3 97 for Windows 95 screen, and methods for creating and modifying 1-2-3 worksheets.

If you are an experienced 1-2-3 user and have upgraded to 1-2-3 97 for Windows 95, you learn about the new features of this version and how to apply them as you develop worksheet applications. In addition to the new features provided in 1-2-3 97, you'll also learn how to perform common procedures using new streamlined methods. Lotus has updated many of the menus and dialog boxes in 1-2-3 97 to make learning and using key 1-2-3 features and procedures much easier.

What's New in 1-2-3 97?

1-2-3 97 incorporates several new features that enable you to communicate more effectively with other people, and increase your productivity. Listed below are some of the key new (or enhanced) features included with 1-2-3 97. The specified chapter numbers indicate where you can look in *Special Edition Using 1-2-3 97* to find more detailed information on these features.

- *TeamConsolidate* enables users to collaborate with others to expedite tasks such as group budgeting, forecasting, planning, and review. With *TeamMail*, users can send messages or worksheets to others, or route a range of worksheet data to a list of people. *See Chapter 30.*
- *Internet access* is provided on the File and Help menus. Users can open a file from the Internet, save a file to the Internet, and quickly access Lotus support on the Internet. *See Chapter 30.*
- *The Lotus InfoBox* provides a quick method of formatting and changing the properties of worksheet data. Changes you make in the InfoBox are immediately reflected in the worksheet. *See Chapters 4, 10, and 32.*
- *Outlining* enables users to automatically expand and collapse selected groups of rows and columns, so that you can view or print only the data you need. *See Chapter 15.*
- *Dynamic Preview* displays the worksheet and print preview of that worksheet onscreen at the same time. Changes made in the worksheet immediately appear in the preview window. *See Chapter 10.*
- *QuickDemos* are animated demonstrations that show you how to perform common 1-2-3 tasks. *See Chapter 1.*
- *LotusScript* is a cross-platform, object-oriented programming language that easily integrates with Microsoft Visual Basic to automate processes. LotusScript offers developers many enhancements that allow for automation between applications, and the ability to use teams to develop scripts. *See Chapters 37, 38, and 39.*
- *Full OLE 2.0 Support.* Visual editing, drag and drop, and OLE 2.0 Automation are supported. *See Chapters 28 and 29.*
- *Lotus Chart* is a shared tool that Lotus plans to use in all SmartSuite applications. New chart types in 1-2-3 97 include true 3D XYZ Bar, XYZ Line, XYZ Area, and multiple pie charts. *See Chapter 14.*

- *NotesFlow*, an extension of Notes/FX technology, provides an interface that enables users to easily customize menus in 1-2-3 and Notes. This feature also allows developers to modify information in a Notes form and have it automatically update in all embedded 1-2-3 worksheets. *See Chapter 29.*

A Quick Tour of This Book

Special Edition Using 1-2-3 97 is organized to follow the natural flow of learning and using 1-2-3. The following sections describe the organization of this book.

Part I: Everyday Worksheet Tasks

Chapter 1, "Getting Around in 1-2-3 and Windows," introduces the general concepts you need to understand to use 1-2-3. You learn how to manipulate and display multiple windows as well as use menus, dialog boxes, SmartIcons, and the mouse to improve your efficiency.

Chapter 2, "Navigating and Selecting in 1-2-3," introduces worksheets and files and teaches you how to move the cell pointer around the worksheet. You also learn how to work with ranges of data in the worksheet.

Chapter 3, "Entering and Editing Data," shows you how to enter and edit data in the worksheet, how to fill ranges with a series of data, and how to find and replace data. This chapter also covers how to erase cells and ranges, spell check your data, and use the Undo feature. In addition, you learn how to insert and delete cells, rows, and columns.

Chapter 4, "Formatting Worksheets," shows you how to change the way data appears onscreen, including the way values, formulas, and text display. You also learn how to set column widths and row heights, suppress the display of zeros, and how to use named styles, and style galleries to quickly format data.

Chapter 5, "Working with Formulas," discusses how to create and enter worksheet formulas, and how to correct errors. In addition, you learn how to specify the method and order of recalculation and how to handle unwanted circular references in the worksheet.

Chapter 6, "Using Functions," explains how to enter and use functions. The chapter provides a description of all the functions available in the following categories: Calendar, Database, Engineering, Financial, Information, Logical, Lookup, Mathematical, Statistical, and Text.

Chapter 7, "Moving or Copying Data," shows you a variety of techniques for moving and copying worksheet data. These include drag and drop, which allows you simply to drag information from one location to another, and using the Windows Clipboard together with 1-2-3 commands to reposition information on your worksheet.

Chapter 8, "Reorganizing Worksheets," explains how you can organize your data more efficiently by using the multiple-worksheet feature to include up to 256 worksheets in a single worksheet file. You learn how to insert, delete, rename, and group worksheets in a multiple-worksheet file.

Chapter 9, "Managing Files," covers the commands related to creating, saving, closing, opening, deleting, and listing files. You also learn how to change directories and protect files. In addition, this chapter teaches you how to enter and view file information.

Chapter 10, "Printing Worksheets," shows you how to preview reports before you print them, specify a print range, print reports of different sizes, and enhance reports with page setup options.

Part II: Working with Charts and Maps

Chapter 11, "Creating Charts," teaches you the different methods for creating charts from worksheet data. You learn how to create charts automatically from data in a worksheet file and to define a chart's data ranges manually. You also learn how to preview and print charts.

Chapter 12, "Modifying Charts," explains how to manipulate the elements in a chart, including resizing the whole chart or parts of the chart, adding and deleting elements, editing the titles and legends, and other tasks.

Chapter 13, "Formatting Charts," covers how to change colors, patterns, number format, and text attributes, as well as how to annotate a chart. In addition, you learn how to add symbols to line charts, format a chart frame, and explode pie slices.

Chapter 14, "Building Complex Charts and Mapping Data," shows you how to create the more complicated chart types offered by 1-2-3 (such as XY, XYZ, HLCO, Mixed, and Radar), as well as how to import graphics into a chart. You also learn how to use the mapping feature to illustrate worksheet data.

Part III: Optimizing 1-2-3

Chapter 15, "Managing the Worksheet Display," shows you how to freeze worksheet titles, split and scroll worksheet windows, display worksheets using different views, zoom the worksheet display, and hide columns, rows, and ranges. You'll also learn how to use the new outlining feature in 1-2-3 97.

Chapter 16, "Adding Graphics to Worksheets," covers how to add text boxes, lines, arrows, ellipses, and other graphic elements to worksheets. You also learn how to rearrange graphic objects in the worksheet.

Chapter 17, "Developing Business Presentations," focuses on using spreadsheet-publishing techniques to create computer, slide, and overhead presentations. Examples include how to combine text, graphics, and clip art effectively on a single page.

Part IV: Analyzing the Worksheet

Chapter 18, "Manipulating and Analyzing Data," covers how to combine whole and partial units of text, use formulas that make decisions, analyze and obtain data from tables, and create what-if tables.

Chapter 19, "Linking and Consolidating Worksheets," discusses the benefits of using multiple-worksheet files, and shows you how to enter formulas that link worksheets and files, and how to combine and consolidate worksheets.

Chapter 20, "Solving Problems with Backsolver," shows you how to use Backsolver to find and evaluate solutions to "what-if" scenarios. Examples illustrate how Backsolver is used in practical business situations.

Chapter 21, "Managing Multiple Solutions with Version Manager," shows you how to use the Version Manager feature to keep track of the changing information in worksheets—and how to share this information with others. You learn how to create and display different versions of data in a named range and how to group versions together into scenarios.

Part V: Managing Databases

Chapter 22, "Creating a Database," introduces the simplified 1-2-3 97 database features. This chapter shows you how to define, design, and create a 1-2-3 database.

Chapter 23, "Entering and Editing Data in a Database," shows you how to add and delete database records, edit records, insert and delete fields, move a field, and divide and combine fields.

Chapter 24, "Sorting Data," discusses how to sort data in a worksheet according to one, two, or more columns of data. This chapter also explains how to restore worksheet data to its original order if you make a mistake when sorting or need a copy of the original data prior to sorting.

Chapter 25, "Finding and Extracting Data," explains how to search a worksheet to find data. You learn the ways you can list, extract, and delete records in a 1-2-3 database. Also, the chapter explains the different methods for defining the criteria upon which to conduct a search.

Chapter 26, "Understanding Advanced Data Management," covers some of the more advanced database features such as joining multiple databases and using crosstabs and aggregates. You also learn how to create frequency distributions, perform regression analysis, and analyze matrices.

Chapter 27, "Retrieving Data from External Databases," explains how to create a query table from data in an external database, update or add data to an external table from 1-2-3, create a new external table, and import data from other programs to a 1-2-3 worksheet and "parse" it into columns.

Part VI: Integrating 1-2-3

Chapter 28, "Using 1-2-3 with SmartSuite Applications," explains how to use the more advanced DDE, OLE, and OLE 2.0 capabilities of Lotus SmartSuite applications (1-2-3, Word Pro, Approach, and Freelance Graphics) to dynamically link data between applications.

Chapter 29, "Using 1-2-3 with Lotus Notes," shows you how to use 1-2-3 effectively with Lotus Notes—a "groupware" application that manages data and information for many users. You learn how to use DDE/OLE between 1-2-3 and Notes, import and export 1-2-3 data with Notes, and use Application Field Exchange.

Chapter 30, "Using the Team Computing Features," shows you how to use Lotus' Team Computing technology to more effectively communicate with your coworkers and others. You'll learn about the following 1-2-3 97 features: TeamMail, TeamReview, TeamConsolidate, NotesFlow, and the Internet access options.

Chapter 31, "Integrating 1-2-3 with DOS Applications," explains how to copy and paste information between 1-2-3 and DOS applications, save 1-2-3 worksheets in file formats readable by other applications, and transfer data to and from 1-2-3 and DOS applications by using text files.

Part VII: Customizing 1-2-3

Chapter 32, "Customizing the 1-2-3 Screen," teaches you how to customize the 1-2-3 screen by controlling which elements appear on the 1-2-3 screen, controlling the appearance of the worksheet grid, changing the screen's color scheme, and modifying the desktop.

Chapter 33, "Customizing SmartIcons," shows you how to use and customize 1-2-3's SmartIcons. Specifically, you learn how to switch SmartIcon bars, hide and display SmartIcons, move and rearrange SmartIcons, create custom SmartIcons, and create custom SmartIcon bars.

Chapter 34, "Working with Templates," shows you how to use the 1-2-3 SmartMaster templates, use and design custom templates, and create autoloading worksheets.

Chapter 35, "Creating Custom Dialog Boxes," explains how to use the Lotus Dialog Editor to design custom dialog boxes for use with 1-2-3 scripts and macros.

Chapter 36, "Writing 1-2-3 Macros," is an introduction to the powerful macro capabilities of 1-2-3. This chapter teaches you how to plan, create, format, name, and run macros, as well as how to document and protect macros.

Appendixes

Appendix A, "Finding Optimal Solutions with the Solver," discusses how you can obtain and use the latest version of the Solver. Although the Solver included with earlier versions of 1-2-3 is no longer supported, you can obtain a more powerful version of Solver for 1-2-3 97 with added capabilities from other vendors.

Appendix B, "Programming 1-2-3 97 with LotusScript," discusses how to move or copy data and formats to a new location and how to change a cell reference in a formula so that it is absolute or mixed. Use this appendix to fine-tune your formulas for error-free moving and copying.

Special Index

The "Index of Common Problems," includes a table that categorizes the most common 1-2-3 problems and provides page numbers referencing the location of solutions to these problems in this book.

Conventions Used in This Book

Certain conventions are used in *Special Edition Using 1-2-3 97* to help you more easily use this book and understand 1-2-3's concepts. The following sections include examples of these conventions to help you distinguish among the different elements.

Special Typefaces and Representations

Special typefaces used in this book include the following:

Type	Meaning
italics	New terms or phrases when initially defined; function, script, and macro command syntax variables
<u>underline</u>	Menu and dialog box options that appear underlined on-screen
boldface	Information you are asked to type
`special type`	Direct quotations of words that appear on-screen or in a figure; script and macro code

Elements printed in uppercase include range names such as SALES, functions such as @FIND, and cell references such as A:B19. Also presented in uppercase letters are file names such as STATUS. Mode and status indicators such as Ready and End are printed in initial cap, as they appear on-screen.

In most cases, keys are represented as they appear on the keyboard. The arrow keys usually are represented by name (for example, ***the up-arrow key***). The Delete key is abbreviated Del, Insert is Ins, and so on. On your keyboard, these key names may be spelled out or abbreviated differently.

When two keys appear together with a plus sign, such as Shift+Ins, press and hold the first key as you press the second key. When two keys appear together without a plus sign, such as End Home, press and release the first key before you press the second key.

Special Elements

This book includes notes, tips, and cautions as indicated and described below.

NOTE This paragraph format indicates additional information that may help you avoid problems or that should be considered in using the described features.

TIP This paragraph format suggests easier or alternative methods of performing a procedure.

CAUTION

This paragraph format warns you of hazardous procedures (for example, activities that delete files).

Margin Icons

1-2-3 SmartIcons appear in the margin to indicate that the procedure described in the text includes instructions for using the pictured SmartIcons. In some instances, a SmartIcon may appear in the margin to indicate an alternative method to that described in the text.

Cross-References

Special Edition Using 1-2-3 97 includes cross-references to help you access other parts of the book. Following the relevant paragraphs, related tasks you may need to perform or reference are listed by section name and page number, as shown here:

▶ **See** "Entering Functions," **p. 154**

Troubleshooting Elements

Troubleshooting elements are provided in most chapters to help you find solutions to common problems encountered with the 1-2-3 procedures covered in that section of the book. An example of a troubleshooting element is shown here:

TROUBLESHOOTING

My auto-execute macro will not run when I load a workbook. Why is this? Make certain that the Run Autoexecute Macros check box is selected in the 1-2-3 Preferences dialog box. Choose File, User Setup, 1-2-3 Preferences to access this dialog box.

PART I

Everyday Worksheet Tasks

CHAPTER 1

Getting Around in 1-2-3 and Windows

by Joyce J. Nielsen

This chapter provides an introduction to using Lotus 1-2-3 97 in the Windows 95 environment. 1-2-3 97 is a 32-bit spreadsheet that takes full advantage of the improved speed and memory management of the Windows 95 operating system. If you have used earlier versions of 1-2-3, you will also be impressed with how much easier it is to use 1-2-3 97. Some of these improvements include a more graphical and context-sensitive interface. You can apply the ideas and concepts you learn in this chapter to all your 1-2-3 operations.

In this chapter, you learn how to start and exit 1-2-3, and you become familiar with the screen elements. You'll also learn how to use the mouse or keyboard to choose menu commands, access the shortcut menu, make selections in dialog boxes, and access the 1-2-3 Help system. In addition, this chapter shows you how to manipulate windows so that you can access and use multiple workbooks at once.

Starting and exiting 1-2-3

Learn several methods for starting and exiting 1-2-3, as well as how to automatically load a workbook when you start 1-2-3.

Using 1-2-3 menus and dialog boxes

Menus and dialog boxes provide the commands you need to perform actions on your worksheets, such as copying and moving data, creating charts, and customizing worksheets.

Using SmartIcons

1-2-3's SmartIcons enable you to quickly perform common commands or procedures by clicking a button.

Manipulating windows

You can easily regulate how your windows appear on-screen so that you can view your worksheet data in different ways.

Getting Help

1-2-3 97 includes several methods for accessing Help information, such as Lotus Assistants, QuickDemos, and detailed online Help screens.

NOTE If you purchased 1-2-3 97 as part of Lotus SmartSuite 97, you'll discover that many features described in this book work in a way that is similar to the other SmartSuite applications. For detailed information on how to effectively use 1-2-3 with other SmartSuite applications, such as Word Pro and Freelance, refer to Chapter 28, "Using 1-2-3 with SmartSuite Applications." ■

▶ **See** "Using Common Lotus Tools and Interfaces," **p. 633**

Starting and Exiting 1-2-3

The most common way to start a Windows 95 application is to use the Windows 95 Start button. To start 1-2-3 97 using the Start button, follow these steps:

1. Click the Start button in the Windows 95 Taskbar.
2. Move the mouse pointer over the Programs command.
3. In the Programs menu, move the mouse pointer over the Lotus SmartSuite option.
4. In the Lotus SmartSuite menu, click the Lotus 1-2-3 97 option (see fig. 1.1). The 1-2-3 97 program starts.

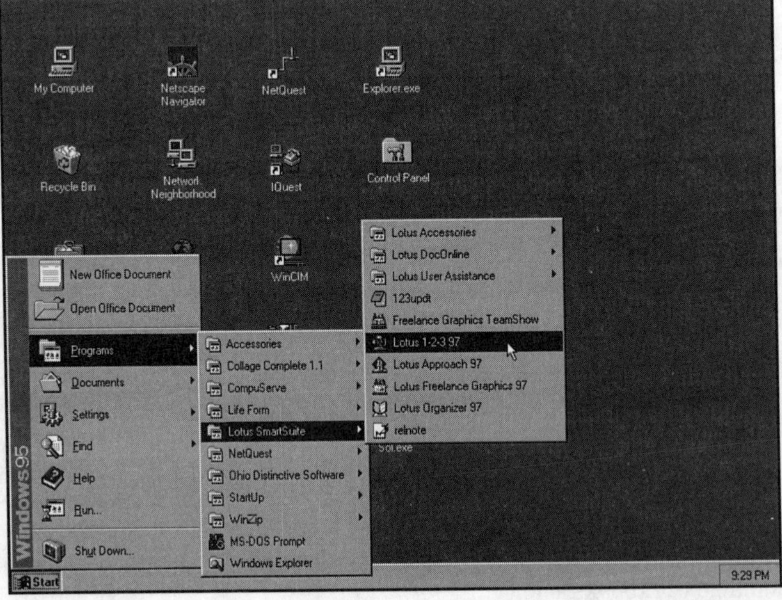

Fig. 1.1
Use the Start button on the Windows 95 Taskbar to access and start 1-2-3.

If the Start button method seems too tedious, you can create an application shortcut icon on your Windows 95 desktop that you can double-click to start 1-2-3. To create the shortcut icon, use the right mouse button to drag the 1-2-3 application icon from the Windows Explorer and then drop it on the desktop. Then, from the resulting shortcut menu click Create Shortcut(s) Here.

NOTE If you use 1-2-3 on a daily basis, you might want to have 1-2-3 start automatically when Windows 95 starts. To do this, you need to copy the 1-2-3 icon to the StartUp folder. Start Windows Explorer, then open the Windows folder, the Start Menu folder, the Programs folder, and the StartUp folder. Locate the 1-2-3 application icon, then press Ctrl and drag the 1-2-3 application icon into the StartUp folder.

TIP To start 1-2-3 and automatically open a specific workbook, you can double-click the workbook file name in Windows Explorer. 1-2-3 starts, then opens the file you double-clicked.

Or, if you have used the 1-2-3 workbook recently, a faster method is to click the Start button, move the mouse pointer over Documents, and click the file name you want to open. If 1-2-3 isn't already running, this action starts 1-2-3 and loads the file you clicked.

1-2-3 enables you to close individual workbooks or to exit from 1-2-3 entirely, closing all open workbooks at one time. To exit from 1-2-3 and close all open workbooks, follow these steps:

1. If you are using a mouse, click the File menu, and then click Exit 1-2-3; or click the X (Close button) in the upper-right corner of the 1-2-3 screen. To choose this command using the keyboard, press Alt+F, and then press X.
2. If you have saved all recent changes in the open workbook(s), 1-2-3 closes. If you have not saved changes to open workbooks, a confirmation box appears, prompting you to save your changes.

   Select Yes to save the current workbook before exiting; choose No to exit without saving the file; choose Cancel to cancel the exit command and return to 1-2-3; or choose Save All if you have multiple workbooks open and want to save all of them before exiting.

Using the mouse, you also can double-click the 1-2-3 Control menu icon (in the upper-left corner of the 1-2-3 screen) to close 1-2-3; the Exit confirmation box appears. Make your selection as outlined in step 2 above.

Creating a New Workbook or Opening an Existing Workbook

When you start 1-2-3, the Welcome to 1-2-3 dialog box shown in figure 1.2 appears.

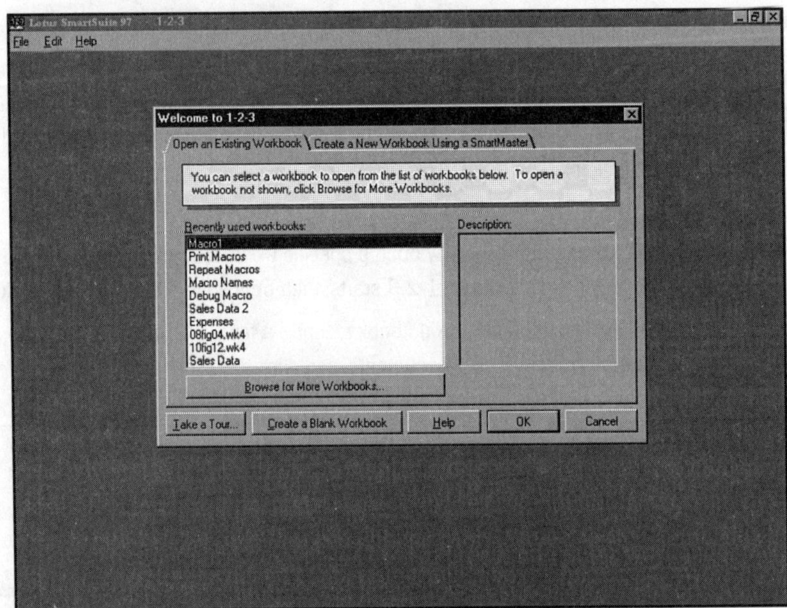

Fig. 1.2
You can choose to create a new workbook or open an existing one from the Welcome to 1-2-3 dialog box.

The Welcome to 1-2-3 dialog box provides the following choices:

- *Open an Existing Workbook.* If you want to open a file that you recently worked on, click the file name in the Recently Used Workbooks list box. If you don't see this list box, click the Open an Existing Workbook tab. Alternatively, you can choose Browse for More Workbooks if the workbook you want to open doesn't appear in the list.
- *Create a New Workbook Using a SmartMaster.* Click this tab if you want to create a new workbook that is based on a 1-2-3 SmartMaster template. *SmartMasters* are worksheets that have been predesigned for many common applications. They contain text, formatting, and formulas, so that all you need to do is enter your specific information into the worksheet. Select the desired SmartMaster from the SmartMaster Templates list box. You can choose More SmartMaster Templates if the template you want to use doesn't appear in the list box. Chapter 34, "Working with Templates," discusses SmartMaster templates in more detail.
- *Create a Blank Workbook.* When you choose this button, you open a blank, untitled workbook that you can use to create a new workbook.

- *Take a Tour.* This starts the online tutorial that leads you through the basic functions of 1-2-3.

▶ **See** "Opening Existing Workbooks," **p. 271**

▶ **See** "Creating a New Workbook," **p. 264**

NOTE If you do not want to see the Welcome to 1-2-3 dialog box every time you start 1-2-3, choose File, User Setup, 1-2-3 Preferences, and then deselect the Show Welcome Dialog check box. Click OK to close the dialog box and save your changes. ■

Understanding the 1-2-3 Screen

Access to all of 1-2-3's features is accomplished using various screen elements. All Windows 95 applications have some common screen elements. Once you learn how to work with the common features, you can master other Windows applications easily. Figure 1.3 shows a blank workbook in 1-2-3, with common Windows 95 elements labeled. Table 1.1 describes these standard Windows 95 screen elements.

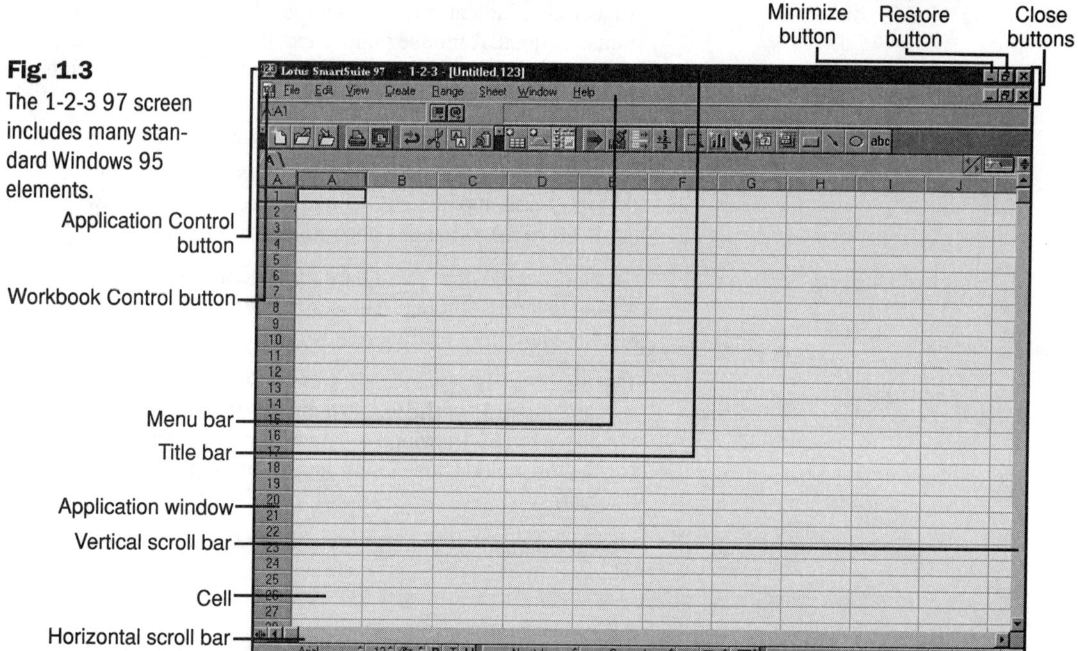

Fig. 1.3
The 1-2-3 97 screen includes many standard Windows 95 elements.

Table 1.1 Standard Windows 95 Screen Elements

Part	Description
Application Control icon	Opens a menu that enables you to control the application window.
Application window	1-2-3 runs in this window.
Close icon	The X that appears on the right side of a title bar, window, or dialog box. Click the Close icon to close the application, window, or dialog box.
Maximize icon	A box, located near the upper-right corner of all windows (before they are maximized), which enlarges the application or window to fill the available screen display. After you click the Maximize icon, it is replaced with a Restore icon.
Menu bar	A list of menu names displayed below the title bar of an application.
Minimize icon	An underscore, located near the upper-right corner of all windows, that reduces an application window to an application button in the Windows 95 Taskbar, or a worksheet window to a button at the bottom of the worksheet area.
Mouse pointer	An icon that indicates the current location affected by your mouse actions. A mouse pointer can take on various shapes, such as an arrow, cross, or I-beam, depending on the action you are performing.
Restore icon	A double box, located near the upper-right corner of all windows, that restores the window to its previous size (before it was maximized). When you restore a window, the Restore icon changes back to a Maximize icon.
Scroll bars	Gray horizontal or vertical bars that enable you to scroll the screen using the mouse. The scroll box in the bar shows the display's current position, relative to the entire worksheet.
Title bar	The bar at the top of an application or window, which usually contains the title of the window and/or the name of the file displayed in the window. The Minimize, Maximize (or Restore), and Close icons appear on the right side of a title bar.
Workbook Control icon	Opens a menu that enables you to control the Workbook window.

Other parts of the screen are specific to the 1-2-3 program. Together, these parts enable you to work with and display worksheets and charts. Figure 1.4 shows some of the screen elements that are specific to 1-2-3. Table 1.2 describes these screen elements.

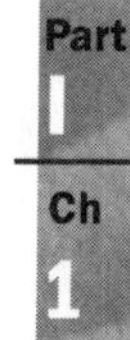

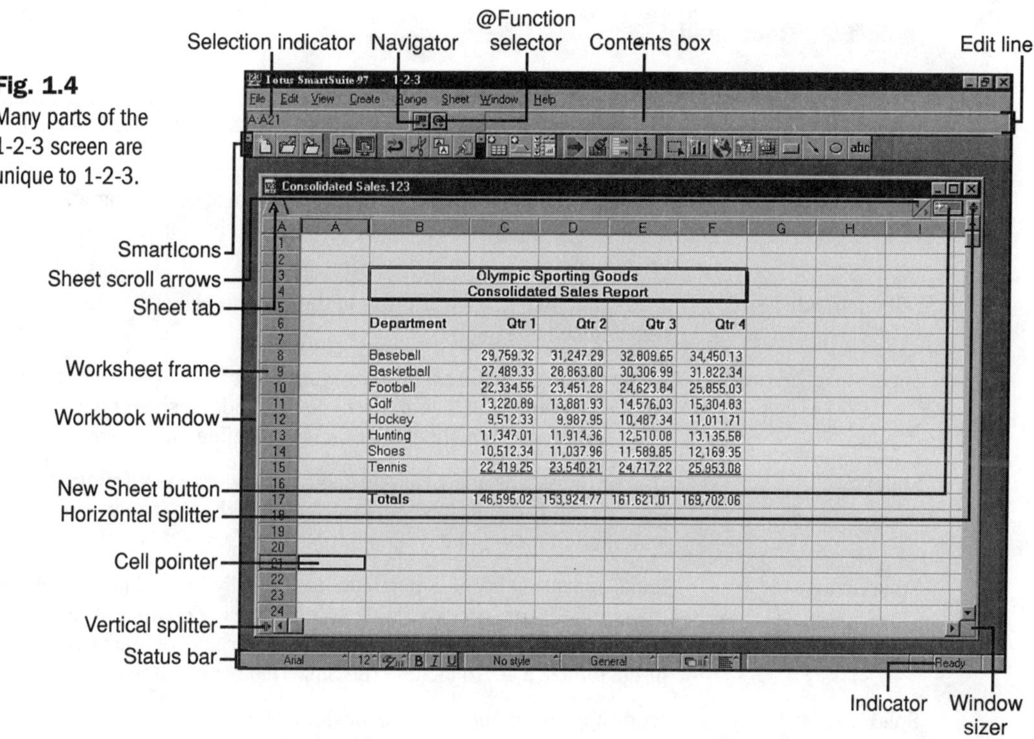

Fig. 1.4
Many parts of the 1-2-3 screen are unique to 1-2-3.

Table 1.2 1-2-3 Screen Elements

Part	Description
Cell	The intersection of a column and row in the worksheet. All worksheet data is stored in individual cells.
Cell pointer	Marks the location of the selected cell.
Contents box	A box on the right side of the edit line, which displays the contents of the selected cell. When you enter information into a 1-2-3 worksheet, the information appears both in the contents box and in the selected cell.
Edit line	The row appearing just below the menu bar, which includes the selection indicator, navigator, @function selector, and the contents box.
@Function selector	Displays a list of functions available in 1-2-3. You can use this tool to insert functions into a formula that you are typing.
Indicators	Various mode and status indicators appear on the right side of the status bar. These display modes of operation, such as Edit, when you are editing the contents of a cell.

continues

Table 1.2 Continued

Part	Description
Navigator	Displays a list of all named ranges and objects in the worksheet, if any exist.
New Sheet button	An icon located above the right edge of the worksheet frame. Click this button to add new sheets to the active (or *current*) workbook.
Selection indicator	A box that displays the address of the current selection (the selected cell or range).
Sheet scroll arrows	Arrow icons appearing above the worksheet frame (just left of the New Sheet button). Click these to display hidden sheet tabs when you need to access a sheet tab that is not visible on-screen.
Sheet tab	One or more tabs appearing just above the worksheet frame, which identify different sheets within a workbook. These provide a method of moving between multiple sheets.
SmartIcons	Icons appearing in the SmartIcon bar (usually located just below the edit line) that provide quick access to many commands and tools available in 1-2-3. You can display other sets of SmartIcons, or customize a set to include the SmartIcons you choose.
Splitters	Icons appearing above the vertical scroll bar and to the left of the horizontal scroll bar that can divide a sheet into two panes (when you drag them). This enables you to view two different areas of a sheet at one time.
Status bar	A bar at the bottom of the screen that provides information as well as a means of quickly changing fonts, sizes, colors, alignment, and other formatting options. Click one of the status bar buttons to display a pop-up list, then select the desired option. The status bar elements may sometimes change, depending on the current action you are performing.
Window sizer	The icon that appears to the right of the horizontal scroll bar, which enables you to quickly adjust the size of a non-maximized window.
Workbook window	A window within the 1-2-3 application that displays a specific workbook with cells into which you can enter data. There may be multiple workbooks open on-screen at one time.
Worksheet frame	The horizontal gray bar containing the sheet letter and column letters, and the vertical gray bar containing the row numbers (just above and left of the worksheet area).

Using the Status Bar

The *status bar* is the bottom line of the 1-2-3 screen. This bar displays information about the attributes of the current cell, such as the font applied to the cell and the number of decimal places displayed. As you move from one cell to another in the worksheet, the status bar changes to reflect the attributes of each cell. In addition, the contents of the status bar sometimes change when you select certain items, such as a text block or a line shape.

The status bar also provides a quick method of changing cell attributes. Simply click a formatting attribute displayed in the status bar to display a pop-up list of options for that attribute (see fig. 1.5). The bold, italic, and underline buttons in the status bar do not display a pop-up list—you just click them to apply the attribute to the selected cell(s).

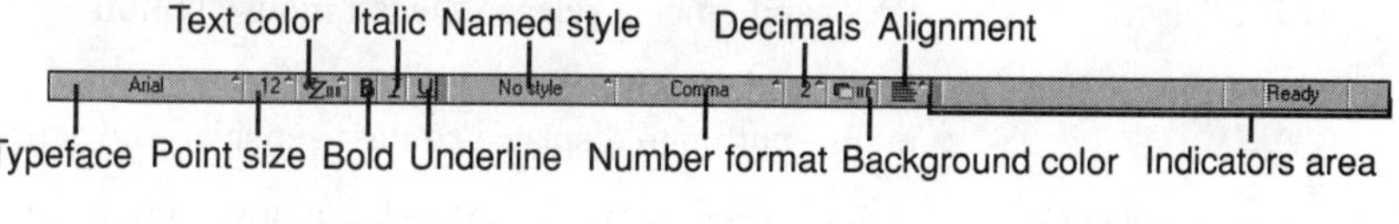

Fig. 1.5
Click one of the buttons in the status bar to change the attributes of the selected cell(s).

The status bar displays other information in the special indicators area on the right side of the bar. Mode and status indicators appear at various times to tell you what mode 1-2-3 is in (such as Ready), and the status of certain keys that you pressed (if applicable). Also, when you save a file or open an existing file, the status bar is temporarily replaced with the *progress indicator*, which indicates the percentage of the file saved or opened. The status bar reappears after the file has finished saving or opening.

NOTE If you select two or more cells that contain different attributes, portions of the status bar appear blank, indicating that several attributes apply to the selection. If you choose a new attribute for the selection, the attribute applies to all the selected cells. ■

Using the Mouse with 1-2-3

As with the keyboard, the mouse enables you to choose commands and manipulate objects on-screen. You can perform many tasks more quickly with the mouse, such as moving through windows, setting column widths, and moving around in dialog boxes. Some tasks in 1-2-3 can be performed *only* with a mouse—using SmartIcons, selecting individual elements in a chart, selecting collections of data, and using shortcut menus.

Most pointing devices have a left and a right button. You use the left button to select cells and ranges, use menus, and enter information in dialog boxes. Clicking the right mouse button displays a context-sensitive shortcut menu that helps you with certain tasks. Some of these include selecting a range of cells, or working with the SmartIcon bar and the worksheet frame. The right mouse button can also help you if you need to manipulate an object in a chart. Table 1.3 describes the mouse terminology you need to know as you read this book.

Table 1.3 Mouse Terminology

Term	Meaning
Point	Place the mouse pointer over the menu, cell, or data that you want to select or move.
Click	Press and quickly release the left mouse button.
Right-click	Position the mouse pointer in the desired location and click the right mouse button to display a context-sensitive shortcut menu.
Double-click	Quickly press and release the left mouse button twice.
Drag	Press and hold down the left mouse button and then move the mouse. This action, which is also called click-and-drag, is usually performed to highlight a range of cells or to move an object.
Select	To select a range of cells, click and drag the mouse pointer over the range. To select an object, click the mouse pointer on the object.

Usually, the mouse pointer is in the shape of an arrow. As you perform different tasks in 1-2-3, however, the mouse pointer changes shape. In the Help window, for example, the mouse pointer becomes a hand with an extended index finger, indicating that you can select highlighted Help topics.

Using 1-2-3 Menus

Almost every task you perform in 1-2-3 is part of a *command*. Commands help you copy, move, and format data, create charts, open and close workbooks, and customize worksheets with colors and fonts, and so on. You also choose commands from dialog boxes and InfoBoxes, which are described later in this chapter.

Following are the different types of menus available in 1-2-3:

- *Main menu*. The main menu appears in the menu bar near the top of the 1-2-3 screen, and includes items that enable you to access the 1-2-3 commands. The main menu changes from time to time, depending on your actions. For example, when you work with charts, the Range menu changes to the Chart menu to provide you with commands specific to charting.

- *Shortcut menu.* This type of menu appears only when you press the right mouse button. It consolidates commands from several of the 1-2-3 main menu selections onto one easy-to-use menu. The shortcut menus contain different commands, depending on what is selected in the worksheet.
- *1-2-3 Classic menu.* This is the classic 1-2-3 Release 3.1 menu and is available to make the transition to 1-2-3 97 easier for experienced users of 1-2-3 for DOS. Some of the commands on the classic menu are obsolete, and do not work with 1-2-3 97, however. This book does not discuss the options on the 1-2-3 Classic menu. Refer to the 1-2-3 online Help if you need more information.

Choosing Commands from the Menu

All the commands on the 1-2-3 main menu lead to pull-down menus; many (but not all) pull-down menus lead to cascade menus that appear beside the pull-down menu. Other menu options open dialog boxes (described later in this chapter).

1-2-3 uses the standard Windows techniques for choosing commands from the menus. You can choose commands with the mouse arrow keys, keystrokes, or shortcut keys. Many users mix the way they select commands based on a specific situation. If your hands are on the keyboard while you are initially entering data into a worksheet, you might want to select commands with keystrokes. However, if you are editing and revising a worksheet and your hand is on the mouse, use the mouse techniques to select commands.

To display a pull-down menu, use one of these methods:

- Use the mouse to click the command you want; 1-2-3 automatically activates the menu and displays the pull-down menu options.
- Activate the main menu by pressing the Alt key. Use the arrow keys to move the menu pointer to the name of the command and then press Enter or the down-arrow key to see the pull-down menu.

  When you activate the main menu and press the right- or left-arrow key, the menu pointer moves across the menu bar and highlights commands.
- Press and hold down the Alt key and type the underlined letter of the command. For example, to choose the File menu, hold down Alt and type **F**. The Alt key activates the menu, **F** selects the File menu option.

When you choose a command from the main menu, the resulting pull-down menu appears. Menu items in the pull-down menu can appear with a triangle, an *ellipsis* (...), or nothing beside them (see fig. 1.6). If the menu item has a triangle, the item results in a cascade menu when selected. If the menu item has an ellipsis, 1-2-3 needs more information to complete the command and displays a *dialog box* or *InfoBox* for you to complete. If the menu item has no marker, the item is usually the last selection in the command sequence: if you click the command (or highlight it and press Enter), 1-2-3 executes the selected command.

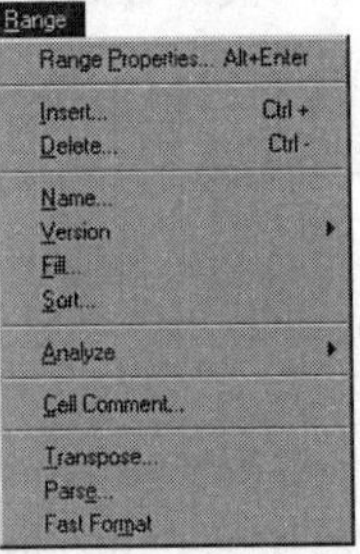

Fig. 1.6
Arrowheads indicate a cascade menu, while an ellipsis indicates that a dialog box will appear if you select the command.

To choose a command from the pull-down or cascade menus, use one of these techniques:

- Use the mouse to click the command you want. 1-2-3 performs the command, or displays a cascade menu, dialog box, or InfoBox, depending on the situation.
- Use the up or down arrow keys to highlight the command and then press Enter.
- Type the underlined letter of the command. For example, to choose Name from the Range menu, type **N**. The Range menu must already be open (pulled down).

You can explore command menus without actually executing the commands. Highlight a menu option on the main menu or a pull-down menu and read the command description in the title bar to find out more about the selected option. For more detailed information about a command, move the menu pointer to the command and press F1 (Help).

TROUBLESHOOTING

I pull down a menu and choose a gray option but nothing happens. Grayed out menu selections are standard in all Windows applications. It means that the particular menu selection is not available or is not appropriate at this time. Many commands require you to select an area of the worksheet before you can issue a command. Another example is that Edit, Paste may be gray if you have not copied anything.

Canceling a Command

If you make a mistake while choosing menu commands, press Esc to return to the preceding menu. If you press Esc at the main menu, you deactivate the menu and return to Ready mode.

If you click a main menu item by mistake, click the same main menu item again. The menu disappears.

If you execute a command accidentally, you usually can undo the action of that command. For example, if you erase a range by mistake, you can choose the Edit, Undo command or click the Undo SmartIcon to recover the erased range.

▶ **See** "Using the Undo Feature," **p. 89**

Saving Time with Shortcut Menus

A 1-2-3 shortcut menu combines commands from various menus to make them available in a single location as you work in the worksheet. Shortcut menus provide all the commands you are likely to require for the current activity and they appear right in the worksheet location, so that you don't have to move the mouse up to the top of the screen to choose commands.

To access a shortcut menu, follow these steps:

1. Select a range of cells in the worksheet if you want to perform a command on the range.
2. Click the right mouse button *inside* the cell, range, column or row heading, or other worksheet or graphic element with which you are working.

The shortcut menu that appears is appropriate for the selected element. For example, figure 1.7 shows the shortcut menu that appears when you select a range of cells.

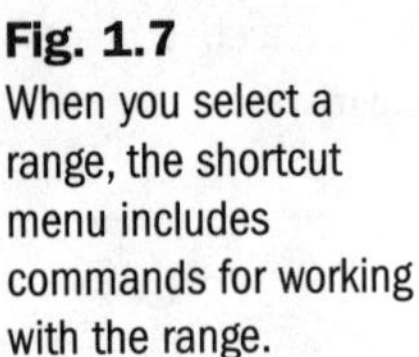

Fig. 1.7
When you select a range, the shortcut menu includes commands for working with the range.

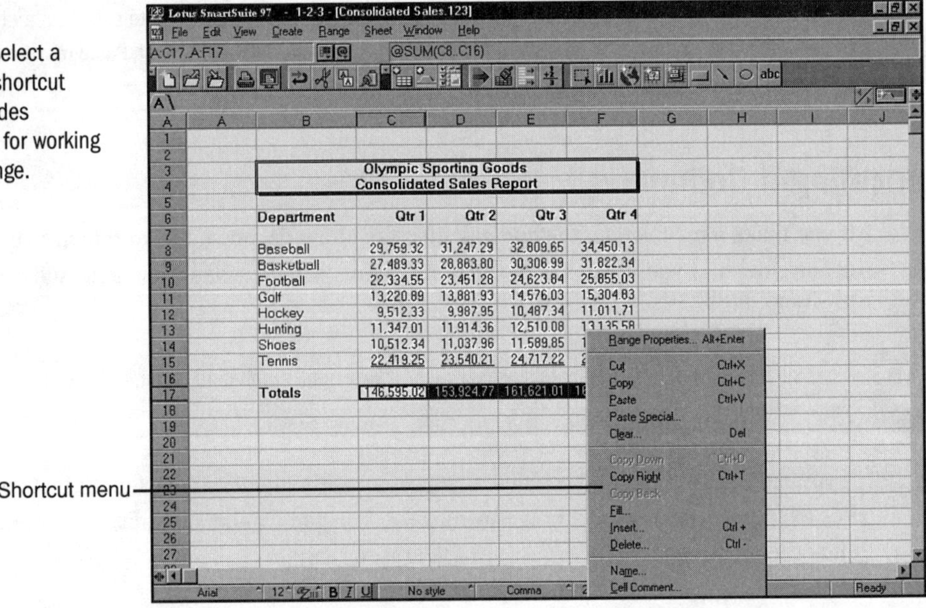

Working with Dialog Boxes

As mentioned earlier in this chapter, commands listed in pull-down menus that require additional information are followed by an ellipsis (...). When you choose one of these commands, 1-2-3 displays a dialog box. You must supply the necessary information in the dialog box to execute the command.

NOTE In 1-2-3 97, you can use an InfoBox to quickly and easily format and change the properties of worksheet data. You select items in an InfoBox in the same manner that you select dialog box options. There are a few differences between dialog boxes and an InfoBox, however. Changes you make in an InfoBox are immediately reflected in the worksheet. Also, unlike dialog boxes, you can keep an InfoBox on-screen while working in the worksheet. You will learn more about how to use an InfoBox in Chapter 4, "Formatting Worksheets," Chapter 10, "Printing Worksheets," and Chapter 32, "Customizing the 1-2-3 Screen." ■

A dialog box contains many sections so that you can read and enter information easily. Each dialog box in 1-2-3 differs from another, but every dialog box has a *title bar* and *command buttons*. The title bar displays the name of the dialog box. When one dialog box appears in front of another, the title bar of the active dialog box is highlighted.

TIP Occasionally, a dialog box covers worksheet data you need to see to complete the command. To see the worksheet data, you have to move the dialog box. Drag the title bar of the dialog box to move it to another location.

There are several different types of items included in dialog boxes (see fig. 1.8). These items, which are explained in more detail later in this section, include the following:

- *Command button.* A button that executes or cancels a command, such as OK or Cancel. The names on some buttons are followed by an ellipsis to indicate that an additional dialog box appears if you select the button.
- *Option button.* A button that you use to select one choice from a group of two or more options. You cannot select more than one option button in a single group.
- *Check box.* A square box that you can select (turn on) or deselect (turn off). In many cases, several check boxes can be selected at once.
- *List box.* A box containing a list of items from which you can select the desired item. A drop-down list appears when you click an arrow beside a list box. You can scroll a drop-down list to see all available items.
- *Text box.* A box in which you can type and edit information, such as text, numbers, and dates. Some text boxes, such as the Number of Copies text box shown in figure 1.7, include up and down arrows beside them, which you can use to increment or decrement a value in a text box. This is sometimes called a *spinner* or a *spin box*.
- *Combo box.* A box that is the combination of a list box and a text box. You can either type an entry in the text box, or select an item from the list box.
- *Range selector.* A special button that sometimes appears beside a text box and enables you to temporarily exit the dialog box in order to select a range of cells in the worksheet. After you select the range, you are returned to the dialog box, and the range you selected appears in the accompanying text box.

You rarely need to fill in every item in a dialog box. For example, the dialog box shown in figure 1.7 has several options. To print multiple copies of a worksheet, increase the number in the Number of Copies text box and choose Print to print the worksheet. You don't have to select specific pages, a page range, or Page Setup, if these items are already set the way you want them.

Some dialog boxes in 1-2-3 include tabbed sections, with multiple tabs appearing at the top of the dialog box (similar to cards in a card file). All options grouped on each tab are related. You click a tab to select it. Figure 1.9 shows the Workbook Properties dialog box, with the View tab displayed. Click another tab, such as the General tab, to display a different panel with additional options.

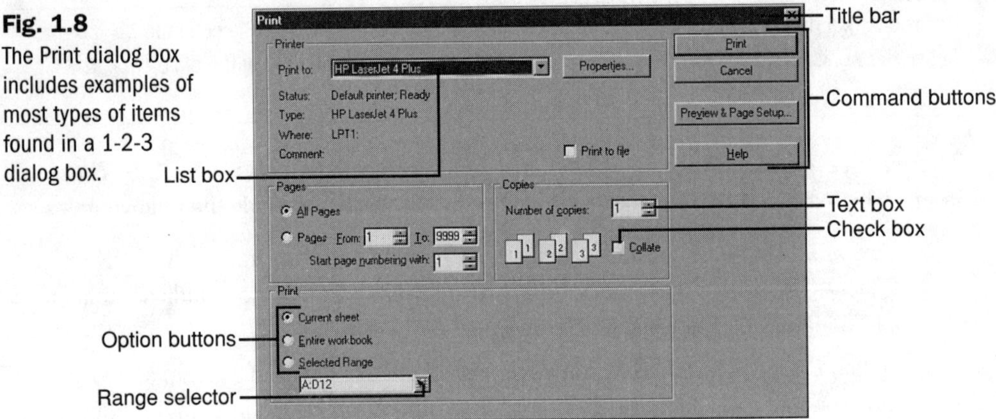

Fig. 1.8
The Print dialog box includes examples of most types of items found in a 1-2-3 dialog box.

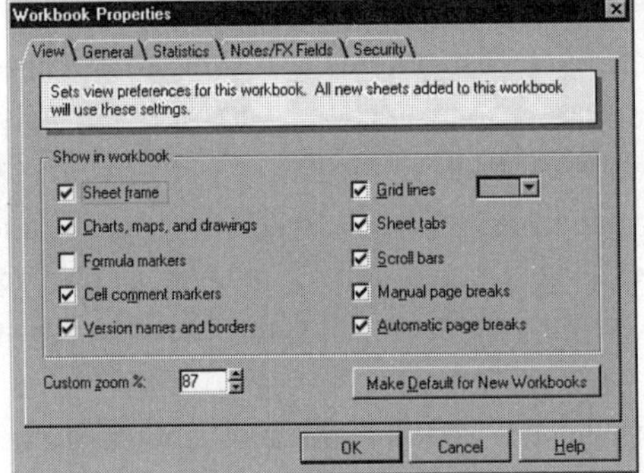

Fig. 1.9
A few 1-2-3 dialog boxes include tabbed sections, with additional options appearing on each tab.

Selecting Check Boxes and Option Buttons

Check boxes turn choices on or off. If a choice is turned on, a check mark appears in the box. Several (or all) check boxes in a dialog box can be selected at once.

To select or deselect a check box, use one of these techniques:

- Click the check box to select or deselect it.
- Press and hold down the Alt key, and then press the underlined letter of the check box option.
- Use the Tab key to move to the check box. Then, press the space bar to toggle between selecting or clearing the check box.

Option buttons (sometimes called *radio buttons*) indicate choices within a group of mutually exclusive items. You can select only one option button at a time within a group. In the Print dialog box, for example, you can choose only one of the option buttons in the Print area near the bottom of the dialog box (refer to fig. 1.8). You can choose C_u_rrent Sheet, _E_ntire Workbook, or _S_elected Range, but not more than one of these items.

To select an option button, use one of these techniques:

- Click the option button to select it.
- Press and hold down the Alt key, and then press the underlined letter of the option button.
- Use the Tab key to move to the option button. Then, use the direction keys (such as ↑ or ↓) to move through the choices. Stop when you get to the option you want to choose.

Entering Information in Text Boxes

A text box is a box in which you type information, such as worksheet ranges or file names. 1-2-3 includes several types of text boxes in which you can type and edit text. Text boxes can appear with or without arrows or a range selector (described in the next section). When text boxes appear alone, you enter information in the box. Sometimes, 1-2-3 places a default entry in a text box, which you can change as needed.

Use Tab to move to a text box. The suggested text entry is highlighted so that you can easily type over it.

Use one of these techniques to enter information into a text box:

- If the text box is empty, click it. Then, type the information into it.
- To add text to an existing entry, click the location in which you want to make changes. Then, begin typing.
- If an existing text box entry is highlighted, you can begin typing to erase the existing entry and replace it with what you type.
- Double-click a word in a text box and begin typing to replace only that word. Or, you can click and drag across any letters in a text box that you want to type over, and begin typing to replace only those letters with new text.

NOTE If a text box includes arrows beside it (such as the Number of _C_opies option shown in figure 1.8), you can either type a new number directly into the text box (using one of the methods described above), or you can click the up or down arrow next to the box to increase or decrease the number.

Using the Range Selector

Some text boxes include a range selector, as shown below the Selected Range option in figure 1.8. This means that you can either click the text box and type a range from the worksheet (for example A1..Z20); or you can click the range selector to select a range from the worksheet with the mouse.

To use the range selector to fill in a text box, follow these steps:

1. Click the range selector. 1-2-3 switches temporarily to your worksheet.
2. Move the mouse pointer over the first cell in the range you want to select. Press and hold down the mouse button and drag over the range you want to select.
3. When you release the mouse button, 1-2-3 switches back to the dialog box and the range you selected appears in the text box. You can repeat these steps if you want to choose a different range.

Selecting Items from List Boxes

List boxes display lists of choices. You can select only one choice from a list box. If the item you want to choose in a list box is visible, click it to select it.

If a list box has more choices than it can display, you can scroll through the list box and see all the choices. Click the scroll arrows (the up and down arrows) or drag the scroll box in the scroll bar, or click the scroll bar to scroll the list. When you see the option you want, click it to select it.

Some list boxes display an arrow to the right of the list box instead of a scroll bar. Click the arrow to display a drop-down list of choices. Select the desired choice from the drop-down list to select it and move it to the list box.

SmartIcon Basics

SmartIcons are on-screen buttons that you can use to access many 1-2-3 tasks quickly and easily. Instead of moving through several layers of menus to choose commands, you can click a SmartIcon to initiate the action. You need a mouse to use SmartIcons; they cannot be accessed from the keyboard.

The SmartIcon bar appears at the top of the screen by default. To move a SmartIcon bar, position the mouse pointer over the blue bar (on the left side of a group of SmartIcons), and drag the bar to another edge of the screen. You can also drag a SmartIcon bar onto the worksheet to create a floating bar.

▶ **See** "Using SmartIcon Bars," **p. 766**

1-2-3 provides approximately 300 different SmartIcons for your use. Many commonly used SmartIcons are grouped together into bars that you can display on-screen. You can usually fit more than one group of SmartIcons within the SmartIcon bar. When you start 1-2-3 97, both the Universal SmartIcons and the Sheet SmartIcons appear in the SmartIcon bar.

The default SmartIcons that appear on-screen sometimes change, depending on the action you are performing. For example, when you add a chart to the worksheet (or click an existing chart), the Chart SmartIcons automatically appear in the SmartIcon bar. You aren't limited to the SmartIcons displayed by default; you can add existing SmartIcons to the SmartIcon bar, or you can create custom SmartIcons to execute macros that you create.

▶ **See** "Customizing the SmartIcons," **p. 768**

To use a SmartIcon, follow these steps:

1. Depending on the purpose of the SmartIcon, select the data, rows, columns, or other worksheet element that you want to work on, if applicable.
2. Place the mouse pointer over the SmartIcon. A short description of the SmartIcon's function appears in a yellow "bubble" on-screen (see fig. 1.10).
3. Click the left mouse button to invoke the SmartIcon's action.

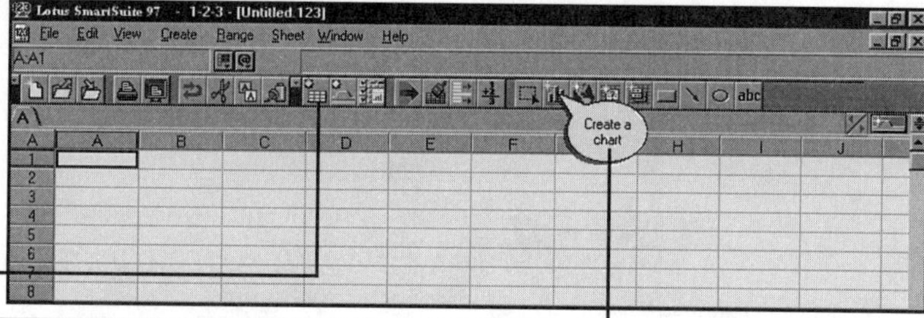

Fig. 1.10
The customizable SmartIcon bar allowed us to add the Range Properties button. Yours may look different.

Manipulating Windows

You use the 1-2-3 application window to display and work with 1-2-3 workbooks. You can change the size and position of the 1-2-3 window or a Workbook window by using the mouse or the keyboard. You can enlarge a window to fill the entire screen, reduce the window to a smaller size, or shrink the window to an icon. 1-2-3 also enables you to easily move a window, switch among windows, and close a window. In addition, you can arrange the windows for easier viewing by cascading or tiling the windows.

Because Windows enables you to display and run multiple applications at one time, you may also want to display windows from other applications as you use 1-2-3. In addition to

1-2-3 97, for example, you may also want to run other applications such as Word Pro 97 and Windows Explorer. To use all these applications together effectively, you need to understand how to organize and manipulate your Windows applications and 1-2-3 workbooks.

Switching Between Applications

You can work in an application or workbook only when the window is active. An active window has a dark title bar. If you are running 1-2-3 97 with other applications, Windows 95 enables you to easily switch between these applications by using the Taskbar (see fig. 1.11). The Windows 95 Taskbar normally appears on-screen by default, unless you (or someone else) has selected an option to hide the Taskbar.

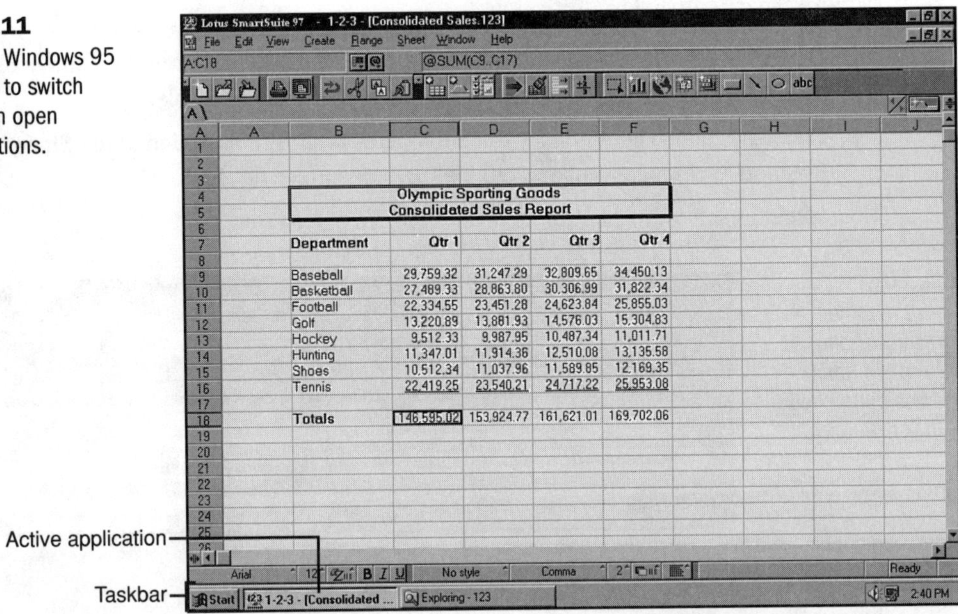

Fig. 1.11
Use the Windows 95 Taskbar to switch between open applications.

NOTE If you don't see the Windows 95 Taskbar at the bottom of your screen while you are running 1-2-3 97 (look for the Start button in the lower-left corner), move the mouse pointer to the bottom of the screen and pause. If the Taskbar still doesn't appear, press Ctrl+Esc to display the Taskbar along with the available Start menu options. ■

The Windows 95 Taskbar displays a button for each open application. To switch to another open application, click the appropriate button on the Taskbar. If you need to access an application that is not currently open, click the Start button on the Taskbar, navigate to the program you want to open, and click the name of the program. Refer to your Windows

95 documentation or on-screen Help if you need more specific information (click the Start button on the Taskbar, then click the Help option).

You can cycle among open applications by holding down the Alt key, and pressing Tab until you see the application you want to activate. Then release both keys.

If your display shows multiple application windows on-screen at one time, you can switch to another application window by clicking the window to activate it.

Switching Between Windows

When you choose the Window command from the main menu, 1-2-3 lists up to nine open windows at the bottom of the Window menu; a check mark appears next to the active window's name. To make another window active, type the number displayed next to the window name, or click the number in the menu with the mouse. If you have more than nine open windows, you can display the names of the additional windows by using the Window, More Windows command (which appears only if more than nine windows are open).

You can make another window active without using the Window menu. To cycle through the open windows in the 1-2-3 window, activating each window in turn, press Ctrl+F6 (Next). You also can activate a window (if it is visible on-screen) by clicking anywhere in that window.

Using the Control Menu

Every window in 1-2-3 has a Control menu in the upper-left corner of the window. This menu is similar to the Control menu available in other Windows 95 applications. The *1-2-3 Control menu* (also called the *Application Control menu*) enables you to manipulate the size and position of the 1-2-3 window, and close the 1-2-3 window (see fig. 1.12).

The menu shown in figure 1.11 has six options, but Move, Size, and Maximize are *dimmed* (or *grayed*); this means that their functions are currently unavailable. Because 1-2-3 is running as a full-screen application (that is, it is *maximized*) in this figure, the three grayed choices are inappropriate. If you are running 1-2-3 in a partial-screen window or have reduced it to an icon (that is, you have *minimized* the window), different choices on this menu are dimmed, indicating that they are currently unavailable.

To access the 1-2-3 Control menu with the mouse, click the 1-2-3 Control menu icon and then click the command you want to activate.

To access the 1-2-3 Control menu with the keyboard, follow these steps:

1. Press Alt and then the space bar.

2. Type the underlined letter of the command; or, use the arrow keys to highlight the command and then press Enter.
3. If you chose a command such as Move or Size, use the direction keys to move or size the 1-2-3 window.

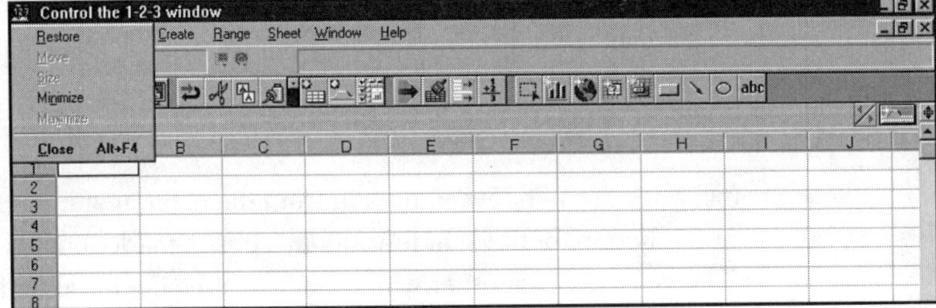

Fig. 1.12
Use the 1-2-3 Control menu to manipulate the 1-2-3 window.

To close the 1-2-3 Control menu by using the keyboard, press Esc twice. To close the 1-2-3 Control menu with the mouse, click anywhere outside the menu.

The *Workbook Control menu* controls the size and position of the Workbook window. You can access it through the *Workbook Control menu icon* in the upper-left corner of the Workbook window. Although similar to the 1-2-3 Control menu, the Workbook Control menu applies only to its own Workbook window. The Workbook Control menu includes an additional option, the Next option (which switches between active 1-2-3 Workbook windows). Figure 1.13 shows the Workbook Control menu.

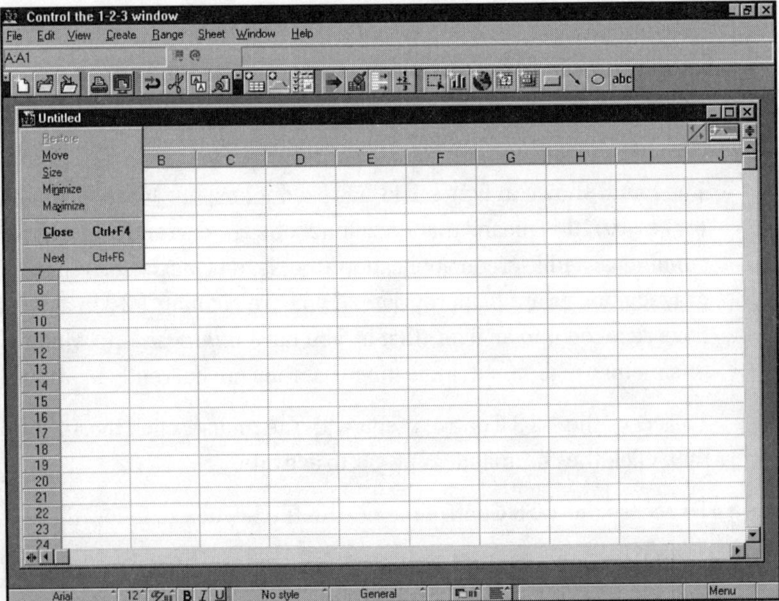

Fig. 1.13
Use the Workbook Control menu to move and size a specific Workbook window.

The 1-2-3 Control menu controls the 1-2-3 window; the Workbook Control menu controls a single Workbook window within the 1-2-3 window.

To activate the Workbook Control menu with the mouse, click the Workbook Control menu icon and then click the command you want to activate.

To access the Workbook Control menu with the keyboard, press Alt+ - (hyphen). To select a command, type the underlined letter of the command; or, use the arrow keys to highlight the command and then press Enter.

To close the Workbook Control menu by using the keyboard, press Esc twice. To close the Workbook Control menu with the mouse, click anywhere outside the menu.

Minimizing, Maximizing, and Restoring Windows

If you typically open many applications or workbooks at one time, you might find that your computer desktop often becomes too cluttered. To gain more space, you can store applications or Workbook windows by minimizing them so that they become small buttons at the bottom of the screen.

When you need one of the applications or workbooks that has been minimized, you can restore the button to its former window location and size. When you want a window to fill the entire available display area, you can maximize it. The icons for minimizing and maximizing are shown in figure 1.3, earlier in this chapter.

To maximize an application or Workbook window using the mouse, click the Maximize icon for the active window or double-click the title bar of the window. To maximize an application or Workbook window using the keyboard, press Alt+ - (hyphen) to display the Workbook Control menu, or press Alt+space bar to display the Application Control menu, and then choose the Maximize command.

You can minimize application or Workbook windows so that they are stored temporarily at the bottom of the screen. To minimize a window using the mouse, click the Minimize icon. Using the keyboard, press Alt+ - (hyphen) to display the Workbook Control menu or press Alt+space bar to display the Application Control menu, and then choose the Minimize command.

You can restore 1-2-3 and Workbook windows from their maximized or minimized sizes to their preceding window size and location. If 1-2-3 or a workbook has been converted to a button at the bottom of the screen, click it. If 1-2-3 or a Workbook window is maximized, click the Restore (double box) icon at the right side of the 1-2-3 or workbook title bar to restore it to its earlier window size. Using the keyboard, press Alt+space bar to select the

1-2-3 Control menu, or press Alt+ - (hyphen) to select the Workbook Control menu, and then choose the Restore command.

TROUBLESHOOTING

My Workbook window suddenly disappeared—where did it go? You might have accidentally minimized the window containing the workbook. Depending on what other workbooks are open, you might not be able to see the minimized window. The easiest way to find your workbook again is to open the Window menu and choose the workbook from the list at the bottom of the menu.

Moving Windows

If a window obstructs part of the screen you want to see, you may want to temporarily move it to another area of the display. You cannot move an application or Workbook window that is maximized; you must either minimize or restore a window before you can move it.

To move a window using the mouse, click the title bar and drag the window to its new location. Release the mouse button to fix the window in its new location.

To move a window using the keyboard, activate the Control menu (for the application or window you want to move), and choose the Move command. When the black four-headed arrow appears, use the direction keys to move the outline of the window. Press Enter to fix the window in its new location, or press Esc to retain its original location.

Sizing Windows

You can change the size of a window if you only want to see part of an application or Workbook window. You cannot size an application or Workbook window that is maximized; you must either minimize or restore a window before you can size it.

To size a window using the mouse, drag the window's edge or corner to the location you want, and then release the mouse button.

To size a window using the keyboard, activate the Control menu (for the application or window you want to size), and choose the Size command. When the black four-headed arrow appears, press the arrow key that points to the edge you want to move. Press the arrow keys to move that edge to its new location. Press Enter to fix the window in its new location, or press Esc to retain its original location.

Cascading Windows

Choose the Window, Cascade command or click the Cascade Windows SmartIcon to arrange open windows so that they appear on top of one another, with only their title bars and the left edges of the windows showing (see fig. 1.14). The active window always appears on top. To use the keyboard to switch between cascaded windows, press Ctrl+F6 (Next). To use the mouse, click the title bar or the edge of the window you want to see. You can change the size and location of the cascaded windows as described in the preceding sections.

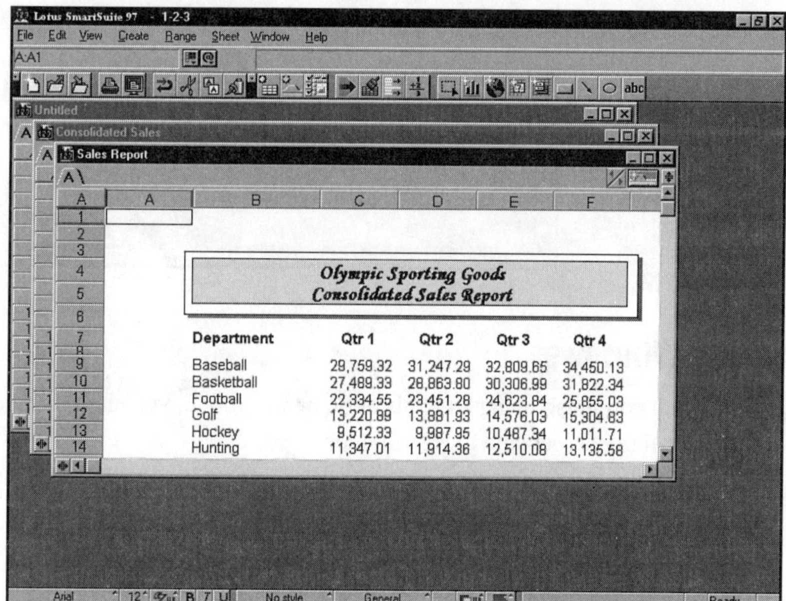

Fig. 1.14
Use Window, Cascade to display overlapping windows.

Tiling Windows

When you select Window, Tile Left-Right, or Window, Tile Top-Bottom (or click one of the corresponding SmartIcons), 1-2-3 sizes and arranges all open windows side by side, like floor tiles. The Window, Tile Left-Right command arranges all open windows vertically; the Window, Tile Top-Bottom command arranges all open windows horizontally (see fig. 1.15). The active window's title bar has a dark background. To use the keyboard to switch between tiled windows, press Ctrl+F6 (Next); to use the mouse, click the window you want. You can change the size and location of the tiled windows as described earlier in this chapter.

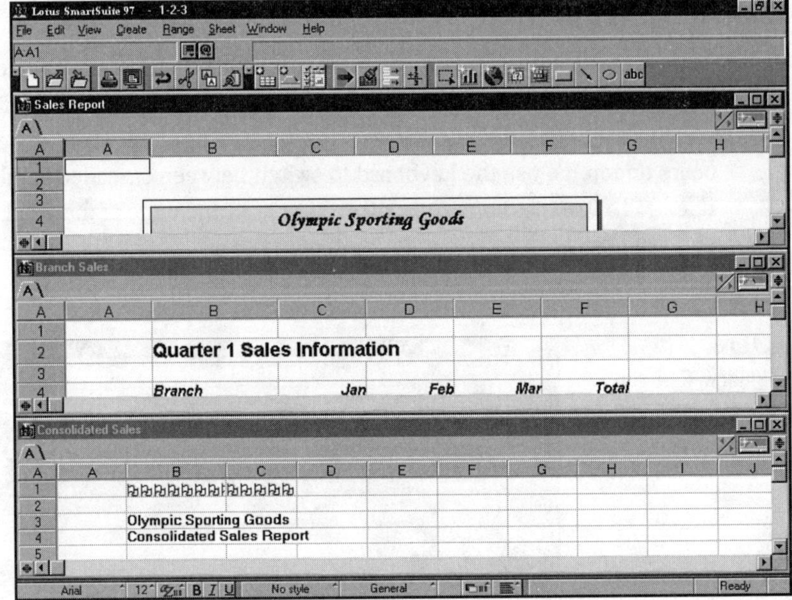

Fig. 1.15
You can tile windows to see portions of each open Workbook window on-screen.

Closing Windows

When you finish using an application or workbook, you should close its window to remove it from the screen and to free memory.

To close an active workbook using a mouse, click the Close icon (the X) that appears at the right end of the Workbook window (or at the right end of the menu bar, if the Workbook window is maximized). You also can double-click the Workbook Control icon to close the active workbook.

To close an active workbook using the keyboard, press Alt+ - (hyphen) to select the Workbook Control menu, and then choose the Close command.

If you have made any changes since the last time you saved the workbook, 1-2-3 displays an alert dialog box, as shown in figure 1.16, asking whether you want to save your work before closing.

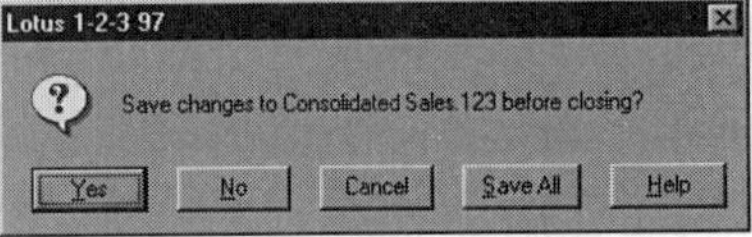

Fig. 1.16
If you try to close a window without saving the latest changes, 1-2-3 prompts you to save the file.

CAUTION

The difference between closing a Workbook window and closing an entire workbook is important. If more than one window is open on a workbook, you can close the active window without closing the file. However, if there is only one workbook window or if you choose File, Close, you also close the file that contains the entire workbook.

▶ **See** "Closing Workbooks," **p. 270**

Getting Help

1-2-3 provides many different forms of Help information to assist you:

- *1-2-3 Guided Tour*. The guided tour is an animated presentation that shows you some of the major features available in 1-2-3. You can access it by choosing Help, Tour from within 1-2-3.
- *Lotus Assistants*. Use Lotus Assistants when you need to complete certain more complex tasks, such as creating dynamic crosstabs. Assistants provide detailed instructions each step of the way.
- *QuickDemos*. The QuickDemos are animated demonstrations that provide a visual alternative for learning how to use specific tasks in 1-2-3.
- *Online Help*. This is the online, context-sensitive help that you can access at any time while using 1-2-3. You can be in the middle of any operation and press F1 (Help) to display one or more screens of explanations and advice.

Lotus also provides additional support information via the Internet. You can access some of these Lotus Internet sites directly from within 1-2-3. Choose Help, Lotus Internet Support from the 1-2-3 main menu. In the resulting cascade menu, choose the desired option: Lotus Home Page, Lotus Customer Support, or Lotus FTP Site.

The following sections provide more detailed information on using Lotus Assistants, QuickDemos, and the online Help system.

Using Lotus Assistants

Lotus Assistants provide on-screen, step-by-step guidance throughout more complex tasks, as you are completing the task. You can easily move forward and backward between the steps of a task, redo a previous step, or exit the assistant at any time. Some of the more complex assistants use tabbed dialog boxes to provide more detailed information on a task.

Using QuickDemos

You can access the QuickDemo animated demonstration by selecting Demo Catalog from the Help Contents tab, or by clicking "Show me a demo" from specific Help topics themselves (see fig. 1.17). When you start a demo, you see a screen similar to the one shown in figure 1.18 (depending on the topic you choose).

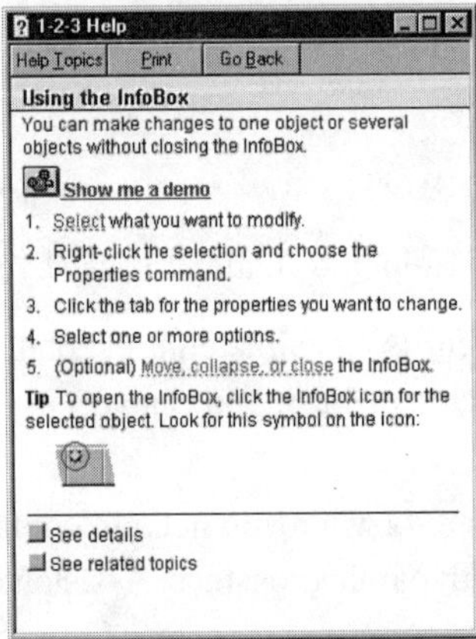

Fig. 1.17
Click "Show me a Demo" in a Help screen to access animated Help for a specific task.

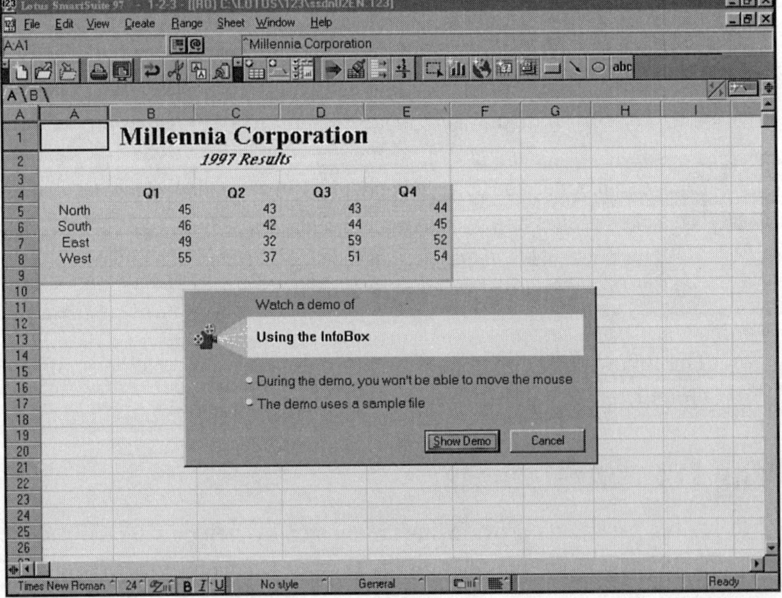

Fig. 1.18
A screen such as this appears when you start a demo.

1-2-3 97 includes demos for common tasks such as the following:

- *Using the InfoBox and SmartIcons.* Using the InfoBox, adding an icon to a set of SmartIcons.
- *Entering, annotating, and calculating data.* Filling a range using drag-and-fill, filling a range with dates, creating a cell comment, summing a range automatically.
- *Copying and moving data.* Copying and moving in a sheet, copying down to fill a range.
- *Naming sheets and ranges.* Naming a sheet, naming a range using adjacent labels.
- *Changing columns and rows.* Sizing columns, fitting the widest column entry, hiding columns, sizing rows, freezing columns and rows as titles.
- *Ordering and outlining data.* Sorting data, collapsing an outline to show less detail, expanding an outline to show more detail, demoting rows and columns.
- *Working with versions and version groups.* Creating a version, creating a version group.
- *Working with graphic objects.* Creating a text block, creating a map, adding an overlay.

Online Help

1-2-3 97 also provides extensive online Help information to guide you through commands and procedures. At any point in time, you can access Help to provide assistance, definitions of common tools, and tips you can use to perform a task quicker.

To look up a Help topic, choose Help, Help Topics (or press F1). The Help Topics window appears (see fig. 1.19). Click the Contents tab, then double-click the desired Help category. Continue double-clicking subtopics until the Help information you need appears on-screen. To print the displayed information, click the Print button. To close the 1-2-3 Help window, click the Close icon in the upper-right corner of the window.

You can press F1 at almost any time, even while you choose a command or edit a cell. The Help information that you receive is context-sensitive. If, for example, you are in the process of sorting a range of data and you press F1, 1-2-3 displays a Help window titled "Sorting Data."

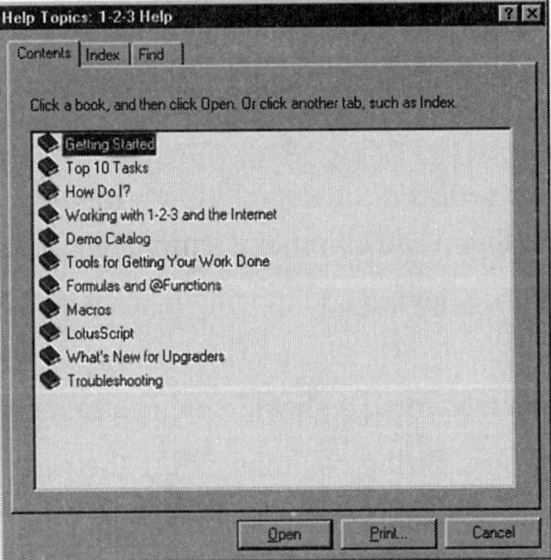

Fig. 1.19 Choose Help, Help Topics or press F1 to see the table of contents for the Help screens.

All Windows Help systems have a series of buttons across the top of the Help window that enable you to navigate in the Help screens. Choose a button by clicking it or pressing Alt followed by the underlined character. These buttons are described in the following table:

Button	Action
Help Topics	Shows the main screen of the Help Topics window.
Print	Displays the Print dialog box, enabling you to quickly print the contents of the displayed Help window.
Go Back	Returns to the preceding Help topic. If no previous Help topic exists, this button appears dimmed and is unavailable.

Searching for a Help Topic One of the most useful features of the Windows Help system is the capability to search for specific words or topics. To search for a specific topic in the Help screens, follow these steps:

1. Choose Help, Help Topics; then click the Find tab.

NOTE The first time you use Find, 1-2-3 builds a listing of Help terms. Follow the instructions provided with the Find Setup Wizard to complete the setup. This procedure may take a few minutes.

2. Type the word(s) you want to find in the top text box.
3. In the list box in the middle of the dialog box, select a word or phrase to narrow your search (see fig. 1.19).
4. The bottom list box displays topics related to the selected word or phrase. Select a topic and choose Display to jump to that topic, or double-click the topic in the bottom list to jump directly to it.

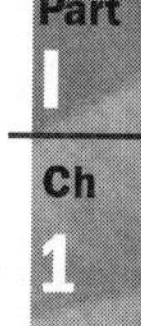

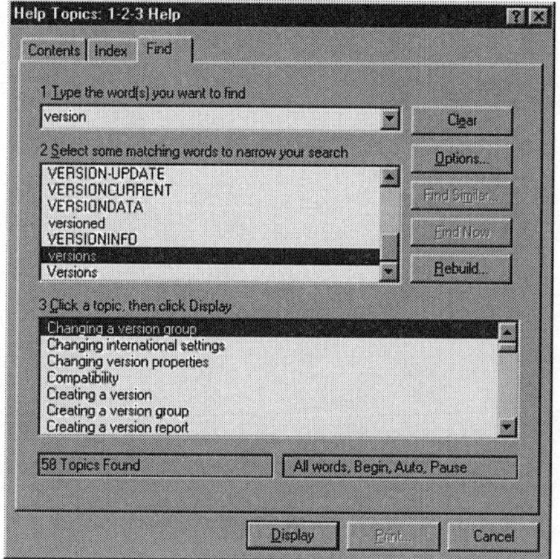

Fig. 1.20
Use the Find tab in the Help Topics dialog box to search for Help information on a specific topic.

NOTE You also can click the Index tab in step 1 (above) to access an alphabetical listing of all 1-2-3 Help topics. Type the first few letters of the topic you want Help on, and related topics appear in the bottom window. Select the topic you want to see and choose the Display button, or double-click the topic.

Jumping Between Help Topics Certain Help topics appear in a color or intensity different from the rest of the Help window (refer to fig. 1.16). If you place the mouse pointer on a colored topic, the pointer changes from an arrow to a hand with a pointing index finger. To see more information about one of these topics, click that topic.

Some of the different color topics have a dashed underline. These are glossary terms. If you click one of these topics, a definition of the term appears.

Getting Help in Dialog Boxes and InfoBoxes To display Help information for a dialog box while it is displayed, either press F1 (Help), or click the Help button in the dialog box (if one exists).

To display Help information for an InfoBox while it is displayed, either press F1 (Help), or click the question mark button in the upper-right corner of the InfoBox.

Closing the Help Window Because the Help information actually appears in a window, you need to close the Help window when you are finished with it. To close the Help window with the mouse, click the Close icon in the upper-right corner of the window. To close the Help window with the keyboard, activate the window and press Esc; or press Alt+space bar to activate the Control menu, and then choose Close.

CHAPTER 2

Navigating and Selecting 1-2-3

by Joyce J. Nielsen

All of your work in 1-2-3 is contained in *worksheets*; one or more worksheets comprise a *workbook*. In this chapter, you learn how to create a new workbook, as well as how to save and open workbooks. You also learn how to create workbooks containing multiple worksheets.

To use 1-2-3 skillfully, you need to be able to maneuver from cell to cell and worksheet to worksheet with ease. In this chapter, you also learn a variety of methods for moving the cell pointer around in a workbook.

At various times when you are using 1-2-3, you will need to refer to rectangular collections of cells, called *ranges*. You can define ranges by their cell addresses, as well as through a method called "naming ranges," assigning descriptive text such as "Qtr4" or "Western Region" to represent these rectangular collections. ■

Understanding workbooks and worksheets

A 1-2-3 workbook is composed of one or more worksheets. You will learn how to open and save workbooks, and use and display multiple worksheets in a workbook.

Moving around in a worksheet

1-2-3 provides many options for navigating the worksheet, whether you prefer using the keyboard or the mouse.

Working with cells and ranges

You will learn how to select cells and ranges so you can then perform actions on the selection. If you assign a name to a cell or range, you can reference the name in formulas.

Understanding Workbooks and Worksheets

You can think of a worksheet as the electronic version of one page of a large ledger pad or one piece of graph paper: it is a page containing boxes (or *cells*) into which you can place information. The ledger pad itself would be considered the *workbook*, containing multiple pages, or *worksheets*. To create a new, blank workbook when you start 1-2-3, you choose the Create a Blank Workbook button in the Welcome to 1-2-3 dialog box. The blank workbook appears with the name `Untitled` (see fig. 2.1).

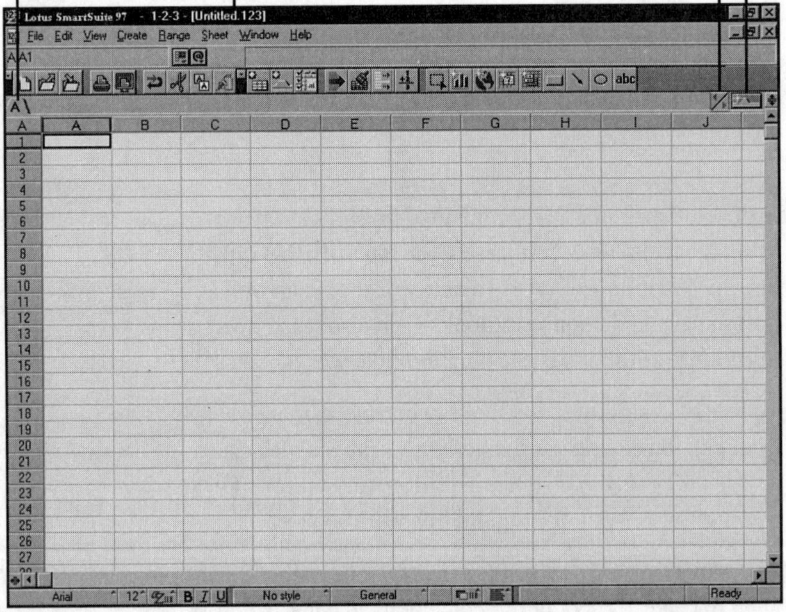

Worksheet tab

Name of worksheet

Tab-scroll arrows

New Sheet button

Fig. 2.1
A new, blank workbook as it appears when you start 1-2-3 and choose Create a Blank Workbook.

▶ **See** "Starting and Exiting 1-2-3," **p. 14**

▶ **See** "Saving Workbooks," **p. 265**

Notice that a *worksheet tab* containing the letter `A` appears above the top left corner of the workbook. You can add as many as 255 more worksheets (also called *sheets*) to the workbook. Each additional worksheet is identified by a different letter. The identification scheme is similar to the scheme used for worksheet columns; columns are labeled A through Z, then AA through AZ, BA through BZ, and so on, out to column IV, 256 columns to the right. Similarly, the first worksheet is A; the second is B; the 27th is AA; and so on. The sequence continues to IV, the 256th worksheet in the file. Together, these 256 (or fewer) worksheets are considered to be a workbook. You can enter data into one or more worksheets in a workbook and then save your work in a file on disk using a single file name for the entire workbook. After you save the workbook, the title bar displays the file name.

Figure 2.2 shows the workbook named Quarterly Sales, which contains two worksheets, labeled A and B. The section titled "Using Multiple Worksheets," which appears later in this chapter, includes information on how to change the tabs so that, instead of displaying the worksheet letters, they can display more descriptive information like "Jan," "Feb," "Mar," or "North," "South," and so on.

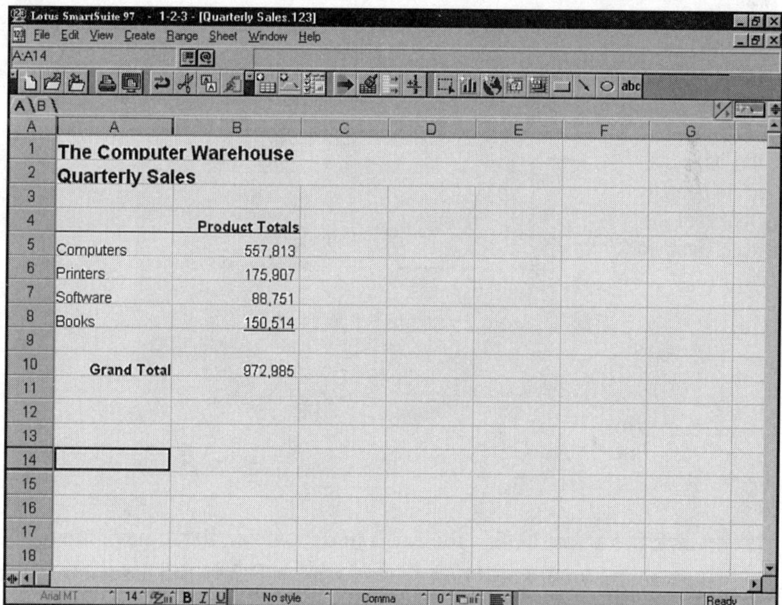

Fig. 2.2
This Quarterly Sales workbook contains two worksheets.

Opening and Saving a Workbook

Although you can create a blank workbook when you start 1-2-3, you will eventually need to open other (existing) workbooks. You also may need to start a new workbook and save it for future use. In 1-2-3, you can open a workbook at any time and even view two or more separate workbooks at the same time.

NOTE The following sections briefly explain the procedures for opening and saving workbooks. These procedures are described in greater detail in Chapter 9, "Managing Files."

Opening New and Existing Workbooks If you are beginning a new fiscal year, you might decide to start a new workbook, rather than add another worksheet to an existing workbook. To start a new, blank workbook, choose the File, New Workbook command or click the Create a New Workbook SmartIcon. 1-2-3 displays a new workbook without removing any other open files from memory. The new workbook initially includes only one worksheet. As explained in Chapter 1, you can rearrange individual workbooks (windows) and even minimize them to accommodate multiple files in the 1-2-3 window.

▶ **See** "Manipulating Windows," **p. 31**

You also can open workbooks that you created and saved previously. To open an existing file, choose the OpenFile, Open command or click the Open an Existing File SmartIcon. The Open dialog box appears (see fig. 2.3).

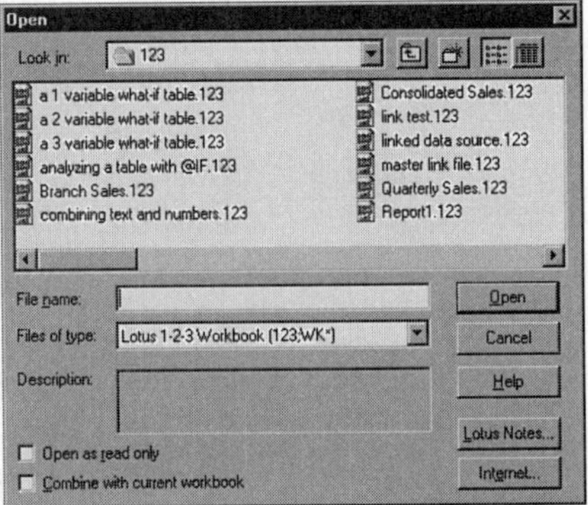

Fig. 2.3
Use the Open dialog box to open a workbook that you already created and saved.

Click the arrow beside the Look In drop-down list to navigate to the drive and directory containing your workbook (if necessary). Select the file name; the name appears in the File Name text box. Choose the Open button to open the workbook. Alternatively, you can double-click the file name when it appears in the window just below the Look In drop-down list.

▶ **See** "Opening Existing Workbooks," **p. 271**

▶ **See** "Saving Workbooks," **p. 265**

TROUBLESHOOTING

I want to open a workbook that I created in an earlier version of 1-2-3, but I don't see it in the Open dialog box. Where did it go? 1-2-3 97 uses a different default directory than previous versions, so your older files won't automatically appear when you display the Open dialog box. Click the Look In drop-down list in the Open dialog box to switch to the drive and directory containing the file.

Saving Workbooks When you build a new workbook or make changes in an existing one, all the new work exists only in the computer's memory. If you do not save new worksheets or changes before you quit 1-2-3, you lose that work. (1-2-3 provides a warning, asking you whether you want to save the file before closing.)

When you *save* a file, you copy the file in memory to the disk and give the file a name. The file remains on disk after you quit 1-2-3 or turn off the computer.

To save changes in an existing file, choose File, Save, or click the Save the Current File SmartIcon. 1-2-3 automatically updates the file on disk to include whatever alterations you made.

When you want to name a new file, or when you want to save an existing file with a new name while keeping the old file intact, use the File, Save As command. 1-2-3 displays the Save As dialog box that enables you to save the file (see fig. 2.4).

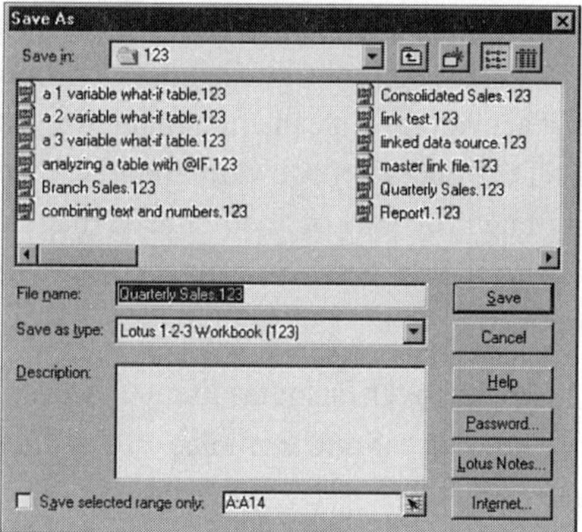

Fig. 2.4
Use the Save As dialog box to assign a name to a new workbook.

Using Multiple Worksheets

Occasionally, you need only one worksheet to analyze and store data. At other times, however, you need to use multiple worksheets to organize your information effectively. Some applications are especially well-suited to multiple worksheets. For example, multiple worksheets are ideal for consolidations. If you need a worksheet that tracks data for several departments, you can create a separate worksheet for each department and store all the worksheets as individual sheets in the same file. Each worksheet is smaller (and easier to understand and use) than a large worksheet containing all the data for all of the departments. You can enter into a cell in any worksheet a formula that refers to cells in the other worksheets.

▶ **See** "Linking Worksheets and Files with Formulas," **p. 483**

Use multiple worksheets for any consolidations that contain separate parts, such as products, countries, projects, or quarterly data. Although you can accomplish many of these objectives by putting data in separate files, creating and maintaining separate files is more difficult than keeping all the data in a single workbook with multiple sheets.

Another example of a multiple sheet workbook is a file in which each worksheet represents the activity for a month. Twelve worksheets contain the data for an entire year; and a 13th worksheet, placed before or after the others, represents a consolidation of data for all 12 months.

You also can use multiple worksheets to place separate sections of data in separate worksheets. You can, for example, place input areas, data ranges, formulas, assumptions, constants, and macros in separate worksheets. You then can customize each worksheet for a particular purpose. This technique of organizing data includes using global formats and setting column widths and row heights, as described in Chapter 4, "Formatting Worksheets."

Breaking your large applications into separate sheets in a workbook has other advantages. As long as Group mode is not activated, you can change one worksheet without accidentally changing the others. If all the data is in one worksheet, you could insert or delete a row or column in one area and destroy part of another area that shares the same row or column. If you use multiple worksheets, however, you can insert and delete rows and columns anywhere without affecting other parts of the file.

Another common accident is writing over formulas in input areas. When you use multiple worksheets, you can separate input areas and formulas so that this error is less likely to occur.

Commands or actions related to multiple worksheets include the following:

- *Insert one or more woorksheets* before or after the current worksheet by choosing Create, Sheet. A fast way to insert a worksheet after the current worksheet is to click the Insert a Sheet SmartIcon.

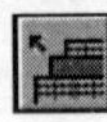

- *Remove a worksheet* by choosing Sheet, Delete Sheet after first selecting the worksheet you want to delete. You can delete selected worksheets quickly by clicking the Delete Selected Sheets SmartIcon.
- *Assign descriptive names to the tabs* by double-clicking the worksheet tab, typing a name, and pressing Enter. Move among the various worksheets by clicking their worksheet tabs.
- *Show or hide the worksheet tabs* by choosing View, Set View Preferences. Then select or deselect the Sheet Tabs option on the View tab in the Workbook Properties dialog box.

- *Group several or all worksheets in a workbook* so that some commands affect the whole group, not just the current worksheet, by using the Sheet, Group Sheets command and then specifying the sheets you want to group in the Group Sheets dialog box.

  ▶ **See** "Grouping Worksheets," **p. 258**

- *Customize a worksheet's tab* by double-clicking the tab and then typing the desired name. For example, you might name the sheets Jan, Feb, Mar, and so on. You can enter as many as 255 characters, but it's best to use short, descriptive names.

Moving Around in a Worksheet

You can enter data only at the location of the cell pointer. Because you can display only a small part of the worksheet at one time, you must know how to move the cell pointer to see other parts of the worksheet. The following sections focus on moving the cell pointer within a single worksheet and between worksheets in a workbook.

Navigating with the Mouse

To use the mouse to scroll the worksheet without moving the cell pointer, click one of the arrows in the scroll bars at the right and bottom edges of the worksheet. If you click an arrow one time, the worksheet scrolls one column or row in the direction of the arrow, and the cell pointer doesn't move. If you click an arrow and hold down the mouse button, the worksheet scrolls continuously in the direction of the arrow until you release the mouse button.

As you click the left or right arrows in the horizontal scroll bar, you will notice a small square, the scroll box, slide along the scroll bar. You can also scroll from side to side by dragging this box along the scroll bar and releasing it in a new position. As you drag a scroll box, a small box appears on-screen, which indicates the current position of the row or column. Finally, if you click the scroll bar to the right or left of the scroll box, you will shift your view one full screen to the right or left. You can perform the analogous tasks using the vertical scroll bar, located on the right side of the screen.

Navigating with the Keyboard

The arrow keys that move the cell pointer are located in the numeric keypad (or also in a separate keypad on an enhanced keyboard). The cell pointer moves in the direction of the arrow on the key. If you hold down the arrow key, the cell pointer continues to move in the direction of the arrow key. When the cell pointer reaches the edge of the screen, the worksheet continues to scroll in the direction of the arrow, with the cell pointer visible on-screen.

NOTE If you press an arrow key to move the cell pointer and your screen moves in an unexpected manner, you may have pressed the Scroll Lock key accidentally. Check to see if the Scroll Lock indicator on your keyboard is lit. If it is, press Scroll Lock once to deactivate this feature. ■

You can use several other direction keys to move around the current worksheet one screen at a time. Press the PgUp or PgDn key to move up or down one screen. Press Ctrl+→ to move one screen to the right; press Ctrl+← to move one screen to the left. The size of one screen depends on the size of the worksheet window.

Pressing the Home key moves the cell pointer directly to the *home position*, usually cell A1 of the current worksheet. In Chapter 15, you learn how to lock titles on-screen. Locked titles affect the location of the home position. Pressing End and then Home moves the cell pointer to the last active cell in the current worksheet.

▶ **See** "Freezing Worksheet Titles," **p. 392**

Two direction keys, PgUp and PgDn, are especially important for moving around a workbook. Ctrl+PgUp moves the cell pointer to the last highlighted cell in the following worksheet, and Ctrl+PgDn moves the cell pointer to the last highlighted cell in the preceding worksheet.

End Ctrl+Home moves the cell pointer to the end of the active area of the last worksheet in a file (similar to End+Home in a single worksheet).

End Ctrl+PgUp and End Ctrl+PgDn move the cell pointer up or down through the worksheets to the next cell that contains data (similar to End+↑ and End+↓ in a single worksheet).

The End key is used to move to the intersections of blank cells and cells that contain data. Suppose cells A5 through A50 *all* contain data. If your cell pointer is in cell A5 and you press the End key and then the down arrow key, the cell pointer will move to cell A50, the last cell containing data, just before a blank cell. If you then press End and the up arrow, you will move to cell A5, again the last cell containing data, just before a blank cell. If you start at A1 and press End and the down arrow, the cell pointer will move to cell A5, the first filled-in cell after blank cells. The End key works the same with the left- and up-arrow keys.

Tables 2.1 and 2.2 summarize the keys you can use to navigate your worksheets and workbooks.

Table 2.1 Direction Keys

Keys	Action
→ or ←	Moves right or left one column
↑ or ↓	Moves up or down one row
Ctrl+←	Moves left one worksheet screen
Ctrl+→	Moves right one worksheet screen
Ctrl+Home	Moves to the home position (usually cell A:A1) in the current workbook
PgUp or PgDn	Moves up or down one worksheet screen
Home	Moves to the home position in the current worksheet (usually cell A1)
End Home	Moves to the bottom right corner of the worksheet's active area
Ctrl+PgUp	Moves to the last highlighted cell in the following worksheet
Ctrl+PgDn	Moves to the last highlighted cell in the preceding worksheet
End+→	Moves right to the next intersection between a blank cell and a cell that contains data
End+←	Moves left to the next intersection between a blank cell and a cell that contains data
End+↑	Moves up to a cell that contains data and is next to a blank cell
End+↓	Moves down to a cell that contains data and is next to a blank cell
End Ctrl+Home	Moves to the bottom right corner of the current file's active area
End Ctrl+PgUp	Staying in the same row and column, moves back through worksheets to the next intersection between a blank cell and a cell that contains data
End Ctrl+PgDn	Staying in the same row and column, moves forward through worksheets to the next intersection between a blank cell and a cell that contains data

Table 2.2 Workbook Navigation Keys

Keys	Action
Ctrl+End Home	Moves to the cell last highlighted in the first open workbook
Ctrl+End End	Moves to the cell last highlighted in the last open workbook
Ctrl+End, Ctrl+PgUp	Moves to the cell last highlighted in the next open workbook
Ctrl+End, Ctrl+PgDn	Moves to the cell last highlighted in the preceding open workbook
Ctrl+F6	Makes the next open worksheet, graph, or transcript window active

Using the Goto Feature

The Goto feature enables you to jump directly to a specified cell in the current worksheet, to cells in other worksheets of the current workbook, or to any cell in any worksheet of any other open workbook. You can use *range names* with Goto so that you do not need to remember cell addresses. A *range* is a rectangular group of cells and can be three-dimensional, spanning several worksheets in a file. (For more information about ranges and range names, see "Working with Cells and Ranges" later in this chapter.)

You can access the Goto feature by choosing the Edit, Go To command, or pressing F5. When you choose Edit, Go To, the Go To dialog box appears (see fig. 2.5). In this dialog box, you specify in the Type of Object box what you want to find: a range, sheet, chart, map, drawn object, or other item. The specified ranges for that type of item appear in the list box in the center of the dialog box; you can select the name from this list. If you are moving to a range that you previously named with Range, Name, select the range name in the list box. When you choose OK, the cell pointer moves directly to this address.

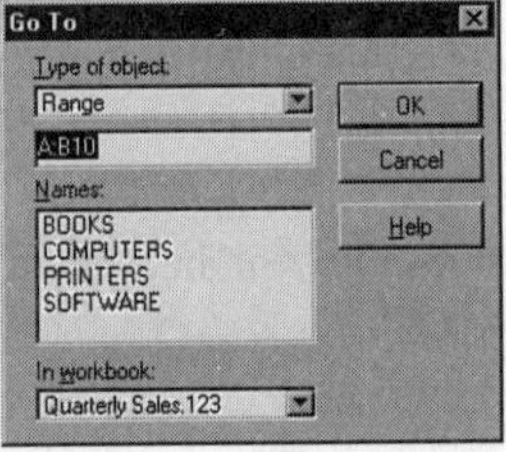

Fig. 2.5
The Go To dialog box enables you to quickly jump to a specified address or range name.

To move quickly to the desired range, double-click it in the list.

The Go To dialog box also contains the names of other open workbooks; to move the cell pointer to another file, choose the file name from the In Workbook list. All previously named ranges in the selected file appear in the Go To list box.

When you are in the Go To dialog box, to move to a specific cell in a specific worksheet in the chosen file, you need to type the worksheet letter and cell address. To move to cell B3 in worksheet C of the existing file, for example, type **C:B3** in the Range text box and choose OK.

An easier way to move to another workbook is to click the file (if the file is visible). If the file is hidden behind another window, press Ctrl+F6 repeatedly to cycle through the open windows until the file you want appears. Or, choose Window, and select the desired file name from the bottom of the drop-down menu.

Working with Cells and Ranges

A *range* is a rectangular group of cells in a worksheet. A single cell can be defined as a range. A column or row of adjacent cells can be defined as a range. A block of cells spanning worksheets in a file can also be defined as a range.

You define a range with the cell addresses of any two diagonally opposite corners of the range. When you specify a range address, you separate the cell addresses with one or two periods when typing, but two periods always appear when 1-2-3 displays the dimensions of a range. Notice in figure 2.6 that a range can be a single cell (E1..E1), part of a row (A1..C1), part of a column (G1..G5 and F14..F21), or a rectangle that spans multiple rows and columns (B4..E9 and A13..C15).

If you were to drag the cell pointer from A5 to B10, cell A5, the beginning cell of the range, is called the *anchor cell.* Cell B10, the end point of the range, is called the *free cell.* Whenever you highlight a range, the cell diagonally opposite the *anchor cell* is the *free cell.*

A range can also be three-dimensional, spanning two or more worksheets. A three-dimensional range includes the corresponding cells in each worksheet. When you use a three-dimensional range, you must include the worksheet letters with the cell addresses. For example, if cells A3 through D3 are highlighted in worksheets A, B, and C, the address of this range is A:A3..C:D3. For more information on three-dimensional ranges, see the "Using Three-Dimensional Ranges" section later in this chapter.

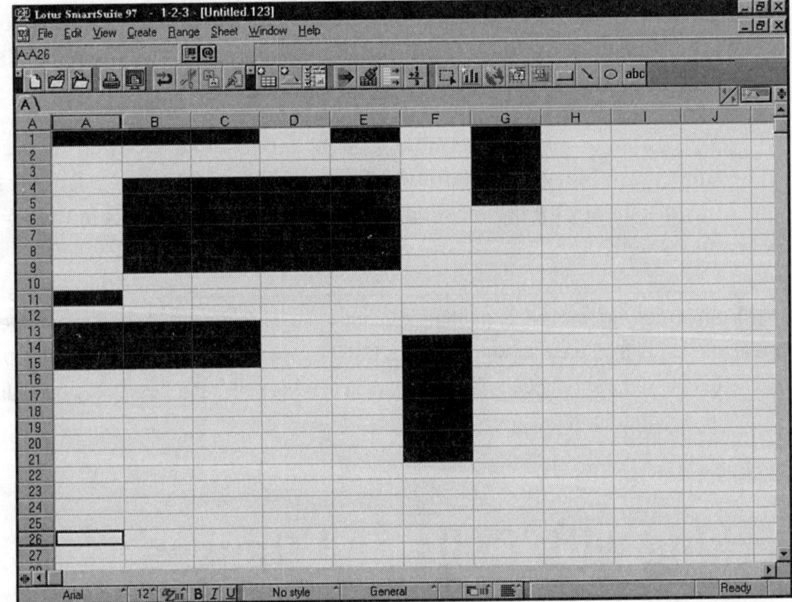

Fig. 2.6
You can use several different types of ranges in a worksheet.

Selecting a Single Cell

To select a single cell in a worksheet with the mouse (the easiest method), just click the cell you want to select. You may need to navigate to the portion of the worksheet containing the cell before you can use this method.

With the keyboard, use the keys listed in Table 2.1 to move to the desired cell.

Selecting a Range of Cells

Many commands act on ranges. For example, the Range, Sort command prompts you for the range you want to sort. When 1-2-3 prompts you for a range, you can respond in one of these ways:

- Highlight the range with the keyboard or the mouse either before or after you select the command.
- Highlight a group of ranges (a collection) with the keyboard or mouse, before or after you choose the command.
- Type the cell addresses of two of the opposite corners of the range or of the cells in the ranges. Separate the two references with two periods. For example, the range that includes cells A1, A2, B1, and B2 can be specified as A1..B2, B2..A1, A2..B1, or B1..A2. Normally, however, you indicate a range address by first specifying the cell

in the upper-left corner, followed by two periods, and then the cell in the bottom right corner (such as A1..B2, in this example).

The following sections describe these options in detail. If you have already assigned a name to a range, you can also specify the range name when prompted for a range. This topic is covered later in this chapter, in the section titled "Naming Ranges."

Highlighting a Range You can highlight a range by clicking the mouse pointer on a cell and dragging to highlight a range. This action is the most popular method of selecting a range. You can highlight a range with the keyboard or the mouse either before or after you issue a command. Special considerations for highlighting ranges in functions are covered in Chapter 6, "Using Functions."

1-2-3 enables you to highlight cells before you issue a command. When you *preselect cells* and then issue a command, the address automatically appears in the dialog box. You need not reenter the address.

To use the keyboard to preselect a range, press F4 and highlight the range by using the arrow keys. When you finish specifying the range, press Enter. Alternatively, using the Shift key can make the selection process even faster (this method also works if you select the range after you issue the command). Just move to the beginning of the range, press and hold the Shift key, and press the arrow keys as necessary to highlight the rest of the range. When finished, release the Shift key.

If you have a large range of contiguous cells containing data you want to highlight, use the End key along with the Shift key. Move to the beginning of the range (that is, its upper left cell) and press and hold the Shift key. Then press End, the right arrow, End again, and the down arrow. This technique assumes that the range is surrounded by blank cells and has no blank cells in either the top row nor the last column.

To highlight a range with the mouse, just click any corner of the range and drag to the diagonally opposite corner. All cells between the corners are highlighted. You also can click a corner once, press and hold the Shift key, and click the opposite corner once.

Highlighting Groups of Ranges You can highlight a group of ranges, called a *collection*. Highlight the first range using any method you like, and then press and hold the Ctrl key as you highlight other ranges. All ranges are highlighted as a collection. (Refer to fig. 2.6 to see a collection of highlighted ranges.)

When you press the Enter key, you move from cell to cell within the collection. Press Shift+Enter and you move backward within the collection.

To specify a collection as a reference (such as when you want to sum the numbers in A1..C1, E1, and G1..G5), you must separate each distinct range reference with a semicolon. For example, you can enter **A1..C1;E1;G1..G5;B4..E9;A11;A13..C15;F14..F21** to specify the collection shown in figure 2.6.

It is easier and more efficient to highlight a range before you issue a command, but if you forget to select a range, you can select one after you issue the command. When the command leads to a dialog box, you can type or point to the range by using the range selector within the dialog box. The range selector is described in Chapter 1.

Typing Range Addresses Typing the range address is probably the least used method of specifying ranges, because it is most prone to error. With this method, you type the addresses of any two cells in diagonally opposite corners of the range, separating the two addresses with one or two periods. (If you type only one period, 1-2-3 automatically inserts a second period to separate the addresses.) For example, to specify the range B4..E9, you can type **B4..E9** or **B4.E9**, or **E9..B4** or **E9.B4**. Or you can specify the other two corners: **E4..B9** (**E4.B9**), or **B9..E4** (**B9.E4**). No matter how you type the range, 1-2-3 stores it as B4..E9.

Naming Ranges

Another way to specify a range is to refer to the range by name. Range names, which should be descriptive, can include as many as 15 characters and can be used in formulas, functions, and commands. You can apply a range name by using the Range, Name command; a list of existing range names can be viewed by using the navigator on the edit line.

You can type or refer to a range name by using any combination of uppercase and lowercase letters, but 1-2-3 stores all range names as uppercase letters. Note the following rules and precautions for naming ranges:

- Do not use spaces, commas, semicolons, or the following characters:
  + - * / & > < @ # ? . {

NOTE Actually, range names can contain spaces, but they cannot begin with a space or an ! (exclamation point).

- You can use numbers in range names, but don't start the name with a number. TOTAL1 is okay, but 1TOTAL is not.
- Do not use range names that are also cell addresses, column letters, or row numbers (such as A2, IV, or 100), names of keys (such as GoTo), function names (such as @SUM), or macro commands (such as FORM).

Using range names has a number of advantages: Range names are easier to remember than addresses. Using a range name is usually faster than pointing to a range in another part of the worksheet. You can, for example, remember more easily that the sales totals are in a range named TOTALS instead of in cells G5..G12. Also, if you highlight a named range by dragging across it, its name appears in the selection indicator, below the menu bar.

Range names also make formulas easier to understand. For example, if you want to calculate a grand total from subtotals, you can give the range containing the subtotals a name and then use the range name in a formula that adds all the subtotals. As an example, you can enter into the contents box (on the edit line) the formula `@SUM(TOTALS)`. Because this formula uses a range name, it is equivalent to but easier to understand than the formula @SUM(A:G5..A:G12).

Whenever 1-2-3 expects the address of a cell or range, you can specify a range name, if one already exists. Three ways to specify a range name are available. You can type the range name in the dialog box, press F3 (Name) to display existing range names in all active workbooks, or click the navigator on the edit line. The navigator lists the range names in alphabetical order (see fig. 2.7). When you edit a formula and choose a range name from the navigator's range list, the range name is inserted into the formula.

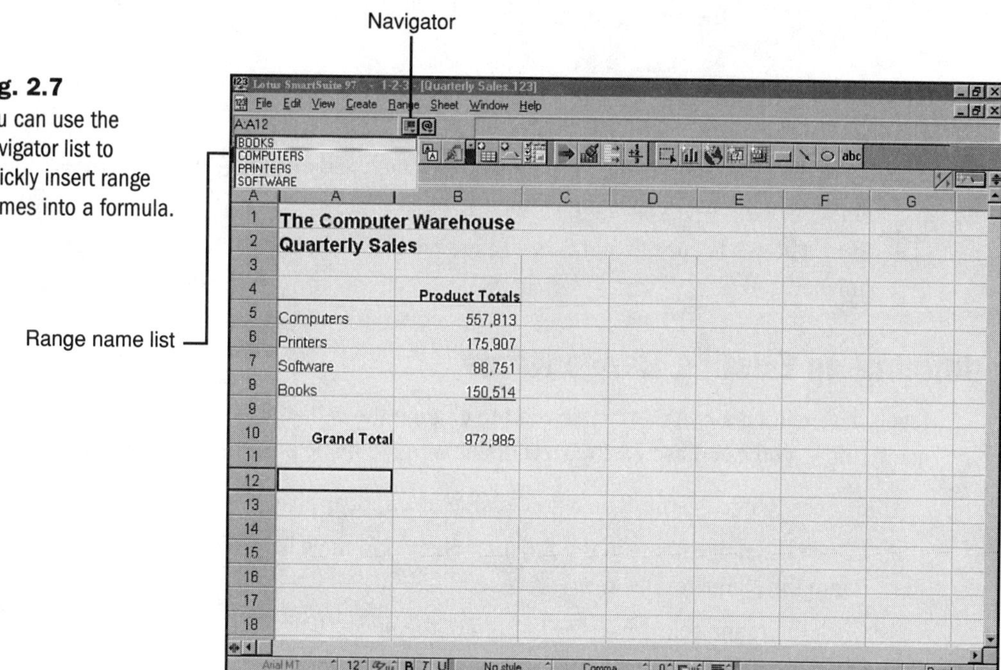

Fig. 2.7
You can use the navigator list to quickly insert range names into a formula.

Because a single cell is considered a valid range, you can name a single cell as a range. If a command or action, such as F5 (GoTo), calls for a single-cell address, you can specify the cell by typing its range name. If you type a range name that refers to a multiple-cell range when 1-2-3 calls for a single-cell address, 1-2-3 uses the upper-left corner of the range.

NOTE If you type a nonexistent range name, 1-2-3 displays an error message. Choose OK or press Esc to clear the error. Errors may occur when you use range names in formulas.

To create a range name, follow these steps:

1. Select the cell or range you want to name.
2. Choose Range, Name. The Name dialog box appears (see fig. 2.8).

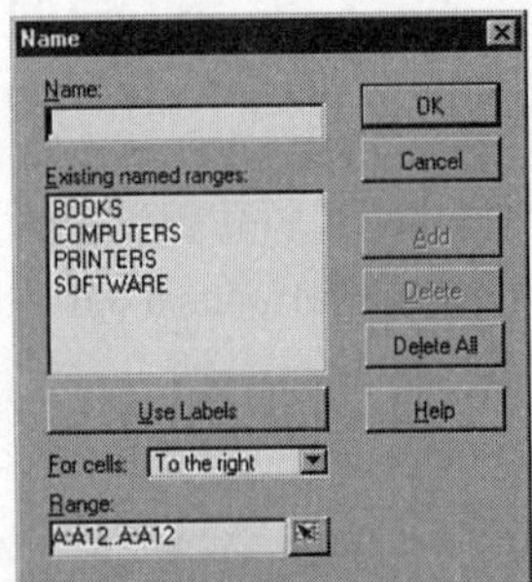

Fig. 2.8
Use the Name dialog box to create new range names.

3. Type the new range name in the Name text box, and choose Add. The range name appears in the list of Existing Named Ranges.
4. Repeat step 3 to specify additional range names, and choose OK when you are finished.

Redefining an Existing Range Name

If you have named a range but later want to change the cell addresses to which the range name refers, you can do so easily. To redefine a range name's address, follow these steps:

1. Choose Range, Name. The Name dialog box appears (refer to fig. 2.8).
2. Locate the range name in the Existing Named Ranges list. Click the name to insert it into the Name text box.
3. Click the range selector at the bottom of the dialog box.
4. Use any method to select the new range on the worksheet.

5. Choose OK to close the Name dialog box. The existing range name now refers to the new range of cells.

Creating Range Names from Labels

You can use the Range, Name command to create range names from labels already typed into the worksheet. In figure 2.9, for example, you can use the labels in cells A5..A8 to name the cells with sales data in B5..B8.

By choosing the Use Labels button in the Name dialog box, you can automatically create range names using column and row labels in the highlighted range. With the For Cells drop-down list in the Name dialog box, specify whether the cells to be named appear Above, Below, To the Right, or To the Left of the labels you want to use as range names.

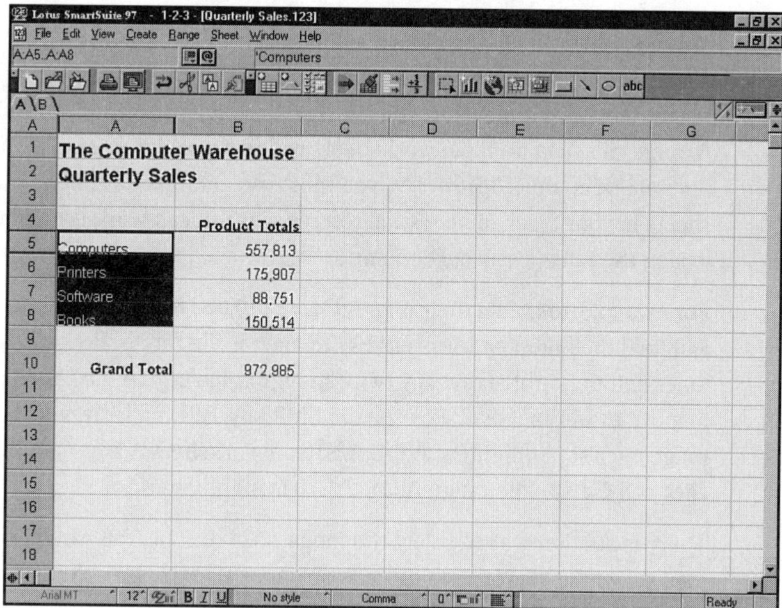

Fig. 2.9
The labels in the range A5..A8 can be used to name the cells in the adjacent column.

Suppose that you want to name the cells to the right of the labels in figure 2.9. In other words, you want to assign the range name "Computers" to cell B5, "Printers" to cell B6, and so on. Select cells A5..A8. Choose Range, Name, click the Use Labels button in the Name dialog box, and select To the Right from the For Cells list box. Then press Enter. You could also have selected the range after using the command but before choosing OK in the dialog box.

When you specify cells that contain labels you want to use as range names, only cells that contain labels are used. If you specify cells that are blank or that include numbers or formulas, 1-2-3 ignores them when it uses labels to name ranges. If you specified the range A4..A9 in the preceding example (see fig. 2.9), the blank cells in A4 and A9 are ignored.

To delete an unwanted range name, choose Range, Name and then select the name from the list of Existing Named Ranges. Then choose the Delete button. To delete all range names in a workbook, choose the Delete All button.

Using Three-Dimensional Ranges

Three-dimensional ranges are useful when you build consolidation worksheets. Consolidations are worksheets that combine data from different files, each of which contains data from one department, region, product, and so on.

A three-dimensional range has the shape of a three-dimensional rectangle. The first two dimensions include the height (number of rows) and width (number of columns) in the range. The third dimension, the depth, occurs when you add worksheets to the range. A range can span multiple worksheets within a workbook, giving you a range that goes several levels "deep." However, you must use contiguous sheets. That is, you cannot skip sheets in your three-dimensional references. You can work around this limitation by selecting the ranges as a collection.

For example, to create the range A:C4..C:E10, move the cell pointer to cell A:C4. Press and hold the Shift key (or press F4) to anchor the range. Press the down-arrow key six times and the right-arrow key twice to highlight A:C4..A:E10; then press Ctrl+PgUp twice to move to worksheet C. Release the Shift key. Alternatively, you can highlight the entire range by first highlighting A:C4..A:E10 on worksheet A and then hold the Shift key and click cell C:E10. The range A:C4..C:E10 is highlighted.

There is another way to select the range A:C4..C:E10. You can highlight A:C4..A:E10 and then select the corresponding cells on pages B and C by holding the Shift key and clicking the C worksheet tab.

You also can select three-dimensional ranges by first grouping worksheets together. When worksheets are grouped, range selections applied to one worksheet occur in all the worksheets simultaneously. Using this feature, you can avoid moving between worksheets and can use the mouse more easily.

▶ **See** "Grouping Worksheets," **p. 258**

Highlighting a three-dimensional range is much easier than typing the corner addresses. If you do type the addresses, make sure that you use the correct worksheet letters. The corners of a three-dimensional range are diagonally opposite; usually, this means the upper-left corner cell in the first worksheet and the lower-right corner cell in the last worksheet.

Entering Data in a Range

When you highlight a range in a worksheet, the cell pointer remains within that range as you type information into the cells. When you press Enter to complete an entry, the cell pointer moves to the next cell inside the highlighted range. Until you press an arrow key or click the mouse outside the range, pressing Enter simply moves the cell pointer within the highlighted area. This arrangement can be useful for entering numeric values down a column.

The order 1-2-3 uses in moving around in a highlighted range is as follows: 1-2-3 begins in the upper-left corner cell of the range, moves down until the first column is completed, moves to the top of the next column to the right, completes that column, and so on. After the cell pointer reaches the bottom right corner of the highlighted range, 1-2-3 returns to the upper left corner of the range. The fill area is two-dimensional only; even if the specified range is three-dimensional, 1-2-3 fills only the specified range in the current worksheet.

▶ **See** "Filling Ranges," **p. 72**

NOTE To make successive entries down a column, first highlight the column. The cell pointer is in the top cell. Type information into the first cell and press Enter. The column remains highlighted, but the cell pointer moves to the next cell in the range. You can continue to make entries in these cells by typing each entry and pressing Enter, rather than having to use the arrow keys. ■

CHAPTER 3

Entering and Editing Data

by Joyce J. Nielsen

This chapter presents the skills you need to start creating your own worksheets. You enter data into worksheet cells by typing the data or by using a Fill command to enter sequential numbers, month names, dates, and so on, into the worksheet. Once you have entered data into a worksheet, you need to know how to edit the data, erase entries, and reorganize the worksheet by inserting or deleting rows and columns.

1-2-3 also includes some features similar to those provided in a word processing program. You can check the spelling of data in a worksheet, for example, or use a find and replace command to search for specific data and replace it with new information. ■

Entering and editing worksheet data

1-2-3 provides several easy methods for entering and editing text, numbers, and dates.

Finding and replacing text

1-2-3 enables you to find specified text in your worksheet, and optionally, replace it with another string of text.

Inserting and deleting cells, rows, and columns

You can reorganize your worksheet data or make room for additional data by inserting or deleting rows, columns, and cells.

Undoing previous actions

Many actions you perform in 1-2-3 can be reversed if you use the Undo command before you perform another action.

Checking the spelling of text in your worksheet

You can use the Spelling feature of 1-2-3 to easily check the spelling of your worksheet data and make corrections as needed.

Entering Data

The first way that you can enter data into a worksheet is to type the data. You can create two kinds of cell entries: labels and values. A *label* is a text entry, and a *value* is a number or formula. 1-2-3 determines the kind of cell entry from the first character you type. When you type the first character, the mode indicator changes from `Ready` to either `Value` or `Label`.

1-2-3 considers an entry to be a value (a number or formula) if the entry begins with one of the following characters:

0 1 2 3 4 5 6 7 8 9 + - = (@ # . $

If the entry begins with any other character, 1-2-3 considers the entry to be a label.

NOTE If you begin a cell entry with a dollar sign ($), 1-2-3 initially displays `Label` in the status bar. However, when you type a number following the dollar sign and press Enter, the entry is converted to a value.

To enter data into a worksheet, follow these steps:

1. Select the cell in which you want to enter data.

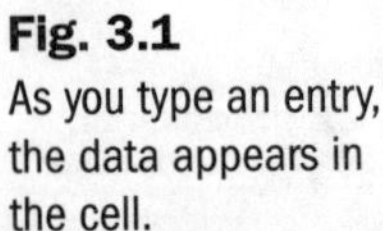

TIP Avoid starting your worksheet in cell A1. Leave an extra row or two at the top of the worksheet and an extra column at the left side to make your worksheets easier to read.

2. Type the entry.

   As you type, the text appears in the cell (see fig. 3.1). While you are typing the entry, you can press the Backspace key to back up and correct your typing, or you can press Esc to cancel your entry.

3. To complete the entry, press Enter. The entry is now placed in the cell, and the cell pointer automatically moves down one cell.

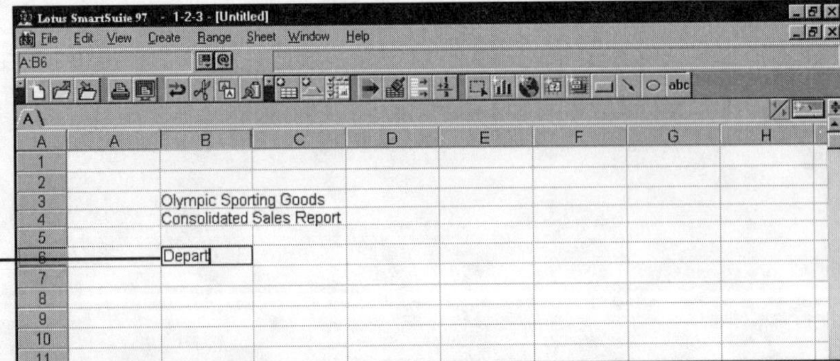

Fig. 3.1
As you type an entry, the data appears in the cell.

You also can enter data by using the contents box in the edit line. You may opt for this method if you prefer using the mouse. To enter data using the contents box, follow these steps:

1. Select the cell in which you want to enter data.
2. Click the contents box of the edit line.
3. Type the entry.

   As you type, the entry appears in the contents box (see fig. 3.2). While the data is still on the edit line, you can press the Backspace key to back up and correct your typing, or you can click the Cancel button if you want to cancel your entry.
4. To complete the entry, click the Confirm button. The entry is now placed in the cell, and the cell pointer moves down one cell.

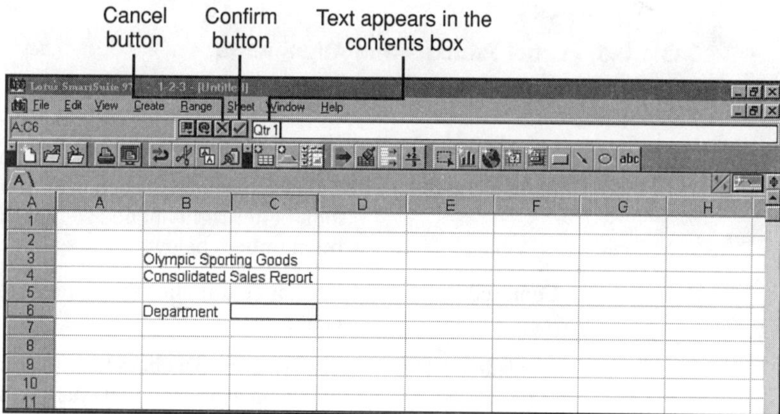

Fig. 3.2
You can also use the contents box in the edit line to enter data.

Another way to enter information into a cell is to double-click the cell. Double-clicking places the *cursor* (the flashing bar) inside the cell, and you can begin typing. Press Enter to complete the entry. Using this method easily enables you to edit a text entry as you are first entering it in a cell.

CAUTION

Be sure to check which cell is selected before you begin typing. If you type data into a cell that already contains information, your typing replaces the original text. If you make this mistake, you can reverse the error if you immediately choose Edit, Undo Cell Contents.

Entering Text

Labels, or text entries, make the numbers and formulas in your worksheets understandable by providing titles, row and column headings, and descriptive text. The text in a single cell can be a string of up to 512 characters.

When you enter a label, 1-2-3 adds a *label prefix* to the cell entry. 1-2-3 uses the label prefix to identify the entry as a label and to determine how to display and print the entry. By default, the program uses an apostrophe (') for a left-aligned label, meaning that labels are automatically lined up at the left edge of the cell. To place your label in the center or right edge of a cell, type one of the label prefixes shown in Table 3.1 as the first character of the label. The table also provides examples of when you might use the different label prefix characters. Figure 3.3 shows examples of their uses; notice that the label prefix is not visible in the worksheet, but appears in the contents box when you select a cell containing text.

Table 3.1 Label Prefixes and Alignments

Prefix	Alignment	Usage
'	Left aligned	Use for normal text (the default).
"	Right-aligned	Column headings placed over numeric columns often look better right-aligned so that the labels line up over the numbers below.
^	Centered	Use for column headings and other text you want centered.
\	Repeating	Use with special characters to create borders and other effects in a sheet. If you change the column width, 1-2-3 changes the length of a repeating label to fill the new column width.

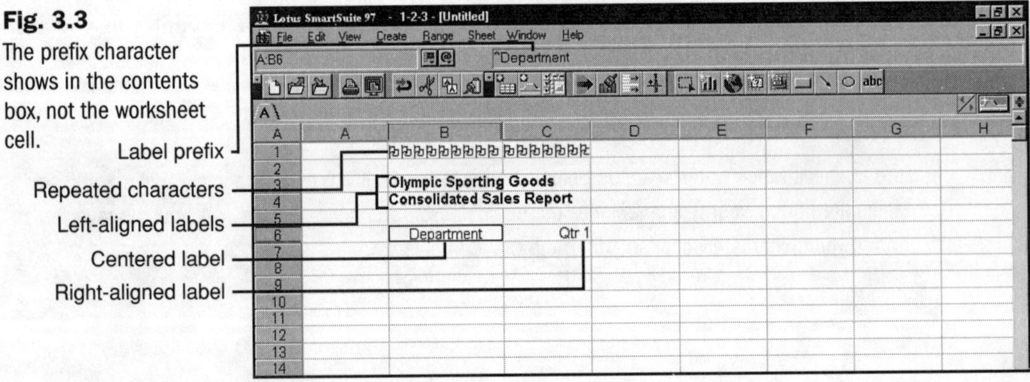

Fig. 3.3
The prefix character shows in the contents box, not the worksheet cell.

In figure 3.3, the text in cell B6 is centered, while text in cell C6 is right-aligned. Because numbers and numeric formulas are always right-aligned, you will probably want to also right-align the headings above columns of numbers.

NOTE When an entry fills the cell width, the alignments do not make a noticeable difference in the appearance of that cell. ■

Cells in the ranges B1..C1 in figure 3.3 show the use of a repeated character. In this case, the character is a "wingding," a special font that consists entirely of symbols. By repeating a wingding character, you can create a fancy border.

NOTE If you want a label prefix character (or certain other special characters) to appear as the first character of a label, you first must type the label prefix and then type *another* label prefix as the first character of the label. If you type **\015** in a cell, for example, 1-2-3 displays `015015015015015015` as a repeating label, rather than \015. You first must type another label prefix–here, an apostrophe ('). Therefore, you must type **'\015** to display `\015` in the cell. ■

Part I Ch 3

In addition to typing label prefixes, you can align labels and values using two other methods. You can click the Alignment button in the status bar and choose the desired alignment, or you can click the appropriate buttons on the Alignment tab of the Range Properties InfoBox. This topic is covered in Chapter 4, "Formatting Worksheets."

▶ **See** "Changing Fonts and Attributes," **p. 125**

▶ **See** "Aligning Labels and Values," **p. 127**

Typing Dates, Phone Numbers, and Social Security Numbers Some types of data may look like numbers, but should really be entered as labels. Dates, phone numbers, and Social Security numbers fall into this category. If the data you need to type contains only numbers, but the entry really is not a number, you must type a label prefix before typing the entry. If you do not type a prefix, when you type the numeric character, 1-2-3 switches to Value mode and expects a valid number or formula to follow.

TIP Type dates with slashes (11/6/97), and 1-2-3 automatically stores them as a date format.

Let's look at some examples. If you type a telephone number such as **317-555-6100**, 1-2-3 evaluates the entry as a formula and subtracts the second two numbers from the first. Similarly, if you type **9-30-97** to refer to a date, 1-2-3 evaluates the entry as a formula and displays the result `-118`. 1-2-3 considers a date entry of **9/30/97**, however, to be valid, and the program stores that entry as a date serial number.

▶ **See** "Calendar Functions," **p. 159**

NOTE If the entry contains any character that is not interpreted as an appropriate character in a value or formula, 1-2-3 recognizes the entry as a label. For example, if you type a phone number and place a space between the area code and the rest of the number, 1-2-3 enters the phone number as a label. When you type an address, like **123 Oak Street**, 1-2-3 recognizes it as a label because it contains spaces and alphabetic characters.

If you have many phone numbers to type, you can preformat a range to contain labels by selecting the range, then clicking the Number Format button in the status bar and choosing Label.

Typing Long Labels If a label is longer than a cell's width, 1-2-3 displays the label across blank cells to the right of the cell. The data is not actually filling all these cells but is spilling across them. A long text entry may spill across several blank cells. For example, the label "Consolidated Sales Report," entered in cell B4 of figure 3.3, extends into cells C4 and D4.

If the cells to the right of the label cell are not blank, 1-2-3 truncates the display of the label entry at the cell border. The program still stores the complete entry, however, and displays the full entry in the contents box when you select the cell.

NOTE To display the entire label in the worksheet, you can insert blank columns to the right of the cell containing the long label, or you can widen the column. Widening the column is easy when you use the mouse; simply move the mouse pointer over the column border to the right of the column letter and drag the border to the desired width. To automatically widen the column to fit the widest entry in the column, double-click the border to the right of the column letter.

▶ **See** "Enhancing the Appearance of Data," **p. 125**

▶ **See** "Setting Column Widths," **p. 94**

Entering Numbers

To enter a valid number in a worksheet, you can type any of the 10 digits (0 through 9). You can precede a numeric entry with certain other characters, such as a plus sign (+), minus sign (-), dollar sign ($), period (.), comma (,) or percent sign (%).

If you type a number that includes a dollar sign, comma, or percent sign, 1-2-3 automatically formats the cell to have those characteristics. This is because 1-2-3 formats a cell based on the data you enter into it. If you enter 24% into a cell, for example, 1-2-3 displays 24% in the cell, and automatically formats the cell as Percent format. If you change the entry in that same cell (or any other cell, for that matter) to $749, 1-2-3 displays $749 in the cell and changes the format from Percent to US Dollar.

▶ **See** "Working with Number Formats," **p. 110**

1-2-3 stores only 15 digits of any number. If you enter a number with more than 15 digits, 1-2-3 rounds the number after the 15th digit. When displaying numbers on-screen, the program stores the complete number (up to 15 digits) but displays only what fits in the cell. If the number is too long to display in the cell, 1-2-3 tries to display as much of the number as possible. If the cell uses the default General format and the integer part of the number fits into the cell, 1-2-3 rounds the decimal characters that don't fit. If the integer part of the number doesn't fit in the cell, the program displays the number in *scientific (exponential) notation*. If the cell uses a format other than General or the cell width is too narrow to display in scientific notation and the number cannot fit into the cell, 1-2-3 displays asterisks. Figure 3.4 shows a worksheet where some of the columns are not wide enough to display the cell entries.

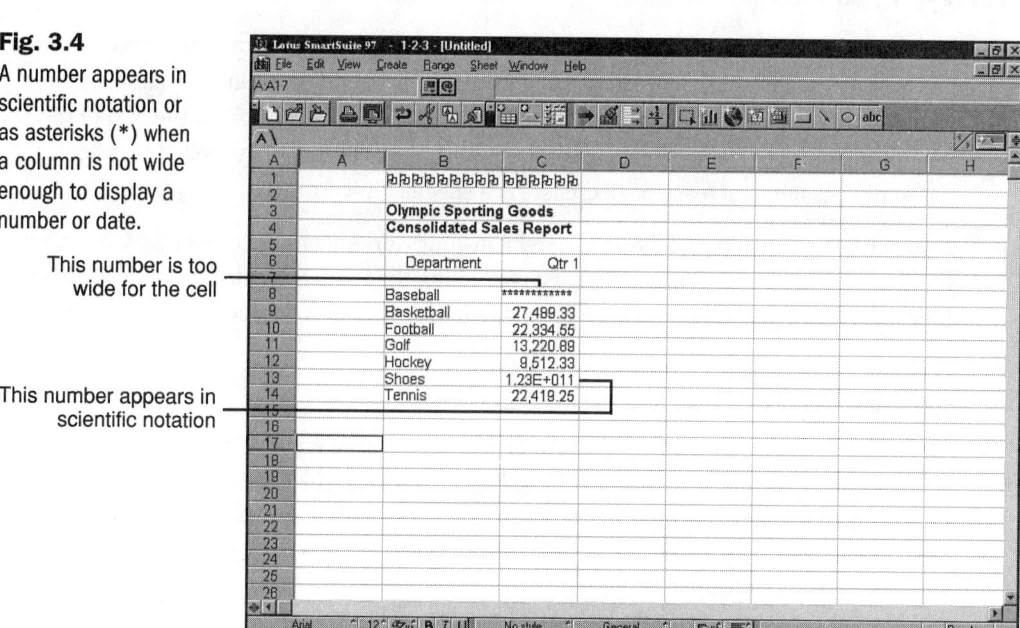

Fig. 3.4
A number appears in scientific notation or as asterisks (*) when a column is not wide enough to display a number or date.

1-2-3 stores a number in scientific notation only if it contains 8 or more digits *preceding* the decimal point. If you enter a number with more than 15 total digits, 1-2-3 rounds the number to end with one or more zeroes. You can actually type a number by using scientific notation, but 1-2-3 still rounds to 15 digits.

The appearance of a number in the worksheet depends on the cell's format, font, and column width. When you use the default font (12-point Arial) and the default column width (9), 1-2-3 displays the number 1234567890 as `1.23E+009`. If you use a column width of 10 or higher, however, 1-2-3 displays the number as entered.

▶ **See** "Setting Column Widths," **p. 94**
▶ **See** "Working with Number Formats," **p. 110**

You can make the process of entering data into a worksheet easier by preselecting the range in which you want to enter the data. After you preselect the range, type the entry in the first cell and press Enter. 1-2-3 automatically moves down to the next cell in the selected range and, when appropriate, wraps around to the top of the next column.

You can correct an entry before you have entered it by using the Backspace key, but do not use an arrow key or you will deselect the range.

Filling Ranges

You can use 1-2-3 to automatically fill a range with a sequence of data. For example, you can quickly create column headings such as month names by entering the name of the first month, then using the mouse (or the Range, Fill command) to fill in the rest of the headings. You can also use this feature to fill a range of cells with a series of numbers, dates, or times that increase or decrease by a specified increment.

If you create certain lists of data repeatedly in your worksheets, such as company branch locations, you can create a SmartFill list containing the branch names so that 1-2-3 knows how to automatically fill a sequence of data that includes one of these names.

Using Drag and Fill

The quickest and easiest way to fill a range is with the drag and fill technique, which enables you to accomplish the fill by dragging the mouse. This feature is also sometimes referred to as "fill-by-example." The critical part of using this method is entering the initial value (or values). The fill uses the initial values as an example for filling a selected range with information.

To use the drag and fill technique, follow these steps:

1. Enter the first item of the sequence into the first cell of the range. If you want to fill a range with an unusual pattern, type the first two or three entries to establish the pattern.
2. Select the cell(s) containing the initial entries.
3. Move the mouse pointer over the lower-right corner of the selected cell(s), until the mouse pointer displays four arrowheads (see fig. 3.5).
4. Drag the mouse to select the rest of the range you want to fill, then release the mouse pointer. 1-2-3 fills the range with data.

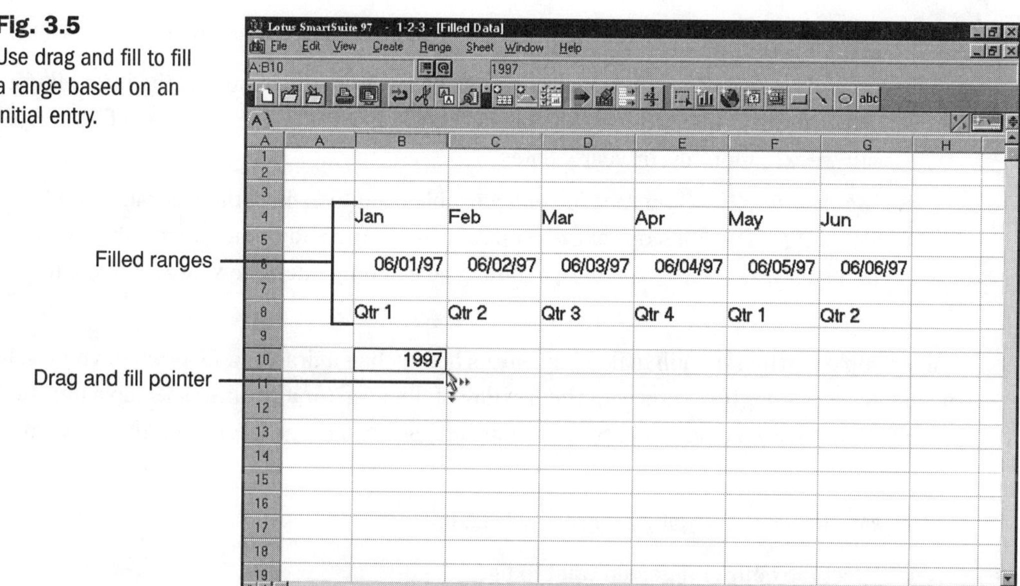

Fig. 3.5
Use drag and fill to fill a range based on an initial entry.

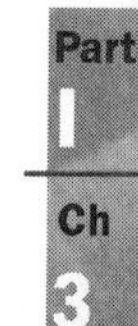

Using Range Fill for More Control

An alternative to using drag and fill is the Range, Fill command. This command enables you to choose additional options, such as the Fill Type, and the Start At, Increment By, and Stop At values in the Fill dialog box (see fig. 3.6).

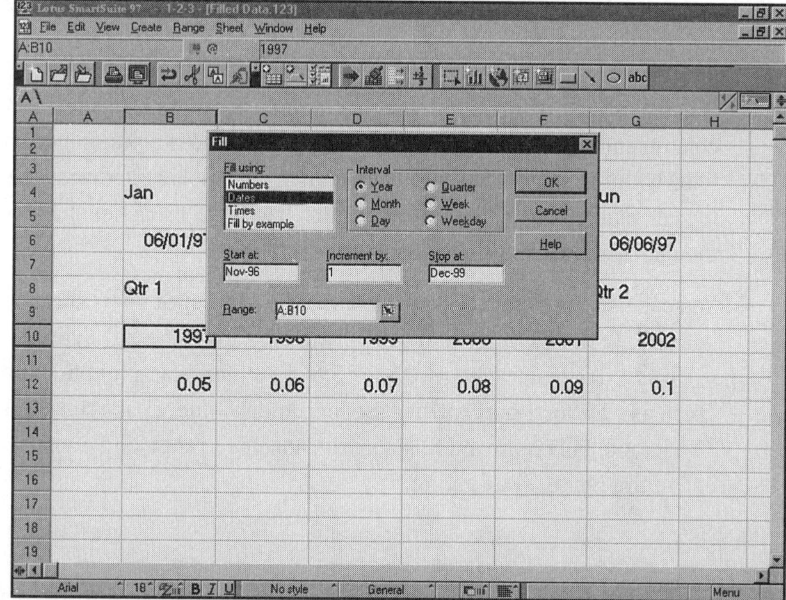

Fig. 3.6
Use the Fill dialog box to choose the type of fill and the start, increment, and stop values.

The Fill dialog box provides two primary advantages over using drag and fill:

- *Interval options*. The Fill dialog box provides a variety of options for the interval (for date values and time values), so that you do not have to type examples to fill a range with weekly, monthly, or yearly dates.
- *Stop At value*. The Stop At value entry enables you to control the last value in the filled range. The Fill stops at the Stop At value or the end of the range, whichever comes first. When you use drag and fill, you can only guess how large a range to select.

An example of when the Fill dialog box works better than a drag and fill is when you want to create a calendar that ends with the last day of the year (or any other specific date). Just type the last desired date as the Stop At value and select a range large enough to extend past the last date.

To fill a range using the Range, Fill command, follow these steps:

1. Select the entire range you want to fill.
2. Choose Range, Fill. The Fill dialog box appears (refer to fig. 3.6).
3. Choose the type of fill from the Fill Type list box. The available fill types are: Numbers, Date Values, Time Values, and Fill by Example.
4. Select an interval (if applicable) from the Interval area of the dialog box.
5. Type a starting value in the Start At text box.
6. Type an increment in the Increment By text box.
7. If desired, type an ending value in the Stop At text box.
8. Choose OK to fill the range.

When a range that includes several columns or rows is selected, 1-2-3 fills down the first column and then wraps around to the top of the next column in the range. The first cell is filled with the start value, and each subsequent cell is filled with the value in the preceding cell plus the increment. Filling stops when 1-2-3 reaches the stop value or the end of the fill range, whichever happens first.

You can use the Range, Fill command to build a list of interest rates (see fig. 3.7). After you specify the fill range and select Numbers from the Fill Type list, enter the starting value as a decimal fraction (**.05** for 5 percent, for example) and another decimal fraction (such as **.01**, for 1 percent) for the increment value. Leave the default stop value at 32767. The Range, Fill command fills only the specified range and doesn't fill cells beyond the end of the range (see fig. 3.8).

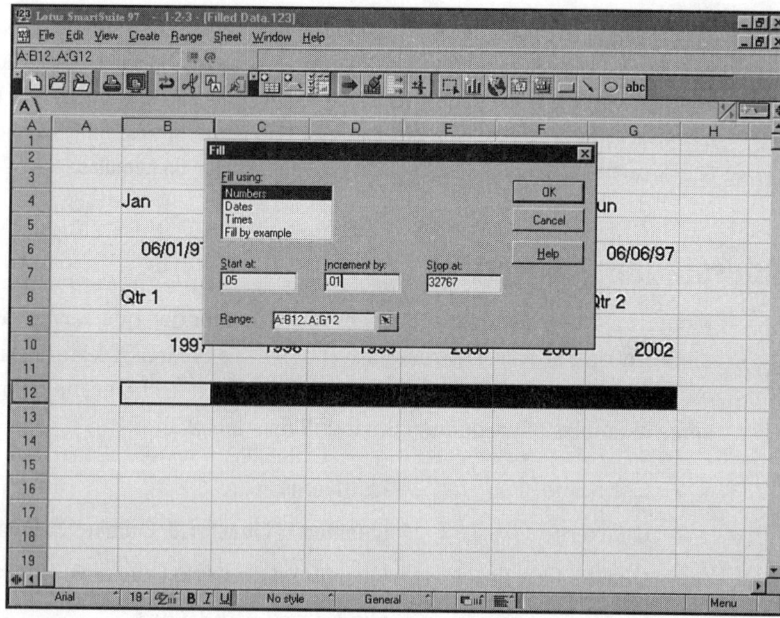

Fig. 3.7
Use the Start At and Increment By values to accomplish any type of numeric fill.

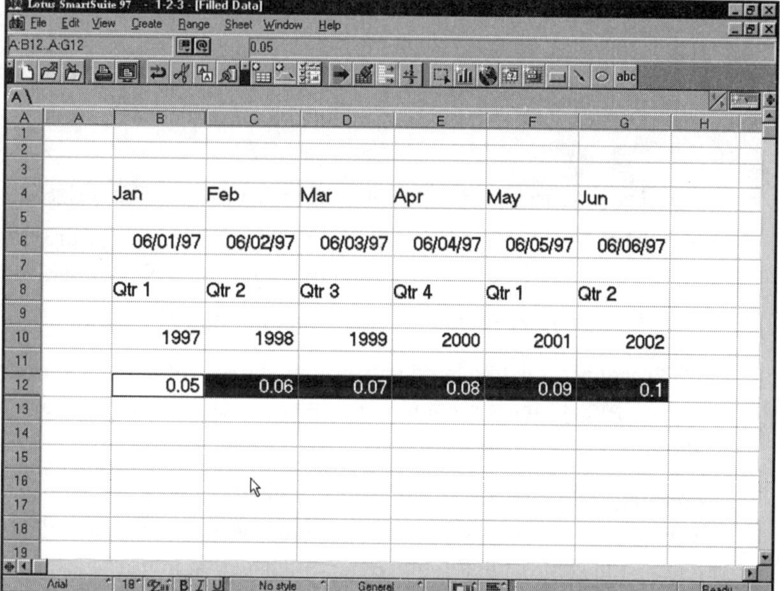

Fig. 3.8
The result of using the Fill dialog box to enter interest rates.

The Range, Fill command cannot be used to fill all types of series, such as a series of numbers that increase geometrically (1, 10, 100, 1000,...). However, you can still accomplish this fill by using formulas. Place the starting value in a cell; for example, type **1** in cell A1. Then, enter a formula in the second cell (for example, **+A1*10**) and copy this formula to the range. See "Creating Formulas" in Chapter 5 for more information on formulas.

Understanding SmartFill

Many commonly used fill sequences, such as months, quarters, years, and simple numeric entries, are already recognized by 1-2-3's SmartFill feature. You can also enter your own custom SmartFill lists, as detailed in the next section. The following table shows some examples of predefined SmartFill lists in 1-2-3.

List Name	List Items
Quarters	Quarter 1, Quarter 2, Quarter 3, Quarter 4
Quarters No Space	Quarter1, Quarter2, Quarter3, Quarter4
Qtrs	Qtr 1, Qtr 2, Qtr 3, Qtr 4
Qtrs No Space	Qtr1, Qtr2, Qtr3, Qtr4
Qs	Q 1, Q 2, Q 3, Q 4
Qs No Space	Q1, Q2, Q3, Q4
Days	Sunday, Monday, Tuesday, Wednesday, Thursday, Friday, Saturday
Days Abbreviated	Sun, Mon, Tue, Wed, Thu, Fri, Sat
Months	January, February, March, April, May, June, July, August, September, October, November, December
Months Abbreviated	Jan, Feb, Mar, Apr, May, Jun, Jul, Aug, Sep, Oct, Nov, Dec

1-2-3 recognizes date-related entries and starts over at the end of a year, quarter, month, or day. If 1-2-3 cannot recognize a pattern in your examples, drag and fill copies the original entries into the selected cells.

Creating a Custom SmartFill List If you often enter the same set of labels in your worksheets, you may want to create your own custom SmartFill list for use with the Range, Fill command. Custom SmartFill lists that might be useful include region names, store locations, and sales representatives' names. You can create any custom fill sequence you need for values that you frequently use in your worksheets.

To create a custom SmartFill list, follow these steps:

1. Choose File, User Setup, SmartFill Setup. The SmartFill Setup dialog box appears (see fig. 3.9).

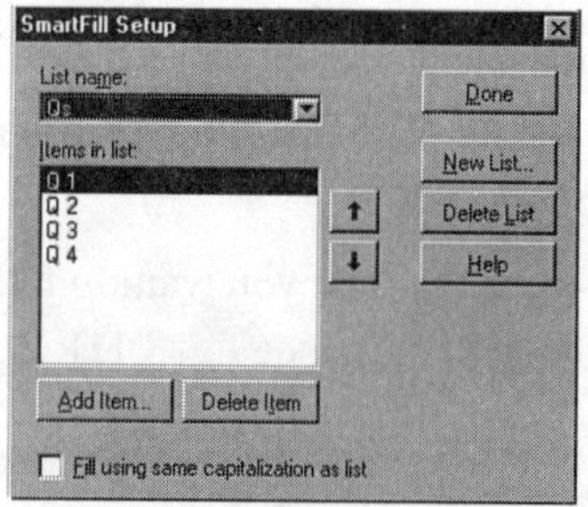

Fig. 3.9
You can use the SmartFill Setup dialog box to create your own custom lists.

2. Choose New List.
3. In the New SmartFill List dialog box, type a name for the custom list in the New List Name text box. Then, choose OK to return to the SmartFill Setup dialog box.
4. Choose Add Item.
5. In the Add Item dialog box, type a name for the first item in your custom list in the New Item text box. Then, choose OK to return to the SmartFill Setup dialog box.
6. Repeat steps 4 and 5 until you have added all items you want to include in the custom SmartFill list. Figure 3.10 shows five items added to a custom list named Branch Locations.

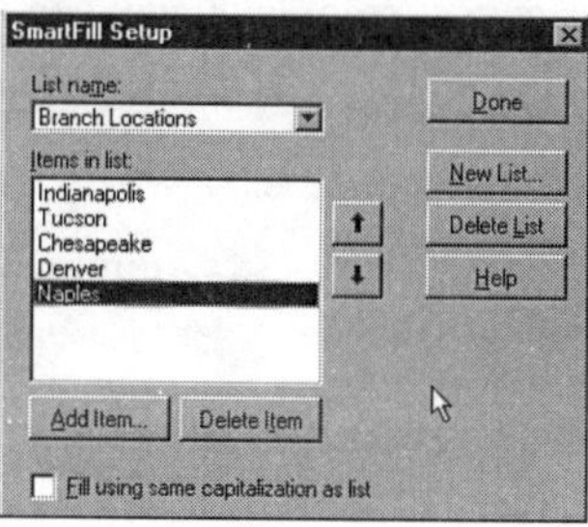

Fig. 3.10
A custom list of five items has been created.

If you want 1-2-3 to always use the same capitalization you used when you created the list, select the Fill Using Same Capitalization As List check box.

7. Click Done to exit the SmartFill Setup dialog box.

Using a Custom SmartFill List To use a custom SmartFill that you have already created, follow these steps:

1. In your worksheet, enter one of the items from the custom SmartFill list you created.
2. Select the cell containing the initial item.
3. Move the mouse pointer over the lower-right corner of the selected cell(s), until the mouse pointer displays four arrowheads.
4. Drag the mouse to select the rest of the range you want to fill, then release the mouse pointer. 1-2-3 fills the range with data (see fig. 3.11).

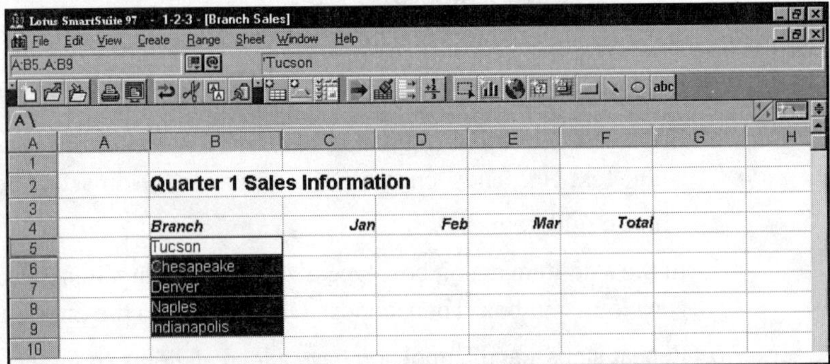

Fig. 3.11
Data from a custom SmartFill list has automatically been entered in the selected range.

Modifying a SmartFill List After you've created and begun using a custom SmartFill list, you may decide that you want to add or delete items, or rearrange the order of the items in the list. In addition to modifying your own custom lists, you can also modify 1-2-3's predefined SmartFill lists.

To modify an existing SmartFill list, follow these steps:

1. Choose File, User Setup, SmartFill Setup. The SmartFill Setup dialog box appears (refer to fig. 3.9).
2. From the List Name drop-down list, select the name of the list you want to modify.
3. Modify the list, as desired:

   To add an item to the list, choose the Add Item button, enter the new item name, and choose OK.

   To delete an item from the list, select the item you want to delete, and choose the Delete Item button.

   To rearrange the items in the list, use the up and down arrows or drag the items to their desired locations.
4. Choose Done when you are finished.

To delete an entire SmartFill list that you no longer need, choose File, User Setup, SmartFill Setup. From the List Name drop-down list, select the name of the list you want to delete, and click the Delete List button. Choose Done to exit the dialog box.

TROUBLESHOOTING

When I tried to use Range, Fill to enter numbers in a range, only part of the range was filled. Why wasn't the entire range filled, as I expected? Range, Fill fills the selected range until all the cells are filled or until the stop value is reached. You may have forgotten to make the stop value large enough to accommodate the entire range that you wanted to fill.

Why did 1-2-3 drag-and-fill the entire range with the same labels that I entered in the first two cells of the range? If drag-and-fill cannot recognize the correct pattern to use for incrementing labels, it copies the existing label(s) to the entire range. Make certain that the existing labels are ones that 1-2-3 can recognize (for example, Qtr 1 or January), or create a custom-fill sequence so that 1-2-3 knows how you want to fill the range.

When I fill a range in my worksheet, I get dates or percents instead of the numbers I expected. If the range you fill previously contained dates or percents, the cells are still formatted that way. Change the range to a numeric format using the Format button on the status bar.

Editing Data

After you enter data in a cell, you may want to change the data. Perhaps you misspelled a word in a label or created an incorrect formula, or you have more current information. You can change an existing entry in either of two ways:

- *Type over.* You can replace the contents of a cell by typing a new entry into the cell.
- *Edit.* You can change part of a cell's contents by editing the cell.

Typing Over Existing Entries

The quickest way to make a change to a short entry is to just type over the old data. Follow these steps:

1. Select the cell you want to change.
2. Type the new data.
3. Press Enter.

If you type over a cell accidentally, use Edit, Undo Cell Contents or the Undo SmartIcon immediately to undo the typing.

Editing Entries

If you need to make a correction to a long entry or a formula in the worksheet, you might want to edit the existing entry instead of typing over it. This enables you to add or delete characters in the entry, the same way you do in a word processing program.

There are three ways to enter Edit mode so that you can modify a cell entry. Use one of these techniques:

- Select the cell and press F2 (Edit).
- Double-click the cell.
- Select the cell, then move the mouse pointer to the contents box. Move the I-beam pointer to the area you want to change, then click the mouse button to place an insertion point in the text.

When 1-2-3 is in Edit mode, a cursor flashes in the cell (or in the contents box, if you are editing the entry there). You can then use the keys shown in Table 3.2 to move around the entry and make changes to the entry. When you press Enter or move to another cell, the edited information is entered into the worksheet.

Table 3.2 Editing Keys

Key	Action
← or →	Moves to previous or next character.
Ctrl+←	Moves to previous word.
Ctrl+→	Moves to next word.
Home	Moves to start of entry.
End	Moves to end of entry.
Any character	Inserts character at insertion point.
Del	Deletes character to right of insertion point.
Backspace	Deletes character to left of insertion point.
Insert	Switches to overtype mode to type over existing characters.
Enter	Enters the revised text into the cell.
↑ or ↓	Enters revised text and moves to next cell (up or down).
Esc	Cancels Edit mode without changing the cell entry.

Finding and Replacing Data

When you need to make the same change to several entries in a worksheet, use the Edit, Find & Replace command or the Find and Replace Data SmartIcon to find and replace characters in a range of labels and formulas. The command works much like the search and replace feature in many word processing programs. When you choose Edit, Find & Replace, the Find and Replace dialog box appears. You can specify what data to search for, what kind of data to search through, what characters to find or replace, and which range to search.

NOTE You should first save the file before choosing Edit, Find & Replace, even though you can undo an incorrect search.

Suppose that you have a list of department names as labels and you want to shorten the labels from *Department* to *Dept.* To find and replace the data, follow these steps:

1. Choose Edit, Find & Replace or click the Find and Replace Data SmartIcon. The Find and Replace dialog box appears.
2. Type the text you want to find in the Find text box. In this example, type **Department**.
3. Type the new text in the Replace With text box. In this example, type **Dept.** (remember to include the period). See figure 3.12.

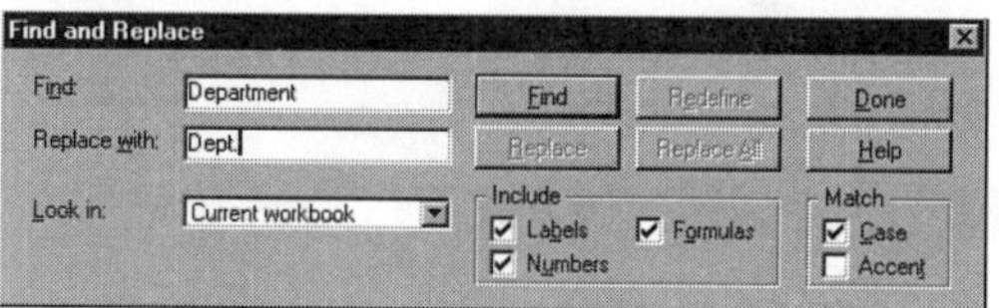

Fig. 3.12
You can use the Find and Replace dialog box to replace one text string with another.

TIP You can also use the Find and Replace dialog box to locate information in the worksheet without changing it. Just enter the text you want to find in the Find text box and keep the Replace With text box in the Find and Replace dialog box blank. Choose the Find button one or more times to find the text you want to search for.

4. (Optional) In the Look In drop-down list, specify where you want to look when performing the search. The default selection is Current Workbook.
5. (Optional) Select the type of text you want to search: Labels, Numbers, or Formulas. Each of these check boxes is selected by default—this works for most situations, unless you specifically want to restrict the search to labels, numbers, or formulas.

6. Choose the Find button. 1-2-3 highlights the first cell that contains the text you entered in the Find text box.
7. Choose the Replace button to replace the text and move to the next occurrence of the text you are searching for; or choose the Find button again to skip this occurrence (without replacing the text) and move to the next occurrence.

Choose Replace for the first occurrence to make sure the change is correct, and then choose Replace All if you want to replace all occurrences quickly. You can use the Redefine button if you want to modify some of the search options while you are performing the search.

8. If 1-2-3 displays the dialog box message `No more matching strings`, choose OK.
9. Choose the Done button in the Find and Replace dialog box to end the search.

You also can use Edit, Find & Replace to modify formulas. If you have many formulas that round to two decimal places, such as @ROUND(A2*B2,2), you can change the formulas to round to four decimal places with a search string of `,2)` and a replace string of `,4)`.

▶ **See** "Entering Formulas," **p. 137**

▶ **See** "Entering Functions," **p. 154**

CAUTION

Be extremely careful when you replace numbers in formulas. If you just replace `2` with `4` in this example, the formula @ROUND(A2*B2,2) becomes @ROUND(A4*B4,4).

Erasing Cells and Ranges

As you correct and revise your worksheet, you probably will need to erase some cell entries. Any data you erase is removed from memory, but these changes don't affect the file on disk until you save the current version of the file to disk.

Any of the following techniques can be used to erase (clear) cell entries:

- *Delete key.* Select the cell or range and press the Delete key. This clears the contents of the cell(s) but leaves the format (like dollar signs, commas, or percents).
- *Delete SmartIcon.* Select the cell or range and click the Delete SmartIcon to clear the contents of the cell.
- *Edit, Clear.* Select the cell or range and choose Edit, Clear from the main menu or Clear from the shortcut menu. This displays the Clear dialog box that enables you to clear the cell contents or format. For example, if a cell previously contained a

percent and you no longer want it to contain a percent, use Edit, Clear and check the Contents check box and the Styles and Number Formats check box.

- *Edit, Cut*. Select the cell or range and choose Edit, Cut from the main menu or Cut from the shortcut menu. This places the data in the Windows Clipboard so that it can later be pasted back into the worksheet at a different location. Chapter 7, "Moving or Copying Data," covers moving and copying data in more detail.

NOTE You might think that an easy way to clear or blank out the contents of a cell is to move to the cell and type a space into the cell. This does *appear* to clear the cell, but the cell is not empty; it contains a space character. This is considered to be a filled cell and takes up memory and space on disk when you save the worksheet. It also can create problems in calculations. For example, the @AVG function ignores empty cells when it averages a range of values. But a cell with a space in it is counted as zero and makes the average inaccurate!

To clear the contents or formatting from a cell with the Edit, Clear command, follow these steps:

1. Select the cell or range you want to clear.
2. Choose Edit, Clear or click the right mouse button and choose Clear from the shortcut menu. The Clear dialog box appears (see fig. 3.13).
3. Select the check boxes that describe what you want to clear. By default, only the Contents check box is selected.

   The Contents option clears just the data from the cell, so it has the same effect as using the Delete key to erase a cell. The Styles and Number Format option clears only the styles from the cell. Styles include any type of formatting or enhancements including numeric formats (dollar signs or percent signs), alignments (center or right), and enhancements (bold or italic). You also can choose options to remove Borders and Designer Frames, Cell Comments, and Scripts attached to the selected cell(s).
4. Choose OK.

TIP If you accidentally clear a cell's contents, styles, or both, choose Edit, Undo Clear or the Undo SmartIcon to restore the entry, styles, or both.

CAUTION

Many users make the mistake of choosing Range, Delete instead of Edit, Clear when they want to clear a cell or range. These commands perform very different functions. The Edit, Clear command leaves cells in place and just clears the contents (or styles). The Range, Delete command affects the structure of the worksheet. Range, Delete removes the selected cells from the worksheet, like pulling bricks out of a wall. Adjacent cells are moved up or to the left to fill the void.

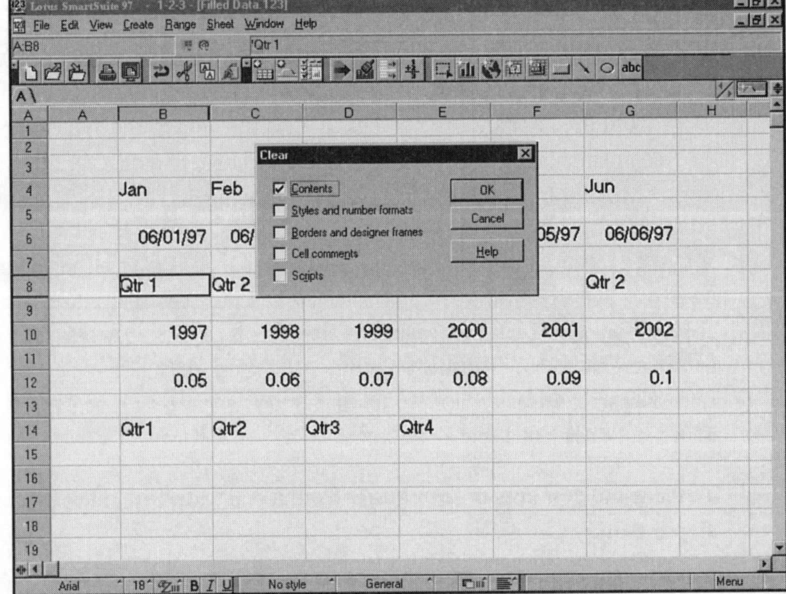

Fig. 3.13
Use the Clear dialog box to clear contents or styles (formats) from a cell.

Inserting and Deleting Cells, Rows, and Columns

After you have created a worksheet, you may discover that you forgot to include an item. This is easily fixed by inserting cells, rows, or columns into the worksheet with the Range, Insert command or Insert SmartIcons.

When you insert rows, all rows at and below the cell pointer move down. When you insert columns, all columns at and to the right of the cell pointer move to the right. You can even insert a cell or cells into the worksheet and move adjacent cells to the right or down. This is helpful when you forget a cell entry and enter data into the wrong cell.

Similarly, you may also find that you want to delete unwanted data in an entire row or column, or in individual cells. When you delete rows, all rows below the deleted rows move up to fill the gap. When you delete columns, all columns to the right of the deleted columns move to the left. If you delete selected cells, the adjacent cells move to the left or up to fill the gap.

> **CAUTION**
>
> If your workbook contains multiple worksheets that you have grouped (by using the Sheet, Group Sheets command), and you insert or delete columns or rows in one worksheet, those changes are reflected in every worksheet in the file. Be sure to ungroup your sheets if you don't want these changes to occur in all of the grouped sheets.

▶ **See** "Grouping Worksheets," **p. 258**

Inserting Rows or Columns

The quickest way to insert a row or column is to select the entire row or column first.

To insert rows or columns, follow these steps:

1. Select the entire row(s) or column(s) at the location where you want the new row(s) or column(s) to appear by clicking the row or column header(s). Figure 3.14 shows a worksheet with an entire row selected.

Fig. 3.14
Click the row or column header to select an entire row or column, then choose insert.

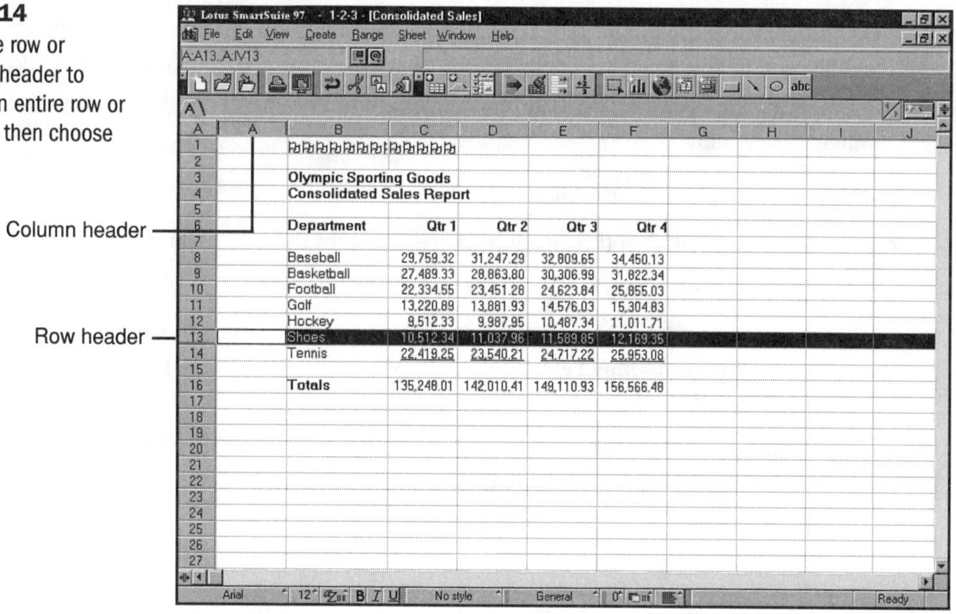
Column header
Row header
Lotus SmartSuite 97 - 1-2-3 - [Consolidated Sales]
File Edit View Create Range Sheet Window Help
A:A13..A:IV13
Olympic Sporting Goods
Consolidated Sales Report
Department Qtr 1 Qtr 2 Qtr 3 Qtr 4
Baseball 29,759.32 31,247.29 32,809.65 34,450.13
Basketball 27,489.33 28,863.80 30,306.99 31,822.34
Football 22,334.55 23,451.28 24,623.84 25,855.03
Golf 13,220.89 13,881.93 14,576.03 15,304.83
Hockey 9,512.33 9,987.95 10,487.34 11,011.71
Shoes 10,512.34 11,037.96 11,589.85 12,169.35
Tennis 22,419.25 23,540.21 24,717.22 25,953.08
Totals 135,248.01 142,010.41 149,110.93 156,566.48
Arial 12 No style General Ready

> **TIP** To insert multiple adjacent rows or columns, drag across several row or column headers.

2. Choose Range, Insert Rows; or use the shortcut menu to choose Insert Rows (or Insert Columns, as appropriate). A new blank row (or column) is inserted at the selected location.

NOTE If you forget to select an entire row or column in Step 1, the Insert dialog box displays and you can choose Rows or Columns from this box to insert a row or column at the current location.

You can save even more time when you use the shortcut menu to insert a row or column. You don't even need to preselect the row or column first, just click the row or column header with the right mouse button to both select the row or column and access the shortcut menu.

You may worry that inserting rows or columns into a worksheet requires you to redo existing formulas. If you insert a row or column within the borders of a range, the range expands to accommodate the new rows or columns. For example, if you have the range A1..B4 referenced in a formula, and insert a row above row 4, the reference would read A1..B5.

Inserting Cells

Occasionally, you may want to insert an individual cell or range into the worksheet. This enables you to add new blank cells into the worksheet and push existing entries down or to the right. This is especially handy when you have missed an entry while typing a column or row of data.

To insert a cell or range of cells into the worksheet, follow these steps:

1. Select the cell(s) at the location where you want the new cells inserted.
2. Choose Range, Insert. The Insert dialog box appears.
3. Select the Insert in Selected Range Only check box. Also, either select the Rows option button (to move existing cells down) or the Columns option button (to move existing cells to the right).

   Figure 3.15 shows the Insert dialog box filled in to insert a cell at C7 in the worksheet and move the two numbers down. Figure 3.16 shows the worksheet after the insertion.
4. Choose OK.

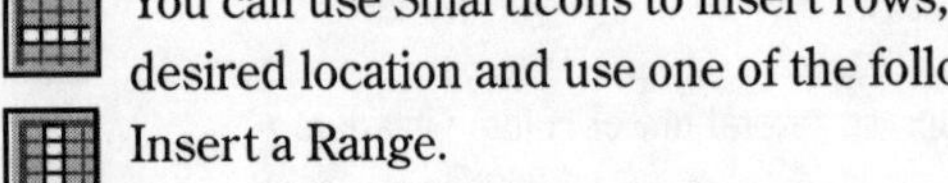

You can use SmartIcons to insert rows, columns, or cells. Select a cell or range at the desired location and use one of the following SmartIcons: Insert Rows, Insert Columns, or Insert a Range.

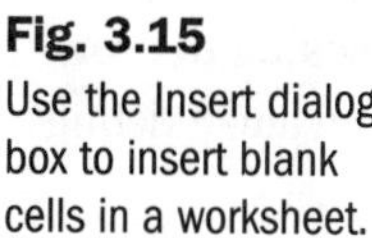

Fig. 3.15
Use the Insert dialog box to insert blank cells in a worksheet.

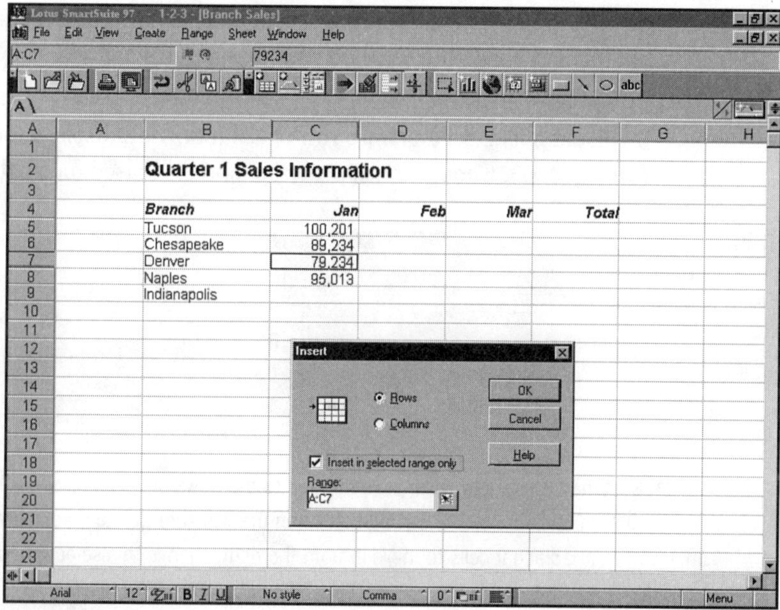

Fig. 3.16
When you insert a cell using the Rows option, existing data moves down.

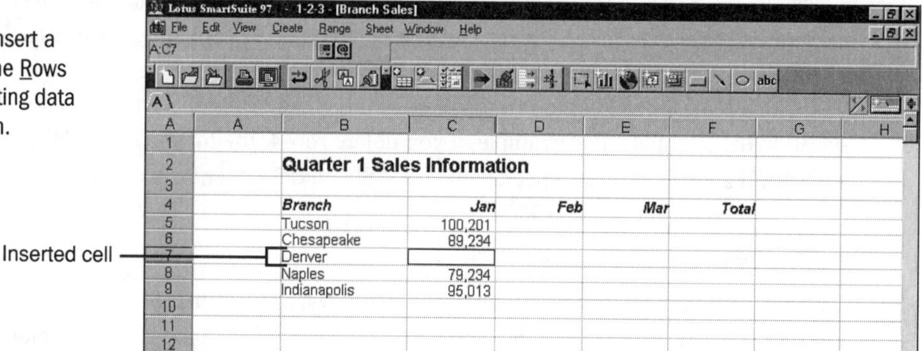

Deleting Rows, Columns, or Cells

When you erase cells with Edit, Clear or Edit, Cut, the cells still exist in the worksheet, but they are empty. In contrast, when you delete a cell, row, or column, 1-2-3 removes the entire cell, row, or column and moves others to fill the gap created by the deletion. 1-2-3 also updates cell addresses, such as those used in formulas.

To delete a row, column, or cell, follow these steps:

1. Select the row, column, or cells you want to delete.

2. Choose Range, Delete. If you selected an entire row or column by clicking the row or column header, the selected row or column is automatically deleted and existing rows or columns move up or left, respectively.

   If you did not select an entire row or column, 1-2-3 displays the Delete dialog box (see fig. 3.17). Choose the appropriate options, based on what you want to delete.

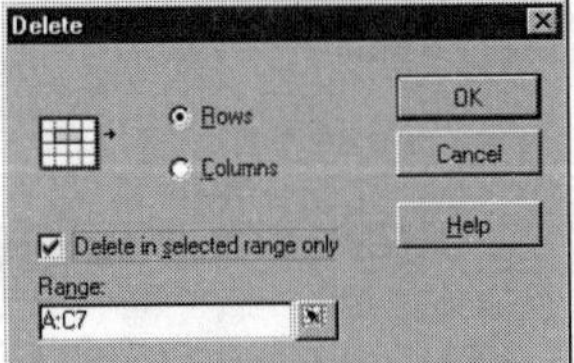

Fig. 3.17
Choose what you want to delete in the Delete dialog box.

NOTE When you delete cells, pay attention to the Rows or Columns selection. The default selection is Rows, meaning that when the cells are deleted, adjacent cells are moved up. If you want adjacent cells to move in from the right, change this selection to Columns.

NOTE If you did not select the item to be deleted or were in the wrong location in the worksheet, you can use the Range text box in the Delete dialog box to specify the range you want to delete. You can type the address or highlight cells using the range selector.

Range references in formulas are adjusted when you delete cells, rows, or columns referenced in the formulas. For example, if you delete row 4, the formula +A3+A6 becomes +A3+A5. If a formula refers specifically to a cell you deleted, however, the formula may result in an error message (ERR).

▶ **See** "Correcting Errors in Formulas," **p. 145**

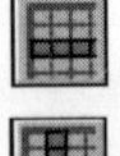

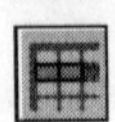

You can also use SmartIcons to delete ranges, rows, or columns. Select cells at the desired location in the worksheet and use one of the following SmartIcons: Delete Selected Rows, Delete Selected Columns, or Delete a Selected Range.

CAUTION

Deleting rows or columns usually affects only the current worksheet. If, however, you have grouped together several worksheets and you delete rows or columns in one worksheet, you delete the same rows or columns in all the grouped worksheets.

TROUBLESHOOTING

I meant to insert an entire row into my worksheet, but only one cell was inserted and now some entries in my worksheet don't line up correctly. You probably forgot to choose Rows in the Insert dialog box and only a single cell was inserted into the worksheet, shifting existing entries down. Use Edit, Undo to undo the insertion. If it is too late to undo the insertion, select the inserted cell and choose Range, Delete to delete the cell and return the worksheet to the way it was originally. Then, select an entire row before choosing Range, Insert Rows again.

I deleted a row from my worksheet and now one of my formulas shows ERR. Although 1-2-3 does its best to revise formulas to account for insertions and deletions, if you delete a cell that was specifically referenced in a formula, you may lose your calculation and see ERR in the cell. You need to edit the formula to replace the ERR with a valid cell reference.

Using the Undo Feature

When you type an entry, edit a cell, or issue a command, you change the worksheet. If you change the worksheet in error, you can undo your last change by using one of these techniques:

- Choose the Edit, Undo command.
- Click the Undo SmartIcon.

If you type over an existing entry, you can undo the new entry and restore the old one. The Undo feature undoes only the last action performed, such as entering data or choosing a command.

NOTE When you use the Undo feature, 1-2-3 must remember the most recent action that changed the worksheet. This feature requires computer memory; how much memory depends on the different actions involved. If you run low on memory, you can disable the Undo feature by choosing the File, User Setup, 1-2-3 Preferences command and deselecting the Undo check box on the General tab.

The Undo feature is powerful. To use Undo properly, you must understand what 1-2-3 considers to be a change. A change occurs between the time 1-2-3 is in Ready mode and the next time 1-2-3 is in Ready mode.

Suppose that you press F2 (Edit) to go into Edit mode to change a cell. You can make changes in the cell and then press Enter to save the changes and return to Ready mode. If you choose Undo at that point, 1-2-3 returns the worksheet to the condition the worksheet was in during the last Ready mode. The cell returns to the state it was in before you performed the edit.

NOTE If you've just completed an action, Undo on the Edit menu is specific about what action it will undo. For example, if you've just deleted several rows of data, Undo shows up as Undo Delete Rows on the Edit menu. Also, if you have just saved the workbook, the Undo command is dimmed, saying Can't Undo. ■

Some commands and actions cannot be canceled, including the Undo command. If you use Undo at the wrong time and cancel an entry, you cannot recover the entry. Other commands and actions that cannot be canceled include the following:

- A previous use of Edit, Undo
- All commands in the Control menus
- Changes to files on disk
- Actions that move the cell pointer or scroll the worksheet
- Formula recalculations that result when you press F9 (Calc)

Checking Your Spelling

1-2-3 includes a spell check utility that reviews and helps you correct spelling throughout your worksheets. The spell check utility checks the words in your worksheet against a dictionary and flags words that are not found. You then have the opportunity to replace the incorrect word with a suggested word or move on to the next spelling error.

To use the spelling checker, follow these steps:

1. Choose Edit, Check Spelling or click the Check Spelling SmartIcon. The Check Spelling dialog box appears (see fig. 3.18).
2. In the Look In drop-down list, select the area of the worksheet that you want to spell check (the default selection is Current Workbook).
3. (Optional) Choose the Options button if you want to change any global spell check settings, such as whether or not to check for repeated words. These options are detailed later in this section.

   After making any desired changes, choose OK to return to the Check Spelling dialog box.

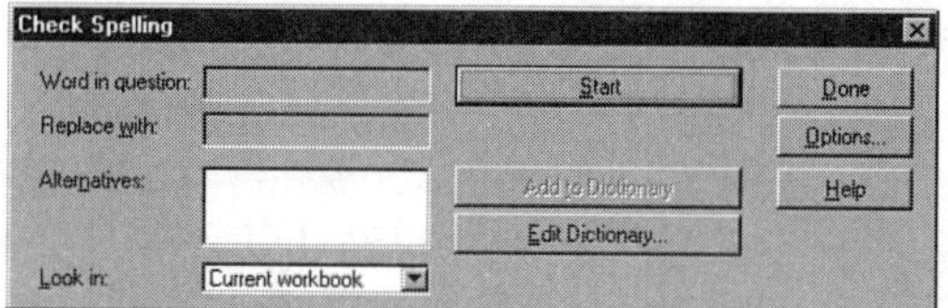

Fig. 3.18
Use the Check Spelling dialog box to indicate whether you want to check the entire worksheet or part of the worksheet.

4. Choose Start to begin the spell check.
5. If the spelling checker finds an unknown word, a dialog box like the one shown in figure 3.19 appears. Select the appropriate option from the dialog box, described as follows:

Option	**Action**
Replace	Replace the incorrect word with the word in the Replace With box. You can type a word into this box, or choose one of the words in the Alternatives list.
Replace All	Replace all occurrences of the misspelled word with the word in the Replace With box.
Skip	Skip this word and proceed to the next misspelling.
Skip All	Skip all occurrences of this word.
Add to Dictionary	Add this word to the user dictionary so that 1-2-3 will not flag it as misspelled again.
Edit Dictionary	Add or delete words from your 1-2-3 user dictionary.

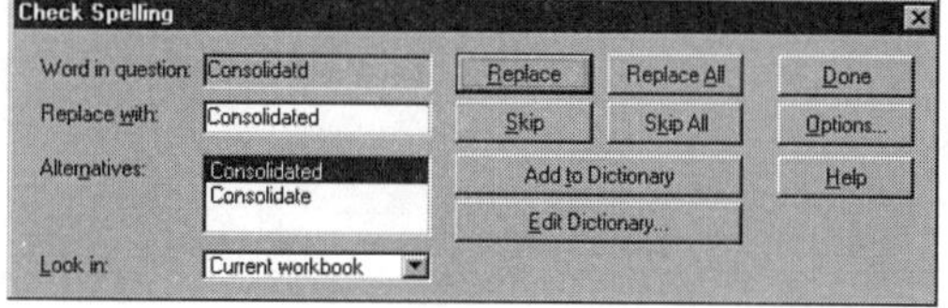

Fig. 3.19
Correct your spelling with the second Spell Check dialog box.

TIP You can drag the title bar to move the dialog box, so that you can see the misspelled word in context.

6. 1-2-3 continues the spell check. When 1-2-3 displays the dialog box message Search completed, click OK.
7. Choose the Done button in the Check Spelling dialog box to end the spell check.

TIP A quick way to select a replacement word is to double-click the desired alternative in the list.

The spelling checker may flag some correctly spelled words as incorrect, simply because those words are not in 1-2-3's dictionary. You can add those words to the dictionary by using the Add to Dictionary button. By adding words to the dictionary, you begin to create your own personal dictionary for repeated use. If the word is flagged, but you don't want to add it to your dictionary, use the Skip command to skip the word or the Skip All command to skip all occurrences of the word throughout this spell check session.

Remember, the spell check only checks for spelling, not for usage. As long as a word is in the dictionary, the spell check program thinks that the word is correct. So, if you type "too" instead of "to," the spell check does not flag it. Or if you type "far" instead of "car," the spell check thinks it is correct. The bottom line is that you still need to proofread your worksheet!

The Options button in the first Spell Check dialog box enables you to specify your preferences about how the spelling checker works and includes these choices (all of which are selected by default):

- *Repeated Words*. When this check box is selected, the spell check flags repeated words (such as "the the").
- *Words with Numbers*. Deselect this check box if you do not want the spell check to flag words that contain numbers as incorrect.
- *Words with Initial Caps*. Deselect this check box if you do not want the spell check to flag proper names as incorrect.
- *Macro/@Function Keywords, Punctuation*. Deselect this check box if you do not want the spell check to include a dictionary of special macro and @function words.
- *User Dictionary*. Deselect this check box if you do not want the spell check to list words that you have added to the dictionary in the list of Alternatives.

CHAPTER 4

Formatting Worksheets

by Jan Snyder

Although you can create a perfectly acceptable worksheet for your personal use by using a plain worksheet template with default font and color settings, 1-2-3 provides many features that let you format your worksheets so that they present your data in a professional, easy-to-read fashion. When you first create a workbook by starting 1-2-3 or by choosing File, New Workbook, 1-2-3 gives you the option of choosing from the available SmartMasters. These are templates for common business tasks that pre-format your worksheets, charts, and forms. After you assign a SmartMaster, you can use the InfoBox, SmartIcons, and status bar buttons to customize your worksheet. You also can choose to create a blank workbook, and then format your data as you enter it, also using commands in the InfoBox, SmartIcons, and formatting buttons on the status bar. ■

Work with column width and row height

Adjust column width and row height by entering a number, by dragging, or by double-clicking to change automatically.

Set styles with the new InfoBox

Change all your range and worksheet styles in this new multiple-panel dialog box.

Set workbook and worksheet style defaults

Change defaults that apply to most of your workbook or worksheet.

Format text and numbers

Use the InfoBox or status bar to format cell contents.

Change colors and add borders to cells and ranges

Dress up the appearance of your worksheets.

Work with styles

Create your own named styles or use the Style Gallery.

▶ **See** "Using SmartIcon Bars," **p. 766**

Setting Column Widths

When you start a new, blank workbook (and do not assign a SmartMaster template), the default column width of all columns is nine characters. You may have to change the width of a column or the height of a row to display data properly. If columns are too narrow, asterisks appear rather than numbers in the cells, and labels are truncated if the cell to the right of a long label contains data. If columns are too wide, you may not be able to see enough data on-screen or print enough data on one page.

NOTE 1-2-3 may display more or fewer characters than you expect in a cell. The column-width number approximates the number of characters that can be displayed. The actual display depends on the typeface and point size of the cell and the individual characters you have entered in the cell. ■

You can change the width of all the columns in the worksheet or the width of individual columns. To change the default column width for new workbooks, refer to the "Setting Workbook Style Defaults" section in this chapter.

Whether a number can fit into a cell depends on both the column width and the format of the number. For example, some worksheets are formatted so that negative numbers appear with parentheses. This makes every negative number two extra characters long. If a number appears as a row of asterisks, you can change the column width, the format, or both to display the number itself.

Changing the Default Column Width

You can change the column width for the entire worksheet by choosing Sheet, Sheet Properties or by clicking the Sheet Properties SmartIcon to open the Sheet InfoBox. Click the Basics tab (see fig. 4.1), and then specify the new column width, from one to 240 characters, in the Default column width spin box. The new setting is applied as the default column width for the current worksheet; any columns you insert use the new width. 1-2-3 also immediately adjusts the widths of all columns in the worksheet not formatted locally (set earlier to specific individual widths). Close the InfoBox by clicking the Close button in its top-right corner.

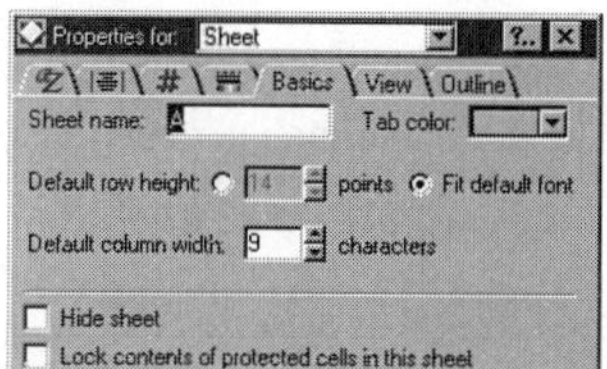

Fig. 4.1
Adjust the default column width for the current worksheet in the Basics panel of the Sheet InfoBox.

NOTE Individual column-width settings override the default column width. If you change the default column width after changing the width of individual columns, the individual columns retain their previously adjusted widths.

Changing Individual Column Widths

You can change the width of one or more columns by using the keyboard and the Range, Range Properties command. Alternatively, you can use the mouse to change the width of one or more columns.

To change the width of an individual column or a range of columns, follow these steps:

1. Select a cell or range in the column you want to change.

2. Choose Range, Range Properties or click the Range Properties SmartIcon. The Range InfoBox appears.

TIP You also can choose Range Properties from the shortcut menu after right-clicking the selected range.

3. Click the Basics tab. The Basics panel is displayed (see fig. 4.2).

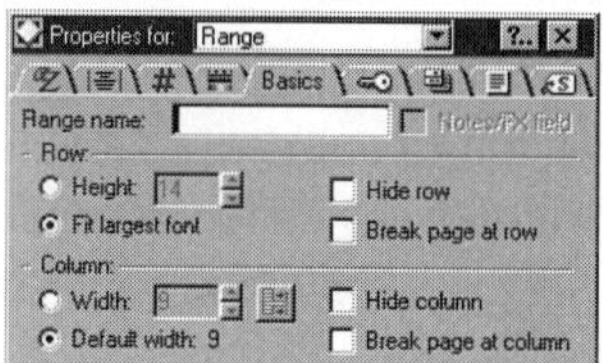

Fig. 4.2
Use the Range InfoBox to change the column width for individual columns.

4. Select the Width option button and type the new column width, from one to 240 characters, in the Width spin box or use the spin arrows to set the new value.

   The selected columns widen (or narrow) immediately as the Width value changes.

If you set the column width to 0, the columns in the selected range will be hidden. Refer to Chapter 15 "Managing the Worksheet Display" for more information about hiding columns.

▶ **See** "Hiding Worksheets, Columns, and Rows," **p. 401**

5. Close the InfoBox by clicking the Close button in its top-right corner.

To temporarily display the width of a column in the worksheet, position the mouse pointer on the right border of a column heading (the mouse pointer changes to a double-arrow pointing horizontally) and then hold down the left mouse button. The number of characters is displayed in a box. Release the mouse button to discontinue the display.

You can change the width of several columns by selecting a range that includes these columns before you issue the command. All columns represented in the range are affected when you use the InfoBox to change the column width.

To change the width of an individual column by dragging with the mouse, use these steps:

1. Move the mouse pointer to the column border (to the right of the column letter in the worksheet frame) until the mouse pointer changes to a double-arrow pointing horizontally.
2. Press and hold the left mouse button. The current width for that column is displayed in a box (see fig. 4.3).
3. Drag the column border to the left or right to its new position and release the mouse button.

When you use the mouse to change the width of a column, 1-2-3 displays a solid vertical line that moves with the mouse pointer to show you the position of the new column border.

You can change several columns at once with the mouse by clicking the first column's heading (for example, the letter C for column C) and dragging to highlight additional columns (see fig. 4.4). Then adjust the width of any one of the highlighted columns, and the widths of all the columns change to match the width of the column whose border you drag.

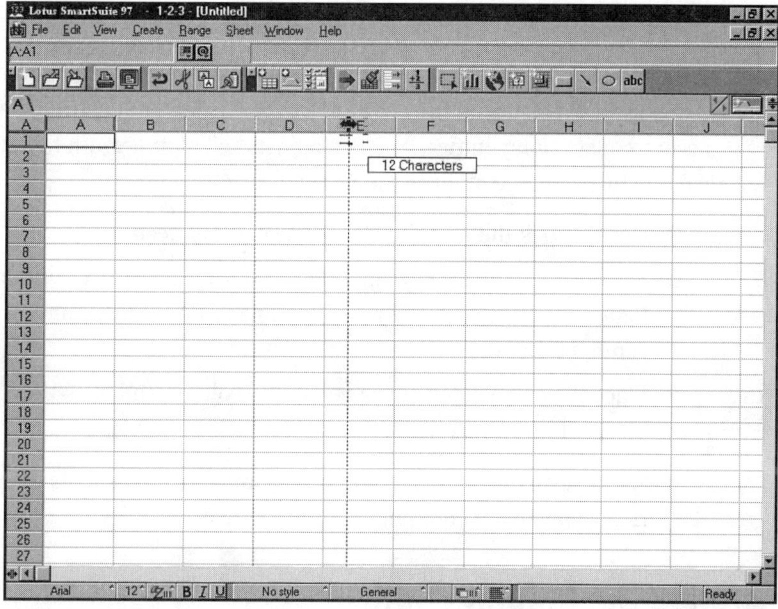

Fig. 4.3
Clicking the right border of a column header displays the current column width.

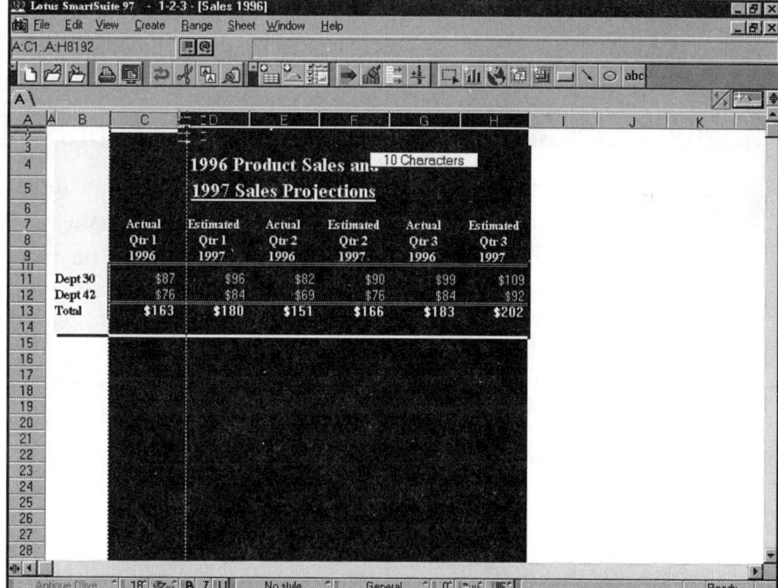

Fig. 4.4
Change the width of several columns at once using the mouse.

Fitting the Column Width to the Data

You can set up a column in a 1-2-3 worksheet so that its width automatically conforms to the longest data entry in the column. Using this feature ensures that every column width accommodates long entries. You can adjust the column width to fit the widest entry in the column by using one of three methods:

- Double-click the right border of the column heading.

- Select the column you want to fit to the widest entry. In the Basics panel of the Range InfoBox, click the Size Columns to Fit Widest Entry button (located near the center of the panel).

- Place the cell pointer in any cell in the column and click the Size Columns to Fit Widest Entry SmartIcon.

When you use any of these methods, 1-2-3 immediately adjusts the column width to match the widest entry in the column.

Restoring the Default Width

To restore a column's width to the worksheet default column width, choose Range, Range Properties. In the Basics panel of the InfoBox, select the Default width option button. The column or range of columns you selected are reset to the worksheet default column width.

Changing Column Widths for a Group of Sheets

Individual column widths and worksheet column widths can apply to several worksheets if you first group the sheets together. When you group worksheets, you can change column widths of every sheet in the group at the same time based on changes made to a single worksheet's column settings.

Group worksheets when you want all of the worksheets in a workbook to have the same format—for example, when each worksheet contains the same data for a different department or division. When you group worksheets, any formatting change (such as setting column widths) made to one worksheet in the group affects all the worksheets in that group.

To group sheets, choose Sheet, Group Sheets. In the Group Sheets dialog box, specify a worksheet letter for the First sheet of group, Last sheet of group, and Copy styles from this sheet (see fig. 4.5). Refer to Chapter 8, "Reorganizing Worksheets" for more information on grouping sheets.

▶ **See** "Grouping Worksheets," **p. 258**

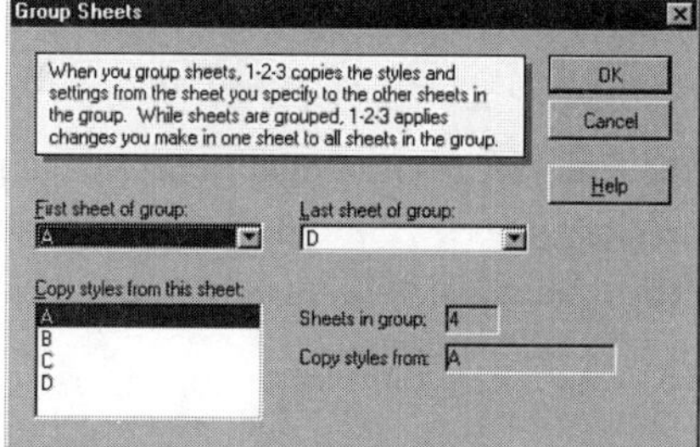

Fig. 4.5
Group a range of similar worksheets to apply formatting changes in the original sheet to all sheets in the group.

CAUTION

You cannot group noncontiguous worksheets in a workbook. The group includes sheets from the first to last specified in the Group Sheets dialog box.

Any changes you make to one worksheet apply to all worksheets in the group. You should therefore exercise caution when grouping sheets.

TROUBLESHOOTING

I changed the default column width for the entire worksheet, but some columns did not change. Any columns you have manually adjusted are not affected by the default column width changes. You can reset any column to the worksheet default by selecting any cell in the column and then choosing the Default width option button in the Basics panel of the Range InfoBox.

Do I have to expand a column's width just because text entries spill over the edge of the column? No. Text can spill over the edge of a column without problems. However, if the next column contains data, that data will hide any data that doesn't fit in the current column width.

I want to adjust the widths of several nonadjacent columns at once. Select nonadjacent columns by holding the Ctrl key as you click the column headings. Then adjust the width of any one column to affect them all.

Setting Row Height

By adjusting row height, you can make worksheet entries more attractive and easier to understand. The default row height, which depends on the default font, changes if you change the default font. For example, if the default worksheet font is 12-point Arial, the default row height is 14 points. If you change the global font to 14-point Arial, the default row height changes automatically to 17 points. A point is approximately 1/72 of an inch when printed; therefore, 12-point type is about 1/6 of an inch high when printed.

1-2-3 adjusts row height automatically to accommodate changes in point size. Occasionally, however, you may need to change a row's height—for example, to add more white space between rows of data. The following sections describe the process of changing row height.

Setting the Default Row Height

You can change the row height for the entire worksheet by choosing Sheet, Sheet Properties or by clicking the Sheet Properties SmartIcon to open the Sheet InfoBox. Click the Basics tab, and then type the new row height (in points) in the Default row height spin box or click the scroll arrows (see fig. 4.6). The new setting is applied as the default row height for the current worksheet; any rows you insert use the new height. 1-2-3 immediately adjusts the heights of all rows in the worksheet not formatted locally (set earlier to specific individual heights). Close the InfoBox by clicking the Close button in its top-right corner.

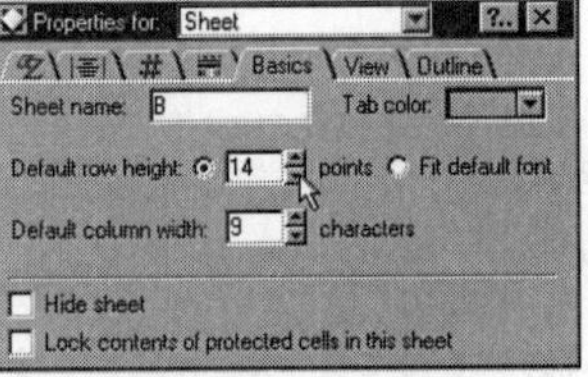

Fig. 4.6
Use the Basics panel of the Sheet InfoBox to adjust the default row height for the current worksheet.

Setting Individual Row Height

You can change the height of one or more rows by choosing Range, Range Properties to open the Range InfoBox. Choose the Basics tab and select the Height option button (it may already be selected). Type the new row height, in points, in the Height spin box or use the spin arrows to set the new value. The rows heights change immediately as the Height value changes.

If you set the row height to 0, the rows in the selected range will be hidden. Refer to Chapter 15 for more information about hiding rows.

▶ **See** "Hiding Worksheets, Columns, and Rows," **p. 401**

You can change the height of several rows by selecting a range that includes all the rows. The selected rows appear in the Range name text box in the Basics panel of the InfoBox. All rows represented in the range are affected when you set the Height in the InfoBox.

1-2-3 shows the row height if you press the left mouse button while the mouse pointer is positioned on the lower border of a row heading.

To change the height of an individual row with the mouse, use these steps:

1. Move the mouse pointer to the row border (below the row number in the worksheet frame) until the mouse pointer changes to a double-arrow pointing vertically.
2. Press and hold the left mouse button.
3. Drag the row border up or down to its new position and release the mouse button.

   When you use the mouse to change the height of a row, 1-2-3 displays a dotted horizontal line that moves with the mouse pointer to show the position of the new row border.

You can change several rows at once with the mouse by clicking the first row's number (for example, the number 1 for row 1) and dragging to highlight additional rows. Then adjust the height of any one of the highlighted rows. All highlighted rows comply with the changes made to the individual row.

Fitting the Row Height to the Font

You can automatically fit the row height to the largest font in the row by using the Fit Largest Font option in the Basics panel of the Range InfoBox (see fig. 4.7). With this option selected, 1-2-3 automatically locates the largest font in the row and adjusts the row's height to fit that font. Because row heights automatically fit your font selections as you make them, the only reason you would need to select this option is when you have set the normal row height to a specific size.

You can adjust the height of one or more selected rows to fit each row's tallest entry by double-clicking the lower border of one of the row headings.

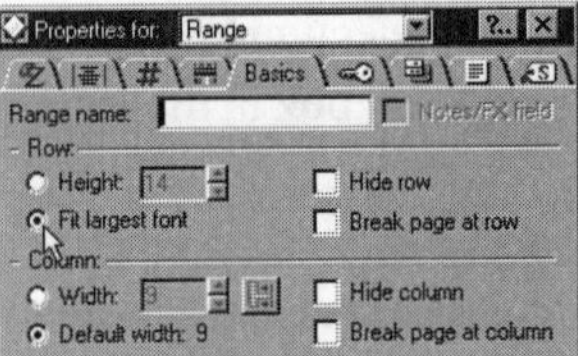

Fig. 4.7
The Fit Largest Font option is in the Basics panel of the Range InfoBox.

Changing Row Height for a Group of Sheets

Individual row height can apply to several worksheets if you first group them together by choosing Sheets, Group Sheets, as described in the earlier section, "Changing Column Widths for a Group of Sheets." If worksheets are grouped, all the sheets change row height at the same time based on changes made to a single worksheet's row settings.

Group sheets when several worksheets have the same format—for example, when each worksheet contains the same data for a different department or division. When you group worksheets, any formatting change (such as setting row heights) made to one worksheet in the group affects all the worksheets in that group. Therefore, you should be sure that you want to apply any formatting changes to all worksheets before you group them.

▶ **See** "Grouping Worksheets," **p. 258**

Setting Range Properties with the InfoBox

Earlier in this chapter you were introduced to the InfoBox to set column width and row height. The InfoBox is a comprehensive dialog box that enables you to change the many properties to style your 1-2-3 workbooks (see fig. 4.8). With Windows 95, the term *properties* came into widespread use, and refers to the many characteristics that define or describe a particular feature or object.

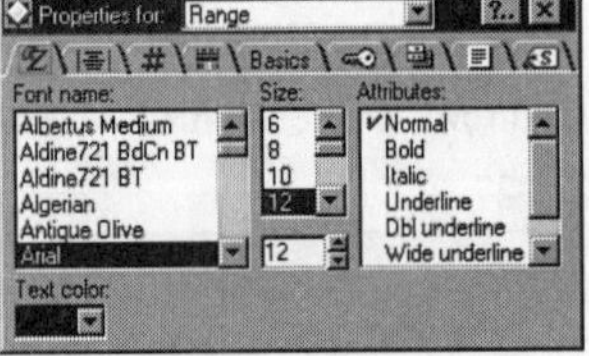

Fig. 4.8
The InfoBox is a quick tool for changing range or sheet properties, such as fonts and attributes.

With the InfoBox, you can change several of a selection's properties without closing and reopening the InfoBox. There is no OK button to confirm your changes—all changes are applied immediately, and the InfoBox is displayed until you close it or collapse it. You also can select other ranges or change properties for an entire worksheet.

To display the InfoBox, first select the cell or range and then display the InfoBox by any of the following methods:

- Choose Range, Range Properties.
- Right-click the cell or range and then choose Range Properties from the shortcut menu that appears.

- Click the Range Properties SmartIcon.
- Press Alt+Enter.

Because you chose range properties, the Properties For drop-down list at the top of the InfoBox shows `Range` selected. Properties you change apply to the range address displayed in the Range name text box in the Basics panel of the InfoBox.

NOTE You can change default properties for an entire worksheet by first selecting Sheet in the Properties For drop-down list at the top of the InfoBox. See the section, "Setting Worksheet Style Defaults," later in this chapter.

Choosing InfoBox Tabs

How can so many properties fit in the InfoBox without taking up too much space onscreen? The InfoBox is organized into several panels, accessed by clicking tabs at the top edge of the panels. This keeps the InfoBox compact, but if it blocks your view of the area of the worksheet you want to style, you can always move it out of the way by dragging its title bar.

Figure 4.9 shows the tabs for the Range InfoBox. The Sheet InfoBox has several of the same tabs for setting default properties for the worksheet styles. Table 4.1 shows the properties available on each tab of the Range InfoBox.

Balloon help is available for the InfoBox tabs. Simply position the mouse pointer over a tab; balloon help appears with a brief description of the tab's panel. This book uses the balloon help description when referring to a tab or panel that does not already show a word.

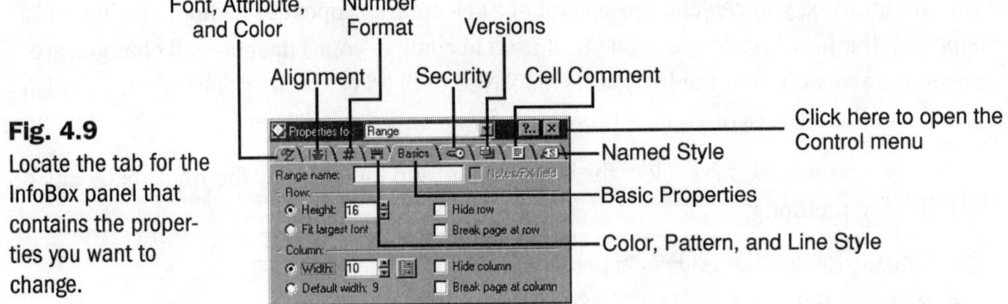

Fig. 4.9
Locate the tab for the InfoBox panel that contains the properties you want to change.

Table 4.1 Range InfoBox Properties

Tab	Properties
Font, Attribute, and Color	Font name, Size, Style, Text color
Alignment	Horizontal alignment, Vertical alignment, Align across columns, Wrap Text in cell, Orientation
Number Format	Category, Current format, Parentheses, Show in Frequently Used list
Color, Pattern, and Line Style	Pattern, Pattern color, Background color, Text color, Negative values in red, Border, Line style, Line color, Designer frame
Basics	Range name, Notes/FX field, Row height, Fit largest font, Hide row, Break page at row, Column width, Default width, Hide column, Break page at column
Security	Hide cell contents, Protect cell contents from changes
Versions	Name of current version, Comment, Show name and borders, Keep style with version, Protection
Cell Comment	Cell comment, Name and Date Stamp button
Named Style	Style name (buttons to create and manage styles)

Changing a Range's Properties

This chapter focuses on use of the InfoBox range properties for formatting worksheets. The InfoBox is convenient and enables you to accomplish multiple style changes without repeating menu options to open dialog boxes. You use the controls in the InfoBox the same way you use controls in other dialog boxes: selecting options, entering text, or clicking buttons. The surprising effect is that you see the properties applied to the selected range immediately, allowing you to further change it, or even revert to the way it was, without closing the InfoBox.

When you have finished assigning properties, you can:

- Keep the InfoBox open for later use as you work. Move it to a new location by dragging its title bar. You also can move the InfoBox choosing Move from the InfoBox Control menu and using the arrow keys to reposition it.
- Close the InfoBox by clicking the Close button or by choosing Close from the InfoBox Control menu.
- Collapse the InfoBox by choosing Collapse from the InfoBox Control menu. The InfoBox shrinks, revealing only its title bar and tabs. (Click a tab or choose Restore from the same menu to display the entire InfoBox again.)

Another way to collapse or restore the InfoBox is to double-click its title bar.

Understanding Style

Beginning with 1-2-3 97 Edition for Windows 95, you use the InfoBox to set styles in your worksheets. The term *style* refers to virtually any type of formatting you can apply to data in a cell, such as currency symbols; commas and decimal places; a new font or point size; bold, underline, or italic; or the alignment of data in a cell. It also includes setting row height and column width, as discussed earlier in this chapter.

While the InfoBox is the most complete collection for making multiple style changes to your worksheets, 1-2-3 continues to feature the status bar buttons and SmartIcons for selecting some styles. When style characteristics are applied to a cell, the entry in the cell reflects those characteristics; indicators for certain of the style properties appear on the status bar.

For example, in figure 4.10, the entry in cell C11 displays a formula result `($2,775)` in currency format, complete with a dollar sign, comma, and zero decimal places—in a 14-point sans-serif font. The status bar displays the indicators `US Dollar` (the number format), `0` (the number of decimal places), `Arial` (the font), and `14` (the point size).

Fig. 4.10
Indicators for several style properties appear on the status bar.

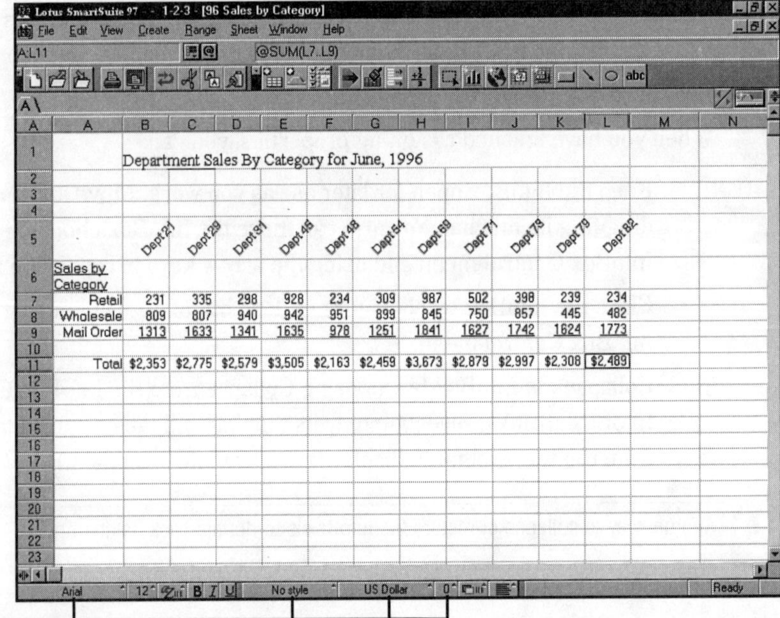

Status bar style indicators

To change the style properties of a cell or a range of cells, first select the cell or range and then display the InfoBox by any of the methods described in the section, "Setting Range Properties with the InfoBox," in this chapter. After the InfoBox is displayed, choose the tab that accesses the panel of properties you want to change, as described earlier in the chapter in the section, "Choosing InfoBox Tabs." On each panel, properties are available for entry or selection, as with usual dialog boxes.

You also can use the status bar to change the named style, cell color, number format, decimal places, text alignment, text attributes, font, and point size of a cell or range. At first glance, you might not realize that the boxes making up the status bar are actually buttons, or *selectors*. For example, if you click the font selector, 1-2-3 displays a pop-up list of other fonts (see fig. 4.11). The status bar selectors let you quickly change certain style properties for the selected cell or range without choosing InfoBox options. (For a complete discussion of the status bar, see Chapter 1, "Getting Around in 1-2-3 and Worksheets.") Use the mouse or the arrow keys and the Enter key to choose an item from the pop-up list.

▶ **See** "Understanding the 1-2-3 Screen," **p. 17**

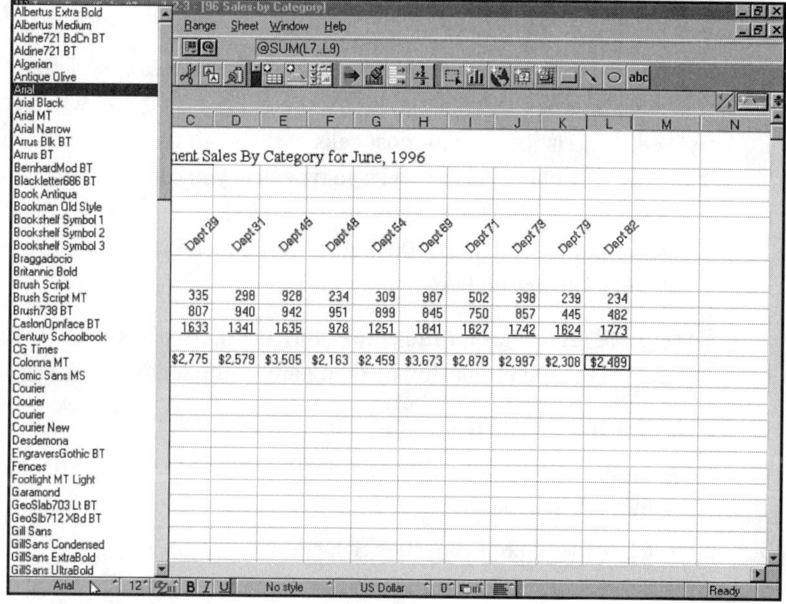

Fig. 4.11
You can see what font is currently selected in the status bar, and click the font selector to choose another font.

Setting Workbook Style Defaults

1-2-3 provides a number of default settings that determine how the program operates under most circumstances. When you choose File, User Setup, 1-2-3 Preferences, you access the 1-2-3 Preferences dialog box. Use this dialog box to change many of the default settings that affect the display and behavior of 1-2-3 in the current session and all future sessions. The following options, all located in the New Workbook Defaults panel of the dialog box (see fig. 4.12), affect the formatting of data in new workbooks created in 1-2-3:

- Text Format: Font name, Size, Text color, and Background color
- Column and row size: Column width and row height

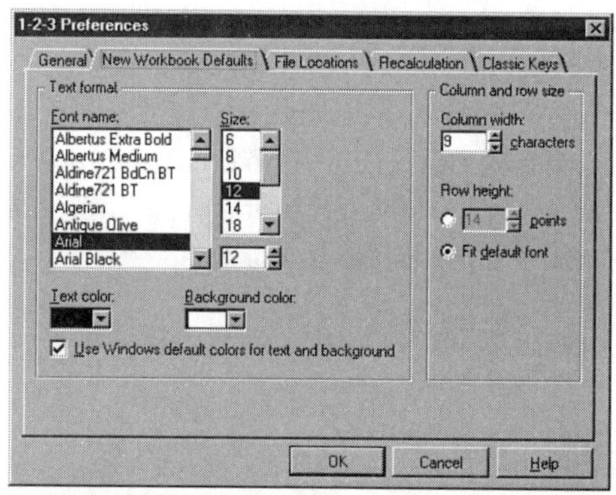

Fig. 4.12
A few style properties can be set as defaults for new workbooks.

Setting Worksheet Style Defaults

In 1-2-3, you can set certain style properties for an entire worksheet or workbook before you begin entering data. Set styles for the entire worksheet when you want to specify the style characteristics used in most cells of the worksheet. For example, if you want the data in the worksheet to appear in a large typeface, you can specify a point size of 14 for the entire worksheet. If all the values in the worksheet represent dollars, you can apply the US Dollar number format to the entire worksheet. Later you can override the default format on a cell-by-cell basis.

To set style properties for the entire worksheet, use the Sheet InfoBox (see fig. 4.13). You access the Sheet InfoBox by doing any of the following:

- Choose Sheet, Sheet Properties.
- Right-click the worksheet tab and then choose Sheet Properties from the shortcut menu that appears.

- Click the Sheet Properties SmartIcon.

TIP If the InfoBox is already displayed for changing Range Properties, display Sheet Properties by choosing Sheet in the Properties For drop-down list at the top of the InfoBox.

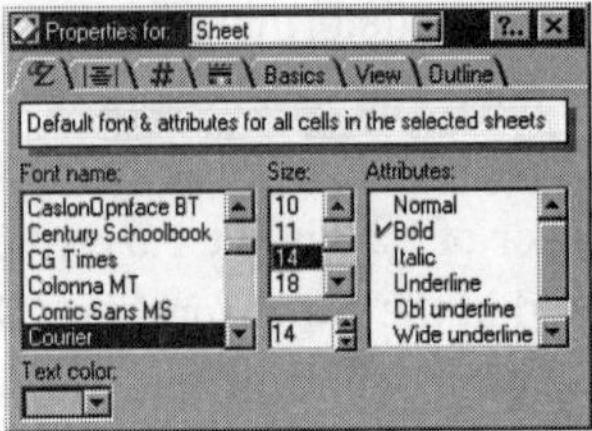

Fig. 4.13
Use the Sheet InfoBox to set default style properties for the entire worksheet.

Using the Sheet InfoBox, you can specify the font, number format, colors, and other options for the entire worksheet. The options in this dialog box are the same as the options that you can specify for an individual cell or range (with the exception of the worksheet tab color specification). For detailed descriptions of these options, refer to "Working with Number Formats," "Changing Fonts and Attributes," and "Formatting Cells with Color and Borders," later in this chapter. If you intend to create multiple worksheets for the current workbook, you can apply the style properties to all worksheets in the workbook by grouping the sheets, as described earlier in this chapter.

NOTE You can set the color of an individual worksheet tab by selecting a color from the Tab color drop-down palette in the Basics panel of the Sheet InfoBox (refer to fig. 4.13). To set the color for each worksheet tab in a workbook, you select each worksheet tab, then select a Tab color in the Sheet InfoBox.

The remainder of this chapter describes all the style properties you can apply to individual cells or to entire worksheets.

Understanding the Difference Between Content and Format

Cell formatting changes the *appearance* of data, not its actual value. For example, some formats display a number as a rounded value. However, even when a number appears rounded in the cell, 1-2-3 stores the exact value of the number and uses the exact value in formulas and calculations. For example, if you format 1234.5 in Fixed format with 0 decimal places, the number appears as 1235, but 1-2-3 uses the exact value 1234.5 in formulas.

In figure 4.14, the sales total in cell C11 looks like an addition error. The formula in cell C9 is +B9*1.1, resulting in 95.7. Cell C9 displays 96, however, because it is formatted as Fixed with 0 decimal places. The result of a similar formula in cell C10 is 83.6, but the cell displays 84. The result of the formula in cell C11 is 179.3, but the cell displays 179. The formula appears to add as follows: 96+84=179, when the equation should result in 180. This apparent error is produced by rounding the displayed values without rounding the actual values.

Part I Ch 4

To avoid rounding errors, round the *actual value* of the numbers used in formulas, not just their displayed value. To round values in a formula, use the @ROUND function. For example, to eliminate the rounding error in figure 4.16, change the formula in cell C9 to @ROUND((B9*1.1),0). Then copy the formula to cell C10. When you round the numbers in the formula with this technique, the @SUM function in cell C11 correctly results in 180. For complete information on functions, see Chapter 6, "Using Functions."

NOTE 1-2-3 displays numbers with as many as 15 decimal places. By default, negative numbers have a minus sign and decimal values have leading zeroes. The following section "Working with Number Formats" tells you how to change these number format settings.

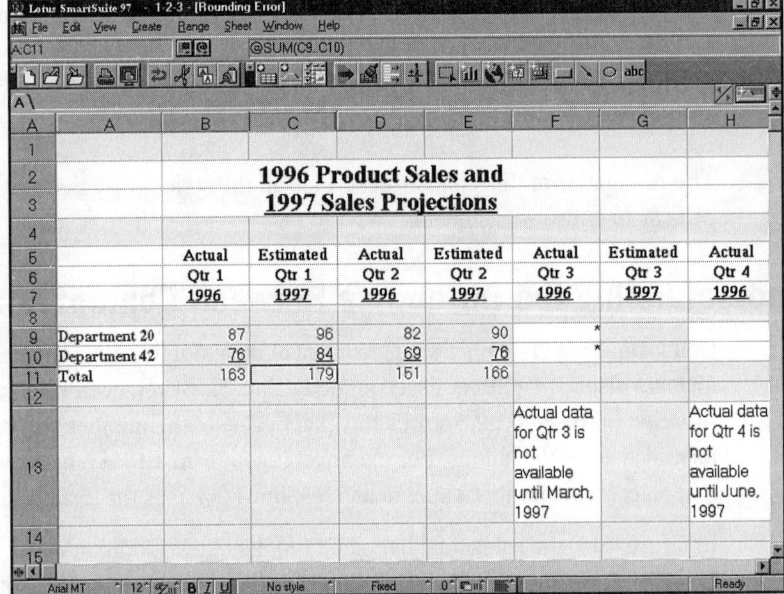

Lotus SmartSuite 97 - 1-2-3 - [Rounding Error]
File Edit View Create Range Sheet Window Help
A:C11
@SUM(C9..C10)
1996 Product Sales and
1997 Sales Projections
Actual Qtr 1 1996
Estimated Qtr 1 1997
Actual Qtr 2 1996
Estimated Qtr 2 1997
Actual Qtr 3 1996
Estimated Qtr 3 1997
Actual Qtr 4 1996
Department 20 87 96 82 90
Department 42 76 84 69 76
Total 163 179 151 166
Actual data for Qtr 3 is not available until March, 1997
Actual data for Qtr 4 is not available until June, 1997
Arial MT
No style
Fixed
Ready

Fig. 4.14
The value in cell C11 is the result of a rounding error.

Working with Number Formats

The third tab of the 1-2-3 InfoBox is Number Format. You use this panel to assign a specific number format to a cell or range of cells. Assigning a format to cells maintains consistency throughout the worksheet and saves you the effort of typing symbols (dollar signs, commas, parentheses, and so on) along with the cell value.

Number formats apply only to numeric data (numeric formulas and numbers). If you format a label as Fixed or Scientific, for example, the number format has no effect on how a label appears.

To simplify locating the number formats, 1-2-3 97 categorizes the number formats. The categories are: Frequently Used, Number, Currency, ISO Currency, Date, Time, and Text. Table 4.2 shows samples of some of the available cell formats and how each one changes the appearance of data. Date formats in this table assume that the current year is 1996. For a discussion of available currency formats, see "Changing the Currency Format" later in this chapter.

Table 4.2 Number Formats

Format	Entry	Displayed
General	**1234**	1234
General	**1234.5**	1234.5
Fixed, 2 decimal places	**1234.5**	1234.50
Fixed, 0 decimal places	**1234.5**	1235
Comma, 2 decimal places	**1234.5**	1,234.50
US Dollar, 2 decimal places	**1234.5**	$1,234.50
ISO US Dollar, 2 decimal places	**1234.5**	USD 1,2345.50
Percent, 1 decimal place	**0.364**	36.4%
Scientific, 4 decimal places	**1234.5**	1.2345E+003
31-Dec-96 (date format)	**2/14/97**	14-Feb-97
31-Dec (date format)	**2/14/97**	14-Feb
Dec-96 (date format)	**2/14/97**	Feb-97
12/31/96 (date format)	**2/14/97**	02/14/97
12/31 (date format)	**2/14/97**	02/14
11:59:59 PM (time format)	**1:15**	01:15:00 AM
11:59 PM (time format)	**1:15**	01:15 AM
23:59:59 (time format)	**1:15**	01:15:00
23:59 (time format)	**1:15**	01:15
1:59 PM (time format)	**1:15**	1:15 AM
Formula (text format)	**+C6**	+C6
Label (text format)	**57 Main St.**	57 Main St.

NOTE General format is the default format that 1-2-3 uses whenever you create a new worksheet. This format is discussed in detail later in this chapter.

If a column isn't wide enough to display a formatted numeric entry, asterisks fill the cell. If the numeric entry is unformatted and too long to fit in the cell, 1-2-3 converts the entry to scientific notation. To display the data, you must change the format or the column width. See "Setting Column Widths," earlier in this chapter, for instructions on changing column width.

NOTE If you have a color monitor, you can display negative numbers in the worksheet in red. For details, see the section "Formatting Cells with Color and Borders" later in this chapter.

Click the Reset to Sheet Format button in the Number Format panel of the Range InfoBox to return a cell value to the default format for the worksheet.

Handling Zeroes

By default, 1-2-3 displays a zero (0) in any cell that contains an entry of zero or a formula that evaluates to zero. Using the Number Format panel of the Sheet InfoBox, you can control how 1-2-3 displays zeroes in your worksheet. You have the option of changing the Display zeroes as setting so that 1-2-3 displays a blank cell or a label that you specify. (A *label* is defined as any entry that begins with a letter or a label-prefix character, such as ' for left-alignment or " for right-alignment.) To have 1-2-3 display a blank cell, deselect the check box next to the Display zeroes as text box. To have 1-2-3 display a label (such as the word *zero*), type the label in the Display zeroes as text box, and be sure the check box also is selected.

Assigning Number Formats

To change the format of a cell or range, access the Number Format panel of the Range InfoBox by choosing Range, Range Properties. If you preselected a range, that range is listed in the Range name text box in the Basics panel of the InfoBox; if you did not preselect a range, you may select the range while the InfoBox is displayed. Select the Number Format tab, and then choose the type of format from the Category list box. When you select a Category, the Current format list box displays the formats assigned to that category (see fig. 4.15). Select the format you want from the Current format list box. The format of the range changes immediately to the format you specified.

Some of the more common number formats appear not only in their own category, but in the Frequently Used category. To add other formats to the Frequently Used category, highlight the format, and then select the Show in Frequently Used list check box in the Number Format panel of the Range InfoBox.

If you choose the Currency, ISO Currency, or Number category (except General), you can specify the number of decimal places or use the default number, 2, shown in the Decimals spin box. To change the number of decimal places, type another number between 0 and 15 or use the scroll arrows (spinners) to change the number.

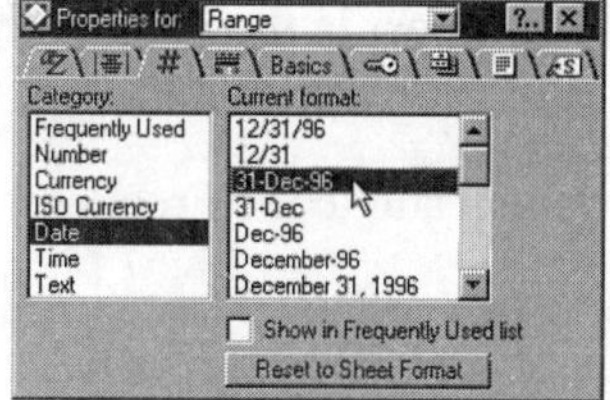

Fig. 4.15
To change the date format of a cell or range, select Date in the Category list box and then select the specific date format you want in the Current format list box.

The format button on the status bar displays the format of the current cell (see fig. 4.16). For example, `Fixed` appears on the format button when the current cell is formatted with the Fixed format. The number of decimal places for the current cell appears on the decimal button. In figure 4.16, the status bar shows `Fixed` on the format button and `0` on the decimal button. You can use the format button to select a number format for the highlighted cell or range.

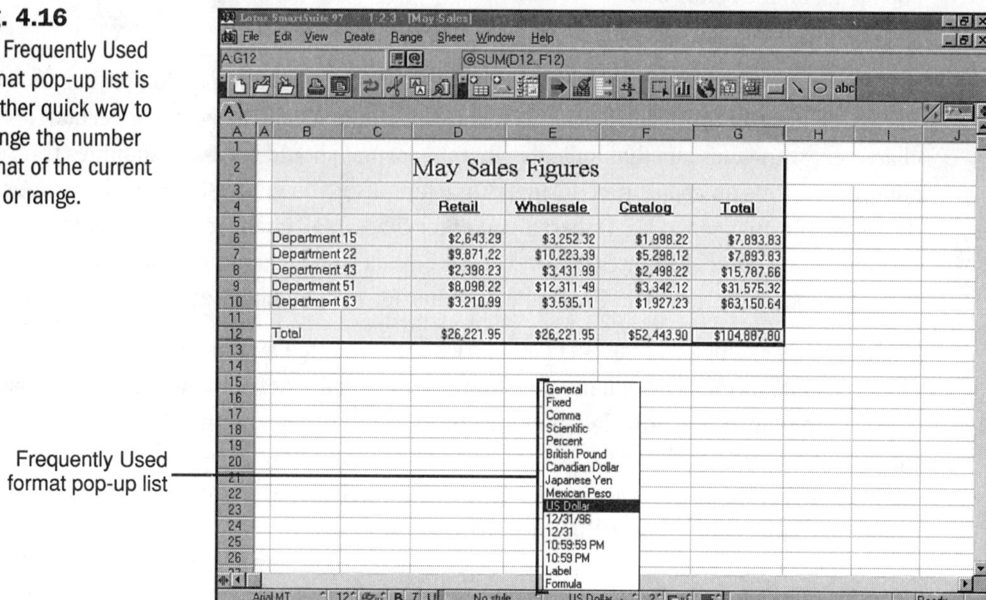

Fig. 4.16
The Frequently Used format pop-up list is another quick way to change the number format of the current cell or range.

The format button on the status button pops up a list that includes only the formats that have been added to the Frequently Used category (common formats have already been added for you). To change the formats that appear in the Frequently Used format pop-up list, do the following:

1. Select a cell with the format you want to add to the Frequently Used list.
2. Open the Range InfoBox.
3. Choose the Number Format tab. You see the current format highlighted in the Current format list box.
4. Select the Show in Frequently Used list check box.

The new format is added to the format pop-up list on the status bar, as well as to the Frequently Used category in the Category list in the Number Format panel of the InfoBox.

TIP You also can remove formats you never use from the Frequently Used list by locating them in the InfoBox and clearing the Show in Frequently Used list check box.

The following sections describe the formats available in the InfoBox and from the format pop-up list on the status bar.

▶ **See** "Entering Data," **p. 66**

Setting the Number Format Automatically While 1-2-3 97 Edition no longer has the Automatic number format, cells can be formatted automatically by entering certain characters with your data that indicate what the format should be. 1-2-3 examines the entry and selects an appropriate format. For example, if you enter **$325**, 1-2-3 changes the format for that cell to US Dollar; if you enter **50%**, 1-2-3 changes the format to Percent. If you enter **325** or **50**, however, 1-2-3 makes no change to the format, and the cell remains formatted as General or another format you have set.

Table 4.3 lists examples of how certain entries are formatted automatically when you enter data into a cell. (The cell has a column width of 9; the default font is 12-point Arial.) The first column shows how the entry was typed. The second column shows the number format 1-2-3 assigns to the entry. The third column shows how the entry is stored in the worksheet; the fourth column shows how the data is displayed in the worksheet. Date examples in this table assume that the current year is 1997.

Table 4.3 Automatic Effects of Entries on Number Format

Typed Entry	Cell Format	Data Stored	Display Result
1,258	Comma, 0	1258	`1,258`
1,258.00	Comma, 2	1258	`1,258.00`

Typed Entry	Cell Format	Data Stored	Display Result
87.00	General (not changed)	87	87
$258.00	US Dollar, 2	258	$258.00
25%	Percent, 0	0.25	25%
2.50%	Percent, 2	0.025	2.50%
1.2e4	Scientific, 1	12000	1.2E+004
2.587e-16	Scientific, 3	2.587E-016	2.587E-016
25.87e-17	Scientific, 2	2.587E-016	2.59E-016
20-Oct-97	31-Dec-96	35723	20-Oct-97
20-Oct	31-Dec	35723*	20-Oct
Oct-97	Dec-96	35704	Oct-97
10/20/97	12/31/96	35723	10/20/97
10/15	General (not changed)	0.666666666666667	0.666667
6:23:57 AM	11:59:59 PM	0.266631944444444	**************
6:23:57	23:59:59	0.266631944444444	06:23:57
6:23:57 PM	1:59:59 PM	0.766631944444444	**************
6:23 AM	1:59 PM	0.265972222222222	6:23 AM
6:23	23:59	0.265972222222222	06:23
6:23 PM	1:59 PM	0.765972222222222	6:23 PM
18:23:57	23:59:59	0.766631944444444	18:23:57
18:23	23:59	0.765972222222222	18:23

After you enter a number into a cell and 1-2-3 applies a format, the format stays with the cell unless you enter another number that can automatically reformat the cell. For example, if you type **$250.00** into a cell, its format changes to US Dollar format with two decimal places. If you later type **25%** into the cell, 1-2-3 automatically changes the cell format to Percent. This feature is new to 1-2-3 97 Edition.

If you type an invalid number in a cell, such as **57 Main Street**, 1-2-3 precedes the invalid entry with a label prefix and considers the entry a label. The cell's current number format is unchanged.

If the number looks like one of the date or time formats, 1-2-3 uses that date or time format. However, 1-2-3 does not recognize the date format 12/31; it stores 12/31 as a formula (12 divided by 31).

1-2-3 formats a cell automatically only when you enter a number with certain automatic conditions, as illustrated in Table 4.3. If you enter a label or a formula in a cell, the number format does not change. If you later enter a number into the cell, 1-2-3 reformats the cell if one of the automatic conditions is present.

Currency Format and ISO Currency Format 1-2-3 provides 43 possible currency formats, as well as the ISO (International Standards Organization) codes for the 43 countries in the ISO Currency format list. You select the default currency for 1-2-3 (and other programs) in the Regional Settings of the Windows 95 Control Panel. Numbers formatted as any of the 86 currencies can have from 0 to 15 decimal places. Thousands are separated by a comma (or other specified international separator). Negative numbers appear with a minus sign or in parentheses—depending on the current setting in the Windows 95 Control Panel.

NOTE The Default Currency SmartIcon formats numbers in the current default currency. The default currency is set in the Windows 95 Control Panel. Open the Regional Settings properties and then use the Regional Settings tab to select a country, and the Number and Currency tabs to define options for the country you selected. Refer to Windows 95 documentation for more information about changing the Regional Settings.

1-2-3 also provides three SmartIcons to quickly format a number in US Dollars ($), Japanese yen (¥), or British pounds (£). These SmartIcons format with the default thousands separator and decimal places (two for the pound and the dollar, zero for the yen). First select the range to format and then click the SmartIcon.

NOTE If a SmartIcon does not appear in your SmartIcons set, choose File, User Setup, SmartIcons Setup to add it to the icon set you work with. For more information about SmartIcons, see "Customizing the SmartIcons," in Chapter 34.

To choose a Currency or ISO Currency format, open the InfoBox and select the Number Format tab. Select Currency or ISO Currency in the Category list box, and then choose the country currency in the Current format list box. Table 4.4 shows several examples of currency formats in cells that have a column width of 9 and the default font of 12-point Arial. The examples include international currency symbols in addition to the dollar sign. USD is the ISO code for US Dollar.

Table 4.4 Examples of Different Currency Formats

Typed Entry	Format	Decimal Places	Display Result
123	US Dollar	2	`$123.00`
123	ISO US Dollar	2	`USD 123.00`
123	Japanese Yen	2	`¥123`
123	British Pound	2	`£123.00`
-123.124	US Dollar	0	`($123)` or `-$123`
1234.12	US Dollar	0	`$1,234`
1234567.12	US Dollar	2	`**************`

To change the currency symbol or the ISO code for a currency format (or to change the position of the symbol), choose the Currency Option button on the Number Format panel.

Date and Time Formats All the formats discussed so far deal with regular numeric values. You use *date and time formats* when you work with date and time calculations or functions (see Chapter 6, "Using Functions"). For example, the Dec-96 format is used to format a date as Month-Year. 8/29/97, therefore, appears as `Aug-97`.

In the Number Format panel of the InfoBox, there are Date and Time categories. Choose Date or Time to display the list of available formats.

Date Formats When you use date functions, 1-2-3 stores the date as a number representing the number of days since December 31, 1899. The date number for January 1, 1900 is 1. The date number for January 15, 1996 is 35079. The latest date 1-2-3 can display is December 31, 2099 (that date has the date number 73050).

CAUTION

All the date numbers starting with March 1, 1900 are off by one day. The calendar inside 1-2-3 treats 1900 as a leap year; it isn't. A date number of 60 appears as `02/29/00`—a date that never existed. Unless you compare dates before February 28, 1900 to dates after February 28, 1900, this error has no effect on the worksheets. Dates can be off by one day, however, if you export data to a database program.

If the number in a cell formatted with a date format is less than 1 or greater than 73050, the date appears as asterisks. Date formats ignore fractions; the value 35723.99 in a cell with the 12/31/96 date format appears as `10/20/96`. The fraction represents the time—a fractional portion of a 24-hour clock.

To format a cell as a date, select the Number Format tab in the InfoBox and select one of the date formats. To quickly choose a date format, click the format selector in the status bar and choose a format from the Frequently Used format pop-up list.

To enter a date, you do not have to know the date number or the date and time functions. Type what looks like a date in any of the 1-2-3 date formats that begin with a number. That is, type an entry like 10/20/97 or 20-Oct-97 or 20-Oct. (If you enter a date without the year, 1-2-3 assumes you want the current year, which is drawn from the current system date.) 1-2-3 converts the entry to a date number and, if you have not yet formatted the range with a date format, 1-2-3 changes the Automatic format to the appropriate date format. The contents box in the edit line displays the date number, and the cell displays the formatted date. If you have already formatted the range, the date appears according to the format you specified.

Don't be concerned with which date number refers to which date. Let 1-2-3 format the date number to appear as a textual date.

You can quickly update the system date and time in Windows 95 by double-clicking the clock, at the right side of the taskbar. In the Date/Time Properties dialog box, highlight the current date, update the time, and then click OK.

Table 4.5 shows several examples of dates in cells that have a column width of 9 and the default font of 12-point Arial. In each case, the cell format shown was applied to the cell after the entry was typed. (Remember, 1-2-3 automatically formats a date entry it recognizes.) This table assumes that the current year is 1997.

Table 4.5 Examples of Date Formats

Typed Entry	Cell Format	Data Stored	Display Result
10/20/97	31-Dec-96	35723	20-Oct-97
10/20/97	31-Dec	35723	20-Oct
10/20/97	Dec-96	35723	Oct-97
10/20/97	12/31/96	35723	10/20/97
10/20/97	12/31	35723	10/20
20-Oct	31-Dec-96	35723	20-Oct-97

TIP  You can quickly enter today's date in the current cell by clicking the Insert Date icon. 1-2-3 automatically applies the 12/31/96 date format to the cell.

Time Formats When you use a time function, such as @NOW, 1-2-3 stores the time as a *time fraction*. You can format a time fraction so that it looks like a time of day by choosing any of the time formats in the Number Format dialog box or by clicking the format selector in the status bar and choosing a time format.

▶ **See** "Calendar Functions," **p. 159**

When you enter a specific time, such as 3:00 AM, 12:00 PM, or 6:00 PM, 1-2-3 applies the correct time format to the entry but stores the entry as a time fraction. For example, 3:00 AM is stored as 0.125; 12:00 PM is stored as 0.5; and 6:00 PM is stored as 0.75. If you type 6:23, 6:23:00, 6:23AM, or 6:23:00 AM, 1-2-3 converts the entry to the time fraction 0.265972... (to 15 decimal places). If you type 6:23:57 or 6:23:57 AM, 1-2-3 converts the entry to the time fraction 0.26663194... (to 15 decimal places).

1-2-3 uses a 24-hour clock system; noon is regarded as 12:00 and midnight as 00:00. Times between midnight and 1:00 A.M. are displayed as 00:01, 00:02:00, and so on. You don't have to type **AM** for times before noon. For times after noon, however, type **PM** or type the hour using the numbers 12 to 23.

NOTE You can type the letters *AM* or *PM* in either uppercase or lowercase; it isn't necessary to type a space between the time and the AM or PM designator.

Table 4.6 shows several examples of time formats in cells that have a column width of 9 and the font of 12-point Arial. The Data Stored column displays only 10 of the 15 decimal places that 1-2-3 stores.

Table 4.6 Examples of Time Formats

Typed Entry	Cell Format	Data Stored	Display Result
6:23:57	1:59:59 PM	0.2666319444	6:23:57 AM
6:23:57 PM	1:59:59 PM	0.7666319444	6:23:57 PM
6:23	01:59 PM	0.2659722222	06:23 AM
6:23:57	23:59:59	0.2666319444	06:23:57
6:23:57 PM	23:59:59	0.7666319444	18:23:57
6:23	23:59	0.2659722222	06:23
6:23 PM	23:59	0.7659722222	18:23

Fixed Format You use *Fixed format* when you want to display numbers with a fixed number of decimal points. Table 4.7 shows several examples of Fixed format in cells that have a column width of 9 and the default font of 12-point Arial. In all cases, the full number in the cell is used in calculations, even though the displayed value may be rounded, or asterisks may appear.

Table 4.7 Examples of Fixed Format

Typed Entry	Number of Decimal Places	Display Result
123.46	0	123
123.46	1	123.5
–123.46	2	-123.46
123.46	4	123.4600
1234567.89	4	**************
123456789	2	**************

Scientific Format You use *Scientific format* to display very large or very small numbers. Such numbers usually have a few significant digits and many zeroes as placeholders to show how large or small the number is.

A number in scientific notation has two parts; a *mantissa* and an *exponent.* The mantissa is a number from 1 to 10 that contains the significant digits. The exponent tells you how many places to move the decimal point to get the actual value of the number.

1-2-3 displays numbers in Scientific format in powers of 10, with 0 to 15 decimal places, and an exponent from –308 to +308. If a number has more significant digits than the number you specify in the format, the number is rounded on the display, although 1-2-3 uses the full value for formulas and calculations.

1230000000000 appears as `1.23E+012` in Scientific format with two decimal places. E+012 signifies that you must move the decimal point 12 places to the right to get the actual number. 0.000000000237 appears as `2.4E-010` in Scientific format with one decimal place. E-010 means that you must move the decimal point 10 places to the left to get the actual number.

NOTE A number too large to appear in a cell in General format appears in Scientific format.

Table 4.8 shows several examples of Scientific format in cells that have the default column width of 9 and the default font of 12-point Arial.

Table 4.8 Examples of Scientific Format

Typed Entry	Number of Decimal Places	Display Result
1632116750000	2	1.63E+012
16321167500000	2	1.63E+013
–1632116750000	1	-1.6E+012
–1632116750000	2	-1.63E+012
00000000012	2	1.20E+001
–.00000000012	0	-1E-010

Comma Format Like the Fixed format, the *Comma format* displays data with a fixed number of decimal places (from 0 to 15). The Comma format separates the thousands with commas (or another symbol specified in the Regional Settings of the Windows 95 Control Panel). Negative numbers appear with a minus sign or in parentheses—depending on the current setting in the International dialog box. Positive numbers less than 1,000 appear the same way in Fixed format and Comma format.

TIP For large numbers, use the Comma format instead of the Fixed format. The number 12,300,000.00 is easier to read than 12300000.00.

Table 4.9 shows several examples of Comma format in cells that have a column width of 9 and the default font of 12-point Arial.

Table 4.9 Examples of Comma Format

Typed Entry	Number of Decimal Places	Display Result
123.46	0	123
1234.6	2	1,234.60
–1234.6	0	(1,235) or -1,235
–12345678	2	**************

To apply the default thousands separator (for example, a comma) and zero decimal places to selected cells, click the Comma 0 SmartIcon.

General Format Numbers in *General format* have no thousands separators and no trailing zeroes to the right of the decimal point. Negative numbers are preceded by a minus sign; if the number contains decimal digits, it can contain a decimal point. If a number contains too many digits to the right of the decimal point to fit within the column width, the decimal portion is rounded. If a number has too many digits to the left of a decimal point, the number appears in Scientific format. For example, 1234000000 appears as 1.2E+009.

Table 4.10 shows several examples of General format in cells that have a column width of 9 and the default font of 12-point Arial.

Table 4.10 Examples of General Format

Typed Entry	Display Result
123.46	123.46
–123.36	-123.36
1.2345678912	1.234568
15000000000	1.5E+10
–.000000026378	-2.6E-08

Percent Format You use *Percent format* to display percentages. A number formatted as a percentage can have from 0 to 15 decimal places. The number displayed is the value of the cell multiplied by 100, followed by a percent sign (%). Notice that the number of decimal places you specify is the number as a percent: For example, only two decimal places are needed to display .2456 as 24.56% in Percent format.

The number displayed is multiplied by 100, but the value of the cell is unchanged. To display 50% in a cell, type **.5** and use the Percent format. If you type **50** and use the Percent format with 0 decimal places, `5000%` appears. If you simply type **50%**, 1-2-3 automatically assigns the Percent format to the cell and displays 50%.

To apply the percent format with two decimal places to selected cells, click the Percent 2 SmartIcon.

Table 4.11 shows several examples of Percent format in cells that have a column width of 9 and the default font of 12-point Arial.

Table 4.11 Examples of Percent Format

Typed Entry	Number of Decimal Places	Display Result
2	2	`200.00%`
-.3528	2	`-35.28%`
30	0	`3000%`
300	4	`**************`

Formula Format You use *Formula format* to display numeric and text formulas instead of their results. Numbers formatted as Formula appear the same way as they do in General format. If a formula is too long to appear in the column width, the formula is truncated unless the cell to the immediate right is blank. In this case, the formula spills over and is displayed in full in the cell or cells to the right.

Formula format is useful for criteria ranges (covered in Chapter 25, "Finding and Extracting Data"). You also can use Formula format when you enter or debug complex formulas.

The Formula format is accessed by choosing the Text category in the Number Format panel of the InfoBox, and then choosing Formula in the Current format list box. It is also on the Frequently Used list, and therefore available in the Frequently Used format pop-up list on the status bar.

Label Format You use *Label format* on blank cells to make numbers that are labels easier to enter. In Label format, all entries are considered labels; 1-2-3 precedes the entry with the default label prefix. You can easily enter a label that looks like a number or a formula—either of which begins with a numeric character.

In a worksheet where cells are still formatted with the default General format, suppose that you type the label **57 Main Street** and press Enter. Because the entry contains letters, 1-2-3 considers the entry a label and inserts a label prefix. The format type remains General. Now suppose that you type the label **10/15** and press Enter. 1-2-3 considers 10/15 a formula (10 divided by 15), converts the entry to a number, and displays `0.66666667`.

In both preceding examples, if you format the range as Label before you type the entry, 1-2-3 precedes the entry with a label prefix, and the entry becomes a text label.

If you format numeric entries with the Label format, they do not become labels, even though the format is changed. For example, after the Label format is applied, the entry 0.666667 remains the same until you retype the entry **10/15**. At that point, the entry appears as the label `10/15` in the cell.

The Label format is accessed by choosing the Text category in the Number Format panel of the InfoBox, and then choosing Label in the Current format list box. It is also on the Frequently Used list, and therefore available in the Frequently Used format pop-up list on the status bar.

▶ **See** "Entering Text," **p. 68**

The Parenthesis Option The parenthesis option is a style property that is available in the Number Format panel of the InfoBox. You choose the Parenthesis check box when you want 1-2-3 to enclose negative numbers in parentheses. This option adds parentheses to negative numbers that use any of 1-2-3's number formats (labels are unaffected). When you want to use parentheses for every unformatted cell in the current worksheet, select the Parentheses option in Sheet InfoBox. (Refer to the section "Setting Worksheet Style Defaults" earlier in this chapter.) To use parentheses with a specific cell or range, select the range and then select the Parenthesis option and the number format in the Number Format panel of the Range InfoBox.

The Parenthesis option can produce confusing results, so use it with care. For example, if you apply the Parenthesis option with the General format to the number 456, the number appears in the cell as `(456)`. If you apply parentheses to a negative number, the number still appears as negative—but with varying results depending on the number format used. With the General format, –1234 appears as `(-1234)`; with the Comma format, –1234 appears as `((1,234))`; with the US Dollar format, –1234 appears as `(($1,234))`.

TROUBLESHOOTING

When I enter and format a date, why does 1-2-3 display the wrong date? 1-2-3 can format a date correctly only if you enter it in a format 1-2-3 recognizes. If the date you enter is in some other format, 1-2-3 interprets the entry as a label or a formula. If you enter **12-31-96**, for example, 1-2-3 recognizes the hyphens as minus signs and returns -115. However, if you enter **31-Dec-96**, 1-2-3 formats the entry correctly because 31-Dec-96 is a valid date format.

When I enter time and date numbers, why doesn't 1-2-3 display a recognizable time or date? Unless the cell is already formatted with a date or time format, 1-2-3 interprets the number as an integer.

How can I perform mathematical operations on dates and times? You construct the formula just like you do for any other values in the worksheet. Remember that 1-2-3 stores dates and times as numbers and uses these numbers to perform the calculation you specify.

Enhancing the Appearance of Data

The InfoBox provides options for enhancing the appearance of data in the worksheet. These enhancements include changes to the worksheet fonts; the addition of borders, lines, shading, and colors; and changes to the alignment of data in worksheet cells. You use the Font, Attribute, Color, Pattern, Line Style, and Alignment panels in the Range InfoBox to change these properties for a cell or range of cells.

NOTE You can specify a default set of worksheet styles (typeface, point size, default cell alignment, column width, default number format, and text and cell background colors) with the Sheet InfoBox. These settings apply to the current worksheet (or all the worksheets in the workbook if you group the sheets). For more details, see "Setting Worksheet Style Defaults," earlier in this chapter.

Changing Fonts and Attributes

A *typeface* is a particular style of type, such as Arial MT or TimesNewRoman PS. Typefaces can have different *attributes*, such as weight (regular, bold, italic) and underline. Most typefaces are available in a number of point sizes. The *point size* describes the height of the characters (there are 72 points in an inch). The most commonly used point sizes for "standard" print are 10-point and 12-point. Titles and headings are often set in 14-point or 18-point type.

A typeface of a given point size with a given set of attributes is called a *font*. In practice, many people use the terms *typeface* and *font* interchangeably, although they have different meanings. In 1-2-3 97 Edition, you select a font name and a size.

To change the font and attributes for a cell or range, use one of the following methods:

- Open the Range InfoBox and choose the Font, Attribute, and Color tab or click the Font, size, and color SmartIcon to open the Font, Attribute, and Color tab of the Range InfoBox (see fig. 4.17). Change the settings as desired for the Font name, Size, Style (attributes and underline), and Text color. If you have data in the selected cells, you see instantly how the changes affect the worksheet.

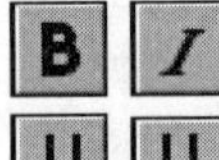

- To apply boldface, italic, or underline to a selected cell or range, click the Boldface, Italics, Single Underline, or Double Underline SmartIcon. You can apply several attributes by clicking more than one of these formatting SmartIcons.
- Select the cell or range to change and click the font selector or point-size selector in the status bar to reveal a pop-up list of choices. Select the font and point size from the list with the mouse or arrow keys.

TIP You can choose the text color by using the text color indicator in the status bar.

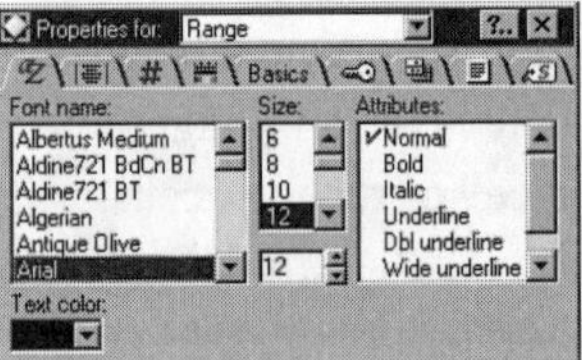

Fig. 4.17 Use the Font, Attribute, and Color panel of the InfoBox to change fonts and attributes.

If necessary, 1-2-3 enlarges the row height to fit the selected fonts. However, 1-2-3 does not adjust column widths automatically. After you change a font, numeric data may no longer fit in the columns; numeric data may display as asterisks. Change the column widths as needed to correctly display the data (see "Setting Column Widths," earlier in this chapter).

You can restore the previous font and attributes to selected cells by choosing Edit, Undo immediately after applying a new font or attribute. If you have made other editing changes already, you can change the fonts and attributes using the same methods described.

TIP Use formatting to improve the appearance and legibility of the worksheet, but don't make so many changes that the worksheet becomes difficult to read.

To remove boldface, underline, and italic all at once from selected cells, click the Normal Format SmartIcon. To remove these properties individually, click the appropriate SmartIcon.

Use the Delete Style SmartIcon to delete all styles and formats from selected cells, but leave the data intact.

Aligning Labels and Values

By default, 1-2-3 aligns labels to the left and values (numbers and formulas) to the right of the cell. You can change the default worksheet alignment of labels or values to the left, right, or center by choosing Sheet, Sheet Properties to open the Sheet InfoBox. In the Alignment panel, choose the desired alignment option. The alignment property is applied immediately to all cells in the worksheet.

To change the alignment of a cell or range of entries, select the range and then use the Alignment panel of the Range InfoBox (see fig. 4.18).

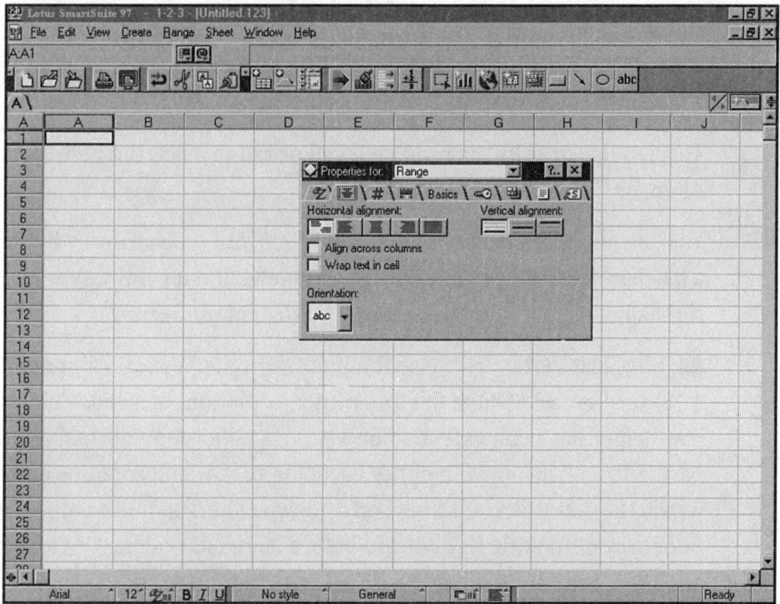

Fig. 4.18
The Alignment Panel of the Range InfoBox enables you to change orientation and wrap text, too.

The following sections describe the options in the Alignment panel you can use to align text horizontally and vertically and to align across columns, wrap, orient, and rotate text.

Aligning Labels Horizontally Use the buttons in the Horizontal Alignment option to align data. The face of each button illustrates the purpose of the button. The General button is the default that left-aligns all labels and right-aligns all numbers in the selected range. The Left, Center, and Right buttons align data at the left of the cell, in the center of a cell, and at the right of a cell, respectively. The Evenly Spaced button adds spaces, if necessary, between characters so that label entries fill the selected cell from edge to edge (like justifying text with a word processing program). The Evenly Spaced option is ignored if the label ends with a period (.), colon (:), question mark (?), or exclamation point (!). The Evenly Spaced button has no effect on numbers.

NOTE Any spaces that are included at the beginning or end of an entry are considered valid characters when 1-2-3 aligns the data. For instance, if you type the entry **"Sales Projections"** in a right-aligned cell and the entry includes two extra spaces at the end as shown, the entry will not appear to be properly right-aligned. (The same is true if extra spaces appear at the beginning of an entry in a left-aligned cell.) When extra spaces appear in an entry that is centered, the spaces also affect where 1-2-3 centers the entry in the cell. To ensure that data is properly aligned, remove all unnecessary spaces from cell entries. ■

When centering a long entry, 1-2-3 will allow the label to spill over and be displayed in the cells to the immediate right and immediate left of the current cell if those cells are blank. If the adjacent cells are not blank, 1-2-3 still centers the entry but the label is truncated where data appears in an adjacent cell.

To align data quickly in a selected cell or range, click the Left Align, Center Align, Right Align, or Even Align SmartIcon.

You can also align data automatically when you type an entry by preceding the entry with a label prefix. Type an apostrophe (') to left-align an entry, type a quotation mark (") to right-align an entry, or type a caret (^) to center an entry.

Aligning Text Vertically Use the buttons in the Vertical Alignment option (refer to fig. 4.18) to align cell data at the top, center, or bottom of a cell. This option is useful when the row height has been extended or when a smaller-than-normal font has been used in a particular cell in a row. In either case, the row or cell contains extra vertical space within which the entry can be moved up or down. The Top button aligns data along the top boundary of the cell, the Bottom button aligns data along the lower boundary of the cell, and the Center button centers data between the top and bottom boundaries of the cell. By default, 1-2-3 uses bottom alignment in worksheet cells.

Aligning Text across Multiple Columns When you center or right-align text, the alignment is relative to the column width of the cell. If you select the Align Across Columns check box in the Alignment panel of the InfoBox, the label is aligned relative to all selected columns. This option can be handy when you want to center a title over a worksheet. When you align across columns, you can specify whether the label should be aligned Left, Center, Right, or Evenly Spaced. You can also click the Center text across columns SmartIcon as a shortcut for opening the InfoBox.

Wrapping Text in a Cell Sometimes you have to include a large section of text in a worksheet but you don't want it to extend across columns. Instead, you want the text to continue line by line (*wrap*) within that cell rather than across adjacent columns. In this case, you can use the Wrap Text in Cell check box in the Alignment panel of the InfoBox. 1-2-3 automatically wraps text at the right edge of the column and carries it to the next line in the cell. 1-2-3 also increases the cell height automatically, if necessary.

Changing the Text Orientation You can alter the direction in which characters appear in a cell or range (the *orientation* of the text) by using the options in the Orientation section of the Alignment dialog box. This option can be useful for labeling a worksheet as shown in figure 4.19. In the figure, the labels in column A use a horizontal orientation. The year labels across row 5 use a diagonal orientation of 45 degrees. Choose the option in the Orientation drop-down list that looks like it is angled at 45 degrees.

Part I Ch 4

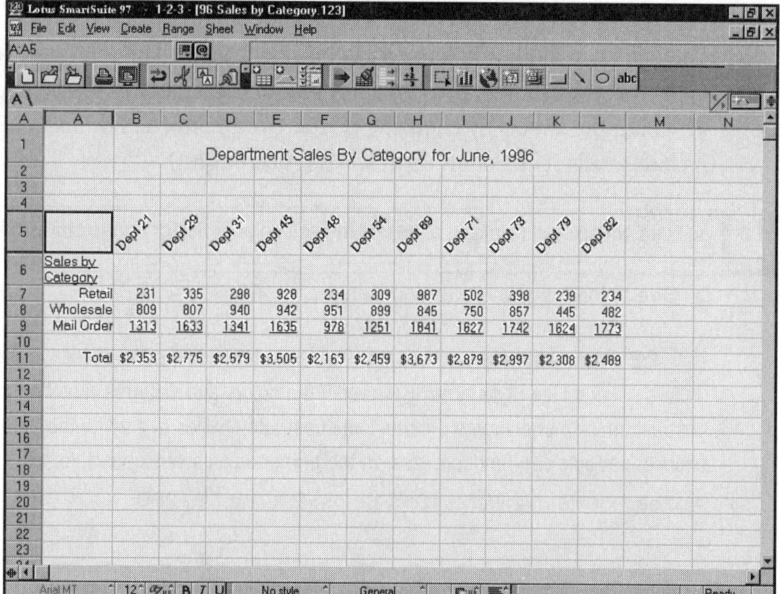

Fig. 4.19
A worksheet that uses the 45-degree angle orientation option. Also, notice that the title uses the Center text across columns option.

To quickly change data in a selected cell to a 45-degree orientation, click the Rotate Text SmartIcon. The other options in the Orientation list rotate text at 90 degrees or 270 degrees, or wrap each letter to appear stacked vertically. You also can specify the exact degree of rotation in the Angle spin box. The Angle box appears in the Alignment panel after you choose the angled Orientation.

Formatting Cells with Color and Borders

The Color, Pattern, and Line Style panel of the InfoBox, shown in figure 4.20, enables you to enhance and emphasize data in a worksheet by choosing colors, specifying borders, and adding frames. To access the Color, Pattern, and Line Style panel, open the Range InfoBox or click the Change Color, Pattern, and Line Style SmartIcon. As you make changes, they will appear in the worksheet.

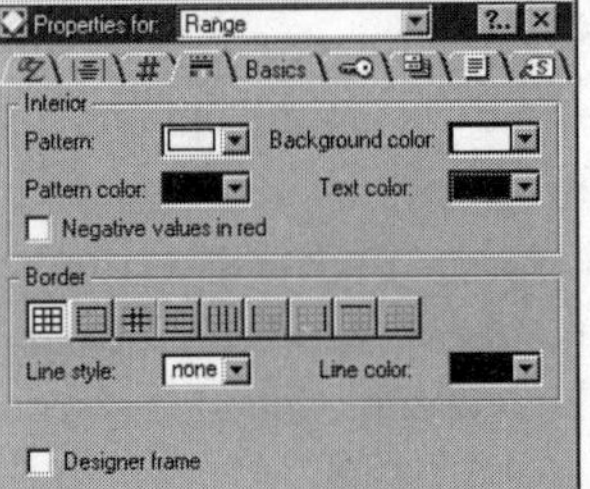

Fig. 4.20
The Color, Pattern, and Line Style panel contains options for colors and borders to enhance the appearance of your worksheet.

You can keep the InfoBox open as you select the cell or cell range to which you want to apply these attributes. You can apply any of the attributes to all sheets in a workbook after grouping the sheets by choosing Sheet, Group Sheets. For instance, the range A:A1..D:F9 includes cells A1 through F9 in sheets A through D.

TIP You can change cell colors by choosing the cell color indicator on the status bar.

▶ **See** "Working with Cells and Ranges" **p. 55**

NOTE You must have a color printer to accurately print colors chosen in the Color, Pattern, and Line Style panel. However, if the colors and patterns you choose contain enough contrast, many monochrome printers can substitute shades of gray for the different colors you choose; patterns can be duplicated on the printer as closely as possible. ■

▶ **See** "Previewing Worksheets Before Printing," **p. 290**

The settings in the Interior section of the Color, Pattern, and Line Style panel let you specify a Background color, Pattern, Pattern color, and Text color for any cells or ranges in the worksheet. The background color is the color that fills the cell (white by default). If you choose a pattern, it appears in black unless you choose a pattern color. Text appears in black as well, unless you choose a text color.

Use the buttons in the Border section of the Color, Pattern, and Line Style panel to draw lines above, below, on the sides of, and around cells in a range. You also can outline all cells in a selected range (as if they were one object), choose the second Border button or click the Add a Border to a Range SmartIcon. To outline individual cells in the selected range, choose the first Border button. Choose a style and color for the border from the Line Style and Line Color drop-down boxes.

You can add a drop shadow to a cell or selected range by clicking the Add Border and Drop Shadow to a Range SmartIcon.

To further enhance borders, you can click the Designer Frame check box to choose from a collection of specially designed frames. After you choose a frame style from the Frame style drop-down list, choose a color from the Frame color drop-down list. Figure 4.21 shows an example of a designer frame used in a worksheet.

▶ **See** "Developing Multiple-Page Presentations" **p. 427**

Fig. 4.21
An example of a designer frame.

May Sales Figures

	Retail	Wholesale	Catalog	Total
Department 15	$2,643.29	$3,252.32	$1,998.22	$7,893.83
Department 22	$9,871.22	$10,223.39	$5,298.12	$7,893.83
Department 43	$2,398.23	$3,431.99	$2,498.22	$15,787.66
Department 51	$8,098.22	$12,311.49	$3,342.12	$31,575.32
Department 63	$3,210.99	$3,535.11	$1,927.23	$63,150.64
Total	$26,221.95	$26,221.95	$52,443.90	$104,887.80

TROUBLESHOOTING

How do I change the alignment of data in a cell by using the edit line? 1-2-3 uses label prefixes to identify the alignment of label entries. The label prefix is visible in the edit line but not in the cell itself. You can use the edit line to change the alignment of a label by erasing the old prefix and typing a new one just in front of the entry. Type an apostrophe (') for left alignment, a caret (^) for center alignment, and a quotation mark (") for right alignment. You must use the InfoBox or SmartIcon to evenly space an entry across a cell or range.

continues

continued

I used the Del key to delete a long text entry from a cell formatted with the Wrap text in cell option. I want the new entry to display into the next column, but it wraps, too. I know I can turn off the Wrap text in cell option, but isn't there a better way to solve this problem? When you use the Del key to delete an entry, you delete only the contents of the cell, not the style. You can use Edit, Clear to display the Clear dialog box where you can delete the cell Contents only, the Styles and number format, or both. If you select both check boxes, 1-2-3 clears the cell contents as well as the wrap-text style.

When I deleted a long text entry from a cell that used the Wrap text in cell option, the row height was not readjusted. Did I do something wrong? No. When you use the Wrap text in cell option for a long text entry, 1-2-3 adjusts the row height to accommodate the entire entry. When you delete the cell contents, style, or both, 1-2-3 doesn't assume that you want the row height readjusted. You can readjust the row height quickly by choosing the Fit largest font option in the Basics panel of the InfoBox.

Using Named Styles

Another way to assign styles (groups of formats) is to name them. Using a *named style* is especially helpful when a cell or range has several style properties attached to it. You can assign names to many different sets of styles with the Named Style panel of the InfoBox. Use this panel to define styles and to apply a style to a selected cell or range. You also can access this panel by clicking the Change Named Styles SmartIcon.

A named style includes all style properties (font, point size, number format, decimal places, color, border, and so on) to be assigned to the selected cell or range. To define a named style, do the following:

1. Select the cell or cell range that represents all the style characteristics you want to name.
2. Choose Range, Range Properties and then the Named Style tab to display the Named Style panel.
3. Choose the Create Style button. The Create Style dialog box appears.
4. In the Style name text box, enter a name for the style.
5. Choose OK. The Create Style dialog box closes and you are returned to the InfoBox. The new named style appears in the Style name list box in the Named Style panel.

When you define named styles, a status bar button becomes the style selector. (This selector displays `No Style` until you create named styles.) To apply a named style, select the cell or range to which you want to apply the style, then click the style selector. 1-2-3 pops up a list of all named styles. Click a style from the list to apply all attributes of the style to the selected range. You can also apply a named style to a cell or range by selecting the cells, then choosing a style from the Style name list box in the Named Style panel of the InfoBox.

You can quickly remove all styles from a selected range of cells by clicking the Delete Formatting from a Range SmartIcon. This removes styles only; the data in the cells remains intact.

To delete a named style from the list of named styles, follow these steps:

1. Display the Named Style panel of the InfoBox.
2. In the Style name list box, choose the style you want to delete.
3. Choose the Manage Styles button. The Manage Style dialog box opens.
4. Choose Delete and then click OK.

You also can Rename a style in the Manage Style dialog box.

Using the Style Gallery

Like the named-style feature, the Style Gallery command (or Style Gallery SmartIcon) enables you to apply styles quickly to a selected range of cells. The difference between the named-style feature and the Style Gallery is that the Style Gallery contains 14 predesigned style templates. Just choose a template from the list in the Gallery dialog box and all the style characteristics that make up the template are applied to the selected range.

To remove a template from the selected range, choose Edit, Clear. In the Clear dialog box, select the Styles and number formats check box, and if applicable, the Borders and designer frames check box. Deselect the other check boxes and then choose OK.

To use the Style Gallery:

1. Select the range you want to style.
2. Open the Range InfoBox.
3. In the Named Style panel, choose the Style Gallery button. The Style Gallery dialog box is displayed (see fig. 4.22).

4. Choose a style from the Style templates list box.
5. Refer to the Sample area in the dialog box to preview each template before applying it to the selected range.

   In figure 4.22, the Chisel1 template is shown in the Sample box. The worksheet underneath the dialog box is formatted with the Chisel1 template.
6. Choose OK to close the Style Gallery dialog box. The selected style is applied to the range.

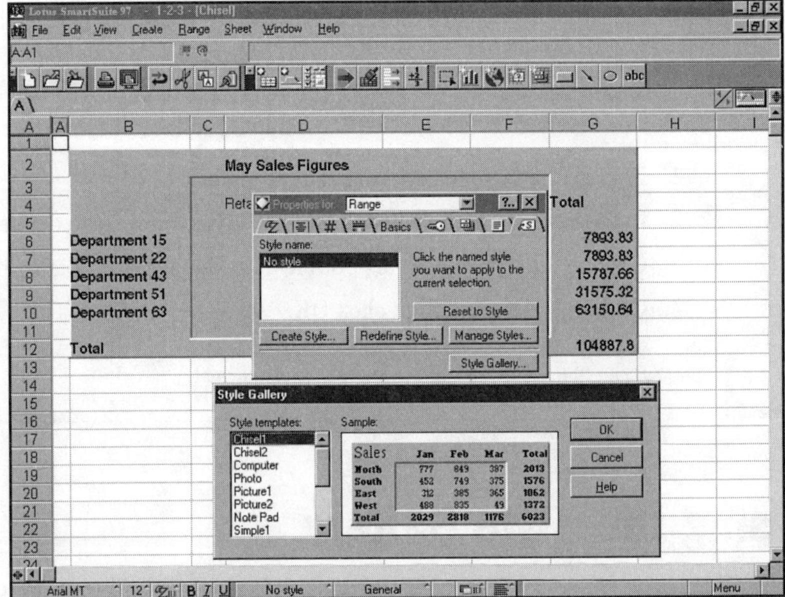

Fig. 4.22
The Style Gallery dialog box.

CHAPTER 5

Working with Formulas

by Jan Snyder

Probably the single most basic and important characteristic of spreadsheet programs is that after you've created a worksheet by using formulas, when you change any number on the worksheet, all formulas that depend on that number change automatically.

To use 1-2-3 effectively, you must be able to create many types of formulas to help you analyze the data on your worksheets. This chapter shows you a variety of methods for creating and editing formulas. You also explore techniques to deal with incorrectly written formulas.

On particularly complex worksheets or worksheets with a large number of complex formulas, 1-2-3's automatic recalculation feature can take some time to recalculate all formulas. While it is recalculating, you cannot continue to enter other data on your worksheet. This chapter teaches you how to turn off the automatic recalculation feature so that 1-2-3 only recalculates your worksheet when you tell it to do so.

Enter formulas into cells

You'll learn the rules and methods for entering formulas.

Use operators in numeric, text, and logical formulas

Operators are used to construct simple to complex formulas.

Sum values automatically without entering a formula

Type **Total** to create the formulas for totaling rows or columns of values.

Point at cells when creating a formula

You can prevent errors by pointing to cells instead of typing their references.

Edit formulas

Find out how to correct errors in formulas.

Modify the method 1-2-3 uses when recalculating a worksheet

You can change the order in which 1-2-3 calculates.

Identify, locate, and modify circular references

Circular references are usually created in error.

Creating Formulas

Because 1-2-3 is used primarily for financial and scientific applications, its capability to use formulas is one of its most sophisticated yet easy-to-use features. You can create a simple formula that adds the values in two cells on the same worksheet:

+A1+B1

This formula indicates that the value stored in cell A1 is to be added to the value stored in cell B1. The formula that adds the values in A1 and B1 is recalculated if you enter new data into either of those cells. For example, if A1 originally contains the value 4 and B1 contains the value 3, the formula results in the value 7. If you change the value in A1 to 5, the formula is recalculated to result in 8.

You create formulas with symbols called *operators*:

+ addition

– subtraction

* multiplication

/ division

Logical formulas use *logical operators*:

< less than

> greater than

= equal to

You can also combine the operators:

<= less than or equal to

>= greater than or equal to

<> not equal to

Operators tell 1-2-3 the relationship between numbers.

The power of 1-2-3 formulas, however, is best showcased by the program's capability to link data across worksheets and workbooks. By referencing cells in other worksheets and workbooks, formulas can calculate results from many worksheet applications. To create a formula that links data across worksheets, you first specify the worksheet in which the data is located, followed by a colon (:), and the cell address. The following example shows a formula that links data across three worksheets (A, B, and D):

+A:B3+B:C6+D:B4

This formula adds the contents of cell B3 on worksheet A, cell C6 on worksheet B, and cell B4 on worksheet D.

If the formula links data across workbooks, include the workbook name, surrounded by double angle-brackets. For example, the following formula adds the contents of cell C6 on worksheet A of the current workbook to the contents of cell C6 on worksheet A in the workbook named SALES1.123.

+A:C6+<<SALES1.123>>A:C6

If the workbooks you want to link are open, click the cells you want to include in the formula. When you do this, 1-2-3 inserts the workbook name, worksheet name, and cell address for you.

▶ **See** "Linking Worksheets and Files with Formulas," **p. 483**

Entering Formulas

The real power of 1-2-3 comes from the program's capability to calculate formulas. Formulas make 1-2-3 an electronic worksheet, not just a computerized way to assemble data. You enter the numbers and formulas into the worksheet, and 1-2-3 calculates the results of all the formulas. As you add or change data, you do not need to recalculate the worksheet to reflect the changes; 1-2-3 recalculates the data for you.

In the example shown in figure 5.1, if you change the value of Sales or Variable Costs, 1-2-3 recalculates Variable Margin.

You can enter formulas that perform calculations on numbers, labels, and other cells in the worksheet. As with a label, a formula can contain as many as 512 characters. A formula can include numbers, text, operators, cell and range addresses, range names, and functions. A formula cannot include spaces except within a range name or a text string.

You can create four kinds of formulas: numeric, text, logical, and function. *Numeric formulas* work with numbers, other numeric formulas, and numeric functions. *Text formulas* (known as *string formulas* in previous versions of 1-2-3) work with labels, other text formulas, and text functions. *Logical formulas* are true-or-false tests for numeric or text values.

This chapter covers numeric and text formulas, which are the kinds you are likely to use for most of the speadsheets you create.

▶ **See** "Understanding 1-2-3 Functions," **p. 152**

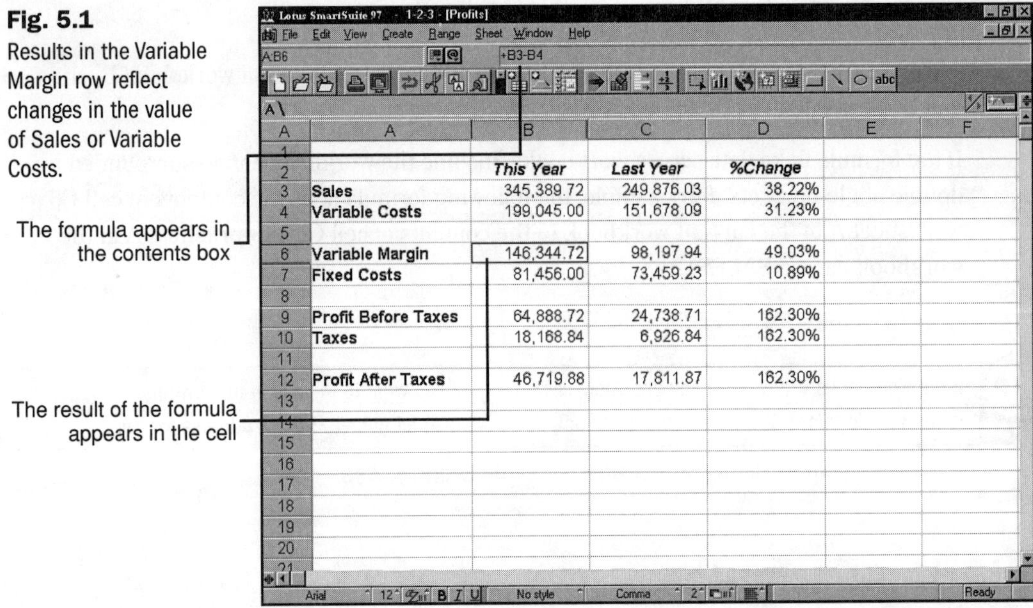

The formula appears in the contents box
The result of the formula appears in the cell
Lotus SmartSuite 97 - 1-2-3 - [Profits]
File Edit View Create Range Sheet Window Help
A:B6
+B3-B4
This Year
Last Year
%Change
Sales 345,389.72 249,876.03 38.22%
Variable Costs 199,045.00 151,678.09 31.23%
Variable Margin 146,344.72 98,197.94 49.03%
Fixed Costs 81,456.00 73,459.23 10.89%
Profit Before Taxes 64,888.72 24,738.71 162.30%
Taxes 18,168.84 6,926.84 162.30%
Profit After Taxes 46,719.88 17,811.87 162.30%
Arial
No style
Comma
Ready

Fig. 5.1
Results in the Variable Margin row reflect changes in the value of Sales or Variable Costs.

Formulas can operate on numbers or on the contents of cells. The formula 8+26 uses 1-2-3 as a calculator. A more useful formula involves cell references in the calculation. In figure 5.2, the formula in cell F16 is +B16+C16+D16+E16. The contents box shows the formula, and the worksheet shows the result of the calculation: 183. The result in cell F16 changes when you change any number in the other cells. This automatic recalculation capability is the basis of the power of the 1-2-3 worksheet.

Notice that the formula begins with a plus sign (+). If the formula begins with B16, 1-2-3 assumes that you are entering a label and performs no calculations.

You can add a row or column of values quickly by placing the cell pointer in the blank cell at the bottom of a column (or at the right end of a row) and then clicking the Sum SmartIcon to calculate the result. You can also add a row or column of values by entering **total** in the column to the left of the column of values or in the row above a row of values. See "Totaling Ranges Automatically" later in this chapter.

A formula is an instruction to 1-2-3 to perform a calculation. All formulas begin with a number, a decimal point, +, –, @, $, #, or (.

Any entry that begins with any other character is treated as a label by 1-2-3.

Fig. 5.2
The result, not the formula, appears in the worksheet. The formula appears in the contents box, near the top of the screen.

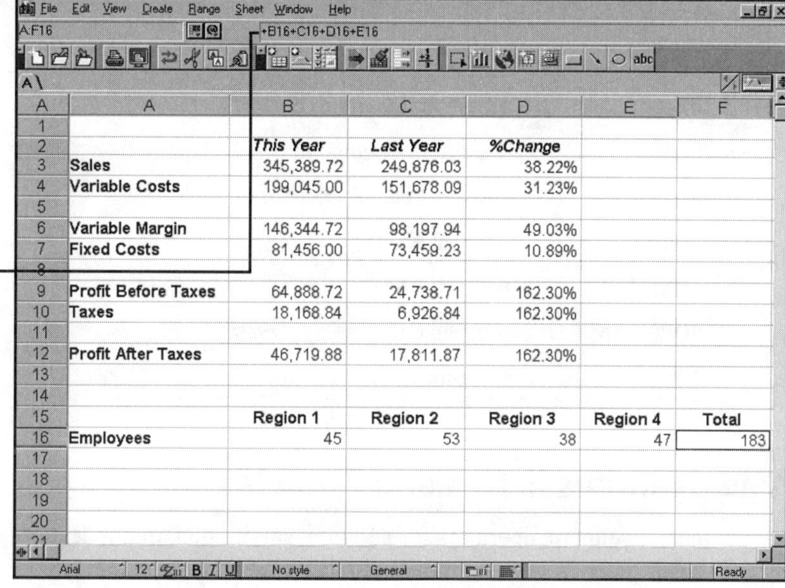

Contents box

> **CAUTION**
>
> Be sure you begin formulas with one of the symbols shown in the preceding text. If you don't, 1-2-3 will treat what you type as text and enter it into a cell preceded by an apostrophe ('), a label prefix. To correct the entry so that it becomes a formula, you need either to retype the formula or to delete the apostrophe and replace it with one of the numeric indicators shown here.

You use operators in numeric, text, and logical formulas to specify the calculations to be performed, and in what order they are performed. Table 5.1 lists the operators in the order of precedence in which 1-2-3 uses them.

Table 5.1 Operators and Their Order of Precedence

Operator	Operation	Precedence
^	Exponentiation	1
–, +	Negative, positive value	2
*, /	Multiplication, division	3
+, –	Addition, subtraction	4
=, <>	Equal to, not equal to	5

continues

Table 5.1 Continued

Operator	Operation	Precedence
<, >	Less than, greater than	5
<=	Less than or equal to	5
>=	Greater than or equal to	5
#NOT#	Logical NOT	6
#AND#	Logical AND	7
#OR#	Logical OR	7
&	Text formula	7

Using Operators in Numeric Formulas

You use numeric operators for addition, subtraction, multiplication, division, and *exponentiation* (raising a number to a power). The simplest kind of formula is a simple reference, such as the following:

+C4

You can enter this formula into any cell except C4. It takes whatever is in C4 and reproduces it in the cell containing this formula. That way, if the content of C4 changes, the cell containing the formula also changes.

Another formula might be

+C4+C5

This formula adds the values in two cells: C4 and C5.

You might include a constant value if needed, such as in the following example:

+C4+C5+100

In this formula, the value 100 is constant but the values in cells C4 and C5 are variable; those values depend on the numbers that currently appear in those cells.

If a formula uses all the operators shown in Table 5.1, 1-2-3 calculates the exponentials first and then works down the list. If two operators are equal in precedence, 1-2-3 can calculate either one first. The order of precedence affects the result of many formulas. To override the order of precedence, use parentheses; 1-2-3 always calculates operations within a set of parentheses first.

Table 5.2 shows how 1-2-3 uses parentheses and the order of precedence to evaluate complex formulas. The examples use numbers instead of cell references to make the calculations easier to follow.

Table 5.2 Evaluating Complex Formulas in 1-2-3

Formula	Evaluation	Result
5+3*2	(5+(3*2))	11
(5+3)*2	(5+3)*2	16
–3^2*2	–(3^2)*2	–18
–3^(2*2)	–(3^(2*2))	–81
5+4*8/4–3	5+((4*8)/4)–3	10
5+4*8/(4–3)	5+((4*8)/(4–3))	37
(5+4)*8/(4–3)	((5+4)*8)/(4–3)	72
(5+4)*8/4–3	((5+4)*(8/4))–3	15
5+3*4^2/6–2*3^4	(5+(3*(4^2)/6))–(2*(3^4))	–149

TROUBLESHOOTING

After pressing Enter to enter a formula, 1-2-3 displays ERR in the cell. Although you began the formula with a symbol 1-2-3 recognized as a formula indicator, somewhere in the formula you have made an error, and the formula cannot be interpreted or evaluated. Common errors include neglecting to put in an operator where one is necessary (A1B1 rather than A1*B1), or typing a cell reference incorrectly (for example, 1A rather than A1). If you easily can spot the error, move the cursor to the location of the error and correct it. If you can't spot your error, the easiest solution is to reenter the formula, this time pointing at the cells with your mouse pointer rather than typing in cell addresses.

Totaling Ranges Automatically

As described previously in this section, you can sum a column or row of numbers by clicking the Sum SmartIcon. 1-2-3 places the formula—the @SUM function—in the active cell or range. 1-2-3 97 has enhanced this automatic summing feature with a new shortcut for totaling rows and columns of numbers.

Instead of typing a formula in a cell to add the numbers in the column, simply type either the word **Total** or **Totals** in a cell next to the row or column where you want the totals to appear. 1-2-3 supplies the formulas for each row or column of numbers adjacent to the Total (or Totals) label and displays the results instantly.

To sum a row or column using automatic summing:

1. Enter a range of values to be totaled in the worksheet. You can sum rows or columns or both, but do not enter the formulas.
2. To sum the columns, type **Total** in the cell one row down and to the left of the range where you want to create the totals.

   To sum the rows, type **Total** in the cell one column to the right and above the range where you want to create the totals, as shown in figure 5.3.
3. Press Enter. 1-2-3 places @SUM formulas in the cells where you indicated you want totals.

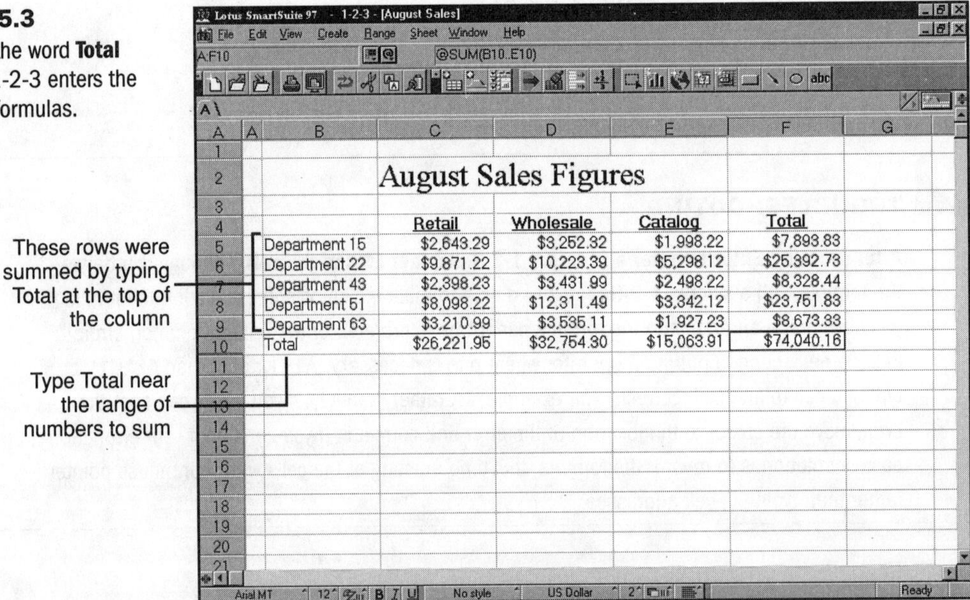

Lotus SmartSuite 97 - 1-2-3 - [August Sales]
File Edit View Create Range Sheet Window Help
A:F10
@SUM(B10..E10)
August Sales Figures
Retail
Wholesale
Catalog
Total
Department 15 $2,643.29 $3,252.32 $1,998.22 $7,893.83
Department 22 $9,871.22 $10,223.39 $5,298.12 $25,392.73
Department 43 $2,398.23 $3,431.99 $2,498.22 $8,328.44
Department 51 $8,098.22 $12,311.49 $3,342.12 $23,751.83
Department 63 $3,210.99 $3,535.11 $1,927.23 $8,673.33
Total $26,221.95 $32,754.30 $15,063.91 $74,040.16
These rows were summed by typing Total at the top of the column
Type Total near the range of numbers to sum
Arial MT
No style
US Dollar
Ready

Fig. 5.3
Type the word **Total** and 1-2-3 enters the sum formulas.

NOTE You can have up to 10 blank rows above the Total label when you sum columns, and up to 10 blank columns to the left of the Total label when you sum rows. However, the numbers you want to sum should not be adjacent to other cells that contain numbers.

You can turn off the automatic summing feature by choosing File, User Setup, 1-2-3 Preferences, General tab. Deactivate the Use "Total" to Sum Automatically check box.

Using Operators in Text Formulas

The rules for text (or string) formulas are different from the rules for numeric formulas. A string is a label or a text formula. Only two text operators exist, so you can perform only two operations with text formulas: repeat a text string or *concatenate* (join) two or more text strings.

The simplest text formula uses only the plus sign (+) to repeat the text in another cell:

+C4

In this example, cell C4 contains a text label, which is reproduced in the cell containing this formula.

The text string concatenation operator is the ampersand (&), as used in this example:

+A4&B4

If, for example, cells A4 and B4 contain the text strings *New* and *York,* respectively, the result of the formula is the concatenated text string, *NewYork,* with no space between the words.

The first operator in a text formula must be a plus sign; all other operators in the formula must be ampersands. If you do not use the ampersand but use any of the numeric operators, 1-2-3 considers the formula to be a numeric formula and calculates the data in the cells as numeric values. A cell that contains text is considered to have a numeric value of 0 (zero).

If you use an ampersand in a formula, 1-2-3 considers the formula to be a text formula. If you also use any numeric operators (after the plus sign at the beginning), the formula results in ERR. The formula +A3&B3+C3, for example, results in ERR.

In many text formulas, you need to put a space between the various parts of the formula. You can insert a space directly into a text formula by placing the space inside double quotation marks (" "). If cells A4 and B4 contain the text *New* and *York,* for example, you can enter the formula **+A4&" "&B4** to get the result *New York* instead of *NewYork.*

NOTE You can insert text, as well as spaces between entries in a text formula. Suppose, for example, that cell A1 contains the name *Dan Snyder,* B1 contains *Chesapeake,* and C1 contains *Virginia,* and this formula is entered into D1:

```
+A1&" lives in the city of "&B1&" in the state of "&C1
```

The result is the following entry:

```
Dan Snyder lives in the city of Chesapeake in the state of Virginia
```

continues

continued

Note the spaces in the formula, including the one between the opening quotation mark and the word *lives*. If that space were not included in the formula, the result in the cell would, in part, look like this

```
Dan Snyderlives in...
```

with no space between *Snyder* and *lives*. ■

Text formulas are the only formulas in which spaces are allowed and then only when the spaces are enclosed within quotation marks.

To write more complex text formulas, you can use text functions. For a detailed discussion of these functions, see Chapter 6, "Using Functions."

Using Operators in Logical Formulas

Logical formulas are true/false tests. A logical formula compares two values and returns 1 if the test is true or 0 if the test is false.

Pointing to Cell References

Formulas consist mainly of operators and cell references. The formula +C4+C5+C6+C7, for example, has four cell references. You can type each reference, but there is an easier way to enter them. When 1-2-3 expects a cell address, you can use the direction keys or the mouse to point to the cell or range. When you move the cell pointer, 1-2-3 changes to POINT mode, and the address of the cell pointer appears in the formula in the contents box.

To point to a cell when entering a formula, you can use the arrow keys to move the cell pointer to the correct cell, or you can click the cell. If this location marks the end of the formula, press Enter. If the formula contains more terms (or parts of the equation), type the next operator and continue the process until you finish; then press Enter.

You can type some addresses and point to others. You cannot tell in a completed formula whether the cell references were entered by typing or pointing.

In formulas, you also can refer to cells in other worksheets in the workbook. To refer to a cell in another worksheet, include the worksheet letter (or custom tab label) in the cell address. To refer to cell C4 in worksheet B, for example, type **+B:C4**. To point to a cell in another worksheet, type + and then use the direction keys, including Ctrl+PgUp and

Ctrl+PgDn. To move the cell pointer to other worksheets, you also can click the worksheet tab.

Because typing an incorrect address in a formula is easy, pointing to a cell usually is faster and more accurate than typing the cell's address. The only time when typing an address is easier is when the cell reference is far from the current cell and you happen to remember the address. If you enter a formula in cell Z238 and want to refer to cell K23, typing **K23** may be faster than pointing to cell K23.

You also can use range names instead of cell addresses in formulas. Experienced 1-2-3 users rarely type cell addresses and frequently use range names.

▶ **See** "Working with Cells and Ranges," **p. 55**

Correcting Errors in Formulas

If you accidentally enter a formula that 1-2-3 cannot evaluate properly, the program either enters the formula as a label or displays ERR in the cell.

Common errors that make a formula invalid are extra or missing parentheses, misspelled function names, and incorrect arguments in functions. Following are a few examples of common errors:

Formula	Error
+A1(A2*A3)	Missing an operator between A1 and the product in parentheses
@SIM(A1..A3)	Misspelled @SUM function
@IF(A1>200,200)	Missing argument in function

If you cannot find, or do not know how to fix, the error in the formula, you can use the Help system to check the format of the function.

Because all labels are valid entries, instead of deleting the entire formula and starting over again, 1-2-3 often converts the erroneous formula to a label. This allows you to continue working until you have the time or information to determine the error in the formula. After you have corrected the formula, you can delete the label prefix and change the entry back to a formula.

You can use the Help system again or look at another part of the worksheet that has a similar formula. When you find the error, correct the formula and remove the apostrophe.

NOTE 1-2-3 corrects certain types of errors for you. For example, if you type **@SUM(A1..A5** and forget to close the parentheses before you press Enter, 1-2-3 closes the parentheses for you and enters the formula into the cell. The result may not always be what you expect, however, since 1-2-3 places the closing parentheses at the end of the formula if possible even if this was not your intent. ■

▶ **See** "Editing Data," **p. 79**

Recalculating a Worksheet

When a value in a cell changes, 1-2-3 recalculates every cell that depends on the changed value. This recalculation demonstrates the power of an electronic spreadsheet. Usually, 1-2-3 recalculates a worksheet automatically when a cell changes. If you prefer, you can tell 1-2-3 you want to recalculate manually.

Unless you specify otherwise, 1-2-3 recalculates only those formulas whose values have changed since the last recalculation. If you change the data in one cell and that cell is used in one formula, 1-2-3 recalculates only that formula.

CAUTION

If you have set manual recalculation on a worksheet, be sure you make this known to those who share the worksheet. Place a notation on the worksheet reminding users to recalculate the worksheet if changes are made.

Specifying the Recalculation Method

You can tell 1-2-3 not to recalculate the worksheet automatically by choosing File, User Setup, 1-2-3 Preferences, choosing the Recalculation tab in the 1-2-3 Preferences dialog box, and selecting the Manual option button (see fig. 5.4). (If you followed along with this example, repeat this procedure, choosing the Automatic option button to reset 1-2-3 to Automatic recalculation.)

After recalculation is set to manual, you can use any of the following methods to recalculate the worksheet:

- Press F9 (Calc)
- Click the Calc indicator in the status bar
- Click the Recalculate SmartIcon

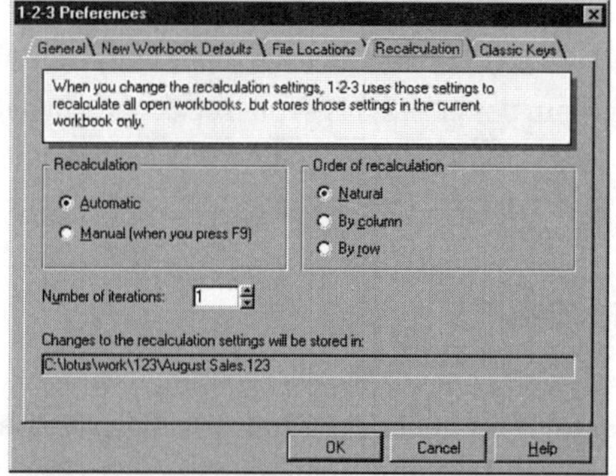

Fig. 5.4
Use File, User Setup, 1-2-3 Preferences, Recalculation to change to and from manual and automatic recalculation.

NOTE Generally, manual recalculation is used only if you have a large workbook that contains many complex formulas. In that case, 1-2-3 could take some time—seconds to perhaps minutes or more—to recalculate each time you enter a value into a cell. In cases like this, it is sensible to turn on manual recalculation, enter all of the values you want to change, and then use one of the techniques described earlier to recalculate all formulas.

Specifying the Recalculation Order

You can control the order in which 1-2-3 recalculates. By default, 1-2-3 recalculates in natural order. In natural order recalculation, 1-2-3 determines which formulas depend on which cells and then sets up a recalculation order to produce the correct results.

If you prefer, you can tell 1-2-3 to recalculate by row or by column. Row recalculation starts in cell A1 and continues across the cells in row 1, then row 2, and so on. Columnar recalculation starts in cell A1 and continues down the cells in column A, then column B, and so on.

To change the order of recalculation, choose File, User Setup, 1-2-3 Preferences, and then choose the Recalculation tab in the 1-2-3 Preferences dialog box. Select either By Column or By Row, as shown in figure 5.4.

NOTE Unless you have a specific reason for being sure one cell is calculated before another, let 1-2-3 recalculate in natural order. When calculating by row or by column, 1-2-3 must sweep through columns and rows several times to make sure that formulas produce correct results. Natural order is faster because 1-2-3 first determines which cells have changed and then recalculates them in one sweep.

If you specify By Row or By Column, you should tell 1-2-3 the number of iterations to perform (how many times to recalculate). Specify a number from 1 (the default) to 50 in the Number of Iterations spin box. If 1-2-3 is set to recalculate in natural order and no circular references exist, 1-2-3 may stop calculating before it reaches the number of iterations indicated.

Handling Circular References

The natural order of recalculation is not always accurate if a circular reference exists. A *circular reference* is a formula that depends, either directly or indirectly, on its own value. Whenever 1-2-3 performs a recalculation and finds a circular reference, the Circ indicator appears on the circular-reference button in the status bar. A circular reference is almost always an error, and you should correct it immediately. Figure 5.5 shows an erroneous circular reference in which the cell containing the @SUM function includes itself.

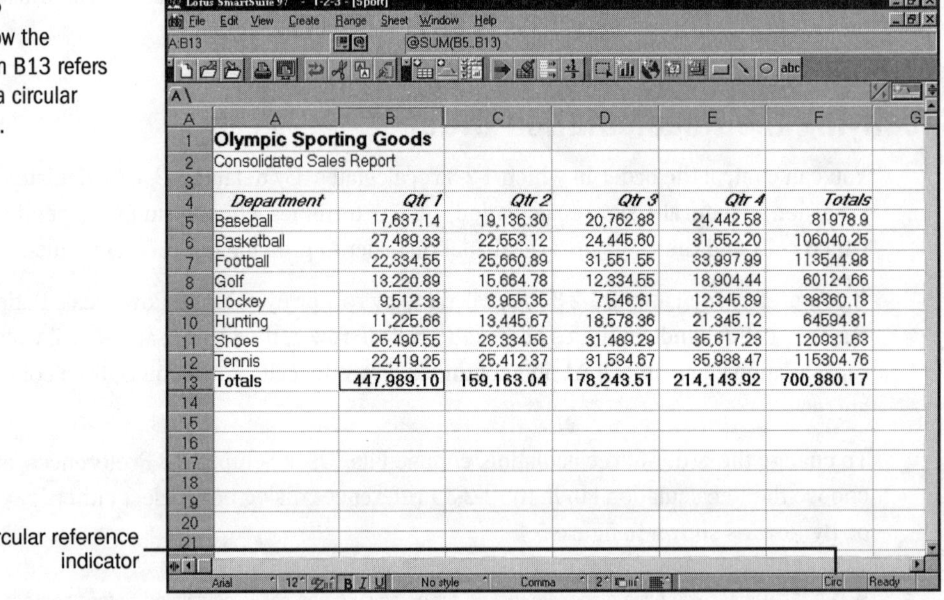

	A	B	C	D	E	F
1	**Olympic Sporting Goods**					
2	Consolidated Sales Report					
3						
4	*Department*	*Qtr 1*	*Qtr 2*	*Qtr 3*	*Qtr 4*	*Totals*
5	Baseball	17,637.14	19,136.30	20,762.88	24,442.58	81978.9
6	Basketball	27,489.33	22,553.12	24,445.60	31,552.20	106040.25
7	Football	22,334.55	25,660.89	31,551.55	33,997.99	113544.98
8	Golf	13,220.89	15,664.78	12,334.55	18,904.44	60124.66
9	Hockey	9,512.33	8,955.35	7,546.61	12,345.89	38360.18
10	Hunting	11,225.66	13,445.67	18,578.36	21,345.12	64594.81
11	Shoes	25,490.55	28,334.56	31,489.29	35,617.23	120931.63
12	Tennis	22,419.25	25,412.37	31,534.67	35,938.47	115304.76
13	**Totals**	**447,989.10**	**159,163.04**	**178,243.51**	**214,143.92**	**700,880.17**

Fig. 5.5 Notice how the formula in B13 refers to itself: a circular reference.

In some cases, a circular reference is deliberate. Figure 5.5 shows a worksheet with such a reference. In this example, a company has set aside 10 percent of its net profit for employee bonuses. The bonuses themselves, however, represent an expense that reduces net profit. The formula in cell C5 shows that the amount of bonuses is net profit (in cell D5) multiplied by 0.1 (10 percent). But net profit (the formula in cell D5) is profit after bonuses (B5 minus C5). The value of employee bonuses depends on the value of net profit, and the value of net profit depends on the value of employee bonuses. In figure 5.6, C5 depends on D5, and D5 depends on C5. This situation is a classic circular reference.

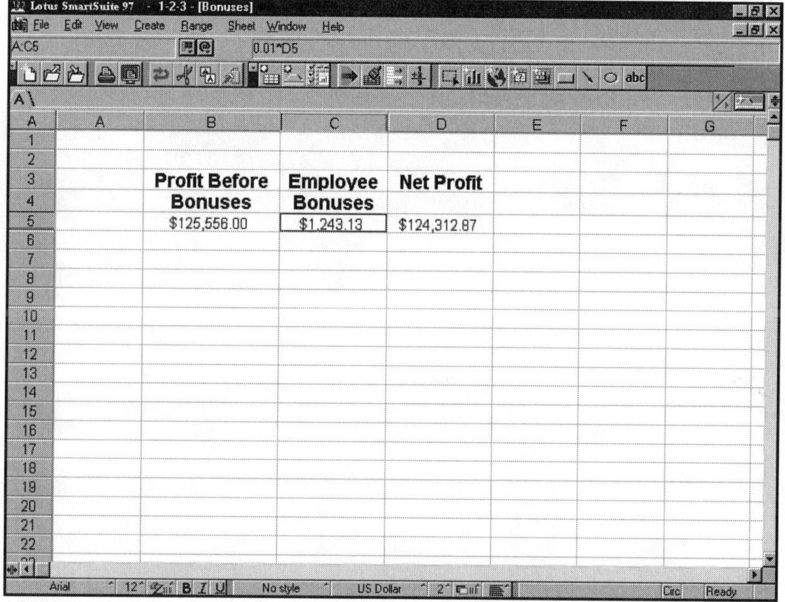

Fig. 5.6
A worksheet with a deliberate circular reference.

If a deliberate circular reference exists, each time you recalculate the worksheet, the values change by a smaller amount. Eventually, the changes become insignificant. This reduction is called *convergence*. Notice that the erroneous circular reference in figure 5.5 never converges, and the @SUM result is bigger every time you recalculate.

The worksheet in figure 5.6 needs three recalculations before the changes become less than one cent. After you establish this number, you can tell 1-2-3 to recalculate the worksheet five times every time it recalculates by specifying 5 in the Number of Iterations spin box in the Recalculation panel of the 1-2-3 Preferences dialog box. In most cases, you can calculate a converging circular reference with a macro. ●

CHAPTER 6

Using Functions

by Jan Snyder

In addition to creating your own formulas in a worksheet, you can take advantage of 1-2-3's predefined formulas, or functions. Functions can perform math, text, and logical calculations as well as determine information about the worksheet.

By using a function rather than writing a formula, you speed your work and avoid typing errors. To find the average of the amounts in five cells, for example, you could enter the formula +(A3+B3+C3+D3+E3)/5. It is faster and simpler, however, to use the @AVG function, @AVG(A3..E3). You can enter a function by typing it in a cell or using the @function selector.

Basic concepts about functions

Discover the power of functions to speed your calculations.

How to enter functions

Select a function, and 1-2-3 supplies the arguments for you to fill in.

How to customize the @function-selector list

Prepare frequently used functions for easy selection.

Syntax and arguments for commonly used functions

Examples illustrate how to use the most popular functions.

1-2-3 provides more than 230 built-in functions broken into the following 10 categories:

- Calendar
- Database
- Engineering
- Financial
- Information
- Logical
- Lookup
- Mathematical
- Statistical
- Text

This chapter describes the general steps you follow to use 1-2-3 functions and then provides discussions and examples of specific functions in each category. ■

Understanding 1-2-3 Functions

A *function* is a preprogrammed set of instructions that returns a value. You can use a function as an independent formula that shows results based on information in the function—for example, the @NOW function returns the value of the current date and time. You also can use a function as a component of another formula or function—for example:

```
@IF(@NOW<@DATE(2000,1,1),"This is still the 20th century","The 21st century")
```

In this formula, the text string that the @IF function returns depends on the values returned by the functions it contains: @NOW and @DATE.

Functions have a general format, which includes the following:

- The @ symbol, which tells 1-2-3 that what follows is a function.
- The name of the function. (There is no space between the @ symbol and the function name.)
- Arguments, which appear in parentheses.

TIP If an argument is a text string, you must enclose the text in quotation marks (" "). Otherwise, 1-2-3 assumes that the text is a range name.

Arguments are information that the function needs to complete its task. This information can be provided by you when you enter the function, or by a formula or other function.

Some functions do not require arguments. Most functions require one or more arguments; many have optional arguments as well. If a function contains multiple arguments, the arguments are separated by commas.

NOTE You also can use a period (.) or semicolon (;) to separate arguments, but the argument separator should never be the same as the decimal separator in the worksheet. This restriction rules out the period separator used in the United States. If the worksheet will be used internationally, the semicolon is the best separator to use. ■

Ten new functions have been added in 1-2-3 97 for Windows 95. Table 6.1 lists the new functions. For further details on the use of these functions, refer to the 1-2-3 Help system.

Table 6.1 New Functions in 1-2-3 97

Function	Description
@DECILE	Decile for a given range and tile
@FORECAST	Forecast value based on the linear trend between values in two ranges
@FVAMOUNT	Future value of a lump sum invested at a given rate for a number of periods
@ISBETWEEN	Logical true if value is between given bounds
@NSUM	Adds every *n*th values starting a given offset in a list of values
@PUREMEDIAN	Median of values in list, ignoring blanks, labels, and string valued formulas
@PVAMOUNT	Present value of a lump sum to be received a given number of periods in the future discounted at a given rate
@QUARTILE	Quartile for a given range and tile
@XIRR	Internal rate of return for a series of inflows and outflows
@XNPV	Net present value of a series of inflows and outflows

Entering Functions

You can use two methods to enter functions in a worksheet. After you click the cell that should contain the function, you can:

- Use the @function selector
- Use the @Function List dialog box
- Type the function in the cell

Whichever method you use, the function appears both in the current cell and in the contents box as you enter it. When you finish, press Enter or click the Confirm button to complete the entry.

Using the @function selector or the @Function List dialog box helps you prevent errors you might introduce if you type the function in the cell.

Using the @Function Selector and @Function List Dialog Box

The @function selector lets you choose a common function or open the @Function List dialog box, which automates your entry of functions. To use the @function selector, follow these steps:

1. Click the @function selector, which is the second icon in the edit line. A short drop-down list of common functions appears, as shown in figure 6.1. This list includes at least two sections separated by a solid line.

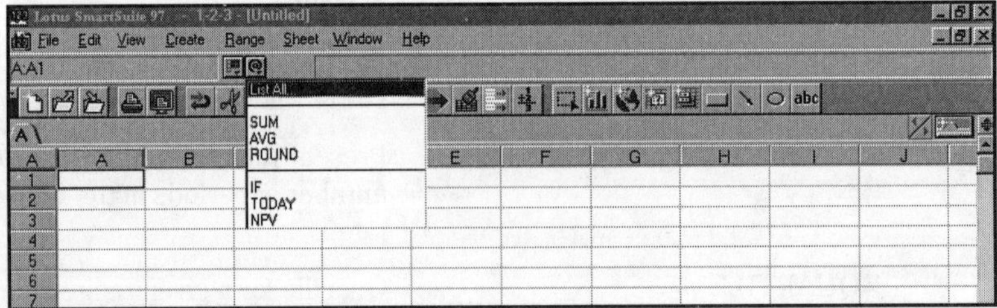

Fig. 6.1 When you click the @function selector, a short list of common functions appears.

2. If the function you need appears in the short list, you can select it. 1-2-3 enters the function, with the proper argument syntax, in the current cell and in the contents box. (Skip to step 6.)

   If the function you need is not in the short list, click the List All option at the top of the drop-down list. The @Function List dialog box appears, listing all the available functions (see fig. 6.2).

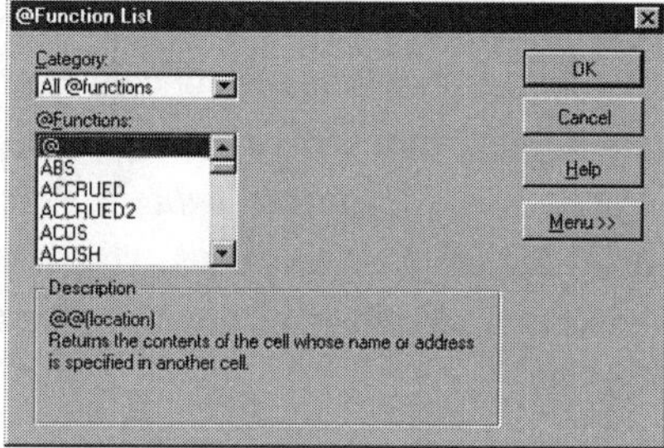

Fig. 6.2
The Function List dialog box lists all the functions.

TIP If you know the category of functions you want to see, you can select that category quickly by typing its first letter.

3. You can look through the list of functions to find the function you want, or you can use the Category drop-down list to display only functions in a certain category—for example, the financial functions. When you select a category, only functions of that type appear in the functions list.
4. Scroll through the list, using the scroll bars, or type the first letter of the function name and then scroll through the functions that begin with that letter. As you highlight different functions in the list, the Description box at the bottom of the dialog box displays the correct syntax and a brief description of the highlighted function.

NOTE When you look for a function in the @Function List dialog box by typing its name, you cannot type the entire function name. If you type the second letter of the name, 1-2-3 moves the highlight to the function in the list that starts with this letter.

5. When you find the correct function, highlight it and choose OK, or simply double-click it. 1-2-3 closes the dialog box and enters the function, with the proper argument syntax, in the current cell (see fig. 6.3).

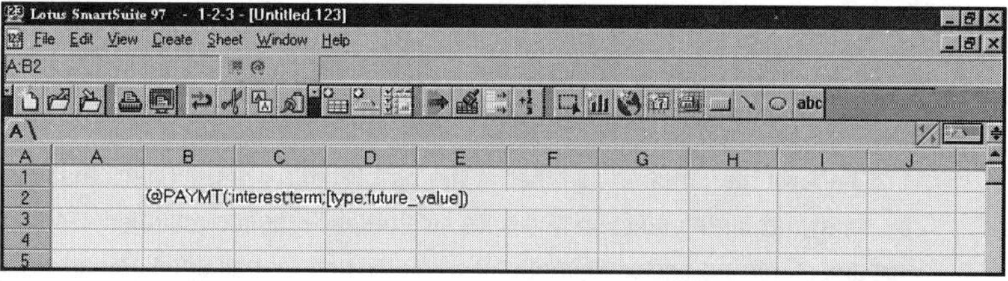

Fig. 6.3
1-2-3 places the function in the current cell.

6. Replace the argument names in the function with the necessary information. Highlight the argument name and then type the specific information, or select the appropriate cells or ranges with the mouse. For example, the @PAYMT function appears as @PAYMT(*;interest;term;[type;future_value]*). Replace the arguments with the list or range of cells that contain the values. The first argument is not shown by name, but the insertion point is in position for you to enter the argument (in this case, the principal).

If you point to a range that has been named, 1-2-3 uses the range name, rather than the cell addresses, in the function formula.

7. When the function is complete, press Enter or click the Confirm button to complete the entry. 1-2-3 displays the result of the function in the cell.

If you have used previous versions of 1-2-3, you may be in the habit of entering functions by typing @ and then pressing the F3 key. You can continue to use this method as you start entering functions in 1-2-3 97 for Windows 95.

When you type the @ symbol and then press F3, the @Function List dialog box appears.

Typing the Function

You can type the entire function, including its arguments. Save this method for simple functions that you use repeatedly (and thus remember their argument requirements). Typing a function may be the fastest method of entry, as long as you remember and use the proper syntax.

TROUBLESHOOTING

I have entered all of the required arguments for a function as well as the last optional argument. Why won't 1-2-3 accept the function formula? If you are using optional arguments in a function, you must use them sequentially. That means that to use the last optional argument, you must also enter all previous optional arguments. (You can specify the default values for these previous arguments, which won't change your results.)

1-2-3 shows the function as label in the cell. What's wrong? Check that you have used the proper syntax for the function and have included all required arguments. Also make sure that text arguments are enclosed in quotation marks and that all opening and closing parentheses are in place. If you are nesting functions, it is especially easy to forget an opening or closing parenthesis.

Customizing the @Function-Selector List

When you click the @function selector, a drop-down list of common functions appears. 1-2-3 lets you to customize this list so that it includes the functions you use most frequently. In addition to adding and removing functions, you can add and remove separator lines. These lines let you group the functions in the list in the way that's most useful to you.

To customize the @function-selector list, follow these steps:

1. Click the @function selector and select List All to display the @Function List dialog box.
2. Click the Menu button. The dialog box expands to include the Current Menu list and the >>, <<, and Separator buttons (see fig. 6.4). The Current Menu list contains all the functions that currently appear in the @function-selector list.

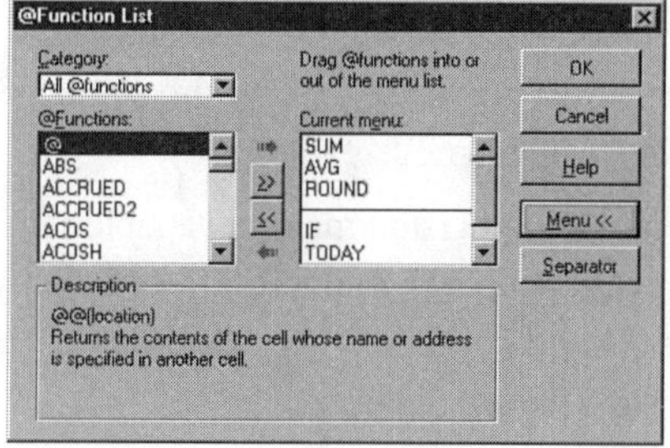

Fig. 6.4
You can customize the @function-selector list by using the expanded @Function List dialog box.

3. To add a new function, highlight it in the @Functions list. In the Current Menu list, highlight the function that you want the new function to follow. Finally, click the >> button. 1-2-3 adds the new function after the highlighted function in the Current Menu list.
4. To add a separator, highlight the function in the Current Menu list that you want the separator to follow, and click the Separator button.
5. To remove a function from the list, highlight it in the Current Menu list, and click the << button. To remove a separator, click and drag it away from the list.
6. When you are satisfied with the Current Menu list, click OK. The last function you added to the list is then placed in the active cell.

1-2-3 Function Dictionary

1-2-3's functions are divided into 10 categories:

- *Calendar functions* provide a set of conversion tools that let you perform date and time arithmetic. These functions are valuable for worksheets that use logic based on dates and times; they also are useful for calculations that show the number of days, months, or years between specific events.
- *Database functions* perform statistical calculations as well as queries in worksheets and external databases based on criteria that you specify.
- *Engineering functions* perform advanced mathematical operations, numeric-type conversions, and specific engineering calculations.
- *Financial functions* aid you in many business worksheets. With these functions, you can discount cash flow, calculate depreciation, and find the interest rate necessary for an annuity to grow to a future value. This set of functions provides great flexibility in investment analysis as well as cash-planning strategies.
- *Information functions* provide a quick way to find the status of cells and ranges, the system, and errors in the worksheet.
- *Logical functions* lets you to add decision-making capabilities to the worksheet. With logical functions, you can test whether a condition—one that you have defined in a worksheet or a 1-2-3 predefined condition—is true or false. Logical tests are important for formulas that need to make decisions.
- *Lookup functions* find and return the contents of a cell. These functions are used primarily in conjunction with logical functions in macros to determine the information contained in a cell, making your worksheets more efficient and valuable.
- *Mathematical functions* complement engineering functions. These tools are useful in complex and simple worksheets because they perform a variety of standard arithmetic operations, such as rounding values and calculating square roots.
- *Statistical functions* let you perform all the standard statistical calculations on data in the worksheet or database. You can find minimum and maximum values, calculate averages, and compute standard deviations and variances.
- *Text functions* provide a means to manipulate text. Text functions (also called *string functions*) are used to repeat characters; convert letters to uppercase, lowercase, or proper case; and change characters to numbers and numbers into text or strings. Text functions can be important when you are converting data for use by other programs, such as word processor mailing lists.

The following sections discuss each category and describe the most commonly used functions.

To get help on any function, open the @Function List dialog box, highlight the function in the @Function list, and choose Help or press F1.

Calendar Functions

1-2-3 stores dates as date numbers that represent a date between January 1, 1900 and December 31, 2099. For example, 1 is the date number for January 1, 1900; and 33554 is the date number for November 12, 1991. 1-2-3 stores times as time numbers that range from .0 for 12:00:00 A.M. to .9999884 for 11:59:59. By using these date and time numbers, you can use dates and times in calculations such as elapsed time or days.

The 1-2-3 calendar functions let you convert dates and times to date and time numbers so that you can use them in worksheet calculations.

NOTE 1-2-3 expresses time as a decimal fraction of a full day. For example, 0.5 is equal to 12 hours (or 12:00 P.M.). In addition, 1-2-3 works on international time: 10:00 P.M. in U.S. time is 22:00 in international time.

@DAYS360*(start_date,end_date)* and @D360*(start_date,end_date)*

@D360 returns the number of days between two dates, based on 12 months, each with 30 days—a 360-day year.

@DAYS360 is a more technical version of @D360. @DAYS360 has the same format as @D360; it, too, returns the difference between two dates based on a 360-day year. The @DAYS360 function, however, bases its calculations on the Security Industries Association's 1990 modifications to the 1986 edition of the *Standard Security Calculation Methods*. This is the standard in the securities industry for calculating the difference between two dates based on a 360-day year.

The two functions generally return different answers for the same data whenever the `start_date` or `end_date` arguments are the last day of the month. You should use @DAYS360 to calculate the number of days between two dates based on a 360-day year unless you must use calculations that are consistent with earlier worksheets in which the @D360 function was used.

Limits: Both date arguments must be expressed as valid date numbers, or the function returns `ERR`. If the `end_date` occurs before the `start_date`, 1-2-3 returns a negative number.

Example: @DAYS360(33554,B5) or @D360(33554,B5) returns `881`, where 33554 is the date number for 11/12/91 and cell B5 contains the date 4/23/94. There were 881 days between these two dates.

@DATE(*year,month,day*)

@DATE works with all algebraic symbols. For example, the syntax for adding a day to the @DATE function is @DATE(*year,month,day*)+1.

@DATE returns the date number for the day specified by the arguments. You can enter numbers for the arguments or reference cells containing the values or formulas that calculate the values.

Limits: You must enter numbers that are valid to represent the year, month, and day. For example, the `day` argument for February cannot be 30 or 31.

1-2-3 returns date numbers for dates between January 1, 1900 and December 31, 2099. Enter years from 1900 to 2099 either by entering all four digits or by entering from 00 (for 1900) to 199 (for 2099). Enter months from 1 to 12, and days from 1 to 31 (or the last day of the specified month).

Example: Both @DATE(51,04,06) and @DATE(51,4,6) return the date number for April 6, 1951: 18724. If the cell has a date format, the result appears in that date format. If the cell format is General, the date number appears.

NOTE Even though 1900 wasn't a leap year, 1-2-3 assigns the date number 60 to the date February 29, 1900 (a date that never existed). Although this assignment should not be a problem, you may have difficulty if you transfer data between 1-2-3 and other programs. In that case, you must adjust for this error yourself.

@DATEVALUE(*text*)

@DATEVALUE computes the date number for a date entered in one of the date formats that 1-2-3 recognizes. Click the Number Format button in the status bar or display the Number Format panel in the InfoBox to display the acceptable formats. If 1-2-3 does not recognize the format, @DATEVALUE results in ERR.

Be sure to enclose the date text in quotation marks when you specify the date as the `text` argument. Alternatively, you can specify a cell address of a cell that contains the date text as the `text` argument.

Limits: 1-2-3 returns date numbers for dates between January 1, 1900 and December 31, 2099. Enter years from 1900 to 2099 either by entering all four digits or by entering from 00 (for 1900) to 199 (for 2099). Enter days from 1 to 31.

You cannot use the "3-digit" format for specifying the years 2000 and beyond. That is, an entry such as @DATEVALUE ("1-Jan-199") will not work correctly. The year part of the text argument must be either 2-digit or 4-digit.

Example: If cell A1 contains the formatted date 31-Dec-2099, you can use @DATEVALUE(A1) to return the date number 73050. Alternatively, you can use @DATEVALUE("31-Dec-2099") to return the same date number.

NOTE If you reset the default date format so that you can use regional date formats, make sure that the *text* argument is in one of the date formats for the country you selected. To change the default date format, open Regional Settings in the Windows 95 Control Panel, and then choose the Date tab. In the Short Date Style drop-down list or the Long Date Style drop-down list, choose the date format that you would like.

@DATESTRING(*date*)

@DATESTRING computes the date from the date number and displays it as a label using the default regional date format. To change the default regional date format, open Regional Settings in the Windows 95 Control Panel, and then choose the Date tab. In the Short Date Style drop-down list, choose the date format that you would like.

Limits: The `date` argument must be expressed as a valid date number or the function returns ERR.

Example: @DATESTRING(32780) returns 09/29/89 when the default regional date format is MM/dd/yy.

@DAY(*date_number*)

@DAY converts a date number to a numeric day of the month. The function accepts a valid date number as its single argument and returns a number ranging from 1 to 31. You can use a cell reference or another function (such as @TODAY) to supply the value for the `date_number` argument.

Limits: The date number must range from 1 (January 1, 1900) to 73050 (December 31, 2099).

Examples: @DAY(32780) returns 29 as the day of the month, because this date number represents September 29, 1989. @DAY(B3) returns 29 when cell B3 contains the date 29-Sep-89.

@MONTH(*date_number*)

@MONTH converts a date number to a numeric month. The function accepts a valid date number as its single argument and returns a number ranging from 1 (January) to 12 (December). You can use a cell reference or another function (such as @DATE) to supply the value for the `date_number` argument.

Limits: The date number must range from 1 (January 1, 1900) to 73050 (December 31, 2099).

Examples: @MONTH(32780) returns 9 (September) as the month, because this date number represents September 29, 1989. @MONTH(B3) returns 9 (September) when cell B3 contains the date 29-Sep-89. @MONTH(@DATE(89,9,29)) also returns 9 (September).

@YEAR(*date_number*)

@YEAR converts a date number to a numeric year. The function accepts a valid date number as its single argument and returns a number ranging from 0 (for 1900) to 199 (for 2099). You can use a cell reference or another function (such as @DATE or @NOW) to supply the value for the `date_number` argument.

Limits: The date number must range from 1 (January 1, 1900) to 73050 (December 31, 2099).

To convert @YEAR results to four-digit years, add 1900 to the formula. For example, @YEAR(@DATE(89,9,29))+1900 returns 1989.

Examples: @YEAR(32780) returns 89 as the year, because this date number represents September 29, 1989. @YEAR(B3) returns 89 when cell B3 contains the date 29-Sep-89. @MONTH(@NOW) returns the current year.

@NOW

@NOW retrieves the current system date and time as date-and-time numbers. The integers to the left of the decimal point specify the date; those to the right of the decimal point specify the time.

@NOW is a convenient tool for recording the date and time when a worksheet is modified or printed. 1-2-3 recalculates @NOW every time you recalculate your work. If you selected automatic recalculation (choose File, User Setup, 1-2-3 Preferences; click the Recalculation tab and select Automatic) 1-2-3 recalculates @NOW every time it recalculates any value.

If you format the cell containing @NOW as a date, only the date portion of the result appears. If you format the cell as a time, only the time portion appears. To change formats, click the Number Format button in the status bar or choose a format in the Number Format panel of the InfoBox.

Example: On March 25, 1996, at 9:27:36 P.M., @NOW returns 35149.8942. 35149 is the date number for March 25, 1996, and .8942 is the time number for 9:27:36 P.M.

NOTE Use the @INT function to calculate the date or time portion of the @NOW function. To extract the date portion of the @NOW function, use @INT(@NOW); the result is the same as the result of @TODAY. To extract the time portion, use @NOW-@INT(@NOW); the result is the same as the result of @NOW-@TODAY. ■

@TODAY

@TODAY retrieves the current system date (not the system time) as a date number. This function is a convenient tool for recording the date when a worksheet is modified or printed. 1-2-3 recalculates @TODAY every time you recalculate your work. If you selected automatic recalculation (choose File, User Setup, 1-2-3 Preferences; click the Recalculation tab and select Automatic), 1-2-3 recalculates @TODAY every time it recalculates any value.

You can format the cell containing @TODAY as a date. To change formats, click the Number Format button in the status bar or open the InfoBox and choose a format in the Number Format panel.

Example: On March 25, 1996, @TODAY returns 35149, which is the date number for that date.

@TIME(*hour,minutes,seconds*)

@TIME returns the time number for the time specified by the arguments. You can enter numbers for the arguments or reference cells containing the values or formulas that calculate the values. You can use @TIME to calculate the time period between events.

Limits: Enter hours from 0 (for midnight) to 23 (for 11 P.M.), minutes from 0 to 59, and seconds from 0 to 59.

Example: @TIME(14,0,0) returns the time number for 2:00:00 P.M.: .583333. If the cell has a time format, the result appears in that time format. If the cell format is General, the time number appears.

One way to produce a range of times is to use the Range, Fill command. The following steps produce a table that can be used as an event calendar for the period 8:00 A.M. to 7:30 P.M., in 30-minute increments:

1. Select the range in which you want the times to appear. For this example, select the range A4..A19.
2. Open the Range menu and choose the Fill command.
3. In the Fill Type box, choose Times.
4. In the Interval box, choose the Minute option.
5. Select the start text in the Start At box; type **8:00**.
6. Select the increment text in the Increment By box; type **30**.
7. Select the stop text in the Stop At box; type **4:00pm**.
8. Click OK. 1-2-3 fills the range A4..A19 with time-conversion numbers.

9. 1-2-3 formats the range of cells with the default time format. To change the time format for the selected range, open the InfoBox and choose the Number Format panel. In the Category box, select Time, and then select the time format 01:59AM and choose OK. 1-2-3 converts the cells in the selected range to this format.

@TIMEVALUE(*text*)

Like @DATEVALUE and @DATE, @TIMEVALUE is a variation on @TIME. Like @TIME, @TIMEVALUE produces a time number from the hour, minute, and second information you supply. Unlike @TIME, however, @TIMEVALUE uses text arguments rather than numeric arguments.

You must enter the time text in one of the time formats that 1-2-3 recognizes. To display the acceptable formats, click the Number Format button in the status bar or open the InfoBox and choose the Number Format panel. If 1-2-3 does not recognize the format, @TIMEVALUE results in ERR.

Be sure to enclose the time text in quotation marks when you specify the time as the `text` argument. Alternatively, you can specify the cell address of a cell that contains the time text as the `text` argument.

Limits: Enter hours from 0 (for midnight) to 23 (for 11 P.M.), hours from 0 to 59, and seconds from 0 to 59.

Examples: If cell A1 contains the formatted date `02:00 pm`, you can use @TIMEVALUE(A1) to return the time number `.583333`. Alternatively, you can use @TIMEVALUE("02:00 pm") to return the same time number.

NOTE If you reset the default time format so that you can use international time formats, make sure that the `text` argument is in one of the time formats for the country you selected. To change the default regional time format, open Regional Settings in the Windows 95 Control Panel, and then choose the Time tab. In the Time Style drop-down list, choose the time format that you would like.

@SECOND(*time_number*)

@SECOND extracts the seconds from a time number. The function accepts a valid time number as its single argument and returns a number ranging from 0 to 59. You can use a cell reference or another function (such as @TIME) to supply the value for the `time_number` argument.

Limits: The time number must range from .000000 (for midnight) to .999988 (for 11:59:59 P.M.).

Examples: @SECOND(.590394) returns `10` as the seconds, because this time number represents 02:10:10 P.M. @SECOND(B3) returns `10` when cell B3 contains the time 02:10:10. @SECOND(@TIME(02,10,10)) also returns `10`.

@MINUTE(*time_number*)

@MINUTE extracts the minutes from a time number. The function accepts a valid time number as its single argument and returns a number ranging from 0 to 59. You can use a cell reference or another function (such as @TIME) to supply the value for the `time_number` argument.

Limits: The time number must range from .000000 (for midnight) to .999988 (for 11:59:59 P.M.).

Examples: @MINUTE(.590394) returns `10` as the minutes, because this time number represents 02:10:10 P.M. @MINUTE(B3) returns `10` when cell B3 contains the time 02:10:10. @MINUTE(@TIME(02,10,10)) also returns `10`.

@HOUR(*time_number*)

@HOUR extracts the hours from a time number. The function accepts a valid time number as its single argument and returns a number ranging from 0 to 23. You can use a cell reference or another function (such as @TIME) to supply the value for the *time_number* argument.

@HOUR is useful for calculations that involve hours, such as calculating hourly wages or elapsed hours.

Limits:	The time number must range from .000000 (for midnight) to .999988 (for 11:59:59 P.M.).
Examples:	@HOUR(.590394) returns `14` (2:00 P.M.) as the hour because this time number represents 02:10:10 P.M. @HOUR(B3) returns `14` when cell B3 contains the time 02:10:10. @HOUR(@TIME(02,10,10) also returns `14`.

Database Functions

1-2-3 database functions manipulate database fields. Like other functions, the database functions perform—in one simple statement—calculations that otherwise would require a complex series of operations. The efficiency and ease of application make these functions excellent tools for examining database records in either worksheet databases or external database tables (see Part V, "Managing Databases," for details about working with databases).

Following is the general syntax of all database functions except @DQUERY:

@DSUM(*input,field,criteria*)

The `input` argument specifies the database or part of a database to be scanned; it can be the address or name of a single-worksheet range that contains a database table or the name of an external database table. You can use more than one `input` argument in a database function by separating the `input` arguments with commas. 1-2-3 reads database-function arguments from right to left, so it uses the last argument as the criteria, the next-to-last argument as the field, and the remaining arguments as input. You can use an unlimited number of `input` arguments, provided that you do not exceed 512 characters in the cell that contains the function. You do not need to identify an `input` (using the Create, Database, Query Table command) before you use it as an `input` argument in a database function.

The `criteria` argument specifies which records are to be selected. The `criteria` argument can be a criteria formula, a range address, or a range name of a range containing a criteria formula.

The `field` argument is the field name from the database table, enclosed in quotation marks. If you use just one `input` argument, you can represent the `field` argument with an offset number. If you use more than one `input` argument, and the field name you want to use as the `field` argument appears in more than one of the input ranges, the field must be entered as the name of the input, followed by a period, and the field name, enclosed in quotation marks. For example, if you have two input ranges named SALES (A1..E20) and BUDGET (A22..E42), each of which has a field called DEPARTMENT, you can refer to the DEPARTMENT field in the SALES range this way:

"SALES.DEPARTMENT" or "A1..E20.DEPARTMENT"

Database functions are similar to statistical functions, but database functions process only data items that meet the criteria you specify. For example, if you have a list of employees, the departments where they work, and their annual salaries, you can use @AVG to calculate the average of all salaries. Use @DAVG to calculate the average salaries of any subgroup, such as the Sales department, without first extracting the Sales department records.

Figure 6.5 shows a few examples of common database functions.

Fig. 6.5
Database functions manipulate database fields.

	A	B	C	D	E
1	*Input Range*				*Criteria Range*
2	Name	Department	Salary		Department
3	Arron, R.	Shipping	16,600		<>Shipping
4	Abbot, D.	Customer Support	36,600		
5	Beheler, S.	Shipping	22,400		*Criteria Range for @DGET*
6	Bonkers, D.	Marketing	32,500		SALARY
7	Roche, D.	Administration	42,300		39,100
8	Smokey, T.B.	Sales	40,250		
9	Williamson, J.	Administration	39,100		
10	Williamson, B.	Administration	33,300		
11	**Database @Functions**		**Returns**		
12	@DAVG($A$2..$C$10,"Salary",$E$2..$E$3)		37,342		
13	@DCOUNT($A$2..$C$10,"Salary",$E$2..$E$3)		6		
14	@DGET($A$2..$C$10,"Name",$E$6..$E$7)		Williamson, J.		
15	@DMAX($A$2..$C$10,"Salary",$E$2..$E$3)		42,300		
16	@DMIN($A$2..$C$10,"Salary",$E$2..$E$3)		32,500		
17	@DSTD($A$2..$C$10,"Salary",$E$2..$E$3)		3,570		
18	@DSTDS($A$2..$C$10,"Salary",$E$2..$E$3)		3,911		
19	@DSUM($A$2..$C$10,"Salary",$E$2..$E$3)		224,050		
20	@DVAR($A$2..$C$10,"Salary",$E$2..$E$3)		12,743,681		
21	@DVARS($A$2..$C$10,"Salary",$E$2..$E$3)		15,292,417		

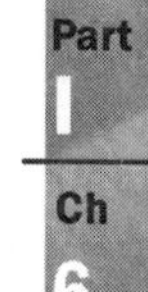

@DAVG(*input,field,criteria*)

@DAVG calculates the average of the values in a field of the `input` argument for records that match the criteria.

Example: In figure 6.5, the average in the Salary field for records that match the non-Shipping department criteria is 37,342.

@DCOUNT(*input,field,criteria*)

@DCOUNT counts the ***nonblank cells***—cells that contain data—in a field of the `input` argument for records that match the criteria.

Example: In figure 6.5, the number of cells containing data in the Salary field for records that match the non-Shipping department criteria is 6.

@DGET(*input,field,criteria*)

Although @DGET uses the same three arguments as most other database functions, @DGET performs a different function. @DGET returns the value of the `field` argument for the record that matches the condition set in the `criteria` argument. Because @DGET returns `ERR` if no records match or if more than one record matches the criteria, @DGET often requires a more selective `criteria` argument.

Example: In figure 6.5, the criteria used for @DGET specifies the single record where the Salary field value equals 39,100; the value returned for the Name field is `Williamson, J.`

@DMAX(*input,field,criteria*)

@DMAX finds the largest value in a field for records that match the criteria.

Example: In figure 6.5, the maximum in the Salary field for records that match the non-Shipping department criteria is 42,300.

@DMIN(*input,field,criteria*)

@DMIN finds the smallest value in a field for records that match the criteria.

Example: In figure 6.5, the minimum in the Salary field for records that match the non-Shipping department criteria is 32,500.

@DSTD(*input,field,criteria*)

@DSTD calculates the population standard deviation of values in a field for records that match the criteria.

Example: In figure 6.5, the standard deviation of the Salary field for records that match the non-Shipping department criteria is 3,570.

@DSTDS(*input,field,criteria*)

@DSTDS calculates the sample standard deviation of values in a field for records that match the criteria.

Example: In figure 6.5, the standard deviation of a sample population of the Salary field for records that match the non-Shipping department criteria is 3,911.

@DSUM(*input,field,criteria*)

@DSUM totals the values in a field for records that match the criteria.

Example: In figure 6.5, the sum of the Salary field for records that match the non-Shipping department criteria is 224,050.

@DVAR(*input,field,criteria*)

@DVAR calculates the population variance of values in a field for records that match the criteria.

Example: In figure 6.5, the population variance of the Salary field for records that match the non-Shipping department criteria is 12,743,681.

@DVARS(*input,field,criteria*)

@DVARS calculates the variance of sample values in a field for records that match the criteria.

Example: In figure 6.5, the variance of sample values of the Salary field for records that match the non-Shipping department criteria is 15,292,417.

Engineering Functions

The engineering functions provide solutions for Bessel calculations, hex-to-decimal conversions, error-function calculations, and power-series summations.

Bessel functions are used in calculations dealing with cylindrical symmetry. You use these functions in conjunction with diffusion, elasticity, wave propagation, and fluid motion:

- @BESSELI(*x*,*n*) calculates the modified Bessel function of integer order I*n*(*x*). This function approximates to within +/-5*10^-8.
- @BESSELJ(*x*,*n*) calculates the Bessel function of integer order J*n*(*x*). This function approximates to within +/-5*10^-8.
- @BESSELK(*x*,*n*) calculates the modified Bessel function of integer order K*n*(*x*). This function approximates to within +/-5*10^-8.
- @BESSELY(*x*,*n*) calculates the Bessel function of integer order Y*n*(*x*). This function sometimes is called the Neumann function. This function approximates to within +/-5*10^-8.

In each of these functions, the `x` argument is the value at which to evaluate the function; it can be any value. The `n` argument is the order of the function, which can be any positive integer or (for @BESSELI and @BESSELJ) 0.

@BETA(*z*,*w*)

@BETA calculates the Beta function to within at least six significant digits. The `z` and `w` arguments can be any value.

Example: @BETA(.5,.5) returns `3.141593`.

@BETAI(*a*,*b*,*x*)

@BETAI calculates the incomplete Beta function to within at least six significant digits. The `a` and `b` arguments can be any value. The `x` argument must be a value ranging from 0 through 1.

Example: @BETAI(.5,.5,.668271) returns `0.609257`.

@DECIMAL(*hexadecimal*)

@DECIMAL converts a hexadecimal value to its signed decimal equivalent. The `hexadecimal` argument, which you enter as text, can be a value ranging from 00000000 through FFFFFFFF. The value 0 and all positive hexadecimal numbers are in the range 00000000 through 7FFFFFFF. Negative hexadecimal numbers are in the range 80000000 through FFFFFFFF.

Limits: The argument can contain only valid hexadecimal digits and letters. Valid digits range from 0 through 9; valid letters range from A through F. The letters are not case-sensitive.

Example: @DECIMAL("1A") returns `26`.

@ERF(*lower_limit,[upper_limit]*)

@ERF is an approximation function that calculates the error function integrated between the lower limit and the upper limit. The approximation is within +/-1.2x10^7.

The `lower_limit` argument is the lower boundary for integrating @ERF; it can be any value. The optional `upper_limit` argument specifies the upper boundary for integrating @ERF; it can be any value greater than or equal to the `lower_limit` value. If you omit the `upper_limit` argument, @ERF integrates between 0 and `lower_limit`.

Examples: @ERF(.7) returns `0.677801`, and @ERF(.8) returns `0.742101`. Notice that @ERF(.7,.8) returns `0.0643` and is the difference between the first two examples.

@ERFC(*x*)

@ERFC calculates the complementary error function integrated between the argument and infinity. The @ERFC function is 1-@ERF(*x*), which approximates the complementary error function to within +/-3*10^-7. The *x* argument can be any error-function value.

Example: @ERFC(0.7) returns `0.322199`.

@ERFD(*x*)

@ERFD calculates the derivative of the error function, using the formula (2/SQRT(@PI)) *@EXP(-*x*^2). The `x` argument can be an error-function value ranging from approximately -106.56 to 106.56. If the argument falls outside this range, 1-2-3 returns `ERR`. If the argument is outside the boundaries -15.102 to 15.102, 1-2-3 can calculate and store the value for use in other calculations, although it cannot display the value in the cell (a series of asterisks appears instead).

Example: @ERFD(0.7) returns `0.691275`.

@GAMMA(*x*)

@GAMMA approximates the Gamma distribution accurately to within six significant figures. The *x* argument can be any positive value greater than 0.

Examples: @GAMMA(.5) returns `1.772454`, and @GAMMA(3.6) returns `3.717024`.

@GAMMAI(*a,x,[complement]*)

@GAMMAI calculates the incomplete Gamma function and is accurate to within six significant figures. The `a` argument can be any positive value. The `x` argument can be any positive value or 0.

The optional `complement` argument controls how 1-2-3 calculates @GAMMAI; you can set this value to 0 or 1. If you use 0, 1-2-3 calculates P(*a*,*x*). (This is the default if you omit the `complement` argument.) If you use 1, 1-2-3 calculates Q(*a*,*x*) or 1-P(*a*,*x*).

Example: The value of @GAMMAI(7.5,12.4497,1) is `0.051311`.

@GAMMALN(*x*)

@GAMMALN calculates the natural log of the gamma function to within six significant digits. The `x` argument can be any value greater than 0.

Example: @GAMMALN(0.5) returns `0.572365`.

@HEX(*decimal*)

The @HEX function converts a decimal value to its signed hexadecimal equivalent. The `decimal` argument can be a value ranging from -2,147,483,648 through 2,147,483,647. Enter the argument as a value; if it is not an integer, 1-2-3 truncates it to an integer.

Example: @HEX(162) returns `A2`.

@SERIESSUM(*x,n,m,coefficients*)

@SERIESSUM calculates the sum of a power series. The `x` argument is the power series' input value. The `n` argument's value is the initial power to which to raise x. The `m` argument's value is the increment to increase n for each term in the series.

The `coefficients` argument is a range that contains the coefficients by which 1-2-3 multiplies each successive power of *x*. The number of terms in the series is determined by the number of cells in the `coefficients` argument. For example, if coefficients contains eight cells, the power series contains eight terms.

Example: Suppose that a range called INPUT contains the values 0.2, 0.7, and 1.3 for the `coefficients` argument. @SERIESSUM(3.5,2,1,INPUT) returns `227.5438`.

Financial Functions

1-2-3 provides a series of financial functions that calculate discounted cash flow, loan amortization, depreciation, investment analysis, and annuities. The 1-2-3 financial functions are categorized into the following five groups, so that you can find the best type of function quickly:

- Annuities
- Bonds
- Capital-Budgeting Tools
- Depreciation
- Single-Sum Compounding

Annuity Functions You use annuity functions as financial-analysis tools. These functions give you full-range capability to calculate current payments, future values, and interest rates. You can use this information to make prudent financial decisions.

@ FV(*payments, interest, term*) and @FVAL(*payments, interestterm,[type],[present_value]*)

@FV calculates the future value of an investment based on a specific interest rate and a fixed number of regular investment payments. @FVAL calculates the future value of an investment based on a specific interest rate, a fixed number of regular payments, the optional position of the period in which the payments are made, and the optional starting amount of the investment. @FV and @FVAL are helpful for estimating the future balances of savings accounts, college funds, and investments.

The `payment` argument is the amount of each equal payment. The `interest` argument is the periodic interest rate. The `term` argument is the total number of payments.

When payment is made at the end of the period, you are calculating an ordinary annuity. When payment is made at the beginning of the period, you are calculating an annuity due.

For @FVAL, the optional `type` argument can be 0 or 1. A value of 0 causes 1-2-3 to calculate based on payments being made at the end of the period. This value is the default value if you omit the `type` argument. A value of 1 causes 1-2-3 to calculate based on payments being made at the beginning of the period.

For @FVAL, the optional `present_value` argument indicates the current value of the series of future payments. It can be any value. If you omit the `present_value` argument, 1-2-3 assumes a value of 0.

Limits: The interest argument must be greater than -1.

You must use the same period for the `payment`, `interest`, and `term` arguments. Therefore, if you are calculating a monthly payment, use monthly increments for *interest* and *term*. This means you need to divide the annual interest rate by 12 and multiply the number of years by 12. If you keep the `interest` and `term` arguments annual, increase the `payment` argument to a yearly amount by multiplying the monthly payment by 12.

Example: You start your three-year-old's college-education fund with $2,000, and you plan monthly contributions of $200 at the end of the period. The annual interest rate is 6 percent, and the time period is 15 years. Use the function @FVAL(200,0.06/12,15*12,0,2000) to calculate the result of your savings at the end of the term: $63,071.93.

NOTE When entering optional arguments, you must enter all the optional arguments before the optional argument that you want to use. For example, for @FVAL(*payments, interest, term,[type],[present_value]*), to use the `present_value` argument, you first must enter a `type` argument.

@IPAYMT(*principal,interest,term,start_period,[end_period],[type],[future_value]*) and @PPAYMT(*principal,interest,term,start_period,[end_period],[type],[future_value]*)

Performing loan analysis can be very beneficial when you are looking for a loan. @IPAYMT and @PPAYMT are complementary functions: @IPAYMT calculates the interest on payments that you make on a loan, and @PPAYMT calculates the principal contributed to the loan you are paying off.

The `principal` argument is the amount of the loan. The `interest` argument is the periodic interest rate. The `term` argument is the number of payment periods for the loan (frequently, the number of months or years). The `start_period` argument is the point in the term when you want to begin calculating interest or principal.

The optional `end_period` argument is the point in the term when you want to stop calculating interest or principal. If you omit this argument, 1-2-3 assumes that the `start_period` and `end_period` arguments are the same.

The optional `type` argument can be 0 or 1. A value of 0 causes 1-2-3 to calculate based on payments being made at the end of the period. This value is the default value if you omit the `type` argument. A value of 1 causes 1-2-3 to calculate based on payments being made at the beginning of the period.

The optional `future_value` argument indicates the future value of the series of payments; it can be any value. If you omit the `future_value` argument, 1-2-3 assumes a value of 0.

You can enter interest rates in the function as a percentage. 1-2-3 converts the percentage to the decimal format it requires. If you enter **5%**, for example, 1-2-3 enters `0.05` in the function.

Limits: The `interest` argument must be greater than -1.

The `term` argument can be any value except 0.

The `start_period` argument can be any value greater than or equal to 1, but it cannot be greater than the `term` value.

You must use the same period for the `interest` and `term` arguments. Therefore, if you are calculating a monthly payment, use monthly increments for interest and term. This means you need to divide the annual interest rate by 12 and multiply the number of years by 12.

Example: You have a $5,000 loan at 10.25 percent, to be paid back in two years (24 months). To determine the interest amount for the 12th month, use @IPAYMT(5000,0.1025/12,24,12), which returns `$24.21` (when rounded for Currency format). To determine the principal amount for the 12th month, use @PPAYMT(5000,0.1025/12,24,12), which returns `$207.09` (when rounded for Currency format).

@IRATE(*term,payment,present_value,[type],[future_value],[guess]*)

@IRATE calculates the rate of interest necessary for an investment to grow to a specific future value. This function is useful for determining the interest rate necessary to maintain the principal amount of an investment while generating a specific amount in interest—for example, for a trust or retirement fund.

The `term` argument is the number of payments. The `payment` argument is the payment amount. The `present_value` argument is the starting amount of the investment.

The optional `type` argument can be 0 or 1. A value of 0 causes 1-2-3 to calculate based on payments being made at the end of the period. This value is the default value if you omit the `type` argument. A value of 1 causes 1-2-3 to calculate based on payments being made at the beginning of the period.

The optional `future_value` argument indicates the future value of the series of payments; it can be any value. If you omit the `future_value` argument, 1-2-3 assumes a value of 0.

The optional `guess` argument is your estimate of the interest rate; it can be a value between 0 and 1. If you omit this argument, 1-2-3 assumes a value of .1 (10%).

Limits: You must use the same period for the `term` and `payment` arguments. Therefore, to find an annual interest rate, enter the term in years and multiply the monthly payment by 12 to use a yearly payment figure.

Example: You have a $200,000 retirement fund, from which you want to withdraw $2,000 monthly for 25 years. Use @IRATE(25*12,2000,200000) * 12 to determine that your investment needs an interest rate of 11.27 percent.

@TERM(*payments,interest,future_value*) and @NPER(*payments,interest,future_value,[type],[present_value]*)

@TERM calculates the number of periods required to accumulate a specified future value by making equal payments into an interest-bearing account at the end of each period. The number of periods is the term for an ordinary annuity.

@NPER performs the same calculation, with a slight twist: It allows for optional `present_value` and `type` arguments. These arguments provide flexibility by adjusting the starting amount and the time of the period within the estimation.

You can calculate the term necessary to pay back a loan by using a negative *future_value* argument with @TERM.

The `payment` argument is the amount of each payment. The `interest` argument is the periodic interest rate. The `future_value` argument is the amount you want to have at the end of the payment schedule.

For @NPER, the optional `type` argument can be 0 or 1. A value of 0 causes 1-2-3 to calculate based on payments being made at the end of the period. This value is the default value if you omit the `type` argument. A value of 1 causes 1-2-3 to calculate based on payments being made at the beginning of the period.

For @NPER, the optional `present_value` argument indicates the current value (the starting balance); it can be any value. If you omit the `present_value` argument, 1-2-3 assumes a value of 0.

Limits: The `interest` argument must be greater than -1.

The `payment` argument can be any value except 0.

Examples: To determine how long it will take to accumulate $5,000 by making a monthly payment of $50 into an account that pays 8 percent annual interest compounded monthly (0.67 percent per month), use @TERM(50,0.0067,5000), which returns `76.80` (months).

If you have $200 saved and want to start with that amount, use @NPER(50,0.0067,5000,0,200), which returns `72.84` (months).

@PMT(*principal,interest,term*) and
@PAYMT(*principal,interest,term,[type],[future_value]*)

TIP @PMTC is similar to @PMT, except that it supports Canadian mortgage conventions.

@PMT and @PAYMT calculate the periodic payments necessary to pay the entire principal on an amortizing loan. @PMT assumes that the payments are made at the end of each period, whereas @PAYMT lets you specify that payments are made at the beginning or the end of each period. In addition, @PAYMT includes an optional argument for the future value.

The `principal` argument is the amount of the loan. The `interest` argument is the periodic interest rate. The `term` argument is the number of payment periods for the loan.

For @PAYMT, the optional `type` argument can be 0 or 1. A value of 0 causes 1-2-3 to calculate based on payments being made at the end of the period. This value is the default value if you omit the `type` argument. A value of 1 causes 1-2-3 to calculate based on payments being made at the beginning of the period.

For @PAYMT, the optional `future_value` argument indicates the future value of a series of payments; it can be any value. If you omit the `future_value` argument, 1-2-3 assumes a value of 0.

Limits: The `interest` argument must be greater than -1.

You must use the same period for the `interest` and `term` arguments. Therefore, if you are calculating a monthly payment, use monthly increments for interest and term. This means you need to divide the annual interest rate by 12 and multiply the number of years by 12.

Examples: To calculate the monthly payments on a $10,000 five-year loan with an interest rate of 9 percent and payments due on the last day of the month, use @PMT(10000,0.09/12,60), which returns a figure of `$207.58` (when rounded for Currency format). If payment is due on the first day of the month, use @PAYMT(10000,0.09/12,60,1), which returns a figure of `$206.04` (when rounded for Currency format).

NOTE If you make monthly payments, enter the interest rate as the monthly interest rate (annual rate divided by 12) and the term as the number of months for which you make payments (number of years multiplied by 12). Alternatively, if you make annual payments, enter the interest rate as the annual interest rate and the term as the number of years for which you make payments.

@PV(*payments,interest,term*) and @PVAL(*payments,interest,term,[type],[future_value]*)

Use @PV in conjunction with @PMT to create an amortization table.

@PV and @PVAL calculate the present value of an investment made as a series of equal payments. Use @PV and @PVAL to compare different investments. For example, you can compare a single-payment investment with a pension fund that has multiple equal payments.

The `payment` argument is the amount of the payments. The `interest` argument is the periodic interest rate. The `term` argument is the number of payment periods for the investment.

For @PVAL, the optional `type` argument can be 0 or 1. A value of 0 causes 1-2-3 to calculate based on payments being made at the end of the period. This value is the default value if you omit the `type` argument. A value of 1 causes 1-2-3 to calculate based on payments being made at the beginning of the period.

For @PVAL, the optional `future_value` argument indicates the future value of the payments; it can be any value. If you omit the `future_value` argument, 1-2-3 assumes a value of 0.

Limits: The `interest` argument must be greater than -1.

You must use the same period for the `interest` and `term` arguments. Therefore, if you are calculating a monthly payment, use monthly increments for `interest` and `term`. This means you need to divide the annual interest rate by 12 and multiply the number of years by 12.

Examples: To calculate the present value of 20 yearly payments of $1,000 invested at 5 percent and paid at the end of each period, use @PV(1000,0.05,20), which returns a figure of `$12,462.21` (when rounded for Currency format). If payments are made at the beginning of each period, use @PVAL(1000,0.05,20,1), which returns a figure of `$13,085.32` (when rounded for Currency format).

Bonds Functions Bonds functions provide the tools you need to analyze investments. With these tools, you can make better investment judgments and (ideally) increase your scope of investments.

@ACCRUED(*settlement,issue,first_interest,coupon,[par],[frequency],[basis]*)

@ACCRUED calculates the accrued interest for securities that have periodic interest payments. You can use @ACCRUED for short, standard, and long coupon periods.

Following are this function's arguments and limits:

settlement	A date number that represents the settlement date, or date of ownership, for the security.
issue	The date number of the security's issue or dated date.
first_interest	The date number of the security's first interest date; it must be greater than or equal to the `issue` argument.
coupon	The annual coupon rate for the security; it can be any positive value or 0.
[*par*]	An optional argument that represents the value of the security's principal when paid at maturity. 1-2-3 assumes the value of 100 if this argument is omitted. If a value is included, it must be positive.
[*frequency*]	An optional argument that represents the number of coupon payments per year. This argument has four options:

Frequency	**Representing**
1	Annual
2	Semiannual (the default if you omit the argument)
4	Quarterly
12	Monthly

[*basis*]	An optional argument specifying the type of day count (*days_per_month/days_per_year*) to use. This argument has four options:

Basis	**Days_per_Month/ Days_per_Year**
0	30/360 (the default if you omit the argument)
1	Actual/Actual
2	Actual/360
3	Actual/365

Use @DATE to specify the date numbers within @ACCRUED. @DATE converts the dates that you enter in a valid 1-2-3 date format to the date number that @ACCRUED requires.

Example: A bond has a settlement date of May 1, 1990, an issue date of January 1, 1990, and a first-interest date of April 1, 1990. The semiannual coupon rate is 6 percent, with 100 par value and a 30/360 day count (that is, the default for all optional arguments is appropriate). To calculate the accrued interest use @ACCRUED(@DATE(90,5,1),@DATE(90,1,1),@DATE(90,4,1),0.06), which returns `0.5`.

@PRICE(*settlement,maturity,coupon,yield,[redemption],[frequency],[basis]*)

@PRICE calculates the price per $100 face value on installments that have periodic interest payments and a maturity date.

Following are this function's arguments and limits:

settlement A date number that represents the settlement date, or date of ownership, for the security.

maturity The date number for the security's maturity date. The maturity date must be greater than the settlement date.

coupon The annual coupon rate for the coupon; it must be a positive value or 0.

yield The annual yield on the security; it must be a positive value.

[*redemption*] An optional argument that specifies the redemption value of the security per $100 face value. If used, [*redemption*] must be a positive number; if [*redemption*] is omitted from the argument list, 1-2-3 assumes that the value is 100.

[*frequency*] An optional argument that represents the number of coupon payments per year. This argument has four options:

Frequency	Representing
1	Annual
2	Semiannual (the default if you omit the argument)
4	Quarterly
12	Monthly

[basis]	An optional argument specifying the type of day count (*days_per_month/days_per_year*) to use. This argument has four options:

Basis	Days_per_Month/ Days_per_Year
0	30/360 (the default if you omit the argument)
1	Actual/Actual
2	Actual/360
3	Actual/365

Example: A bond has a settlement date of May 1, 1990 and a maturity date of December 1, 1995. The semiannual coupon rate is 6 percent and the annual yield is 6.11 percent, with a 30/360 day-count basis (that is, the default for all optional arguments is appropriate). To calculate the price, use @PRICE(@DATE(90,5,1),@DATE(95,12,1),0.06,0.0611), which returns `99.47989`.

@YIELD(*settlement,maturity,coupon, price,[redemption],[frequency],[basis]*)

@YIELD calculates the price per $100 face value on instruments that have periodic interest payments and a maturity date.

Following are this function's arguments and limits:

settlement	A date number that represents the settlement date, or date of ownership, for the security.
maturity	The date number for the security's maturity date. The maturity date must be greater than the settlement date.
coupon	The annual coupon rate for the coupon; it must be a positive value or 0.
price	The price per $100 of face value; it must be a positive value.
[redemption]	An optional argument that specifies the redemption value of the security per $100 face value. If used, *[redemption]* must be a positive number; if *[redemption]* is omitted from the argument list, 1-2-3 assumes that the value is 100.
[frequency]	An optional argument that represents the number of coupon payments per year. This argument has four options:

Frequency	Value
1	Annual
2	Semiannual (the default if you omit the argument)
4	Quarterly
12	Monthly

[*basis*] An optional argument specifying the type of day count (*days_per_month/days_per_year*) to use. This argument has four options:

Basis	Days_per_Month/ Days_per_Year
0	30/360 (the default if you omit the argument)
1	Actual/Actual
2	Actual/360
3	Actual/365

Example: A bond has a settlement date of May 1, 1990 and a maturity date of December 1, 1995. The semiannual coupon rate is 6 percent. The bond cost $99. It has a $100 redemption value and a 30/360 day-count basis (that is, the default for all optional arguments is appropriate). To calculate the price, use @YIELD(@DATE(90,5,1),@DATE(95,12,1),0.06,99), which returns `0.62133`.

Capital-Budgeting Tools Functions These functions work with cash flows and rates of return.

@IRR(*guess,range*)

The @IRR function calculates the internal rate of return on an investment.

If you calculate several rates, use @AVG to determine the internal rate of return.

The `guess` argument typically should be an estimate of the internal rate of return. Because it is an interest rate (and, therefore, a percentage value), the `guess` argument should be a decimal between 0 (0%) and 1 (100%).

You should start the calculation with an estimated interest rate as close as possible to the internal rate of return on your investment. From this guess, 1-2-3 attempts to converge on a correct interest rate with .0000001 precision within 30 iterations. If the program cannot do so, the @IRR function returns `ERR`. When that happens, try again with another `guess` argument.

The `range` argument is the address or range name that contains the cash flows. Initial cash flow at time 0 is negative (because the cash flows out from you). Cash flows in the range after that may be negative (payments by you) or positive (payments to you). Cash flows occur at the end of equally spaced periods, with the initial payment by you being at time 0. 1-2-3 assigns the value of 0 to empty cells and labels in the range of cash flows. (Ranges can span more than one column, but remember about empty cells.)

Limits: The `guess` argument should be a decimal between 0 and 1.

Example: Figure 6.6 shows the @IRR function calculating the internal rate of return on an investment with uneven cash flows. Notice that during the same period, the investor injected additional cash into the investment. Notice also that multiplying the monthly amount by 12 converts the monthly internal rate of return to an annual rate.

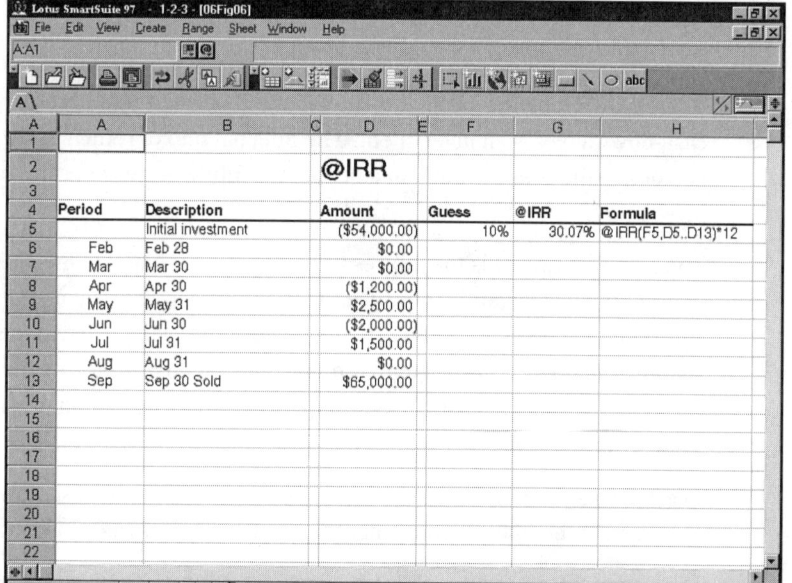

Period	Description	Amount	Guess	@IRR	Formula
	Initial investment	($54,000.00)	10%	30.07%	@IRR(F5,D5..D13)*12
Feb	Feb 28	$0.00			
Mar	Mar 30	$0.00			
Apr	Apr 30	($1,200.00)			
May	May 31	$2,500.00			
Jun	Jun 30	($2,000.00)			
Jul	Jul 31	$1,500.00			
Aug	Aug 31	$0.00			
Sep	Sep 30 Sold	$65,000.00			

Fig. 6.6 Use the @IRR function to calculate the internal rate of return on an investment.

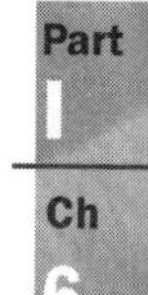

A Warning About the Internal Rate of Return Method

Although the internal-rate-of-return profit measure is widely used, you should be aware that the formula has multiple detriments when used to analyze investments. The problem is with the internal-rate-of-return method, not with 1-2-3's @IRR function.

One problem is evident when you use the internal-rate-of-return measure for an investment that has multiple internal rates of return. In theory, the formula for calculating the internal rate of return for an investment with cash flows over 10 years is a 10th-root polynomial equation with up to 10 correct solutions. In practice, an investment may have as many correct internal rates of return as sign changes in the cash flows.

A *sign change* occurs when the cash flow changes from positive to negative (or vice versa) between periods. Accordingly, even if the @IRR function returns an internal rate of return with your first guess, try other guesses to see whether another correct internal-rate-of-return answer is evident; you probably should not use the measure when it delivers multiple solutions.

A serious problem with the @IRR method is that it tends to overestimate a positive rate of return from the investment and neglects to account for additional outside investments that must be injected into the investment over its life span. The overestimate on return occurs because the @IRR method assumes that positive cash flows are reinvested at the same rate of return earned by the total investment. Actually, a small return rarely can be reinvested at the same high rate as that of a large investment. This feature is especially true when you are analyzing large fixed assets and land investments.

@MIRR(*range,finance_rate,reinvest_rate,[type]***)**

The @MIRR function calculates the modified internal rate of return from a range of cash-flow values in an investment. The internal rate of return is the percentage rate that equates to the present value of an expected future series of cash flows to the initial investment.

The `range` argument is the address or range name that contains the cash flows. Initial cash flow at time 0 is negative (because the cash flows out from you). Cash flows in the range after that may be negative (payments by you) or positive (payments to you). 1-2-3 assumes cash flows occur at regular equal intervals. 1-2-3 assigns the value as before and labels in the range of cash flows. (Ranges can span more than one column, but remember about empty cells.)

The `finance_rate` argument is the rate of interest paid on cash flows. The `reinvest_rate` argument is the interest rate you receive on cash flows as you reinvest them.

The optional `type` argument can be 0 or 1. A value of 0 causes 1-2-3 to calculate based on payments being made at the end of the period. A value of 1 causes 1-2-3 to calculate based on payments being made at the beginning of the period. This value is the default value if you omit the `type` argument.

Limit: The range must contain at least one positive and one negative value. `Finance_rate` and `reinvest_rate` can be any values.

Example: Figure 6.7 calculates the profit from a small used-car dealership, for which an initial payment of $100,000 was made. Over the next five years, the investor made a living from the sale of cars and logged the profits in a range called INCOME. The interest rate on the initial loan is 9.5 percent; because of the investor's skill, he or she has been earning 13.18 percent return on the profits.

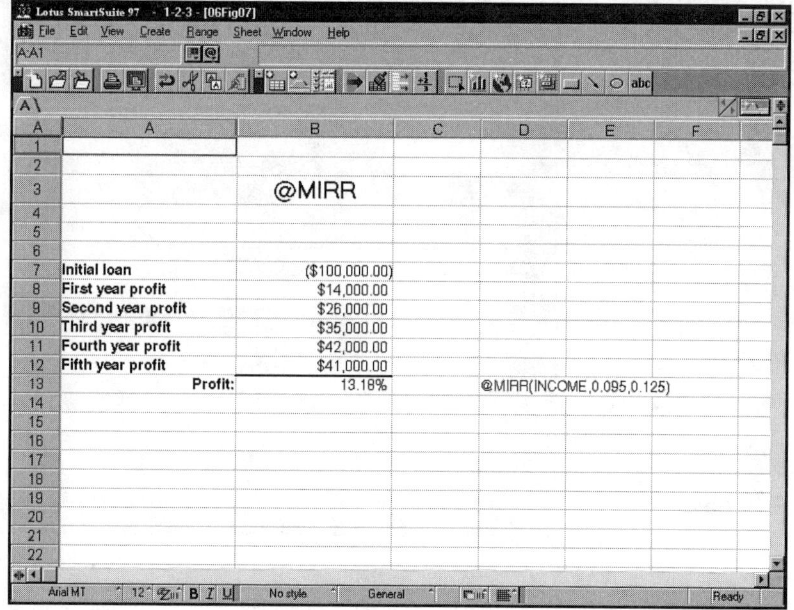

Fig. 6.7 Use the @MIRR function to calculate the modified internal rate of return on an investment.

@NPV(*interest,range(,[type]*)

@NPV is similar to @PV, except that @NPV can calculate the present value of a varying, or changing, range of cash flows. @NPV assumes that cash outflows occur at the same time in each subsequent period.

The `interest` argument is the interest rate. The `range` argument is the address or name of the range that contains the cash flows.

The optional `type` argument can be a 0 or 1. A value of 0 causes 1-2-3 to calculate based on payments being made at the end of the period. This value is the default value if you omit the `type` argument. A value of 1 causes 1-2-3 to calculate based on payments being made at the beginning of the period.

Limits: @NPV returns `ERR` if the `range` argument contains more than one row or column. The `interest` argument must be greater than -1.

Example: Figure 6.8 shows how you can use @NPV to calculate the present value of a stream of varying cash flows with cash outflows made at the end of the period. In the figure, the range CASH is B10..B17.

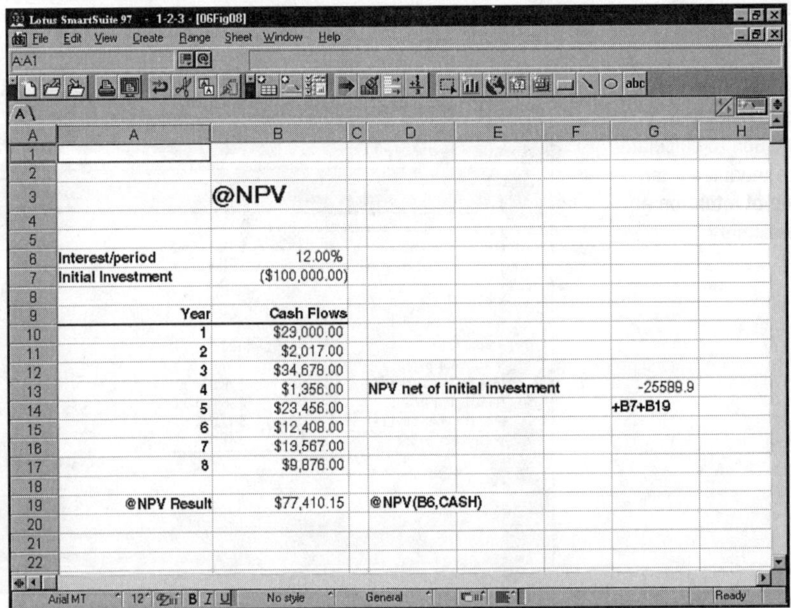

	A	B	C	D	E	F	G
3		@NPV					
6	Interest/period	12.00%					
7	Initial Investment	($100,000.00)					
9	Year	Cash Flows					
10	1	$23,000.00					
11	2	$2,017.00					
12	3	$34,678.00					
13	4	$1,356.00		NPV net of initial investment			-25589.9
14	5	$23,456.00					+B7+B19
15	6	$12,408.00					
16	7	$19,567.00					
17	8	$9,876.00					
19	@NPV Result	$77,410.15		@NPV(B6,CASH)			

Fig. 6.8 Use the @NPV function to calculate the present value of varying cash flows.

NOTE Accountants and financial analysts use the term *net present value* to refer to a measure of an investment's profitability by including the initial cash outlay for the investment. To calculate the actual profitability measure, or net present value, subtract the initial investment from the result of @NPV. When you construct a formula that uses @NPV in this way, you essentially test whether the investment meets, beats, or falls short of the interest rate specified in @NPV. Such a formula can be the following:

```
+INITL_AMOUNT+@NPV(interest,range)
```

The value in the cell named INITL_AMOUNT is negative because the amount is money you paid out. The formula in G14 in figure 6.8 is:

```
+B7+B19
```

If the calculated result of the preceding formula is a positive amount, the investment produces an investment return that beats the interest rate specified in @NPV. If the calculated result equals 0, the investment produces an investment return that equals the interest rate specified in @NPV. If the calculated result is a negative amount, the investment produces an investment return that falls short of the interest rate specified in @NPV.

Depreciation Functions Depreciation functions allow for asset management. The following functions let you calculate different methods of depreciation.

@DB(*cost,salvage,life,period*)

@DB calculates the depreciation allowance of an asset with an initial value of *cost*, an expected useful *life*, and a final *salvage* value for a specified *period* of time. @DB uses the fixed-declining-balance method.

The `cost` argument is the amount paid for the asset; it is a positive value. If cost is 0, the value of @DB also is 0. The `salvage` argument is the estimated value of the asset at the end of its useful life; it is a positive value. If salvage is larger than cost, the value of @DB is negative. The `life` argument is the number of periods the asset takes to depreciate to its salvage value. The `period` argument is the time period for which you want to find the depreciation allowance; it is a value greater than or equal to 1.

Limits: The `cost` and `salvage` arguments must be positive values or 0. The `life` and `period` arguments can be any value greater than or equal to 1. The `life` and `period` arguments must be in the same units of time, which usually is years.

Example: Figure 6.9 shows how you can use @DB to calculate the depreciation allowance, by year, for a $10,000 piece of equipment.

@SLN(*cost,salvage,life*)

@SLN calculates straight-line depreciation for an asset, given the asset's cost, salvage value, and depreciable life. Straight-line depreciation divides the depreciable cost (the cost minus the salvage value) into equal periods (typically, years) for the useful life of the asset.

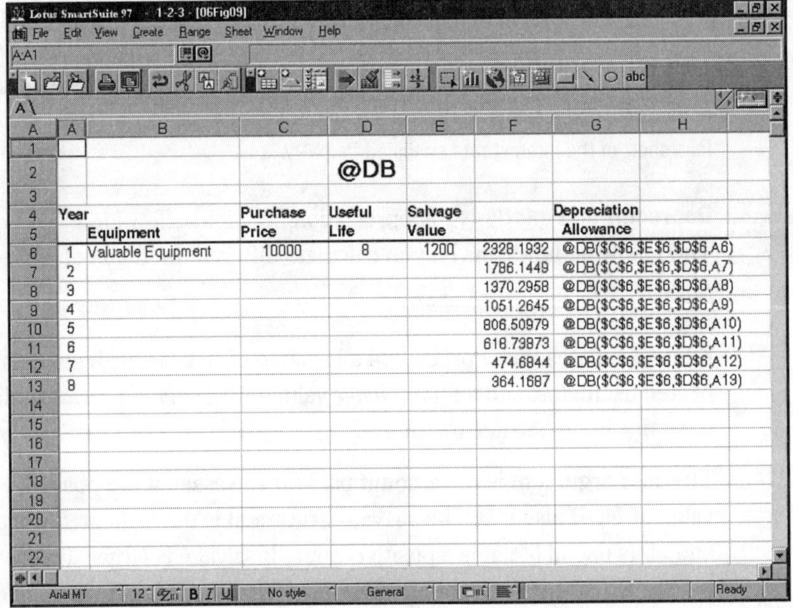

Fig. 6.9
Use the @DB function to calculate the depreciation allowance.

The `cost` argument is the amount paid for the asset. The `salvage` argument is the estimated value of the asset at the end of its useful life. The `life` argument is the number of periods the asset takes to depreciate to its salvage value.

Limits: `Cost` and `salvage` can be any value. `Life` can be any value except 0.

Example: Suppose that you purchased, for $10,000, a machine that has a useful life of eight years and a salvage value estimated at 12 percent of the purchase price ($1,200) at the end of the machine's useful life. Use @SLN(10000,1200,8) to determine the straight-line depreciation for the machine, which is $1,100 per year.

@SYD(*cost,salvage,life,period*)

The @SYD function calculates depreciation by the sum-of-the-years'-digits method. This method accelerates depreciation so that earlier periods of the item's life reflect greater depreciation than later periods do.

The *cost* argument is the purchase cost of the asset. The `salvage` argument is the estimated value of the asset at the end of its depreciable life. The `life` argument is the depreciable life of the asset. The `period` argument is the period for which depreciation is to be computed.

Limits: *Cost* and *salvage* can be any value. *Life* and *period* can be any value greater than or equal to 1.

Example: Figure 6.10 shows how you can use @SYD to calculate depreciation for an asset that cost $10,000, with a depreciable life of eight years and an estimated salvage value of $1,200.

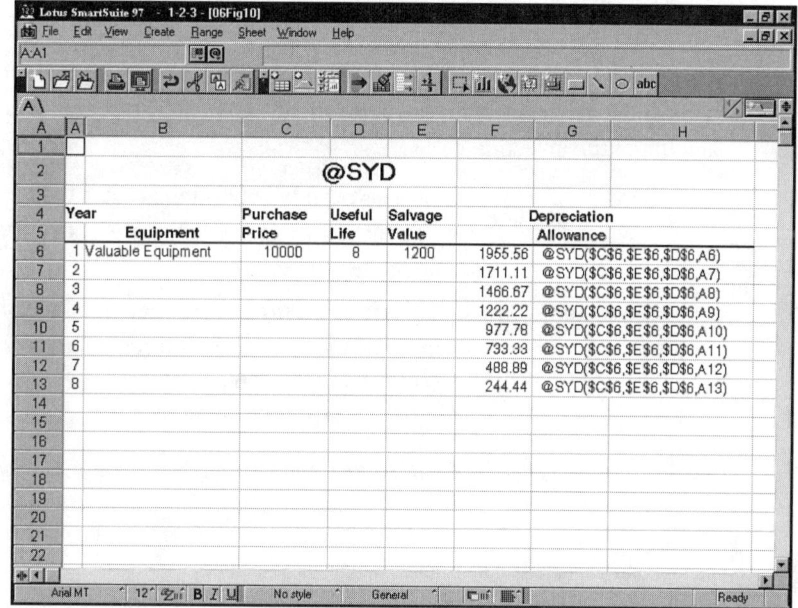

@SYD

Year	Equipment	Purchase Price	Useful Life	Salvage Value	Depreciation Allowance	
1	Valuable Equipment	10000	8	1200	1955.56	@SYD($C$6,$E$6,$D$6,A6)
2					1711.11	@SYD($C$6,$E$6,$D$6,A7)
3					1466.67	@SYD($C$6,$E$6,$D$6,A8)
4					1222.22	@SYD($C$6,$E$6,$D$6,A9)
5					977.78	@SYD($C$6,$E$6,$D$6,A10)
6					733.33	@SYD($C$6,$E$6,$D$6,A11)
7					488.89	@SYD($C$6,$E$6,$D$6,A12)
8					244.44	@SYD($C$6,$E$6,$D$6,A13)

Fig. 6.10
Use the @SYD function to calculate sum-of-the-years'-digits depreciation.

NOTE @SYD calculates depreciation with the following formula:

```
(cost-salvage)*(life-period+1)
life*(life+1)/2
```

The expression *(life-period+1)* in the numerator shows the life of the depreciation in the first period, decreased by 1 in each subsequent period. This expression reflects the declining pattern of depreciation over time. The expression in the denominator, *life*(life+1)/2*, is equal to the sum of the digits, as in the following expression:

1 + 2 +...+ *life*

The name *sum-of-the-years'-digits* originated from this expression.

Single-Sum Compounding Functions The single-sum compounding functions deal with growing your investment. Use these functions to monitor and work with future values.

@CTERM(*interest,future_value,present_value*)

NOTE Use @TERM to calculate the number of periods needed for a series of payments to grow to a future value. Use @CTERM to calculate the number of periods needed for an initial amount (its *present_value*) to grow to a future value.

@CTERM calculates the number of periods required for an initial investment that earns a specified interest rate to grow to a specified future value.

The `interest` argument is the interest rate for the investment. The `future_value` argument is the value you want the investment to reach. The `present_value` argument is the amount of the investment.

Limits: `Interest` can be any value greater than 1. Both `present_value` and `future_value` must be either positive or negative values.

Example: To determine how many years it takes for $2,000 invested in an IRA at 10 percent interest to grow to $10,000, use @CTERM(0.1,10000,2000), which returns `16.89`—just over 16 years and 10 months.

@RATE(*future_value,present_value,term*)

@RATE also is useful in forecasting applications that calculate the compound growth rate between current and projected future revenue, earnings, and so on.

@RATE calculates the compound growth rate for an initial investment that grows to a specified future value over a specified number of periods. The rate calculated is the periodic interest rate; it is not necessarily an annual rate.

The `future_value` argument is the amount you want the investment to reach. The `present_value` argument is the amount of the investment. The *term* argument is the length of the investment.

Example: You can use @RATE to determine the yield of a zero-coupon bond sold at a discount from its face value. Suppose that for $350, you purchase a zero-coupon bond with a $1,000 face value that matures in 10 years. Use @RATE(1000,350,10) to determine the implied annual interest rate: 11.07 percent.

Information Functions

The information functions return information about cells, ranges, the operating system, Version Manager, and Solver.

@CELL(*attribute,location*) and @CELLPOINTER(*attribute*)

@CELL and @CELLPOINTER provide an efficient way to determine the nature of a cell. These functions return information on one of 42 cell characteristics, such as a cell's number or value, color, or width.

Because you want to examine a cell's attributes, both functions have `attribute` as a text argument. @CELL, however, also requires the specification of a range as the `location` argument. If you specify a single cell, such as A6, 1-2-3 changes it to a range format (A6..A6) and returns the attribute of the single-cell range. If you define a larger range, 1-2-3 evaluates the cell in the top-left corner of the range.

Before you use @CELL or @CELLPOINTER, press F9 (Calc) to make sure that the results are correct.

@CELLPOINTER works with the current cell—the cell where the cell pointer was positioned the last time the worksheet was recalculated. The result remains the same as long as the current position of the cell pointer does not change and you do not recalculate the worksheet by entering a value or by pressing F9 (Calc).

The `attribute` argument is a text string and must be enclosed in quotation marks. If a range of cells is specified for the `location` argument in the @CELL function, the returned value refers to the top-left cell in the range.

Refer to the 1-2-3 Help system to view the full set of more than 40 attributes that you can examine with @CELL and @CELLPOINTER.

Limit:	You can address only one attribute at a time in any @CELL or @CELLPOINTER function. The *attribute* argument is a text string and must be enclosed in quotation marks.
Example:	If the range named SALES is C187..E187, use @CELL("address",sales) to find the address of the top-left cell in the range, $C$187. This function is particularly useful for listing range addresses in the worksheet.

Use @CELL("format",A10) to find the format of cell A10. 1-2-3 returns a text string using the same notation as that used in the worksheet—for example, C2 for Currency format with two decimal places.

@COLS(*range*), @ROWS(*range*), and @SHEETS(*range*)

@COLS, @ROWS, and @SHEETS describe the dimensions of ranges. These functions are useful in macros to determine the size of a range. After you determine the size of a range, you can use FOR loops to step the macro through all the cells in the range.

The `range` argument is a range address or range name. If you specify one cell (such as C3) as the argument, 1-2-3 changes the argument to range format (C3..C3), and the function returns the value `1`.

Example: Suppose that you want to determine the number of columns in the range PRICE_TABLES, which has the cell coordinates A:D4..C:G50. You also want to display that value in the current cell. To determine the number of columns, use @COLS(PRICE_TABLES). Similarly, you can use @ROWS(PRICE_TABLES) to display the number of rows in the range and @SHEETS(PRICE_TABLES) to display the number of worksheets in the range.

@COORD(*worksheets,column,row,absolute*)

You use @COORD to create an absolute, relative, or mixed cell address. When you use @COORD, it returns the actual address, not a value.

The `worksheet` argument corresponds to the worksheet containing the referenced cell. The `column` and `row` arguments refer to the column and row that contain the cell address. The `absolute` argument refers to the exact type of reference (absolute, relative, or mixed) that you want the function to return.

Limits: The `worksheet` argument is a number from 1 to 256. Use 1 for worksheet A, 2 for worksheet B, and so on up to 256 for worksheet IV. The `column` argument is a number from 1 to 256. Use 1 for column A, 2 for column B, and so on up to 256 for column IV. The `row` argument is a number from 1 to 8192. The `absolute` argument is a number from 1 to 8.

Example: To change the cell address A:A1 to the mixed address A:A$1, use @COORD(1,1,1,6), which returns the address `A:A$1`.

@INFO(*attribute*)

Before using @INFO, you should recalculate your work to ensure accurate results.

@INFO lets you tap 30 types of system information for the current session.

The `attribute` argument is a text string and must be enclosed in quotation marks. Refer to the 1-2-3 Help system to view a list of the attributes you can check with @INFO.

Also, the `attribute` argument can be any Info component. Info components store information about the 1-2-3 session, such as the default background color, the current data sort range, or the current state of Edit Undo. When you use an info component as the @INFO attribute argument, you can find out the value of that Info component.

The values returned by @INFO are useful in macros that monitor such things as application memory size, the current mode, and the current directory. After the macro obtains this information, it can warn users to make changes in their activities, upgrade their systems, and so on. When used in conjunction with @IF, this function can tell 1-2-3 what to do under specific conditions—for example, to close active files when memory is low.

@ERR and @NA

@ERR and @NA let you flag errors in data entry or calculations. You rarely use these functions by themselves; instead, you can use them with @IF to return ERR or NA when a certain condition exists, such as an unacceptable entry in a cell.

Example: Suppose that you are developing a checkbook-balancing macro in which checks with values less than or equal to 0 are unacceptable. One way to indicate the unacceptability of such checks is to use @ERR to signal that fact. You can use the following version of the @IF function to check the value of the check and to invoke @ERR if the value is less than 0:

```
@IF(B9<=0,@ERR,B9)
```

In plain English, this statement says, "If the amount in cell B9 is less than or equal to 0, display ERR on-screen." Another approach is to display a message to the operator that indicates the specific error, as in the following example:

```
@IF(B9<=0,"Enter positive amounts",B9)
```

NOTE 1-2-3 also uses ERR as a signal for unacceptable numbers–for example, if you divide by 0 or mistakenly delete cells. ERR often shows up temporarily when you reorganize the cells in a worksheet. If ERR persists, you may have to do some careful analysis to figure out why.

1-2-3 displays ERR (as it does NA) in any cells that depend on a cell with an ERR value. Sometimes, the ERR cascades through other dependent cells. To return the worksheet to the way it was before the change, open the Edit menu and choose Undo, or press Ctrl+Z. For more information about the Undo command, refer to Chapter 3, "Entering and Editing Data."

Logical Functions

The logical functions let you use Boolean logic within worksheets. Most logical functions test whether a condition is true or false. The test—and what the function returns based on the test—are built into the function. For one of the logical functions—@IF—you describe the test and what the function result should be, based on the test.

@IF(*condition,true_result,false_result*)

@IF tests a condition and returns one value or label if the test is true and another value or label if the test is false.

@IF is a powerful tool, one that you can use to manipulate text within worksheets and to affect calculations. Use this function to add decision-making logic to a worksheet. For example, you can use the @IF function to test the condition "Is the inventory on hand below 1,000 units?" and then return one value or text string if the answer to the question is true and another value or text string if the answer is false.

The `condition` argument is the condition that should be tested. The logical test can be based on text or numeric comparison.

The `true_result` and `false_result` arguments are what 1-2-3 should return when the condition is true or false, respectively. These arguments can be text enclosed in quotation marks or names of cells that contain values or labels.

You can use any of six operators when you use @IF to test conditions. Table 6.2 summarizes these operators.

Table 6.2 Logical Test Operators

Operator	Description
<	Less than
<=	Less than or equal to
=	Equal to
>=	Greater than or equal to
>	Greater than
<>	Not equal to

You can expand the power of @IF by using compound tests. You also can perform complex conditional tests by using @IF with logical operators that let you test multiple conditions in one @IF function. Table 6.3 summarizes these complex operators.

Table 6.3 Complex Operators

Operator	Description
#AND#	Used to test two conditions, both of which must be true for the entire test to be true
#NOT#	Used to test that a condition is *not* true
#OR#	Used to test two conditions; if either condition is true, the entire test condition is true

Example: You can check whether cell A6 contains a value greater than 4 by using @IF(A6>4,"Valid","Not Valid"). If the A6 value is greater than 4, 1-2-3 returns `Valid`; otherwise, the program returns `Not Valid`.

A simple but valuable use for complex @IF functions is to test whether data entries are in the correct range of numbers. Consider the following formula:

```
@IF(A15=A12#OR#A15=A13,"Send a Card","There is Still Time")
```

This formula compares the contents of cell A15 with those of two other cells (A12 and A13). If the value in A15 is the same as the value in either A12 or A13, the text `Send a Card` is inserted into the current cell. If the value A15 does not equal either A12 or A13, the text `There is Still Time` appears in the current cell.

NOTE Within @IF, you can use another @IF function as the *true_result* or *false_result* argument. Putting @IF functions inside other @IF functions is a common and important logical tool. This technique, called a *nested @IF*, lets you construct sophisticated logical tests and operations in your 1-2-3 worksheets.

Part I Ch 6

@ISEMPTY(*location*)

@ISEMPTY tests a location for a blank cell and returns a `1` if the cell is empty and a `0` if it is not. 1-2-3 considers a cell blank if it contains no letters, numbers, spaces, or label prefix character (such as an apostrophe for a left-aligned label or a caret for a centered label).

The `location` argument is the name or address of a single cell. If you enter a name for a range as the `location` argument, 1-2-3 returns 0 (false).

Example: @ISEMPTY(B3) returns 1 if cell B3 is blank or 0 if cell B3 contains a number or label.

@ISERR(*cell_reference*) and @ISNA(*cell_reference*)

@ISERR tests whether the argument equals `ERR`. If the test is true, @ISERR returns the value `1`; if the test is false, it returns the value `0`.

@ISNA works in a similar way, testing whether the argument is equal to `NA`. If the test is true, @ISNA returns the value `1`; if the test is false, it returns the value `0`.

@ISERR and @ISNA are handy, because you can use them to trap errors produced in one location that may cause more drastic results in other locations.

The `cell_reference` argument can be any value, location, text, or condition. The argument can be as simple as a cell reference, or it can perform some simple arithmetic (such as divide two cells to determine whether an error exists before the actual division result is displayed in the cell).

Example: Figure 6.11 shows how to use @ISERR and @ISNA with @IF to trap a possible division-by-zero error or a serious data-entry error that can cause an error to appear on-screen or in the printout.

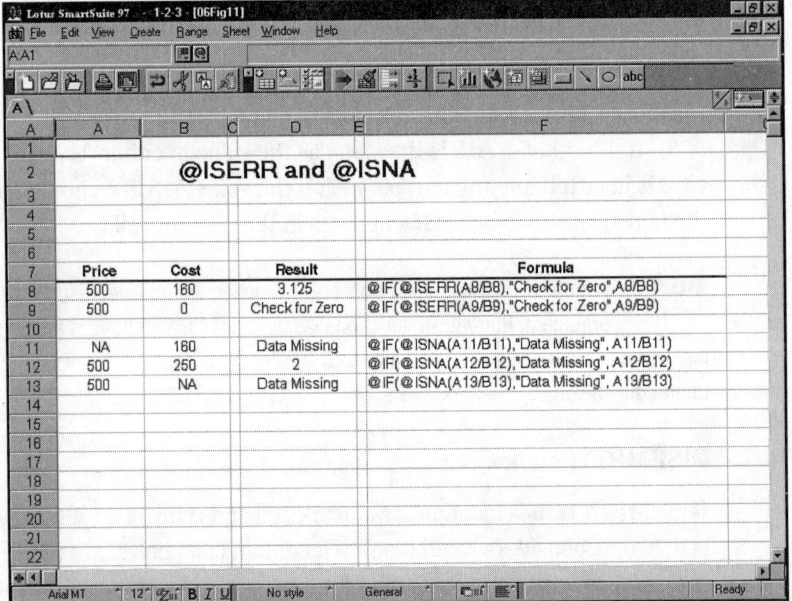

Price	Cost	Result	Formula
500	160	3.125	@IF(@ISERR(A8/B8),"Check for Zero",A8/B8)
500	0	Check for Zero	@IF(@ISERR(A9/B9),"Check for Zero",A9/B9)
NA	160	Data Missing	@IF(@ISNA(A11/B11),"Data Missing", A11/B11)
500	250	2	@IF(@ISNA(A12/B12),"Data Missing", A12/B12)
500	NA	Data Missing	@IF(@ISNA(A13/B13),"Data Missing", A13/B13)

Fig. 6.11
Use @ISERR and @ISNA to test for errors.

@TRUE and @FALSE

Use the @TRUE and @FALSE functions to check for errors. Neither function requires arguments. These functions are useful for providing documentation for formulas and advanced macro commands. @TRUE returns the value `1`, which is the Boolean logical value for true. @FALSE returns the value `0`, which is the Boolean logical value for false.

Lookup Functions

1-2-3 provides a group of functions that service the contents of a cell or a group of cells. These functions are very useful in a variety of situations, from locating the contents of a cell in a macro to matching the contents of a cell.

@@(*location*)

@@ provides a way to reference one cell indirectly through the contents of another cell.

If the location argument refers to a cell that contains a formula, press F9 (Calc) to update @@ after automatic recalculation; otherwise, @@ returns `0`.

The `location` argument must be a cell reference for a cell that contains an address. This address is an *indirect address*. Similarly, the cell referenced in the `location` argument must contain a text value that evaluates to a cell reference. This cell can contain a label, a text formula, or a reference to another cell, as long as the resulting text value is a cell reference.

@@ is useful primarily when several formulas have the same argument and the argument must be changed from time to time during the course of the application. 1-2-3 lets you to specify the argument of each formula through a common indirect address, as shown in figure 6.12.

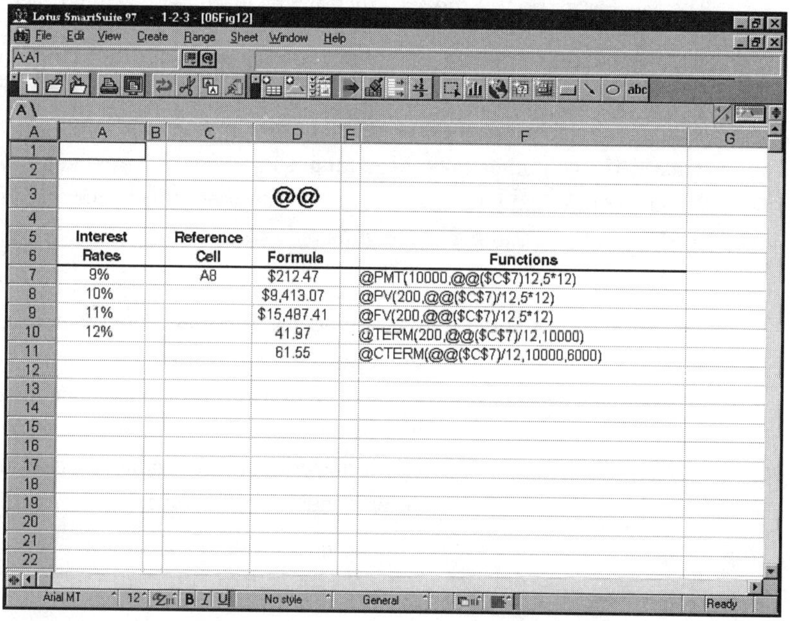

Fig. 6.12
Use @@ to reference one cell indirectly through another cell.

Interest Rates	Reference Cell	Formula	Functions
9%	A8	$212.47	@PMT(10000,@@($C$7)12,5*12)
10%		$9,413.07	@PV(200,@@($C$7)/12,5*12)
11%		$15,487.41	@FV(200,@@($C$7)/12,5*12)
12%		41.97	@TERM(200,@@($C$7)/12,10000)
		61.55	@CTERM(@@($C$7)/12,10000,6000)

Examples: If cell A1 contains the label `'A2` and cell A2 contains the number `5`, the function @@(A1) returns the value `5`. If the label in cell A1 is changed to `'B10`, and if cell B10 contains the label `'hi there`, @@(A1) returns the text value `hi there`.

In figure 6.12, column F contains a variety of financial functions, all of which use @@ to indirectly reference one of seven interest rates in column A through cell C7. When you are ready to change the cell being referenced, you change only the label in cell C7 instead of editing all five formulas in column F.

@HLOOKUP(*key,range,row_offset*) and @VLOOKUP(*key,range,column_offset*)

@HLOOKUP and @VLOOKUP retrieve a text string or value from a table, based on a specified key used to find the information. The operation and format of the two functions are essentially the same, except that @HLOOKUP looks through *horizontal* tables (hence, the *H* in the function's name) and @VLOOKUP looks through *vertical* tables (the source of the *V* in its name).

The `key` argument is either a value or text, depending on what the first row/column of the lookup table includes. If the first row or column contains values, `key` can be any value equal to or greater than the first value in the range. If the first row or column contains labels, `key` can be text enclosed in quotation marks, a formula that returns text, or the address or name of a cell that contains a label or a formula that returns a label.

The `range` argument is the area that makes up the entire lookup table.

The `row_offset` or `column_offset` argument specifies which row or column contains the data you are looking up. This argument always is a number, ranging (in ascending order) from 0 to the greatest number of columns or rows in the lookup table. The offset number 0 marks the column or row that contains `key` data. The next column or row is 1, the next is 2, and so on. When you specify an offset number, the number cannot be negative or exceed the correct number of columns or rows.

Limits: If the `key` argument is text, it must be enclosed in quotation marks. The `key` argument must match the contents of a cell in the first row/column of the range; text key arguments are case-sensitive. When you use numeric `key` arguments, make sure that the `key` values in the table range are in ascending order; otherwise, you may get an incorrect value. By contrast, if the `key` arguments are text strings, they can be listed in any order.

If the `range` argument specifies a 3-D range, 1-2-3 uses only the first worksheet in the range.

Example: Suppose that you want to create a worksheet that figures out the state tax for all employees of your company. This seems straightforward except that for some reason, employees are continually changing their filing status. When the filing status changes, you must change the formula that computes the tax. Figure 6.13 shows a @VLOOKUP table that solves your problem. You can see how to use @VLOOKUP (or @HLOOKUP) to find any type of value that you may have to look up manually in a table, such as price changes in inventory items, tax rates, shipping zones, or interest charges.

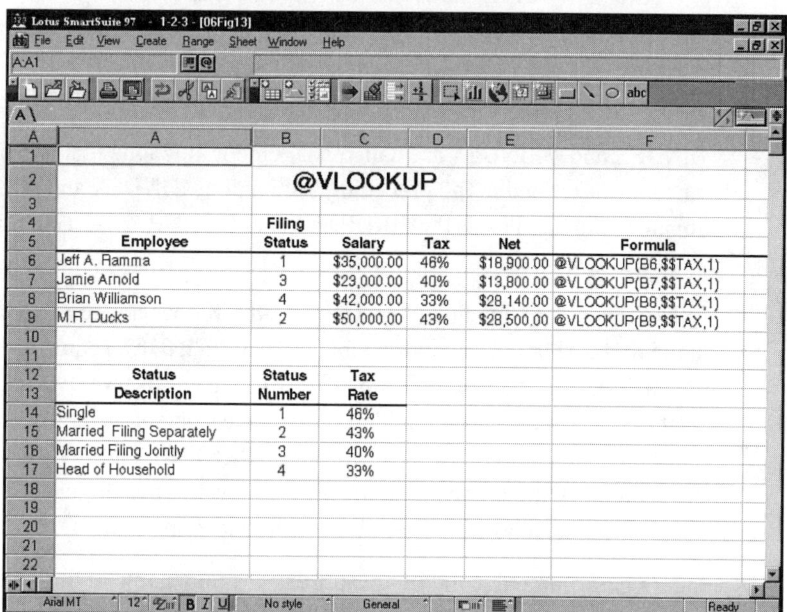

@VLOOKUP

Employee	Filing Status	Salary	Tax	Net	Formula
Jeff A. Ramma	1	$35,000.00	46%	$18,900.00	@VLOOKUP(B6,$$TAX,1)
Jamie Arnold	3	$23,000.00	40%	$13,800.00	@VLOOKUP(B7,$$TAX,1)
Brian Williamson	4	$42,000.00	33%	$28,140.00	@VLOOKUP(B8,$$TAX,1)
M.R. Ducks	2	$50,000.00	43%	$28,500.00	@VLOOKUP(B9,$$TAX,1)

Status Description	Status Number	Tax Rate
Single	1	46%
Married Filing Separately	2	43%
Married Filing Jointly	3	40%
Head of Household	4	33%

Fig. 6.13 Use @VLOOKUP to retrieve text strings and values from a vertical lookup table.

Watch for These Three Common Errors When You Construct @HLOOKUP and @VLOOKUP Functions:

- When you use a text string as the `key` argument, the lookup function returns `ERR` if it cannot find the text in the lookup table. If @HLOOKUP or @VLOOKUP with a text `key` returns `ERR`, make sure that you didn't misspell the text in the function or in the lookup table.

continues

continued

- If you fail to include the columns or rows that contain the *key* text strings or values in the *range* argument for the lookup table, the result is ERR. The example shown in figure 6.13 uses cell addresses to define the lookup table so that you can understand the example easily; you probably will name your lookup tables instead. Be aware that naming lookup tables can make spotting missing rows or columns more difficult.
- Do not place the *key* argument's text strings or values in the wrong row or column. Remember that the *key* argument's strings or values belong in the first column or row of the lookup table; column and row numbering starts at 0 (at the row or column that contains the *key*). Accordingly, the first row or column offset is 0 (the row or column that contains the *key*); the second row or column is 1; the third is 2, and so on.

@INDEX(*range,column_offset,row_offset,[worksheet_offset]*) and @XINDEX(*range,column_heading,row_heading,[worksheet_heading]*)

@INDEX and @XINDEX are data-management functions that are similar to the lookup functions described in the preceding section, but @INDEX and @XINDEX have some unique features. Like @HLOOKUP and @VLOOKUP, @INDEX and @XINDEX find a value within a table.

Unlike the lookup functions, however, @INDEX does not compare a key value with values in the first row or column of the table. Instead, @INDEX requires you to indicate the column offset, row offset, and (optionally) worksheet offset of the range from which you want to retrieve data. The function returns the value of the cell at the intersection of these offset locations. @XINDEX is more like @HLOOKUP and @VLOOKUP in that you specify the contents of the first column or row—that is, the headings—to indicate which column, row, and (optionally) worksheet 1-2-3 should look in.

The `range` argument is the range address or range name of the area that makes up the table.

For @INDEX, the offset arguments use number offsets to refer to the columns, rows, and worksheets; 0 corresponds to the first column/row/worksheet; 1 corresponds to the second column/row/worksheet; and so on. If you leave out the optional `worksheet_offset` argument, 1-2-3 assumes the first worksheet of the range. For example, using 3 for the `column_offset` argument and 2 for the `row_offset` argument indicates that you want an item from the fourth column, third row.

For @XINDEX, you can use number offset numbers or the value or text in the column and row headings and the first cell of the range (for the `worksheet_heading` argument).

Limits: With both @INDEX and @XINDEX, you cannot use column, row, or worksheet numbers outside the specified range. Using negative numbers or numbers that are too large for the range causes 1-2-3 to return `ERR`.

Example: Figure 6.14 shows an example of an @INDEX function that returns the employee's name (`M.R. Ducks`) in E13 and salary (`$28,500.00`) in E16.

Lotus SmartSuite 97 - 1-2-3 - [06Fig14]

	A	B	C	D	E	F
1						
2			@INDEX			
3						
4		Filing				
5	Employee	Status	Salary	Tax	Net	Formula
6	Jeff A. Ramma	1	$35,000.00	46%	$18,900.00	@VLOOKUP(B6,$$TAX,1)
7	Jamie Arnold	3	$23,000.00	40%	$13,800.00	@VLOOKUP(B7,$$TAX,1)
8	Brian Williamson	4	$42,000.00	33%	$28,140.00	@VLOOKUP(B8,$$TAX,1)
9	M.R. Ducks	2	$50,000.00	43%	$28,500.00	@VLOOKUP(B9,$$TAX,1)
10						
11						
12	Status	Status	Tax		Employee	
13	Description	Number	Rate		M.R. Ducks	
14	Single	1	46%		@INDEX(A6..E9,0,3)	
15	Married Filing Separately	2	43%		Salary	
16	Married Filing Jointly	3	40%		$28,500.00	
17	Head of Household	4	33%		@INDEX(A6..E9,4,3)	

Fig. 6.14
Use @INDEX to return the value of a cell specified by column, row, and worksheet offset numbers.

@MATCH(*cell_contents,range,[type]*)

@MATCH returns the location of the cell whose contents match what you are searching for. You can search for either text or a number value.

@MATCH searches the rows of a column from top to bottom and the columns from left to right until it finds a match. @MATCH returns a numerical value that indicates the offset from the top-left cell of the range you are searching. (The cells in the range are numbered down the columns and then across the rows. In the range A1..D4—a 16-cell range—an offset of 4 refers to cell B1.)

The `cell_contents` argument is the value of the information for which you are searching. The value can be text (enclosed in quotation marks) or numeric. If the value is text, you can include wild cards to aid in your search.

The range argument is the range name or address of the data for which you are searching.

The optional type argument indicates how you want 1-2-3 to look for the data. Type can be 0, 1, or 2. A value of 0 indicates that 1-2-3 should return the first cell whose contents match the cell_contents argument. A value of 1 indicates that 1-2-3 should return the first cell whose contents are less than or equal to the cell_contents argument. If you omit the type argument, 1-2-3 assumes 1. A value of 2 indicates that 1-2-3 should return the first cell whose contents are greater than or equal to the cell_contents argument.

Example: Figure 6.15 shows how you can use @MATCH to locate data.

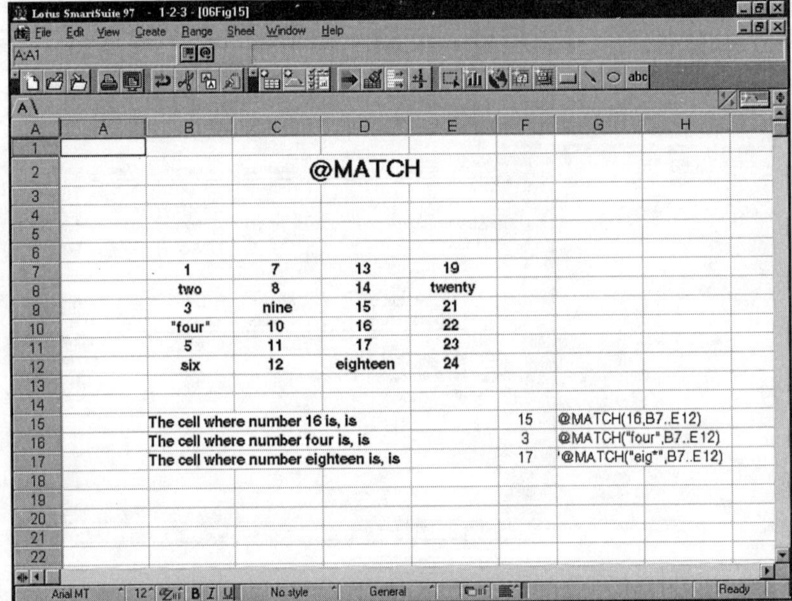

Fig. 6.15
Use @MATCH to locate values in a table.

Mathematical Functions

1-2-3 provides mathematical functions that perform most of the common—and some of the more specialized—mathematical operations. To simplify calculations, 1-2-3 offers five general mathematical categories of functions: general, conversion, hyperbolic, rounding, and trigonometric. The following sections discuss some of the most commonly used mathematical functions.

General Mathematical Functions

@ABS(*x*)

@ABS calculates the absolute value of a number. The result of @ABS is the positive value of its argument. @ABS converts a negative value to a positive value. @ABS has no effect on positive values.

@ABS is useful for showing the difference between two values, regardless of whether the difference is positive or negative. @ABS can be helpful if used with @IF to determine whether two numbers are within a specific range, regardless of which number is greater. In data-entry macros, use @ABS to ensure that an entered number results in a positive or negative number, regardless of what the user typed. @ABS also can be helpful in some trigonometric calculations.

The x argument can be a numeric value or the cell reference of a numeric value.

To force the @ABS result to be negative, use -@ABS.

Examples: If A6 contains 9 and B6 contains -9, @ABS(A6) returns 9 and @ABS(B6) returns 9.

@EXP(*x*) and @EXP2(*x*)

@EXP calculates *e* (approximately 2.718282), raised to the power of the x argument. @EXP2 calculates *e* (approximately 2.718282), raised to the power (*x*^2).

Limits: For @EXP, do not use an argument larger than 709. With @EXP, you can create very large numbers quickly. If the function's resulting value is too large to be displayed, 1-2-3 displays asterisks.

For @EXP2, do not use an argument larger than approximately 106.57 or one smaller than -106.57; if you do, the calculation results in ERR.

@FACT(*x*)

@FACT calculates the factorial of a number. The *factorial* of a number is the product of all positive integers from 1 to that number (the x argument). The x argument can be any positive integer or 0.

Limits: If *x* is greater than or equal to the integer 1755, the result is ERR because the result is too large for 1-2-3 to store. If *x* is greater than or equal to 70, 1-2-3 can calculate and store the result but cannot display it.

Examples: @FACT(3) returns 6; @FACT(10) returns 3628800.

@FACTLN(*x*)

@FACTLN calculates the natural log of the factorial of a number. The x argument can be any positive integer or 0.

Example: @FACTLN(3) returns 1.791759; @FACTLN(10) returns 15.10441.

@INT(*x*)

@INT converts a decimal number to an integer by truncating the decimal portion of a number. @INT is useful for computations in which the decimal portion of a number is irrelevant or insignificant.

The x argument can be a numeric value or the cell reference of a numeric value.

Examples: @INT(3.1) returns 3; @INT(4.5) returns 4; @INT(5.9) returns 5.

If you have $1,000 to invest in XYZ Company and shares of XYZ sell for $17 each, you divide 1,000 by 17 to compute the total number of shares that you can purchase. Because you cannot purchase a fractional share, you can use @INT to truncate the decimal portion.

NOTE Do not confuse the @INT and @ROUND functions. @ROUND rounds decimal numbers to the nearest integer; @INT cuts off the decimal portion, leaving the integer. ■

@LOG(*x*) and @LN(*x*)

@LOG computes the base-10 logarithm. @LN computes the natural, or base-*e*, logarithm. For both @LOG and @LN, the x argument is any value greater than 0.

Limit: If the x argument is negative, @LOG and @LN return ERR.

Examples: @LOG(5) returns 0.69897; @LN(5) returns 1.609438.

@MOD(*x*,*y*)

@MOD computes the remainder (or *modulus*) when two numbers are divided—that is, *x*/*y*.

Both the x and y arguments can be numeric values or cell references. The sign of the x argument (+ or -) determines the sign of the result.

Limit: The y argument cannot be 0, or @MOD returns ERR.

Examples: @MOD(11,5) returns 1; @MOD(11,3) returns 2.

@SIGN(*x*)

@SIGN determines whether a value in a cell is positive, 0, or negative. If the value or cell reference is positive, @SIGN returns 1. If the value is 0, @SIGN returns 0. If the value is negative, @SIGN returns -1. The x argument can be any value or a cell reference.

Examples: @SIGN(A6) returns 1 if A6 contains 9 and -1 if A6 contains -9.

@SQRT(*x*)

The @SQRT function is equivalent to using the ^ (exponentiation) operator with an exponent of 0.5. For example, @SQRT(25) and 25^0.5 both calculate the square root of 25, which is 5.

@SQRT calculates the square root of a positive number. The x argument must be a non-negative numeric value or a cell reference to such a value.

Limit: If @SQRT is a negative value, it returns ERR.

Example: @SQRT(20) returns 4.472136; @SQRT(25) returns 5.

Hyperbolic Functions

NOTE @DEGTORAD and @RADTODEG convert angular measurements. @DEGTORAD converts degrees to radians, and @RADTODEG converts radians to degrees. You can use these functions to convert the values returned by hyperbolic functions.

@ACOSH(*angle*)

@ACOSH calculates the inverse (arc) hyperbolic cosine of an angle, using the hyperbolic cosine value of the angle being calculated. The function returns a result in radians.

Example: If the value of the hyperbolic cosine of an angle is 3, @ACOSH(3) results in 1.762747 (radians).

@ACOTH(*angle*)

@ACOTH calculates the inverse (arc) hyperbolic cotangent of an angle, using the hyperbolic cotangent value of the angle being calculated. The function returns a result in radians.

Example: If the value of the hyperbolic cotangent of an angle is 3, @ACOTH(3) results in .346574 (radians).

@ACSCH(*angle*)

@ACSCH calculates the inverse (arc) hyperbolic cosecant of an angle, using the hyperbolic cosecant value of the angle being calculated. The function returns a result in radians.

Example: If the value of the hyperbolic cosecant of an angle is 2.54, @ACSCH(2.54) results in .38418 (radians).

@ASECH(*angle*)

@ASECH calculates the inverse (arc) hyperbolic secant of an angle, using the hyperbolic secant value of the angle being calculated. The function returns a result in radians.

Example: If the value of the hyperbolic secant of an angle is .25, @ASECH(.25) results in 2.063437 (radians).

@ASINH(*angle*)

@ASINH calculates the inverse (arc) hyperbolic sine of an angle, using the hyperbolic sine value of the angle being calculated. The function returns a result in radians.

Example: If the value of the hyperbolic sine of an angle is 3, @ASINH(3) results in .1.818440 (radians).

@ATANH(*angle*)

@ATANH calculates the inverse (arc) hyperbolic tangent of an angle, using the hyperbolic tangent value of the angle being calculated. The function returns a result in radians.

Example: If the value of the hyperbolic tangent of an angle is .6223, @ATANH(.6223) results in .72875 (radians).

@COSH(*angle*)

@COSH calculates the hyperbolic cosine of an angle, measured in radians. The function returns a result in radians. The result of @COSH is a value greater than 1.

The `angle` argument (the value in the cell or the value of the cell reference) must be in radians instead of an angular measurement. The value in radians can be between -11355.1371 and 11355.1371, although it cannot be the value 0. Use @DEGTORAD to convert an angle to radians before using @COSH.

Example: @COSH(@DEGTORAD(30)) returns 1.140238 (radians).

@COTH(*angle*)

@COTH calculates the hyperbolic cotangent of an angle. The function returns a result in radians.

The `angle` argument (the value in the cell or the value of the cell reference) must be in radians instead of an angular measurement. The value in radians can be between -11355.1371 and 11355.1371, although it cannot be the value 0. Use @DEGTORAD to convert an angle to radians before using @COTH.

Example: @COTH(@DEGTORAD(30)) returns `2.081283` (radians).

@CSCH(*angle*)

@CSCH calculates the hyperbolic cosecant of an angle. The function returns a result in radians.

The `angle` argument (the value in the cell or the value of the cell reference) must be in radians instead of an angular measurement. The value in radians can be between -11355.1371 and 11355.1371, although it cannot be the value 0. Use @DEGTORAD to convert an angle to radians before using @.

Example: @CSCH(@DEGTORAD(30)) returns `1.825306` (radians).

@SECH(*angle*)

@SECH calculates the hyperbolic secant of an angle. The function returns a result in radians.

The `angle` argument (the value in the cell or the value of the cell reference) must be in radians instead of an angular measurement. The value in radians can be between -11355.1371 and 11355.1371, although it cannot be the value 0. Use @DEGTORAD to convert an angle to radians before using @SECH.

Example: @SECH(@DEGTORAD(30)) returns `.87701` (radians).

@SINH(*angle*)

@SINH calculates the hyperbolic sine of an angle. The function returns a result in radians.

The `angle` argument (the value in the cell or the value of the cell reference) must be in radians instead of an angular measurement. The value in radians can be between -11355.1371 and 11355.1371, although it cannot be the value 0. Use @DEGTORAD to convert an angle to radians before using @SINH.

Example: @SINH(@DEGTORAD(30)) returns `.547853` (radians).

@TANH(*angle*)

@TANH calculates the hyperbolic tangent of an angle. The function returns a result in radians.

The `angle` argument (the value in the cell or the value of the cell reference) must be in radians instead of an angular measurement. The value in radians can be between -11355.1371 and 11355.1371, although it cannot be the value 0. Use @DEGTORAD to convert an angle to radians before using @TANH.

Example: @TANH(@DEGTORAD(30)) returns `.480473` (radians).

Rounding Functions The rounding functions let the user control the scope of values. The functions do this by allowing the user to round up, round down, or truncate numerical values.

@ROUND(*number,precision*)

@ROUND rounds values to a precision that you specify. @ROUND rounds a number according to the old standard rule: Numbers less than 0.5 are rounded down; numbers equal to or greater than 0.5 are rounded up. @ROUND is most useful for rounding a value used in other formulas or functions.

The `number` argument is the number you want to round or a cell reference to the cell that contains the number.

The `precision` argument determines the number of decimal places to which you round. This argument can be a numeric value between -100 and +100. Use positive *precision* values to specify places to the right of the decimal place; use negative values to specify places to the left of the decimal place. A *precision* value of 0 rounds decimal values to the nearest integer.

NOTE @ROUND and the InfoBox Number Format settings do different things. @ROUND actually changes the contents of a cell; the Number Format settings change only how 1-2-3 displays the cell's contents.

In 1-2-3, the formatted number you see on-screen or in print may not be the number used in calculations. This difference can cause errors of thousands of dollars in worksheets such as mortgage tables. To prevent errors, use @ROUND to round formula results or the numbers feeding into formulas so that the numbers used in calculations are the same as those in the display.

Examples: @ROUND(123.456,2) returns 123.46; @ROUND(123.456,0) returns 123; @ROUND(123.456,-2) returns 100.

NOTE If you want to round up to the nearest integer, you can do so by adding a number a little less than 0.5 to the number you want to round. If you work with numbers to two decimal places, add .49. If you work with numbers to four decimal places, add .4999.

@EVEN(*x*) and @ODD(*x*)

@EVEN rounds the value in the argument to the nearest even integer value away from 0. This means that positive values are made larger and negative values are made smaller.

@ODD rounds the value in the argument to the nearest odd integer value away from 0. This means that positive values are made larger and negative values are made smaller.

Examples: @EVEN(4.4) returns 6; @EVEN(5) returns 6; @ODD(4.4) returns 5; @ODD(3.1) returns 5.

@TRUNC(*x,[precision]*)

Like other rounding functions, @TRUNC modifies the values in the worksheet by truncating the value to the number of decimal places specified by the `precision` argument.

The `x` argument is any value or a cell reference to a cell that contains the value.

The optional `precision` argument can be a value between -100 and +100. If the *precision* value is negative, the integer portion of *x* is rounded to the value of the decimal position, starting from the left of the decimal point. If you omit the `precision` argument, @TRUNC truncates to the nearest integer.

Examples: @TRUNC(5849.8204) returns 5849; @TRUNC(5849.8204,2) returns 5849.82; @TRUNC(5849.8204,-2) returns 5800; @TRUNC(-5849.8204) returns -5849; @TRUNC(-5849.8204,-3) returns 5000.

NOTE Compare @TRUNC with @ROUND. @TRUNC(5849.8204) returns 5849, whereas @ROUND(5849.8204) returns 5850.

Trigonometric Functions 1-2-3 provides the standard trigonometric functions, which are described in this section.

@ACOS(*angle*), @ASIN(*angle*), @ATAN(*angle*), and @ATAN2(*x,y*)

@ACOS, @ASIN, @ATAN, and @ATAN2 calculate the arccosine, the arcsine, the arctangent, and the four-quadrant arctangent, respectively. @ACOS computes the inverse of cosine. @ASIN computes the inverse of sine, returning a radians angle between $-\pi/2$ and $\pi/2$ (-90 and +90 degrees). @ATAN computes the inverse of tangent, returning a radians angle between $-\pi/2$ and $\pi/2$ (-90 and +90 degrees). @ATAN2 calculates the four-quadrant arctangent, using the ratio of its two arguments.

To convert the values from radians to degrees, use @RADTODEG.

Because all cosine and sine values lie between -1 and 1, @ACOS and @ASIN work only with values between -1 and 1. This means that the angular measurements in the argument will be in radians. Either function returns ERR if you use an argument outside this range. @ASIN returns angles between $-\pi/2$ and $+\pi/2$; @ACOS returns angles between 0 and $\pi/2$.

For @ATAN, the `angle` argument can be any number, and the function returns a value between - /2 and + /2.

@ATAN2 computes the angle whose tangent is specified by the `x` and `y` arguments. At least one of the arguments must be a number other than 0. @ATAN2 returns radians angles between - and + .

@ACOT(*angle*), @ACSC(*angle*), and @ASEC(*angle*)

@ACOT, @ACSC, and @ASEC calculate the arccotangent, the arccosecant, and the arcsecant, respectively, of an angle. The results of the calculations are in radians. @ACOT computes the inverse of cotangent. @ASEC computes the inverse of secant, returning a radians angle between 0 and (0 and +180 degr ees). @ACSC computes the inverse of cosecant, returning a radians angle between - /2 and /2 (-90 and +90 degr ees).

@COT(*angle*), @CSC(*angle*), and @SEC(*angle*)

Be sure to convert angle measurements to radians before you use @COT, @CSC, @SEC, @COS, @SIN, and @TAN. You can accomplish this task quickly by using the @DEGTORAD function described earlier in this chapter.

@COT, @CSC, and @SEC calculate the cotangent, cosecant, and secant, respectively, of an angle. For each function, the `angle` argument is measured in radians.

@COS(*angle*), @SIN(*angle*), and @TAN(*angle*)

@COS, @SIN, and @TAN calculate the cosine, sine, and tangent, respectively, of an angle. For each function, the `angle` argument is measured in radians.

@PI

@PI results in the value 3.14159265358979324. Use @PI in calculations for the area of circles and the volume of spheres. You also can use @PI to convert angle measurements in degrees to angle measurements in radians (if you prefer to make this calculation on your own instead of using @DEGTORAD).

Statistical Functions

1-2-3 provides five statistical function categories: forecasting, general, probability, ranking, and significance tests.

Many statistical functions use the `list` argument. This argument can contain individually specified values, cell addresses, a range of cells, multiple ranges of cells, or range names. For example, 1-2-3 considers each of the following formats to be a valid `list` argument:

```
@SUM(1,2,3,4)
@SUM(B1,B2,B3,B4)
@SUM(B1..B4)
@SUM(A1..B2,B3..E10)
@SUM(NAME)
```

Labels can be used as valid items within the group of cells in a range or range name. 1-2-3 assigns a 0 to the position occupied by the label in the group.

CAUTION

1-2-3 ignores blank cells embedded within a range in calculations. If the blank cells in a list are referenced as specific items in the list, however, the function counts and uses them. For example, the @AVG function can use either of these two *list* formats: (A1..A3) or (A1,A2,A3). In both *list* formats, assume that cell A1 is blank (that is, it has nothing in it). The @AVG(A1..A3) function does not include cell A1 as a value or position and divides by 2. In @AVG(A1,A2,A3), cell A1 is counted and @AVG divides by 3.

Forecasting Functions You can create forecasts by performing regression analysis. This section explores @REGRESSION.

@REGRESSION(*x_range,y_range,attribute,[compute]*)

@REGRESSION performs multiple linear regression on ranges of values and returns the statistic.

Following are this function's arguments and limits:

x_range	Also known as the ***independent variable,*** the `x_range` argument can be a range name or an address that contains up to 75 columns and 8,192 rows.
y_range	Also known as the ***dependent variable,*** the `y_range` argument can be a range name or an address that has a single column and the same number of rows as the `x_range`.
attribute	Specifies which regression output value to calculate. Following are the available attributes:

Attribute	Calculation Performed
1	Constant
2	Standard error of Y estimate
3	R squared
4	Number of observations

continues

continued

Attribute	Calculation Performed
5	Degrees of freedom
101 to 175	X coefficient (slope) for the independent variable specified by attribute
201 to 275	Standard error of coefficient for the independent variable specified by attribute

[*compute*] An optional argument that specifies the Y-intercept. This argument has the following options:

Compute	1-2-3
0	Uses 0 as the Y-intercept
1	Calculates the Y-intercept and is the default if omitted from the argument

1-2-3 numbers the independent variables in the *x_range*, starting with the number 1, from top to bottom in a column, and in columns from left to right. If the *x_range* is A1..C10, you can find the X coefficient for the independent variable in A2 by using the attribute 102. Using the same *x_range*, you can find the standard error of coefficient for the independent variable in A5 by using the attribute 205.

For the same data, @REGRESSION returns the same result as the Range menu's Analyze Regression command.

General Statistical Functions 1-2-3's general statistical functions help you perform standard statistical analysis. The following sections describe some of the commonly used general statistical functions.

@AVG(*list*) and @PUREAVG(*list*)

Essentially, @AVG produces the same result as if you divided @SUM(*list*) by @COUNT(*list*)—two functions described later in this section.

To calculate the average of a set of values, you add all the values and then divide the sum by the number of values. @AVG calculates this arithmetic mean for a list of values. For @AVG, if a label is specified in the list as a cell value, 1-2-3 counts that cell in the @AVG calculation.

Like @AVG, @PUREAVG calculates the average of a set of values. @PUREAVG, however, has the added feature of ignoring cells in the list that are labels, rather than converting them to zero.

The `list` argument can be values, cell addresses, cell names, cell ranges, range names, or a combination of all these formats.

Examples: Suppose that cells A5 through A12 contain the values January, 5, 4, 5, February, 5, 6, and 4. @AVG(A5..A12) returns `3.625` because it adds the numbers (using 0 for the two labels January and February) and divides by 8. @PUREAVG(A5..A12) returns `4.833` because it ignores the labels, adds only the numbers, and divides by 6.

@COUNT(*list*) and @PURECOUNT

@COUNT totals the number of cells that contain nonblank entries of any kind, including labels, label-prefix characters, and the values ERR and NA. @PURECOUNT totals the number of cells that contain nonblank entries that are values only.

For both @COUNT and @PURECOUNT, the `list` argument can be values, cell addresses, cell names, cell ranges, range names, or a combination of these formats—including ERR and NA. @PURECOUNT, however, counts only the cells that contain values.

Limits: Include only ranges as the argument in @COUNT. If you specify an individual cell, 1-2-3 counts that cell as though it has an entry, even if the cell is empty. If you absolutely must specify a cell individually, but want that cell to be counted only if it actually contains an entry, use @PURECOUNT.

NOTE 1-2-3 considers ERR and NA to be values. Also, be aware that different situations call for the use of different functions. Use @COUNT to include all cells, no matter what is included in those cells; use @PURECOUNT to include only cells that contain values. Make sure that the result reflects what you are trying to accomplish.

@GRANDTOTAL(*list*) and @SUBTOTAL(*list*)

@GRANDTOTAL calculates the sum of all cells that contain the @SUBTOTAL function. @SUBTOTAL adds a list of values and returns the sum. This function is a tool that lets you mark values—most commonly, for use with @GRANDTOTAL.

For @SUBTOTAL, the `list` argument can be numbers, numeric formulas, and range addresses or range names that contain numbers or formulas.

For @GRANDTOTAL, the `list` argument is a group or range of @SUBTOTAL formulas. Notice that if the range of cells for @GRANDTOTAL includes cells that contain @SUM formulas, 1-2-3 ignores the @SUM formulas.

Example: Figure 6.16 shows how @SUBTOTAL and @GRANDTOTAL can be used.

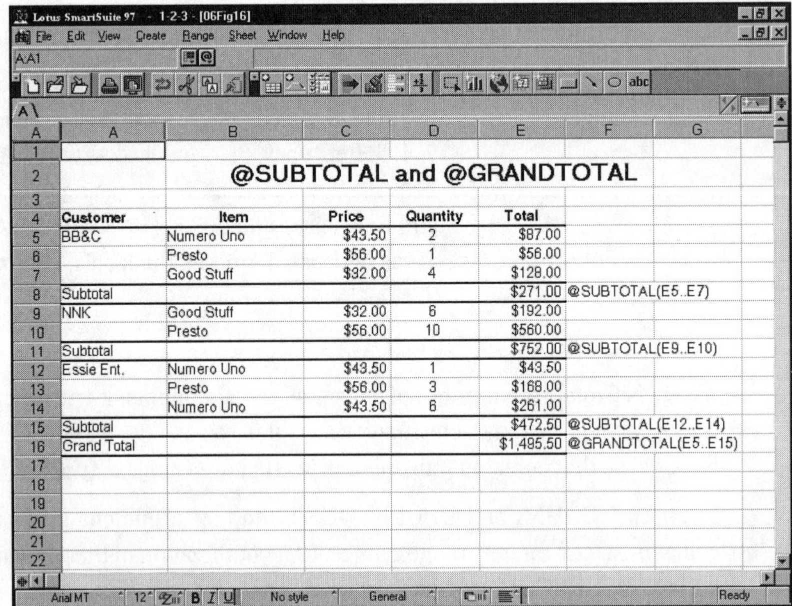

	A	B	C	D	E	F
1						
2	@SUBTOTAL and @GRANDTOTAL					
3						
4	Customer	Item	Price	Quantity	Total	
5	BB&C	Numero Uno	$43.50	2	$87.00	
6		Presto	$56.00	1	$56.00	
7		Good Stuff	$32.00	4	$128.00	
8	Subtotal				$271.00	@SUBTOTAL(E5..E7)
9	NNK	Good Stuff	$32.00	6	$192.00	
10		Presto	$56.00	10	$560.00	
11	Subtotal				$752.00	@SUBTOTAL(E9..E10)
12	Essie Ent.	Numero Uno	$43.50	1	$43.50	
13		Presto	$56.00	3	$168.00	
14		Numero Uno	$43.50	6	$261.00	
15	Subtotal				$472.50	@SUBTOTAL(E12..E14)
16	Grand Total				$1,495.50	@GRANDTOTAL(E5..E15)

Fig. 6.16 Use @SUBTOTAL to mark values to be gathered into a grand total by @GRANDTOTAL.

NOTE @SUBTOTAL and @SUM both sum a series of values and return the same results. If you want to use @GRANDTOTAL to calculate a grand total, however, you must sum values with @SUBTOTAL, because @GRANDTOTAL ignores @SUM values.

@MAX(*list*), @MIN(*list*), @PUREMAX(*list*), and @PUREMIN(*list*)

@MAX finds the largest value in the `list` argument; @MIN finds the smallest value in the `list` argument. Both functions assign a value of 0 to a label and include the label in their evaluation. @PUREMAX and @PUREMIN also find the largest and smallest value, respectively, in the `list` argument, but both functions ignore cells that contain labels and do not include those cells in their evaluations.

The `list` argument can be numbers, numeric formulas, and range addresses or range names that contain numbers or formulas. Any blank cells are ignored. For @MAX and @MIN, any cell with a label is given the value 0. For @PUREMAX and @PUREMIN, any cell with a label is ignored.

Examples: Suppose that you have a range named PRICES that contains the entries 35, 43, unknown, 43, 55, and 23. @MAX(PRICES) and @PUREMAX(PRICES) return `55`, the largest value.

@MIN(PRICES) returns 0, because the label *unknown* is evaluated as 0. @PUREMIN(PRICES) returns 23 because it ignores the label *unknown*.

NOTE If you are familiar with statistics, you may recognize that the @MAX and @MIN functions provide the two pieces of data you need to calculate a popular statistical measure: a range. A *range*—which is one measure of variability in a list of values—is the difference between the highest value and the lowest value in a list of values. (A range as a statistical measurement is not the same thing as a worksheet range, which is a rectangular block of cells.)

@MEDIAN(*list*)

@MEDIAN returns either the middle value in a list or the arithmetic average of the list. 1-2-3 looks at the number of values in a list; if the number of physical entries is odd, the result of @MEDIAN is the middle value of the list. If the number of physical entries is even, the result is the arithmetical average of the two middle values in the list.

The `list` argument can be values, cell addresses, cell names, cell ranges, range names, or a combination of all these formats. Blank cells are ignored.

Examples: Suppose that the GENERIC range contains the values 3, 3, a blank cell, 9, 8, 15, 2, and 1; the @MEDIAN value is 3. If you enter **5** in the blank cell, the @MEDIAN value is 4.

@PRODUCT(*list*)

@PRODUCT multiplies the values in the argument list. This function works exactly like a calculator, multiplying the values in the *list* argument to return the result. The key portion of the preceding sentence is *exactly like a calculator*. If you include a 0 or a label in the list, the result is 0.

The `list` argument can be values, cell addresses, cell names, cell ranges, range names, or a combination of all these formats. Blank cells are ignored.

@STD(*list*), @STDS(*list*), @PURESTD(*list*), and @PURESTDS(*list*)

@STD uses the *n*, or population, method of calculating standard deviation; the @STDS function uses the *n*-1, or sample population, method of calculating the standard deviation. Both functions assign a value of 0 to a label and include the label in their evaluations. @PURESTD and @PURESTDS also use the population and sample methods, respectively, of calculating the standard deviation, but both functions ignore cells that contain labels and do not include those cells in their evaluations.

The `list` argument can be values, cell addresses, cell names, cell ranges, range names, or a combination of all these formats. Blank cells are ignored. For @STD and @STDS, any cell that contains a label is given the value 0. For @PURESTD and @PURESTDS, any cell that contains a label is ignored.

Examples: Suppose that you have a range named PRICES that contains the entries 35, 43, unknown, 43, 55, and 23. @STD(PRICES) returns `17.68631`, and @STDS returns `19.37438`. The difference reflects the adjustment that @STDS makes, because that function assumes a sample of the population. @PURESTD(PRICES) returns `10.55272`, and @PURESTDS(PRICES) returns `11.7983`. The differences between these results and those of @STD and @STDS reflect the fact that the PURE functions ignore the label *unknown* rather than include it (as 0) in their calculations.

NOTE Essentially, the standard deviation is a measure of how individual values vary from the mean or average of all of the values in the list. A smaller standard deviation indicates that values are grouped closely around the mean; a larger standard deviation indicates that values are widely dispersed from the mean. Perhaps not surprisingly, a standard deviation of 0 indicates no dispersion—that is, every value in the list of values is the same.

To choose the correct function, you need to know whether you are dealing with the entire population or with a sample. If you are measuring, or including, every value in a calculation, you are working with a population. If you are measuring, or including, only a subset or a portion of the values in a calculation, you are working with a sample. @STDS and @PURESTDS use the *n*-1, or sample population, method to calculate standard deviation for sample populations. This method adjusts the standard deviation so that it is slightly higher to compensate for possible errors because the entire population was not used.

@SUM(*list*)

Use the SmartSum SmartIcon to enter the @SUM function automatically. The list argument is the range address or name of cells containing values either above or to the left of the current cell. You also can sum a range of numbers automatically by typing the label **Total** or **Totals** in a cell next to the range. 1-2-3 enters the @SUM functions for you.

@SUM provides a convenient way to add a list of values. Of all the functions that 1-2-3 provides, @SUM is the one that you probably will use most often. You can calculate a total of cell values by typing a formula that uses the cell addresses, as follows:

+E5+E6+E7+E8+E9

This method, however, is inefficient and conducive to typing errors. A more efficient way to total the values is to use the following formula:

@SUM(E5..E9)

The `list` argument can be numbers, numeric formulas, and range addresses or range names that contain numbers or formulas.

NOTE When you sum a range of cells and include the horizontal totaling line in the @SUM formula, you can insert cells into or delete cells from the range and keep the formula intact and working perfectly; you never have to adjust the range. If you include a *placeholder* (a blank or text-filled cell) at the top or bottom of the range of cells being summed, maintaining the worksheet is easier. The placeholder cell does not affect the total, because the cell is text and adds as 0. ■

@SUMPRODUCT(*list*), @SUMNEGATIVE(*list*) and @SUMPOSITIVE(*list*)

@SUMNEGATIVE sums only the negative values in the specified list, and @SUMPOSITIVE sums only the positive values in the specified list.

The `list` argument can be numbers, numeric formulas, and range addresses or range names that contain numbers or formulas. Separate the elements of the list with argument separators (such as commas or semicolons).

Example: @SUMNEGATIVE(3,-5,7,9,-10,1) returns `-15`.
@SUMPOSITIVE(3,-5,7,9,-10,1) returns `20`.

@SUMPRODUCT gets its name because it sums the products of corresponding cells in multiple ranges.

The `list` argument can be any combination of ranges that are the same size and shape. If the ranges are not the same size and shape, @SUMPRODUCT returns `ERR`. If the ranges in the list are rows, @SUMPRODUCT multiplies by columns. If the ranges are columns or span more than one column, @SUMPRODUCT multiplies by rows.

Example: Figure 6.17 shows how you can use @SUMPRODUCT to calculate the total dollar value of inventory.

@VAR(*list*), @VARS(*list*), @PUREVAR(*list*), and @PUREVARS(*list*)

The *variance*, like the standard deviation, is a measure of how much the individual values within the measurement vary from the mean or average. @VAR calculates the variance by using the population, or *n*, method. @VARS calculates the variance by using the sample population, or *n*-1, method. Both functions give a label a value of 0 and include the label in their evaluations. @PUREVAR and @PUREVARS also use the population and sample methods, respectively, of calculating the variance, but both functions ignore cells that contain labels and do not include those cells in their evaluations.

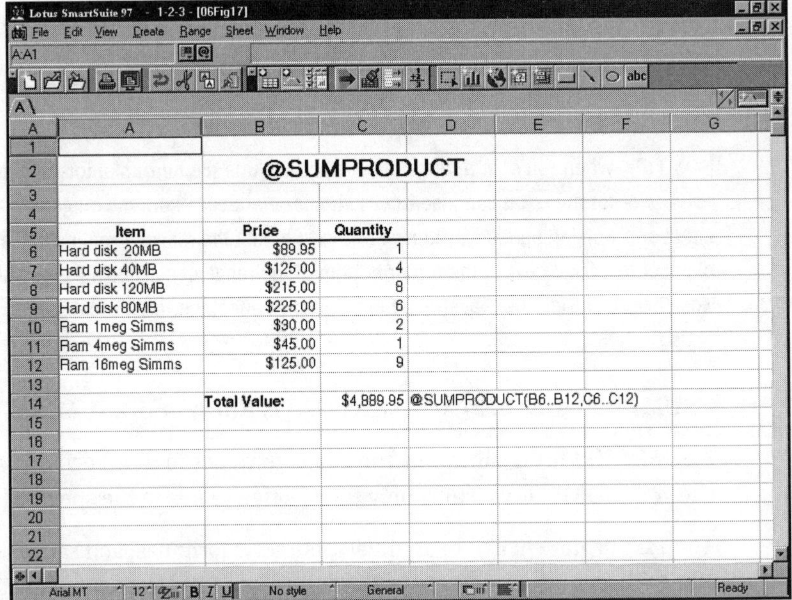

Fig. 6.17
Use @SUMPRODUCT to sum the products of corresponding cells in multiple ranges.

The `list` argument can be values, cell addresses, cell names, cell ranges, range names, or a combination of all these formats. Blank cells are ignored. For @VAR and @VARS, any cell that contains a label is given the value 0. For @PUREVAR and @PUREVARS, any cell that contains a label is ignored.

Examples: Suppose that you have a range named PRICES that contains the entries 35, 43, unknown, 43, 55, and 23. @VAR(PRICES) returns `312.8056`, and @VARS(PRICES) returns `375.3667`. The difference reflects the adjustment that @VARS makes because it assumes a sample of the population. @PUREVAR(PRICES) returns `111.36`, and @PUREVARS(PRICES) returns `139.2`. The differences between these results and the @VAR and @VARS results reflect the fact that the PURE functions ignore the label *unknown* rather than include it (as 0) in their calculations.

@WEIGHTAVG(*range1,range2*)

@WEIGHTAVG calculates the weighted average of a list by multiplying the values in corresponding cells in multiple ranges, summing the products, and finally dividing by the number of values in the list.

The ranges in the arguments must be the same shape and size; if they are not, @WEIGHTAVG returns ERR. If the ranges are columns, @WEIGHTAVG multiplies by rows; otherwise, the function multiplies by columns. If each list spans more than one column, @WEIGHTAVG multiplies by rows.

Example: Suppose that you run a real estate office and want to calculate the weighted average of the sales commissions payable to an agent for a month's house sales. The data obtained from the computer gives you the following information:

SOLD	COMMIS
$25,000	.04
$34,580	.04
$77,325	.05

You can use @WEIGHTAVG(SOLD,COMMIS) to determine the agent's monthly commission amount: $48,072.69.

Probability Functions

@BINOMIAL (*trials,successes,probability,[type]*)

@BINOMIAL calculates the binomial probability mass function or the cumulative binomial distribution. The function approximates the cumulative binomial distribution to within +/-3*10^-7.

Following are this function's arguments and limits:

trials — The number of independent trials. This value must be a positive nonzero integer. If *trials* is not entered as an integer, 1-2-3 truncates the value to an integer.

successes — The number of successes in *trials*. This value can be any positive integer or 0, but it must be less than or equal to *trials*. If *successes* is not entered as an integer, 1-2-3 truncates the value to an integer.

probability — The probability of success on each trial. This value must be any valid probability between 0 and 1.

[*type*] — This optional argument specifies whether 1-2-3 calculates the probability mass function or the cumulative binomial distribution. This argument has three switch options:

Type	Switch Value
0	The probability of the exact number of successes specified by the succeses argument (the default if [type] is omitted)
1	The probability of the most number of successes specified by the successes argument
2	The probability of at least the numbers of successes specified by the successes argument.

Examples: Suppose that you want to know how many people prefer Cola A over Cola B in a blind taste test. You set up a polling booth at the local mall and call the local TV station. Ten random entrants appear; you hand each person two glasses of cola. There is no difference in the glasses except for the code on the bottom, which identifies which glass contains which cola. Because the people showed up at random, there should be a probability of 50 percent of the participants liking either cola.

To determine the probability that *exactly* 7 of 10 will prefer Cola A, use @BINOMIAL(10,7,.5), which returns `0.117188`. To determine the probability that *at most* 7 of 10 will prefer Cola A, use @BINOMIAL(10,7,.5,1), which returns `0.945313`. To determine the probability that *at least* 7 of 10 will prefer Cola A, use @BINOMIAL(10,7,.5,2), which returns `0.171875`.

@CHIDIST(*x,degrees_of_freedom,[type]*)

@CHIDIST calculates the chi-square distribution. The *chi-square distribution* is a continuous, single-parameter distribution derived as a special case of the gamma distribution. The chi-square distribution is approximated to within +/-3*10^-7; if the result is not approximated to within .0000001 after 100 attempts, @CHIDIST returns `ERR`.

Following are this function's arguments and limits:

x The value at which to evaluate the chi-squared distribution. The value of *x* depends on the optional [*type*] argument. You have two choices for *x*:

0	This value is the upper boundary for the value of the chi-squared cumulative distribution random variable and is a value greater than or equal to 0 (the default if [*type*] is omitted).
1	A significance level, or probability, between 0 and 1.

degrees_of_freedom The number of degrees of freedom for the sample. This argument is a positive integer. If the value is not entered as an integer, 1-2-3 truncates it to an integer.

[*type*] This optional argument specifies how the @CHIDIST is calculated. You have two options:

Type	How Calculated
0	The significance level corresponding to x (the default if [*type*] is omitted)
1	The critical value that corresponds to the significance level

@COMBIN(*n,r*)

The binomial coefficient is the number of ways that *r* can be selected from *n*, without regard to order. @COMBIN approximates the binomial coefficient to within +/-3*10^-7.

Following are this function's arguments and limits:

n The number of values. This argument can be any positive integer or 0.

r The number of values in each combination. This argument can be any positive integer less than or equal to *n* and can be 0.

Example: Suppose that a cup contains six pennies, each with a different date and mint mark. You pick two at random. As you pick a penny from the cup, you do not replace it. To determine the number of date combinations you could have, use @COMBIN(6,2), which returns 15.

@NORMAL(*x,[mean],[std],[type]*)

@NORMAL calculates the normal distribution factor for *x*.

Following are this function's arguments and limits:

x	The upper boundary for the value of the cumulative normal distribution. The value of *x* used in the calculation is the absolute value of the number used as the argument.
[*mean*]	This optional argument specifies the mean of the distribution. If used, [*mean*] must be a positive value; if *[mean]* is omitted, 1-2-3 defaults to 0.
[*std*]	This optional argument specifies the standard deviation of the distribution. If used, [*std*] must be positive or 0; if *[std]* is omitted, 1-2-3 defaults to 1.
[*type*]	This optional argument specifies the function you want @NORMAL to calculate. You have three options:

Type	What Is Calculated
0	Cumulative distribution function (the default if [type] is omitted)
1	Inverse cumulative distribution function
2	Probability density function

@PERMUT(*n,r*)

@PERMUT calculates the permutations of *r* selected from *n*.

The `n` and `r` arguments must be integers; otherwise, 1-2-3 truncates them to integers for the calculations. The `n` argument is any positive integer or 0. The `r` argument is any positive integer or 0; it cannot be greater than the `n` argument.

Example:	Suppose that meetings scheduled for 9:00, 10:00, and 11:00 are to be conducted by three of the five vice presidents of your company. To calculate the number of possible combinations (which vice president conducts which meeting), use @PERMUT(5,3), which returns `60`.

Ranking Functions

@PERCENTILE(*x,range*)

@PERCENTILE calculates the *x*th sample percentile among the values in a range.

The `x` argument is the percentage you want to find; it can be a value from 0 to 1. The `range` argument is the range name or address of the values. In the range, blank cells are ignored and cells with labels are assigned the value of 0.

Example: Suppose that you have given a test and gathered the scores. The scores are entered in a range named SCORES in a worksheet and have the following values: 98, 80, 59, 77, 97, 88, 69, and 89. To determine the 95th percentile, use @PERCENTILE(.95,SCORES), which returns `97.65`.

@RANK(*item,range,[order]*)

@RANK calculates the relative size or position of a value in a range, relative to other values in the range. 1-2-3 assigns the same rank to duplicate numbers in the range, although duplicate numbers affect the rank of subsequent numbers in the range.

The `item` argument is the value whose rank you want to determine. The `range` argument is the range name or address of a group of values. The `item` argument must be part of the range.

The optional `order` argument specifies how to rank items. This value can be 0 or 1. The value 0 indicates descending order (9 to 1) of ranking. If you omit the `order` argument, 1-2-3 assumes 0. The value 1 indicates ascending order (1 to 9) of ranking.

Examples: Suppose that you have given a test and gathered the scores. The scores are entered in a range named SCORES in a worksheet and have the following values: 98, 80, 59, 77, 97, 88, 69, and 89. To determine the highest ranking of the score of 88, use @RANK(88,SCORES), which returns `4`. To determine the lowest ranking of the score of 88, use @RANK(88,SCORES,1), which returns `5`.

Significance Tests

@CHITEST(*range1,range2*)

@CHITEST performs a chi-square test.

The argument list contains two ranges of values that must be the same size and can contain only values. If the ranges are not the same size, @CHITEST returns `ERR`. If the ranges are blank, contain labels, or have text formulas, @CHITEST returns `ERR`.

@FTEST(*range1,range2*)

@FTEST performs an F-test on two ranges to determine whether two samples have different variances. The probability of @FTEST is approximated to within +/-3*10^-7. The range arguments contain the values for the test. The ranges do not have to be the same size.

@TTEST(*range1,range2,[type],[tails]*)

@TTEST performs a student's T-test on the data in two ranges and returns the associated probability.

Following are this function's arguments and limits:

range1	Contains values. If *range1* contains labels, text formulas, or blank cells, 1-2-3 returns ERR.
range2	Contains values. If *range2* contains labels, text formulas, or blank cells, 1-2-3 returns ERR.
[*type*]	This optional argument specifies what type of T-test to perform. You have three options:

Type	**T-Test**
0	A T-test for samples drawn from populations with the same variance (homoscedastic populations); range1 and range2 do not have to contain the same number of cells (the default if [type] is omitted)
1	A T-test for samples drawn from populations with unequal variances (heteroscedastic populations); range1 and range2 do not have to contain the same number of cells
2	A paired T-test; range1 and range2 must contain the same number of cells

[*tails*]	This optional argument specifies the direction of the T-test. You have two options:

Tails	**How Calculated**
1	One-tailed T-test
2	Two-tailed T-test (the default if [tails] is omitted)

Text Functions

1-2-3 offers a variety of functions that give you significant power to manipulate text strings. The program provides a few special functions for working with the 1-2-3 character set (the IBM PC Multilingual code page—code page 850).

Strings are labels or portions of text. More specifically, strings are data that consist of characters (alphabetical, numeric, blank, and special) enclosed in quotation marks—for example, "total". The functions specifically designated as string functions are not the only 1-2-3 functions that take advantage of the power and flexibility of strings; logical, error-trapping, and special functions also use strings as well as values. The text functions, however, are specifically designed to manipulate text strings.

You can link text to other text by using the concatenation operator (&). The discussion of the individual text functions in this section shows several examples of the use of the concatenation operator. Keep in mind that you cannot link text to cells that contain numeric values or that are empty. If you try, 1-2-3 returns ERR.

Avoid mixing data types in text functions. Some functions produce text, but other functions produce numeric results. If a function's result is not the data type you need, use @STRING to convert a numeric value to a text string; use @VALUE to convert a text string to a numeric value.

The numbering scheme for positioning characters in a string begins with 0 and continues to the number that corresponds to the last character in the label. The label prefix (') is not counted for numeric positioning. In the label *'dog*, for example, *d* is position 0, *o* is position 1, and *g* is position 2. You cannot use negative position numbers.

@CHAR(*number*) and @CODE(*text*)

@CHAR takes a code-page number that specifies a character and returns that character. @CODE does the opposite; it takes an IBM multilingual character and returns a code-page number. Keep in mind that uppercase and lowercase characters have different codes.

Example: Figure 6.18 shows several examples of the use of @CHAR and @CODE.

NOTE 1-2-3 does not support some numerical-equivalent characters; these characters return a symbol that does not match the code-page symbol. Character number 200 in figure 6.18 shows a different character from the one presented in the code-page examples in your Lotus documentation.

@FIND(*search_text,text,start_number*)

@FIND locates the starting position of one set of characters within another set of characters. When @FIND cannot find a match, the result is ERR.

The `search_text` argument is the text you want to locate; it can be one or more characters long. The `text` argument is the text in which to locate the `search_text`. Both `search_text` and `text` can be text enclosed in quotation marks, a formula that returns text, or an address of a cell that contains text or a formula that returns text. @FIND's comparison of the `search_text` and the `text` arguments is case-sensitive. For example, @FIND will not find the `search_text` *j* in the text *Jim*.

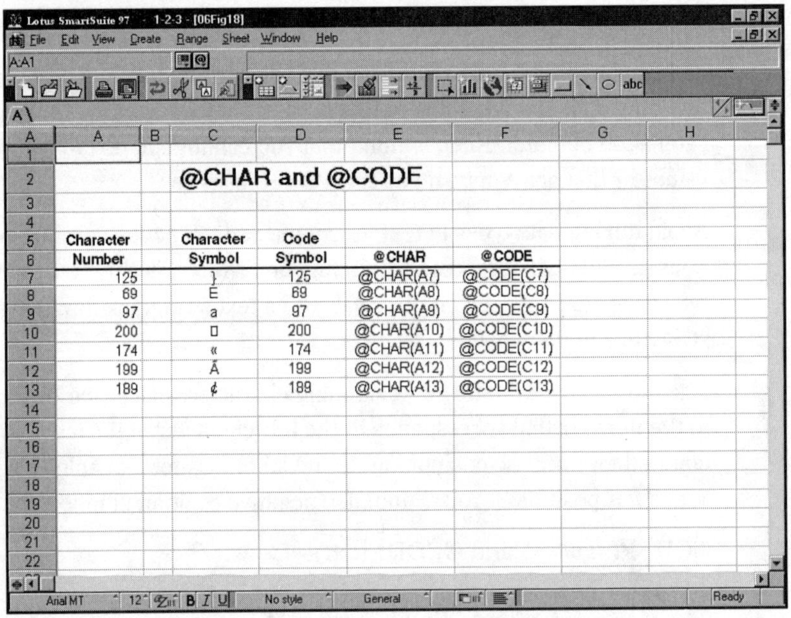

Fig. 6.18
Use @CHAR and @CODE to convert character and code-page equivalents.

@CHAR and @CODE

Character Number	Character Symbol	Code Symbol	@CHAR	@CODE
125	}	125	@CHAR(A7)	@CODE(C7)
69	E	69	@CHAR(A8)	@CODE(C8)
97	a	97	@CHAR(A9)	@CODE(C9)
200	□	200	@CHAR(A10)	@CODE(C10)
174	«	174	@CHAR(A11)	@CODE(C11)
199	Ã	199	@CHAR(A12)	@CODE(C12)
189	¢	189	@CHAR(A13)	@CODE(C13)

The `start_number` argument is the position number in *text* at which you want to start the search. Remember that the first character in the text is counted as 0, not 1.

Example: To determine the position of the blank space within the text *Jim Johnson*, which appears in cell A6, use @FIND(" ",A6,0). Here, the search text is " " (a blank space enclosed in parentheses). The 0 indicates the search should begin at the first character of the text being searched. @FIND(" ",A6,0) returns the value 3.

NOTE You can search for a second occurrence of *search_text* by adding 1 to the result of the first @FIND function and using that value as the *start_number* argument. This action starts the next @FIND operation at the character location after the blank space already found. The following formula searches for the character position of the second blank space for the text in cell A6:

```
@FIND(" ",A6,@FIND(" ",A6,1)+1)
```

@MID(*text,start_number,number*)

@MID extracts one text string from another.

The `start_number` argument is a number that represents the character position in *text* at which you want to begin extracting characters. The `number` argument indicates the length of the *text* to be extracted; it is the number of characters to extract.

Example: To extract the first name from a label containing the full name *Mary Baggett*, use @MID("Mary Baggett",0,4). This function extracts the *text* starting in position 0 (the first character) and continuing for four characters—through the text *Mary*.

@LEFT(*text,number*) and @RIGHT(*text,number*)

The @LEFT and @RIGHT functions are variations of @MID; you use them to extract one text string from another, beginning at the leftmost and rightmost positions in the text.

The *text* argument is the text string from which you want to extract characters. The `number` argument is the number of characters to be extracted.

Example: If you want to extract the ZIP code from the text "Cincinnati, Ohio 45243", use @RIGHT("Cincinnati, Ohio 45243",5); To extract the city, use @LEFT("Cincinnati, Ohio 45243",10).

@REPLACE(*original_text,start_number,length,new_text*)

@REPLACE replaces one group of characters in a text string with another group of characters. @REPLACE is a valuable tool for correcting a frequent incorrect text entry without retyping the entry.

Example: If you need to change to all phone numbers in a database that have area codes 301 to 407, you could use @REPLACE("301",0,3,"407").

The `start_number` argument indicates the position at which 1-2-3 should begin removing characters from `original_text`. The `length` argument shows how many characters to remove. The `new_text` argument contains the new characters that will replace the removed ones. @REPLACE starts counting character positions in a text string at 0 and continues to the end of the string (up to 511).

@LENGTH(*text*)

@LENGTH calculates the number of characters in *text*. @LENGTH frequently is used to calculate the length of a text string being extracted from another text string. You also can use this function to check for data-entry errors. @LENGTH returns `ERR` as the length of numeric values or formulas, empty cells, and null strings.

Example: @LENGTH("welcome back") returns `12`.

@EXACT(*text1,text2*)

@EXACT compares two sets of characters and returns `1` (true) if the two sets are the same or `0` (false) if the sets are different. @EXACT checks for an exact match that distinguishes between uppercase and lowercase characters.

The `text1` and `text2` arguments can be text, the result of text formulas, or references to cells that contain text or text formulas.

NOTE The @EXACT function's method of comparison is similar to the = operator in formulas (except that the = operator checks for a match regardless of uppercase and lowercase characters). If cell B7 holds the text *Wrench* and cell D7 holds the text *wrench*, the logical value of B7=D7 is 1, because the two text strings are an approximate match. The value of @EXACT(B7,D7), however, is 0, because the two functions are not an exact match; their cases are different.

@EXACT cannot compare nontext arguments. In fact, if either argument is a nontext value of any type (including numbers) or is blank, 1-2-3 returns `ERR`. (You can use the @S function, which is explained later in this chapter, to ensure that the arguments used within @EXACT have text values.) When you use = to compare a text string with a number or a blank cell, the string is treated as the number 0, as is a blank cell. This means that if you use the = formula, any string is equal to a blank cell or to a cell that contains the number 0.

Example: Figure 6.19 demonstrates the use of @EXACT.

@LOWER(*text*), @UPPER(*text*), and @PROPER(*text*)

1-2-3 offers three functions for converting the case of a text value. @LOWER converts all letters in a text string to lowercase, @UPPER converts all letters in a text string to uppercase, and @PROPER capitalizes the first letter in each word of a label and the remaining letters in each word to lowercase. (Words are defined as groups of characters separated by blank spaces or nonletter characters.)

The `text` argument can be a set of characters enclosed in quotation marks or a cell reference to a cell that contains text. If a cell contains a number or a null string (" "), 1-2-3 returns `ERR`. (You can use the @S function, which is explained later in this chapter, to ensure that the arguments of these functions have text values.)

Examples: If cell A6 contains the text *welcome BACK*, @UPPER(A6) returns `WELCOME BACK`, @LOWER(A6) returns `welcome back`, and @PROPER(A6) returns `Welcome Back`.

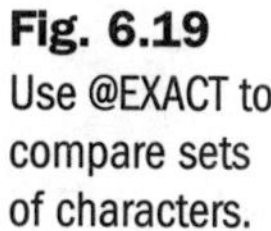

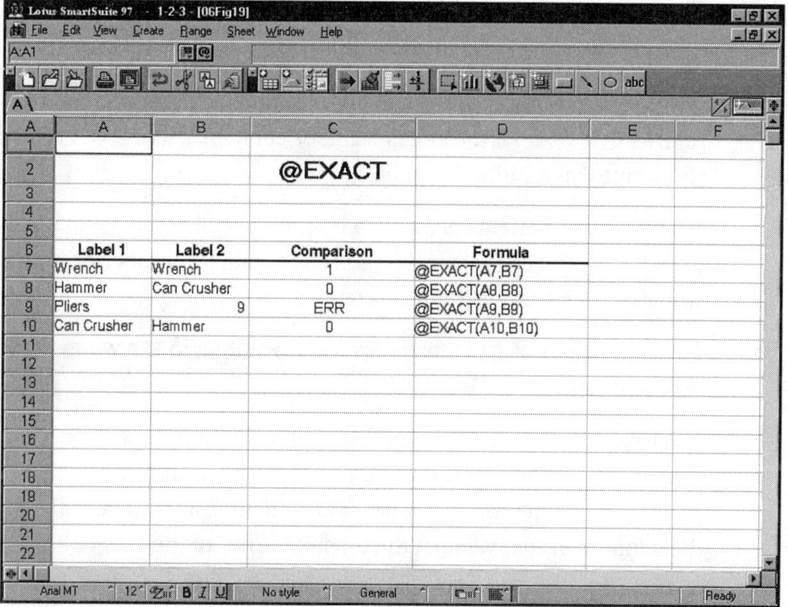

Fig. 6.19
Use @EXACT to compare sets of characters.

NOTE Use @LOWER, @UPPER, or @PROPER to modify the contents of a database so that all entries in a field have the same capitalization. This technique produces consistent reports. Capitalization also affects the sorting order: Uppercase and lowercase letters do not sort together. To ensure that data with different capitalization sorts together, create a column (use one of the functions that references the data) and then sort on this new column.

@REPEAT(*text,number*)

@REPEAT repeats text a specified number of times, much as the backslash (\) repeats text to fill a cell. @REPEAT, however, has some distinct advantages over the backslash. With @REPEAT, you can repeat the text the precise number of times you want. If the result is wider than the cell width, the result is displayed in empty adjacent cells to the right.

The *text* argument is the set of characters you want repeated. The `number` argument indicates the number of times you want to repeat *text* in the cell.

Example: If you want to repeat the characters `=**=` three times, use @REPEAT("==",3). The resulting text is `=**=**=**=`.

@N(*range*) and @S(*range*)

@N and @S ensure that a cell contains numeric values or text values. These functions are important when you use other functions that operate on numeric values only or on text values only. When you are unsure whether a cell contains a numeric or text value, use @N or @S to force the contents to become a number or text.

@N forces the contents of a cell to be a number. If the cell contains a numeric value, @N returns that value. If the cell is blank or contains a label, @N returns the value `0`. @N always returns a numeric value.

@S forces the contents of a cell to text. If the cell contains text or a formula that evaluates to text, @S returns that text. If the cell contains a number or is empty, @S returns the null string (" "). @S always returns a text value.

These functions prevent formulas from resulting in `ERR` when data in a cell is not of the expected type.

The `range` argument must be a range or a single-cell reference. If you use a single-cell reference, 1-2-3 adjusts the argument to range format and returns the numeric or text value of the single cell. If the `range` argument is a multiple cell range, @N or @S returns the numeric or text value of the top-left corner of the range.

@STRING(*value,format*)

@STRING lets you convert a number to its text-string equivalent. @STRING formats this label as Fixed, Comma, Scientific, or General format, according to the `format` argument's value.

@STRING ignores all numeric formats placed on the cell you are converting and operates on just the numeric contents of the cell.

The *value* argument is any value. The `format` argument specifies how 1-2-3 should format the resulting label. The possible `format` arguments values are:

Value	Format
0 through 116	Fixed; with *value* decimal places
1000 through 1116	Comma; with *value*-1000 decimal places
-18 through -1	Scientific; with @ABS(*value*) digits
10001 through 10512	General; with up to *value*-10000 characters

Example: If cell A6 contains 12345.678, @STRING(A6,2) returns `12345.68`, @STRING(A6,1002) returns `12,345.68`, and @STRING(A6,-1) returns `1E+04`.

@VALUE(*text*)

@VALUE converts a number that is entered as text to a numeric value that can be used in calculations.

The `text` argument must be text or a label made up only of numbers and numeric formatting characters, such as the comma, decimal point, and dollar sign. The text cannot contain other alphabetical characters or an illegal number format (such as 1,23.99); it can include leading or trailing spaces and can begin with a currency symbol (such as $). Do not include spaces between the currency symbol and the numbers in the text.

A nice feature of @VALUE is that it converts text fractions to decimal numbers. This function is useful, therefore, for converting stock data from databases or wire services to numbers that you can analyze and chart.

Example: If cell A6 contains the label 2 3/4, @VALUE(A6) returns `2.75`.

@TRIM(*text*)

@TRIM eliminates unwanted blank spaces from the beginning, end, or middle of a text string. If a string contains multiple adjacent spaces, the function reduces them to one space.

@TRIM is useful for trimming spaces from data as it is entered into a macro or for trimming unwanted spaces from data in a database. Such spaces in a database can cause the sort order to be different from what you expect.

The `text` argument can be text enclosed in quotation marks, a formula that results in text, or a cell reference to a cell containing text or a formula resulting in text.

Example: If cell A6 contains the text `welcome back`, @TRIM(A6) returns `welcome back`.

@CLEAN(*text*)

When you import text into 1-2-3 from other programs, particularly files transmitted with a modem, the text sometimes contain nonprintable characters. @CLEAN removes the nonprintable characters from the text.

The `text` argument can be text enclosed in quotation marks, a formula that results in text, or a cell reference to a cell containing text or a formula resulting in text. 1-2-3 cannot accept a cell entry that contains @CLEAN with a range argument specified. ●

CHAPTER 7

Moving or Copying Data

by Jan Snyder

As you develop more and more sophisticated models on 1-2-3, you will need to duplicate or move data or formulas from one location to another. In this chapter, you learn some techniques for handling these procedures. You also learn about absolute and relative cell references and the part they play in copying formulas. ■

Move or copy data to a new location

Use drag and drop or the Windows Clipboard.

Move or copy a formula to a new location

1-2-3 automatically adjusts cell references for you.

Move or copy a format to a new location

Transfer various aspects of a cell's formatting and style attributes to another cell or range.

Change a cell reference in a formula so that it is absolute or mixed

Fine-tune your formulas for correct moving and copying.

Moving Data

1-2-3 provides a number of ways to move data, including dragging the cell or range with the mouse, using commands or shortcut keys from the Edit menu, and using SmartIcons.

In a move operation, the data being moved is called the *source*; the location to which you are moving the data is called the *target* or *destination*. When you move data, the source data disappears from its original location and reappears at the target location.

The following sections describe all the available methods used for moving and discuss how 1-2-3 handles the movement of formulas or data used in formulas and the movement of formatting and style attributes.

Remember that you can use the Edit, Undo command to correct a mistake in moving a range, press Ctrl+Z (Undo), or click the Undo SmartIcon.

Dragging a Range to a New Location

Dragging the cell or range is the simplest way to move data. You can use this technique to move a single cell or a range of cells to another location on the same worksheet, to another worksheet in the same workbook, or even to a range in another workbook. You cannot drag a collection (two or more separate ranges) with the mouse.

You also can drag and drop data between 1-2-3 and other programs that support OLE 2.0.

To drag a range to another location in a worksheet, first highlight the range you want to move and position the mouse pointer so it is at one of the edges of the range—anywhere other than the bottom-right corner of the cell or range. When you move the mouse pointer to the edge of a range, or to the edge of a single cell containing the cell pointer, the pointer changes to a hand (see fig. 7.1).

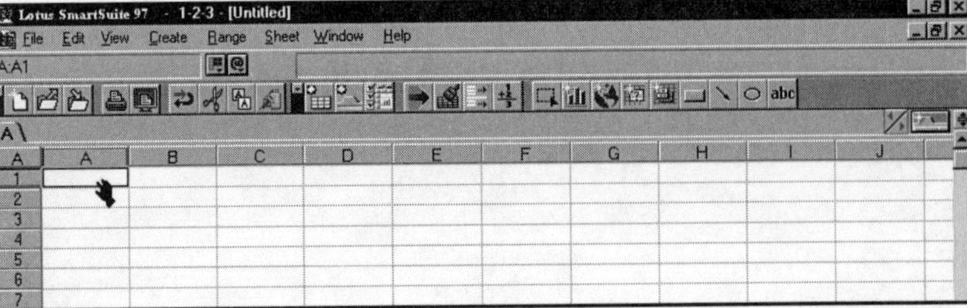

Fig. 7.1
When you move the mouse pointer to the edge—other than the bottom-right corner—of a cell or range, the mouse pointer changes to a hand.

Then, click and hold down the left mouse button.

When you click and hold down the left mouse button while the mouse pointer is shaped like a hand, the mouse pointer changes to a hand grasping a rectangle. This indicates that 1-2-3 is in drag mode. Drag the range to another location.

Often the new location will be on the same worksheet. If you want to drag to another worksheet in the workbook, you can have the other worksheet visible on the screen by using one of the View, Split options (refer to Chapter 15 for more information on View, Split), and then drag the range, as before, to the new worksheet.

If you move the mouse pointer to the bottom-right corner of a selected range, the mouse pointer changes shape, not to a hand, but to the drag-and-fill pointer, shown in figure 7.2. This pointer is used to fill ranges with data.

▶ **See** "Filling Ranges," **p. 72**

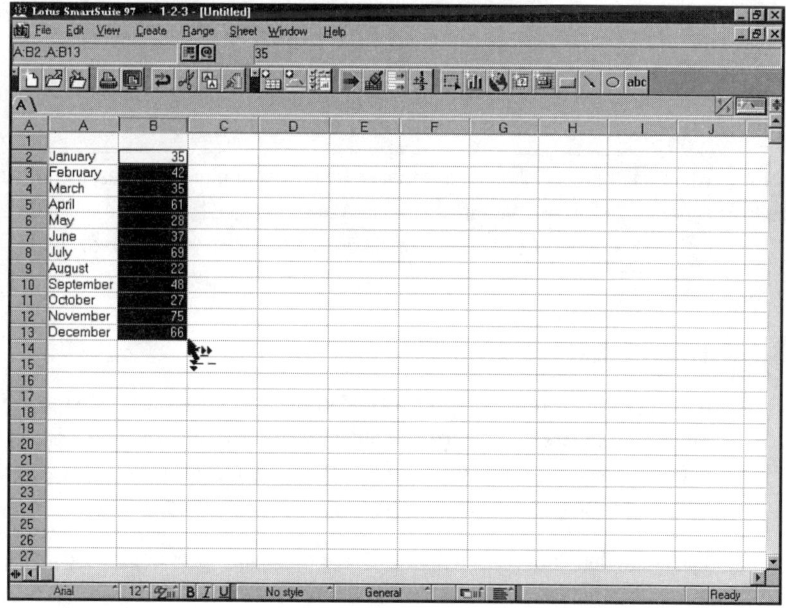

Fig. 7.2
At the bottom-right corner of a cell or selected range, the mouse pointer changes to drag-and-fill, not the correct pointer for dragging to a new location.

If you have not split the screen you can still drag information to another worksheet in the same workbook, but when the mouse pointer changes into a hand grasping a rectangle, drag to the tab indicating the worksheet on which you want the information placed. That worksheet appears and you can position the mouse pointer anywhere on that worksheet, and then release the mouse button when the data is positioned correctly.

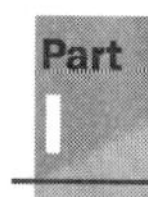

To drag information from one workbook to another, both workbooks must be open and visible on the screen. You can use the Window, Tile Left-Right; Window, Tile Top-Bottom; or Window, Cascade options to display both workbooks. When both workbooks are visible, you can drag a range from one workbook to the other, as discussed previously.

▶ **See** "Tiling Windows," **p. 37**

Occasionally, you may accidentally drag and drop a range onto another range that already contains information. If you are about to do so, 1-2-3 warns you by displaying the dialog box shown in figure 7.3.

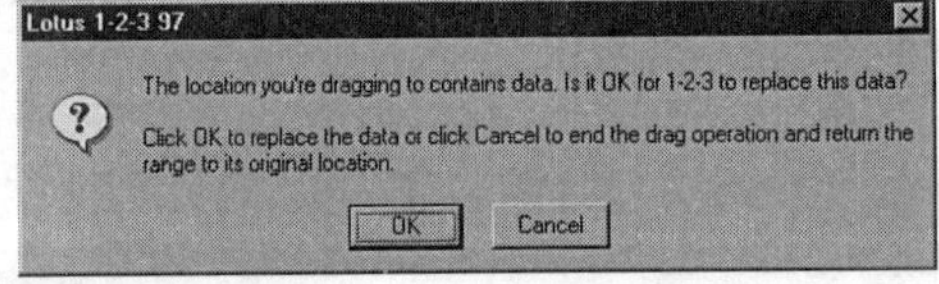

Fig. 7.3
The confirmation dialog box that appears if you attempt to drag and drop information onto a range that already contains information.

When you move a cell or a range that contains one or more formulas, the formulas stay intact. For example, say you have the formula +A1+B1 in cell C1. If you move cell C1 to C5, the formula in C5 will also be +A1+B1. The formula does not change when moved.

TROUBLESHOOTING

Nothing happens when I try to drag and drop. I don't even see the hand appear when I move the mouse pointer to the edge of a highlighted area. Drag and drop may not be enabled. To check to see whether it is, choose File, User Setup, 1-2-3 Preferences General tab. Under Options, the Drag and drop cells check box must be checked.

I accidentally "dragged and dropped" one range on top of another, and the new one overwrote what was originally there. Is there a way to prevent this from happening in the future? You can have 1-2-3 warn you if you are about to drag and drop information on top of other information. To do so, choose File, User Setup, 1-2-3 Preferences General tab. Under Options, click the check box to the left of Confirm overwrite for drag and drop. Click the OK button to make this warning mode the default.

Cutting and Pasting a Range

To move data by cutting and pasting, you cut the data from the worksheet to the Clipboard (a Windows holding area in memory), then you paste the data from the Clipboard to a new location in the same worksheet, to a different worksheet in the same workbook, to a different workbook, or to a different Windows application. You can move entire columns, rows, or worksheets with this method, but you cannot use this technique to move a column so it becomes a row, a row so it becomes a column, or a worksheet or workbook so it becomes a column or row.

You can paste data many times if you want to copy the same information to many different locations. If you want to copy data to many different places, however, do not interrupt the pasting operation by cutting or copying other data to the Clipboard. Pasting makes a copy of whatever is on the Clipboard, and only the contents of the most recent copy or cut operation are stored on the Clipboard.

To cut and paste data, follow these steps:

1. Highlight the range or cell you want to cut and paste.
2. Choose Edit, Cut, press Ctrl+X, or click the Cut SmartIcon.
3. Move the cell pointer to the first cell of the destination range.

4. Choose Edit, Paste, press Ctrl+V, or click on the Paste SmartIcon.
5. To paste the data in another location also, move the cell pointer or select the target range and either press Ctrl+V or click on the Paste SmartIcon. Pressing Enter does not paste the information in the new location, as is the case immediately after you have cut or copied information to the Clipboard.

You also can choose Cut, Copy, Paste, and Paste Special from the shortcut menu after clicking the right mouse button on the cell or range.

TROUBLESHOOTING

When I paste data, I don't get the correct information copied into the cells. Be certain when you copy or cut information to the Clipboard that you immediately paste it into the destination cells. If you don't do so immediately, you may inadvertently copy additional data to the Clipboard, wiping out what you meant to copy.

continues

continued

When I pasted data onto my worksheet, it overwrote other information that was already there. When you paste data onto your worksheet, it overwrites information already in that area. Be certain when you are pasting information onto your worksheet that there is adequate room into which to place the information. Otherwise, information is overwritten. If necessary, insert extra columns or rows to make room for your information.

Note that the Confirm overwrite of drag and drop warning discussed in the Troubleshooting note in the previous section does not apply to this paste/overwrite situation. Even if Confirm overwrite for drag and drop is checked, pasted data will still overwrite other information with no warning.

▶ **See** "Inserting Rows or Columns," **p. 85**

Moving a Formula

If you move one corner of a range used in a formula, the range expands or contracts and the formula is adjusted. Figure 7.4 shows a range of data that includes formulas. Figure 7.5 shows what happens after you move the range F2..H6 to G2. Notice that 1-2-3 adjusted the range in the @SUM formula (shown in the contents box of the edit line in both figures). In figure 7.4, the formula in cell G3 is @SUM(D3..F3). The move changed the formula (now in cell H3) to @SUM(D3..G3). The @SUM in both formulas starts with cell D3. Because this cell did not move, that portion of the range was not altered. But, the @SUM range expanded to include D3..G3. A common use of this kind of range movement is to make room for a new row or column in the range of data.

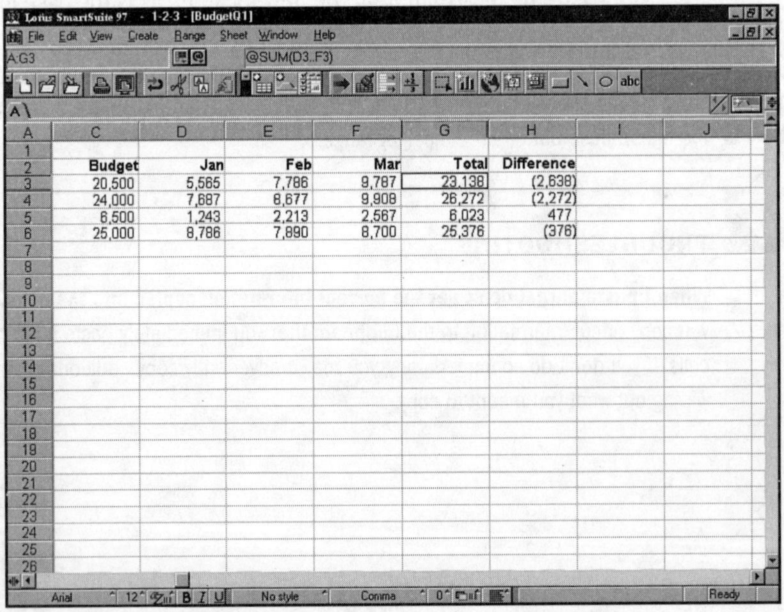

Fig. 7.4
A worksheet before cells F2..H6 are moved to cell G2.

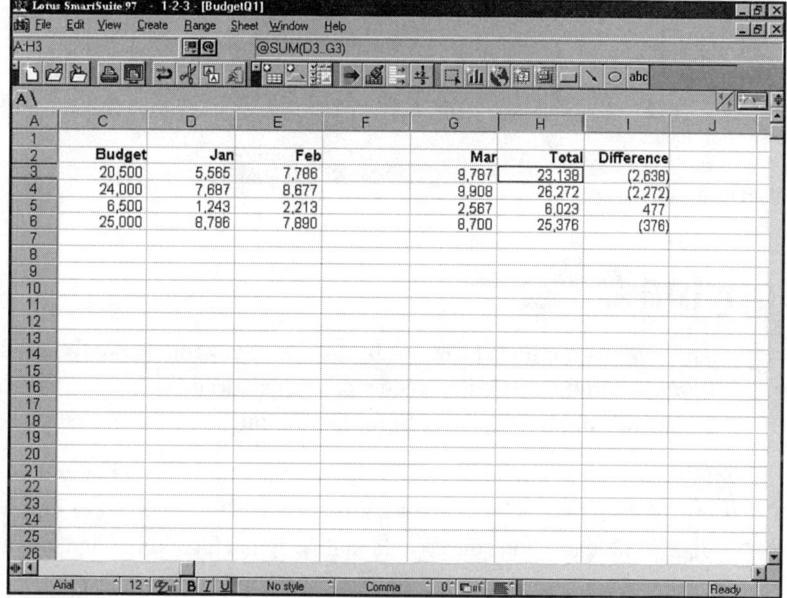

Fig. 7.5
Notice how the @SUM formula, now in cell H3, changes after cells F2..H6 are moved to G2.

If you move the range G2..I6 in figure 7.5 back to cell F2, the formula reverts to the one shown in figure 7.4. ERR does not appear even though part of the range is eliminated.

> **CAUTION**
>
> Be careful when moving cells that are referenced in formulas without also moving the formulas. If you move a portion of a range without its formula, the resulting formula might not be accurate.

Moving Formats and Data Types

If you want to move just the formatting and style attributes of a cell or range to another cell or range, choose Edit, Paste Special instead of Edit, Paste. In the Paste Special dialog box, shown in figure 7.6, you can select one or more of the following check boxes:

- *Contents* pastes the contents of the selection.
- *Formulas as values* converts formulas into values when pasting.

- *Styles and number formats* pastes the styles and number formats of the selection.
- *Borders* pastes the same borders as in the selection.
- *Cell Comments* pastes the cell comments from the selection.

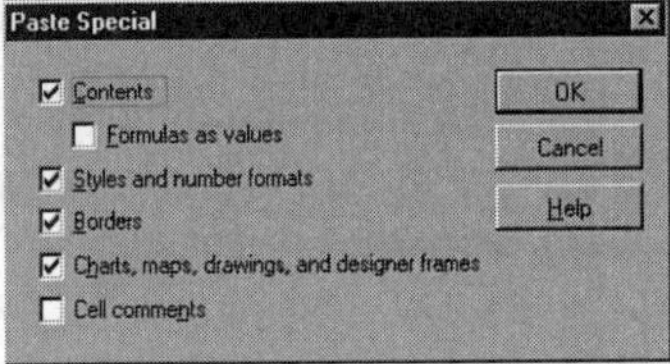

Fig. 7.6
The Paste Special dialog box enables you to move the format and style attributes of a cell or a range to another location.

Copying Data

The copying methods provided by 1-2-3 are very much like the methods used for moving described in the preceding sections. You can drag the cell or range with the mouse, use commands or shortcut keys from the Edit menu, or use SmartIcons.

In a copy operation, just as in a move operation, the data being copied is called the *source*; the location to which you move the data is called the *target* or *destination*. When you copy data, 1-2-3 leaves the source data in its original location and places a copy of the data in the target location—in other words, the copied data appears in both places. Copied data includes the same labels and values—as well as the same formats, fonts, colors, protection status, and borders—as the original data. You do not, however, copy the column width or row height. You can use Edit, Copy with Edit, Paste Special to paste only some of the properties or types of data that were copied.

Remember that you can use the Edit, Undo command to correct a mistake in copying a range, press Ctrl+Z (Undo), or click the Undo SmartIcon.

Whenever you need to copy data, the drag and drop technique is probably the right choice. The Edit, Copy command is primarily for copying data to and from other applications or when you want to copy the same data to a number of different locations. The Edit, Copy command is also helpful when dragging would be tedious because you're copying data across large areas of the worksheet.

Copying is one of the most frequently performed actions in 1-2-3, and the copy operation can be simple and straightforward or more complex. The following sections begin with basic examples of copy procedures and progress to more complex ones.

Copying with Drag and Drop

Copying a cell or range by using drag and drop is very similar to moving data by using drag and drop. The only difference is that you press the Ctrl key as you drag to the new location to copy.

To copy a cell or range by using the drag and drop technique, follow these steps:

1. Highlight the cell or range you want to copy.
2. Move the mouse pointer to any edge of the selection, other than the lower-right corner, so the mouse pointer changes to a hand.
3. Press and hold the Ctrl key as you click and drag the selection to its new location.
4. When you reach the destination, release the mouse button and the Ctrl key. The data is copied to the new location without changing the original.

If you have activated Confirm overwrite for the drag and drop option in the General panel of the 1-2-3 Preferences dialog box, your drag and drop copy process will overwrite already existing information. You see the warning shown in figure 7.3 and have to confirm that you want to complete the process.

Copying with the Clipboard

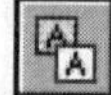

You can use commands and SmartIcons to copy data. The Edit, Copy command and the Copy SmartIcon use the Clipboard to copy data. No dialog box appears; 1-2-3 just copies the source data to the Clipboard. Notice that when you copy data to the Clipboard, the 1-2-3 title bar displays the message `Select destination and press ENTER or choose Edit Paste`. To complete the copying action, you paste the source data with the Edit, Paste command or the Paste SmartIcon, or you can press Enter. You also can copy data from and to other Windows applications by using the Edit, Copy and Edit, Paste commands.

To copy data with commands or SmartIcons, follow these steps:

1. Highlight the range or cell you want to copy.

2. Choose Edit, Copy, press Ctrl+Ins or Ctrl+C, or click the Copy SmartIcon.
3. Move the cell pointer to the first cell of the destination range.

4. Press Enter, choose Edit, Paste, press Ctrl+V, or click the Paste SmartIcon.

Pressing Enter to paste information in a new location only works *immediately* after you copy information to the Clipboard. If you perform *any* other task, such as entering new data, deleting information, and so on, the press Enter to paste information option becomes inoperative, and you must complete the task by using one of the other pasting techniques, Edit, Paste, press Ctrl+V, or click the Paste SmartIcon.

Copying Formulas

The real power of copying becomes evident when you copy formulas. When you copy a formula, 1-2-3 adjusts the new formula so that its cell references are in the same location relative to the original formula. *Relative addressing* is one of the most important concepts in 1-2-3.

The best way to understand relative addressing is to understand how 1-2-3 stores addresses in formulas. The formula @SUM(A1..A5) means to add the contents of all the cells in the range from cell A1 to cell A5, but that's not the way 1-2-3 stores it. If this formula is in cell A6, for example, 1-2-3 reads the formula as "Add the contents of the five cells directly above this one," as illustrated in figure 7.7. When you copy this formula from cell A6 to cell B6, 1-2-3 uses the same relative formula but displays it as @SUM(B1..B5), as shown in figure 7.8.

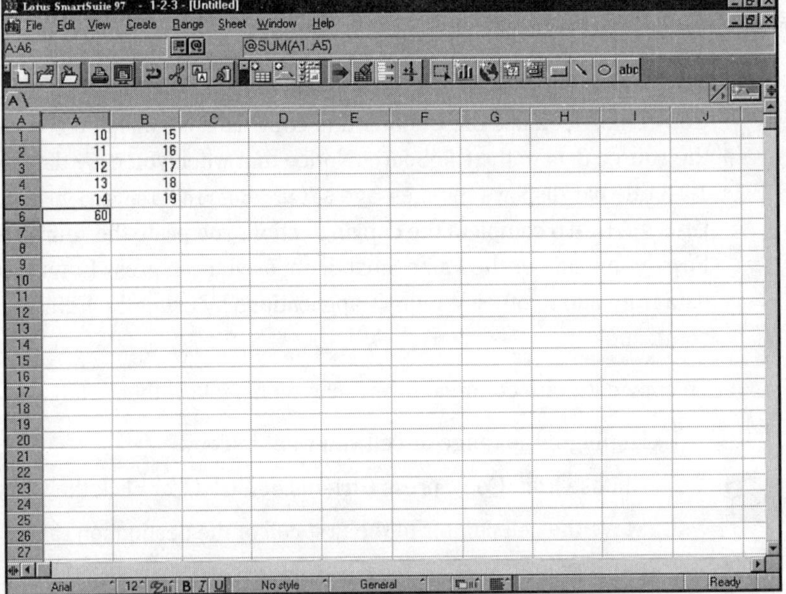

Fig. 7.7
1-2-3 interprets the formula in cell A6 as "Add the contents of the five cells directly above this one."

In most cases, when you copy a formula, you want the addresses adjusted automatically. At times, however, you do not want some addresses to be adjusted, or you may want only part of an address to be adjusted. These cases are examined in the next sections.

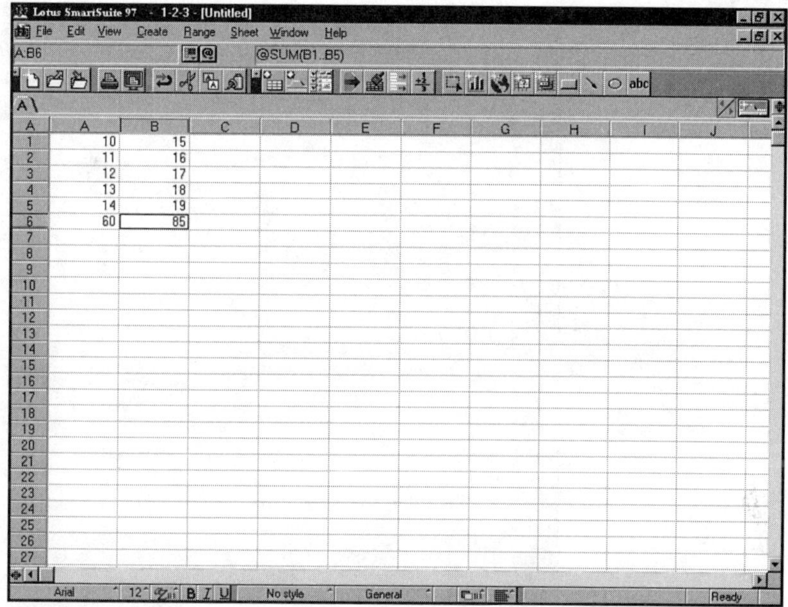

Fig. 7.8
When the formula in cell A6 is copied to cell B6, 1-2-3 maintains the same relative interpretation, "Add the contents of the five cells directly above this one."

You can use drag-and-fill to copy a formula to an adjacent range. With the cell pointer on the formula to be copied, position the mouse pointer in the lower-right corner of the cell, where it changes to a drag-and-fill pointer (as shown in figure 7.2, not the hand pointer). Click and drag to copy the formula to the adjacent range. 1-2-3 adjusts the formulas according to the cell addressing you have entered.

Copying a Formula with Absolute Addressing In figure 7.9, the formula in cell D9 is +D7/G7. This figure represents January's sales as a percent of the total. 1-2-3 interprets this formula as "Take the number two rows above this cell (D7), and divide it by the number two rows above and three columns to the right of this cell (G7)."

Suppose you want to figure out February's sales as a percent of the total sales. If you copy the formula in cell D9 to cell E9, the resulting formula is +E7/H7, which maintains the same relative interpretation as the original formula, as shown in figure 7.10. The E7 part of the formula, which represents the sales for February, is correct. The H7 portion (which refers to the difference between the budgeted amount and the actual amount), however, is incorrect, even though it is two rows above and three columns to the right of the cell containing the formula.

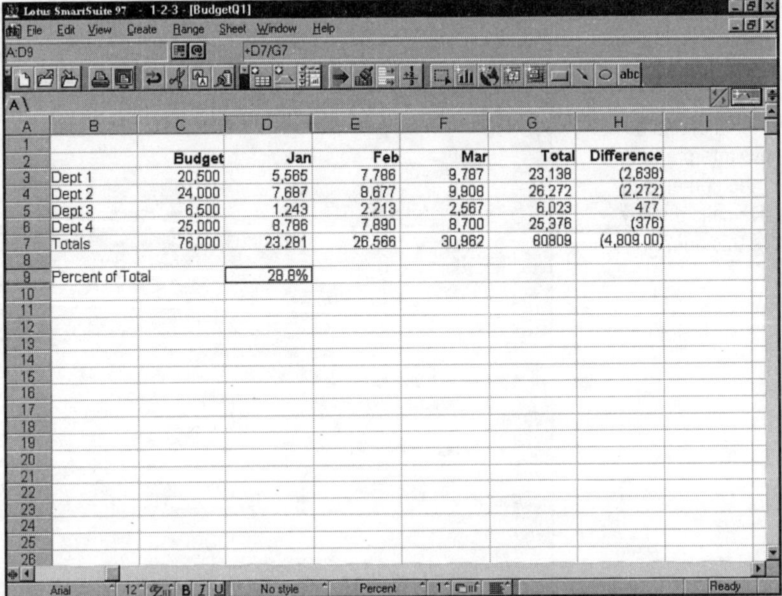

Fig. 7.9
A formula with a relative address.

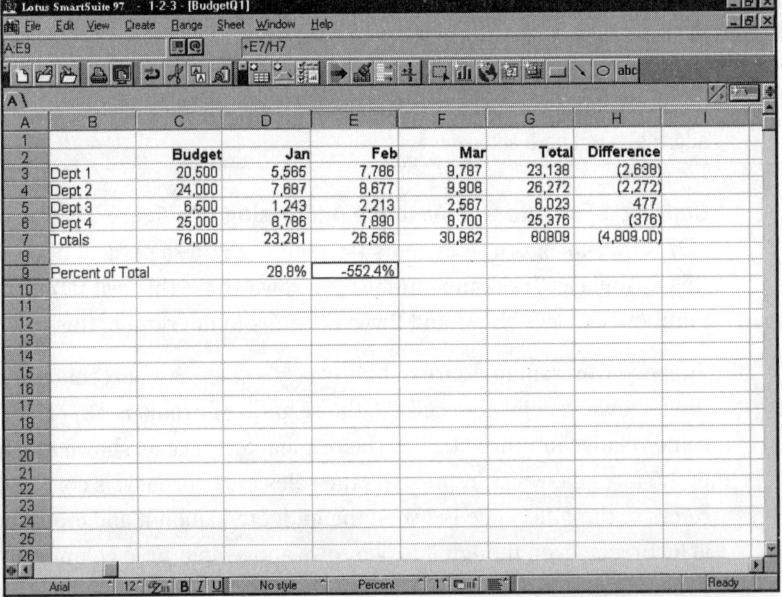

Fig. 7.10
When a formula containing relative references is copied, the relative relationships are maintained, even if they should not be.

To solve this problem, you must copy the G7 address (the total sales) as an *absolute address* when you copy the formula from cell D9 so that the G7 address (the total sales) doesn't change.

To specify an absolute address, type a dollar sign ($) before each part of the address (worksheet, column, and row) you want to remain absolutely the same. The formula in cell D9 should be +D7/$G$7. When you copy this formula to cell E9, the formula becomes +E7/$G$7.

You also can specify an absolute address without typing dollar signs. After you type (or point to) the address, press F4 (Abs); the address changes to absolute. After copying the absolute formula +D7/$G$7 in cell D9 to cells E9..G9, the worksheet appears as shown in figure 7.11.

If you make an error and forget to make an address absolute, *be sure the cell pointer is in the correct cell and* press F2 (Edit), move the insertion point in the contents box to the address you want to make absolute, and press F4 (Abs).

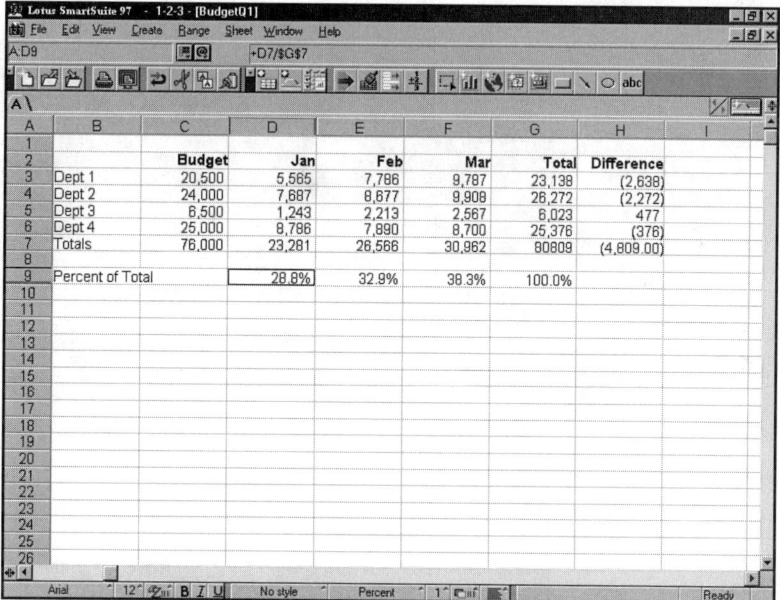

Fig. 7.11
The result after copying a formula with an absolute address.

If you want to change an absolute reference back to a relative reference, press F2 (Edit), move the insertion point to the reference, and then press F4 (Abs) as many times as necessary until the address contains no dollar signs. Press Enter to reenter the formula. You can also edit a formula containing dollar signs by deleting the dollar signs as you would any other character.

Copying a Formula with Mixed Addressing In some cases, you must use formulas with a mix of absolute and relative references if you want the formula to copy correctly. The example presented in this section shows you how to keep a row reference absolute while letting the column reference change during the copy.

Figure 7.12 shows a price-forecasting worksheet with a different price increase percentage for each year. When you copy the formula in cell C3 down column C, you do not want the reference to cell C1 to change, but when you copy the formula across row 3, you want the reference to change for each column. The mixed reference is relative for the column and absolute for the row. The formula in cell C3 is +B3*(1+C$1). When you copy this formula down one row to cell C4, the formula becomes +B4*(1+C$1). The relative address B3 becomes B4, but the mixed address C$1 is unchanged. When you copy this formula to cell D3, the formula becomes +C3*(1+D$1). The relative address B3 becomes C3, and the mixed address C$1 becomes D$1. You can copy this mixed-address formula from cell C3 to C3..F10 for correct results throughout the worksheet.

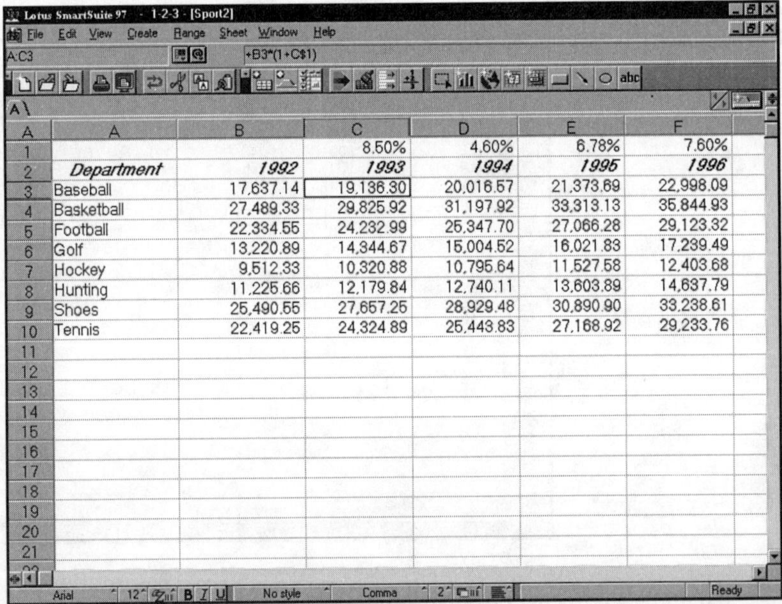

Fig. 7.12
A formula with a mixed address.

To make an address mixed without typing the dollar signs, use F4 (Abs). The first time you press F4, the address becomes absolute. If you continue to press F4, the address cycles through all the possible mixed addresses and returns to relative. The complete list of relative, absolute, and mixed addresses is found in Table 7.1. To change the relative address C1 to the mixed address C$1 shown in figure 7.12, press F4 twice.

Table 7.1 Using F4 (Abs) to Change the Address Type

Address	Status
$A:$D$1	Completely absolute
$A:D$1	Absolute worksheet and row
$A:$D1	Absolute worksheet and column
$A:D1	Absolute worksheet
A:$D$1	Absolute column and row
A:D$1	Absolute row
A:$D1	Absolute column
A:D1	Relative

When you work with multiple worksheets, be careful with absolute and mixed addresses. When you first press F4, the worksheet label is made absolute. In many cases, you do not want this effect. Consider the worksheet in figure 7.12. If you changed the formula in cell C3 to +B3*(1+$A:C$1), the absolute address of the worksheet identifier (the $A: part of the formula) would force the C$1 reference to remain in worksheet A. If you planned to expand this model to multiple worksheets, you would want each worksheet to reference the growth range for that worksheet. You would want the worksheet letter to change relative to its new worksheet; therefore, you would want the formula to use the mixed address A:C$1, not $A:C$1, so that the A: worksheet is not always referenced as you copy to other worksheets. In this case, the correct formula to place in cell C3 before copying it would be +B3*(1+A:C$1).

Copying One Cell to a Range

When copying and pasting, you can copy a single cell to a range of cells by highlighting the destination range before using the Edit, Paste command.

▶ **See** "Working with Cells and Ranges," **p. 55**

You also can copy a single cell to larger ranges in multiple rows and columns. In the price-forecasting model in figure 7.13, the current prices are in column B. The formula in cell C3 increases the price by the percentage in cell B1. To copy this formula throughout the table in worksheet A, use Edit, Copy to copy cell C3 to the Clipboard, select range C3..F10, and then choose Edit, Paste to paste the Clipboard contents to the selected range. Figure 7.14 shows the result.

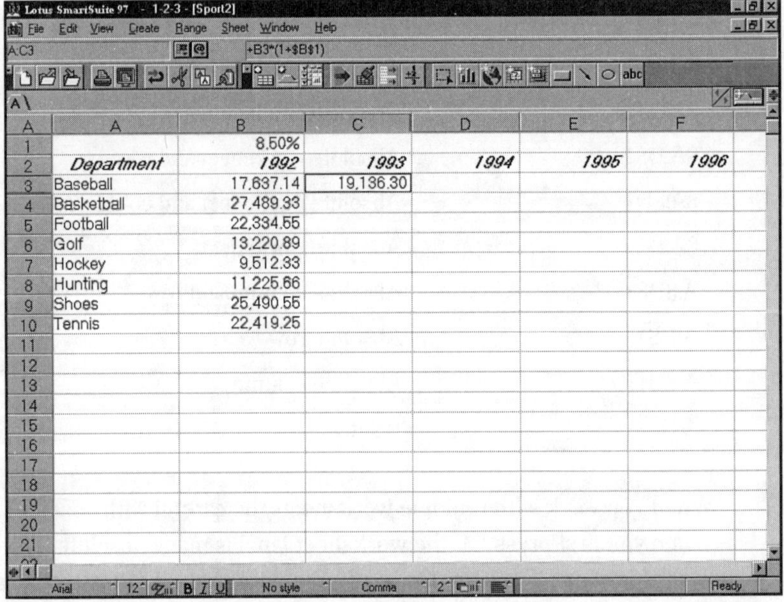

Fig. 7.13
A formula in cell C3 before being copied.

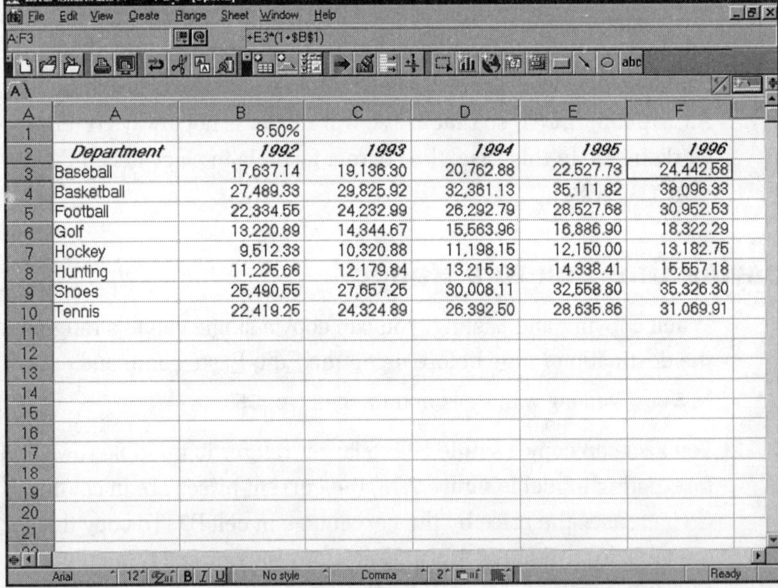

Fig. 7.14
The results of copying cell C3 to the range C3..F10.

In addition, you can copy a cell to multiple rows and columns in different worksheets. For example, if the same price-forecasting model for different departments is found in different worksheets, you can fill in multiple worksheets with one three-dimensional copy. Just copy the original cell, and then select a three-dimensional range as the destination for the Edit, Paste command.

You can copy a range of cells to a bigger range by copying the original range and then selecting the bigger range before you perform the paste.

If you want to copy a cell across a row or down a column, you might find the Edit, Copy Right and Edit, Copy Down commands useful. Just highlight the original cell and any blank cells to the right or below; then use the Edit, Copy Right or Edit, Copy Down command to copy the cell into the blank area. You can also use the following SmartIcons for this purpose:

Use...	**To...**
	Copy Topmost Row to Range (same as Edit, Copy Down)
	Copy Leftmost Column to Range (same as Edit, Copy Right)
	Copy Top Left Cell to Range (row or column)

Using Paste Special to Copy Styles

When you use the Edit, Copy command, 1-2-3 copies all aspects of the cell or range, including the underlying values and the formats. If you want to paste only one aspect of the copied data, use the Edit, Paste Special command instead of Edit, Paste. The Paste Special command enables you to copy just the formatting of cells instead of data and formats. Formatting includes the following attributes: cell format, font, border (including lines and drop shadows), color, and shading.

You also can choose the Formulas as Values option to convert formulas into their underlying values when pasting. This option can be useful when you have to reference the values elsewhere in the worksheet without the underlying formulas in place.

CAUTION

1-2-3 does not recalculate formulas before it converts the formulas to values. If recalculation is set to manual or if the Calc indicator appears in the status bar, press F9 (Calc), click the Calc button in the status bar, or click the Recalculate SmartIcon before you use the Formulas as Values option.

TROUBLESHOOTING

The Paste command is grayed out when I try to use it. You haven't copied anything to the Clipboard. The Edit, Paste command is only available if you previously used either the Edit, Copy or the Edit, Cut commands (or their keyboard shortcuts or the corresponding SmartIcons) to place something on the Clipboard.

Transposing Ranges

The Range, Transpose command and Transpose Data SmartIcon provide another way to copy data. This operation converts rows to columns or columns to rows and changes formulas to values at the same time. In figure 7.15, the range A1..H9 is to be transposed to the range A12..I19.

To perform the transposition,

1. Highlight the range from which you want to transpose data, in this case, A1..H9.
2. Select Range, Transpose, or click on the Transpose SmartIcon, if it appears on the current SmartIcon palette.
3. The Transpose dialog box, shown in figure 7.15 appears. This dialog box provides the Transpose the range and Put the results in text boxes.
4. In the Put the results in text box, indicate the top-left corner of the range where you want the transposed data placed. In this example, the location is cell A12.
5. The resulting transposed information is shown in figure 7.16; the rows and columns are transposed, and the formulas in row 9 become numbers in column I.

The Range, Transpose command copies formats, fonts, colors, and shading but does not copy shadow boxes or border lines.

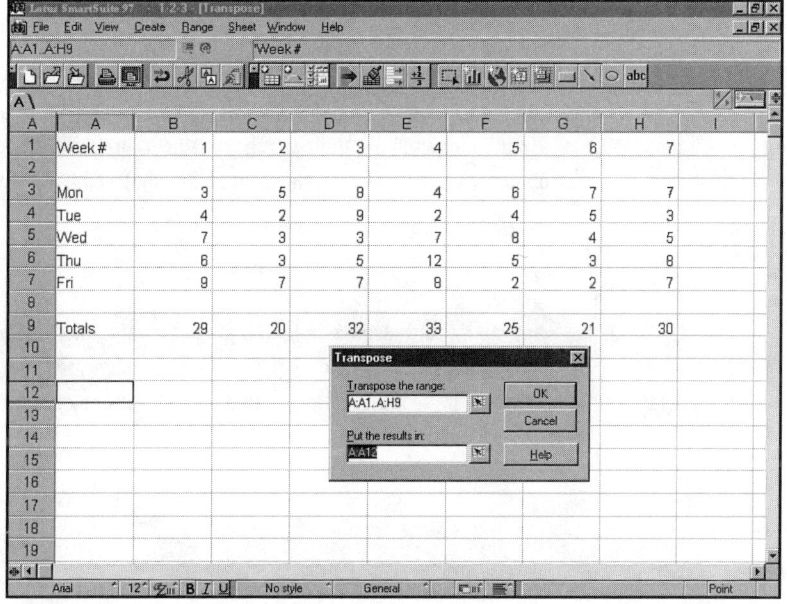

Fig. 7.15
The Transpose dialog box used to transpose the range A1..H9 to A12.

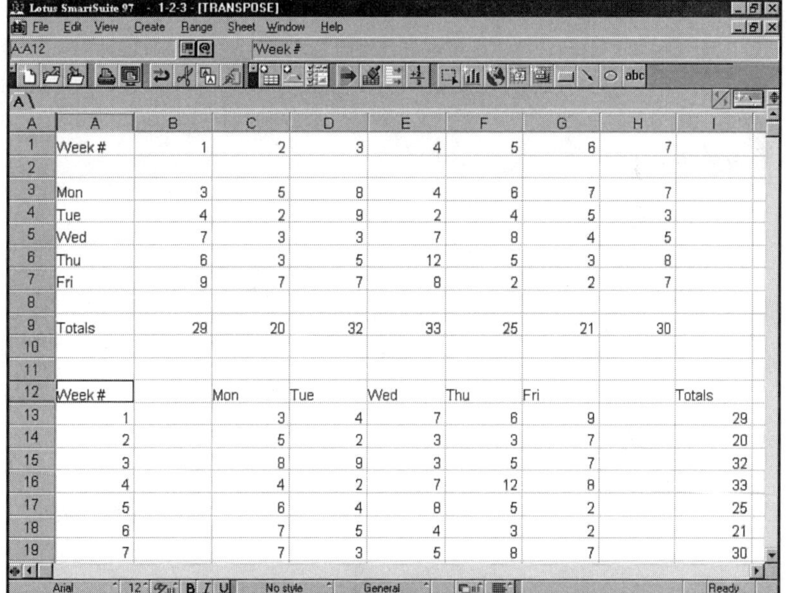

Fig. 7.16
The result of transposing A1..H9 to the range A12..I19. Only the top-left corner of the To range (A12) needs to be specified.

CAUTION

Range, Transpose doesn't recalculate the worksheet before transposing data. You can freeze incorrect values if you execute the command without recalculating. Always recalculate the worksheet before you transpose a range. If the range you are transposing contains formulas linked to data in other workbooks, you must update these formulas by choosing Edit, Manage Links.

CAUTION

1-2-3 does not warn you if you transpose data to a range that already contains information. 1-2-3 overwrites information already in the range when you do so. Be sure you have adequate blank space in the range to which you are transposing data so you don't inadvertently overwrite other information.

CHAPTER 8

Reorganizing Worksheets

by Joyce J. Nielsen

By default, a new workbook in 1-2-3 includes a single worksheet. However, you can use as many as 256 worksheets in a single workbook. With multiple-sheet workbooks, you can organize your data more efficiently than you can using a single worksheet. For example, you can create a separate worksheet for each sales region, and then consolidate sales figures in a worksheet that calculates total sales for all regions. You might also create 12 separate worksheets to track company activity for each month of the year, and then create a 13th worksheet to consolidate those figures into a yearly report.

This chapter teaches you the basics of creating and managing multiple-worksheet files. ■

Inserting and deleting worksheets

1-2-3 enables you to insert worksheets in a workbook, including as many as 256 total worksheets. You also can delete any worksheet in a workbook.

Renaming individual worksheets

You can assign descriptive names to your worksheets, such as *Sales* or *Budget Information*.

Grouping worksheets

If you temporarily group multiple worksheets, you can then apply formatting changes that automatically affect all worksheets in the group.

Inserting and Deleting Worksheets

Just as you can insert and delete columns and rows in a worksheet, you also can insert and delete any worksheet in a workbook. As you create new workbooks, you may find that you want to expand the workbook to include more information by adding one or more worksheets. Or, you may want to delete a worksheet that you no longer need. The following sections show you how to perform these tasks.

Display the Sheet SmartIcon bar if you need to make multiple changes to the structure of your workbooks. Choose File, User Setup, SmartIcons Setup. Then, select Sheet from the Bar Name drop-down list and choose OK.

Inserting a Worksheet

To insert one worksheet at a time *after* the current worksheet, click the New Sheet button at the top-right corner of the worksheet window (see fig. 8.1). Each time you click the New Sheet button, a new worksheet is added to the workbook. You should only insert as many worksheets as you think you will need, however, because each worksheet you add requires additional memory. In the section titled "Renaming Worksheets," later in this chapter, you will learn how to assign unique names to each worksheet.

You can use the Create Sheet dialog box to insert multiple worksheets at a time, either before or after the current worksheet.

NOTE The Create Sheet dialog box provides the only method for inserting one or more worksheets *before* the current worksheet.

To insert a worksheet using the Create Sheet dialog box, follow these steps:

1. Choose Create, Sheet. The Create Sheet dialog box appears (see fig. 8.1).

You also can click the Create a Sheet SmartIcon (which appears on the Sheet SmartIcon bar) to display the Create Sheet dialog box.

2. In the Number of Sheets text box, type the number of worksheets you want to insert, or use the scroll arrows to select the desired number. Remember that a workbook can contain no more than 256 worksheets.

3. In the Place area, select the After Current Sheet option button to insert the specified number of sheets after the current worksheet; or select the Before Current Sheet option button to insert the sheet(s) before the current worksheet.
4. Click OK.

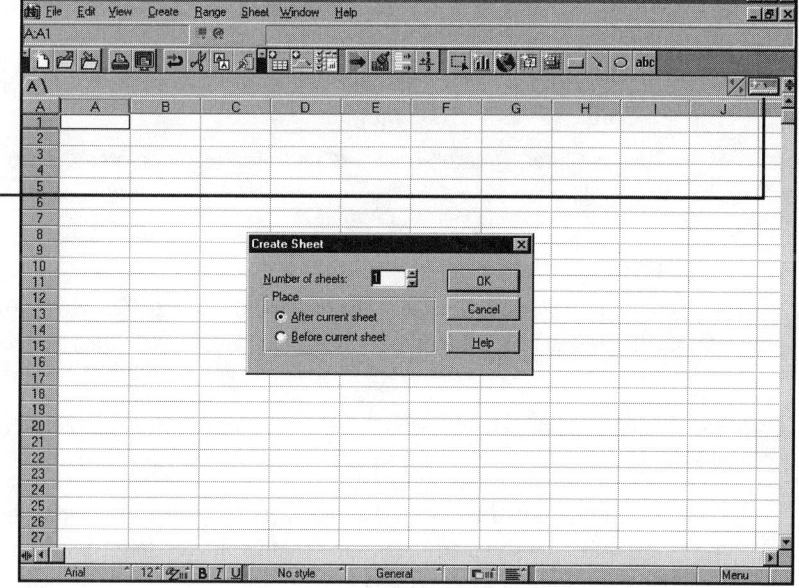

Fig. 8.1
Use the Create Sheet dialog box to insert more than one worksheet at a time.

When you insert a worksheet or worksheets, 1-2-3 assigns new worksheet letters to all the worksheets behind the worksheets you insert. For example, if you insert a new worksheet after worksheet A, and worksheet B already exists, the new worksheet becomes B, the former worksheet B becomes worksheet C, and so on. 1-2-3 also adjusts all addresses and formulas in the worksheets automatically.

If you insert a worksheet within a formula range that spans worksheets, the range expands automatically to accommodate the new worksheet. Formulas referring to that range include the new cells. However, if you insert a worksheet after a range that spans worksheets A, B, and C, the new worksheet (D) will not be considered part of the range unless you redefine the range.

Deleting a Worksheet

When you erase a range in a worksheet with Edit, Clear or Edit, Cut, the cells still exist in the worksheet, but they are empty. In contrast, when you delete a worksheet, 1-2-3 removes the entire worksheet and moves other existing worksheets to fill the gap created by the deletion. 1-2-3 also updates all cell addresses and range names used in formulas.

▶ **See** "Understanding Workbooks and Worksheets," **p. 46**

To delete a worksheet, follow these steps:

1. Select the worksheet(s) you want to delete.
2. Choose Sheet, Delete Sheet. 1-2-3 automatically deletes the worksheet(s) you selected.

CAUTION

Be sure you have correctly selected the worksheets you want to delete before you choose the Sheet, Delete Sheet command. 1-2-3 does not prompt you before deleting the selected worksheets.

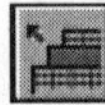

You also can use the Delete Selected Sheets SmartIcon to automatically delete all selected worksheets.

When you delete a worksheet, 1-2-3 moves up the remaining worksheets, and adjusts the range references in formulas. For example, if you delete worksheet A, the formula +B:C3+B:C6 becomes +A:C3+A:C6.

If you delete worksheets that are part of a named range, the named range then includes a smaller range of worksheets. If you delete an entire named range, 1-2-3 deletes the range and its name so that formulas that refer to that range name result in an ERR message.

Use the Undo SmartIcon or choose Edit, Undo to reverse a worksheet deletion.

TROUBLESHOOTING

When I delete a worksheet, some of the formulas in my other worksheets evaluate to ERR.
Before you delete a worksheet, make sure that none of the formulas in the remaining worksheets rely on values in the worksheet to be deleted. Undo the worksheet deletion (if it is not too late) and modify the formulas, as necessary.

Renaming Worksheets

By default, 1-2-3 names the worksheets you add to a workbook A, B, C, and so on. It includes these worksheet names on the worksheet tabs. However, you can give worksheets meaningful names to make it easier to navigate to different parts of a multiple-worksheet file. For example, you might name the worksheet that includes first quarter sales totals *Quarter 1*, the worksheet for the second quarter *Quarter 2*, and so on. You might also name a fifth consolidation worksheet *Annual Total* (see fig. 8.2).

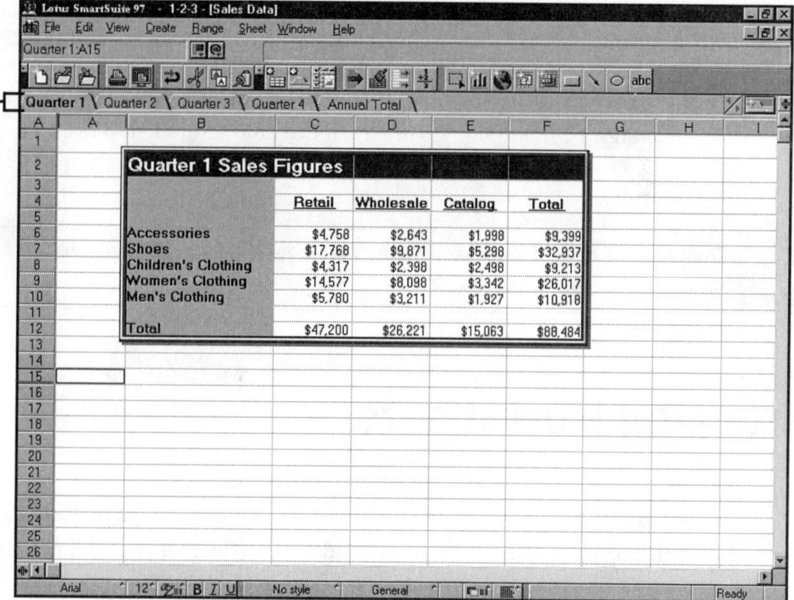

Fig. 8.2 This workbook includes multiple worksheets with descriptive worksheet names.

▶ **See** "Applying Different Colors to the Worksheet Tabs," **p. 756**

To rename a worksheet, double-click the worksheet tab, type the new name, and then press Enter. You also can rename a worksheet using the Basics tab of the Sheet Properties InfoBox. A name can be as many as 15 characters long, but it's best to use something short and descriptive so that you and any other users that share the file can navigate easily from worksheet to worksheet. You can use the Basics tab of the Sheet Properties InfoBox to distinguish the worksheets even further by applying different colors to the worksheet tabs.

1-2-3 automatically names worksheets you insert before or after a worksheet whose name 1-2-3 recognizes as part of a fill sequence. For more information about fill sequences, see "Filling Ranges" in Chapter 3.

When you name a worksheet, remember these rules:

- Avoid ambiguous names, such as C:, because 1-2-3 does not distinguish between upper- and lowercase letters in names and might confuse a worksheet of that name with the third worksheet in a file (worksheet C).
- Don't create worksheet names that resemble cell addresses, @function names, key names, or macro commands.
- Don't start a worksheet name with an exclamation point (!), a dollar sign ($), or the at sign (@), and don't use any of the characters listed here in a worksheet name:

  + * – / & > ^ < @ # { ? (,) =

To restore the original letter name of the worksheet (for example, A), double-click the tab, press Delete or Backspace, and press Enter.

Grouping Worksheets

With 1-2-3, you can group contiguous worksheets in a worksheet file so that settings you make to one worksheet affect all the other selected worksheets. This feature is especially useful when you are creating consolidated worksheets that all use the same worksheet layout.

You can use the group feature to apply the following settings to grouped worksheets simultaneously:

- Number formats
- Font and text attributes
- Text alignment
- Colors
- Column width
- Row height
- Protection settings
- Frozen worksheet titles
- Page breaks
- Outlines

To group worksheets, follow these steps:

1. Choose Sheet, Group Sheets. The Group Sheets dialog box appears (see fig. 8.3).

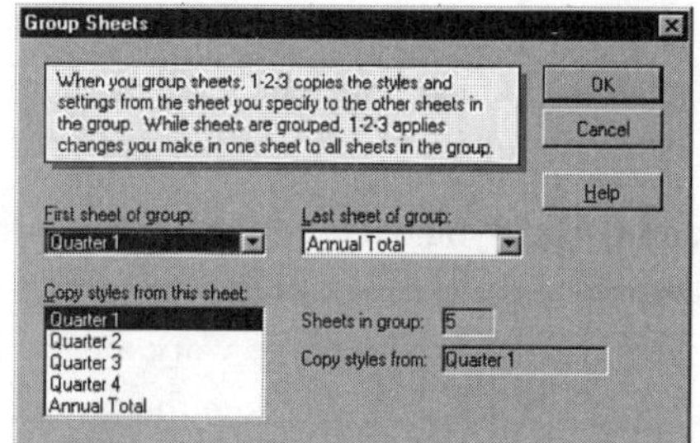

Fig. 8.3
Use the Group Sheets dialog box to specify which worksheets you want to group.

2. In the First Sheet of Group drop-down list, select the first worksheet you want to group.
3. In the Last Sheet of Group drop-down list, select the last worksheet you want to group.
4. In the Copy Styles from This Sheet list box, select the worksheet whose formatting you want to apply to the group of worksheets.
5. Click OK.

When you close the dialog box, the names on the worksheet tabs of the grouped worksheets appear in italics. In addition, the Group mode (Grp) indicator appears in the status bar at the bottom of the screen when one of the grouped worksheets is current (see fig. 8.4).

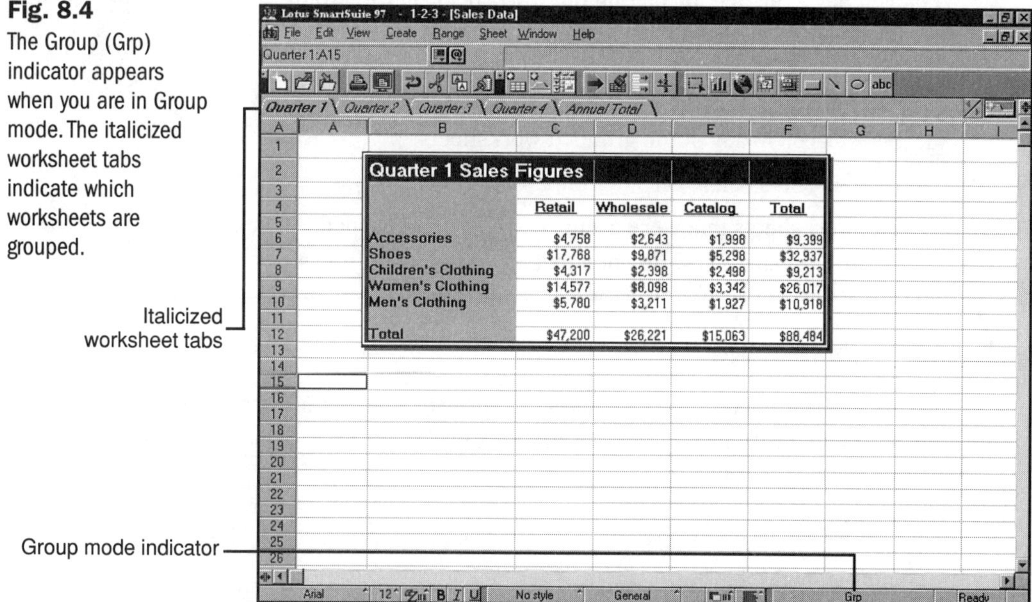

Fig. 8.4
The Group (Grp) indicator appears when you are in Group mode. The italicized worksheet tabs indicate which worksheets are grouped.

When you select a cell or range in one worksheet in a group, 1-2-3 selects the same area in all of the worksheets in that group. When you format a cell or range in one worksheet, the corresponding cell or range is formatted in all of the other grouped worksheets.

Similarly, if 1-2-3 is in Group mode, and you use a command that prompts you for a cell address or range, 1-2-3 does not need the address of the three-dimensional selection that spans the group—it just needs the range in one of the worksheets. When you complete the command, the effect takes place in all worksheets in the group, even though you only referred to cells in one of the worksheets.

If you add a worksheet within an existing group using the Create, Sheet command or the New Sheet button, the new worksheet takes on the formatting and attributes of the active worksheet. However, 1-2-3 does not copy any data from the active worksheet in a group to the other worksheets; it only copies cell formats and attributes. If Group mode is not selected before you insert a new worksheet, 1-2-3 does not copy the current worksheet's formats and settings to the new worksheet.

CAUTION

Be careful not to lose important data while worksheets are grouped. For example, if Group mode is active and you delete rows or columns in one worksheet, you will also delete the same rows or columns in all the other worksheets in the group.

When you have finished formatting the worksheets in the group, you will want to ungroup the worksheets to begin entering data.

To ungroup worksheets, follow these steps:

1. Select a cell in any of the grouped worksheets.
2. Choose Sheet, Clear Sheet Group.

   The worksheets that were grouped are now ungrouped. Any changes you make to a single worksheet now do not affect any other worksheets.

TROUBLESHOOTING

When I type data into one of the worksheets in a grouped worksheet file, nothing appears in the other worksheets. Group mode does not duplicate data you enter–it only duplicates formatting and style changes.

I want to reformat my consolidation worksheet so that the totals are more prominent. However, I want to keep the formatting of the other, monthly worksheets the same. To reformat a single worksheet, you need to turn off Group mode so that the formatting changes apply to one worksheet only. To turn off Group mode, select a cell in one of the grouped worksheets, and then choose Sheet, Clear Sheet Group.

CHAPTER 9

Managing Files

by Jan Snyder

The commands on the 1-2-3 File menu provide many capabilities for file management, modification, and protection. Some commands, such as File, Open; File, Save; and File, Save As; are similar to commands in other Windows applications. Other commands are related to specific 1-2-3 tasks and applications. This chapter discusses the File commands and good file management techniques for 1-2-3. ■

Create and open workbooks

Start with a blank workbook, choose a SmartMaster template, or open an existing workbook. Open files from other programs, too.

Close and save workbooks

Use the new long file names to better describe your workbook contents. Save files in other formats.

Enter and display workbook information

Describe the workbook and display workbook statistics.

Protect workbooks

Assign passwords and protect workbooks or ranges.

Delete workbooks

Use Windows Explorer to remove unwanted workbooks.

Understanding File Types

The type of file you create most often in 1-2-3 97 is a *workbook*. This edition of 1-2-3 begins the use of the term *workbook*, instead of *worksheet file*, to refer to a collection of worksheets. 1-2-3 workbooks are stored in a single file format with the 123 extension. A workbook saves all the data, formulas, and text you enter into its worksheets, as well as the format of cells, the alignment of text, range names, and settings for ranges that are protected. 1-2-3 97 also can read the following file formats:

- WKS, WK1, WK3, WK4, FMT, FM3, ALL files (1-2-3, all releases)
- 12M, WT4 files (1-2-3 SmartMaster Template)
- LSS, LSO files (LotusScript)
- XLS, XLT, XLW files (Excel, all releases)
- DBF files (dBASE)
- DB files (Paradox)
- HTM, HTML files (HTML)
- WQ1, WB1, WB2 files (Quattro Pro)
- TXT, PRN, CSV, DAT, OUT, ASC files (text files)
- WMF, BMP, CGM, PIC files (graphics files)

If you use Lotus Notes, you also can open and save Notes Release 4 shared (NS4) files containing versions and scenarios created with the Version Manager. See Chapter 21, "Managing Multiple Solutions with Version Manager," and Chapter 29, "Using 1-2-3 with Lotus Notes," for more information on sharing 1-2-3 files with Lotus Notes and using the Version Manager.

▶ **See** "Understanding Workbooks and Worksheets," **p. 46**

Creating a New Workbook

When you start 1-2-3, the Welcome to 1-2-3 dialog box presents tabs for opening an existing workbook and for creating a new workbook using a SmartMaster. To create a workbook based on a predefined template, select the Create a New Workbook Using a SmartMaster tab. Select a template from the SmartMaster templates and then choose OK. For more information about SmartMasters, see Chapter 34, "Working with Templates."

To create a workbook with default worksheet settings, click the Create a Blank Workbook button at the bottom of the Welcome to 1-2-3 dialog box.

If you want to create additional new workbooks during the same work session, choose File, New Workbook or click the Create File SmartIcon or the Create a Plain New File SmartIcon. The File, New Workbook command and the Create File SmartIcon open the New Workbook dialog box. The Create a Plain New File SmartIcon opens a new workbook with a blank worksheet in the current window. Any workbooks that are open when you choose File, New Workbook or click the Create File or Create a Plain New File SmartIcon remain open. The new workbook becomes an open workbook and is listed on the Window menu. 1-2-3 assigns temporary file names to new workbooks you create, as described in the next section.

Saving Workbooks

When you create a new workbook or when you make changes to an existing workbook, your work exists only in the computer's memory. If you don't save a new workbook or the changes you make before you exit 1-2-3, you lose your work. Saving a workbook copies the file from memory onto the disk.

To save your work, choose File, Save or File, Save As, or click the Save File SmartIcon. If you select File, Save or click the Save File SmartIcon and the workbook has been saved previously, 1-2-3 saves the workbook under the current file name without displaying a dialog box. If you select File, Save As (or if you are saving a new workbook for the first time and use File, Save or click the Save File SmartIcon), 1-2-3 displays the Save As dialog box shown in figure 9.1.

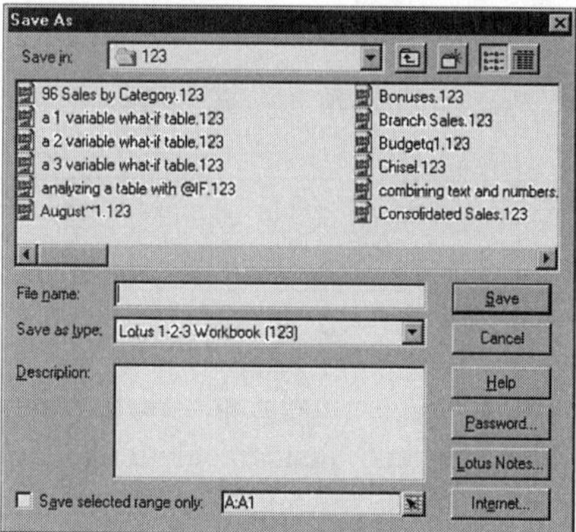

Fig. 9.1
The Save As dialog box is where you specify the workbook's name, drive, folder, and file type.

If you have saved files in other Windows 95 programs, the buttons and boxes in this dialog box should look familiar. After you specify the file information, choose Save or press Enter. If an existing workbook already uses the file name you entered in the Save As dialog box, 1-2-3 displays a message saying that the file already exists. Choose Replace to overwrite the existing file; choose Backup if you want 1-2-3 to make a backup copy of the file; or choose Cancel to cancel the save operation.

NOTE You also use the Save As dialog box to assign a password or to save only a selected range of cells in the current worksheet. These features are discussed later in this chapter.

Naming Workbooks

When you create a new file, 1-2-3 automatically assigns the file a temporary file name, UNTITLED*n*.123, where *n* is replaced with a number (after the first temporary file name). The first temporary file name is UNTITLED.123. If you create additional new files, 1-2-3 names these files UNTITLED1.123, UNTITLED2.123, and so on, incrementing the numeric portion of the file name with each new file (see fig. 9.2). You can save your work using the temporary file names 1-2-3 assigns, or you can choose a descriptive name.

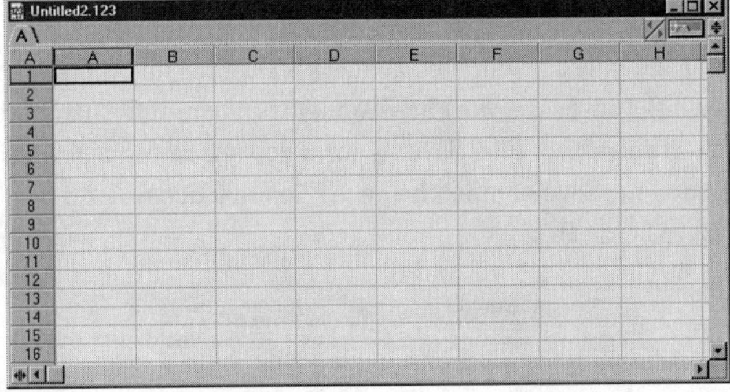

Fig. 9.2 New workbooks—UNTITLED, UNTITLED1, UNTITLED2—created during one work session.

Give all your workbooks descriptive names. Descriptive names make it easy to identify the contents of the workbook.

With Windows 95, the combined length of a path and file name can be as many as 255 characters; it is not limited to the DOS rule of eight characters plus a three-character extension. A file name can contain any combination of letters, numbers, spaces, hyphens, periods, and underscores. You cannot use the following characters for a file name in Windows 95:

\?:*,“<>|

The standard file extension for 1-2-3 97 workbooks is 123. When you open or save a file, type only the descriptive part of the name; 1-2-3 supplies the appropriate file extension for you. 1-2-3 97 recognizes the file extensions shown in Table 9.1. If you type one of these extensions, 1-2-3 will save the workbook as the appropriate file type.

Table 9.1 File Save Extensions and Types

Extension	Type
123	1-2-3 97 Edition workbook
WK1	1-2-3 for DOS Release 2 workbook
WK3	1-2-3 for Windows Release 1 workbook or 1-2-3 for DOS Release 3 workbook
WK4	1-2-3 Release 4 or Release 5 for Windows workbook
12M	1-2-3 for Windows 95 SmartMaster template
WT4	1-2-3 Release 4 or Release 5 for Windows SmartMaster template
TXT	A text file
DB	Paradox file
DBF	dBASE IV file
XLS	Excel worksheet file
XLW	Excel workbook

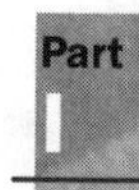

You can override these standard extensions and type your own, but keep in mind that file extensions help identify the file type. If you use File, Open to open the file BUDGET.WK1, for example, you can tell by the file extension that the file is a 1-2-3 for DOS Release 2 workbook. If you rename the file to BUDGET.JAN, 1-2-3 can still identify and translate the file type, but you cannot readily identify the file as a 1-2-3 workbook.

When you choose File, Open or click the Open File SmartIcon, 1-2-3 lists all the files with extensions of 123 or that begin with WK. To open a file that has a different extension, you must type the complete file name and extension or use *wild cards* (see "Using Wild Cards to Open Workbooks" later in this chapter).

NOTE Sometimes you may want to save a file with a nonstandard extension so that the file does not automatically appear when the Open File dialog box lists files in the current folder. For example, you may want to assign a nonstandard extension to a file that is part of a macro-controlled system so that you don't accidentally open the file outside the macro. The nonstandard extension "hides" the file from the standard list of workbooks.

Saving a Portion of a Workbook

The Save Selected Range Only option in the Save As dialog box (refer to fig. 9.1) saves data from a cell, range, or worksheet to a new or existing workbook. You might use this command to save part of a workbook before you change it, to break a large workbook into smaller workbooks, to create a partial workbook for someone else to work on, or to send information to another workbook. For example, you may want to use this feature to break a large budget workbook into separate workbooks, each one containing information about a single department's budget. This technique is useful when you need to work with portions of a worksheet's data in separate workbooks.

The Save Selected Range Only option copies all settings associated with the copied cells, including styles, formats, protection status, range names, column widths, row heights, fonts, and font attributes.

To save a selected range, follow these steps:

1. Open the workbook that contains the range you want to save.
2. Select the range.
3. Choose File, Save As to display the Save As dialog box.
4. In the File Name box, enter a name for the workbook in which you want to save the range.
5. Select the Save Selected Range Only check box in the Save As dialog box. The range address you selected appears in the text box. You can use the range selector button next to the text box to select a different range if needed.
6. Choose Save. 1-2-3 displays the Save Selected Range dialog box (see fig. 9.3).

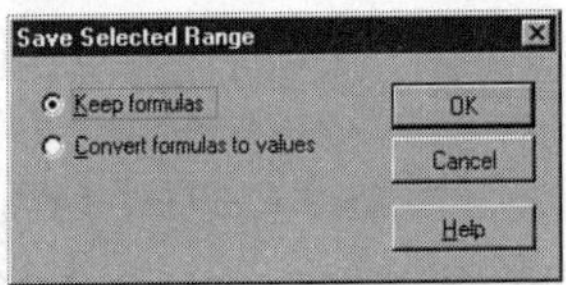

Fig. 9.3 Specify whether to keep formulas or values in the Save Selected Range dialog box.

7. Select either the Keep Formulas option or the Convert Formulas to Values option. When you save a range with the Keep Formulas option, 1-2-3 adjusts the addresses in formulas to reflect their new locations in the destination workbook. The Convert Formulas to Values option, on the other hand, saves all calculated cells as values.

NOTE If you save a range that contains a formula, be certain to include all the cells that the formula refers to; otherwise, the formula does not calculate correctly. If the cells you are saving are part of a named range, you must select the entire range; otherwise, the range name does not refer to the correct cell addresses.

8. Choose OK or press Enter to complete the saving process. 1-2-3 saves the specified range in the specified workbook. 1-2-3 *doesn't* automatically open the workbook. To view the workbook, use File, Open to open the workbook.

Remember that 1-2-3 also enables you to copy and move data between workbooks with the Edit, Cut; Edit, Copy; Edit, Paste; and Edit, Paste Special commands. In some cases, using these commands may be just as easy as saving a range of cells. For more information about these commands, see Chapter 7, "Moving or Copying Data."

Saving Workbooks in Other 1-2-3 Formats

1-2-3 enables you to save files in file formats used by previous releases of 1-2-3. This feature is useful if you need to send a workbook to someone who is using an earlier release of 1-2-3. To use this feature, choose File, Save As to open the Save As dialog box. Then choose the appropriate file format from the Save As Type drop-down list box (see fig. 9.4). For example, you can save a 1-2-3 97 workbook in a WK1 (1-2-3 for DOS Release 2) format by choosing the 1-2-3 (WK1) option. Refer to Table 9.1 for a list of the other 1-2-3 file types and their extensions. If you prefer, you can type the file name with the WK1 or other extension in the File Name text box.

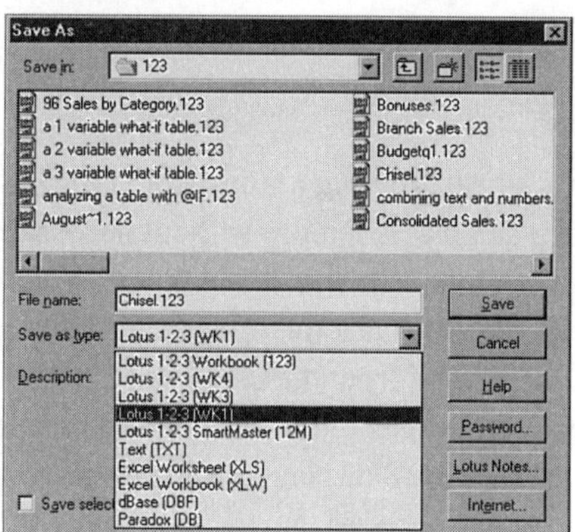

Fig. 9.4
Save a workbook in another file type by selecting from the Save As Type drop-down list box in the Save As dialog box.

Although saving 1-2-3 97 files in 1-2-3 WK1 or other previous release formats is possible, you lose some of the worksheet information in the conversion because 1-2-3 97 supports features that earlier releases of 1-2-3 do not support. When you save the file, 1-2-3 warns you that you may lose some worksheet information. Following is some of the information you could lose:

- For a WK1 file, versions and scenarios created with the Version Manager
- Worksheets other than the first worksheet in a workbook

- Queries and query tables
- Drawn objects (not including charts)
- Embedded data from other Windows applications
- Worksheet settings (including tabs for a WK1 file, range names, default text, and cell background colors)

You can also save a workbook as a SmartMaster template with a 12M file extension. To do so, choose SmartMaster (12M) from the Save As Type drop-down list in the Save As dialog box. Then type a file name, and press Enter or click Save.

▶ **See** "Creating a SmartMaster," **p. 790**

TROUBLESHOOTING

I want to use 1-2-3 97 to rename a workbook without returning to the Windows 95 Explorer, but can't find the command to rename a file. Use the File, Open command to display the Open dialog box. Right-click the workbook you want to rename and select Rename. Type the new name for the workbook, but don't change the extension. Press Enter to apply the new name. Select Open to open the renamed file, or Cancel to close the dialog box without opening the file.

Closing Workbooks

Closing a workbook is not the same as saving a workbook. *Closing* a workbook removes the workbook from the screen and from memory without necessarily saving it. *Saving* a workbook saves the changes and keeps the workbook open. When you finish working with a workbook, choose File, Close or click the Close Window SmartIcon to remove the current workbook from the screen and from the list of open workbooks on the Window menu. If you have made unsaved changes to the workbook when you select File, Close or click the Close Window SmartIcon, 1-2-3 displays a warning that allows you to save the recent changes. Choose Yes to save changes, No to close the workbook without saving changes, or Cancel to return to working on the workbook.

Another common method of closing a workbook is to click the Close button (the x button) in the upper-right corner of the workbook window. Be careful not to click the application Close button if you are attempting to close only the active workbook.

You can use File, Exit 1-2-3 or the End 1-2-3 Session SmartIcon to exit the 1-2-3 program; these commands don't automatically close all open workbooks, however. If you choose File, Exit 1-2-3 or click the End 1-2-3 Session SmartIcon while workbooks are still open, 1-2-3 gives you the opportunity to save any open workbooks that have been changed but not yet saved.

TIP If you are working with many workbooks at one time, close any workbooks that you are finished with. Closing workbooks frees up memory, enabling you to work more efficiently with the workbooks that remain open.

Opening Existing Workbooks

When you start 1-2-3, the Welcome to 1-2-3 dialog box displays its Open an Existing Workbook panel. In the Recently Used Workbooks list box, you can select a workbook. If the workbook you want to open is not displayed, click the Browse for More Workbooks button. The Open File dialog box opens, the same dialog box you see if you choose File, Open during a 1-2-3 session.

By using the File, Open command, you can open an existing workbook without closing the current workbook. 1-2-3 displays the workbook you open in the current window. The workbook that was current before you opened the new workbook remains active, but the new workbook becomes the current workbook in the current window. If other workbooks are open, they remain open and are unaffected by the workbook you open. (All open workbooks are listed on the Window menu.)

To look at but avoid making accidental changes to a workbook, check the Open As Read Only check box in the Open File dialog box. A workbook opened with this check box selected will display (RO) before the workbook name in the title bar. While you may make temporary changes to this workbook, you will not be able to save the changes.

To open a workbook, choose File, Open or click the Open Existing File SmartIcon to display the Open dialog box (see fig. 9.5). The current folder is shown in the Look In drop-down list box. In fig. 9.5, the current folder is 123. To view the path to that folder, drop down the list. In this example, the 123 folder is located in C:\lotus\Work\. Changing to other folders and specifying the working folder are discussed later in this chapter.

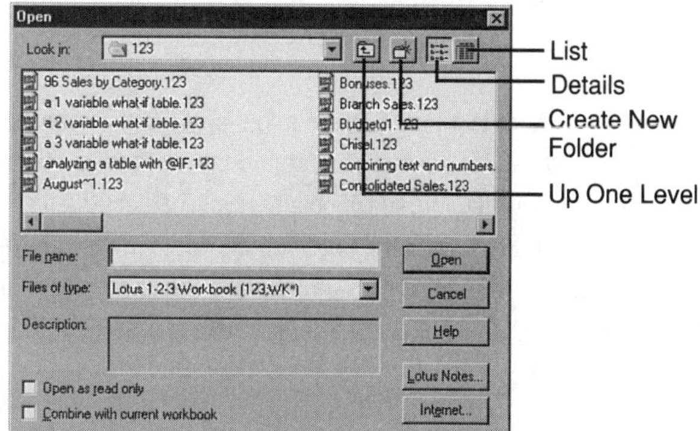

Fig. 9.5 The Open dialog box displays existing workbooks for the current folder.

The workbooks for the current folder are shown in the list box. Click the name of the workbook you want to open, or type the workbook name in the File Name text box. Then click Open to open the workbook.

TIP You can click the Details button in the Open File dialog box to change the view of the workbook names to include the size, type, and modified date and time. Using the List button (the default) lists only the workbook names.

Opening Multiple Workbooks at Once

You can also use the Open File dialog box to open multiple workbooks at once—as many as 32 at one time. Note, however, that the workbooks must all be in the same folder. You also are limited by the amount of computer memory available.

To open multiple workbooks, choose one of the following procedures:

- Type a series of workbook names in the File Name text box, enclosing each name in quotation marks (") and separating each name with a space.

NOTE Because Windows 95 permits spaces and additional periods in file names, you must enclose multiple file names in quotes to separate each name. Otherwise, 1-2-3 interprets the entry as a single workbook name, and displays a `File does not exist` message.

- Click a workbook name to select it; then press and hold Ctrl and click any additional workbook names (up to 32).
- Click the first in a series of workbook names to select it; then press and hold Shift, and click the last workbook name in the series. 1-2-3 selects all the workbooks between and including the two workbook names you selected.

After you have typed in or selected the names of the workbooks you want to open, click Open to open the workbooks. 1-2-3 opens multiple workbooks alphabetically by workbook name.

NOTE You can incorporate data from another file into an open workbook. Select the cell where you want to begin placement of data from the other file, then choose File, Open. (If the file is not a 1-2-3 workbook, specify the file type.) Select the file you want to combine, browsing until you find it, or type the path and file name in the File Name text box. Click Combine in the Open File dialog box. The Combine 1-2-3 File dialog box opens. (If you opened a text file, the Text File Options dialog box opens instead.) Select options in the dialog box and choose OK.

Opening Workbooks from Folders and Other Drives

Often, the workbook you want to open is stored in a different folder, so the workbook name isn't currently shown in the list box in the Open File dialog box. To display the workbook name in the list box, you must first select the correct folder name from the Look in drop-down list box.

The folder where the workbook is stored could be a parent folder to the current folder, or it could be a subfolder to the current folder. To select a parent folder, click the Up One Level button, which is located next to the Look in box (refer to fig. 9.5). To select a subfolder, double-click the folder name which is displayed in the list box.

When you have selected the correct folder by double-clicking it, 1-2-3 lists all files with a 123 or wk* extension in that folder. (If necessary, use the scroll bar or arrow keys to display all entries.) To list *all* files in the current subdirectory, select All(*) in the Files of type drop-down list. Alternatively, you can display all files of a different file type by selecting the type from the Files of type drop-down list. Select the file you want to open, and then click Open.

If the workbook you want to open is stored on another drive, select the appropriate drive in the Look in drop-down list. When you select a different drive, 1-2-3 displays all files with a 123 or wk* file extension in the last subdirectory you used on that drive. To select a different subdirectory, follow the guidelines in the previous paragraph.

NOTE You also can use the Look in drop-down list to locate files that are elsewhere on a drive, not a nearby parent or subdirectory. For example, if you want to locate an Excel workbook to open in 1-2-3, click the drive letter in the Look in drop-down list (or repeatedly click the Up One Level button until you reach the root folder of the current drive). Folders and files appear in the list box. Double-click the folder where the Excel workbook is located. You will probably double-click more than one level of folder to reach your file. Remember to select All(*) or a specific file type in the Files of type drop-down list if you are looking for files from other programs. ■

Using Wild Cards to Open Workbooks

In the Open File dialog box, you can include an asterisk (*) or a question mark (?) as *wild card characters* (often just called *wild cards*) in the File Name box. Wild cards act as placeholders that match one character or any number of characters in sequence. The ? wild card matches any one character in the file name. The * matches any number of characters in sequence. When you use wild cards in a File Name text box, 1-2-3 lists only the files whose names match the wild card.

The (123;WK*) in the Files of type box tells 1-2-3 to list all files with file extensions of 123 and those that begin with WK followed by any number of other characters. You can further narrow the selection by using wild cards in the File name text box. Suppose that you type **????tree.wk*** in the File name text box. 1-2-3 lists all the file names that start with any four characters, followed by TREE and an extension beginning with WK; examples are AUDITREE.WK4, BACKTREE.WK3, SOLVTREE.WK1, and VIEWTREE.WK. If you type **budget*.***, 1-2-3 lists all the file names that start with budget (upper- or lowercase), such as BUDGET.WK4, BUDGET1.TXT, and Budget 1996.123. Notice that, although Windows 95 enables you to use upper- and lowercase in file names, the wild card search finds files with both cases regardless of which case you type (case-insensitive).

Opening a Workbook Automatically When You Start 1-2-3

When you start 1-2-3, you can display a blank worksheet or a worksheet based on a SmartMaster (see the earlier section "Creating a New Workbook"). However, if you usually begin a work session using the same workbook, you can tell 1-2-3 to automatically display that workbook when the program starts.

To open a specific workbook upon starting 1-2-3, you can do any of the following:

- Store the workbook in the \lotus\123\auto folder
- Double-click an icon copy (or shortcut) of the workbook on the Windows 95 desktop
- Double-click the workbook name in Windows 95 Explorer

If you store a workbook in the \lotus\123\auto folder, the workbook opens each time you start 1-2-3. You can change the default folder for automatically opening workbooks by choosing File, User Setup, 1-2-3 Preferences. In the File Locations panel, type a different path in the Automatically Opened Files text box.

NOTE If the auto folder does not exist, you can create it. Click the Create New Folder button in the Save As dialog box. A folder named New Folder appears in the workbook list box, with the name highlighted. Type **auto** to change the name. A folder named auto is created in the current path.

If you frequently open the same workbook, you can put an icon for that workbook directly on the Windows 95 desktop. When you double-click the icon, 1-2-3 will start and then automatically open the workbook represented by the icon. To create the icon copy of a workbook on the desktop:

1. Open Windows Explorer and locate the workbook name you want to start automatically.

2. With the right mouse button, drag the workbook name to the Windows desktop, and then release the mouse button. An icon and shortcut menu appear (see fig. 9.6).
3. Select Copy Here in the shortcut menu. The shortcut menu closes and a larger 1-2-3 icon with the workbook name below it appears on the desktop.
4. You can drag the icon to another location on the desktop if you want to.

Use this workbook icon to start 1-2-3 instead of starting 1-2-3 with its usual program icon. 1-2-3 starts and opens this workbook, bypassing the Welcome to 1-2-3 dialog box. You also can start 1-2-3 with a specific workbook by double-clicking its file name in Windows Explorer (see fig. 9.6). Because the file you select has an extension of 123, it is associated with the 1-2-3 program. When you double-click the file name, the Windows Explorer starts 1-2-3 and opens the file.

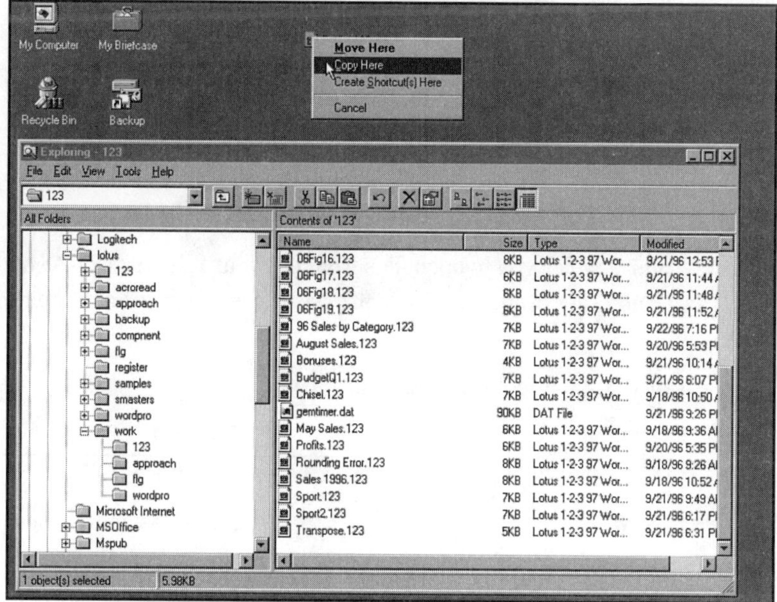

Fig. 9.6
Create an icon on the desktop or double-click the name of a 1-2-3 file in the File Manager to start 1-2-3 and open the file in one step.

Opening Recently Used Workbooks

1-2-3 provides a convenient feature that enables you to quickly open the workbooks you used most recently. This feature saves you the trouble of selecting a workbook name from the Open File dialog box when you want to open a workbook. By default, 1-2-3 lists the five most recently read workbooks at the bottom of the File menu. To open a recently read workbook, you click its name.

To change the number of workbooks displayed, choose File, User Setup, 1-2-3 Preferences. In the General panel (see fig. 9.7), enter a number between 0 and 10 in the Number of Recent Files to Show spin box, and then click the OK button. 1-2-3 adds the names of the workbooks (up to the number you specify) at the bottom of the File menu. To open a workbook, simply click the workbook name on the File menu.

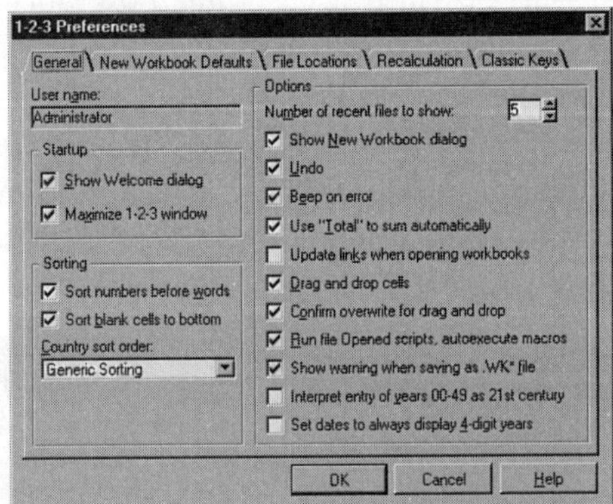

Fig. 9.7
Select the number of recently used workbooks that appear at the bottom of the File menu.

Opening Spreadsheets from Other Programs

1-2-3 97 enables you to open files from previous releases of 1-2-3 and from Excel, Quattro Pro, and other programs. Table 9.2 lists these programs and their file extensions.

Table 9.2 File Types 1-2-3 Can Open

Extension	Program
123, WK4, WK3, WK1	1-2-3 Workbook
12M, WT4	SmartMaster Template
TXT, PRN, CSV, DAT, OUT, ASC	Text
XLS, XLT, XLW	Excel
WQ1, WB1, WB2	Quattro Pro
DBF	dBASE
DB	Paradox
WMF	Windows metafile
BMP	Bitmap
CGM	ANSI metafile
PIC	1-2-3 PIC

To open any of these files, select the file from the correct folder in the Open File dialog box, and then click Open. You can save 1-2-3 and other files in their original file formats, or you can save them as 1-2-3 97 (with 123 extension). Keep in mind, however, that if you add features to the file that are available only in 1-2-3 97, these features are lost when you save the file in its original file format. See "Saving Workbooks in Other 1-2-3 Formats" earlier in this chapter for more information.

TROUBLESHOOTING

I tried to open a 1-2-3 workbook from Windows 95 Explorer and got an error message `Windows cannot find 123w.exe`. You tried to open a workbook that 1-2-3 cannot open or display. You must choose a valid file with a 123 file extension or other format that 1-2-3 understands. Try again, using the correct file type.

I tried to open a workbook by clicking the workbook name listed at the bottom of the File menu, but 1-2-3 says `File does not exist`. What's wrong? The workbook is no longer available from the location in which you last opened it. It has been deleted, renamed, or moved to a different folder. If the workbook has not been deleted, open the workbook by using File, Open, and 1-2-3 will remember its new location the next time you select the workbook name from the File menu.

Changing Your Working Folder

A hard disk is divided into a hierarchy of folders that store related data files. The list of folders that leads from the root folder (usually c:\) to the file you want is the *path* or *path name*.

If you installed 1-2-3 97 using the default installation settings, your workbooks are stored in the path c:\lotus\Work\123. This folder is called your *working folder*. Each time you choose File, Open; File, Save; or File, Save As, 1-2-3 automatically assumes you want to save workbooks or open workbooks in your working folder.

To organize your work, you may have created other folders and subfolders under 123. If so, you might want 1-2-3 to save workbooks automatically to a different folder. Choose File, User Setup, 1-2-3 Preferences to specify a new working folder. In the File Locations panel, enter a new path name in the Workbook Files text box, and then choose OK to change the working folder for the current and all future work sessions.

Entering and Viewing Workbook Information

You can keep track of useful information about workbooks by using the Workbook Properties dialog box. To enter or view information, choose File, Workbook Properties or click the Workbook Properties SmartIcon. To enter general information about a workbook, such as title, subject, and description, select the General tab (see fig. 9.8).

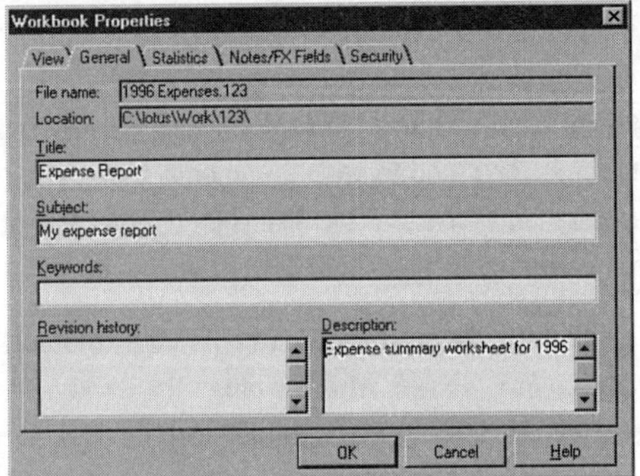

Fig. 9.8
Enter descriptive information about a workbook in the General panel of the Workbook Properties dialog box.

The information in the Description box also appears in the Description box of the Open File dialog box, thus helping you remember the purpose of a selected workbook before opening it. The Description box in the Save As dialog box contains the same information, which can be entered there or in the Workbook Properties dialog box—the text appears in all three places.

In the General panel, you can also enter a keyword or keywords to share file information with Lotus Notes. For more information about keywords, see Chapter 29, "Using 1-2-3 with Lotus Notes."

The Statistics panel of the Workbook Properties dialog box displays statistics about the workbook, including the file size and number of worksheets, revision information, and total editing time. You cannot directly edit the information in the Statistics panel.

Protecting Workbooks

1-2-3 offers two methods of protecting workbooks. You can protect confidential workbooks by assigning a *password* when you save the workbook, or you can *lock* a workbook to prevent unauthorized changes. When you save a workbook with a password, no one can open, copy, or print the workbook without first issuing the password. When you lock a workbook, no one can make changes to a workbook's reservation status or to the data, graphics objects, structure, versions, and styles in the workbook.

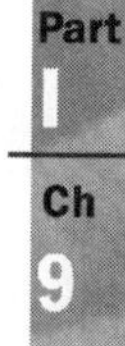

Assigning Passwords

You assign a password to a workbook by using the Save As dialog box, as explained in the following steps:

1. Open the workbook you want to protect.
2. Choose File, Save As to display the Save As dialog box (see fig. 9.9).

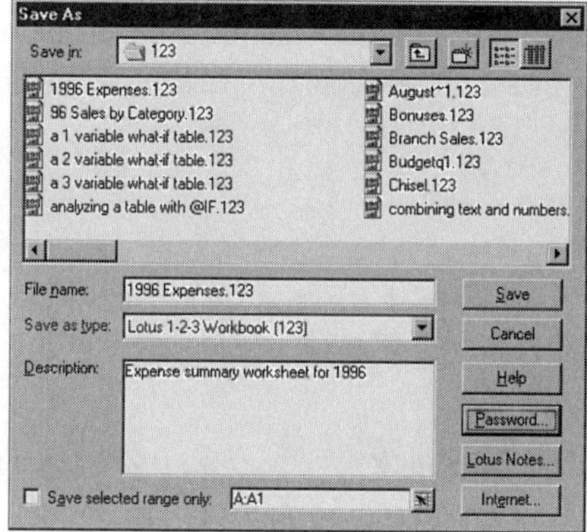

Fig. 9.9
Select Password in the Save As dialog box to protect your workbook with a password.

3. Type a new workbook name in the File Name text box or leave the workbook name unchanged.
4. Select the Password. 1-2-3 displays the Set Password dialog box (see fig. 9.10).

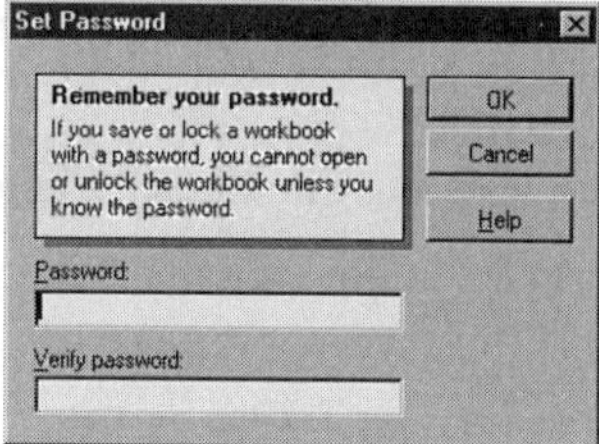

Fig. 9.10
Setting a password for a workbook prevents unauthorized opening of the workbook.

5. In the Password text box, type a password of up to 15 characters. For security, 1-2-3 displays an asterisk (*) for each character you type.
6. In the Verify Password text box, type the password again exactly as you typed it before. Again, 1-2-3 displays asterisks in place of the characters you type.
7. Select OK.

If, in the File Name box, you enter a workbook name that already exists, 1-2-3 asks whether you want to replace the existing workbook, back up the existing workbook, or cancel saving the workbook. You must select Replace or Backup to save the workbook with the password. If you select Cancel, 1-2-3 doesn't assign the password and returns to the Worksheet window. If the workbook doesn't already exist, the password is assigned after you complete the Set Password dialog box.

A password can contain any combination of uppercase or lowercase characters. It's best not to use obvious passwords such as your birthdate, license plate number, children's or pets' names. Because longer passwords are more difficult for someone to guess, phrases with no spaces between words (such as **itrainsinapril**) work well. As you enter the password, 1-2-3 displays an asterisk for each character you type. Remember that passwords are case-sensitive; if you specify **JustForMe** as the password, typing **justforme** to open the workbook does not work.

CAUTION

Remember your password exactly as you type it. You cannot open the workbook again unless you enter the password in precisely the same way.

Opening a Password-Protected Workbook When you try to open a password-protected workbook by using File, Open, 1-2-3 prompts you for the password. You must enter the password exactly as you originally entered it, with the correct upper- and lowercase letters. If you make an error as you enter the password, an error message appears, saying that you entered an incorrect password. Try opening the workbook again, using the correct password.

Changing and Deleting Passwords You can change or delete a workbook's password at any time, provided you know the current password. To change a password, follow these steps:

1. Choose File, Open or use the Open Existing File SmartIcon to open the workbook.
2. Type the name of the current password in the Password dialog box and click OK. 1-2-3 opens the workbook.
3. Choose File, Save As and then click Password.
4. Type a new password in the Password and Verify Password text boxes and choose OK. The new password is set.

Locking a Workbook to Prevent Changes

Locking a workbook prevents a user from changing data, styles, or other settings used in the workbook. When a workbook is locked, you cannot insert or delete columns, show hidden worksheets or columns, change, add, or delete range names, page breaks, frozen titles, graphics, or set new formats, column widths, row heights, or cell alignments.

You lock a workbook when you want other users to be able to open and read the workbook, but not change it. A locked workbook is also password-protected. Although you can open and read the workbook without knowing the password, you must know the password to change the workbook in any way. The password protection on a locked workbook allows you to give read access—permission to look at the workbook but not to make changes—to a large group of users while giving only one or a few users the authority to change the workbook. (Without the password protection, only the user who creates the workbook can change it.)

To lock a workbook, follow these steps:

1. Choose File, Workbook Properties or click the Workbook Properties SmartIcon to display the Workbook Properties dialog box.
2. Click the Security tab and select the Lock Workbook check box (see fig. 9.11). 1-2-3 displays the Set Password dialog box, the same dialog box used to save a workbook with a password (see fig. 9.10).
3. In the Set Password dialog box, type the password in the Password text box, and then type the password a second time in the Verify Password text box. Just like when you save a workbook with a password, you can use any combination of upper- and lowercase characters in the password.
4. Click OK to set the password. The Set Password dialog box closes.
5. Click OK to lock the workbook. The Workbook Properties dialog box closes.

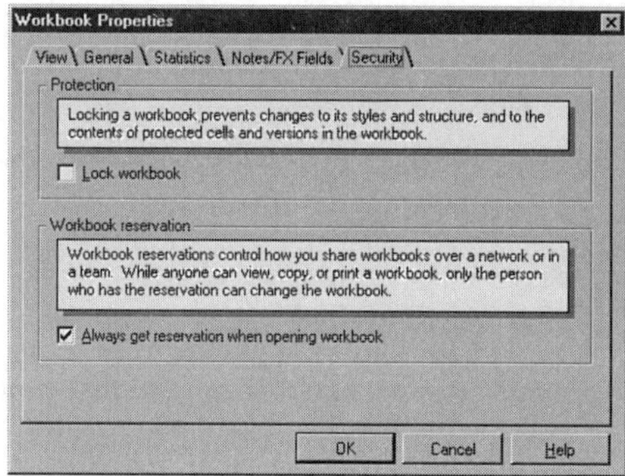

Fig. 9.11
Lock the Workbook in the Workbook Properties dialog box.

To unlock the workbook:

1. Open the Workbook Properties dialog box.
2. Click the Security tab and turn off the Lock Workbook check box.
3. Click OK. 1-2-3 displays the Password dialog box.
4. Type the password in the Password text box, and then click OK.

Protecting Selected Cells or a Range

In some cases, you may want users to be able to change certain cells in a workbook, even though the workbook is locked. For example, you can create a data entry form or a script in which you want the user to be able to enter information, but not change or delete data entry prompts or parts of a script. You can leave certain cells unprotected by using the Security panel of the Range InfoBox *before* you lock the workbook. First, select the cells you want unprotected, and then choose Range, Range Properties to display the Range InfoBox. Select the Security tab, shown in figure 9.12.

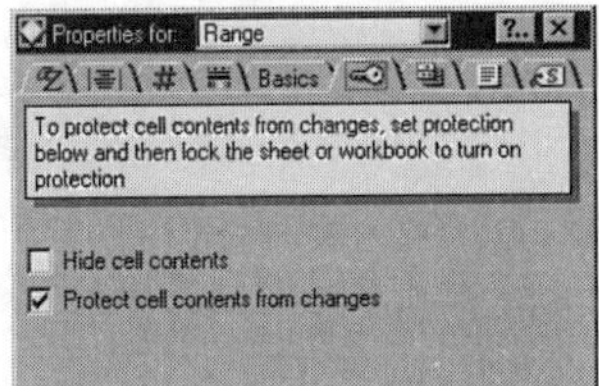

Fig. 9.12
Unprotect a selected range before locking the workbook.

Turn off the Protect Cell Contents From Changes check box, and then click OK. Now that a range of cells has been set as unprotected, you can lock the workbook by using the steps outlined in the preceding section. When a locked workbook contains unprotected cells, the status bar displays `Pr` when the cell pointer is in a protected cell and `U` when the cell pointer is in an unprotected cell.

Remember that locking a workbook is different from protecting a workbook with a password. Saving a workbook with a password prevents *all* access to the workbook unless the user knows the password. When the workbook is open, however, a user can change it. When you lock a workbook, other users can open and read the workbook and make changes to any unprotected cells. Without a password, however, they cannot change data, styles, or other settings in protected cells.

Reserving Shared Files

If you use 1-2-3 on a network, two or more people can read the same workbook at the same time. If more than one person can change a workbook at the same time, the result can be inaccurate data or formulas. To avoid multiple updates of the same shared workbook, 1-2-3 has a *reservation* system. 1-2-3 also enables you to hide and protect confidential data in a shared workbook.

The Always Get Reservation When Opening Workbook option is located in the Security panel of the Workbook Properties dialog box (refer to fig. 9.11). With this option turned on (the default), 1-2-3 gives you the reservation when you open a workbook. If you try to open a workbook that someone else is currently working on, 1-2-3 displays a message box that asks whether you want to open the workbook without having the reservation. If you select Yes, you can read the workbook and change the data, but you cannot save the changes to the same workbook name. You can, however, save the workbook with another name so that your changes are preserved.

If you have the reservation for a workbook, you keep the reservation until you close the workbook, or you can release the reservation by choosing File, Release Reservation. The workbook is still open on your computer, but you cannot save the workbook under the same name because you no longer have the reservation.

You can change the setting for a workbook so that a user must get the reservation manually instead of automatically. To change the default, deselect the Always Get Reservation When Opening Workbook check box. Now, anyone who opens the workbook has read-only access until one user reserves the workbook using the File, Get Reservation command.

You can lock a workbook's reservation setting after you change it so that no one else can change the setting. Choose File, Workbook Properties and select the Security tab. Select the Lock Workbook check box. When 1-2-3 displays the Password dialog box, enter a password in the Password and Verify Password text boxes. (Passwords are case-sensitive.) Remember the password exactly as you type it. If you or someone else later tries to change the reservation setting, 1-2-3 prompts for the password.

TROUBLESHOOTING

How can I lock one worksheet in a workbook that contains multiple worksheets? 1-2-3 allows you to lock individual worksheets in a workbook; however, no password is applied so this kind of lock only prevents accidental changes to the worksheet. To lock a worksheet, select the Lock Contents of Protected Cells in this Sheet check box in the Basics panel of the Sheet InfoBox.

I can't remember the password for a workbook I created some time ago. How can I display a list of all the current passwords? You can't. Passwords are intended to restrict `all` access to a workbook and, therefore, are not recorded anywhere except with the *workbook* itself. If you forget the password, you can't reopen the workbook; all you can do is re-create the workbook.

I am trying to open an Excel file (XLS) in 1-2-3 but can't open the file. What's wrong? Check to see whether the Excel file is password-protected. If so, remove the password from the Excel file before opening it in 1-2-3.

Deleting Files

When you create and save a workbook, the file occupies disk space. Eventually, you run out of disk space if you do not occasionally delete old, unneeded files from the disk. Even if you have disk space left, you have more difficulty finding the files you want to open if the disk contains many obsolete files.

Before you delete old files, you may want to save them to a floppy disk in case you need them again.

You can use the Open dialog box to delete files. Select File, Open to display the dialog box. Right-click the file you want to delete and select Delete. Select Yes to send the file to the Recycle Bin. Deleted files are moved to the Recycle Bin and are retrievable until you empty the Recycle Bin. ●

CHAPTER 10

Printing Worksheets

by Joyce J. Nielsen

1-2-3 gives you considerable control over the design of printed output—from one-page reports to longer reports that incorporate data from multiple worksheets and sophisticated charts.

Many features you may associate with printing are actually part of the worksheet. For example, boldface, italic, and underlining are selected from the Range Properties InfoBox, not through a print command. When you are ready to print, these attributes automatically print with the worksheet data. With 1-2-3, you are always in a WYSIWYG (What-You-See-Is-What-You-Get) environment—what you see on-screen closely resembles the printed output. ■

Previewing reports

Learn how to preview data you want to print, so you can make any necessary adjustments before printing.

Printing reports

With 1-2-3 you can print both simple and complex worksheets quickly and easily.

Enhancing reports

Use 1-2-3's printing options to enhance the look of your report. For example, you can change the margin settings and page orientation, add a header and footer, center the print range, and print worksheet grid lines.

Enhancing Printed Worksheets

Usually, you will want to format a worksheet so that it is attractive, readable, and professional looking before you print it. 1-2-3 offers a number of features that let you enhance printed worksheets. You can use different fonts; you can also add borders, drop shadows, and colors. These formatting options are for highlighting important areas of the worksheet and improving its readability. However, if you use too many formatting options, your audience may be overwhelmed: a printed worksheet that's too busy may be difficult to read.

▶ **See** "Setting Range Properties with the InfoBox," **102**

▶ **See** "Enhancing the Appearance of Data," **125**

To save yourself time when you format a worksheet, use one of the style templates included with 1-2-3. Click the Named Style tab (the tab with the "S") in the Range Properties InfoBox and then click the Style Gallery button. Select one of the preformatted templates in the list. Figure 10.1 shows a worksheet formatted with the Picture2 style template.

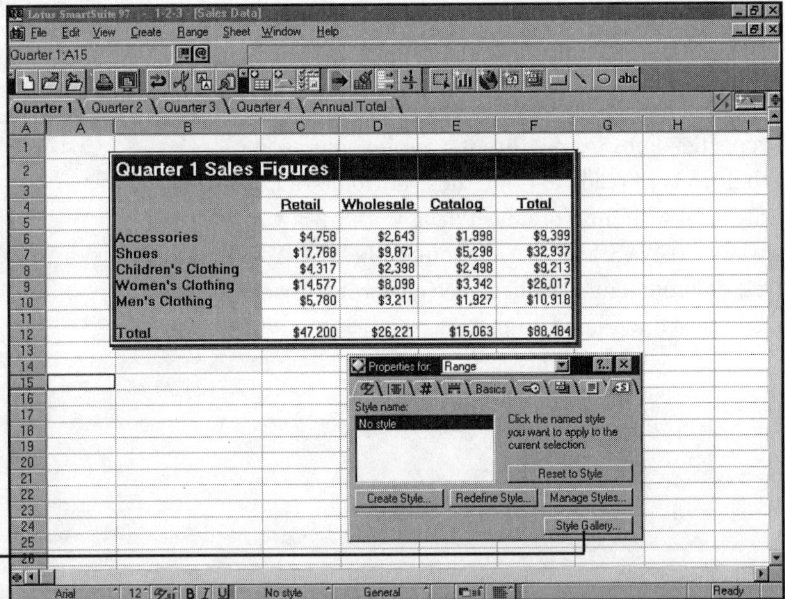

Fig. 10.1 This worksheet was formatted with the Picture2 template from the Style Gallery.

Using the Default Printer Settings

Because you are using Windows 95, many printer settings are already in place. The Windows 95 environment retains basic information about the printer, such as resolution, paper size, and amount of memory. This information is available to all of your Windows 95 applications, including 1-2-3.

By using the Windows 95 Control Panel, you can change the hardware-specific printer defaults. You can add or delete printer drivers and set other printer defaults (such as the kind of paper feed, orientation, and paper size). Refer to the Windows 95 documentation for details on changing these defaults.

You also can change many of the default printer settings from within 1-2-3. Choose File, Print, and then click the Properties button. Make any desired changes in the Properties dialog box, and then click OK.

Reviewing the Printing Options

In 1-2-3, the File menu contains two different commands that you can use to control printed output: Print, and Preview & Page Setup. When you choose File, Print or when you click the Print SmartIcon, 1-2-3 displays the Print dialog box (see fig. 10.2). Use this dialog box to specify the pages you want to print, the number of copies you need, the range you want to print, and so on. You choose the Print button in the Print dialog box when you are ready to print the worksheet.

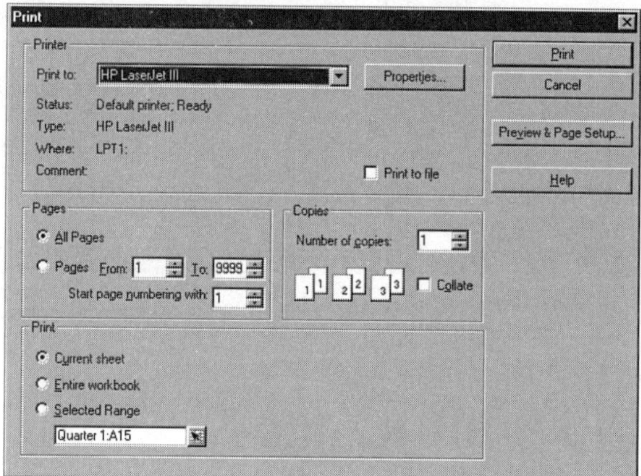

Fig. 10.2
You can access most 1-2-3 printing options through the Print dialog box.

To get an idea of what your report looks like before you print it, you can preview each page on-screen. The Preview & Page Setup button in the Print dialog box accesses the Preview window. The Preview window also appears when you choose File, Preview & Page Setup from the 1-2-3 main menu, or when you click the Preview SmartIcon.

In 1-2-3 97, the new dynamic preview feature enables you to preview your work while you make changes to the worksheet. When you access the Preview feature, a Preview window (which shows how the printed worksheet will look) appears beside the Worksheet window. In addition, 1-2-3 displays the Print Preview SmartIcon bar (beside the Universal SmartIcon bar) as well as the Preview & Page Setup Properties InfoBox (see fig. 10.3). As you will learn later in this chapter, you can use the InfoBox to change several print settings. These settings include the margins, print orientation (portrait or landscape), headers and footers, centering on the page, and so on. When you like how the preview looks, you can print the worksheet from the preview.

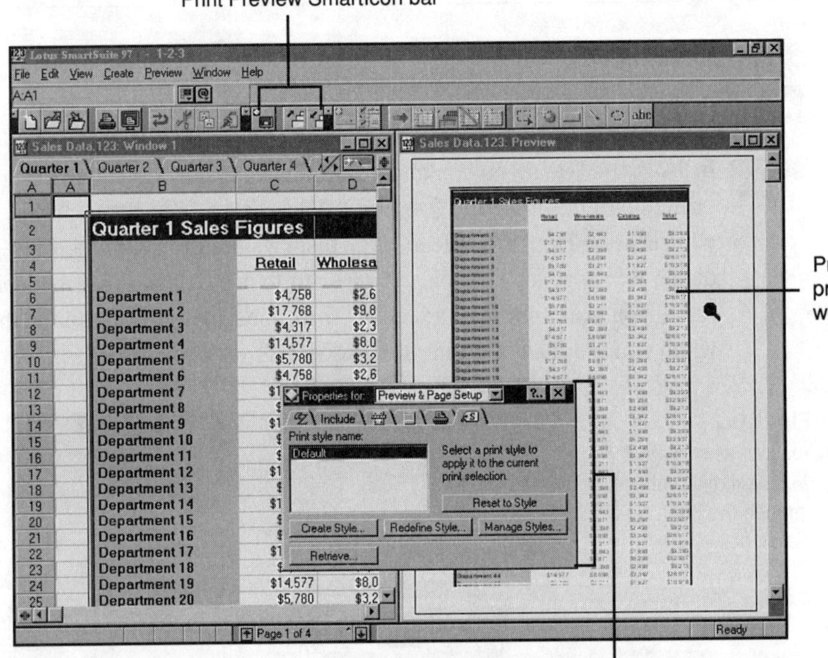

Fig. 10.3
The Preview window shows you how the printed worksheet fits on the page.

Specifying the Print Range

You specify a print range in the same way you specify other ranges: You can select the print range before using the File, Print command or the Print SmartIcon, or you can specify the range from the Print dialog box. If you do not specify a print range, 1-2-3 prints the entire worksheet by default.

Specifying a Single Print Range

To preselect a print range before you choose a print command, highlight the range with the mouse or keyboard.

If you forget to preselect the range you want to print, you can specify the range in the Selected Range text box of the Print dialog box (refer to fig. 10.2). You can type the cell addresses, enter a range name, or highlight the range from this text box. To highlight the print range, first click the range selector (the button to the right of the Selected Range text box) and then select the range in the worksheet using the mouse or keyboard.

For many reports, a *two-dimensional range*—that is, a rectangular area in a worksheet—is all you need to specify. The next section describes how to specify multiple (nonadjacent) ranges for a single print job.

Printing Multiple Ranges

Most reports require only a single print range. You can, however, specify that a single print job include a *collection*—that is, several ranges in one or more worksheets.

▶ **See** "Working with Cells and Ranges," **p. 55**

Specifying multiple print ranges is similar to specifying a single range in a single worksheet: Preselect the range or specify the range address or range name in the Print dialog box. If you are typing several print ranges in the Selected Range text box, type a comma or semicolon between each range. If you want to highlight a range that spans multiple worksheets or highlight multiple ranges in the same worksheet, you *must* preselect the ranges; the Print dialog box does not permit you to highlight multiple ranges.

To preselect a three-dimensional range across contiguous worksheets, highlight the range in the first worksheet and then hold down the Shift key as you click the last worksheet tab you want to select; the same range is selected in the group of worksheets. To preselect multiple ranges, highlight the first range, then hold down the Ctrl key as you highlight each additional range; click the worksheet tab to move to other worksheets.

NOTE If you forget to hold down the Ctrl key when selecting ranges, all currently selected ranges are deselected. ■

You can specify any combination of two-dimensional and three-dimensional print ranges. 1-2-3 prints the ranges in the order in which you enter the range addresses or select the ranges. Before you print multiple ranges, always preview the report, as detailed in the next section.

Previewing Worksheets Before Printing

Previewing a worksheet on-screen before sending it to the printer can save paper, printer toner (or ink or ribbon), and time. You can find and fix many minor errors before printing if you use the 1-2-3 Print Preview feature. With Print Preview, you can see how 1-2-3 breaks up a large print range over several pages, how multiple ranges fit on one or more pages, whether the specified margins are appropriate, and so on.

To preview a print job, you can use any of the following methods:

- Choose File, Preview & Page Setup.
- Choose File, Print. From the resulting Print dialog box, choose the Preview & Page Setup button.

- Click the Preview SmartIcon.

All these methods display the Preview window (refer to fig. 10.3). You can use the Preview window to preview any of the worksheets in a workbook. The following sections describe how to use the options in the Preview window.

Navigating the Preview

As you preview a multiple-page report, you may want to see more than just the first page. The Display Next Page and Display Previous Page SmartIcons in the Preview window let you browse through the pages in a multiple-page report (see fig. 10.4). The up and down Preview arrows in the status bar perform the same function. You can also use the scroll bar to scroll up and down a previewed report.

Previewing Multiple Pages at a Time

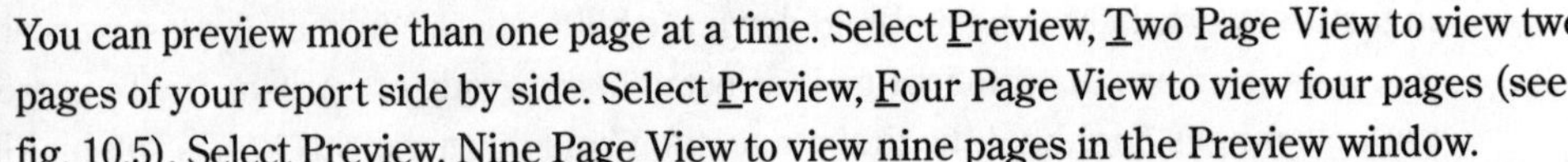

You can preview more than one page at a time. Select Preview, Two Page View to view two pages of your report side by side. Select Preview, Four Page View to view four pages (see fig. 10.5). Select Preview, Nine Page View to view nine pages in the Preview window.

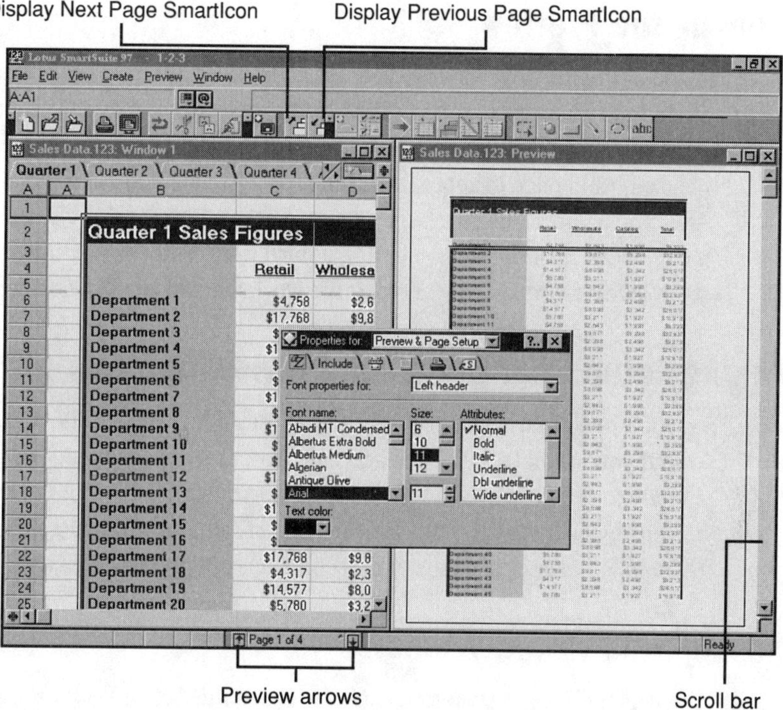

Fig. 10.4
1-2-3 provides several methods for previewing all pages of a multiple-page report.

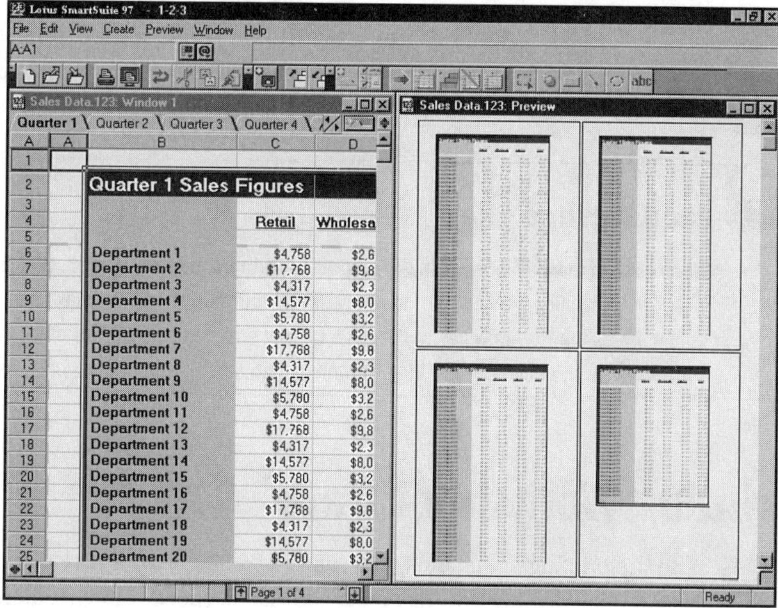

Fig. 10.5
You can preview up to nine pages of a report at once. This Preview window displays four pages.

Zooming the Preview

While in the Preview window, you can zoom in on the preview so that you can more easily read the worksheet text. 1-2-3 provides three levels of magnification. Move the mouse pointer over the Preview window; the pointer changes to a magnifying glass. Click the mouse button once to zoom in on the preview; click it again to enlarge the text even more. After you zoom in, use the arrow keys to navigate around the page. To return to the original preview, click the mouse button a third time. You can continue to cycle through the zoom levels by repeatedly clicking the worksheet in the Preview window.

Making Setup Changes While Previewing

As you preview a report, you may sometimes discover that the margins aren't quite right or that you forgot to specify headers or footers. For these types of changes, you can go directly to the Preview & Page Setup Properties InfoBox (if it doesn't already appear on-screen) by clicking the Print Preview SmartIcon. As you make changes in the InfoBox (as detailed in later sections of this chapter), the preview adjusts to reflect your changes.

Closing the Preview Window

To clear the Preview window, click the Close the Active Window SmartIcon. Or, you can click the Close icon of the Preview window (the x that appears on the far right side of the Preview window's title bar). 1-2-3 returns to the full-screen worksheet display.

You can print the worksheet while the Preview window is displayed by clicking the Print SmartIcon and then choosing Print in the Print dialog box.

TROUBLESHOOTING

When I zoom in while previewing my report, nothing shows on-screen. Why is this? The zoom-in feature magnifies the center of the page. If the report is short, you may see nothing on the screen. Press the Up Arrow key or the Page Up key until you see the top of the report. Use the arrow keys (or the Page Up and Page Down keys) to see all parts of the page as you zoom.

Printing Worksheet Data

With the printing commands, you can print a simple or a very complex worksheet. To print a range quickly (for data that requires no special enhancements, such as headers, footers, or different margin settings) use the File, Print command or the Print SmartIcon.

The following procedure shows you how to print reports quickly and efficiently. In subsequent sections of this chapter, you learn how to include headers and footers in reports, compress a report to fit on one page, add grid lines, column letters and row numbers, and repeat certain columns or rows (as column or row labels) on each page.

To print worksheet data, follow these steps:

1. Check that the printer is online and that the paper is properly positioned.
2. Select the print range.

3. Choose File, Print; or click the Print SmartIcon. The Print dialog box appears (refer to fig. 10.2).
4. Choose the Print button or press Enter to send the report to the printer.

If the print range contains more rows or columns than can fit on a page, 1-2-3 prints the report on multiple pages. Figure 10.6 shows how 1-2-3 indicates a split print range—the vertical and horizontal thick gray lines show the page boundaries or *page breaks*. The numbers of rows and columns that fit on a page depend on the fonts, individual column widths and row heights, and whether you have chosen to compress the worksheet.

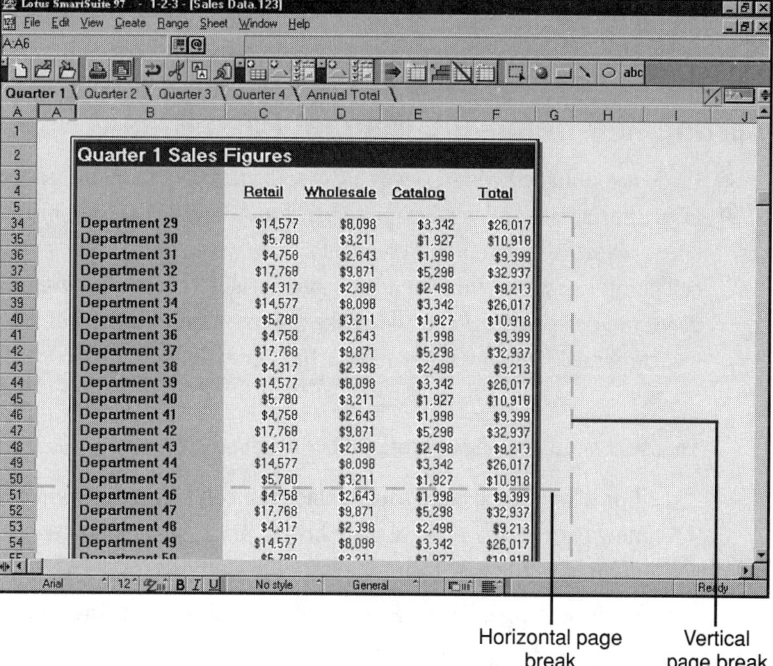

Fig. 10.6
Dashed lines indicate where the page breaks will be when the worksheet is printed.

NOTE When you print a multiple-page report, you must pay attention to where 1-2-3 splits the worksheet between pages—vertically *and* horizontally. 1-2-3 can split pages at inappropriate locations, resulting in a report that is hard to read or understand. By previewing the report, you can see exactly how 1-2-3 will print a large range. You can then insert manual page breaks that override the automatic page breaks, specify print titles that appear on every page, change the page orientation, compress the worksheet, or make other changes to improve the look of the report. The next section describes the options for changing the format of the report. ■

Enhancing Reports with Page Setup Options

A printed report that contains numbers without descriptive headings is difficult, if not impossible, to interpret. You can make a report easier to understand by using 1-2-3 features that help you fit an entire report on a single page by changing the orientation. You can specify that specific data ranges print on each page of a multiple-page report (these ranges are called *row* or *column titles*). You also can print the worksheet frame (the row numbers and the column letters). The sections that follow show you how to create headers and footers, repeat row and column headings on subsequent pages, and print the worksheet frame and grid lines. You also learn how to set margins and save the print settings.

Inserting and Removing Manual Page Breaks

If you are unhappy with the way 1-2-3 splits the data in a long report, you can manually insert horizontal and vertical page breaks. A horizontal page break controls a long worksheet; a vertical page break controls a wide worksheet. To insert a page break, move the cell pointer to where you want the page break to occur. Horizontal breaks are inserted *above* the cell pointer; vertical breaks are inserted to the *left* of the cell pointer. When you insert manual page breaks, you see thick gray lines that represent the placement of these breaks.

To insert a manual page break, follow these steps:

1. For a horizontal page break, place the cell pointer anywhere in the first row of the new page. For a vertical page break, place the cell pointer anywhere in the first column of the new page.
2. Choose Range, Range Properties to display the Range Properties InfoBox.
3. Click the Basics tab.
4. To insert a horizontal page break, select the Break Page at Row check box. To insert a vertical page break, select the Break Page at Column check box.

1-2-3 immediately displays a thick gray line indicating the location of the page break in the worksheet.

You also can click the Horizontal Page Break SmartIcon or the Vertical Page Break SmartIcon to quickly insert a page break. Be sure to position the cell pointer before you click the SmartIcon.

To remove a manual page break, follow these steps:

1. Position the cell pointer in the row just below or the column just to the right of the manual page break you want to remove.
2. Choose Range, Range Properties to display the Range Properties InfoBox.
3. Click the Basics tab.
4. To remove a horizontal page break, deselect the Break Page at Row check box. To remove a vertical page break, deselect the Break Page at Column check box.

Hiding Segments in the Print Range

Sometimes data appears in a worksheet that you don't want to appear in a printed report. For example, you may have a column of data in the middle of the worksheet that is necessary for a calculation but not important to view on a report. Or, your report might include a row of confidential sales information that you don't want others to see. 1-2-3 97 offers different ways to exclude data from a printout, depending on whether you want to hide a row, a column, a cell, or a range of cells. 1-2-3 also provides a new outlining feature that enables you to automatically expand and collapse rows and columns, so that you can print only the data you need. For more information on outlining, refer to Chapter 15, "Managing the Worksheet Display."

Excluding Rows from a Print Range To exclude a row from the print range, follow these steps:

1. Position the cell pointer in the row you want to exclude from the print range. If you want to exclude multiple adjacent rows, select a cell from each row you want to exclude.

If you want to exclude multiple rows that are not adjacent, you can use Ctrl+click to click the row numbers for rows you want to exclude.

2. Choose Range, Range Properties to display the Range Properties InfoBox.
3. Click the Basics tab.
4. To exclude the selected rows, select the Hide Row check box.

To restore the hidden rows after printing, select the row numbers in the worksheet frame that span the hidden row(s). For example, if rows 8 and 10 are hidden, select rows 7 through 11. Then, deselect the Hide Row check box in the Range Properties InfoBox.

Excluding Columns from a Print Range To exclude a column from the print range, follow these steps:

1. Position the cell pointer in the column you want to exclude from the print range. If you want to exclude multiple adjacent columns, select a cell from each column you want to exclude.

If you want to exclude multiple columns that are not adjacent, you can use Ctrl+click to click the column letters for columns you want to exclude.

2. Choose Range, Range Properties to display the Range Properties InfoBox.
3. Click the Basics tab.
4. To exclude the selected columns, select the Hide Column check box.

To restore the hidden columns after printing, select the column letters in the worksheet frame that span the hidden column(s). For example, if columns B and D are hidden, select columns A through E. Then, deselect the Hide Column check box in the Range Properties InfoBox.

NOTE Another way to hide a column is to set its width to zero. A quick way to do this is to drag the right border of the column so that it touches (or crosses) the left border. Similarly, you can also hide a row by changing its row height to zero. Use the same method described previously to restore the hidden column(s) or row(s). ■

Excluding Cells and Ranges from a Print Range A worksheet may include information you want to save on disk but omit from a printed report. For example, you may want to omit an employee name from a printout of an expense report. To hide single cells or a range of cells, follow these steps:

1. Select the cell or range of cells in the worksheet that you want to hide.
2. Choose Range, Range Properties to display the Range Properties InfoBox.
3. Click the Security tab (the tab with the key on it).
4. To hide the selected cells, select the Hide Cell Contents check box.

To restore the hidden data after you finish printing, follow these steps:

1. Select the hidden cells in the worksheet that you want to display.
2. Choose Range, Range Properties to display the Range Properties InfoBox.

3. Click the Security tab (the tab with the key on it).
4. To display the data in hidden cells, deselect the Hide Cell Contents check box.

If you find yourself repeating certain print operations, you can save time by creating and using print macros. For more information on creating basic macros, see Chapter 36, "Writing 1-2-3 Macros."

TROUBLESHOOTING

I'm trying to select multiple print ranges from the Print dialog box, but 1-2-3 won't let me. As soon as I define the first range, I return to the Print dialog box. What am I doing wrong?
Nothing. 1-2-3 won't let you select multiple ranges when defining the print range from the Print dialog box. You must either type the range addresses (separated by commas or semicolons) in the Selected Range text box or preselect the ranges before you access the Print dialog box.

Changing the Page Orientation

One way to get a wide report to fit on a single page is to change the *orientation* (direction) of the printing. Normally you print in *portrait orientation*; that is, the text prints across the narrower part of the page. If you want to print horizontally on the page (across the longer width of the page), use *landscape orientation*.

To switch between portrait and landscape orientation, follow these steps:

1. Select the data in the worksheet that you want to print.
2. Choose File, Preview & Page Setup.
3. Click the Margins, Orientation, and Placement tab of the Preview & Page Setup Properties InfoBox (the third tab from the left).

NOTE If the Preview & Page Setup Properties InfoBox doesn't already appear on-screen, choose Preview, Preview & Page Setup Properties.

4. In the Orientation area of the Margins, Orientation, and Placement tab, switch between portrait orientation (the vertical page on the right) or landscape orientation (the horizontal page on the left).

Figure 10.7 shows an expense report displayed in the Preview window with landscape orientation.

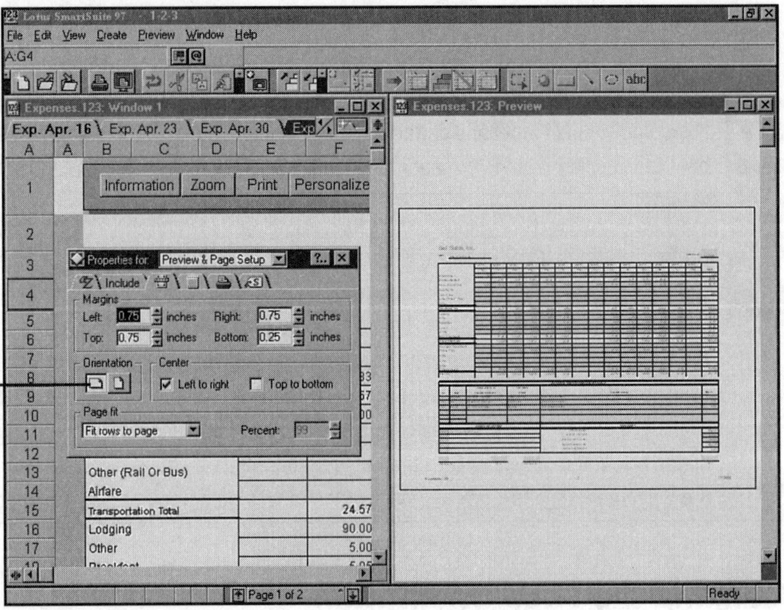

Fig. 10.7
If your worksheet includes several columns of data, you may want to use the landscape orientation.

Change the page orientation here

You also can use the Portrait or Landscape SmartIcons to switch page orientations. The SmartIcon showing a vertical page selects portrait orientation; the SmartIcon showing a horizontal page selects landscape orientation.

Changing Margin Settings

To make your worksheet data fit better on the printed page, you may want to change one or more of the page margins. Margins are measured from the edge of the page inward. You can change the margin settings for the left, right, top, and bottom margins of your report. The default settings are 0.5 inches for each margin.

To change the margin settings, follow these steps:

1. Select the data in the worksheet that you want to print.
2. Choose File, Preview & Page Setup.
3. Click the Margins, Orientation, and Placement tab of the Preview & Page Setup Properties InfoBox (the third tab from the left).
4. In the Margins area, use the Left, Right, Top, and Bottom text boxes to specify the margin width in inches (refer to fig. 10.7). You can type the desired setting, or use the scroll arrows beside each text box.

You can change the unit of measurement for margin settings by using the Windows Control Panel. Click Start, then choose Settings, Control Panel. Double-click the Regional Settings icon, then click the Number tab. Choose the desired option from the Measurement System drop-down list, then choose OK.

NOTE If your report has a header, it appears *after* (not within) the top margin, and footer text appears above the bottom margin. If you didn't specify a header, the report begins printing immediately after the top margin. See "Adding Headers and Footers" later in this chapter for more information on headers and footers.

Compressing and Expanding the Report

If your report doesn't fit on one page, you can have 1-2-3 automatically shrink the data using the Margins, Orientation, and Placement tab of the Preview & Page Setup Properties InfoBox. Five sizes are available:

- *Actual* (the default). 1-2-3 makes no attempt to alter the size of the printed output; that is, the data is not compressed at all.
- *Fit all to page.* 1-2-3 compresses the print range, in an attempt to fit all the information on one page. If the print range still does not fit, 1-2-3 prints the first page with the most compression possible and subsequent pages with the same compression.
- *Fit rows to page.* 1-2-3 compresses just the rows (not the columns) in an attempt to fit all the data on a single page.
- *Fit columns to page.* 1-2-3 compresses just the columns (not the rows) in an attempt to fit all the data on a single page.
- *Custom.* You also may enter a specific percentage by choosing the Custom option. If you select this option, you then enter a percentage in the Percent text box; this number can be as low as 15 (representing 15 percent of normal size) or as high as 1,000 (representing 1,000 percent, or 10 times the normal size).

There are also SmartIcons available for fitting the print range on a single page: Fit All to Page, Fit Rows to Page, and Fit Columns to Page.

▶ **See** "Setting Column Widths," **p. 94**

There are several other ways to fit more of your worksheet on a printed page. One way is to narrow the column widths or row heights as much as possible, either globally or individually. You can also print the report in landscape orientation or set smaller margins. See "Changing the Page Orientation" and "Changing Margin Settings" earlier in this chapter for details.

Centering a Print Range on the Page

1-2-3 provides options in the Preview & Page Setup Properties InfoBox that let you center your report horizontally, vertically, or both on the page. Choose File, Preview & Page Setup to display the Preview & Page Setup Properties InfoBox. Then, click the Margins, Orientation, and Placement tab, and select the Left to Right check box or the Top to Bottom check box; or you can select both check boxes (refer to fig. 10.7).

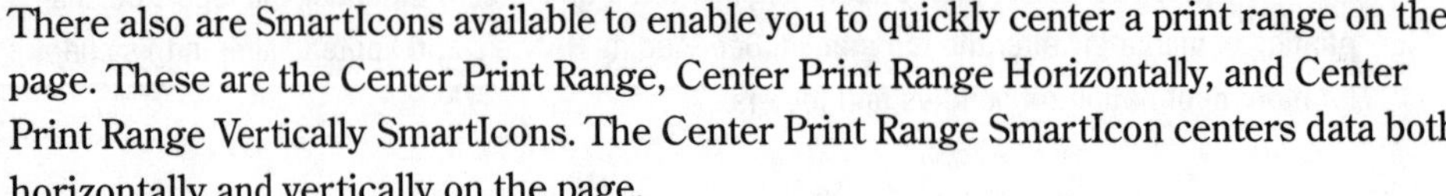

There also are SmartIcons available to enable you to quickly center a print range on the page. These are the Center Print Range, Center Print Range Horizontally, and Center Print Range Vertically SmartIcons. The Center Print Range SmartIcon centers data both horizontally and vertically on the page.

Adding Headers and Footers

A *header* is a single line of text that prints at the top of every page in your report; a *footer* prints at the bottom of each page. You can use headers and footers to print page numbers, the worksheet file name, the report date and time, the report title, and so on. The header text, which is printed on the first line after the top margin, is followed by two blank header lines preceding the report (for spacing). The footer text is printed above the bottom margin and below two blank footer lines (again, for spacing).

You specify a header or footer in the Preview & Page Setup Properties InfoBox. Choose File, Preview & Page Setup to display the Preview & Page Setup Properties InfoBox. Click the Headers and Footers tab (the fourth tab from the left). A header or footer can have three parts: left-aligned, centered, and right-aligned text. There are boxes provided for each of these three parts (three for a header, and three for a footer) in the Preview & Page Setup Properties InfoBox (see fig. 10.8). Whatever is entered in the first box is aligned at the left margin; the text in the second box is centered between the left and right margins; the text in the third box is aligned at the right margin. The header and footer text is printed in the worksheet's default typeface and size.

To change the font of a header or footer, click the Font, Attribute, and Color tab (the first tab) in the Preview & Page Setup Properties InfoBox. Select the appropriate header or footer option in the Font Properties drop-down list; then change the Font Name, Size, Attributes, or Text Color settings, as desired.

In addition to any text you enter, the header or footer can include codes for inserting page numbers, the date or time of printing, the file name, or the contents of a cell. First, place the cursor in the appropriate text box (left, center, or right; header or footer) in the Preview & Page Setup Properties InfoBox. The insert icons immediately become active. Then specify the codes you want to use from the following list (see fig. 10.8):

Fig. 10.8
Use the Preview & Page Setup Properties InfoBox to add headers and footers; in this figure, a footer has been added.

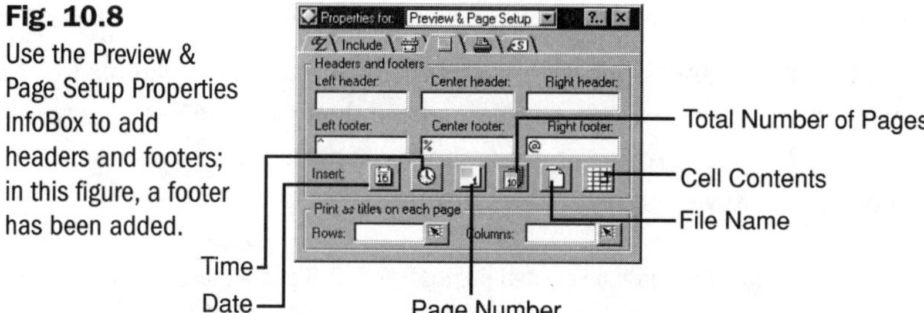

- To print the current date, type an at sign (@) or click the Date icon (the first icon).
- To print the current time, type a plus sign (+) or click the Time icon (the second icon).
- To number pages sequentially (starting with 1), type a pound sign (#) or click the Page Number icon (the third icon).
- To insert the total number of pages in the printed worksheet, type a percent sign (%) or click the Total Number of Pages icon (the fourth icon).
- To insert the file name, type a caret symbol (^) or click the File Name icon (the fifth icon).
- To use the contents of a cell as a header or footer, type a backslash (\) or click the Cell Contents icon (the sixth icon). Then type the address or range name of the cell that contains the text you want to include in the header or footer. The specified cell address or range name can contain a formula. If you specify a range name, 1-2-3 uses the contents of only the first cell in the range.

Printing Worksheet Titles

To make a multiple-page printed report more understandable, you can add headings from row or column worksheet ranges to each page of the printout by using the Headers and Footers tab (the fourth tab) of the Preview & Page Setup Properties InfoBox (refer to fig. 10.8). To specify row titles in the Rows text box of the Preview & Page Setup Properties InfoBox, use the range selector (beside the Rows text box) to select one or more rows of labels to print above each print range, at the top of all pages. To specify column titles in the Columns text box of the Preview & Page Setup Properties InfoBox, use the range selector (beside the Columns text box) to designate one or more columns of labels to print to the left of every print range, at the left edge of all pages.

Setting titles in a printout is similar to freezing titles in the worksheet. The Rows option produces a printed border similar to a frozen horizontal title display; the Columns option produces a printed border similar to a frozen vertical title display.

▶ **See** "Freezing Worksheet Titles," **p. 392**

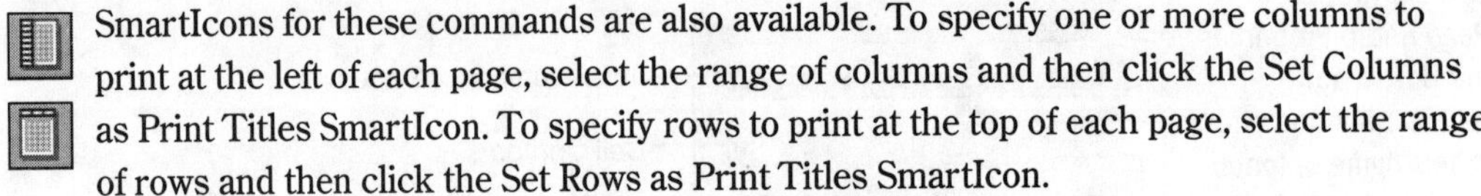

SmartIcons for these commands are also available. To specify one or more columns to print at the left of each page, select the range of columns and then click the Set Columns as Print Titles SmartIcon. To specify rows to print at the top of each page, select the range of rows and then click the Set Rows as Print Titles SmartIcon.

NOTE If you also include the print titles in the selected print range, 1-2-3 prints these elements twice. Be careful, therefore, not to include the range containing the print titles in the print range.

To cancel a print title, clear the entry in the Columns or Rows text box in the Preview & Page Setup Properties InfoBox.

Printing the Worksheet Frame and Grid Lines

Printing the worksheet frame is particularly useful during worksheet development, when you want the printouts to show the location of data in a large worksheet. In the Include tab of the Preview & Page Setup Properties InfoBox, you can use the Show list box to make selections to print the grid lines or the worksheet frame. The Sheet Row and Column Frames option prints column letters across the top of a worksheet and row numbers down the side of the worksheet. The Sheet Grid Lines option prints lines between all cells in the print range (see fig. 10.9).

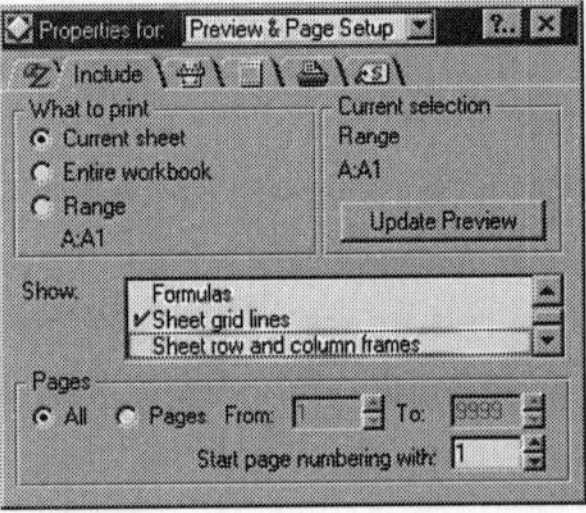

Fig. 10.9
You can add the worksheet frame or grid lines to your printout. In this example, grid lines have been added.

TIP You also can print cell comments, formulas, or an outline frame by selecting these items from the Show list box in the Preview & Page Setup Properties InfoBox.

Naming and Saving the Current Print Settings

When you have several worksheet reports with a similar layout, you may want to save the page setup so that you can retrieve the settings for other files. Saving the page setup options keeps you from having to specify the same settings over and over again. The Named Style tab of the Preview & Page Setup Properties InfoBox offers options for saving and retrieving page settings.

To assign a named style to the current print settings, follow these steps:

1. Choose File, Preview & Page Setup.
2. Click the Named Style tab (the tab with the "S") in the Preview & Page Setup Properties InfoBox.
3. Select the Create Style button. The Create Style dialog box appears.
4. In the Print Style Name text box, type a name for the style. If desired, type a description of the style in the Description text box (see fig. 10.10). If you always want to use these settings for the selected print range, select the Save print selection as part of the style check box.

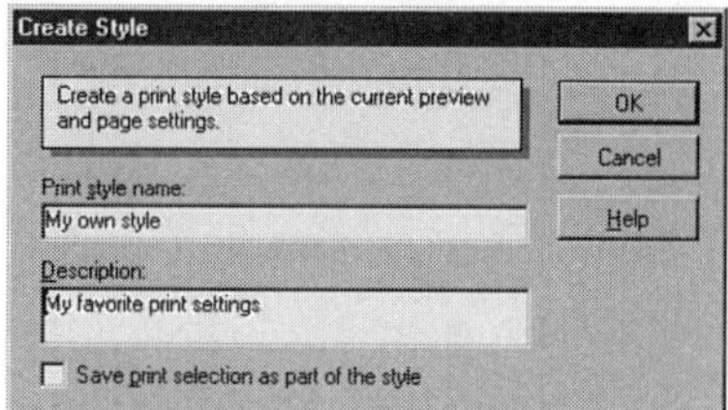

Fig. 10.10
Use the Create Style dialog box to specify a named style for your print settings.

5. Click OK to return to the Preview & Page Setup Properties InfoBox.

NOTE When you want to retrieve named page settings from earlier versions of 1-2-3, select the Retrieve button on the Named Style tab of the Preview & Page Setup Properties InfoBox. Then select the file name from the Retrieve Named Settings dialog box, and click Open.

TROUBLESHOOTING

I want to print my report on legal-sized paper, but I can't find an option for specifying the paper size in the Preview & Page Setup Properties InfoBox. Click the Printer tab in the Preview & Page Setup Properties InfoBox. Then, click the Printer button, and click the Properties button in the Print dialog box. Select the desired option, and click OK twice to return to the Preview & Page Setup Properties InfoBox.

I have two different printers installed, and want to print certain worksheets to the non-default printer. How do I do this? Choose File, Print and select the printer name from the Print To drop-down list. Or, if you are in the Preview window, you can click the Printer and Paper Size tab in the Preview & Page Setup Properties InfoBox. Then, click the Printer button, and click the desired printer name in the Print To drop-down list of the Printer dialog box. Click OK to return to the Preview & Page Setup Properties InfoBox.

PART II

Working with Charts and Maps

CHAPTER 11

Creating Charts

by Sue Plumley

Even if 1-2-3 provided only worksheet capabilities, the program would be extremely powerful. Despite the importance of keeping detailed worksheets that show real or projected data, however, data that is difficult to understand can be worthless.

Drawing conclusions from countless rows of numeric data is often difficult. To make data more readily understandable, 1-2-3 offers graphics capabilities that enable you to display data graphically. The program offers several types of business charts and sophisticated options for enhancing the appearance of charts. The real strength of 1-2-3 for Windows' graphics, however, lies in the graphics' integration with the worksheet. When you create a chart in the worksheet file, the chart is linked to the file. When you change data in the graphed range, the chart is automatically updated to reflect the change. ■

Create charts automatically from data in a worksheet file

When you create a chart automatically in 1-2-3, you create a professional-looking chart that includes a legend, title, data labels, and other chart elements.

Define a chart's data ranges manually

You can select specific ranges to use in a chart, even if the ranges are not contiguous in your worksheet, making it easy for you to create a chart with any data range necessary.

Add charts to worksheet files

In 1-2-3, you can create your charts within a worksheet file so you can better identify, reference, and illustrate your figures.

Understanding Common Chart Elements

When you create a chart, 1-2-3 includes several elements. Figure 11.1 shows a bar chart with these elements; the default chart type is a bar chart. Except for pie charts, all charts have a *y-axis* (a vertical left edge) and an *x-axis* (a horizontal bottom edge). In horizontally oriented charts, the y-axis is the bottom edge, and the x-axis is the left edge. 1-2-3 also enables you to use an optional second y-axis along the right side of a chart.

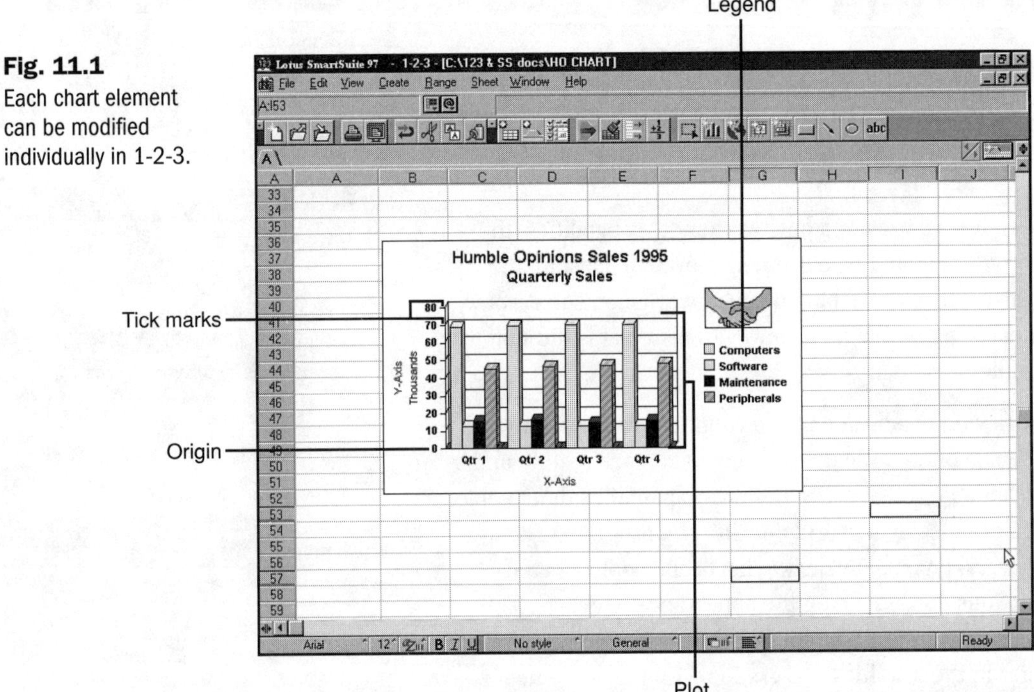

Fig. 11.1
Each chart element can be modified individually in 1-2-3.

1-2-3 divides the axes with *tick marks* and scales the numbers on the y-axis based on the minimum and maximum numbers in the associated data range. The intersection of the y-axis and the x-axis is the *origin*. Although you can plot charts with a nonzero origin, using a zero origin makes a chart easier to compare and understand.

A chart is made up of one or more *data series,* each of which reflects a category of data. The first category of data is always series A, the second is series B, and so on. Some chart types use a limited number of data ranges; for example, pie charts use one data range, and XY charts use two. Other chart types, such as line and bar charts, can graph up to 23 data ranges. When a chart has more than one data series, a *legend* is necessary to describe each of the data series.

The main part of the chart is called the *plot.* The plot includes the axes and their labels and titles and all the data plotted on the axes. A pie chart's plot is the pie and data labels. The plot does not include the legend, titles, or footnotes.

Selecting Worksheet Cells to Be Charted

To create a chart, you first must open the worksheet file that contains the data you want to plot. The examples in this chapter are based on the quarterly sales report shown in figure 11.2.

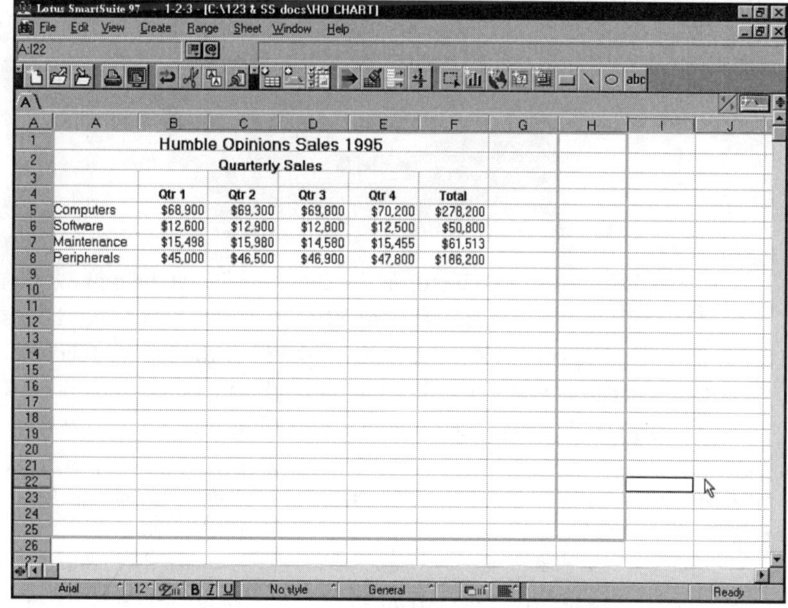

Fig. 11.2
A sample worksheet will be used throughout this chapter to illustrate the charting features.

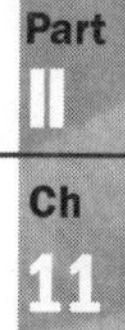

To graph information from the sales report, you must know which data you want to plot and which data you want to use to label the chart. In figure 11.2, the labels in rows 1 and 2 are suitable for the chart titles. Time-period labels are listed across row 4; these labels will go on the x-axis. Category identifiers are located in column A; these labels will become part of the legend. The numeric entries in rows 5 through 8 contain four different data series.

Creating an Automatic Chart

Suppose you're about to attend a meeting and you'd like to have a chart that illustrates those sales figures. You don't really have time to create a chart, or do you? Using automatic charting, you can quickly create a chart to meet your needs. If your worksheet is set up properly (as described in the section "Understanding the Rules for Automatic Charting," later in this chapter) creating an automatic chart is a very simple process:

1. Choose Create, Chart; or click the Create Chart SmartIcon. The Chart Assistant dialog box appears (see fig. 11.3). It shows and describes the steps to create the chart.

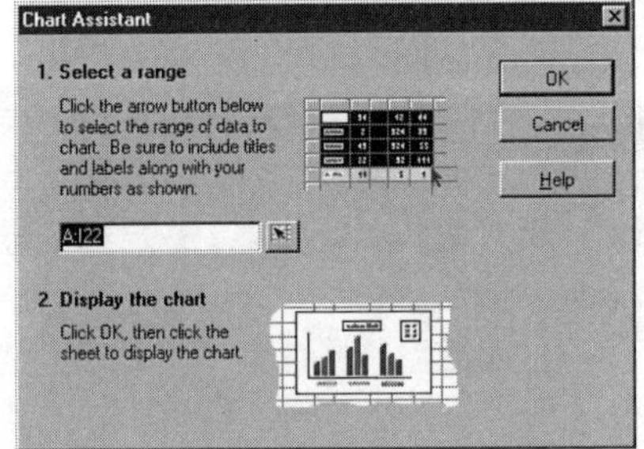

Fig. 11.3
The Chart Assistant dialog box coaches you through the automatic chart creation process.

2. Click the range selector in the Chart Assistant dialog box, then select the range of cells to be charted, including titles, legend labels, x-axis labels, and the numeric data. You can select the range with either the mouse (click and drag) or the keyboard (use the arrow keys to highlight the range, then press Enter). For example, you could select the range A1..E8 in figure 11.2.

TIP Don't chart the totals column with the rest of the data; the large sums in that column will throw off the comparisons.

3. The range you selected appears in the Range text box. To create a chart with this range, click the OK button. The Chart Assistant dialog box disappears and the mouse pointer changes to the chart pointer, which looks like a cross. The message at the top of the window tells you to click where you want to display the chart.
4. Indicate where you want to place the chart in the worksheet.

TIP Preselect the range you want to chart before you click the Create Chart SmartIcon or select the Chart command from the Create menu; this lets you create the chart without displaying the Chart dialog box.

There are two ways you can indicate placement of the chart. If you just click the chart pointer on the upper-left corner of where you want to place the chart, it will be inserted at a default size (about 4 by 2.5 inches). Alternatively, you can click and drag a box, indicating the size of your chart. Either way, the chart is inserted into the worksheet as soon as you release the mouse button.

▶ **See** "Changing the Chart Type and Style," **p. 325**

The Default Automatic Chart

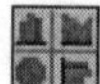

Figure 11.4 shows the default automatic chart created for the worksheet range A1..E8. Notice that the default chart type is a bar chart. To change the type (for example, to a line or pie chart), use the Chart, Chart Type command or the Select Chart Type SmartIcon. Chart types are discussed in more detail in the next chapter.

▶ **See** "Changing the Chart Type and Style," **p. 325**

▶ **See** "Building Complex Charts and Mapping Data," **p. 357**

When 1-2-3 creates the chart, it is automatically *selected*; that is, you can move, resize, and manipulate the chart in other ways. You can see that the chart is selected because it has *selection handles*—small black boxes that appear around the border of the chart (see figure 11.4).

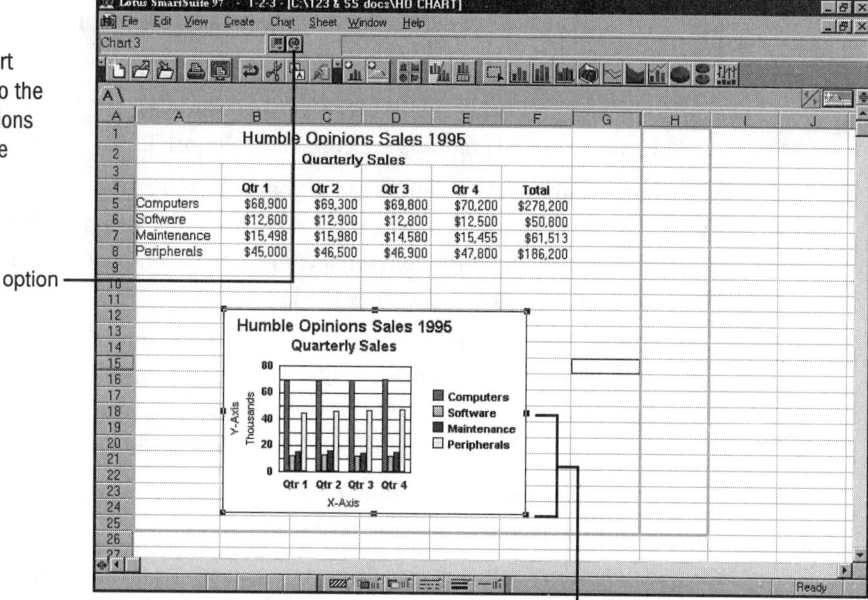

Fig. 11.4
When a chart is selected, the Chart option is added to the menu and all actions taken relate to the selected chart.

Here are a few other things to notice about the default chart:

- The title and subtitle are centered at the top of the chart.
- The legend is located to the right of the plot.
- Default axis titles (X-Axis and Y-Axis) are inserted.

Also notice that after you create a chart, a new menu, Chart, replaces Range in the menu bar. This menu displays only if the chart, or an element in the chart, is selected. Chapters 12, 13, and 14 cover how to manipulate and change these chart elements.

CAUTION

If you click a worksheet cell, the chart is no longer selected and the Chart menu option disappears. To access the Chart menu again, you must select an element on the chart by clicking it; you then see selection handles around the object, and the Chart menu returns.

Understanding the Rules for Automatic Charting

If you know the rules 1-2-3 uses to create a chart automatically, you can make sure that your worksheet is set up in such a way that the chart will look the way you want it to. Here are the rules 1-2-3 follows when it creates the chart:

Rule 1. If a title is anywhere in the first row of the selected range, it becomes the chart title.

Rule 2. If a title is anywhere in the second row, it becomes the chart's subtitle.

Rule 3. Blank rows and columns are completely ignored.

Rule 4. If more rows than columns are in your selected range, 1-2-3 plots the data by column. The first column becomes the x-axis labels, the second column becomes the first data series, the third column becomes the second data series, and so forth. The first row after any titles becomes the legend labels.

Rule 5. If more columns than rows are in the selected range, 1-2-3 plots the data by rows. The first row (after any titles or blank rows) becomes the x-axis labels; the second row becomes the first data series; the next row becomes the second data series; and so on. The first column becomes the legend labels.

Rule 6. If there are the same number of columns and rows in the selected range, 1-2-3 plots the data by column. (See rule 4.)

Rule 7. If you select only numeric data when you create a chart, 1-2-3 follows rules 4 and 5 to determine how to lay out the chart (by column or by row). 1-2-3 creates a default heading and legend, and default axis titles (see fig. 11.5); you can modify this default text by double-clicking the appropriate chart element. You then see the appropriate InfoBox (Headings, X-Axis, Y-Axis, or Legend) in which you can change the text. These InfoBoxes are discussed in Chapter 12, "Modifying Charts."

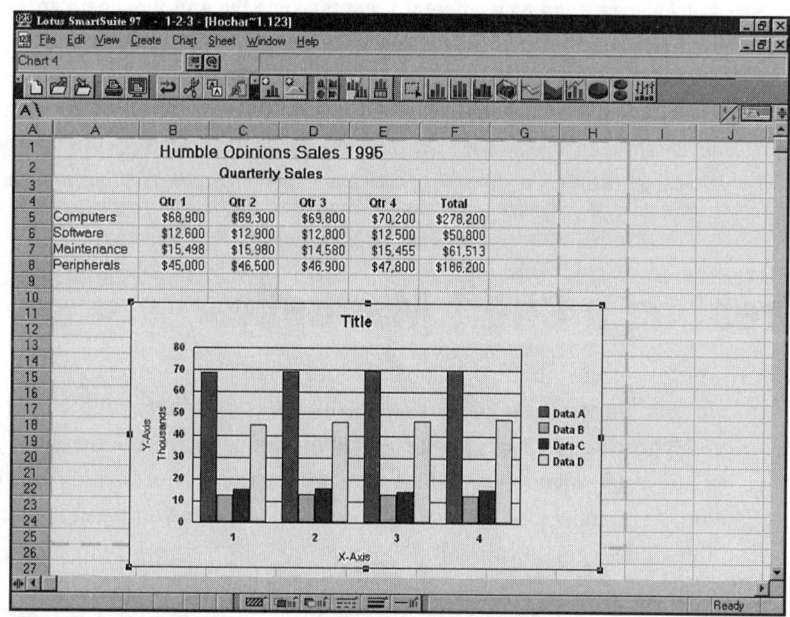

Fig. 11.5
1-2-3 creates default titles and legend labels when you have only values in the chart range.

Although it may seem that there are a lot of rules for creating automatic charts, you do have quite a bit of flexibility. 1-2-3 is smart when it looks at your selected range. 1-2-3 ignores blank rows and columns and can determine whether a row contains a title for the heading, labels for the x-axis or legends, or numbers to be plotted. If you don't include the legend labels or x-axis labels in your chart range, 1-2-3 does not use the first row or column of numeric values as your labels—it leaves the row or column blank so that you can specify the range later. The labels are undefined until you specify the range.

TROUBLESHOOTING

I created an automatic chart by preselecting the range and choosing Create, Chart. However, the chart isn't set up the way I want it. The legends and x-axis labels are switched. Is there a way to fix this? When 1-2-3 produces automatic charts, it looks at your preselected range and uses its rules for determining how to set up your chart ranges. To switch your legends and data labels, choose Chart, Ranges to display the Properties for Chart InfoBox. Choose the Ranges tab and then select the Options button to display the Range Options dialog box. In Assign Ranges,

continues

continued

choose either Series by Row or Series by Column. A sample layout shows how the data will look. Choose OK to close the dialog box and the selected range assignment appears in your chart.

Can I place a chart on a different sheet than one the worksheet data appears on? Yes. First, create the new sheet for the chart if it doesn't already exist (click the New Sheet button or choose Create, Sheet). Then move to the sheet with the data and perform the steps to select the chart data ranges. When the mouse pointer changes to the chart pointer (a cross), click the tab for the sheet on which you want to place the chart and click the cell in which you want the upper-left corner of the chart to begin, or click and drag to make the chart a size other than the default.

Creating a Chart Manually

As you learned in the previous section, when you preselect the range, 1-2-3 uses the data in your worksheet to produce a default chart. But that isn't the only way to create a chart. 1-2-3 provides a Chart menu so that you can define the elements of your chart (see fig. 11.6). You'll want to go to this menu if your worksheet isn't laid out in the prescribed fashion, if you must modify any of the ranges, or if you would just rather define the data series, titles, and legends yourself.

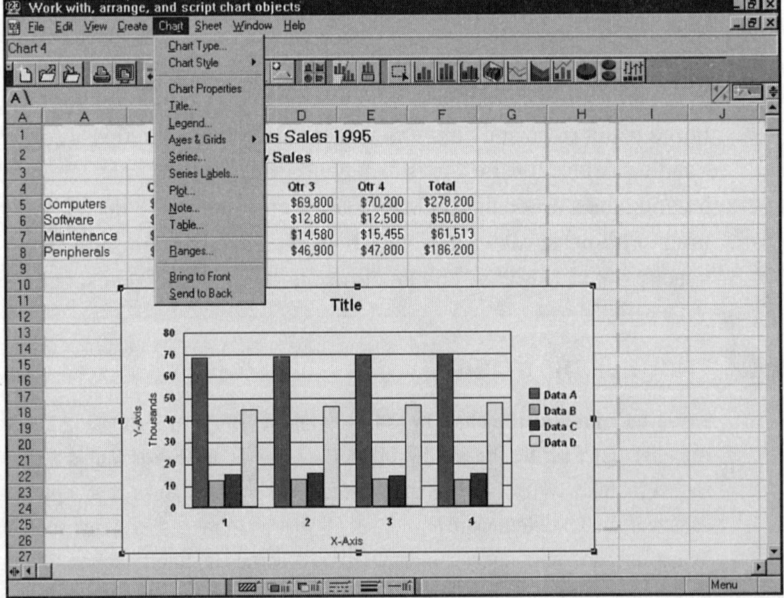

Fig. 11.6
Use the Chart menu to define specific elements of a selected chart.

To create a chart from scratch, first select the range using either the mouse or the keyboard. Next, choose either Create, Chart or click the Create Chart SmartIcon. The mouse pointer changes to the cross you use to create the chart. Click or click and drag the mouse to indicate the size and placement of the chart. The default bar chart appears with the selected data.

Your next step is to define the ranges containing your x-axis labels and your data series. The Properties InfoBox lets you define or modify your chart's x-axis labels and data series ranges, as well as many other properties of your chart. Figure 11.7 shows the Ranges tab of the Properties InfoBox. Display the InfoBox by selecting the chart and then choosing Chart, Chart Properties; alternatively, double-click the chart.

▶ **See** "Changing the Chart Type and Style," **p. 325**

▶ **See** "Modifying Other Elements of a Chart," **p. 334**

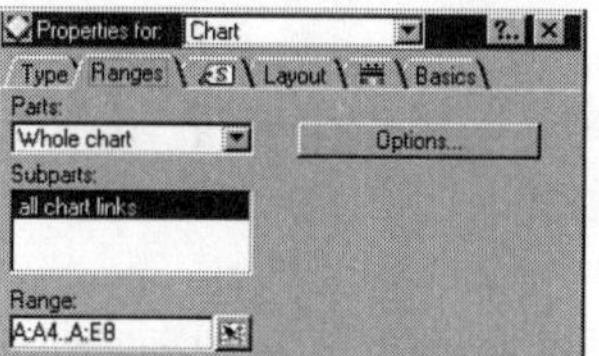

Fig. 11.7
You can define or modify chart ranges by using the Ranges tab.

To define a range, you first select the chart element from the Parts list in the Ranges tab. You can choose from such elements as Data, Legend, Title, X Axis Title, X Axis Labels, and so on, although you can only change the ranges of the following: Data, Data Labels, Legend, or X, Y, or ZY Axis Labels.

After you select a part, related elements appear in the Subparts list. For example, if you choose Data as a part, its related subparts are All Series, Series 1, Series 2, and so on, up to Series 30. Select any series within the Subparts list to display its range in the Range box.

If you want to change the range for any series, select the series in the Subparts list and then enter the new range in the Range text box. You can, alternatively, click the range selector and then select the range on your worksheet.

You can also define a chart's ranges by row or by column, to indicate how you want the data series displayed within the chart. In the Ranges tab of the InfoBox, choose the Data Parts, then choose All Series in the Subparts list. Choose the Options button; the Range Options dialog box appears (see fig. 11.8). To change the range assignment, click the Assign Ranges drop-down box and choose Series by Columns or Series by Rows. Choose OK to accept and view the change in your chart.

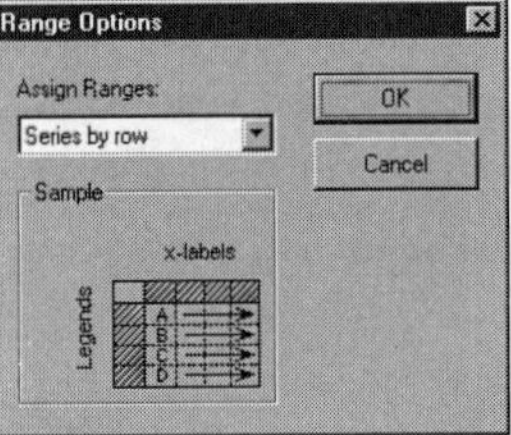

Fig. 11.8
A sample worksheet grid shows the way 1-2-3 assigns the data series when you choose Series By Row for Assign Ranges.

If you redisplay your chart, the legend labels appear next to each series letter, assuming you included the labels in the range you defined. If you didn't include the legend labels, the generic names (Data A, Data B, and so on) appear in the legend.

Defining the ranges individually requires more work but is sometimes the only way to define chart ranges. When you don't want to plot certain columns or rows that are in the middle of a range, you must define the series one at a time. For example, if you want to graph computer sales (refer to row 5 of fig. 11.2) versus peripherals sales (refer to row 8 of fig. 11.2), you must define the series individually so that you don't plot the other sales figures (refer to rows 6 and 7 of fig. 11.2).

NOTE If the ranges for the chart are not next to each other, you can still create the chart automatically by selecting the collection of ranges for the chart before you click on the Create Chart SmartIcon or choose Create, Chart. To select a collection of ranges, press Ctrl while you select additional ranges for the collection.

Naming and Finding Charts

1-2-3 automatically names your charts as you create them (Chart 1, Chart 2, and so forth). The name of the selected chart (or the last one you selected) appears in the selection indicator on the edit line. To give your charts more descriptive names, use the Chart Properties InfoBox. Select the Basics tab in the InfoBox (see fig. 11.9).

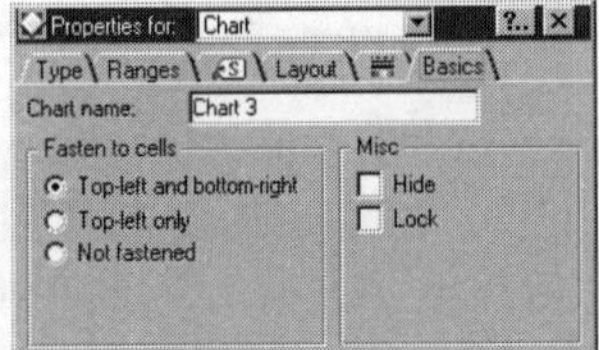

Fig. 11.9
The Chart Properties InfoBox can assign descriptive names to your charts.

Use the Basics tab of the InfoBox to name your chart. In the Chart Name text box, enter a new name for the chart; you can use any letter or number characters, punctuation, and spaces in the name. Press Enter to complete the name.

NOTE You also can use the Basics tab of the Chart InfoBox to anchor the chart, hide the chart, or lock the chart. ■

To display a chart associated with a name, press F5 (GoTo) or choose Edit, Go To to open the Go To dialog box. In the drop-down list box, choose Chart. A list of chart names appears in the item list box. Select the chart name and choose OK to go to that chart. The dialog box closes and the chart appears on-screen, selected.

Creating Multiple Charts in a File

1-2-3 lets you create an unlimited number of charts in each worksheet file. You can define new charts and place them in different parts of the worksheet. For organizational purposes, you might want to place each chart in its own sheet; use the New Sheet button to insert a sheet after the current one.

Previewing and Printing Charts

You can easily view on-screen a chart you create in 1-2-3 for Windows, but often you need to print copies of charts to share with coworkers. You can preview and print charts the way you print worksheets—by using the Print command on the File menu.

Printing a Chart

Before printing a chart, select it—any element on the chart will suffice. Then choose File, Print or click the Print SmartIcon. The Print dialog box shows the name of the selected chart in the Selected chart field. Figure 11.10 shows the dialog box with the name `1995 Sales` as the Selected Chart; if you have not renamed the chart, Chart 1 or Chart 2 will appear in the Selected Chart area. When you choose OK, the chart prints at the size it appears in the worksheet.

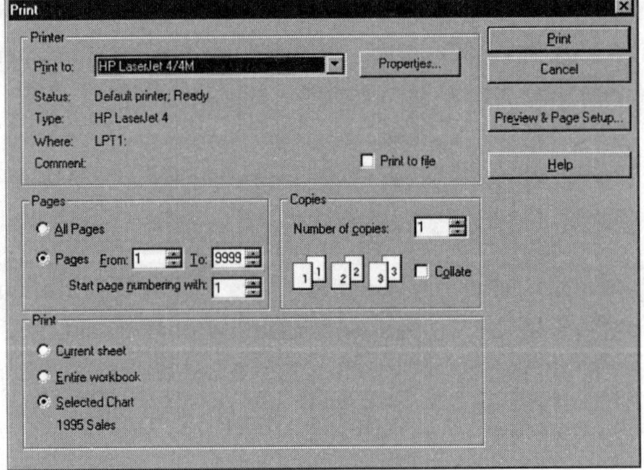

Fig. 11.10
Print the selected chart instead of the current sheet or entire workbook.

Printing a Chart Full Page In some cases, you may want a chart to fill a printed page—such as when you are printing charts for a presentation. 1-2-3 provides a command that automatically enlarges a chart to fill a page, adjusting the size of all elements and the point size of text proportionally. To use this option, select the chart; then choose File, Preview & Page Setup. (You can also display the Page Setup InfoBox by clicking the Preview & Page Setup button in the Print dialog box.)

The chart appears in print preview and the Properties for Preview & Page Setup InfoBox appears with the Size tab showing. At the bottom of the Size tab is the Page Fit drop-down box, which has four settings for charts: Actual, Fill Page, Fill Page But Keep Proportions, and Custom.

- Actual is the default size or the size the chart was drawn originally.
- Fill Page enlarges or reduces the chart until it fills the page.
- Because Fill Page may produce a distorted chart, a better choice is often Fill Page But Keep Proportions. This chart prints as large as possible without any distortion.
- Custom enables you to set a percentage, such as 50 percent or 300 percent to enlarge or reduce the chart (100 percent is the default size). Press Enter to see the results of the percentage you selected.

Depending on the chart, the Fill Page But Keep Proportions option is often more effective when you change the Orientation setting to landscape (in the Size tab of the InfoBox).

Printing Charts and Worksheet Data on the Same Page

To add white space between a worksheet data and chart, include blank rows as part of the range(s) to be printed.

You can print a chart and its supporting data on separate pages and then collate them to produce a report. However, printing a chart and its worksheet together on one page can sometimes be easier for your coworkers to read. How you print this type of report depends on where the chart is located in the worksheet in relation to its supporting data.

- If the chart and data are placed exactly where you want them in the report, you can define a single print range: select the range of cells that includes the data and the chart. (Even though 1-2-3 for Windows highlights the cells behind the chart without appearing to select the chart, the chart is selected when you select *all* the cells behind it.)
- If the data is in one part of the worksheet and the chart is in another, you must define two print ranges. To define multiple ranges, type the ranges, separated by commas or semicolons. To point to the ranges, you must preselect them; remember to hold down the Ctrl key as you select the second and subsequent ranges.

Selecting a Chart with Draw Objects If you have used Create, Drawing to add any text or objects to your chart, they will not print if you simply select the chart name in the Print dialog box. To print the chart and objects you have added to it, you must use the Select Objects SmartIcon to "lasso" the chart. Then, when you display the Print dialog box, the word `Collection` appears in the Selected Drawn Object field. This means that 1-2-3 will print the chart with all the graphic elements you selected.

▶ **See** "Annotating a Chart," **p. 368**

▶ **See** "Working with Graphics," **p. 415**

Previewing a Chart

You can preview a chart before you print it. Previewing can save you time and paper, enabling you to make all necessary adjustments and changes before you print. To preview a chart, select the chart, and then choose File, Preview & Page Setup or click the Preview SmartIcon. You also can select the Preview & Page Setup button from the Print dialog box.

When you add a chart to a worksheet, you specify the size of the chart and the location at which it appears on the page. By previewing the chart, you can determine how the chart fits on the printed page. You then can decide whether you should use one of the Size options described earlier in this chapter. Figure 11.11 shows a previewed chart in portrait orientation, with the Fill Page option selected.

Fig. 11.11
Use preview to adjust the chart size and position.

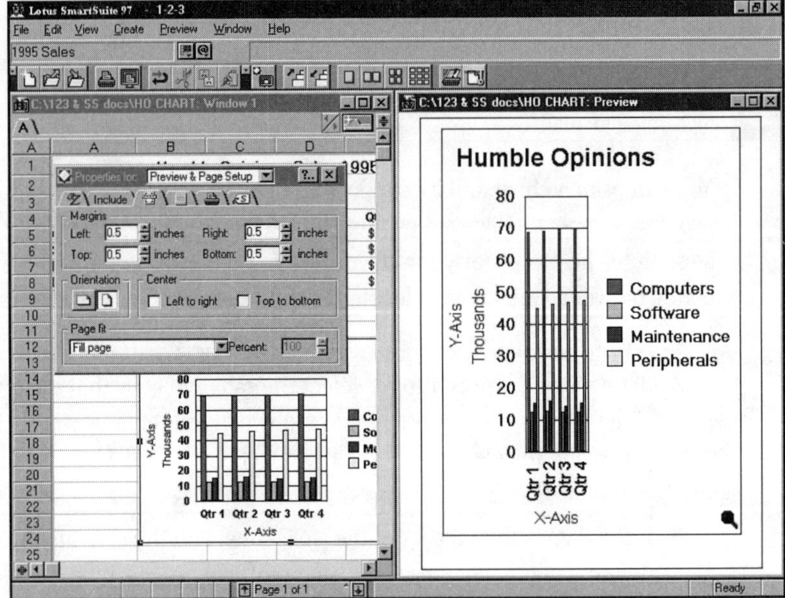

Printing Color Charts on a Black-and-White Printer

If you try to use a black-and-white printer to print a color chart, items in color print in black or grays and the background colors are often ignored. Many grays in the chart make it difficult to discern between your data series.

For greater control over the way the chart appears in black and white, you can change the solid colors to shades of gray or black-and-white hatch patterns. Also, be sure to include symbols in your line charts to make the data series easier to distinguish.

▶ **See** "Changing Data Series Colors and Patterns," **p. 350**

TROUBLESHOOTING

I'm having trouble selecting the worksheet data and two charts that I want to print on one page. Remember to press and hold the Ctrl key while you use the mouse to highlight the worksheet range and click the charts.

I want to put some white space on the printed page between the worksheet data at the top of the page and a chart at the bottom. How do I do it? If there are blank rows below the worksheet range, select those rows to provide the white space. If not, select the worksheet range, select another blank range in the worksheet for the white space, then select the chart.

CHAPTER 12

Modifying Charts

by Sue Plumley

In Chapter 11, you saw how easy it was to create a chart from worksheet data. Although the default bar chart may suit your needs perfectly, you may find that a different kind of chart would illustrate your data more effectively, or you may want to add titles or notes to make your chart's message more clear.

1-2-3 offers many different chart types and styles that you can select with a click of the mouse. You can also move and resize chart elements, add titles and notes, and exercise more advanced control over the way 1-2-3 graphs the data, such as changing the scale of the y-axis. ■

Select and manipulate chart objects

You can change the size and position of a chart's elements—such as a data series, legend, title, and so on—and otherwise manipulate chart objects after you select them.

Select an appropriate chart type and style

1-2-3 provides many types of charts, such as bar, pie, line, and so on, that you can create. This chapter shows you how to choose the type of chart that best suits your data.

Change the default chart type and style

Customize the type and style of chart that displays by default when you create a chart, thus saving you time and energy.

Modify chart elements

Change a variety of chart elements—including orientation, legend, titles, axis titles, axis scale, and tick marks—so your chart better represents the data in your worksheet.

Add elements to a chart

You can better represent data if you include such elements as notes, a background grid, data labels, and a table of values to your charts. This chapter shows you how.

Manipulating Chart Elements

One beneficial aspect of 1-2-3's charts is how flexible they are. You can select individual elements on the chart, and then move, size, delete, or format them. It's this flexibility that makes it so easy to build charts in 1-2-3.

Resizing the Entire Chart

The printed dimensions of a chart correspond to its size in the worksheet. However, you might discover that the default size or the size for which you initially made the chart does not meet your needs. Resizing a chart is straightforward. First, click the chart frame so that you see selection handles surrounding the chart. Next, drag one of the handles until the chart is the desired size. While you drag the handles, the mouse pointer changes to a four-headed arrow.

Options for Resizing The way that 1-2-3 resizes depends on which handle you drag:

- If you drag a corner handle, you change both the height and width of the chart.
- By dragging a middle handle on the right or left side of the chart, you change just the width.
- If you drag a middle handle on the top or bottom of the chart, you adjust the height only.
- If you want to size the chart proportionally, hold down the Shift key as you drag.

If a chart is too large to fit on-screen, choose View, Zoom To, and select 50% to show more of the worksheet.

Selecting Chart Objects

Before you can copy, delete, rearrange, move, or otherwise manipulate an object, you must select it. You can select one or several objects. When an object is selected, selection handles appear around the object.

To select an object, just click it. To select several objects with the mouse, click the Select Objects SmartIcon, which enables you to draw a rectangle around the objects you want to select; after selecting the icon, drag the mouse until you surround all the objects. As you drag, you see a box with a dotted outline. When you release the mouse button, all the objects that were in this box will have selection handles. Figure 12.1 shows a data series selected; note all corresponding bars are selected, as well as the matching legend item, when you select only one bar in the chart.

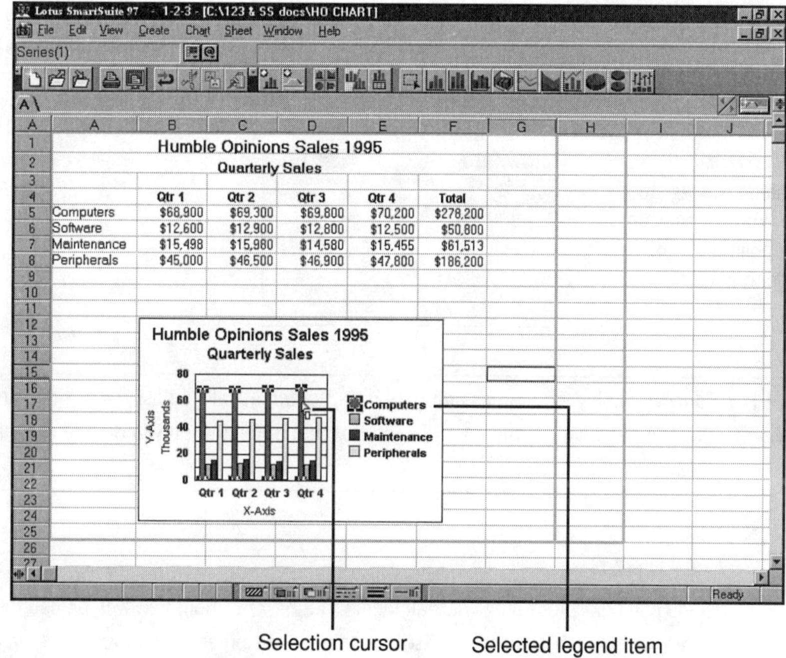

Fig. 12.1
Select any chart item by clicking it; corresponding items also become selected.

Because a chart contains so many different elements, it can be difficult sometimes to determine whether the mouse pointer is actually on the object you want to select. To help you select objects, the mouse pointer reflects what you are pointing to. For example, when you point to text, the mouse pointer has a capital A underneath it. When you are pointing to a line, you see a diagonal line underneath the mouse pointer; when you are pointing to a bar, the pointer has a hollow rectangle underneath it. A circle underneath the mouse pointer indicates that you are pointing to a data point.

To deselect all selected items, position the mouse pointer on any blank area on the chart and click the mouse. To deselect one item when several items are selected, position the mouse pointer on the item, and then press and hold down Shift while you click the mouse.

Moving Objects

You can move objects in the chart by dragging them with the mouse or, in some cases, by selecting an available position from a dialog box. For example, the Properties for Legend InfoBox presents options for placing the legend to the top, bottom, right, left, or corner of the plot, but you are not restricted to these places (see fig. 12.2). You can move the legend anywhere inside the chart frame. You can also move the plot, the titles, the footnotes, the entire chart, and any objects that you added by using the Drawing commands on the Create menu. (For more information about using dialog boxes to move the legend and titles, see "Specifying or Changing the Legend" and "Customizing the Chart Titles and Adding Notes" later in this chapter.)

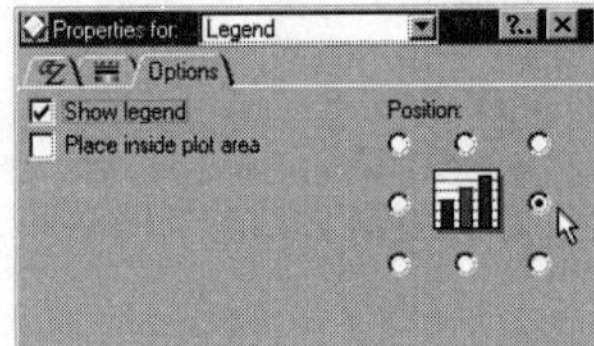

Fig. 12.2
Position the legend in the chart by selecting the position in the Legend InfoBox.

To move the legend or titles and have 1-2-3 automatically adjust the positions of other objects, first try the positions offered in the InfoBox that appear when you double-click the legend or titles.

CAUTION

You can select and drag chart elements to a new position; however, be careful to select all related items. Also, 1-2-3 doesn't reposition other chart elements when you move an item in the chart box; you'll have to do that yourself.

To move an object, perform the following steps:

1. Select the object you want to move by clicking it; make sure selection handles are on the desired object or you might move the wrong thing.
2. Place the mouse pointer inside the object and begin dragging the object by moving the mouse. As you drag the object, a dotted box appears around the object and is moved to the new location. (A dotted line appears on lines and arrows).
3. When you finish moving the object, release the mouse button. The dotted box disappears and the object is moved to the new location.

Resizing Objects in the Chart

To change the size of an object, select it and then place the mouse pointer on one of the selection handles. Before dragging, make sure you see a four-headed arrow, which is generally the mouse pointer for sizing an object; although with some objects you'll use a two-headed arrow, and with others, the normal mouse pointer works for resizing. To define the new size, drag the selection handle until the object is the desired size. Release the mouse button when you are done.

Resizing a frame that contains centered text, such as the titles or legend, works a little differently. As you drag a selection handle, both sides of the box expand or contract. For example, if you drag a right-hand handle to the right, the frame expands on the right and the left, keeping the text inside centered within the frame. This applies to title, footnote, and legend frames only.

Deleting Objects

If the chart contains an element you don't want, delete it by selecting the object and pressing the Del key. 1-2-3 lets you delete the title frame (along with its contents), the legend, axis titles, the footnote frame (and its contents), the unit indicator, individual data series, the entire chart, and any objects that you added by using the Drawing commands on the Create menu. You cannot delete the plot, x-axis labels, or the y-axis scale. Also, you cannot delete a frame's contents without deleting the entire frame.

If you accidentally delete an object, choose Edit, Undo, click the Undo SmartIcon, or press Ctrl+Z.

TROUBLESHOOTING

How can I tell whether the chart and the worksheet data it comes from will both fit on a page? You can open the File menu and choose the Preview & Page Setup command.

I enlarged the title frame to accommodate the length of the chart title and now the title frame does not fit in the chart frame. Enlarge the size of the entire chart until the title frame is completely displayed.

Changing the Chart Type and Style

Although the default chart that 1-2-3 creates may suit your needs, you may need to change the chart to make it more appropriate for your report or presentation. Sometimes a different type of chart can present the data more effectively. This section describes the many chart types that are available in 1-2-3, as well as how to change the chart type and select different styles for each chart type.

NOTE Most of the modifications you make to a chart can be executed using the Properties InfoBox. Whether you choose a command from the Chart menu or double-click a chart element, the Properties InfoBox will appear. You can leave the InfoBox open for use throughout this chapter, changing the elements using the drop-down list box in the title bar.

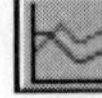

By default, 1-2-3 displays a bar chart when you create a chart. To change the type of chart that 1-2-3 displays, you can click one of the SmartIcons that directly selects a new chart type (such as the Change to Line Chart SmartIcon or the Change to 3D Pie Chart SmartIcon), choose Chart, Chart Type, or, you can display the Properties for Chart InfoBox and choose from the Type tab.

In the Type tab of the Chart Properties InfoBox (see fig. 12.3), you can choose from all chart types, select one of the styles available for the selected chart type, and change from vertical to horizontal orientation. When you choose the type of chart from the list on the left, 1-2-3 changes the display on the right to reflect your choice. Additionally, any changes in chart type you make in the InfoBox take immediate effect on-screen so you can see if the change is what you want.

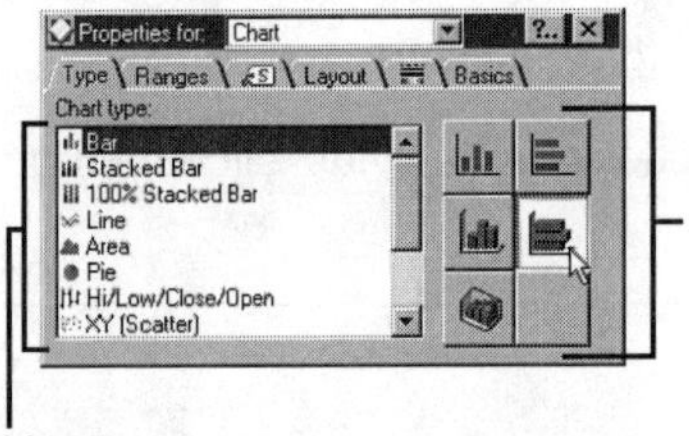

Fig. 12.3
Experiment with different chart types to see which one best conveys your data by making selections in the Type dialog box.

Chart styles for selected type

Chart types

Selecting the Chart Style

To the right of the Chart Type list in the Type tab, several large buttons showing the different styles for the current type of chart appear. In figure 12.3, five styles of bar charts are displayed. The upper-left style button is used to select a standard bar chart. The button to the right produces a vertical bar chart. You also can choose any of three three-dimensional bar charts. Additionally, you can select from various types of Stacked Bar and 100% Stacked Bar chart types. In a stacked bar chart, for example, the sections of a bar represent the individual data ranges, and the top of the bar shows the total of the data ranges.

To select one of the chart style buttons, click it with the mouse. 1-2-3 immediately changes the chart type, leaving the InfoBox open for you to continue editing the chart.

Selecting the Chart Type

The type of chart you choose depends on the type of data you are using. If, for example, you're comparing pieces of data to the whole—such as quarterly sales for the year—a pie chart would best represent your data. Table 12.1 lists the chart types you can create in

1-2-3 and offers some guidelines for using each type. The next sections discuss each chart type in more detail.

Table 12.1 Chart Types

Type	Description
Line	Shows the trend of numeric data over time.
Area	Shows broad trends in data that occur over time.
Bar	Compares related data at a certain time or shows the trend of numeric data over time.
Pie	Graphs a single data range, showing what percentage of the total each data point contributes. Do not use this type of chart if the data contains negative numbers.
Multiple pie	Shows the relationship between two or more data ranges, each represented by an individual pie and its pieces.
XY (Scatter)	Shows the relationship between one independent variable and one or more dependent variables.
HLCO (High-Low-Close-Open)	Shows fluctuations in data over time, such as the high, low, close, and open prices of a stock.
Mixed bar/line	Shows a bar chart for the first three ranges and a line chart for three additional ranges.
Radar	Wraps a line chart around a central point, showing the symmetry or uniformity of data.
Number Grid	Creates a table from the data and organizes it in columns and rows.
Donut	Similar to a pie chart in that it shows the relationship between each piece and the whole.

To select a chart type, select the type from the list on the left in the Type tab of the Properties for Chart InfoBox. The next sections describe the most common types of charts: Line and 3D Line, Area and 3D Area, Bar and 3D Bar, Pie and 3D Pie.

▶ **See** "Creating Special Charts," **p. 358**

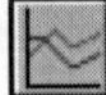

Line Charts Line charts are ideal for displaying trends and changes in data over time. Figure 12.4 shows the styles available for line charts, with the first style applied to the Humble Opinions Sales for 1995. The first style in the left column has lines with symbols located at each data point, so it's easy to find each point, the next style down has lines with no symbols, and the last style has lines only with a 3D effect.

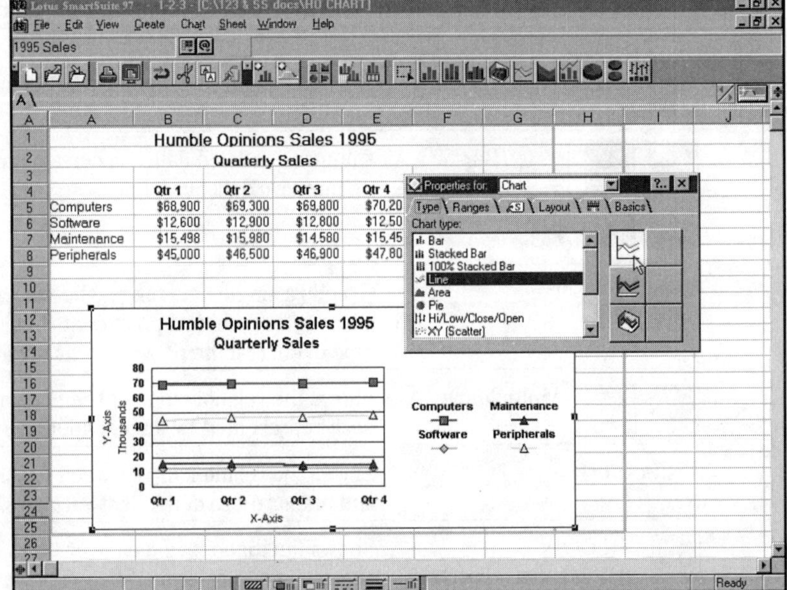

Fig. 12.4
The line chart styles are ideal for showing changes over time.

Area Charts An area chart, which emphasizes broad trends, is similar to a line chart except that the area between data ranges is filled with a different color or pattern. The two-dimensional area chart has three basic styles: one 2D and two 3D; choose the style that best represents your data. Figure 12.5 shows the choices for an area chart with the second option applied to the sample chart.

If you want to show the total of all series at each data point, use the standard area chart or the 3D stacked area chart. To compare the individual data series, use the 3D area chart that displays one data series behind another; however, in order to see all the data series, the data series in front needs to have smaller values than the data series in the back. You might arrange your data in the worksheet from smallest to largest before plotting this type of chart.

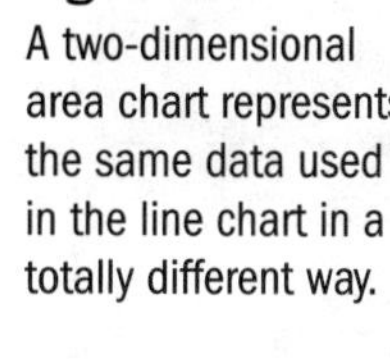

Fig. 12.5
A two-dimensional area chart represents the same data used in the line chart in a totally different way.

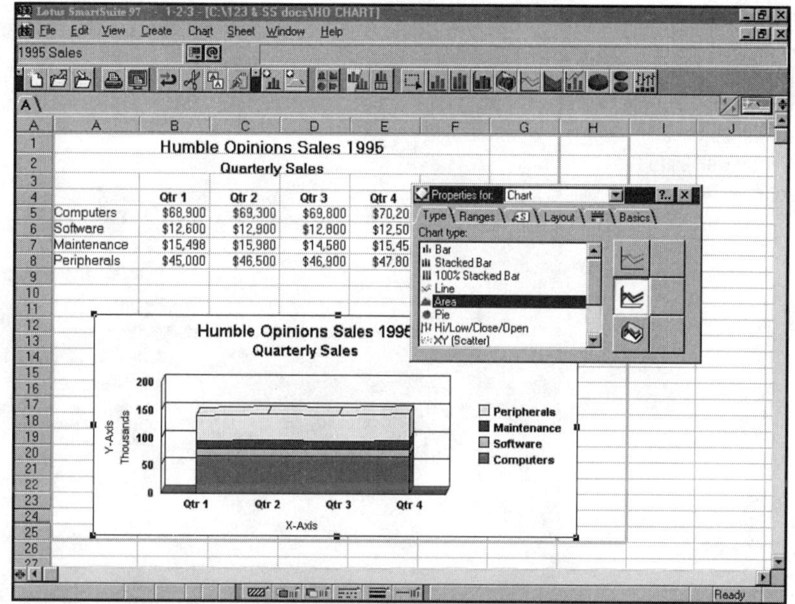

Bar Charts Although Standard Bar is the default chart type, you might want to make a trip to the InfoBox to choose a different style of bar chart (for example, a stacked bar), to select a 3D Bar type, or to change the chart's orientation.

The Bar chart type offers three types: Bar, Stacked Bar, and 100% Stacked Bar. Within each of these types are five styles, both 2-dimensional and 3-dimensional. The standard bar chart, the default, places the bars side by side. A *stacked bar chart* shows data as a series of bars piled on top of one another. The 100% stacked bar presents columns that are the same size with each data series claiming its share of the column (see fig. 12.6).

Stacked bar charts are useful for showing the portion that data series contribute to each other, to the whole, and for comparing totals over time. 100% stacked bar charts serve the same purpose, as well as show trends between the portions over time.

Figures 12.7, 12.8, and 12.9 plot the same data, comparing the quarterly sales of each department. However, these three charts present different messages. The bar chart in figure 12.7 compares the relative sales in dollars of the departments. The stacked bar chart in figure 12.8 compares each department's contribution to the combined sales. The 100% stacked bar chart in figure 12.9 is the same as figure 12.8, except that the 100% bars help to show changes in the individual data series.

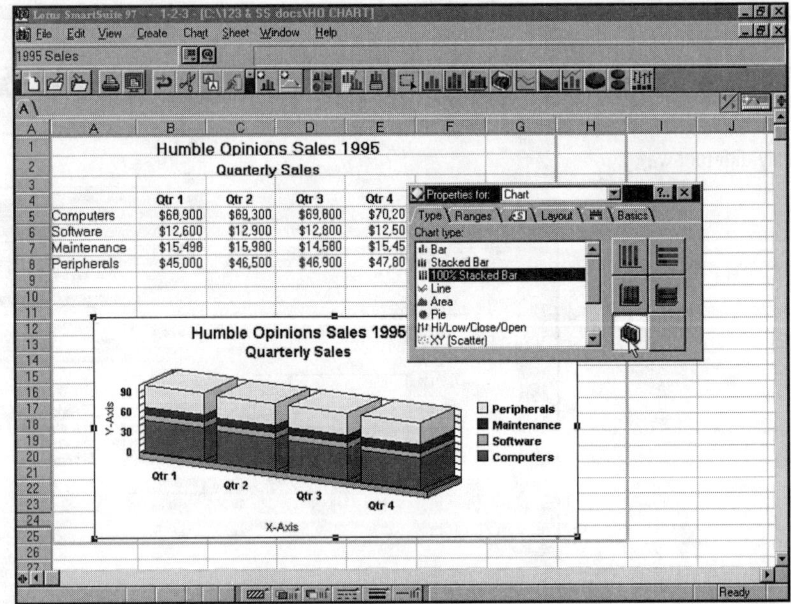

Fig. 12.6
The 3D 100% bar chart enables you to compare two or more data series to each other as well as to the whole.

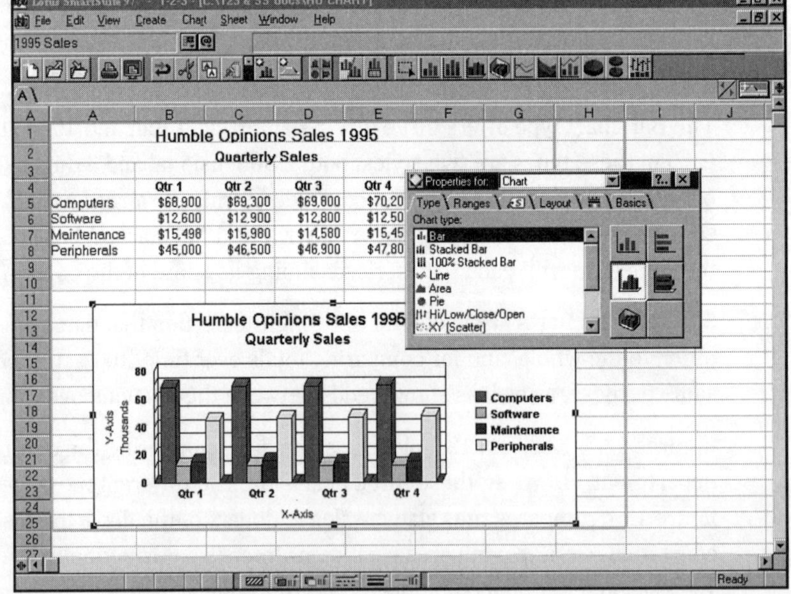

Fig. 12.7
A standard bar chart of the sales data worksheet shows each product category for each quarter in a single bar.

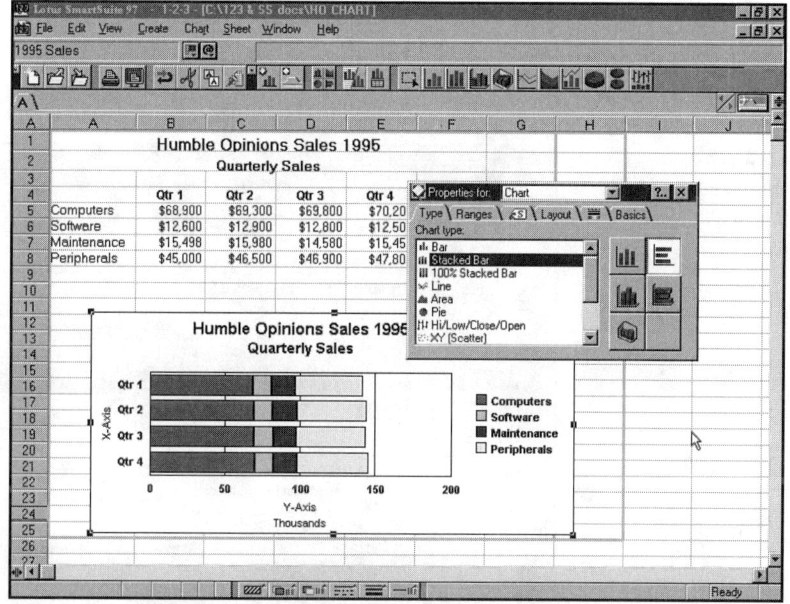

Fig. 12.8
A stacked bar chart of the sales data worksheet shows each product category as a part of the total sales for the quarter.

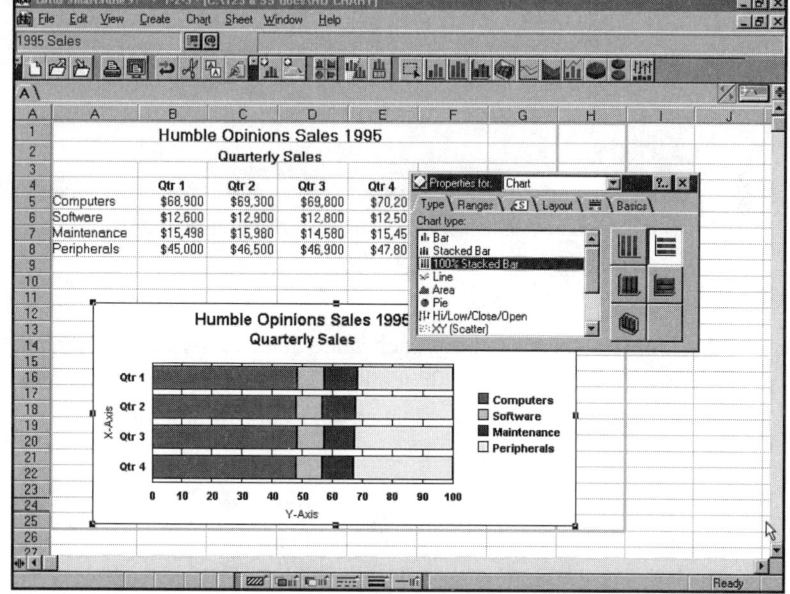

Fig. 12.9
The 100% stacked bars show trends over time for the individual data series.

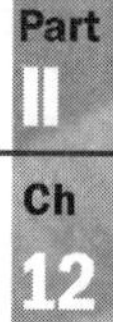

Figure 12.10 shows a 3D bar chart that represents the same data in a different way. As you can see, you must be careful when using the 3D charts; the larger bars sometimes hide smaller ones.

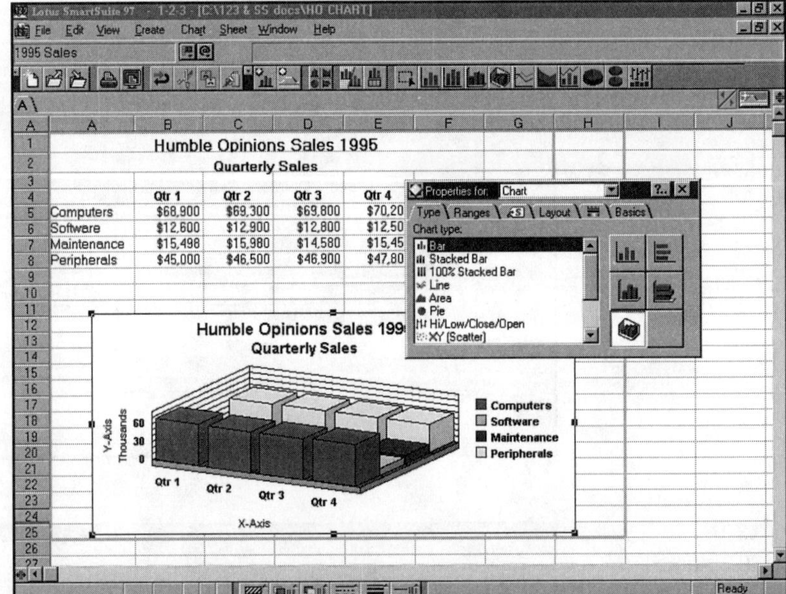

Fig. 12.10
A 3D bar chart puts a different slant on the data.

> **CAUTION**
>
> Each chart type presents a different view of your data; so different, in fact, that the data could be misinterpreted by your audience. Make sure the chart type you choose accurately depicts the data in your worksheet.

Pie Charts In a pie chart, each value determines the size of a pie slice and represents a percentage of the total. Unlike other chart types, pie charts can have only one data series (the A data range). If you select an adjacent row or column of labels, 1-2-3 uses it as the legend to identify the pie slices.

Suppose that you want to graph the percentage of department sales during the first quarter. Figure 12.11 shows a pie chart and the data used to create the chart. The data included in the chart ranges from cell A4 to B8 in the sample worksheet.

1-2-3 automatically calculates and displays the percentages of the whole represented by each slice. Instead of percentages, you can display the actual values or other information (see "Showing the Values and Percentages of Pie Slices" later in this chapter).

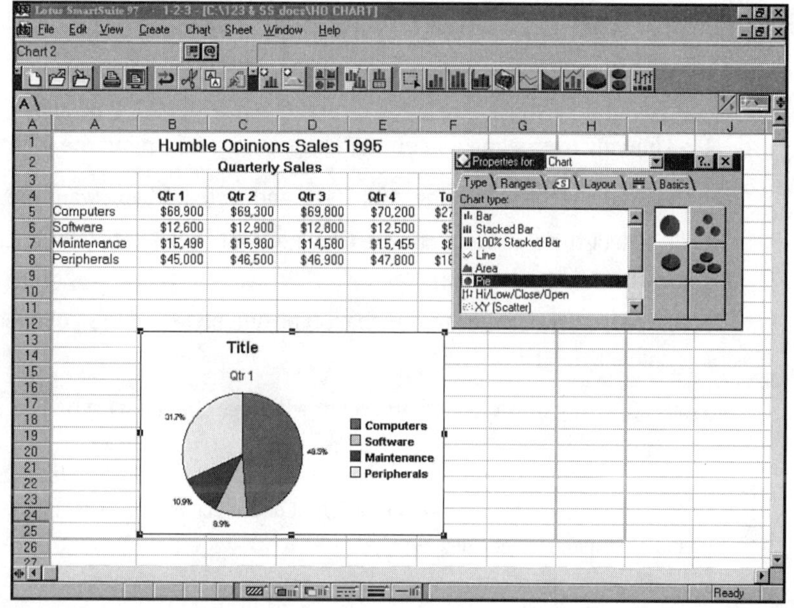

Fig. 12.11
The pie chart shows the relationships between the parts and the whole, as well as between parts.

The 3D pie chart style represents the data in the same manner as the 2D, but with depth. The multiple pie and 3D multiple pie charts enable you to compare several different data series. Figure 12.12 shows the four-quarter sales figures represented in a multiple 3D pie chart.

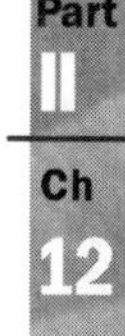

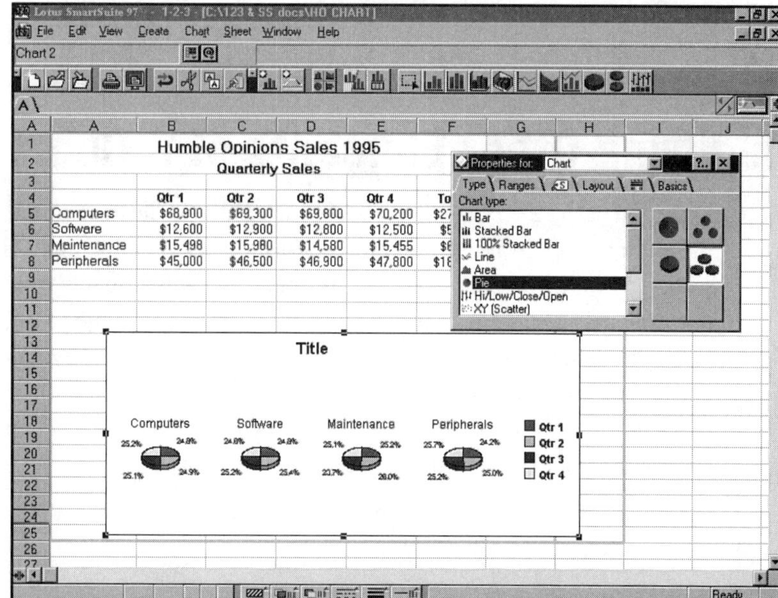

Fig. 12.12
The multiple pie chart lets you compare the parts to the whole in several data series.

Setting the Default Chart Type and Style

As was previously mentioned, the default chart type is a standard bar. If you use a different type or style more often, you can change the default type and style (the kind of chart 1-2-3 initially uses when you create a chart) by performing the following steps:

1. Create a chart with the chart type and style that you want the default to be.
2. Select the chart and choose Chart, Chart Style, Set Default Chart. The Set Default Chart dialog box appears.
3. Make any changes to the chart type and style and then choose OK to set the default chart.

Thereafter, any new charts you create will have that chart type and style by default.

NOTE The default (or preferred) chart setting controls only the type (such as line or area) and style (for instance, 2D or 3D). It doesn't control other settings such as orientation, legend placement, or grid lines.

TROUBLESHOOTING

I want to show expenditures for salaries and health benefits as parts of the whole compensation package for the past five years. I thought I wanted to use a pie chart, but I have more than one data series, so what kind of chart should I use? You should use either an area chart or a stacked bar chart to show salaries and health benefits as parts of the whole compensation package. Make sure the years form the x-data series so that the chart shows change over time.

Modifying Other Elements of a Chart

Once you select the type and style of chart that best illustrates your data, you can modify the chart in other ways so that it presents the data effectively and clearly points out information you want others to see. For example, you will probably want your chart to have a title. You may also want your chart to have a legend. In some cases, the layout of your data in the worksheet may make it necessary to enter the legend by hand, or you may want to change one of the legend labels. In some charts, you may want to change the default scale of the y-axis to make the values easier to read. The rest of this chapter explains how to control these and other attributes of charts in 1-2-3.

Specifying or Changing the Legend

When you graph a data range, 1-2-3 uses colors, symbols, or patterns to identify data ranges. The *legend* shows which data range each color, symbol, or pattern represents. By default, 1-2-3 places legend labels in an invisible frame to the right of the chart.

The Properties for Legend InfoBox (see fig. 12.13) enables you to add or edit legend labels or change the position of the legend box. To access this InfoBox, choose Chart, Legend. Alternatively, you can choose Legend from the drop-down list box in the Properties InfoBox. Finally, you can double-click the legend in the chart to display the Properties for Legend InfoBox.

To show the legend, if it's not already displayed, choose the Show Legend option in the Options tab of the Legend InfoBox.

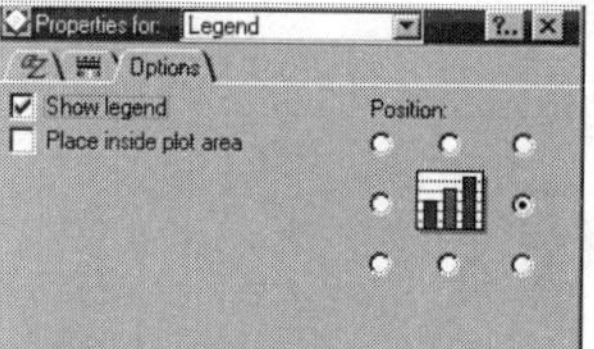

Fig. 12.13
The Legend InfoBox lets you control the position of the Legend box in the Options tab.

To change any label in the legend box, double-click the text and enter the new legend. Press Enter when you're done.

In the Options tab of the Legend InfoBox, you can choose the location of the legend by clicking one of the radio buttons in the Position area. The legend will immediately move to the new position. If you want, you can choose a different position or leave it as is.

CAUTION

Depending on the size of the legend and the new location, the rest of the chart may become distorted to accommodate the legend placement when you use the Legend InfoBox Position options. You can adjust for some of the distortion by enlarging the chart box; however, the text and other elements may then become distorted.

Another way to move the legend is by selecting it and dragging it to another location. When you move the legend using the mouse, the rest of the chart remains in place and proportionately sized.

TIP When you manually position a legend, the chart does not automatically move to accommodate the legend. You can select the plot and drag it so that it doesn't overlap the legend.

Customizing Chart Titles and Adding Notes

You use the Properties InfoBoxes for Title and for Note to add text to your chart. You can add up to three titles to a chart and up to three notes. The default location for the titles you add is centered near the top of the chart box. The default positioning of the notes is in the lower-right corner of the chart box. You can, however, change the position of a title or note by choosing a position in the Options tab of the InfoBox or by dragging the element to a new location. You can also select and format the text in the title or note.

▶ **See** "Formatting Text Attributes," **p. 350**

Figure 12.14 shows the Options tab of the Title InfoBox with three text boxes for titles or headings. Additionally, you can choose one position for the titles: left, center, or right.

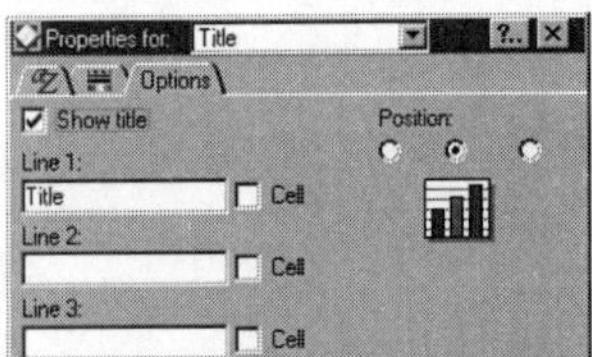

Fig. 12.14
Enter up to three lines of text for a title and select the position.

Entering Title and Note Text To enter titles, open the Properties for Title InfoBox and choose the Options tab. In the text box for Line 1, 2, or 3, you can type the text directly in the text box or select the Cell check box and enter the address of the cell that contains the label or number to be used as the title or note. You can either type the cell address or use the Range Selector to point to the cell.

To enter notes, open the Properties for Note InfoBox and choose the Options tab, which looks and acts the same as the Options tab for titles. Enter the note in the text box or use the Cell option as explained previously.

To edit a title or note, double-click on the title or note in the chart to display the Properties InfoBox. Replace existing text by highlighting the appropriate text box and typing in the new text. To delete text, press Del while the text box is highlighted. Another way to delete a title or note is to select the text on the chart and press Del.

Selecting Title and Note Positions By default, titles are centered at the top of the chart and notes are right-aligned at the bottom of the chart. You can left-align, right-align, or center-align titles and notes by choosing an option from the Options tab of the Properties InfoBox. Another way to change the position of titles and notes is to select the text you want to move by clicking it, and then drag the block anywhere inside the chart frame. When you move a title, all titles move as well; when you move one note, all notes move.

Changing the Axis Titles and Orientation

By default, 1-2-3 inserts X-Axis and Y-Axis as your axis titles. To change these axis titles to something more descriptive, choose Chart, Axes and Grids and select one of the following: X-Axis & Grids or Y-Axis & Grids. If the chart is a 3D chart, you can also select Z-Axis & Grids. Alternatively, select the appropriate axis from the Properties InfoBox's drop-down list. Choose the Titles tab and enter a title or subtitle in the text boxes; press Enter to display the title in your chart.

The placement of axis titles depends on whether the chart is horizontally or vertically oriented. In a vertical chart (the default chart orientation), the y-axis title appears left of the y-axis; the x-axis title is centered below the x-axis; and the second y-axis title appears to the right of the second y-axis. In a horizontal chart, the y-axis title appears above the y-axis; the x-axis title appears to the left of the x-axis; and the second y-axis appears below the second y-axis.

You can also choose orientation for the Y-axis titles, rotating the text to best suit the data in the chart.

Figure 12.15 is a chart with a rotated Y-axis title and an X-axis title and subtitle. Notice the Properties for Y-axis InfoBox shows the Titles tab.

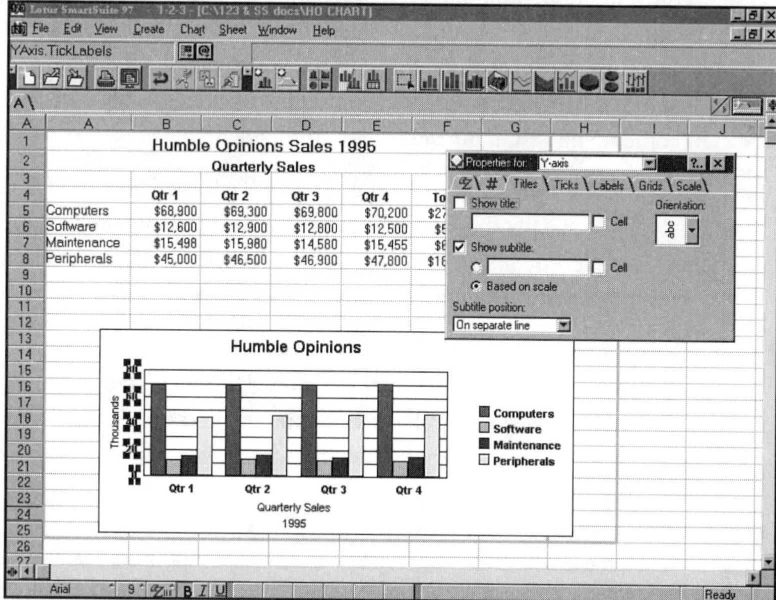

Fig. 12.15
Add axis titles and subtitles, change position and orientation, as well.

Controlling the Axis Scale

When you create a chart, 1-2-3 automatically sets the *scale* (the minimum to maximum range) of the y-axis based on the smallest and largest numbers in the data range(s) plotted. This default also applies to the second y-axis when you use it. For XY charts, 1-2-3 also establishes the x-axis scale based on values in the X-data range.

▶ **See** "Creating Special Charts," **p. 358**

To modify an axis scale, open the Chart menu, choose Axes & Grids, and then choose the command that corresponds to the axis whose scale you want to modify: X-Axis & Grids or Y-Axis and Grids. When the Properties InfoBox appears, open to the appropriate axis. Choose the Scale tab (see fig. 12.16). The Y-Axis, X-Axis, and 2nd Y-Axis Scale tabs offer the same settings.

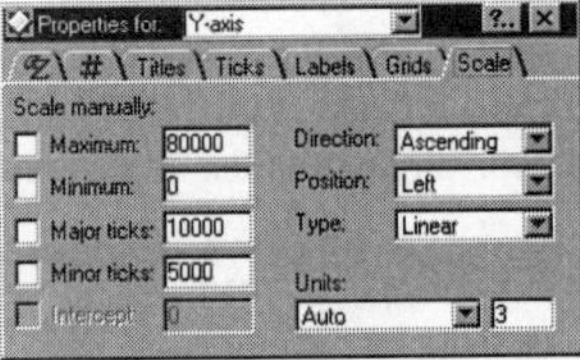

Fig. 12.16
The Scale tab of the Y-Axis InfoBox lets you control the axis scale upper and lower limits and tick mark intervals and display.

Setting the Minimum and Maximum Values You can change the scale by selecting options in the Scale Manually fields. These fields initially contain the values that 1-2-3 determines are appropriate for your data. You can change the scale by specifying different numbers in the Maximum and Minimum text boxes. Only data that falls between the Maximum and Minimum values are graphed.

Changing the Tick Marks Use the Major Ticks and Minor Ticks text boxes under Scale Manually to specify the increments between tick marks. For example, the automatic scale may have increments of 100 on the y-axis (100, 200, 300, 400, and so on). If you want fewer increments, you can change the Major interval setting to an increment such as 200; the major tick marks will then be labeled 200, 400, 600, and so on.

To control the display of tick marks, choose the Ticks tab of the InfoBox and choose Major Intervals, Minor Intervals, or both options in the Show Tick Marks At area of the tab. You also can choose whether to position the tick marks Outside, Inside, or Across the chart.

If your chart does not contain enough tick marks to tell what values the data series represent, decrease the value in the Major Ticks field and/or display Minor Interval tick marks.

Returning to Automatic Scaling To return to automatic scaling, deselect all the check boxes on the Scale tab—you don't have to clear out the values or return options to their original values.

Changing Other Scale Options The Scale tab also contains other options you might need to set: Direction, Position, Type, and Units. These options govern the selected axis.

Direction can be set to Ascending or Descending. Ascending, the default, displays the axis scale from low to high; descending switches the scale so it's high to low, for example. Note that your data series also switches directions if you change the direction of the axis scale.

Position enables you to place the axis scale to the left or right or the top or bottom, or to display the scale in both positions. The Type of scale field determines whether a Standard (linear), Log (logarithmic), or 100% scale is used. On a logarithmic scale, each unit of distance represents 10 times the value of the preceding unit; the scale is labeled 1, 10, 100, 1000, and so forth.

If your chart contains widely fluctuating data, use a logarithmic scale. For example, if the minimum value you are plotting is 1,000 and the maximum value is 10,000,000, the smaller data points are virtually invisible on a standard linear scale (they are so close to zero that they lie on the x-axis). By using a logarithmic (log) scale, you can show all the data points. Figure 12.17 shows a chart that has a linear scale, and figure 12.18 shows the same data plotted with a logarithmic scale.

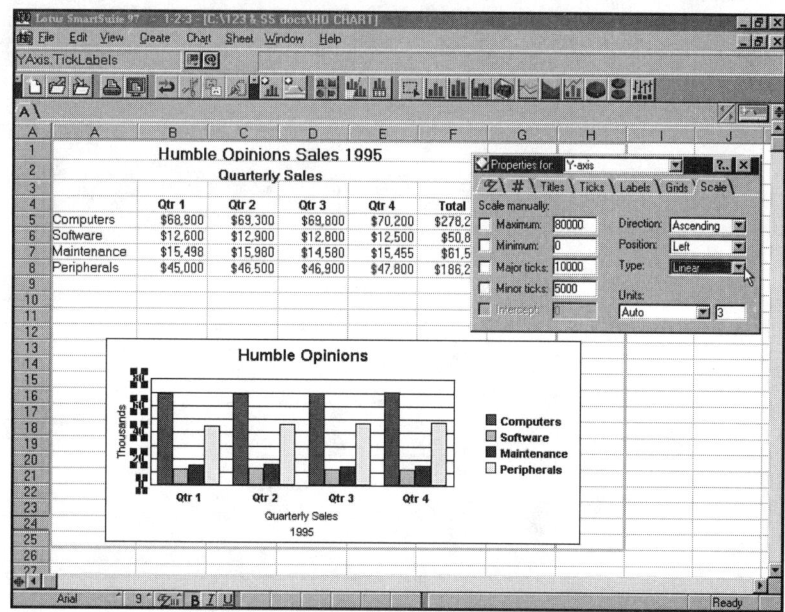

Fig. 12.17
With a linear y-axis scale, some of the values are relatively so small that the data points lie on the x-axis.

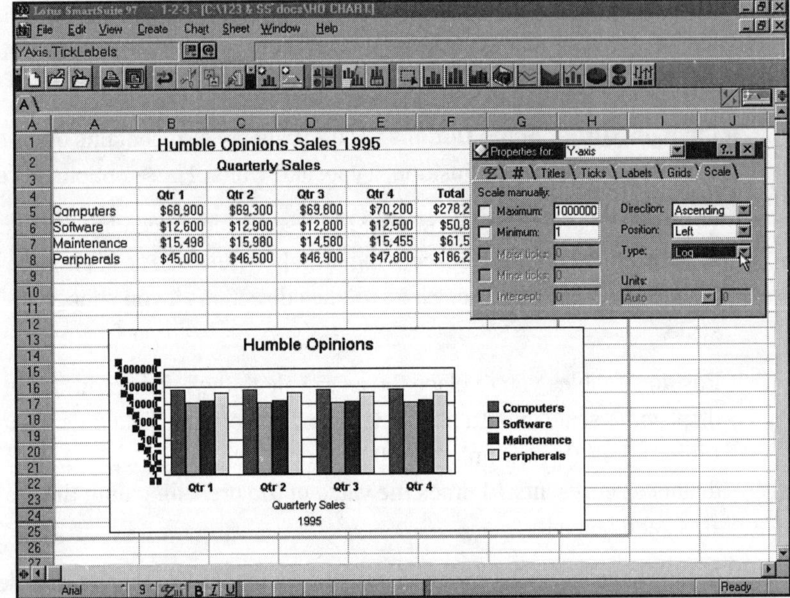

Fig. 12.18
With a logarithmic scale, you can clearly see all data points.

A 100% scale is similar to a pie chart in that it shows the relative portion that each series is of the total; the scale is labeled from 0 to 100 percent. A 100% scale is most appropriate for bar, stacked bar, and 100% bar charts, as shown in figure 12.19.

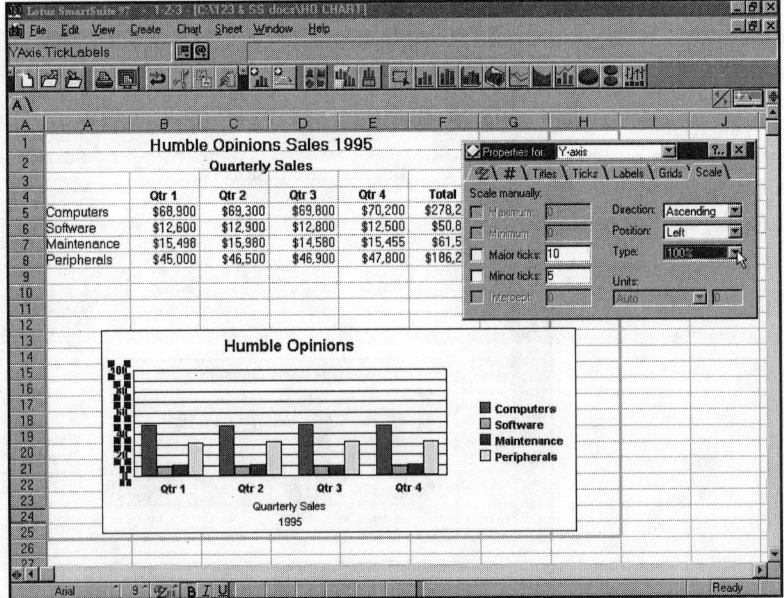

Fig. 12.19
The bar chart with a 100% scale represents the data in a different manner.

In the Units field, you can set the order of magnitude (power of 10) used to scale the values. Usually, 1-2-3 does this automatically.

In some cases, changing the units can make the chart easier to interpret. For example, the automatic scale on your chart might range from 0 to 4,000 and the automatic units title might read *Thousands*. In other words, 4,000 actually represents 4,000,000. If you specify Millions, the scale would range from 0 to 4; with a units title that says *Millions*, the chart would be much easier to understand.

Sometimes 1-2-3 uses an exponent on your axis when you would rather show the exact values. For example, the scale might have the labels 1, 2, 3, 4,... with Thousands as the units title. If you would rather have the scale show 1,000, 2,000, 3,000, 4,000,..., choose None for the axis units.

Adjusting the Display of Axis Labels

When your axis is crowded with many labels, you can use the Show scale labels every [__] ticks field in the Y-Axis, X-Axis, or 2nd Y-Axis dialog box to determine how many axis labels appear. This option is found in the Labels tab of the InfoBox. For example, if the value in this field is 2, every second label appears (see fig. 12.20).

Skip tick mark labels only if the axis contains values or units of time so that it's obvious what the missing labels are.

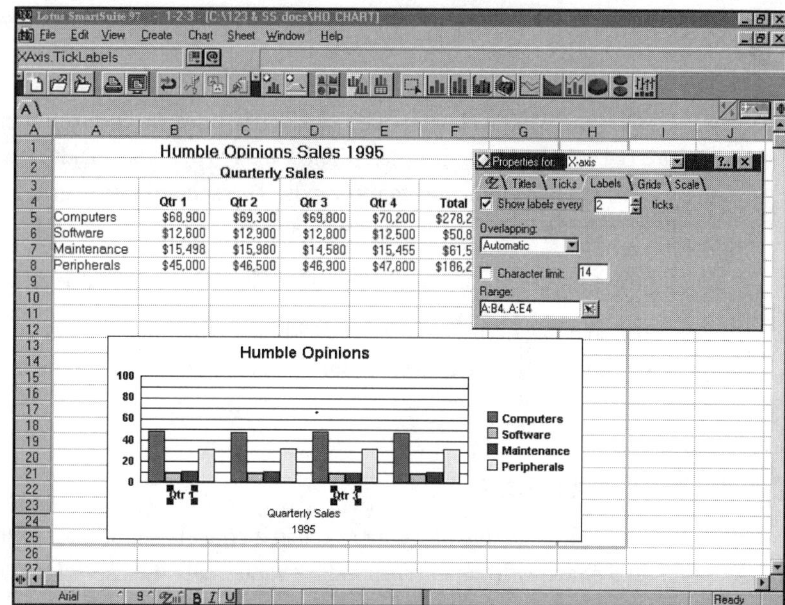

Fig. 12.20
Every other label is displayed on the x-axis.

Displaying a Background Grid

Grids often make it easier to interpret the data points in charts, especially if the data points are far from the x-axis and y-axis labels. Use the Grids tab of the InfoBox to set grid lines in your chart. The chart in figure 12.21, for example, uses horizontal and vertical grid lines to make the data easier to interpret.

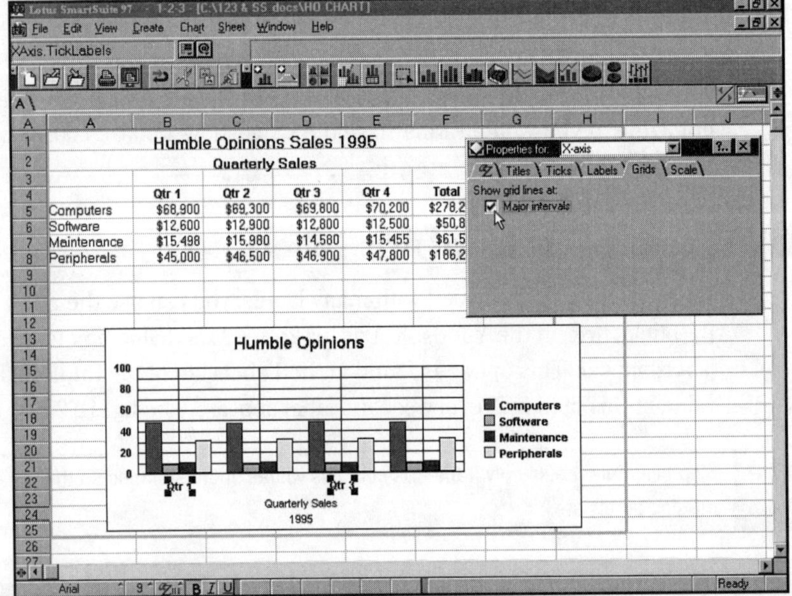

Fig. 12.21
A chart with grid lines added to make it easier to determine the values represented by the bars.

You can create horizontal and vertical grid lines for charts that have axes (Line, Bar, Area, XY, HLCO, and Mixed charts). The x-axis grid lines extend from tick marks on the x-axis and are perpendicular to the x-axis. The y-axis grid lines (major) extend from y-axis tick marks and are perpendicular to the y-axis. The second y-axis grid lines (minor) extend from the tick marks on the second y-axis.

To turn on grid lines, choose the settings: Major intervals and/or Minor intervals.

You can also choose the Show Extra Grid Lines option and enter the number of grid lines, the line number, and the line value for each grid line in the Grids tab of the Y-axis InfoBox.

Adding Series Labels

Knowing the exact value of a data range in a chart is sometimes helpful. To label series points in a chart with the corresponding value (called *series labels*), choose Chart, Series Labels; the Properties for Series Labels InfoBox appears, as shown in figure 12.22.

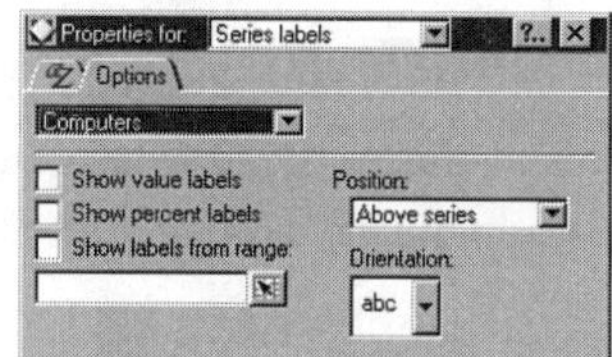

Fig. 12.22
The Series Labels enables you to modify the labels used for specific data.

To specify a series label, follow these steps:

1. Choose the Options tab and select the series you want to modify from the drop-down list box.
2. Choose one or more of the following options:

   Show Value Labels. Displays a value for each data bar, bar segment, or data point.

   Show Percent Labels. Displays the percentage for each data bar, bar segment, or data point.

   Show Labels from Range. Select a range in the worksheet to use as a label.
3. Use the Position drop-down list to choose to display the selected labels either Above or Below the series.
4. Select the orientation you want from the Orientation drop-down list.
5. Repeat this process for each series.

As you make your selections in the InfoBox, 1-2-3 displays in the chart the exact value of each data range. Figure 12.23 shows a chart with series labels on one data series.

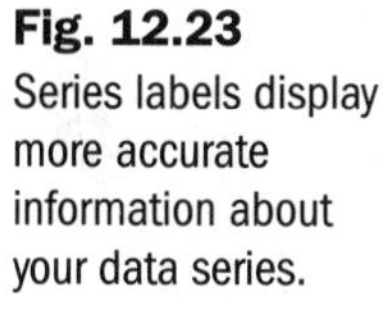

Fig. 12.23
Series labels display more accurate information about your data series.

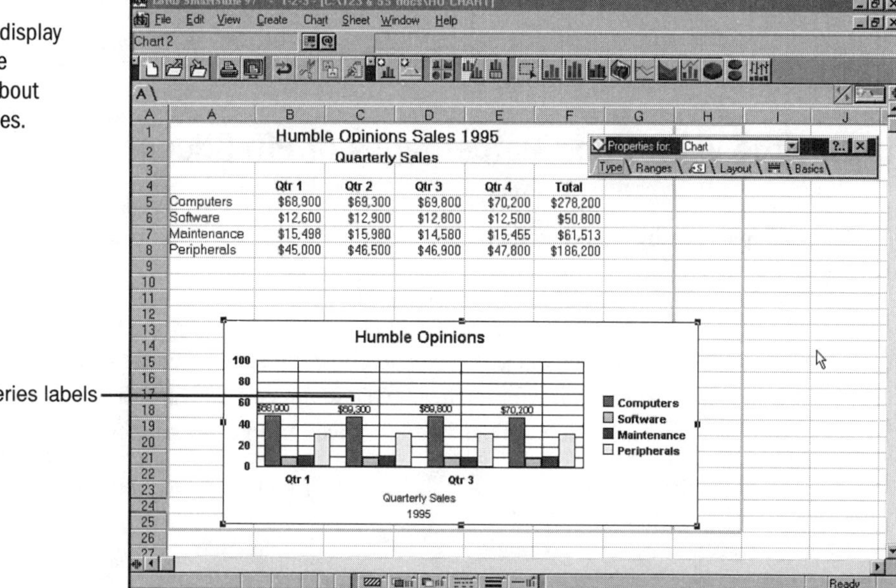

Including a Table of Values in the Chart

Series Labels can be difficult to read and can clutter the chart. An alternative method of displaying the data values being graphed is to display a table of the data series at the bottom of the chart box.

To add a table to the chart, choose Table in the Properties for drop-down list and choose the Options tab. Figure 12.24 shows the Options tab in the InfoBox and a chart with a table of data added.

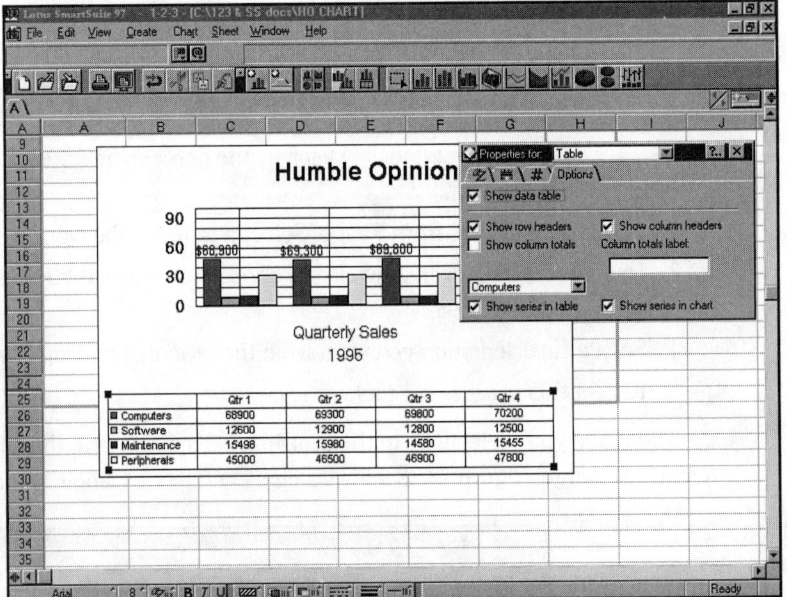

Fig. 12.24
A chart using a table of values rather than data labels.

Showing the Values and Percentages of Pie Slices

If you create a pie chart, you can show the values and/or percentages corresponding to each pie slice by choosing the Properties for Pie Labels, Options tab, as shown in figure 12.25.

By default, 1-2-3 displays the percentages of the whole represented by each slice. You can also display the values of each slice and show the slice labels as well as select the position as Inside or Outside for each. The pie in figure 12.26 shows values, percentages, and the slice labels. The legend has been removed from this chart because it is no longer necessary.

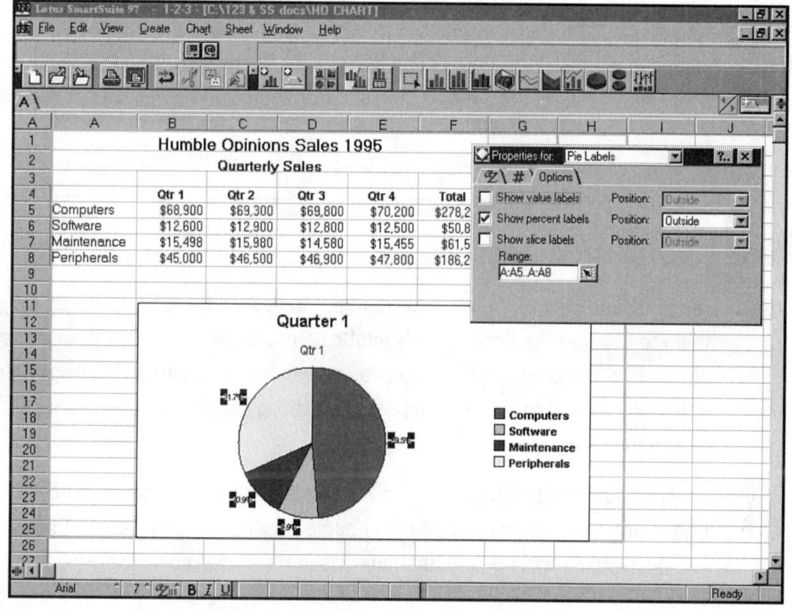

Fig. 12.25
The Options tab of the InfoBox for pie labels lets you specify what information the labels include.

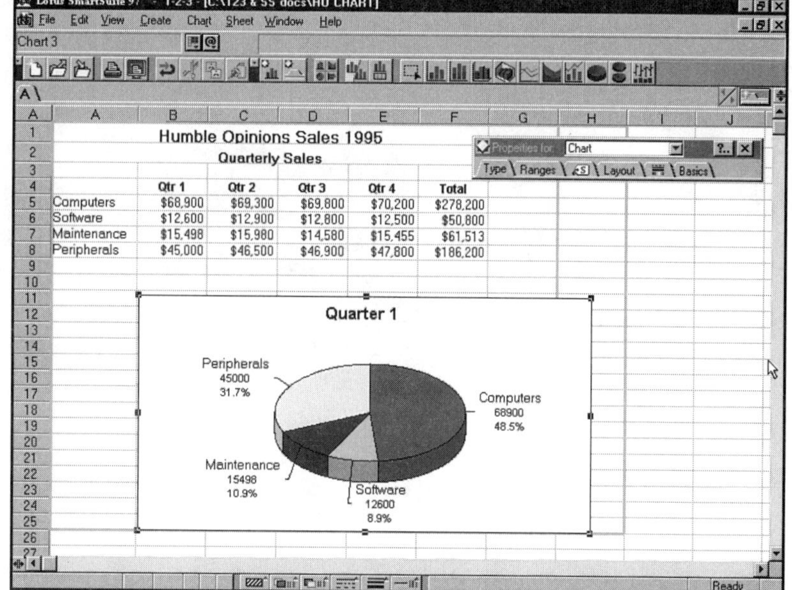

Fig. 12.26
A pie with values, percentages, and slice labels.

You can open the Properties for Slices InfoBox and choose the Options tab, then select any slice of the pie and hide it by deselecting Show Slice. The remaining slices take up the extra room in the chart. Of course, the pie may then show misleading data because of the missing piece.

▶ **See** "Exploding Pie Slices," **p. 354**

TROUBLESHOOTING

My pie slices aren't labeled, even though I indicated them as my x-axis range. How can I get them to display? The Series Labels InfoBox, Options tab, has check boxes for controlling the display of x-axis labels, values, and percentages next to each slice. To display the x-axis labels, double-click the slices in your chart. In the Options tab, choose the appropriate check box to display the labels.

My chart has overlapping labels on the x-axis. Is there any way to relieve this crowding? Open the X-Axis Properties InfoBox by double-clicking the x-axis labels. Choose the Labels tab and then enter a value greater than the one in the Show Labels Every [__] ticks field.

CHAPTER 13

Formatting Charts

by Sue Plumley

1-2-3 includes many ways to format and enhance charts. For example, to call attention to a particular data series, you might want to "explode" a pie slice (that is, move it slightly outward from the rest of the pie) or display it in a special color. With 1-2-3, you can change the attributes and colors of chart text, lines, and areas the same way you format ranges in the worksheet. You also can add special effects to your charts such as design frames. These options help you create more attractive charts and communicate the message in the data more effectively.

Change the typeface, point size, and attributes of the titles and labels

You can change any font in the chart to make it easier to read or more attractive by using the Properties InfoBox.

Change the color of any chart element

Use color to attract attention and differentiate between data series in a chart. You can view the colors on-screen in the chart and in the printed copy if you have a color printer.

Choose a pattern for a data series

If you're printing in black and white, using various patterns to represent the data series makes the printed copy of a chart easier to read and understand.

Explode pie slices

Separate pie slices by pulling them out from the rest of the pie, also called *exploding* the pie slices.

Create and save styles of charts

Using chart styles, just like using text styles, saves time and energy when formatting charts. Use one style over and over again without formatting each individual chart.

Enhancing the Chart

Just as a Property InfoBox lets you change the settings for many worksheet items—number formats, font attributes and size, colors, and line styles—it also gives you flexibility in formatting charts. Figure 13.1 shows a chart with these changes made using the Properties InfoBox: different typeface, size, and attributes of text, different colors of chart elements, new patterns for data series, different style and width of the lines. The chart also draws attention to one slice.

Double-click on any item in a chart to open the Properties InfoBox. If you leave the InfoBox open as you format the chart, just click once on the element to be formatted and the appropriate item appears in the InfoBox.

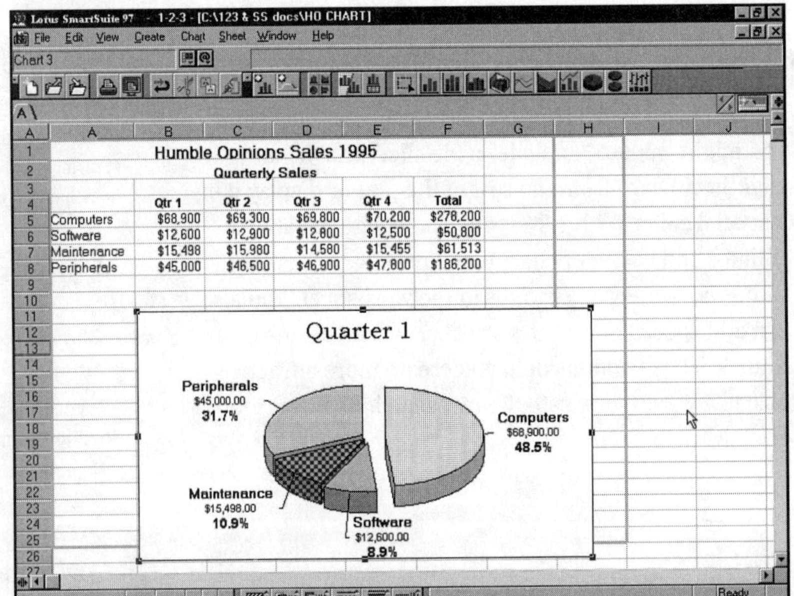

Fig. 13.1
A chart with a new title typeface, enlarged label type, slice patterns, and an exploded pie slice.

Changing the Format of Numbers

By default, 1-2-3 displays numbers in a chart in General format, which is also the default format for worksheet values. You can display x-axis, y-axis, or the second y-axis labels, series labels, or pie labels in any of 1-2-3's numeric formats.

To change the format of numbers in a chart, double-click one of the numbers you want to format; the group of numbers is selected and the Properties InfoBox appears with the labels tabs showing. Then choose the Numbers tab and select the desired format from the list. Some formats require that you specify a number of decimal places, and date and time formats require that you specify format types for those entries. Figure 13.2 shows the pie chart with the currency format type used.

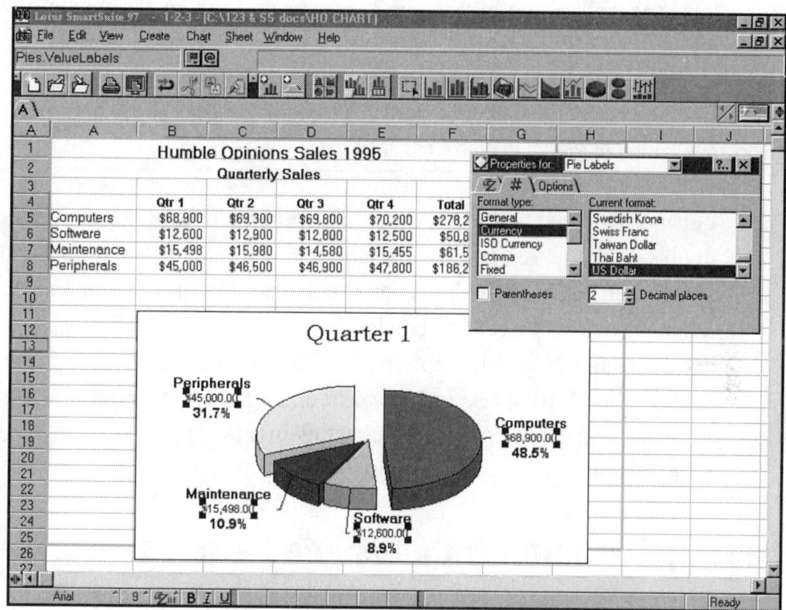

Fig. 13.2
Using a number format makes the labels more descriptive.

See "Working with Number Formats," **p. 110**

TROUBLESHOOTING

My y-axis scale shows single digit numbers (1, 2, 3,...) with a unit indicator of Thousands, but I would prefer to see the actual numbers (1000, 2000, 3000,...). How can I do this? Choose Chart, Axes and Grids, and then select Y-Axis and Grids. In the Y-Axis InfoBox, select the Scale tab and set the Units to None.

Even though the numbers in my worksheet are formatted for currency, the y-axis scale in the chart doesn't show the dollar sign. 1-2-3 does not automatically use worksheet formatting in charts. To change the number format of the y-axis scale to currency, select one of the numbers on the y-axis to display the Properties for Y-axis InfoBox. In the Number Format tab, choose Currency under the Format Type and US Dollar under Current Format. Additionally, you can choose the number of Decimal places to display.

Formatting Text Attributes

You can change the typeface, point size, color, and attributes (boldface, italic, and so on) of any text on a chart. You also can format the chart titles, legend text, data labels, and axis labels as well as text blocks you created with the Create, Drawing command or the Create a Text Block SmartIcon.

When you resize the chart by dragging the frame, 1-2-3 does not automatically change the font size, so you may want to do so manually.

Formatting chart text is not much different from formatting worksheet cells. First, double-click the text you want to change. If you are formatting a group of objects (such as all the data labels or the labels on the x-axis), double-click one of the labels and 1-2-3 automatically selects all related labels. In the Properties InfoBox, choose the Font, Attribute, and Color tab. Notice the options for Font, Size, Style, and Text Color are the same as those for formatting text in a worksheet. You also can use the Status bar to choose lines, patterns, and colors for various chart elements.

▶ **See** "Enhancing the Appearance of Data," **p. 125**

Changing Data Series Colors and Patterns

With 1-2-3 you easily can select colors for each of the data series on a chart. You can change the color and pattern of lines, bars, areas, and individual pie slices.

Unless your printer can print in color, you may be better off using hatch (or line) patterns, shades of gray, or symbols to differentiate data ranges.

To change the format of a series, first click on any data point of that series. For example, if you are changing the color of a line, click the line or one of the data points on the line. If you are choosing a different color for one of the data series in a bar chart, click one of the bars. 1-2-3 then selects all the bar or bar segments in that series. Another way to change the color of a series is to click on the appropriate color box in the legend. The appropriate item appears in the title bar of the Properties InfoBox and you can then choose the Lines & Color tab (see fig. 13.3).

The Interior area of the Lines & Color tab lets you choose the pattern, pattern color, or the background color of your data series. When you click the down arrow beside any of these options, a palette of choices appears; to choose a pattern or color, click any box in the palette.

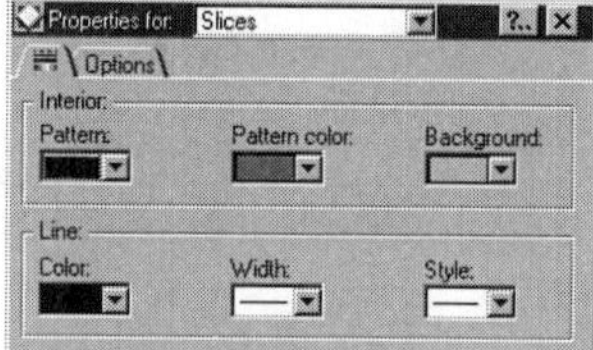

Fig. 13.3
The Lines & Color tab presents options for formatting data series.

The Interior Pattern applies to the selected data series; if the series has a color assigned to it, the pattern displays over the color as lines or hatches. Choose a different color, if you want, from the Pattern Color palette and choose a color from the Background palette to apply to area behind the pattern in the data series. Refer to figure 13.1 to view a chart with various grays and patterns applied to the data series.

TIP When you print the chart on a black and white printer, it is often a good idea to alternate light and dark colors or shades of gray for bars or pie slices that are next to each other.

The Line area of the Color, Pattern, and Line Style tab applies to the outline of the data series, such as the bars of a chart or to the lines in a line chart, although the options differ slightly.

For the bars, pie slices, area charts, and so on, you can apply various colors to the outline as well as different widths and styles of lines. Use the Color palette to choose a color to apply to the outline of a data series. The Width drop-down box presents seven varying widths to apply to the outline and the Style drop-down list presents solid, dashed, dotted, and other variations for the line, as well as the no outline option.

If you're formatting a line chart, you have more choices for modifying the lines. Figure 13.4 shows the Properties InfoBox for modifying the lines and color of a line chart. After selecting the chart, choose Chart, Series and in the InfoBox, choose the Lines and Colors tab.

Table 13.1 describes the options for modifying the lines in a line chart.

Table 13.1 Color, Pattern, and Line Style for Line Charts

Option	Description
Connect Points	Select this option to display a line that joins all data points in the line chart; deselect this option to display only the data points.
Line Color	Select a color from the palette to represent the selected series.
Line Width	Change the width of the line of the selected series.

continues

Table 13.1 Continued

Option	Description
Line Style	Choose a solid, dashed, dotted, or other style of line to represent the selected series.
Show Marker	Select this option to display a symbol at the appropriate points on the line chart; deselect to display only the line.
Marker Symbol	Select a symbol to represent the selected data series.
Marker Color	Select a color in which to display the marker symbol.

Figure 13.5 shows a modified line chart.

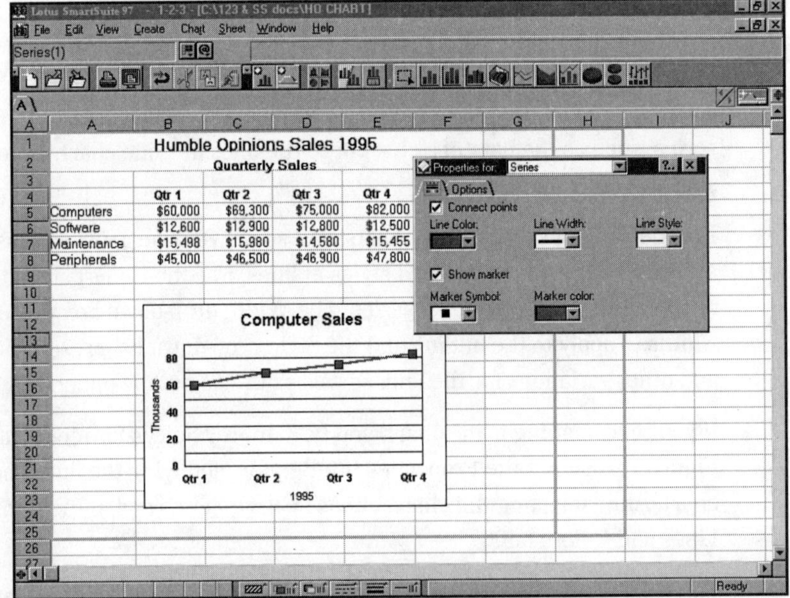

Fig. 13.4
Choose from various line colors, widths, and styles for a line chart.

Formatting a Frame

By default, the chart is enclosed in a *frame*, or *box*. To change the format of a frame, select it to display the Lines & Color tab of the Chart InfoBox.

In the Lines & Color tab, you'll notice the Border area and a Designer Frame area (see figure 13.6); the Designer Frame area options appear when you select the Designer Frame check box. Use the Border Line Color, Line Style, and Line Width boxes to choose options for the chart frame. Alternatively, select the Designer Frame check box and choose a Frame Style from the drop-down box. Next, choose a color from the Frame Color drop-down palette.

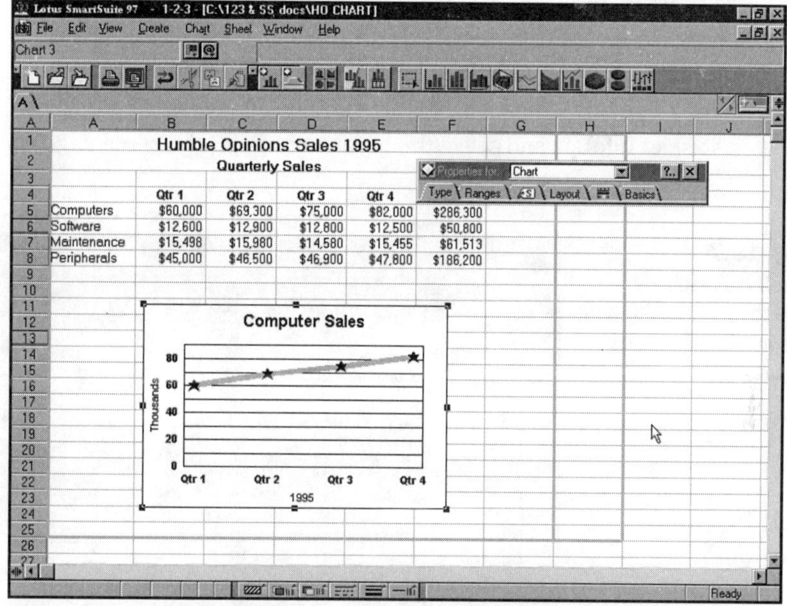

Fig. 13.5
Make your line charts stand out by modifying lines and color.

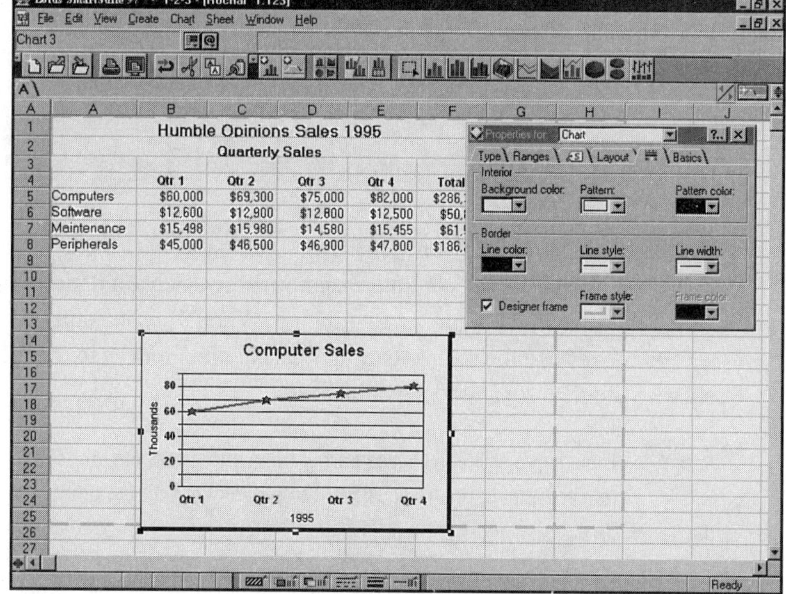

Fig. 13.6
Choose a fancier border by selecting the Designer Frame check box; this example shows a drop-shadow frame.

▶ **See** "Enhancing the Appearance of Data," **p. 125**

Exploding Pie Slices

You can separate pie slices for a better look at the sections by exploding a pie slice. For example, figure 13.7 shows a pie with slices exploded at 30 percent. Naturally, the higher the percentage, the further apart the slices. To separate pie slices, choose the Properties for Plot InfoBox and select the Layout tab. Enter the percentage you want to explode the slices by.

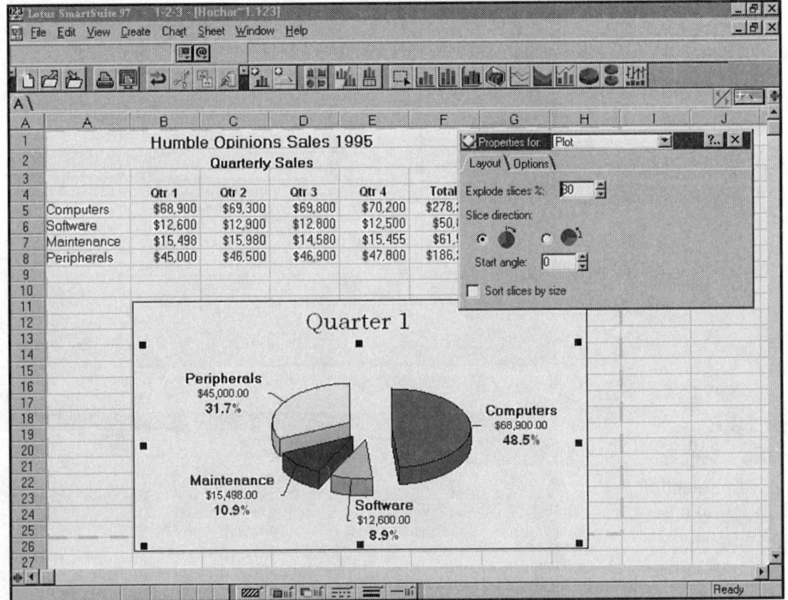

Fig. 13.7
A 3-D Pie graph with exploded slices makes the relationship easier to see.

You also can separate any one slice from the rest by clicking it and dragging the slice away from the pie. A selected pie slice has three selection handles on it. As you drag the slice, it has a dotted outline surrounding it. When the slice outline is where you want the slice to be, release the mouse button; the slice then moves to that position. Figure 13.8 shows a pie slice separated from the rest.

NOTE Exploding a slice may cause part of the pie to disappear, or be cropped from the frame; if that happens, you'll want to experiment with the other slices to fit them all in the frame.

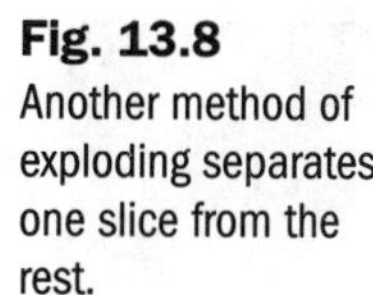

Fig. 13.8
Another method of exploding separates one slice from the rest.

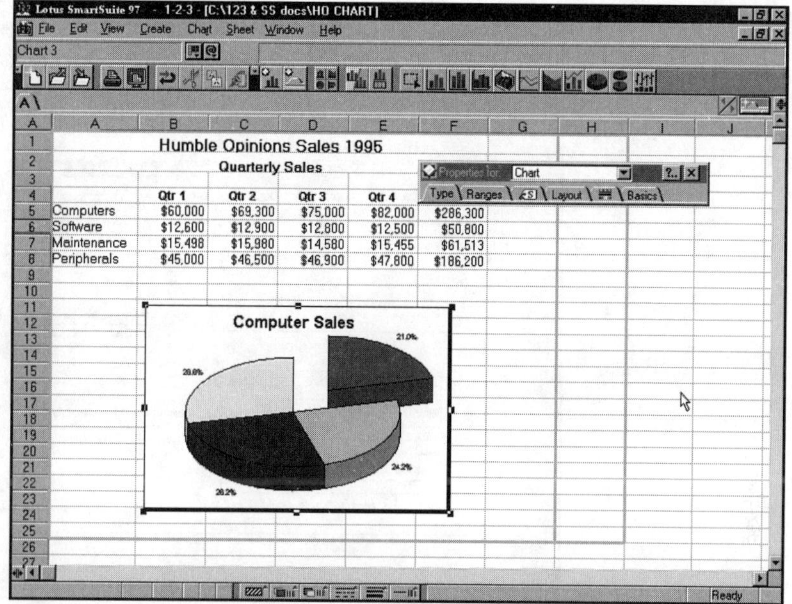

Using and Creating Chart Styles

After you format a chart—changing number formatting, text, grids, frames, and so on—you can save the formatting as a chart style to use over again in your worksheets.

TIP All charts you display in one business report, presentation, or other business document should be formatted similarly for consistency and a professional look.

To create a chart style, format the chart elements the way you want the chart to appear. Then, follow these steps:

1. Open the Properties for Chart InfoBox and choose the Style tab (see fig. 13.9).
2. Choose the Create Style button; the Create Chart Style dialog box appears.
3. Choose OK to save the style. The Save As dialog box appears.
4. Enter a name for the style and choose the Save button. 1-2-3 saves the chart style in the Style tab of the Chart InfoBox.

Anytime you want to use the style you've created, select the chart and then choose the Style tab in the Chart InfoBox. Select the style and choose the Apply button.

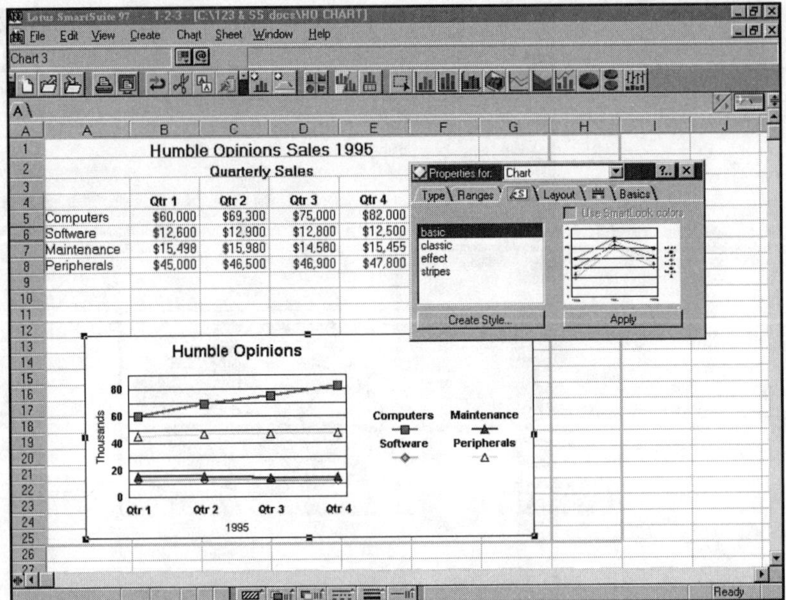

Fig. 13.9
Create a chart style to use in this worksheet and in others.

CHAPTER 14

Building Complex Charts and Mapping Data

by Sue Plumley

Chapters 11, 12, and 13 covered how to create, format, enhance, and print the most commonly used chart types. In most cases, these chart types and styles are sufficient to show trends, track changes, show relationships, and visually emphasize other information.

Some business and scientific purposes, however, require special charts to illustrate specific kinds of data. For example, stockbrokers often work with high-low-close-open charts to track stock prices, and scientists use XY charts to show the relationship between independent and dependent variables. 1-2-3 enables you to create these and other types of charts for special purposes as easily as you create basic line, bar, area, and pie charts. In addition, you can create charts that mix the basic chart types and plot data against a second y-axis.

Create XY charts, mixed charts, HLCO charts, radar charts, and second y-axis charts

Create and edit special charts to illustrate text in reports and other business documents.

Annotate charts

Use annotations with your charts to illustrate your data and to add a professional touch.

Use clip art with charts

Add interest and emphasis to your charts with clip art.

Illustrate data with maps

Use 1-2-3's mapping feature to illustrate data relating to geographical locations; anytime you can add an image to your data, you're making it easier to understand and remember.

You also might want to make a chart more complex by adding an arrow or another device to catch the reader's attention. You may want to add your company's logo or to include clip art or graphics from another program. Ideally, these elements help convey the chart's message.

Another way that you can illustrate data in 1-2-3 is with maps. Suppose that you have sales figures for each state in the United States. In 1-2-3 97, you can create a map that automatically assigns six colors to indicate the sales levels in each state. You can create maps of the world or regions in many individual countries. ■

Creating Special Charts

The following sections discuss when and how to create XY charts, mixed charts, HLCO charts, radar charts, and second y-axis charts. One thing that these charts have in common is that they use data series in very specific ways, so you need to make sure that you set up the charts properly.

XY Charts

An XY chart, or *scatter chart,* is a variation on a line chart. Like a line chart, an XY chart has values plotted as points, but an XY chart uses numeric values rather than labels on its x-axis. XY charts are most useful for scientific or statistical data.

Some relationships that would be well-illustrated by XY charts are population density versus number of crimes, luxury purchases versus age, or quantity of algae per water sample versus oxygen and nitrogen levels.

XY charts show the correlation between two or more sets of data. To use XY charts effectively, you must understand two terms: independent variables and dependent variables. One data range represents the ***independent variable,*** which is data that you can change or control. The other data ranges, the ***dependent variables,*** depend on the independent variable; you cannot control or change the dependent variables. For example, the worksheet shown in figure 14.1 has average daily temperatures in column A. Column B contains ice cream sales on days that had corresponding average daily temperatures. The temperature is the independent variable, and ice cream sales are the dependent variable. The XY chart beside the worksheet data in figure 14.1 illustrates the relationship between the temperature and ice cream sales. Each data point represents ice cream sales for a particular average daily temperature.

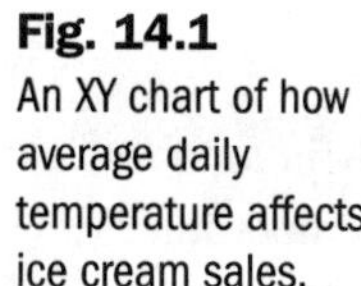

Fig. 14.1
An XY chart of how average daily temperature affects ice cream sales.

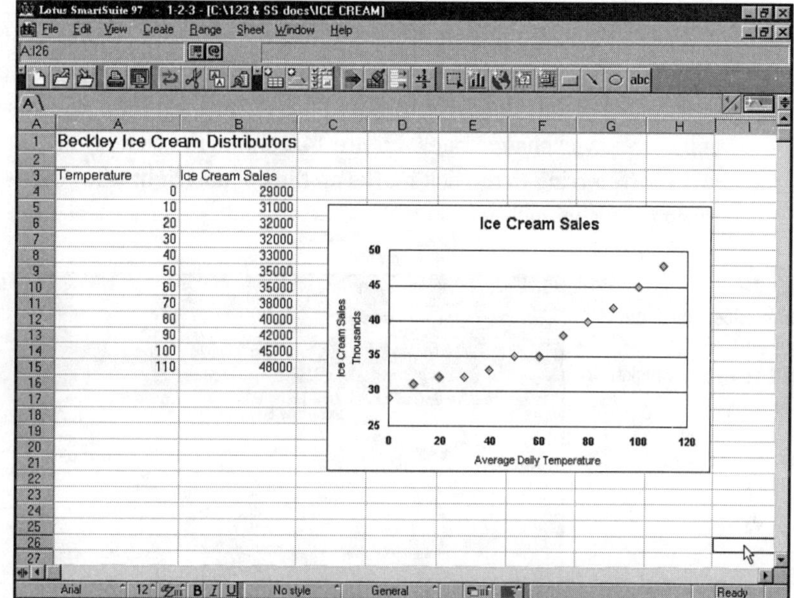

Usually, the independent variable is plotted against the x-axis and the dependent variable(s) is plotted against the y-axis. Create an XY chart by following these steps:

1. Select the data and choose Create, Chart; alternatively, click the Create a Chart SmartIcon.
2. Drag the chart cursor to create a frame for the chart or click the mouse and let 1-2-3 create and size the chart for you; the chart data may look strange when you first create the chart because 1-2-3 defaults to the bar chart.
3. Double-click the chart to display the Properties for Chart InfoBox.
4. In the Type tab, choose the XY (Scatter) chart; there is only one type of XY chart you can choose.
5. Format the chart elements, such as legend, axes, title, and so on.

▶ **See** "Changing the Chart Type and Style," **p. 325**

▶ **See** "Enhancing the Chart," **p. 348**

NOTE Legends are required only in XY charts that have more than two data series. For an XY chart with only X and A data series, use the x- and y-axis titles to identify the data, and delete the legend.

HLCO (High-Low-Close-Open) Charts

HLCO charts are specialized for stock-market information, but you can use them to track other kinds of data that have high and low values over time, such as daily temperatures and currency-exchange rates. Figure 14.2 shows the standard HLCO chart style, called *whisker* (referring to the tick marks on the left and right sides of the vertical lines, which resemble an animal's whiskers).

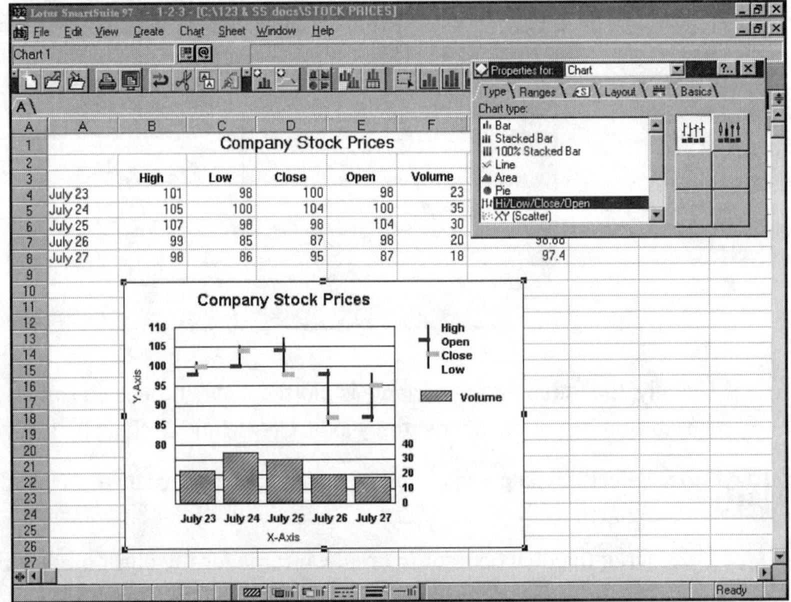

Fig. 14.2
Stock-price worksheet data and an HLCO chart using the whisker style.

An HLCO chart typically has four series, representing high, low, close, and open values. This data is represented on the chart as a vertical line; the line extends from the *low value* to the *high value*. A tick mark extending to the right of the line represents the *close value*, and a tick mark extending to the left represents the *open value*. The total number of lines in the chart depends on the number of time periods included. Following are the meanings of the four values:

High	The stock's highest price during the given period
Low	Thc stock's lowest price during the given period
Close	The stock's price at the end, or close, of the period
Open	The stock's price at the start, or open, of the period

An HLCO chart can include a set of bars below the HLCO section of the chart and one or more lines across the HLCO section. In the financial world, the bars often are used to represent the daily trading volume for the stock; the line can represent a changing stock-price average.

You can use 1-2-3's automatic chart feature if your worksheet ranges are set up in the following order: The first four data series (A through D) represent the high, low, close, and open values, respectively. If you specify a fifth set of data, the E range appears as bars plotted against a second y-axis on the right side of the chart's frame. Any additional ranges appear as lines plotted against the y-axis.

1-2-3 offers a second style of HLCO chart, called *candlestick*. The only difference between the two styles is in the way that the open and close data is illustrated. Instead of using tick marks, the candlestick style spans the range between the open and close value. The bar is empty if the close value is lower than the open value; otherwise, it is filled in.

If you want to emphasize the open and close values, use the candlestick style; otherwise, use the default whisker style.

Figure 14.3 shows an example of the candlestick style. The candlestick style places more emphasis on the open and close data; as you can see, the open/close bars in figure 14.3 are much more prominent than the tiny tick marks of the whisker style shown in figure 14.2.

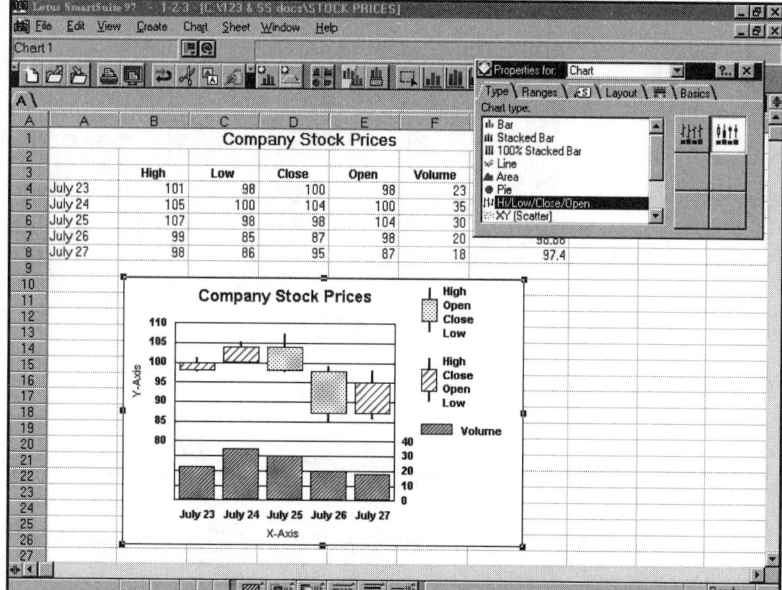

Fig. 14.3
A candlestick-style HLCO chart emphasizes open and close values.

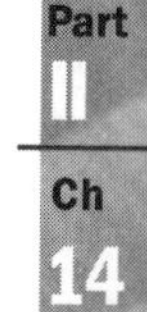

NOTE Stock-market figures often are downloaded from online information services as text labels, in the format '45 3/8. To change these labels to values for use in an HLCO chart, use @VALUE, as described in Chapter 6, "Using Functions." ■

Mixed Charts

The mixed chart type enables you to use two or three different chart types in a single chart. When you choose the Mixed type in the Chart InfoBox, you can assign the appropriate type (line, area, or bar) to each data series. Follow these steps:

1. Select the data and then choose Create, Chart.
2. Define the area for the chart.
3. Open the Properties for Chart InfoBox and choose the Mixed Type; then select either a 2D line and bar chart or one of the two 3D line and bar charts.
4. To complete the chart, you may have to define the range for one of the axes; for example, in figure 14.4, the temperature range was defined for the x-axis by choosing the Ranges tab of the Charts InfoBox.

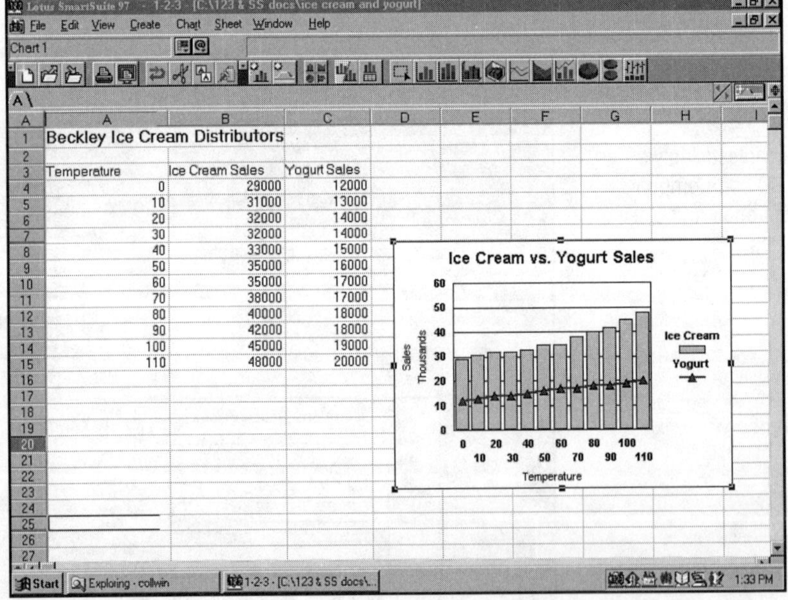

Fig. 14.4
A mixed line and bar chart may need some modifications before it is complete.

5. Format the chart any way you want: text, labels, lines and patterns, and so on.

One common use for a mixed chart is to show an average or trend line in a bar chart. Suppose that you are plotting temperature levels over the past three decades. First, you could plot as bars the temperatures for the 1960s, 1970s, and 1980s; then you could plot the average temperature during the measured time span and display this series as a line. Mixed charts also are useful in charts that have a second y-axis.

Radar Charts

A radar chart plots data as a function of distance from a central point, with each spoke representing a set of data points. This chart is perfect for comparing parts to the whole and to each other. Figure 14.5 shows a radar chart.

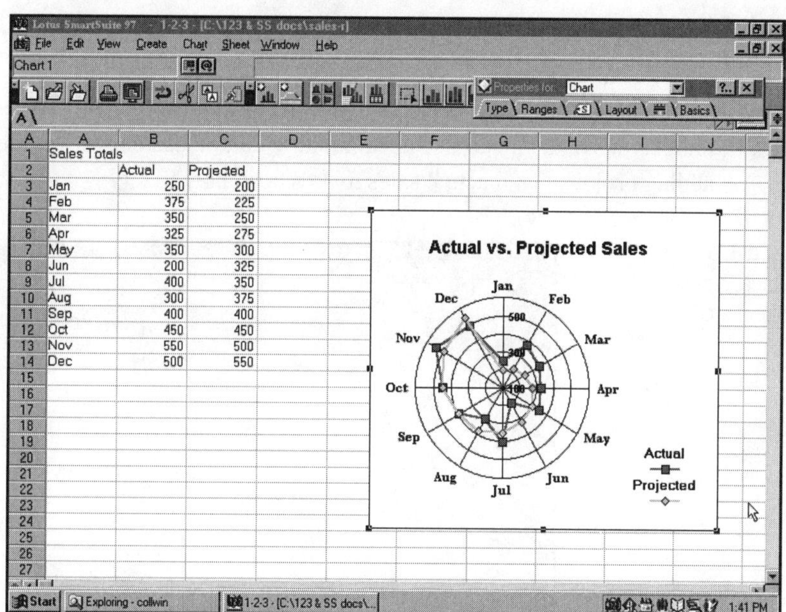

Fig. 14.5
A radar chart shows how close the actual sales are to the projected sales.

The radar chart in figure 14.5 illustrates the basic characteristics of radar charts:

- The central point from which each value is measured from is 0,0 (unless you change the minimum value of the y-axis).
- All spokes that extend from the central point are labeled with what typically are used as x-axis labels. In figure 14.5, the spokes are labeled with months.
- The data points for each series are connected, forming a spiral, or a "bent" circle, around the central point.

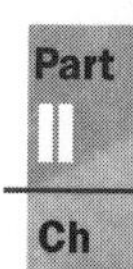

- For each major interval on the y-axis, 1-2-3 draws a dotted circle around the central point. Figure 14.5, for example, shows circles at 100, 200, 300, 400, 500, and 600. These circles function like grid lines, helping readers interpret the values of the data points.

You can gather two pieces of information from a radar chart. First, you can compare the data series; the greater the distance between the data points in each spoke, the greater the difference between the series. Second, you can see how much the data fluctuates; a smooth spiral indicates a steady increase, and a jagged spiral indicates more variability. In figure 14.5, notice how smooth the spiral for the projected series is (a steady increase was predicted) and how the spiral for the actual series jumps around (sales increased during some months and decreased in others).

The Type tab of the Chart InfoBox offers two styles of radar charts. The first style is the one shown in figure 14.5. The second style stacks the series and fills in the area between spirals. Figure 14.6 shows a chart with the stacked-area style. This style is not appropriate for all types of data, because accumulating data doesn't always make sense. For example, adding projected and actual sales makes no sense.

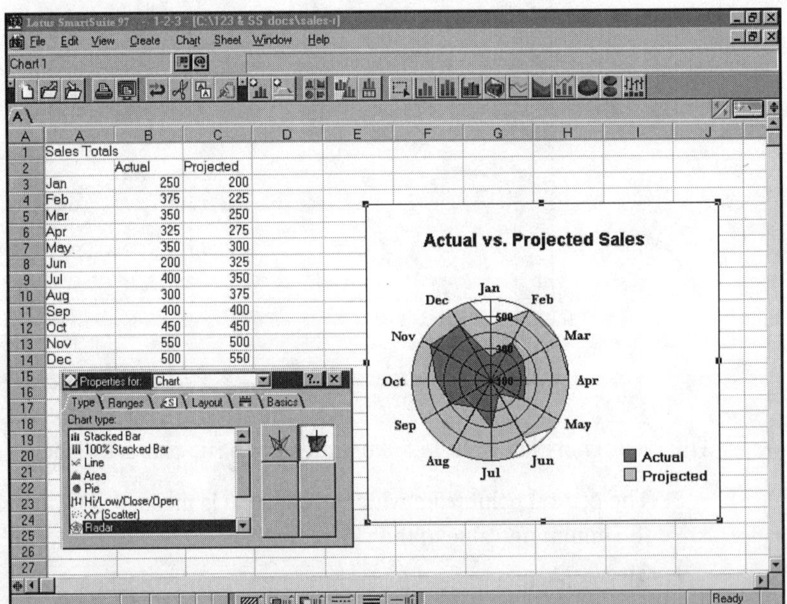

Fig. 14.6
A stacked-area-style radar chart.

Adding a Second Y-Axis to a Chart

Sometimes you may want to chart two kinds of data in a single chart to show how the two are related. The worksheet shown in figure 14.7 shows sales data for an ice cream company. Notice that the worksheet also contains a column for average monthly temperatures.

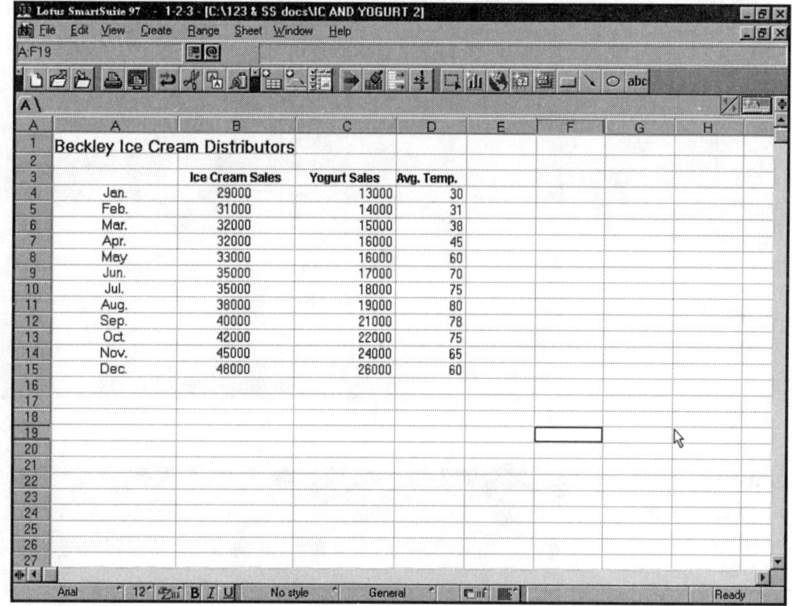

	A	B	C	D
1	Beckley Ice Cream Distributors			
2				
3		Ice Cream Sales	Yogurt Sales	Avg. Temp.
4	Jan.	29000	13000	30
5	Feb.	31000	14000	31
6	Mar.	32000	15000	38
7	Apr.	32000	16000	45
8	May	33000	16000	60
9	Jun.	35000	17000	70
10	Jul.	35000	18000	75
11	Aug.	38000	19000	80
12	Sep.	40000	21000	78
13	Oct.	42000	22000	75
14	Nov.	45000	24000	65
15	Dec.	48000	26000	60

Fig. 14.7
Data for ice cream sales and average temperatures each month.

TIP You should use a second y-axis only to plot two different types of data in the same chart.

The company is interested in finding out whether there is a relationship between the temperature and sales. Figure 14.8 shows a line chart created with this data. Because temperature is a much smaller number than ice cream and frozen yogurt sales, the temperature line barely registers in the chart. Creating another scale to display the temperatures would be helpful. To create this scale, add a second y-axis to the chart.

Figure 14.9 shows the same chart with a second y-axis scale on the right to plot the temperatures. Notice that the chart also is a mixed chart. Using a mixed chart to display a second y-axis scale helps to cue the reader that the chart contains two types of data.

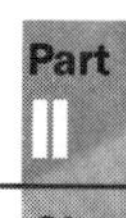

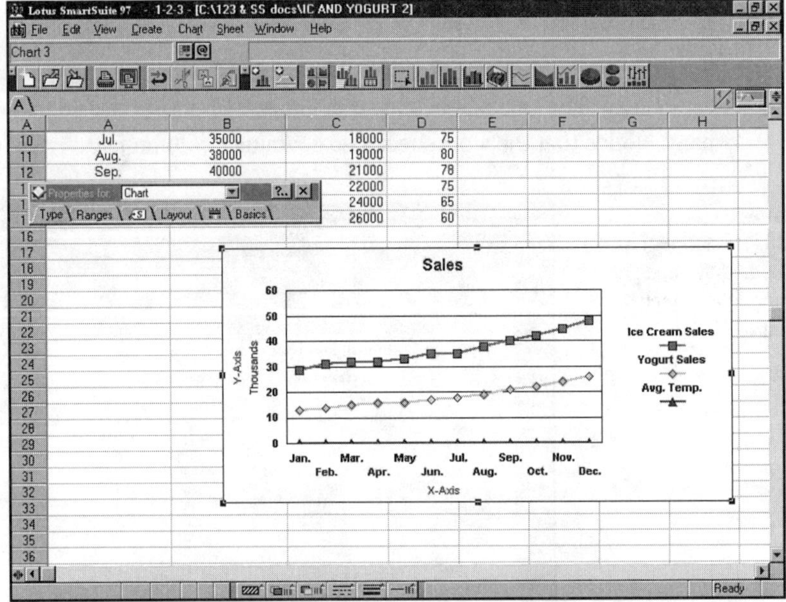

Fig. 14.8
Temperature and sales values are too different to be plotted against the same y-axis scale.

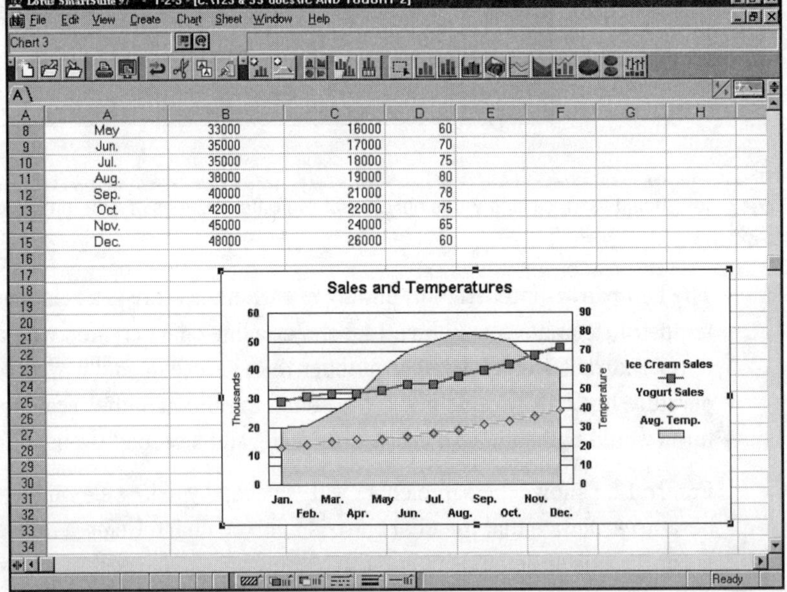

Fig. 14.9
A mixed chart with a second y-axis accurately plots both sales and temperature values.

To create a second y-axis chart, select the data series range or range(s) that you want to plot on a second y-axis, and then follow these steps:

1. Create a line, area, or bar chart and then select the chart.
2. Choose Chart, Series to open the Properties for Series InfoBox.
3. In the drop-down list box, choose the data series you want to plot on the second y-axis.
4. Choose the Options tab and select Plot Against 2nd Y-axis.
5. In Mixed Type, choose Line, Area, or Bar. Figure 14.10 shows the Properties for Series InfoBox set with the second Y-Axis for the chart shown in figure 14.9.

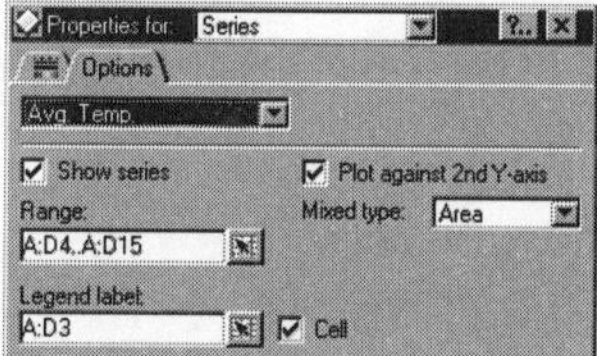

Fig. 14.10 Selections in the Options tab for a mixed chart with a second y-axis.

It is very important to use the y-axis and second y-axis titles to indicate which data series are plotted against which y-axis.

▶ **See** "Changing the Axis Titles and Orientation," **p. 337**

▶ **See** "Controlling the Axis Scale," **p. 338**

After you add the second y-axis, you can treat it the way you treat a regular y-axis: you can give it a title, format the numbers, adjust the scale, and so on. To make any of these changes, use the Properties InfoBox.

TROUBLESHOOTING

I'm having trouble creating an XY chart. I preselected the range and created an automatic chart, but the ranges are all wrong. 1-2-3 used the x-axis values as series A and the y-axis values as series B. How do I solve this problem? Because of the rules that 1-2-3 follows when producing an automatic chart, you can't use this feature successfully when you create XY charts. 1-2-3 gets confused, because the x-axis labels in an XY chart must be values. The best way to create an XY chart is to create a chart from scratch and define the ranges yourself.

I chose the Mixed chart type, but all my data series display as bars. How can I get one of them to display as a line? Open the Properties for Series InfoBox, select the series you want to chart, and then choose Line from the Mixed Type drop-down box.

Adding Graphics and Clip Art to Charts

You may want to use graphics to make your charts more attractive or to highlight specific data. In 1-2-3, you can choose Create, Drawing and the various drawing SmartIcons to create graphics. You also can import graphics or clip art from other programs into your charts. The following sections explain how to accomplish these tasks.

Annotating a Chart

In 1-2-3, you can add descriptive labels, lines, objects, and arrows to existing charts. For example, you might want to explain why a data point is particularly high or low, or to state a conclusion illustrated by the chart. Figure 14.11 shows a chart annotation created with the Text Block SmartIcon and the Draw Arrow SmartIcon. You create this annotation by opening the Create menu and choosing the Drawing command; and then choosing the item you want to draw.

▶ **See** "Working with Graphics Text," **p. 411**

▶ **See** "Working with Graphics," **p. 415**

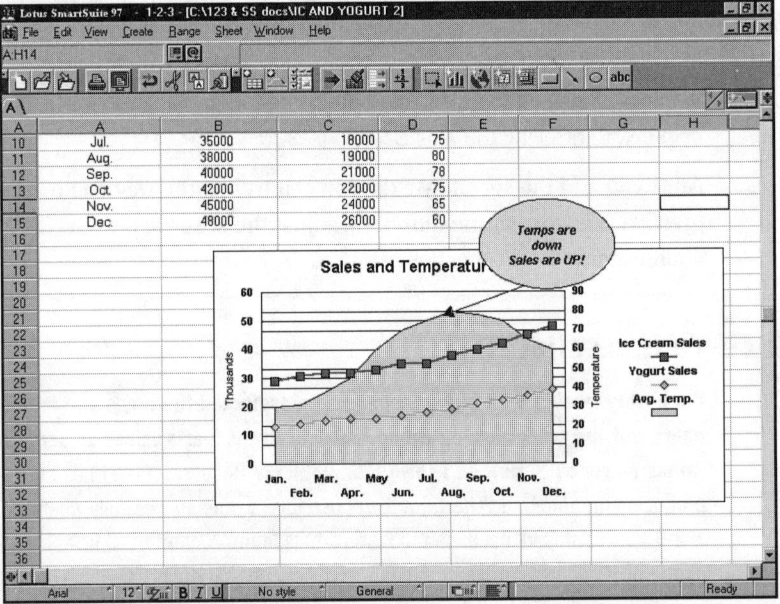

Fig. 14.11
A chart annotated with the drawing commands adds pizzazz.

Adding Clip Art

You might want to enhance your charts and worksheets further by using *clip art*—graphics imported from other programs. You can bring in clip art easily by using the Windows Clipboard or you can use the Create command. Using the Create command limits you to the following file types: bitmap (BMP), Windows metafile (WMF), 1-2-3 PIC, and ANSI metafile (CGM).

To add a graphic to a 1-2-3 chart using the Clipboard, perform the following steps:

1. Copy the graphic to the Windows Clipboard from any application in Windows.
2. In 1-2-3, select a range of cells in the worksheet in which to paste the graphic.
3. In 1-2-3, choose Edit, Paste to copy the graphic into the selected worksheet cells; alternatively, click the Paste from Clipboard SmartIcon. (If you did not preselect a range, the graphic is pasted into a single cell.)

4. Drag the graphic into your chart.
5. Resize the graphic as necessary by dragging the selection handles.

To add clip art by inserting it through the Create menu, follow these steps:

1. Choose Create, Drawing, Picture. The Picture dialog box appears (see fig. 14.12).

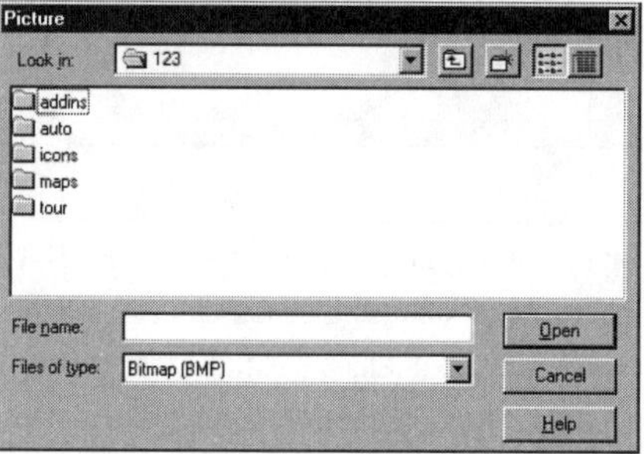

Fig. 14.12 Choose the picture from your disk to insert to your chart.

2. Select the file type in the Files of Type drop-down list.
3. Select the folder and file you want to insert.
4. Choose the Open button to insert the picture.

NOTE 1-2-3 automatically adds a visible frame around imported graphics. To remove the frame, double-click the art to open the Properties for Draw Object InfoBox; in the Color, Pattern, and Line Style tab, choose None for the Line Style.

Graphic elements in 1-2-3 are stacked on top of one another. To change the stacking order, open the Drawing menu and choose the appropriate command: Bring to Front or Send to Back.

Figure 14.13 shows a chart that displays clip art—a drawing of hands shaking—above the legend. The drawing was pasted into the worksheet and then moved into the chart.

Fig. 14.13
Graphics make the chart more interesting to look at.

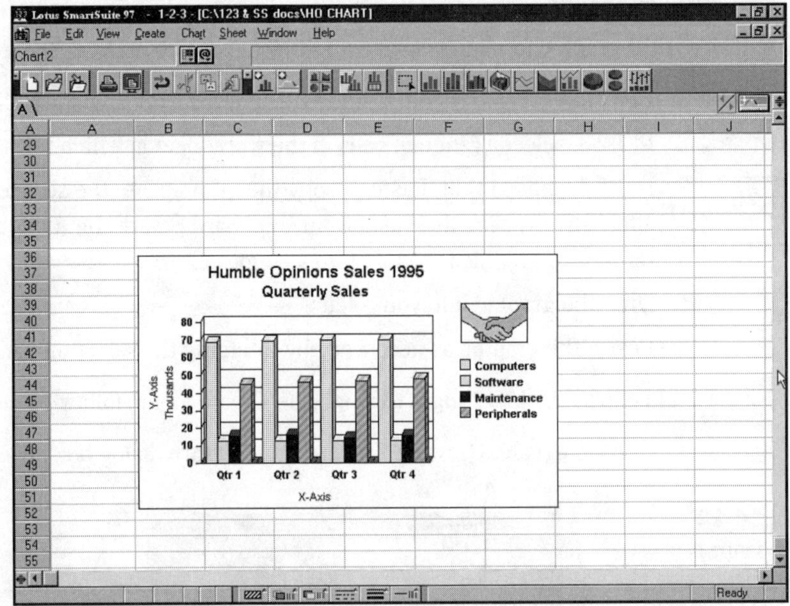

Where does clip art come from? Many drawing programs, such as CorelDRAW! and Lotus Freelance Graphics, come with a collection of images that you can use in other programs. You also can purchase packages of clip art from companies such as Masterclip Graphics, 3G Graphics, TMaker, and Image Club. Lotus Development Corporation offers its own clip-art package, called SmartPics. For more information on SmartPics for Windows, call Lotus Selects at 1-800-635-6887.

TROUBLESHOOTING

When I use the Create command to insert a picture, I can't find any compatible files to import; I know there are files somewhere but I can't find them. Leave the Picture dialog box up and choose Windows' Find, Files or Folders command from the Start menu. In the Name & Location tab, enter *.BMP, *.WMF, or *.CGM. In the Look In box, choose to search your entire hard disk and choose the Find Now button. Windows lists the files it finds and you can make note of their name and location to use in the Picture dialog box.

Illustrating Data with Maps

1-2-3 offers a useful feature: maps that illustrate data in the worksheet. Suppose that you have compiled sales figures for each state in your sales area. Instead of trying to create a bar chart, you can link the data to colors in a map. As figure 14.14 shows, 1-2-3 evaluates the worksheet data and automatically assigns each state a color, depending on the sales figure for the state. You also can illustrate a second kind of data with as many as six patterns; in this case, the map shows sales volumes in colors and sales regions in patterns. You can create maps of this type for other countries and regions in the world, as well as for the entire United States or just specific areas of the United States.

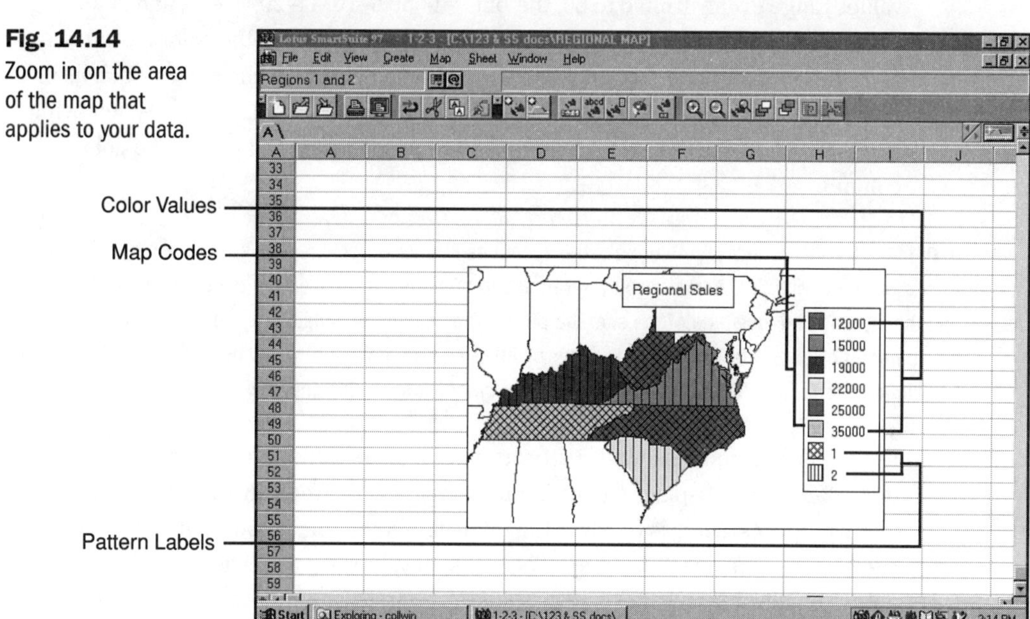

Fig. 14.14
Zoom in on the area of the map that applies to your data.

Setting Up the Map Data Ranges

Before you can create a map, you need to set up the data ranges in the way that 1-2-3 can interpret them to create a map. To do so, follow these rules:

- In the first column, identify the geographic regions you want to illustrate in the map. The regions can be countries in the world, U.S. states, Canadian provinces, or other provincial regions throughout the world. To identify the regions, you can either enter the name of the country, state, or province or use a two-letter map code. 1-2-3

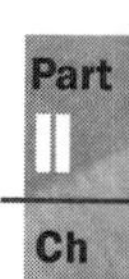

recognizes as map codes the standard two-letter post office abbreviations for U.S. states, but you will probably have to look up the two-letter map codes for other regions or countries.

If you use labels instead of values to determine colors or patterns, each label can be as short as one or two characters or as long as you like in the legend.

- In the second column, place the color values; these are the values that 1-2-3 uses to display regions in different colors. The range of values is unlimited; 1-2-3 will always divide the range into six bins that are illustrated by six colors. For example, if the values range evenly from 0 to 60, the bins will be 0–10, 11–20, 21–30, and so on. The value 25 falls into the 21–30 bin and will be illustrated by the color assigned to all values in that range. You can also use labels to determine the colors, such as in a map to illustrate U.S. states with Democratic or Republican majorities. When using labels to determine the color, you are limited to six different labels in the color column.

NOTE 1-2-3 also lets you point out exact locations in a geographic region, such as a city, by specifying the character you want to use to mark the site (called the *pin character*) and the latitude and longitude of the site. The pin character, latitude, longitude, and (optional) pin character color may be entered in the fourth, fifth, and sixth columns, respectively. This technique is covered in "Showing Pin Characters in a Map," later in this chapter.

- In the third column, place the pattern values or labels; these are the values or labels that 1-2-3 uses to display regions in different patterns. You can use this column for many purposes, such as dividing the total area in the map into regions or showing another set of values in the map. The range of values for patterns is unlimited; 1-2-3 always divides these values into six bins. You can use no more than six labels in the pattern column, however.

Creating the Map

You can create a map as easily as you can create a chart: automatically, as long as you set up the map data ranges following the rules in the previous section, "Setting Up the Map Data Ranges."

To create a map automatically, do the following:

1. Select the range that contains all the data ranges for the map: the map codes column, color column, and (optionally) pattern column. Do not select the headings for the columns, such as Sales or Region.

2. Choose Create, Map; the mouse cursor changes to a cross and the title bar indicates you should click the worksheet to display the map.
3. Click the worksheet where you want 1-2-3 to place the upper-left corner of the map.

It may take a moment for 1-2-3 to evaluate the data and develop the map. When this process is complete, 1-2-3 inserts the map in the default size. Figure 14.15 shows a map created from the data in figure 14.14. Notice that the map automatically includes a legend that identifies the colors and patterns; the values in the legend are the highest number in each bin. The default title is determined by the map. The selection handles around the map frame indicate that the map is selected.

Each map that you create with 1-2-3 is a single embedded OLE object. The sections that follow tell you how you can change the title and control other aspects of the map.

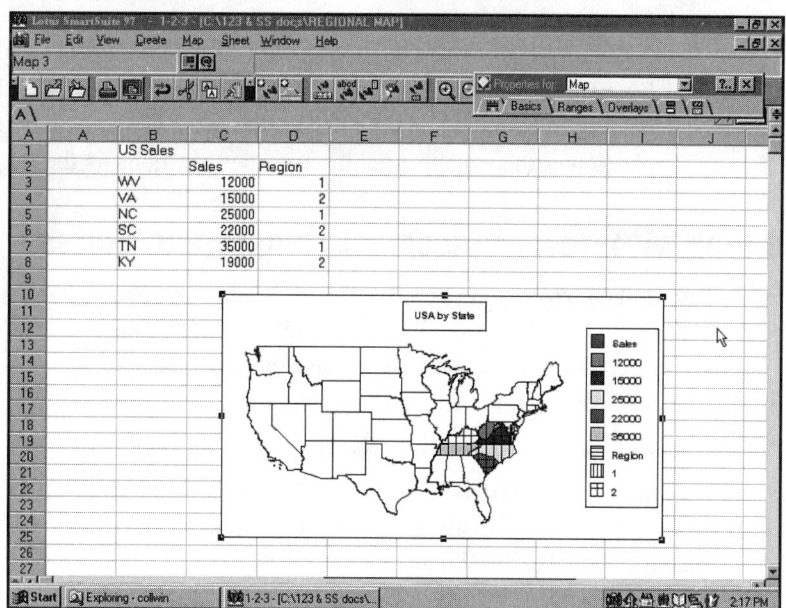

Fig. 14.15
After the map is created, you can edit it, just as you edit a chart.

The following list explains how 1-2-3 handles the data when it creates the map:

- 1-2-3 evaluates the map codes to determine which map to use.
- When the color column contains values, 1-2-3 determines the highest and lowest values, then divides the range of values into six bins. For example, if the numbers range from 0 to 60, the bins might be 0–10, 11–20, 21–30, 31–40, 41–50, and 51–60. In figure 14.16, the numbers range from 7,000 to 56,000, so 1-2-3 created the bins 0–9400, 9401–18800, and so on. (For information on changing the bins, see

"Changing the Bin Definitions," later in this chapter.) Alternatively, when the color column contains labels, 1-2-3 evaluates how many different labels there are to determine how many colors to use in the map; the maximum is six.

- 1-2-3 evaluates the pattern column (if any) in the same way it evaluates the color column: it divides the range of values into six bins or determines the number of labels to see how many patterns to use; the maximum is six. (For information on changing the bins, see "Changing the Bin Definitions," later in this chapter.)
- If you have entered pin characters, the latitude and longitude of the sites for the characters, and (optional) pin character color in the fourth, fifth, and sixth columns, respectively, 1-2-3 calculates the locations for the pin characters. (In most cases, you will add pin characters to an existing map. For more information about this option, see "Adding Pin Characters to a Map," later in this chapter.)
- Finally, 1-2-3 draws the map, assigning each state, province, or country in the map code column a color based on its value or label in the color column and a pattern based on its value or label in the pattern column (if any). The legend shows the colors and patterns and their associated bin value upper limit and/or label. The pin characters (if any) appear at the specified locations on the map.

Dealing with New or Incorrect Geographic Codes

During the map creation process, if 1-2-3 encounters geographic codes that do not belong in the same map or a code that it does not recognize (one that does not match any of geographic codes in the system), it displays the Region Check dialog box to give you a chance to correct the error and complete the map creation process.

Suppose, for example, that you are creating a map of the United States, and misspelled the code for Virginia (VA) as VL. You select the map data ranges and choose Create, Map. 1-2-3 begins to develop the map, but encounters the geographic code VL in cell A:A4; this code is not part of the U.S. map.

1-2-3 displays the Region Check dialog box (see fig. 14.16).

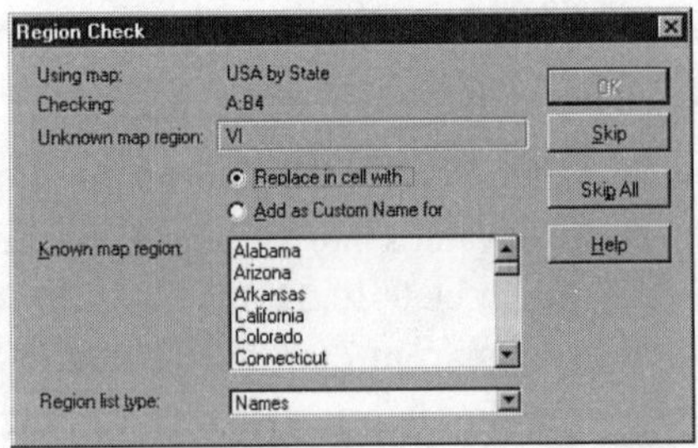

Fig. 14.16
1-2-3 will not create the map with an unrecognized region.

Notice that the cell and the incorrect code are displayed in the top two fields of the Region Check dialog box.

If the entry is a misspelling that you want to correct in the worksheet so that you can create the map, perform the following steps to change the entry in the cell and continue to create the map with the correct map region:

1. Select the Replace in Cell With option.
2. In the Known Map Region list, select the state or other region you want to substitute. You can choose to change to a code in the Region List Type drop-down list, if you prefer.
3. If your region name is correct but is a previously created custom name, choose the Add as Custom Name for option and choose Custom Names from the Region List Type list. Select the name in the Known Map Region list.

   Alternatively, you can choose the Skip button to skip the region; 1-2-3 doesn't add skipped regions to your map.
4. Click OK to change the cell entry to your selection and continue to create the map with the corrected information.

Moving and Resizing the Map

You can move the entire map the way you move a chart or other graphic object in a worksheet. Click the map frame so that the selection handles appear around it; then drag the map to the new position.

CAUTION

If you click the map instead of the frame, you'll move the map around in the frame.

To resize the entire map, click it to select it. Point to one of the selection handles; the mouse pointer should change to a four-headed arrow. Then drag the selection handle in the direction in which you want to change the size. If you want to maintain the map's current proportions, drag a corner handle.

Modifying a Map

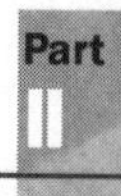

1-2-3 uses default colors and patterns, which you can change. You can also edit the legend labels, change the bin definitions, and supply a new title for the map. All of these elements are controlled with the commands on the Map menu and Properties InfoBox and are described in the following sections.

Changing the Title By default, a map's title comes from the graphic that 1-2-3 used to create the map. To change the title, double-click the title and enter a new one. Alternatively, select the map and then choose Map, Title. The Properties for Title InfoBox appears, as shown in figure 14.17. You can enter a new title in the Basics tab, as well as two additional lines for subtitles. You can also change the position of the title in the Basics tab.

NOTE You can also use the Font, Attribute, and Color tab of the Properties for Title InfoBox to change the title's formatting.

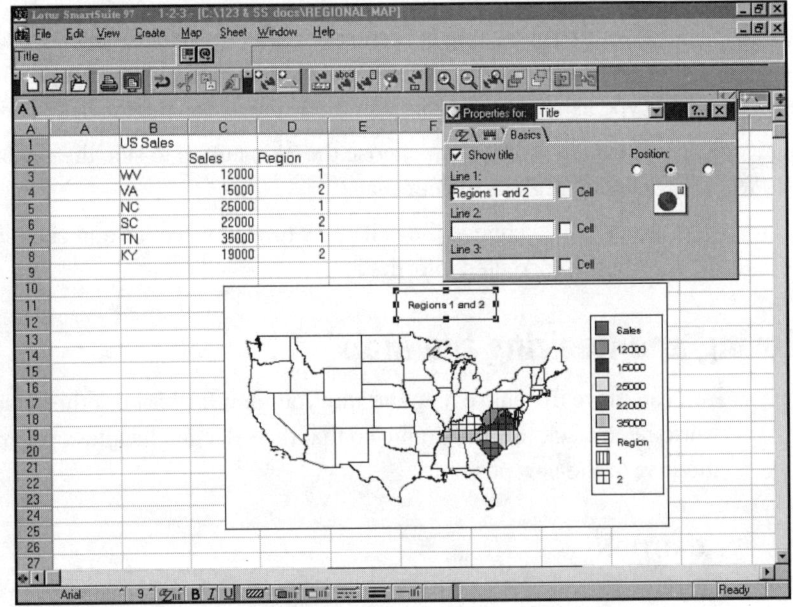

Fig. 14.17
Enter a new title plus subtitles for the map from the Title InfoBox.

Changing the Data Ranges You can change the ranges that define the map. You may want to add more items at the bottom of the list, for example, or change the map so that it shows only some of the regions. Choose Map, Ranges to display the Map InfoBox, Ranges tab.

TIP To find out the code, name, or coordinates of any state, province, or country in a map, right-click the area. The Quick menu displays the information after the Plot Properties command.

Choose the Range button for any of the following to select a new range in your worksheet:

Map Region Names or Codes. Displays the data range currently specified for the region names or codes.

Data to Map with Colors. Displays the data range currently specified to be mapped with colors.

Data to Map with Patterns. Displays the data range currently specified to be mapped with patterns.

Pin Characters, Latitude and Longitude. Displays the data range currently specified for the pin characters; see "Adding Pin Characters to a Map," later in this chapter.

Choosing Other Colors and Patterns You may want to use different colors or patterns in a map, perhaps to provide better contrast when the map is printed on a black-and-white printer. Or you may want to modify the bin definitions to divide the values into bins that are more relevant to the way you view the data. To control the colors and patterns and how they are assigned, select the map; then open the Map menu and choose either:

- Color Bins. Displays the Properties for Map InfoBox with the Colors tab displaying (see fig. 14.18).
- Pattern Bins. Displays the Properties for Map InfoBox with the Patterns tab displaying (see fig. 14.19).

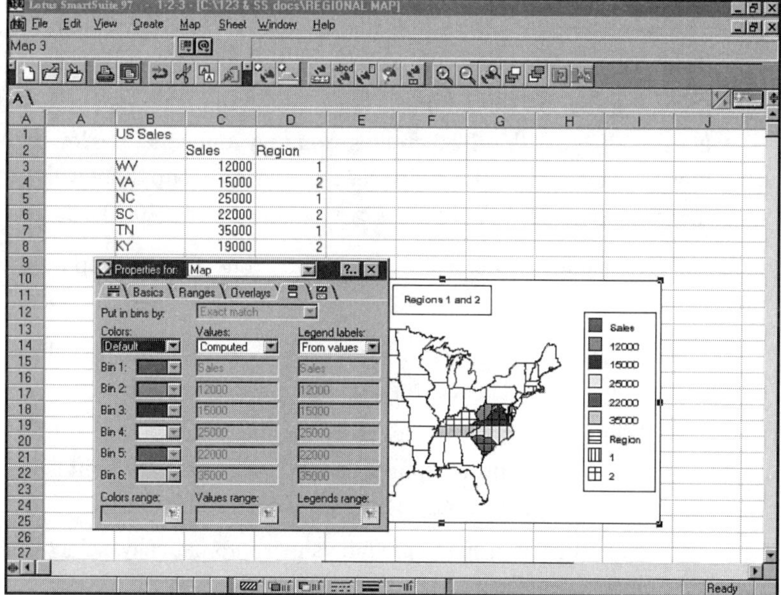

Fig. 14.18
Set the colors to default or manually change colors and values.

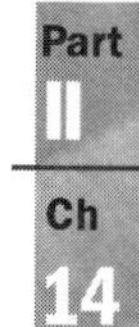

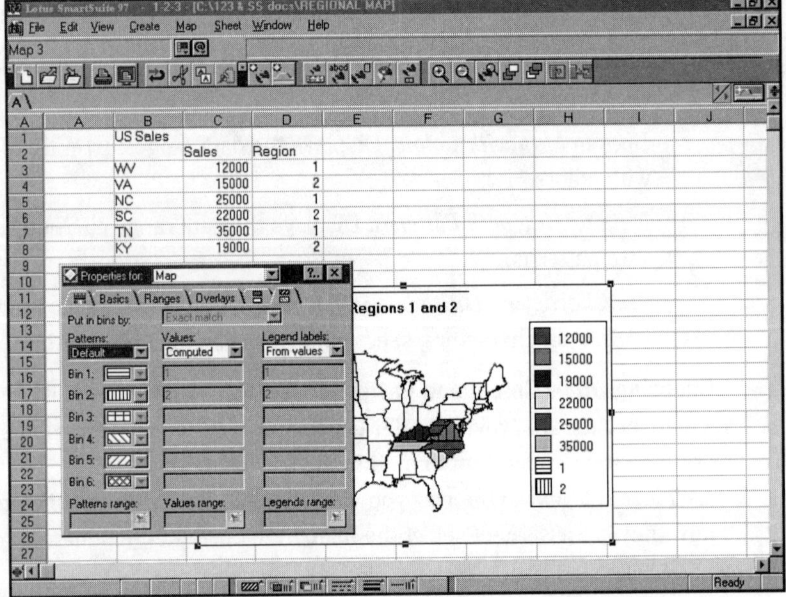

Fig. 14.19
Choose the patterns you want to represent your pattern labels.

As you can see in figures 14.18 and 14.19, changing the colors and patterns is essentially the same. These figures show the default settings. Notice that the values, legend labels, colors, and patterns are automatically assigned by default.

To change a color or pattern, choose Manual from the Patterns or Colors drop-down list box and then select the new color or pattern from the Bin's drop-down list.

Changing the Bin Definitions Sometimes, you may want to define the bin values instead of using the ones that 1-2-3 creates. You may know that the lowest numbers in the color range are exceptions, for example, and want to group them with higher numbers, or you may want the bins to be defined by round numbers (10,000, 20,000, 30,000, and so on).

You can change the bin definitions in the Properties for Map InfoBox, Colors or Patterns tab.

- To enter your own bin values, select Manual from the Values drop-down list, and type the bin values in the text boxes for bins 1 through 6.
- To use a worksheet range to define the bin values, select From Range from the Values drop-down list; then use the range selector to indicate the range in the worksheet that contains the bin values.
- To let 1-2-3 determine the bin values automatically, select Computed from the Values drop-down list.

The Put in Bins By drop-down list at the top of the Colors and Patterns tabs controls the way 1-2-3 uses the bin values. By default, the bin values are Exact Match. You can, however, tell 1-2-3 to use the Upper Limit to color the states or countries by choosing that option. When the Exact Match option is selected, 1-2-3 colors only those states or countries whose values match the value in any of the bin text boxes.

If the color or pattern column contains labels instead of values, however, 1-2-3 matches the labels by using the upper limit.

Changing the Legend Labels By default, 1-2-3 automatically uses the values in the bin text boxes as the legend labels, whether these values are determined automatically, manually, or from a range. If you want to edit or change these labels, you can do one of the following things in either the Colors or Patterns tab of the Map InfoBox:

- Select Manual from the Legend Labels drop-down list, and then type new labels in the text boxes. You can either enter entirely new labels, or add text or currency symbols to the automatically generated labels.
- Select From Range from the Legend Labels drop-down list, and then use the range selector to indicate the range in the worksheet that contains the labels.
- Select From Values from the Legend Labels drop-down list to use values or labels in the Values text boxes as the legend labels.

Selecting Other Colors You can control the colors in the map individually by using the Colors tab of the Map Properties InfoBox. Choose Manual under Colors and select the drop-down box beside the Bin you want to modify. A color palette appears from which you can select a new color for the bin.

For greater control of the way the map appears printed in black and white, change the map colors to shades of gray.

You can select the From Range option in the Colors tab, and then use the range selector to indicate the range in the worksheet that contains the color values. 1-2-3 associates numbers with the colors in the color palette; for example, the numbers 0 through 15 represent the colors in the top row of the color palette from left to right.

Selecting Other Patterns You can control the patterns in the map individually by using the Patterns tab of the Map Properties InfoBox. Choose Manual under Patterns and select the drop-down box beside the Bin you want to modify. A pattern palette appears from which you can select a new pattern for the bin.

You can select From Range from the Patterns drop-down list, and then use the range selector to indicate the range in the worksheet that contains the pattern values. The pattern values can be a number from 1 to 6, representing the six available patterns.

Changing the Redraw Preference

By default, 1-2-3 automatically redraws the map whenever you make changes in a map dialog box or in the data ranges that define the map. However, if you are making several changes, you may not want 1-2-3 to redraw the map after each change. You can change 1-2-3's redraw preference from automatic to manual. Choose the Basics tab in the Properties for Map InfoBox and deselect the Redraw Map Automatically When Data Changes check box.

Editing the Map Graphic

Similar to a chart, you can select and manipulate elements individually within a map. You can change position of the title and legend, format fonts, show only parts of the map, and overlay other maps.

Changing the Text Attributes The two map elements that contain text are the title and the legend. You can change the font and attributes of this text. To change the actual text of the title or the legend labels, use the Properties for Legends and the Properties for Titles InfoBoxes. (Refer to "Changing the Title" and "Changing the Legend Labels" earlier in this chapter.)

▶ **See** "Enhancing the Appearance of Data," **p. 125**

To change the font and attributes of the title or legend labels, select the appropriate element in the map and select the Font, Attribute, and Color tab of the appropriate InfoBox. This InfoBox works the same way as any Font tab, enabling you to change the typeface, style, size, and other attributes of the text.

Moving, Resizing, or Deleting the Title and Legend You can drag the map title and legend to other positions within the map frame; simply select the item so that the handles appear and then drag the item with the mouse to the new position. To change the sizes of these items, select the frame so the handles show; then drag the handles to enlarge or reduce the frame.

To delete the title or legend, you can use a number of methods. The simplest way is to select the title or legend and press the Delete key.

Showing Part of the Map You can change the size of the map itself (as separate from the frame, title, and labels) by zooming in and out. To make the map a little smaller (as it appears in fig. 14.20), open the Map menu and choose the Zoom Out command. The map becomes a little smaller within the frame, but the title and legend do not change. You can repeat this command several times to make the map even smaller.

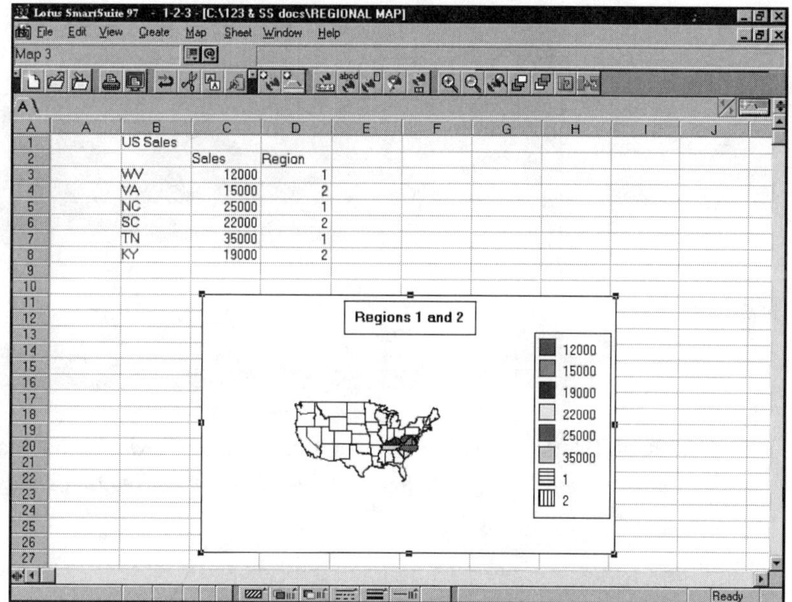

Fig. 14.20
Reduce the map if you want to fit a large region into a smaller space.

You may want to show only part of the map that 1-2-3 draws. You can zoom in on part of the map by opening the Map menu and choosing the Zoom In command. The map becomes larger in the frame. When the map becomes too big to fit in the frame, you see only the part that fits. You can repeat this command several times to make the map larger in the frame.

When you zoom in, you may lose sight of the regions you want to show; right-click the map and choose Recenter to take care of that problem. Figure 14.21 shows the map of the enlarged region.

To return the map to its original size, right-click the map and choose Reset to Original View.

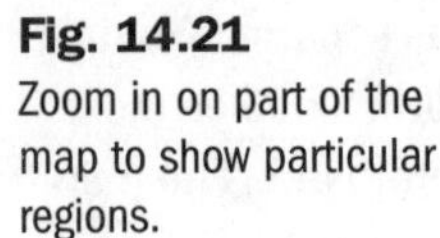

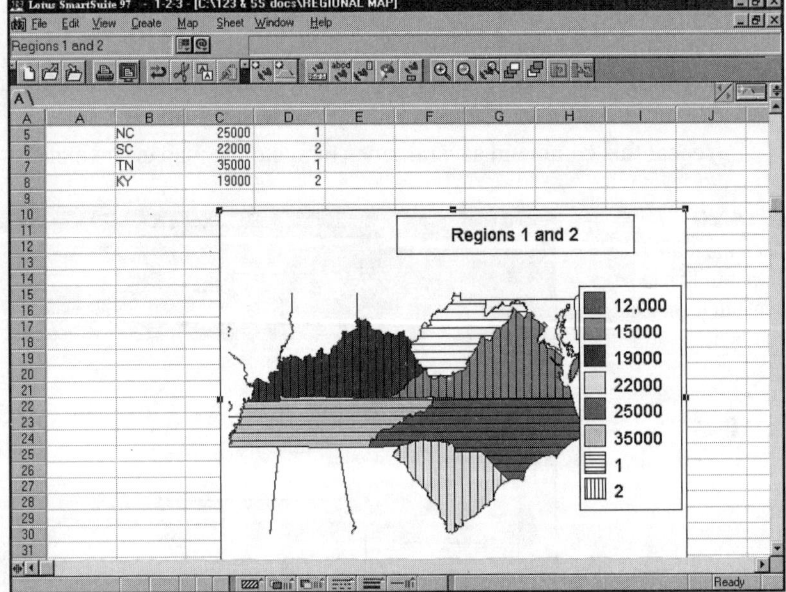

Fig. 14.21
Zoom in on part of the map to show particular regions.

Adding an Overlay Sometimes, you may want to show adjacent maps for which you are not illustrating data. You can achieve this effect by *adding an overlay*—placing another map over the map graphic.

To add a map overlay, open the Map InfoBox and choose the Overlays tab; alternatively, choose Map, Overlays. Choose the Add button to display the Add Overlay dialog box (which looks just like the Open dialog box. Select the map (with TV extensions) you want to add and choose the Open button. 1-2-3 displays the outline of the map (without color) over your map. You may need to zoom out to view the map overlay.

Adding Pin Characters to a Map

Suppose that you want to show the location of capital cities in the United States or flag the countries in which you have recently opened sales offices. On a paper map on a wall, you would use push pins to show the specific sites. In a 1-2-3 map, you can use pin characters—characters that you add to a map by telling 1-2-3 what character to use, the latitude and longitude of the site, and (optionally) the color you want the pin character to be.

Setting Up the Coordinates Data Before You Create the Map To set up your pin characters before you create the map, you must set up data ranges, as follows:

- The first column contains the character or label you want to display in the map. You create the characters by formatting letters with symbol fonts such as Wingdings, ZapfChancery, or Symbol. You can use a different character for each site or use the same character for each site you flag in the map.
- The second column contains the latitude of the pin character site.
- The third column contains the longitude of the pin character site.
- 1-2-3 automatically selects a color that contrasts with the background color of the region in which the pin character is placed. If you want to select a different color, enter the number for the color in the fourth column. 1-2-3 associates numbers with the colors in the color palette; for example, the numbers 0 through 15 represent the colors in the top row of the color palette from left to right.

You can find the latitude and longitude of each site by following these steps:

1. Display the map on which you want to add pins.
2. Point the mouse arrow at the site where you want to put a pin character.
3. Right-click the mouse button to display the quick menu; choose the Copy Coordinates command. The coordinates are copied to the Clipboard.
4. Click the mouse in the cell you want to paste the coordinates and choose Edit, Paste. The latitude and longitude are copied to the worksheet cells.

Where you set up the pin character data ranges in the worksheet depends on where and how many pin characters you want. If there will only be one pin character per geographic region, such as state capitals, it is probably easiest to place the pin character data in the columns immediately to the right of the map data so that each pin character site is in the same row as the region in which it falls. You do not need to include a pin character in every region.

Suppose that you want to mark the site of each international sales office and you have more than one office in some countries. In a situation like this, it would be easier to place the pin character data in a separate part of the worksheet; the pin character data does not need to line up in rows with the map regions. The character and coordinates for each pin character need only appear in consecutive rows and columns.

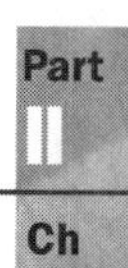

Adding the Coordinates to the Map Definition After you set up the pin character's data ranges, you need to add the ranges to the definition of the map ranges. Perform the following steps:

1. Select the map.
2. Choose Map, Ranges to display the Properties for Map InfoBox, Ranges tab.

3. In Pin Characters, Latitude and Longitude, either type the range that includes the pin character, latitude, longitude, and optional pin character columns in the Range text box or select the range with the range selector.
4. Choose OK to redraw the map with the pin characters in it.

Changing and Deleting Pin Characters To change the pin character to a different character or label, enter a new character or label in the worksheet cell containing the pin character you want to change; when 1-2-3 redraws the map, it will display the new character or label.

To delete a pin character, delete the latitude and longitude from the worksheet cell as well as the representative pin character from the worksheet; when 1-2-3 redraws the map, it will no longer appear.

Enhancing the Map with Other Text and Graphics

▶ **See** "Enhancing the Chart," **p. 348**

▶ **See** "Working With Graphics," **p. 415**

Just as you can enhance worksheets and charts by adding text blocks and graphics (such as lines and arrows), you can add these elements to enhance a map and make its meaning clearer. For example, you may want to add a title to the legend or change the map frame.

To add graphics elements to the map, you can use the following 1-2-3 features:

- To add a text block, choose Create, Text.
- To add an arrow, choose Create, Drawing, Arrow.

- To change the background color of the map graphic and/or the frame style and color, open the Properties for Map InfoBox and choose the Color, Pattern, and Line Style tab.

Previewing a Map

▶ **See** "Previewing Worksheets Before Printing," **p. 290**

▶ **See** "Previewing and Printing Charts," **p. 317**

▶ **See** "Working with Graphics" **p. 415**

Before you print a map, you can preview it. Previewing can save you time and paper, enabling you to make all necessary adjustments and changes before you print. To preview a map, select the map, and then choose the File, Preview & Page Setup command. You also can click the Preview & Page Setup button in the Print dialog box.

Printing a Map

You can preview and print maps the way you print worksheets and charts: by choosing the File, Print command.

Before printing a map, select it; then choose the File, Print command. When a map is selected, the Print dialog box displays the map name (such as Map 1) in the Selected Map field (see fig. 14.22). When you choose OK, the map prints at the size it appears in the worksheet.

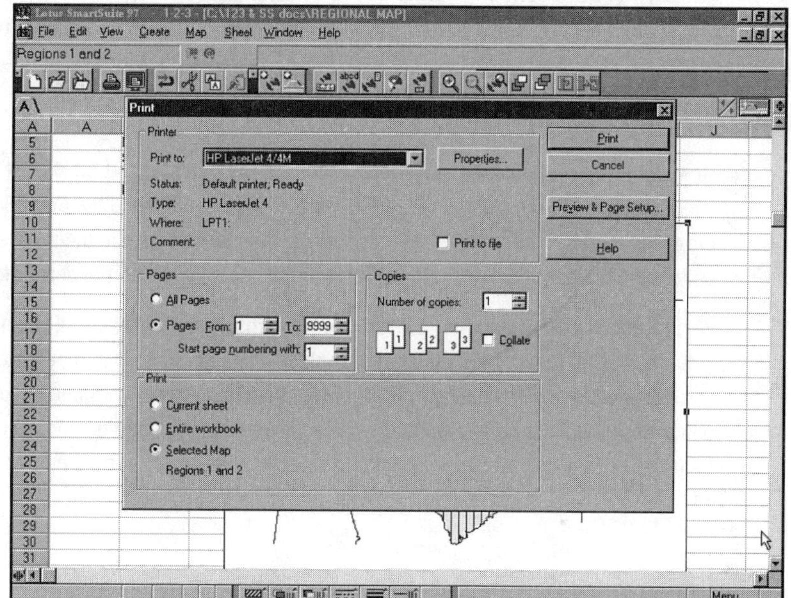

Fig. 14.22
Make sure your map is selected by finding its name in the Print area, under the Selected Map option.

You have the same options for printing maps as for printing charts. You can do any of the following things:

- Print it full-page. Select the chart; then choose the File, Preview & Page Setup command. The Page Fit option in the Properties for Preview & Page Setup InfoBox has four settings for maps and charts: Actual, Fill Page, Fill Page But Keep Proportions, and Custom.

To add white space between a worksheet data and map, include blank rows as part of the range(s) to be printed.

- Print the map and its worksheet data together on one page. If the map and data are placed exactly where you want them to appear in the report, you can define a single print range: Select the range of cells that includes the data and the map. If the data is in one part of the worksheet and the map is in another, you must define two print ranges. To define multiple ranges, type the ranges, separated by commas or semicolons. To point to the ranges, you must preselect them; remember to hold down the Ctrl key as you select the second and subsequent ranges.

- If you added any text or drawing objects to your map, those elements will not print if you simply click the map in the worksheet to select it. To print the map and added objects, you must click the Select Several Objects SmartIcon to "lasso" the map.

TROUBLESHOOTING

How can I add commas and currency symbols to the color legend labels? Select the map; choose Map, Color Bins to open the Properties for Map InfoBox and the Color Bins tab. In Values or Legend Labels, choose Manual. Next, position the mouse cursor in the numbers and enter a dollar sign, comma, or other character you want to show. Press Enter to complete each text box.

When I created my map, it did not include patterns. Now I want to add them. Create a range in the worksheet that contains the pattern values or labels. Make sure that there is one pattern value or label for each map region code. Select the map; open the Properties for Map InfoBox and choose the Patterns tab. In Patterns, choose Manual and enter the range in the Patterns Range text box or use the range selector to select the range you want to apply patterns to.

PART III

Optimizing 1-2-3

CHAPTER 15

Managing the Worksheet Display

by Elaine Marmel

Each 1-2-3 97 file appears in a window within the 1-2-3 window. Occasionally, you may want to compare data in two or more files. Or, you may need to open utility windows within a worksheet or chart. You can control the way 1-2-3 for Windows displays multiple windows.

You also can change the way you view an individual file. For example, you can freeze titles on-screen, split a worksheet window, or reduce or enlarge the displayed worksheet.

Outlining, a new feature to 1-2-3 97, helps you view or hide details of worksheet data. When you are preparing budget information, for example, outlining helps you view the details of a Utilities category such as Heat, Light, Gas, Electricity, and Water. Or, using the Outlining feature, you can hide these details and view the total for the Utilities category.

Displaying multiple workbooks

1-2-3 enables you to simultaneously open and work in more than one workbook.

Freezing worksheet titles

Using this feature, you can keep in view the labels you use for rows and columns while you scroll around the worksheet.

Hiding worksheet data

Suppose a column contains formulas necessary for the calculation of another column, but that formula column doesn't need to appear on a printout. You can hide information.

Outlining a worksheet

Often worksheets contain rows and columns that summarize other sets of rows and columns. By outlining a worksheet, you can display just the summarized information; or, you can display both the details and the summary information.

Displaying Multiple Workbooks

Suppose you're working in one worksheet file and you realize you need information contained in another worksheet file. "Well, that's simple," you say. "I'm working in Windows, so I'll just open the other file and get the information I need. Then I can close the second file and return to work on the first file." But perhaps you'd like to compare the files simultaneously. You can open both files and display them on-screen together—and control the way 1-2-3 97 displays multiple windows for those occasions.

You also can use traditional Windows commands to resize windows.

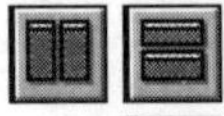

Using the commands on the Window menu or SmartIcons, you can display more than one worksheet simultaneously. In figure 15.1, two different worksheet files are open and displayed Tile, Left-Right. In figure 15.2, they are displayed Tile, Top-Bottom. And in figure 15.3, they are displayed Cascade.

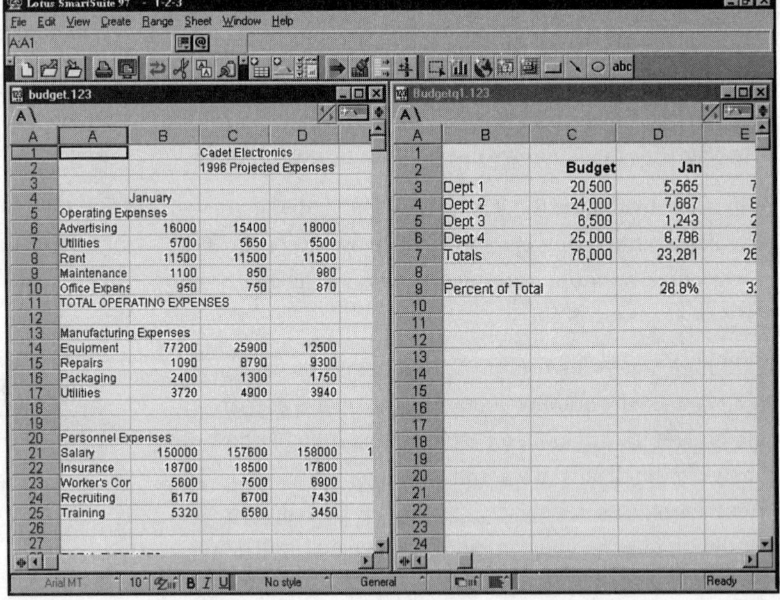

Fig. 15.1
When you choose Window, Tile Left-Right, the current workbook appears on the left.

If you want to switch the position of the workbooks, place the cell pointer in the workbook you want on the left and choose Window, Tile Left-Right again. Or place the cell pointer in the workbook you want on top and choose Window, Tile Top-Bottom again. You can control which workbook appears in front by making it the active workbook when you choose Window, Cascade.

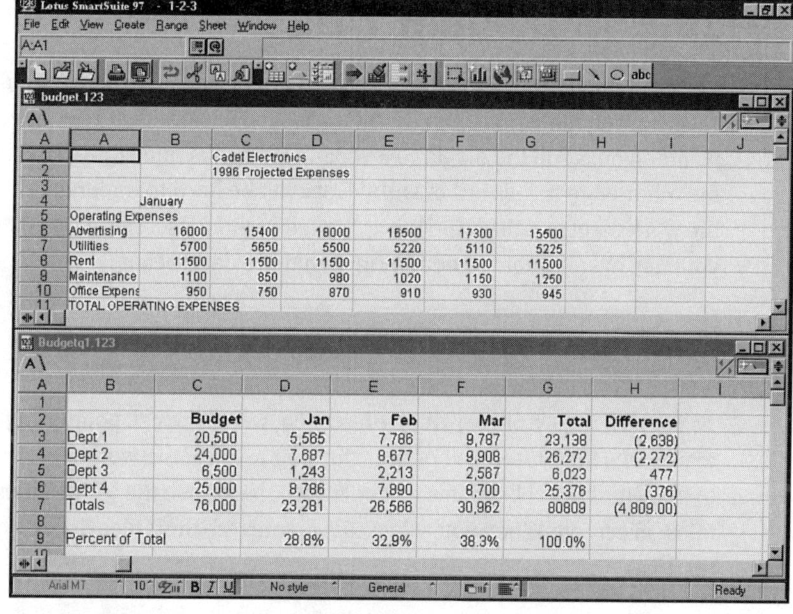

	A	B	C	D	E	F	G
1			Cadet Electronics				
2			1996 Projected Expenses				
3							
4	January						
5	Operating Expenses						
6	Advertising	16000	15400	18000	16500	17300	15500
7	Utilities	5700	5650	5500	5220	5110	5225
8	Rent	11500	11500	11500	11500	11500	11500
9	Maintenance	1100	850	980	1020	1150	1250
10	Office Expens	950	750	870	910	930	945
11	TOTAL OPERATING EXPENSES						

	B	C	D	E	F	G	H
1							
2		Budget	Jan	Feb	Mar	Total	Difference
3	Dept 1	20,500	5,565	7,786	9,787	23,138	(2,638)
4	Dept 2	24,000	7,687	8,677	9,908	26,272	(2,272)
5	Dept 3	6,500	1,243	2,213	2,567	6,023	477
6	Dept 4	25,000	8,786	7,890	8,700	25,376	(376)
7	Totals	76,000	23,281	26,566	30,962	80809	(4,809.00)
8							
9	Percent of Total		28.8%	32.9%	38.3%	100.0%	

Fig. 15.2
When you choose Window, Tile Top-Bottom, the current workbook appears on the top.

budget.123

	A	B	C	D	E	F	G
1			Cadet Electronics				
2			1996 Projected Expenses				
3							
4	January						
5	Operating Expenses						
6	Advertising	16000	15400	18000	16500	17300	15500
7	Utilities	5700	5650	5500	5220	5110	5225
8	Rent	11500	11500	11500	11500	11500	11500
9	Maintenance	1100	850	980	1020	1150	1250
10	Office Expens	950	750	870	910	930	945
11	TOTAL OPERATING EXPENSES						
12							
13	Manufacturing Expenses						
14	Equipment	77200	25900	12500	65900	54000	31400
15	Repairs	1090	8790	9300	7540	6350	4870
16	Packaging	2400	1300	1750	2520	1780	1930
17	Utilities	3720	4900	3940	4780	4320	4180

Fig. 15.3
When you cascade workbooks, you can see information only in the workbook that appears in front. You can switch to the other workbook by clicking anywhere on it.

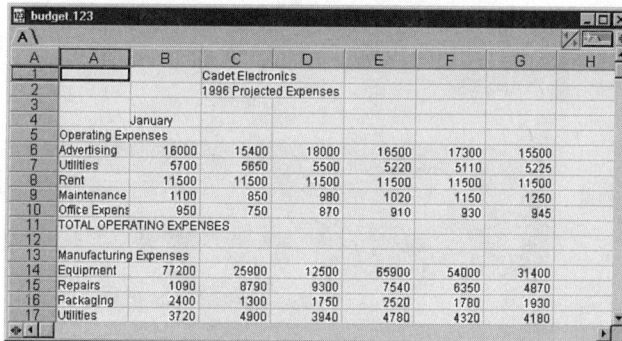

To move among the workbooks on-screen, press Ctrl+PgUp or Ctrl+PgDn. Each time you press a key combination, 1-2-3 makes a new file the active file on-screen.

NOTE To stop viewing multiple worksheets simultaneously, click the worksheet in which you want to work and maximize it using the Maximize button (middle button in the upper-right corner of the worksheet window).

Freezing Worksheet Titles

This section focuses on working within one file and controlling the display. Most worksheets are much larger than can be displayed on-screen at one time. As you move the cell pointer, you scroll the display. New data appears at one edge of the display as the data at the other edge scrolls out of sight. Data can be hard to understand when titles at the top of the worksheet and descriptions at the left scroll off-screen. Without the titles to refer to, you may have trouble remembering what the data means.

Freeze titles to keep them on-screen when you scroll the worksheet file.

To prevent titles from scrolling off-screen, move the cell pointer to the row and column that marks the top-left cell of the "working area" of the worksheet. Everything above and to the left of the cell pointer will be frozen. Next, use the View, Titles command to lock titles on-screen. When you select this command, the Titles dialog box appears (see fig. 15.4).

CAUTION

If you don't position the pointer correctly, your titles may not freeze. Place the pointer below the last row you want to freeze and to the right of the last column you want to freeze.

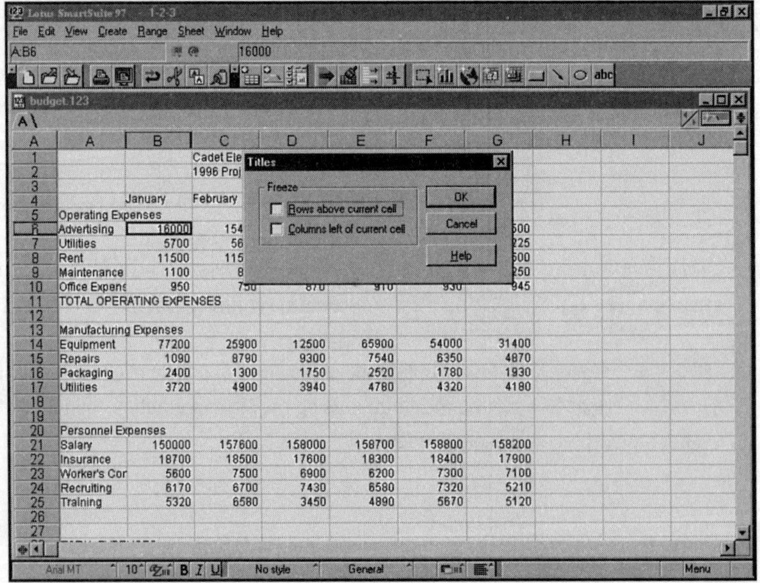

Fig. 15.4
With a few simple clicks, you can freeze titles on-screen.

You can freeze the top rows of the worksheet with the Rows above current cell option or the leftmost columns with Columns left of current cell. To freeze both rows and columns, check both boxes. To unfreeze the titles, open the Titles dialog box and remove the check marks.

If you use Group mode, freezing titles affects all worksheets in the group. When you clear the titles, the titles of all worksheets are released.

▶ **See** "Grouping Worksheets," **p. 258**

To freeze titles in Rows 1–2 and Column A, for example, follow these steps:

1. Position the worksheet so that you can see at least part of Rows 1 and 2 and Column A.
2. Move the cell pointer to cell B3—the first row below the titles and the first column to the right of the titles you want to freeze.
3. Choose View, Titles. In the Titles dialog box, check the Rows above current cell box to freeze horizontal titles and check the Columns left of current cell box to freeze vertical titles.

These steps freeze the titles in Rows 1–2 and Column A. 1-2-3 removes the gridlines from frozen rows and columns, helping you to visually identify which rows and columns are frozen on-screen. When you move the pointer downward through the file, as shown in figure 15.5, the top titles remain in place. If you move the pointer off-screen to the right, the titles in column A would remain frozen in place.

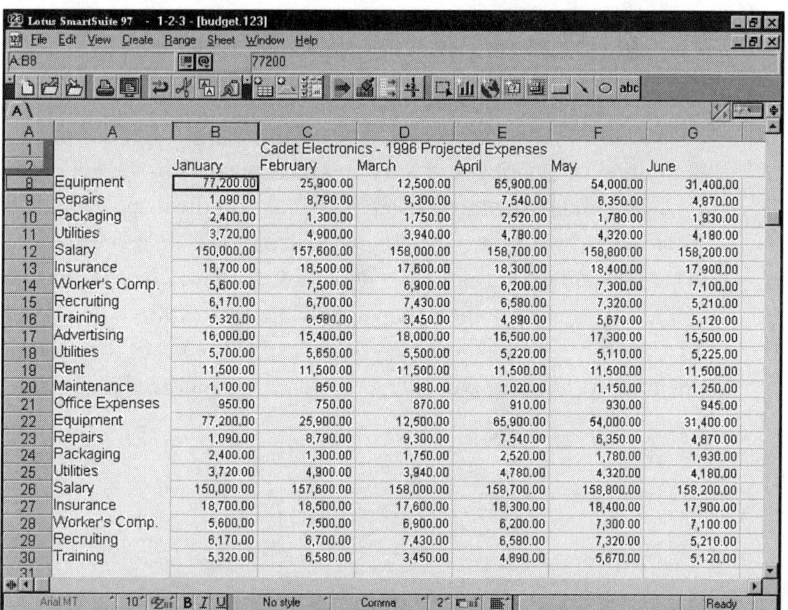

A	A	B	C	D	E	F	G
1			Cadet Electronics - 1996 Projected Expenses				
2		January	February	March	April	May	June
8	Equipment	77,200.00	25,900.00	12,500.00	65,900.00	54,000.00	31,400.00
9	Repairs	1,090.00	8,790.00	9,300.00	7,540.00	6,350.00	4,870.00
10	Packaging	2,400.00	1,300.00	1,750.00	2,520.00	1,780.00	1,930.00
11	Utilities	3,720.00	4,900.00	3,940.00	4,780.00	4,320.00	4,180.00
12	Salary	150,000.00	157,600.00	158,000.00	158,700.00	158,800.00	158,200.00
13	Insurance	18,700.00	18,500.00	17,600.00	18,300.00	18,400.00	17,900.00
14	Worker's Comp.	5,600.00	7,500.00	6,900.00	6,200.00	7,300.00	7,100.00
15	Recruiting	6,170.00	6,700.00	7,430.00	6,580.00	7,320.00	5,210.00
16	Training	5,320.00	6,580.00	3,450.00	4,890.00	5,670.00	5,120.00
17	Advertising	16,000.00	15,400.00	18,000.00	16,500.00	17,300.00	15,500.00
18	Utilities	5,700.00	5,650.00	5,500.00	5,220.00	5,110.00	5,225.00
19	Rent	11,500.00	11,500.00	11,500.00	11,500.00	11,500.00	11,500.00
20	Maintenance	1,100.00	850.00	980.00	1,020.00	1,150.00	1,250.00
21	Office Expenses	950.00	750.00	870.00	910.00	930.00	945.00
22	Equipment	77,200.00	25,900.00	12,500.00	65,900.00	54,000.00	31,400.00
23	Repairs	1,090.00	8,790.00	9,300.00	7,540.00	6,350.00	4,870.00
24	Packaging	2,400.00	1,300.00	1,750.00	2,520.00	1,780.00	1,930.00
25	Utilities	3,720.00	4,900.00	3,940.00	4,780.00	4,320.00	4,180.00
26	Salary	150,000.00	157,600.00	158,000.00	158,700.00	158,800.00	158,200.00
27	Insurance	18,700.00	18,500.00	17,600.00	18,300.00	18,400.00	17,900.00
28	Worker's Comp.	5,600.00	7,500.00	6,900.00	6,200.00	7,300.00	7,100.00
29	Recruiting	6,170.00	6,700.00	7,430.00	6,580.00	7,320.00	5,210.00
30	Training	5,320.00	6,580.00	3,450.00	4,890.00	5,670.00	5,120.00
31							

Fig. 15.5
Those titles aren't going anywhere.

If you press Home when titles are frozen, the cell pointer moves to the position below and to the right of the titles rather than to cell A1. You can, however, move to cell A1 by clicking, using the arrow keys, or using the Go To dialog box (F5). And, you can edit cells in the frozen title area. Just move to the cell and type.

Splitting the Worksheet Window

When you need to compare two different portions of the same worksheet, you can split the worksheet window into *panes* and move through the sections independently or together. A pane is simply a segment of the worksheet window.

In a split window, you can change data in one pane and see how the change affects data in the other pane. This capability is useful for what-if analysis. A split window also is useful when you write macros. You can write the macro in one pane and see the data that the macro is working on in the other pane.

Suppose that you want to see how a change in data affects totals located in an area of the worksheet off-screen. You can split the window to see the data and the totals at the same time. If the worksheet is designed so that totals are in a column to the right, split the window vertically (see fig. 15.6). If the worksheet displays totals in a row at the bottom, split the window horizontally.

NOTE You can display multiple files and even split a worksheet window at the same time.

TIP In a split window, freezing titles affects only the current pane.

You can divide a worksheet window horizontally so that one pane appears in the top half of the worksheet window and the other pane appears in the bottom half. If you split a window vertically, you have one pane on the left side of the display and another on the right. If you create a four-way split, 1-2-3 creates four windows on-screen. All cells above and to the left of the cell pointer appear in the upper-left window. All cells above and to the right of the cell pointer appear in the upper-right window. As you would expect, the lower-left window contains the cells that appeared below and to the left of the cell pointer. And, of course, the lower-right window contains the cells that appeared below and to the right of the cell pointer.

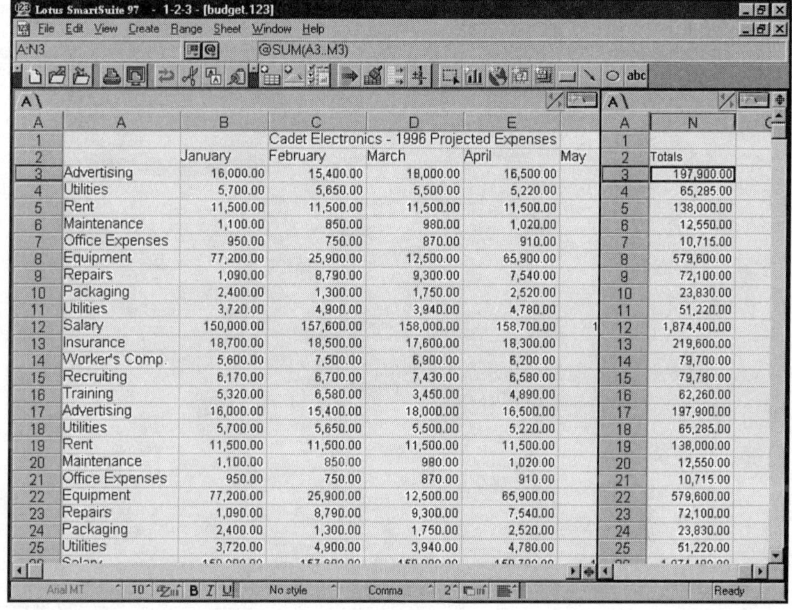

Fig. 15.6
A window split into two vertical panes enables you to see distant parts of the worksheet at the same time.

Be sure to position the pointer at the point you want to split the window before you split the window.

The first step in splitting your worksheet display involves positioning the pointer. Click a cell in the row or column that you want to appear first in the new window. If you want to split the window horizontally, click the row you want to appear at the top of the new window. If you are splitting the window vertically, click the column you want to appear at the left edge of the new window.

Using the Split Dialog Box to Divide the Window

After you have positioned the pointer, use the View, Split command. The Split dialog box appears (see fig. 15.7). Choose whether you want to split the window Top-Bottom (horizontally), Left-Right (vertically), or Four-way. Then click OK. 1-2-3 divides the window at the pointer location.

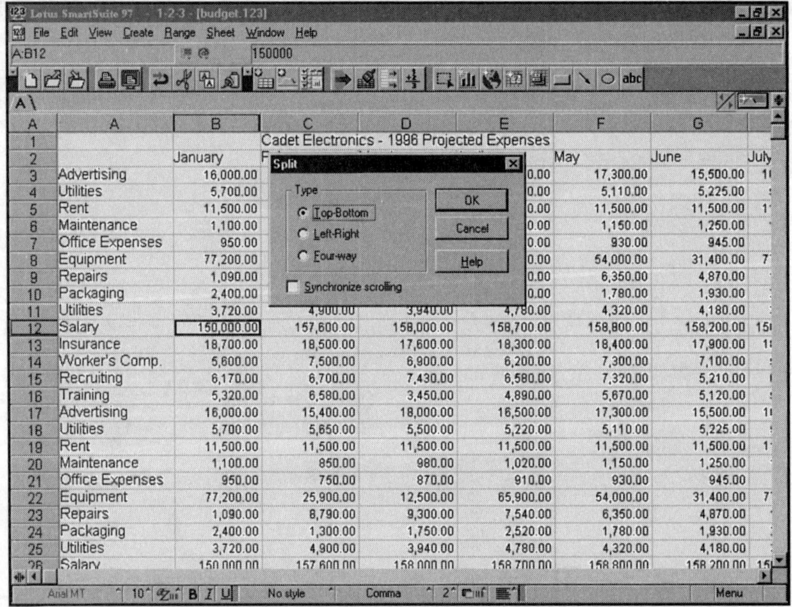

Fig. 15.7
Splitting windows with the Split dialog box.

Dragging to Divide the Window

1-2-3 provides tools you can use to split the window at any time without opening the Split dialog box. In the upper-right corner and the lower-left corner of the worksheet window, you see small buttons called *splitters*. To use a splitter to divide the window, position the pointer and then drag the splitter. Use the lower-left splitter to split the window vertically and the upper-right splitter to split the window horizontally. Figure 15.8 shows a splitter used to divide the window horizontally.

Because a split window displays at least two frames, you cannot display as much data at one time as you can with a full window. To add more space to a split view, remove the worksheet frame. To remove the frame, choose View, Set View Preferences and deselect the Sheet Frame option in the Workbook Properties dialog box.

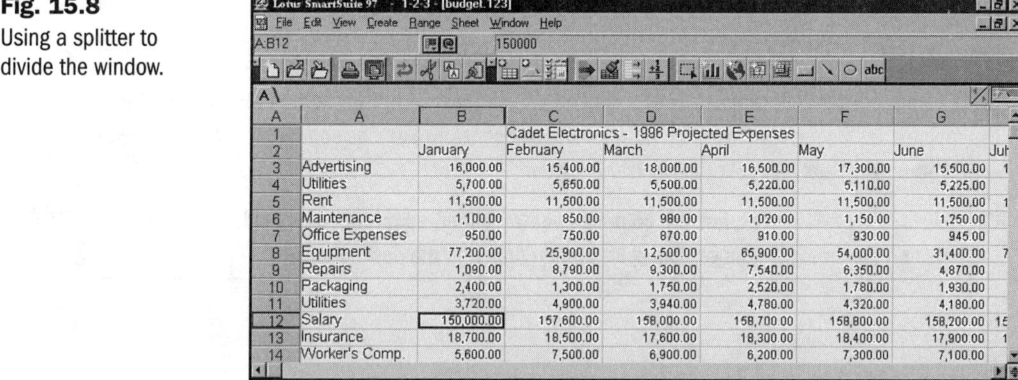

Fig. 15.8
Using a splitter to divide the window.

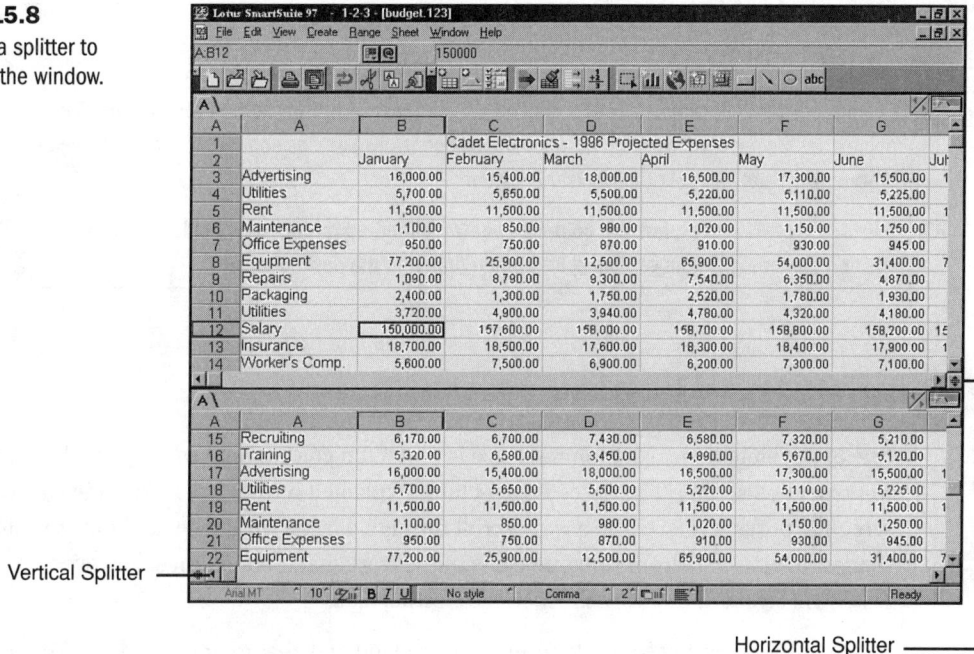

Scrolling Split Windows

NOTE When scrolling is synchronized, both panes move together as you scroll the worksheet.

At times, you may want to see two unrelated views of the same worksheet. For example, you may want to see data in one pane and macros in the other pane. In this case, you want the two panes to scroll separately. Use the View, Unsynchronize Split command; select the View, Synchronize Split if you want to restore synchronized scrolling.

To move between panes, press the F6 (Pane) key or click the other window with the mouse.

Clearing Split Windows

To clear a split window and return to a single pane, use View, Clear Split. No matter which pane the cell pointer is in when you choose this command, the cell pointer moves to the left pane (in a vertically split window) or to the upper pane (in a horizontally split window) when you clear a split window.

TROUBLESHOOTING

I displayed the Split dialog box and clicked on Top-Bottom, but my screen didn't split. The pointer determines the boundary at which the screen is divided. Position the pointer in the center of your worksheet and split the worksheet again.

I divided the worksheet, but the column I wanted ended up on the wrong side of the split. Position the mouse on the vertical splitter; then drag it to the desired location.

Zooming the Display

One of the limitations of a monitor's size is that often you cannot see very much of the worksheet on-screen. The preceding sections explained how to freeze specific data on-screen to provide references as you scroll through a large worksheet and how to split a window to view data from separate parts of the worksheet. Sometimes, however, you want to see the layout of the worksheet, not the actual data.

By using the View, Set View Preferences command and changing the Custom Zoom % setting in the Workbook Properties dialog box View tab, you can specify a percentage (anywhere from 25 to 400) by which to shrink or enlarge the worksheet display. Select 25 to make the display shrink to one-fourth its normal size; select 400 to make the worksheet four times larger. If you reduce the display, the resulting image is barely readable, but it gives you a view of many cells. In figure 15.9, where 25 percent reduction was used, the screen shows about 80 rows and about 300 characters across a row. The readability of these settings varies from monitor to monitor.

Be aware that the size of the 1-2-3 screen is affected by the monitor's resolution setting in Windows. If the monitor is displaying in 1024×768, switching to 800×600 or 640×480 can make a big difference in what you see.

You also can use View, Zoom to or the Zoom SmartIcons to switch among different zoom percentages. From the Zoom To submenu, you can zoom the display to 25%, 50%, 75%, 100%, or 200%.

To return the display to the default size, click the Zoom to Custom Level SmartIcon or choose View, Zoom to Custom level. 1-2-3 returns the display to the default zoom percentage in the Workbook Properties dialog box.

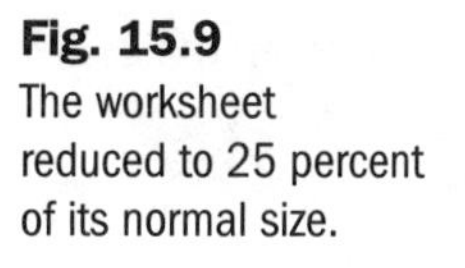

Fig. 15.9
The worksheet reduced to 25 percent of its normal size.

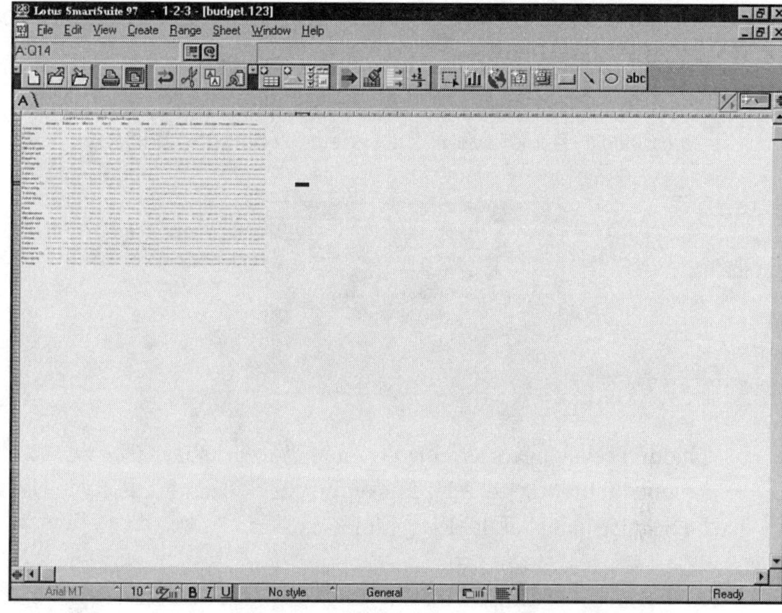

NOTE There is no relationship between the size of the worksheet as displayed on the screen and the size you get when printing. To enlarge or reduce the printed worksheet, use the File, Preview & Page Setup command with the Size options. Refer to Chapter 10, "Printing Worksheets" for more information.

Hiding Worksheet Data

Some worksheets you create may include sensitive information or data not meant for inquiring minds. On some worksheets—particularly those to be used by other people—you may want to protect certain formulas, labels, or data values so they cannot be changed. This section shows you how to suppress or hide the display of items in your worksheet.

Hiding Cells and Ranges

Sometimes you want to do more than just stop someone from changing data or formulas; you want to prevent other users from even seeing the information. To hide a cell or range, follow these steps:

1. Select the cell or range of cells you want to hide.

2. Choose Range, Range Properties or click the Range Properties SmartIcon to display the Range InfoBox.
3. Click the Security tab of the Range InfoBox (see fig. 15.10).
4. Place a check mark in the Hide cell contents check box.

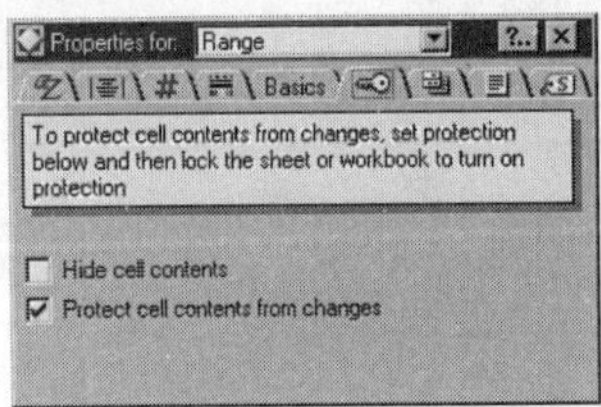

Fig. 15.10 The Security tab of the Range InfoBox.

A hidden cell appears as a blank cell in the worksheet (see fig. 15.11). To redisplay the cell contents in the worksheet, remove the check from the Hide cell contents check box on the Security panel of the Range InfoBox.

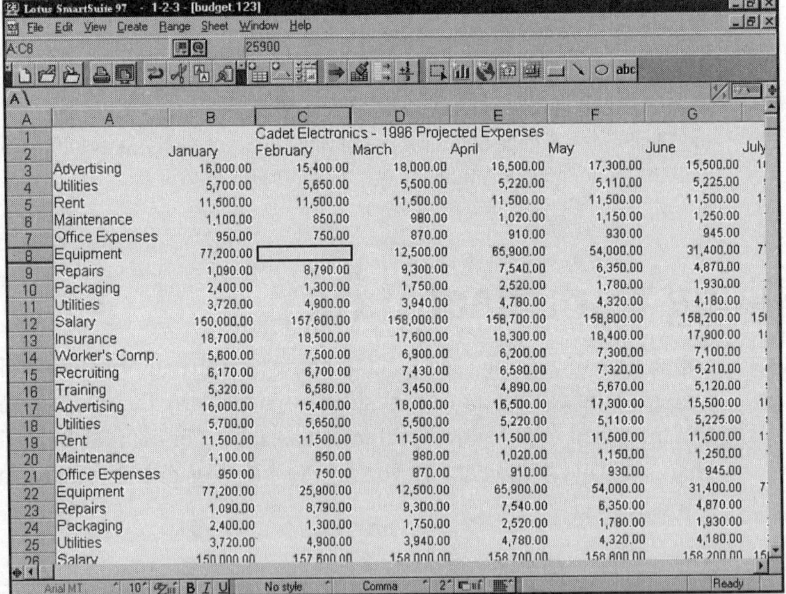

	A	B	C	D	E	F	G
1			Cadet Electronics - 1996 Projected Expenses				
2		January	February	March	April	May	June
3	Advertising	16,000.00	15,400.00	18,000.00	16,500.00	17,300.00	15,500.00
4	Utilities	5,700.00	5,650.00	5,500.00	5,220.00	5,110.00	5,225.00
5	Rent	11,500.00	11,500.00	11,500.00	11,500.00	11,500.00	11,500.00
6	Maintenance	1,100.00	850.00	980.00	1,020.00	1,150.00	1,250.00
7	Office Expenses	950.00	750.00	870.00	910.00	930.00	945.00
8	Equipment	77,200.00		12,500.00	65,900.00	54,000.00	31,400.00
9	Repairs	1,090.00	8,790.00	9,300.00	7,540.00	6,350.00	4,870.00
10	Packaging	2,400.00	1,300.00	1,750.00	2,520.00	1,780.00	1,930.00
11	Utilities	3,720.00	4,900.00	3,940.00	4,780.00	4,320.00	4,180.00
12	Salary	150,000.00	157,600.00	158,000.00	158,700.00	158,800.00	158,200.00
13	Insurance	18,700.00	18,500.00	17,600.00	18,300.00	18,400.00	17,900.00
14	Worker's Comp.	5,600.00	7,500.00	6,900.00	6,200.00	7,300.00	7,100.00
15	Recruiting	6,170.00	6,700.00	7,430.00	6,580.00	7,320.00	5,210.00
16	Training	5,320.00	6,580.00	3,450.00	4,890.00	5,670.00	5,120.00
17	Advertising	16,000.00	15,400.00	18,000.00	16,500.00	17,300.00	15,500.00
18	Utilities	5,700.00	5,650.00	5,500.00	5,220.00	5,110.00	5,225.00
19	Rent	11,500.00	11,500.00	11,500.00	11,500.00	11,500.00	11,500.00
20	Maintenance	1,100.00	850.00	980.00	1,020.00	1,150.00	1,250.00
21	Office Expenses	950.00	750.00	870.00	910.00	930.00	945.00
22	Equipment	77,200.00	25,900.00	12,500.00	65,900.00	54,000.00	31,400.00
23	Repairs	1,090.00	8,790.00	9,300.00	7,540.00	6,350.00	4,870.00
24	Packaging	2,400.00	1,300.00	1,750.00	2,520.00	1,780.00	1,930.00
25	Utilities	3,720.00	4,900.00	3,940.00	4,780.00	4,320.00	4,180.00
26	Salary	150,000.00	157,600.00	158,000.00	158,700.00	158,800.00	158,200.00

Fig. 15.11 A hidden cell appears blank.

CAUTION

You can hide data so that it's not easily visible, but you cannot prevent someone from seeing hidden data if that person knows how to use 1-2-3 for Windows. The only way to keep data truly confidential is to save the file with a password (see Chapter 9, "Managing Files").

You cannot hide data completely. If you move the cell pointer to a hidden cell, you can see the contents of the cell in the contents box. And remember that all you have to do to redisplay the contents of the cell is to remove the check mark in the Hide cell contents check box for that cell. If the file is locked, however, you cannot change the format or view the contents of the cell in the edit line.

▶ **See** "Protecting Workbooks," **p. 278**

NOTE When you print a range containing hidden cells, columns, or worksheets, the hidden text does not appear in the printout.

CAUTION

Hidden cells appear empty; protect the cells and seal the file to prevent users from accidentally typing over the contents of hidden cells or reformatting the cells.

Hiding Worksheets, Columns, and Rows

When you hide worksheets, columns, and rows, they retain their letters and numbers but 1-2-3 doesn't display the hidden sheets, columns, or rows. For example, if you hide columns B and C, 1-2-3 97 displays columns A, D, E, and so on.

Hiding Worksheets To hide a worksheet, move the cell pointer to the worksheet you want to hide, choose Sheet, Hide. 1-2-3 97 removes the worksheet from the screen, and the cell pointer moves to the next worksheet.

To display a hidden worksheet, choose Sheet, Unhide. In the Unhide dialog box that appears (see fig. 15.12), select the sheet you want to display in the list box, and choose OK.

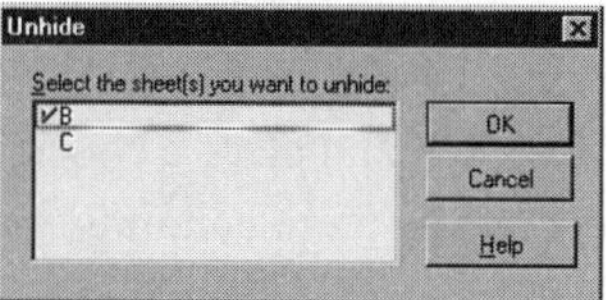

Fig. 15.12
Choose the sheet(s) you want to display from the Select the sheet(s) you want to unhide list box.

Although a hidden worksheet does not appear on-screen, formulas that refer to the worksheet remain valid and intact. For example, if you hide worksheet A, and worksheet B includes a reference to worksheet A in a formula, the formula is not affected. The worksheet is actually still part of the file—it's just invisible.

Hiding Columns A hidden column does not appear in the worksheet, but the column letter is retained. Formulas that refer to cells in hidden columns are calculated correctly, and 1-2-3 for Windows continues to store the full value of hidden data.

Figure 15.13 shows a worksheet after columns are hidden. Notice that in the worksheet frame, column letters B, C, and D are missing. The columns are still there, but they do not appear and you cannot move the cell pointer to them. When you print a range that contains hidden columns, the hidden columns do not print.

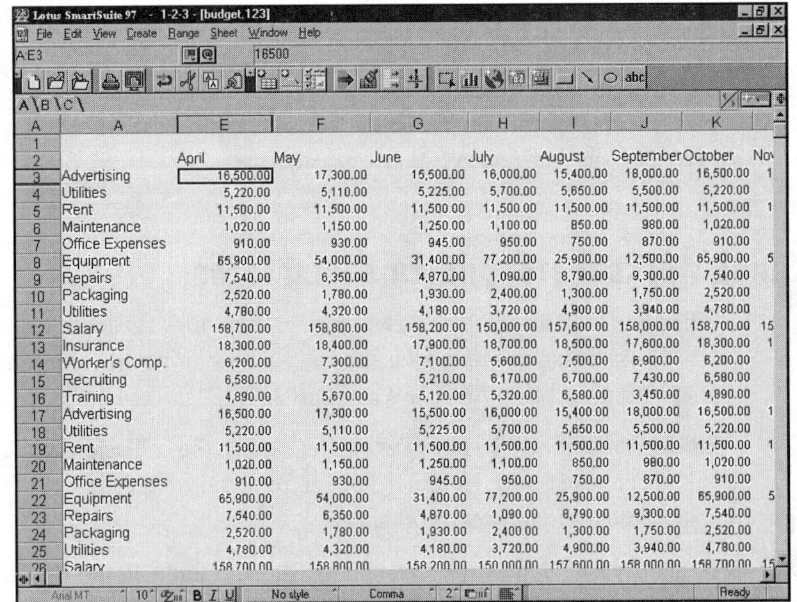

Fig. 15.13
When you hide worksheet columns, their missing column letters show that they are hidden.

To hide a column, move the cell pointer to a cell in the column you want to hide. Then, display the Basics panel of the Range Properties InfoBox (use the Range Properties SmartIcon or choose Range, Range Properties) and place a check mark in the Hide Column check box. If you don't preselect one or more columns, you can type a column address in the Range name text box. To redisplay hidden columns, select a range that includes the hidden columns. Then, display the Basics panel of the Range Properties InfoBox. The Hide column check box appears gray—it's very faint on-screen, so you may need to look hard to notice that it's gray (see fig. 15.14). Choose it to redisplay the hidden columns.

TIP If you hid Column A, select the entire sheet to unhide Column A.

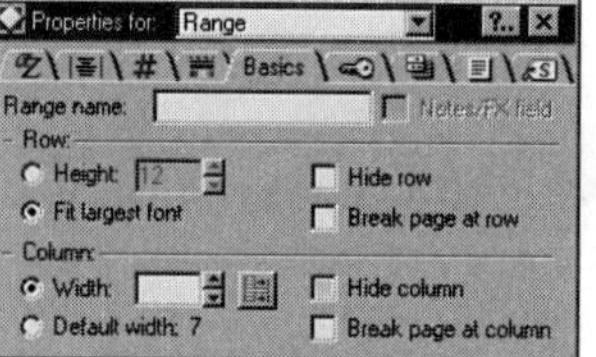

Fig. 15.14
When you select a range containing hidden columns, the Column check box in the Range Properties InfoBox appears gray.

Hiding Rows As with hidden columns, you won't see hidden rows on-screen, but 1-2-3 retains the row number, and formulas that refer to cells in hidden rows are calculated correctly. 1-2-3 97 continues to store the full value of hidden data. When you print a range that contains hidden rows, the hidden rows do not print.

You hide rows in the same way you hid columns. Follow these steps:

1. Select a cell in the row you want to hide. To hide more than one row, select the rows you want to hide.

2. Open the Range Properties InfoBox.
3. Display the Basics panel.
4. Place a check mark in the Hide row check box.

You redisplay hidden rows the same way you redisplayed hidden columns. Select a range that includes the hidden rows. Then, display the Basics panel of the Range Properties InfoBox. The Hide row check box appears gray. Choose it to redisplay the hidden rows.

If you hid row 1, select the entire worksheet to unhide row 1.

TROUBLESHOOTING

I hid sensitive data, but you can still tell by the missing letters and numbers in the worksheet frame that I hid the data. Use the File, Workbook Properties command to display the Workbook Properties dialog box. Then, on the View tab, deselect the Sheet frame option to hide the frame around the worksheet. The casual observer then finds it difficult to know that you have hidden columns or rows.

That works fine if I hide columns or rows, but what if I want to hide a sheet? How do I disguise the hidden sheet from the viewer? Again, use the Workbook Properties dialog box, but this time, deselect the Sheet tabs check box.

Outlining a Worksheet

Suppose you create a budget worksheet, and in your budget worksheet, you create categories for expenses. For example, you might create a category called Utilities that includes Heat, Light, Water, Gas, Electricity, and Telephone. Suppose you've got another category called Entertainment, and it includes Movies, Video Rentals, and Book Purchases. You might have a worksheet that looks like the one in figure 15.15.

Fig. 15.15
Sample budget worksheet.

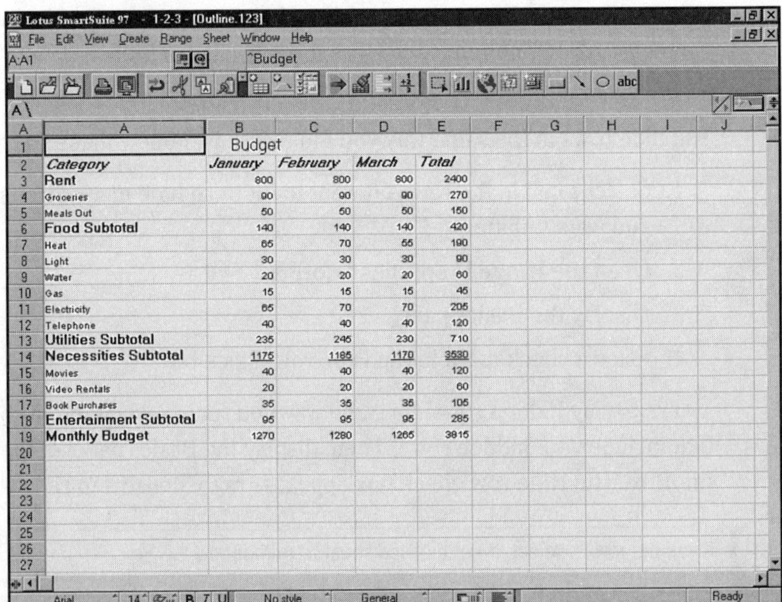

Wouldn't it be great if you could look at all the detail, as in Figure 15.15, but also just view the subtotal categories? Outlining in 1-2-3 lets you do exactly that—view and print your data both in detail and summarized by sets of subtotals.

Understanding Outlines

Because worksheets are "freeform"—that is, you determine the layout of the worksheet—you have to analyze your worksheet to set up outlining. You need to know:

- If your worksheet contains summary rows or summary columns or both.
- Which rows and columns contain summary data.
- If summary rows appear above or below detail rows.
- If summary columns appear to the left or right of detail columns.

The example in figure 15.15 contains both summary rows and summary columns. Column E is a summary column and Rows 6, 13, 14, 18, and 19 are all summary rows. In this worksheet, summary rows appear below detail rows, and the summary column appears to the right of the detail columns.

TIP Rows marked in bold are shown when you summarize. Notice that Row 3 is bold, but technically, it's not a summary row because there are no details that comprise it.

You can create an outline that contains as many as eight levels of rows and columns. To keep things simple, the outline in the figure contains only two levels.

Setting Up an Outline

Use the Sheet Properties InfoBox to set up outline properties. The outline properties you set tell 1-2-3 where summary rows and columns appear in relation to detail rows and columns.

CAUTION

Be aware that the properties you set apply to all outlines you create within a sheet. If you need summary rows to appear above details in one outline and below details in another outline, move the information for one of the outlines to a different sheet.

To set up the worksheet for outlining, follow these steps:

1. Display the Sheet Properties InfoBox using the SmartIcon or by choosing Sheet, Sheet Properties.
2. Display the Outline tab (see fig. 15.16).

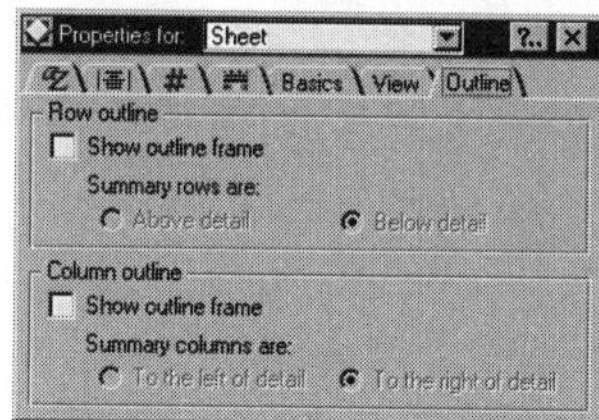

Fig. 15.16 Use the Outline panel of the Sheet InfoBox to set up outlining for the worksheet.

3. Place a check mark in the Show outline frame check box in the Row outline section. Choose the appropriate option button for summary rows.
4. Repeat step 3 for the Column outline section of the tab.
5. Close or collapse the Sheet Properties InfoBox.

Notice that 1-2-3 places small dots to the left and above the worksheet frame. This is the outline frame.

Manipulating an Outline

Now you're ready to identify for 1-2-3 the detail rows and columns you want to summarize. In the example, Rows 4–5, 7–12, and 15–17 all contain detail rows that you want to summarize. In addition, Rows 3–13 comprise a second level of details you can summarize, the Necessities Subtotal. Follow these steps:

1. Select the first set of rows or columns you want to summarize. You can select the entire row or column or just some cells in the row or column.
2. Choose Sheet, Outline, Demote. The Demote dialog box appears. Choose Rows if you are marking rows as details, or Columns if you are marking columns as details. Then, choose OK.
3. Repeat these steps for all other sets of rows and columns you want to mark as details.

1-2-3 automatically creates levels for your outline if you demote detail rows or columns within another set of detail rows or columns.

When you finish, 1-2-3 has changed the outline frame to identify the rows and columns you marked as details (see fig. 15.17).

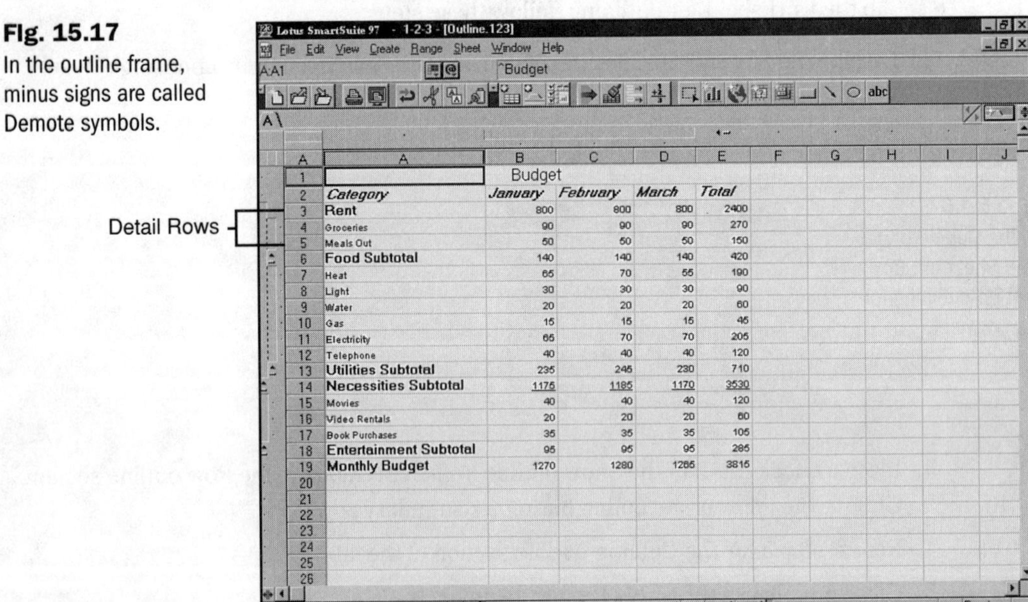

Fig. 15.17
In the outline frame, minus signs are called Demote symbols.

NOTE The Demote and Promote symbols, as used in the following text, don't promote and demote heading levels; they expand and collapse sections of the outline.

To take advantage of outline mode and view your worksheet summarized, click a Demote symbol that appears next to a summary row. 1-2-3 changes the Demote symbol to a Promote symbol (plus sign) and collapses the worksheet to hide the detail rows and display only the summary row. Repeat the process as many times as necessary to show only a summarized version of the worksheet. Figure 15.18 is summarized to the top level of detail, showing only three totals—Necessities, Entertainment, and the Monthly Budget. To summarize to this level, click the Demote symbols next to Necessities and Entertainment.

Figure 15.19 is summarized to the second level of detail—showing the breakdown of Necessities into Rent, Food, and Utilities. Click the Promote symbol next to Necessities and then click the Demote symbols next to Food Subtotal and Utilities Subtotal to get this. Notice that Rent, on Row 3, appears but was not part of any set of rows selected for summarizing.

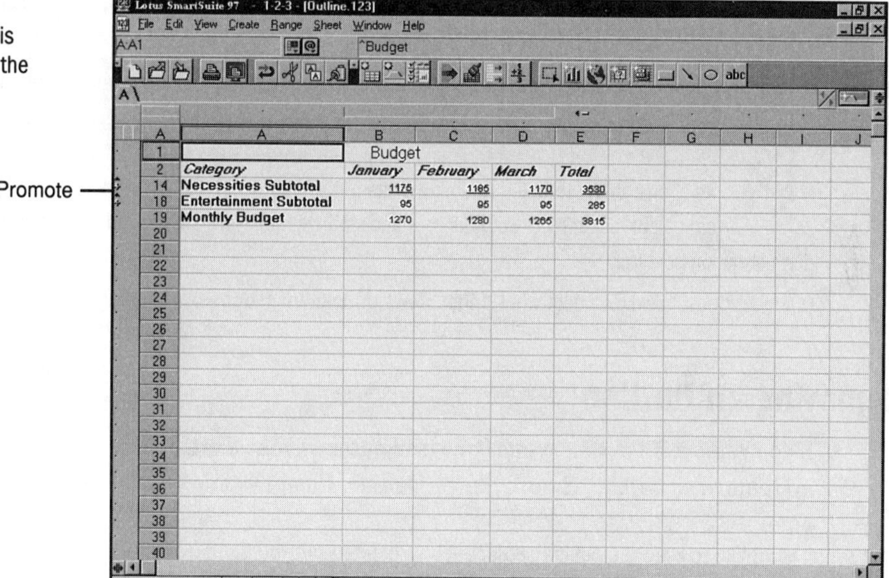

Fig. 15.18
This worksheet is summarized to the top level.

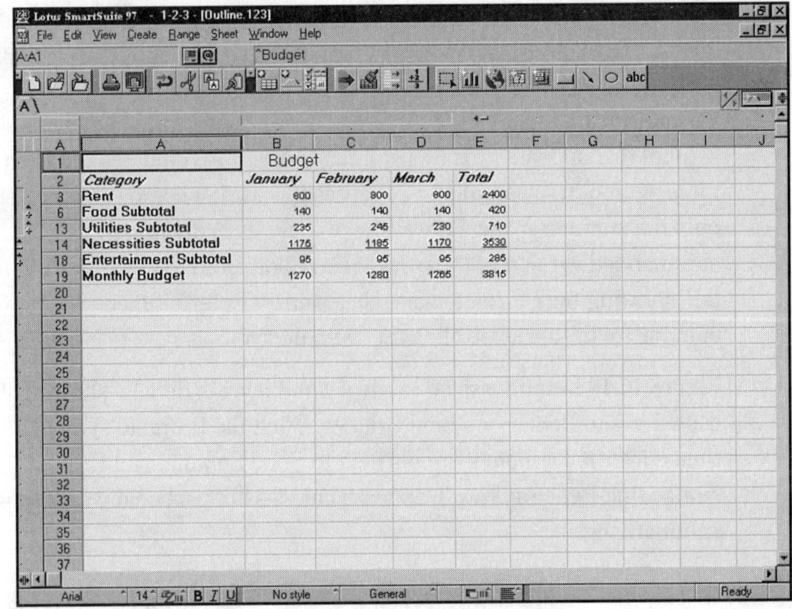

Fig. 15.19
This worksheet is summarized only to the second level.

TIP To redisplay details, click the Promote symbol that appears near the summary row or column.

NOTE As shown in figure 5.18, outlining does not affect the way 1-2-3 performs mathematical calculations. The subtotals for Food and Utilities were still added even though they don't show on-screen.

Outlining does, however, affect what prints. Rows or columns hidden by outlining *do not* print.

Removing an Outline

If you remove an outline, you remove all outlines you've created in the worksheet. To remove an outline, choose Sheet, Outline, Clear Outline.

If you'd like to keep the outline settings you've created but you don't want to see the outline, use the Sheet Properties InfoBox to hide the outline frame. That way, you can reinstate the outline at any time. On the Outline tab of the Sheet Properties InfoBox, remove the check marks from both Show outline frame check boxes.

CHAPTER 16

Adding Graphics to Worksheets

by Elaine Marmel

Included with 1-2-3 for Windows is a set of basic drawing tools that you can use to enhance your worksheets, maps, and charts. There are tools for drawing shapes (such as ellipses, rectangles, and polygons), lines, arrows, and arcs. There is also a tool that enables you to type text anywhere on the chart.

You can use the drawing tools to add lines and arrows that point out specific items in your chart, add a rectangle to a selected cell range in a worksheet to call attention to important data, draw a simple logo, or add note text to charts. Figure 16.1 shows a rectangle and arrow used to point out the data to which a chart refers. ■

Working with graphics text

1-2-3 enables you to add graphics text, for example, to clarify something on a chart.

Adding graphics

You can draw lines and shapes in a worksheet that may help you emphasize information.

Rearranging graphics

As you add graphics to a worksheet, the graphics may overlap—but you can rearrange them to control the appearance of an image.

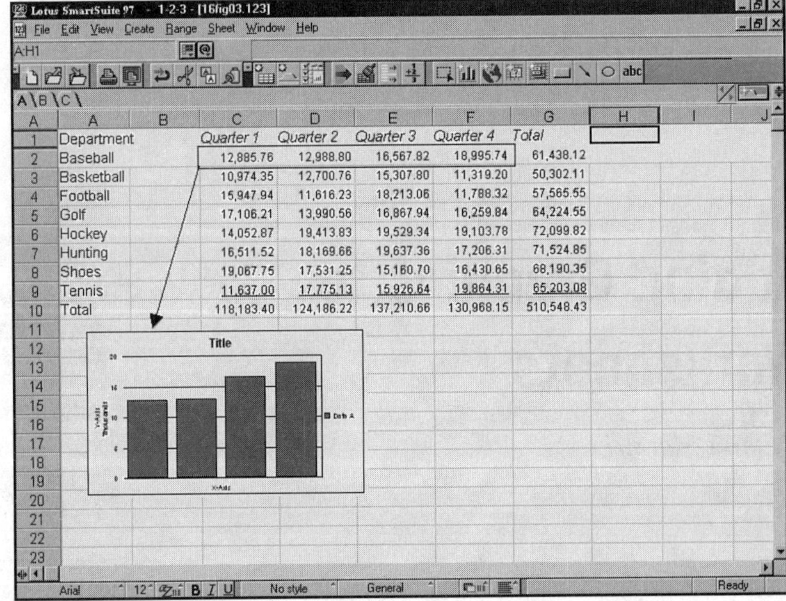

	A	C	D	E	F	G
1	Department	Quarter 1	Quarter 2	Quarter 3	Quarter 4	Total
2	Baseball	12,885.76	12,988.80	16,567.82	18,995.74	61,438.12
3	Basketball	10,974.35	12,700.76	15,307.80	11,319.20	50,302.11
4	Football	15,947.94	11,616.23	18,213.06	11,788.32	57,565.55
5	Golf	17,106.21	13,990.56	16,867.94	16,259.84	64,224.55
6	Hockey	14,052.87	19,413.83	19,529.34	19,103.78	72,099.82
7	Hunting	16,511.52	18,169.66	19,637.36	17,206.31	71,524.85
8	Shoes	19,067.75	17,531.25	15,160.70	16,430.65	68,190.35
9	Tennis	11,637.00	17,775.13	15,926.64	19,864.31	65,203.08
10	Total	118,183.40	124,186.22	137,210.66	130,968.15	510,548.43

Fig. 16.1
Two drawn objects—a rectangle and an arrow—used in a spreadsheet.

Displaying the Drawing Tools

To display the drawing tools, open the Create menu and choose Drawing. A cascade menu appears that contains the drawing tools (see fig. 16.2).

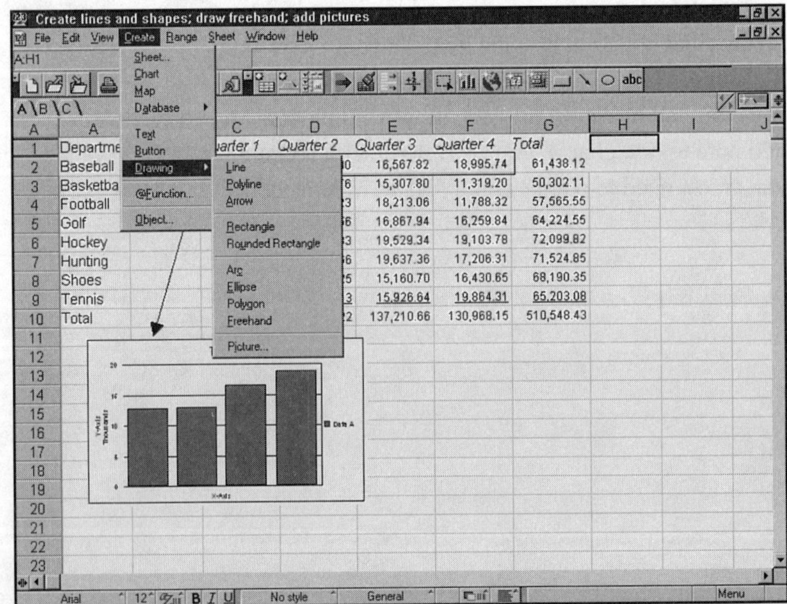

Fig. 16.2
Use the Create menu to display the drawing tools to add drawings to your worksheets.

You can also use one of the many drawing SmartIcons to add graphics to your worksheets and charts. Table 16.1 shows the these SmartIcons and provides a description of each.

Table 16.1 The Drawing SmartIcons

SmartIcon	Description
	Draws a line
	Draws a segmented line
	Draws a forward-pointing arrow
	Draws a double-headed arrow
	Draws a rectangle or square
	Draws a rounded rectangle
	Draws an arc
	Draws an ellipse or circle
	Draws a polygon
	Lets you draw freehand lines
abc	Lets you add graphics text

If you use these tools often, add the Drawing SmartIcon bar to those you can easily display. For more information, see Chapter 33, "Customizing SmartIcons."

Working with Graphics Text

Graphics text may be one of the first additions you make to your worksheets. You might want to add a note, for example, to clarify a chart you've added on the worksheet.

When you choose Create, Text or click the Text Block SmartIcon, you are ready to click and drag to create a text block. A *text block* is the container for your descriptive text.

To add graphics text:

1. Choose Create, Text or click the Create a Text Block SmartIcon.
2. Click the spot where you want the upper-left corner of the text block to appear and drag down and to the right to create a text block the approximate height and width that you want. Don't worry too much about the size and placement because it's easy enough to move and resize the text block later.

If you simply click the spot where you want the upper-left corner of the text block to appear, 123 creates a default-sized block there.

3. Release the mouse button. A flashing text cursor appears in the box.
4. Type the text.

To enter multiple lines of text, you can either let the text wrap or press Enter after each line.

Figure 16.3 shows a worksheet after graphics text has been added.

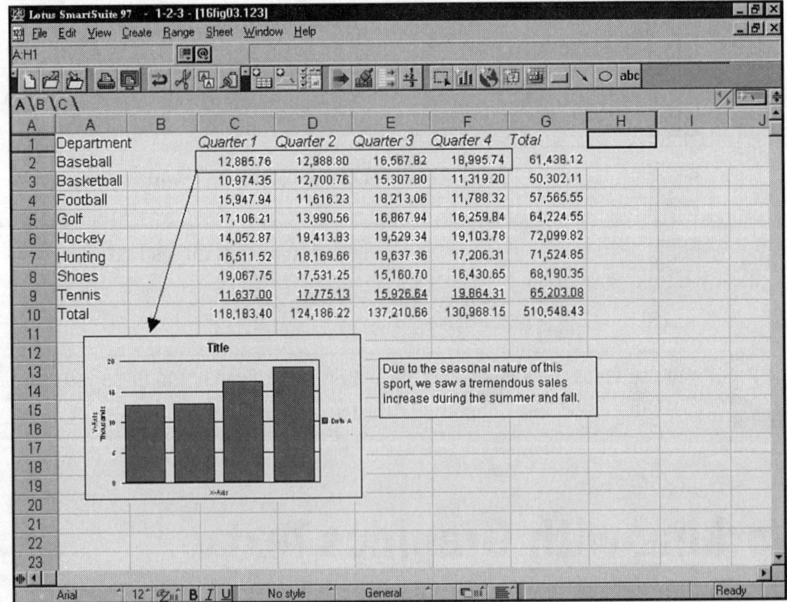

A	A	B	C	D	E	F	G
1	Department		Quarter 1	Quarter 2	Quarter 3	Quarter 4	Total
2	Baseball		12,885.76	12,988.80	16,567.82	18,995.74	61,438.12
3	Basketball		10,974.35	12,700.76	15,307.80	11,319.20	50,302.11
4	Football		15,947.94	11,616.23	18,213.06	11,788.32	57,565.55
5	Golf		17,106.21	13,990.56	16,867.94	16,259.84	64,224.55
6	Hockey		14,052.87	19,413.83	19,529.34	19,103.78	72,099.82
7	Hunting		16,511.52	18,169.66	19,637.36	17,206.31	71,524.85
8	Shoes		19,067.75	17,531.25	15,160.70	16,430.65	68,190.35
9	Tennis		11,637.00	17,775.13	15,926.64	19,864.31	65,203.08
10	Total		118,183.40	124,186.22	137,210.66	130,968.15	510,548.43

Fig. 16.3
Graphics text added to the worksheet.

By default, the text block is surrounded by a frame with a white background. To change the interior color or to format the frame, use the Draw Object Properties InfoBox. Click the Lines & Color SmartIcon. Or, position the mouse pointer over the drawing object and press the right-mouse button. 1-2-3 selects the block (you'll see selection handles around the frame), and displays a quick menu (see fig. 16.4). Choose Draw Object Properties from the quick menu, and the Draw Object Properties InfoBox appears (see fig. 16.5).

CAUTION

Be careful not to change colors to the same color as the worksheet background, or the object seems to vanish. It's actually there, but you can't see it.

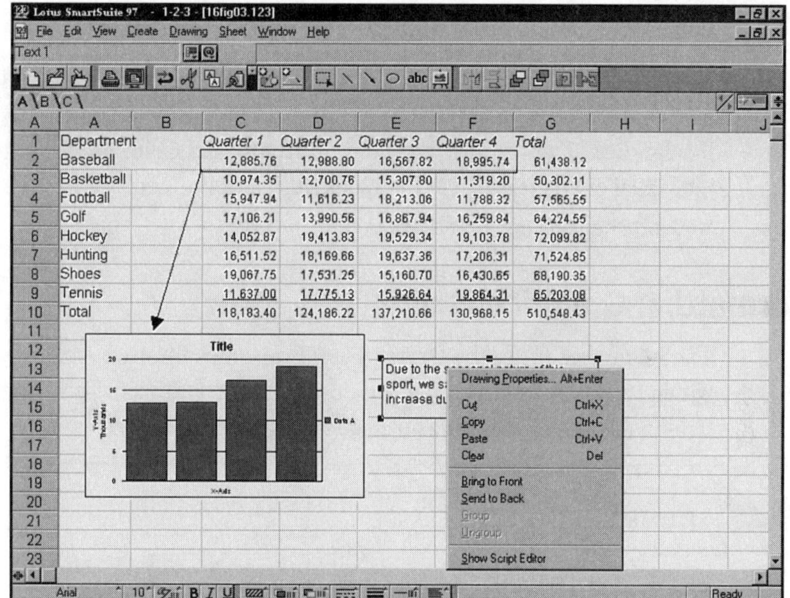

Fig. 16.4
Click the right button on an object to display the quick menu.

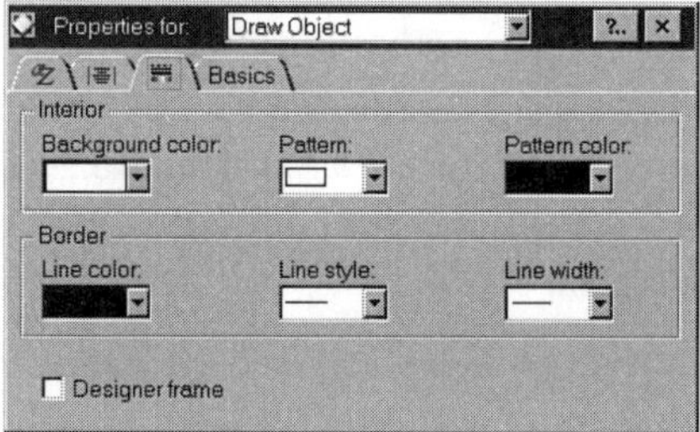

Fig. 16.5
The Draw Object Properties InfoBox has four tabs—use them to control the properties of any drawing object.

If you are adding a block of text to a chart, for example, you might want to change the interior color of the text block so that it has the same background color as the plot. To do this, choose the Lines & Color tab in the Drawing InfoBox (refer to fig. 16.5), open the Interior Background color list box, and choose the same color as your plot background.

To eliminate the frame from a text block, click the down arrow beside the Border Line Style box and choose None.

▶ **See** "Formatting Text Attributes" **p. 350**

Editing Graphics Text

Suppose you need to change the text you typed. To edit the text, double-click the text block. A cursor appears at the beginning of the text. Use the mouse or arrow keys to position the cursor and make your corrections.

To change the typeface, point size, and attributes of the text, select the text block (make sure that selection handles are around the text block) and open the Draw Object Properties InfoBox. Then choose the Font, Attribute, and Color tab. Note that you cannot format individual characters inside the block; it's all or nothing.

▶ **See** "Changing Fonts and Attributes," **p. 125**

Formatting Graphics Text

The Alignment tab of the Draw Object Properties InfoBox enables you to align the text within its frame. For instance, for a multiple-line text block, you might want to center the lines inside the block. You can also left-align or justify text.

TROUBLESHOOTING

I was entering text when the characters I had typed disappeared. If you don't make your text block long enough, your text may scroll out of view after you type another line. If this happens, you must lengthen the block by dragging the center handle at the top, bottom, or the side of the selected text block.

I want to change the style of my text object, but I can't get the right InfoBox to display. I keep getting the Range InfoBox. Before you can make any changes to a text object, you need to tell 1-2-3 what text you want to work with. Select the text block by clicking it before you try to display the Draw Object Properties InfoBox.

Working with Graphics

If you've ever used a simple graphics program—like Windows Paint—you may be familiar with the way graphics tools work. You click the tool and draw the shape on-screen. 1-2-3 for Windows includes a number of graphics tools you can use to add shapes and freehand lines to your worksheets and charts.

Drawing Lines and Arrows

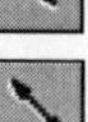
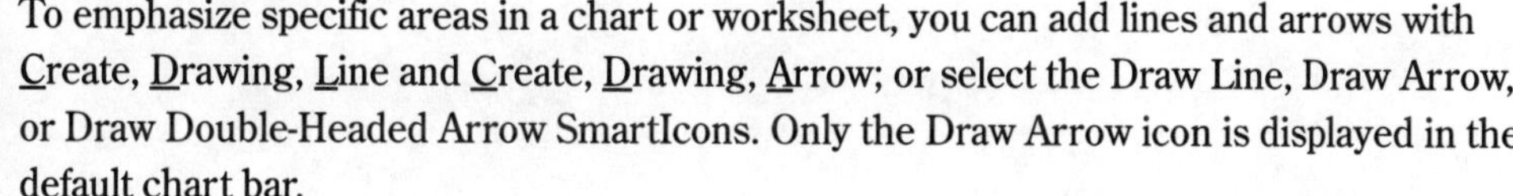

To emphasize specific areas in a chart or worksheet, you can add lines and arrows with Create, Drawing, Line and Create, Drawing, Arrow; or select the Draw Line, Draw Arrow, or Draw Double-Headed Arrow SmartIcons. Only the Draw Arrow icon is displayed in the default chart bar.

Be aware that, when printing lines, your printer determines whether diagonal arrows or lines print as smooth lines or jagged ones.

To create the line or arrow:

1. Click the Line or Arrow tool. 1-2-3 changes the shape of the mouse pointer to a plus sign and prompts you, in the title bar, to click and drag.
2. Slide the mouse so that the pointer appears at the location where you want one end of the line or arrow to appear, and then click and drag in the direction you want to draw the line or arrow.
3. When you reach the end of the line, release the mouse button.

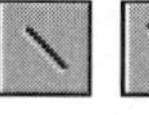

If you are creating an arrow, the final data point displays an arrowhead. If you are creating the double-headed arrow, arrowheads appear on both ends of the line.

1-2-3 displays a line or arrow on the chart or worksheet, with selection handles to indicate that the line or arrow is selected. While selected, the line or arrow can be moved or changed. Notice also that the Default SmartIcon bar is replaced with a new bar—this one is called the Default Draw bar. The SmartIcons in the new bar provide you with tools you need to edit and arrange the lines and shapes you draw (see fig. 16.6).

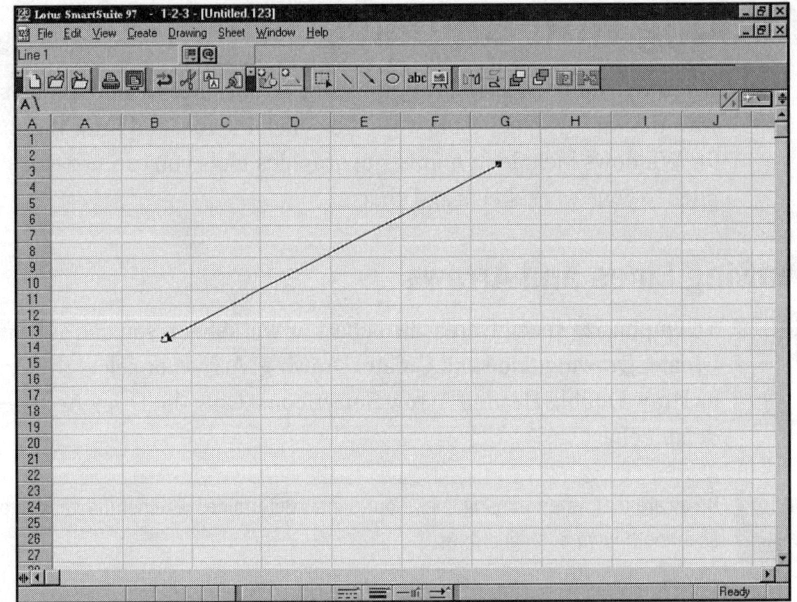

Fig. 16.6
The Default Draw SmartIcon bar appears after you draw a line or shape.

Connecting Lines To connect two or more line segments, use the Create Drawing Polyline command or the Draw a Polyline SmartIcon. Click at the beginning of the first line, and then click at the end of the line. The next segment automatically begins at the end of the first segment. Each time you click, one segment ends and the next begins (see fig. 16.7). When you are finished, double-click.

When would you want to use a polyline? Perhaps if you want to trace a number to its corresponding position on a chart and, simultaneously, to a comment.

To draw a horizontal, vertical, or diagonal line, hold down Shift as you draw. The Shift key restricts the line to increments of 45 degrees.

Editing Lines To change the style, width, and color of the line, you can use the Lines & Color panel of the Draw Object Properties InfoBox. Select the object and press the right-mouse button. From the quick menu that appears, choose Drawing Properties. When the Draw Object Properties InfoBox appears, click the Color, Pattern, and Line Style tab. Change the color, style, and width of lines using the Line color, Line style, and Line width list boxes.

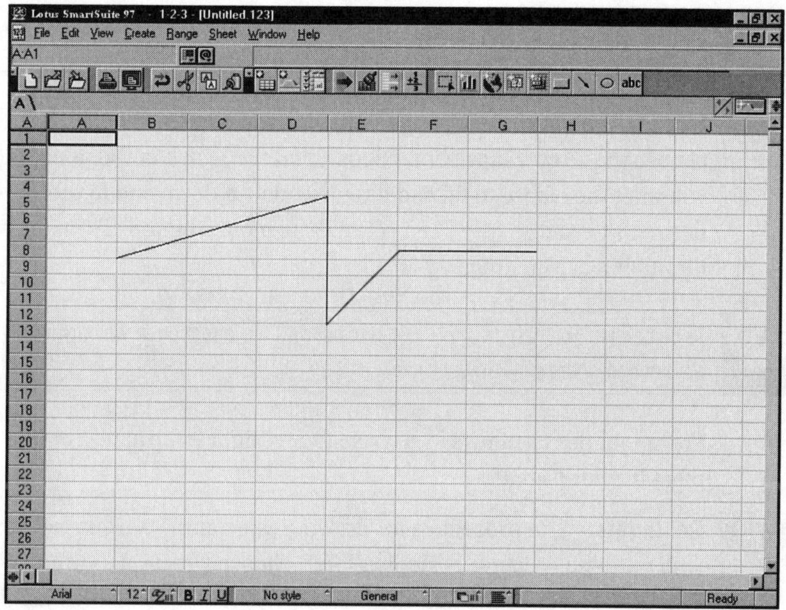

Fig. 16.7
Using the polyline tool.

You can use the Arrowhead list box on the Lines and Colors panel to move the arrowhead to the opposite end of the line, to place arrowheads at both ends of the line, and to add or remove the arrowhead. To change the size and direction of a line or arrow, use the mouse.

▶ **See** "Manipulating Chart Elements" **p. 322**

Drawing Arcs

An arc is a curved line and, in fact, drawing an arc is just like creating a line except you use a different tool. To create an arc, use the Create, Drawing, Arc command or the Draw Arc SmartIcon. Then click and drag in the direction you want the arc to curve. The shape of the arc is controlled by the way you move the mouse. When the arc is the size and shape you want, release the mouse button.

Drawing Shapes

1-2-3 has four tools for drawing enclosed shapes: Ellipse, Rectangle, Rounded Rectangle, and Polygon.

To draw a perfect circle or square, press and hold Shift while drawing the shape.

Ellipse To draw an ellipse (also known as an oval), choose Create, Drawing, Ellipse (or choose the Draw Ellipse SmartIcon), and then click in the upper-left corner of the area you want the ellipse to fill and drag the mouse down and to the right until the ellipse is the desired size and shape. Then release the mouse button. To create a perfect circle, hold down Shift as you drag.

To be precise, you can drag in any direction, and the direction in which you choose to drag determines where you'll initially click.

You might use an ellipse or a circle to highlight information or add a special design element to your page.

Rectangle The procedure for drawing a rectangle or rounded rectangle (a rectangle with rounded corners) is similar. First, choose Create, Drawing, Rectangle (or Rounded Rectangle) or click the Draw Rectangle or Draw Rounded Rectangle SmartIcon. Then, click where you want the upper-left corner of the rectangle to appear and drag the mouse down and to the right until the rectangle is the desired size. Release the mouse button to complete the rectangle. By holding down Shift as you drag, you create a square.

You might use a square or rectangle to highlight worksheet cells, call attention to a specific portion of a chart, draw a background shaded box for text or other graphics, or provide a customized legend or shaded area for selected cells.

You might find it helpful to zoom the worksheet before surrounding something with a box, to be sure that the box is positioned correctly. Grid lines help, too.

Polygon A polygon is a multisided object. The object can have as many connecting lines as you want.

To create a polygon, follow these steps:

1. Choose the Create, Drawing, Polygon command; or click the Draw Polygon SmartIcon.
2. Place the mouse pointer where you want the first point of the polygon to be and click the mouse button.

3. Move the pointer (you don't need to drag) to the opposite end of the first line and click again.
4. Continue clicking at each point of the polygon, and double-click when you are finished.

You don't need to concern yourself with connecting the last point with the first because 1-2-3 automatically connects these points for you when you double-click.

TIP Holding down Shift as you create a polygon restricts the angle to increments of 45 degrees.

Changing Shape Color and Style The object's interior is white; to change the color (for example, to the color of the plot background), use the Lines & Colors panel of the Draw Object Properties InfoBox. You can also use the Color, Pattern, and Line Style panel, shown in figure 16.8, to change the style, color, or width of the object's outline.

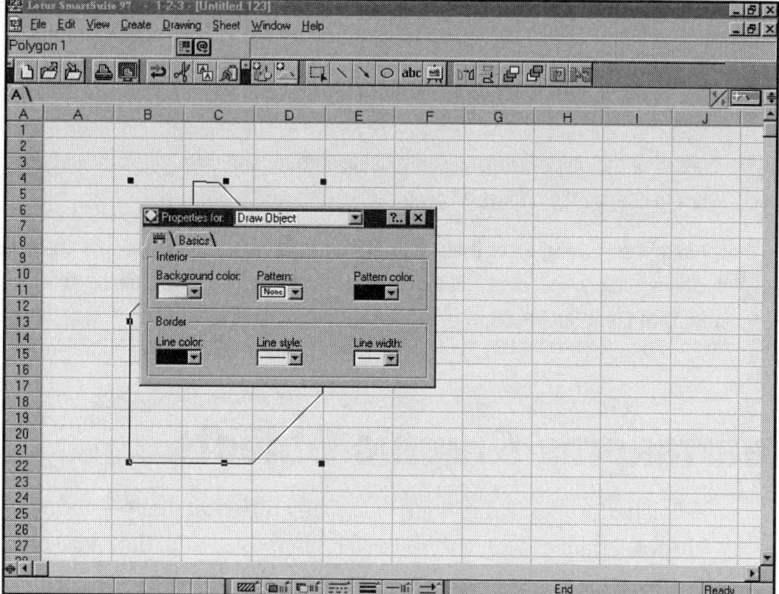

Fig. 16.8 Changing the color and style of shapes.

To change the color and appearance of the inside of a shape, use the Interior settings on the Color, Pattern, and Line Style panel of the Draw Object Properties InfoBox. To change the color inside the shape, use the Background color list box. To apply a pattern to the inside of the shape, use the Pattern list box. To apply a color to a pattern, use the Pattern color list box.

Drawing Freehand

When you use the Freehand tool, it's as if someone gave you a pencil and let you draw on the screen. However, if you're like me and you have limited artistic ability, freehand drawing looks more like freehand scribbling.

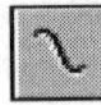

To activate this tool, choose Create, Drawing, Freehand; or select the Freehand Drawing SmartIcon. The mouse pointer then turns into a crosshair. Place the intersection of the crosshair where you want to begin and click and drag to draw. Release the mouse button when you are finished drawing.

TROUBLESHOOTING

I created a polygon but don't like the way it looks. You can instantly remove any shape you just added by choosing Edit Undo. Or, delete any shape by selecting it and pressing the Del key. Or, edit the shape by first "showing its points." You select the polygon, then select Show Points in the Basic tab of the Infobox. Now, each corner of the polygon is movable by dragging them with the mouse.

I drew a line with a single arrow, but I meant to draw a double-headed arrow. Click the line, right-click the mouse while the pointer rests over the selected line, and choose Drawing Properties from the quick menu. Click the Color, Pattern, and Line Style tab, and use the Arrowhead list box to change the arrowhead style.

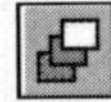

I added a rectangle but it blocks out half my chart. Objects on your chart are displayed on different layers. The chart is behind the rectangle you added. Click the chart, and then click the Bring to Front SmartIcon.

Rearranging Graphic Objects

A finished worksheet may include many different items—numbers in cells, charts, shapes, graphics text, and so on. The more you add, the more crowded things get. To control how items are displayed—which item is placed on top of another item, which box goes behind a chart, and so on—you need to be able to work with the different layers on your worksheet. You also need to be able to move the graphics you create. 1-2-3 lets you flip graphics horizontally or vertically. Finally, you can put all the objects you create together into a group and lock them in place to prevent accidental changes. You'll find all these options in the Drawing menu, which appears when you select any drawn object. Table 16.2 explains the rearranging options.

Table 16.2 Rearranging Graphics

Option	Description
Bring to Front	Moves selected object in front of other objects
Send to Back	Moves selected object in back of other objects
Group	Joins a number of selected individual objects into a single group
Ungroup	Removes all objects from a group and returns to treating them as individual objects
Flip Left-Right	Flips the selected object horizontally
Flip Top-Bottom	Flips the selected object vertically

Understanding Layering

All objects you create are stacked on top of one another, in the order you create them. If your chart is on the bottom layer, for example, any objects you draw or text blocks you create inside the chart boundaries are layered on top of the chart. If you draw an object on top of a text block, the text in the text block is hidden unless you change the stacking order.

Changing the Stacking Order

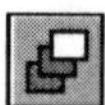
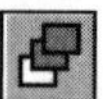

You can change the stacking order of objects in your worksheet by using the Bring to Front SmartIcon and the Send to Back SmartIcon or by using commands on the Drawing menu, which appears when you select a drawn object.

These commands send an object all the way to the back or bring it all the way to the front; there is no way to move an object forward or backward one layer.

Change the stacking order quickly by positioning the mouse pointer on the selected object, pressing the right-mouse button, and choosing Bring to Front or Send to Back from the quick menu.

Flipping Graphics Objects

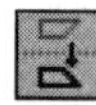

\If you want to flip an object you've created, click the object to select it; then open the Drawing menu. Choose Flip Left-Right if you want to flip the graphic horizontally and choose Flip Top-Bottom to flip the object vertically. If you prefer, you can use the Flip Horizontal SmartIcon or Flip Vertical SmartIcon to make the change.

Grouping and Locking Graphics Objects

Grouping allows you to select multiple objects and put them all together in one group. This is helpful, for example, when you've created a logo out of several different shapes. Whenever you move the logo, if the items are not grouped, you have to move each shape individually. After you group the objects, you can move, resize, cut, and paste the group as a single graphic.

To select multiple items to group, press Shift while clicking each object desired.

To group items, select the items you want to group. Choose the Drawing, Group command.

The handles on the individual items disappear and the objects are treated as a single object. Later, you can ungroup the objects by selecting the grouped objects and choosing Drawing, Ungroup.

After you put the objects together as a group, you may want to lock the image to keep if from accidentally being altered. Select the object(s) and open the Draw Object Properties InfoBox. On the Basics panel, place a check in the Lock check box. ●

CHAPTER 17

Developing Business Presentations

by Elaine Marmel

You can use the charting, graphic, and printing capabilities of 1-2-3 in many creative ways to report worksheet data. This chapter discusses using 1-2-3 to create high-quality presentation slides, overheads, and screen shows. ■

Setting up workbooks to create slides

To use 1-2-3 to prepare slides for a presentation, you should make certain adjustments to 1-2-3's appearance.

Slide concepts

Creating a slide is one issue, but creating a good, effective slide is another.

Printing slides

Typically, you'll use slides on a computer during a presentation, but you can print them and use them as handouts for your audience.

Presentation Possibilities

The way in which you present your information will have some effect on the type of presentation you create. If you are creating handouts and transparencies, you can move through the pages as quickly or slowly as you like, allowing plenty of time for audience questions. You can print slides and graphics, using black-and-white or color printers, directly on transparent overhead-projector film, resulting in colorful and persuasive overhead presentations. If you don't have a color printer, you can print the presentation to a file and send the file to a slide-generating service.

You also can use your computer to display presentation pages on-screen. This technique is often called a *computer screen show*. If you are working with a computerized presentation, you can design your presentation to advance pages automatically or to advance only when you click the mouse or press Enter on the keyboard. Screen-show capabilities are available in many presentation graphics packages, such as Lotus Freelance Graphics, but 1-2-3 provides many of the same capabilities and can create a visually interesting screen show.

If you have access to both 1-2-3 and Freelance, say through Lotus SmartSuite, you might want to consider using them together to create a presentation. And, if you have SmartSuite, you also can use WordPro to help you prepare your presentation. See Que's *Special Edition Using Lotus SmartSuite for Windows 95*.

For the majority of this chapter, we'll focus on using 1-2-3 effectively to create images you can print on transparencies. Throughout this chapter, you'll notice that the figures don't include grid lines. At the end of this chapter, we'll show you how to turn off grid lines and other settings that help you set up the 1-2-3 display to use it in a computerized screen show.

Setting Up Workbooks to Create Slide Presentations

To use 1-2-3 to create overhead transparencies (or slides or a computerized slide show), you'll find it easiest to think of a worksheet as one slide. In this section, you'll learn the basics of creating a slide layout template. Then, we'll cover some techniques for efficient handling of multiple-page presentations.

Creating a Slide Layout

Creating slides in 1-2-3 is as easy as typing the text in worksheet cells. Depending on the nature and length of your presentation, you might want to set up one basic slide format that you use repeatedly; or you might want to create a few different formats that you use depending on the information on the slides.

What kind of slides do you need? Table 17.1 lists the four basic presentation slide types.

Table 17.1 Presentation Slide Types

Slide	Description	Use For
Title slide	Shows title and subtitle of presentation	First slide of presentation; parts slides between presentation sections
Bullet slide	Displays slide title and bulleted list of information	Slides in which you introduce a series of steps, options, or ideas
Chart slide	Shows slide title and a 1-2-3 chart	Slides that require a large display of charted information
Text and graphics slide	Shows slide title, text, and clip art or custom graphics	Text slides that need illustration (or chart)

You can create a basic layout for each type of slide you'll use in your presentation. Then you can use the settings in that worksheet as a template and copy the settings from slide to slide as necessary.

▶ **See** "Setting Column Widths," **p. 94**

The key to creating the slide layout is setting up the appropriate column widths for text, bullets, and graphics. Organizing the columns in this manner enables you to indent bullets and other text easily. Figure 17.1 shows how you can use 1-2-3 to set up a template for a bullet slide.

In this example, the column widths appear in the first row of the worksheet. The differences in the column widths help you align the title, subtitle, bullets, and bullet text. You can simply move from one column to the next, rather than use the space bar within the same column, to get characters to line up.

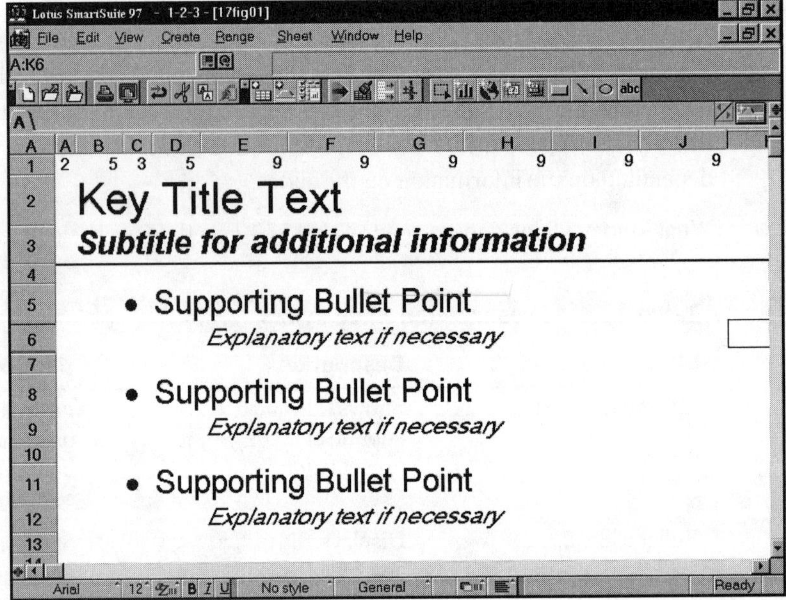

Fig. 17.1
A template for a bullet page in 1-2-3.

Here's how the columns in figure 17.1 were set up:

Skip a row between bullet points to leave space between lines of text.

Column	Width	Description
A	2	Space to separate the overall slide contents from the slide frame
B	5	Indentation for subtitles below the title
C	3	Space for the bullet characters
D	5	Indentation for text below bullet items

To add text, highlight the appropriate cell and type the new information. Long labels will appear across the adjacent columns. Press the arrow keys as necessary to move the cell pointer.

Larger typefaces and other attributes, such as bold, italics, and lines, make the information clearer for your audience.

After you add the text, you can use the settings in the Range InfoBox panels, the status bar, and the quick menus (displayed when you click the right mouse button) to make the text more readable.

Developing Multiple-Page Presentations

Most presentations take up more than one page or worksheet screen; 1-2-3 can accommodate presentations of almost any length. Using the worksheet tabs of a workbook, you create individual slides one to a page and simultaneously put the slides together as a group the way you would a series of worksheet files. You then can move among the slides by clicking the tabs at the top of the slides. Simply click the tab you want, and that slide is displayed. Figure 17.2 shows a presentation using the worksheet tabs.

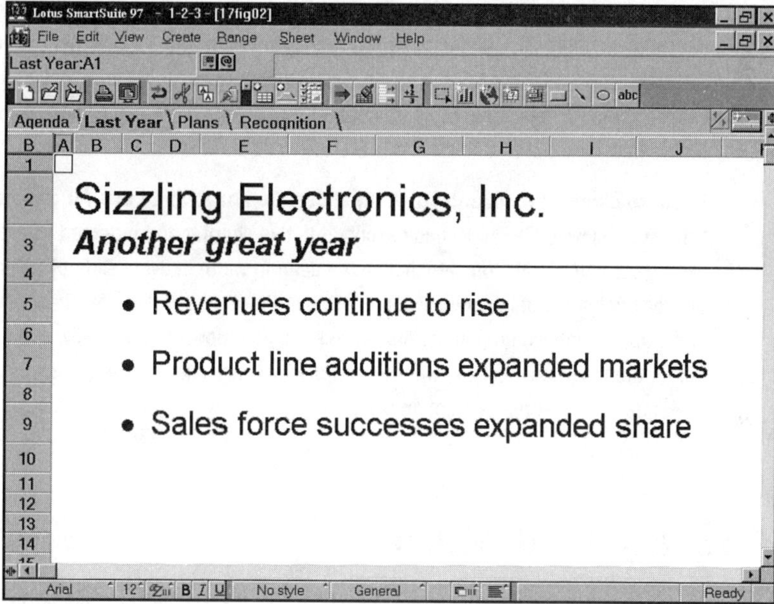

Fig. 17.2
Using the 1-2-3 worksheet tabs to organize slides on multiple pages.

Set the font colors and other formats on one slide and then enable Group mode. This procedure copies the same format settings to any new worksheets you create in that group. Disable Group mode to alter the format settings of individual worksheets.

The Group mode feature enables you to use the format of one worksheet to format all the pages in multiple worksheets. The formats applied across the worksheets include column widths and spreadsheet publishing formats. To enable Group mode, choose the Sheet, Group Sheets command. Then select the first sheet in the workbook to serve as the model for all subsequent sheets.

▶ **See** "Understanding Style," **p. 105**

TROUBLESHOOTING

I turned on Group mode so I could preserve the same column widths from sheet to sheet, but when I click File, New Workbook, a separate workbook appears. Add a new worksheet by clicking the New Sheet button, not by using File, New Workbook.

I used a few standard text formats for my first slide. Is there an easy way to apply these formats to other slides in my presentation? You can create named styles that contain all the style information you need. Place the cell pointer in the cell from which you want to define the named style. Right click and choose Range Properties from the quick menu. Click the Named Style tab; choose Create Style, type a Style name and choose OK. You now can use the style by clicking the style selector in the status bar or by opening the Range Properties InfoBox, displaying the Named Style panel, and choosing the Style you want to apply.

I want to change the indents in all my slides. Do I have to do this for every slide individually? No, if you followed the guidelines described in this chapter and indented your bullets by using varying column widths. You can change the column width in every slide by selecting a three-dimensional range of columns. Open the Range Properties dialog box. Then, place the cell pointer in the appropriate column in the first worksheet, hold down the Shift key, and click the worksheet tab for the last worksheet you want to format. You have selected the same column in every worksheet. Now set the new column width.

Anatomy of a Slide

You'll find yourself using two basic types of slides: slides that contain text only (see fig. 17.3), and slides that contain text and graphics (see fig. 17.4).

▶ **See** Understanding Style," **p. 105**

Regardless of whether the slide contains only text or a combination of text and graphics, you'll want to focus on creating clear, persuasive, and successful presentations. The visibility of your slide and the clarity of your ideas should be your primary focus.

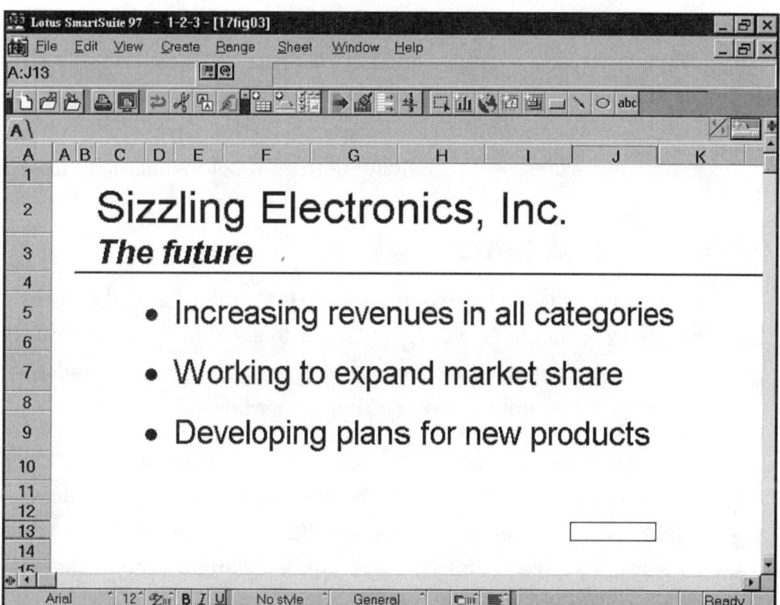

Fig. 17.3
Some slides contain only text...

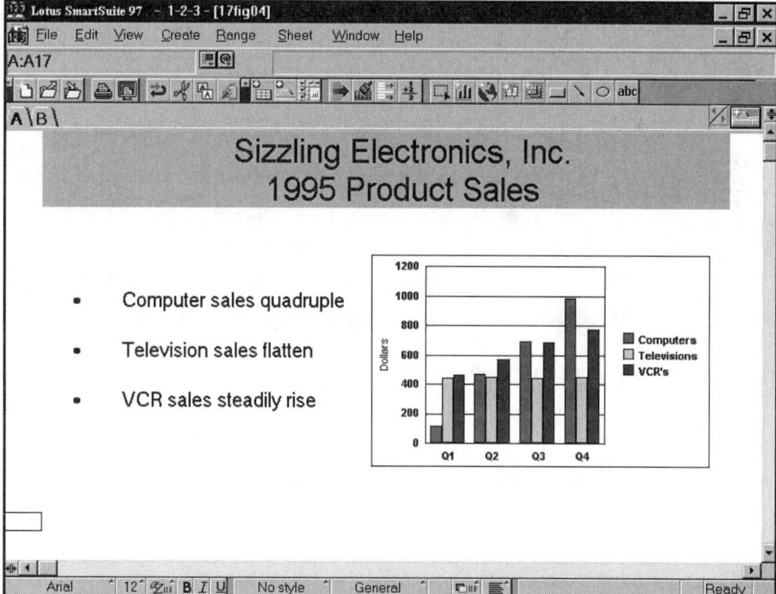

Fig. 17.4
...while other slides contain both text and graphics.

1-2-3 provides great flexibility in text size and font, emphasis such as boldface and italics, colors, lines, and shading. The key to a successful presentation, however, is using these elements in moderation. By following a few guidelines, you can create impressive and effective presentations. In the following sections, we'll focus on presenting text and graphics on your slides, and enhancing both with colors and designer frames.

Preparing a Text Slide

Your focus, particularly when creating text slides, should be presenting your ideas in the most comprehensible way. The danger to avoid in a text slide is "busy-ness." Keep your slides as short and simple as possible to ensure that your audience concentrates on understanding your points, not on reading your slide.

Most text slides consist of two parts: a title area and a body area. The title area can contain both a title and subtitle. The body area typically contains bullets or numbered lists, making the presentation easier for your audience to follow. And, even on text slides, you find formatting such as boldface, italics, underlining, and color that shape the visibility and clarity of the slide.

In this section, we'll focus on presenting your ideas, making sure that your slides are readable, and enhancing text with boldface and italics. We'll postpone discussing color on slides until after we've talked about preparing slides that contain graphics. Why? Because you might want to add color to both text slides and graphic slides.

Presenting Ideas Slides should not be narratives of the entire presentation. Instead, use the titles, subtitles, and bullet items to present the essential points clearly. Rely on the spoken presentation to explain the basic information that the slides present.

Adding another slide is always better than crowding too much information into a single slide.

Effective slides contain a title and no more than four or five bullet points. Don't crowd information onto a slide. If the bullets require sub-bullets, make sure that the slide contains no more than three main bullets and five or six total bullets, including sub-bullets. Limit the sub-bullets to two or three lines at most.

Depending on the bullet character you choose, you might need to make it one or two point sizes larger than the accompanying text to make the character easy to see.

You can precede text items with bullet symbols, such as diamonds, arrows, or check marks. These symbols are available in the Windows Wingdings, Monotype Sorts, Zapf

Dingbats, and Symbols typefaces. You create a symbol by placing the appropriate character in a cell and formatting the cell with the appropriate font. Choose a point size for the symbol that corresponds to the adjacent text. For example, if the bullet text is set to 18-point, the bullet should also be set to at least 18 points.

You can create bullets by using the Windows Character Map to copy a bullet character from one of these typefaces to the Windows Clipboard. Then, switch to 1-2-3 and paste the character in the appropriate cell. The Character Map (see fig. 17.5) is an accessory that comes with Windows 95—if you don't see it in the Accessories folder, you need to add it. See the sidebar to learn to use the Character Map.

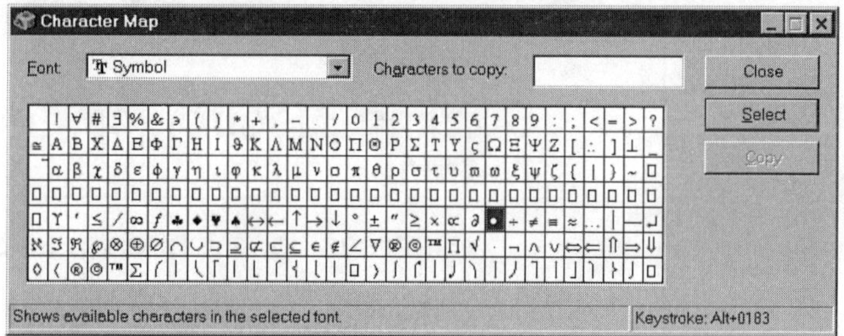

Fig. 17.5 Use the Windows Character Map applet to insert bullet characters.

The Windows Accessory Character Map

The Windows accessory Character Map provides an easy way to add special characters to Windows applications. To add special characters with the Windows Character Map, follow these steps:

1. Click the Start button, select Programs, Accessories, Character Map.
2. Select a font in the Font drop-down list and highlight the symbol you want to use. The bottom-right corner of the dialog box displays the keystroke for the highlighted item.
3. Double-click the symbol, press Enter, or choose Select. The character appears in the Characters to Copy text box. Repeat this process until the Characters to Copy box contains all the characters you want to use.
4. Choose the Copy button to copy the characters to the Clipboard and then choose Close to close the Character Map.
5. Switch back to 1-2-3, and place the cell pointer in the appropriate cell.
6. Set the font to the font you selected in step 2; then paste the contents of the Clipboard using the Paste SmartIcon or the Edit Paste command. The character(s) appear in your worksheet.

In 1-2-3, you also can type the keystroke for the character you saw displayed in the lower right corner of the Character Map window.

To make the points easier to understand, use the same grammatical construction for all bullets in a slide. Bullets can start with a noun or a verb of any tense, but all the bullets should use the same structure. The slide shown in figure 17.6 shows bullet items that use parallel structure. Compare this slide with the one shown in figure 17.7, which does not use parallel structure. A parallel construction creates a tighter presentation and conveys information more clearly.

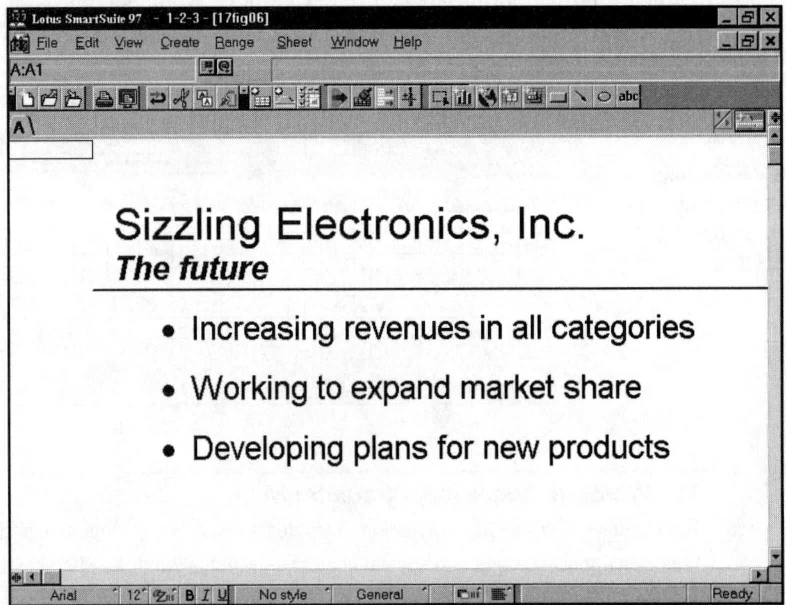

Fig. 17.6
Use bullets that are parallel for better understanding.

Assuring Visibility Because an audience reads presentations from a distance, slides must be clear, in large type, and contain as few words as possible. Use fonts that can be read from a distance. For titles, use a 24-point font or larger, and text in the body of the slide should be at least 14 points. Use the Text Format panel of the Range Properties InfoBox to choose font sizes.

TIP Be consistent with text style and size. Use the same size and style for titles and the same size for bullets, from slide to slide.

Slides convey information better when the title is easy to locate and read. You can use a solid line below the title to separate the title from the body of the slide. If a slide has both a title and subtitle, underline the subtitle to separate the title area of the slide from the body of the slide (refer to figure 17.7). Use the Lines & Colors tab of the Range Properties InfoBox to place a solid line under the slide title area.

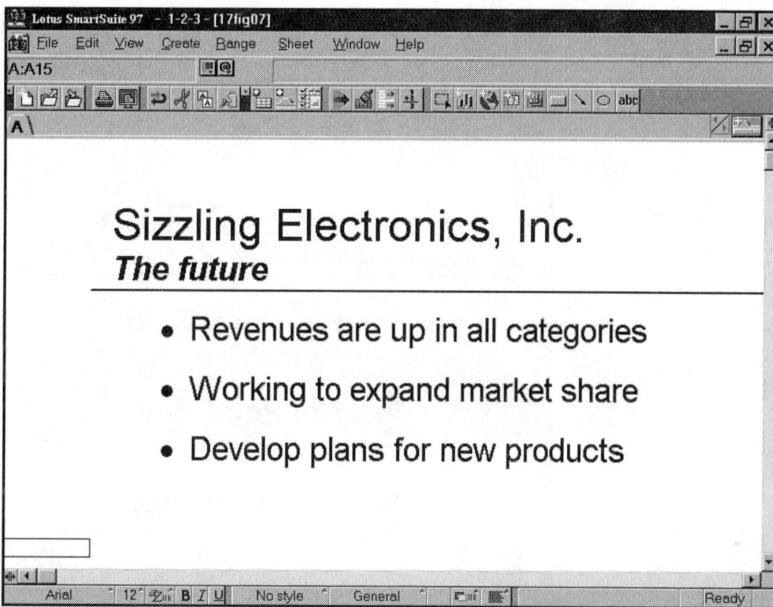

Fig. 17.7
Avoid bullets that aren't parallel.

Although 1-2-3 enables you to use up to eight different fonts on a page, the best slides use only one or two typefaces in up to three point sizes. If you use too many different type styles, you'll make the slide difficult to read and reduce the impact of the slide's message. Never make text in the body of the slide smaller than 14 points.

Format slide text in a sans-serif typeface such as Arial or Helvetica. Serif typefaces such as Times New Roman may be appropriate with longer lines of text, but sans-serif text is most appropriate for headlines, which are what appear most on your slides. Notice that newspapers typically use a sans-serif font for the headline and serif fonts for the body of an article. Use the Text Format panel of the Range Properties InfoBox to select font styles.

Figure 17.8 shows a slide with effective font selections. Figure 17.9, on the other hand, contains too many typefaces and type styles. The viewer is distracted by a multitude of fonts and loses focus on the slide's message.

▶ **See** "Changing Fonts and Attributes," **p. 125**

Emphasizing Information At a distance, plain type tends to fade into the projection screen and become unreadable. To make slide text easier to read, use boldface for titles, subtitles, and bullets. Be sure, however, to apply the boldface consistently.

A subtitle message usually supports or expands on the title message. You can differentiate the subtitle from the title by using a smaller point size and italics.

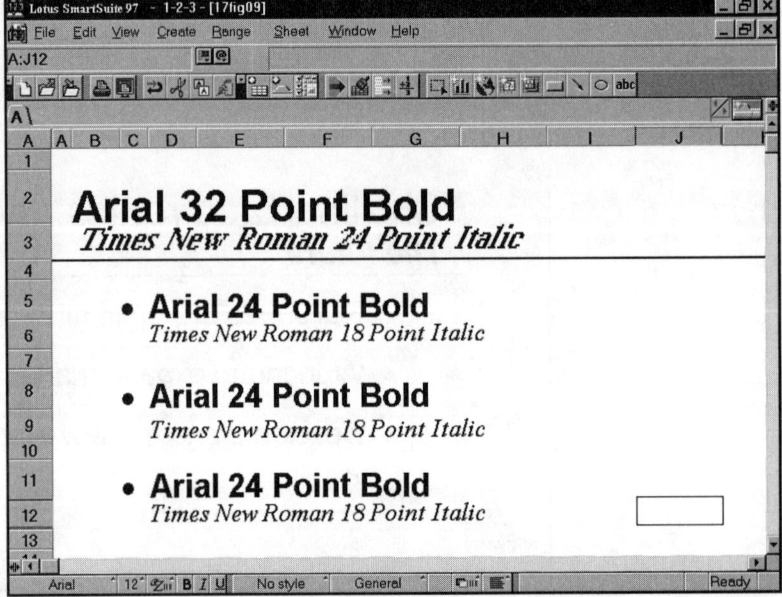

Fig. 17.8
Use fonts that work together for clarity of presentation.

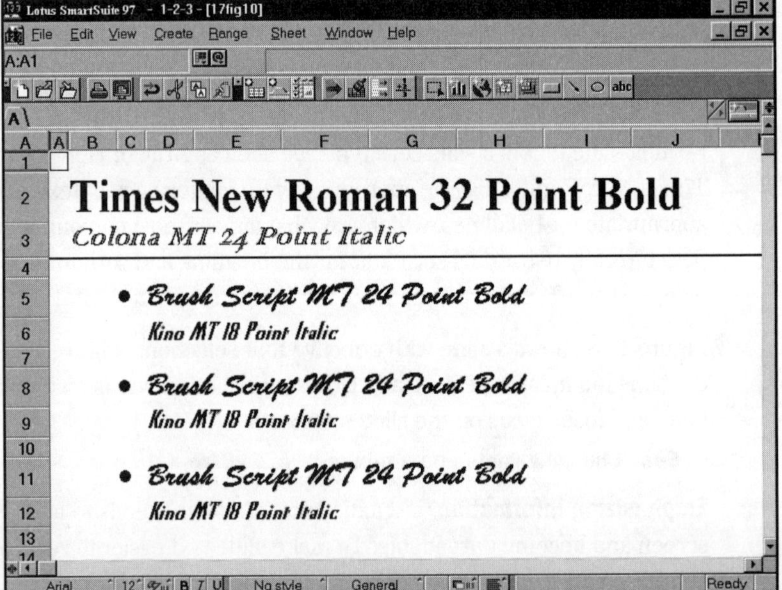

Fig. 17.9
Don't use fonts that make the slide hard to read and understand.

TIP Use bold italic to make italicized text stand out.

You also can use italics to separate the parts of the slide and to show that text has special meaning. Italics are effective for emphasizing direct or indirect quotations, for example.

Figures 17.10 and 17.11 show different ways of using bold and italics to add emphasis and clarity to slides.

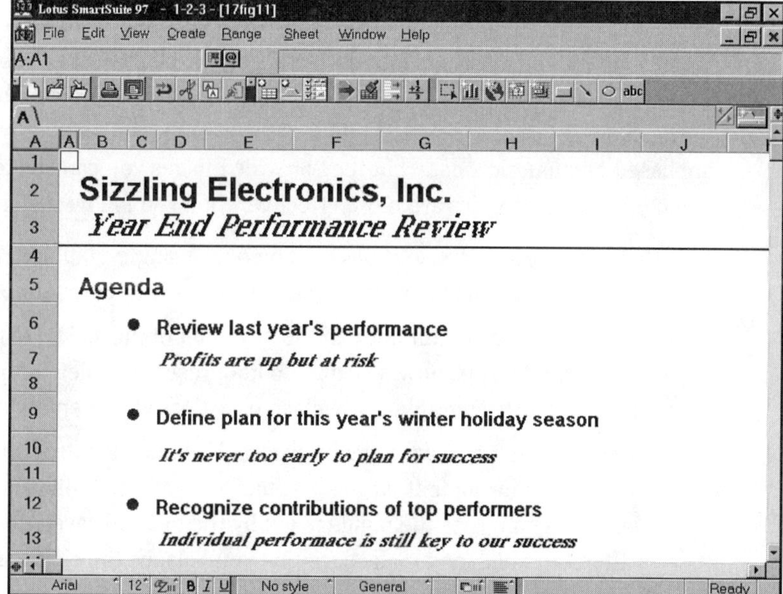

Fig. 17.10
You can use boldface symbols with italic subtext.

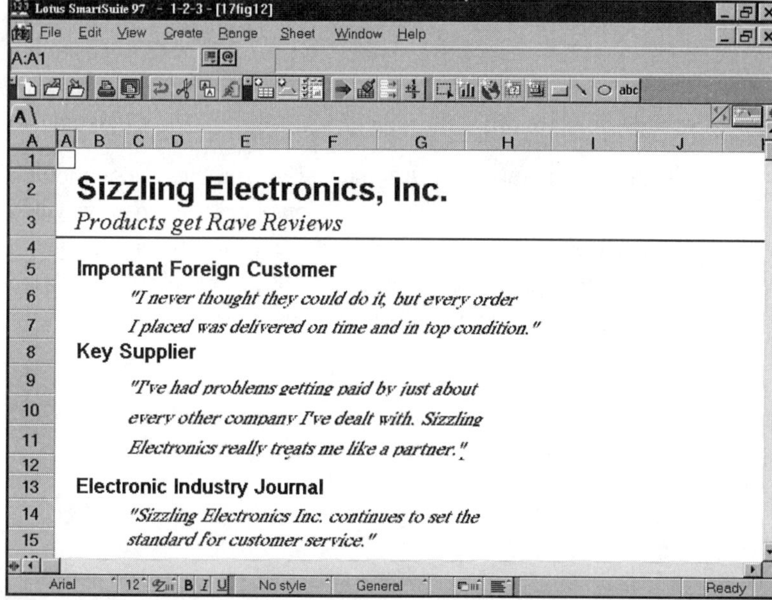

Fig. 17.11
Another effective technique is to use boldface italics for quotations.

Show the screen show to friends or coworkers before you present it to make sure the text is readable and understandable.

Preparing a Slide Containing Graphics

To make presentation slides more effective and persuasive, you can use graphic images. Graphic images fall basically into three categories: charts (like those you can produce by using your 1-2-3 data), clip art, and drawings. Charts can be data tables of numbers, or they can be the graphic representation of those numbers. Neither clip art nor drawings are based on numerical data, but they provide images you can use to liven up your presentation. Like text, graphics are more effective when you follow certain guidelines:

- In most cases, effective slides contain only a single graphic. The key to an effective slide presentation is to present the key points with clear, simple illustrations.
- A graphic can draw attention to the key point of the slide. Do not try to encompass too many concepts, however, and do not present detailed information in a single graphic. The best graphics are clear, easy-to-read presentations of a single key point.
- Effective graphics have a clear purpose. Use titles to introduce the key message and to establish the context for the graphic. You can use bullets in your graphics to clarify or emphasize the points made by the text; however, do not overload the page with information, and make sure that you balance the elements of the overall layout.

In figure 17.12, the information is poorly organized and the slide is unbalanced. Figure 17.13 presents the same information clearly.

Graphics add substance to a slide. However, you need to position a graphic to balance the page. Center a graphic if the slide contains little text; otherwise, position the graphic to the right or left to offset the weight of the other slide elements (refer to fig. 17.13).

Presenting Concepts with Graphics Use graphics of common objects to convey new ideas. Look at your environment for metaphors that effectively communicate your message. Building blocks, for example, can show the addition of new products over time. Pie charts can show that a combination of various parts make a whole (see fig. 17.14). A bridge can represent the joining of two separate entities.

Make sure that your graphics fit your message.

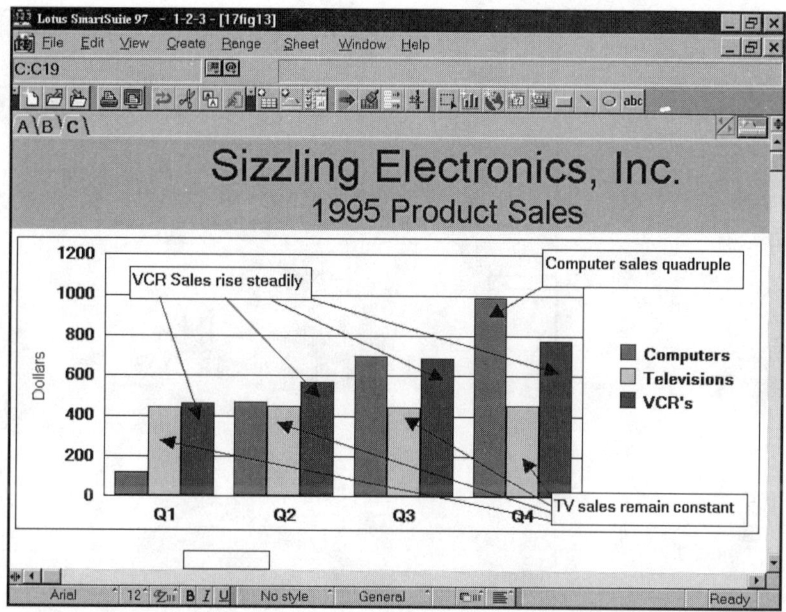

Fig. 17.12
An unbalanced presentation of graphics makes the slide difficult to understand.

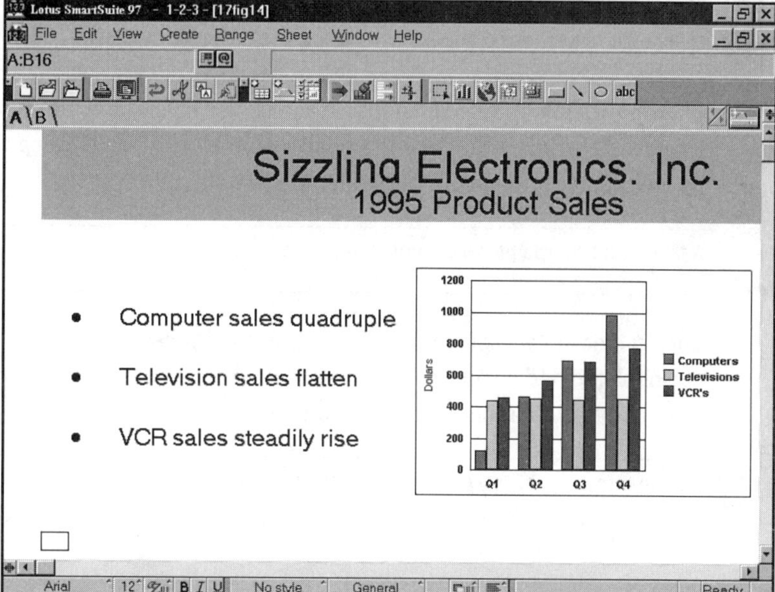

Fig. 17.13
Use bullets to explain the chart and balance it in the slide.

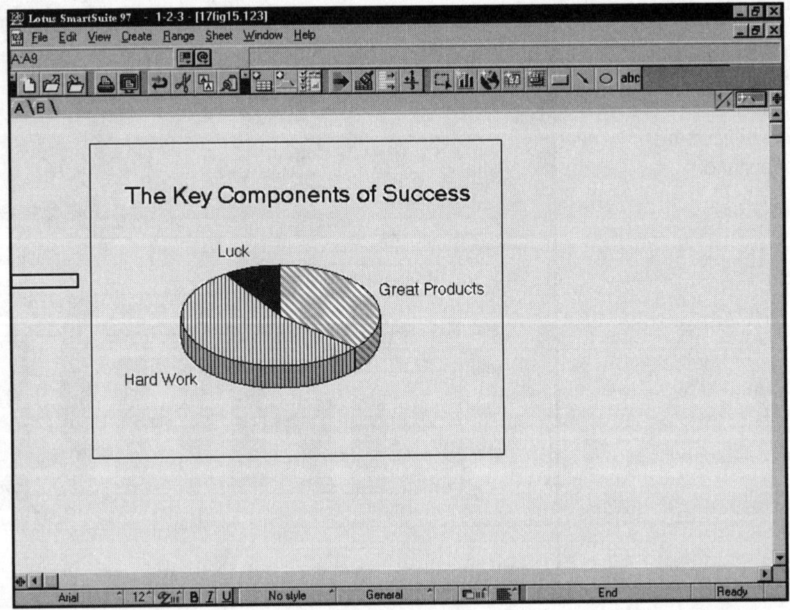

Fig. 17.14
A pie chart representing proportions can show data effectively.

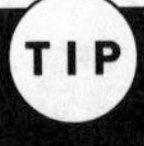

When creating charts like the one in fig. 17.14, be sure to use distinguishable colors or patterns so that the viewer has no trouble determining where one pie slice ends and another begins.

Showing Trends or Relationships You can use charts and tables on slides to illustrate key trends in data or to show the relationship among items. Keep charts and tables simple by limiting the amount of information they contain.

A table can help you present information in a new way.

Long tables of data seldom are effective in slide presentations and, in most cases, should be supplemented or replaced by charts. A table on a slide should be no more than four rows and four columns, with one row and one column used for labels.

Choose a preset table style to create a table quickly.

Rows and columns of numbers and labels can be very hard to read, but 1-2-3 provides a gallery of predefined table formats. These table formats are a quick way to create an easy-to-read worksheet table. The table in figure 17.15 was formatted using a table style.

▶ **See** "Using the Style Gallery," **p. 133**

And, you can draw attention to the trends and relationships among data items by supplying lines and arrows that you add using the Create menu's Drawing commands. When you must include a table in your presentation, like the one shown in figure 17.15, use it to provide the information for a chart that illustrates the data graphically like the chart shown in figure 17.16. (The chart in figure 17.16, for example, clearly shows the trends in product sales.)

▶ **See** "Creating Charts," **p. 307**

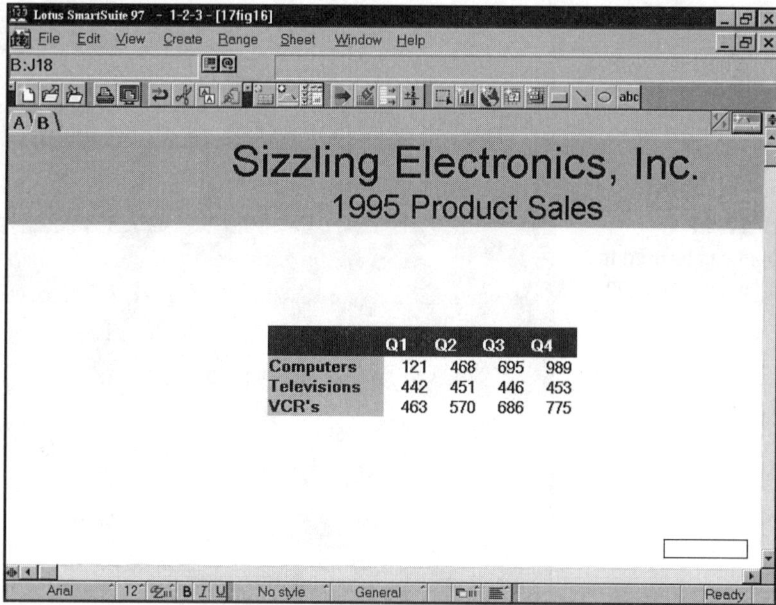

	Q1	Q2	Q3	Q4
Computers	121	468	695	989
Televisions	442	451	446	453
VCR's	463	570	686	775

Fig. 17.15
Use worksheet data in a slide to point out key information in a worksheet table.

Adding Visual Interest with Clip Art You can use commercially available clip art to make the presentation more interesting. You can paste clip art in Windows metafile format directly into the 1-2-3 worksheet. Choose images that support your presentation's theme and are appropriate to the setting (see fig. 17.17).

▶ **See** "Adding Clip Art," **p. 369**

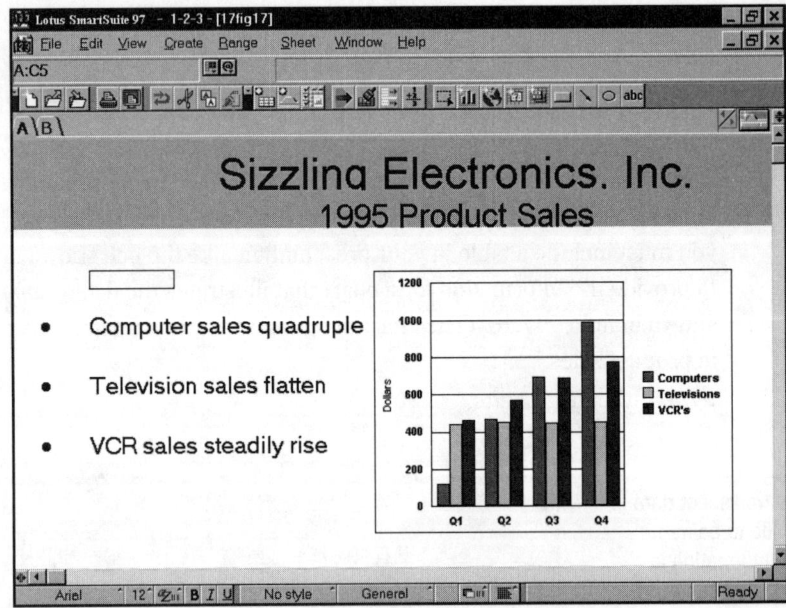

Fig. 17.16
Add a 1-2-3 chart to a slide to show data more effectively.

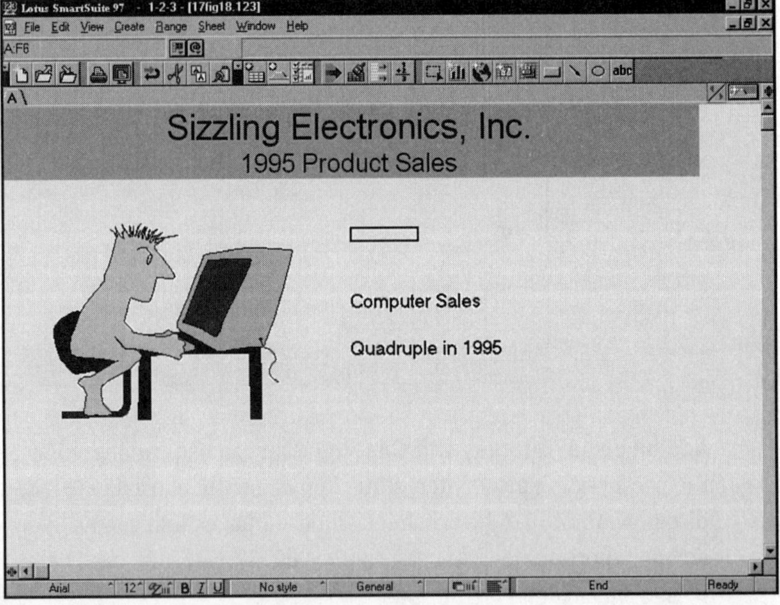

Fig. 17.17
Clip art can be used to enliven a presentation.

Virtually any image seems to be available as clip art in the Windows metafile format. Clip art adds interest to a slide presentation and often communicates key concepts.

Using Drawings on a Slide You can add graphics drawings anywhere in the 1-2-3 worksheet area. Use the Create menu's Drawing commands or the drawing SmartIcons to draw in the worksheet. You can use a drawing to explain difficult concepts or to illustrate key points presented in the slide. Figure 17.18 shows an example of an organizational chart created by adding rectangles to the draw layer.

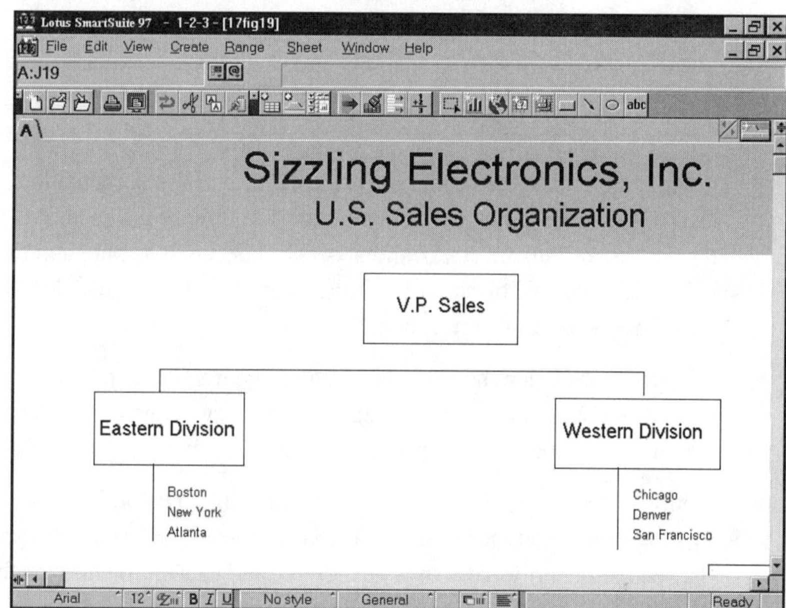

Fig. 17.18
An organizational chart drawn in the worksheet draw layer.

Enhancing Slides with Colors and Designer Frames

You can use color and borders to enhance presentations. You've already seen, in the last section, how lines can add interest to slides; colors can also add interest to slides and even direct attention to key data.

NOTE To present in color, you must be able to print to a color printer or use a computer with a color monitor to give the presentation as a screen show. On black-and-white printers, colors print as different shades of gray, which also can create a useful effect.

▶ **See** "Formatting Cells with Color and Borders," **p. 130**

1-2-3 enables you to choose the color of cell backgrounds, text, lines, and drawing objects from 256 color choices. 1-2-3 also allows you to add lines and borders to cells or slides.

In the following sections, we'll talk about using color in your presentation slides and adding designer borders to frame your presentation slides.

Using Color to Highlight Presentation Elements and Suggest Meaning In a presentation, you can use colors in several ways. The most obvious method of adding color is by using a different color for the main point in the presentation. Yet you can choose among several other common ways to use color.

Keep your colors consistent to help viewers understand what they represent.

Color can enhance the organizational structure of the presentation. Using a standard color layout makes the slides easy to understand and more interesting to read. Choose consistent colors for the different regions of the slide, such as blue text for the titles, red for the bullet symbols, and black for the bullet text. You also can use different background colors for different sections of the slide.

Because many colors have common connotations, you can use color to convey meaning in a presentation. In business, for example, red represents a monetary loss or negative number, and black represents a profit or positive number.

Figure 17.19 shows a slide that easily could contain color. If the third bullet of the slide in this figure were red, for example, the viewer would suspect that expenses (mentioned in the second bullet) were actually excessive and caused the loss for the company.

Choose colors that show up well, even at a distance. Use Print Preview to help you.

Red also can suggest danger. Blue, generally considered to be a peaceful and even soothing color, can imply tranquillity or coolness. Green—the color of U.S. currency and the stoplight color for GO—often implies profit or advancement. Yellow often means caution, a message that also comes from traffic lights and road signs.

NOTE With most printers, 1-2-3 prints different colors in different shades of gray. However, you also can directly select shades of gray with the Lines & Colors panel of the Range Properties InfoBox. The Pattern Color, Background Color, and Text Color drop-down boxes include gray shades in the far-right column. ■

▶ **See** "Changing Fonts and Attributes," **p. 125**

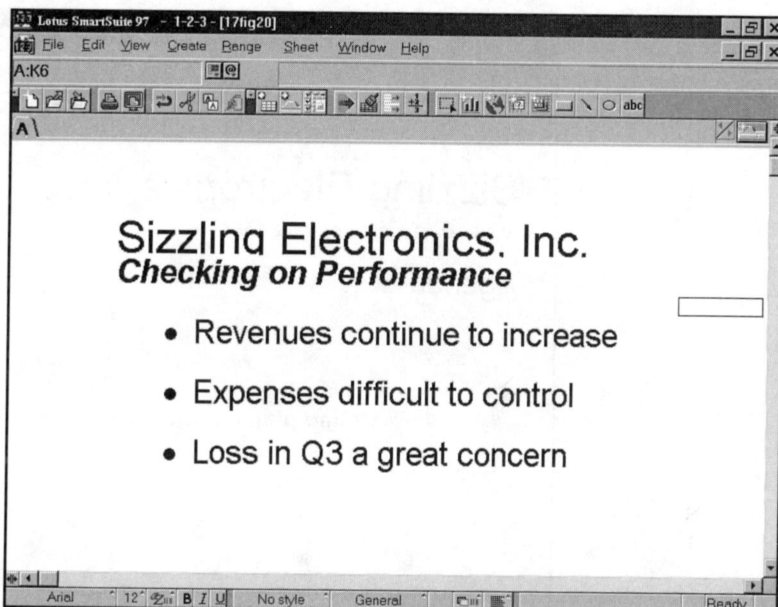

Fig. 17.19
A slide that can use red to convey monetary loss.

Most presentations start with an agenda. You can tie a presentation together by repeating the agenda slide before switching to the next topic. This method is more effective if you also highlight the topic that follows. One way to highlight the topic is to use color.

Figure 17.20 shows the slide you might use to introduce the second topic (*Define plan for upcoming year*). In this example, the first and third bullets are shaded gray with the gray scale choices you'll find on the Color, Pattern, and Line Style panel of the in the Range Properties InfoBox.

Set the background color before setting the text color.

In 1-2-3, you can select the color of the cell background and the cell contents. This way, you can emphasize text or areas of the presentation file. Open the Range Properties InfoBox by choosing the Range Properties SmartIcon, by choosing Range, Range Properties, or by choosing Range Properties from the quick menu you see when you right click.

Click the Color, Pattern, and Line Style tab and use the Background Color list box to set the background color of the cells (see fig. 17.21). To set the color of text, use the Text Color list box.

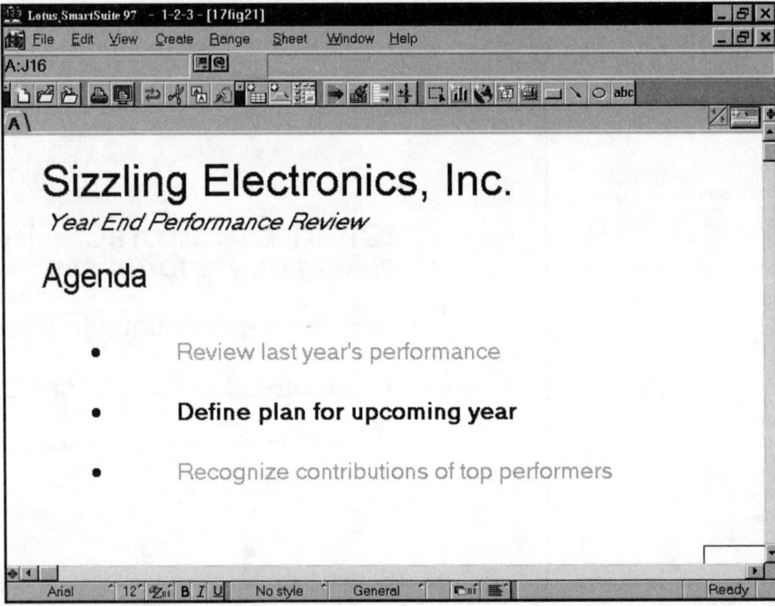

Fig. 17.20
Introduce the next topic by emphasizing a bullet item.

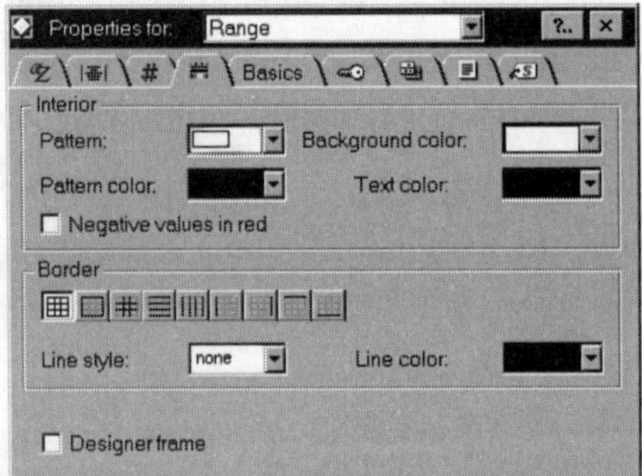

Fig. 17.21
Use the list boxes on this panel of the Range Properties InfoBox to set text color, background color, and shading.

The Text Color list box on the Text Format panel of the Range Properties InfoBox also sets text color. After you've set colors, you might want to use Print Preview to help you determine whether the colors are compatible.

Adding Designer Frames to Slides You can frame a slide on a page or a printout with a border by using a designer frame. Figure 17.22 shows a slide with a corporate-mission statement set off from the worksheet by a designer frame.

▶ **See** "Formatting Cells with Color and Borders," **p. 130**

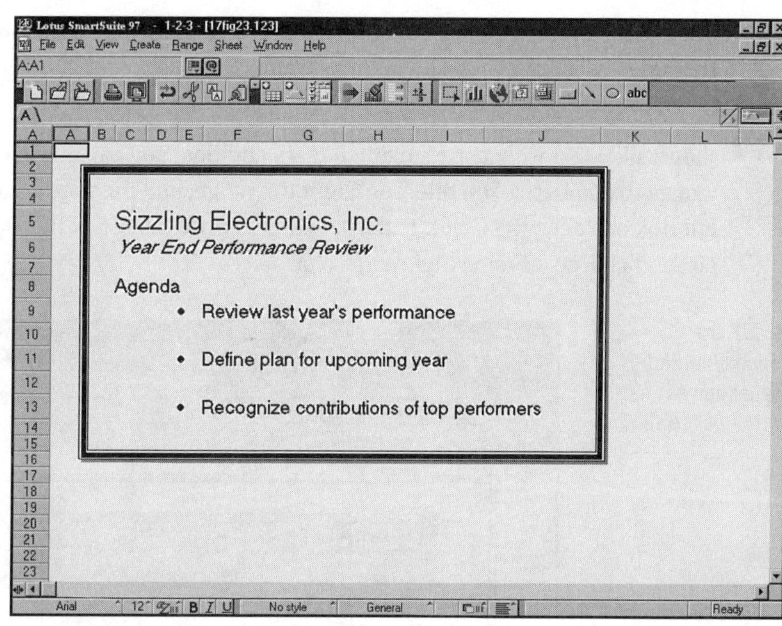

Fig. 17.22
You can use a designer frame to frame your slides.

To frame a slide with a border, open the Range Properties InfoBox and click the Color, Pattern, and Line Style tab. Place a check in the Designer Frame check box to display the Frame Style and Frame Color list boxes (see fig. 17.23).

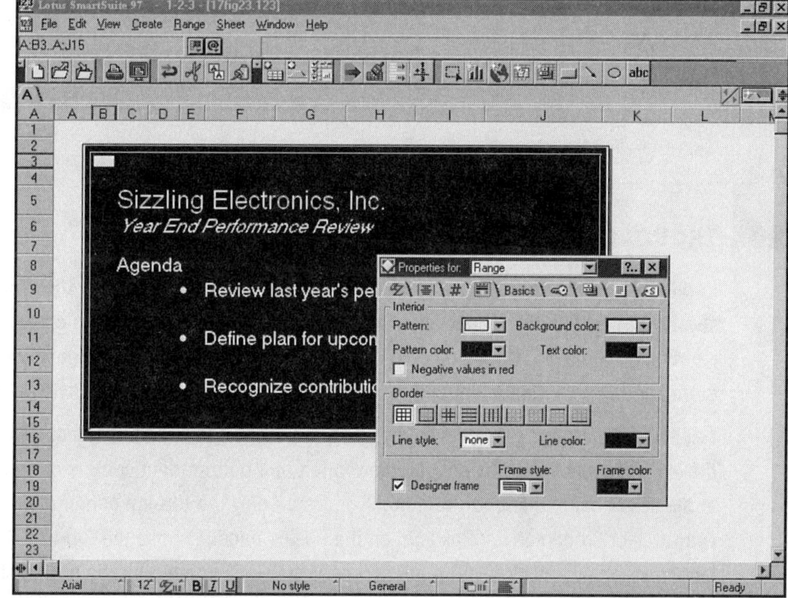

Fig. 17.23
After placing a check in the Designer Frame check box, 1-2-3 displays both the Frame Style and Frame Color list boxes.

Open these list boxes to display the pop-up list of frame choices. You can choose among 16 frame styles, and you can make the frame any color.

You also can emphasize a slide title by enclosing the text in a colored box. Figure 17.24 shows slide text with a shaded title box. In addition, you can use one of the designer frames to emphasize the title. Highlight the range, and then open the Range Properties InfoBox and click the Color, Pattern, and Line Style tab. Click the Designer Frames check box and choose a Frame Style and Color.

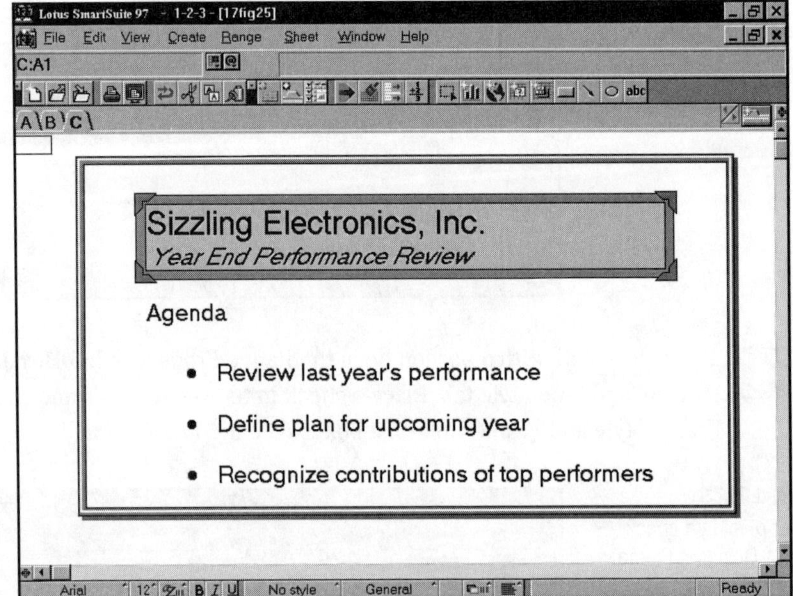

Fig. 17.24
A shaded box and designer frame emphasizes the slide title.

TROUBLESHOOTING

I added a clip art image to my worksheet, but I want the cells under the Windows metafile to show through. The default background for a metafile is opaque. You can choose to allow cell information to display through the clip art image. Select the clip art image; click the right mouse button and choose Document Properties. Set the Pattern and the Line Style to None.

I added some drawing objects to my slide, but when I insert columns or change widths, my drawings move around. By default, the top-left and bottom-right corners of objects are fastened to the cells behind them. You can, however, fasten only the top-left corner of an object. Open the Draw Object Properties InfoBox and, on the Basics panel, choose the Top-Left Only button to fasten the object only in the top-left corner or the Not Fastened button to unfasten the object entirely.

I want to show a general growth trend in a chart, but I don't have any real data. Do I have to draw the entire chart with the draw tools? You can draw the chart if you want, but you might find it easier to create dummy data from which to draw the chart. Type a starting value, such as 10, in a cell. If you want 10 percent growth, type in the cell next to it a formula that multiplies the first cell by 1.1. Copy the formula to the right for as many cells as you need in your chart; then create a chart from this range.

I've been trying to put borders in my slides with the designer frames, but they turn out looking really dark and uninteresting. What am I doing wrong? You probably are using black as the frame color. Display the Lines & Color panel of the Range Properties InfoBox by opening the Range menu and choosing the Range Properties command. Click the Lines & Colors tab, and open the Frame Color list box. Select gray or some other light color to give more contrast to your frame.

Printing Slides

You also can print handouts or create collaborative materials so that viewers can read your presentation later. Most presentations ultimately are printed for distribution or duplication on overhead transparencies. You can use the 1-2-3 print commands to print slides created on-screen.

Use the File, Preview and Page Setup command to choose landscape orientation for printing slides.

▶ **See** "Previewing Worksheets Before Printing," **p. 290**

A slide formatted to fit the screen does not fill a printed page. You can enlarge the slide, however. Open the Preview & Page Setup Properties InfoBox by choosing the File, Preview & Page Setup or by clicking the Print Preview Properties SmartIcon. On the Layout panel, open the Page Fit list box and choose Fit All To Page.

If you need to insert page breaks because you didn't create one slide to a worksheet page, position the cell pointer just below the last row you want included on the current page. Open the Range Properties InfoBox. On the Basics panel, place a check in the Break Page at Row check box.

To get out of Print Preview, click the X in the Print Preview window to close it.

Setting Up the Presentation Display for a Slide Show

Although the standard 1-2-3 screen looks nothing like a presentation, you can easily set up the 1-2-3 screen so that you can give an effective computerized screen show. How do you give 1-2-3 the appearance of a presentation-graphics screen?

First, hide the SmartIcons, the Status Bar, and the Edit Line. You'll find three commands on the View menu that perform these functions (see fig. 17.25).

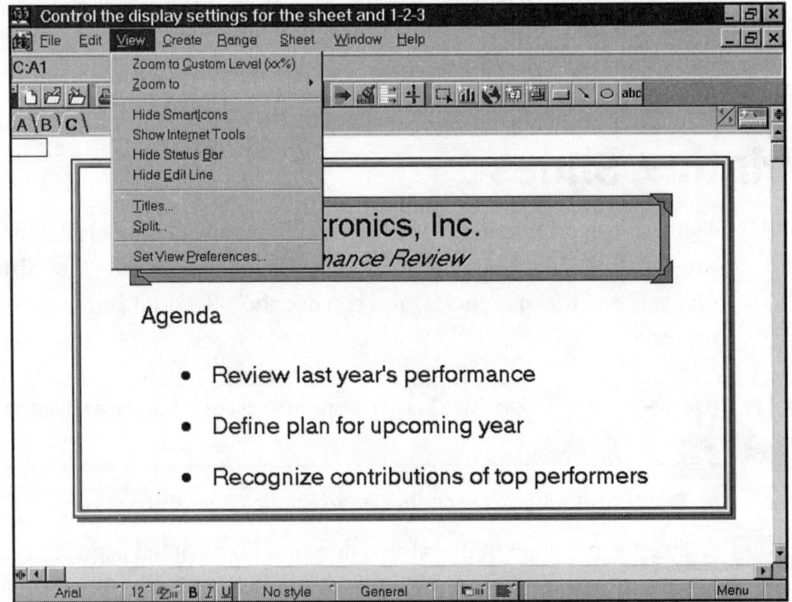

Fig. 17.25
On the View menu, you'll find the three commands you need to select to hide the SmartIcons, the Status Bar, and the Edit Line.

Next, open the File menu and choose the Workbook Properties command to change the way 1-2-3 elements are displayed on-screen. In the Workbook Properties dialog box (see fig. 17.26), make the following changes to the View tab:

- Uncheck the Sheet frame check box.
- Uncheck the Grid lines check box.
- Uncheck the Scroll bars check box.

Keep Sheet Tabs displayed so you have an easy way to move from slide to slide.

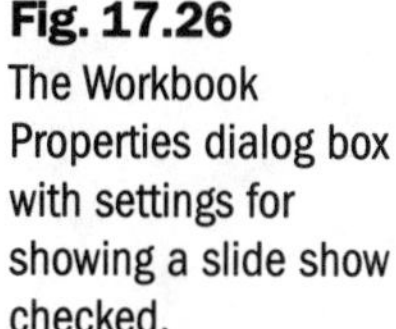

Fig. 17.26
The Workbook Properties dialog box with settings for showing a slide show checked.

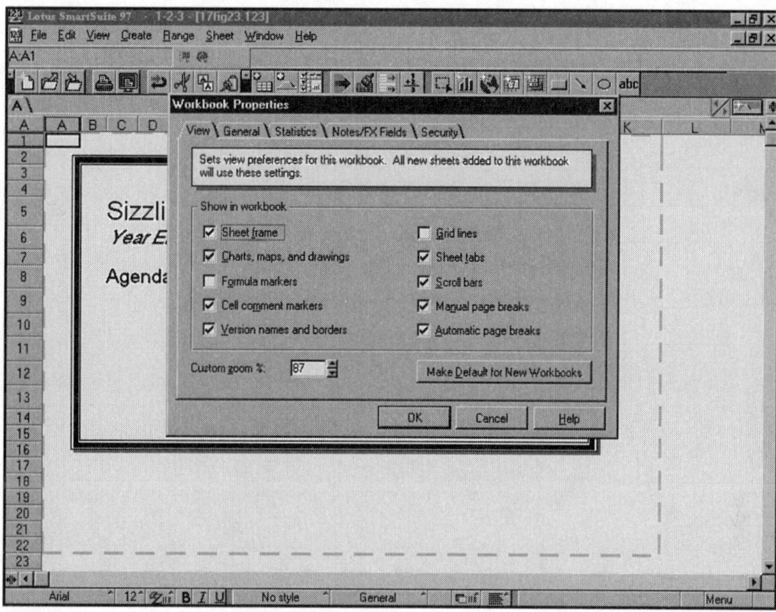

Click the OK button to apply the settings to the current worksheet. These settings are saved for each worksheet file, so open the File menu and choose the Save command to save the settings in the worksheet file.

Figure 17.27 shows what your screen would look like if you set it up the way we described.

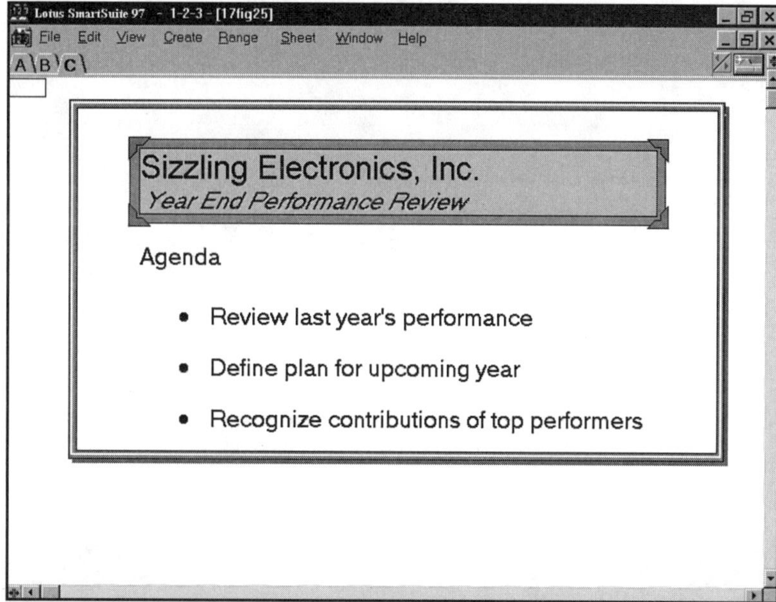

Fig. 17.27
As you can see, hiding the items we described makes your screen most effective for presenting a computerized slide show.

PART IV

Analyzing the Worksheet

CHAPTER 18

Manipulating and Analyzing Data

by Brian Underdahl

In this chapter, you learn key skills for manipulating and analyzing data to develop answers that you and your business want. Whether your data is mainly text, mixed text and numeric values, or totally numeric, you need to know the proper techniques to obtain the answers you need. 1-2-3 offers many powerful methods of analyzing your data—knowing which methods to use will save you much time and effort. ■

Combine text values

Combining text makes it possible to more effectively use data such as the information in an address database.

Combine text and numeric values

Simple techniques enable you to use text and numbers together to provide more meaningful results.

Use formulas that make decisions

Using conditional formulas, you can produce answers which are dependent upon conditions you specify for the input data.

Analyze and obtain data from tables

Select data from tables based on selection criteria.

Create what-if tables

Examine the many possible outcomes produced by a variety of input data.

Manipulating Text

You can combine and manipulate text by using text formulas. Using the text functions discussed in Chapter 6, you can perform powerful manipulations of text data such as finding specified text strings, changing one text string to another, determining the length of a text string, or even converting a numeric value into a text string so it can be combined with other text strings.

You may be surprised to learn that you cannot combine text strings and numeric values directly. 1-2-3 makes a clear distinction between the two types of data—text and numbers. Fortunately, you can easily overcome this problem by using text functions that convert between the two types of data. See "Combining Text and Numbers" later in this chapter for more information on using text and numeric data together.

Combining Text

Text formulas are also often called string formulas, because they work with text strings.

In a single worksheet cell, you can combine text from two or more sources by following these rules:

- Always begin the cell entry with a + (plus sign) to indicate that you are entering a formula.
- Use the & (ampersand), not a plus sign, to combine the different elements of the text string. With the exception of the single plus sign that starts a text formula, the only operator allowed in a text formula is the ampersand.
- If you type any text directly into the formula, enclose the text in " " (double quotes). Include any punctuation or spaces you want included in the string within the quotes as well.
- To include a copy of the text contained in another cell, enter the cell address without quotes (but don't forget the ampersand).

Figure 18.1 shows several examples of combining text using text formulas. For each example, column C shows the result of combining text, and column B shows the text formula which was entered to get the result. Cells B4..B7 contain the text to be combined.

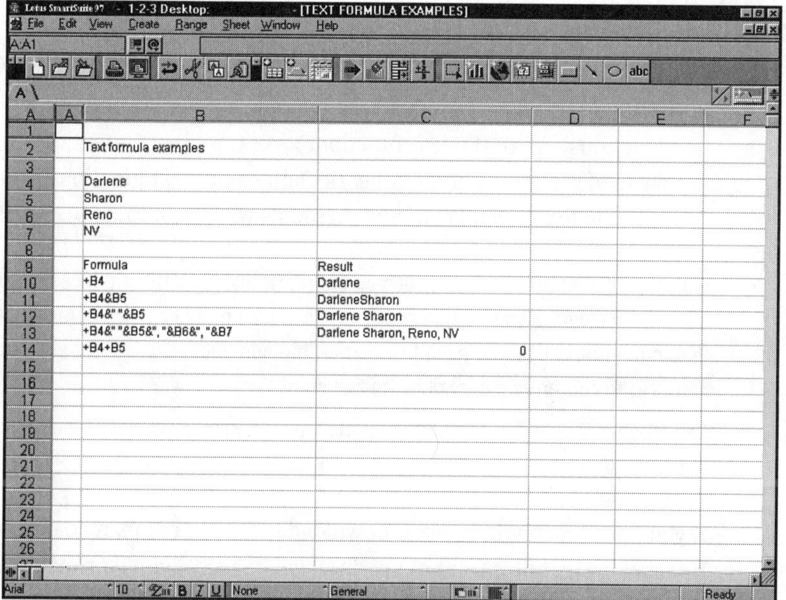

Fig. 18.1
Use text formulas to combine text from different sources.

Cell C10 shows an example of the simplest kind of text formula: a cell address preceded by a plus sign. You use this type of formula to copy the contents of a cell containing text, just as you do to copy the contents of a cell containing a numeric value. You must start the formula with a plus sign so that 1-2-3 understands that you are entering a formula.

Cells C11..C13 show examples of *concatenation*—combining two or more text strings using a text formula. In each case the formula begins with a plus sign and the ampersand is used to combine the text strings.

Notice the difference between the results in rows 11 and 12. To include a space between the two text strings, the formula in cell C12 includes an extra element—a space enclosed in double quotes. Cell C13 takes this idea one step further by including punctuation as well.

The result displayed in cell C14 provides a graphic example of what happens if you attempt to use the plus sign in place of the ampersand to concatenate text strings. Notice that the only difference between the formulas in cells C11 and C14 is the ampersand between the two cell references in C11 and the plus sign in C14. Because the formula in C14 includes a plus sign between the cell references, 1-2-3 interprets the formula as a numeric formula, not a text formula. Since cells B4 and B5 both contain text, the numeric value of both cells is zero (text strings are considered to be equal to zero), so the formula in C14 results in 0.

Changing Text

Of course, 1-2-3 can do more than simply combine text entries. You can use *text functions* in your text formulas to modify text even more (see Chapter 6 for a listing of the major text functions). With the text functions, you can create a text formula that selects or modifies parts of the text in other cells. Because most text functions produce a text result, you can also use text functions in text formulas which combine text strings.

NOTE Some text functions, such as @LENGTH and @VALUE, produce numeric, rather than text results. If you want to combine the results of these types of functions with functions that return text values, you must first convert the numeric results to text strings. You can use @STRING to convert numeric values to text strings.

See Chapter 6 for more information on the types of values you can expect from many of the text functions.

If you use files that have been downloaded from a company database, transferred over the Internet, or text files from many different sources, you'll probably find that the data in those files is not quite ready to use. Mainframe data files, as an example, may store all text in uppercase characters—not exactly the most readable format nor one you're likely to choose for professional looking reports. Fortunately, 1-2-3 provides a broad range of text functions you can use to clean up text regardless of the source. Figure 18.2 demonstrates a few of the 1-2-3 text functions you'll find quite useful.

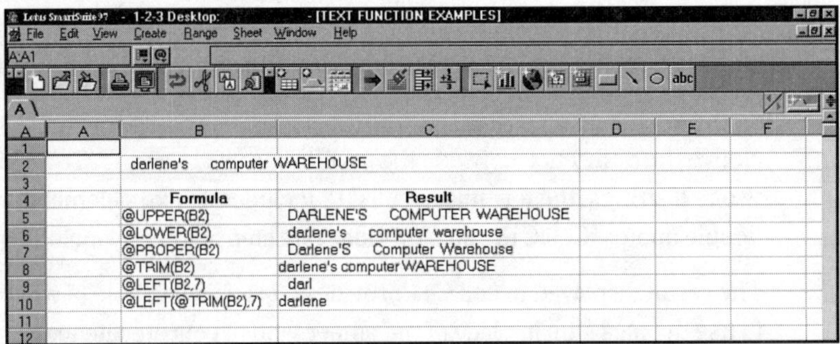

Fig. 18.2 With text functions, you can easily modify text to suit your needs.

In figure 18.2, cell B2 holds a text string which displays several types of problems you may need to solve. The text is partially lowercase, partially uppercase, and includes numerous extra spaces. This example does not cover the complete range of text string problems you may encounter, but it does demonstrate several common ones.

Rows 5, 6, and 7 demonstrate how the @UPPER, @LOWER, and @PROPER functions can be used to standardize the capitalization of a text string. These functions convert a text string to all uppercase, all lowercase, or lowercase with the first letter of each word capitalized.

CAUTION

Notice in figure 18.2 that the @PROPER function in row 7 incorrectly displays "Darlene'S" instead of "Darlene's" as you would expect (both 1-2-3 and Excel exhibit this same error). While it is possible to write a formula using such text functions as @IF, @FIND, and @REPLACE to correct this error, keep in mind that the same error may occur more than once in a text string.

Row 8 demonstrates how you can use the @TRIM function to remove extra spaces from a text string, while rows 9 and 10 show one reason you may need to use this function. In row 9, the leading spaces remain when the @LEFT function displays the first seven characters from the source string. Because @TRIM removes all leading, trailing, and multiple spaces within a text string, combining @LEFT and @TRIM in row 10 produces the desired result.

Combining Text and Numbers

It's often useful to be able to combine text and numbers, but that can be difficult to accomplish since 1-2-3 does not allow the two different types of data to be combined directly. For example, you may want to combine the description of an item along with the sales price of the item. The key to this common task is simple; you must convert any numeric data into a text string before combining the data.

You use the @STRING function to convert numeric data into a text string, which can then be combined with other text strings. Figure 18.3 shows what happens when you try to combine text strings and numeric values. Let's examine each attempt to combine these two types of values to determine how 1-2-3 is arriving at its results.

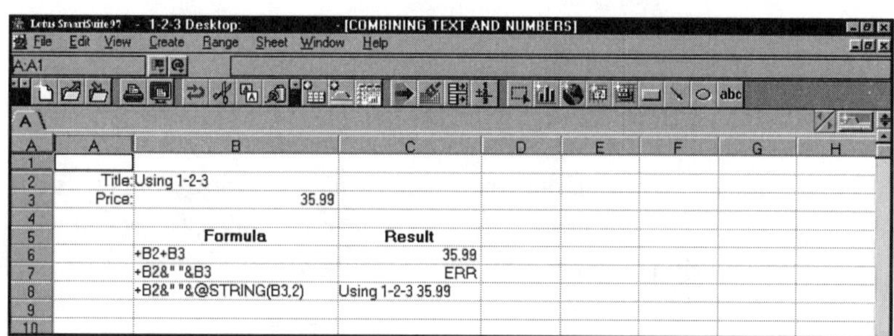

Fig. 18.3 To combine text and numbers correctly, you must first convert the numbers into text strings.

In row 6, an attempt has been made to add the text string in cell B2 to the numeric value in B3 by using a plus sign. The plus sign between the two cell references causes 1-2-3 to treat the formula as a numeric formula rather than a text formula. The result is 35.99, the numeric sum of the two values (remember, labels have a numeric value of zero).

In row 7, an attempt was made to combine the two values as text strings. The ampersand concatenation operator causes 1-2-3 to treat the formula as a text formula, but the result is ERR because cell B3 contains a numeric value, not a text string.

Finally, row 8 has it right. Here we're using @STRING to convert the numeric value in B3 into a text string, which we can then combine with the text string from cell B2. As you can see in cell C8, the result is exactly what we want.

The text functions provide solutions to many problems you'll encounter as you use 1-2-3. Be sure to examine the text functions that are discussed in chapter 6.

Using Formulas to Make Decisions

You may not realize it, but you use formulas to make decisions all the time. When you plan a trip, you probably decide to travel by car for short distances, but by plane for longer distances. When you shop for groceries, you probably decide to buy steaks if they're on sale, and hamburger if the steak is too expensive. These are both examples of using a formula that says "if certain conditions exist, I'll take choice one, otherwise I'll take choice two."

In 1-2-3, you use *logical* functions, such as @IF, to make these same types of decisions. In this section we'll examine some of the uses of the @IF function in making decisions.

▶ **See** "Logical Functions," **p. 194**

The @IF function has three arguments:

- A logical *condition*, which must be either true or false
- The *if-true* value
- The *if-false* value

1-2-3 evaluates the @IF function by first determining whether the *condition* is true or false. In the case of planning a vacation, this condition might be something like "is the trip over 400 miles?" If *condition* is true, the result is the *if-true* value; otherwise, the result is the *if-false* value. Therefore, if the trip is over 400 miles, the result would be that you would travel by air. For shorter trips, you would drive.

To express conditions in @IF functions, you can use any one or more of the logical operators summarized below.

Operator	Description
<	Less than
<=	Less than or equal to
=	Equal to
>=	Greater than or equal to
>	Greater than
<>	Not equal to
#AND#	Used to test two conditions, both of which must be true for the entire test to be true
#OR#	Used to test two conditions; if either condition is true, the entire test condition is true
#NOT#	Used to test that a condition is *not* true

It's generally easier to create and certainly easier to understand @IF functions that use a single logical operator rather than a combination of several operators. When possible, simplify the logical testing as much as possible—that way you'll find it much more straightforward to correct any errors in your formulas.

Using @IF to Analyze Tables of Data

There are many uses for functions such as @IF. Let's have a look at how you can use @IF to analyze data contained in a table. Imagine that you run a small business such as a doctor's office, and you need some method of keeping track of customers who are past due on their payments. Figure 18.4 demonstrates one way you can use the @IF function to analyze your receivables to determine who is behind in their payments.

In this example, column A contains the customer names, column B contains the amounts of their bills, and column C contains the dates of those bills. Column D is the status column, and contains the formulas that determine whether a customer is current or past due. Let's have a closer look at the formula in cell D3:

```
@IF(C3<@TODAY-45,+"$"&@STRING(B3,2)&" past due","Current")
```

This formula starts out by analyzing whether the customer's billing date was 45 or more days before the current date. This condition is specified by the logical test:

```
C3<@TODAY-45
```

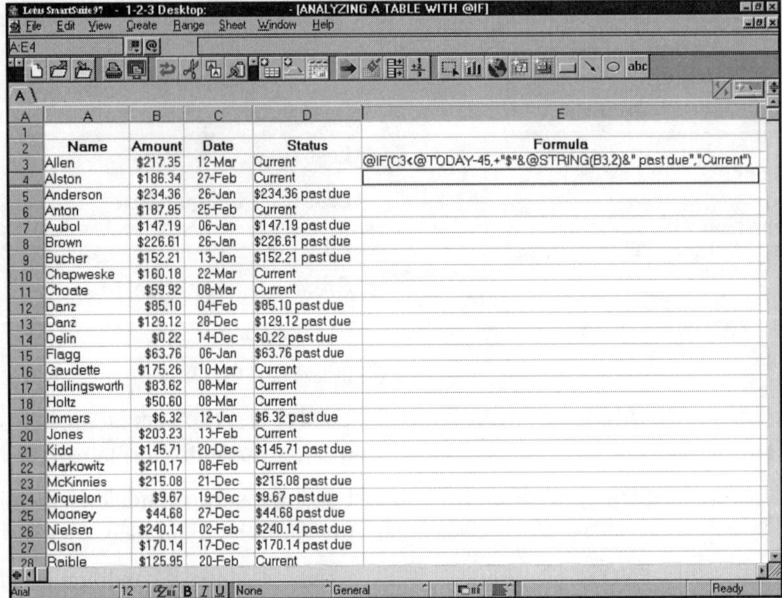

	A	B	C	D	E
1					
2	Name	Amount	Date	Status	Formula
3	Allen	$217.35	12-Mar	Current	@IF(C3<@TODAY-45,+"$"&@STRING(B3,2)&" past due","Current")
4	Alston	$186.34	27-Feb	Current	
5	Anderson	$234.36	26-Jan	$234.36 past due	
6	Anton	$187.95	25-Feb	Current	
7	Aubol	$147.19	06-Jan	$147.19 past due	
8	Brown	$226.61	26-Jan	$226.61 past due	
9	Bucher	$152.21	13-Jan	$152.21 past due	
10	Chapweske	$160.18	22-Mar	Current	
11	Choate	$59.92	08-Mar	Current	
12	Danz	$85.10	04-Feb	$85.10 past due	
13	Danz	$129.12	28-Dec	$129.12 past due	
14	Delin	$0.22	14-Dec	$0.22 past due	
15	Flagg	$63.76	06-Jan	$63.76 past due	
16	Gaudette	$175.26	10-Mar	Current	
17	Hollingsworth	$83.62	08-Mar	Current	
18	Holtz	$50.60	08-Mar	Current	
19	Immers	$6.32	12-Jan	$6.32 past due	
20	Jones	$203.23	13-Feb	Current	
21	Kidd	$145.71	20-Dec	$145.71 past due	
22	Markowitz	$210.17	08-Feb	Current	
23	McKinnies	$215.08	21-Dec	$215.08 past due	
24	Miquelon	$9.67	19-Dec	$9.67 past due	
25	Mooney	$44.68	27-Dec	$44.68 past due	
26	Nielsen	$240.14	02-Feb	$240.14 past due	
27	Olson	$170.14	17-Dec	$170.14 past due	
28	Raible	$125.95	20-Feb	Current	

Fig. 18.4
Use @IF to find customers who are late paying their bills.

If this condition is true—that is, the customer's bill is over 45 days old—the second part of the @IF function provides the result:

```
+"$"&@STRING(B3,2)&" past due"
```

This is simply a text formula which concatenates a dollar sign, the value of the bill, and the words *past due*, to show how much the customer owes. Because the amount of the bill is a numeric value, the @STRING function is used to convert the value into a text string which can be combined with the rest of the string.

If the customer's bill is less than 45 days old, the third part of the @IF function provides the result:

```
"Current"
```

Using Nested @IF Functions

TIP Multiply @IF power and flexibility by using a technique known as *nesting*. Anywhere in an @IF argument where you can place a value, you can instead place a function that delivers a value.

While this simple example certainly tells you which customers are past due, you may want to expand on the idea and provide even more information. For example, while the model does show which customers are 45 or more days past due, you may want a bit more flexibility in dealing with customers. You may want to send a gentle reminder to customers who are 45 days past due, but you may want to send a stronger note to customers who are 90 days past due. The way to accomplish this is to nest an additional @IF function within the first @IF function. For example, you might use the following formula:

```
@IF(C3<@TODAY-45,@IF(C3<@TODAY-90,+"$"&@STRING(B3,2)
➥&" over 90 days past due, start collections process now",+"$"
➥&@STRING(B3,2)&" past due"),"Current")
```

This nested formula really isn't too complex, but let's take a closer look at it to see how you may be surprised by one portion of the new formula. Let's look at the nested @IF function which replaces the second part of the original formula:

```
@IF(C3<@TODAY-90,+"$"&@STRING(B3,2)
➥&" over 90 days past due, start collections process now",+"$"
➥&@STRING(B3,2)&" past due")
```

Notice that the nested @IF function contains the second part of the original formula:

```
+"$"&@STRING(B3,2)&" past due"
```

It's important to understand why this piece of the original function has become a part of the nested function. The nested function is active if the original @IF test is true, that is, if the bill is over 45 days old. But the nested @IF function performs an additional test to see if the bill is also over 90 days old. If this test fails, the nested @IF function must be able to display the "over 45 day but under 90 day" message, so the second part of the original formula must now be the third part of the nested function. You must understand this concept fully in order to create effective formulas which use nested @IF functions. If you're unsure of yourself, create a formula using nested @IF functions and try out different conditions until you're certain you know how these useful functions actually work—you'll be glad you took the time to learn this subject.

Using Functions to Find and Analyze Data in Tables

1-2-3 offers you an extensive set of tools for obtaining and analyzing data in tables. With the functions discussed in chapter 6, you can obtain data contained in tables and develop valuable new information that the tables do not display, through the data-analysis powers of these functions.

As with other tools, you can multiply the power and value of these functions by using them in combination with other tools and powers of 1-2-3. For example, from a giant sales-department data table with many columns of data on sales to every customer, you can extract a concise table of regional sales totals by product line and turn it into a bar graph.

▶ **See** "Lookup Functions," **p. 197**

▶ **See** "Database Functions," **p. 166**

Using Functions to Find Data in Tables

1-2-3 offers you four lookup functions: @HLOOKUP, @VLOOKUP, @INDEX, and @XINDEX. Of these, @XINDEX is the most flexible, and has the very important advantage of permitting you to specify both column and row in whatever headings are most meaningful to you. And compared to @HLOOKUP and @VLOOKUP, @XINDEX also has the advantage of applicability for three-dimensional multi-worksheet tables.

To make effective use of these functions—and also to make your data tables themselves as clear as possible when you and others look at them—you should first make sure that the data table has meaningful headings for both the columns and the rows. Figure 18.5 shows a table with meaningful headings.

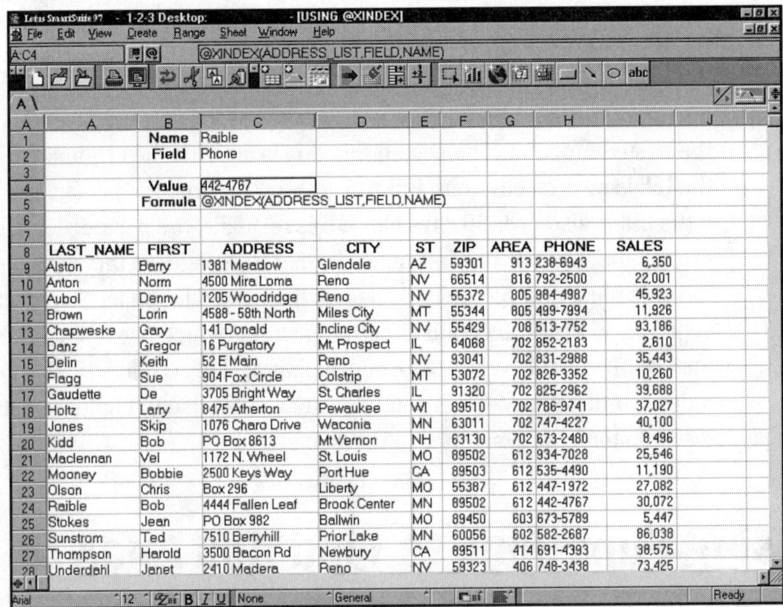

LAST_NAME	FIRST	ADDRESS	CITY	ST	ZIP	AREA	PHONE	SALES
Alston	Barry	1381 Meadow	Glendale	AZ	59301	913	238-6943	6,350
Anton	Norm	4500 Mira Loma	Reno	NV	66514	816	792-2500	22,001
Aubol	Denny	1205 Woodridge	Reno	NV	55372	805	984-4987	45,923
Brown	Lorin	4588 - 58th North	Miles City	MT	55344	805	499-7994	11,926
Chapweske	Gary	141 Donald	Incline City	NV	55429	708	513-7752	93,186
Danz	Gregor	16 Purgatory	Mt. Prospect	IL	64068	702	852-2183	2,610
Delin	Keith	52 E Main	Reno	NV	93041	702	831-2988	35,443
Flagg	Sue	904 Fox Circle	Colstrip	MT	53072	702	826-3352	10,260
Gaudette	De	3705 Bright Way	St. Charles	IL	91320	702	825-2962	39,688
Holtz	Larry	8475 Atherton	Pewaukee	WI	89510	702	786-9741	37,027
Jones	Skip	1076 Charo Drive	Waconia	MN	63011	702	747-4227	40,100
Kidd	Bob	PO Box 8613	Mt Vernon	NH	63130	702	673-2480	8,496
Maclennan	Vel	1172 N. Wheel	St. Louis	MO	89502	612	934-7028	25,546
Mooney	Bobbie	2500 Keys Way	Port Hue	CA	89503	612	535-4490	11,190
Olson	Chris	Box 296	Liberty	MO	55387	612	447-1972	27,082
Raible	Bob	4444 Fallen Leaf	Brook Center	MN	89502	612	442-4767	30,072
Stokes	Jean	PO Box 982	Ballwin	MO	89450	603	673-5789	5,447
Sunstrom	Ted	7510 Berryhill	Prior Lake	MN	60056	602	582-2687	86,038
Thompson	Harold	3500 Bacon Rd	Newbury	CA	89511	414	691-4393	38,575
Underdahl	Janet	2410 Madera	Reno	NV	59323	406	748-3438	73,425

Fig. 18.5
Use the @XINDEX function to get the data from any column and row.

Using @XINDEX to Find Data from a Specified Column and Row Figure 18.5 also demonstrates another very important technique you should always try to work into your 1-2-3 models—flexibility. Notice that rather than "hard coding" information into the formula, the formula refers to cells C1..C2 to see which information you want. By taking this extra step in setting up your worksheet models, you save considerable time when you use them to look up information. If you want Chapweske's address rather than Raible's phone number, all you need to do is enter new information in C1 and C2.

This @XINDEX function entry delivers the contents of a cell in the row titled `Raible` and the column titled `Phone` in range named ADDRESS_LIST.

You can make it easier to use functions with data tables by using range names. Instead of having to determine and type in the table's upper-left and lower-right cell addresses, such as A8..I333, each time you use a function with the table, you can just enter the table's range name. In this example, cell C1 was named NAME and C2 was named FIELD. As a result, the formula is much easier to understand, since it displays range names rather than the more cryptic cell addresses.

You may deal with data tables in which the column headings correspond to the column numbers—1 for first column, 2 for the second, 3 for the third, and so on. Or the row headings may match row numbers. This may be true for both the columns and the rows. Figure 18.6 shows a table of price-discount percentages for a fastener company in which both the column headings and the row headings correspond to the columns' and rows' numbers.

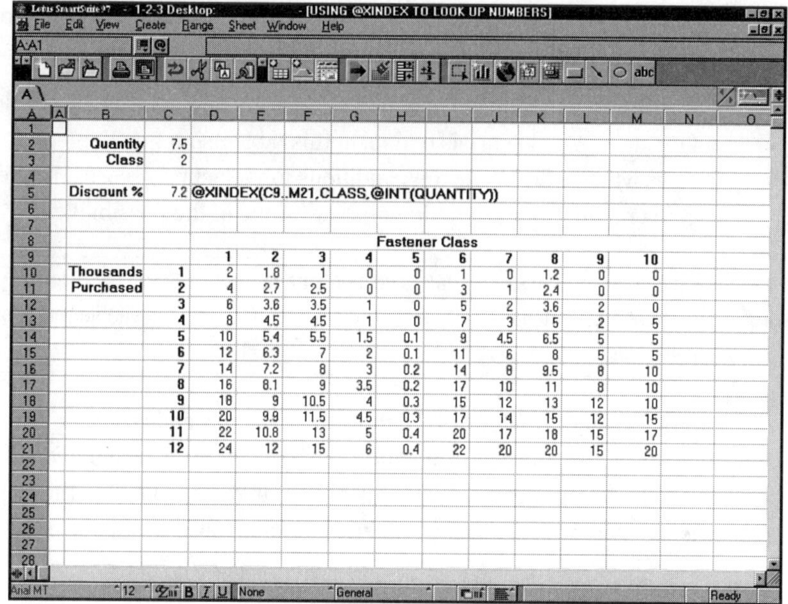

	B	C	D	E	F	G	H	I	J	K	L	M
2	Quantity	7.5										
3	Class	2										
5	Discount %	7.2	@XINDEX(C9..M21,CLASS,@INT(QUANTITY))									
8							Fastener Class					
9			1	2	3	4	5	6	7	8	9	10
10	Thousands	1	2	1.8	1	0	0	1	0	1.2	0	0
11	Purchased	2	4	2.7	2.5	0	0	3	1	2.4	0	0
12		3	6	3.6	3.5	1	0	5	2	3.6	2	0
13		4	8	4.5	4.5	1	0	7	3	5	2	5
14		5	10	5.4	5.5	1.5	0.1	9	4.5	6.5	5	5
15		6	12	6.3	7	2	0.1	11	6	8	5	5
16		7	14	7.2	8	3	0.2	14	8	9.5	8	10
17		8	16	8.1	9	3.5	0.2	17	10	11	8	10
18		9	18	9	10.5	4	0.3	15	12	13	12	10
19		10	20	9.9	11.5	4.5	0.3	17	14	15	12	15
20		11	22	10.8	13	5	0.4	20	17	18	15	17
21		12	24	12	15	6	0.4	22	20	20	15	20

Fig. 18.6
Get data from a column and row with @XINDEX when the columns and rows are numbered 1, 2, 3, and so on.

Notice in figure 18.6 that the @XINDEX function is used differently than in figure 18.5. Rather than simply looking up a matching value for the quantity purchased, the quantity is rounded down to the closest integer by nesting an @INT function in the formula. Unlike @HLOOKUP and @VLOOKUP, @XINDEX only works with an exact match. To make certain @XINDEX returns the correct answer rather than ERR, you must make certain each of the lookup values exactly matches one of the column or row headings—whether those headings are labels or numbers.

Using Functions with Criteria Arguments to Find Data Although the lookup functions are powerful, they're not the only way you can extract useful data from tables. In many cases, it's better to use the database functions, such as @DGET, @DMIN, or @DMAX. In fact, database functions can often be a better choice because a single formula can provide important information about either the entire data set, or about selected records within the table. The key to this power is the way database functions use *criteria* to select specified records. For example, a sales database might have many different records, each recording sales for a specific sales representative. In order that the data be useful in paying out commissions, you'd probably want to know the total sales for each sales representative, not just the total of all sales.

When using @XINDEX (or other lookup functions), the arguments you specify are range (table), column, and row. With the database functions, the first two arguments are also range (table) and column (which database functions call field). But the third argument is not row—it is *criteria*, which you can define as a test of the contents of any cell in any column of rows, and in which you can use logical operators.

Figure 18.7 shows a table in which a company maintains current sales-related records. As a first step toward analysis of data in this table using functions, you should create criteria ranges which will specify the conditions for selecting records. In this case, three different criteria ranges are used to demonstrate some of the possibilities.

Even though you can specify data selection criteria within a database function, you should always create separate criteria ranges as shown in figure 18.7. This will enable you to quickly set new criteria without the need to edit your formulas.

Rows 3, 4, and 5 of figure 18.7 show the formulas and results of using @DGET, @DMIN, and @DMAX to analyze the data. Notice that in each case the formula refers to a criteria range to determine which records to select. You can include the criteria argument within the formula, as in the following line, but doing so is very poor practice:

```
@DGET(TABLE1,"SALESMAN",PRODUCT1>60000)
```

The reason for this is simple; if you need to change the criteria and you've included the criteria in the formula, you must edit the formula—risking the great possibility that you'll introduce an error which won't be easily discovered or corrected. When the selection criteria are specified in the formula itself, you can only see the criteria when the formula itself is highlighted. If you use a criteria range, it's easy to see what criteria were specified. It's also much easier to change the criteria, since all you have to do is enter your new criteria in the criteria range.

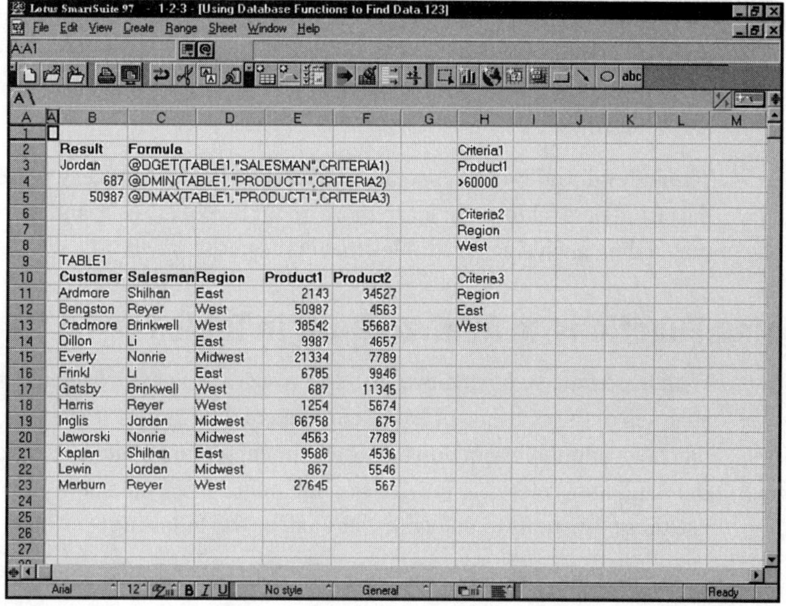

	B	C	D	E	F	G	H
1							
2	**Result**	**Formula**					Criteria1
3	Jordan	@DGET(TABLE1,"SALESMAN",CRITERIA1)					Product1
4	687	@DMIN(TABLE1,"PRODUCT1",CRITERIA2)					>60000
5	50987	@DMAX(TABLE1,"PRODUCT1",CRITERIA3)					
6							Criteria2
7							Region
8							West
9	TABLE1						
10	**Customer**	**Salesman**	**Region**	**Product1**	**Product2**		Criteria3
11	Ardmore	Shilhan	East	2143	34527		Region
12	Bengston	Reyer	West	50987	4563		East
13	Cradmore	Brinkwell	West	38542	55687		West
14	Dillon	Li	East	9987	4657		
15	Everly	Nonrie	Midwest	21334	7789		
16	Frinkl	Li	East	6785	9946		
17	Gatsby	Brinkwell	West	687	11345		
18	Harris	Reyer	West	1254	5674		
19	Inglis	Jordan	Midwest	66758	675		
20	Jaworski	Nonrie	Midwest	4563	7789		
21	Kaplan	Shilhan	East	9586	4536		
22	Lewin	Jordan	Midwest	867	5546		
23	Marburn	Reyer	West	27645	567		

Fig. 18.7
Get data from data table cells with functions using criteria.

To create a criteria range, place the field name in the top row, and the selection criteria in the row immediately below. If you want more than one value to be acceptable, you specify the values in different rows of the criteria range such as in Criteria3 in figure 18.7. This type of selection is a logical OR, since the value in either H12 OR the value in H13 are acceptable.

This @DGET example is a basic illustration of the power of database function criteria that you can apply very quickly and easily. You may, however, encounter a problem using @DGET if your selection criteria do not result in a unique result. @DGET must be able to find one record, but only one record that matches the specified selection criteria. If either no records, or more than one record matches the selection criteria, @DGET cannot determine which record to select, and displays ERR to indicate an error. For example, if you were to specify either >70000 or >50000 as the selection criteria, @DGET would show ERR as the answer.

In database functions which return numeric values, such as the @DMIN function, multiple matching records are not a problem, because the function will still return the correct answer. Therefore the criteria argument does not have to be narrow enough to designate a single record. If the table in figure 18.7 had several records with sales of 687 for Product1, the answer displayed in cell B4 would still be 687. Similarly, the @DMAX function delivers the largest value in the set of records defined by its arguments.

In the @DMAX example in figure 18.7 row 5, the criteria argument has two tests joined by the OR operator in the range Criteria3. This selection includes items from all the rows where either of these two tests is met—in this case, it includes data from both East rows and West rows.

Through full and creative use of criteria, you can develop very powerful abilities to extract data from data tables. You learn more about use of criteria, and see more examples, in the material on analyzing data tables that comes next.

Using Functions to Analyze Data in Tables

With the database functions that 1-2-3 provides, you can very quickly and easily perform analyses of the contents of entire columns of data tables. (For basic information on these functions and their common trio of arguments—range, field, criteria—see Chapter 6 and the @function reference in 1-2-3's online help.) For a data table column (field), you can use these functions to determine or analyze the following:

Number of items	@DCOUNT delivers total item-count.
	@DPURECOUNT counts the records that actually contain values.
Total of values	@DSUM delivers total of values.
Average of values	@DAVG delivers average of values.
Statistical analysis of values	@DSTD and @DSTDS deliver standard deviation of values, and @DVAR and @DVARS deliver variance of values. You use @DSTD and @DVAR if the data includes all of the values, and @DSTDS or @DVARS if the data includes only samples of the entire set.

These functions provide you with tools for very quick and easy access to data-field analysis answers that could otherwise require much more work to get. By making multiple use of these functions for data analysis reports, and by using these functions in combination with other powers of 1-2-3, you can use these functions to develop fullest business information value from data tables. Figure 18.8 shows a variation on the data analysis themes shown in figure 18.7. By simply replacing the function names in the formulas, and adjusting the values in the criteria ranges, entirely different data analysis functions were quickly added to the model. In the next section you'll learn how to perform even more sophisticated types of analysis by using what-if tables.

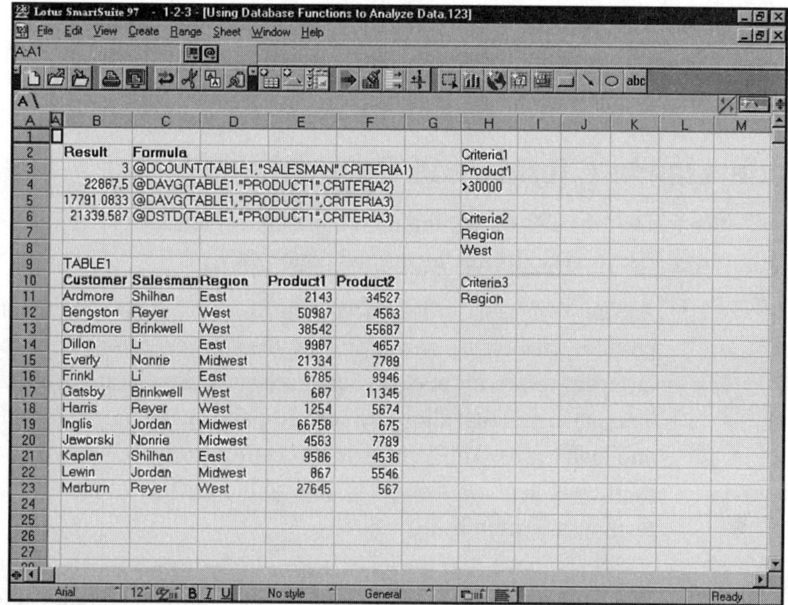

	B	C	D	E	F	H
2	Result	Formula				Criteria1
3	3	@DCOUNT(TABLE1,"SALESMAN",CRITERIA1)				Product1
4	22867.5	@DAVG(TABLE1,"PRODUCT1",CRITERIA2)				>30000
5	17791.0833	@DAVG(TABLE1,"PRODUCT1",CRITERIA3)				
6	21339.587	@DSTD(TABLE1,"PRODUCT1",CRITERIA3)				Criteria2
7						Region
8						West
9	TABLE1					
10	Customer	Salesman	Region	Product1	Product2	Criteria3
11	Ardmore	Shilhan	East	2143	34527	Region
12	Bengston	Reyer	West	50987	4563	
13	Cradmore	Brinkwell	West	38542	55687	
14	Dillon	Li	East	9987	4657	
15	Everly	Nonrie	Midwest	21334	7789	
16	Frinkl	Li	East	6785	9946	
17	Gatsby	Brinkwell	West	687	11345	
18	Harris	Reyer	West	1254	5674	
19	Inglis	Jordan	Midwest	66758	675	
20	Jaworski	Nonrie	Midwest	4563	7789	
21	Kaplan	Shilhan	East	9586	4536	
22	Lewin	Jordan	Midwest	867	5546	
23	Marburn	Reyer	West	27645	567	

Fig. 18.8
Analyze data in tables using database functions.

Creating What-If Tables

Of all the powers offered by 1-2-3 and all the things it enables or helps you do, the greatest potential value to businesses may be what-if analysis to explore future possibilities. By using formulas that calculate key results (such as profit and cash flow) for various combinations of things a business decides (such as a marketing plan) and predicts (such as resulting sales), and then changing numbers to explore what-ifs, a business can do better at choosing the key decisions that promise the best for the future, and at preparing for what the results may be.

What-if analysis can also be quite useful in helping you make personal financial decisions, such as home and auto purchase and financing, stock and other investments, and overall financial planning. There's no reason you shouldn't benefit from the same tools and techniques used by successful businesses when doing your personal financial planning!

For summarizing maximum what-if power most concisely and clearly, one of the most useful of all the tools offered by 1-2-3 is the what-if table. In a what-if table, you can see the effects on one or more goal-results (such as profit and cash flow) of numerous possibilities for one key factor (such as sales); or you can see effects on one goal-result (such as profit) of many possible combinations of two or three key factors (such as sales, cost-per-unit, and advertising expense).

Creating what-if tables is a straightforward process as long as you understand the basics. We'll start by defining the terms used with what-if tables, and then go on to create several different examples.

Understanding Terms and Concepts

To follow the rules for setting up the worksheet for use of the What-if dialog box, you need to understand some terms and concepts:

- A *what-if table* is a table in a worksheet which shows you a number of different possible results. These varying results are generated using combinations of different values for one, two, or three variables. As an example, consider a table of loan payments that shows what your payment would be for different interest rates and loan terms. The term "what-if" comes from the way you use the table—you might wonder "*what* would be my payment *if* the interest rate was 8 percent and the term was 60 months?"
- A *what-if table range* is a worksheet range that contains a what-if table. You don't actually have to create a range name for your what-if table, but you'll probably find your formulas are easier to understand and audit if you create range names for all variables you use with your what-if table.
- A *variable* is a formula component whose value can change. In a loan what-if table, these would include the interest rate, the term, and possibly the loan amount.
- An *input cell* is a worksheet cell used by 1-2-3 for temporary storage of the variable values during calculation of a what-if table. One input cell is required for each variable in the what-if table formula. Input cells should have range names which will then appear in the formulas.
- An *input value* is a specific value that 1-2-3 uses for a variable during the what-if table calculations.
- The *results area* is the portion of a what-if table in which the calculation results are placed. One result is generated for each combination of input values. The results area of a what-if table must be unprotected, so that 1-2-3 can place the results in the table. The values generated by the what-if and placed in the results area are static. To see the effects of changing some of the what-if conditions, you must generate a new set of values using the Range, Analyze, What-if Table command.

The formulas used in what-if tables can contain values, strings, cell addresses, and functions. You should not use logical formulas because this type of formula always evaluates to either 0 or 1. Although the use of a logical formula in a what-if table does not cause an error, the results generally are meaningless.

Understanding the Three Types of What-If Tables

With the What-if dialog box, there are three types of what-if tables that 1-2-3 can generate. The three table types differ in the numbers of formulas and variables they can reflect. Descriptions of the table types follow:

1 variable	For various values of one variable, shows resulting values of one or more formulas. A 1 variable what-if table is the only type of what-if table which can show the results of more than one formula in a single table.
2 variables	For various combinations of values of two variables, shows resulting values of one formula.
3 variables	For various combinations of values of three variables, shows resulting values of one formula.

Each type of what-if table serves a slightly different purpose. 1 variable what-if tables can show you several related types of analysis of the same data using a variety of formulas. 2 and 3 variable what-if tables use a single formula to produce either a 2- or 3-dimensional results table, depending on the number of variables.

Creating a 1 Variable What-If Table

A 1 variable what-if table shows how changing one variable affects the results of one or more formulas. This type of what-if table is uniquely suited to showing more than one type of analysis of the same data. 1 variable what-if tables provide you the opportunity to see how results from the same data affect the outcome of different formulas.

If your data analysis consists primarily of examining the effects of two or more changing factors, i.e., interest rate and term, using the same formula, you'll find it easier and quicker to use 2 or 3 variable what-if tables rather than several copies of the same formula in a 1 variable what-if table.

Let's have a look at how you can use a 1 variable what-if table to analyze the payments on a loan. Suppose you want to know what part of each of your loan payments is going toward interest and how much of the principal is being paid off with each payment. These are two related calculations that clearly show the value of a 1 variable what-if table.

Begin by setting up your worksheet as shown in figure 18.9. Both the @IPAYMT function for calculating the interest portion of a payment and the @PPAYMT function for calculating the principal portion of a payment use the same four arguments: principal, interest rate, loan term, and payment number. In this example, the first three arguments are static—they remain the same throughout the loan term. The payment number is the variable, because you want to know how the interest and principal portion of your payments vary over the life of the loan. Therefore, the input cell will take the place of the payment number argument in the formulas.

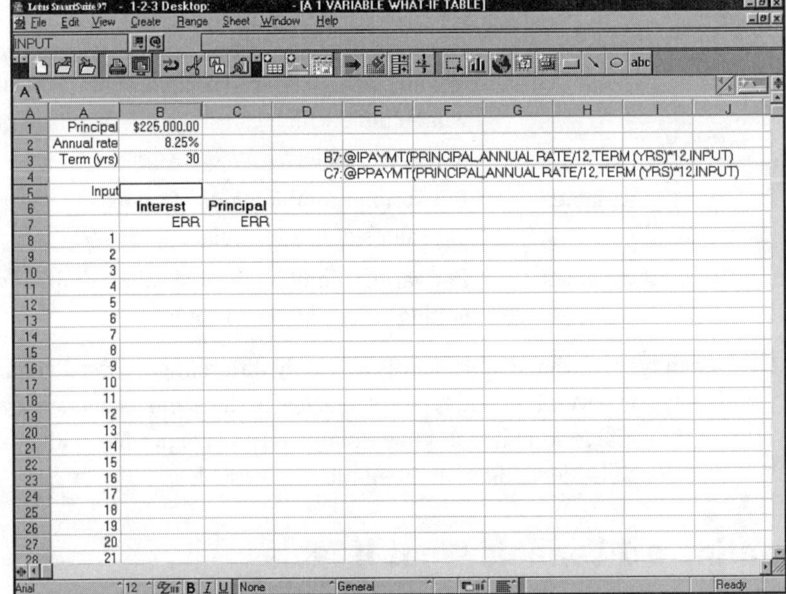

Fig. 18.9
Set up a 1 variable what-if table by making worksheet entries including the formulas in the top row of the table.

Notice that cells B7..C7 show ERR. Because the required payment number argument is blank, these formulas will always display ERR, but this has no effect on the calculations. Here are the two formulas that are actually entered in these cells:

```
B7: @IPAYMT(PRINCIPAL,ANNUAL RATE/12,TERM (YRS)*12,INPUT)
C7: @PPAYMT(PRINCIPAL,ANNUAL RATE/12,TERM (YRS)*12,INPUT)
```

Cells B1..B3, and B5 were all named using the Range, Name, Use labels command so that range names, rather than cell addresses, would appear in the formulas. Also, remember to divide the annual interest rate by 12 to obtain the correct monthly interest rate, and multiply the number of years by 12 to obtain the correct term in months. If your loan has different payment terms, make certain you adjust both of these arguments correctly to reflect the actual loan terms. You'll probably want to use the correct principal, interest rate, and term for your loan rather than the sample figures shown in the figure.

Once you have set up your worksheet, select the Range, Analyze, What-if Table command to display the What-if dialog box as shown in figure 18.10.

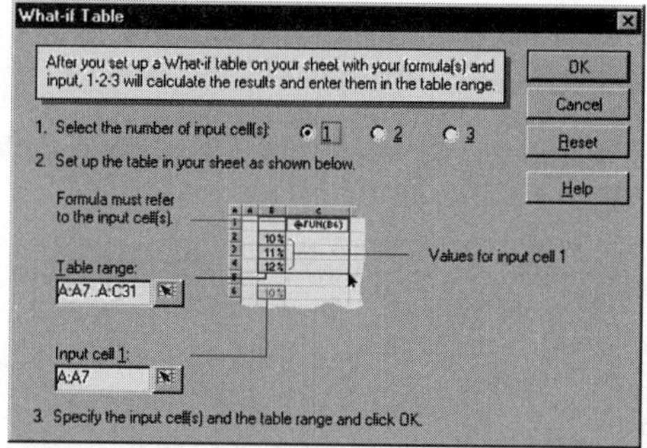

Fig. 18.10
Use the What-if dialog box to define your 1 variable what-if table.

To use the What-if dialog box, start by specifying the number of variables—in this case, 1. Next, specify the Input cell 1, which 1-2-3 will use as it calculates the results. Remember, this is the blank cell referred to by each of the formulas as the location of the missing argument. 1-2-3 will substitute the values in the leftmost column of the what-if table for the value of the input cell as it generates the table results. Specify the cell addresses or range name for the what-if table in the Table range list box. Select OK to generate the what-if table results.

Figure 18.11 shows the what-if table after the results area has been formatted to more clearly show the information. If you don't apply an appropriate numeric format to the results, the table will be quite difficult to understand. See Chapter 4, "Formatting Worksheets," for more information on applying formats.

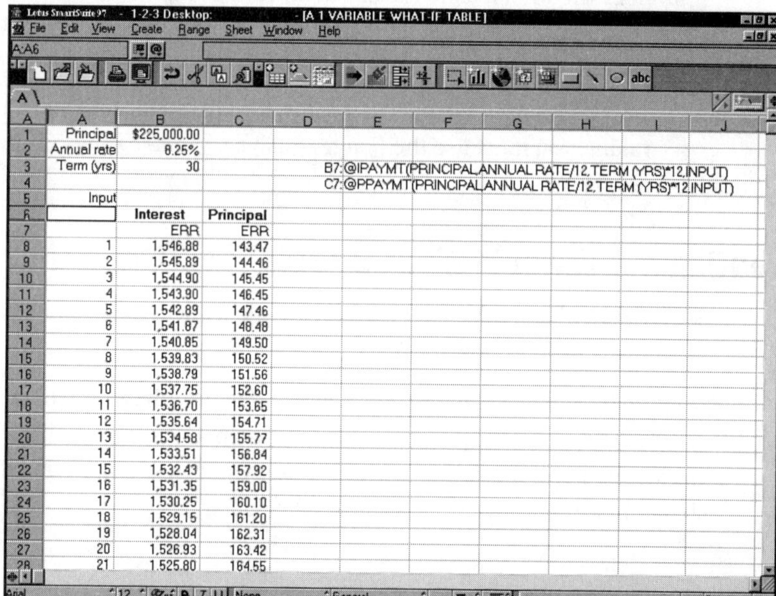

	A	B	C
1	Principal	$225,000.00	
2	Annual rate	8.25%	
3	Term (yrs)	30	
4			
5	Input		
6		Interest	Principal
7		ERR	ERR
8	1	1,546.88	143.47
9	2	1,545.89	144.46
10	3	1,544.90	145.45
11	4	1,543.90	146.45
12	5	1,542.89	147.46
13	6	1,541.87	148.48
14	7	1,540.85	149.50
15	8	1,539.83	150.52
16	9	1,538.79	151.56
17	10	1,537.75	152.60
18	11	1,536.70	153.65
19	12	1,535.64	154.71
20	13	1,534.58	155.77
21	14	1,533.51	156.84
22	15	1,532.43	157.92
23	16	1,531.35	159.00
24	17	1,530.25	160.10
25	18	1,529.15	161.20
26	19	1,528.04	162.31
27	20	1,526.93	163.42
28	21	1,525.80	164.55

Fig. 18.11
The completed 1 variable what-if table (after formatting) shows two related analyses of the loan.

You can set up the kind of table shown in these figures using the What-if dialog box by following rules and procedures described next.

Before using the What-if dialog box, you must set up the what-if table range and a single input cell.

The input cell can be a blank cell anywhere in the worksheet. The best practice is to identify the input cell by entering an appropriate label either above or to the left of the input cell.

The what-if table range is a rectangular worksheet area that can be placed in any empty worksheet location. The size of the what-if table range can be calculated as follows:

- The range has one more column than the number of formulas being evaluated (the leftmost column contains the values of the variable).
- The range has one more row than the number of input values being evaluated (the top row contains the formulas).

The general structure of a 1 variable what-if table range is as follows:

- The top-left cell in the what-if table range is empty.
- The formulas to be evaluated are entered across the first row. Each formula must refer to the input cell.
- The input values to be plugged into the formulas are entered down the first column.
- After the what-if table is calculated, each cell in the results range contains the result obtained by evaluating the formula at the top of that column with the input value at the left of that row.
- 1-2-3 does not place formulas in the results range, so if you change any of the input values, you must use the Range, Analyze, What-if Table, OK command to generate new results.

Creating a 2 Variable What-If Table

A 2 variable what-if table enables you to evaluate a single formula based on changes in two variables.

Suppose that you want to create a what-if table that shows the monthly payments on a $12,000 loan at several interest rates and loan periods. Figure 18.12 shows the worksheet entries you make to create a table of these results using the What-if dialog box and also shows the results after you have used the dialog box.

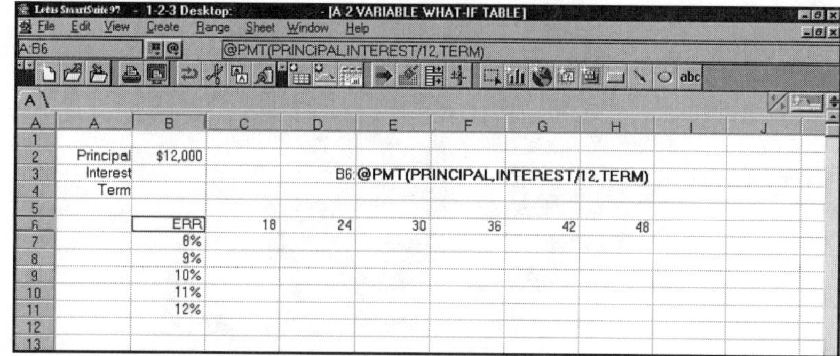

Fig. 18.12
Set up the worksheet for a 2 variable what-if table.

To create the 2 variable what-if table, you carry out the following steps:

To use a 2 variable what-if table, you need two blank input cells—one for each variable. They can be located anywhere in the worksheet and need not be adjacent to each other. In this example, cells B3 and B4 are the input cells, and they are labeled to show their purpose in the worksheet.

The size of the what-if table range depends on the number of values of each variable you want to evaluate. The range is one column wider than the number of values of one variable and one row longer than the number of values of the other variable.

A major difference between a 1 variable and a 2 variable what-if table is the location of the formula to be evaluated. In a 1 variable table, the formulas are placed along the top row of the table, and the upper-left corner is blank. In a 2 variable what-if table, the upper-left cell of the what-if table range contains the single formula to be evaluated. This formula must refer to the input cells.

The Input cell **1** text box specifies the input cell that will use the values in the column below the formula. The Input cell **2** text box specifies the input cell that will use the values in the row to the right of the formula. In this case, Input cell **1** specifies the values for interest, and Input cell **2** specifies the values for term. Be sure that the formula refers correctly to the two input cells so that the proper input values are plugged into the correct part of the formula. Figure 18.13 shows the completed What-if dialog box for a 2 variable what-if table.

Once you have completed the entries in the What-if dialog box, select OK to generate the table of results. Apply an appropriate numeric format to make the data more understandable. Figure 18.14 shows the completed 2 variable what-if table.

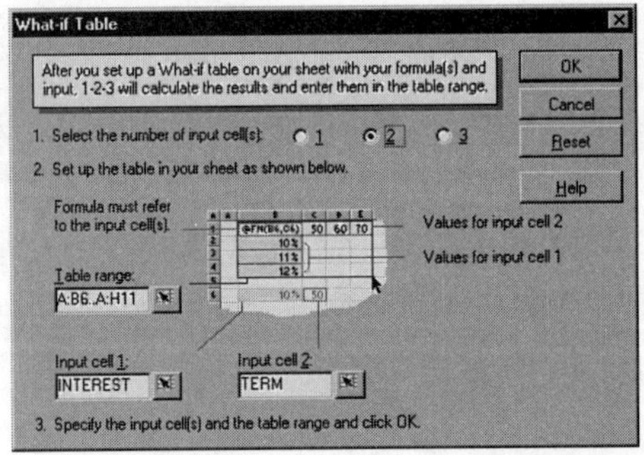

Fig. 18.13
The completed What-if dialog box for a 2 variable what-if table includes two input cells, one for each variable.

Lotus SmartSuite 97 - 1-2-3 Desktop: - [A 2 VARIABLE WHAT-IF TABLE]

File Edit View Create Range Sheet Window Help

A:B6 @PMT(PRINCIPAL,INTEREST/12,TERM)

A	A	B	C	D	E	F	G	H	I	J
1										
2	Principal	$12,000								
3	Interest				B6:@PMT(PRINCIPAL,INTEREST/12,TERM)					
4	Term									
5										
6		ERR	18	24	30	36	42	48		
7		8%	709.68	542.73	442.66	376.04	328.52	292.96		
8		9%	715.17	548.22	448.18	381.60	334.13	298.62		
9		10%	720.68	553.74	453.74	387.21	339.80	304.35		
10		11%	726.22	559.29	459.34	392.86	345.53	310.15		
11		12%	731.78	564.88	464.98	398.57	351.31	316.01		
12										
13										

Fig. 18.14
Use an appropriate numeric format to make the completed 2 variable what-if table easier to understand.

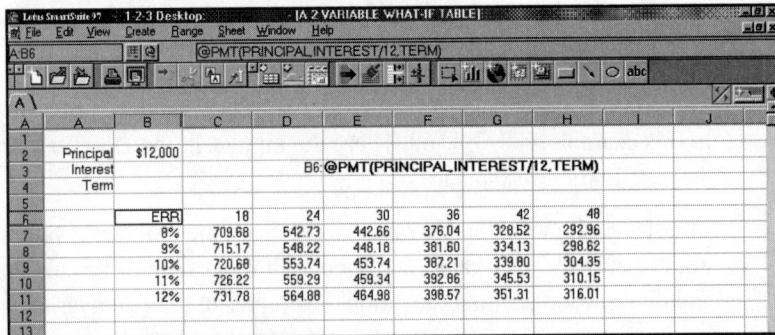

After the what-if table is calculated, each cell in the table range contains the result obtained by evaluating the formula with the input values in that cell's row and column. In figure 18.14, for example, cell F9 contains the value for a loan payment using a 10 percent interest rate and a 36-month term.

Creating a 3 Variable What-If Table

A 3 variable what-if table shows the effects of changing three variables in a single formula. The three dimensions of a 3 variable what-if table are represented by a three-dimensional worksheet range: the table spans two or more worksheets.

Calculating loan payments is a perfect application for a 3 variable what-if table because the relevant formula uses three variables: principal, interest rate, and term. You can create a what-if table that calculates monthly payments for several principal amounts, interest rates, and loan periods.

The structure of a 3 variable what-if table is an extension of the 2 variable what-if table structure. But just as the 2 variable what-if table has a different layout than the 1 variable what-if table, so too does the 3 variable what-if table differ from the other two types. In a 3 variable what-if table, the values of the third variable are located in the upper-left corners of the what-if table range; the different values of the third variable are each located on different worksheets.

A 3 variable what-if table range spans a three-dimensional region. The size of the region is determined as follows:

Number of rows = (values of variable 1) + 1

Number of columns = (values of variable 2) + 1

Number of worksheets = (values of variable 3)

You also need three input cells. These cells can be located anywhere in any worksheet but are often grouped together for convenience. You should identify the input cells with labels in adjacent cells, and use those labels to create range names which will then appear in the formula.

The formula evaluated in a 3 variable what-if table must correctly refer to all three input cells. When you fill out the What-if dialog box, the Input cell **1** text box refers to the values in the first column of the what-if table range. Input cell **2** refers to the values in the first row of the what-if table range. Input cell **3** refers to the values in the upper-left corners of the what-if table range in each worksheet.

Figure 18.15 shows a simple example of a 3 variable what-if table. The three input cells, A:B1..B3, have been given descriptive names using the Range, Name, Use labels command. The formula in cell A:D2 is displayed in the Text Formula format; otherwise, the formula would display ERR since it refers to the three blank input cells.

To establish a 3 variable what-if table range similar to the one shown in figure 18.15, follow these steps:

Insert the additional worksheet you need for this application by selecting Create, Sheet and entering the number of new worksheets you need using the Number of sheets spin control. You'll need one worksheet for each value of the third variable. Select OK.

If you want to view more than one worksheet at the same time, move the cell selector down to slightly below the last row of the what-if table, and select View, Split, Top-Bottom, and click OK to view the active worksheets. If you have more than two values for the third variable, you may prefer to use the Four-way split option. If your what-if table is quite large, it may be more sensible to simply view one worksheet at a time, and move to the remaining worksheets as necessary.

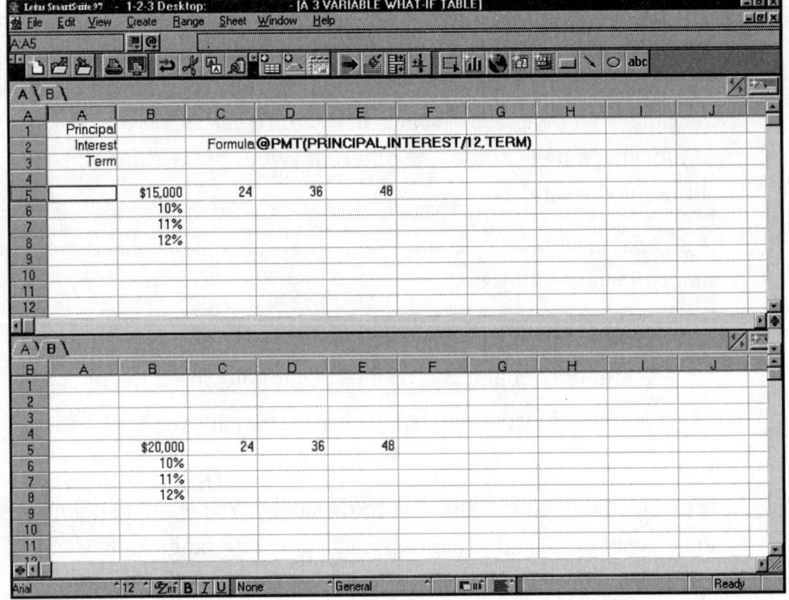

Fig. 18.15 Set up your worksheets for creating a 3 variable what-if table by including one worksheet for each value of the third variable.

Enter labels for the three input cells and then use the Range, Name, Use labels command to name the cells. Enter the formula in a cell outside the what-if table range. In this case, the formula calculates loan payments based on the three variables:

```
@PMT(PRINCIPAL,INTEREST/12,TERM)
```

Next, create the basic what-if table by entering the values for the first variable in the first column of the what-if table range. Enter the values for the second variable in the top row of the range. For now, leave the upper-left corner blank—this is where you'll soon place the values for the third variable. Select the what-if table, and then use Edit, Copy to copy the table to the Clipboard. Select the upper-left corner of the what-if table range in each of the remaining worksheets (click the first destination cell, hold down the Shift key, and click the final destination cell to select more than one worksheet at a time) and the select Edit, Paste to place identical copies of the what-if table in each worksheet.

Place one of the values for the third variable in the upper-left corner of each of the what-if tables contained on the different worksheets. You are now ready to select Range, Analyze, What-if Table and specify the locations of the what-if table elements. Figure 18.16 shows the What-if dialog box with each of the elements specified correctly for the what-if table shown in figure 18.15.

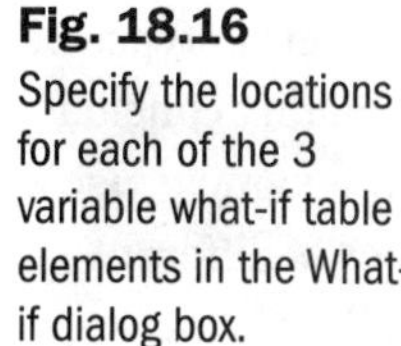

Fig. 18.16
Specify the locations for each of the 3 variable what-if table elements in the What-if dialog box.

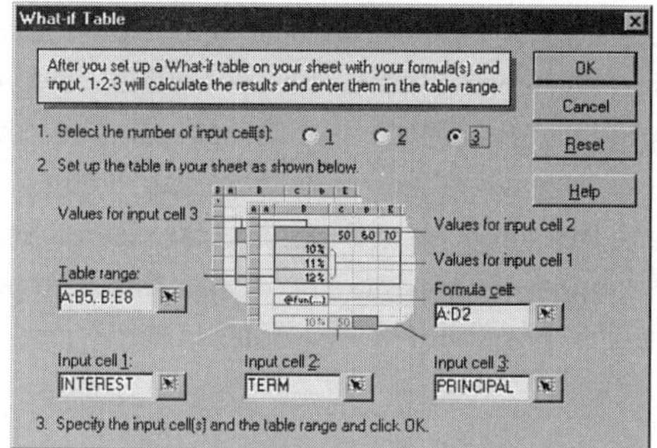

Notice that the 3 variable what-if table requires two additional entries in the What-if dialog box. Input cell 3 and the Formula Cell must be specified for a 3 variable what-if table. Remember that the input cell text boxes refer to the input cells referred to by the formula, not to the actual cells containing the values for the variables.

Once you have completed all the entries in the What-if dialog box, select OK to generate the what-if table results and return to the worksheet. Figure 18.17 shows the completed 3 variable what-if table.

Fig. 18.17
The 3 variable what-if table has separate what-if tables on each worksheet in the workbook.

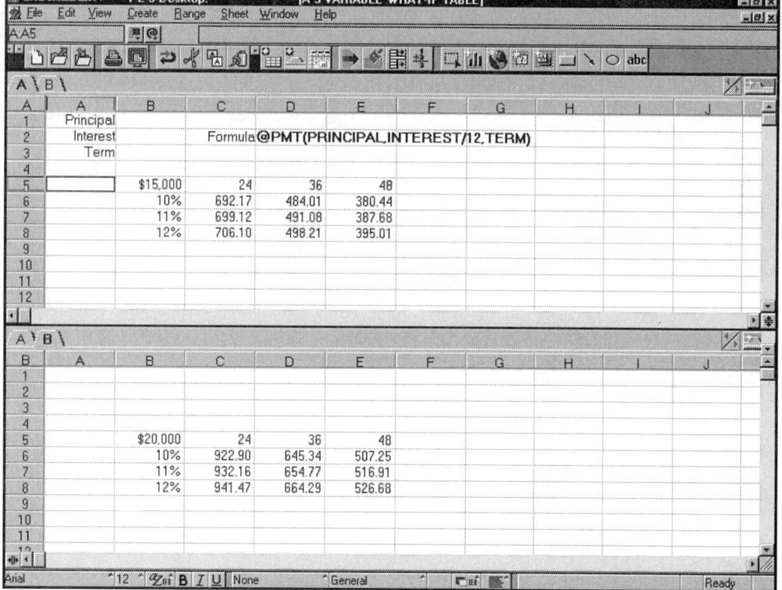

What-if tables are powerful analytical tools you can use to examine many different types of problems. In this chapter you've seen a few of the possibilities, but you shouldn't conclude that these examples showed all possible uses for these tools. You could, for example, use a 1 variable what-if table to analyze scientific experiment data using a number of different types of formulas applied to the same set of experimental results. You could use 2 or 3 variable what-if tables to examine the potential profits for different products based on sales and cost projections. The possibilities are endless. ●

CHAPTER 19

Linking and Consolidating Worksheets

by Brian Underdahl

Information comes from many different sources, and it is seldom packaged in a ready to use format. To use the information effectively, you must be able to link to the sources of information and consolidate your data. In 1-2-3, information sources are usually worksheets. In essentially the same way that you can relate data in different cells in a worksheet, you can relate data in cells of different worksheets, not only within a workbook but also in worksheets of different files. ■

Use multiple worksheets and files

Organize information in the most efficient way possible using the 3-dimensional capabilities of 1-2-3.

Enter formulas that link worksheets and files

Connect to the sources of information to report on widely scattered data.

Combine and consolidate worksheets

You can use information produced by outside sources, such as other departments or divisions.

Why Use Multiple Worksheets and Files?

1-2-3 uses the term *worksheet* to denote a single page in a *workbook*. All of the worksheets in a workbook are saved in a single *file*. Each worksheet is two-dimensional—you can move up and down rows, or left and right across columns. When you add additional worksheets to a workbook, you begin working in three dimensions—you can now move between pages, too. For most worksheet applications, you can multiply your worksheet power by using multiple worksheets and, in some cases, files.

By going beyond the standard two-dimensional worksheet view, thinking of your worksheets and your projects in 3-D, you can improve every quality of your spreadsheet work, from data organization to analysis to management and information control.

Think about how worksheet value is multiplied by the second dimension. With a single dimension (columns), spreadsheet use is limited; adding the second dimension (rows) truly multiplies spreadsheet value. With multiple worksheets, you add a third dimension to multiply power and value again. For your work on larger data systems and analyses, going from two dimensions to three can be as valuable as going from one to two.

To use the most important capability of worksheets—relating items of data through formulas—in a single 2-D worksheet you use cell references to reach left to right and up and down to locate a data item. You reach left and right with column letters, and up and down with row numbers. In the same way, by including worksheet and file specifications in references to data items, you can extend your reach from two dimensions to three.

In addition, for any project or body of information, the third dimension of multiple worksheets and files gives you powers of organization and management that single-worksheet columns and rows do not provide. When you use the third dimension, you can organize and control the project or information by creating separate worksheet files, a 3-D set of worksheets in a single workbook file, or multiple 3-D sets of worksheets grouped in separate files.

When Should You Use Multiple Worksheets and Files?

Types of work in which you can gain major benefits by using multiple worksheets include the following:

For fullest display of multiple worksheets and files, choose View, Set View Preferences and eliminate unneeded screen items. (For display of linked files, however, keep the status bar. See "Updating and Recalculating File Links" later in this chapter.) Depending on the size of your monitor, you may also want to adjust the zoom level to a lower value.

- *Multiple similar reports.* If you are dealing with numerous identical-format reports, such as reports for several products or divisions of a company or reports for a sequence of months, using a separate worksheet for each report enables you to organize and handle the reports easily. For example, you can give each report item the same address in every report worksheet, such as C3 for each product's sales. You can display and manipulate multiple reports easily and clearly by splitting the screen for worksheets within a file or by tiling or cascading the file windows, using worksheet tabs or file-window title bars for clear report-by-report labeling (see fig. 19.1).

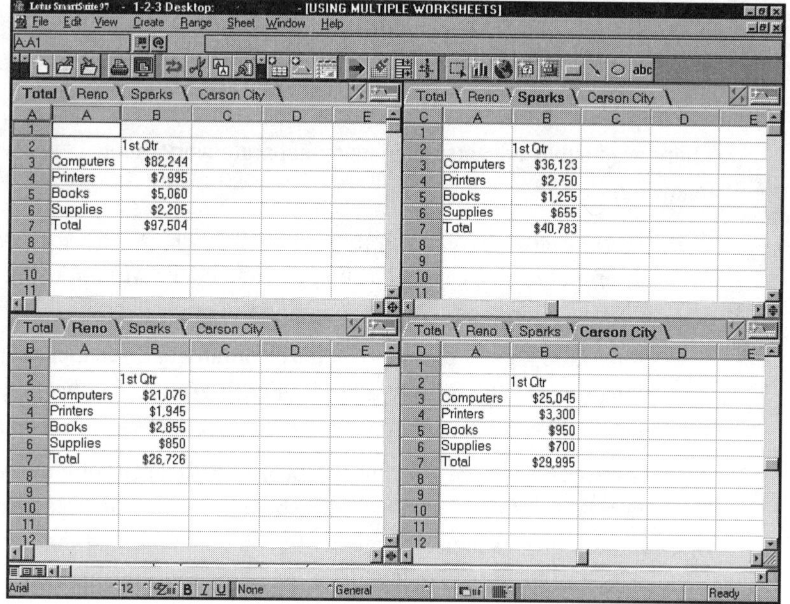

Fig. 19.1
For reports on several divisions or months, with multiple worksheets you can give each item the same cell in every report, and use worksheet tabs or file title bars for report names.

Make it your policy to use multiple worksheets for each project that you may refer to later. A single worksheet encourages hard-to-follow entry structure, whereas multiple worksheets encourage clear organization and structure.

- *Complex analysis.* If you are developing a complex analysis, you can use multiple worksheets to organize the analysis and output for other people. For a complex what-if analysis, you can use one or more worksheets for the output that managers will see; you can use other worksheets to keep your underlying analysis organized—for example, using one worksheet for input plans and assumptions, another for output goal measures, a third for the formulas and other entries that translate inputs into outputs, and a fourth for tables of data used in the calculations (such as tax rates).

  Compared with a single giant worksheet analysis, smaller modules are easier to design, understand, and test. By keeping assumptions that you and others may want to change in a worksheet separate from formulas that calculate results, you can eliminate or reduce the risk of accidental damage to the formulas. If you lay out an analysis in different worksheets, you have more flexibility to make each worksheet's column widths right for its contents. By entering names in the worksheet file tabs, you can organize the project in seconds.
- *Multiple contributors.* If different people are responsible for different parts of the whole, each person can work in their worksheet without disturbing work that the other people are doing.

There are further advantages in using separate worksheets in separate files, including the following:

- *Separate locations.* If different parts of the data system are developed or managed at different locations, each location can use its file without using up disk space for the other locations and without changing the other files.
- *Protection.* If parts of the project are confidential, you can keep those parts private. Besides ensuring privacy, providing each group a file that contains only nonconfidential data eliminates accidental changes of that data.
- *Large worksheet projects.* For any project with large computer-memory requirements, use of multiple files can be beneficial. For multiple users of various parts, you can give each user a smaller file that contains just the parts that they need. This is especially important if you are using modems to share data over long distance connections.

For almost every worksheet project of any size, it is worthwhile to consider these factors and to think about using multiple worksheets and possibly multiple files.

Linking Worksheets and Files with Formulas

To use multiple 1-2-3 files, the essential skill to learn is using formulas that link files. These formulas are so similar to those that link worksheets that you should think of all multiple-worksheet linkings—single file and multiple files—as a single technique applied in two slightly different ways.

▶ **See** "Entering Formulas," **p. 137**

Figure 19.2 shows formulas for identical uses of data in other worksheets, for multiple worksheets within the *same* file and in *different* files. Cell A:B2 in the workbook named Master Link File is linking to cell A:B2 in the workbook named Linked Data Source, while cell A:B3 in the workbook named Master Link File is linking to cell B:B2 in the second worksheet of the Master Link File workbook.

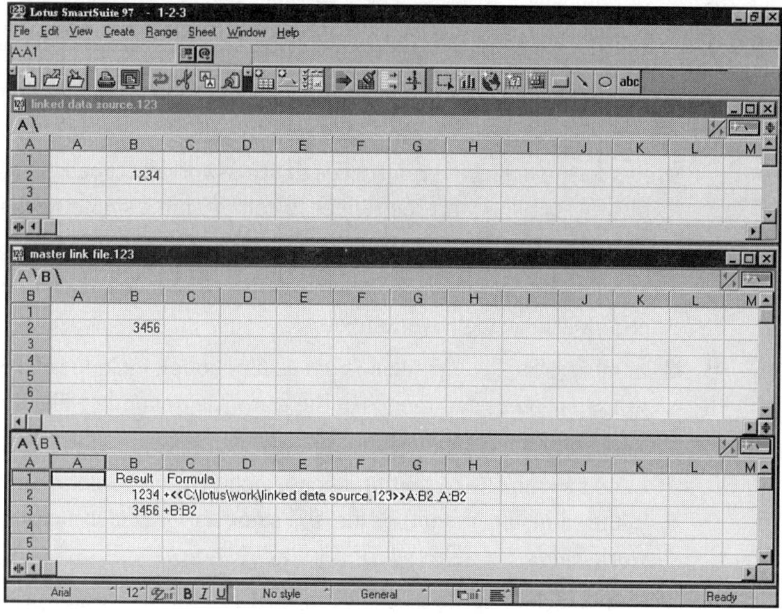

Fig. 19.2
You can use formulas to link to cells in other worksheets, whether they are in the same or a different workbook file.

These two formulas also show that you refer to cells in other worksheets and files in essentially the same way that you refer to cells in the same worksheet. Compared with the way you make the cell references when all the cells are in the same worksheet, the only differences are these:

- When referring to cells in *another worksheet within the same file*, each reference to a cell in another worksheet precedes the cell address with the worksheet name, followed by a colon to specify which worksheet contains the cells.

- When referring to cells in ***another workbook file***, each reference to a cell in another workbook precedes the worksheet name and cell/range reference with the file path and workbook filename inside double angle-brackets to specify which file contains the worksheet with the cell or range.

Usually, the best way for you to enter formula references to another file is to display the file that contains the data you want to reference and then select the cell or range that contains that data. When you do this, 1-2-3 enters the file reference in the formula for you. In figure 19.2, for example, 1-2-3 entered the formula as:

```
+<<C:\LOTUS\work\LINKED DATA SOURCE.123>>A:B2..A:B2
```

This method of entering references is generally much faster and easier than other methods, and it eliminates the likelihood of typos or omitted reference elements.

Once you have created a linking formula in a worksheet, you can copy, edit, or move the formula using the same techniques you use with formulas referring to cells in a single worksheet.

Using linking formulas, you can accomplish a number of tasks, including the following examples:

- In a formula, include references to other-worksheet cells in the same file or another file, the same as with references to cells within a single worksheet.
- Copy formulas that contain references to other-worksheet cells in the same or another file, taking advantage of relative references, the same as with references to cells within a single worksheet.
- In more complex formulas (such as functions), include references to other-worksheet cells and ranges in the same file or another file, the same as with references to cells within a single worksheet.
- In text formulas and text functions, include references to other-worksheet text cells in the same file or another file, the same as with references to cells within a single worksheet.

Wherever you can refer to a cell or range of cells in the same worksheet, you can refer to a cell or range in another worksheet within the same workbook file or in another workbook file.

Understanding Linking Formulas

Linking formulas have their own subtleties which you must understand if you want your results to be as you expect. If you aren't careful, or if you don't understand how linking formulas work, you may be surprised by the way linking formulas actually work. Figure 19.3 shows some examples which will help you better understand these types of formulas.

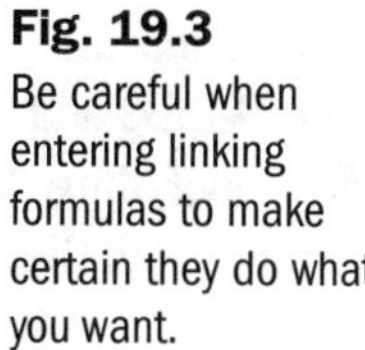

Fig. 19.3
Be careful when entering linking formulas to make certain they do what you want.

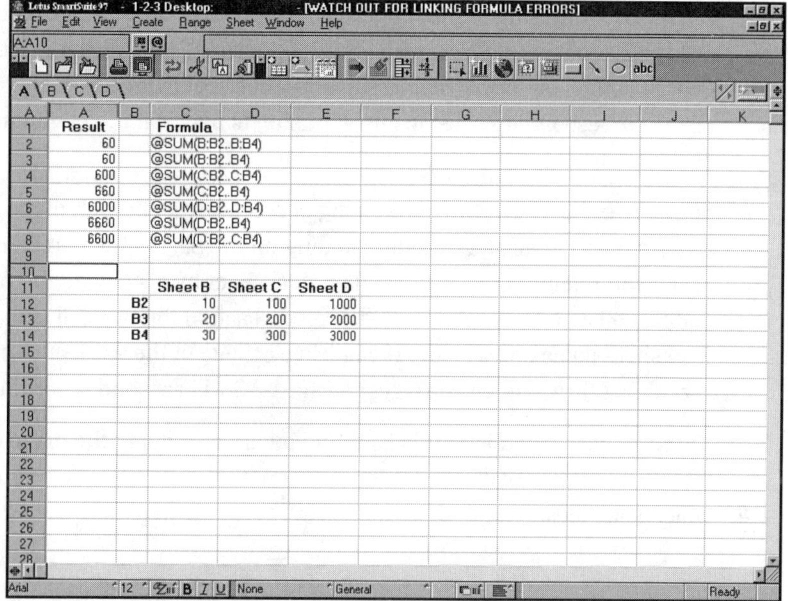

In figure 19.3, cells B11..E14 show the values entered in cells B2..B4 of worksheets B, C, and D. The linking formulas are shown in cells C2..C8, and the results appear in A2..A8. Let's have a look at each of the formulas to see why they produce the results shown.

The formula in row 2, @SUM(B:B2..B:B4), returns the expected result, 60, which is the sum of cells B:B2, B:B3, and B:B4. The slightly different formula in row 3, @SUM(B:B2..B4), produces the same result, which might lead you to believe that both methods of specifying the range B:B2..B:B4 and B:B2..B4 are the same. As you'll soon see, this result is deceptive.

Let's look at the formulas in rows 4 and 5. In row 4, @SUM(C:B2..C:B4) produces the correct sum for cells C:B2, C:B3, and C:B4—600. But the formula in row 5, @SUM(C:B2..B4) produces a result of 660, which probably is 60 more than you would expect.

To solve the problem, let's look a little further. The formula in row 6 shows a result of 6000, which is correct, but the formula in row 7 shows 6660, which is 660 more than you might expect. The formula in row 8 provides a clue to the apparent discrepancy. Here the result is 6600, the sum of the values from sheets C and D.

Although you may feel that 1-2-3 is producing inconsistent answers, in reality, these examples simply show one more facet of 1-2-3's flexibility. Notice that in each of the formulas which seem to be producing unusual results (rows 3, 5, and 7), that the range specification includes a worksheet reference for the beginning of the range, but skips the reference for the end of the range. That is, B:B2..B:B4 specifies that the range begins at cell B:B2 and ends at B:B4, while B:B2..B4 specifies that the range begins at cell B:B2 and ends at cell B4 *on the current worksheet*—thus specifying a 3-dimensional range including all the corresponding cells on any worksheets between the beginning of the range and the current worksheet.

So you see, 1-2-3 actually is producing correct results in each of the formulas. What seem like errors are really a misunderstanding on the part of the person entering the formulas. When you refer to a range in another worksheet by specifying the range's beginning and ending cell addresses, you should precede each of the two cell addresses with the worksheet name and a colon. If you leave off one of the worksheet references, you've specified a three-dimensional range, and 1-2-3 will respond accordingly.

There is one exception to this rule—if you are specifying the name of another workbook file, 1-2-3 knows that any cell references are to that file, because you cannot create ranges which span files.

Updating and Recalculating File Links

When you use a file which has links to a *source* file, you generally want the active file's data to reflect the source file's current data. You can control the default behavior using two settings in the 1-2-3 Preferences dialog box. To make certain 1-2-3 automatically updates links to closed workbook files on disk, select File, User Setup, 1-2-3 Preferences to display the General tab of the 1-2-3 Preferences dialog box (see figure 19.4). Make certain the Update links when opening workbooks check box is checked.

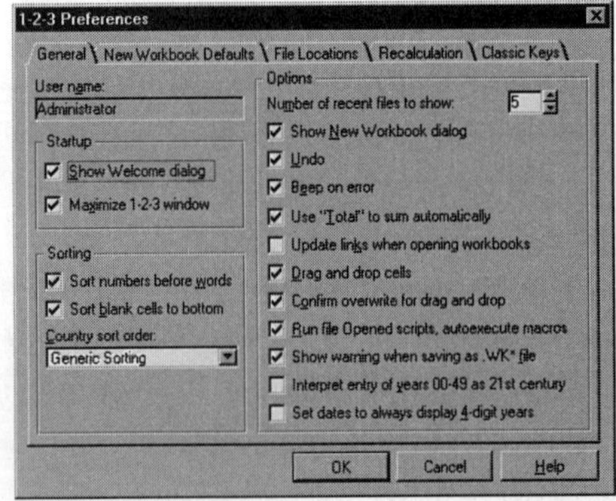

Fig. 19.4
Make certain the Update links when opening workbooks check box is checked in the 1-2-3 Preferences dialog box.

To make certain 1-2-3 automatically updates file reference links to open workbook files whenever those files are changed, select the Recalculation tab of the 1-2-3 Preferences dialog box (see figure 19.5). Make certain the Automatic radio button is selected. Because 1-2-3 stores the recalculation settings with the current workbook file, it is especially important to check this setting when the file containing the linking formulas is the active workbook.

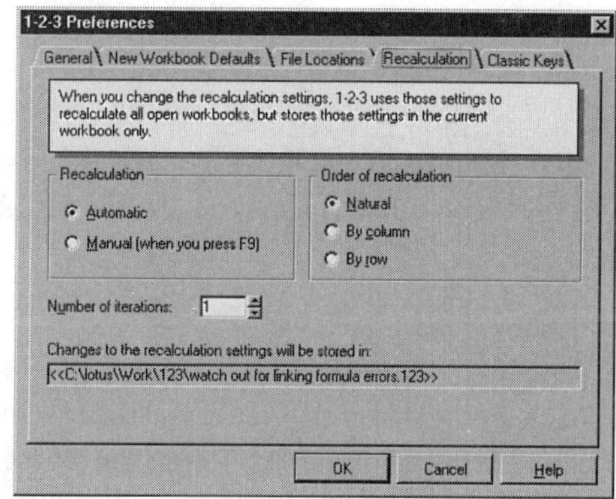

Fig. 19.5
Make certain the Automatic radio button is selected in the 1-2-3 Preferences dialog box.

If you maintain these settings, a file with links to source files will always use current data from any source file that is either open or on disk in the computer (assuming correct file links).

CAUTION

If you move a source file, 1-2-3 will not be able to automatically update the file references in the linking formulas. You'll need to edit the file references to re-establish the links.

If you don't want to mark the Update Links When Opening Files check box (if, for example, the source file might not be available), after you open a user file with links to a source file that is on disk but not open, follow these steps to ensure that the user file is using current data from the source file.

1. Select Edit, Manage Links to display the Manage Links dialog box (see fig. 19.6).
2. Select 1-2-3 file links in the Link Type list box.
3. Select the link to update, and then select Update All Now.

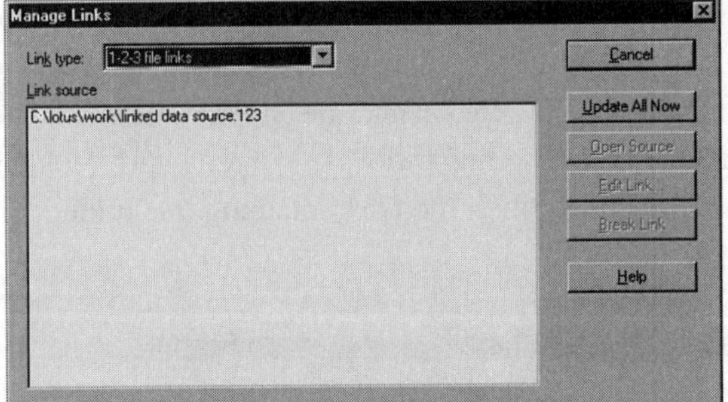

Fig. 19.6
Select the Update All Now button to update links to closed workbook files on disk.

If you want Recalculation set to Manual instead of Automatic, keep an eye on the status bar's Calc indicator. Whenever the word `Calc` appears, press F9 (Calc) or click the Calc indicator for current data.

CAUTION

Each file contains a Recalculation setting, either Automatic or Manual, and whenever multiple files are open, 1-2-3 applies the Recalculation setting of the most recently opened file to all open files. For example, if you open file A, which has Automatic recalculation, and then open file B, which has Manual recalculation, if you change data in file A, file A will not recalculate the effects of the data change until you issue a Calc command.

So whenever you are using multiple open files, if any of the files have Manual recalculation, keep the status bar displayed and watch the Calc indicator so that you know when a Calc command is needed to make all cells reflect current data.

Combining and Consolidating Data

Linking files using file reference formulas isn't your only option when you want to combine or consolidate data from more than one 1-2-3 workbook file. Another option which often is a better solution is to use the Combine 1-2-3 file dialog box (see fig. 19.7).

When you combine data using the Combine 1-2-3 file dialog box, no file reference linking formulas are used, so once you've combined the data, there's no danger that moving or deleting the source file can corrupt or destroy the link. In fact, once you've used the Combine 1-2-3 file dialog box to combine data, there really is no link between the source file and your active workbook file. You manipulate and modify the data completely within your active workbook file.

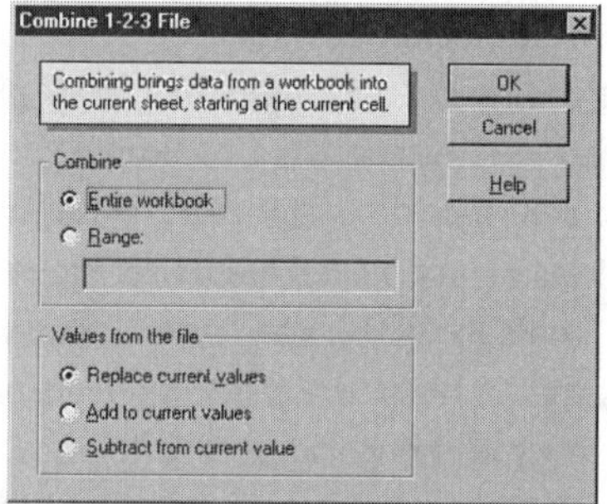

Fig. 19.7
For certain current-file uses of data from other files on disk, you may find the Combine 1-2-3 File dialog box convenient.

Notice in figure 19.7 that the Combine 1-2-3 file dialog box offers you three options for combining data. You can replace the data in the active workbook with the data from the source workbook, add the data from the source workbook to the data in the active workbook, or subtract the source file data from the values in the active workbook. Of course, only numeric data can be added or subtracted, so any labels in the active workbook will remain unchanged. 1-2-3 also protects formulas in the active workbook—incoming data which would overwrite a formula is ignored.

Before attempting to use the Combine 1-2-3 file dialog box, make certain that the source workbook has a compatible layout to that of the active workbook. In addition, you must make certain the cell selector is in the correct cell of the active workbook—where the incoming data lands is completely dependent on the current location of the cell selector. For example, suppose the cell selector is in cell B:B2 in the active workbook, worksheet B is totally blank, and that the source workbook contains the value 123 in cell A:B2. If you combine the data using either the replace or add options, cell B:C4 in the active workbook will contain the value 123. In other words, 1-2-3 treats the current location of the cell selector in the active workbook as if it were cell A:A1, and uses that location as the first cell where combined data may appear.

CAUTION

Before you combine data from a source file into the active workbook, save the current file. If you make a mistake combining the data, you can then simply revert to your original data by reopening the active workbook's file.

To use the Combine 1-2-3 file dialog box to combine data from a source file into the active workbook, first make certain you have the cell selector in the correct cell. Then select File, Open, choose the file you wish to combine, and select the Combine with current workbook check box. Then select Combine to display the Combine 1-2-3 file dialog box. Next select whether you want to combine the Entire workbook or a specified Range. Select the type of combine operation, Replace current values, Add to current values, or Subtract from current value. Select OK to combine the data and return to the worksheet.

It cannot be stressed too highly how important it is that the source data layout be compatible with the data layout in the active file. Even a single misplaced piece of data can render the entire process meaningless, or even destructive. Consider a simple example. Suppose you produce a report which combines sales data from several different company stores. In each case, your original worksheet layout placed computer sales for the first quarter in A:B10, furniture sales in A:B11, tools in A:B12, and so on. Imagine, however, that the manager of one of your stores felt that in his store, sales of televisions were the most important, and he rearranged his copy of the worksheet so television sales were in A:B10, telephones were in A:B11, and so on. If you didn't notice that he had been making such changes and simply went ahead with combining the data from each store into your master workbook, your results would be misleading at best.

TROUBLESHOOTING

When I display the source file for a combine operation and make revisions to it, the Combine 1-2-3 file dialog box keeps ignoring my revisions. The dialog box gets the source-file data from the disk version of the source file, not from your display of the source file.

If you make revisions in the source file when you display it to find its range for use in the Combine 1-2-3 file dialog box, you should save the revised source file to disk before opening the dialog box.

When I use the Combine 1-2-3 file dialog box to combine results from separate files for several company divisions or several months, I often lose track of which source files I have added in and which I haven't. Does 1-2-3 provide any record of what I have combined? No. That is one reason why it may be better to use formula file linking to combine files.

Is there a good system that I can set up to keep track of the source files I have added in? Pick a cell that is blank in all the files but is easy to include in the combine ranges. Use this cell to number the source files.

To make the numbers easy to interpret, you could give each source file's number one zero more than the preceding one. Number the first source file 1, the second 20, the third 300, and so on. With this system, by looking at the number in the current file, you can tell which source files have been added in and which have not. For example, if the number in the current file is 7604341, you added in source file 2 twice and skipped source file 5.

It may not always be immediately clear which method of combining data will work best for your circumstance. Let's look at an example which will help you decide which method is appropriate for you.

Imagine that you must combine data for six divisions within your company. The following sections describe each method of combining the data and the likely result.

Combining Division Figures with the Combine Box

If you use the Combine 1-2-3 file dialog box, each month you carry out these steps:

1. Collect each of the six division files, and place on your hard disk.
2. Open your whole-company worksheet.
3. Place the cell selector in the correct cell.
4. Select File, Open, and select a division's file.
5. Select Combine with Current Workbook and then Combine to display the Combine 1-2-3 file dialog box.
6. Select the Range radio button and enter the range to combine.
7. Select the Add to Current Values radio button.
8. Click OK.

Repeat steps 4-8 for each of divisions 2 through 6.

Combining Division Figures with Formula File Linking

If you use formula file linking, you must enter the file reference linking formulas into the master workbook. For example, if each division's workbook contains a range named DIVDATA, you might enter the formula like this (assuming you copied the division workbooks DIV1 through DIV6 into the current directory):

+<<DIV1.123>>DIVDATA+<<DIV2.123>>DIVDATA
+<<DIV3.123>>DIVDATA+<<DIV4.123>>DIVDATA
+<<DIV5.123>>DIVDATA+<<DIV6.123>>DIVDATA

Copy this formula down and right to all cells in the division results range of your total-company worksheet.

For each month you take these steps:

1. Put the six division files on your hard disk.
2. Open your whole-company worksheet file.

Comparing the Methods

Notice that although setting up the workbooks to use file reference linking formulas takes a bit more effort, in the long run, using linking formulas has several advantages, including these:

- *Monthly work is much quicker and simpler.* In the examples, you can see that using the Combine 1-2-3 file dialog box you have many more steps to carry out each month. Using formula file linking will take you less time each month.

- *Verifiably correct results*. This is a very important advantage of using formula file linking. Using the Combine 1-2-3 file dialog box, you risk making a mistake in either cell pointer location in the total-company file or the range you enter for the division file. When you use the Combine 1-2-3 file dialog box, your worksheet provides you no record of how your total-company numbers have been calculated. After you've done your combining, neither you nor anyone else can find worksheet verification of how the your total-company worksheet calculated the numbers it contains.

By contrast, when you use formula file linking, every cell in your total-company worksheet contains the formula showing how the worksheet calculated its number. Compared to using the Combine 1-2-3 file dialog box, the risk of your making mistakes in updating your formula file links is vastly less because the steps are far fewer and simpler. In addition, there are better safeguards: if you type a source file's name wrong so the file-link formulas cannot find that file, your total-company worksheet's cells will not show you incorrect numbers. Instead, every cell will show ERR. ●

CHAPTER 20

Solving Problems with Backsolver

by Brian Underdahl

People often have the need to achieve a specific result even though they cannot determine the exact conditions necessary to meet their goal. This task, called *goal seeking,* is an important function you can perform using 1-2-3's Backsolver tool. With Backsolver, you can specify the number you want for a result and see what some other number or range of numbers have to be to produce that result.

Before you can use Backsolver effectively, you must understand the basics of using 1-2-3. In fact, you must be able to describe the problem using the many formula and function options available in the 1-2-3 toolkit before you even begin using Backsolver.

Once you have effectively defined the problem in a 1-2-3 workbook, you can apply Backsolver to help you find alternatives to the predefined set of conditions which lead to the current results. For example, if you want to know how you can increase your profits from their current level to a new figure you specify, you first start by creating your worksheet using your current results. Once you know your model is correct, you can then use Backsolver to determine what must be done to reach your new goal.

Identify ways to meet a goal

To solve complex problems, you must determine the best ways to meet your goals. For example, is it more reasonable to increase sales or reduce the workforce?

Determine how to best specify a problem

You need to determine how you can specify a problem so Backsolver can show you ways to reach the desired results.

Prepare goal-focused decision analyses

You must analyze the problems by keeping your efforts focused on the best means to reach your goals. You must understand how to structure a problem so the solution not only produces the desired results, but represents a realistic approach.

You may want to think of Backsolver as performing a reverse analysis of a problem. While you normally attack a problem by entering all the current data and seeing the result, Backsolver adjusts the input data to produce a desired result. This allows you to see how the data must change to meet your goal.

NOTE Previous versions of 1-2-3 included another powerful problem solving tool, Solver. This tool, which was used to find optimal solutions to very complex problems, is not included in 1-2-3 97, but is available as an add-in. See Appendix A, "Finding Optimal Solutions with the Solver," for more information. ■

Understanding How Backsolver Works

Backsolver is a simple tool to use and understand. At the most basic level, a worksheet that uses Backsolver to find out how to reach a goal can have as few as two active cells—one cell for the formula that produces the result, and one cell containing the data that must be changed to produce that result. Of course, most problems are much more complex, but the basic idea remains the same. You tell Backsolver which cell to adjust to produce a specified result in another cell.

For example, imagine that your company produces a product that has a raw materials cost of $80 per unit, a labor cost that varies depending on how many pieces are produced, and certain fixed costs. You know that you can sell the product for $125 per unit, and your company president wants to know how many pieces must be produced and sold so he will be able to afford a new $50,000 boat in six months. With all the variable factors, it looks like a real case of trial and error as you attempt to find the answer. Compare how you might solve this problem using standard spreadsheet techniques with what you can do with Backsolver:

- In standard worksheet use, after entering a formula to determine net profit, you enter a prediction for sales and let 1-2-3 tell you the resulting profit. After you see the results, you adjust the sales figure to produce a net profit figure closer to your goal. You continue to make adjustments as you narrow in on your goal, a technique which will probably require quite a few attempts before you find the correct answer.
- With Backsolver, you start by entering the same set of formulas you would use in the manual technique, but then you tell Backsolver your goal for profit ($50,000), and let Backsolver adjust the sales in the worksheet to tell you what sales have to be to meet your profit goal. Rather than making a whole series of guesses, you let Backsolver quickly find the solution.

Using the Backsolver really is that simple. The Backsolver is extremely valuable for almost every project in business planning and decision analysis (and personal financial planning). For a business plan, you can enter the profit goal and see what is required to meet it. For a decision such as a company investment, you can enter the company's minimum acceptable return-on-investment rate and see what any number in the investment plan has to be to meet that standard. If you are building a nest egg for retirement, you can enter the amount of nest egg you want to build and see what you have to add each year to build the desired sum.

Using Backsolver to Change a Single Cell

Once you've entered a plan or analysis, using Backsolver with the plan is as easy as saving the plan. For example, use the following steps to use Backsolver with the simple product example introduced previously.

The first step is to create a worksheet to use with Backsolver. You can use Backsolver with any plan or analysis that has these two components:

- *Input numbers*. One or more cells containing numbers (not formulas) that are used to calculate results in one or more other cells with formulas. In business planning, these input numbers are often called ***assumptions***.
- *Output formulas*. One or more cells containing formulas that use one or more of the input numbers to calculate results.

The simplified worksheet shown in figure 20.1 meets both of these requirements. Note that for clarity, this worksheet does not address all possible factors which could effect a business plan. You might need to include additional items such as taxes, production constraints, quantity discounts, and so on in your real world model, but the basic methods of using Backsolver would remain the same.

In figure 20.1, each of the factors involved in the final net profit are shown individually and labeled to clearly show their purpose in the model. Column C shows each of the four formulas included in the corresponding row in column B. Ultimately, the goal of this example is to produce $50,000 in profits at the end of six months by adjusting the number of units produced and sold (it's assumed that every unit produced is sold).

In this plan, cell B2 contains the input number (sales) used in the output formula for six-month profit entered in B11. Cell B11 meets the output formula requirement: It contains a formula that uses the input number to calculate a result.

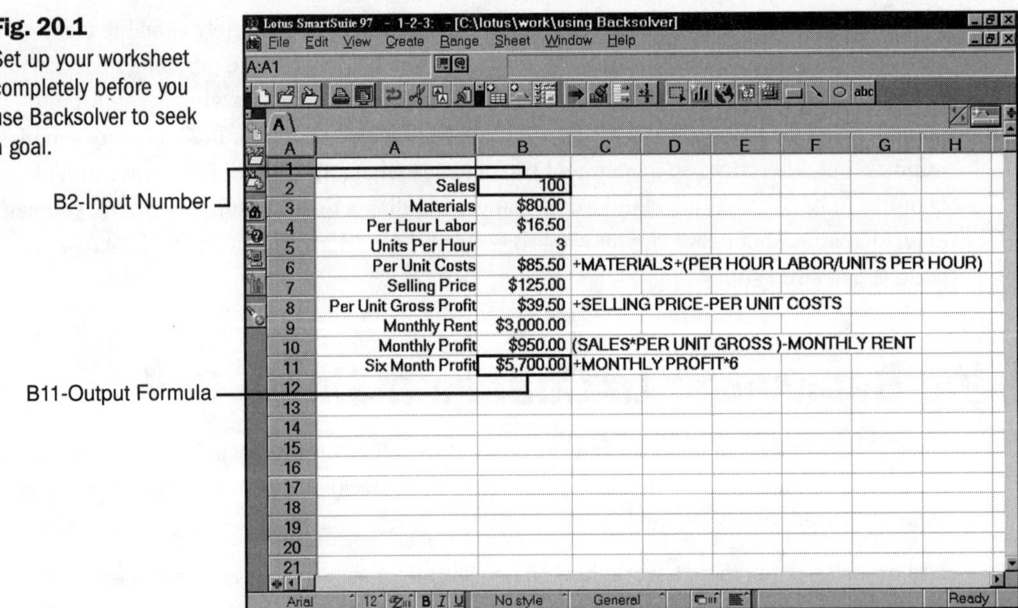

Fig. 20.1
Set up your worksheet completely before you use Backsolver to seek a goal.

Since these are the two basic elements of all spreadsheet what-if analyses, and virtually every worksheet business plan or decision analysis has them, you can use Backsolver with practically every business plan or decision analysis you already have.

CAUTION

Before using Backsolver, save your plan. When Backsolver acts, it replaces an input number (or range of input numbers) in your plan. And when it does so, the worksheet recalculates all cells with formulas dependent on what Backsolver changed.

Once you have your plan or analysis in the worksheet, follow these steps to use Backsolver:

1. Select Range, Analyze, Backsolver to display the Backsolver dialog box (see figure 20.2).
2. In the Make the Formula in this Cell text box, enter the address of the goal's output formula cell. For this example, the goal is the six-month profit goal in cell B11, so you enter **B11**.
3. In the Equal to this Value text box, enter the result that you want for that goal. For this example, enter the desired profit result, **50000**.

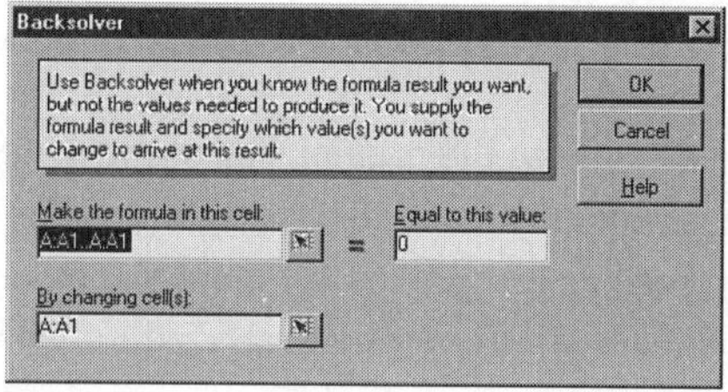

Fig. 20.2
Use the Backsolver dialog box to specify how to reach the desired goal.

4. In the By Changing Cell(s) text box, enter the cell address of the input number that you want Backsolver to change so that your goal is met. In this example, you want the input number for sales changed to meet your profit goal, so enter its cell address, **B2**.
5. Select OK to solve the problem and return to the worksheet.

If you use Backsolver without saving your plan first, you can restore the numbers Backsolver changes by choosing Edit, Undo Backsolve immediately after Backsolver is finished.

Backsolver figures out and enters the input number required so that the output formula returns the result you want (see figure 20.3). In this example, for six-month profit to be $50,000, monthly sales must be 286.9. Of course, your customers will probably insist on buying complete units, so you'll likely have to sell 1,722 units in six months, rather than 1,721.5 (monthly sales times 6). Maybe your boss will give you the extra $20 in profits as a bonus!

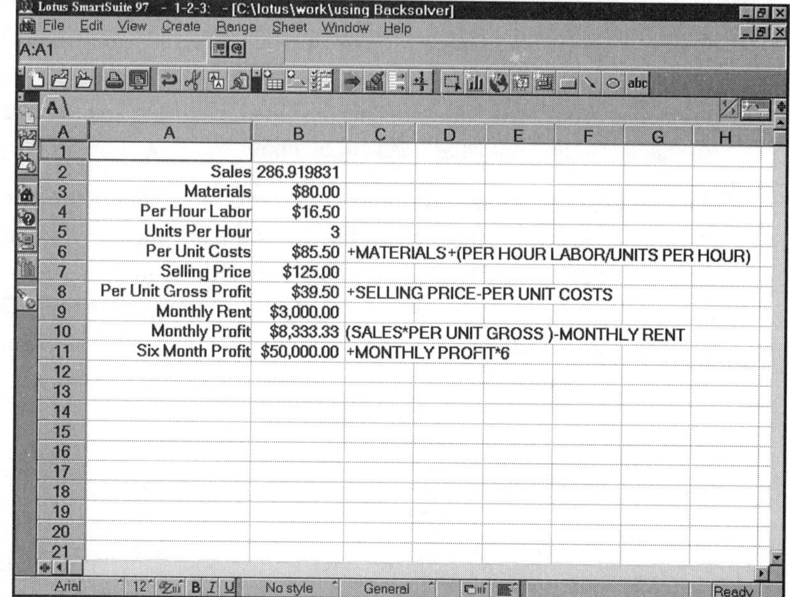

Fig. 20.3
Backsolver determines how to change the input values to meet your stated goal.

Using Backsolver to Change a Range

Most problems aren't quite as simple as the previous example. Often, there isn't a single value which can be changed independently of all others, but rather a series of values which all must be adjusted to reach a reasonable solution. For example, in the previous example, imagine how your factory workers would respond if they were told they had to adjust the production by changing only one month's output, rather than changing the output for everyone of the six months evenly. Needless to say, you probably would not have had a happy crew!

Fortunately, you can tell Backsolver to change an entire range of numbers when finding a solution for your goal. If you do, Backsolver changes all numbers in the range by the same percentage. In other words, Backsolver figures out the percentage change that, when applied to every number in the range, makes the result formula return the goal you entered. Backsolver then changes all numbers in the range by that percentage. In the production example we accomplished this same result by assuming that each month's production would be the same, but this does not have to be the case when you specify a range of numbers to change.

Changing Entries in a One-Dimensional Range

Figure 20.4 shows an example of using Backsolver to meet a goal by changing a range of input numbers. As you can see, this example uses an example similar to the earlier one, but now several additional factors have been added to the plan. Because this is a new product, you've decided that sales will likely improve each month and the number of units produced per hour will likely increase as the workers become familiar with the product. You've also decided to give the workers small monthly raises as an incentive to improve production. Your boss still wants his new boat, however, so once again we'll call on Backsolver to find out what needs to be done.

Once you've created and saved the worksheet, select Range, Analyze, Backsolver to display the Backsolver dialog box. In the Make the Formula in This Cell text box, enter **B14**, the address of the goal's output formula cell. In the Equal to This Value text box, enter **50000**, the result that you want for that goal. In the By Changing Cell(s) text box, enter **B3..G3**, the cell addresses of the input numbers that you want Backsolver to change so that your goal is met. Figure 20.5 shows the completed Backsolver dialog box.

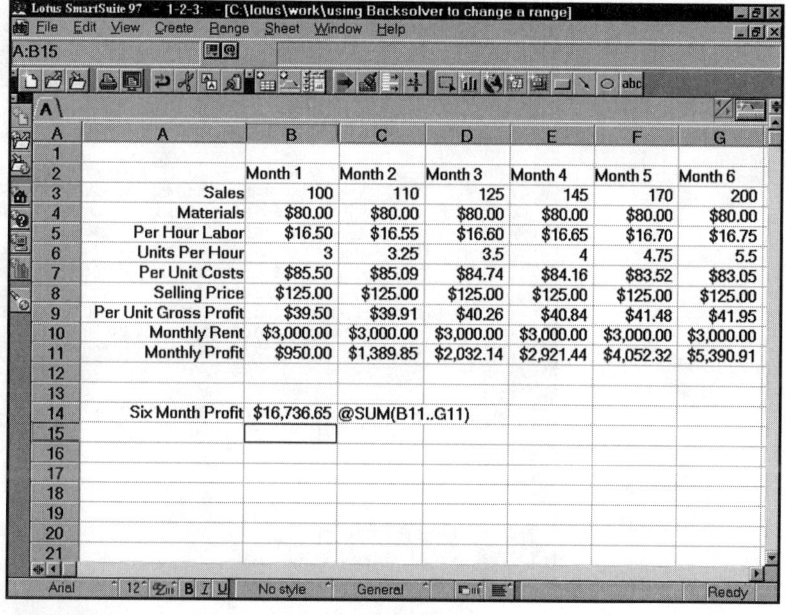

	A	B	C	D	E	F	G
1							
2		Month 1	Month 2	Month 3	Month 4	Month 5	Month 6
3	Sales	100	110	125	145	170	200
4	Materials	$80.00	$80.00	$80.00	$80.00	$80.00	$80.00
5	Per Hour Labor	$16.50	$16.55	$16.60	$16.65	$16.70	$16.75
6	Units Per Hour	3	3.25	3.5	4	4.75	5.5
7	Per Unit Costs	$85.50	$85.09	$84.74	$84.16	$83.52	$83.05
8	Selling Price	$125.00	$125.00	$125.00	$125.00	$125.00	$125.00
9	Per Unit Gross Profit	$39.50	$39.91	$40.26	$40.84	$41.48	$41.95
10	Monthly Rent	$3,000.00	$3,000.00	$3,000.00	$3,000.00	$3,000.00	$3,000.00
11	Monthly Profit	$950.00	$1,389.85	$2,032.14	$2,921.44	$4,052.32	$5,390.91
12							
13							
14	Six Month Profit	$16,736.65	@SUM(B11..G11)				

Fig. 20.4
Use Backsolver to meet a goal by changing an entire row of numbers in the plan.

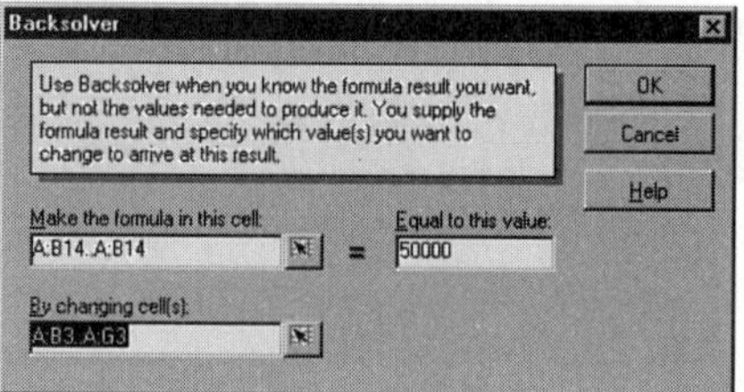

Fig. 20.5
Use Backsolver's options to specify the problem cells when you want to change an entire row of numbers in the plan.

Select OK to solve the problem and return to the worksheet. Figure 20.6 shows Backsolver's solution for this more complex example.

Notice that in figure 20.6, Backsolver has still specified partial unit production for each month. Because you can only produce and sell complete units, you'll probably have to adjust the Backsolver solution manually to correct this problem. While it would be possible to try forcing Backsolver to produce a more reasonable answer, it might not really be practical. To understand why, consider what would happen if you added a row to your model immediately below the sales row, and added the formula +@INT(B3) in the new blank cell B4. You could then copy this formula across the row. Finally, you would edit the monthly profit formulas to use this integer value, rather than the decimal values calculated by Backsolver. Figure 20.7 shows the result you'd likely encounter after asking Backsolver to find the new answer.

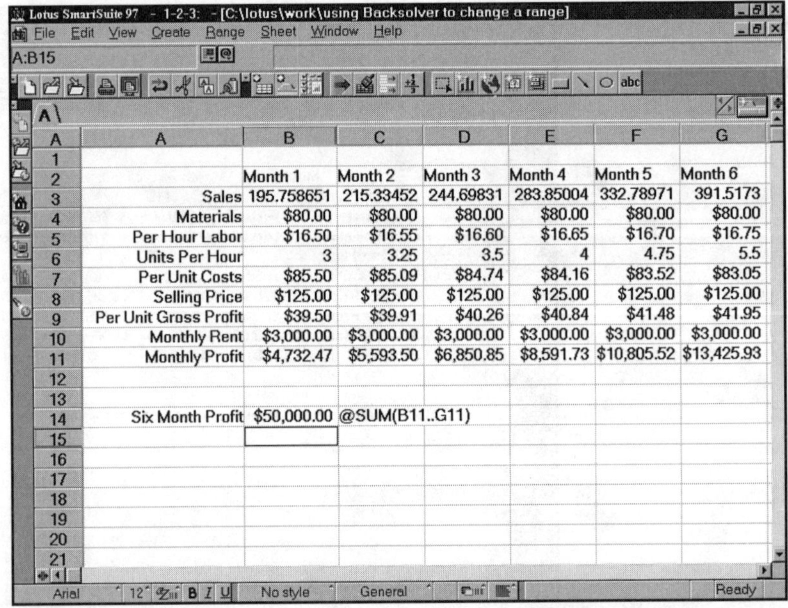

A	B	C	D	E	F	G
	Month 1	Month 2	Month 3	Month 4	Month 5	Month 6
Sales	195.758651	215.33452	244.69831	283.85004	332.78971	391.5173
Materials	$80.00	$80.00	$80.00	$80.00	$80.00	$80.00
Per Hour Labor	$16.50	$16.55	$16.60	$16.65	$16.70	$16.75
Units Per Hour	3	3.25	3.5	4	4.75	5.5
Per Unit Costs	$85.50	$85.09	$84.74	$84.16	$83.52	$83.05
Selling Price	$125.00	$125.00	$125.00	$125.00	$125.00	$125.00
Per Unit Gross Profit	$39.50	$39.91	$40.26	$40.84	$41.48	$41.95
Monthly Rent	$3,000.00	$3,000.00	$3,000.00	$3,000.00	$3,000.00	$3,000.00
Monthly Profit	$4,732.47	$5,593.50	$6,850.85	$8,591.73	$10,805.52	$13,425.93
Six Month Profit	$50,000.00	@SUM(B11..G11)				

Fig. 20.6
Backsolver can change all the numbers in a range to arrive at the specified goal.

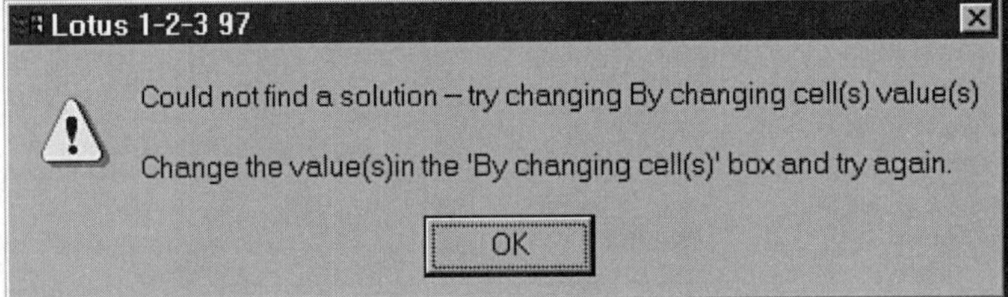

Fig. 20.7
Sometimes Backsolver cannot arrive at the specified goal.

This Backsolver error message tells you that there is no answer that correctly solves the problem. No matter how hard Backsolver tries, it is not possible to make cell B14 exactly equal $50,000.00 if production and sales must always be integer values. On the other hand, it probably isn't critical that your profit be exactly $50,000 and that production always be in integer amounts. That's where your ability to make manual adjustments to Backsolver's solution enables you to produce a superior solution to the problem.

Changing Entries in a Two-Dimensional Range

With Backsolver you can also see how to meet a goal by changing all input numbers in a two-dimensional range. This can be quite useful if you have several different product lines, and want to apply the same type of adjustment to each in reaching your specified goal. Let's look at a simple example of how this might work.

Imagine that you just bought an ice cream stand, and the previous owner wasn't as ambitious as you. The sales were okay, but you feel you can do a lot better. Figure 20.8 shows a worksheet with the previous owner's sales projections. You want to increase the six-month sales to $4,000, and have decided to use Backsolver to see how much you'll need to sell of each flavor to reach your goal.

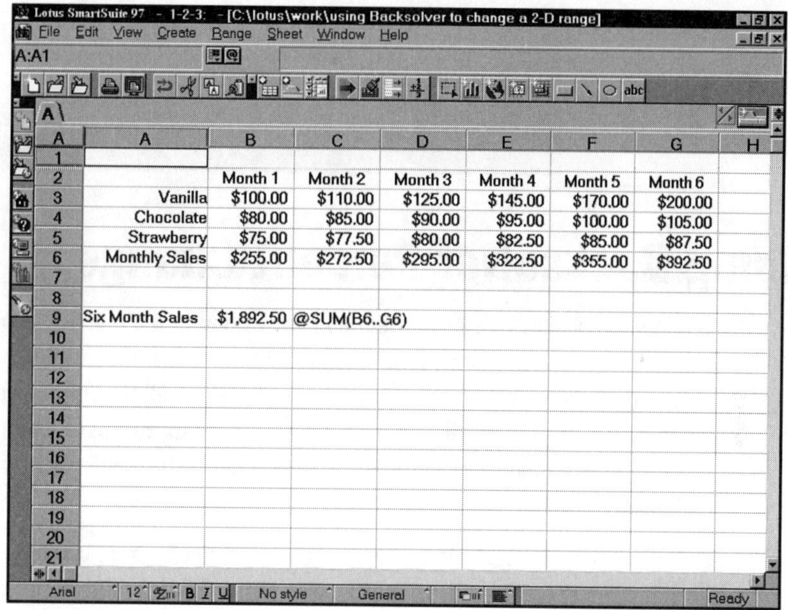

Fig. 20.8
Use Backsolver to meet a goal by changing an entire 2D range of numbers by the same percentage.

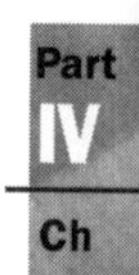

Just as it did when adjusting a single-row range of input values, Backsolver changes all input values in a two-dimensional range by the same percentage. Figure 20.9 shows Backsolver's solution to the problem. In this case, Backsolver was instructed to make cell B9 equal to 4,000 by changing the values in cells B3..G5.

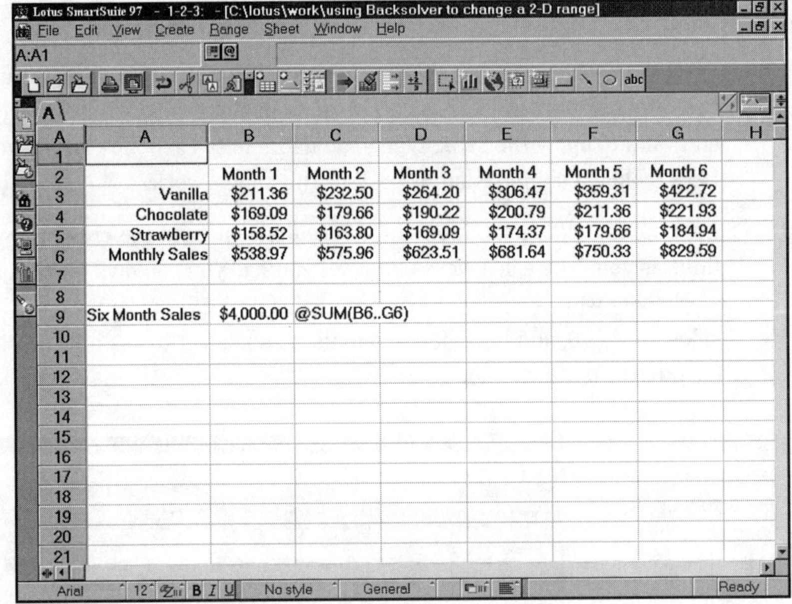

Lotus SmartSuite 97 - 1-2-3: - [C:\lotus\work\using Backsolver to change a 2-D range]
File Edit View Create Range Sheet Window Help
A:A1
Month 1 Month 2 Month 3 Month 4 Month 5 Month 6
Vanilla $211.36 $232.50 $264.20 $306.47 $359.31 $422.72
Chocolate $169.09 $179.66 $190.22 $200.79 $211.36 $221.93
Strawberry $158.52 $163.80 $169.09 $174.37 $179.66 $184.94
Monthly Sales $538.97 $575.96 $623.51 $681.64 $750.33 $829.59
Six Month Sales $4,000.00 @SUM(B6..G6)
Arial 12 No style General Ready

Fig. 20.9
Backsolver changed the values in cells B3..G5 to meet the goal of $4,000 in total sales.

Using Backsolver Percent Change

When you use Backsolver to meet a goal by changing a multicell range, the best way to summarize the route to the goal that Backsolver has found is the percent by which it has changed all the cells to meet the goal. Compared to all the number changes in all the individual cells, it is much easier for people to grasp, compare, and remember alternative ways to meet a goal when each is stated as a single percent change, such as "reduce all expenses by 13%."

Unfortunately, when Backsolver changes a multicell range by some percent to meet a goal, it does not display the percent change it applies to all the cells. But you can very easily make each of your Backsolver-result worksheets display the percent change that Backsolver found and applied to a range of cells to meet the goal.

The key to determining what percent change Backsolver made in the input range cells is to store one of those values before using Backsolver. Since Backsolver makes an identical percent change to all input cells, you only need to compare one before and after value to determine what the change actually was.

Use Edit, Copy to copy one of the input values to a blank cell outside the range of cells you specify in the By changing cell(s) text box. You don't want to use a formula, such as +B3 to copy the value, because the result of the formula will change to the new value of the cell once Backsolver solves the problem. You can then use a simple formula to compare the before and after values. For example, suppose you want to know how much Backsolver changed the input range to arrive at the values shown in figure 20.9. Copy the value from cell G3 to H3 before running Backsolver, and then place the following formula in cell H4:

```
+G3/H3
```

Format cell H4 as Percent, and then run Backsolver. The result shown in H4 will tell you that new values in the input range are 211.4% of the original value.

Before you use Backsolver, cell H4 displays `100%`. After you use Backsolver, this cell displays the change Backsolver applied to cell G3. Since Backsolver solves by applying the same percent change to all cells in the By changing cell(s) range, this number reports the change Backsolver applied to all cells in the entire range to meet your goal.

If you prefer to see the change as the percent difference between the old and new values, simply modify the formula to read +(G3/H3)-1.

Organize sets of Backsolver routes to a goal in Version Manager. See Chapter 21 for more information on using Version Manager.

CHAPTER 21

Managing Multiple Solutions with Version Manager

by Brian Underdahl

People often run into a problem when attempting to analyze data using a spreadsheet—it's difficult to have different versions of a projection available for comparison. 1-2-3's Version Manager is a powerful tool for managing multiple versions of worksheets, making the use of multiple versions of business plans, predictions, and decision analyses quite possible. If you need to compare the outcomes from numerous possible scenarios, you'll find Version Manager very valuable. ■

Create and use versions

Learn how to lay out a worksheet so you can later compare the results from different sets of assumptions.

Manage versions

Group versions to enable more effective analysis of the different results produced by changing conditions.

Create reports

Show your results effectively so others can understand the effects of the different versions.

Managing Business Planning

For business planning, the principal value of Version Manager is in managing multiple what-ifs—multiple variations of a business plan that have specific differences, such as different sales predictions, but are otherwise alike. With Version Manager, you can efficiently create and use multiple sets of data for a plan.

When you use the Version Manager, you set up the structure of your plan once, and then use the same set of formulas to produce the multiple sets of results that demonstrate the range of possible outcomes. Because you're using the same worksheet areas for all of the different versions, you also save time because you only need to apply your preferred formats and styles once, and each version will then have the same appearance—although showing the different sets of results.

Finding Better Plans More Systematically

Managing multiple spreadsheet versions is critical to getting the most from worksheets for business plans and decisions.

Almost every plan or key decision has many possibilities. Worksheets are a marvelous tool for capturing the possibilities and seeing the results. To go from numbers to plans and decisions, you need a system for keeping track of the alternatives in a uniform framework, and for integrating parts from different experts into the overall plan.

Version Manager is such a system. With Version Manager, you can give your planning and decision analysis the following key strengths:

- *Compare and integrate many predictions and other inputs in one planning framework.* With Version Manager you can set up one framework of formulas and reports and then insert and integrate various inputs into various versions.
- *Keep full track of all versions.* Version Manager automatically keeps a record of each version. It also provides a convenient system for labeling and annotating each version: what it represents, who contributed it, assumptions and reasoning behind this prediction, and other notes.
- *Sort and reorganize plan versions.* With Version Manager you can sort plan versions and group them according to various criteria, such as when created or by whom created.

Viewing and Using Version Manager Results

When you use Version Manager, 1-2-3 stores two or more named sets of data, or *versions*, in a range. You can then easily select which version is displayed in the worksheet and used in calculations. Figures 21.1 and 21.2 demonstrate how this works. In figure 21.1, a version named Low Costs is selected, showing the results on company profit when the cost of production is low. Figure 21.2 shows the same worksheet, but with the version called High Costs displayed. You can quickly see the effect on the company's profits when going from a low cost to a high cost of production.

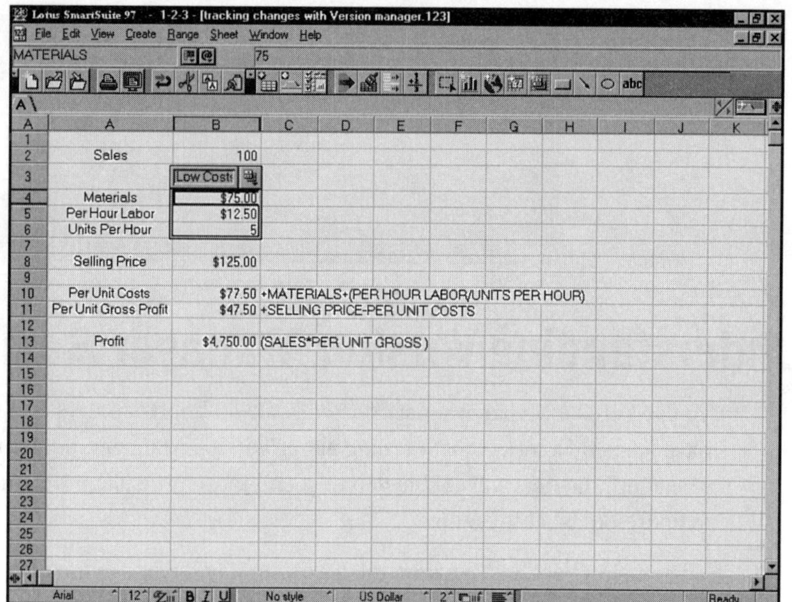

Fig. 21.1
Version Manager displays the results of selecting the version named Low Costs.

Notice in figures 21.1 and 21.2 that Version Manager has added a box around the worksheet cells containing the costs. The title bar of this box displays the name of the currently selected version. To see a list of current version names, you click the arrow button at the right side of the version title bar. When you choose a version, the worksheet changes to reflect the selected version in the version box, and also in other cells dependent on those values.

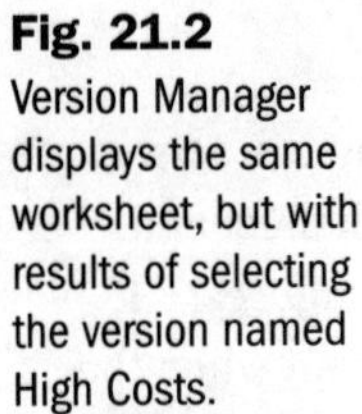

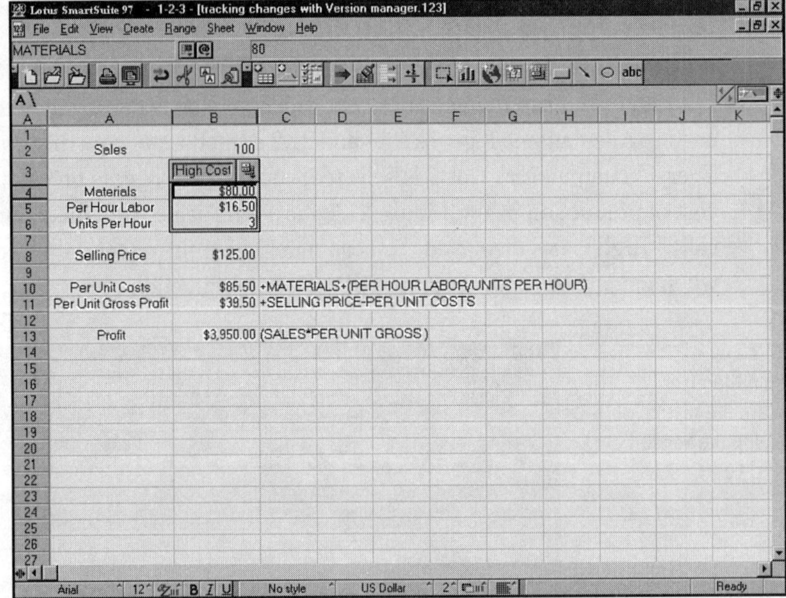

Fig. 21.2 Version Manager displays the same worksheet, but with results of selecting the version named High Costs.

Understanding Version Manager Basics

To use Version Manager most effectively, it will help to understand the basics. You don't have to spend a lot of time learning about Version Manager, but knowing how Version Manager functions will enable you to spend more time using the tool, rather than trying to figure out what to do next.

When using Version Manager, the following key terms are important:

- *Named range*. You can create different sets of data only for named ranges. You can use Version Manager to simultaneously assign a name to a range and create a version of that named range—it isn't necessary to name version ranges before using Version Manager.
- *Version*. When you create different sets of data for a named range, you assign each set a name, such as HIGH SALES or LOW SALES. Each named set of data for a range is called a *version* of that range. When you create a version of a range, Version Manager stores the current contents of the range as well as other information including your name, the date, and the time you created the version and an optional comment.

You can create versions for any range in a workbook file. For example, if you want to compare different combinations of revenues and expenses, you can create different versions of both ranges, and use Version Manager to display the different combinations.

- *Group.* After you create versions, you can treat selected versions of different named ranges as a group. For example, you can group the HIGH SALES version of the REVENUES range with the LOW EXPENSES version of the EXPENSES range to create a group named BEST CASE. You also can create a WORST CASE group that contains the LOW SALES version of REVENUES and the HIGH EXPENSES version of EXPENSES.

A version's range can contain anything you can enter in a cell: values, labels, formulas, functions, and even macros.

The Version Manager displays several different dialog boxes, depending on which Version Manager function you select. For example, if you select a single cell range, and then select Range, Version, New Version, Version Manager will display the Version Assistant dialog box (see fig. 21.3).

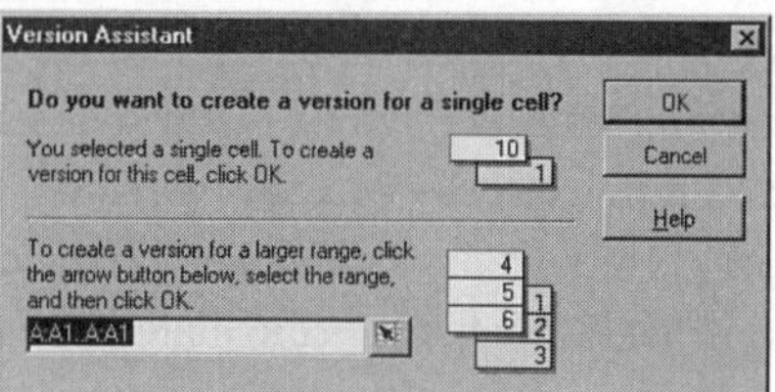

Fig. 21.3
The Version Manager displays the Version Assistant dialog box if you attempt to create a single cell version range.

Other Version Manager dialog boxes you'll see include these:

- The *New Version* dialog box, which you use to define new versions. You can create new versions for ranges which already have named versions, or start new version ranges.
- The *Display Version* dialog box, which you can use to select which versions are displayed in the workbook. Although you can select versions directly in the workbook, the Display Version dialog box enables you to select the displayed versions for all version ranges at one time.
- The *Delete Version* dialog box, which enables you to discard versions which you no longer need.

- The *Version Groups* dialog box, which enables you to group sets of named versions. This enables you to combine several versions in different ranges into named groups.
- The *Version Report* dialog box, which lets you see how the different versions each affect the workbook, as well as enabling you to see when the versions were created.

You'll see each of these dialog boxes in use in later sections of this chapter.

Using Version Manager

You use the Version Manager to create, display, update, modify, and delete versions. In this section, you learn how to use the Version Manager to create versions of named ranges in a worksheet.

Understanding the New Version Dialog Box

When you select Range, Version, New Version, 1-2-3 displays either the Version Assistant dialog box shown in figure 21.3, or the New Version dialog box shown in figures 21.4 and 21.5. If you do not select a multiple cell range before selecting the command, 1-2-3 displays the Version Assistant dialog box, giving you a chance to create a version in the active cell, or to select the range you really want to use. If you select a range first, 1-2-3 displays the New Version dialog box. This dialog box has two different appearances depending on whether the selected range already contains versions. If the selected range does not already contain versions, 1-2-3 displays the dialog box shown in figure 21.4. If the range does contain existing versions, 1-2-3 displays the dialog box shown in figure 21.5. Although the two variations of the dialog box show different messages, the only real functional difference between them is whether you can create a new range name for the selected range.

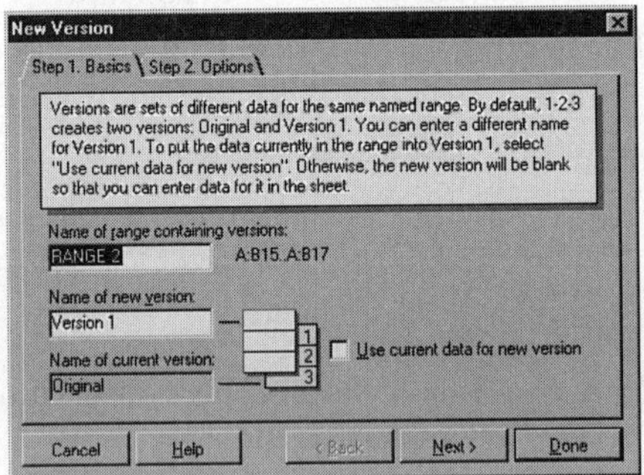

Fig. 21.4
The Version Manager displays this New Version dialog box if you attempt to create a new version in a new range.

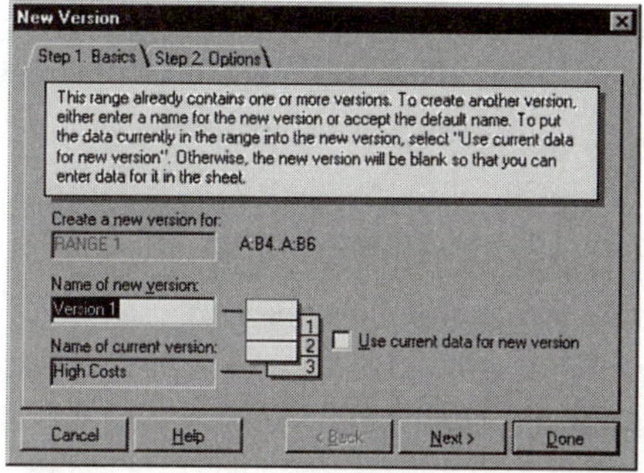

Fig. 21.5
The Version Manager displays this New Version dialog box if you attempt to create a new version in a range that already contains versions.

variations on the New Version dialog box are so similar, we'll use figure

the worksheet we'll use for our example. You can use Version Manager
ults of different strategies for reaching the goal of maximum profits
le range of possibilities.

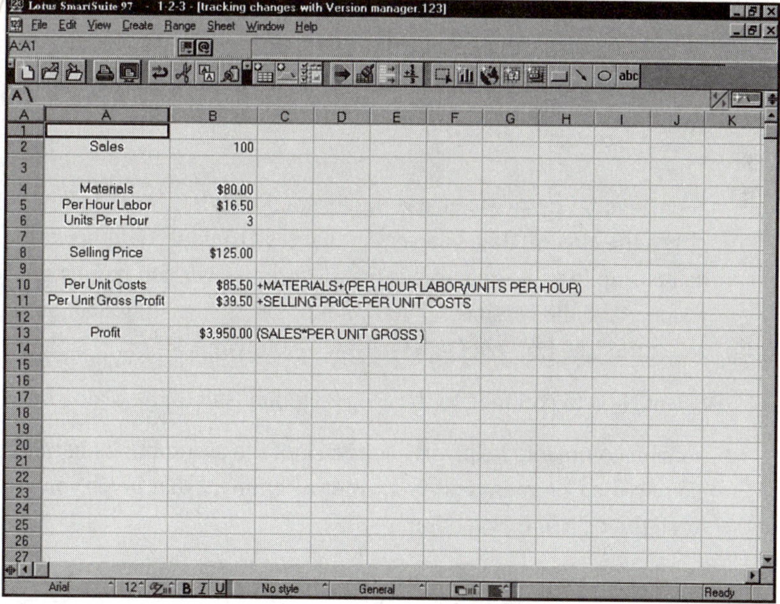

Fig. 21.6
Use Version Manager to see the effects of different assumptions on the bottom line.

The first step in creating a version of a range is to enter the data for the version. If the range already contains data you want to preserve, begin by creating a version that contains the data currently stored in the range. This action saves that data so that you don't lose the original data when you enter different sets of data for the range. In fact, 1-2-3 offers to name the existing data set as Original.

For example, to explore different assumptions, begin by creating a version that contains the data currently stored in the range B4..B6. First, select cells B4..B6, and then select Range, Version, New Version to display the New Version dialog box as shown in figure 21.4.

Next, you must assign a range name to the selected range. You can either enter a new name in the Name of range containing versions text box, or accept the default name of RANGE 1. As you create additional version ranges, the default name 1-2-3 offers will increment by one each time; RANGE 2, RANGE 3, and so on.

Each version must also have a name, which you enter in the Name of New Version text box. Here, too, you have the option of accepting a default name for the version (Version 1, Version 2, and so on), or entering your own, more descriptive version name. It's a good idea to create your own version names, because this will make it easier to select the versions you want to try, and also will make the Version Manager's reports easier to understand.

NOTE When you create versions, each named range you use as the basis for a version must contain fewer than 2000 cells. ■

You can enter new data or use the existing data for the new version. By default, 1-2-3 places the current data in a version named Original. Whether or not you want to use this name is up to you—remember that descriptive version names are very useful in helping you manage the versions. If you want to use the existing data but use a new version name, select the Use Current Data for New Version check box.

Select Next to continue to the Step 2 Options tab of the dialog box (see figure 21.7).

Version comments help you keep track of the assumptions behind the data in each version. In the Comment text box, enter a comment that helps you remember why you entered the data in this version.

Use the Show Name and Border Around Version check box to control whether 1-2-3 includes the Version Manager title bar and border around the version range. If you include this, you can select different versions by clicking the down arrow at the right side of the Version Manager title bar, and choosing a version from the list of versions.

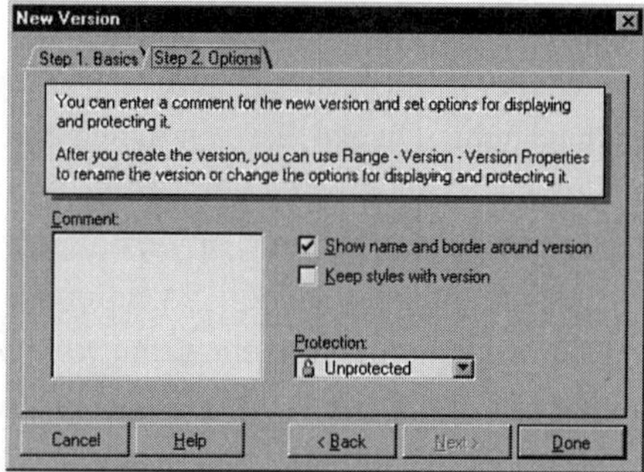

Fig. 21.7
Use the Options tab to enter comments, set the display style, and control the Protection setting.

Use the Keep styles with version check box to indicate whether or not each version in a range should have its own styles. Usually you'll want to apply the same style to all versions in a range, so you should leave this check box blank.

The Protection options are most useful when you use Version Manager to share data with other users. Unprotected is the default sharing option. Choose the Protected option to protect versions so that other users can't change them; choose the Hidden option to hide versions so that other users can't display them.

When you complete the New Version dialog box, click the Done button to create the version and return to the worksheet.

CAUTION

If you didn't select the Use current data for new version check box, don't be surprised to find formulas that show ERR or 0. Leaving this check box blank causes 1-2-3 to erase the existing data, so formulas that depend on the data will not evaluate correctly until you add new data.

To create a second version of a range, again select Range, Version, New Version to display the New Version dialog box. Enter the new version name, any options such as comments, and select Done. Make certain you do not select the Use current data for new version check box, because you want to enter new data.

Displaying Versions

After you create several versions of a range, you can display the versions in the worksheet. To display a version of a range in the worksheet, select the desired version from the drop-down list box by clicking the down arrow on the range's Version Manager title bar, and then selecting the version from the list box.

Although the drop-down list boxes on the Version Manager title bars are quite handy for selecting a version for a single range, you'll probably want to use the Range, Version, Display Version command to display the Display Version dialog box if you have more than one range containing versions in a workbook (see figure 21.8). When you use this dialog box, you can select which version to display for each range before you leave the dialog box. That way you'll know for certain that all the correct versions are displayed together. You also can group sets of versions if you often use the same versions together. See "Creating, Displaying, and Modifying Groups" later in this chapter for more details on using groups.

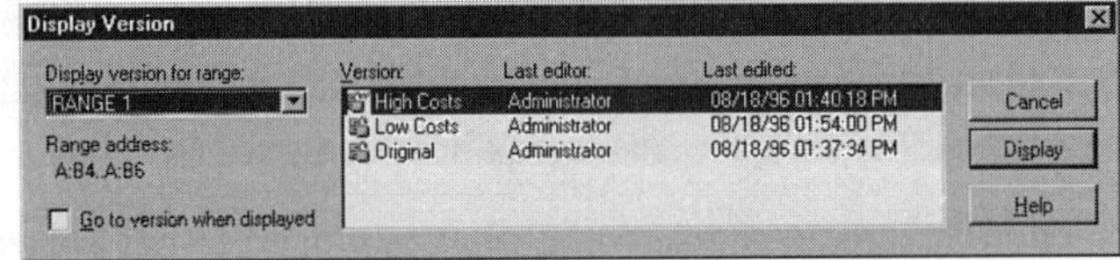

Fig. 21.8
Use the Display Version dialog box to make certain the correct version is displayed for all version ranges.

As soon as you select the version or versions to display in the worksheet, 1-2-3 replaces any existing data with the data from the selected version. If you want to save the existing data, first create a version for that data, and be sure to select the Use Current Data for New Version check box to keep the data.

Modifying and Updating Versions

After you create a version, you can change it in several ways. You can modify the data to reflect new information, you can delete a version, or you can add new versions to a range to examine even more possibilities.

To change the data in a version, first display the version in the worksheet. Then enter the new data for the version, and save the workbook. Rather than changing the data in an existing version, however, you may find it is a better idea to create a new version and retain the old data.

CAUTION

When you update a version, you replace the original data stored in the version with the data currently in the worksheet.

To delete a version you no longer need, thus preventing its data from being used accidentally, select Range, Version, Delete Version to display the Delete Version dialog box (see fig. 21.9). Select the proper range and then the version you wish to remove, and then select Delete. Select Done to return to the worksheet.

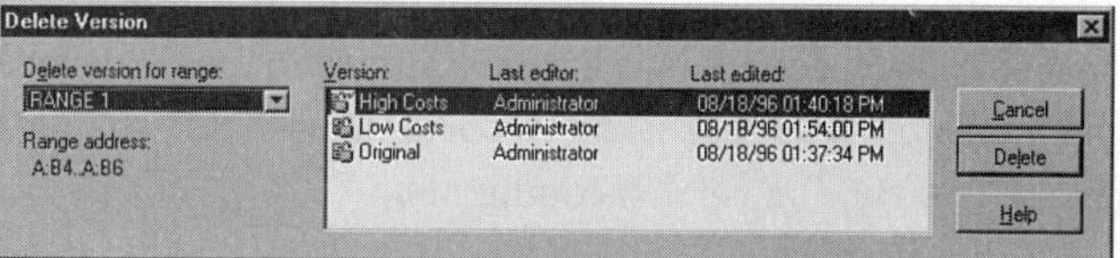

Fig. 21.9
Use the Delete Version dialog box to remove versions you no longer want in the workbook.

To change a version's name, comment, protection options, and style-retention setting, display the version in the worksheet and then select Range, Range Properties (or right-click the version range and choose Version Properties in the shortcut menu) to display the InfoBox. Select the Versions tab to change any of these settings (see fig. 21.10).

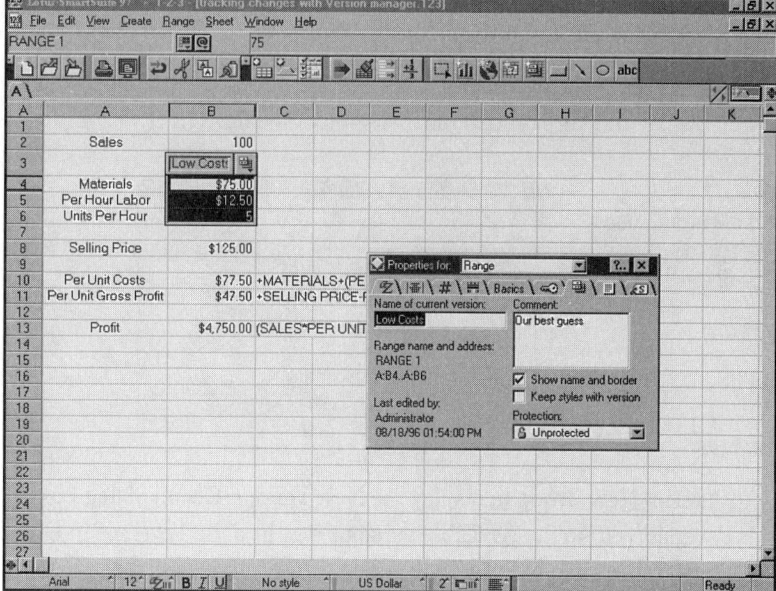

Fig. 21.10
Use the Versions tab of the InfoBox to modify version names, comments, and other related settings.

Displaying Version Comments

Version comments enable you to include extra information that explains the assumptions you used to create a version. To display the comments for the current version, use the Range, Range Properties command (or right-click the version range and choose Version Properties in the shortcut menu) to display the InfoBox. The Comment box on the Versions tab displays any comments entered for the version. You can also include all version comments in a report. See "Creating Reports" later in this chapter for more information on this method of viewing version comments.

Creating, Displaying, and Modifying Groups

Groups are named sets of versions you want to display together. When you create groups, you can quickly select the exact versions you want to use by simply selecting the appropriate group. For example, you might create a group called Most Optimistic that displays the lowest manufacturing costs version, the highest sales version, and the highest price version. You might go on to create additional groups such as Worst Case, Most Likely, and We Can Manage. Each of these groups would contain the particular set of versions that best suits the assumptions for the group.

To create, display, modify, or delete a group, select Range, Version, Version Groups to display the Version Groups dialog box (see fig. 21.11).

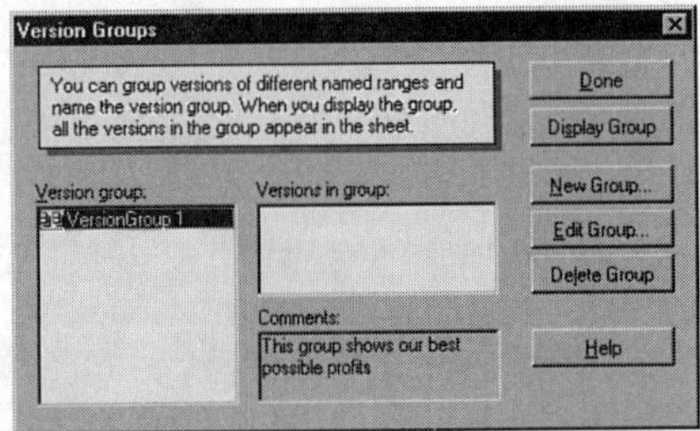

Fig. 21.11
Use the Version Groups dialog box to manage groups of versions.

Select New Group to display the New Version Group dialog box (see fig. 21.12). Drag versions from the Available versions box into the Versions in Group box to add them to a group. You can only add one version from each version range to a group. You can add one version from each version range, but this is not required. For example, if you want to use the best costs and the highest sales price in a group, but don't want to be locked into using the highest sales Figures, don't add a version from the SALES range to the group.

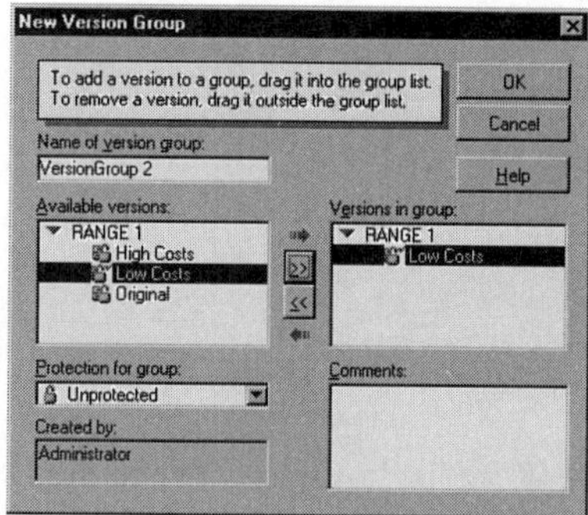

Fig. 21.12
Use the New Version Group dialog box to create groups of versions.

Comments you add in the New Version Group dialog box apply to the group, not to individual versions. Likewise, any protection you apply to the group does not affect the individual versions' protection settings.

To display a group in the worksheet, select the Display Group button in the Version Groups dialog box. 1-2-3 will then display all the versions contained in the group, but won't change the display for any version ranges not included in the selected group.

To modify an existing group, select the Edit Group button in the Version Groups dialog box. This will display the Edit Version Group dialog box, which is nearly identical to the New Version Group dialog box. Use the same drag and drop techniques to move versions in and out of the group as you did to create the group originally.

If you no longer need a group, you can delete a version group by selecting it in the Version Groups dialog box and selecting Delete Group. 1-2-3 does not prompt you for confirmation, but simply deletes the group immediately. If you make a mistake and accidentally delete a group in error, select Done to close the Version Groups dialog box, and then immediately select Edit, Undo Version Group.

Creating Reports

In addition to displaying versions and groups in the worksheet, you may want to create reports that show the data in different versions of a range or the effects of different versions on formulas in the worksheet.

To create a report showing the data and audit information for versions of a range—as well as the effects of the versions on formulas in the worksheet—select Range, Version, Report to display the Version Report dialog box (see fig. 21.13).

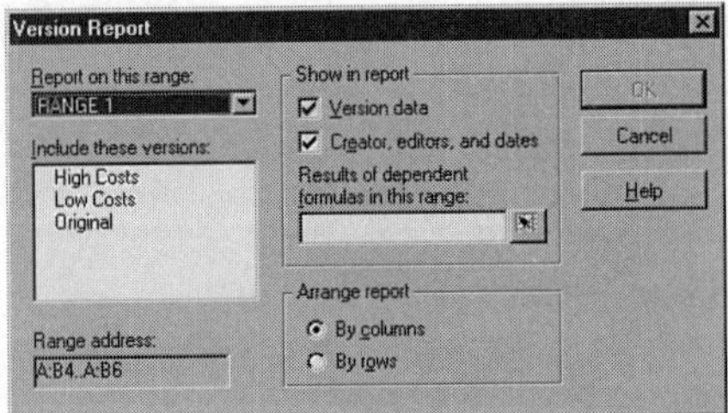

Fig. 21.13
Use the Version Report dialog box to report on the effects of the various versions.

In the Report on This Range drop-down list box, select the named range for which you want to create a report. Then select one or more versions of the range from the Include These Versions list box. A check mark appears next to versions you have selected.

If you want the report to include the effects of the different versions on a range of formulas in the worksheet, specify the range in the Results of Dependent Formulas in this Range text box. You can use point mode to select this range.

In the Show in Report section of the dialog box, select the Version Data check box to include in the report the data in each version; select the Creator, Editors, and Dates check box to include the name of the creator or modifier, date, and time. The default setting selects both these options. In the Arrange Report area of the dialog box, select By Columns or By Rows to choose the orientation of data in the report.

When you choose OK, 1-2-3 creates the report in a new workbook file which will be named REPORT1.123 when you save the file. Figure 21.14 shows the report that results from the selections shown in the Version Report dialog box in figure 21.13.

NOTE You can create customized reports using the @VERSIONDATA, @VERSIONINFO, and @SCENARIOINFO functions. (Functions are described in the @function reference of the 1-2-3 online help system.)

CAUTION

When you use the Version Report dialog box, and you specify a range in the Results of Dependent Formulas in this range text box, 1-2-3 recalculates formulas in all active files once for each version you include in the report. If you have several 1-2-3 files open, or if your file takes a long time to recalculate, you may want to create reports at a time when you don't need to use the computer for something else.

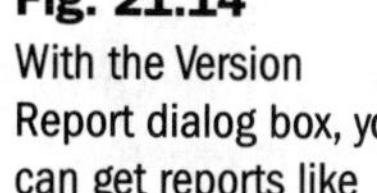

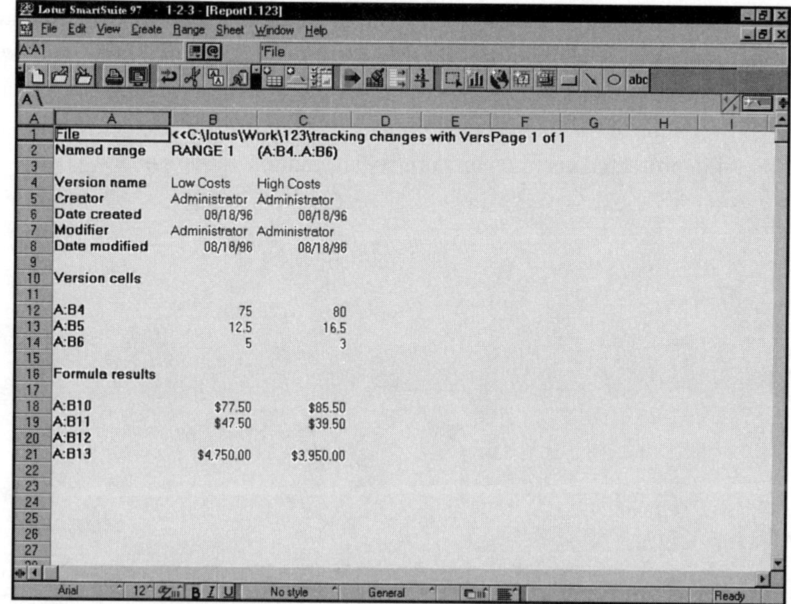

Lotus SmartSuite 97 - 1-2-3 - [Report1.123]
File Edit View Create Range Sheet Window Help
A:A1
File
File
<<C:\lotus\Work\123\tracking changes with VersPage 1 of 1
Named range
RANGE 1 (A:B4..A:B6)
Version name
Low Costs
High Costs
Creator
Administrator
Administrator
Date created
08/18/96
08/18/96
Modifier
Administrator
Administrator
Date modified
08/18/96
08/18/96
Version cells
A:B4
75
80
A:B5
12.5
16.5
A:B6
5
3
Formula results
A:B10
$77.50
$85.50
A:B11
$47.50
$39.50
A:B12
A:B13
$4,750.00
$3,950.00
Arial
12
No style
General
Ready

Fig. 21.14
With the Version Report dialog box, you can get reports like this. This report results from the Version Report dialog box selections shown in figure 21.13.

Using Version Manager To Share Data

In addition to enabling you to create and maintain different versions of data in your own worksheets, Version Manager makes it easier than ever to share data with other 1-2-3 users. Several users can enter versions in the same file without writing over each other's data. Version Manager provides audit information so that you always know who entered which version.

If you have a local area network, you can share data by keeping a file on a network file server. Users can add versions to the same file along with comments explaining the thinking behind each version. For example, different people can enter revenue forecasts based on their individual expertise. Coworkers can review each other's versions, use the comments section to add suggestions or ask questions, and perhaps create new versions based on someone else's ideas.

Chapter 30, "Using the Team Computing Features," has more information on how you can share 1-2-3 workbooks with other members of your working team. By using the Version Manager effectively, you can keep a complete record of who made changes, when they made them, and if everyone uses the version comment feature, why they made their changes.

Any time you share a file, whether on a network or not, you may want to unprotect the ranges in which you want others to create versions and then seal the file with a password. This arrangement prevents other people from rearranging the file but lets them create versions in the unprotected ranges. Sealing the file also prevents other users from changing protected versions or from seeing hidden versions. ●

PART V

Managing Databases

CHAPTER 22

Creating a Database

by David Plotkin

Building a database in 1-2-3

1-2-3 enables you to build a database using standard spreadsheet features.

Capabilities of a 1-2-3 database

You learn to sort your data in any order, as well as create queries to find specific information, such as "Tell me all customers who have bought more than $1,000 in merchandise during the month of May."

Entering data into a 1-2-3 database

You learn how to enter data into a 1-2-3 database.

A *database* is a collection of related information—data organized so that you can list, sort, or search it. The list of data may contain any kind of information, from addresses to tax-deductible expenditures. Telephone books, Rolodexes, and checkbooks are common examples of databases. Most businesses have databases to keep track of their employees, customers, inventory, and vendors. Figure 22.1 shows an example of an employee database built in 1-2-3.

The advantage to computerizing a database is the ease and speed of data retrieval. Suppose you would like to know which customers purchased more than $30,000 of products from you last year. If you had to manually go through a cabinet full of customer files, it could take you days to compile this data. With a computerized database, you could locate this information in minutes. Anyone who has ever had to manually sort a stack of index cards or file folders can attest to how tedious this task is. But with a computerized database, the Sort command operates so fast that if you blink you might not see it happen! ■

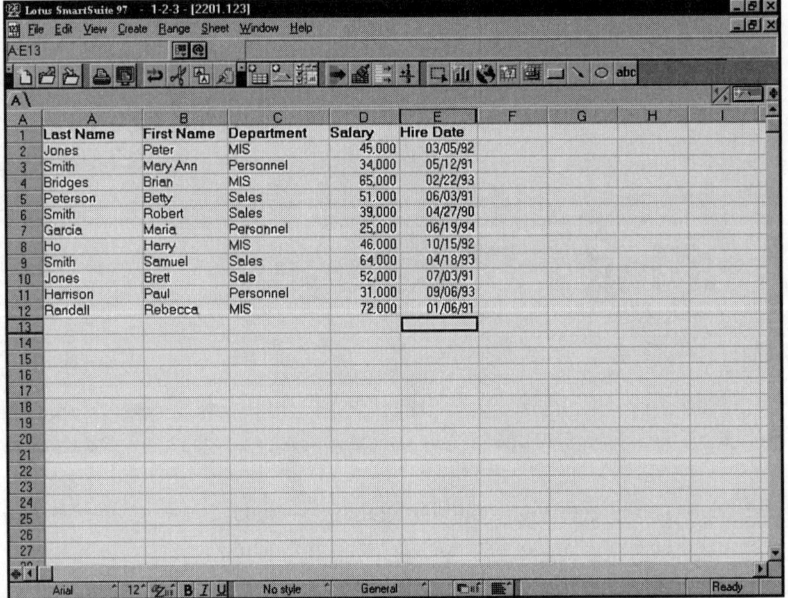

Last Name	First Name	Department	Salary	Hire Date
Jones	Peter	MIS	45,000	03/05/92
Smith	Mary Ann	Personnel	34,000	05/12/91
Bridges	Brian	MIS	65,000	02/22/93
Peterson	Betty	Sales	51,000	06/03/91
Smith	Robert	Sales	39,000	04/27/90
Garcia	Maria	Personnel	25,000	06/19/94
Ho	Harry	MIS	46,000	10/15/92
Smith	Samuel	Sales	64,000	04/18/93
Jones	Brett	Sale	52,000	07/03/91
Harrison	Paul	Personnel	31,000	09/06/93
Randall	Rebecca	MIS	72,000	01/06/91

Fig. 22.1
This is an example of a database you can create in 1-2-3 for Windows.

Understanding 1-2-3 Databases

1-2-3 provides true database management commands and functions so that you can sort, query, extract, and perform analysis on data and even access and manipulate data from an external database. One important advantage of 1-2-3 database functionality over independent database products is that 1-2-3's database commands are similar to the other commands used in the 1-2-3 program. As a result, you have a running start on using the 1-2-3 database manager.

1-2-3 can handle both *flat-file* (where all the data is stored in one "table" or worksheet) and *relational* databases. A relational database spreads the stored information over many tables that are linked together. Relational databases are more efficient than flat-file databases at storing and updating data. In fact, most database applications of any complexity normally use a relational database. Further, relational database programs, such as Lotus Approach, provide functions—form-based queries and cascading deletes/updates—that are more powerful or easier to use than the database capabilities of 1-2-3. However, once you create a database in 1-2-3, you can import it into Approach to use with Approach's advanced database functionality.

▶ **See** "Using 1-2-3 with Approach," **p. 664**

After you build a database table (which is really no different than building any other worksheet application), you can perform a variety of functions on it. You accomplish some of these tasks by using standard 1-2-3 commands. For example, you can add a record to the database by selecting a row (click the row number at the left end of the row) and select the Range, Insert Rows command. Editing the contents of a database record is as easy as editing any other cell: you move the cell pointer to that location and type.

You can access external databases with 1-2-3. You can import records from another database, such as Paradox, into a 1-2-3 worksheet. Using this ability to link to an external database, you can use 1-2-3 to work with data you entered into another database program. You can also move your 1-2-3 data into a more powerful database program.

Organizing Data in a Database

In 1-2-3, the word *database* means a range of cells that spans at least one column and more than one row. Because a database is actually a list, the manner in which database data is organized sets it apart from data in ordinary cells. Just as a list must be organized to be useful, a database must be organized to permit access to the information that it contains.

Databases generally are organized in three ways:

- *A single database contained in a single worksheet.* This organization method is used in most of the examples in this chapter, as well as in most simple real-world applications.
- *Multiple databases in a single worksheet.* Each database occupies a different portion of the worksheet.
- *Multiple databases in two or more worksheets.* Be aware, however, that a single database table cannot span different worksheets. As you learn in Chapter 26, "Understanding Advanced Data Management," you can relate databases that are on different worksheets and thus produce a more efficient overall database structure.

Remember that a 1-2-3 database is similar to any other group of cells. This knowledge may help you as you learn about the different database commands covered in this chapter. In many instances, you can use these commands in what you may consider to be nondatabase applications. For example, you can use the Range, Sort command to sort any range, not just a database range.

Understanding Database Terms

Databases are made up of fields and records. A *field*, or single data item, is the smallest unit in a database. To develop a database of companies with which you do business, for example, you can include the following fields for each company:

Name

Address

City

State

ZIP code

Phone number

A *record* is a set of associated fields. In this example, the accumulation of all data about one company forms one record. The six fields in the preceding paragraph represent one record on one company.

In 1-2-3, a field is a single cell, and a record is a row of cells within a database.

To be useful, a database must be set up so that you can access the information it contains. Retrieval of information usually involves key fields. A database *key field* is any field on which you base a list, sort, or search operation. For example, you can use ZIP code as a key field to sort the data in the company database and to assign contact representatives to specific geographic areas.

One of the most powerful operations you can perform with a database is to retrieve all the records that meet certain criteria. For example, you could list all the records for companies located in New York. This type of data retrieval is called a *query*. Of course, to perform a query, you must store the information on which the query will be based in the database. In the above example, you would have to store a "City" field.

A 1-2-3 database resides in the worksheet's row-and-column format. Figure 22.2 shows the general organization of a 1-2-3 database. Labels, or *field names*, that describe the data items appear as column headings in row 1. Information about each specific data item (field) is entered in a cell in the appropriate column. In figure 22.2, cell B5 represents data (3500 Bacon Ct.) for the second field (ADDRESS) in the database's fourth record, which is in row 5.

Theoretically, the maximum number of records you can have in a 1-2-3 database corresponds to the maximum number of rows in the worksheet (8,192 rows, minus 1 row for the field names). Realistically, however, the number of records in a specific database is limited by the amount of available memory: internal memory (RAM) plus disk storage for virtual memory. You're much better off using Approach than 1-2-3 for very large databases.

When you estimate the maximum database size for your computer equipment, be sure to include enough blank rows to accommodate the maximum output you expect from any operation that requires an area in the worksheet to display its output (e.g., a query). You also may be able to split a large 1-2-3 database into separate database tables on different worksheet levels if all the data does not have to be sorted or searched as a unit. You may, for example, be able to separate a telephone-list database by name (A through M in one file; N through Z in another) or area code.

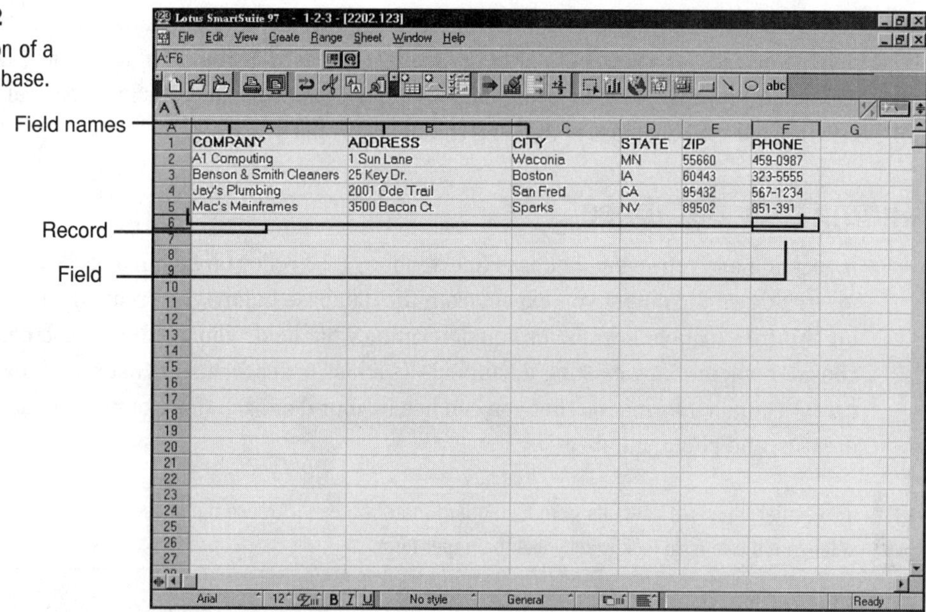

Fig. 22.2
Organization of a 1-2-3 database.

Choosing an Area for Your Database

You can create a database as a new workbook or as part of an existing workbook. If you decide to build a database in an existing worksheet, choose an area of the worksheet that you do not need for any other purpose. This area should be large enough to accommodate the number of records that you plan to enter during the current session and in the future.

A better idea, however, is to add another worksheet to the current workbook so that the database and the existing worksheet don't interfere with each other. To add another worksheet for the new database, click the New Sheet button, click the New Sheet SmartIcon, or use the Create, Sheet command, then select the number of sheets, and select OK.

In addition, you may want to create a separate worksheet to hold a query table so that the query table doesn't overwrite existing data. You may want to add names to the worksheet tabs to make it easy to remember which worksheet holds the database and which holds the query table.

Take advantage of 1-2-3's 3D capabilities by placing the different database elements such as query tables, reports, and so on in their own worksheets.

After you decide which area of the worksheet to use, you create a database by specifying field names across a row and entering data in cells, as you would for any other 1-2-3 application. The mechanics of entering database contents are simple; the most critical step in creating a useful database is defining the fields properly.

Planning Your Database

In locating and retrieving database information, 1-2-3 relies on field names. You may want to write down the output you expect from the database before you create the fields; writing this information down helps you determine what fields you need. You also need to consider whether any existing documents (such as order forms or customer information cards) contain information that you can use in your database (for example, names, addresses, and phone numbers).

If you enter database contents from a standard form, you can increase the speed of data entry by setting up the form to look exactly like the paper form.

When you are setting up the database, you must assign each field a name. 1-2-3 is not strict when it comes to your field names. The names can be as many as 512 characters long (the maximum number of characters that can be entered in a cell) and can contain special symbols and spaces. However, the field names must be labels, even if they are numeric labels ('1, '2, and so on). Of course, field names must be unique—you can't have two fields with the same name. One restriction is that a field name must be entered in a single cell, and all field names must be entered into the same row. For example, if you have a field called *First Name*, do not enter **First** in one cell and **Name** in another.

Although you can use field names of up to 512 characters, it's best to limit them to 15 characters so that you can use range names to refer to the fields. You also should not use spaces, arithmetic operators such as the plus sign (+), nor any of the following:

, . : ; - # ~ !

NOTE While 1-2-3 doesn't allow you to enter field names on multiple rows, you can achieve this look by turning on the Wrap text in cell option in the Range Properties Infobox. You can then increase the height of the row to display several lines of text in a single row. ■

A common error in setting up databases is choosing field names (and entering data) without thinking about the output you want from that field. For example, if you create an address field that contains the city, state, and ZIP code, you are likely to run into problems. You will not be able to sort by ZIP code, nor will you be able to search for a certain state.

A similar problem can crop up if you create a single field for a person's name. If you enter a name as **John Smith**, you will not be able to sort the last names in alphabetical order. While there is a way to search for *Smith* in this example, the procedure is much more complicated than if you had separate fields for first and last names.

When in doubt, separate your data into different fields; you will appreciate the flexibility later as you perform queries and sorts.

While creating your database, you may also want to preformat some of the fields. Your numeric fields should be formatted appropriately (Fixed, Comma, Currency, Percent, and so forth). Label fields do not need to be preformatted unless the data begins with a numeric character. Suppose you are entering Social Security numbers, telephone numbers, or part codes that begin with a number. You'll probably find it helpful to format these fields with Label format so that you do not have to type a label prefix before entering the data. Date fields should be formatted with the particular date format that you prefer; for example, 31-Dec-97, 12/31/97, or 12/31.

While setting up your database, it's helpful to set an appropriate column width for each field. Try to guess what will be the longest piece of data that will go in a field, and set the column width to accommodate this data. Probably the easiest way to set the width is to drag the column borders. Keep in mind that numeric fields may require extra space for punctuation and decimal places, depending on the format you have selected for a field.

▶ **See** "Working with Number Formats," **p. 110**

▶ **See** "Setting Column Widths," **p. 94**

Instead of setting a different column width, some people space out their data by putting a blank column between fields. This is not a good idea because it can interfere with database queries. It is also an inefficient use of space.

Another consideration when defining the database is alignment. If you like, you can preformat the fields to be center- , left-, or right-aligned. By default, labels are left-aligned and numbers and dates are right-aligned.

Building a 1-2-3 Database

After you plan the database, you can build it. To understand how the process works, create a Company database as a new database in a blank worksheet (in READY mode). Enter the field names across a single row (A:A1..A:F1, as shown previously in figure 22.2).

CAUTION

Do not leave a blank row between the field names and the first record. If you do, your query operations may not work correctly. Instead of a blank row, you can separate the field names from the records by increasing the height of the row containing the first record, or formatting the field names differently (bold, italic, bottom border).

Entering Data

After you enter field names, you can add records to the database. To enter the first record, move the cursor to the row directly below the field-name row and then enter the data across the row. To enter the first record shown earlier in figure 22.2, for example, type the following entries in the cells shown:

A:A2:	**A1 Computing**
A:B2:	**'1 Sun Lane**
A:C2:	**Waconia**
A:D2:	**MN**
A:E2:	**'55660**
A:F2:	**'459-0987**

Notice that you enter the contents of the ADDRESS, PHONE, and ZIP fields by typing an apostrophe (') label character. An easier method, however, is simply formatting these fields with Label format.

▶ **See** "Entering Data," **p. 66**

The sample Company database is used periodically throughout this section of the book to demonstrate the effects of various database commands. In this example, the fields are shown in a single screen. In real-life applications, however, you track many more data items. You can maintain 256 fields (the number of columns available) in a single 1-2-3 database. As previously mentioned, the number of records in a specific database is limited by the amount of available memory: internal memory (RAM) plus disk storage for virtual memory.

Assigning a Range Name to the Database

After you have entered all the records into the database, it's a good time to assign a range name to the database. Why bother naming the database range? There are several reasons. If you want to print the database, you won't need to highlight the range—you can just specify the range name as your print range. Secondly, 1-2-3's database queries and functions require you to specify the database range; with a range name, it's very easy to do this. In the example used above, the Range, Name command was used to assign the name COMPANY_DB to the range A1..F5.

▶ **See** "Working with Cells and Ranges," **p. 55**

TROUBLESHOOTING

The leading zero for some of the ZIP codes in my database is not displaying. For example, I typed 06987 but the cell displays 6987. You are losing the leading zero because you have entered the ZIP codes as numbers instead of labels. Either enter a label prefix (such as the apostrophe) before typing each ZIP code or preformat the ZIP code field to Label format.

My database has more records and fields than can fit on-screen at one time. Therefore, it's difficult to enter data when the field names and the data in the first column of the database scroll off-screen. You need to freeze the field names and the first column so that these cells don't scroll off-screen. Place the cell pointer underneath the field names and to the right of the first column, then use the View, Titles and select the check boxes for both Rows Above the Current Cell and Columns Left of Current Cell. Another possibility would be to create a form as discussed in "Other Integrating Methods for Approach and 1-2-3," in Chapter 28.

CHAPTER 23

Entering and Editing Data in a Database

by David Plotkin

After you have created a database, you can easily modify its contents and structure. You can add new records, delete old or duplicate records, and edit the fields in any record. You can modify the structure of the database by inserting, deleting, and moving fields. You can even make significant changes such as dividing one field into two or combining two fields into one. ■

Adding and deleting records

With a 1-2-3 database, you can add records simply by adding rows to the worksheet in the correct position. Deleting records is just as easy—simply delete the record's row.

Adding and removing the fields in a database

If you find that you have left out fields that you need, you can add the fields by inserting a column into the worksheet.

Dividing and combining fields

You can restructure data using 1-2-3's functions. For example, you could split a "Name" field into a "First Name" and a "Last Name" field.

Adding Records to a Database

You can take several approaches to adding records to your database. One way is to type the new record in the first empty row at the bottom of the database. Use this technique, discussed in Chapter 22, "Creating a Database," when you are initially inputting the records.

If you add new records to the bottom of a database, however, they won't automatically be included in the database range name. (As mentioned in Chapter 22, it's wise to assign a range name to your database to save time when printing and using database queries and functions.) You must use the Range, Name command to expand the database range name to include the new records. If you forget to adjust the database range, any commands or formulas that refer to the database name will not include the new records.

You can use two methods to avoid having to manually adjust the database range name when adding records to a named database: you can *insert* them or *append* them.

Inserting Records

The simplest way to add records to a named database range is to insert the new records in the middle of the database; that way, the range name automatically expands to include the new records. The inserted row can be anywhere within the database range. For example, you can insert the row below the first record, above the last record, or anywhere in between. This method does require that you issue a command to insert a row for each new record, however. You can insert a row four ways:

- Click the Insert Rows SmartIcon.
- Click the row number to select the entire row. Press the right-mouse button to display the shortcut Shortmenu and choose Insert Rows. This technique is shown in figure 23.1.
- Click the row number to select the entire row, then choose Range, Insert Rows.
- Press Ctrl++.

If you are going to modify your database often, you may want to display the Editing SmartIcon palette.

▶ **See** "Inserting Rows or Columns," **p. 85**

▶ **See** "Switching SmartIcon Bars," **p. 768**

▶ **See** "Writing 1-2-3 Macros," **p. 811**

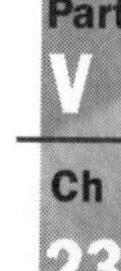

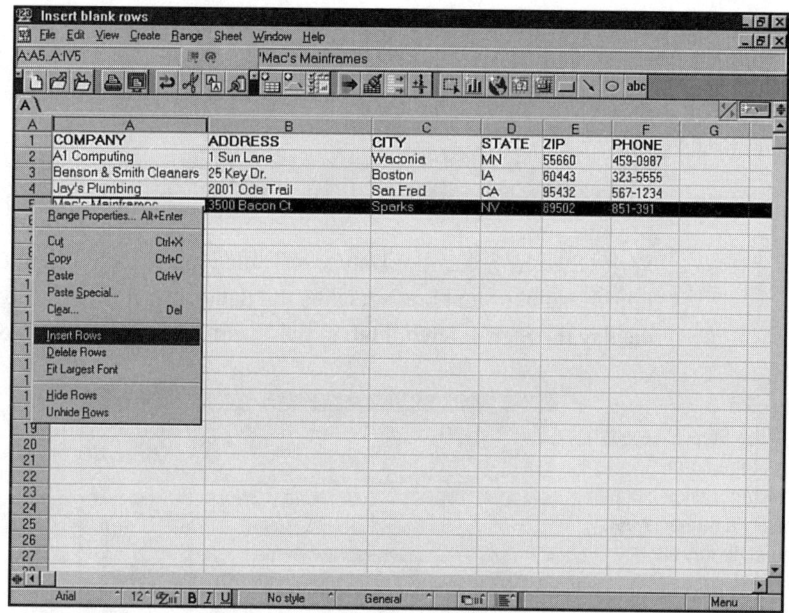

Fig. 23.1
Pressing the right-mouse button displays the shortcut menu; this menu offers a quick way to insert a row for a new database record.

There are two disadvantages to inserting records in the middle of the range. First, the inserted rows may disrupt data to the right of the database. If you have any data to the right of the database, you'll want to move it to another worksheet before inserting records in your database or make certain the Insert in the Selected Range Only checkbox is selected in the Insert dialog box before you insert the new rows. The second disadvantage to this technique is that you aren't putting new records in the most logical place—at the bottom of the database. If this bothers you, add records by using the technique described in the next section.

Appending Records

A better method of adding database records is to use an Approach form. 1-2-3 works with Approach to make maintaining your databases much easier.

Before you use this method, you should assign a range name to the database. Use the Range, Name command to name the database range (cells A:A1..F5 in fig. 23.1). For this exercise, use the range name **COMPANY_DB**. After you have named the database range, follow these steps to create the form:

1. Select the Create, Database, Form command to display the Create Form dialog box (see fig. 23.2).

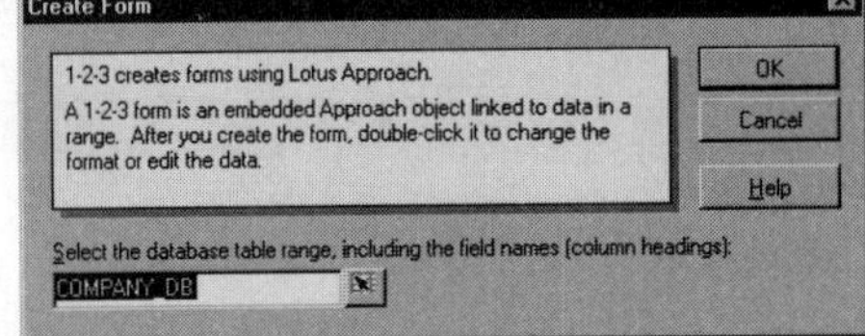

Fig. 23.2
Verify the database table range to insure your form includes the complete database.

2. Verify that the Select the Database Table Range, Including the Field Names (Column Headings) text box specifies the database range correctly and choose OK to display the Step 1: Layout tab of the Form Assistant dialog box (see fig. 23.3).

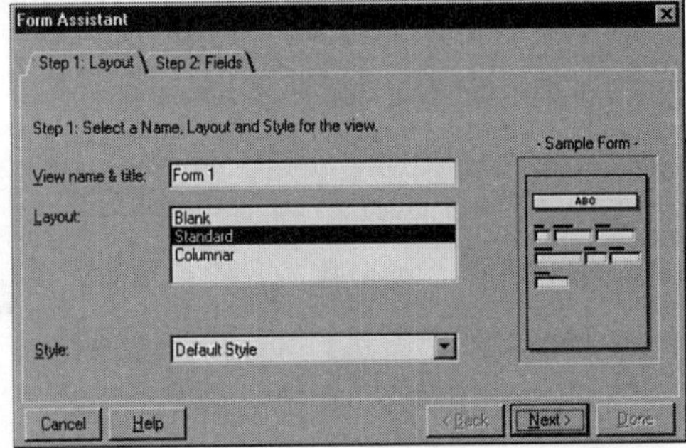

Fig. 23.3
Use the Step 1: Layout tab of the Form Assistant dialog box to specify a name, layout, and style for your form.

3. You can use the default settings for the form or you can use the options on the Step 1: Layout tab of the Form Assistant dialog box to change the form's appearance. For example, you can specify a new name for the form in the View Name & Title text box. When you have completed your selections, choose Next to display the Step 2: Fields tab of the Form Assistant dialog box (see fig. 23.4).

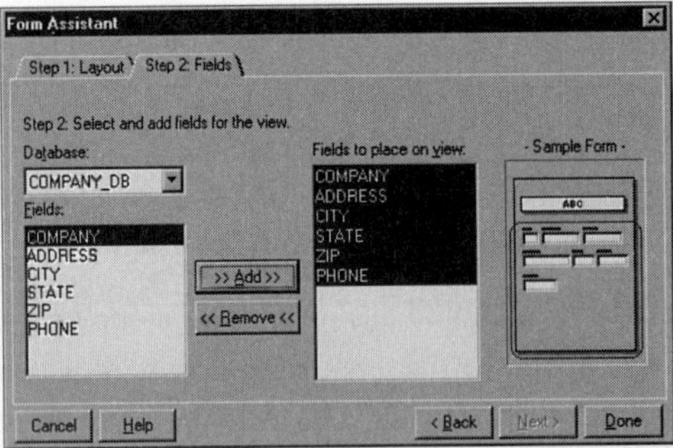

Fig. 23.4
Use the Step 2: Fields tab of the Form Assistant dialog box to specify the fields to appear on your form.

4. Select the fields to appear on your form from the Fields list box and choose >>Add>> to copy the selected fields to the Fields to Place on View list box. Choose Done to confirm the dialog box and add the form to the worksheet.

After the form has been added to the worksheet, you can use the form to add or delete records, modify data in the records, or sort the database. To use the form to view or modify your database, double-click the form if necessary to activate it. Figure 23.5 shows how your screen will appear when the form is active. Notice that the menu and the toolbar are both changed when the form is active.

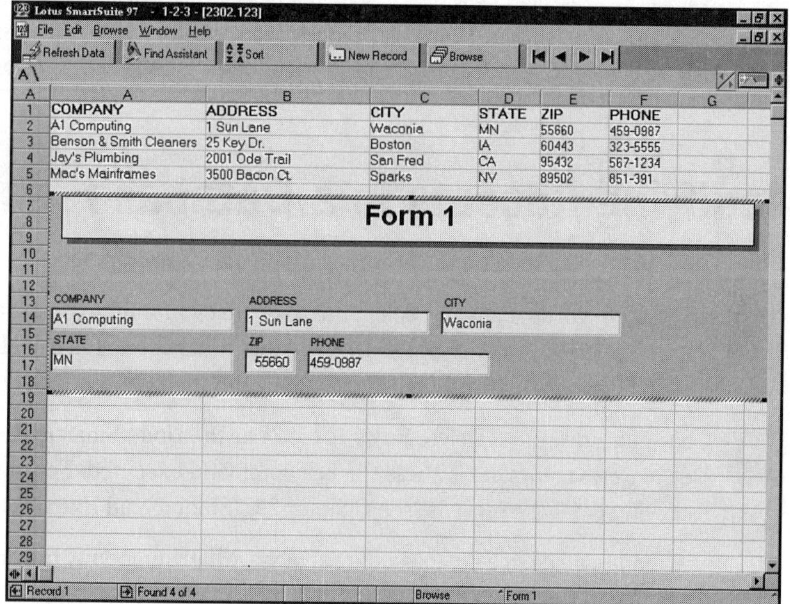

Fig. 23.5
Double-click the form to activate it so you can view and modify your database records.

Here are some of the commands you can use when the form is active to view and modify your database:

Use Browse, New Record to add new records.

Use Browse, Duplicate Record to add an exact duplicate of the currently displayed record. You can then modify the new record to make it unique.

Use Browse, Delete Record to remove a record from the database.

Use the Page Up and Page Down keys to move between records. You can also use the navigator arrows on the right side of the toolbar to navigate between records with your mouse.

The following sections focus on modifying your database manually. For more information on using Approach forms with 1-2-3, see "Using 1-2-3 with Approach" in Chapter 28.

TROUBLESHOOTING

I added new records to my database but when I tell 1-2-3 to print the database range (which I had named DATABASE) the new records don't print. What am I doing wrong? When you add new records manually rather than using a form, the new rows aren't automatically included in the range name. There are several ways to solve this problem. You can manually lengthen the range associated with the name DATABASE, insert new records in the middle of the database so that they are automatically included in the range name, or use the Approach form to add the records.

Modifying Records in a Database

1-2-3 makes maintaining the accuracy of the database contents easy.

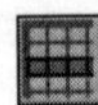

To delete records manually, select the rows that you want to delete and then choose Range, Delete Rows or click the Delete Rows SmartIcon. You can also press the right-mouse button to display the shortcut menu and then choose Delete Rows.

Choosing Edit, Undo Delete Rows (Ctrl+Z) or the Undo SmartIcon can reverse a Range, Delete Rows command if it was the last command executed. For more information on removing database records, see Chapter 25, "Finding and Extracting Data."

You modify fields in a database the same way that you modify the contents of cells. As explained in Chapter 3, you change cell contents either by retyping the cell entry or by pressing the F2 (Edit) key and then editing the entry.

Modifying the Structure of a Database

You can modify the database structure just as easily as the database contents. The database *structure* refers to the set of fields in your database. After you use your database for a while, you may discover that it needs additional fields or that one of the fields is obsolete. You also may find that you prefer the fields to be ordered differently.

Inserting a New Field

To add a new field to a database, click the column letter at the top of the column to select the entire column. Next, choose Range, Insert Columns (or choose Insert Columns from the shortcut menu)or click the Insert Columns SmartIcon; the new column is inserted to the left of the selected column. Alternatively, you can select any cell in a column and then choose Range, Insert (or choose Insert from the shortcut menu). Choose Columns from the Insert dialog box. The new column is inserted to the left of the column in which the selected cell was located.

After you have created a new field, you can fill the field with the appropriate values for each record. To insert a CONTACT field between the ZIP and PHONE fields, for example, position the cell pointer on any cell in the PHONE column, issue the Range, Insert command, and choose Columns from the Insert dialog box. Then, type the new field name (**CONTACT**) in cell A:F1 (see fig. 23.6) and add the contact names.

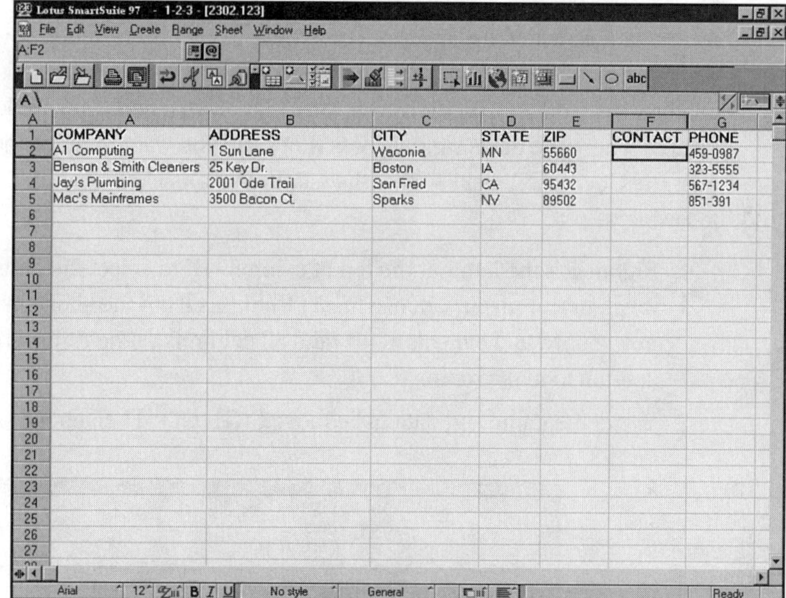

Fig. 23.6
Add a column for a new database field.

▶ **See** "Inserting and Deleting Cells, Rows, and Columns," **p. 84**

As you modify the structure of the database, think about possible effects on the range associated with the database range name. If you insert a field in the middle of the database, the range will automatically expand to accommodate the change. You will run into problems, however, when you insert a field before the first field or after the last field—the new field will not be part of the database range. In this case, you need to respecify the range with the Range, Name command so that the new field is included.

Deleting a Field

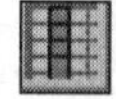

To delete a field, click the column letter at the top of the column to select the entire column. Next, choose Range, Delete Columns (or choose Delete Columns from the shortcut menu) or click the Delete Columns SmartIcon; the column is deleted. Alternatively, you can select any cell in a column and then issue the Range, Delete command (or choose Delete from the shortcut menu). Choose Columns from the Delete dialog box.

When you delete fields, you don't need to be concerned about the database range name. The range will automatically contract when you delete any fields—first, last, or middle fields.

▶ **See** "Inserting and Deleting Cells, Rows, and Columns," **p. 84**

Moving a Field

Moving a field is not just a simple cut-and-paste operation. When you move data in 1-2-3, you must make sure the destination range is empty because any existing data in the destination is overwritten. Furthermore, after you move a field, you are left with an empty column where the data originally was. Let's say you want to move the CONTACT field after the COMPANY field so that the database looks like figure 23.7. To do so, take the following steps:

1. Right-click the letter at the top of column "B" to select the entire column and display the shortcut menu. Choose Insert Columns from the shortcut menu. Column B is now empty, and old column B (and all columns to the right) are "pushed" right one column to make room.
2. Select the name and data to be moved (G1..G6). Then choose Edit, Cut.

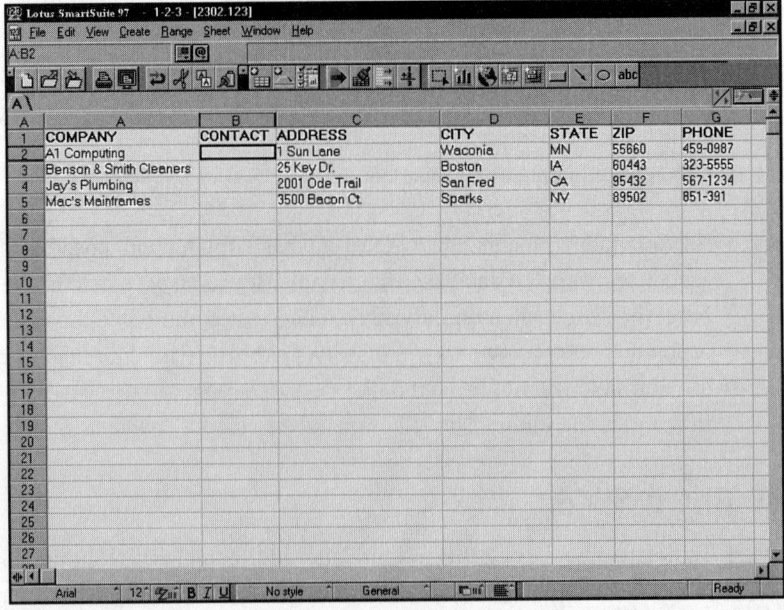

Fig. 23.7
The CONTACT field is moved after the COMPANY field.

3. Place the cell pointer in the field header row of the column you inserted in step 1 (B1). Choose Edit, Paste.
4. Select the column (column G) that previously contained the data that is now empty by right-clicking the letter at the top of the column. Choose Delete Columns from the shortcut menu.

Alternatively, you can move a field with the drag-and-drop method, as follows:

1. Right-click the letter at the top of column "B" to select the entire column and display the shortcut menu. Choose Insert Columns from the shortcut menu. Column B is now empty, and old column B (and all columns to the right) are "pushed" right one column to make room.
2. Select the name and data (G1..G6) to be moved.
3. Place the mouse pointer near the border of the selected range and when you see a hand, press the left-mouse button and drag the data to the destination.
4. Select the column (column G) that previously contained the data that is now empty by right-clicking the letter at the top of the column. Choose Delete Columns from the shortcut menu.

Note that with the drag-and-drop method you still need to do the preparation and clean-up work that was necessary with the cut-and-paste technique.

▶ **See** "Dragging a Range to a New Location," **p. 234**

▶ **See** "Cutting and Pasting a Range," **p. 237**

CAUTION

If you move the first or last field in the database, the range associated with the database name will get scrambled. After moving these fields, make sure you redefine the range with the Range, Name command.

Dividing One Field into Two

Chapter 22 advised you to separate your data into different fields as much as possible so that you have greater flexibility when performing queries and sorts. For example, instead of creating a single NAME field, it's best to create a FIRST NAME and a LAST NAME field. But what if you inherited a database created by another person who didn't follow this rule? Text functions can come to the rescue here.

Text functions, as explained in Chapter 6, allow you to manipulate your labels. With these functions, you can locate a particular string of text in a database field and then extract it and place it in a separate cell. The text functions that help in field subdivision are @FIND, @LENGTH, @LEFT, @MID, and @RIGHT.

To begin, notice that in figure 23.8, the database currently has a field called NAME. Now, suppose you want to extract the first name from the NAME field and place it in the FIRST NAME field, and place the last name in the LAST NAME field. Without text functions, you would have to do this tedious work manually. With text functions, the restructuring takes a matter of minutes—no matter how many records are in your database.

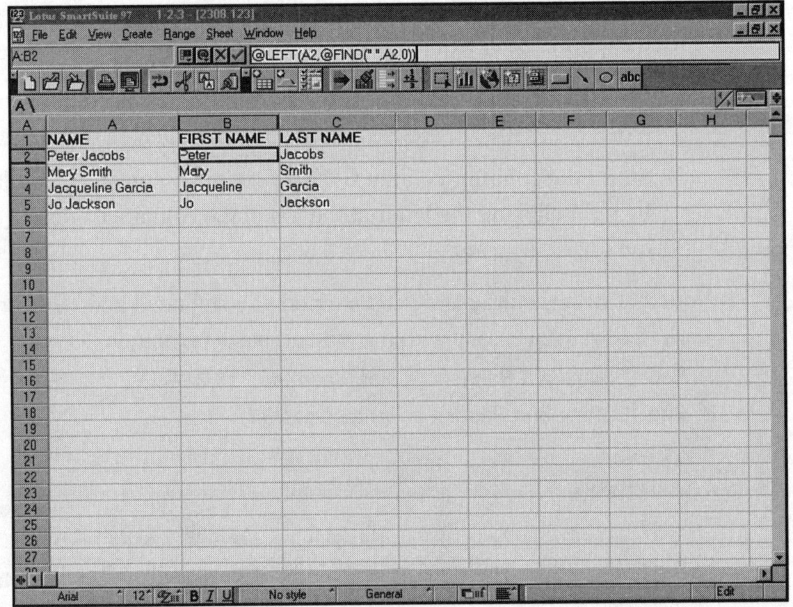

Fig. 23.8
The FIRST NAME and LAST NAME fields were created with text functions.

The formula in B2 reads as follows:

```
@LEFT(A2,@FIND(" ",A2,0))
```

This formula extracts the first name. It looks for the space between the first and last name and then extracts the text from the beginning of the cell up to (but not including) the space.

The formula in C2 is:

```
@MID(A2,@FIND(" ",A2,0)+1,@LENGTH(A2))
```

This formula extracts the last name. Like the previous formula, it locates the space. In this case, however, it extracts text in the middle of the cell.

▶ **See** "Using Functions," **p. 151**

As you may have already guessed, these formulas will not work if the name contains a middle initial or middle name. If all the names contain middle initials, you can modify the formulas to extract this information (though the formulas are more complicated). If, however, some names have middle initials and some don't, or some names have trailing suffixes (e.g., Jr., M.D.) you will need to do some manual editing.

After you have entered the formulas for the first record, you can copy them down to the other records. You now have two choices. You can consider your job done and leave the NAME, FIRST NAME, and LAST NAME fields just as they are. Alternatively, you can delete the NAME field.

If you decide to delete the original data, do not immediately delete the column. If you do, you'll end up with ERRs in the FIRST NAME and LAST NAME fields. This is because the formulas refer to cells that no longer exist. Before deleting the NAME column, you'll need to convert the formulas to values.

Here are the steps for converting the formulas to values:

1. Select the cells containing the text functions (B2..C5 in fig. 23.8).
2. Choose Edit, Copy to copy the formulas to the Clipboard.
3. With the same cells selected, choose Edit, Paste Special.
4. Choose the Formulas as Values checkbox and click OK.

To see the difference in cell contents after this operation, look at the edit line in B2. The cell contents are now simply *Peter* instead of the long text function. The NAME field can now be safely deleted without disturbing the FIRST NAME and LAST NAME fields.

Combining Two Fields into One

For reporting purposes, you may want to combine two fields into one. Suppose you have divided the first and last names into two different fields so that you can easily sort and query the data, but in your report you would like to see the first and last name separated by a space. Figure 23.9 shows this example. The formula in cell C2 is:

```
+A2&" "&B2
```

This formula simply "adds" the first name (in A2), a space, and the last name (in B2). The ampersand, called the *concatenation operator,* is what links each text string. This formula can be copied to the other records.

▶ **See** "Using Functions," **p. 151**

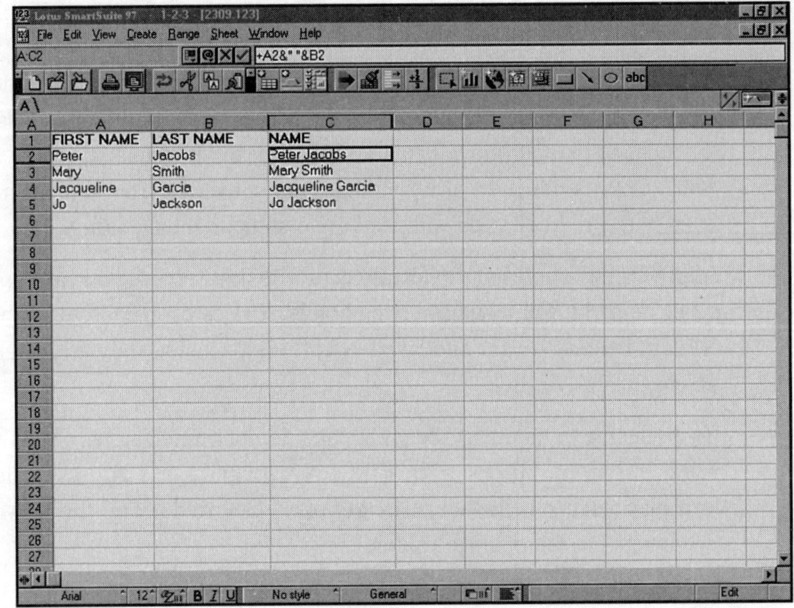

Fig. 23.9
The FIRST and LAST NAME fields were combined into a single field by creating a formula with the concatenation operator (&).

CHAPTER 24

Sorting Data

by David Plotkin

Sorting your records in order

Learn to sort your records in either ascending or descending order. If your data was entered in the right format, you can sort alphabetically, numerically, or even by date (chronologically).

Using keys in your sorts

Learn how to sort on multiple keys to do things like sort by last name, and for people with the same last name, sort by first name.

1-2-3 enables you to change the order of records by sorting them according to the contents of the fields. Sorting a database can provide you with more meaningful information. Frequently, when a database contains people's names or company names, you will want to sort the list in alphabetical order. This reorganization makes it easier to locate information. In a database that contains addresses, you may want to sort by ZIP code to take advantage of bulk mailing rates.

By sorting numerical data, you can answer the following types of questions: Which customers purchased the most from you last year? Who has the highest salary in the marketing department? Which salespeople made the most sales last quarter? In which month were expenses the lowest?

You also can sort dates in chronological order, assuming the dates were entered as numerical dates, not labels. By sorting dates in your database, you quickly can see which employees have worked for the company the longest or which invoices are the oldest.

1-2-3 offers two ways to sort data: using the Range, Sort command directly on the database range or sorting the records in a query table, which does not change the order of the records in the database. ■

Sorting a Range

The Range, Sort command sorts any range, not just a database range. Before issuing this command, select the range to be sorted. This range must include all the records to be sorted as well as all the fields in the database. In figure 24.1, the sort range for the employee database is A1..E12 (with a 1 row header) or A2..E12 (if you don't include the headings).

Unlike earlier versions of 1-2-3, it is perfectly OK to include the field names in the sort range. Just indicate the number of rows that the header comprises in the Sort dialog box (see fig. 24.2).

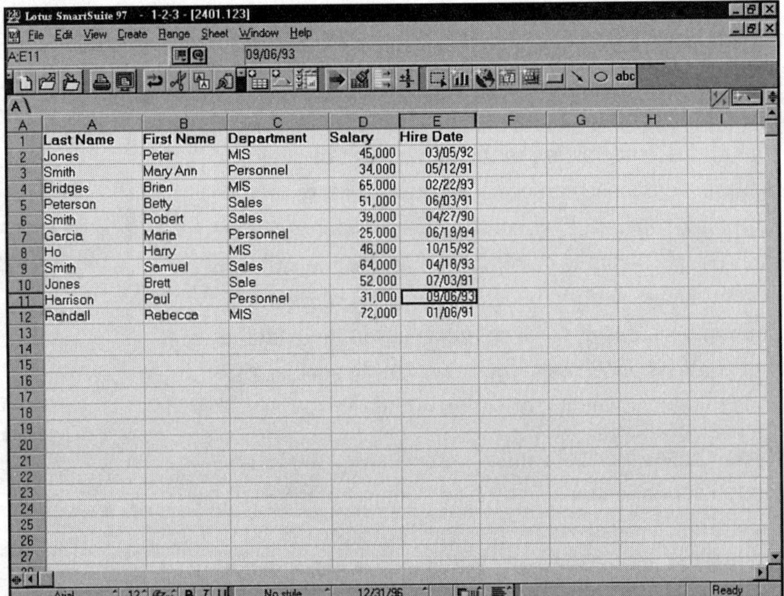

Lotus SmartSuite 97 - 1-2-3 - [2401.123]
File Edit View Create Range Sheet Window Help
A:E11
09/06/93
Last Name First Name Department Salary Hire Date
Jones Peter MIS 45,000 03/05/92
Smith Mary Ann Personnel 34,000 05/12/91
Bridges Brian MIS 65,000 02/22/93
Peterson Betty Sales 51,000 06/03/91
Smith Robert Sales 39,000 04/27/90
Garcia Maria Personnel 25,000 06/19/94
Ho Harry MIS 46,000 10/15/92
Smith Samuel Sales 64,000 04/18/93
Jones Brett Sale 52,000 07/03/91
Harrison Paul Personnel 31,000 09/06/93
Randall Rebecca MIS 72,000 01/06/91
Arial
No style
12/31/96
Ready

Fig. 24.1
The sort range for the employee database is A2..E12.

CAUTION

If you do not include all fields (columns) when sorting, you destroy the integrity of your database because parts of one record will end up with parts of other records. It's easy to think, "I want to sort the last names in alphabetical order so I'll select this column for the sort range." Don't do this! If you do, your names will indeed be in alphabetical order, but the data corresponding to each name will no longer be accurate.

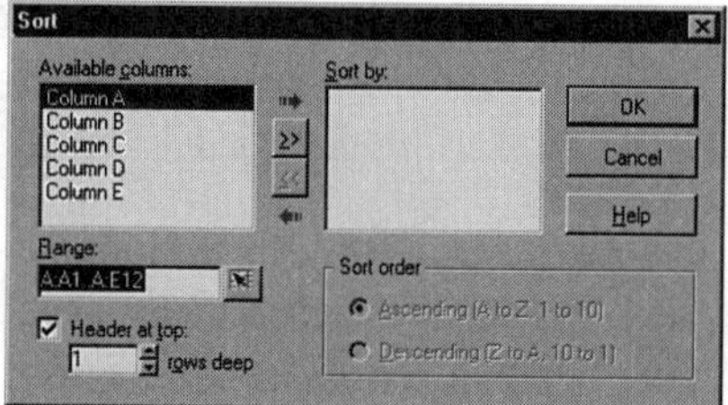

Fig. 24.2
In the Sort By list of the Sort dialog box, specify the column on which you want to sort.

Note that the sort range does not necessarily have to include all records in the database. If part of the database already has the organization you want, or if you do not want to sort all the records, you can sort only a portion of the database.

After selecting the sort range, issue the Range, Sort command. You then see the Sort dialog box shown in figure 24.2. Because you preselected the range, the Range field at the bottom of the dialog box is already filled in. If you had not already selected the range, you could type the range into the Range text box. Alternatively, you can click the range selector (to the right of the Range text box) and then click and drag to specify the range.

If you included the field names at the top of the columns in your range, you need to let 1-2-3 know that so it doesn't sort the field names into the middle of your data. Click in the Header At Top check box, and indicate the number of rows that comprise the header with the Rows Deep spinner.

The next thing you need to indicate are your *sort keys*. The sort key is the column on which you want to sort. To select a sort key, choose a column from the Available Columns list box and click the >> button to move the column into the Sort By list box. In figure 24.1, to sort by the last names, you specify column A. Or, if you wanted to sort by the salaries, you could specify column D.

You can sort the column in Ascending or Descending order. Ascending order sorts labels from A to Z, values from lowest to highest, and dates from earliest to latest. Descending order sorts labels from Z to A, values from highest to lowest, and dates from latest to earliest. If you don't specify a sort order, ascending is the default.

After the sort key is defined, you can click the OK button to sort the data. Figure 24.3 shows the employee database sorted on the last names. Column A was specified in the Sort By list and Ascending order was selected.

To ensure that you can restore the original record order after sorting the database, you can add a Record Number field to the database before sorting. You then can restore the original order by re-sorting on the Record Number field. You can use the Range, Fill command to enter record numbers quickly.

▶ **See** "Filling Ranges," **p. 72**

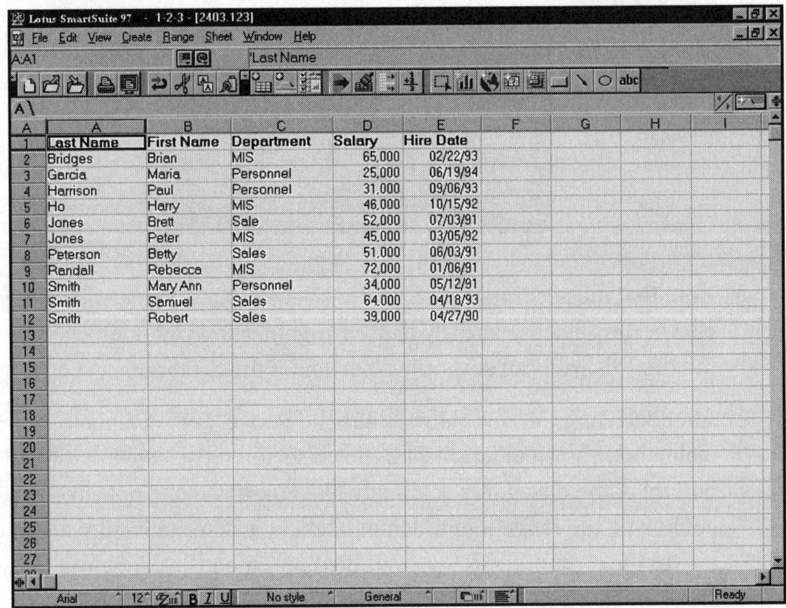

	A	B	C	D	E
1	Last Name	First Name	Department	Salary	Hire Date
2	Bridges	Brian	MIS	65,000	02/22/93
3	Garcia	Maria	Personnel	25,000	06/19/94
4	Harrison	Paul	Personnel	31,000	09/06/93
5	Ho	Harry	MIS	46,000	10/15/92
6	Jones	Brett	Sale	52,000	07/03/91
7	Jones	Peter	MIS	45,000	03/05/92
8	Peterson	Betty	Sales	51,000	06/03/91
9	Randall	Rebecca	MIS	72,000	01/06/91
10	Smith	Mary Ann	Personnel	34,000	05/12/91
11	Smith	Samuel	Sales	64,000	04/18/93
12	Smith	Robert	Sales	39,000	04/27/90

Fig. 24.3
The database is sorted alphabetically by last name.

Using the Sort SmartIcons

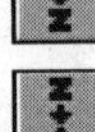

1-2-3 offers two SmartIcons for sorting ranges; one for sorting in ascending order, and the other for sorting in descending order. Both icons are very simple to use. Just place the cell pointer on any cell in the column you want to sort and then click the Ascending Sort or Descending Sort SmartIcon. Note that you do not need to define the sort range—the SmartIcons automatically sort all adjacent columns and rows. These SmartIcons are truly smart in that they know to leave the column headings alone (that is, the headings are not sorted).

Because the Sort SmartIcons are not on any of the palettes, you may want to use the File, User Setup, SmartIcons Setup command to add the icons to the bar(s) you use.

The SmartIcons are probably the fastest way to sort a range, but they are limiting because you cannot specify multiple sort keys, nor can you sort certain records.

Using Multiple Sort Keys

A single sort key works fine if there aren't any duplicate entries in the field you are sorting. But what if you are sorting by last names and there are five Smiths in the database? Or what if you are sorting by city and there are 20 companies in the same city? In these two examples, you would want to use a secondary sort key to serve as a tie breaker. In the first scenario, the primary key would be the LAST NAME field and the secondary key (the tie breaker) might be the FIRST NAME field. In the second scenario, the city field would be the primary key and the company name would be the secondary key.

While it is unlikely you would need to go beyond two or three sort keys, 1-2-3 allows you to define as many as 255. To define multiple sort keys, follow these steps:

1. Select the sort range.
2. Choose Range, Sort.
3. In the Available Columns list, select your primary key column and click the >> button to move it to the Sort By list.
4. Choose Ascending or Descending order.
5. Select your secondary key from the remaining columns in the Available columns list.
6. Click the >> button to move the secondary key to the Sort By list. The second sort key appears below the primary key.
7. Choose Ascending or Descending order.
8. Continue adding keys, as described here.
9. Press Enter or click OK to perform the sort.

NOTE To change the order of a sort key, you can simply drag it to a new position in the Sort By list. ■

Figure 24.4 shows the Sort dialog box with the Last Name field (Column A) as the primary key and the First Name field (Column B) as the secondary key. Ascending order is specified for both keys. After sorting, the range would look like figure 24.5.

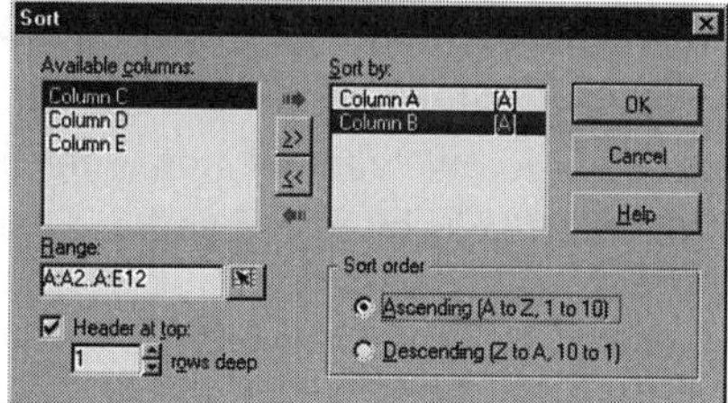

Fig. 24.4
The Sort By list displays the sort keys.

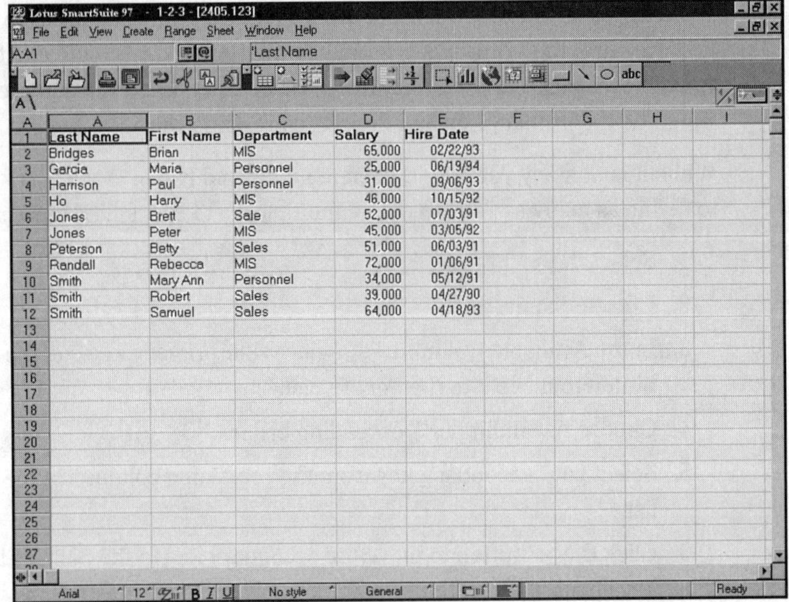

	A	B	C	D	E
1	Last Name	First Name	Department	Salary	Hire Date
2	Bridges	Brian	MIS	65,000	02/22/93
3	Garcia	Maria	Personnel	25,000	06/19/94
4	Harrison	Paul	Personnel	31,000	09/06/93
5	Ho	Harry	MIS	46,000	10/15/92
6	Jones	Brett	Sale	52,000	07/03/91
7	Jones	Peter	MIS	45,000	03/05/92
8	Peterson	Betty	Sales	51,000	06/03/91
9	Randall	Rebecca	MIS	72,000	01/06/91
10	Smith	Mary Ann	Personnel	34,000	05/12/91
11	Smith	Robert	Sales	39,000	04/27/90
12	Smith	Samuel	Sales	64,000	04/18/93

Fig. 24.5
This range was sorted with Last Name (Column A) as the primary key and First Name (Column B) as the secondary key.

Performing Additional Sorts

You can sort a range as many different ways and as many different times as you like. Sometimes you may want the list sorted by last name. Other times you may want the list sorted by department with the last names sorted alphabetically within each department. Or perhaps you need a report in which you can easily determine who is making the most money in each department.

1-2-3 makes it easy to perform additional sorts. There are just two things to remember. First, each time you perform a sort, you do not need to redefine the sort range—1-2-3 remembers the range you defined for the previous sort. Second, 1-2-3 keeps track of the sort keys you previously specified. This is convenient when you have added more records to your database and you now want to sort them in the same order as the previously entered records. If you want to sort by different columns, however, eliminate the old sort keys. You can easily clear out these sort keys by selecting the << button multiple times until the Sort By list is empty.

In figure 24.6, the employee database is sorted by department names, and within each department the last names are alphabetized. The following steps re-sort the database in this order:

1. Select the range A1..E12.
2. Choose Range, Sort.
3. In the Available Columns list box, specify Column C and click the >> button to move it to the Sort By list box.
4. In the Sort By list box, drag column C to the top of the list.
5. Press Enter or click OK. The database should now look like figure 24.6.

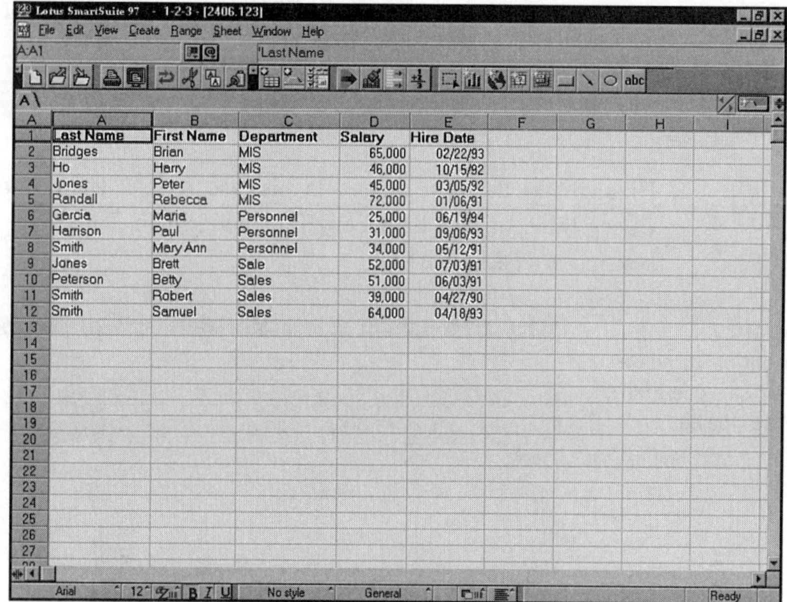

	A	B	C	D	E
1	Last Name	First Name	Department	Salary	Hire Date
2	Bridges	Brian	MIS	65,000	02/22/93
3	Ho	Harry	MIS	46,000	10/15/92
4	Jones	Peter	MIS	45,000	03/05/92
5	Randall	Rebecca	MIS	72,000	01/06/91
6	Garcia	Maria	Personnel	25,000	06/19/94
7	Harrison	Paul	Personnel	31,000	09/06/93
8	Smith	Mary Ann	Personnel	34,000	05/12/91
9	Jones	Brett	Sale	52,000	07/03/91
10	Peterson	Betty	Sales	51,000	06/03/91
11	Smith	Robert	Sales	39,000	04/27/90
12	Smith	Samuel	Sales	64,000	04/18/93

Fig. 24.6
The employee database is sorted by department and within each department the names are alphabetized.

Part V Ch 24

Using a Query Table to Sort Records

1-2-3 offers another way to sort a database: using a query table. *Query tables* are special workspaces in a worksheet that simplify selecting, sorting, and updating database records. In this chapter, you'll see how a query table can be used to sort a database; in Chapter 25, you'll learn how to select and update records using a query table.

Sorting with a query table offers several advantages compared with directly sorting the records in a worksheet database range. First, you don't need to select the sort range because 1-2-3 automatically sorts all the fields and records in the query table. You therefore don't need to worry about defining the range incorrectly and inadvertently making scrambled eggs out of your database. Second, you can sort the records by selecting the field name from a list. Indicating that you want to sort the Last Name field is more intuitive than specifying Column A. Third, you can try several different sort orders without affecting the original database.

Creating a Query Table

Because query tables can overwrite existing worksheet data, it's wise to create a new worksheet for each query table you use. Add a new worksheet before you create the query table.

To create a new query table, follow these steps. Refer to figure 24.7 for the example database.

1. Highlight the database range—in this case, A1..G6. Then choose Create, Database, Query Table, or click the Query Table SmartIcon. The Query Table Assistant dialog box appears (see fig. 24.8).

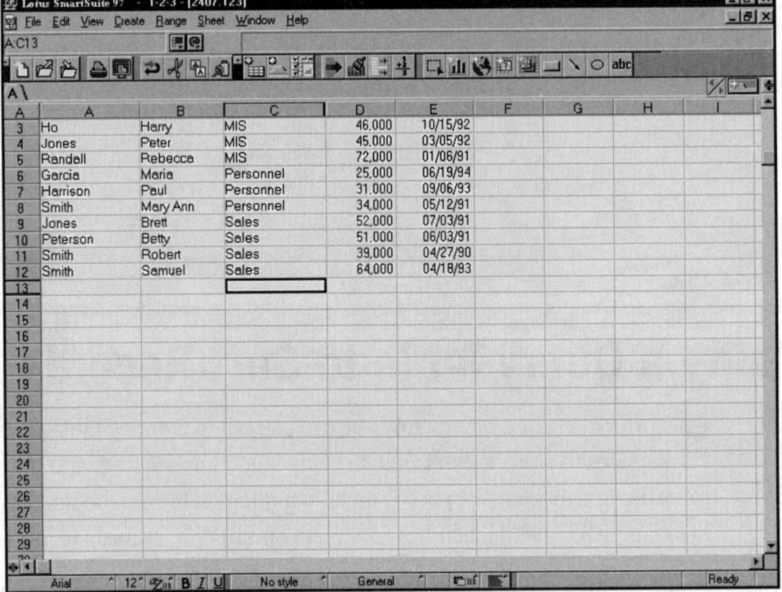

Fig. 24.7
The original database for which a query table will be created.

2. Verify that the correct source range is specified for the input data.
3. Choose OK and then click where you want the query table to appear. After you indicate the location for the query table, the Worksheet Assistant dialog box appears (see fig. 24.9).

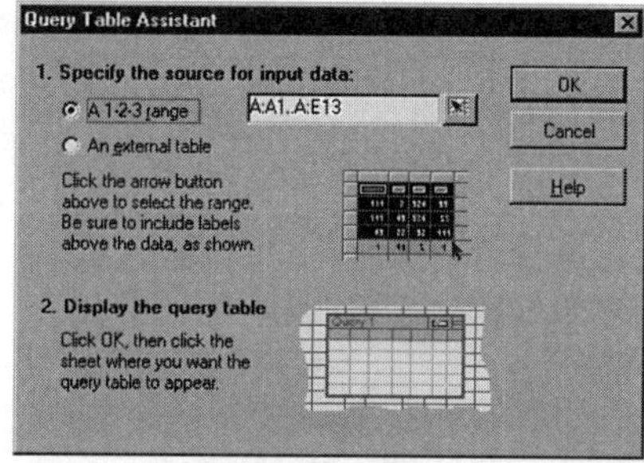

Fig. 24.8
The New Query dialog box.

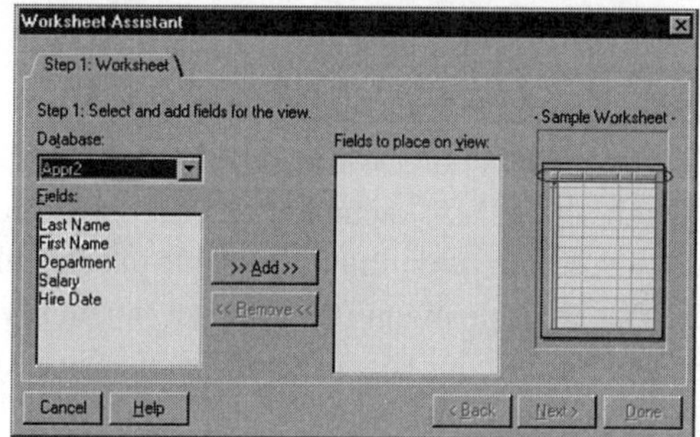

Fig. 24.9
Use the Worksheet Assistant dialog box to specify which fields to include in the query table.

4. In the Fields list box, select the fields to appear on the query table. Choose >>Add>> to copy the selected fields to the Fields To Place On View list box.
5. Choose Done to place the query table in the worksheet (see fig. 24.10).

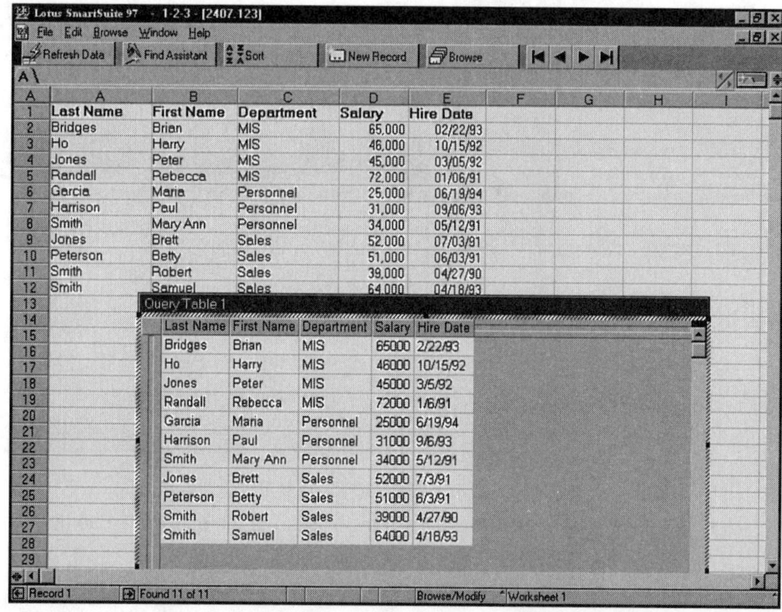

	A	B	C	D	E
1	Last Name	First Name	Department	Salary	Hire Date
2	Bridges	Brian	MIS	65,000	02/22/93
3	Ho	Harry	MIS	46,000	10/15/92
4	Jones	Peter	MIS	45,000	03/05/92
5	Randall	Rebecca	MIS	72,000	01/06/91
6	Garcia	Maria	Personnel	25,000	06/19/94
7	Harrison	Paul	Personnel	31,000	09/06/93
8	Smith	Mary Ann	Personnel	34,000	05/12/91
9	Jones	Brett	Sales	52,000	07/03/91
10	Peterson	Betty	Sales	51,000	06/03/91
11	Smith	Robert	Sales	39,000	04/27/90
12	Smith	Samuel	Sales	64,000	04/18/93

Last Name	First Name	Department	Salary	Hire Date
Bridges	Brian	MIS	65000	2/22/93
Ho	Harry	MIS	46000	10/15/92
Jones	Peter	MIS	45000	3/5/92
Randall	Rebecca	MIS	72000	1/6/91
Garcia	Maria	Personnel	25000	6/19/94
Harrison	Paul	Personnel	31000	9/6/93
Smith	Mary Ann	Personnel	34000	5/12/91
Jones	Brett	Sales	52000	7/3/91
Peterson	Betty	Sales	51000	6/3/91
Smith	Robert	Sales	39000	4/27/90
Smith	Samuel	Sales	64000	4/18/93

Fig. 24.10
Once the query table is created the Approach menus and Toolbars appear at the top of the screen.

6. Click outside the query table to display the Query Table Assistant dialog box (see fig. 24.11). If you wish to copy records from the query table to an output range in 1-2-3, specify the range and click OK. To skip creating an output range, choose Cancel.

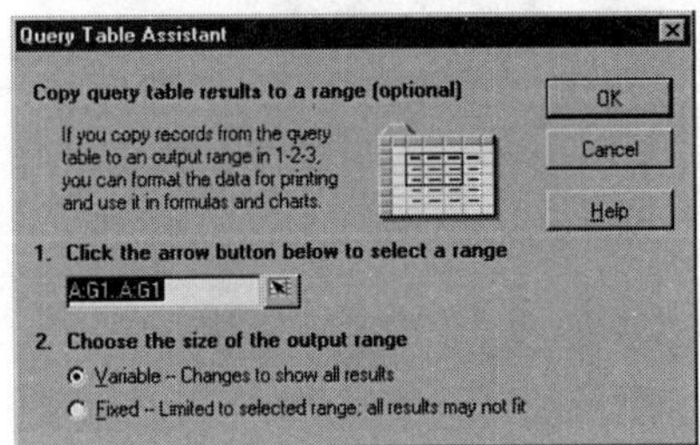

Fig. 24.11
Use the Query Table Assistant dialog box to specify an optional output range.

Notice in figure 24.12 that both the 1-2-3 menu bar and the SmartIcon set change when a query table is selected (click a cell within the query table to select the table). The Range menu is replaced by the Query Table menu (see fig. 24.12), and several standard SmartIcons are replaced by SmartIcons that pertain specifically to query tables. These changes make using a query table even easier.

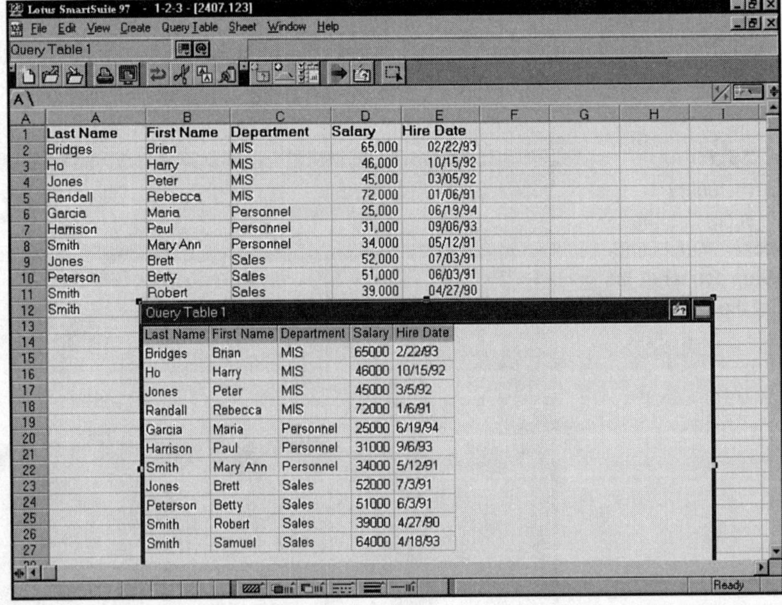

Fig. 24.12
The Query Table menu replaces the Range menu when a query table is selected.

NOTE You can resize the query table by clicking the query table border and dragging the handles. ■

Sorting the Query Table

To sort the query table, follow these steps:

1. First select the query table and choose Query Table, Edit to display the Approach menu as shown in figure 24.10. You can also double-click within the query table to display this menu.
2. Next, click the field you want to sort by.
3. Choose Browse, Sort, Ascending, to sort the query table in ascending order by using the selected field as the sort key. Choose Browse, Sort, Descending, to sort the query table in descending order by using the selected field as the sort key. To sort using more than one sort key, choose Browse, Sort, Define to display the Sort dialog box (see fig. 24.13). This dialog box is similar to the one displayed with the Range, Sort command, with two exceptions. First, the Fields list box displays a list of field names. Second, there is no field for the sort range because 1-2-3 automatically knows what data to sort (everything in the query table except for the field names).

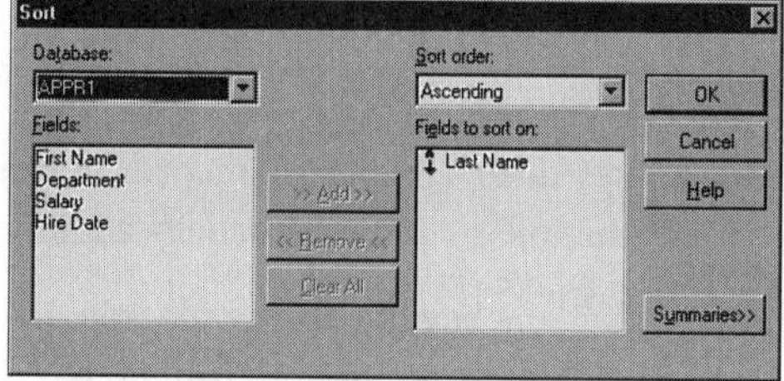

Fig. 24.13
This Sort dialog box is displayed with the Browse, Sort, Define command.

To sort the records, you must specify the key(s) for the sort. As with the Range, Sort command, Browse, Sort, Define can use as many as 255 keys in a sort, but only the first key is required.

Using a One-Key Sort

To specify a single sort key, follow these steps:

1. Click any cell in the query table.
2. Choose Browse, Sort, Ascending or choose Browse, Sort, Descending.

Figure 24.14 shows the query table sorted in Ascending order by Hire Date.

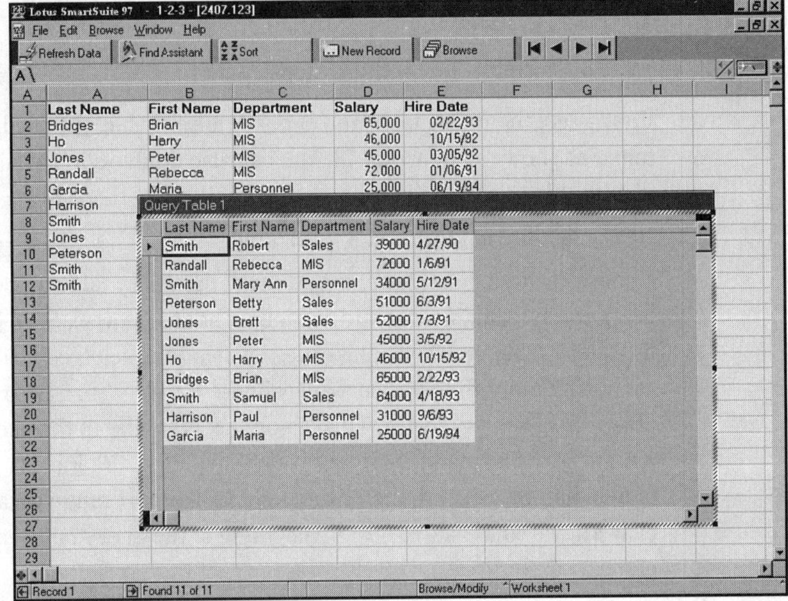

Fig. 24.14
The query table sorted by Hire Date.

Using a Multiple-Key Sort

Sometimes, sorting on a single key does not sort the records in exactly the order you may need. In this case, you can use multiple sort keys to specify additional sorting conditions.

A multiple-key sort uses more than one key to sort the records. In the telephone book's yellow pages, for example, records are sorted first according to business type (the first key) and then by business name (the second key). In the white pages, records are first sorted by last name and then by first name.

To specify additional sort keys, follow these steps:

1. Click any cell in the query table.
2. Choose Browse, Sort, Define to display the Sort dialog box.
3. To specify each sort key, select it from the Fields list box, click the >>Add>> button to move the key to the Fields To Sort On list box, and select the order (Ascending or Descending) in the Sort Order drop-down list box. For this example, Department should already be listed as the first key. For the second sort key, select Salary.
4. Press Enter or click OK.

Figure 24.15 shows the result of the multiple-key sort.

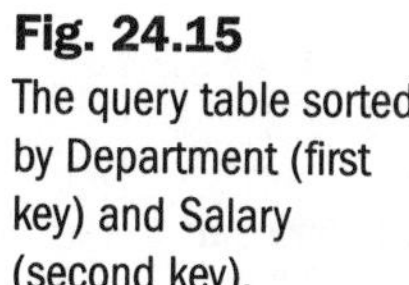

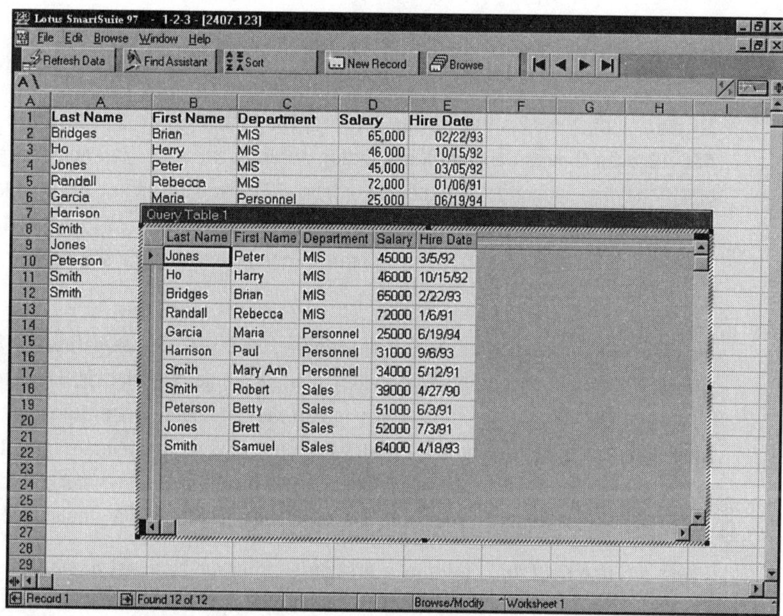

Fig. 24.15
The query table sorted by Department (first key) and Salary (second key).

Determining the Sort Order

When you sort in ascending order, this is the order in which data in the field is sorted:

Blank cells

Labels beginning with a space

Labels beginning with numbers

Labels beginning with letters (lowercase letters before uppercase letters)

Other characters

Values

When you sort in descending order, this sequence is reversed. These sorting rules apply to sorts performed with the Range, Sort command as well as with Browse, Sort. You can use the File, User Setup, 1-2-3 Preferences General Tab Sorting options to exercise additional control over the sort order.

TROUBLESHOOTING

My part number field is not sorting properly. For example, part 1234-AB is sorted before part 456-AB, even though I sorted in ascending order. Because the part numbers are entered as labels, they are not sorted in numerical order. 1-2-3 reads the characters from left to right and determines that 1 is less than 4; it doesn't consider that 456 is less than 1234. A solution is to add enough leading zeros (0) to ensure that all the labels have the same length. For example, specify 0456-AB as the part number.

My dates are not sorting properly. For example, 03-05-97 comes before 12-15-96 even though I sorted in ascending order. When dates are entered as labels, 1-2-3 reads the characters from left to right and sorts by month without regard to the year. You could avoid this problem by entering the year first (**'97-03-05**) but this is a non-standard format. A better solution is to enter the dates as values. This is done automatically when you enter your dates with slashes (**3/5/97**). You can then sort dates in chronological order without a problem.

I have a Name field that contains a first name followed by a last name (for example, Peter Smith). When I sort this field, the first names are alphabetized, not the last names. Is there any way to sort the last names in alphabetical order? No, not without restructuring the database. See Chapter 23 for an explanation on how you can divide one field into two. The problem you are having is a good lesson on the importance of dividing your data into separate fields as much as possible.

CHAPTER 25

Finding and Extracting Data

by Shane Devenshire

Working with query tables

Learn how to modify a query by adding fields to and deleting fields from the query table.

Creating computed fields

You can create more powerful queries through the use of *computed fields*—new fields that are the results of calculations.

Using record selection criteria

Criteria vastly extend the power and usefulness of queries. By adding conditions to a query you can select just records that you want to see.

Deleting records with query tables

You can use queries to quickly delete all records that meet a given set of conditions.

One of the advantages to computerizing a database is the ease and speed with which information can be retrieved. Even in a database containing hundreds or thousands of records, 1-2-3 can locate a particular record in a matter of seconds. You can extract meaningful information from a sea of data. For example, a list of 2,000 records with 15 fields in each is too overwhelming to convey anything of importance. But if you narrow the list to a subset of the database, such as a list of all the customers who have invoices more than 60 days past due, you now have information, not just raw data.

Beginning with 1-2-3 Release 4 for Windows, querying the database became more straightforward and intuitive. Instead of entering formulas in a worksheet (as required in prior versions), you select fields and matching conditions in a dialog box. This chapter shows you how to employ these easy-to-use techniques to analyze your information. The sample database used throughout this chapter is shown in figure 25.1. ■

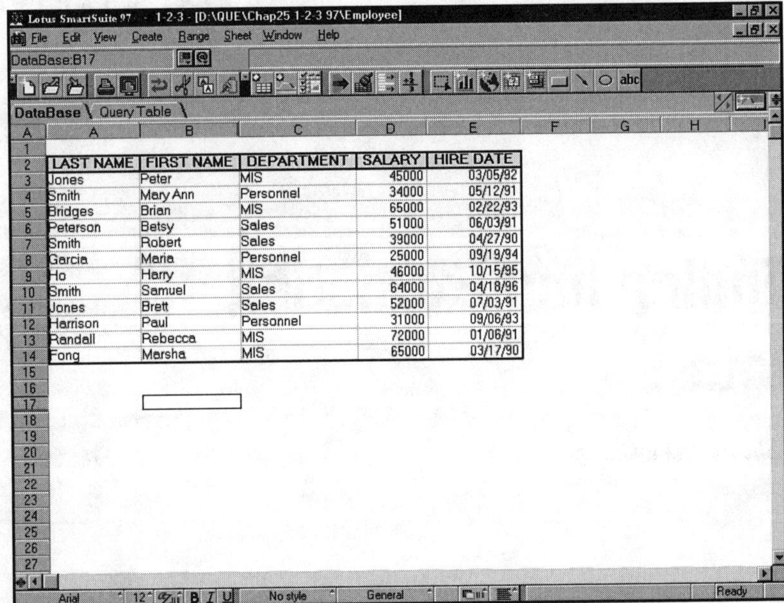

LAST NAME	FIRST NAME	DEPARTMENT	SALARY	HIRE DATE
Jones	Peter	MIS	45000	03/05/92
Smith	Mary Ann	Personnel	34000	05/12/91
Bridges	Brian	MIS	65000	02/22/93
Peterson	Betsy	Sales	51000	06/03/91
Smith	Robert	Sales	39000	04/27/90
Garcia	Maria	Personnel	25000	09/19/94
Ho	Harry	MIS	46000	10/15/95
Smith	Samuel	Sales	64000	04/18/96
Jones	Brett	Sales	52000	07/03/91
Harrison	Paul	Personnel	31000	09/06/93
Randall	Rebecca	MIS	72000	01/06/91
Fong	Marsha	MIS	65000	03/17/90

Fig. 25.1
The employee database is used as an example throughout this chapter.

Using a Query Table

As explained in Chapter 24, "Sorting Data," *query tables* are special workspaces in a worksheet that simplify selecting, sorting, and updating of database records. Query tables work with any database that Lotus 1-2-3 97 can use—a database in a worksheet, or a database contained in external files accessible through Approach (see Chapter 27, "Retrieving Data from External Databases").

▶ **See** "Sorting Data," **p. 545**

Creating a Query Table

Chapter 24 explained how to create a query table, but the steps are repeated here for review:

1. Use the New Sheet button to insert a sheet for the query table. This step is not mandatory, but keeping your database and query table in separate sheets can help you organize your work more efficiently.

2. Highlight the database range (all the fields and records). Then choose Create, Database, Query Table, or click the Create a Query Table SmartIcon. The Query Table Assistant dialog box appears (see fig. 25.2).

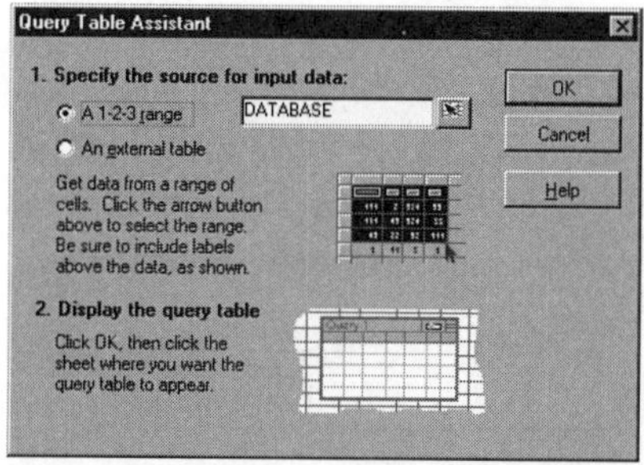

Fig. 25.2 You can indicate the data source with the Query Table Assistant dialog box.

3. If the correct range is already selected, click OK, otherwise, under Specify the Source for Input Data, select your data source. You can choose A 1-2-3 Range or An External Table as your data source. Click OK and the message shown in figure 25.3 appears and your pointer changes to a cross hair.

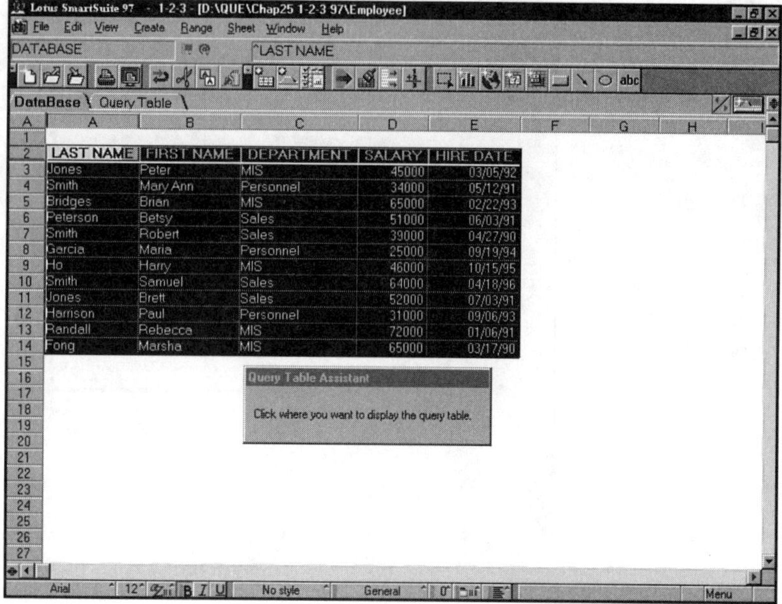

Fig. 25.3 The Query Table Assistant message and pointer, after you choose your data source and click OK.

4. Select and click the location where you want your query table to be placed. You only have to specify a starting cell—you don't need to specify the complete range. The Worksheet Assistant dialog box shown in figure 25.4 appears.

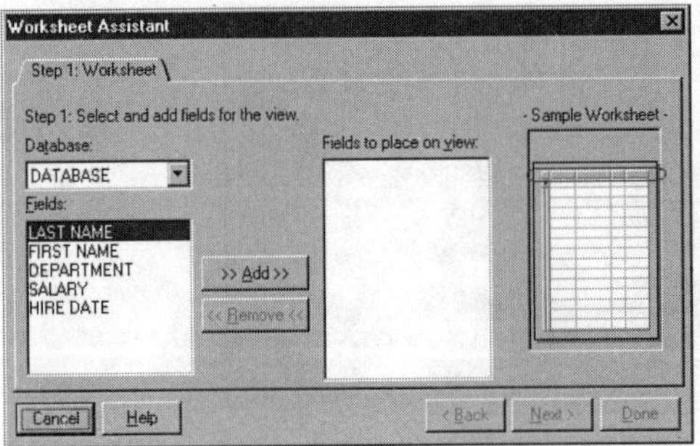

Fig. 25.4
You can specify which fields you want to display in your query table with the Worksheet Assistant.

5. Select the field or fields from the Fields list and click >>Add>> to place them in the Fields to place on view list. Click Done to display the query table. A sample query table is shown in figure 25.5.

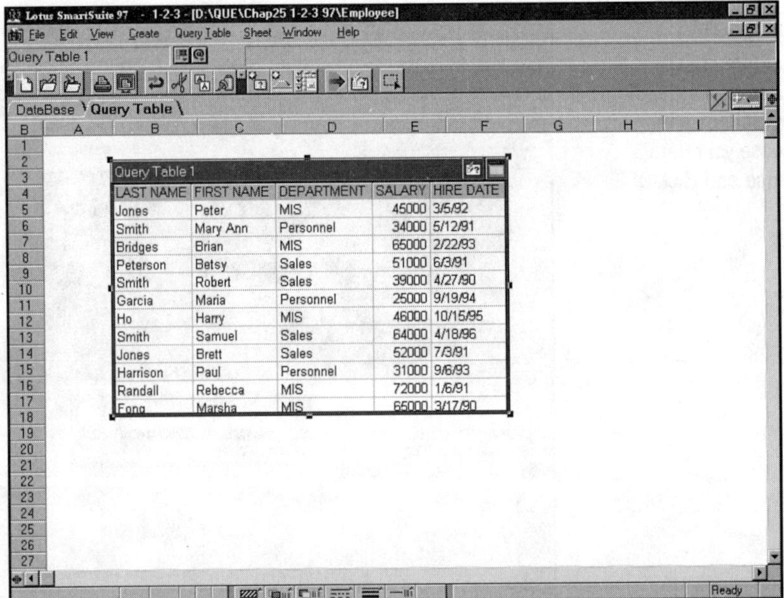

Fig. 25.5
A sample query table in its own worksheet.

TIP To select noncontiguous fields hold down the Ctrl key as you select each field. To select a group of contiguous fields click the first field and Shift click the last field.

Notice in figure 25.5 that both the 1-2-3 97 menu bar and the SmartIcon sets change when the query table is selected. The Range menu is replaced by the Query Table menu, and several standard SmartIcons are replaced by SmartIcons that pertain specifically to query tables. These changes make using a query table even easier.

Setting Query Table Options

Three Query Table menu commands allow you to control various aspects of the query table. These are the Query Table, Properties; Query Table, Edit; and Query Table, Refresh commands.

You can access the query properties with the menu, by right-clicking the title bar of the query table and choosing Query Table Properties or by clicking the Query Table Properties SmartIcon. The Properties InfoBox for the query table is shown in figure 25.6.

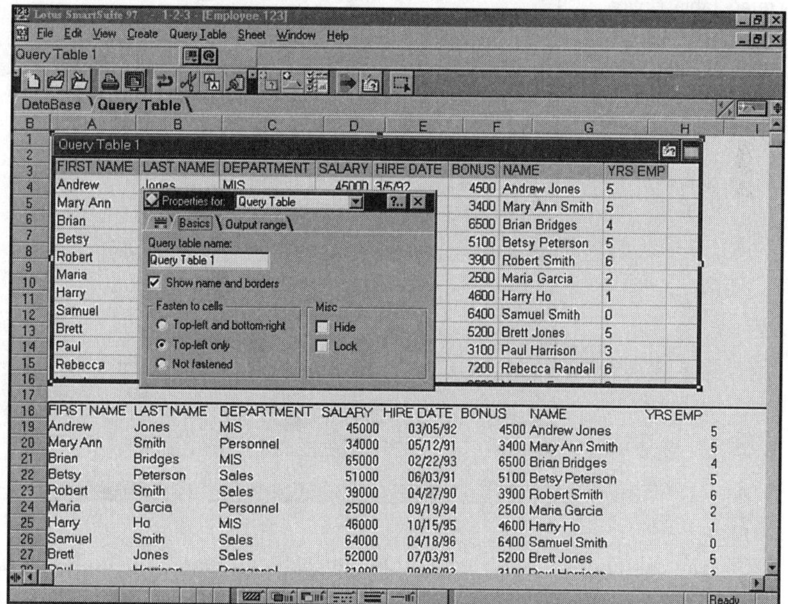

Fig. 25.6 With the Properties InfoBox you can change various aspects of your query table.

In the Basics properties tab you can change the query table name, anchor the table relative to worksheet cells, or hide and lock the table. You can send the query table results to a worksheet range and control table resizing options with the Query results tab. For example, if you want to use the query table's results in a 1-2-3 calculation you will need to send the data to a worksheet range.

TIP If you hide or lose a query table, the easiest way to select it is to choose the Edit, Go To command, Ctrl+G, or F5.

Edit, the second item on the Query Table menu, is used to edit the underlying Approach database using all of the commands available in Approach. You can add and delete fields and records, edit the field names, and change Approach's field definitions. If you want to add a record to your database for a new employee, you can choose the Query Table, Edit command and then right-click anywhere in the query table and choose the Records, New command from the shortcut menu, as shown in figure 25.7, or press Ctrl+N. The new record appears in the original 1-2-3 database and in an output range if you sent the query table data to a worksheet range.

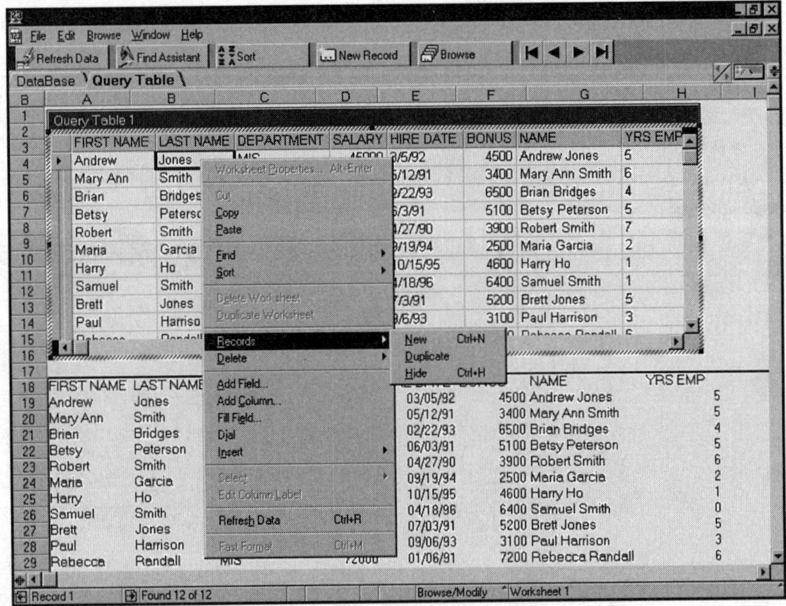

Fig. 25.7
Approach's shortcut menus for modifying the query table. Notice the Approach's menus and toolbars have replaced 1-2-3's.

You can choose the Query Table, Refresh command, or the Refresh the query with latest data SmartIcon, if you want the query to use the most current data from the source database. If the Approach menu is displayed, choose Browse, Refresh Data to update the query table. For example, if you change the department names in your original database, the query table will not reflect the changes until you issue the refresh command. Refreshing the query table will also refresh the output range, if you have one.

Adding, Deleting, and Moving Fields

If the fields in your query table don't meet your needs, you can move, add, or delete them to create the exact results you need. When you want to change a field, select the query table and choose Query Table, Edit. Then choose Approach's Edit, Add Field command to display the Add Field dialog box shown in figure 25.8.

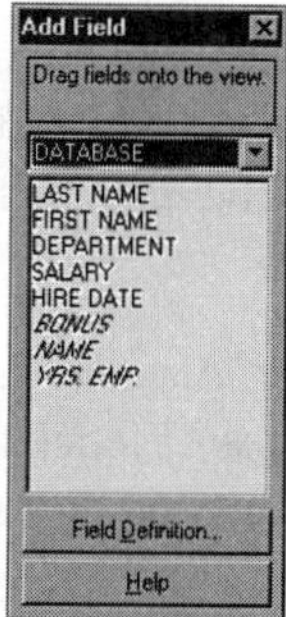

Fig. 25.8
You can drag a field from the Add Field dialog box onto the query table window.

To add a field to your table, drag it from the Add Field dialog box to the place you want to insert it into the query table. When a dark line appears where you want to add the field, release the mouse button.

To delete a field, select the field name while in the edit mode for the query table, drag the field off the query window, and then release the mouse button. Selecting the field name and dragging it are two separate steps—you must release the mouse between the two steps. As you drag the field off the query table the field name icon displays a file folder with a white arrow. When you delete a field in this manner you are only removing it from the query table display (and the query table output range, if you have one), not from the Approach database or your original 1-2-3 database.

To rearrange fields, select the field name(s) while in the query edit mode and then drag them to their new position on the query table.

You also can delete a field from the query table by selecting its field name and pressing Delete.

Creating Computed Fields

From the Add Field dialog box you can move to the Field Definition dialog box and build formulas to create new fields in the query table. For example, in an employee database, you can create a BONUS field that multiplies the SALARY field by 10 percent. You also can create a field that combines two text fields. For example, you can create a NAME field that displays the FIRST NAME followed by the LAST NAME. The easiest way to understand how to build field formulas is to look at some examples:

- `SALARY*0.1`

  Creates a BONUS field by multiplying the SALARY field by 10 percent.

- `Combine("FIRST NAME",' ', "LAST NAME")`

  Creates a NAME field by combining the FIRST NAME and LAST NAME fields.

- `(Today() -"HIRE DATE")/365.25`

  Creates a YEARS EMPLOYED field by subtracting the HIRE DATE field from today's date and then dividing by 365.25 days. The .25 allows the formula to take into account leap years.

Unlike cell formulas, field formulas don't begin with a +. Also, fields are referenced by their names (which makes it easy to build these formulas). Notice from examples shown above that you create a concatenated field—a field combining two labels—by using the Combine function, not the ampersand (&) as you do in a 1-2-3 worksheet. Also, you place single quotation marks around any text you want to include. (In the second example, there are single quotation marks around a space in the second argument of the Combine function.) Figure 25.9 shows the results of these field formulas in the query table and the output range.

▶ **See** "Using Operators in Text Formulas," **p. 143**

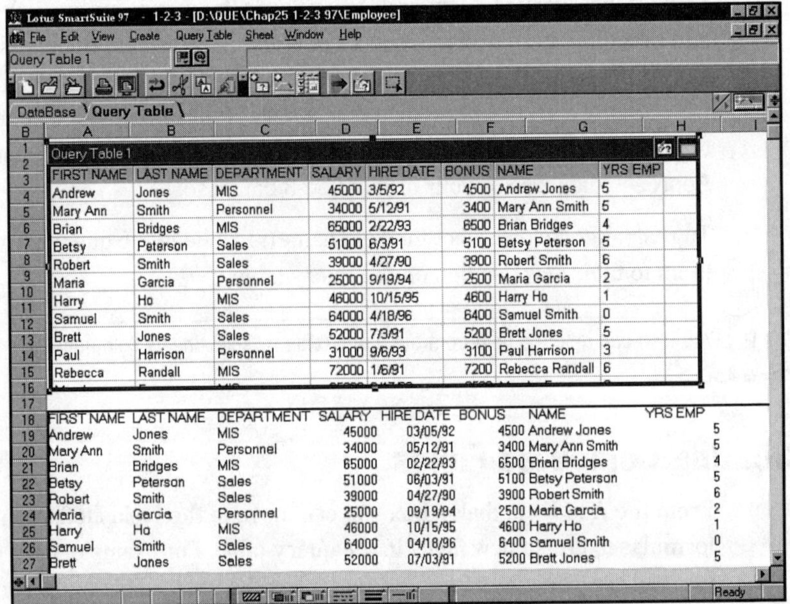

Fig. 25.9
The NAME, BONUS, and YRS. EMP. fields in this query table are new fields calculated with formulas.

To create a computed field follow, these steps:

1. Select the query table and then choose Query Table, Edit.
2. Choose Edit, Add Field or right-click within the query table and choose Add Field from the shortcut menu to display the Add Field dialog box (refer to fig. 25.8).
3. Click the Field Definition button in the Add Field dialog box to display the Field Definition dialog box shown in figure 25.10.

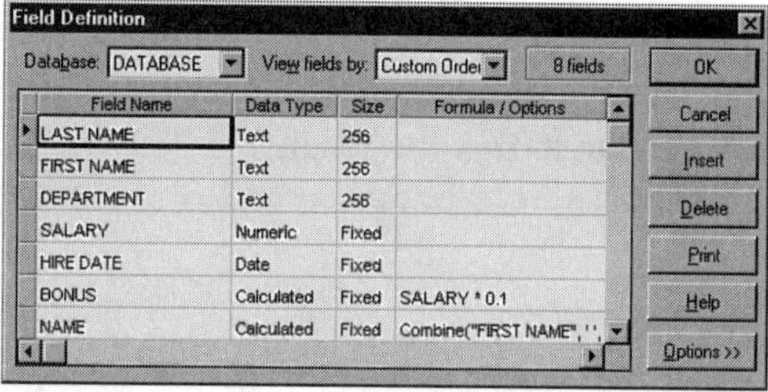

Fig. 25.10
You can create calculated fields in the Field Definition dialog box.

4. Move to the first empty row under the Field Name column and enter a new field name.
5. Move to the Data Type column, click the drop-down arrow that appears, and select Calculated. This modifies the Field Definition dialog box as shown in figure 25.11.

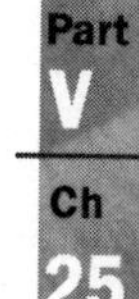

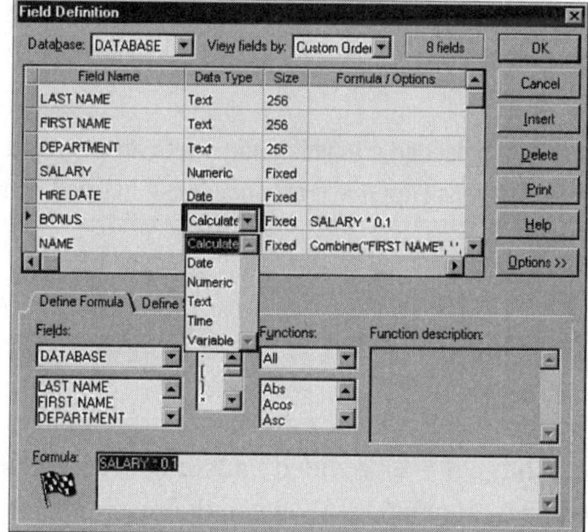

Fig. 25.11
The Field Definition dialog box displaying three calculated fields you might choose to enter.

6. Tab to the Formula/Options column and enter your formula.

Use the Define Formula area at the bottom of the Field Definition dialog box to help you build syntactically correct formulas.

7. When you have entered all the formulas you want, click OK to return to the Add Field dialog box.
8. Add the new field(s) by dragging it from the Add Field dialog box to the query table window. Click the close button to close the Add Field dialog box.
9. Refresh the data. If you are in the edit mode, choose Browse, Refresh Data or press Ctrl+R. If you have the query table selected but you are not in the edit mode, choose Query Table, Refresh.

Note that the fields you create are displayed only in the query table (and the query output range), not in your original database. Computed fields will display as many decimal places as necessary, so you may need to format the results.

TROUBLESHOOTING

After entering a field formula in the Formula dialog box, I got the message `Unable to evaluate the formula specified. Please define a valid formula.` What does this error message mean? You may have misspelled a field name. For example, you typed LASTNAME (one word) instead of LAST NAME (two words).

Another possibility is that you were combining the fields and you entered 1-2-3's concatenation operator (&) instead of using the Combine function. For example, perhaps you typed "FIRST NAME"&""&"LAST NAME" instead of Combine ("FIRST NAME",' ' ,"LAST NAME").

You may also have tried to use one of 1-2-3's functions which is not available in Approach. For example, you might have entered (@NOW()-"HIRE DATE")/365.25 instead of (Today() - "HIRE DATE")/365.25.

Still another possibility is that you preceded a function name with an @ sign, which is what you do in 1-2-3. Remove the @ sign because Approach only needs the function names.

Specifying Record-Selection Criteria

One way to find records that meet specific criteria is to use Approach's Find/Sort Assistant. Several special search types are provided including searches for duplicate records, unique records, and top or bottom values. You can define simple or complex searches using either the Basic Find or Query by Box choices. In all cases you are defining the find criteria for Approach. *Criteria* are conditions that must be satisfied for a record to be displayed in a query table. For example, you may want the query table to list all the employees who make more than $50,000 a year. In this case, your criterion would be SALARY>50000.

The Query by Box method is almost identical to the method used in 1-2-3 Release 5 for establishing query criteria.

The steps for specifying a query criteria using the Query by Box technique are as follows:

1. Select the query table in 1-2-3 and then choose Query Table, Edit.
2. Choose Browse, Find, Find Assistant, or press Ctrl+I to display the Find/Sort Assistant shown in figure 25.12.

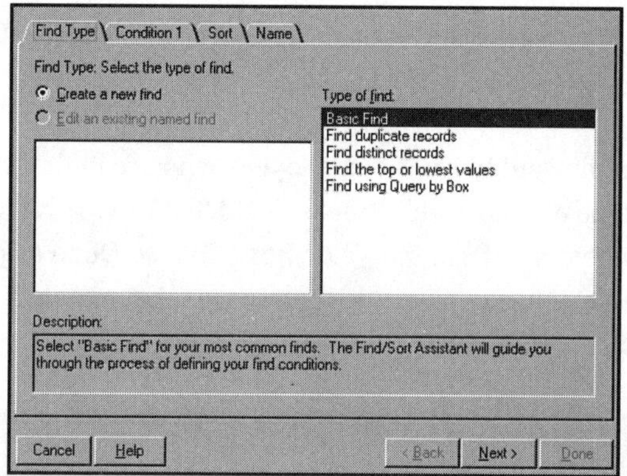

Fig. 25.12
The Find/Sort Assistant helps you through the process of creating queries and sorts.

3. On the Find Type tab select Find using Query by Box from the Type of Find list, and then click Next>. This displays the Query by Box tab shown in figure 25.13.

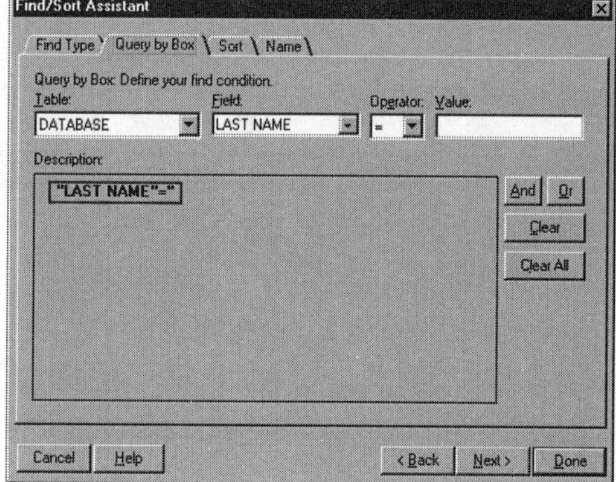

Fig. 25.13
The Query by Box tab of the Find/Sort Assistant is one place you can define your query criteria.

4. In the Query by Box tab, open the Field drop-down list and select the name of the field you want to query.
5. Display the Operator drop-down list and select the appropriate operator.
6. Enter the text or value you are looking for in the Value box. Click Done to run your query.

It doesn't matter whether you enter criteria values in uppercase or lowercase. (JONES matches jones or Jones.)

For example, you might want to list the employees who are in the MIS department. To set the criteria for this type of record selection, select DEPARTMENT from the Field list, = in the Operator list, and enter **MIS** in the Value box. Choose Done or press Enter to run the query. The query table now contains only the records that match the selection criteria, as shown in figure 25.14.

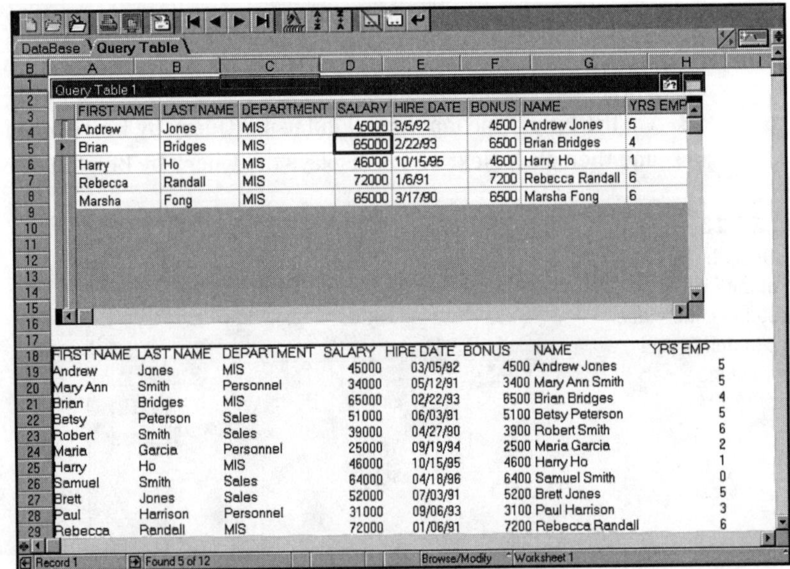

Fig. 25.14 The query table, showing only records that match the specified criteria.

After you locate the information that you want, you can use a refreshed output range to create a report or you can print directly from the Query Table window. You also can copy or cut the information from the query table output range and place that information in a separate section of the worksheet.

Besides searching for an exact match of a single label field, Approach provides several search techniques including: exact matches of numeric fields; exact or partial matches on text fields; searches for range of values; searches that meet multiple conditions; and searches that meet either one condition or another.

Using Operators in Selection Criteria

To set up criteria that query numeric, date, or label fields in the database, you can use the following relational operators (on the Operator drop-down list of the Query by Box tab of the Find/Sort Assistant):

>	Greater than
>=	Greater than or equal to
<	Less than
<=	Less than or equal to
=	Equal to
<>	Not equal to

You create a condition that describes the values of the records you want to select. Approach tests the condition against each record in the database. Here are some examples of valid conditions:

DEPARTMENT<>SALES	Excludes records in which the DEPARTMENT field is not SALES
LAST NAME=SMITH	All records in which the LAST NAME field contains *SMITH*
SALARY>=50000	All records in which the SALARY field is greater than or equal to 50,000
LAST NAME>L	All records in which the LAST NAME field begins with the letters M through Z
HIRE DATE<1/1/92	All records in which the HIRE DATE field contains a date before 1/1/92 (in other words, those who were hired before 1992)

Using Wild Cards to Match Similar Labels

You can use Approach's wild cards to help you find records; however, wild cards cannot be used with the Query by Box approach. In this section you will learn how wild cards work and where you can use them.

Two characters—the question mark (?) and the asterisk (*)—have special meaning when used in criteria. The ? character instructs Approach to accept any character in that specific position; each ? represents one character. The ? also tells Approach that you want to specify the length of the search text. The * character tells Approach to accept any number of characters in that position.

Table 25.1 shows how you can use wild cards in search operations.

Table 25.1 Using Wild Cards in Search Operations

Entry	Search Results
N?	Any two-character label starting with the letter *N* (NC, NJ, NY, and so on)
BO?L?	A five-character label (BOWLE) but not a shorter label (BOWL)
BO?L*	A four-or-more-character label (BOWLE, BOWL, BOLLESON, BOELING, and so on)
J??NSON	A label that starts with the letter *J* followed by any two characters, followed by the letters *NSON* (JOHNSON not JENSON)
SAN*	A three-or-more-character label starting with SAN and followed by any number of characters (SANTA BARBARA and SAN FRANCISCO)
SAN *	A four-or-more-character label starting with SAN, followed by a space, and then followed by any number of characters (SAN FRANCISCO, but not SANTA BARBARA)

Use the ? and * wild-card characters when you are unsure of the spelling or when you need to match several slightly different records.

To create a query using wild cards, follow these steps:

1. If necessary select the query table and choose Query Table, Edit. Then choose Browse, Find, Find using Worksheet. This displays a view with one blank record.
2. Enter the criteria you want under the desired field as shown in figure 25.15.
3. Press Enter and the Query table displays the records that meet your criteria.

TROUBLESHOOTING

I entered the criterion LAST NAME=SMITH using the Query by Box, but my query table didn't display one of the Smiths I know is in my database. What's going on? Try using Find Using Worksheet and changing your criterion to SMITH* or just SMITH. If the elusive Smith appears in this query table, the cell probably has a space after Smith. To see whether this is the problem, go to this field in the database, and press F2 (Edit). If you see extra space after Smith, then press Backspace to eliminate the space.

Some of my records in my mailing list database are missing ZIP codes. I would like to list these records in a query table so that I can easily fill in this information. How can I specify a criterion that will locate all records with an empty ZIP CODE field? Use Query by Box and set the criterion to ZIP CODE=. That is, leave the Value box empty. An empty Value field indicates that you want to find all records with a blank cell in that field.

I am trying to locate last names that end in the letters "son". When I enter the criterion LAST NAME=*SON in the Query by Box, the query table is empty. What am I doing wrong? You cannot use wild cards with the Query by Box approach, because Approach looks for the text ***son**, not things ending in **son**. Wild cards can be used with the Find using Worksheet command.

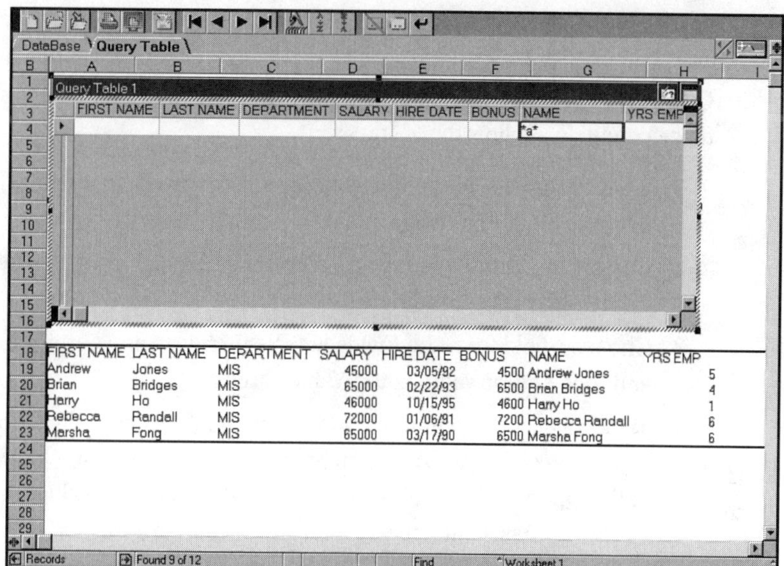

Fig. 25.15
The query worksheet with the wild card ***a***, which would find all names containing the letter "a" anywhere in the NAME field.

Specifying Multiple Criteria

You have seen how to base a selection on only one criterion. In this section, you learn how to use multiple criteria for your queries. You can set up multiple criteria as AND conditions (in which *all* the criteria must be met) or as OR conditions (in which any *one* criterion must be met). For example, searching a music department's library for sheet music requiring drums AND trumpets is likely to produce fewer selections than searching for music appropriate for drums OR trumpets.

NOTE Deciding on whether to use AND or OR can be a little tricky sometimes. For example, suppose you want a list of all companies in California and Nevada. While it may seem logical that you would use the AND connector in this example, OR is the appropriate connector. This is because a single field (STATE in this case) can only contain one value or another. In other words, in a single record the STATE field could not possibly contain two values (CA and NV). ■

Setting Up AND Conditions

To indicate two or more criteria, *all* of which must be met, specify the first condition in the Set Criteria dialog box, choose the And button, and then specify the second condition.

Suppose that you want to retrieve only those records for employees in the Personnel department who make $30,000 or more a year. You can perform this query using either Query by Box, Find Using Worksheet, or by using the method shown here. To specify those conditions, follow these steps:

1. If necessary, select the query table and choose Query Table, Edit. Then choose Browse, Find, Find Assistant.
2. Choose the Find Type tab and then select Basic Find from the Type of Find list. This displays the Condition 1 tab.
3. Choose a field from the Fields list. Next choose an operator from the Operator list and then enter a value in the Values area.
4. To add a second condition choose Find on Another Field. Choose the option Find Fewer Records (AND) option. Select another field in the Fields list and an operator in the Operator list, and type a value in the Values box. Figure 25.16 shows how the Find/Sort Assistant appears after the second criteria has been added. Although, in figure 25.16 you can only see the second condition, you can see that there are two condition tabs.
5. Click Done or press Enter and the query table shows the results of performing the query.

Fig. 25.16
The Find/Sort Assistant dialog box for a Basic Find search after two AND conditions have been set.

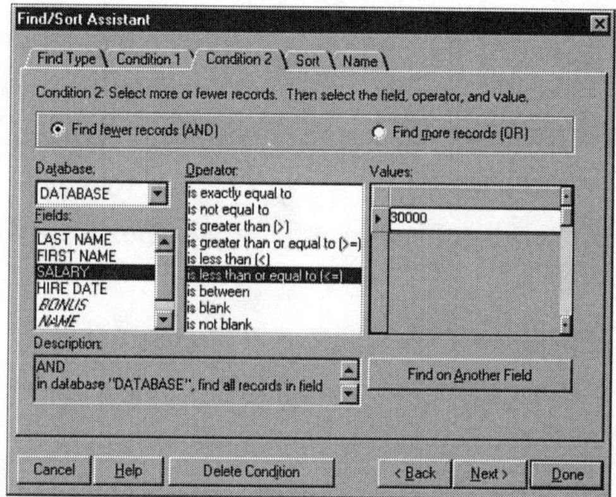

Setting Up OR Conditions

To retrieve records that meet either one condition or another, you combine the conditions by using OR rather than AND. Approach retrieves the records that match either condition. The OR connector is frequently used to search for two possible values in a field, such as DEPARTMENT=MIS OR DEPARTMENT=Personnel. Using Query by Box, the conditions for this query would look like figure 25.17. The two criteria connected with OR result in a list of everyone in the MIS or Personnel department.

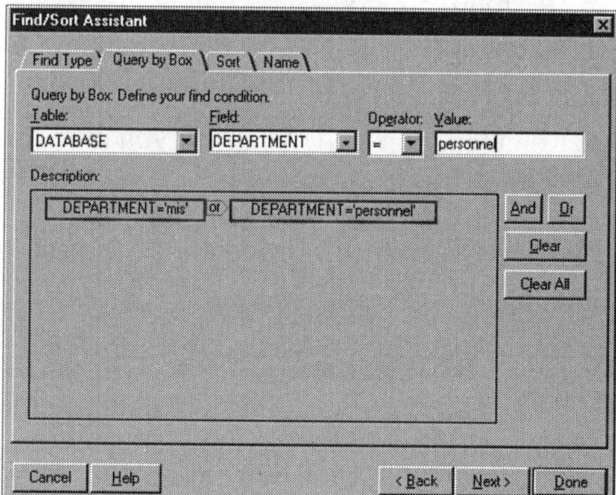

Fig. 25.17
Use OR to combine two criteria with the Query by Box approach.

To set up selection criteria for records containing either MIS or Personnel in the DEPARTMENT field, follow these steps:

1. If necessary, select the query table and choose Query Table, Edit. Then choose Browse, Find, Find Assistant.
2. On the Find Type tab select Find using Query by Box from the Type of Find list, and then click Next.
3. Select DEPARTMENT in the Field list, = in the Operator list, and MIS in the Value list.
4. Click the Or button.
5. Select DEPARTMENT in the Field list and = in the Operator list, and choose Personnel in the Value box.
6. Click Done or press Enter.

Changing Condition Types

Sometimes, you may find that you combined a set of criteria incorrectly. Suppose that you created the criteria set shown in figure 25.16 but later realized that combining the criteria with AND was a mistake. You really wanted to combine the criteria with OR. You could create a new query, but Approach provides an easier method.

As shown in figure 25.16, the Find/Sort Assistant dialog box indicates that the AND condition has been selected. To change the condition type, return to the Assistant by choosing Browse, Find, Find Again. Then select the Condition 2 tab and select the Find More records (OR) option. After changing an AND to an OR you may have to reselect the Operator and reenter the value in the Values area.

You can add as many AND and OR criteria as necessary to select the desired set of records. You may have a little trouble determining the correct set of conditions for very complex selection requirements, but Approach enables you to correct and adjust the criteria until they are perfect.

NOTE If you are having difficulty narrowing down record selection to a precise set in complex situations, try extracting records in stages. First, output a group that contains all the records you want—and also some that you don't want. Then, using the output records as the source, create another query table and output a more precise set of records. If necessary, repeat the process until you have only the records that you need.

NOTE Another way to find data is with the Edit, Find & Replace command. This command looks for the character string you specify. It is more limiting than the Find Records command because you don't have the flexibility of entering different operators, searching for values, using wild cards, or specifying multiple conditions. In certain circumstances, however, you can use Find & Replace to update information in your database. For example, if an employee gets married and changes her name, you can search for her maiden name and replace it with her married name. See Chapter 3, "Entering and Editing Data," for more information.

Deleting Specified Records

As mentioned in Chapter 23, one way to remove records from a database is with the Range, Delete, Rows command. An alternative to this method is to use the Browse, Delete Record command (or press Ctrl+Del) to remove unwanted records from your database. Another alternative is to find all the records you want to delete and then use the Browse, Delete Found Set command. This last method allows you to delete all records that meet a given set of criteria.

▶ **See** "Entering and Editing Data," **p. 65**

Suppose that you want to remove all records with the HIRE DATE between 1/1/91 and 12/31/91. Assuming you already have a query table for your data, follow these steps:

1. If necessary, select the query table and choose Query Table, Edit. Then choose Browse, Find, Find Assistant.
2. In the Find Type tab select Basic Find from the Type of Find list and then click Next>.
3. Select HIRE DATE from the Fields list, and is between from the Operator list. Then enter **1/1/91** and **12/31/91** on the first Values row.
4. Click Done or press Enter. The query table displays all the records you want to delete. If not you should modify your query.
5. If the correct records are displayed choose Browse, Delete Found Set and answer Yes to the prompt. The results of this procedure are shown in figure 25.18. The original data is displayed in the output range below the query table, or you can compare the query table's records with those in figure 25.5 shown earlier in the chapter.

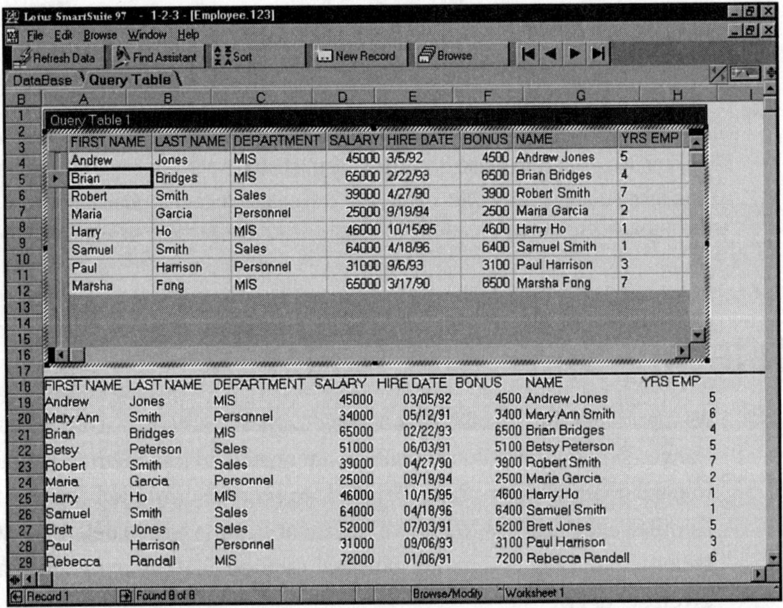

Fig. 25.18
The Delete Found Set command removes unwanted records.

CAUTION

Deleting records is a command you cannot undo.

Modifying Records

Besides finding and deleting database records, you probably will want to modify records. You can modify records directly in the spreadsheet database range, or you can do it in the query table. The query table procedure also enables you to modify records in external databases.

While in the query table edit mode, you can edit records directly in the query table, either by making the changes manually or by using Edit, Find & Replace Text.

If you are proficient with Approach and want to work with all of its features, you can choose the Edit, Open Into Full Window command when you are in the Edit mode for the query table. This brings your query table into Approach, where you could, for example, change number formats, alignments, and fonts. When you finish, choose File, Close & Return to Lotus 1-2-3, which will allow you to bring any changes you have made back into 1-2-3 95. To bring the changes from Approach to 1-2-3 97 you have to refresh the query. ●

CHAPTER 26

Understanding Advanced Data Management

by Shane Devenshire

This chapter builds on the basic database commands introduced in Chapter 25, "Finding and Extracting Data," and covers more advanced data management techniques. You learn how to join databases to take advantage of relationships between them and how to use advanced tools to analyze your data.

After you enter data in a worksheet, it is important to be able to analyze the data. Lotus 1-2-3 97 provides several powerful tools to assist you in this task including the capability to cross tabulate and aggregate data, create frequency distributions (great for analyzing survey results), and perform regression analysis to analyze trends. By mastering these techniques, you can take advantage of some of the most advanced and useful features available to spreadsheet users. ■

Understanding and working with relational databases

In 1-2-3 97 you can work with related data contained in more than one database.

Creating cross tabulation of data

You can use cross tabulation to analyze data stored in any database that 1-2-3 97 can access.

Generating frequency distributions

A frequency distribution can quickly and easily be created to assist you in analyzing and graphing survey results data.

Performing regression analysis

With regression analysis it is easy to project trends in your data to assist in formulating strategies.

Solving linear programming problems

You can solve a linear programming problem using 1-2-3's matrix inversion and multiplication commands.

Joining Multiple Databases

A powerful feature of Lotus 1-2-3 97 is its capability to create a query table that contains fields or calculated columns based on records contained in two or more databases. To do this the two databases must contain fields with similar information. Databases containing common information are said to be related. You join two or more databases that have one or more related fields.

You might wonder why you should keep two or more databases of related information instead of keeping all the information together in one large database. One reason is to increase efficiency. Suppose that you had several business contacts at each of the companies listed in a company database, such as the one shown in figure 26.1. You could add a NAME field to the database and place each contact in a separate record. If you had three contacts at May's Plumbing, for example, you could type three complete records, one for each contact person. Of course, when May's Plumbing moves to a larger building, you have to change the addresses for all three records. On the other hand, if you have one database with the company information and another listing the contact persons with cross-references to their companies, you only have to update one company record to update the addresses for all the contacts you have with that company.

The examples that follow use sample company data, sample contact data, and a query table. If you want to follow along with the examples in this chapter, perform these steps:

1. Insert two new worksheets in the file that contains the sample company data. Enter the data as shown in figure 26.1. You can use the New Sheet button or the Create, Sheet command to add the worksheets.
2. Name the three worksheets Company Data, Contact Data, and Query as shown on the worksheet tabs in figure 26.1.
3. Move the cell pointer to the Contact Data worksheet and enter the information shown in figure 26.2 to create the CONTACTS database. You can type the company name or read the upcoming section "Understanding the Key Field" for some tips on entering the company name.

4. Use the Range, Name command, use the Range name property on the Basics tab of the Range Properties InfoBox, or click the Create and Delete Range Names SmartIcon to name the two database ranges COMPANIES (A:B3..A:H8) and CONTACTS (B:B3..B:D12).

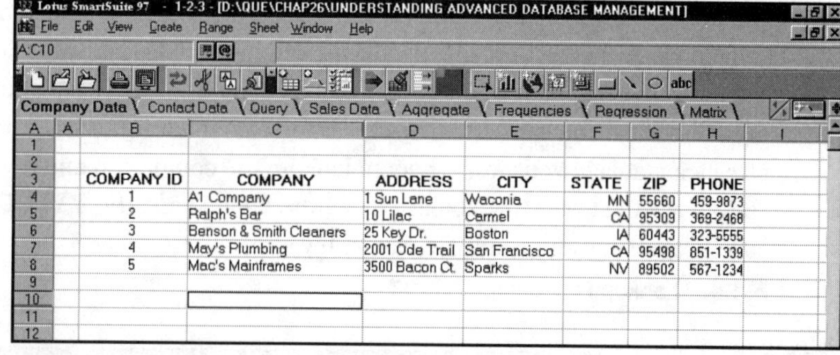

COMPANY ID	COMPANY	ADDRESS	CITY	STATE	ZIP	PHONE
1	A1 Company	1 Sun Lane	Waconia	MN	55660	459-9873
2	Ralph's Bar	10 Lilac	Carmel	CA	95309	369-2468
3	Benson & Smith Cleaners	25 Key Dr.	Boston	IA	60443	323-5555
4	May's Plumbing	2001 Ode Trail	San Francisco	CA	95498	851-1339
5	Mac's Mainframes	3500 Bacon Ct.	Sparks	NV	89502	567-1234

Fig. 26.1
A sample company database has one record for each company.

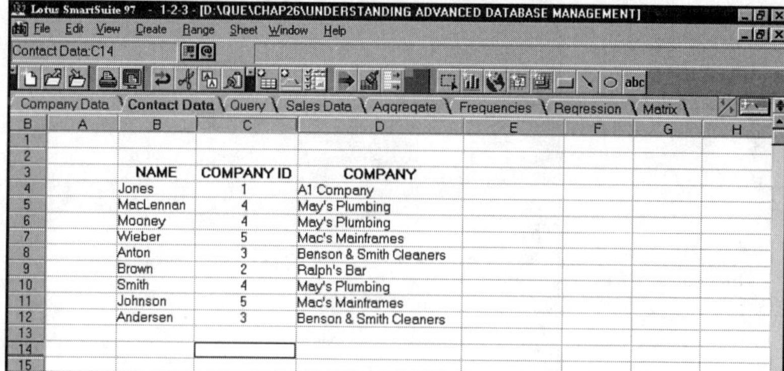

NAME	COMPANY ID	COMPANY
Jones	1	A1 Company
MacLennan	4	May's Plumbing
Mooney	4	May's Plumbing
Wieber	5	Mac's Mainframes
Anton	3	Benson & Smith Cleaners
Brown	2	Ralph's Bar
Smith	4	May's Plumbing
Johnson	5	Mac's Mainframes
Andersen	3	Benson & Smith Cleaners

Fig. 26.2
A sample contacts database contains multiple contacts for each company.

Understanding the Key Field

A *key field* is a field in which the contents are unique for each record in the database. In the sample company database, for example, COMPANY and COMPANY ID are possible key fields because every company has a different name and ID. STATE is not a key field because two companies may be in the same state.

The COMPANY ID is the key field that will be used to join or "match" information from the contacts and company databases. Although you could use the COMPANY field, it would be very important that you enter the company name exactly the same way every time. For example, if one entry says *Mac's Mainframes* and another says *Macs Mainframes*, then the join will not work correctly. Also, there might be more than one company with the same name, for example, how many McDonalds are in New York City? Instead, it is safer to assign a unique ID for each company.

One way to ensure that the entries are exactly the same is to copy them from the Company database to the Contacts database. Another way is to create a lookup table that uses the ID for the company and the full company name. (This also makes entering the data easier because you can just enter the ID instead of having to type the full name.) Then place a formula in your worksheet to look up the company name based on the ID. Figure 26.3 shows the Contacts database using the ID field and the @VLOOKUP formula to speed data entry and eliminate data-entry errors.

▶ **See** "Lookup Functions," **p. 197**

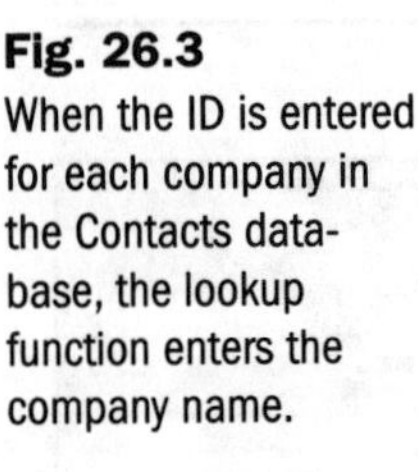

Fig. 26.3
When the ID is entered for each company in the Contacts database, the lookup function enters the company name.

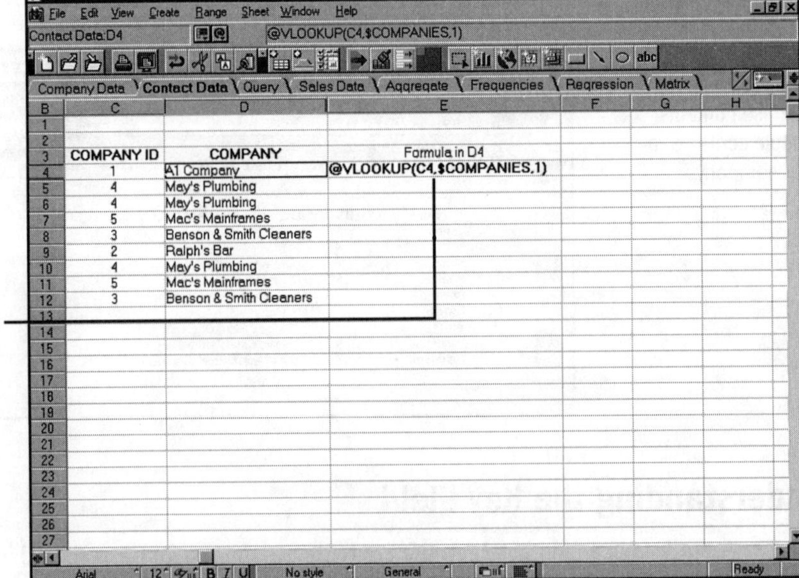

Understanding Database Relationships

Related database tables can have several different types of relationships. Understanding these types of relationships makes it easier to create related databases so that you can join them in a meaningful manner. There are four possible relationships.

- *One-to-one*. For every record in one database, only one record from another database is related to it.
- *One-to-many*. One record in the master database is related to many records in the second database. For example, if the Company database were the master database, its relationship with the Contacts database would be a one-to-many relationship. A single record in the Company database can point to several records in the Contacts database.

- *Many-to-one.* Many records in the master database are related to one value in the second database.
- *Many-to-many.* Many records in the master database are related to many values in the second database.

When you join databases in Lotus 1-2-3 97, you usually want to determine which method of joining databases produces a one-to-many relationship, such as that between the Company and Contacts databases. This kind of relationship results in the highest efficiency. If you create databases with this advantage in mind, you find that you need to enter less data, your databases require less disk space and system memory, and you have better performance.

Performing the Join

Joining two or more Lotus 1-2-3 97 databases requires using Lotus Approach. You can start the process from 1-2-3, or Approach; however, the 1-2-3 file(s) you want to query must be open. Also, you must name the 1-2-3 data ranges you will query.

For example, you might want to create a phone list that contains the contact name, company name, and phone number for each contact. This requires you to combine information from the contacts and company databases. Use the following steps to join two databases. In this example, you will be joining the contacts and company databases to create the phone list.

1. With your file(s) open in 1-2-3 97, open Lotus Approach.
2. Choose the File, Open command in Approach and then select 1-2-3 Ranges(*) from the Files of type list.
3. Select the 1-2-3 Ranges folder from the Look in list. Then pick the file containing your ranges and click Open. This displays a list of all the named ranges in the selected file.
4. Select the range you want to query (in this case Contacts) and click Open. This opens a Lotus 1-2-3 97 range as a new Approach database (see fig. 26.4).
5. Choose Create, Join. This displays the Join window shown in figure 26.5.
6. Choose the Open command and then select 1-2-3 Ranges(*) from the Look In list.
7. Select the range you want to join with (in this case Companies) and click Open. The Join dialog box displays both tables you want to join.
8. To join the key fields, select the desired field from either range and drag it to the equivalent field in the second range. This creates a join line between the two databases as shown in figure 26.6. Click OK.

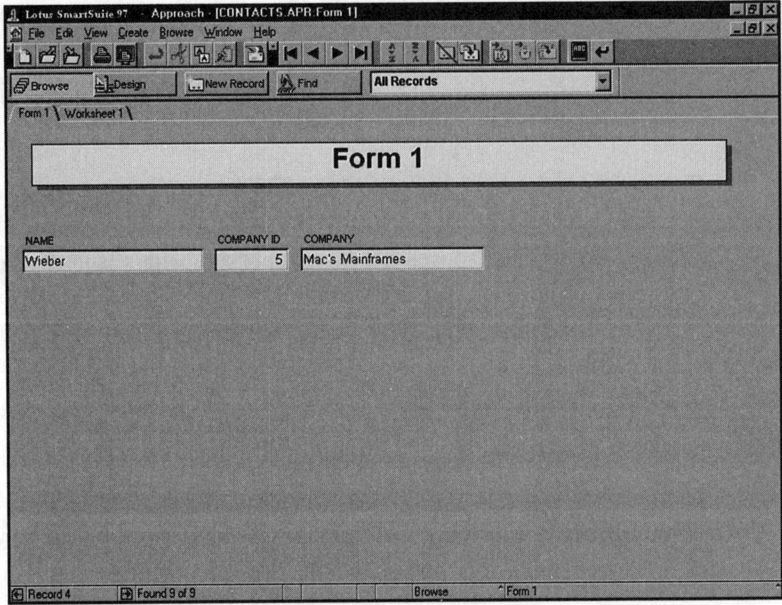

Fig. 26.4 The 1-2-3 Company range displayed in a worksheet view within Approach.

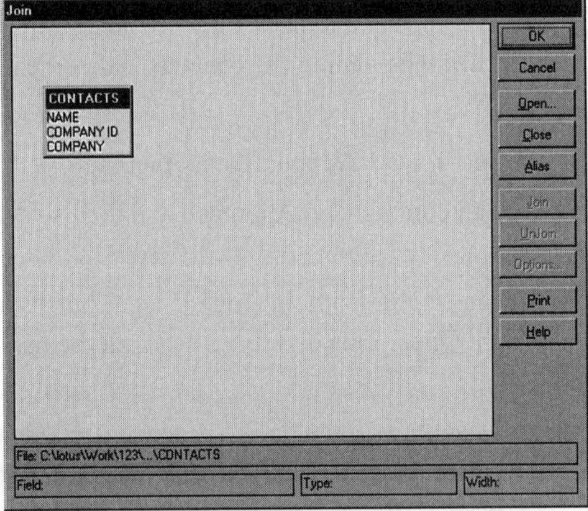

Fig. 26.5 The Join window displays the fields from your current database.

9. To create a worksheet based on both databases, choose Create, Worksheet to display the Worksheet Assistant.
10. From the Database list select one of the 1-2-3 database ranges. Select all the desire fields from the Fields list and click Add. Repeat these steps for each database range from which you want to add fields. The results of this process are shown in the following figure 26.7.

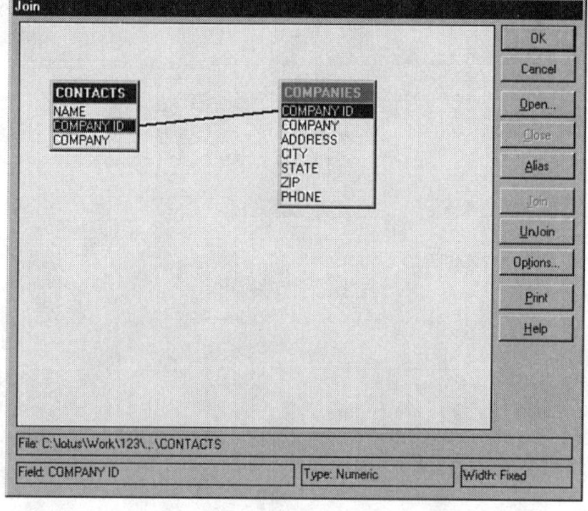

Fig. 26.6
The Join window displaying two database ranges and the join line between them.

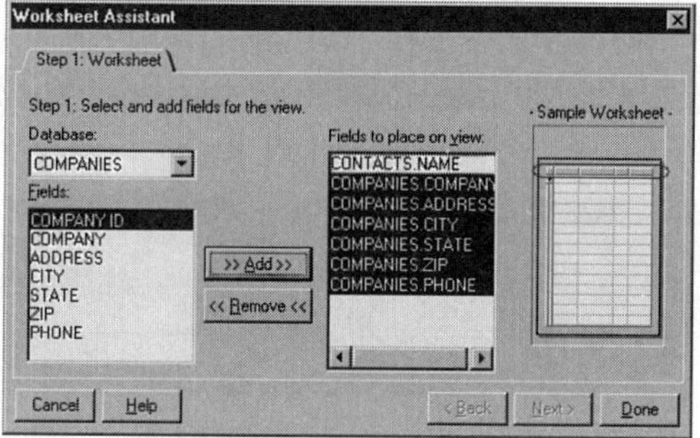

Fig. 26.7
The first step in creating a worksheet view from joined databases.

11. Click Done. This displays the Define Main Database window where you specify which database is the main database. This step controls whether you are creating a one-to-many or a many-to-one relationship. Select the desired database range from the Main database list and click OK. Figure 26.8 shows the resulting worksheet view.

Figure 26.8 shows the results of using the Company database range as the main database. If you follow the same steps but use Contacts as the main database your results would be those shown in figure 26.9.

This example shows how you can join databases that contain related information so that you can have more complete information than what is contained in either database alone. The resulting worksheet view is similar to a single database worksheet view, but is much more useful.

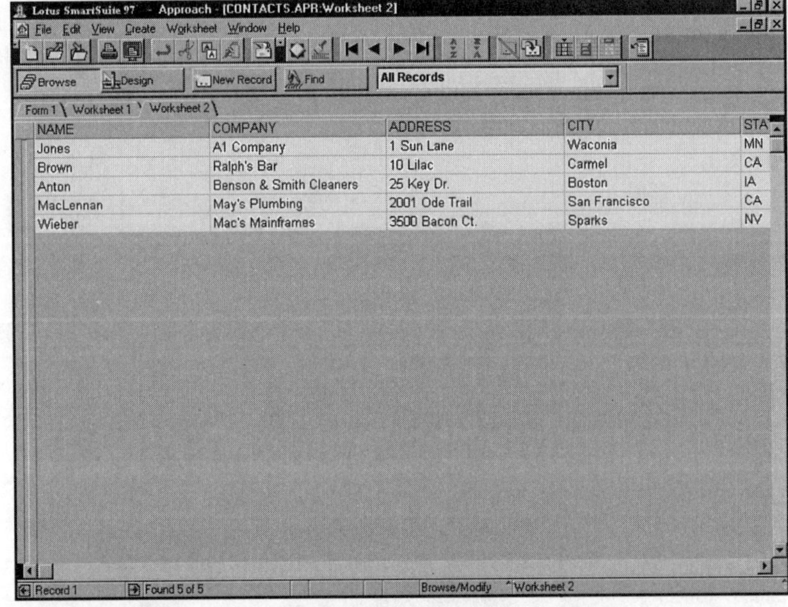

Fig. 26.8
The Approach Worksheet view displaying fields from both 1-2-3 97 ranges using Companies as the main database.

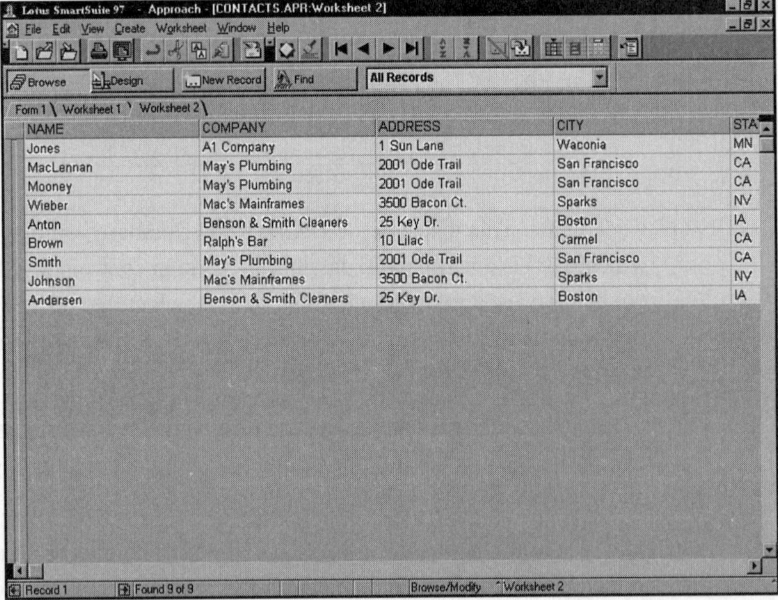

Fig. 26.9
The Approach worksheet view displaying fields from both 1-2-3 97 ranges using Contacts as the main database.

In the next chapter, you learn how to use external database files. The technique of joining databases is even more useful with external databases than it is with worksheet databases, because external databases often hold much larger collections of data. By applying the efficiencies gained through joining related databases, you make better use of disk space and memory.

TROUBLESHOOTING

When I try open my databases in Approach, I can't find any files displayed. Lotus 1-2-3 97 must be open and the files you want to join also must be open.

When I try to open my database from inside Approach I get the error message: `This program has performed an illegal operation and will be shut down.` This problem occurs when you try to open the file from the folder it is stored in within 1-2-3 97 rather than the 1-2-3 Ranges folder.

After receiving the error described above, I tried to open the file from the 1-2-3 Ranges folder but it was not there. Lotus 1-2-3 97 has been closed by the above error and you must reopen it and your file before you can proceed.

Evaluating Data with Cross Tabulations and Aggregate

One of the most useful ways to analyze data is to use a *cross-tabulation table* (or *crosstab*). Cross tabulations summarize data by showing how two factors influence a third factor. For example, the database shown in figure 26.10 tracks the amount of each sale for three different salespersons selling three different categories of products. A cross tabulation shows summary information you can use to analyze how well each salesperson is doing and decide what steps you might take to improve sales.

An *aggregate* is a variation of a cross tabulation that was available in some earlier versions of 1-2-3 for Windows. This command is no longer available in 1-2-3 or Approach, although you can produce the same results using the @DSUM function in 1-2-3 97 or by modifying the Approach command.

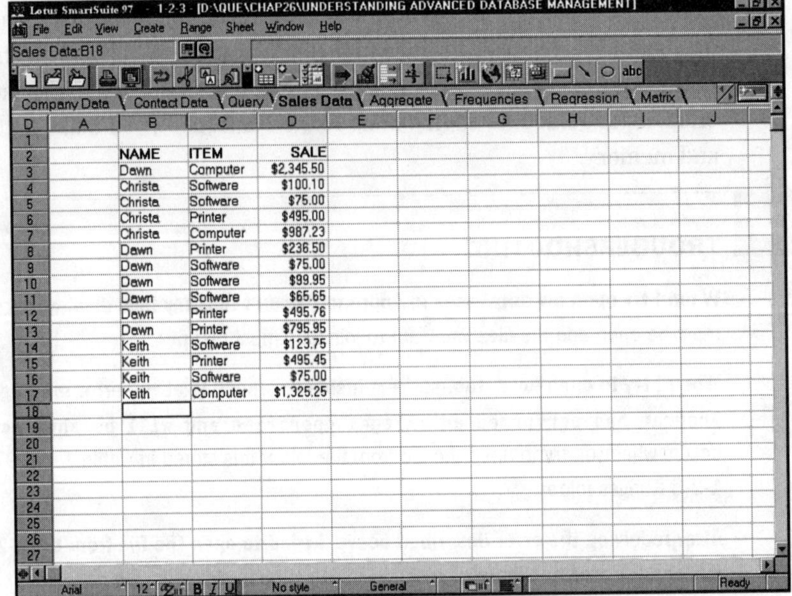

NAME	ITEM	SALE
Dawn	Computer	$2,345.50
Christa	Software	$100.10
Christa	Software	$75.00
Christa	Printer	$495.00
Christa	Computer	$987.23
Dawn	Printer	$236.50
Dawn	Software	$75.00
Dawn	Software	$99.95
Dawn	Software	$65.65
Dawn	Printer	$495.76
Dawn	Printer	$795.95
Keith	Software	$123.75
Keith	Printer	$495.45
Keith	Software	$75.00
Keith	Computer	$1,325.25

Fig. 26.10
A sales database ready to be analyzed using a cross tabulation.

Creating a Cross Tabulation

To create a crosstab table that summarizes the sales data shown in figure 26.10, follow these steps:

1. Select the database range you want to analyze. This range *must* include at least three columns and two rows, one of which is the field names. For example, select B2..D17.

2. Choose the Create, Database, Dynamic Crosstab command; or click the Create an Approach Dynamic Crosstab SmartIcon to display the Dynamic Crosstab dialog box (see fig. 26.11).

3. If the correct range is not selected, choose the range you want in the Select the database table range, including the field names (column headings) list box and then click OK. The mouse pointer becomes a cross hair and the Create message box appears.

4. Move to the sheet you want to place the crosstab on and click the location where you want the top left corner of the table. This displays the Crosstab Assistant shown in figure 26.12.

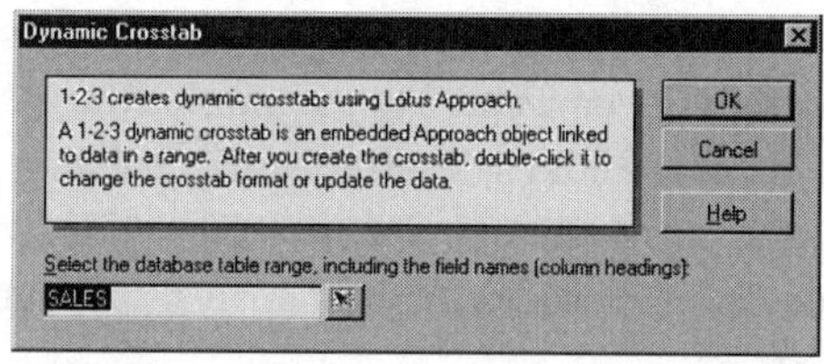

Fig. 26.11
Indicate the database range containing the data you want to cross tabulate in the Dynamic Crosstab dialog box.

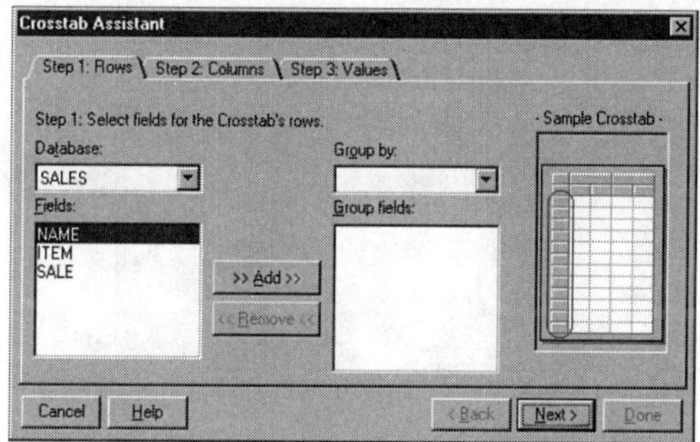

Fig. 26.12
The first step of the Approach Crosstab Assistant enables you to select the crosstab row field.

5. Select the spreadsheet range from the Database list. Select the field you want to use as the rows of your crosstab in the Fields box, and click >>Add>>. Click Next> or click the Step 2: Columns tab to display the second step shown in figure 26.13. For example, the values in the NAME field are to be displayed along the left edge of the cross-tabulation table.

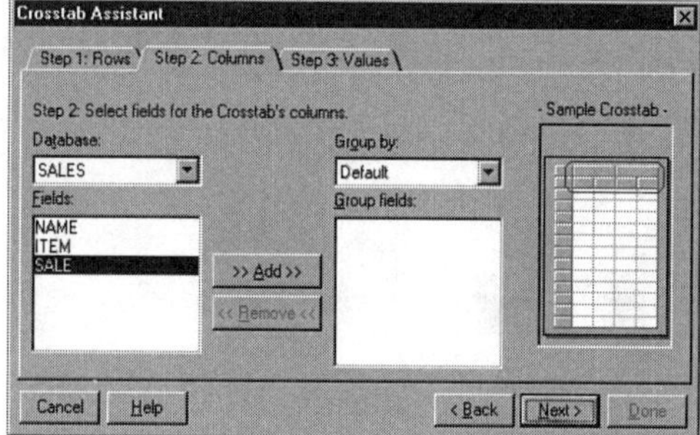

Fig. 26.13
The second step of the Approach Crosstab Assistant allows you to select the crosstab column field.

6. Select the field you want to use for the columns of your crosstab from the Fields list and click >>Add>>, and then Next>.
7. In the third step of the Crosstab Assistant select and add the field you want to use for calculations.

8. Select the type of calculation you want to do from the Calculate the list, shown in figure 26.14. For example, if you wanted to summarize the values in the SALE field by showing their totals, you would select the Sum calculation. You also can select Average, Count, Minimum, Maximum, Standard Deviation, or Variance depending on which type of calculation provides the best analysis of your data.

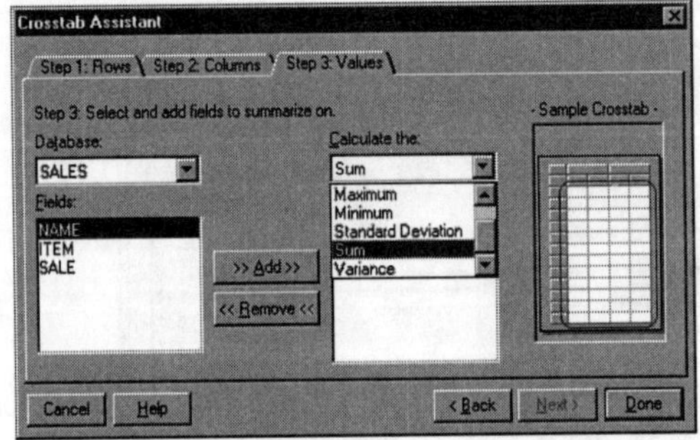

Fig. 26.14 Choose the type of calculation to perform in the Crosstab Assistant dialog box.

9. Click Done, and Approach returns the dynamic crosstab to Lotus 1-2-3 97. Figure 26.15 shows the completed cross-tabulation table. You can double-click on the tab to name the new worksheet Crosstab. Although it is optional, naming the tabs of your spreadsheets is always a good organizational technique.

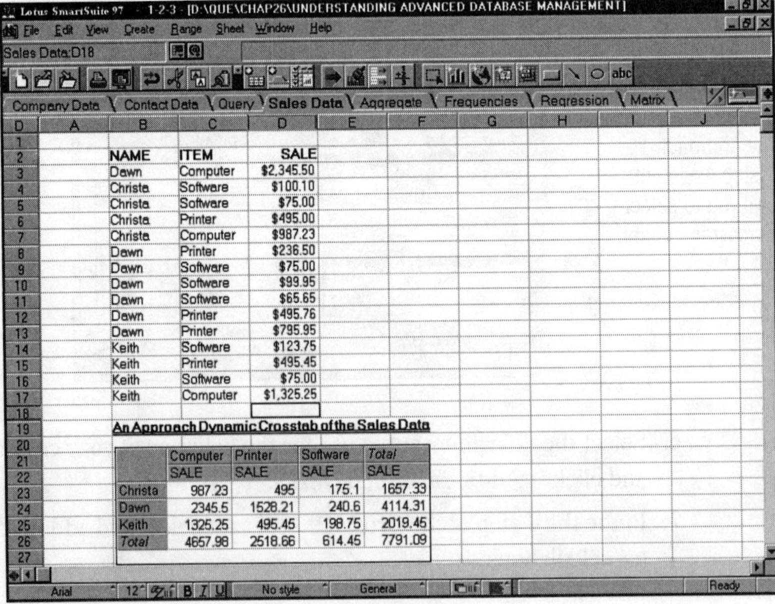

Fig. 26.15 The crosstab results summarize the data into a concise table.

You can enhance the presentation of cross-tabulation data in Approach or by copying the crosstab into the spreadsheet using any of Lotus 1-2-3 97's formatting capabilities. You also can show the analysis of the cross-tabulated data graphically.

Creating an Aggregate

To create an aggregate using Approach follow these steps:

1. Select the database range you want to analyze.

2. Choose the Create, Database, Dynamic Crosstab command; or click the Create an Approach Dynamic Crosstab SmartIcon to display the Crosstab dialog box (refer to fig. 26.11).
3. Choose the range you want in the Database table range box, and then click OK. The mouse pointer becomes a cross hair.
4. Move to the sheet you want to place the crosstab on and click the location where you want the top left corner of the table. This displays the Crosstab Assistant (refer to fig. 26.12).
5. Select the spreadsheet range from the Database list. Then select the fields you want to use as the rows of your crosstab in the Fields box, and click >>Add>>. In our example, you would select both the NAME and ITEM fields for the crosstab rows.
6. Choose the tab Step 3: Values. Here you would not choose any field for the crosstab columns. Select the field you want to calculate on from the Fields list (in this case, SALE), click >>Add>>, and select the type of calculation from the Calculate the list (in this case, sum).
7. Click Done to display the aggregate crosstab in 1-2-3 97 as shown in figure 26.16.

NOTE You can achieve similar results without a dynamic crosstab by using the special Database @functions. This requires you to name your database range and create a criteria range. The @DSUM and @DAVG enable you to sum or average all or part of a database based on the criteria in the criteria ranges. By making the @DSUM or @DAVG the calculation for the Range, Analyze, What-if Table commands, you can produce exactly the same output.

▶ **See** "Using Functions to Find and Analyze Data in Tables," **p. 461**

▶ **See** "Creating What-If Tables," **p. 467**

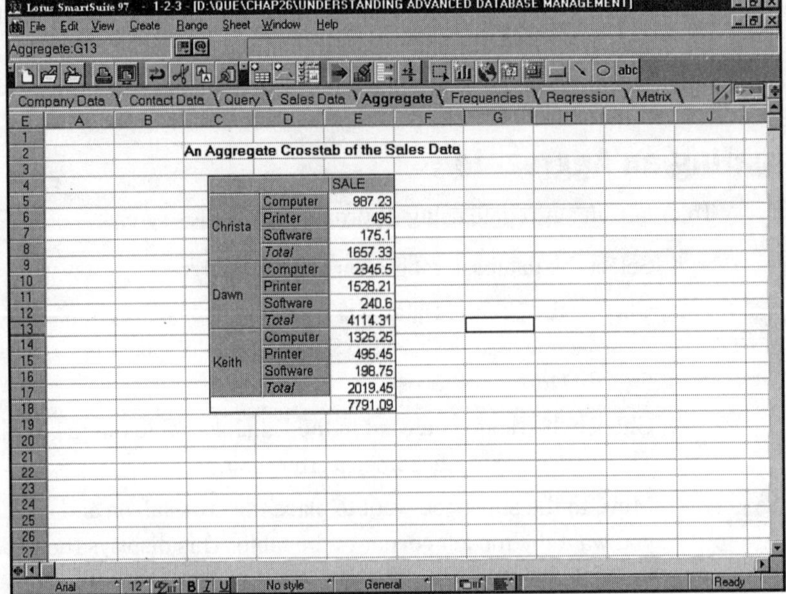

Fig. 26.16
The aggregate crosstab results summarize the data into a columnar table.

Analyzing Data with Frequency Distributions

When you collect certain types of data, such as performance data or survey results, you can analyze it using a frequency distribution. This analysis enables you to see how many people, widgets, or orders per day fit into certain categories that you create. A *frequency distribution* describes the relationship between a set of classes or categories and the number of members in each class. A list of student grades on an examination (shown in fig. 26.17) demonstrates the use of the Range, Analyze, Distribution command to produce a frequency distribution.

For example, figure 26.17 shows a list of students identified by student number in column A, and their letter grades on a particular exam in column B. Column C contains an @VLOOKUP function which returns their numerical grade from the GradeTable range on the far right. You must define the categories or *bins* for 1-2-3 97 to know where to count the scores. This has been done in column E of figure 26.17, and the equivalent letter grade of the bins has been placed in column G. Column F has intentionally been left blank in this example, because the results of the distribution analysis will be placed here.

Fig. 26.17
The setup of the data and the bins to generate a frequency distribution.

Lotus SmartSuite 97 - 1-2-3 - [D:\QUE\CHAP26\UNDERSTANDING ADVANCED DATABASE MANAGEMENT]

Company Data | Contact Data | Query | Sales Data | Aggregate | Frequencies | Regression | Matrix

	A	B	C	D	E	F	G	H	I	J
1									GradeTable	
2	Student ID	Letter Grade	Score		Score	Freq	Grades		Grade	Score
3	1	A	4.00		0.33		F's		A	4.00
4	2	B	3.00		1.33		D's		A-	3.66
5	3	C	2.00		2.33		C's		B+	3.33
6	4	D	1.00		3.33		B's		B	3.00
7	5	F	0.00		4.00		A's		B-	2.66
8	6	A-	3.66						C+	2.33
9	7	C-	1.66						C	2.00
10	8	B+	3.33						C-	1.66
11	9	B-	2.66						D+	1.33
12	10	C+	2.33						D	1.00
13	11	C-	1.66						D-	0.66
14	12	D+	1.33						F+	0.33
15	13	D-	0.66						F	0.00
16	14	F+	0.33							
17	15	D	1.00							
18	16	C	2.00							
19	17	B	3.00							
20	18	F	0.00							
21	19	A	4.00							
22	20	C+	2.33							
23	21	B-	2.66							

Performing the Frequency Distribution

To create a frequency distribution with the Range, Analyze Distribution command, follow these steps:

1. Enter the data you want to analyze, one row per entry. In this example, the data is shown in figure 26.17.
2. Decide the range of intervals or bins for grouping or summarizing the data and enter this information. Figure 26.17 shows this information in column E.

If you have evenly spaced intervals, use the Range, Fill command to enter the values for the bin range.

CAUTION

If there is data to the right of the bins, it is overlaid when you complete the Range, Analyze, Distribution command.

Also, if the values in the bins are not in ascending order, you will get invalid results.

3. Select the range containing the initial values (C3..C23) in this example.
4. Choose Range, Analyze, Distribution. The range selected in step 3 automatically appears in the Range of values to count text box.
5. Enter the bin range in the Bin range text box, in this case E3..F7. Figure 26.18 shows the completed dialog box for this example.

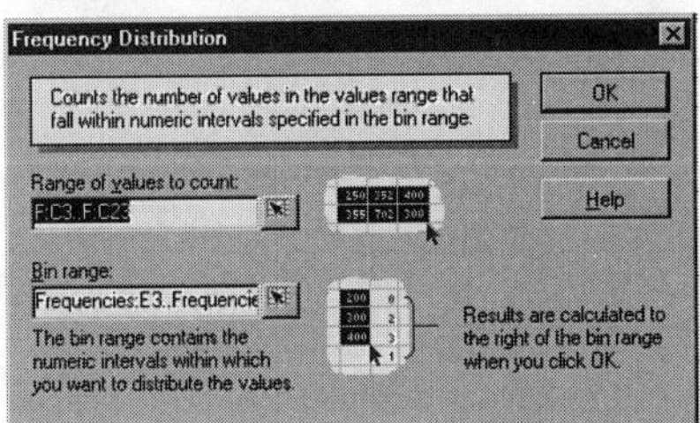

Fig. 26.18
Specify the Range of values and the bin range in the Distribution dialog box.

6. Press Enter or click OK. Lotus 1-2-3 97 creates the results column (F3..F8) to the right of the bin range (E3..E7). The results column, which shows the frequency distribution, is always in the column to the right of the bin range and extends one row below the bin range

The values in the results column represent the frequency of distribution of the numbers in the range of values for each interval. The first interval in the bin range in this example is for values greater than 0 and less than or equal to .33; the second interval is for values greater than .33 and less than or equal to 1.33, and so on. The last value in the results column, in cell F8 of this example, shows the frequency of leftover numbers (the frequency of numbers that do not fit into an interval classification).

TROUBLESHOOTING

I get zeroes as a result of my frequency distribution. If you forget to highlight a range that contains values, the results of the frequency distribution will be zeroes. Or, if the data in your bin range is typed as labels instead of values, the results will be all zeroes.

The results of the frequency distribution don't agree with the input data. If your bin range is not in order you may get inconsistent results. The bin range must be sorted in ascending order.

Analyzing Trends with Regression Analysis

The Range, Analyze, Regression command gives you a multiple linear regression analysis package within Lotus 1-2-3 97. Although most people don't have a need for this advanced feature, if you do need to use it, Lotus 1-2-3 97 will save you the cost and inconvenience of buying a stand-alone statistical package for performing regression analysis.

Use Range, Analyze, Regression when you want to determine the relationship between one set of values (the ***dependent variable***) and one or more other sets of values (the ***independent variables***). Regression analysis has a number of uses in a business setting, including relating sales to price, promotions, and other market factors; relating stock prices to earnings and interest rates; and relating production costs to production levels.

Think of linear regression as a way of determining the best line through a series of data points. Multiple regression does this for several variables simultaneously, determining the best line relating the dependent variable to the set of independent variables. Consider, for example, a data sample showing Annual Earnings versus Age. Figure 26.19 shows the data; figure 26.20 shows the data plotted as an XY graph (using A3..A17 for the X-graph range and B3..B17 for the A-graph range).

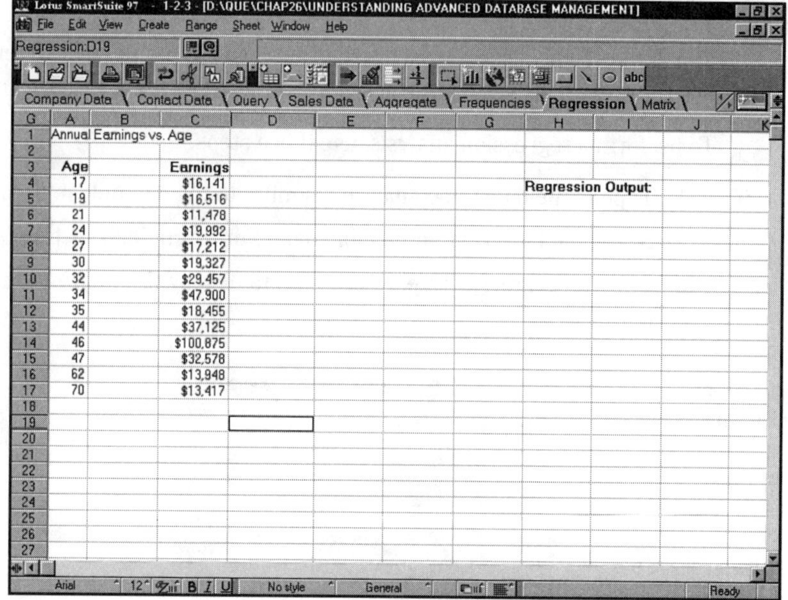

Fig. 26.19
You can use regression analysis to calculate a line that relates the Annual Earnings versus Age data in this worksheet.

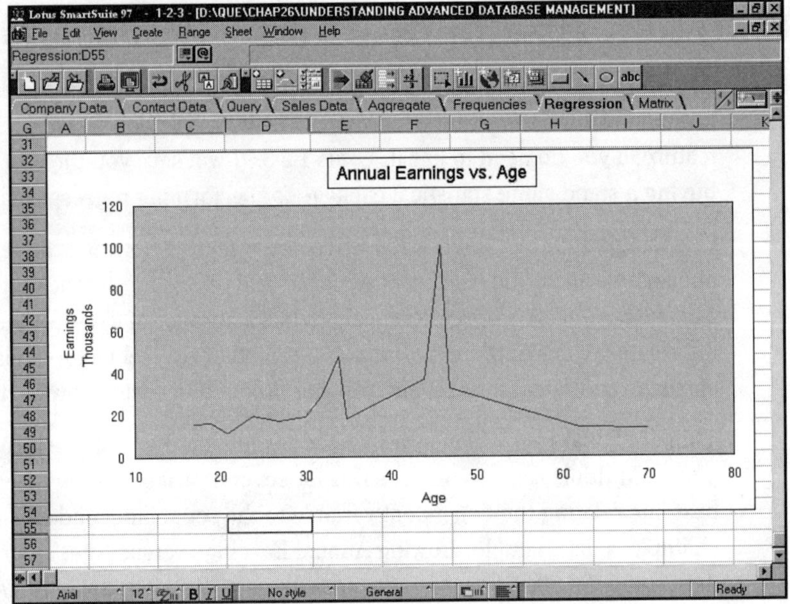

Fig. 26.20 Use the charting capabilities to create a graph of the Annual Earnings versus Age data.

Performing a Regression Analysis

The Range, Analyze, Regression command can simultaneously determine how to draw a line through these data points and how well the line fits the data.

To perform a regression analysis, use these steps:

1. Type in the data to be analyzed, similar to the example in figure 26.19.
2. Select the independent variable data. For example, select A4..A17.
3. Choose Range, Analyze, Regression to display the Regression dialog box shown in figure 26.21.

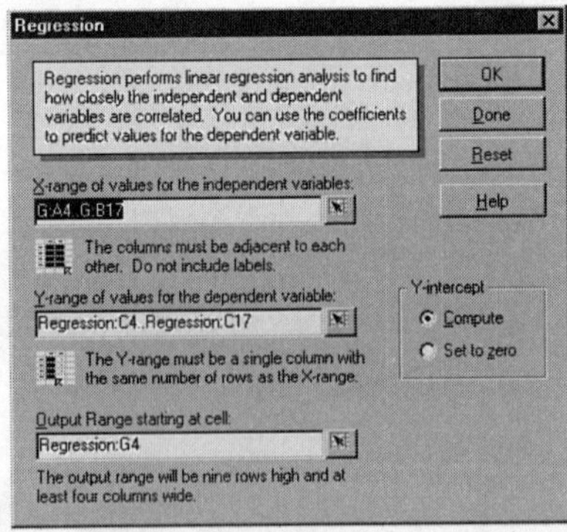

Fig. 26.21 Indicate the independent variable (X-range), dependent variable (Y-range), and output range in the Regression dialog box.

4. Enter the independent variables range in the X-range of values for the independent variables text box. The Range, Analyze, Regression command can use as many as 75 independent variables. If you selected this range in step 2, it automatically appears in the dialog box.
5. Enter the dependent variable range in the Y-range of values for the dependent variable text box. The Y-range must be a single column. In the example, you would select the range C4..C17.
6. Enter the top-left corner cell of the range where you want the results placed in the Output range starting at cell text box. In this example, G4 is specified as the output range.
7. Press Enter or click OK to calculate the regression information. The information is placed in the worksheet at the specified location as shown in figure 26.22.

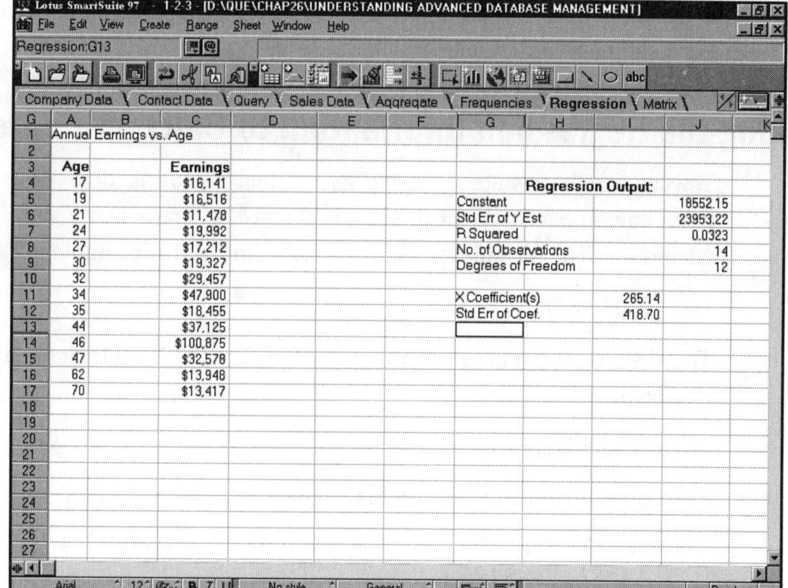

Fig. 26.22 The results of the regression are placed in the worksheet and can be used to calculate a trend or best-fit line.

CAUTION

This output range must be an unused section of the worksheet because the output is written over any existing cell contents.

The Y-intercept options in the Regression dialog box enable you to specify whether or not you want the regression to calculate a constant value. Calculating the constant is the default; in some applications, however, you may need to exclude a constant.

Figure 26.22 shows the results of using the Range, Analyze, Regression command in the Annual Earnings versus Age example. The results include the value of the constant and the coefficient of the single independent variable that was specified with the X-range option. The results also include a number of regression statistics that describe how well the regression line fits the data. In this case, the R-Squared value, the standard errors of the constant, and the regression coefficient all indicate that a linear regression line is not a good estimate of the data.

Using the Regression Information to Calculate a Trend Line

You can use the results of the regression analysis to calculate points on the "best fit" or trend line. The formula for this line is *y=mx+b*, where *m* is the slope of the line and b is the y intercept. The formula for the regression line in this example mx + b would then be:

+A4*$I$11+$J$5

The absolute references are necessary because the X coefficient and constant are always located in cells I11 and J5.

To calculate the regression line, follow these steps:

1. Move to a blank location in the sheet (in this case, cell D4).
2. Type the regression formula, using the pattern *mx+b*, (in this case, **A4*$I$11+$J$5**).
3. Copy the formula down to all applicable rows. The results are shown in figure 26.23.
4. Add the regression line to the chart (see fig. 26.24).

Fig. 26.23
Use a formula to calculate a trend line.

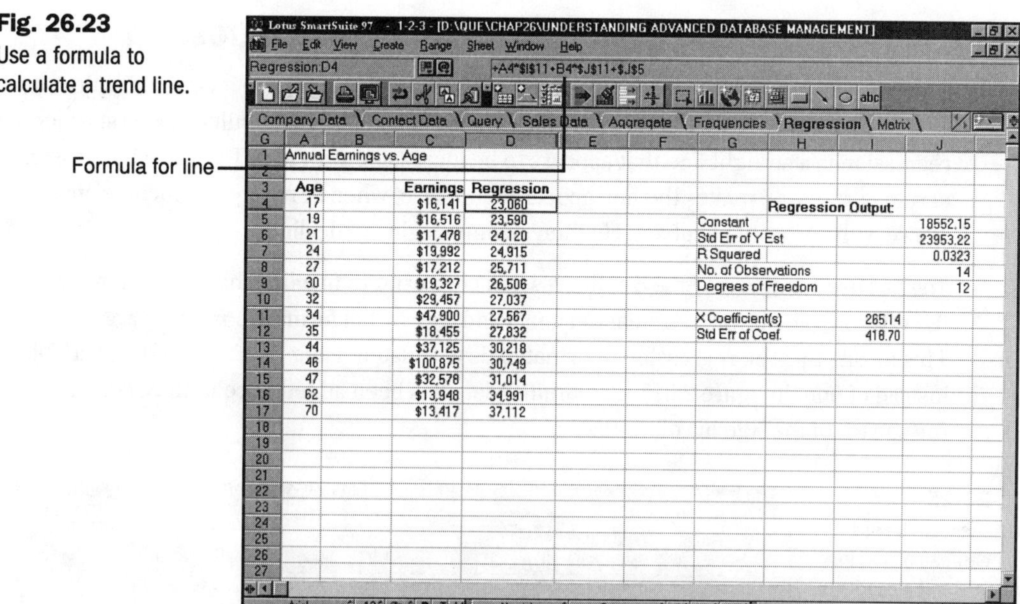

Age	Earnings	Regression
17	$16,141	23,060
19	$16,516	23,590
21	$11,478	24,120
24	$19,992	24,915
27	$17,212	25,711
30	$19,327	26,506
32	$29,457	27,037
34	$47,900	27,567
35	$18,455	27,832
44	$37,125	30,218
46	$100,875	30,749
47	$32,578	31,014
62	$13,948	34,991
70	$13,417	37,112

Fig. 26.24
Add the regression line to a chart of the Annual Earnings versus Age data to see the trend.

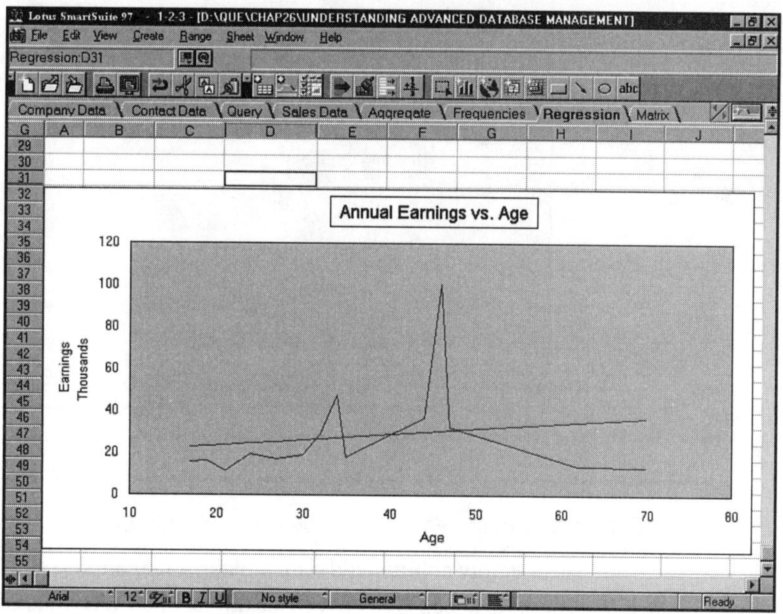

Taking the Analysis One Step Further: Multiple Regression

The regression line calculated in the previous section does not give a valid indication of what is happening to the Annual Earnings versus Age data. The result of the first order regression is a straight line that appears to be increasing with age. The large increase in earnings at age 46 makes the line appear to increase, when in reality, the income appears to rise with age until about age 50; then income begins to decline.

You can use the Range, Analyze, Regression command to fit a line that better describes the relationship between Annual Earnings and Age by performing a ***multiple regression.*** This means that the regression information is calculated using two independent variables instead of one. In figure 26.25, a column of data has been added in column B, containing the square of the Age in column A.

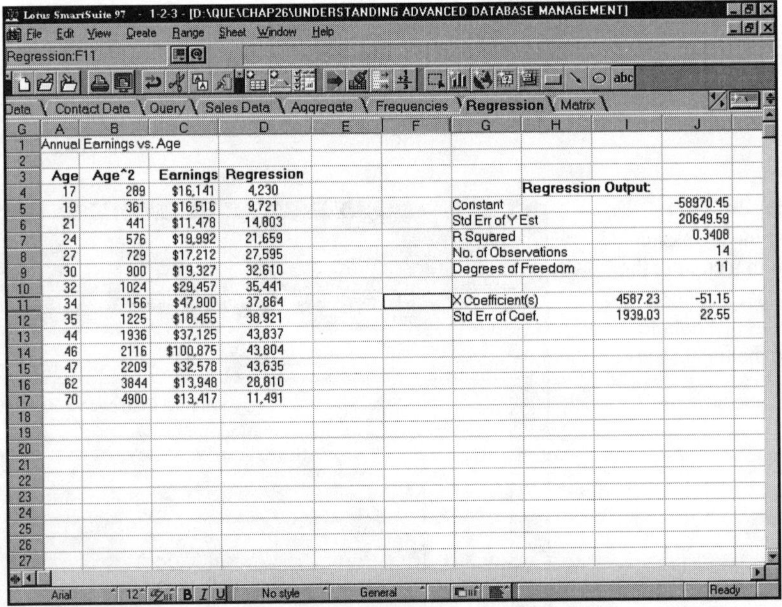

Annual Earnings vs. Age

Age	Age^2	Earnings	Regression
17	289	$16,141	4,230
19	361	$16,516	9,721
21	441	$11,478	14,803
24	576	$19,992	21,659
27	729	$17,212	27,595
30	900	$19,327	32,610
32	1024	$29,457	35,441
34	1156	$47,900	37,864
35	1225	$18,455	38,921
44	1936	$37,125	43,837
46	2116	$100,875	43,804
47	2209	$32,578	43,635
62	3844	$13,948	28,810
70	4900	$13,417	11,491

Regression Output:

Constant		-58970.45
Std Err of Y Est		20649.59
R Squared		0.3408
No. of Observations		14
Degrees of Freedom		11
X Coefficient(s)	4587.23	-51.15
Std Err of Coef.	1939.03	22.55

Fig. 26.25
The square of the Age has been calculated in column B to be used as part of the X-range for multiple regression.

To extend the linear regression previous example, follow these steps:

Enter the data as described in the previous example.

1. In an empty column add a formula to calculate the square of the age. For example, in cell B4 you'd enter the formula +A4^2, and then copy that formula down to B17.

2. Calculate the regression statistics. Select the range A4..B17 and choose Range, Analyze, Regression. Select the range C4..C17 for the Y-range of values for the dependent variable. Enter the cell address G4 for the Output Range starting at cell box and press OK. This results in the new regression data as shown in figure 26.25, starting in G4.
3. Change the formula in cell D4 to:

   +A4*$I$11+B4*$J$11+$J$5

   This results in the new regression data as shown in figure 26.25, starting in G4.
4. Copy the new multiple regression formula down to D17.

Looking at the chart of your new calculations you will notice that the regression statistics are much improved over the original regression of Annual Earnings versus Age. This fact means that the new line fits the data more closely than the old one. (However, the regression statistics indicate that the regression only explains about one-third of the dependent variable variation.) The chart of the new regression line, shown in figure 26.26, is now a parabola that rises until age 45 and then declines. The regression line generated by a multiple regression may or may not be a straight line, depending on the independent variables you use.

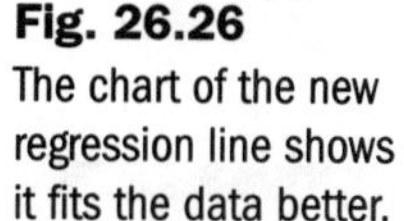

Fig. 26.26 The chart of the new regression line shows it fits the data better.

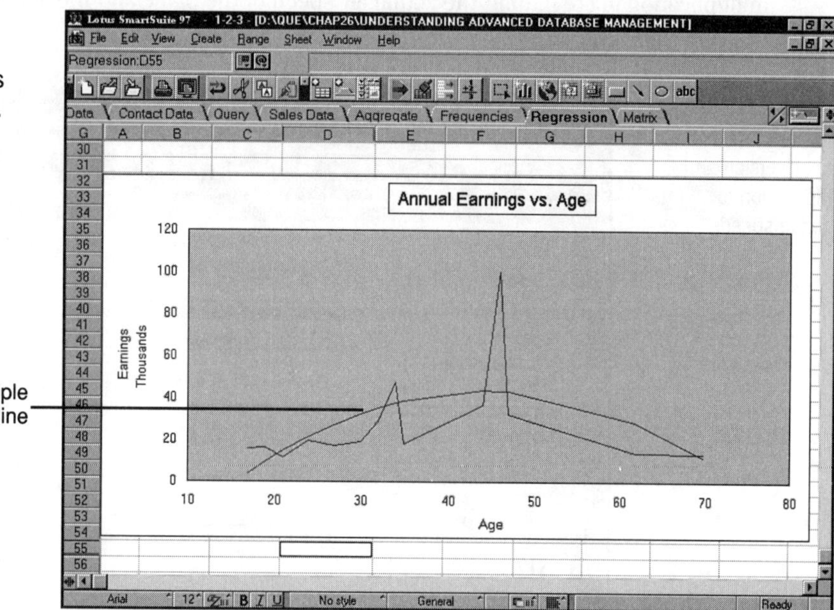

Using the Range Analyze Matrix Commands

The Range, Analyze, Invert Matrix and Range, Analyze, Multiply Matrix commands are specialized mathematical commands that enable you to solve systems of simultaneous linear equations and manipulate the resulting solutions. These commands are powerful but have limited applications in a business setting. If you are using Lotus 1-2-3 97 for certain types of economic analysis or for scientific or engineering calculations, you may find these commands valuable.

The Range, Analyze, Invert Matrix command enables you to invert a nonsingular square matrix of as many as 80 rows and columns. The Range, Analyze, Multiply Matrix command enables you to multiply two rectangular matrices together in accordance with the rules of matrix algebra. The number of columns in the first matrix must equal the number of rows in the second matrix. The resulting matrix has the same number of rows as the first matrix, and the same number of columns as the second.

Figure 26.27 shows the finished results of a sample problem that uses matrix inversion and multiplication to determine an airplane's air speed and the speed of the headwind or tailwind. In this problem, the distance between the two points (cell B1), the time required to travel from point 1 to point 2 (cell B2), the time required to travel from point 2 to point 1 (cell B3), and the relative wind speeds (cells B5 and B6) are known. Matrix inversion and multiplication make finding the actual air speed of the plane and the actual speed of the wind a simple task.

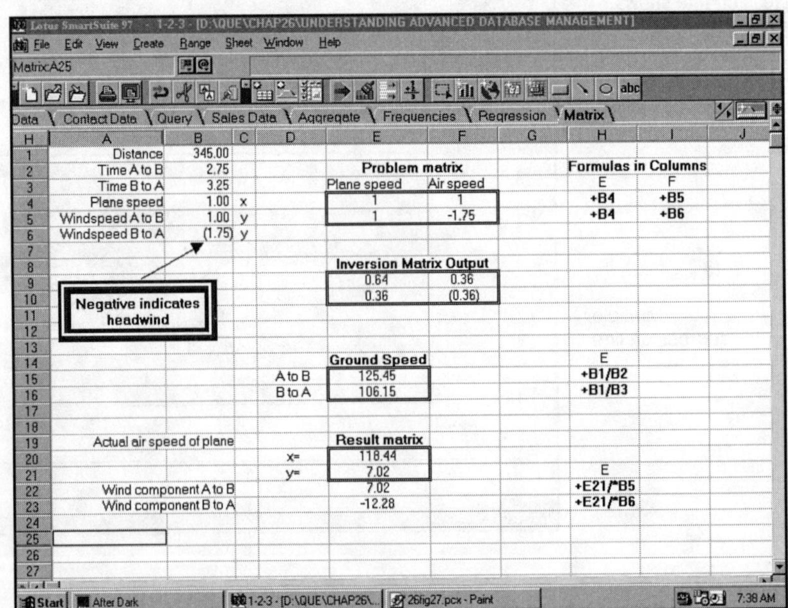

Fig. 26.27
A problem that uses matrix inversion and multiplication to calculate speeds.

To solve this problem using matrix inversion and multiplication, follow these steps:

1. Enter the labels in column A, the data shown in column B, and the formulas in columns E and F (as indicated in columns H and I). The inversion output matrix and the result matrix will be calculated, and should be left blank.
2. Choose Range, Analyze, Invert Matrix to display the Invert Matrix dialog box (see fig. 26.28). Specify **E4..F5** as the From matrix and **E9** as the To matrix. Click OK or press Enter.

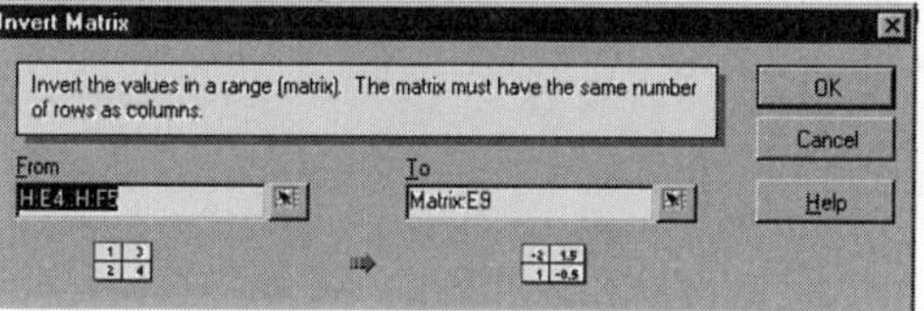

Fig. 26.28
Specify the range containing the original matrix in the From text box and the location for the new matrix in the To text box.

3. Choose Range, Analyze, Multiply Matrix to display the Multiply Matrix dialog box (see fig. 26.29). Specify **E9..F10** as the First Matrix, **E15..E16** as the Second Matrix, and **E20** as the Resulting Matrix. Click OK or press Enter.

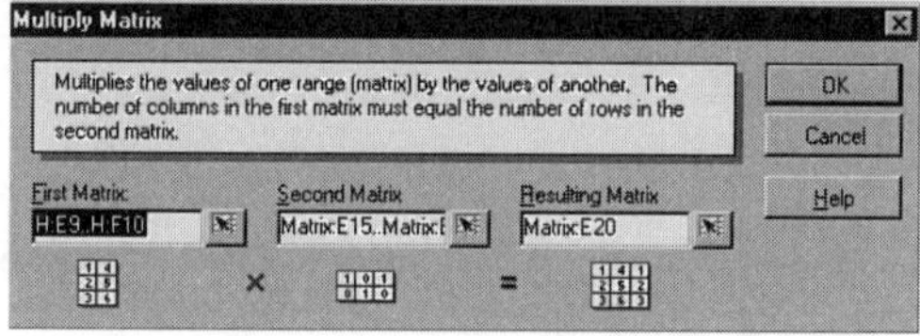

Fig. 26.29
Multiply two matrices by specifying the location of the first matrix, the location of the second matrix, and the location for the resulting matrix.

This problem shows an example of using matrix inversion and multiplication to solve a set of linear equations. The problem matrix (E4..F5) is used to define the equations. When you use Range, Analyze, Invert Matrix to display the Invert Matrix dialog box, the problem matrix is called the *From matrix.* When this matrix is inverted, the *To matrix,* (E9..F10) holds its inverse.

After you perform the matrix inversion, the To matrix becomes the First matrix for the matrix multiplication, and is multiplied by the Second matrix (E15..E16), which contains the ground speed calculations, to produce the Resulting matrix (E20..E21). The Resulting matrix displays the results of solving for the two variables, X (air speed) and Y (wind speed).

When data in a problem changes, remember to select Range, Analyze, Invert Matrix and Range, Analyze, Multiply Matrix again to calculate updated results.

CAUTION

Matrix inversions and multiplications can be time-consuming, especially when you are dealing with large matrices or your system lacks a numeric coprocessor. The 80486DX processor has a built-in numeric coprocessor, but the 80486SX, as well as all 80386 processors, do not.

CHAPTER 27

Additional Database Techniques

by Shane Devenshire

The database tools discussed in Chapters 22 through 26 enable you to create, sort, and query data in 1-2-3, often using Approach. From time to time you may want to use data from database programs such as Paradox, dBASE, or Access. You can create queries in 1-2-3, via Approach, that read the files from these or other databases and bring the data into a worksheet. Databases created in other database programs are called *external databases*.

Most of the querying and extracting techniques discussed in Chapters 25 and 26 require you to use Approach; however, it is possible to use some Classic menu techniques to query 1-2-3 data without resorting to Approach. Databases contained within 1-2-3 are called *internal databases*. This chapter shows you several ways to work with external and internal data.

Opening and using a Paradox or dBASE file in 1-2-3

You can directly open a Paradox or dBASE file into 1-2-3. You can then view the information in rows and columns, update existing data and add new data, and save it back in a Paradox or dBASE format or as a 1-2-3 worksheet.

Querying an external database program

Discover how to create a query table for an external database and work with the data almost as if it were contained in a 1-2-3 worksheet.

Importing and parsing text data

You can work with external data by importing it into a 1-2-3 worksheet as a text file. Depending on how the data in the text file was created, you might then need to *parse* the data (break it up into columns of information) to use it effectively in 1-2-3 97.

Querying a table of 1-2-3 data in 1-2-3

Learn how to extract 1-2-3 data within 1-2-3 and design calculated criteria ranges for querying or extracting data.

Importing Data from Other Programs

Lotus provides several means of importing data from other applications. You can use 1-2-3 97's query table commands as discussed in previous chapters, you can use copy and paste commands, or you can open the file directly into 1-2-3.

Querying an External Database

The process of querying an external database is almost identical to the technique for querying a 1-2-3 database using a query table. You may want to review Chapters 25 and 26 before continuing.

Suppose you want to query an Access database table. You will find that you cannot do this via the File, Open command. One solution is to create a query table, as you did in the prior chapters, but to use an external data source—the Access table. To query an external database, follow these steps:

1. Choose Create, Database, Query Table to display the Query Table Assistant dialog box.
2. Choose the option An External Table and press OK.
3. Click an empty area of your worksheet where you want the table to be placed. 1-2-3 will open the Approach engine and display Approach's Open dialog box.
4. Drop down the Files of Type list and choose Microsoft Access Driver (*.mdb). This will open the Select Database dialog box shown in figure 27.1.

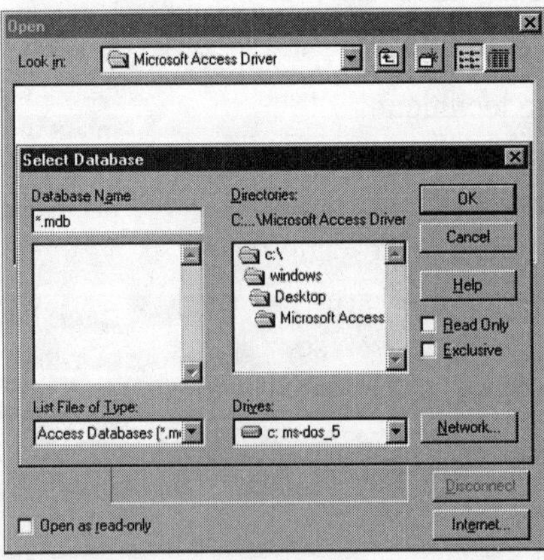

Fig. 27.1
The Select Database dialog box enables you to select the database you want to query.

5. Find and select the drive, folder, and file you want and then choose OK. This will display the admin@ACCESS folder in the Open dialog box.
6. Select the admin@ACCESS folder and choose Open. This will display a list of database folders, as shown in figure 27.2. You may need to open several levels of folders to reach this point.

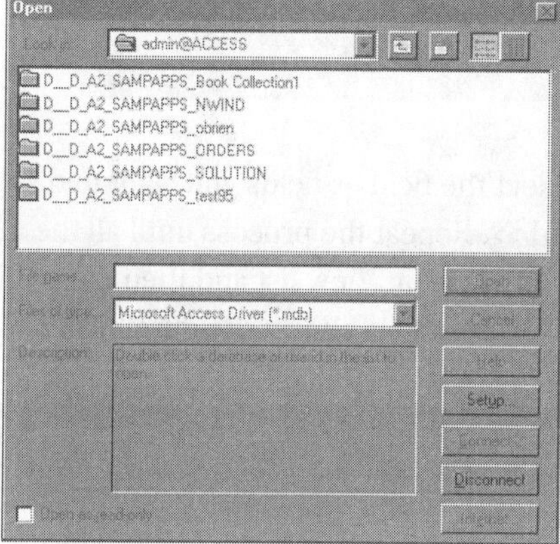

Fig. 27.2
The Open dialog box displays a collection of folders, each representing a specific database.

7. Select the folder containing your database and choose Open to display a list of tables in that database, as shown in figure 27.3.

NOTE An Access database contains tables that are not stored as separate files but as part of the database file; this is not true of all databases.

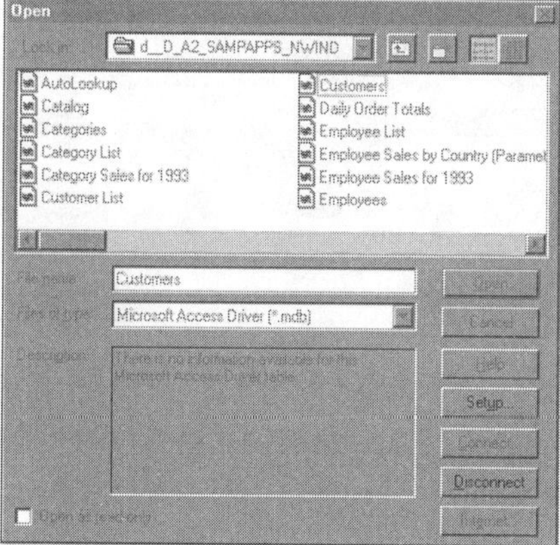

Fig. 27.3
The Open dialog box displays all of the tables in your chosen database.

8. Select the table you want to query and choose Open. This will display Approach's Worksheet Assistant, as shown in figure 27.4.

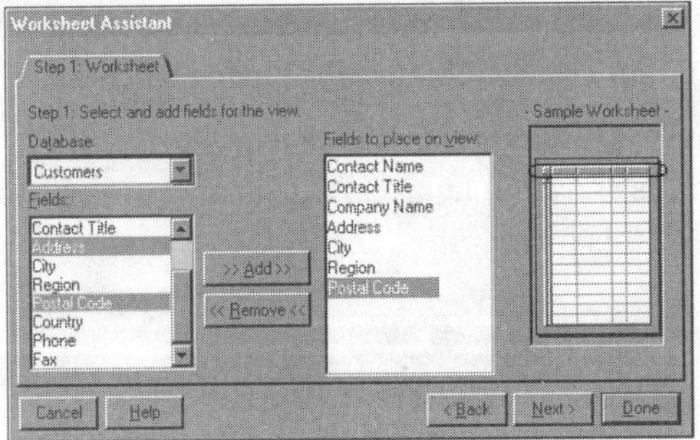

Fig. 27.4
The Worksheet Assistant enables you to pick which fields you want to display in the query table.

9. From the Fields list, select the field or fields you want to display in the query table and then choose >> Add >>. Repeat the process until all the fields you want are displayed in the Fields to Place on View list and then choose Done. A query table will be placed in your worksheet, as shown in figure 27.5.

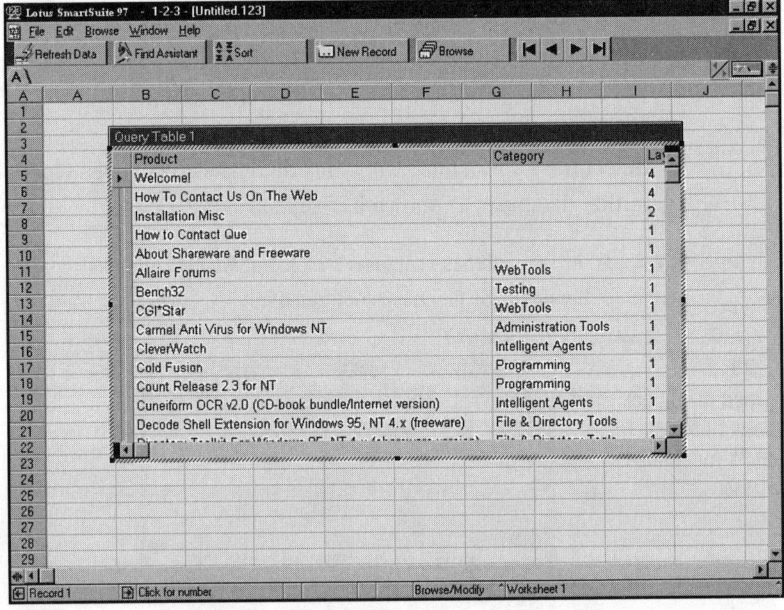

Fig. 27.5
The query table resulting from an Access query is no different from those created in Chapters 25 and 26.

You can use all the techniques you learned in Chapters 25 and 26 to manipulate the query table created when querying an external database.

Using a Paradox or dBASE File

Data management in 1-2-3 97 is powerful and flexible because of 1-2-3 for Window's capability to access data from other sources. If you are a Paradox or dBASE user, 1-2-3 makes it especially easy to work with data you have created in those programs. All you need to do is open the Paradox or dBASE file directly into 1-2-3. After you have opened the file into a worksheet, you can edit, insert or delete records, or add new records to the data. When you save, you have the option of saving back to the original format, or saving the data as a 1-2-3 worksheet.

Opening a Paradox or dBASE File

You can open a Paradox or dBASE file directly into 1-2-3, using these steps:

1. Choose File, Open, or click the Open SmartIcon.
2. From the Files of Type drop down list, choose dBASE (DBF) or Paradox (DB).
3. Type the file name you want in the File Name text box or choose the desired file from the list in the dialog box and then choose OK.

Editing Your Paradox or dBASE File in 1-2-3

Now that you have opened a dBASE or Paradox file in 1-2-3, you can use any editing techniques to edit the file, including any or all of the following:

- Type over existing entries, edit them with the mouse, or use the F2 key.
- Insert new rows in the data or delete existing rows.
- Insert new columns or delete columns.
- Add new rows of data to the bottom of the data range. However, if you do this, use the Range, Name command to display the Name dialog box. In the Existing Named Ranges list box, select the range DATABASE1. Use the range selector next to the Range text box to expand the range downwards to include all of the data in your worksheet. Then when you save the file, the new data will be saved back into the dBASE or Paradox database.

Saving the dBASE or Paradox Data

You have two choices when you save data that originally came from dBASE or Paradox: You can use a normal File, Save command to save the data back to the original database, or you can use File, Save As to save the data as a 1-2-3 worksheet (or into some other format). Just remember to use the Files of Type drop down list in the Save As dialog box to choose the format for the file before you save it.

CAUTION

Be very careful about saving data that you have modified in 1-2-3 97 back into the original Paradox or dBASE file. Database files often have restrictions on the types of data (such as text, integers, dates, or logical values) that are allowed in fields, but 1-2-3 does not prevent you from placing inappropriate data types in a field. If you attempt to save a modified database file containing incorrect data, you could corrupt the database file and destroy data.

Importing Formatted or Unformatted Data

When you use the File, Open command to import data into 1-2-3, the method you use will depend on the type of file that was created in the source program. For example, a large proportion of downloaded data from a mainframe or minicomputer is output to text files. This is usually created in one of two formats:

- *Delimited Data.* This data is organized into records (or rows of data) and fields. The fields are uniquely identifiable because the alphabetic fields are enclosed in quotation marks and the numeric data is separated by commas, blanks, or some other character.
- *Fixed Length Data.* Although each record is on a unique line or row, there are no delimiters to identify the individual fields, so when you import this information into 1-2-3, it comes in as one long label in a single column. You then must disassemble these labels into the appropriate data values or fields by using functions or parsing commands.

You use the same basic steps to import either delimited or fixed length data. But, if the data is fixed length, you will have to parse it (discussed in the next section). Follow these steps to import the data into a 1-2-3 97 worksheet:

1. Choose the File, Open command or click the Open File SmartIcon to import the data stored as a text file.
2. Select Text from the Files of Type list box in the Open File dialog box. See figure 27.6.
3. Select the Combine with Current Workbook check box and then choose Combine. This displays the Text File Options dialog box shown in figure 27.7.

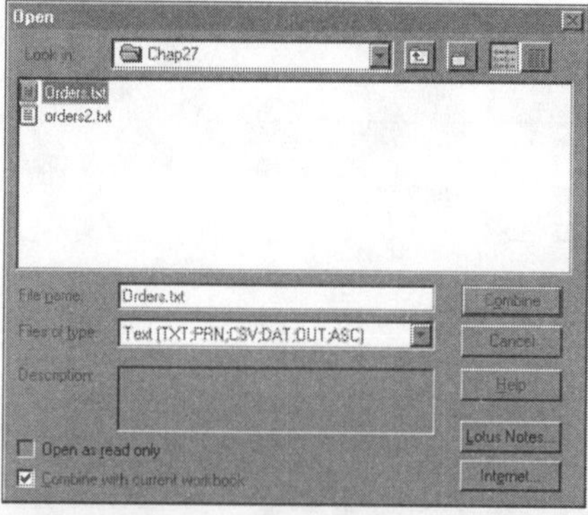

Fig. 27.6
Specify Text in the Files of Type list box to open a text file.

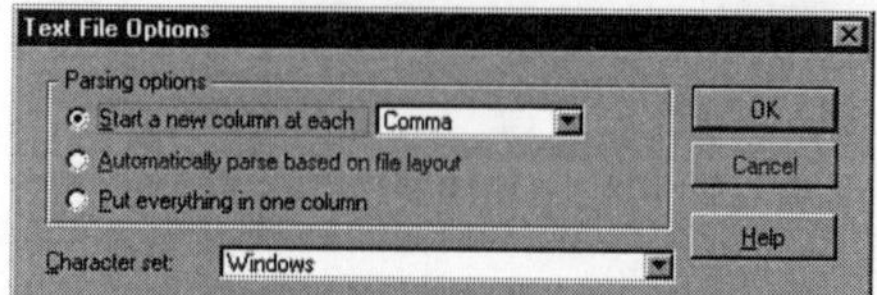

Fig. 27.7
Here you tell 1-2-3 how you would like it to treat the records in the incoming text file.

4. Select the parsing option appropriate for your text file. The following choices enable you to tell 1-2-3 how to separate the data in the text file into unique columns of data in the worksheet:
   - Start a New Column at Each—Choose the character used to separate the fields in the text file.
   - Automatically Parse Based on File Layout—This breaks the data into columns based on the data in the file.
   - Put Everything in One Column—Puts all the text into the first column so you will need to use the parse commands to split it up into separate columns.
5. Choose OK to open the text file into the current cell in the current worksheet. The results might look like figure 27.8. (Put Everything in One Column was selected in this example.)

The results in figure 27.8 illustrate one of the common problems with imported data—the need for data cleanup.

NOTE Figure 27.8 also illustrates that it can be difficult to understand the structure of data when the data is displayed using the default Arial font. In the top half of figure 27.8, the data is displayed using Arial, a proportional font. In the bottom half of the figure the same data is displayed using Courier New, a fixed pitch font. It is much easier to see the actual layout of the fixed length data when you use fixed pitch fonts.

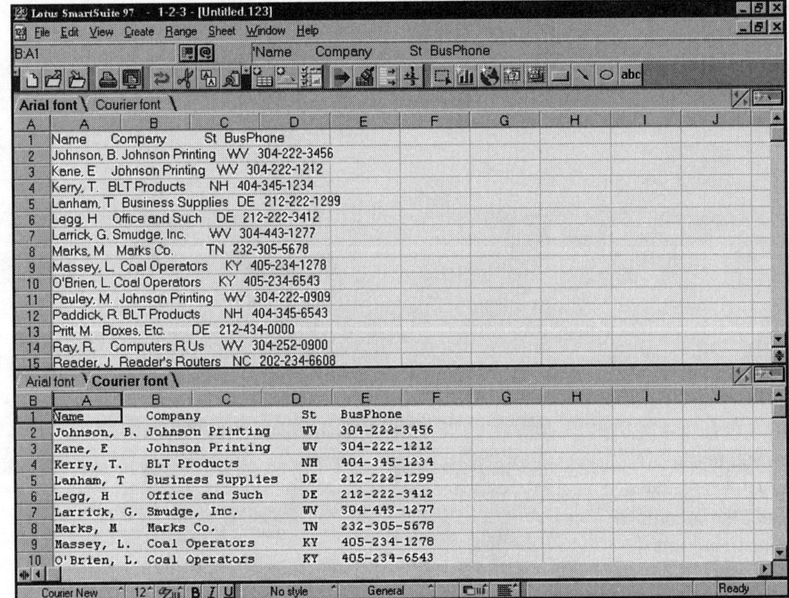

Fig. 27.8
The results of file combining a text file.

Parsing Data

The Range, Parse command is a flexible and easy method of extracting numeric, date, and string data from long labels and placing them in separate columns. Suppose that you printed a report containing important data to a disk file, and now you want to load the ASCII file in 1-2-3. After you load the file by using the File, Open command, Combine with Current Workbook, Combine command and select the Put Everything in One Column option, you must reformat the data with the Range, Parse command.

The File, Open, Combine with Current Workbook, Combine, Put Everything in One Column command loads the data into the first column of a range as shown in figure 27.9 (note the formula line). The current cell-pointer location is B4—all the data is contained as a long label—and not in separate cells as you might assume. Also, the Courier New font has been applied to the entire worksheet.

To parse the long-label columns into fields, follow these steps:

1. Select the range containing the data to be parsed and then choose Range, Parse. The Parse dialog box appears.
2. Choose Guess Format to create a new format line (see fig. 27.10). The Format line specifies the pattern 1-2-3 is to use to split the long labels into numbers, labels, and dates.

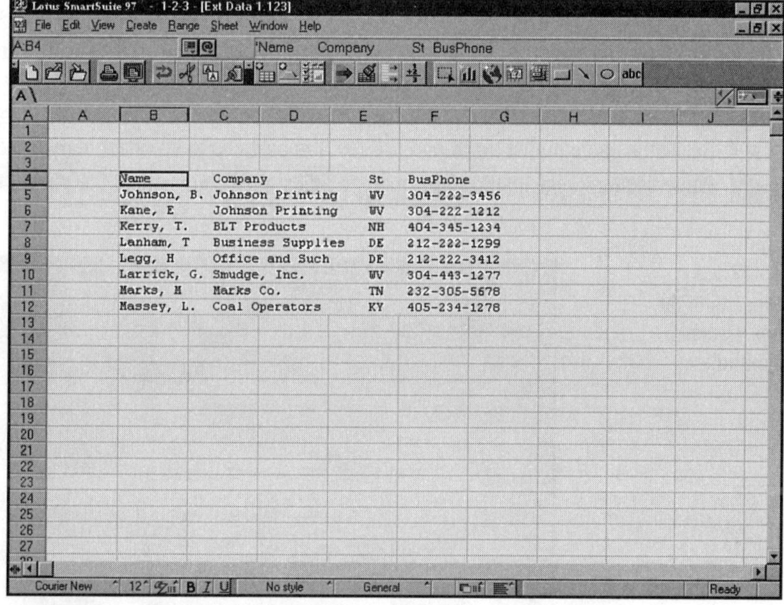

Fig. 27.9
The combined text data is unformatted and placed in a single column.

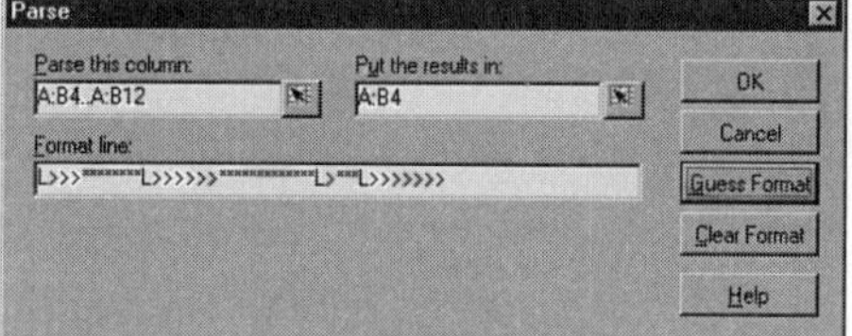

Fig. 27.10
The Parse dialog box enables you to control the parsing process.

3. If the Format line does not accurately reflect how the data should be divided, edit the line using the symbols described in the following section entitled "Using the Format Line to Control the Parse." Use the format line to mark the column positions and the type of data in those positions.
4. Choose Put the Results In and indicate the upper-left corner of the range where you want the parsed data to be placed (a blank area of the worksheet).

CAUTION

Make sure that there are enough empty cells to the right and below that cell to hold the newly parsed data or you might overwrite existing data in the worksheet. The output data has as many rows as there are labels; the number of columns depends on the format line. Also, because the Parse command adds the format line to the worksheet and moves everything else down one row, make sure that you account for this extra row in positioning your output range.

5. Choose OK to parse the data. The suggested format line is inserted above the unformatted data. The newly formatted data appears in the output range as shown in figure 27.11.

Select the entire output range and use the Size columns to fit widest entry button on the Properties for Range InfoBox Basics tab to adjust the columns to fit the parsed data.

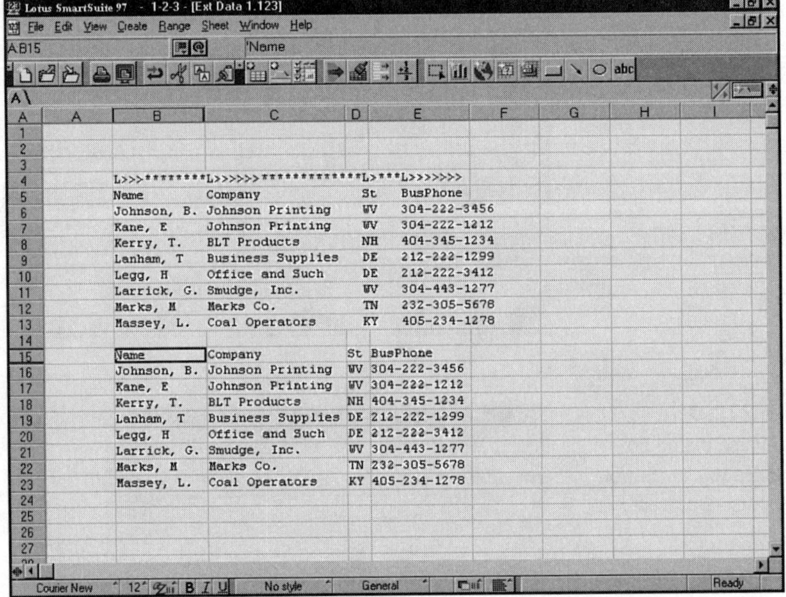

Fig. 27.11
The results of the Range, Parse command.

If 1-2-3 did not guess the correct format line, repeat steps 1 through 4 and then edit the Format line.

TROUBLESHOOTING

When I parse my data, my numeric values are turned into labels. In many real-world situations, you will need to parse the column headings (which are labels) by using one format line; then parse the data with another format line and output range. Different format lines are necessary because all the headings are labels, but the data is a mixture of label, numeric, time, and date data.

Using the Format Line to Control the Parse You use combinations of certain letters and special characters in format lines to control how the data is parsed. The letters denote the beginning position and the type of data; special symbols define the length of a field and the spacing. Table 27.1 explains the letters and symbols typically used in format lines.

Table 27.1 Letters and Symbols Used in Format Lines

Letter/Symbol	Purpose
D	Marks the beginning of a Date field.
L	Marks the beginning of a Label field.
S	Marks the beginning of a Skip position, which instructs 1-2-3 to ignore the data in this position.
T	Marks the beginning of a Time field.
V	Marks the beginning of a Value field.
>	Defines the continuation of a field. Use one > for each position in the field (excluding the first position).
*	Defines blank spaces (in the data below the format line) that may be part of the block of data.

In some cases you may need to add additional format lines to correctly parse the data. For example, if the headings have a different format than the data, two separate parse operations may be necessary.

After parsing is complete, the data displayed in individual cells may not be exactly what you want. You can make a few changes in the format and column width, as shown in figure 27.11, and add or delete information to make the newly parsed data more usable. These enhancements are not part of the Range, Parse command—but they usually are necessary after importing any parsed data.

Using Caution when Parsing Data If you want to parse a value that continues past the end of the field, you should know that 1-2-3 parses the data until it encounters a blank or until the value runs into the next field in the format line. This means that if you parse labels, make sure that the field widths in the format line are wide enough so that you avoid losing data because of blanks. If you parse values, the field widths are less critical.

Experiment on small amounts of data until you are comfortable using the Range, Parse command. After you understand how this important command works, you may find many more applications for it. Every time you develop a new application, consider whether existing data created with another software program can be imported and then changed to 1-2-3 97 format by using the Range, Parse command.

You can use the Edit, Paste command as a shortcut to import and parse data from another Windows application. Try copying the data to the Clipboard in the other application and then using Edit, Paste in 1-2-3 97. You may find that this approach automatically places the data into separate worksheet cells, eliminating the need to use Range, Parse.

▶ **See** "Editing Data," **p. 79**

Querying Within 1-2-3

Querying using 1-2-3's query tools has a number of advantages: 1-2-3 does not need to load Approach, you don't have to learn a new application, and if you already know 1-2-3's Classic /Data, Query command, you're ready to go. If your computer is light on RAM, the first reason may drive your decision to use the Classic method.

Setting Up a 1-2-3 Query Area

To query a 1-2-3 database, all you need to do is set up the database and a criteria area. However, most likely you will also want to set up an extract area. 1-2-3 will copy all the records that meet a given criteria from the database into the extract area. If you don't set up an extract area, the only thing you can do with the /Data, Query command is delete records that meet a given condition.

The database range for the /Data, Query command includes one row of unique field names plus all the rows and columns of data. The criteria range contains a minimum of two rows, the first of which contains some or all of the field names from the database. The remaining rows contain the criteria. Figure 27.12 shows an example of these two ranges with a criteria that would find all names starting with the letter L.

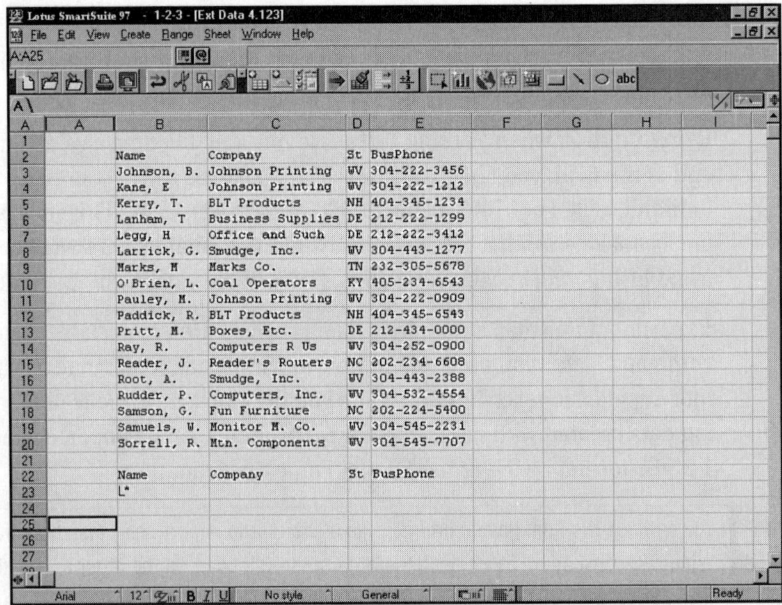

Fig. 27.12
A database and criteria range for a Classic menu query.

Deleting Records from a 1-2-3 Database

One of the things you can do without creating an extract range is delete records from your 1-2-3 database. To delete all records from a database that meet a given condition, follow these steps:

1. Set up a database and criteria range, such as the one shown in figure 27.12. Suppose you wanted to delete all the records for names beginning with L, then you would enter the criteria L* under the Name field in the criteria range.
2. Choose the /Data, Query, Reset command.
3. Choose Input and select the database range including the field names, and press Enter. In figure 27.12 this would be the range B2..E20.
4. Choose Criteria, select the criteria range and press Enter. In figure 27.12 the criteria range is B22..E23.
5. Choose the Del command and then Delete. This will delete all the records that meet the criteria, producing a result similar to figure 27.13. Close the Classic menu by choosing Quit.

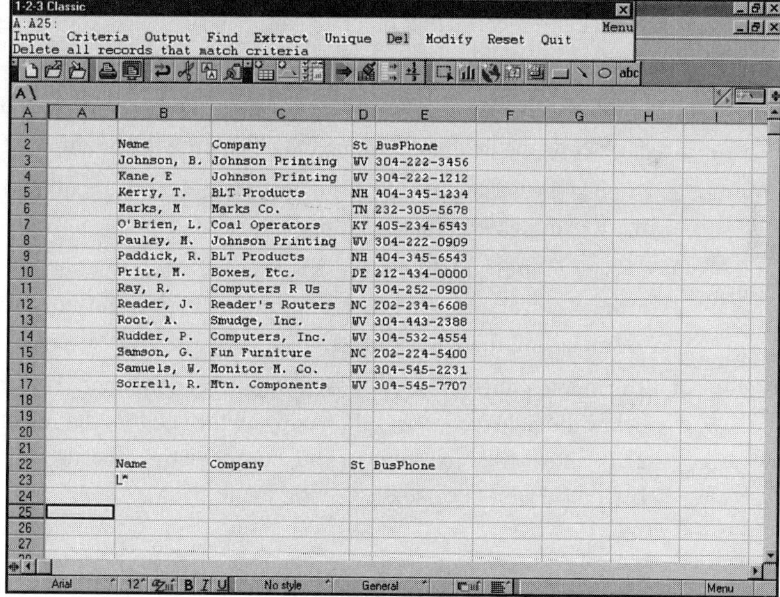

	B	C	D	E
2	Name	Company	St	BusPhone
3	Johnson, B.	Johnson Printing	WV	304-222-3456
4	Kane, E	Johnson Printing	WV	304-222-1212
5	Kerry, T.	BLT Products	NH	404-345-1234
6	Marks, M	Marks Co.	TN	232-305-5678
7	O'Brien, L.	Coal Operators	KY	405-234-6543
8	Pauley, M.	Johnson Printing	WV	304-222-0909
9	Paddick, R.	BLT Products	NH	404-345-6543
10	Pritt, M.	Boxes, Etc.	DE	212-434-0000
11	Ray, R.	Computers R Us	WV	304-252-0900
12	Reader, J.	Reader's Routers	NC	202-234-6608
13	Root, A.	Smudge, Inc.	WV	304-443-2388
14	Rudder, P.	Computers, Inc.	WV	304-532-4554
15	Samson, G.	Fun Furniture	NC	202-224-5400
16	Samuels, W.	Monitor M. Co.	WV	304-545-2231
17	Sorrell, R.	Mtn. Components	WV	304-545-7707
22	Name	Company	St	BusPhone
23	L*			

Fig. 27.13
The database after a delete query has been executed on the data shown in figure 27.12.

If you delete records in error, choose Edit, Undo immediately after closing the 1-2-3 Classic menu (Edit, Undo does not specify an action to undo when you have used the 1-2-3 Classic menu).

Extracting Database Records

One of the most powerful features of the Classic database commands is Extract. When you extract records from a 1-2-3 database, you are copying the records to a new location. This enables you to manipulate the records without harming the original database. 1-2-3 lets you extract, and therefore work with, only those records and fields that are germane to your needs.

Before you can extract records from a 1-2-3 database you must first set up an extract range. The extract range must include the names of fields you want extracted. The field names in the criteria and extract ranges should be exact matches with those in the database.

Copying field names is the safest way to ensure their matching.

To extract all the records that meet a given criteria, follow these steps:

1. After setting up the database and criteria ranges as shown earlier in figure 27.12, set up an extract range with only the field names for the fields you want to see. In this case, copy the fieldname Name to G2, and the fieldname BusPhone to H2.
2. Choose the Classic menu command /Data, Query, Input, highlight the data range—B2..E20 in this example—and press Enter.
3. Choose Criteria, highlight the criteria range, B22..E23 in this example, and press Enter. Then choose Output, highlight the titles of the extract range, G2..H2 in this example, and then press Enter.
4. To complete the extract, choose the Extract command. 1-2-3 will clear anything below the field names and then copy all the records that meet your criteria. Figure 27.14 shows the results when you extract all the records for names beginning with L. Choose Quit to close the Classic menu.

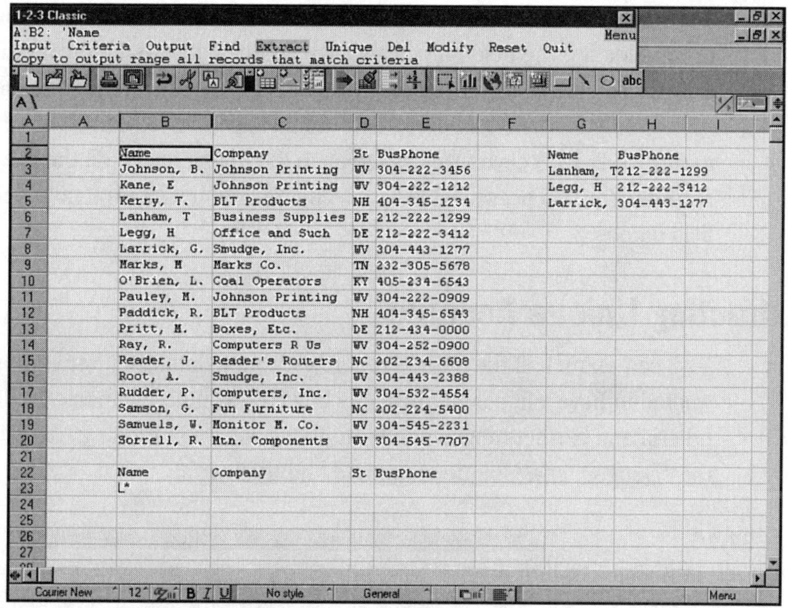

Fig. 27.14
The results of extracting all records that meet the criteria of names beginning with L.

Managing the Output Range

The output range can contain all the field names or any subset. They may be in any order and can even be repeated if necessary. If you wanted to eliminate customers in West Virginia, you could create an extract similar to that shown in figure 27.15.

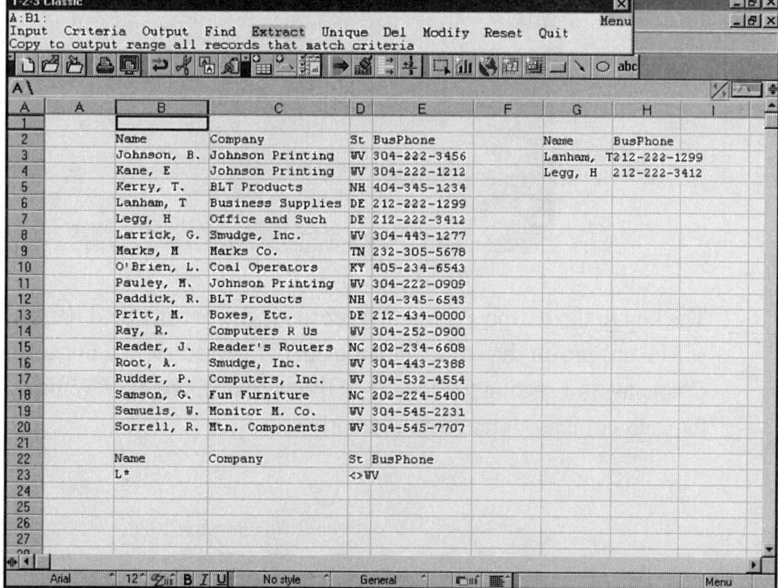

Fig. 27.15
Add additional conditions to further limit the selection of records.

You can specify the output range of an extract two ways: by selecting only the field names or by selecting the field names and any number of rows below them. You may get drastically different results during an extract depending on which of these you choose. If you specify only the field names of the output range, 1-2-3 clears everything below them down to row 8192. 1-2-3 clears this range even if it doesn't need all the rows to output extracted records. You can prevent this by specifying an output range that includes rows below the field names.

Extracting Unique Records

1-2-3 can extract all the unique records within a database. For example, suppose you wanted to have a list of all the states in which you do business. To do this you would set up criteria and extract ranges similar to those shown in figure 27.16. Then you would choose the /Data, Query, Unique command and then Quit.

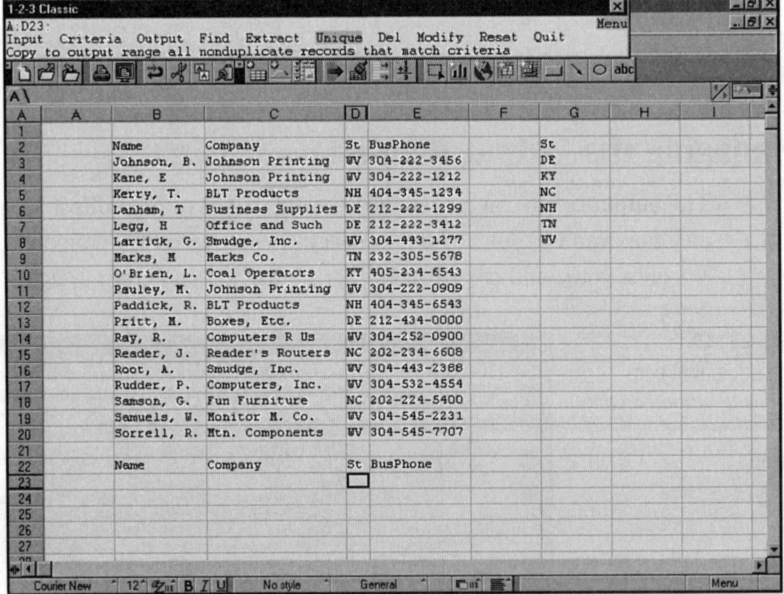

	A	B	C	D	E	F	G
1							
2		Name	Company	St	BusPhone		St
3		Johnson, B.	Johnson Printing	WV	304-222-3456		DE
4		Kane, E	Johnson Printing	WV	304-222-1212		KY
5		Kerry, T.	BLT Products	NH	404-345-1234		NC
6		Lanham, T	Business Supplies	DE	212-222-1299		NH
7		Legg, H	Office and Such	DE	212-222-3412		TN
8		Larrick, G.	Smudge, Inc.	WV	304-443-1277		WV
9		Marks, M	Marks Co.	TN	232-305-5678		
10		O'Brien, L.	Coal Operators	KY	405-234-6543		
11		Pauley, M.	Johnson Printing	WV	304-222-0909		
12		Paddick, R.	BLT Products	NH	404-345-6543		
13		Pritt, M.	Boxes, Etc.	DE	212-434-0000		
14		Ray, R.	Computers R Us	WV	304-252-0900		
15		Reader, J.	Reader's Routers	NC	202-234-6608		
16		Root, A.	Smudge, Inc.	WV	304-443-2388		
17		Rudder, P.	Computers, Inc.	WV	304-532-4554		
18		Samson, G.	Fun Furniture	NC	202-224-5400		
19		Samuels, W.	Monitor M. Co.	WV	304-545-2231		
20		Sorrell, R.	Mtn. Components	WV	304-545-7707		
21							
22		Name	Company	St	BusPhone		

Fig. 27.16
The extract range lists each state only once. Notice that the extract range is in alphabetical order.

The key to the extract of unique records is the extract field names. The extracted records will be unique on the combination of all the extract fields. For example, if you include Company as a second field name in the output range, you would have gotten one record for each company/state combination.

Exploring the Power of Criteria

Criteria provide you with the power to select only the records you need to work with. The previous example demonstrated a number of simple criteria; in the following sections you will work with more complex criteria including AND, OR, and Range criteria as well as a number of calculated criteria.

A number of points to keep in mind:

- In the criteria area, you only need to include the field names of the fields which will contain criteria. Including field names without criteria under them has no effect on the outcome of the query. However, it is often easier to include all the field names so you don't need to add and delete field names before each new query.
- You must include at least one row below the field names when defining the criteria range.
- If you have more than one row of criteria (for example, when using OR—see the next section), you must include all rows with criteria in the criteria range. If you don't, 1-2-3 will ignore the rows outside the defined range.
- Don't include empty rows unless you want to extract all records—1-2-3 assumes a blank row means you have no limiting conditions for your extract.
- Again, remember that the field names must match those in the database.

Working with AND and OR Criteria If you want to query for all records that meet two conditions at the same time, you should use AND criteria. AND criteria are criteria that are on the same row of the criteria range. If you wanted to buy a new car, you would certainly use more than one criterion in making your selection. You might be concerned about gas mileage, color, and price just to name a few. If all of these conditions needed to be met, then the criteria are AND criteria. If only some of them need to be met, you have OR criteria. Suppose you were willing to accept poorer mileage if the price of the car is substantially lower, but in either case the car must be red. In other words, you will settle for a cheap red car or a more expensive red car that has good gas mileage.

Figure 27.17 shows an example of an AND criterion. Here all the companies of interest must have names beginning with B and be located in states which are in the second half of the alphabet—>M.

Figure 27.18 demonstrates an OR criterion. Here all the companies of interest must have names beginning with B or be located in states which are in the second half of the alphabet—>M.

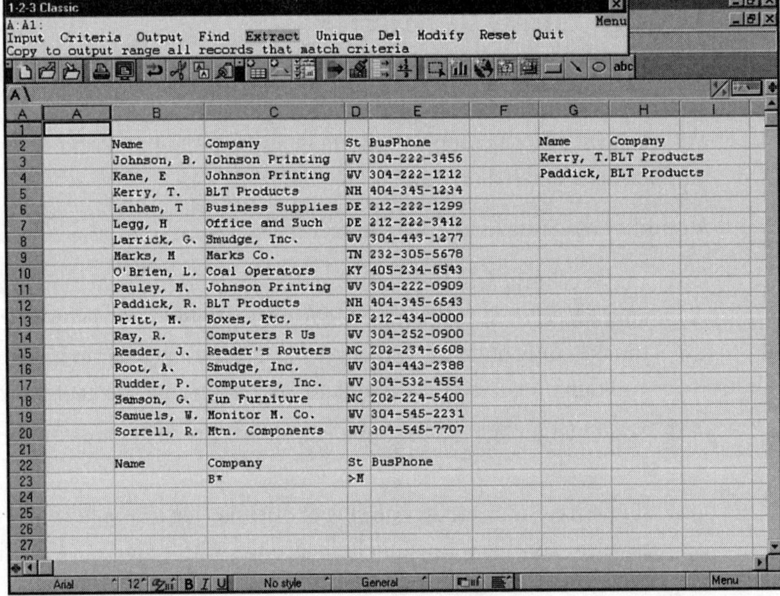

Fig. 27.17
All the conditions for an AND criterion are on the same row.

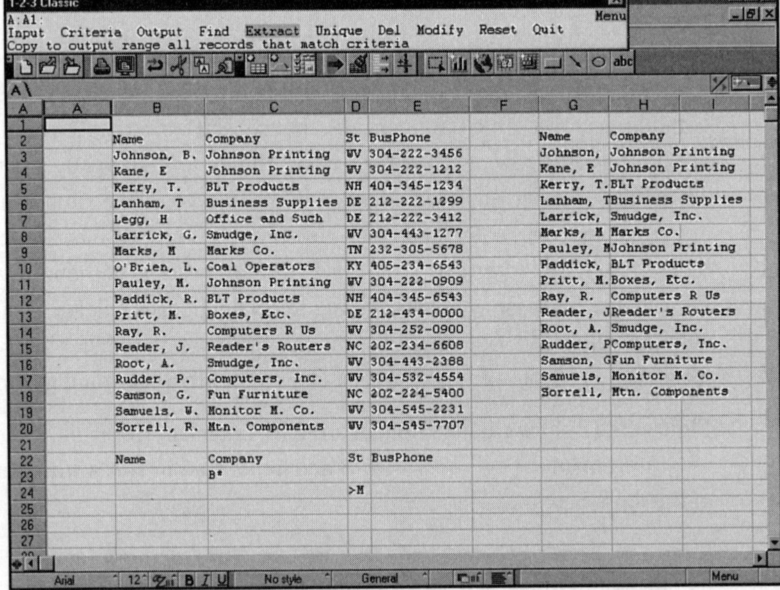

Fig. 27.18
The use of a multi-row OR criterion selects many more records than an AND criterion.

You can repeat the last query by pressing F7.

Using Criteria to Find Ranges of Values It is quite common to want to find all the records that are within a certain range. For example, you might want a list of all the employees hired within the past six months, or a list of all orders placed between 1/1/96 and 6/1/96, or a list of all orders greater than $25.00 but less than $100.00. In each of these cases you are interested in records within a given range. There are two ways to deal with ranges of values—using calculated criteria ranges or by using a modification of the AND criteria range.

The following example demonstrates the second of these approaches. Suppose you want to list all companies that are in states which start with the letters N through V. To do this query set up your criteria range with the field name *St* twice. Then enter the criteria >M under one of the field names and <W under the other. Notice that when you specify that the data must be greater or less than a specified value, you exclude the specified value from the selection. Figure 27.19 shows what this query would look like.

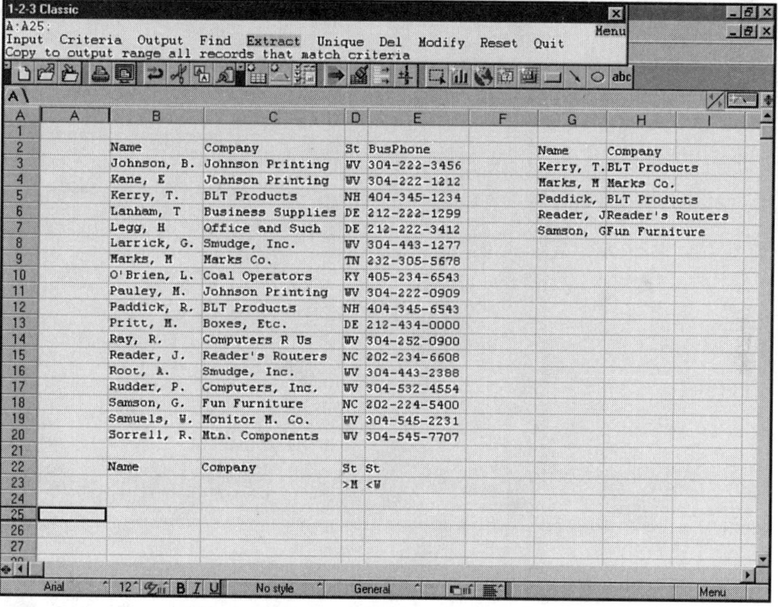

	A	B	C	D	E	F	G	H
1								
2		Name	Company	St	BusPhone		Name	Company
3		Johnson, B.	Johnson Printing	WV	304-222-3456		Kerry, T.	BLT Products
4		Kane, E	Johnson Printing	WV	304-222-1212		Marks, M	Marks Co.
5		Kerry, T.	BLT Products	NH	404-345-1234		Paddick,	BLT Products
6		Lanham, T	Business Supplies	DE	212-222-1299		Reader, J	Reader's Routers
7		Legg, H	Office and Such	DE	212-222-3412		Samson, G	Fun Furniture
8		Larrick, G.	Smudge, Inc.	WV	304-443-1277			
9		Marks, M	Marks Co.	TN	232-305-5678			
10		O'Brien, L.	Coal Operators	KY	405-234-6543			
11		Pauley, M.	Johnson Printing	WV	304-222-0909			
12		Paddick, R.	BLT Products	NH	404-345-6543			
13		Pritt, M.	Boxes, Etc.	DE	212-434-0000			
14		Ray, R.	Computers R Us	WV	304-252-0900			
15		Reader, J.	Reader's Routers	NC	202-234-6608			
16		Root, A.	Smudge, Inc.	WV	304-443-2388			
17		Rudder, P.	Computers, Inc.	WV	304-532-4554			
18		Samson, G.	Fun Furniture	NC	202-224-5400			
19		Samuels, W.	Monitor M. Co.	WV	304-545-2231			
20		Sorrell, R.	Mtn. Components	WV	304-545-7707			
21								
22		Name	Company	St	St			
23				>M	<W			
24								
25								
26								
27								

Fig. 27.19
By using an AND criterion with the same field twice, you can extract a range of values.

You can use any standard operator to specify criteria. When 1-2-3 evaluates the criteria, the result for each record must be either true or false. For example, testing whether a state's name is greater than M results in false for California and true for Nevada. Although you can specify the criteria directly as shown in the preceding examples, in the next section you'll learn how to create calculated criteria, which can be far more flexible to use.

Understanding Calculated Criteria Calculated criteria vastly extend the power of the criteria range. With calculated criteria you can ask to see virtually any subset of records in your database. A calculated criteria is one in which the criteria range contains a formula.

A calculated criteria is a formula example showing 1-2-3 what calculated criteria you want used for each record in the database. This formula example always refers to the first row of the database for any field within the database. For example, if you want to extract all records that contain a payment due greater than the average, you could enter the formula +D3>@AVG($D$3..$D$20) if D3 was the first payment due cell for the first record in the database. (You do not reference the field names.)

In the example in figure 27.20, you want to extract all the records for companies that have a Due amount greater than the average of all the companies. Notice that the average range, D3..D20, is made absolute. The format of cell D23 has been set to Formula. This enables you to quickly note the formula but has no effect on the extract.

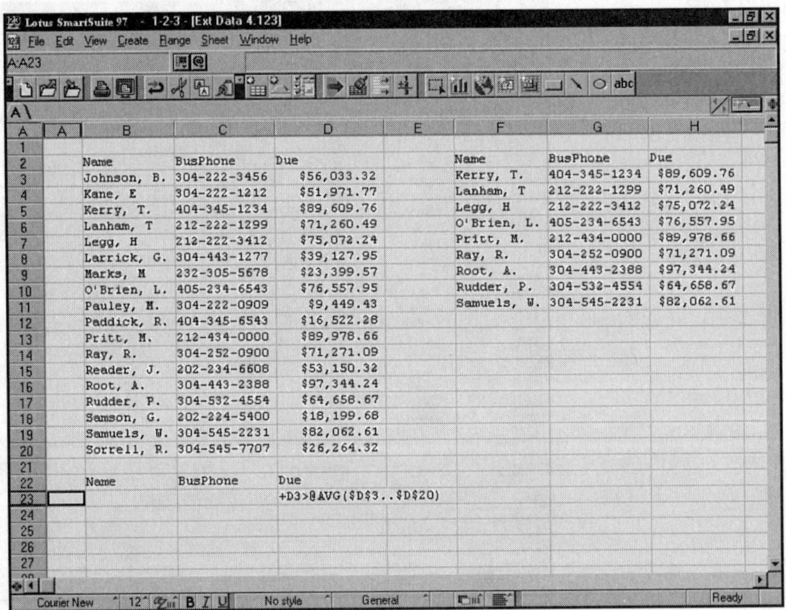

A	A	B	C	D	E	F	G	H
1								
2		Name	BusPhone	Due		Name	BusPhone	Due
3		Johnson, B.	304-222-3456	$56,033.32		Kerry, T.	404-345-1234	$89,609.76
4		Kane, E	304-222-1212	$51,971.77		Lanham, T	212-222-1299	$71,260.49
5		Kerry, T.	404-345-1234	$89,609.76		Legg, H	212-222-3412	$75,072.24
6		Lanham, T	212-222-1299	$71,260.49		O'Brien, L.	405-234-6543	$76,557.95
7		Legg, H	212-222-3412	$75,072.24		Pritt, M.	212-434-0000	$89,978.66
8		Larrick, G.	304-443-1277	$39,127.95		Ray, R.	304-252-0900	$71,271.09
9		Marks, M	232-305-5678	$23,399.57		Root, A.	304-443-2388	$97,344.24
10		O'Brien, L.	405-234-6543	$76,557.95		Rudder, P.	304-532-4554	$64,658.67
11		Pauley, M.	304-222-0909	$9,449.43		Samuels, W.	304-545-2231	$82,062.61
12		Paddick, R.	404-345-6543	$16,522.28				
13		Pritt, M.	212-434-0000	$89,978.66				
14		Ray, R.	304-252-0900	$71,271.09				
15		Reader, J.	202-234-6608	$53,150.32				
16		Root, A.	304-443-2388	$97,344.24				
17		Rudder, P.	304-532-4554	$64,658.67				
18		Samson, G.	202-224-5400	$18,199.68				
19		Samuels, W.	304-545-2231	$82,062.61				
20		Sorrell, R.	304-545-7707	$26,264.32				
21								
22		Name	BusPhone	Due				
23				+D3>@AVG($D$3..$D$20)				
24								
25								
26								
27								

Fig. 27.20 Finding all records with Due amounts above the average.

You can also use calculated criteria to compare one item in the database with another. For example, suppose you have budget figures and actuals. You could extract all those records in which the budget was exceeded. Figure 27.21 shows the criteria range that would extract all records where the gross sales were greater than or equal to budget. Notice that neither reference is absolute. This enables 1-2-3 to compare D3 with C3 and then D4 with

C4, and so on, for each of the records in the database. If you made D3 absolute, then 1-2-3 would compare $D$3 with C3 and then $D$3 with C4, and so on, for each record.

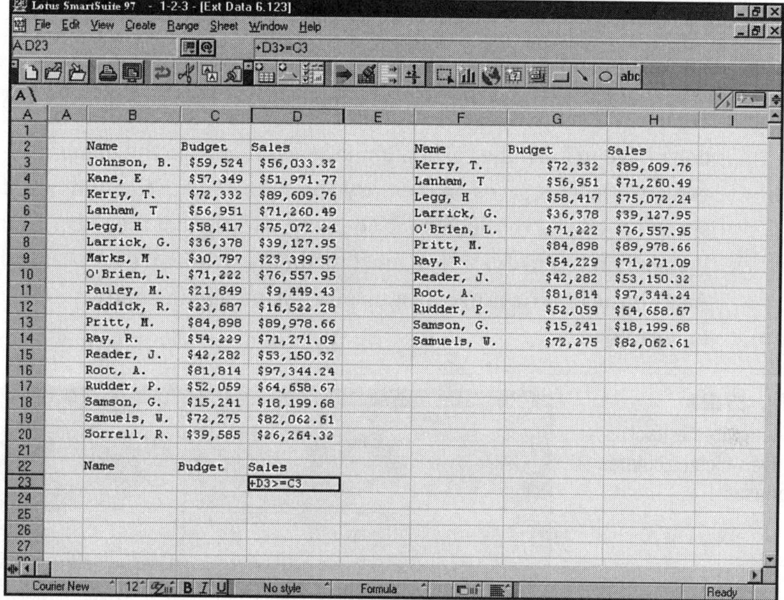

Fig. 27.21
Using a calculated criterion to find all records whose Sales equaled or exceeded Budget.

You can use calculated criteria to easily extract items in date ranges that would otherwise require very complex AND and OR combinations. Suppose you wanted to find all the sales over the past ten years for the month of December. To do this, you need to find all the records where the month number is 12. If column E contains the Date field, and row 3 contains the first record, you could specify the criteria as @MONTH(E3)=12 to extract the desired records.

Because 1-2-3's criteria are not case-sensitive by default, you need to use calculated criteria if you want to extract records in which upper- or lowercase is an issue. This is exactly what the @EXACT function was designed to do. For example, suppose you want to find all companies whose name is *blue sports*, and you want an exact match; you are looking for all *blue sports* that were entered in lowercase. In this case you would specify @EXACT(B3,"blue sports").

▶ **See** "Text Functions" **p. 224**

Creating Computed Extract Ranges In addition to being able to use formulas in criteria ranges, you can also use them in the extract range. This adds another level of sophistication to your database work.

When you use formulas in an extract range you enter them as field names. 1-2-3 will calculate the formula and extract its value for each record in the database that meets your criteria. Suppose bonuses are paid at a rate of 25% when sales exceed budget. To have 1-2-3 calculate the bonuses from your database you would enter a formula of the form:

+ (D3-C3)*0.25

Figure 27.22 shows just such an example. Using a computer extract range means that you don't have to keep the calculation for each record in the database—you only get it when you need it. This saves on memory and, by reducing the number of formulas in a spreadsheet, speeds up recalculation. The down side is that the extract range in non-volatile. It doesn't recalculate, so you must rerun the extract if data changes within the database. As with the criteria range formula, the formula in the extract range has been formatted to Formula.

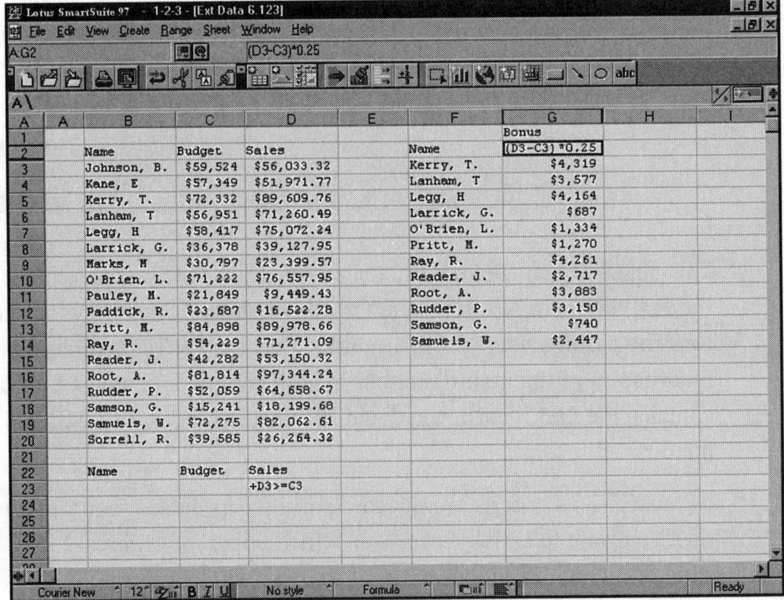

	A	B	C	D	E	F	G
1							Bonus
2		Name	Budget	Sales		Name	(D3-C3)*0.25
3		Johnson, B.	$59,524	$56,033.32		Kerry, T.	$4,319
4		Kane, E	$57,349	$51,971.77		Lanham, T	$3,577
5		Kerry, T.	$72,332	$89,609.76		Legg, H	$4,164
6		Lanham, T	$56,951	$71,260.49		Larrick, G.	$687
7		Legg, H	$58,417	$75,072.24		O'Brien, L.	$1,334
8		Larrick, G.	$36,378	$39,127.95		Pritt, M.	$1,270
9		Marks, M	$30,797	$23,399.57		Ray, R.	$4,261
10		O'Brien, L.	$71,222	$76,557.95		Reader, J.	$2,717
11		Pauley, M.	$21,849	$9,449.43		Root, A.	$3,883
12		Paddick, R.	$23,687	$16,522.28		Rudder, P.	$3,150
13		Pritt, M.	$84,898	$89,978.66		Samson, G.	$740
14		Ray, R.	$54,229	$71,271.09		Samuels, W.	$2,447
15		Reader, J.	$42,282	$53,150.32			
16		Root, A.	$81,814	$97,344.24			
17		Rudder, P.	$52,059	$64,658.67			
18		Samson, G.	$15,241	$18,199.68			
19		Samuels, W.	$72,275	$82,062.61			
20		Sorrell, R.	$39,585	$26,264.32			
21							
22		Name	Budget	Sales			
23				+D3>=C3			

Fig. 27.22
A computed extract range which calculates bonuses.

TROUBLESHOOTING

When I run an extract the results aren't correct. One of the most common problems, and most difficult to find, are hidden spaces. Check for extra spaces in field names or criteria; these will generate incorrect extract results.

I changed the criteria, but 1-2-3 ignored the changes. When you change criteria remember that if you add more rows or columns you must redefine the criteria range.

I've lost a lot of data in my spreadsheet. I had data below an extract range but now it's gone. If you don't specify how many rows 1-2-3 should use in the extract area, 1-2-3 clears all the cells below the field names down to row 8192. When you define the extract range, include rows below the field names. If it's not too late, immediately choose Edit, Undo to restore your data. Otherwise your only choice may be to close the worksheet without saving any changes and then reopen the worksheet.

PART VI

Integrating 1-2-3

CHAPTER 28

Using 1-2-3 with the Lotus SmartSuite

by Sue Plumley

In Windows, data sharing between applications makes it possible to create work in one application and share that work with another application. You can use the numbers in a worksheet to create a chart for a printed report; import a phone list from a database for use in 1-2-3; or even combine the contents of many kinds of documents, in many different applications, to create an annual report.

Sharing data between applications is only the beginning; Windows enables you to set up and maintain active links between the data in the original application and the copies that you transfer to other applications. These links communicate any changes you make, so that the data is updated automatically in every application to which it has been copied. For example, you can use the data-analysis powers of a spreadsheet program, the visual-representation capabilities of a graphics program, and the presentation powers of a word processing program to create a monthly report. Sharing data through linking means your report is always up-to-date and current.

Understand linking and embedding

You can use object linking and embedding (OLE) to share data between applications.

Use object linking and embedding between 1-2-3 and Word Pro

You can link 1-2-3 data to a Word Pro document and then update the link, remove the link, and deactivate the link; additionally, you can create an embedded 1-2-3 object and then edit that object from Word Pro.

Embed a Freelance presentation into a 1-2-3 worksheet

Using OLE, create a presentation you can embed into your 1-2-3 spreadsheet to illustrate your data.

Use 1-2-3 data to create a Freelance chart

Make full use of information-sharing by using data from a 1-2-3 spreadsheet to create a chart in a Freelance presentation.

Use 1-2-3 with Approach to save time and effort in your work

You can import Approach data to 1-2-3 and export 1-2-3 data to Approach to save time when entering databases.

This chapter describes how you can combine the features of 1-2-3 with the strengths of the other SmartSuite programs. SmartSuite contains 1-2-3, the presentation-graphics program Freelance Graphics, the Windows word processing program Word Pro, the relational-database application Approach, and the scheduling program Organizer. This chapter describes the technical features of Windows that make such tight integration possible and offers real-world examples of how you can use the Lotus SmartSuite applications together. ■

NOTE The general techniques you learn in this chapter work for other Lotus Windows applications (such as Lotus cc:Mail, Notes, and Improv) and Windows applications from other software makers (such as Excel, Word, and Access) that support OLE. Consult the user manual for the application to see if it is OLE-compatible. ■

Understanding the Techniques

When sharing data, you know you can copy and paste text, charts, cell contents, entire worksheets, graphics, and more between two Windows applications using the Clipboard. Many Windows applications, however, offer you the option of linking and embedding data as a method of true sharing.

▶ **See** "Copying Data," **p. 240**

When you share data by linking and embedding, you make updating and modifying the shared data easy, efficient, and automatic. Data created in one source application can be linked to many other documents and applications; then when you modify the data at the source, all documents linked to the source are automatically updated. Embedding makes it easy for you to edit data at the source and quickly update the data in the destination application.

NOTE The application in which you created the original data to be shared is called the *source* or *server* application and document. Those applications and documents to which you link or embed the data are called the *destination* or *client* applications or documents. ■

Lotus not only supports OLE in the SmartSuite applications, it makes sharing data between the SmartSuite applications more efficient because of similar tools, interfaces, and commands. After you learn one SmartSuite application, say 1-2-3, you'll find learning and using another SmartSuite application is easier because of similarities between programs.

Using Common Lotus Tools and Interfaces

You are already familiar with most 1-2-3 elements, including the menu bar, SmartIcons, status bar, and so on. As you may know, the other SmartSuite applications share many of these same elements. All of the SmartSuite applications, for example, present menu bars with File, Edit, View, and Help menus in common as well as some of the very same commands found on these menus. All File menus contain Open, Save, Print, and Exit commands; all Edit menus offer these commands: Undo, Cut, Copy, Paste, Paste Special, and so on. Additionally, many dialog boxes contain the same or similar options across the SmartSuite applications. So when you switch between applications, you're already familiar with the program's menu features.

▶ **See** "Understanding the 1-2-3 Screen," **p. 17**

Figure 28.1 shows the Word Pro window and some features it has in common with 1-2-3.

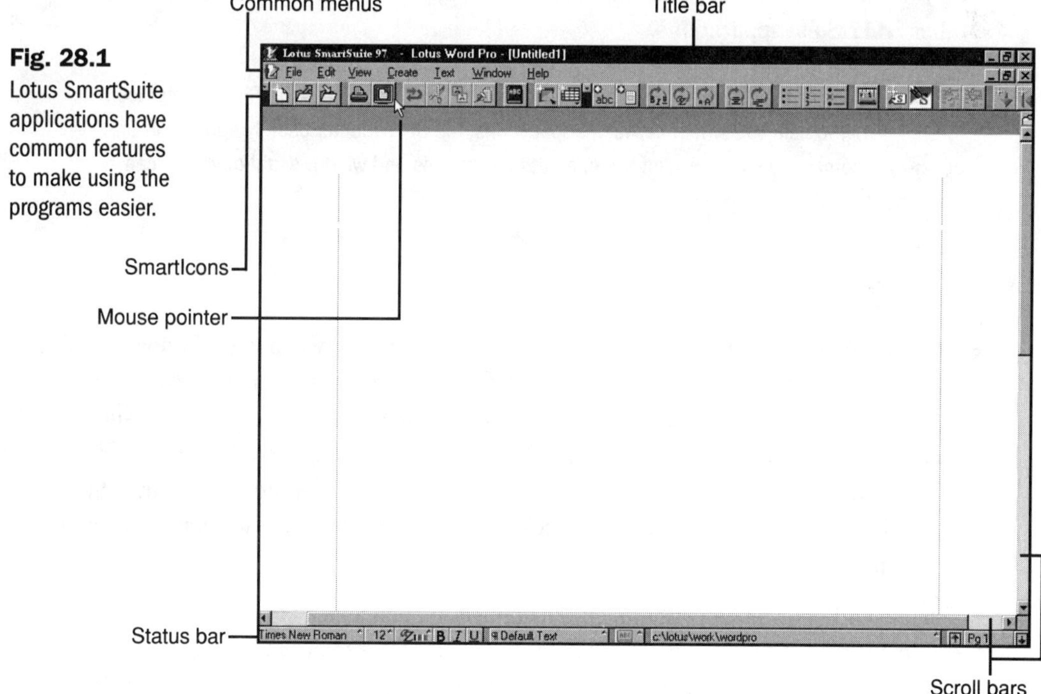

Fig. 28.1 Lotus SmartSuite applications have common features to make using the programs easier.

Here is a list of some of the similarities you'll find in tools and interface between the SmartSuite applications:

- *Title bar.* Presents similar coloring, same Minimize, Maximize, Close, and Control menu buttons, the name of the application, and the name of the current document.
- *SmartIcons.* Open, Save, Print, Undo, Cut, Copy, Paste, and so on are the same throughout the applications; additionally, the use and customization of the SmartIcons is similar.
- *Mouse.* The use of the mouse pointer, hourglass, I-beam, clicks and double-clicks, and so on is similar among all programs.
- *Help feature.* Is the same throughout SmartSuite applications.
- *File management.* Saving, printing, opening, and closing are similar procedures throughout the applications.
- *Features.* Checking spelling, finding and replacing text, and linking and embedding are also similar across the SmartSuite applications.

So you can see, now that you're familiar with 1-2-3, you have a head start on using the other SmartSuite applications.

NOTE If you've installed SmartSuite to your computer, you'll also have the SmartCenter icon bar to help you switch between applications. The SmartCenter usually appears in the upper-right corner of your screen, on top of all other programs and windows, although you can close the SmartCenter if you want.

Using OLE 2

OLE (object linking and embedding) means sharing data between two Windows applications that support OLE. OLE 2 also lets you drag and drop shared data between open documents and applications. OLE 2 makes it easier to edit the objects you link and embed. Suppose you create a worksheet in 1-2-3 that you embed into a Word Pro report. When you edit the worksheet from Word Pro, OLE 2 provides appropriate 1-2-3 menus that enable you to edit the worksheet more quickly and easily than if you switch to the actual source program.

You use OLE to establish either a linked connection between a source and destination document for automatic updating of data; or you use OLE to embed an object into a destination document for quick and efficient editing of the object.

An *object* is a spreadsheet, chart, text, graphic, or other bit of data that has been linked or embedded.

Understanding the Difference Between Linking and Embedding Object linking and object embedding are two related techniques that seem to accomplish similar goals. The difference between the two can be confusing. The main difference between linking and embedding is where the data is stored:

- *Linked* data is stored in a source file.

  When you link an object, a copy of the original data appears in the second (destination) application; the original data remains intact in the first (source) application. If you use object linking to copy a table of numbers from 1-2-3 to Word Pro, for example, the data remains in 1-2-3, but a copy of the table also appears in Word Pro. To change the table in Word Pro, you return to 1-2-3 and change the original numbers. Because a link has been set up between the two applications, any changes to the data in 1-2-3 change the table in Word Pro.

- *Embedded* objects become part of the destination document.

  When you embed an object, you create the object in the source application just as with linking; however, there is only one copy of the object and that resides within the destination document. Say you embed a 1-2-3 chart in a Word Pro document. In Word Pro, you create the object using 1-2-3 menus and tools. You then update the object and exit 1-2-3. When you want to edit the embedded object, you double-click the chart in Word Pro to open the 1-2-3 window in which the object resides.

NOTE Adding an embedded object to a document makes that file larger than linking the data does.

Because embedded data resides in both the source and destination applications, you can move the file that contains the embedded object to another computer. When you take a file with embedded data to a different computer, you don't have to take all the files in which the original data is stored. If the file contained an object linked to a source and you took it to another computer, the link would be broken from the source application.

TIP Windows makes switching between applications easy. To return to the application in which an object was created, simply double-click the object. If the application is not running, Windows will start it for you.

Link data when you want to:

- Automatically update the data in the destination document by modifying only the data in the source application.
- Share the source data with multiple destination documents.

Embed data when you want to:

- Use only one copy of the data.
- Copy the file to disk to use at another computer.

NOTE Whether you're linking or embedding, the computer you're using must have the source application on it to edit the data in the destination document. For example, if you want to embed or link some Word Pro data in a 1-2-3 worksheet, you need to have Word Pro installed on your machine as well as 1-2-3; it's not enough to have 1-2-3.

Linking Data You can link an object from one application to another in several ways, but the easiest way is to follow these steps:

1. Create the object and save the file in the source application.
2. Select the data and copy it to the Windows Clipboard.
3. Switch to the destination application and position the insertion point.
4. Choose Edit, Paste Special. Figure 28.2 shows the Paste Special dialog box from Word Pro.

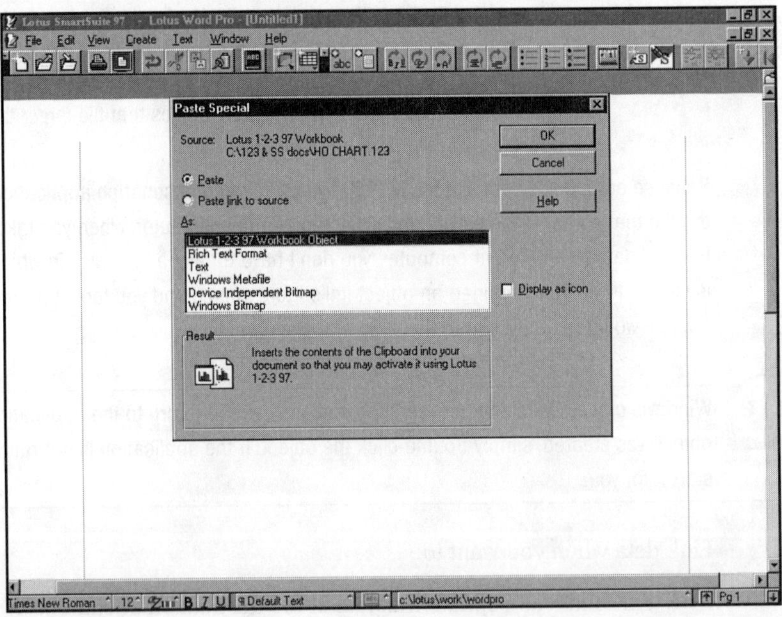

Fig. 28.2
The Paste Special dialog box enables you to paste an object as a link to the source application.

5. Choose the Paste Link to Source option and select the format from the As list box.
6. Choose OK to complete the process.

NOTE In the Paste Special dialog box for most applications, you'll notice the Display as Icon check box. Choose this to display the pasted data or text as an icon; open the icon by double-clicking it in the destination document. Use this option when your reader views your document on the computer, for example. Some formats listed in the As list box do not let you display as an icon.

After you link an object, you can switch to the source application, make a change to the data, and the revision will appear in the destination application when you switch back.

To edit an object that has been linked, you do not need to manually switch to the application that created the object and then load and edit the object, you can simply double-click the object in the destination document. Because Windows tracks the origin of each linked object, you do not have to worry about where an object came from when it needs revision.

NOTE You cannot create an OLE Link between two 1-2-3 worksheets or files. You must use formulas to link worksheets.

▶ **See** "Linking Worksheets and Files with Formulas," **p. 483**

Embedding an Object You can embed an object from one application into another, which means you can easily edit the embedded object from within the destination document. To embed an object, follow these steps:

1. Position the mouse pointer in the destination document.

2. In 1-2-3, choose Create, Object; the Create Object dialog box appears (see fig. 28.3). The types listed are determined by the applications in your system that can provide objects for embedding. The more applications you have, the more object types you see in the list.
3. Choose to either Create a New Object or Create an Object from a File. Use the second option when you want to insert an existing object instead of creating a new one.
4. Select the Object Type from the list and choose OK.
5. Indicate where in the current application and document you want to place the embedded object (usually by clicking the desired upper-left corner, or dragging the mouse to define an area).

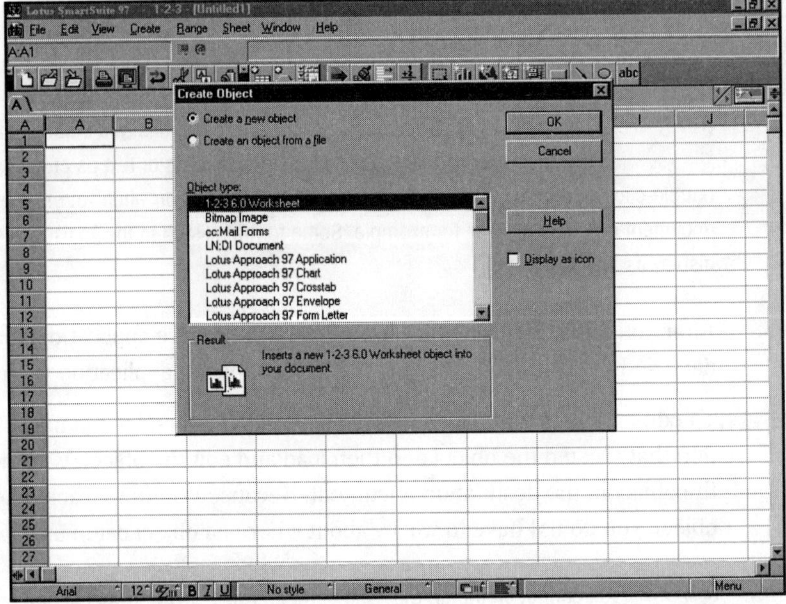

Fig. 28.3 Depending on the applications installed on your computer, you may have many kinds of objects you can create.

6. The source application opens. Create the object, using the source application.
7. When you finish, press Esc or simply click outside of the source application area. The source application closes, and returns to the destination application, with the newly created object in place.

To edit the object, you can double-click it, just as you double-click a linked object. The source application reopens, with the object on-screen and ready for editing.

The remainder of this chapter describes the specific steps you use to link and embed work between particular pairs of Lotus SmartSuite applications.

Using 1-2-3 Data in a Word Pro Document

Word Pro's table feature is sophisticated and easy to use; it enables you to enter text and numbers and format a table quickly. But if you've already entered and calculated a set of data in the cells of a 1-2-3 worksheet, there's no need to manually reproduce that work in a Word Pro table. You can easily transfer a range of cells from a 1-2-3 worksheet to a Word Pro document.

The fastest way to copy a range of data from 1-2-3 is to select the range, copy the data to the Clipboard, switch to Word Pro, and paste the data there. The labels and values in the 1-2-3 range appear in a neatly formatted Word Pro table. You can use all the table-formatting commands in the Word Pro Table menu to change the appearance of the table. If you formatted the range in 1-2-3, that formatting is transferred to Word Pro along with the data. Even formatting applied by using the Properties InfoBox in 1-2-3 transfers to Word Pro.

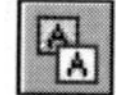

Using the Edit menu's Copy and Paste commands or SmartIcons to transfer a range from 1-2-3 to Word Pro copies only the results of any formulas in the range; the formulas themselves are not copied to Word Pro. Therefore, you cannot recalculate any of the data in the Word Pro table unless you use Word Pro formulas. This is why you might prefer to link or embed the 1-2-3 data instead of simply copying it.

To create a table in Word Pro that you can update if you revise any of the numbers in 1-2-3, you must either link or embed the data.

▶ **See** "Entering Data," **p. 66**

▶ **See** "Enhancing the Appearance of Data," **p. 125**

Linking the Data

Using object linking to copy a range from 1-2-3 to Word Pro sets up a connection between the original range in the worksheet and the data in Word Pro. Changes to the range in 1-2-3 update the Word Pro data too.

Use linking if you want changes to the 1-2-3 data to update in Word Pro. Use embedding if you plan to move the Word Pro document among PCs. The 1-2-3 data is embedded in the Word Pro file.

Linking as Text Paste a link when you want to use Word Pro formatting in your data but maintain a link to 1-2-3. To paste a link, follow these steps:

1. In a 1-2-3 worksheet, enter the data and formulas you need and save the worksheet.
2. In 1-2-3, select the range you want to link. Figure 28.4 shows a sample selected range.

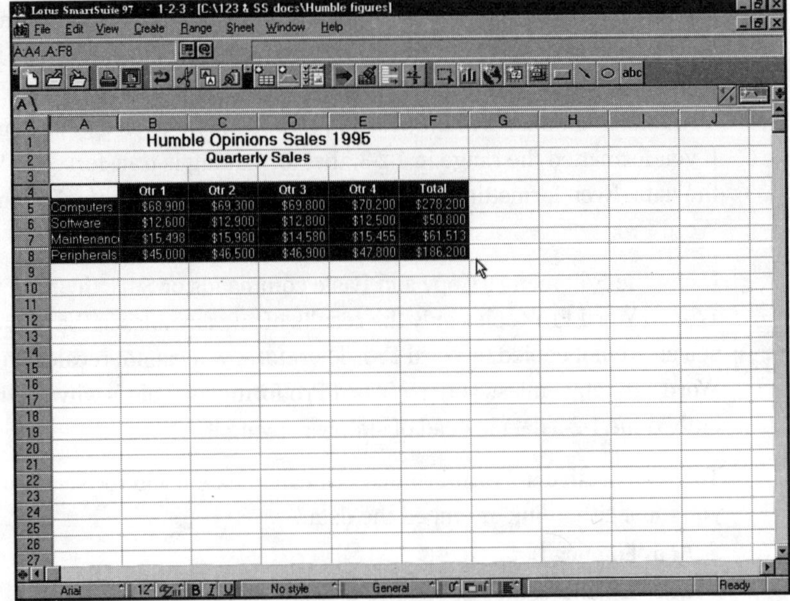

Fig. 28.4
Select one or multiple cells to link to a Word Pro document.

3. Choose Edit, Copy; alternatively, click the Copy SmartIcon.
4. Switch to Word Pro by pressing Alt+Tab.
5. Position the insertion point in the Word Pro document where you want the table to appear.
6. Choose Edit, Paste Special.
7. Choose the Paste Link to Source option and in the As list, choose `Text` and choose OK.

The text and numbers in the range lose all formatting from 1-2-3. You must format the text in Word Pro using the formatting tools on the status bar, the Text Properties InfoBox, or the Text menu. Figure 28.5 shows the 1-2-3 range from figure 28.4, as it appears when linked as a Word Pro table.

CAUTION

After you link a 1-2-3 range with a Word Pro table, you can select any of the data in Word Pro and edit it just as you could if you created the data in Word Pro. But if you make any changes to the original data in 1-2-3, the changes in Word Pro are overwritten when the link is updated.

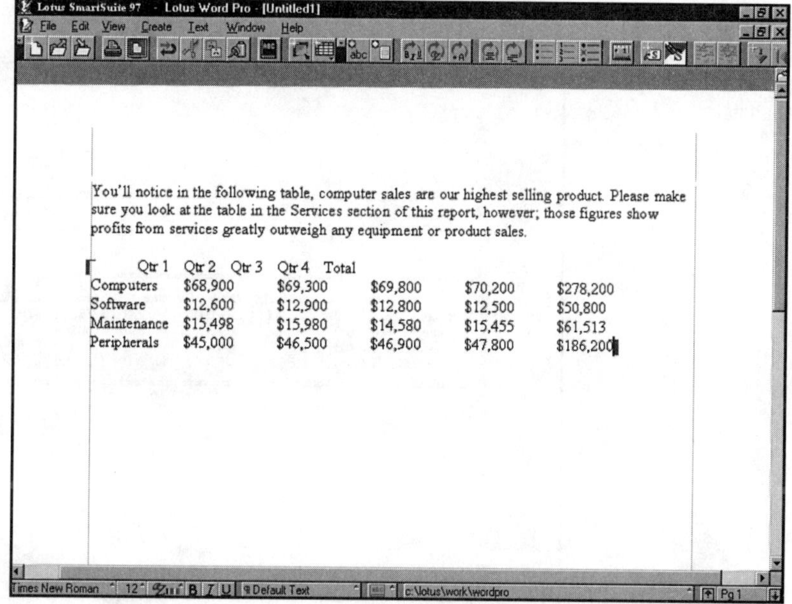

Fig. 28.5
No formatting appears in the data when you choose to paste a text object.

Every time you open a saved Word Pro file that contains a link to 1-2-3 data, Word Pro displays a message box as it updates the links to the file. As Word Pro reads the 1-2-3 worksheet file, it reflects any changes in the data that it finds. You also can manually update data; for example, if you're on a networked system and using other people's data, you would want to update your file with the latest data before printing it. Manually updating links is discussed later in this chapter.

Linking as an Object Another approach to linking 1-2-3 and Word Pro data is linking data as an object. This method copies an image of the 1-2-3 data and its formatting to Word Pro. The method you learned about in the preceding section copies the data to Word Pro, where it takes on Word Pro formatting. When you link data as an object, the result is a table of data in Word Pro that looks the same as the data did in 1-2-3. The data fits in a Word Pro frame, which can have standard frame formatting (such as a line surrounding the frame, a shadow, and rounded or square corners). Figure 28.6 shows how the same range of data from figure 28.4 appears in a Word Pro document when it is linked as an object.

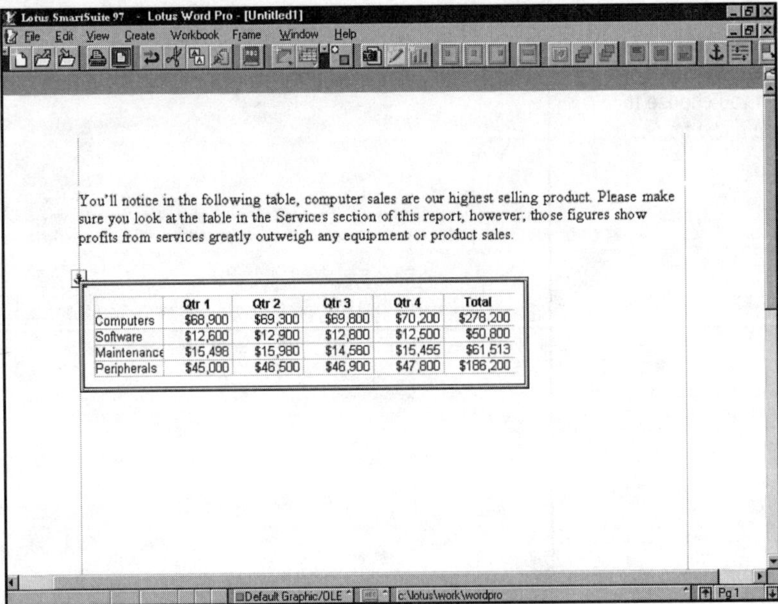

Fig. 28.6
Linking as an object preserves 1-2-3 formatting.

To link data from 1-2-3 to Word Pro as an object, follow the procedure for linking data as text (refer to the preceding section), but when you open the Paste Special dialog box, choose to Paste Link to Source As a Lotus 1-2-3 97 Workbook Object.

If you arrange the 1-2-3 and Word Pro windows side-by-side, you can see the data update in the Word Pro window as soon as you change it in the 1-2-3 window.

You cannot directly edit data linked as an object. Instead, you must double-click the picture of the data to reopen a 1-2-3 window and see the original range of data. Any changes made to the 1-2-3 range are reflected in the Word Pro document immediately.

Updating the Data in 1-2-3 You can update data that has been linked to Word Pro within the source or the destination application. If you linked data as text, any edits you make to the data in Word Pro remain changed in the Word Pro document only, unless and until you choose to update the link. You must manually link the data to update it.

To manually update a link in Word Pro, follow these steps:

1. Choose Edit, Manage Links. The Manage Links dialog box appears (see fig. 28.7), listing all the links in the document.

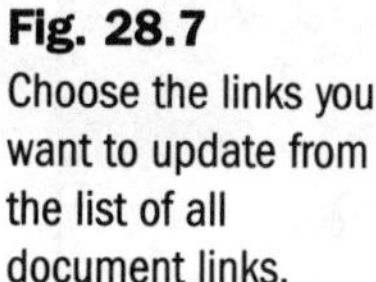

Fig. 28.7
Choose the links you want to update from the list of all document links.

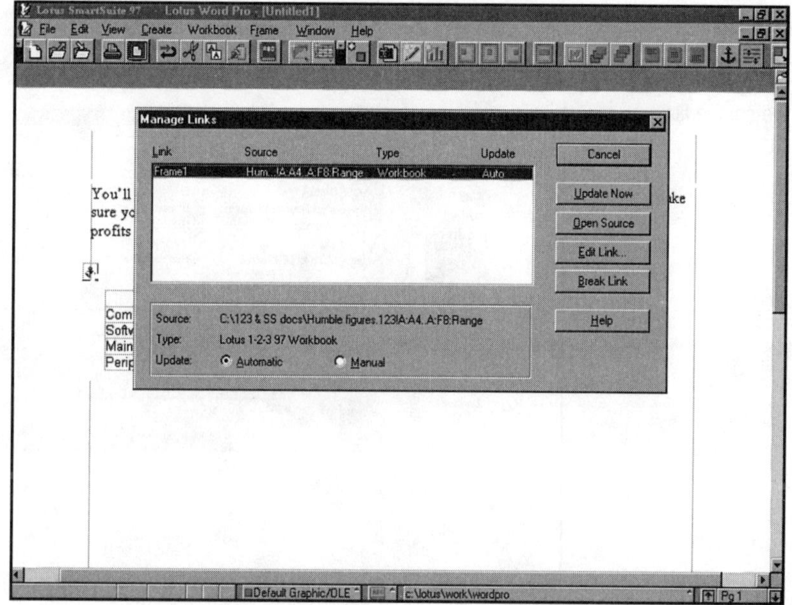

2. Select the link you want to update, and then click Update Now.

Each row of the list in the Manage Links dialog box contains a complete set of information about a link. The following list describes the items:

- *Link*. Specifies the link.
- *Source*. Identifies the range of the link in 1-2-3.
- *Type*. Identifies the type of application you are linked to.
- *Update*. This item identifies the Update option for the specific link: Manual or Auto.

Editing the Link Selecting a link in the Manage Links dialog box and then clicking the Edit Link button also is the way to redirect the link. You can make the link point to different data in another area of the 1-2-3 worksheet or even to a range in a different worksheet. After you click Edit Link, modify the entries in the Item text box of the Edit Link dialog box to link a different range to the Word Pro document. Figure 28.8 shows the Edit Link dialog box.

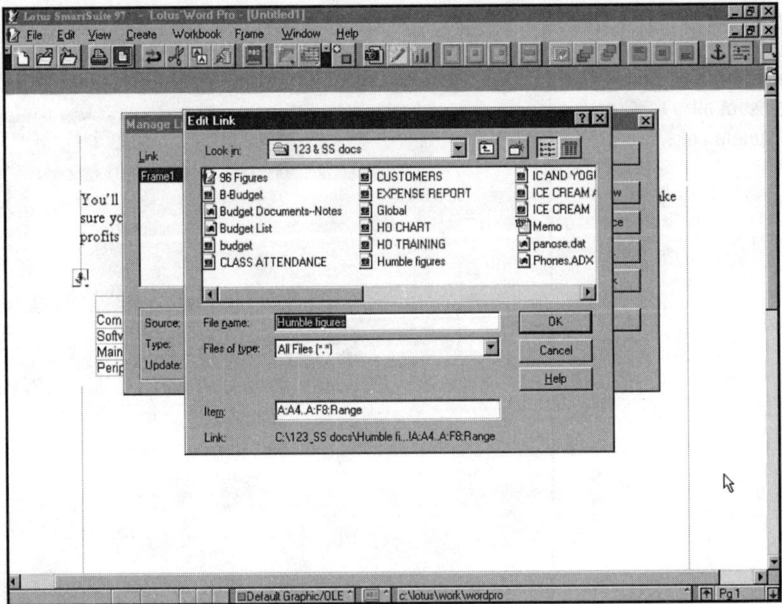

Fig. 28.8
Modify a link if the directory or file name of the source file changes.

Removing the Link To remove a link, select the link in the Manage Links dialog box and then click the Break Link button. There is a warning box that states you are about to break the link. Choose OK to break it. This action removes the link between the original data in 1-2-3 and the copy in Word Pro. Any changes you make to the 1-2-3 data no longer are reflected in Word Pro; the data in Word Pro becomes only a copy of the 1-2-3 data. After you remove a link, you cannot update the link, but you can re-create the link.

Opening the Source You can modify the linked data by selecting the link and choosing the Open Source button in the Manage Links dialog box. Edit the data in the source file, save the changes, and then return to the destination application.

TROUBLESHOOTING

Changing the data in the source application does not change it in the destination application, even though I know the data in two applications is linked. Make sure you chose Paste Link to Source instead of Paste in the Paste Special dialog box. This is a common mistake that's easy to make.

The link may have been removed or deactivated, the source file may have been moved or renamed, or its folder may have been moved or renamed. Select the data again and link it to the destination document.

Embedding the Data

The alternative to linking data to Word Pro is embedding 1-2-3 data in a Word Pro file. In Word Pro, the embedded 1-2-3 data appears as a picture of the data just the way it looked in 1-2-3. The embedded data is automatically placed into a Word Pro frame.

The advantage to embedded 1-2-3 data is that the data is contained in the Word Pro file rather than in the original 1-2-3 worksheet. You can transport the Word Pro file to another computer without also having to transport the 1-2-3 worksheet file. When you need to edit the 1-2-3 data, double-click it; Word Pro uses the facilities of 1-2-3 on the current computer to edit the data, as long as the current computer contains the 1-2-3 application.

You can embed 1-2-3 data in a Word Pro file in two ways:

- Create a new 1-2-3 table while working in Word Pro.
- Embed existing 1-2-3 data in a Word Pro document.

Creating an Embedded Object While Working in Word Pro To create a 1-2-3 table and embed it in a Word Pro document, follow these steps:

1. Position the insertion point in the Word Pro document where you want the table to appear.
2. Choose Create, Object. The Create Object dialog box appears (see fig. 28.9). The Create a New Object option is selected by default.

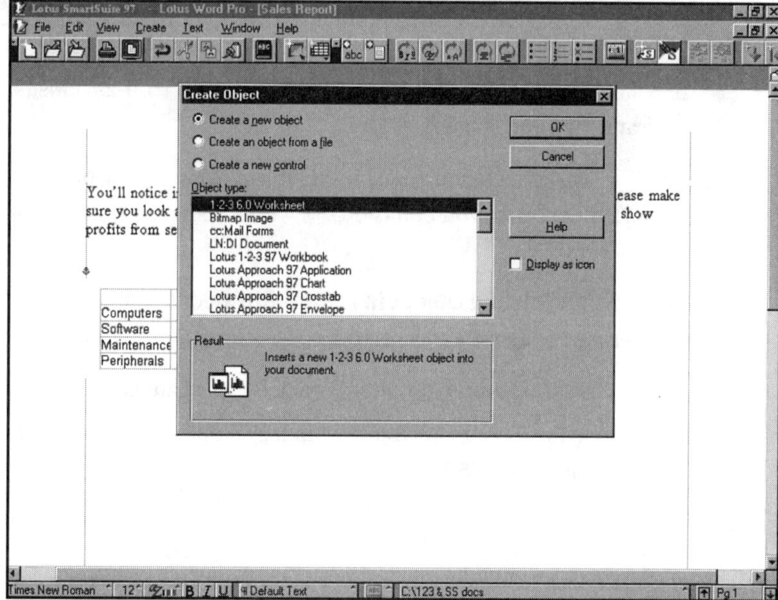

Fig. 28.9
Choose from the list of objects to embed in a Word Pro document.

4. Select Lotus 1-2-3 97 Workbook in the list of object types and choose OK. A frame for the embedded worksheet appears in the Word Pro document, and the 1-2-3 window opens. If necessary, Windows starts the 1-2-3 application.
5. Create the worksheet in 1-2-3. Figure 28.10 shows a sample worksheet created in 1-2-3, ready to be embedded in Word Pro.

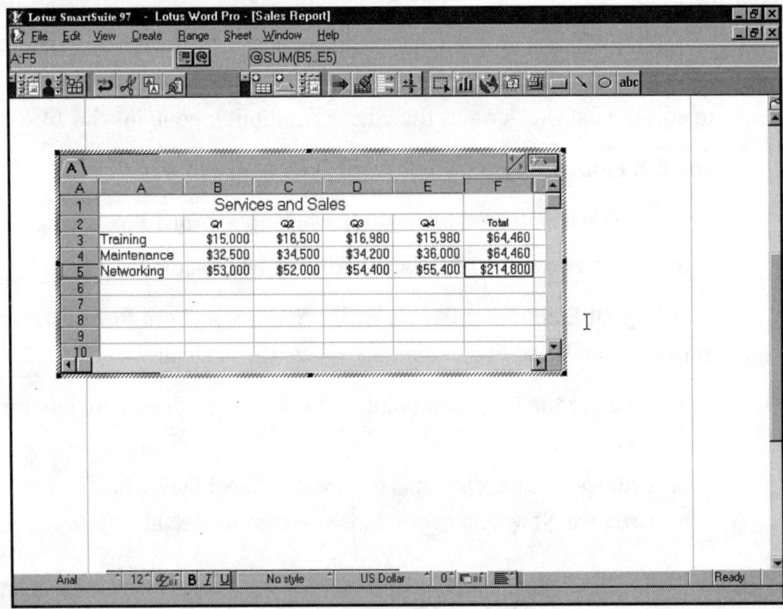

Fig. 28.10
When creating the worksheet, use 1-2-3 tools and features as you normally would.

6. Click outside of the frame to return to Word Pro. 1-2-3 closes, leaving the data in a frame as shown in figure 28.11.

To edit the worksheet, double-click the object. The 1-2-3 window reopens, showing the 1-2-3 worksheet. After you edit the 1-2-3 worksheet, click outside of the object's frame to return to Word Pro.

Embedding an Existing Object in a Word Pro Document If the 1-2-3 worksheet that you want to embed in Word Pro already exists, follow these steps:

1. In Word Pro, choose Create, Object. The Create Object dialog box appears.
2. Choose the Create an Object from a File option and the dialog box changes, as shown in figure 28.12.

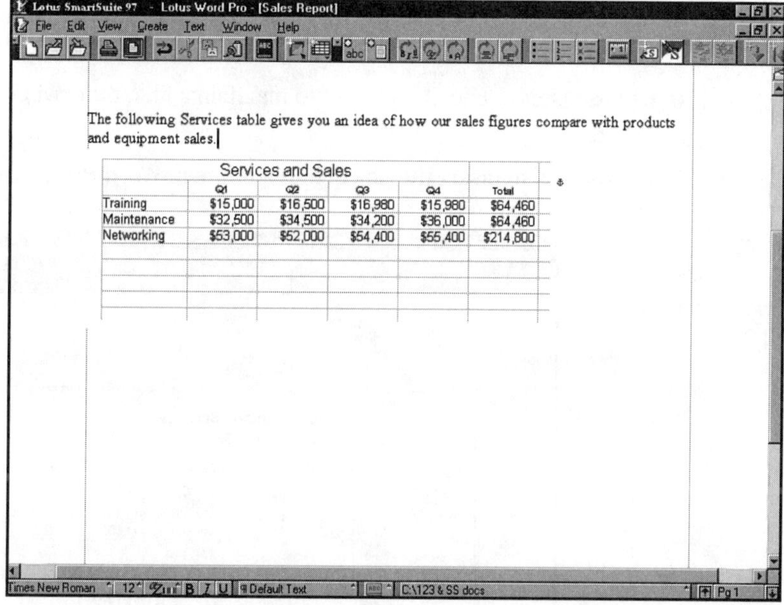

Fig. 28.11
The embedded 1-2-3 object can be moved and/or resized in Word Pro.

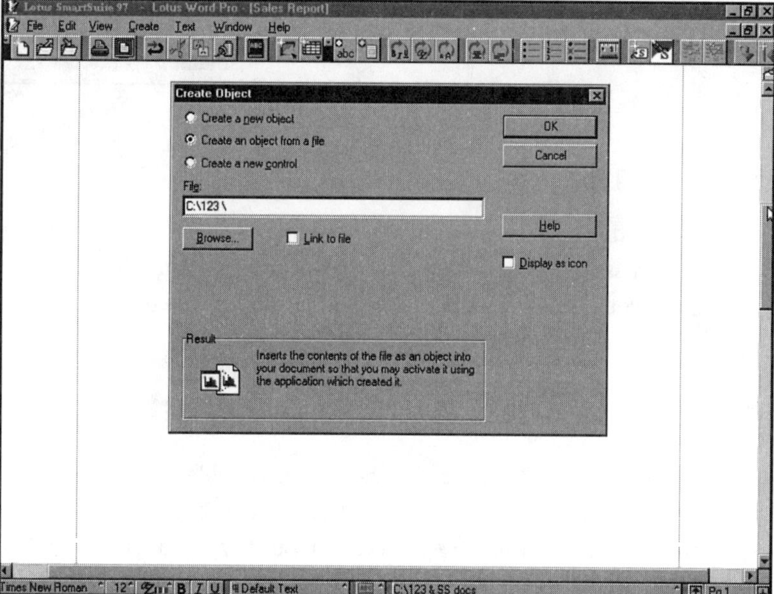

Fig. 28.12
Embed an existing object without affecting the original object.

3. In the File text box, enter the path and file name. If you are unsure, choose the Browse button to locate the file on your disk.
4. Choose Link to File, if you want to maintain a link; otherwise, leave this check box blank.
5. Choose OK to insert the object into a frame in Word Pro (see fig. 28.13).

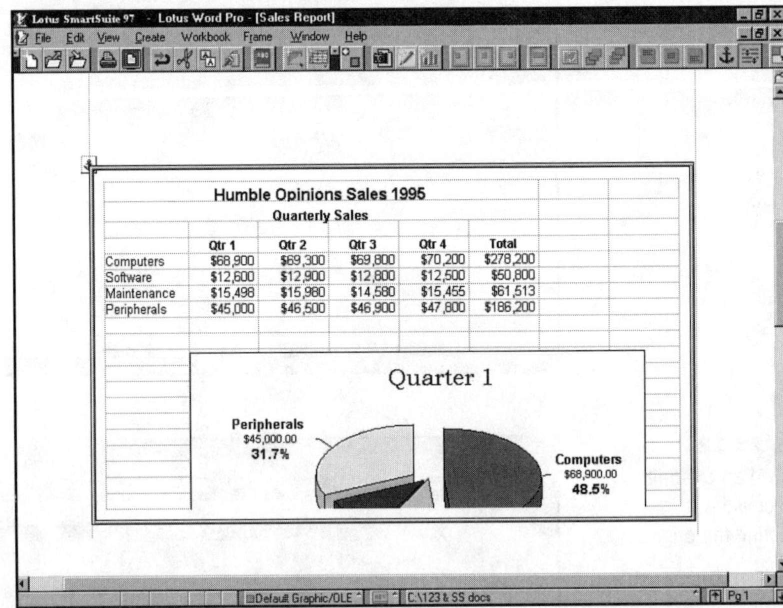

Fig. 28.13
Embed an existing worksheet for use in Word Pro.

To edit the 1-2-3 worksheet data, double-click the frame in Word Pro or select the frame and press Enter. A 1-2-3 window opens, and the data is loaded automatically. After you make your changes, click outside of the 1-2-3 frame to return to Word Pro.

Using a 1-2-3 Chart in a Word Pro Document

Although Word Pro's charting capabilities enable you to create a simple chart, you may want to make use of the superior charting capabilities of a program that is dedicated to chart making. If you have Lotus SmartSuite, you can create sophisticated graphs in Freelance Graphics and copy them into Word Pro documents. You even can link 1-2-3 data to a Freelance graph and then link the Freelance graph to a Word Pro document. If you do not have access to Freelance Graphics, you still can create professional-looking charts in 1-2-3 and use them in Word Pro.

The easiest method to sharing data is to perform a straight copy-and-paste operation by selecting the chart in 1-2-3, copying it to the Windows Clipboard, switching to Word Pro, and then pasting the chart into the document. This method, however, creates no link between the original 1-2-3 data and the chart in Word Pro. To create a link, you must use either linking or embedding.

▶ **See** "Creating a Chart Automatically," **p. 314**

▶ **See** "Manipulating Chart Elements," **p. 322**

Linking a Chart

Use linking to copy a chart from 1-2-3 to Word Pro when you plan for the Word Pro file to remain on the current system, where it always has access to the 1-2-3 file in which you created the chart. When you link a chart from 1-2-3 to Word Pro, the data remains in its original 1-2-3 worksheet file; only an image of the chart is copied to the Word Pro file. To modify the chart, you must return to 1-2-3; any modifications to the 1-2-3 data automatically update the chart in Word Pro, too.

To link a 1-2-3 chart to Word Pro, follow these steps:

1. In 1-2-3, create and format the chart.
2. Save the workbook. This step is mandatory—you cannot link a chart if you have not saved it in a 1-2-3 worksheet file.
3. Click the chart's frame to select it, as shown in figure 28.14.

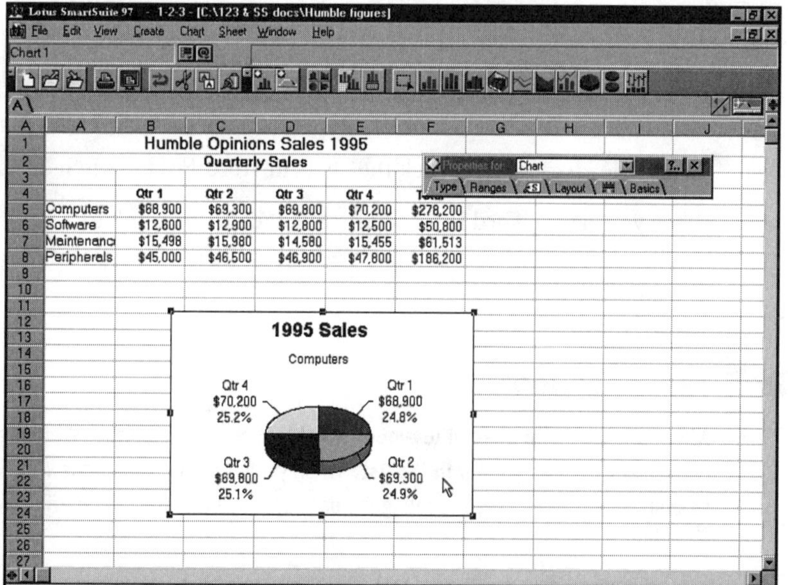

Fig. 28.14
Black handles indicate the chart is selected.

4. Choose Edit, Copy; alternatively, click the Copy SmartIcon.
5. Switch to Word Pro.
6. Position the insertion point in the Word Pro document where you want the chart to appear.
7. Choose Edit, Paste Special. The Paste Special dialog box appears.
8. Choose Paste and select Lotus 1-2-3 97 Workbook Object in the As list.
9. Choose OK. The chart appears in the Word Pro document, as shown in figure 28.15.

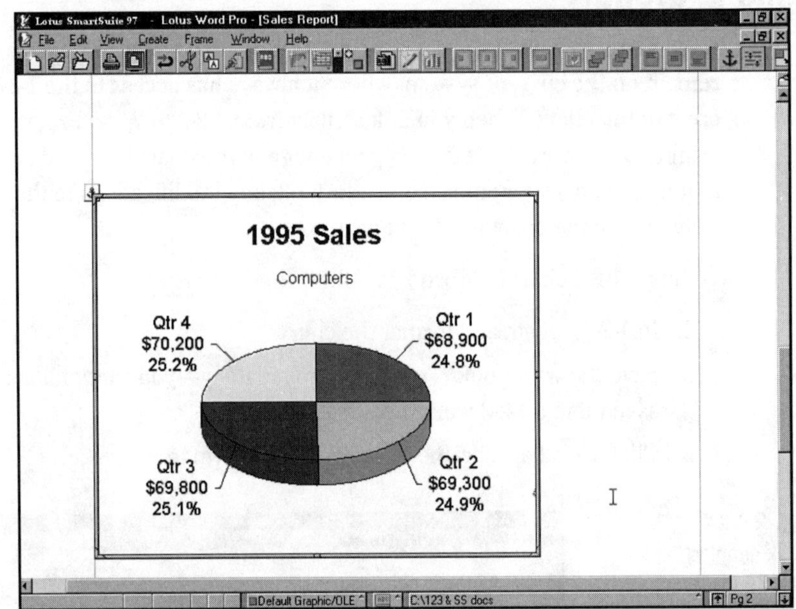

Fig. 28.15
The 1-2-3 chart appears in a frame in the Word Pro document.

To edit the chart, double-click the chart in Word Pro to switch back to 1-2-3 automatically.

When you save a Word Pro document that contains a link to a 1-2-3 chart, the link information is saved in the Word Pro document, but the data is saved in the 1-2-3 worksheet file. The links are updated automatically.

TROUBLESHOOTING

After I choose Paste Special to embed an object copied in another Windows application, why do so many formats appear in the list? When you copy an object to the Windows Clipboard, several different ways of representing the data are copied to the Clipboard simultaneously to ensure that the destination application will find a form of data in the Clipboard that it can accept. For example, when you copy a 1-2-3 table to the Clipboard, the numbers are copied to the Clipboard as text, as Rich Text in a table, and as a picture of the original 1-2-3 formatted table. If the destination application does not have the capability to edit numbers in a table, it can use the plain text or the picture of the 1-2-3 table instead.

Embedding a Chart

If you plan to transport the Word Pro document to another computer (perhaps to copy it to a portable computer), you may want to embed a 1-2-3 chart in the document rather than link it. Embedding has the advantage of incorporating the chart data in the Word Pro file so that you do not need access to the data in the original worksheet if the chart must be updated. You do need access to 1-2-3 on the destination computer to make any changes to the chart, however.

To embed a chart into Word Pro, follow these steps:

1. In Word Pro, choose Create, Object. The Create Object dialog box appears.
2. Choose the Create an Object from a File option to embed an existing chart. Enter the file name and path in the File text box. Choose Link to File and choose OK. The chart and worksheet data appear in the Word Pro document.

   Choose the Create a New Object to produce a chart within Word Pro from 1-2-3. Choose Lotus 1-2-3 97 Workbook from the list of Object Types. Choose OK. The 1-2-3 worksheet, menus, and icons appear within the Word Pro document. Create the worksheet and chart as you would in 1-2-3. Click outside of the worksheet area to return to the Word Pro document.

To edit the chart, double-click the object. The 1-2-3 window opens, displaying the data for the chart. Edit the data and then click outside of the frame to return to Word Pro.

▶ **See** "Creating a Chart Manually," **p. 314**

Embedding a Word Pro Document in a 1-2-3 Worksheet

With object linking, you can link selected text from a Word Pro document to a 1-2-3 cell so that any changes to the text are reflected in the 1-2-3 file automatically. You may find it more useful to embed, rather than link, an entire Word Pro document in a 1-2-3 worksheet file. The document can provide a report on a particular aspect of the data in the 1-2-3 worksheet or add background information that can help another user interpret the worksheet.

When you embed a Word Pro document in a 1-2-3 file, the selected piece of document appears wider than the screen. Double-clicking the embedded document in a 1-2-3 file opens Word Pro so that you can read or print the Word Pro document embedded in the 1-2-3 file. A Word Pro frame appears around the document in 1-2-3. To use the embedded Word Pro information, you do not need the original Word Pro document file on the system; you do need the Word Pro application, however.

To embed a Word Pro document, you can copy an existing document to 1-2-3 or you can create a new object. Either way, double-clicking the embedded item loads the document in Word Pro.

Embedding an Existing Word Pro Document in 1-2-3

When you embed Word Pro text in the following manner, Word Pro marks a Link Bookmark to the text. If you remove the bookmark, you remove the link to 1-2-3.

To embed an existing Word Pro document in a 1-2-3 worksheet, follow these steps:

1. Make sure that the document is saved in a Word Pro file.
2. Select the document. Figure 28.16 shows a selected document.

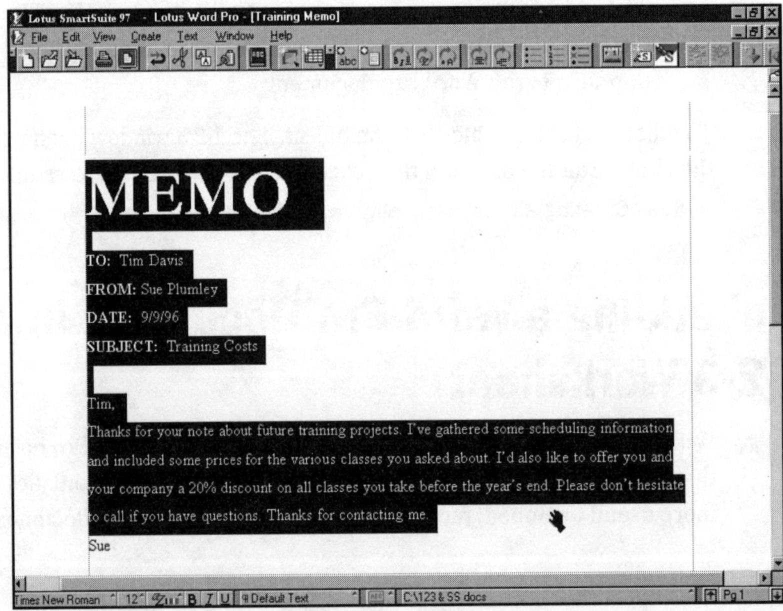

Fig. 28.16
Selected text in a Word Pro document for sharing with 1-2-3.

3. Choose Edit, Copy; or click the Copy SmartIcon.
4. Switch to 1-2-3 by pressing Alt+Tab.
5. Position the cell pointer near the data you want to document with the Word Pro text.
6. Choose Edit, Paste Special. The 1-2-3 Paste Special dialog box appears.
7. Choose the Paste Link to Source option and in the As list, select Lotus Word Pro 97 Document.
8. Choose OK to embed the Word Pro document object. The Word Pro document appears in the 1-2-3 worksheet, as shown in figure 28.17.

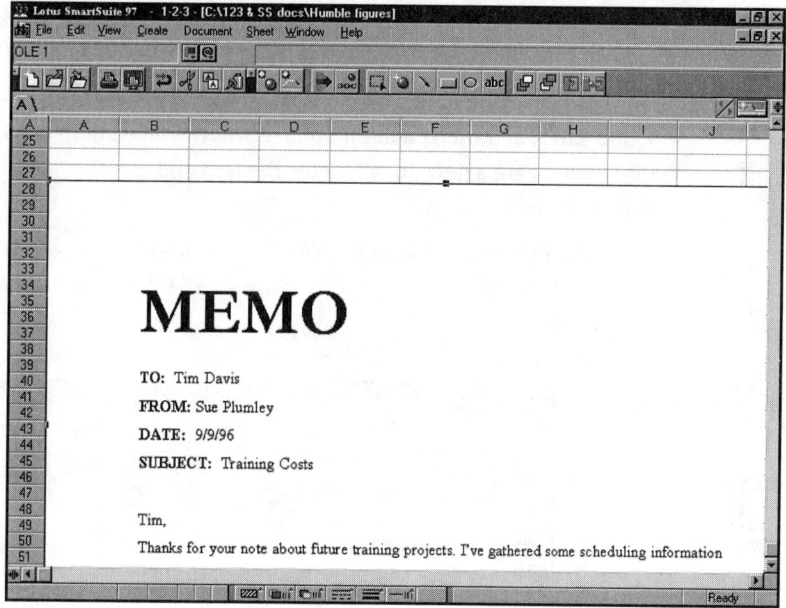

Fig. 28.17
A Word Pro document appears in a 1-2-3 worksheet as an object.

You can reduce the size of the Word Pro document by selecting it and then dragging a corner handle toward the center of the icon. The text in the object frame reduces in size as well. The selected text appears as bookmarked text in the Word Pro document.

Creating and Embedding a Word Pro Document from within 1-2-3

The second method of embedding Word Pro documents in 1-2-3 worksheets is to create a new Word Pro document, so that the document is embedded in the 1-2-3 worksheet you are working on.

To embed a new Word Pro object within 1-2-3, follow these steps:

1. Create or open the 1-2-3 worksheet in which you want to embed the Word Pro object.
2. Position the insertion point in 1-2-3 and choose Create, Object. The Create Object dialog box appears.
3. Choose Create a New Object to produce a Word Pro document within 1-2-3. In Object Type, choose Lotus Word Pro 97 Document.

   Choose Create an Object From a File to use an existing Word Pro document. In the File text box, enter the path and file name of the Word Pro document.

You can embed a sentence, a paragraph or two, or a detailed multi-page document.

4. Choose OK and then click the mouse where you want to place the object. If you chose to create a new object, enter the text and use the Word Pro tools as you normally would.
5. Click the mouse outside of the Word Pro window when you're finished to return to the 1-2-3 worksheet. Figure 28.18 shows a Word Pro document created and embedded in 1-2-3.

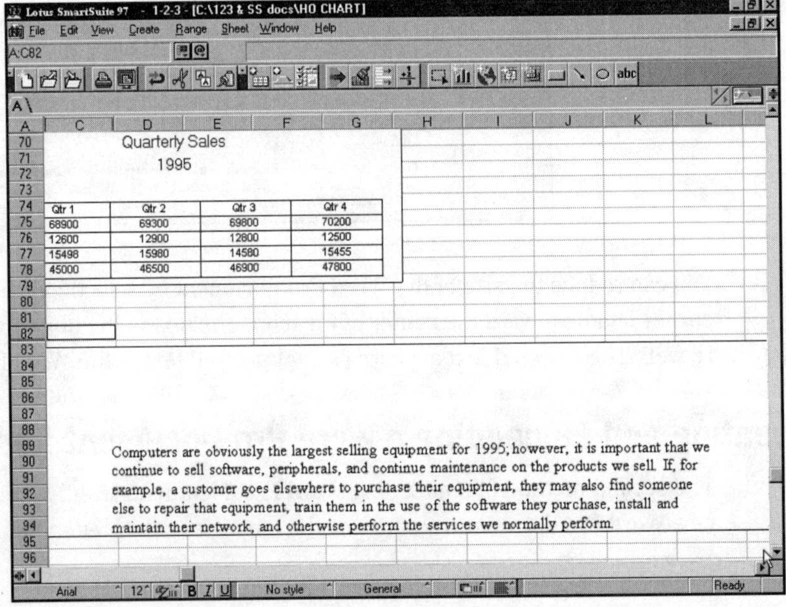

Fig. 28.18
Embed the Word Pro document to help explain your data.

To edit text in the Word Pro object, double-click the text object and the Word Pro window opens. Edit the text as you like and then click outside of the object box to return to the 1-2-3 screen. Click on the Word Pro object once to display handles (refer to fig. 28.18); when selected, you can resize and reposition the object box.

Incorporating Freelance Graphics Art into a 1-2-3 Worksheet

Freelance Graphics, also from Lotus Development Corporation, is an easy-to-use and full-featured presentation graphics application. Freelance makes creating professional-looking presentation handouts, overheads, transparencies, and slides simple and straightforward. In a single file, you can create a series of presentation pages containing text, graphics, organizational charts, table charts, and so on.

Although Freelance excels at creating entire presentations, it also offers a comprehensive set of drawing tools and clip art you can use to create diagrams, designs, and logos. These tools surpass 1-2-3's basic drawing tools. Because Freelance is a Windows application, you easily can transfer a logo drawn in Freelance to a 1-2-3 worksheet. Besides copying a drawn object to 1-2-3, you even can embed an entire Freelance presentation in a worksheet (a topic covered later in this chapter).

To transfer a graphic, such as a logo, drawn in Freelance to a 1-2-3 worksheet, select the art in Freelance, and then choose Edit, Copy. Switch to 1-2-3, place the cell pointer where you want to insert the art, and then choose Edit, Paste command; alternatively, you can use the Copy and Paste SmartIcons. You can move and resize the logo and print it just as it appears in the worksheet.

Embedding a Freelance Presentation in a 1-2-3 Worksheet

Use copying and pasting from Freelance to 1-2-3 so you can transfer a single graphic image; however, you can embed an entire Freelance presentation as an object in a 1-2-3 worksheet file to illustrate your worksheet data. While working in 1-2-3, you (or your customers, staff, or boss) can double-click the presentation object to open Freelance and view the presentation at any time.

Embedding an Existing Presentation To embed an existing Freelance presentation, follow these steps:

1. Create the presentation in Freelance, and save it as a file.
2. Click the Page Sorter tab at the top of the Freelance window, or select View, Page Sorter from the menu to view the presentation in Page Sorter view. You must use Page Sorter view to select the single page to be displayed in 1-2-3, even though the entire presentation will be embedded in 1-2-3.
3. Select the page you want to represent the presentation in 1-2-3. Figure 28.19 shows a presentation in Page Sorter view with the title page selected.

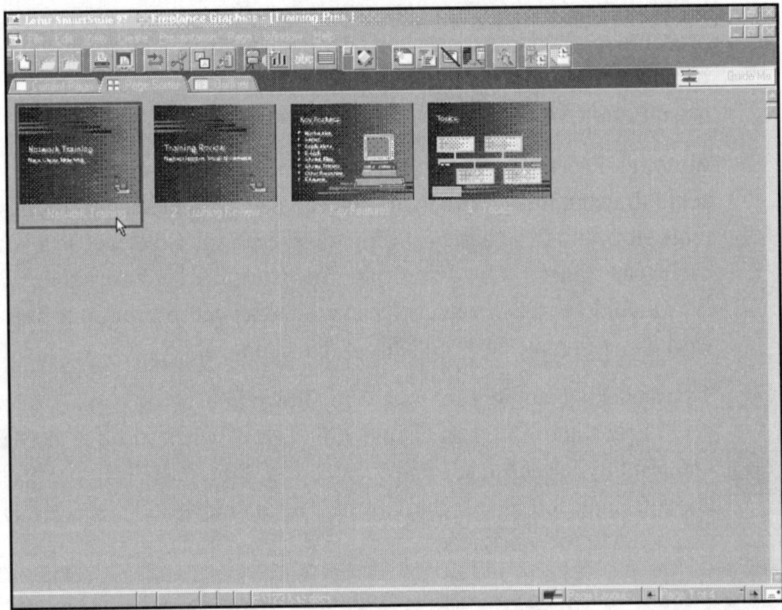

Fig. 28.19 Select one page to represent the presentation.

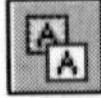

4. Choose Edit, Copy.
5. Switch to 1-2-3 by pressing Alt+Tab.
6. Place the cell pointer in the cell where the presentation object should appear.
7. Choose Edit, Paste Special. The Paste Special dialog box appears.
8. Select Lotus Freelance 97 Presentation, and then click the OK button. The selected page of the presentation appears in the worksheet, as shown in figure 28.20. Use the handles to resize and reposition the page.

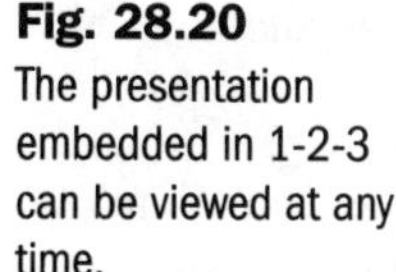

Fig. 28.20
The presentation embedded in 1-2-3 can be viewed at any time.

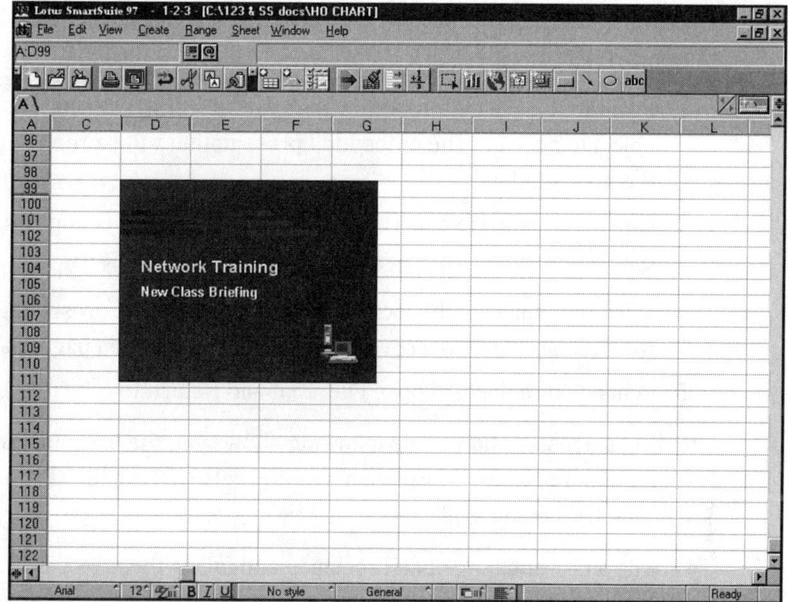

To open the Freelance window and view the presentation, double-click the presentation page in the 1-2-3 worksheet.

NOTE Be sure to close any copies of Freelance that may be open before double-clicking the presentation page.

CAUTION

Because all the Freelance presentation data is embedded in the 1-2-3 worksheet file, the worksheet file grows considerably larger. The advantage of embedding the presentation is that you can transfer the worksheet to another computer and view the presentation there (as long as Freelance Graphics is installed on the other computer) without also transporting the Freelance presentation file. However, the file may be too large to save on disk, depending on the size of the worksheet and the size of the presentation. Additionally, the presentation may run slow if the computer on which you're showing it has a small amount of memory.

Creating an Embedded Freelance Presentation from within 1-2-3 While working in a 1-2-3 worksheet, you can create a presentation that's embedded in the worksheet. From within 1-2-3, you can view the Freelance presentation—complete with charts, tables, graphics, sound, and animation—by double-clicking the presentation page that appears in 1-2-3.

Embedding a New Presentation in 1-2-3 To create a new embedded Freelance presentation from within a 1-2-3 worksheet, follow these steps:

1. Position the cell pointer in the 1-2-3 worksheet where you want the presentation object to appear. (The embedded presentation will be represented by one page from the presentation.)
2. Choose Create, Object. The Create Object dialog box appears.
3. Select Lotus Freelance 97 Presentation as the Object Type, and then click OK.
4. Click the mouse at the location where you want the presentation to appear. When the Freelance window opens, create the presentation pages as you normally would.
5. When you're done, choose File, Exit and Return to return to 1-2-3.

Creating a Presentation The following shows you the basic method of creating a presentation. For more information about Freelance Graphics Presentation program, see online help in the application.

To create a presentation, open Freelance and follow these steps:

1. In the Welcome to Lotus Freelance Graphics dialog box, choose the Create a New Presentation Using a SmartMaster tab and from the number 1, Select the Content Topic list, choose the topic on which you want to base the presentation.
2. In Select a Look of the Create a New Presentation Using a SmartMaster tab, choose a look for the presentation; view samples in the sample box to the right of the Select a Look list box.
3. Choose OK; the New Page dialog box appears. Select the Title page layout, and then click OK.
4. Click the Click Here To Type Meeting Name block and enter the information for the title.
5. Press the down-arrow key to move to the next Click Here block.
6. Enter text and/or clip art to complete the title page. Figure 28.21 shows the completed title page.

To create a second presentation page, follow these steps:

1. Click the New Page button at the top-left corner of the Freelance presentation window. The New Page dialog box appears. Choose the Current Page tab.
2. You might select the Bulleted List page layout—or the charts, table, diagram, or other page—and then click OK.

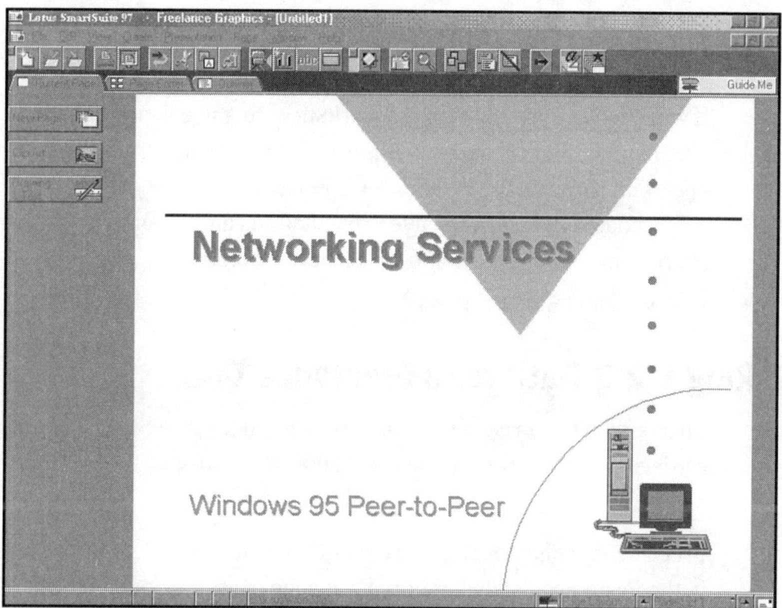

Fig. 28.21
The title page introduces your presentation.

3. Click the Click Here To Type Page Title block, and enter a title for the page.
4. Continue to fill in the text and objects, adding new pages and items as you complete the presentation.

NOTE To use a presentation in a 1-2-3 worksheet, you must first save the presentation (File, Save As). Next, change to Page Sorter view and select the title page, or any page you want to represent the presentation in 1-2-3. Choose Edit, Copy and then switch to 1-2-3.

TROUBLESHOOTING

How do I embed a single object or group of objects from a Freelance page in 1-2-3? You must embed an entire presentation. To transfer a single object, you can use the Edit menu's Copy and Paste commands to transfer the object.

Using 1-2-3 Data in a Freelance Graphics Chart

The charting capabilities of 1-2-3 are sophisticated enough that you may feel no need to use a separate graphics program like Freelance Graphics. But you may want to incorporate data from a 1-2-3 worksheet into a presentation you are preparing in Freelance. If so, you will find it easy to transport the data from 1-2-3 to Freelance and easy to set up an OLE link between the two programs.

If you need to copy data from a worksheet to a Freelance chart and have no concern about whether the chart is updated if the 1-2-3 data changes, a straightforward copy-and-paste operation through the Windows Clipboard can do the job. However, if you want automatically updated data for effective presentations and reports, you can use object linking to share data between 1-2-3 and Freelance Graphics.

▶ **See** "Copying Data," **p. 240**

Linking 1-2-3 Data for a Freelance Chart

To link data to a Freelance chart, use the Edit, Paste Special command in Freelance to retrieve data from the Clipboard. Make sure you save the 1-2-3 file before you copy the data.

Freelance recognizes that the data in the Windows Clipboard is a range of data from 1-2-3; in the Paste Special dialog box, Freelance presents options for importing the data. Figure 28.22 shows the Freelance Paste Special dialog box.

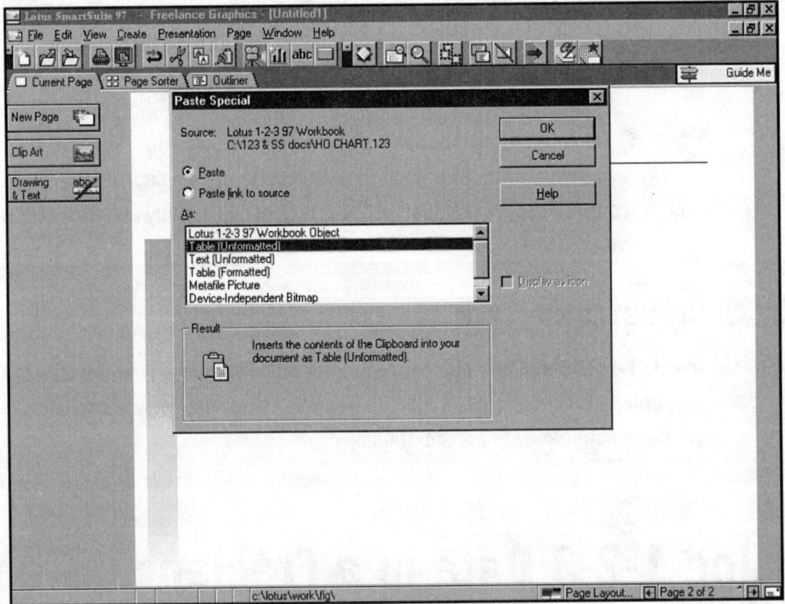

Fig. 28.22
Choose from the options for pasting 1-2-3 data to the presentation.

If you choose to Paste Special the data, you have the following choices in the As list box:

- *Lotus 1-2-3 97 Workbook Object.* Inserts the data as a formatted 1-2-3 worksheet.
- *Table (Unformatted).* Inserts data as an unformatted table.
- *Text (Unformatted).* Inserts data as text with tabs separating columns.
- *Table (Formatted).* Inserts data as a table with formatting similar to applied formatting in 1-2-3.
- *Metafile Picture.* Inserts the data as a Windows Metafile graphic. A metafile is a standardized graphic format that can be read by most Windows applications.
- *Device-Independent Bitmap.* Displays the data as a bitmap allowable on any type of display device. The term "device independent" means that the bitmap specifies pixel color in a form independent of the method used by a display to represent color.
- *Bitmap.* Inserts the data as a bitmap (.bmp) graphic file. A Bitmap graphic is created from a series of dots or pixels.

If you choose to Paste Link to Source, you have only two choices in the As list box: Linked Lotus 1-2-3 97 Workbook Object and Text (Unformatted). Choosing unformatted text means the data is still linked; however you can format the data in Freelance so it looks like the other charts and data in your presentation.

NOTE You also can paste the linked 1-2-3 97 workbook object as an icon, if you prefer. Simply choose Display as Icon.

Figure 28.23 shows the data pasted as unformatted text, before formatting. You can use the handles to enlarge or reduce the size of the object; you can also drag the object to a new location on the page.

TIP Save time and energy by pasting data from 1-2-3 as the Lotus 1-2-3 97 Workbook Object so you don't have to format the data twice.

Linking Data from Several 1-2-3 Worksheets

You can use data from multiple worksheets to create a chart in Freelance Graphics and link the data so updates will be automatic. Sharing data across applications and worksheets, in this manner, makes your work easier and your product more effective.

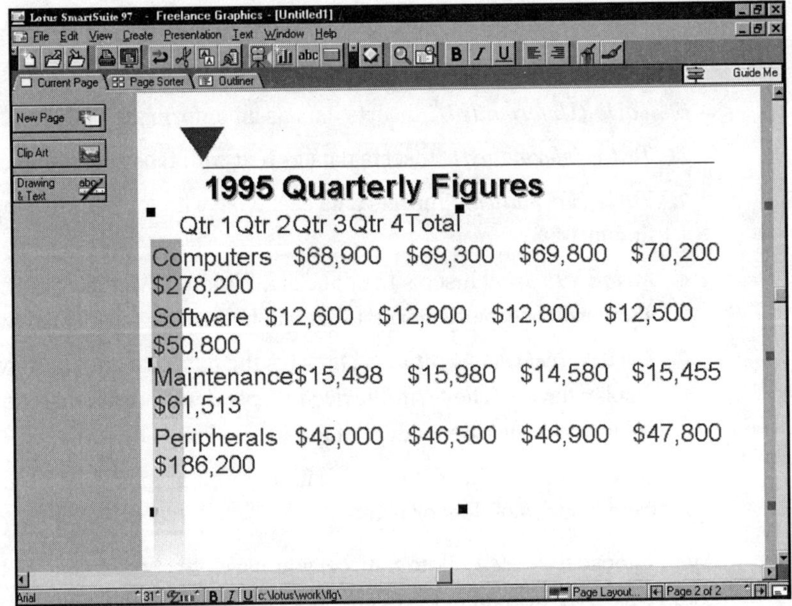

Fig. 28.23
You must format the text so it's readable and easy-to-understand, if you select the Text (unformatted) option in the Paste Special dialog box.

To link data from multiple worksheets to a Freelance chart, follow these steps:

1. In 1-2-3, create or open the first worksheet and save the file.
2. Open Freelance Graphics and create or open the presentation.
3. Select one of the Chart page layouts to quickly and easily create a chart in Freelance.
4. Click the Click Here To Create Chart block. The Create Chart dialog box appears.
5. Choose a chart to create and choose OK. The Edit Data window appears (see fig. 28.24).
6. Choose the Import Data button; the Open dialog box appears.
7. Choose the 1-2-3 file containing the data you want to use and select the Open button. The Edit Links dialog box appears (see fig. 28.25).
8. Select the cells of the worksheet you want to use and then choose one of the following buttons:
   - *Title.* To use the selected data for a title in Freelance.
   - *Legend.* To use the selected data for a legend.
   - *X Axis Labels.* To use the selected data as x-axis labels.

- *Data.* To use the selected data as data.
- *Keep File Links.* Select this check box to link the data between the two programs.

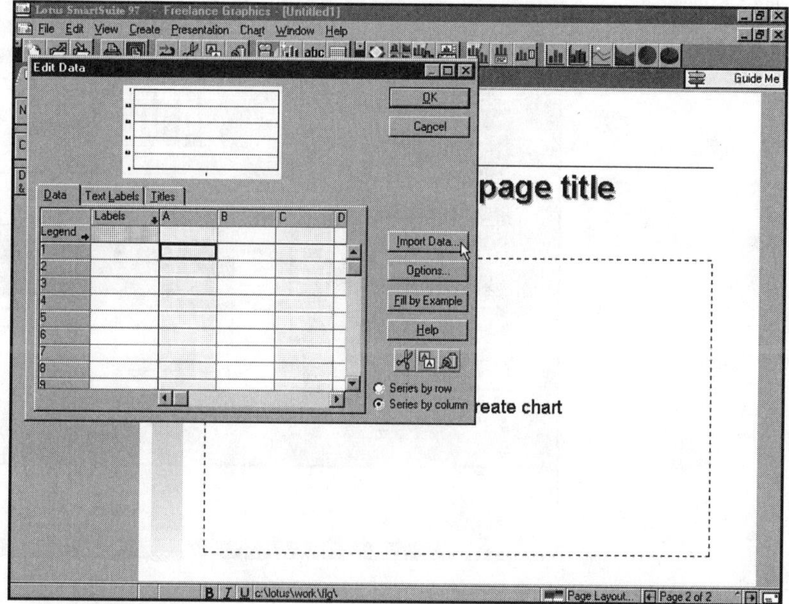

Fig. 28.24 Use the Edit Data window in Freelance to paste the data from 1-2-3.

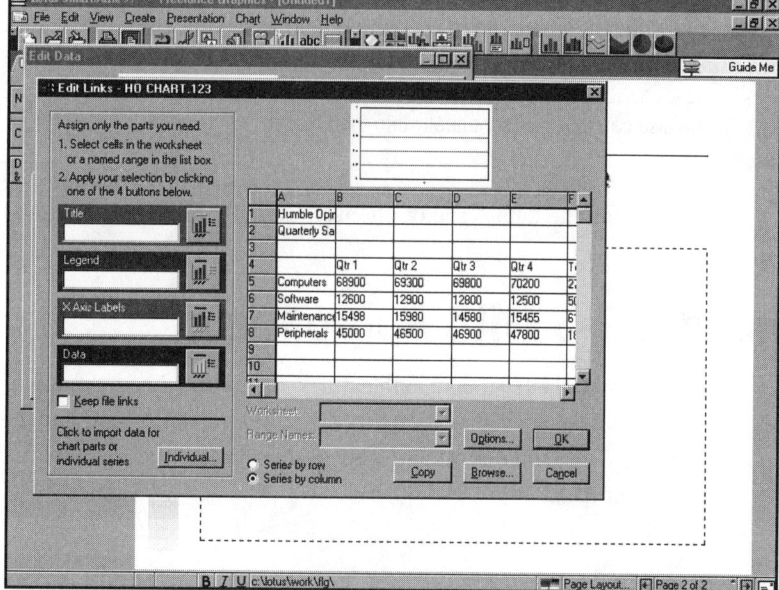

Fig. 28.25 The Edit Links dialog box helps you link 1-2-3 data with a Freelance chart.

9. Click the Individual button to import data for other chart parts (see fig. 28.26). Choose the Groups button to return to the first Edit Links dialog box.

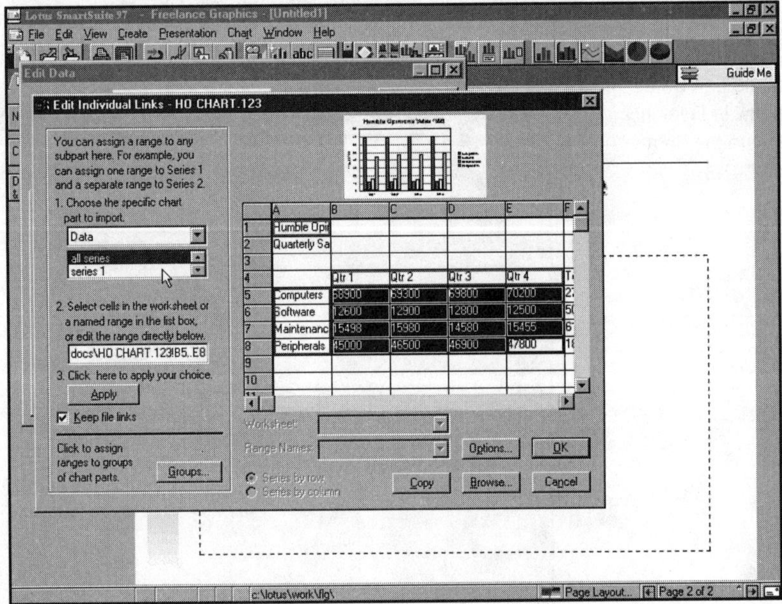

Fig. 28.26
Assign a selected range as a subpart in the chart.

10. Choose OK to enter the data into the Edit Data dialog box.
11. Repeat the process of importing data for any other chart data you want to add to this chart. Be careful to reposition your insertion point in the Edit Data window so you don't overwrite the data you just imported.

You also can enter data manually into the Edit Data window.

12. When the data is ready, choose OK in the Edit Data dialog box to create the chart.

Using 1-2-3 with Approach

Approach is an easy-to-use, full-featured database management application. Approach is a relational database application that promotes versatility and end-user friendliness. With Approach, you can design data-entry forms, create reports, and maintain various views of important data.

Approach does not work directly in a database file; instead, the program uses a view file to create a *picture* of the data. Approach supports a variety of different database file formats so that you can exchange data freely. The easiest way to take advantage of this is simply to open database files created in other database applications, such as Paradox and dBASE.

Approach supports object linking and formatting. You can add graphics, charts, and text created in other applications to your Approach forms, reports, and views. These object elements remain linked to their server applications so that they are updated whenever the source document changes.

▶ **See** "Planning Your Database," **p. 528**

▶ **See** "Modifying the Structure of a Database," **p. 538**

Importing Approach Data into 1-2-3

Approach is a unique database product in that it can create views of another file format but cannot create its own file format. Because Approach does not use a proprietary file format, 1-2-3's Open File dialog box does not include an Approach file format in the Files of Type drop-down list. You can open a desired database file in Approach and then save the file in a format that 1-2-3 can open (Paradox, dBASE, FoxPro, and so on).

▶ **See** "Building a 1-2-3 Database", **p. xx** (Ch. 23)

To import an Approach file into 1-2-3, follow these steps:

1. In Approach, choose File, Open. Open a file and choose the Browse button below the SmartIcon bar if the file is not already in Browse mode (see fig. 28.27).
2. Choose File, Export Data. The Export Data dialog box appears (see fig. 28.28).
3. In the Export Type drop-down list, select Lotus 1-2-3 (*.WK1).
4. Map the desired fields to export to 1-2-3 by selecting each field in the Database Fields list box and then clicking Add to place each selected field in the Fields to Export list box (see fig. 28.29).
5. Select the drive and folder, name the file, and choose Export. The Field Names box will appear, mark the check box if you want the first row to containn field names.
6. Switch to 1-2-3.
7. Open the exported file in 1-2-3. Notice that the records are in row-and-column format.

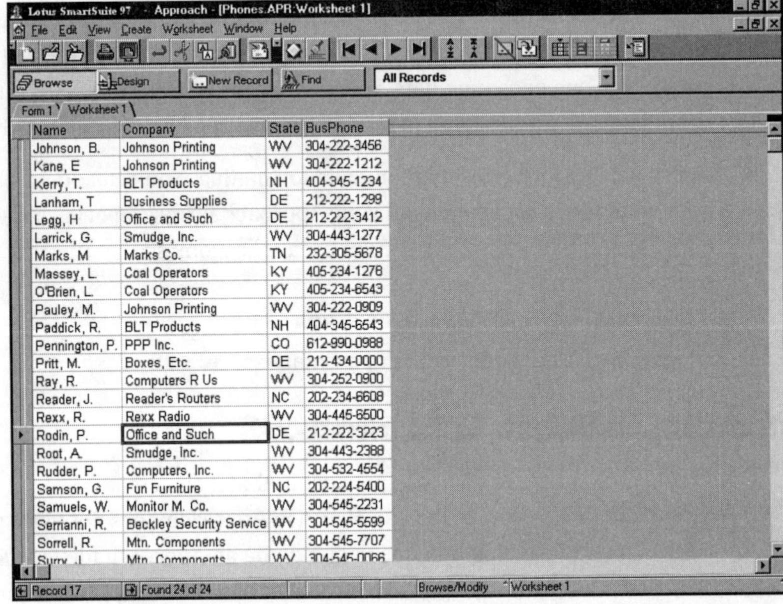

Fig. 28.27
View the records before exporting the data.

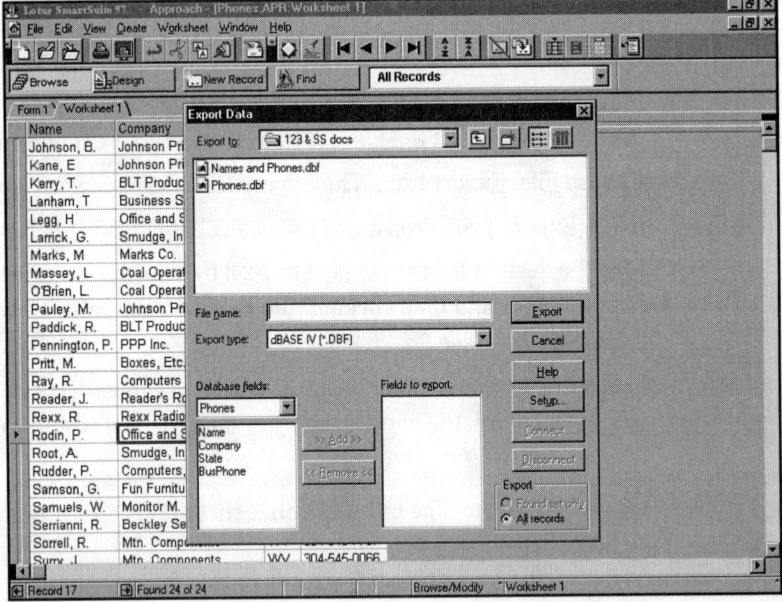

Fig. 28.28
You can choose the file type you want to export in the Export Data dialog box.

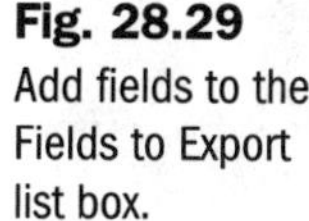

Fig. 28.29
Add fields to the Fields to Export list box.

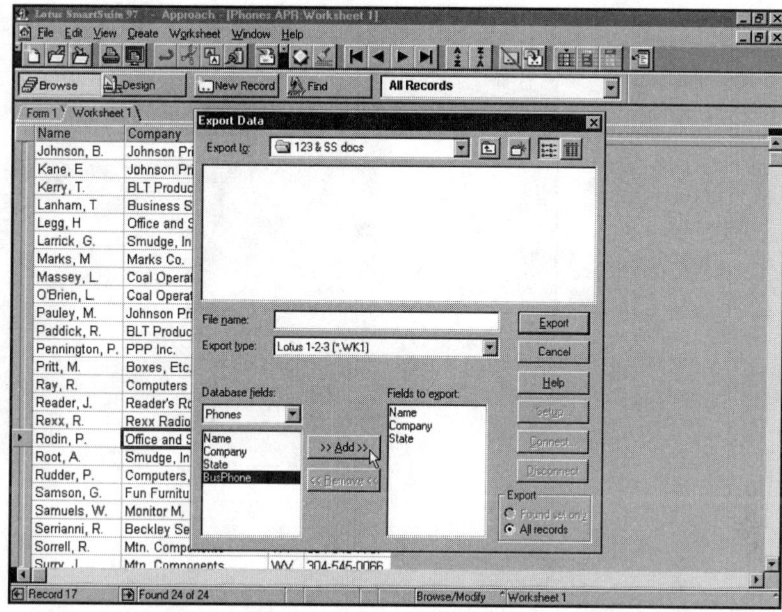

Instead of exporting the Approach file in 1-2-3 file format, you can save the file in Text-Delimited (*.TXT) format. Approach prompts you to select a desired delimiter—commas, semicolons, spaces, tabs, or other character you specify.

You then can open the exported text file in 1-2-3 by choosing Text (TXT;PRN;CSV;DAT;OUT;ASC) as the Files of Type. When you open the file, 1-2-3 displays the Text File Options dialog box (see fig. 28.30). Choose how you want 1-2-3 to handle the delimiters you set when you exported the Approach file and choose OK.

Exporting 1-2-3 Data to Approach

In most cases, you can open and use a database file in Approach without first importing the data. If you want to use data in a 1-2-3 worksheet or text file format, however, you first must create a new database file and then import the worksheet or text file into the new file. This procedure is necessary because Approach does not use a proprietary file format and cannot read a 1-2-3 file format directly.

The initial step to importing 1-2-3 data is to select the type of file you want to import in Approach. Then select the file to be imported, and map the fields in the import file to those in the current Approach database file. Field mapping associates fields in the Approach View file with fields in an underlying database file. The Field Mapping dialog box opens automatically when you try to open a view file that contains fields that need mapping.

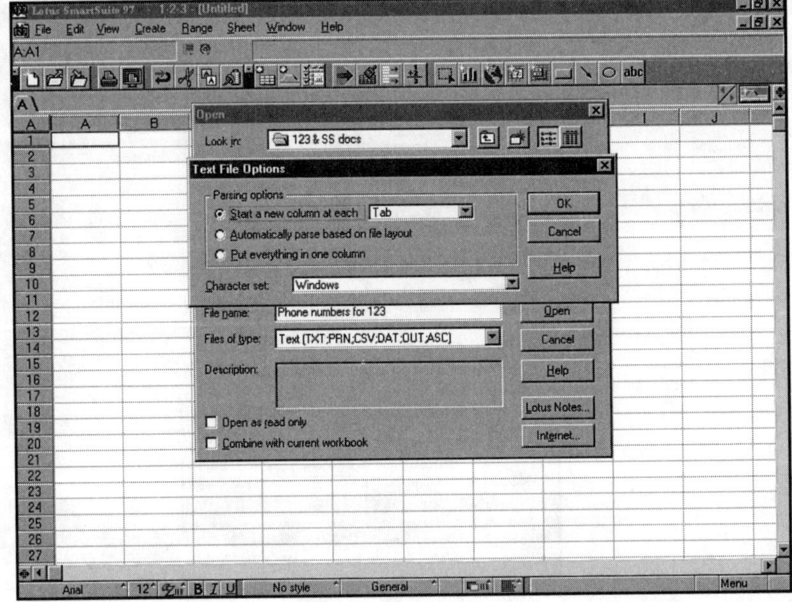

Fig. 28.30 Importing an ASCII text file means choosing a delimiter in Approach and then specifying the delimiter in 1-2-3.

TIP If the fields in the 1-2-3 file match the fields in the new Approach file, Approach maps them for you.

To export a 1-2-3 worksheet to an Approach database file, follow these steps:

1. Create the 1-2-3 worksheet that you want to import, such as the one shown in figure 28.31. After saving the file, make sure you close it.
2. Switch to Approach.
3. Using the File, New Database command, create a new Approach view file. In the first New dialog box, choose Blank Database and then click OK. In the next New dialog box, type a name in the File Name text box and select a file type in the Create Type list box.

TIP Try dBASE IV (*.DBF) as a file type for 1-2-3 database files.

4. Click Create. The Creating New Database dialog box appears, as shown in figure 28.32.
5. Add the fields to be mapped to the 1-2-3 worksheet file using the same fields you used in 1-2-3. Enter the Field Name, choose the Data Type and Size. Figure 28.33 shows sample codes in the Creating New Database dialog box.

Fig. 28.31
Open the 1-2-3 database you want to import.

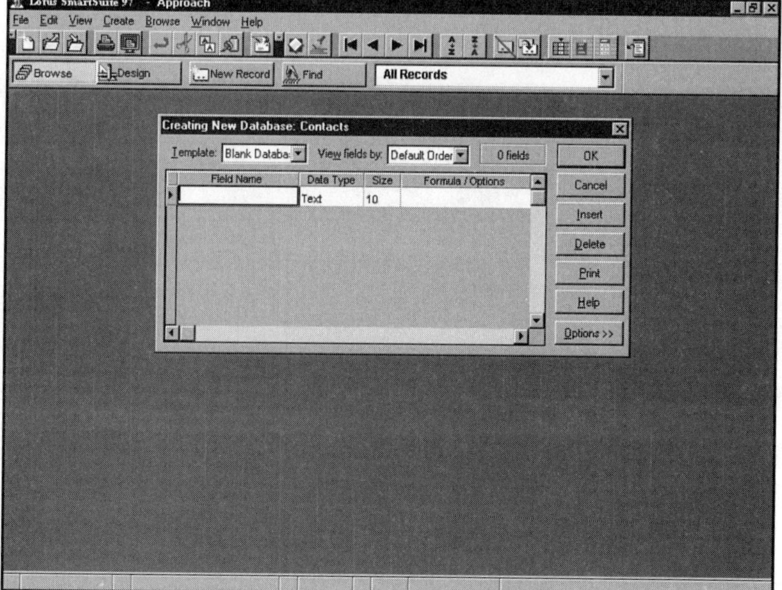

Fig. 28.32
Create fields in a new Approach file.

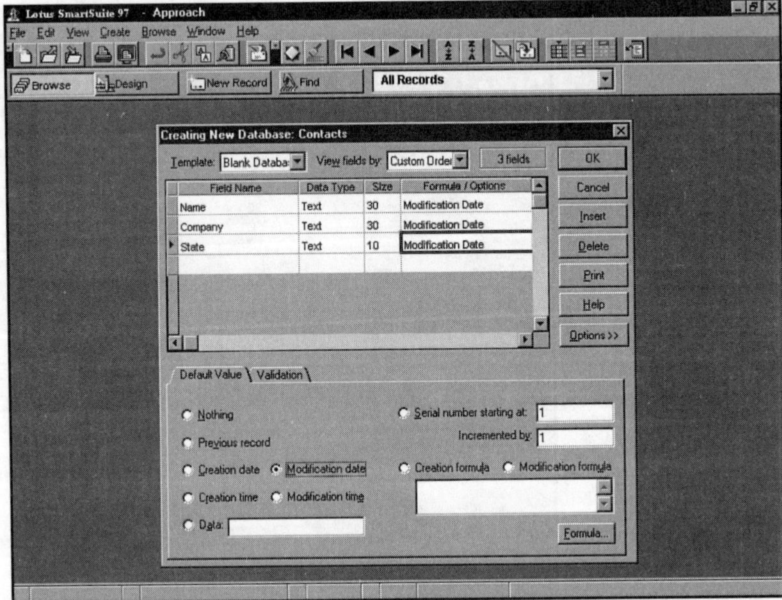

Fig. 28.33
Add the fields for mapping in Approach.

6. Click OK. Approach creates a database form for the file. Figure 28.34 shows the form for the sample data.

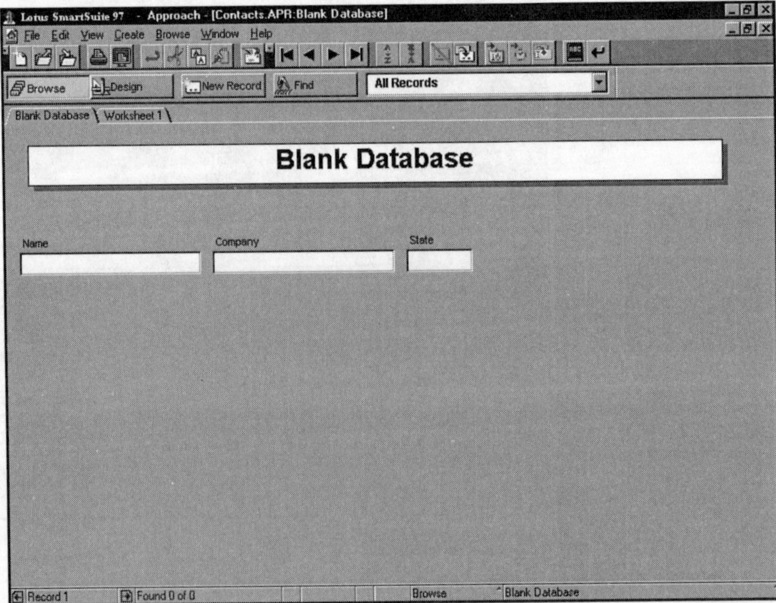

Fig. 28.34
The Approach fields correspond with the 1-2-3 fields.

7. Choose File, Import Data. The Import Data dialog box appears.

Another way to export 1-2-3 data to Approach is to first save the 1-2-3 file as an ASCII text file and then open the text file in Approach.

8. Select the Import Type as Lotus 1-2-3 (*.123,*.WK1), choose the desired 1-2-3 worksheet file, and then click Import. The Field Names dialog box appears, check the First Row contains Field Names box and choose OK. The Import Setup dialog box appears (see fig. 28.35).

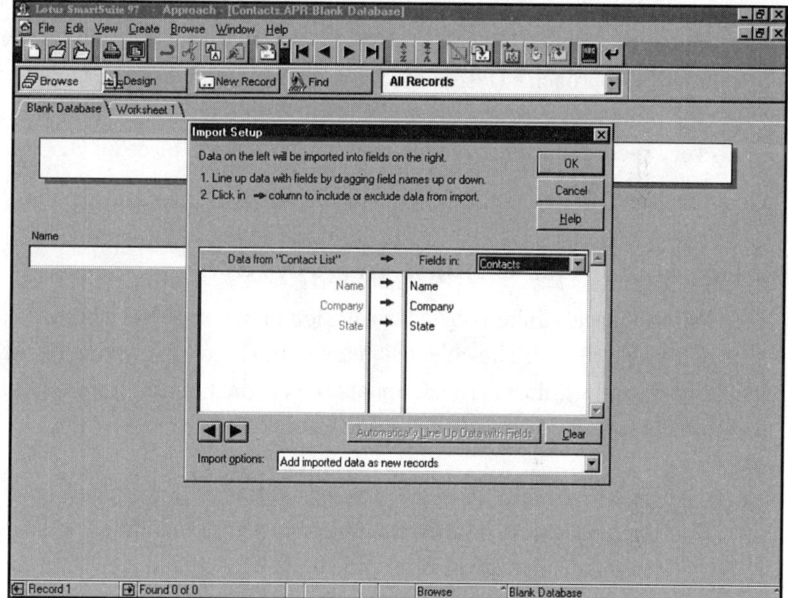

Fig. 28.35
Importing the field information is easy if you set up the fields in Approach ahead of time.

9. Next, you need to map the fields from the 1-2-3 worksheet file to be imported to those in the Approach form. If your fields do not match exactly, you can click the arrow between the two field names to exclude that field. Choose OK when you're ready to import.

NOTE Approach imports the 1-2-3 file, adding the new records to the end of the file. If you import the same file twice, you will get duplicate records. If you don't select the First Row Contains Field Names check box, the first record on the view will be the labels or column headings from the 1-2-3 worksheet.

Understanding OLE Objects in Approach

Approach enables you to include a lot of information in your database, such as graphics, charts, and text from 1-2-3. Depending on the server application, you will see the actual object (such as a Lotus 1-2-3 chart) or an icon that represents the object (such as a Word Pro icon).

If you link a 1-2-3 object to Approach, the object remains in its server application, with a link to the Approach field. You must have 1-2-3 installed to edit the object. Any changes you make to the object automatically update the original.

If you embed an OLE object, the entire object is stored in the field. You can place OLE objects in a PicturePlus field in Approach's Browse mode or directly in a form, report, or letter in Approach's Design mode. If you place the object directly in a Design view, the OLE object appears as a design element. Unless you want the OLE object to appear in every record of a database file, you most often will place an OLE object in a PicturePlus field in Browse mode.

Linking 1-2-3 OLE Objects in Approach

You can place a linked object as a design element in every record or in a PicturePlus field in a single record. The object appears in the record. Any changes you make to the linked object from within Approach update the original object. Before linking, you must create the object in 1-2-3 and copy it to the Clipboard.

To insert a linked object from 1-2-3 into Approach, follow these steps:

1. In 1-2-3, create or open the object you want to link to and select the object—chart, graphic, or range of data, and so on. Copy the object to the Clipboard.
2. Prepare an Approach view file to receive the linked object. Open the view file into which you want to insert the object, and then switch to the form, report, or other view you want to use.

   To paste the 1-2-3 OLE object as a design element, change to Design view: open the View, Design command.

   If you are placing the linked object in a PicturePlus field, change to Browse mode, go to the record, and select the field.
3. Choose Edit, Paste Special. The Paste Special dialog box appears.
4. Choose the 1-2-3 worksheet object format. Click Paste Link and then click OK. Approach displays the object in the current view. A 1-2-3 OLE object appears as an object, as displayed in figure 28.36.

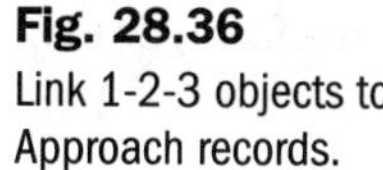

Fig. 28.36
Link 1-2-3 objects to Approach records.

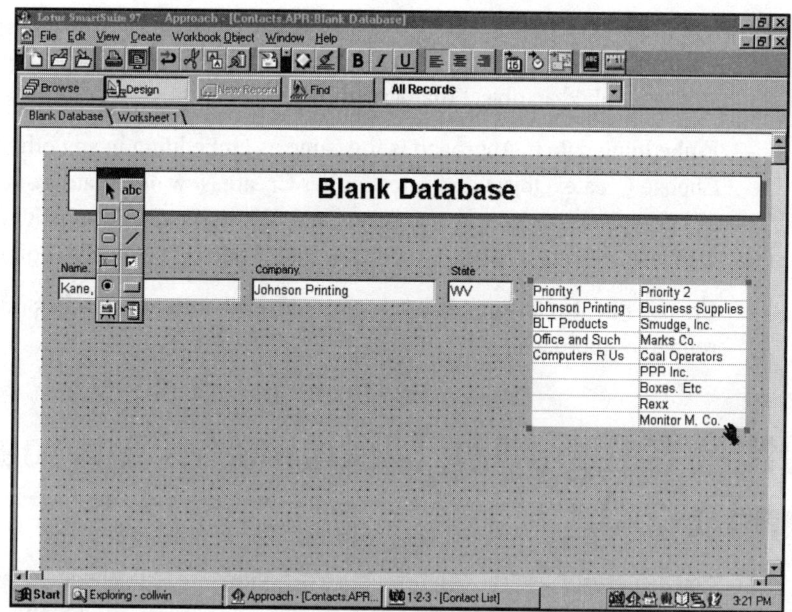

NOTE To delete a linked object, select the object and press the Del key.

Editing a Linked Object

You can modify the data in the linked object from 1-2-3. Then save the updated data to Approach.

To edit a linked 1-2-3 object in Approach, follow these steps:

1. Select the 1-2-3 object. Next, choose Workbook Object, Linked Workbook Object, Edit to switch to 1-2-3.
2. Double-click the 1-2-3 object to open the source document. Edit the object.
3. Switch to Approach. Notice that the object shows your changes.

Embedding 1-2-3 Data in Approach

Embedding a 1-2-3 OLE object in an Approach view file creates a link to 1-2-3 the same way that linking to an object does. The difference between linking and embedding is that an embedded object is the only version of the object, whereas a linked object refers to and can update the original source object.

You can embed an object as a design element in a report or every record of a form, or in a PicturePlus field in a single record. You can embed an object by first creating it in 1-2-3, or you can embed an object that already exists.

Embedding data in Approach is the same as embedding in any other Lotus application. Choose Create, Object and select either Create New or Create from File. Next, choose the object type or the file you want to embed. When the file is embedded into the Approach database, change to Design view and double-click the object to edit it.

Choose File, Update and then choose File, Exit & Return or click outside the object to return to Approach.

Other Integrating Methods for Approach and 1-2-3

You can create several different Approach views in 1-2-3 to display worksheet data—Form, Report, Crosstab, and Mailing Label views—so you can modify the data in Approach while the changes appear in the 1-2-3 range.

Following is a brief summary of the Approach views you can display in 1-2-3:

- *Forms.* This view focuses on a single record in a database. Use Forms view to enter and edit data.
- *Reports.* Use Reports to organize data from multiple records. Reports can show field data, summary information calculated from field data, or a combination of the two.
- *Dynamic Crosstab.* Use this view to categorize and summarize database records. For example, a crosstab might present employees by position, salary, and location.
- *Mailing Labels.* This view displays field data and text in a mailing address format so you can print mailing labels.
- *Form Letter.* This view displays a combination of database fields and text in a letter format. Approach adds the names and addresses from the database to the letter forms so you can print them.

In 1-2-3, you must use column headers for field names; the worksheet cannot exceed 100 columns or 8,192 rows. To display the views, follow these steps:

1. In 1-2-3, select the range of cells you want to use.
2. In 1-2-3, choose Create, Database, and then select Form, Report, Dynamic Crosstab, Mailing Labels, or Form Letter. 1-2-3 starts the Approach Assistant. Figure 28.37 shows the Create dialog box.

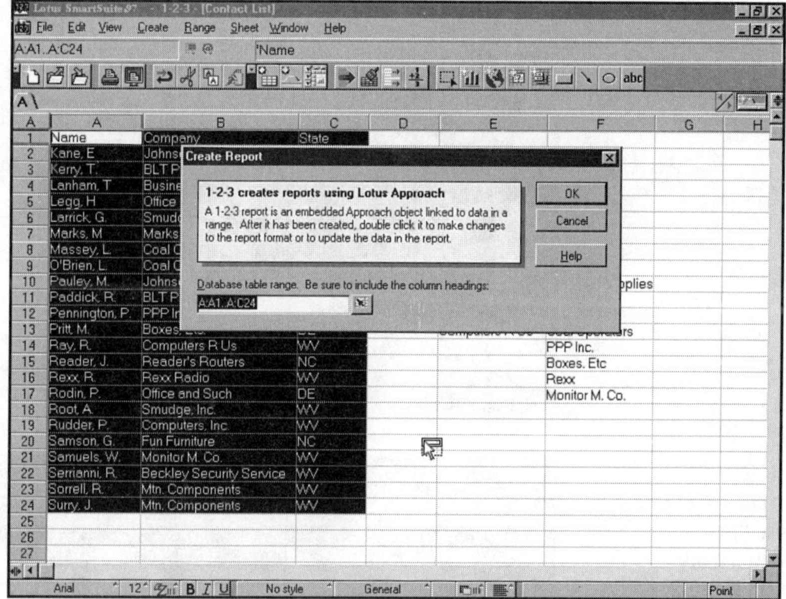

Fig. 28.37
Choose the range.

3. Choose the table range and choose OK. 1-2-3 displays the Create dialog box. You click the mouse pointer, which changes to a cross attached to a database icon, where you want to display the object.
4. 1-2-3 displays the Form Assistant. Select the Approach database file you want to use and choose OK. 1-2-3 displays the Assistant to help you complete the task.
5. Each assistant presents different options; follow the instructions on-screen. Figure 28.38 shows the Report Assistant.
6. When you've completed the steps outlined on-screen, 1-2-3 displays the view, as shown in figure 28.39.
7. To exit a view, click outside the object.

To edit the form, double-click the icon. If you change data in the 1-2-3 database table, Approach updates the form.

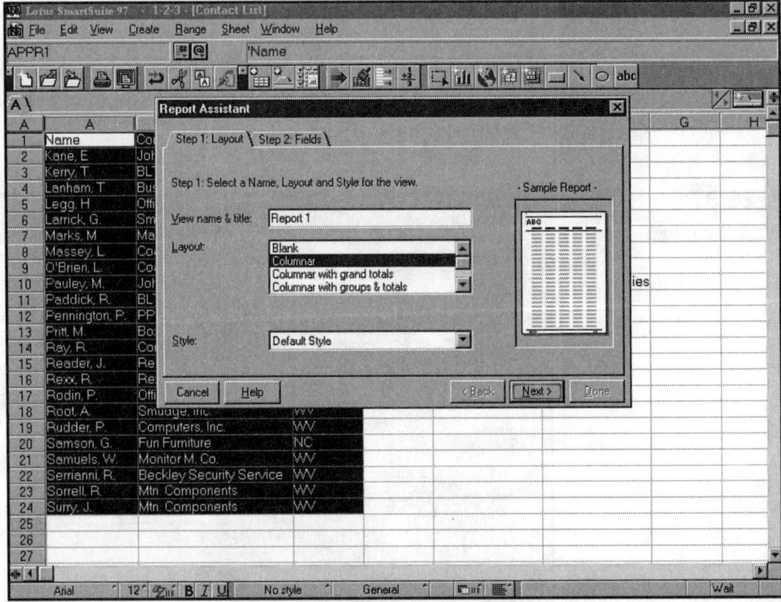

Fig. 28.38
Follow the steps and instructions to create the view you want.

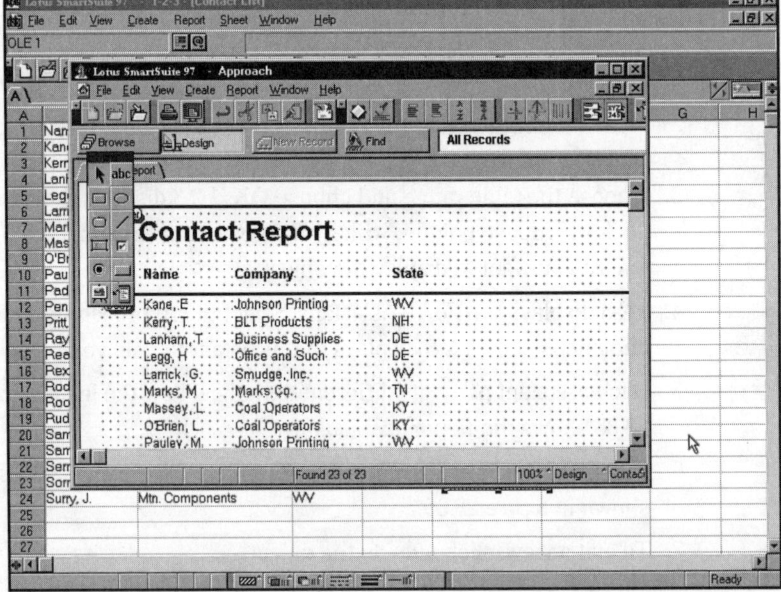

Fig. 28.39
You can resize and move the view as you would any object in 1-2-3.

TROUBLESHOOTING

I've used a PicturePlus field for my 1-2-3 object but it doesn't show up on all records in the database. What can I do? Use PicturePlus fields when you want an object to display on one record only, the record on which you create the field. If you want an object to display on all records, embed the object in the Design view to one record.

I have a 1-2-3 database mailing list with over 10,000 names and addresses. I want to create a Mailing Label view from Approach but I can't get the view to work. What's wrong with it? The range of 1-2-3 cells cannot exceed 100 columns or 8,192 rows. You'll have to break the 1-2-3 file into two files to use the Mailing Label view.

CHAPTER 29

Using 1-2-3 with Lotus Notes

by Sue Plumley

Linking and embedding between 1-2-3 and Notes

Link 1-2-3 data to a Notes database document as well as embed a 1-2-3 object to Notes, and edit these objects quickly and efficiently.

Importing and exporting between 1-2-3 and Notes

You can import worksheets and graphics into a Notes document and export Notes documents to 1-2-3 for later use.

Lotus Notes is a groupware application that manages data and information for many users, enabling them to work together more efficiently. Imagine containers of information that everyone in the organization can access. The containers are Notes databases, which are collections of related documents. In the past, people worked independently and had to exchange data through floppy disks and company pouch mail, now, PCs are linked by local area networks (LANs). Notes enables you to collect and share information—1-2-3 worksheets, text, and graphics, for example—with other users over a network. Additionally, Notes supports larger communications channels, such as the World Wide Web and the Internet.

Workgroup members can use Notes to share documents created in other applications, collaborate on ideas, issue reports, track clients, monitor projects, and customize workgroup processes and reports. ■

Using DDE/OLE Between 1-2-3 and Lotus Notes

Dynamic data exchange (DDE) and object linking and embedding (OLE) are techniques for incorporating data from other programs into 1-2-3, and vice versa. DDE and OLE enable you to paste information created in one Windows application into another Windows application. The distinct advantage of DDE and OLE over normal copy-and-paste procedures is that you can edit the linked or embedded object in its source application without leaving the file that contains the object.

▶ **See** "Using OLE2," **p. 634**

OLE lets you share data between applications by linking or embedding an object to a Notes document. An *object* is a copy of the data from the server application to the client application when embedding or a pointer to the data in the server application for linking to the client. The *server application* is the application in which the data was created; the *client application* is the one receiving the shared data.

DDE is more of a protocol that lets you link data from another application as an object in a Notes document. Both DDE and OLE accomplish the same thing: sharing data between two applications.

To use DDE and OLE, both Windows applications must support the current technology and both applications must be open.

CAUTION

1-2-3 can act as an OLE/DDE client and server, but Notes can act only as a client. Therefore, you can link and embed 1-2-3 objects in Notes documents, but you cannot link or embed Notes objects in 1-2-3 worksheets.

Creating a Linked 1-2-3 for Windows Object in Lotus Notes

A *linked object* is a reference within a DDE/OLE client application file (Notes) to a file in a DDE/OLE server application (1-2-3). When an object is linked with DDE or OLE, the object maintains a relationship with the original source data. If you change or modify the source data, the linked object changes. For example, if you link an object or range created in a 1-2-3 worksheet to a Notes document, and then change the data in the 1-2-3 worksheet, the linked 1-2-3 object in the Notes document reflects those changes.

▶ **See** "Entering Data," **p. 66**

▶ **See** "Enhancing the Appearance of Data," **p. 125**

You should link 1-2-3 information if:

- You want to store 1-2-3 data in a central location.
- The 1-2-3 source file is permanent and will not be moved (for example, a corporate logo).
- The users who need to edit the data have access to the 1-2-3 file and the 1-2-3 application.

To create a 1-2-3 link in Lotus Notes, follow these steps:

1. Open the source worksheet in 1-2-3. These steps use the sample GLOBAL worksheet (see fig. 29.1).

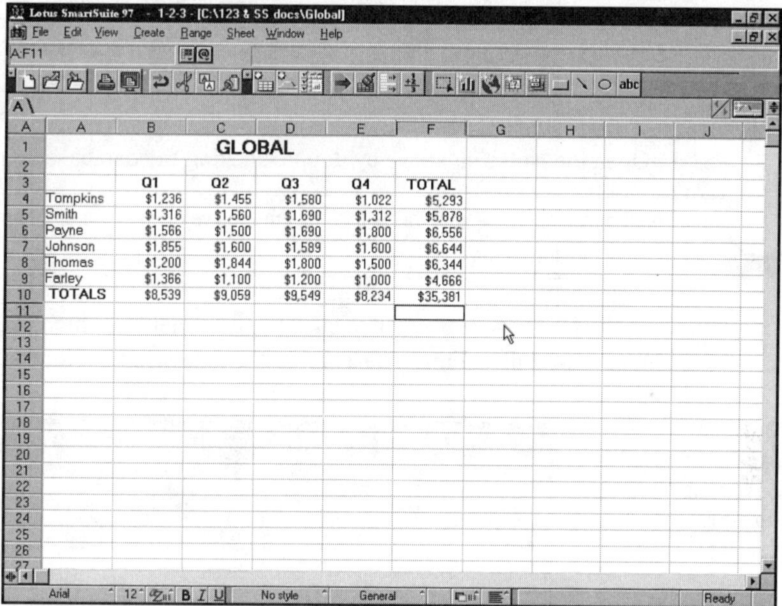

Fig. 29.1
The GLOBAL worksheet can easily be linked to a document in Notes.

2. Select the information you want to use in the object—a range of data, a graph, text, and so on.

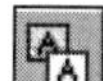

3. Choose Edit, Copy to place the information in the Clipboard.
4. Switch to Notes using the Windows taskbar, pressing Alt+Tab, or by clicking the Notes SmartIcon; alternatively, start the Notes application if it is not running already. Figure 29.2 shows the Notes workspace.

Fig. 29.2
The sample database, Budget 1995, appears on a workspace page created specifically for 1-2-3.

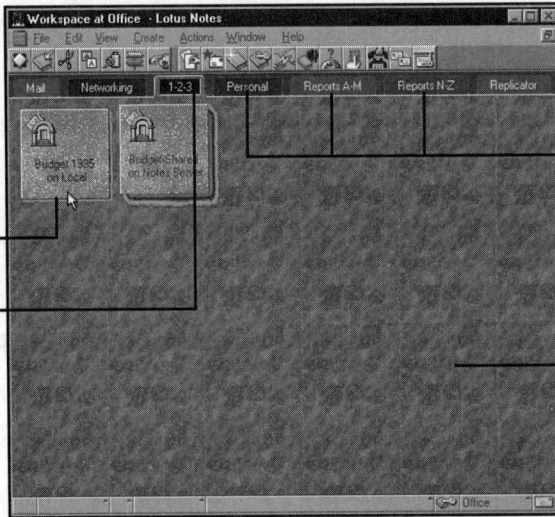

Workspace tabs

Database for use with 1-2-3

1-2-3 tab

Workspace page

5. Open the Notes database by double-clicking the database icon or by pressing Enter.

The About document appears if this is the first time you've opened the database. Press the Esc key to close the document.

6. In the Database view, double-click the document in which you want to place the linked 1-2-3 data. Figure 29.3 shows the database view for the sample data.

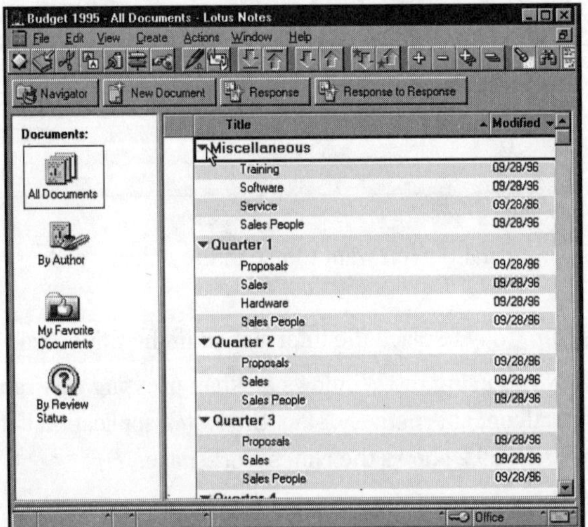

FIG. 29.3
Expand a category if necessary and then double-click a document to open it.

7. Double-click the document to start Edit mode and then position the insertion point in a Rich Text field (see fig. 29.4).

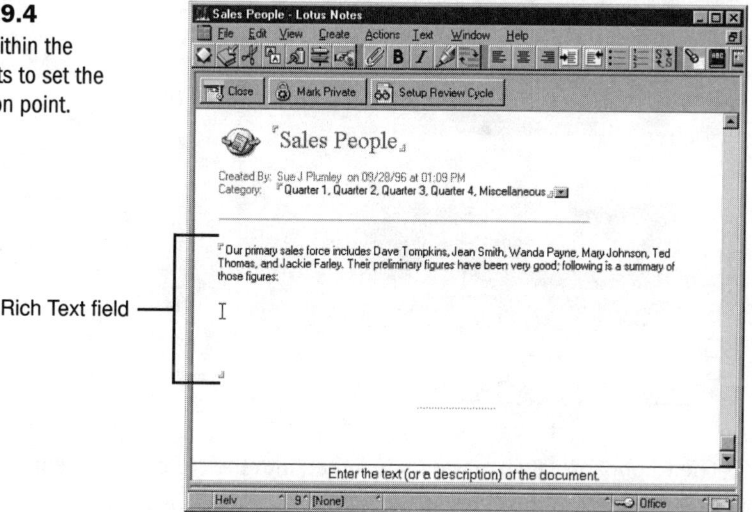

Fig. 29.4
Click within the brackets to set the insertion point.

NOTE Most fields, but not all, are surrounded by tiny brackets or corners, which help you identify the location and size of fields in a document. Rich Text fields enable you to enter words and sentences, but also enable you to make use of different sizes and styles of characters, as well as colors, tables, graphics, pictures, and objects.

CAUTION

Embedded and linked objects need to be inserted into Rich Text fields in Notes documents because plain text fields cannot distinguish formatting and object information.

8. Choose Edit, Paste Special. The Paste Special dialog box appears (see fig. 29.5).
9. Choose Paste Link to Source.
10. In the As list, select the Clipboard format you want to display. The options are determined by the DDE server application (1-2-3). For this example, select Rich Text Format.

TIP Experiment with the various types in the As list to find the format you want to use in the Notes document.

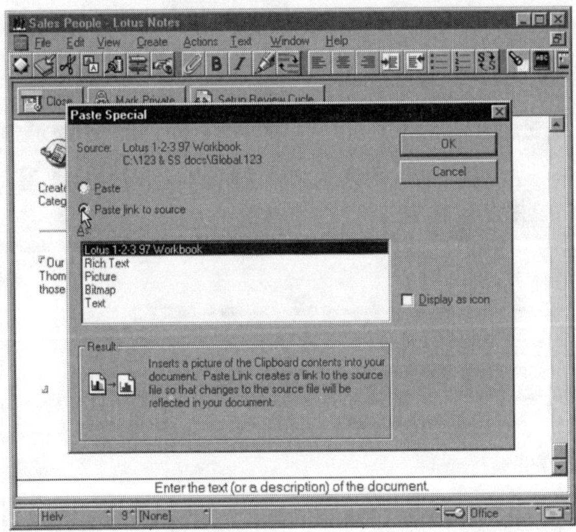

Fig. 29.5
Choose Paste Special to paste a link in a Notes document.

11. Click OK. The Clipboard data is pasted and linked into the Notes document. Page down by using the vertical scroll bar if necessary, because Notes may shift information in the document (see fig. 29.6).

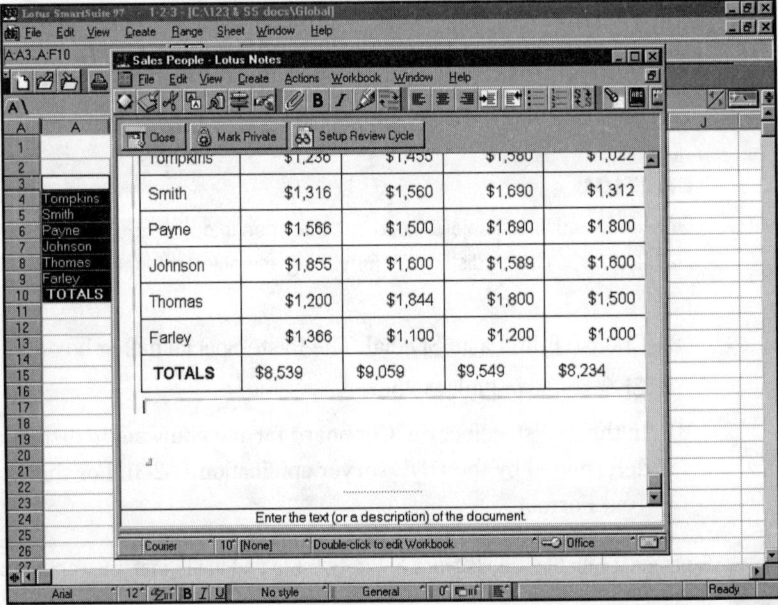

Fig. 29.6
The spreadsheet is larger in Notes than it was in 1-2-3.

12. In Notes, choose File, Save to save the document and the linked data. Make sure you also save the data in the server application.

NOTE To update the linked file, make changes in the server application and save the file under the same name and to the same location. The changes automatically update in the Notes document. See the section "Editing the Linked and Embedded Objects" later in this chapter for more information.

TROUBLESHOOTING

The text in my 1-2-3 object in Notes appears enlarged and is causing word-wrapping. The text in 1-2-3 objects linked to Notes may appear enlarged, depending on the font and text size used in the source 1-2-3 file. You may need to widen columns or decrease font sizes in the source file to prevent cell word-wrapping in the linked object.

My 1-2-3 linked object isn't updating properly. You must save a document before creating a link. If the linked object is not updating properly, make sure that the source file has been saved.

Embedding a 1-2-3 Object in Lotus Notes

Embedding a 1-2-3 object differs from linking a 1-2-3 object, in that the object is not connected to the original worksheet. When a 1-2-3 object is embedded, the client application copies the object, and the connection to 1-2-3 is lost. Therefore, updating the worksheet in 1-2-3 does not update the embedded object within Notes. Instead, you must use OLE to activate 1-2-3 (double-click the 1-2-3 object) and directly edit the embedded copy of the object.

You should use object embedding if:

- You want to use 1-2-3 rather than Notes to edit the copy of the embedded 1-2-3 data in the document. (1-2-3 must be installed on your computer.)
- The document is going to be mailed or otherwise separated from your computer, in which case, any file link would be lost.
- Notes users wouldn't have access to the original 1-2-3 file.

TIP Close the 1-2-3 application; you will open it again within Notes, so you do not want two copies of the application open.

To embed a 1-2-3 object in a Notes, document by creating a new object, follow these steps:

1. In the Notes document where you want to embed the 1-2-3 object, position the insertion point and choose Create, Object. The Create Object dialog box appears (see fig. 29.7).

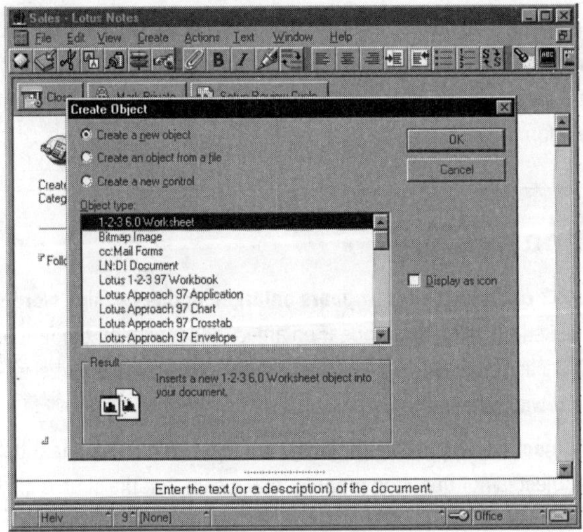

Fig. 29.7
Choose from the list of Object Types to create.

2. Choose Create a New Object. This option enables you to choose the object type and then create the object from within the Notes document.
3. In the list of Object Types, choose Lotus 1-2-3 97 Workbook and choose OK. A 1-2-3 window appears in which you can create the worksheet (see fig. 29.8).

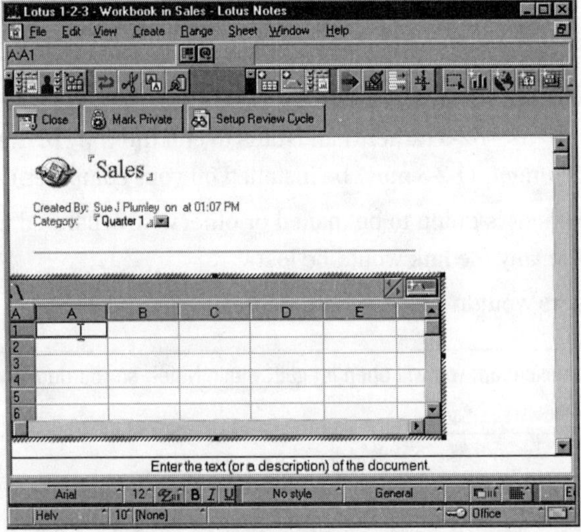

Fig. 29.8
Create a spreadsheet in 1-2-3 as you normally would.

4. Create the worksheet by entering your figures. When you're done, choose File, Close. The 1-2-3 window closes and Notes displays a message asking if you want to save the changes. If you want to use an existing worksheet, see the next set of steps.
5. Choose Yes to save, No to abandon the changes, or Cancel to return to the 1-2-3 worksheet. When you choose Yes, the worksheet appears in the Notes document.

▶ **See** "Working with Cells and Ranges," **p. 55**

To create an object from an existing file, follow these steps:

1. Open the Notes document and position the insertion point.
2. Choose Create, Object. The Create Object dialog box appears.
3. Choose the Create an Object from a File option. The dialog box displays a File text box in which you can enter the path and the file name; alternatively, choose the Browse button to locate the folder and file (see fig. 29.9).

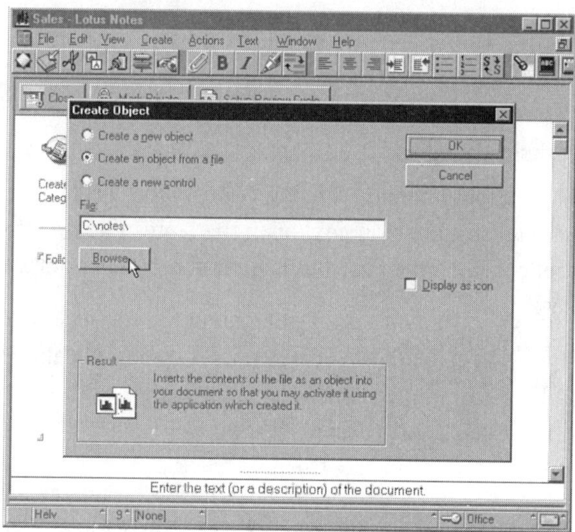

Fig. 29.9
Enter the path or browse for the folder and file you want to embed.

4. Choose OK. The dialog box closes and the object is embedded into your Notes document (see fig. 29.10).

Editing the Linked and Embedded Objects

Linked and embedded 1-2-3 objects behave in different ways. You can see the difference when you modify or edit the linked and embedded objects.

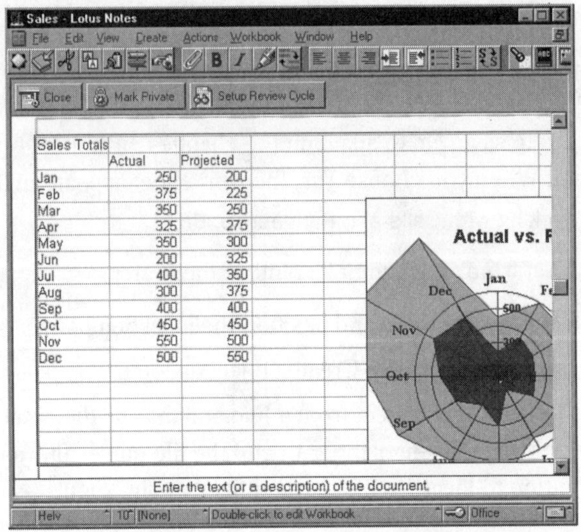

Fig. 29.10
Embedded objects are not linked to any outside source.A linked object maintains a connection to the source. When a change is made in the source worksheet, the change automatically applies to the linked object in Notes.

You can edit a 1-2-3 linked document in Notes in either of two ways:

- Double-click the linked data within Notes to open the server application with the source worksheet in place.
- Open 1-2-3 (without opening or using Notes), edit the 1-2-3 source worksheet, and save the changes. When you next open the Notes document that contains the linked object, it reflects the changes you made in the 1-2-3 worksheet.

A 1-2-3 embedded object in Notes does not maintain a connection with the source worksheet, but you still can edit the object in its server application by double-clicking the object in Notes. This action opens the source application with a *copy or template of the embedded object versus the source document itself.*

Importing and Exporting 1-2-3 Data with Notes

You can import many types of worksheet, word processing, graphics, and text files into Notes documents and views. Because Notes is a Lotus product, it imports 1-2-3 worksheets easily. You also can export Notes views and documents to 1-2-3. These capabilities enable you to share your work with others in your organization more effectively.

You should import 1-2-3 files into Notes rather than use application-sharing tools such as DDE or OLE when:

- The 1-2-3 data file is available to you, but you or other users who need the data do not have access to the 1-2-3 application.
- You want to edit the data in Notes rather than 1-2-3 (for example, you cannot edit linked worksheets in Notes; you can only edit them in the source application).
- The data file is too large for the Clipboard.

Importing a 1-2-3 Worksheet into a Notes Document

One of the most popular uses of Notes and 1-2-3 is to make 1-2-3 worksheets available to an entire organization by means of Notes. When the worksheet file is imported into a document, you can edit and format the text. The imported data is not linked to the original file, so changes made in Notes do not affect the original file.

To import 1-2-3 worksheet data into a Notes document, input the worksheet in a Rich Text field. A Rich Text field is so called because you can enter text and formatting information. You can change color, type style, justification and line spacing, and add tables and graphics to a Notes Rich Text field.

To input the worksheet in a Rich Text field, follow these steps:

CAUTION

Objects and data imported from 1-2-3 worksheets, Word Pro documents, and Freelance Graphics must be placed in a Rich Text field because plain text fields in Notes cannot distinguish formatting and object information.

1. In a Notes database, select or compose a document.
2. Double-click the document to change to Edit mode.
3. Place the insertion point in the Rich Text field where you want the imported file to begin.
4. Choose File, Import. The Import dialog box appears as displayed in figure 29.11.
5. Use the Look In drop-down list to open your work folder.
6. In the Files of Type drop-down list, select Lotus 1-2-3 Worksheet.
7. Select the file you want to import and choose the Import button.
   The 123/Symphony Worksheet Import dialog box appears (see fig. 29.12).

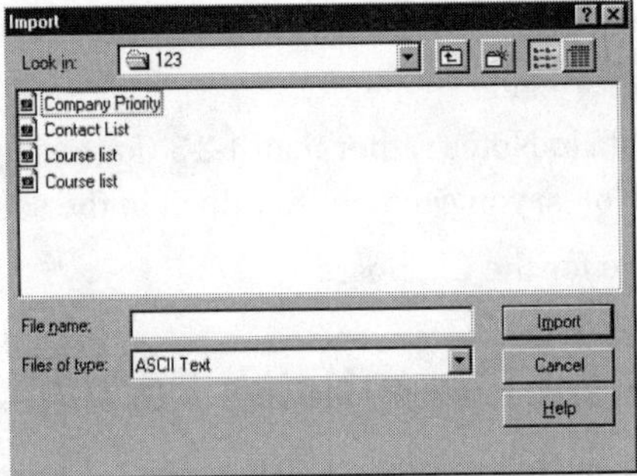

Fig. 29.11
Locate the folder in which you store your 1-2-3 documents.

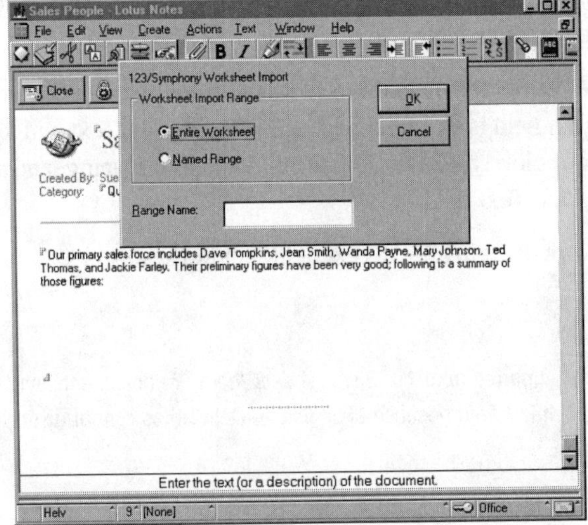

Fig. 29.12
Choose to import a sheet or range.

8. Choose Entire Worksheet or Named Range.

   If you choose Named Range, type the range name in the Range Name text box.

9. Click OK. Notes imports the worksheet into the selected Rich Text field in the document, as shown in figure 29.13.

You now have the capability to edit the data within Notes. You may need to edit the alignment and spacing of the imported worksheet, but the changes will not affect the original 1-2-3 source file.

NOTE To import 1-2-3 data as a database, import it into a Notes view (see "Importing a 1-2-3 Worksheet into a Notes View" later in this chapter). Each worksheet row becomes a document, and each column becomes a field whose contents are the original cell contents.

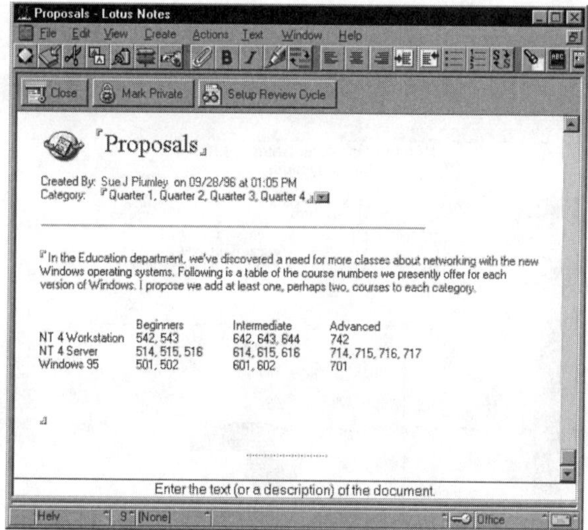

Fig. 29.13
You can edit the worksheet within the Notes document.

Importing a 1-2-3 Graphics File into a Notes Document

Importing a 1-2-3 graphics file or chart into Notes is easy. Sharing 1-2-3 charts and graphs with Notes enables you to distribute important presentations and use Notes as a storage facility for important business graphics. To import a 1-2-3 graphics file into a Notes document, take the following steps:

1. Open the 1-2-3 worksheet that contains the graphic you want to use in Notes.
2. Select the graphic or chart, as displayed in figure 29.14.
3. Open the Edit menu and choose the Copy command to copy the graphic to the Clipboard; alternatively, click the Copy SmartIcon.
4. Switch to Notes; open the database and the document you want to paste the selected graphic into.
5. Place the insertion point in a Rich Text field.

TIP You can use the Edit menu's Paste Special command and the Picture Format option to insert the graphic as an embedded or linked object that you can edit.

6. Open the Edit menu and choose the Paste command. The selected graphic is pasted into the Notes document as shown in figure 29.15.

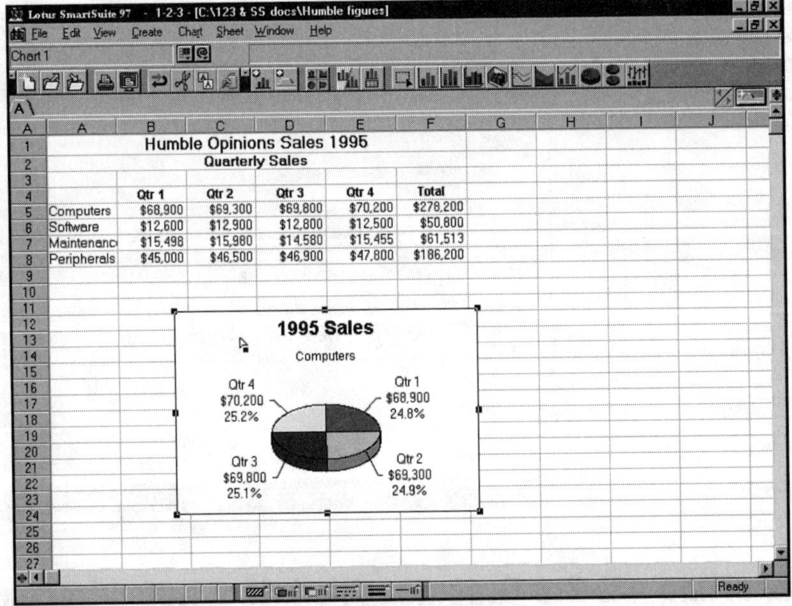

Fig. 29.14
Select the chart you want to import.

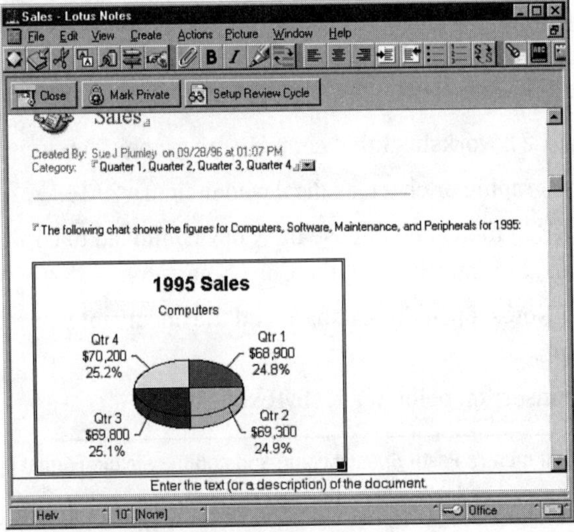

Fig. 29.15
A pasted graphic is the same as an imported graphic.

When you import a graphics file, you can size the object's box but cannot edit the graphic. To size the graphic, drag the handle in the lower-right corner of the imported graphics box.

▶ **See** "Creating an Automatic Chart," **p. 310**

▶ **See** "Manipulating Chart Elements," **p. 322**

TROUBLESHOOTING

My chart looks different in Notes than it did in 1-2-3. Graphics may look different in Notes—colors, fonts, text sizes, and so on—because Notes uses an equivalent to 1-2-3's colors, fonts, and so on. You might try experimenting with the chart in 1-2-3 before importing it to Notes.

I specified a range in my worksheet to import, but only the first page of the range came through. Notes imports only the specified range in the current worksheet; it doesn't import named ranges that span more than one worksheet. You'll have to import the additional pages the range spans, one page at a time.

Exporting Lotus Notes Views to 1-2-3

You can export Notes data so that it can be used in 1-2-3 and other applications. Notes can export a Notes document in text-file format and a Notes view into a worksheet format. For example, you might want to export a list document so you can analyze or format the data in ways that you cannot in Notes.

NOTE No link exists between the exported file and the original Notes view or document, so changes in one file are not reflected in the other.

To export a Notes view to a 1-2-3 file, follow these steps:

1. In Notes, open the database containing the view you want to export. Figure 29.16 shows a sample database in Notes.

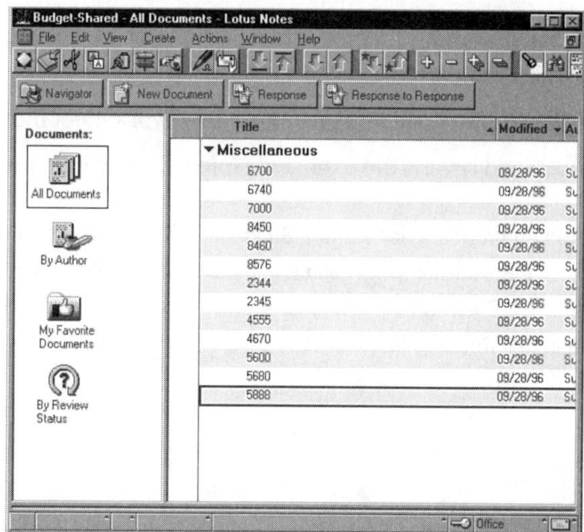

Fig. 29.16
You can export all documents or selected documents.

2. Choose File, Export. The Export dialog box appears, as shown in figure 29.17.

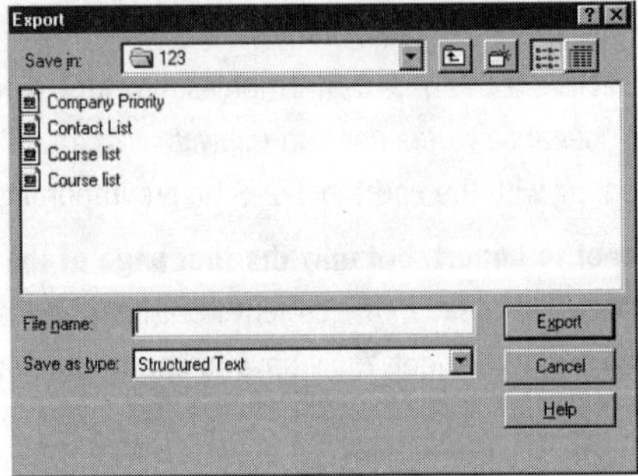

Fig. 29.17
Choose a location and file name for the exported text.

3. In the Save As Type drop-down list, select Lotus 1-2-3 Worksheet. Type the file name and indicate the drive and folder in which you want the file stored and exported.
4. In the File Name box, type a name for the exported file.
5. Choose Export. The 123 Worksheet Export dialog box opens (see fig. 29.18).

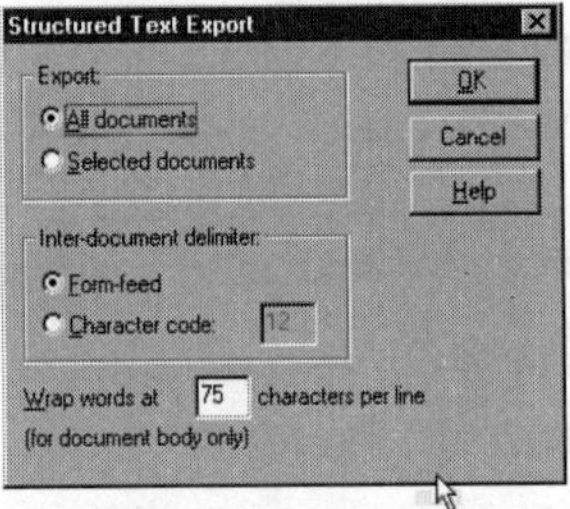

Fig. 29.18
Indicate the options for exporting the document titles.

6. In Export, choose either All Documents or Selected Documents; optionally, choose to Include View Titles.
7. Click OK to export the documents into a 1-2-3 worksheet file.
8. In 1-2-3, open and review the exported Notes document names.

NOTE When you export Notes views to 1-2-3 format, column headings become labels in the first row of the worksheet, and each row in the view becomes a row in the worksheet. Exporting a view to a 1-2-3 worksheet file may be useful if you want to create a graph or chart based on the data in that Notes document.

You can export Notes documents in many different formats. ASCII format is the most common file format that 1-2-3 can read. The process is the same as exporting a Notes view to 1-2-3, except that you must export to ASCII text-file format and then open the file in 1-2-3 as a text file. Follow these steps:

1. In Notes, open the database and the document you want to export text from (see fig. 29.19).

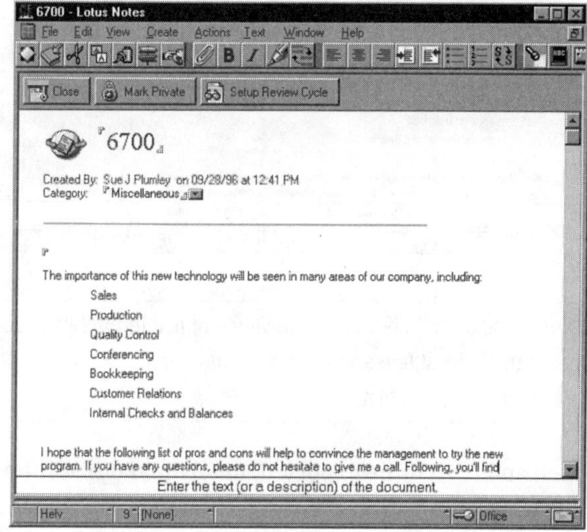

Fig. 29.19
Export an entire Notes document to 1-2-3.

2. Choose File, Export. The Export dialog box appears, as shown in figure 29.20.

If you want to export part of the Notes document instead of the entire document, select the text, then copy and paste it to the 1-2-3 worksheet.

3. In the Save as Type list, select ASCII Text.
4. In the File Name text box, type a name for the file, and then specify the drive and folder in which you want the file to be stored and exported. Select the Export button.
5. The Text File Export dialog box appears. Specify the number of characters that will make a new line or word wrap (see fig. 29.21) and choose OK.

Fig. 29.20
Save the Notes document as an ASCII or other text file.

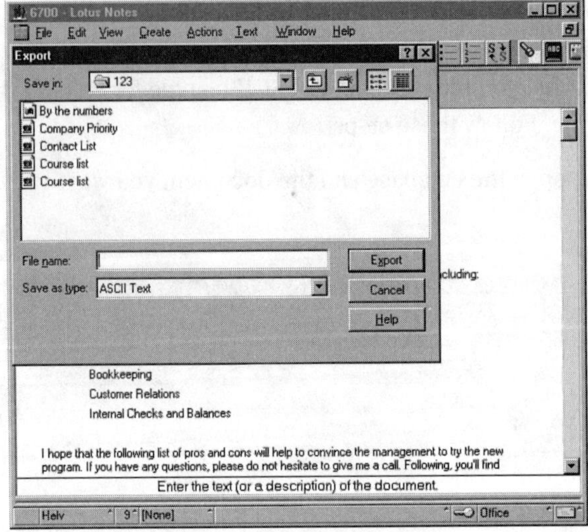

TIP 75 characters per line is the default; however, if the lines of text in the Notes document are longer, you might count the longest line and enter that number in the text box. The font you use may also affect the number of characters.

6. In 1-2-3, open and review the exported, unformatted ASCII text file.

FIG. 29.21
Estimate the number of characters per line for the text.

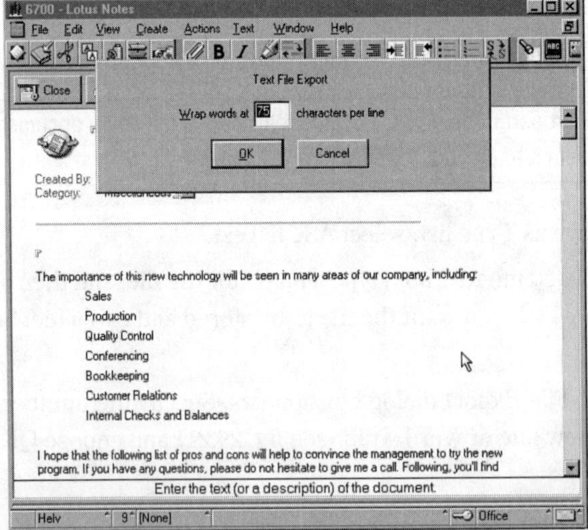

CHAPTER 30

Team Computing

Lotus 1-2-3 97 wasn't developed solely for people to work with worksheets individually. 1-2-3 97 provides tools specially designed for today's crash-and-burn business environment—in which people work together.

1-2-3 provides numerous Team features to enable participants in a project to send messages about files, route files via e-mail or Notes, enter review comments about a worksheet, manage the revisions from the team, and even post a worksheet to the company's Web site.

This chapter covers the most important operations available via the Team features in 1-2-3, highlighting key features along the way. ■

Create an e-mail message using TeamMail

Learn how 1-2-3 97 works with your e-mail software to forward a worksheet as a message or as an attachment.

Consolidate versions from several people

TeamConsolidate lets you use changes received from team members, and the Versions feature enables you to store different sets of changes in a single file.

Share information with Lotus Notes

With Lotus Notes you can share worksheets with team members easily. You have control over who can create, read, or edit the worksheet. This will allow you to include worksheets in your workflow process

Use 1-2-3 with the Internet

You won't be left behind with the impending rush to the Internet. You can save and retrieve worksheets directly from Internet sites, even generate documents for displaying on your company's Web site.

Using TeamMail

Businesses are exploiting the rich capabilities of e-mail in ever-increasing volumes. Employees, contract resources, and customers are sharing e-mail via internal networks, dial-up mail, online services, and the Internet. These connections make it possible to share messages and documents, so that recipients cannot only have a record of when information was received, but also have copies of document files on hand for editing, printing, and more.

Previously, sending an e-mail message—or even sending a message with a file from the 1-2-3 application—required that you switch out of the application, launch your e-mail application, and create the message. The 1-2-3 97 TeamMail feature enables you to create the e-mail message within your worksheet application. After you've completed creating the message, TeamMail sends it directly to the outbox of your e-mail program (for example, Microsoft Exchange on a network) or Notes Mail (used to manage mail with other mail systems and the Internet). Then, you can simply send the message from your e-mail program during a later e-mail session, if your e-mail isn't configured to automatically send messages from the outbox.

Sending or Routing a Message

Sending an e-mail message from within 1-2-3 is easy. You can choose whether to send each message simultaneously to all recipients you list; or, you can route the message, so that the first recipient must review it and comment on it, then send it on to the next recipient, and so on.

Follow these steps to use TeamMail:

1. If you want to send the current worksheet as a message attachment, save it and leave the file open.

   If you want your TeamMail message to include a selection from the current worksheet, drag to make your selection.
2. Choose File, TeamMail. The TeamMail dialog box appears, as shown in figure 30.1.
3. Select whether to send the entire worksheet as an attachment to the message or a message only (and any other available options that you prefer) by clicking the appropriate options in the TeamMail dialog box.
4. Click OK. The Mail Login dialog box showing your mail ID and requesting a password will appear for certain mail applications such as Lotus Notes.

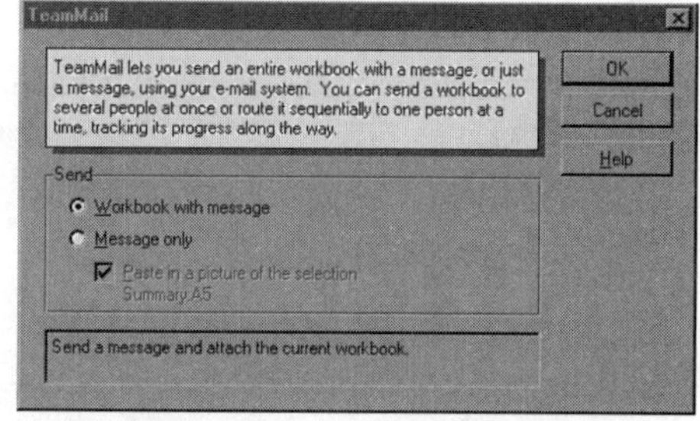

Fig. 30.1
The TeamMail dialog box for 1-2-3 lets you send the whole worksheet file as an attachment to a message (the default option, which is shown selected here) or a message only.

5. The TeamMail dialog box for creating messages appears (see fig. 30.2).
6. Click the letter icon at the far right end of the first Recipient line to add the e-mail addresses of persons to send the message to. The Names dialog box appears (see fig. 30.3).

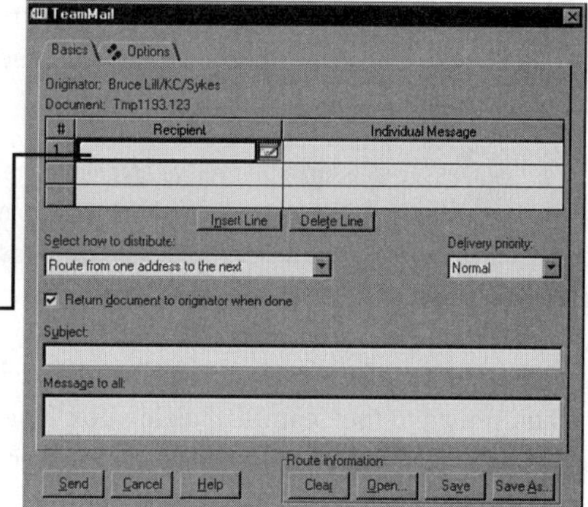

Click here to select recipients

Fig. 30.2
The Basics panel in the TeamMail dialog box enables you to create and address messages.

7. (Optional) If you have more than one address book, click the down-arrow for the Address Book option in the Names dialog box, then click to select the e-mail address book that contains the recipient(s) to whom you want to send the message.
8. Start typing the first name of the recipient in the Find Name box at the top left side of the dialog box. The address box below will automatically go to the first person that starts with the letters you typed. You can use the letter tabs on the right of the address box to select the group of people in the address book who's first initial matches the tabbed letter.

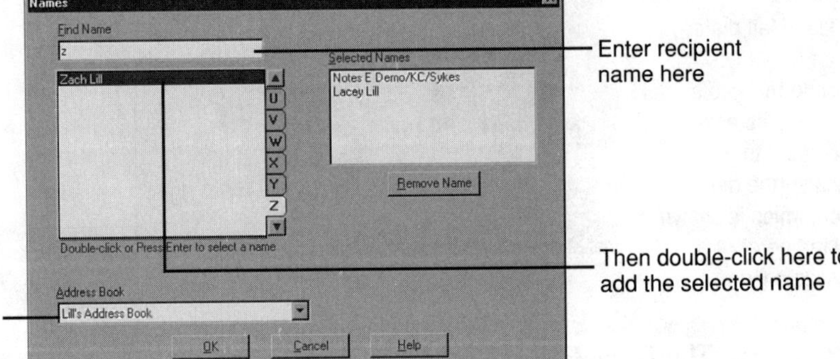

Fig. 30.3
This Names dialog box lets you select recipients from your e-mail address book.

9. Double-click on the name or press enter to add the name to the recipient list at the right side of the dialog box.
10. Repeat steps 7, 8, and 9 as needed to add more recipients to the mailing list. If you're routing the message, make sure you add recipients in the correct routing order. If you're planning to route the message to multiple recipients, the order in the list is the order in which the worksheet will be routed.

NOTE The steps for addressing messages assume that you've entered the recipient names and e-mail addresses you need in your e-mail address book. You cannot mail to a person who is not in your e-mail address book. If the recipient is not in your e-mail address book, you will have to switch to the e-mail program and add the person.

11. When you've finished selecting all the message recipients, click OK to close the Names dialog box and return to the TeamMail dialog box. The TeamMail dialog box will list the recipients you specified, each in its own row under Recipient, as shown in figure 30.4.

TIP If you want to save the list of recipients for reuse later, use the Save buttons at the bottom of the TeamMail dialog box. See the next section for details.

NOTE If you made a mistake entering the order of your recipients, when you are back to the Basics panel of the TeamMail dialog box, you can select a recipient, then click the Insert Line button to add a blank line so you can insert a blank recipient line within the list or the Delete Line button to remove the selected recipient. To change the order of recipients, you will have to delete and insert the names to get the right order. Clicking the Clear button in the Route Information area in the bottom right corner of the dialog box clears all recipients you've entered so you can start over.

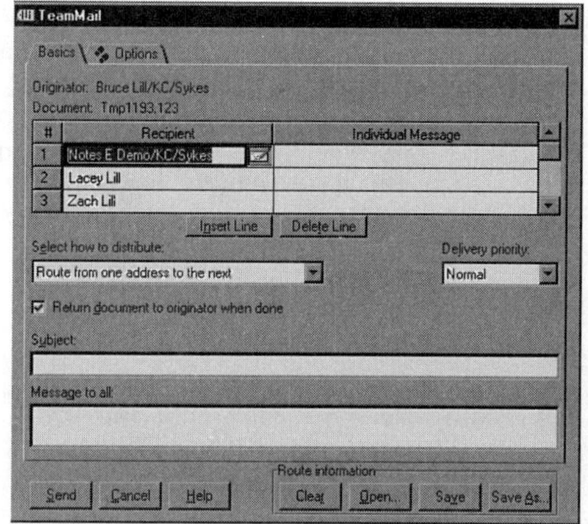

Fig. 30.4
The TeamMail dialog box lists the recipients you specified, each in its own row under Recipient.

12. (Optional) You can send a private message, to each recipient, if needed, using the Individual Message column. The individual message you type beside a recipient's name appears in the message sent to that recipient only, in addition to the general message text and any file attachment added to the message. To add a private message for a recipient, click to position the insertion point in the Individual Message cell beside the appropriate Recipient name, then type a brief message. The character limit is 129 characters.
13. Make a choice from the Select How to Distribute drop-down list box to indicate whether you would like to Route from one address to the next (route the message) or Send to all addresses at once.
14. If the message includes an attached file, specify whether the recipient(s) should Return Document to Originator When Done by leaving the box checked if you would like the recipient(s) to return the file to you with comments or by clicking the check box to clear it if you need not see the file with comments.
15. (Optional) If enabled on your system, use the Delivery Priority drop-down list box to specify whether the message should be treated by recipients as a high, normal, or low priority item.
16. Enter an identifying subject line for the message by clicking in the Subject text box and typing a key phrase recipients can use to screen the message. This will appear as the subject line in the recipients e-mail.
17. Click in the Message to All text box, and type the message text that you want all recipients to receive. This text will appear as the body in the recipients e-mail. At this point, your message might resemble figure 30.5.

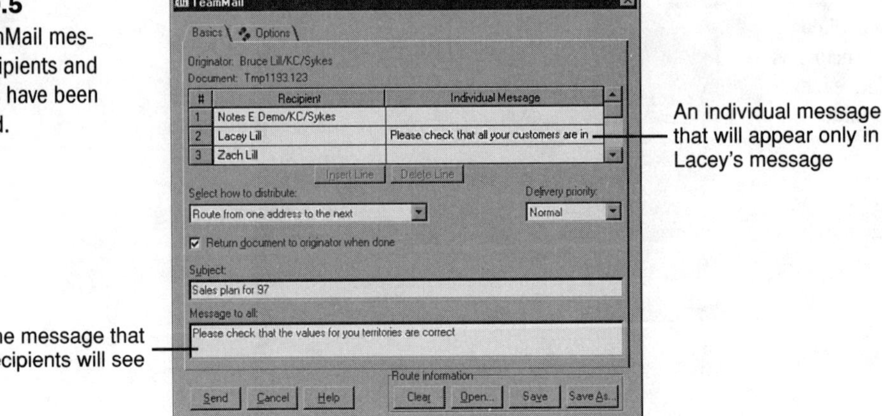

Fig. 30.5
The TeamMail message recipients and contents have been specified.

18. (Optional) Click the Options tab to display additional choices (see fig. 30.6). The check boxes in the top area of the tab labeled To Track Document Progress are only available for routed messages. The check boxes under Mail Message Send Options are available for all messages. Choose the options you want by clicking to check the applicable check box:

    - Send Message to Originator When Document is Forwarded—TeamMail dialog box: Tells your mail system to send you a notification message when each recipient forwards the attached message document.
    - Send Message to Alternate When Document is Forwarded—Rather than notifying you, the mail system can notify another person, such as an assistant, each time the attached document is forwarded. Check this option, then click the icon at the right end of the text box below it to display the Names dialog box so that you can choose the e-mail address for the alternate recipient from your address book.
    - Include Routed Document with Tracking Messages—If you select one of the preceding options, checking this option ensures that the notification message includes a copy of the routed document, so that you can review it for in-progress changes.
    - Allow Recipients to Modify Route—Check this option to enable recipients to change the e-mail addresses included on the routing list.
    - Send Return Mail Receipt when Mail Message is Opened—Select to have your e-mail system notify you when each forwarded message is received and opened, rather than later when the message is forwarded.
    - Save a Copy of this Message—Check this option to ensure that TeamMail saves a copy of the message in your e-mail for your reference.

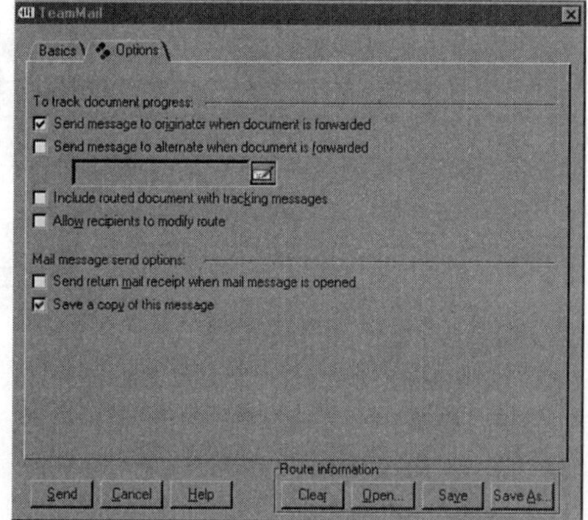

Fig. 30.6
After you've specified the message contents, you can control how it's handled by TeamMail using these options.

19. After you've specified the options you need, click the Send button in the TeamMail dialog box. Then, 1-2-3 97 sends the prepared e-mail message and any file attachment to your e-mail outbox.
20. Use your e-mail system to send the message, if it isn't configured to send outbox messages periodically. For example, you could start Lotus Notes, click the Replicator tab, then click Send & Receive Mail, to send the message.

Once it's been sent from TeamMail to your e-mail system, you can work with the message just as you would a normal message. For example, figure 30.7 shows how the message displayed in figure 30.5 and its attached file appear when received in a recipient's Lotus Notes Mail database. You can use your e-mail commands to reply to or forward the message, and you can open and save file attachments as you normally would. The only technique that requires a slightly different approach is working with a routed message or file, which you'll learn about shortly in the section called "Reviewing a Routed File Attachment."

TROUBLESHOOTING

The TeamMail command is disabled, or I get an error message when I try to send TeamMail. What's wrong? Either your e-mail system isn't compatible with 1-2-3's TeamMail, or you don't have an e-mail system installed. Make sure the e-mail system is a true Windows 95 application, or you'll have problems making it work. You'll need to use the WIN32 version of Lotus Notes for 1-2-3 97 to work together correctly. If you use Microsoft Exchange, then refer to your Windows 95 documentation and Special Edition Using Windows 95 for more about using e-mail and Exchange for Windows 95. For example, even when you have Exchange installed, you have to configure it to work with other services like CompuServe Mail or your Internet e-mail program.

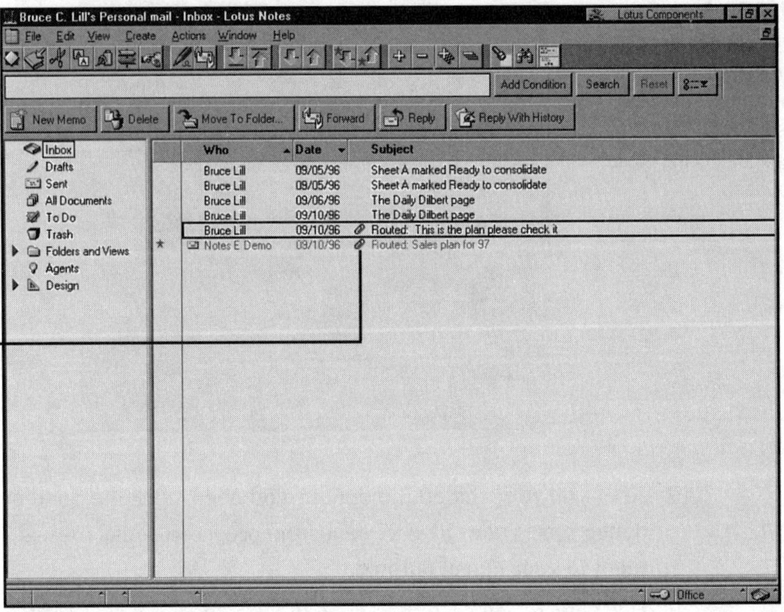

Fig. 30.7
Received TeamMail messages appear in an e-mail inbox like normal messages.

The paper clip indicator identifies the file attachment in Exchange

Saving a Recipient List

If you use e-mail much at all, you know how frequently you send messages to a single group or two of people. Most e-mail applications enable you to save a group of recipient addresses in a mailing list, to save you the time of choosing recipients one by one. Because you address messages in TeamMail, TeamMail also enables you to save lists of recipients. It even saves the recipients in the order in which you entered them, so that you can use the list to correctly route messages. Even though the TeamMail dialog box implies that you only can save routing information, I've found that you can use a saved routing (recipient) list to send a message simultaneously to the recipients.

To save a routing list:

1. Choose File, TeamMail. In the first TeamMail dialog box, specify the basic message options you wish, then click OK.
2. In the Names dialog box, specify the recipients for the message as described earlier in this chapter.
3. Back in the Basics panel of the TeamMail dialog box, click the Save button in the Route Information area in the lower-right corner of the dialog box. The Save dialog box, shown in Figure 30.8, appears. You'll notice that this dialog box resembles many file-saving dialog boxes you'll see throughout 1-2-3.

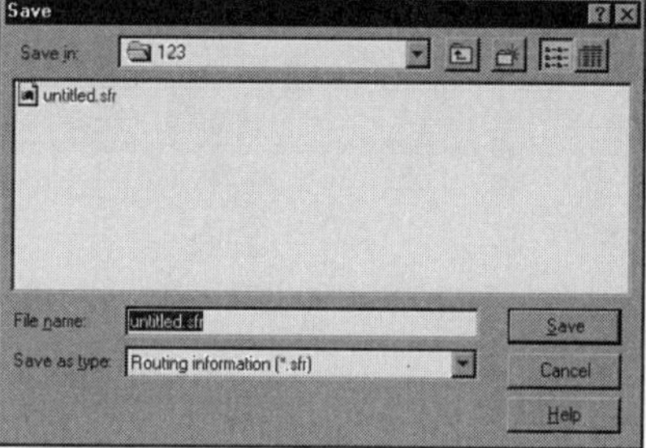

Fig. 30.8
You save and name a routing list file much as you save other 1-2-3 files.

4. (Optional) Use the Save In list box to specify another drive or folder to save the routing information file to.
5. Type the name for the routing file in the File Name text box. For example, if your list holds the names of key decision-makers in your company's sales department, you could type "Sales."
6. Click Save to finish saving the routing list.
7. Finish creating the message and send it, or simply click Cancel to close TeamMail.

To use a routing list once you've saved it, start your TeamMail message as usual. Then, instead of clicking the icon at the right end of the first Recipient line in the TeamMail dialog box, click the Open button in the Route Information area at the lower right corner of the dialog box. Select the routing file you want by clicking its name in the Look In list, then click OK.

After you open a routing list, you can make changes as normal to the list of recipients shown in the TeamMail dialog box. You can save your changes to the routing list by clicking the Save button in the Route information area; or, to save the changed list as a new routing list, click the Save As button, enter a name for the file in the Save As dialog box, then click OK.

Reviewing a Routed File Attachment

To review a file routed with TeamMail, you have to open the worksheet with 1-2-3 97. How you do so depends on the capabilities of your e-mail system. Using some e-mail systems, you may need to save the routed file attachment to a folder on your hard disk. In others, such as Lotus Notes or Microsoft Exchange, you can simply open the e-mail message containing the file attachment, then double-click the icon for the attachment (see Figure 37.9).

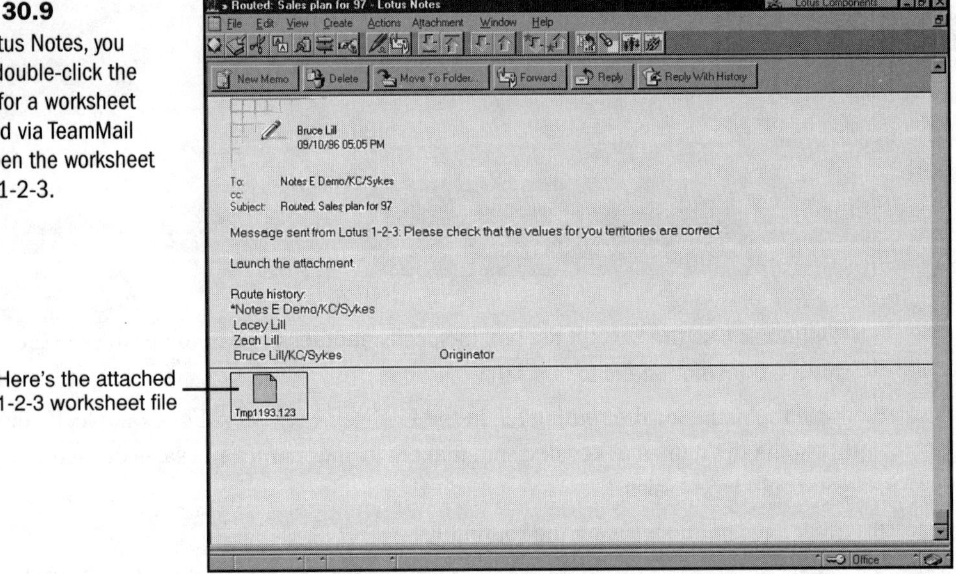

Fig. 30.9
In Lotus Notes, you can double-click the icon for a worksheet routed via TeamMail to open the worksheet with 1-2-3.

No matter which method you use to open the worksheet, when it opens, the TeamMail routing dialog box (see fig. 30.10) appears automatically. Your name will be the top one in the Contributor/Action list, and will be highlighted. If needed, drag the TeamMail dialog box out of the way to review the contents of the routed file.

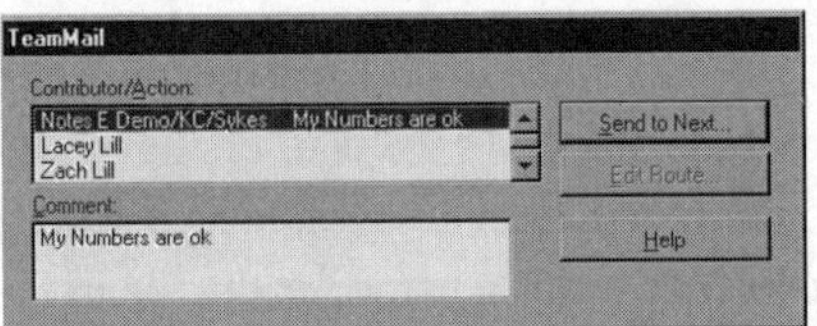

Fig. 30.10
When you open a routed file, this dialog box appears to enable you to comment about the file and send it on to the next recipient.

To route the message to others on the routing list, simply click in the Comment text box in the TeamMail dialog box and type the message you'd like to display in this dialog box for the rest of the reviewers. If the sender selected the Allow Recipients to Modify Route on the Options tab in the TeamMail dialog box (refer to fig. 30.6), then the Edit Route button will be enabled. Clicking the Edit Route button will enable you to select the name of the next recipient. When you're done, click the Send to Next button. A message box will appear, asking you to verify that you want to send the worksheet to the next recipient named on the list. Click OK to continue.

TeamMail creates a message containing the routed worksheet, addresses the message to the next recipient, sends the message to your e-mail outbox, and closes the routed file. If the sender also asks TeamMail to verify when a routed file is opened or forwarded, the appropriate message will be created and added to the outbox, as well. From there, you can use your e-mail program's commands to send the TeamMail messages.

If you open the file directly from an e-mail message, the Save As dialog box appears, so you can save a copy of the worksheet. Type a name in the File Name text box, then click the Save button.

Sending a Worksheet Selection with TeamReview

Preparing a worksheet for TeamReview is straightforward. Basically, TeamReview starts the TeamMail feature, enabling you to distribute a selection from the current worksheet via e-mail. Note that you can't distribute an entire workbook file with TeamReview, only a selection. To send a workbook use the TeamMail feature.

To send a selection from a 1-2-3 worksheet to others for TeamReview, follow these steps:

1. Enter the needed data and save the worksheet.
2. Choose File, TeamReview. The TeamReview Assistant dialog box appears (see fig. 30.11).
3. To select the range of cells that you want to send, click the range selector icon beside the range text box, drag in the worksheet to select the range, then click the enter (check) button to close the range selector dialog box.
4. Click OK to continue. The TeamReview dialog box appears. It verifies the range that you previously selected in the Range text box. If you want to change the range, you can click the button beside the Range text box, then specify a new range as described in the preceding step.

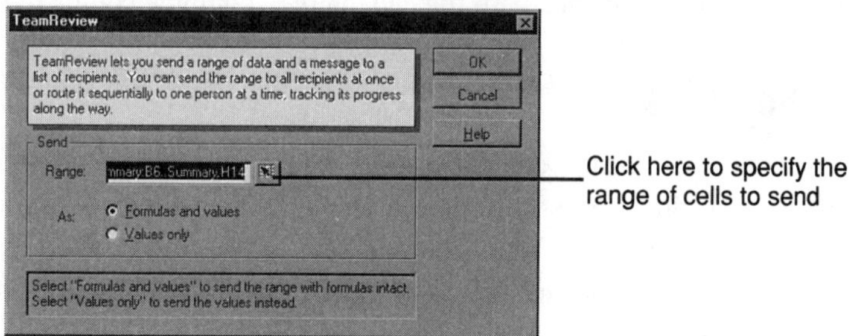

Fig. 30.11
This dialog box in 1-2-3 enables you to specify which cells will be distributed for review.

5. Click the appropriate option to select it. The Formulas and Values choice will send the selected range with formulas intact, so the recipient can see how values are calculated. The Values Only choice converts any cells containing formulas to their displayed values only, so the recipient sees only the values.
6. Click OK. TeamReview displays a message box asking you to verify the send operation. While this dialog box is on-screen, you can work with the worksheet data to make final changes before sending it.
7. Click Send. The TeamMail dialog box appears.
8. Address the TeamReview message as you would any TeamMail message, and enter any message text that you prefer.
9. Click Send. The TeamMail dialog box closes and sends the TeamReview message to your e-mail outbox, from which you should send it on to its recipients.

If you receive and open a TeamReview file in 1-2-3, the TeamMail dialog box appears. You can both edit the worksheet data that appears and enter a comment in the TeamMail dialog box. When you've finished, click the Return to Originator button in the TeamMail dialog box. Click OK in the message box that asks you to verify the send, and use the Save As dialog box if it appears to save the TeamReview file to your hard disk. Then, send the message from your e-mail outbox.

Consolidating Data with TeamConsolidate

After distributing a range for your team to review and revise, you will need to combine the team's changes into one file. Depending upon which method you used to route the range to your team members. If you used TeamReview to route the range of a worksheet, then you will use the Merge Versions feature to combine each reviewer's revisions into the original workbook. With the Share Sheets using Lotus Notes feature, the Lotus Notes database will provide you with the capability to combine completed versions.

Merging Versions

When you receive the data back from the reviewers you'll want to merge their changes into your original worksheet. You will then be able to select which versions you'll want to use in your workbook. This is great for project budgeting, where you'll have team members updating the information at different times. You can then see what the budget was to start with and the changes along the way.

To merge the reviewers data into your workbook follow these steps;

1. Open the original worksheet
2. In your e-mail system launch the attachment in the message from the reviewer. After 1-2-3 loads the file from the reviewer, the TeamMail dialog box appears. You can click the reviewer's name in the Contributor/Action list to see that reviewer's comment below.
3. If you agree with changes from the reviewer and want to merge those changes into your original file, click the Merge button. The TeamReview Merge Data dialog box appears, as in figure 30.12.

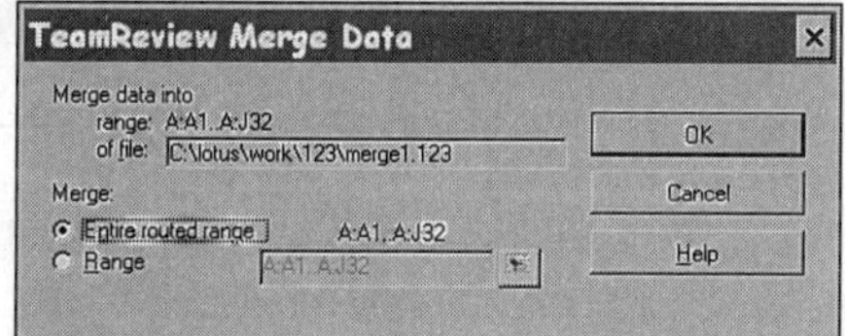

Fig. 30.12
Use this dialog box to merge 1-2-3 revisions from a reviewer.

4. Choose a Merge option:
   - Leaving Entire Routed Range selected merges all the cells from the received message into the original workbook.
   - Click the Range radio button to select a range, click the icon beside its text box, and drag to select the range to merge as shown in figure 30.13.
5. Click OK. If the selected range contains data, a warning message tells you the destination cells already contain data.
6. Click Keep Both to store both versions of the data, or Overwrite to have the reviewer's data simply replace the original data.
7. Now you are back at the TeamReview dialog box where you can select a different reviewer's data to merge in, or close the worksheet if your done.

When you view the worksheet that contains the merged data, there will be a box around the merged range with a title as in figure 30.14. When you click the icon at the right of the title you will see a list of the versions that you can select from. The data from the version selected will be used in the workbook.

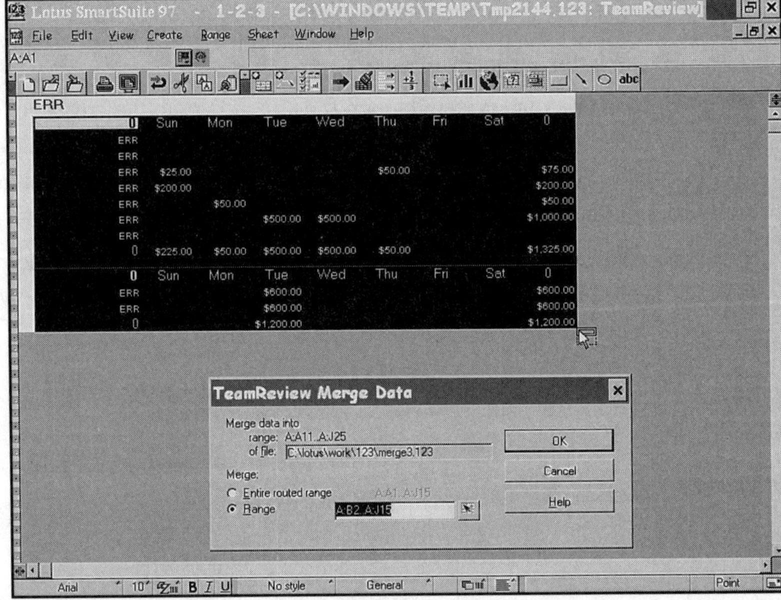

Fig. 30.13 TeamReview Merge Data.

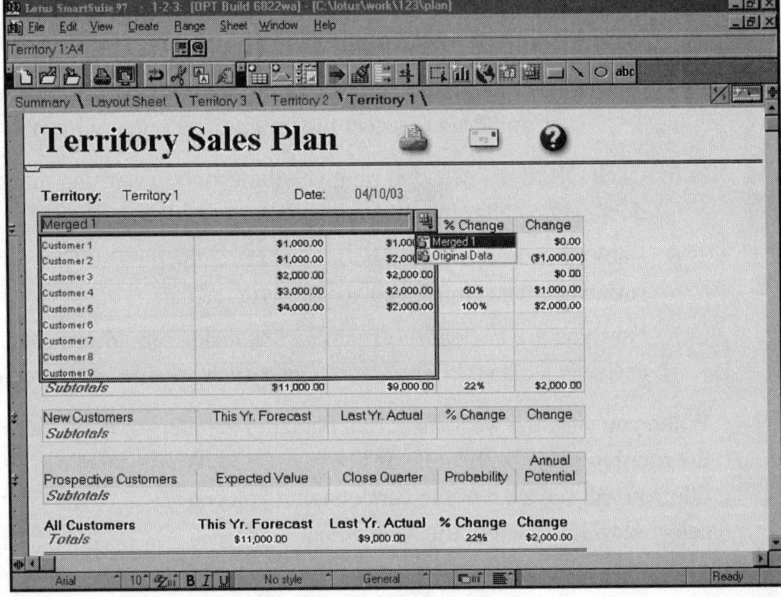

Fig. 30.14 Merged data in a worksheet.

When you have a workbook with merged ranges in it you will see the menu selection File, TeamConsolidate, Merge Versions is now enabled. If you choose Merge Versions when working with a reviewer's file, 1-2-3 presents a dialog box that you can use to merge different versions of the file as shown in figure 30.15. You select the files you want to merge by date.

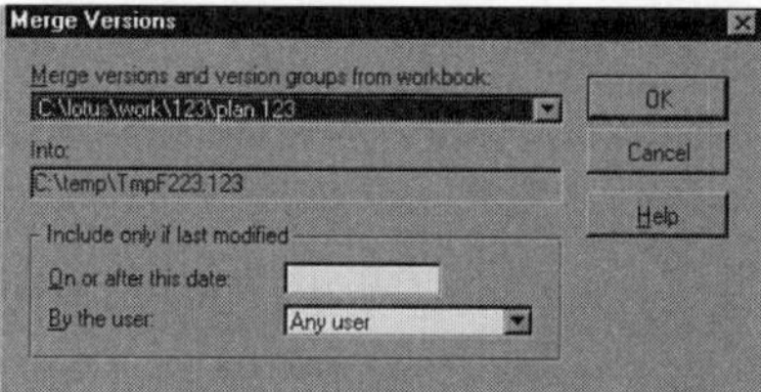

Fig. 30.15
Use this dialog box to merge a version in a workbook.

Use File, Close to close the reviewer's file. The original file appears, with a special window to indicate any data that's been merged (refer to fig. 30.14). Be sure to save your merged file.

Sharing Worksheets with Lotus Notes

You can share a 1-2-3 workbook with other team members by using a Lotus Notes database to hold the workbook and the revisions the team members make. Each team member will access a Notes document to make their changes. This will allow you to build a work flow of the review process. The contributors won't have to know anything about 1-2-3 to make the revisions. The Lotus Notes database that you will use, will be created with the Lotus Notes template file named teamcons.ntf . Teamcons.ntf was copied into your Lotus Notes data directory during the installation of 1-2-3.

Starting the Process Make sure you have Lotus Notes installed on you computer and a database was created with the Teamcons.ntf file. Then, to share a file, do as follows.

NOTE This feature will only work with Lotus Notes versions 4.1 or later. I would highly recommend you have at least 16M of RAM in your computer.

1. In 1-2-3 open the file you want to share, then select File, TeamConsolidate, Share Sheets Using Lotus Notes, this will bring up the Share Sheets using Lotus Notes dialog box. This is shown in figure 30.16.
2. Select Go to Lotus Notes to continue or cancel to exit back to the worksheet. When you select go to Lotus Notes, Lotus Notes will be launched so you can open the database in which you'll store the workbook.

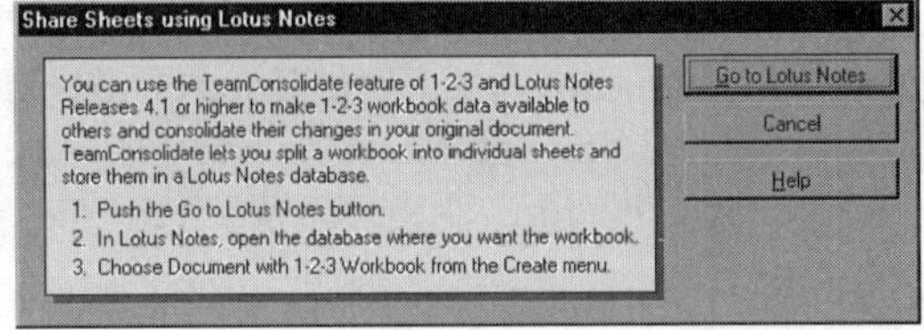

Fig. 30.16
Share Sheets using Lotus Notes.

3. In Lotus Notes open the database that was created with the Teamcons.ntf template. Click the button labeled Create 1-2-3 Workbook Document that appears on the Action bar at the top of the view.

   A new document will be created and the Create Document with 1-2-3 Workbook dialog box appears as shown in figure 30.17.

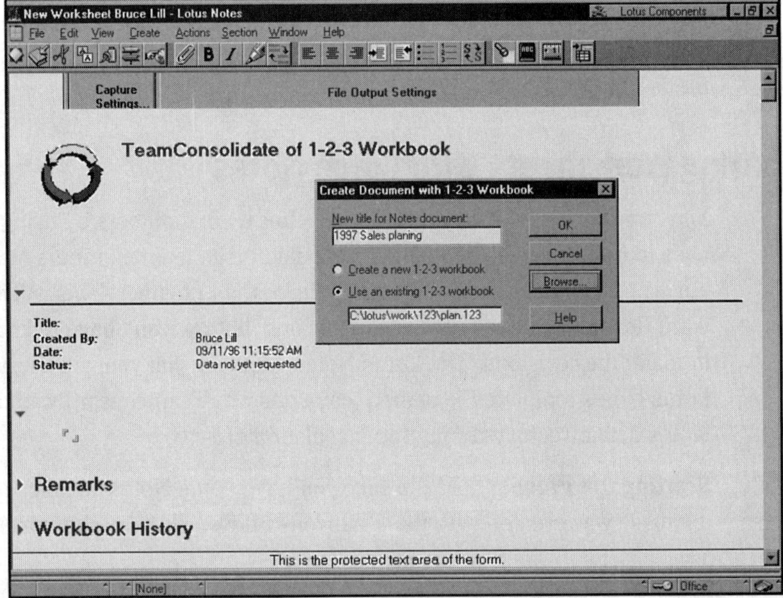

Fig. 30.17
Create Document with 1-2-3.

4. Enter a title for the document in the New Title for Notes Document list box. This title will be used in the Notes database views.
5. Select Create a New 1-2-3 Workbook to be placed back in 1-2-3 with a new workbook or select the default of Use an Existing 1-2-3 Workbook.
6. Enter the name of the existing workbook if you know it or select Browse to bring up the Open a File dialog box.

7. Click OK. The workbook that you selected with be retrieved and stored in the Notes Document as an embedded OLE object. The Shared 1-2-3 Workbook Document Created dialog box will appear if everything was successful. You now have the choice of selecting the team members that will review the workbook now or later. If you select to choose the recipients later, then when you do want to select them use the Request Workbook from the Action menu.
8. Click Now to select how to distribute the workbook. The Request Workbook Data dialog box as shown in figure 30.18 appears.

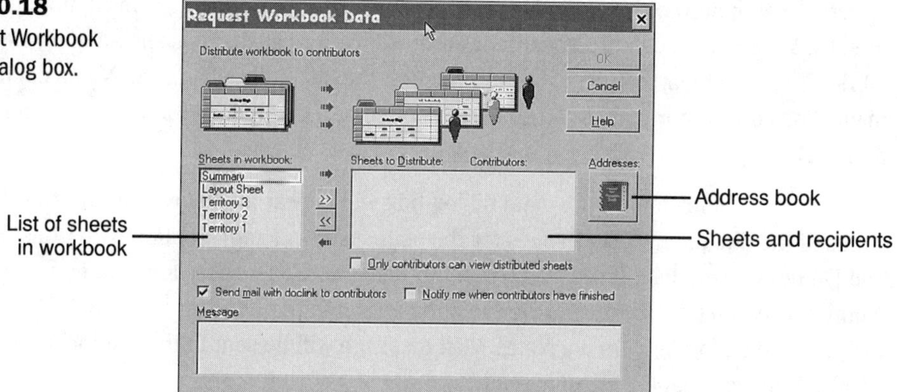

Fig. 30.18
Request Workbook Data dialog box.

9. Select the sheet out of the workbook that you want to distribute by clicking on the sheet's name in the Sheets in Workbook list box on the left. This will cause the sheet's name to move to the Sheets to Distribute list box with the Contributor listed as Enter recipients name.
10. In the Sheets to Distribute list box select the sheet you want to distribute and click the button with the address book on it. This will bring up the Address Book dialog box for you to select the contributor(s) from.
11. Select the desired options in the dialog box:
    - Only Contributor(s) May View Distributed Sheets—This selection will make the contributors documents visible to the group. Anyone else will not see the documents in the database. This can be used for sensitive information, such as salaries, that should be restricted to a few people.
    - Send Mail with Doclink to Contributor(s)—This will cause a Notes mail message to be sent to each contributor with a doclink back to this document. This is a way of notifying them that the worksheet is ready for them. If this is not selected, you will have to notify them that their input is requested some other way.

- Notify Me when Contributors Have Finished—This will cause a Notes Mail message to be sent to you when all of the contributors have completed their changes.
- The Message list box is for you to enter a message for all of the contributors.

12. Click OK. This will create a separate Notes document for each sheet you are going to distribute.

Consolidating Information from Contributors The Contributors will access the Notes Document with their name on it by clicking the doclink in the Notes Mail message (if you selected that option) or by going to the Notes Database and selecting the document directly. When they open the document there will be a worksheet as shown in figure 30.19. This is the neat feature of OLE 2, you edit the sheet directly in the Notes document. The contributor makes the changes needed and then clicks the Done button in the Action Bar.

The Status of Contributor Document dialog box will appear and allow the user to set the status of the document. The choices for the status are: In Progress, Ready to Consolidate, and Do not Consolidate. If the status is set to Ready to Consolidate and you have set the Notify Me When Contributors Have Finished option in the Request Workbook Data (refer to fig. 30.18) dialog box, then a Notes Mail message will be sent to the original requester (you) telling you that the sheet is ready.

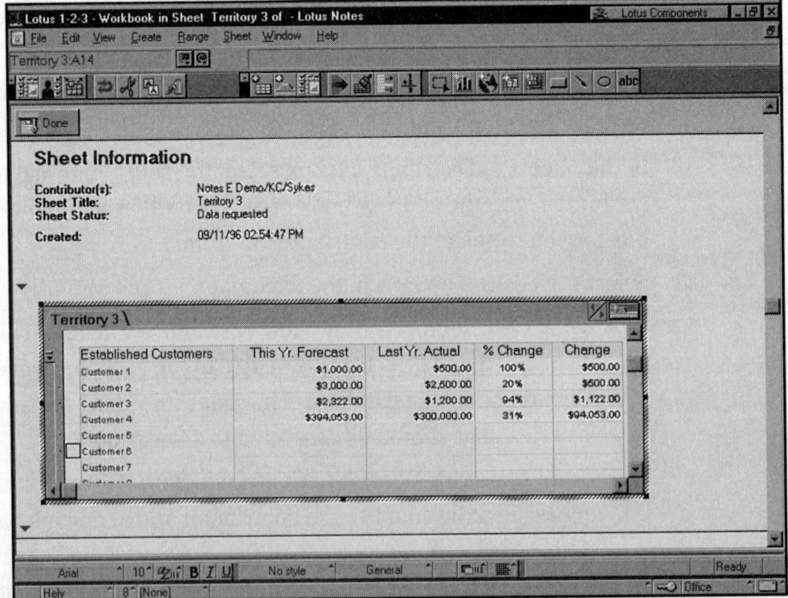

Fig. 30.19
Worksheet as it appears in a Notes document.

When you receive contributor data, you consolidate it by following these steps:

1. To consolidate the changes, open the main document and click the Consolidate Worksheet Data button on the Action bar. The Consolidate Worksheet Data dialog box comes up enabling you to make some choices before consolidation (see figure 30.20):
   - Consolidate Only Documents Marked "Ready to Consolidate"—This is checked by default, so only the documents that the contributors have set the status to Ready to Consolidate are used. If this is not checked then the In Progress documents are also consolidated.
   - Delete Contributors' Documents After Consolidating—The default is not checked and the contributors documents aren't deleted.

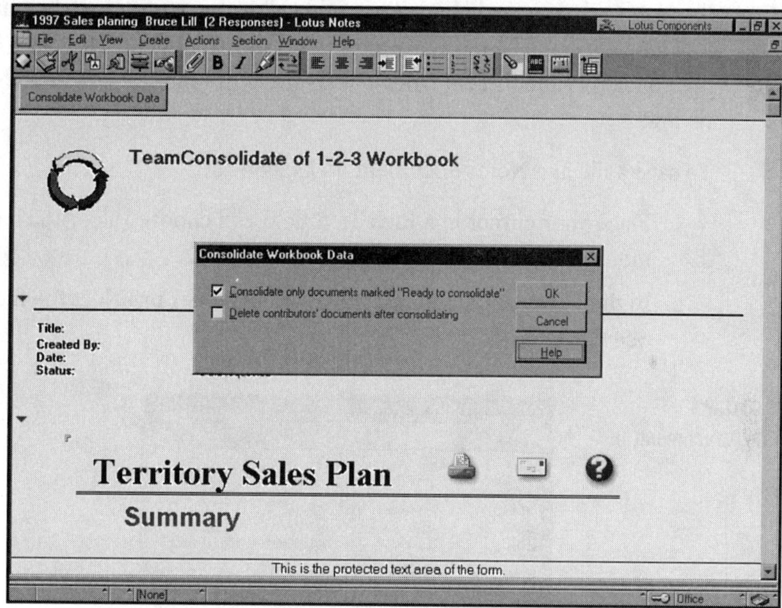

Fig. 30.20 Consolidate Worksheet Data.

2. After setting your options click OK to consolidate the documents. When the consolidation is complete you'll see a dialog box stating that everything is consolidated. The workbook in the main document now has the changes from all the reviewers documents.
3. If you want the workbook saved as a file, then click the Detach 1-2-3 Workbook button that now appears in the Action Bar. The Request Workbook Data button is also visible in the Action Bar. The Request Workbook Data button will let you send requests out again if desired.

Sharing Files Between 1-2-3 and Notes

When you use the TeamMail feature to distribute your worksheets for review, only the originator and the current reviewer know the status of the review. When you use Lotus Notes, everyone can see what is happening to all the worksheets that are being reviewed. You bring the reviewers to the information instead of sending the information to each reviewer. 1-2-3 files can be attached to a Notes document like it was with TeamMail or embedded as an OLE object as it was with the Share Sheets using Lotus Notes feature.

Saving a 1-2-3 File in Notes

1-2-3 files can only be saved in a Rich Text field in the Notes document. To tell if the field is a Rich Text field, put the cursor in the field and look at the status bar at the bottom of the Notes window. Only Rich Text fields allow the font type to be changed, if you see the font name such as Helv, then you are in a Rich Text field. The body field in the Notes Mail memo form is a Rich Text field. This is where TeamMail attached the workbook file for review.

To save a file in a Notes document do as follows;

1. Place your cursor in a Rich Text field and choose File, Attach or click the Attachment SmartIcon.
2. In the Create Attachment(s) dialog box, enter or select the file you want to attach. See figure 30.21.

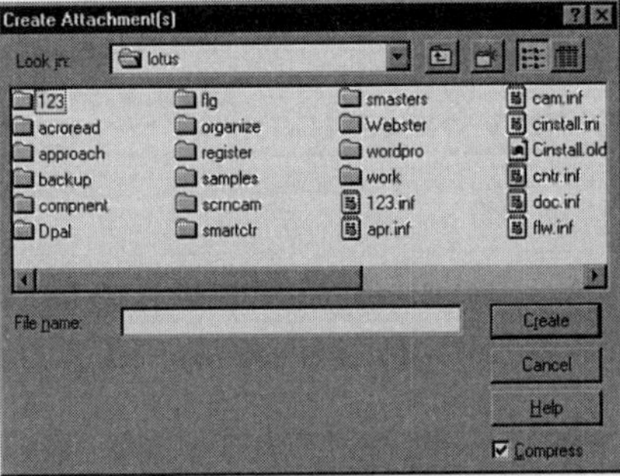

Fig. 30.21
Create Attachment(s).

3. Click Create.
4. The attachment will appear in the document as an icon.
5. Save and exit the document.

Opening an Attachment in Notes

When you open a Notes document that contains a file attachment, you'll have some choices as to what to do with the file. You'll be able to View, Launch, or Detach the file. Lotus Notes V4.x comes with a file viewer built in. It will allow you to look at the contents of a file without having to have the application that created the file. When you double-click a file attachment icon the Properties InfoBox appears (see fig. 30.22).

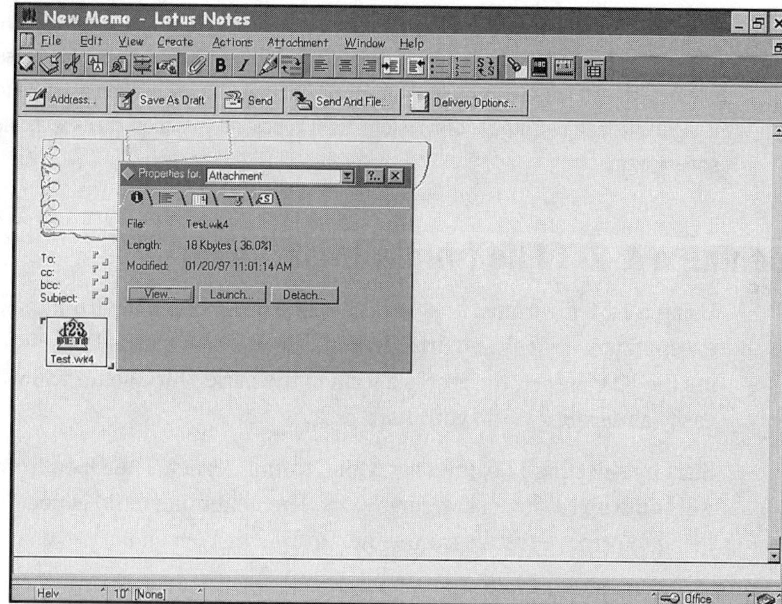

Fig. 30.22
Notes Properties InfoBox.

Choose the desired option:

- View—will open the attachment and display the contents with the Lotus Image Viewer. The viewer supports word processors, spreadsheets, presentations, and graphic files. Press Esc to close the viewer.
- Launch—will launch the application associated with the attachment with the data from the attachment. The changes you make cannot be saved back into the Notes Document. You will have to do a File, Attach to put the updated file in the Notes document.
- Detach—will bring up the Save File dialog box for you to select a location for the file to be saved in.

Working with the Internet

Not only will 1-2-3 allow you to work with your team members remotely with e-mail and Lotus Notes, but also let you work with anyone, anywhere in the world via the Internet. Sit on a nice quite beach in Cancun and update the corporate budgets with only a laptop and cellular phone. The 1-2-3 Internet features allow you to save or open a file from an FTP site or generate an HTML version of the worksheet for viewing on a Web site.

NOTE The Internet features depend upon a TCP/IP connection to the FTP and Web sites. These sites can be on the company's intranet (local network) or accessible via an Internet Service Provider (ISP) to the Internet. The network connection must be in place prior to using these features. If any of this information is beyond you, then check with your network administrator. ■

Opening a 1-2-3 File from a Host Server

Using a 1-2-3 file from a host server is like retrieving a file from the network file server—except that you don't use drive letters. The hardest part is the setup information regarding the FTP server, the rest is a walk in the park. Once setup you will save files just as easily as saving a file to your hard disk.

Start by selecting File, Internet, Open from Internet. The Open from Internet dialog box will come up as shown in figure 30.23. The next thing to do is decide whether you are going to retrieve the file from either an FTP or Web site.

To use an FTP site, follow these steps:

1. Before you can select an FTP site, you will have to enter information on the site by clicking the Host button to open the Hosts dialog box that is shown in figure 30.24.
2. Enter a description of the Host in the Host Description list box. This description will be used in the FTP Server selection list in the Open from Internet dialog box, so make it understandable.
3. In the Host address list box enter the IP address (example: 10.161.1.100) or the name of the site (ftp.lill.com) if you have Domain Name Services (DNS). For most internal FTP sites you will have an IP address to work with.

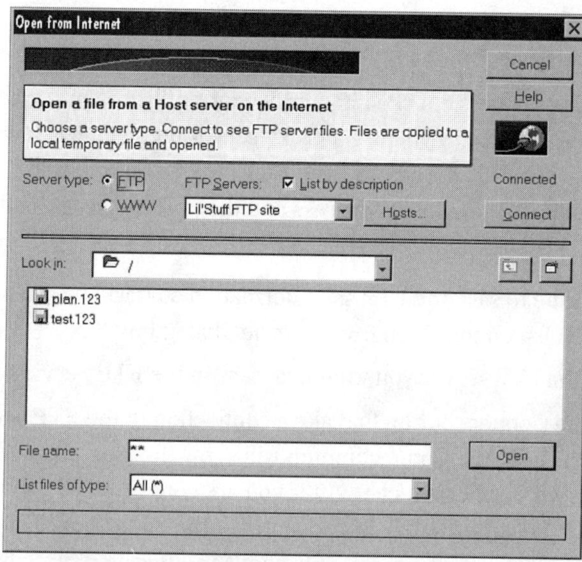

Fig. 30.23
Open from the Internet dialog box.

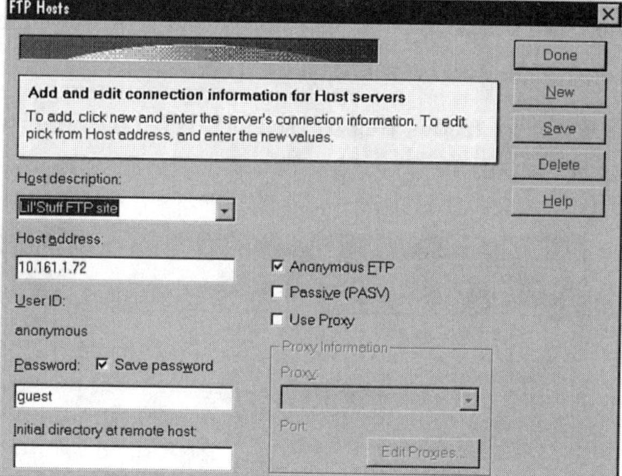

Fig. 30.24
FTP Hosts.

4. Now you need to setup your username and password options:
   - If the FTP site supports anonymous login, check the Anonymous FTP selection, which is the default. The user ID will be set to anonymous and you'll be able to set your password. The password for anonymous login is usually "guest" or your e-mail ID. If your FTP site requires a user ID, uncheck Anonymous FTP selection and enter your user ID in the User ID listbox.

- Passive (PASV) is checked if your network supports passive transfers through the firewall to the Internet.
- Use Proxy is checked if your network utilizes a proxy server as the firewall to the Internet. If you use a proxy server then you will have to enter the proxy server's IP address with the Edit Proxies button. Edit Proxies will let you enter the proxies IP address and the port to use (21 is the default value for the port).

5. Click Done to save the FTP site information so it will be available in the FTP Servers selection list on the Open from Internet dialog box.
6. Select the FTP server you want to access in the FTP Servers listbox.
7. Click the Connect button to make a connection to the FTP site. If you are successful, the icon above the Connect button will show the plug plugged into the world and the caption will read Connected. After you are connected you will see some file names listed in the large list box in the center of the dialog box. This is where you will select your file by clicking the file name or entering it directly into the File name listbox.
8. Click the Open button and the file selected will be retrieved into 1-2-3.

To use the World Wide Web (WWW), follow these steps:

1. To retrieve the file from a Web site select WWW on the Open from Internet dialog box (see fig. 30.25).

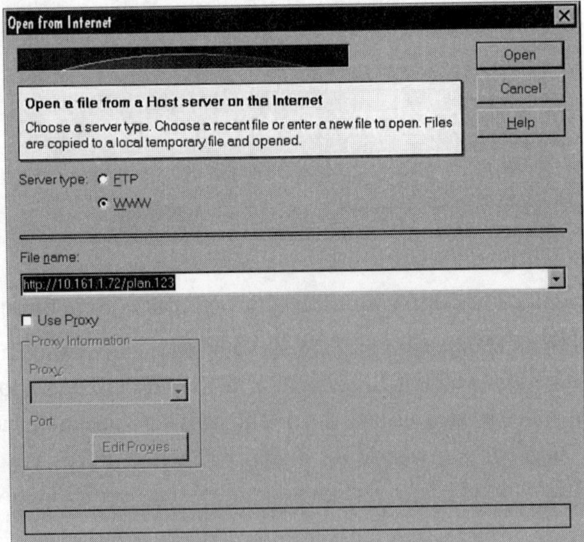

Fig. 30.25
Open from Internet dialog box with WWW selected.

2. In the File name listbox, enter the Universal Resource Locator (URL) of the Web site and file. This URL will be a string such as `www.lill.com/finance/plan.123`. If you just enter the Web site's name you'll end up with the site's home page in your spreadsheet.
3. Use Proxy is checked if your network utilizes a proxy server as the firewall to the Internet. If you use a proxy server then you will have to enter the proxy server's IP address with the Edit Proxies button. Edit Proxies will let you enter the proxy server's IP address and the port to use (21 is the default value for the port).
4. Click OK and the file will be retrieved. A dialog box will be displayed showing the progress of the transfer.

Now you should be looking at a workbook that was retrieved from the Internet.

Saving a 1-2-3 File to a Host Server

You'll be able to save your files to FTP sites only. If you open your file from an FTP site, when you save it, it will be sent to the FTP site automatically. To put a file out on an FTP site, do the following.

1. Select File, Internet, Save to Internet to bring up the Save to Internet dialog box as is shown in figure 30.26

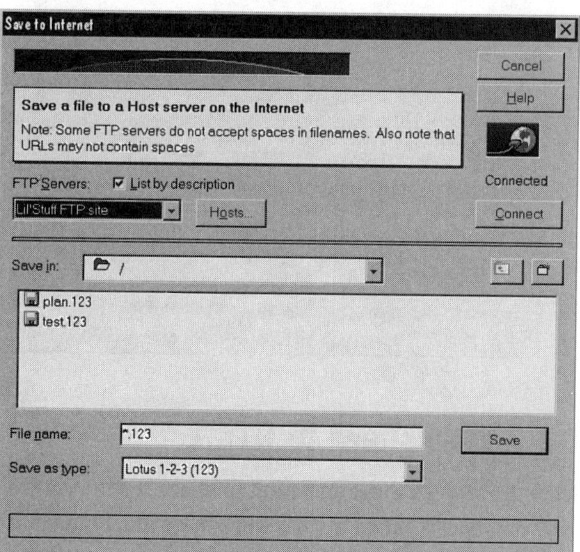

Fig. 30.26
Save to Internet.

2. Select the FTP site from the FTP Servers list box. If the site isn't listed then use the Host button to enter the site information, as discussed in the preceding section.
3. Click the Connect button to connect to the FTP server.

   The Save in: list box shows the current directory on the FTP server. Use the two folder buttons to the right to move up a folder or to create a folder.
4. Select the format of the file, such as 123, DBF, Paradox, in the Save as Type listbox.
5. Enter the name of the file in the File name list box and click the Save button. If everything went well, your file will now be available to everyone on the FTP server.

Setting Internet Options

If you work with an FTP server often, you can have 1-2-3 connect to the server automatically when you select open or save to Internet.

1. Select File, Internet, FTP Connection Setup to Internet to bring up the FTP Connection Setup dialog box shown in figure 30.27.
2. Enable the feature you want and select the FTP server from the list below it. If your server isn't listed click the Host button and setup the host.
3. Click OK. Now when you use the Open from Internet or Save to Internet features, 1-2-3 will automatically connect to the FTP server you selected.

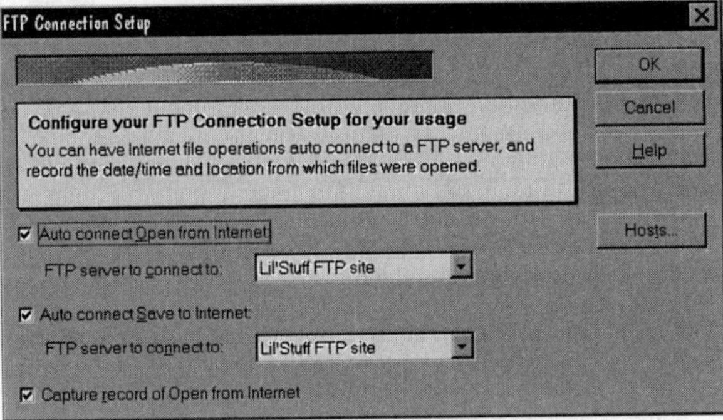

Fig. 30.27
FTP Connection Setup.

Publishing a 1-2-3 Worksheet to HTML

You've created a great worksheet and want to share it with the world, well now you can do it easily. 1-2-3 97 can take a range from a worksheet and convert it to Hypertext Markup Language (HTML) that can be viewed with a Web browser. This will be a trial and error process as you try to make the information look good on the Web.

You just need to follow four simple steps and you're there:

1. Select the range you want to display and select menu options File, Internet, Publish a range to the Internet. The Publish 1-2-3 Range to the Web dialog box shown in Figure 30.28 will appear. To change the range of cells that you want to publish, use the range selector, drag in the worksheet to select the range, then click the enter (check) button to close the range selector dialog box.

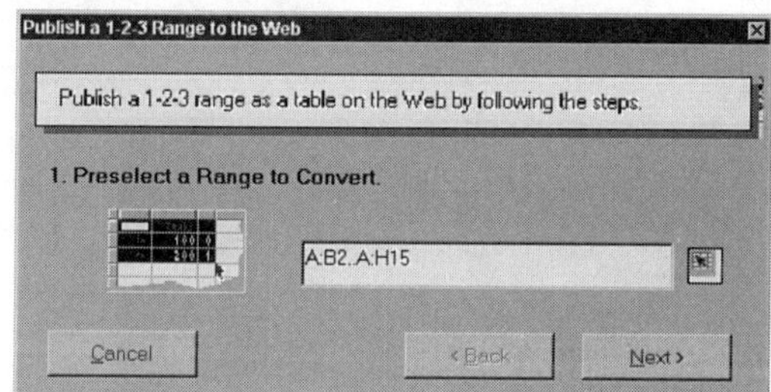

Fig. 30.28
Publish a 1-2-3 Range to the Web.

2. Click Next to go to the next dialog box, step 2 as shown in figure 30.29. The picture on the left will show the results of your choices as you make them:
   - Show Table Title will allow the text added to the listbox to show at the top of the table as a title. If you didn't have a title already in the range, enter it here. It will end up centered in the top row of the table.
   - The Show Cell Borders option will turn on or off the borders of the cells. Remember, if you turn this on, every cell's border will show. If you used empty cells for spacing on the worksheet, they will show up here.
   - Columns Have Equal Width will set every column to the same width.

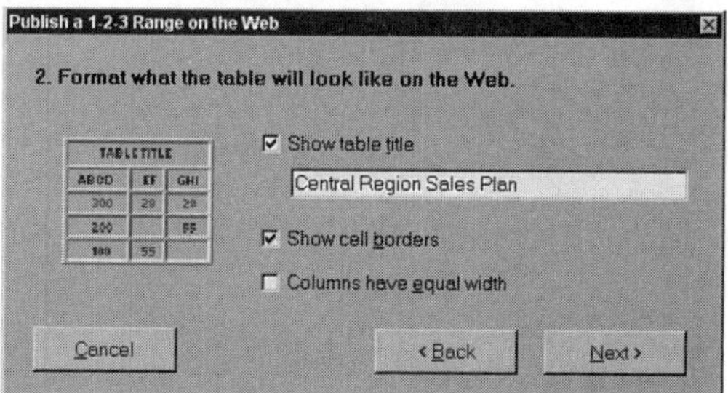

Fig. 30.29
Publish to the Web (step 2).

3. Click Next to go to the next dialog box, step 3 as shown in figure 30.30. Here you be able to enter some additional information that will appear outside of the table on the page. The picture on the left will show the effect of each feature as you select them:

- Enter the title you want to appear in a large bold font at the top of the page in the Page Title listbox.
- The text entered in to the Description text box will appear centered under the table. Use this to explain what the table shows, remember be specific and realize that everyone will be able to read it.
- The last two entries are for the editor's name and e-mail address. This is so everyone will know who to thank (or blame) for the useful information you provided.

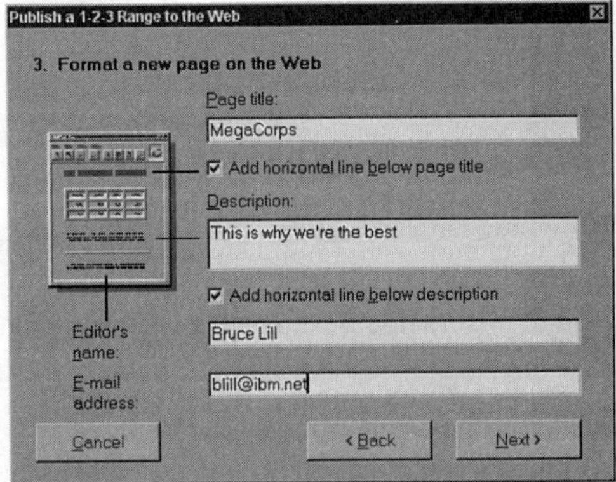

Fig. 30.30
Step 3.

4. Click Next to go to the next dialog box, step 4 as shown in figure 30.31. This is the end. You can save what you created as an HTML file that can be copied over to a Web site, preview your work with a Web Browser, or publish the page to a Web site. I would preview the work first, then go back and change the page to get the look and feel right.

Fig. 30.31
Step 4.

Figure 30.32 is an example of a range publish with all the options turned on. The look will vary with the brand and version of the Web browser you use. The release of 1-2-3 I'm using will not allow you to overwrite a file when saving the HTML as a file.

Fig. 30.32
Final result.

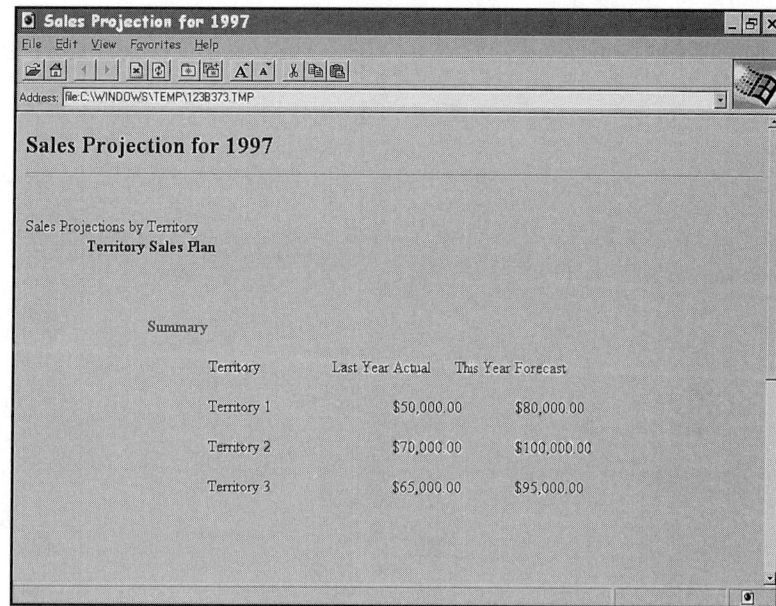

NOTE All of the formatting and graphics features available in 1-2-3 are not available to Web browsers. You will have to go back and forth a few times to get the look right. Web browsers are limited on the type and size of fonts that can be used.

CHAPTER 31

Integrating 1-2-3 with DOS Applications

by David Plotkin

Sharing information with 1-2-3 97 is easy if you use DOS applications such as dBASE, Microsoft Word, Paradox, and WordPerfect. 1-2-3 also allows for the simple transfer and exchange of ASCII (text) files with DOS applications that can read text files.

1-2-3 97 opens, saves, and translates many file formats such as dBASE, Excel, SuperCalc, and previous 1-2-3 releases file formats. 1-2-3 also loads and creates text files for data transfer with applications that do not use one of the common formats as an interchange. ■

Using data from DOS programs in 1-2-3

You can transfer data stored in DOS programs into 1-2-3, and use that data as part of a spreadsheet or database. 1-2-3 supports various formats of data, as well as a common translation format called "Ascii text."

Make your 1-2-3 data available to other programs

1-2-3 can save worksheet data in a variety of formats readable by other programs, making it easy to move the data into another program and use it there.

Seamlessly interchange data between 1-2-3 and DOS applications

You can open DOS applications and 1-2-3 at the same time, and then cut and paste information between them.

NOTE Most popular DOS programs are also available in Windows versions. If you use Excel, Word for Windows, WordPro, Paradox, WordPerfect for Windows, or any other Windows version of an application mentioned in this chapter, use the methods discussed in Chapter 29, "Using 1-2-3 with Lotus Notes," to share data. The instructions in this chapter relate to DOS applications only. ■

Understanding How Windows Runs DOS Applications

Microsoft Windows allows you to run more than one program at a time. The way the programs run—whether they continue processing information when another program is currently being used or stop processing until they are reselected—depends on how you set the Background check box (Misc tab) in the Properties dialog box for the program. If you check the Always Suspend check box, the DOS program will be suspended when it is in the background. Otherwise, it will continue to execute at a speed that is roughly dependent on the Idle Sensitivity setting in the same dialog box. To get to the Properties dialog box, open My Computer or the Windows Explorer, right click on the DOS file icon, and select Properties from the pop-up menu.

You can display DOS applications full-screen or in a window (see fig. 31.1). To switch a running DOS application between a full-screen display and a window, press Alt+Enter.

NOTE When a DOS application is running in a Window, you can use the standard Windows controls to expand the size of the window to a full screen. This is different from "full-screen" display mode in a very important way. When a DOS application is running in a window (even a window that takes up the entire screen), you have access to the editing options as described later in this chapter. However, when a DOS application is running in "full-screen" display mode, you do NOT have access to editing options. Since this chapter concerns itself with performing edits between 1-2-3 and DOS applications, you must be running the DOS application in a window. ■

▶ **See** "Manipulating Windows," **p. 31**

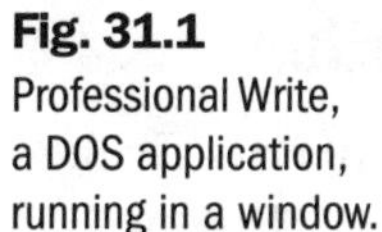

Fig. 31.1
Professional Write, a DOS application, running in a window.

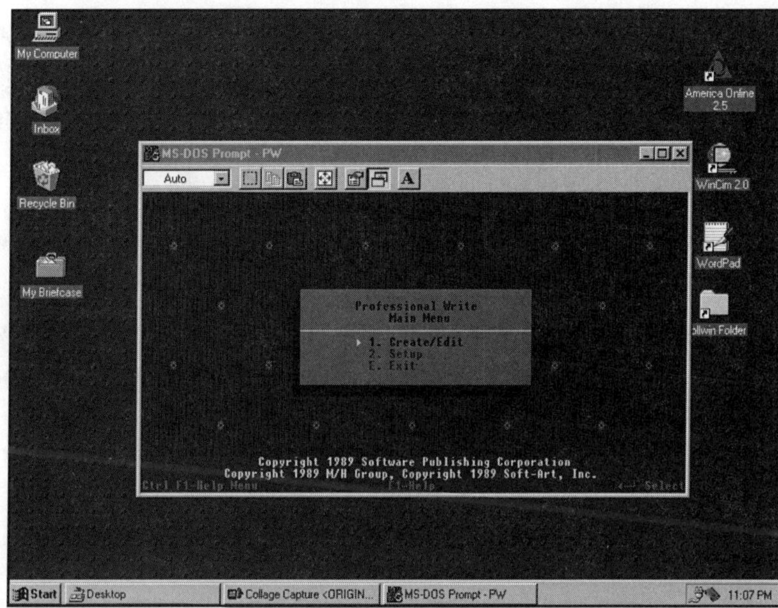

Copying and Pasting Between Applications

The item you use to transfer information between 1-2-3 and DOS applications is called the *Clipboard* (see fig. 31.2).

TIP Display the contents of the Clipboard by clicking the Start button and selecting the Clipboard Viewer from the Programs Accessories menu.

NOTE The Clipboard Viewer may not have been installed by Windows 95. If it was not, you can add it by selecting the Add/Remove Software icon in the Control Panel.

Fig. 31.2
Use the Clipboard Viewer in Windows to see the current contents of the Clipboard.

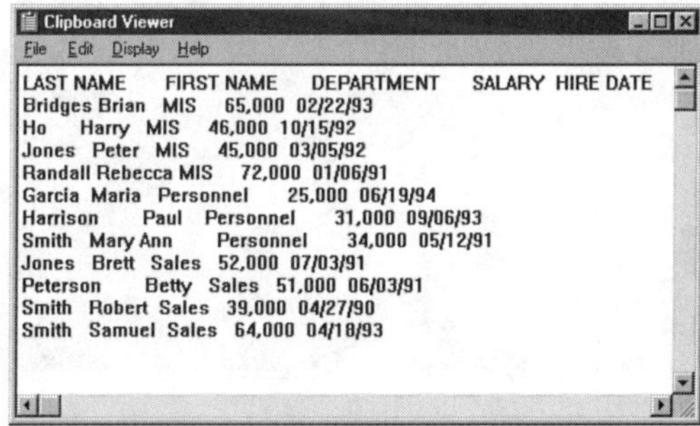

Clipboard Viewer
File Edit Display Help

LAST NAME FIRST NAME DEPARTMENT SALARY HIRE DATE
Bridges Brian MIS 65,000 02/22/93
Ho Harry MIS 46,000 10/15/92
Jones Peter MIS 45,000 03/05/92
Randall Rebecca MIS 72,000 01/06/91
Garcia Maria Personnel 25,000 06/19/94
Harrison Paul Personnel 31,000 09/06/93
Smith Mary Ann Personnel 34,000 05/12/91
Jones Brett Sales 52,000 07/03/91
Peterson Betty Sales 51,000 06/03/91
Smith Robert Sales 39,000 04/27/90
Smith Samuel Sales 64,000 04/18/93

Copying and Pasting Between 1-2-3 and a DOS Application

DOS programs running in a window act just like Windows programs, but you can use the same commands and work with the same display you used when running the DOS program from DOS.

When you run DOS applications in a window, you can copy selected information, the entire desktop, or a single window onto the Clipboard and then switch to another DOS or Windows application to paste the selection.

To copy and paste from a DOS application into 1-2-3, follow these steps:

1. If you are in full-screen mode, press Alt+Enter to toggle the DOS application from full-screen to a window.
2. Click on the MS-DOS button in the upper left corner of the MS-DOS application's window or press Alt+space bar to display the MS-DOS menu. Select Edit, Mark (see fig. 31.3). Mark you to use a keyboard or mouse to select text to move onto the Clipboard. Select the data you want copied by dragging across the data with the mouse. If you are using a keyboard, press the arrow keys to move to one corner of the data you want to select, and then press Shift+arrow keys to select the data (see fig. 31.4).
3. Click on the MS-DOS button in the upper left corner of the MS-DOS application's window or press Alt+space bar to display the MS-DOS menu. Choose Edit, Copy to copy the selected data into the Windows Clipboard (see figure 31.5). You may also choose the Copy button in the toolbar.

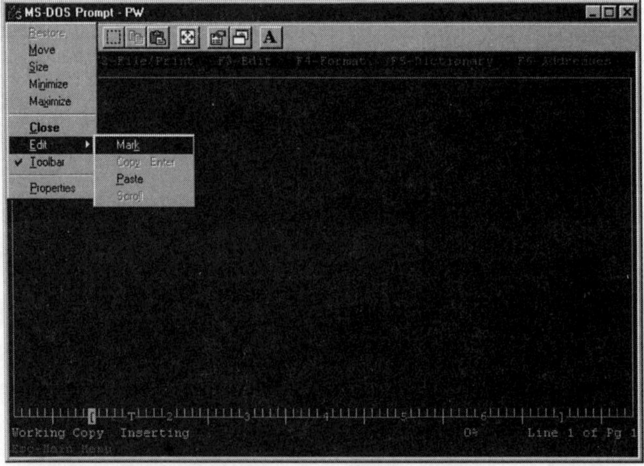

Fig. 31.3
Use Edit, Mark to copy data from a DOS program running in a window to the Clipboard.

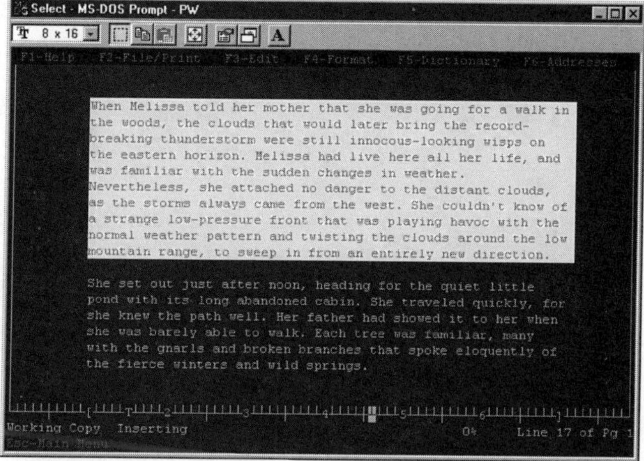

Fig. 31.4
The selected data stands out, ready to be copied.

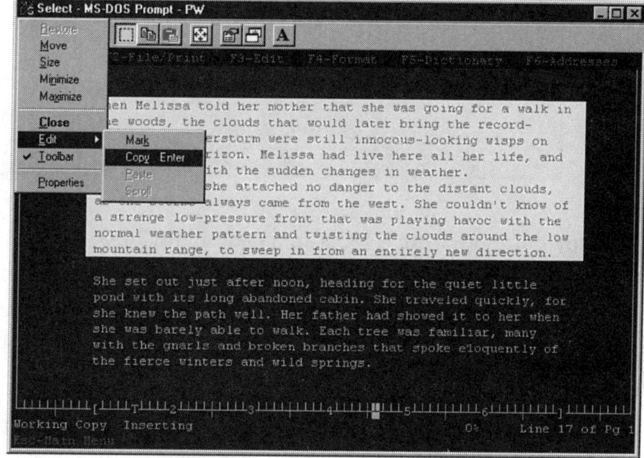

Fig. 31.5
Copying information from Professional Write, a DOS application, to the Windows Clipboard.

NOTE You cannot run a DOS application while in Mar<u>k</u> mode (see Step 2). To return to the DOS application without copying any data to the Windows Clipboard, press Esc to leave the Control menu.

4. If 1-2-3 is running, use the Task Bar along the bottom of the screen to switch it; otherwise, start 1-2-3 now.
5. Select the spreadsheet and cell where you want to paste the data.

6. Choose Edit, Paste, or click the Paste SmartIcon to add the copied data into your 1-2-3 worksheet (see fig. 31.6).

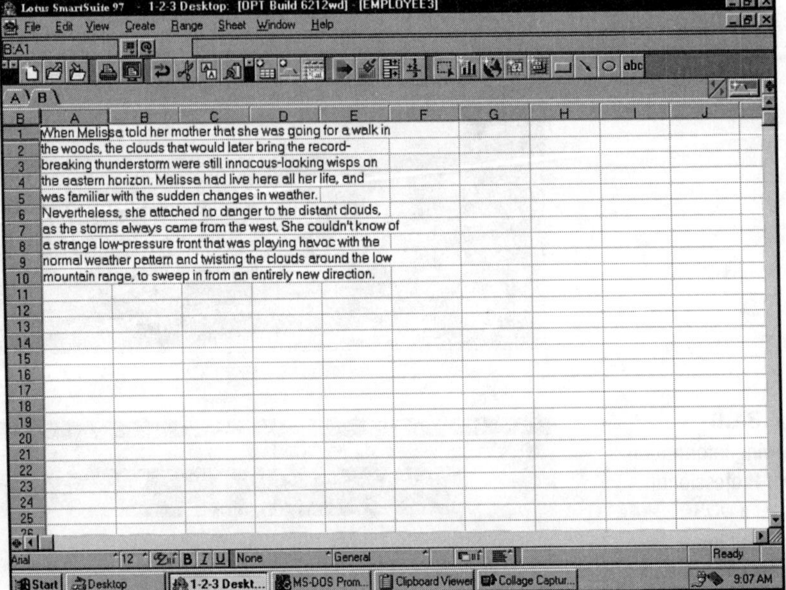

Fig. 31.6
Use the Clipboard to paste DOS program data into 1-2-3.

When you copy numbers from a DOS application into 1-2-3, you can copy a single number or a column of numbers. The numbers or column of numbers are pasted into a single cell or a column of cells. If you copy entire lines, the numbers are not pasted into individual cells in the row. To separate lines of numbers or data into individual cells, you need to parse the data.

To copy data from 1-2-3 and paste it into a DOS application, complete the following steps:

1. Select the cell or range in 1-2-3 that you want to copy.
2. Choose Edit, Copy, or click the Copy SmartIcon.
3. Use the Task Bar at the bottom of the screen to switch to the DOS application, if it is already running; otherwise, start it now.
4. Position the cursor in the application where you want to insert the data.

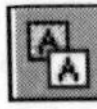

5. Click the MS-DOS button in the upper left corner of the MS-DOS application's window or press Alt+space bar to display the MS-DOS menu. Choose Edit, Paste (see fig. 31.7).

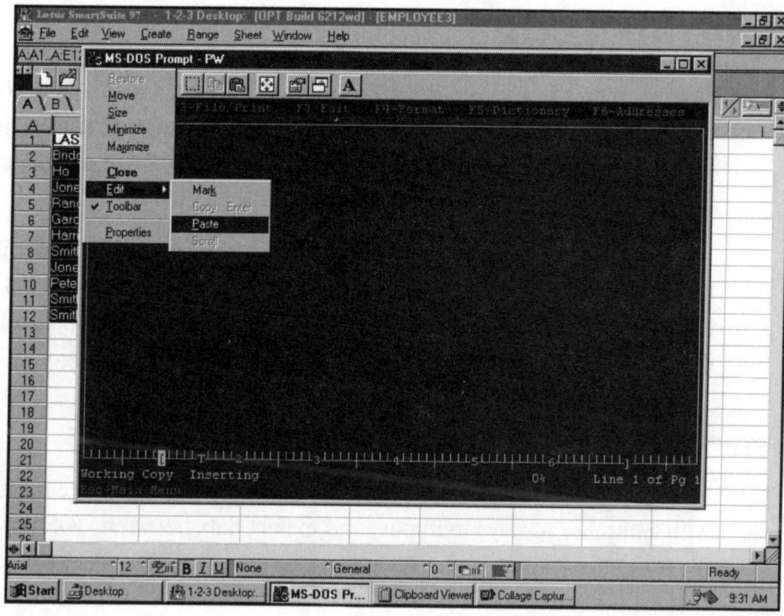

Fig. 31.7
Pasting 1-2-3 data into a DOS application also uses the Clipboard.

The data is inserted into the DOS application (see fig. 31.8) just as though you typed it there.

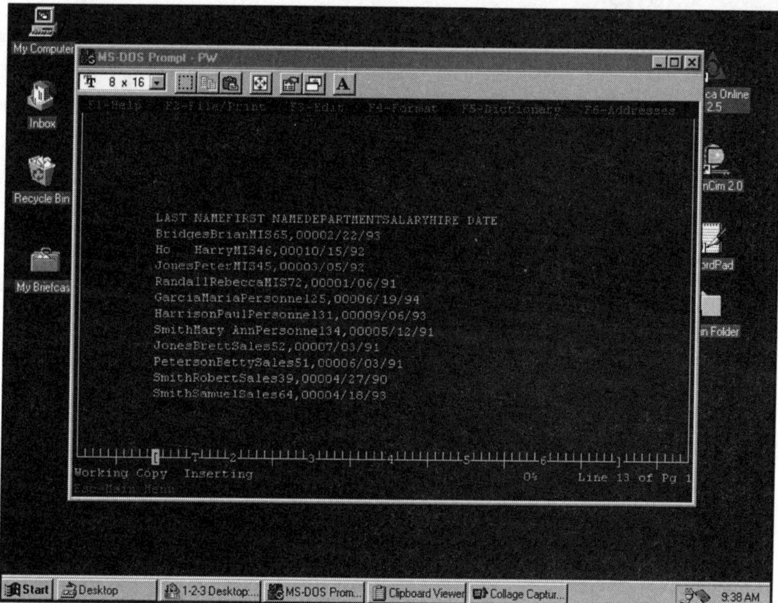

Fig. 31.8
The 1-2-3 data is pasted into a DOS application.

Exporting Data

Exporting data is an easy and efficient way to exchange data between 1-2-3 and DOS applications. Why not use the Clipboard to exchange all of your data? The Clipboard is ideally suited for exchanging small blocks of text or data, while exporting allows you to exchange larger blocks of text in one step.

1-2-3 can share data and charts with other applications. To transfer information between a DOS application and 1-2-3, either export or translate data from 1-2-3 to a file format that the DOS application can read or import data from the DOS application into a file format that 1-2-3 can read, depending on which direction the data is going.

Understanding File Formats

1-2-3 97 includes support for several different file types. This compatibility provides you with a number of ways to import and export data between DOS applications. If no specific file format is available for 1-2-3 to transfer data directly, you can create a text file format that transfers text and numbers. 1-2-3 provides an enhanced method of opening ASCII text files. This capability enables 1-2-3 to automatically parse text files into spreadsheet cells when selecting the File Open command.

CAUTION

By saving a 1-2-3 worksheet to text file format you will only save the text and numbers. The formatting (for example, bold, underline, italics), formulas, charts, and drawn objects will be lost. 1-2-3 will leave blank lines in the text file where the chart or drawn objects would have appeared.

Table 31.1 DOS File Formats Read and Written by 1-2-3

File Extension	Description
WK1	1-2-3 for DOS Release 2 or earlier
WK3	1-2-3 for DOS Release 3
WK4	1-2-3 for Windows, Release 5
XLS	Excel Worksheets
XLT	Excel Templates
XLW	Excel Workbooks
WQ1, WB1, WB2	Quattro Pro

File Extension	Description
TXT, PRN, CSV, DAT, OUT, ASC	Text, ASCII, and Delimited files
BMP	Windows Bitmap (graphics)
WMF	Windows metafile
CGM	ANSI metafile (graphic)
PIC	1-2-3 PIC files
DB	Paradox files
DBF	dBASE III, III+, and IV DBF files

Most DOS programs—including database management programs, spreadsheets, and word processors—can create and read text files. If you have a worksheet or database file from another program that you would like to use in 1-2-3, you can select from the wide range of files that 1-2-3 can read to transfer the file. If 1-2-3 can't read the other program's native file format directly, you might be able to use the other program to save the data in a format that 1-2-3 can read (refer to table 31.1).

Saving 1-2-3 Worksheets in a Different Format

The capability to save 1-2-3 97 worksheets into a different file format can be very useful. For instance, coworkers may need to see your worksheet but they use an earlier DOS release of 1-2-3 requiring you to save the file in WK3 or WK1 file format. Maybe a manager or business client needs your customer address listing to import into Paradox for DOS. The capability to save 1-2-3 worksheets to different file formats enables you to transfer information with other applications easily.

To save 1-2-3 worksheets in a different format, perform the following steps:

1. Choose File, Save As to display the Save As dialog box (see fig. 31.9).
2. Type a file name in the File Name text box (do not add a file extension) and do not press Enter.
3. From the Save as Type drop-down list, select the format in which you want to save these files (see fig. 31.10). Use the Save In drop-down list and folder buttons to select the desired drive and directory in which you want to save the file. Refer back to Table 31.1 for descriptions of the various file formats.
4. Choose the Save button.

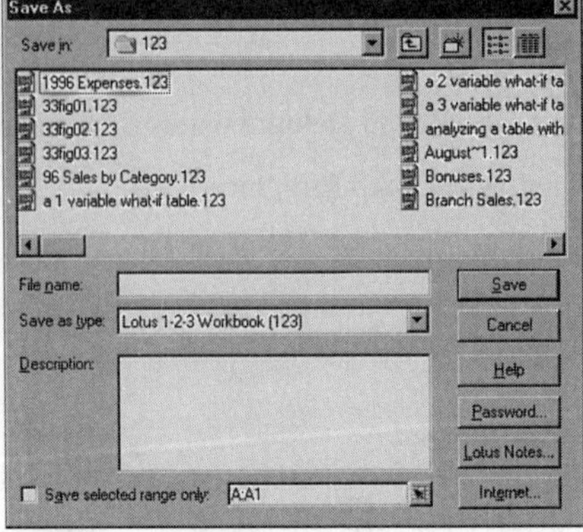

Fig. 31.9
Use the Save As dialog box to save a 1-2-3 worksheet in foreign formats.

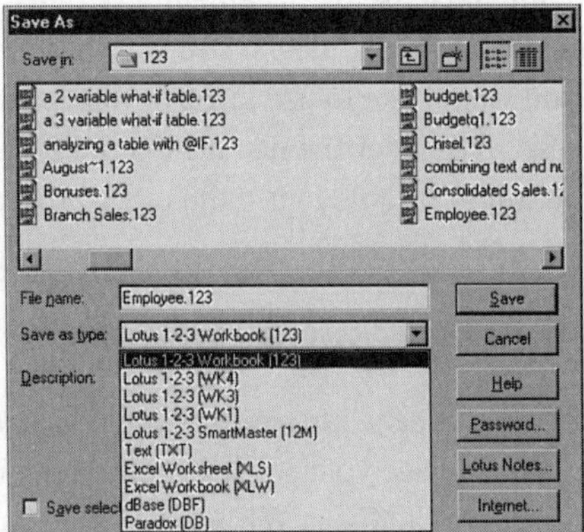

Fig. 31.10
Select the file type in which to save your file.

NOTE If you need to export a file to a format not shown in the Save as Type list box, read your DOS program's manual to find information on the program's capability to read 1-2-3 file formats. Some database management systems and word processing programs, such as Paradox and WordPerfect, can read data directly from 1-2-3 worksheets. This is easier for you because you eliminate the need to save to the proper file format. ■

Saving 1-2-3 Data to Paradox for DOS There are two efficient ways to save and import 1-2-3 data into a Paradox for DOS file. The first method is to use File, Save As in 1-2-3 and specify the Paradox file type. The second method is to save your 1-2-3 97 worksheet in WK1 format and then import the data using the Paradox menu commands. The first method is easier because it saves steps and time.

To save a 1-2-3 worksheet as a Paradox for DOS file using the 1-2-3 Save As dialog box, complete the following steps:

1. Select File, Save As in 1-2-3. The Save As dialog box appears.
2. Specify the Paradox(DB) in the Save as Type drop-down list (see fig. 31.11).
3. Select the drives and directories where you want the file saved, and then press Save.

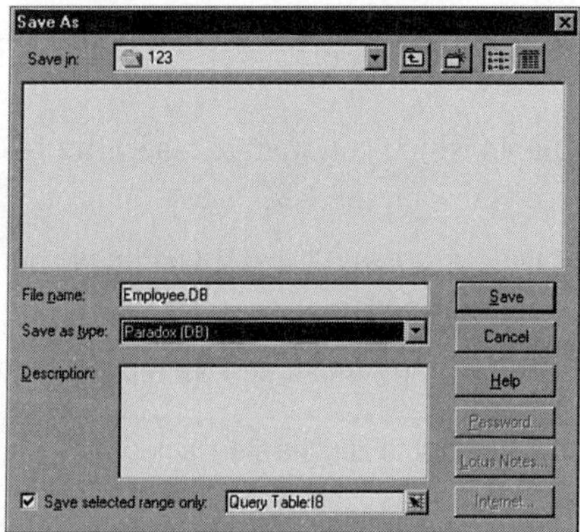

Fig. 31.11
Select Paradox (DB) to save a 1-2-3 file into Paradox for DOS file format.

To save a 1-2-3 worksheet as Paradox for DOS file, by first saving the worksheet into WK1 format, complete the following steps:

1. Save your 1-2-3 97 worksheet in WK1 format.
2. Switch to Paradox if it is already running; otherwise, start it now.
3. Choose Tools, Export, and then select 1-2-3 Release 2 to import a WK1 file format.
4. Type the path and file name.
5. When Paradox asks you to name the new table, type a name of up to eight characters and press Enter.

NOTE Except for delimited ASCII files, data files from other programs can be imported only into new Paradox tables, not into existing tables. ■

CAUTION

Paradox automatically defines the structure of the new table. Only data values, not the formulas, are imported.

Saving 1-2-3 Data to WordPerfect 6.0 for DOS To save and import 1-2-3 data into a WordPerfect 6.0 file, complete the following steps:

1. Save your 1-2-3 worksheet in 1-2-3 WK3 or WK1 format using the steps detailed in the previous section "Saving 1-2-3 Worksheets in a Different Format."
2. Use the Task Bar to select WordPerfect, if it is already running; otherwise, start it now.
3. Open the WordPerfect file in which you want to insert the 1-2-3 data and then position the cursor where you want the 1-2-3 data to appear.
4. Choose the Tools command, or press Alt+F7; then choose Spreadsheet Import. The Spreadsheet Import dialog box appears.
5. Choose Filename, type the full path name, and then press Enter.

You can use WordPerfect's File List or Quicklist to find the file you need.

6. Choose Range, and enter the data range or range name. If you don't specify a data range or range name, the entire worksheet is imported.
7. Choose the Type command, and select Import as Table or Import as Text. You may need to reformat fonts and columns in tables to fit the data on the page.
8. Choose the Import command. WordPerfect inserts the data.

Importing Data

1-2-3 is used by many companies to analyze information and data stored in other applications and file formats. In the past, the only way to import data from another application was to save the application files as text files. Because most applications can work with text files, this format was and still is useful for transfers between vastly different systems. However, Lotus has improved its technologies to import and read other file formats.

1-2-3 enables you to open files saved in another file format using the Open dialog box. Importing data from a different file format is very useful if you need to modify, change, format, or analyze data without having your changes effect the source data in the original file.

Opening Files Saved in Another File Format

The easiest way to import data into 1-2-3 is to import the data in one of the file formats 1-2-3 can read, and then resave the data in 1-2-3 format. The DOS file formats 1-2-3 can read are listed in Table 31.1, shown earlier in this chapter.

To open a non-1-2-3 file, follow these steps:

1. Choose File, Open, or click the Open File SmartIcon to display the Open dialog box (see fig. 31.12).

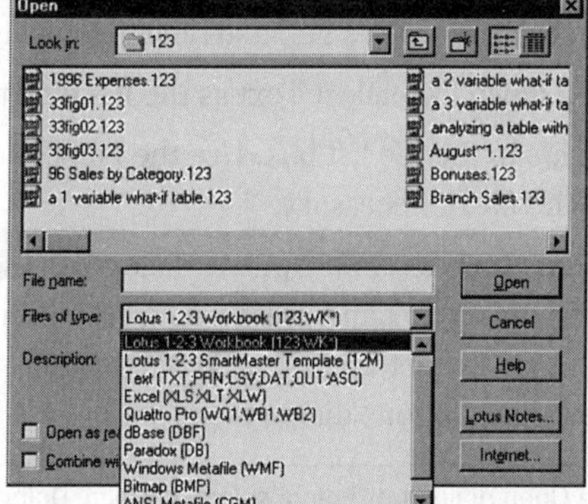

Fig. 31.12
Use the Open dialog box Files of Type drop-down list box to specify the type of file you want to open.

2. Select the file format desired in the Files of Type drop-down list.
3. Select the file you want to import in the File Name list box. Locate the file using Look In drop-down list and directory button, if necessary.
4. Choose the Open button. 1-2-3 imports the file. Generally, 1-2-3 reads and opens the file. In some instances, if you are opening a dBASE or Paradox file, 1-2-3 displays `Connecting dbase c:\path`. After processing and opening, 1-2-3 displays the file name in the title bar.

When 1-2-3 loads a non-1-2-3 file, 1-2-3 remembers the original file format. When you save the file, 1-2-3 displays the Save As dialog box. To save the file in its original non-1-2-3 format, choose the Save button. 1-2-3 prompts you to confirm replacing the original file.

CAUTION

Saving to a non-1-2-3 format can result in the loss of formulas, functions, special features, and formatting that are unique to 1-2-3. Consult your non-1-2-3 application's manual for differences before you save the file.

Importing a Delimited Text File

A *delimited text file* is a file in ASCII format that contains rows of data separated by characters called *delimiters*. A delimiter is a , (comma), space, : (colon), or ; (semicolon) entered between numbers and text in each row. Each row must end with a carriage return.

All labels must be enclosed in quotation marks. For example, `"Jones","Chicago",24,"Engineer",31000` is a line from a delimited text file.

To import data from a delimited text file into 1-2-3 worksheet format, use the following steps:

1. Choose File, Open, or click the Open File SmartIcon to display the Open dialog box.
2. In the Files of type drop-down list, select Text as the file type to open.
3. Select the desired text file in the file list box. Use the Look in drop-down list and the folder button to locate the file, if necessary.
4. Click Open. 1-2-3 presents the Text File Options dialog box (see fig. 31.13). Make your selections from the dialog box and press OK. 1-2-3 automatically separates the data into columns in the worksheet according to the delimiters or the information you supplied in the Text File Options dialog box.

TIP Change the file type to Text in the Open dialog box before selecting Open. Doing this ensures that 1-2-3 recognizes that you are dealing with or opening a text file.

Text File Options is a feature in 1-2-3 that enables you to specify further information about how you want 1-2-3 to open a text file and parse it. The Text File Options dialog box (see fig. 31.13) opens automatically when you load a file of type Text.

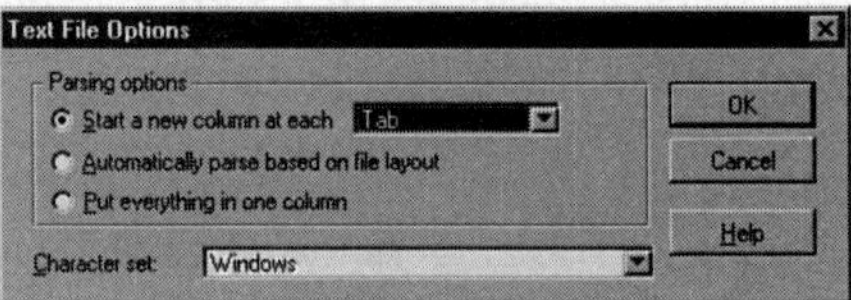

Fig. 31.13
Use the Text File Options dialog box to specify the parsing options for your text file.

To use the Text File Options dialog box, choose one of the Parsing Options:

- Start a New Column at Each specifies the type of separator you want 1-2-3 to use for breaking the text into columns in the worksheet. You can specify Other Character(s) and then enter the separator character in the text box (see fig. 31.14).

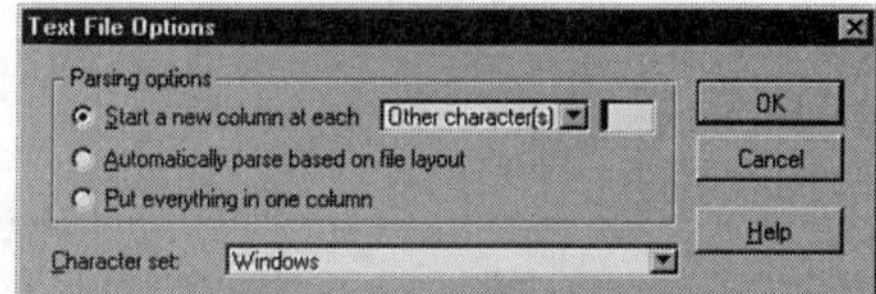

Fig. 31.14 If you select Other character(s), you can specify which character 1-2-3 should parse on.

- Automatically Parse Based on File Layout specifies that you are allowing 1-2-3 to autoparse the text file by determining the breaks and columns.
- Put Everything in One Column does just what it says—puts the entire contents of the text file into a single column

In the Character Set drop-down list, specify the code page you want 1-2-3 to use for interpreting the data in the text file. Generally, you use the Windows (ANSI) or DOS code pages, but this will depend on the source of the data. If the imported text displays strange characters, try importing the text again using a different Character Set.

Using Combine to Import a Text File

When you open or import a text file, the file is entered into a new 1-2-3 worksheet. There might be situations when you need to combine or append data to a current worksheet. You can use 1-2-3 Combine feature to import and open a text file into a current worksheet. This method is easier and faster than importing a text file into its own worksheet and then copying and pasting the information into another worksheet.

To import a text file using the Combine feature:

1. Choose File, Open, or click the Open File SmartIcon to display the Open dialog box.
2. Select Text in the File of Type drop-down list.
3. Choose Combine with current workbook. The Open button changes to read Combine.
4. Choose Combine to display the Text File Options dialog box.
5. Choose the correct Parsing Options for the text file and then OK to add the data to your current worksheet (see fig. 31.15).

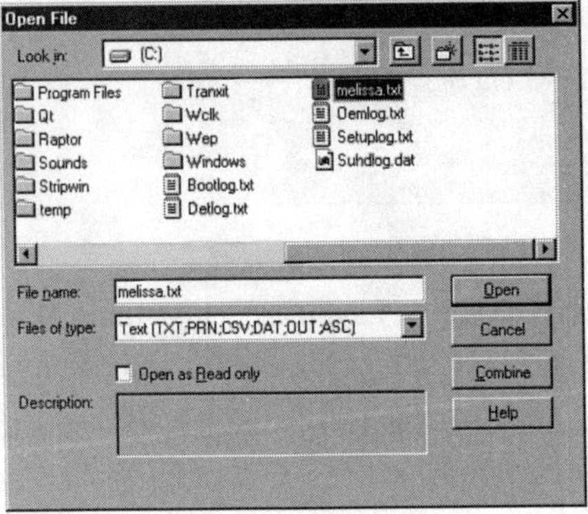

Fig. 31.15
The text file is combined or added to the current worksheet.

Parsing Text into Columns

Occasionally, you may import a text file that is not delimited or is formatted with fixed length records. Each field in a fixed length record occupies the same amount of space in each record. If the data in a field is not long enough to fill the space allotted, the balance of the field length is filled ("padded") with blanks. Thus, if a Last Name field is 20 characters and one record includes a last name of 15 characters, the remaining five characters are padded with blanks. When you open a text file containing fixed length records in a text processor, the fields will line up in columns if you are using a "fixed pitch" font such as Courier New (a fixed pitch font is a font in which each character takes up the same amount of room). If you are working with a text file that consists of fixed length records, Lotus 1-2-3 does a pretty good job of figuring out where the breaks between fields should be if you select the Automatically Parse Based on File Layout option of the Text File Options dialog box. However, sometimes Lotus 1-2-3 is unable to figure out how to parse the text. If this occurs, you need to import the file as single column of data and separate each fixed length record in the imported text file into fields or columns so that you can attain a database in 1-2-3 that consists of rows (records) and columns (fields).

To separate the long lines into cells, you must parse, or separate, each line into its individual parts.

▶ **See** "Parsing Data," **p. 612**

Parsing Text into Columns of Data To parse a text file in 1-2-3, you need to use the Range, Parse command. Range, Parse converts long labels from an imported text file into separate columns of data of one or more types of data (values, dates, time, and labels).

Follow these steps to parse a text file:

1. Open the text file in 1-2-3 via the Open dialog box. In the Text File Options dialog box, select the Put Everything in One Column option.
2. Select the range that contains the long labels or records that you want to parse.
3. Choose Range, Parse to display the Parse dialog box.

NOTE If the first of the input column already contains a format line, the format line appears in the Format line text box, where the format line can be edited. A format line is a line that specifies how to parse the data. ■

4. Select Guess Format. 1-2-3 enters the format line in the Format line text box (see fig. 31.16). The symbols in the format line represent the type of data and the width of each block of data in the first cell of the Parse this column text box.

   The format line instructs 1-2-3 how to parse, or separate, data and enter it in a worksheet. When 1-2-3 creates the format line, it enters a symbol in the format line for each data block in the first line of the input column. Table 31.2 has a listing of available symbols to use in the format line when parsing a range.

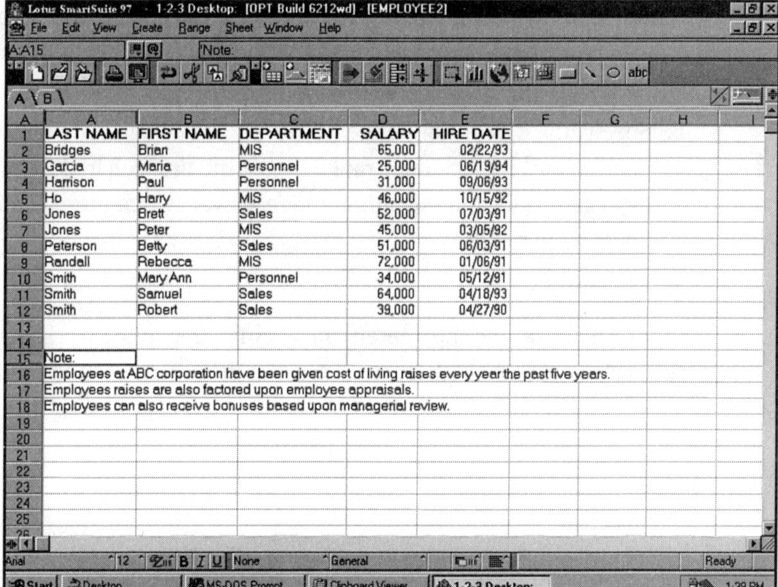

Fig. 31.16
Use the Format line in the Parse dialog box to specify how to parse the data.

Table 31.2 Symbols Used in Range, Parse

Symbol	Description
L	Represents the beginning of a label block
V	Represents the beginning of a value block
D	Represents the beginning of a date block
T	Represents the beginning of a time block
S	Tells 1-2-3 to ignore the data block below the S when it parses the data
>	Represents any character in a data block after the first character
*	Represents a blank space that becomes part of a data block if that block requires extra characters

NOTE When 1-2-3 parses dates, it enters dates as numbers in the worksheet. Format the date values using Number format tab of the Range Info box to display the dates in date format. Select Date from the Category list box, and then select the date format you want from the Current format list box. ■

5. Compare the format line to the data in the worksheet. If the format line does not accurately represent the type of data or length of entries in a data block located in the lines below it, edit the format line.
6. Specify the destination range for the parsed data in the Put the results in text box. You can specify the entire range or just the first cell in the range. 1-2-3 writes over any existing data in the output range, so verify that there is no data that you want to keep in the range.
7. Choose OK.

1-2-3 inserts a row, and then enters the Format Line in the worksheet above the data. The parsed data is entered in the designated Put the results in range (see fig. 31.17).

▶ **See** "Parsing Data," **p. 612**

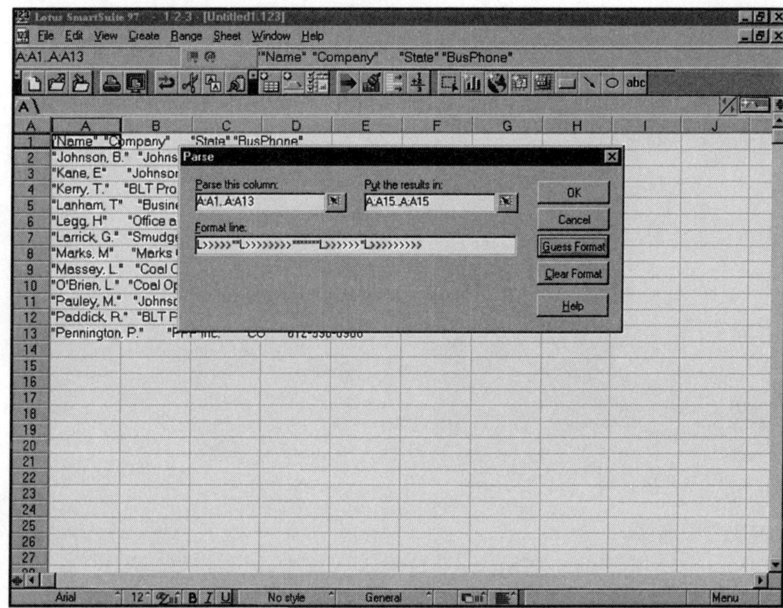

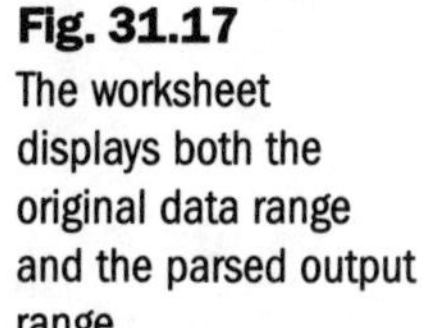
Fig. 31.17
The worksheet displays both the original data range and the parsed output range.

PART VII

Customizing 1-2-3

CHAPTER 32

Customizing the 1-2-3 Screen

by Elaine Marmel

Setting view preferences

Learn how to customize the appearance of the 1-2-3 window to suit your needs.

Changing the colors of the worksheet tabs

Change the colors of worksheet tabs to make them more visible.

Using the Control Panel

Use Windows' Control Panel to modify the way 1-2-3 appears.

The Windows environment invites customization of the screen so that you can accomplish your tasks as easily as possible. As a Windows application, 1-2-3 works with the Windows customization features and adds some of its own. Although there are many ways to customize your work with 1-2-3, this chapter focuses on two tools that control the appearance of the 1-2-3 screen: the 1-2-3 Workbook Properties dialog box and the Windows Control Panel. ■

Setting View Preferences

You can customize the way the 1-2-3 worksheet appears. For example, you may want to hide or display the frame surrounding the worksheet, remove gridlines or change their color, or hide the scroll bars. You can control all of these options—as well as a few others—from the Workbook Properties dialog box. As a shortcut, you can also control some of these items from the Sheet Properties InfoBox.

Using the check boxes on the View tab of the Workbook Properties dialog box, you can display most of the elements that you want to see on-screen and hide other screen elements. The choices you make here determine how much of the worksheet you can see at one time. Your work habits will help you determine which elements you need to see and which you can hide. If you never use the scroll bars, for example, you can turn them off.

Choose the File, Workbook Properties command to display the Workbook Properties dialog box shown in figure 32.1.

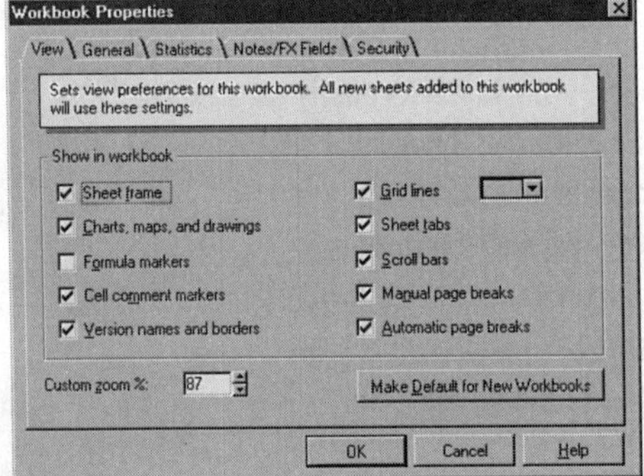

Fig. 32.1
Use the Workbook Properties dialog box to control the elements that appear on the 1-2-3 screen.

To display elements, place a check in the check box that appears next to them on the View tab of the Workbook Properties dialog box. To hide an element, remove checks from the check boxes next to the elements. The changes you make apply only to the current workbook.

You can also control the display of the sheet frame, grid lines, and Charts, Maps, and Drawings from the Sheet Properties InfoBox.

Removing Grid Lines

In some cases, such as when you are creating a data-entry form, a slide show, or a report, you may want to remove the gridlines that divide your worksheet into individual cells.

1-2-3 displays the gridlines by default, but you can remove them by removing the check mark from the Grid Lines check box on the View tab in the Workbook Properties dialog box. Figure 32.2 shows an example of a worksheet with no grid lines.

▶ **See** "Anatomy of a Slide," **p. 428**

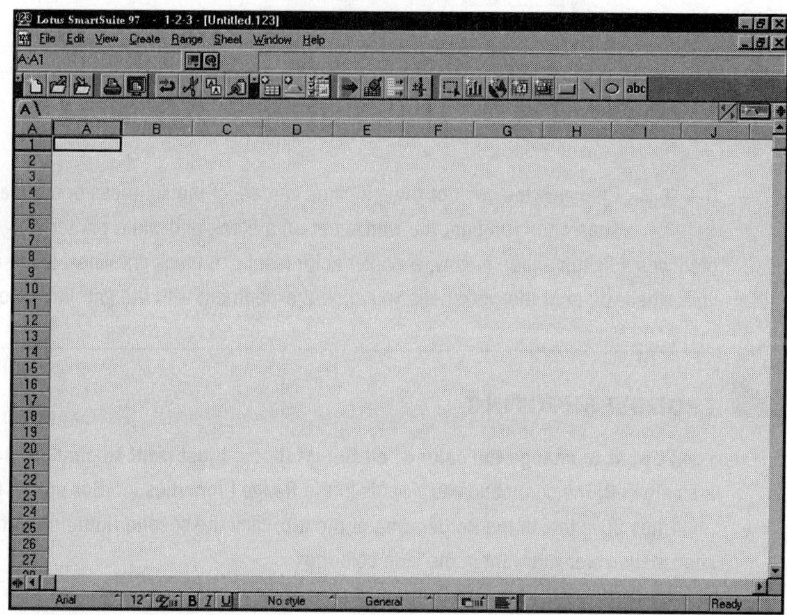

Fig. 32.2
You can remove gridlines to help display data more clearly.

To hide grid lines, you can use the Workbook Properties dialog box, but the Sheet Properties InfoBox may be quicker. Click the Sheet Properties SmartIcon and then display the View tab. Remove the check from the Grid line check box. To redisplay the gridlines, place a check in the Grid lines check box.

Changing the Color of Grid Lines

By default, the worksheet grid is gray. You can change it to any of the available 255 colors. To change the color of the worksheet grid, use either the Sheet Properties InfoBox or the Workbook Properties dialog box.

Click the Sheet Properties SmartIcon and then click the View tab to display the View tab. Make sure a check appears in the Grid Lines check box and open the list box next to the Grid Lines check box to see the color tab (see fig. 32.3).

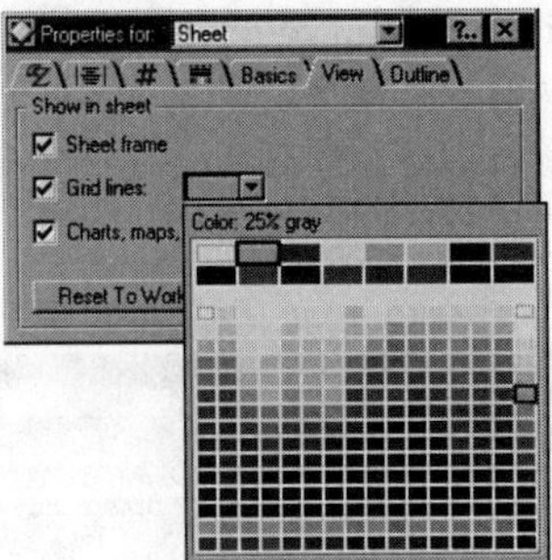

Fig. 32.3 Using the View tab of the Sheet Properties InfoBox, you can change the color of the grid lines in your worksheet.

NOTE Changing the color of the grid lines can affect the lightness or darkness of the grid lines when you print the worksheet on a black-and-white printer. A lighter color produces a lighter shade of gray; a darker color results in black grid lines. If you are printing grid lines when you print the worksheet, you should experiment with the grid-line color.

TROUBLESHOOTING

I don't want to change the color of all the gridlines; I just want to change the outline color of a single cell. The command you want is in the Range Properties InfoBox on the Color, Pattern, and Lines Style tab. In the Border area of the tab, click the second button from the left. Then, choose the color you want in the Line color box.

Hiding and Displaying Scroll Bars

The scroll bars along the right and bottom edges of the worksheet window appear by default when you create a worksheet file. You can hide the scroll bars, if you like, in case you're working with a small spreadsheet that doesn't require scrolling. Hiding the scroll bars also helps you display a larger worksheet on-screen and may keep other users from accessing information in a portion of the file that doesn't appear in the current window.

To hide the scroll bars in your worksheet window, follow these steps:

1. Choose File, Workbook Properties to display the Workbook Properties dialog box.
2. On the View tab, remove the check mark from the Scroll bars check box and choose OK.

When the worksheet redisplays, the scroll bars are hidden (see fig. 32.4). This change affects the current worksheet as well as any other worksheets in a grouped workbook.

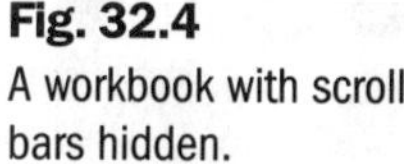

Fig. 32.4
A workbook with scroll bars hidden.

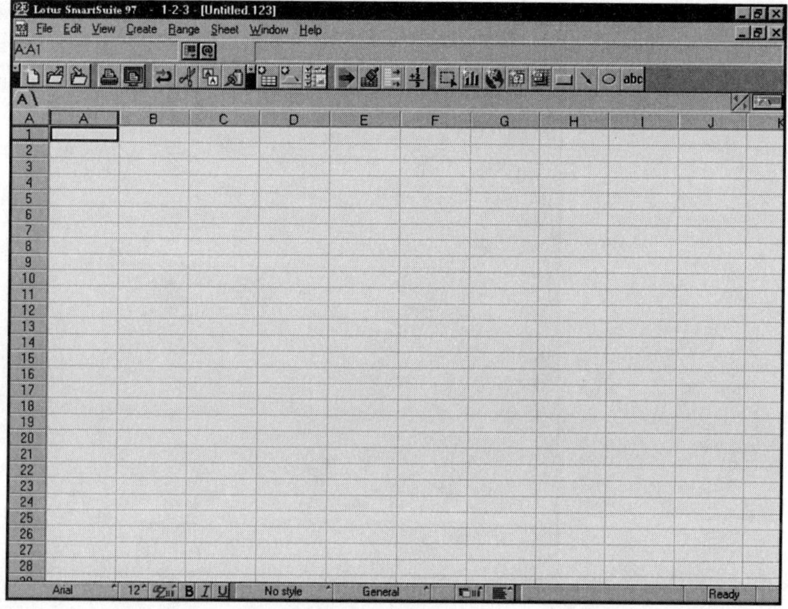

To redisplay the scroll bars, reopen the Workbook Properties dialog box and place a check in the Scroll bars check box; then click OK.

Hiding and Displaying Sheet Tabs

By default, 1-2-3 sequentially identifies new worksheets in a workbook with letters that appear on a worksheet tab. A new workbook contains only one worksheet called A. As you add worksheets, 1-2-3 names them B, C, D, and so on. And, each worksheet tab letter appears on the tab for the worksheet.

You can change worksheet tab names by double-clicking the tab letter and typing a new name. You can hide worksheets, but you may want to hide worksheet tab names without hiding the entire worksheet. Use the Workbook Properties dialog box to hide worksheet tabs.

Choose the File, Workbook Properties command. On the View tab of the Workbook Properties dialog box, remove the check from the Sheet tabs check box and choose OK. Your workbook will then look like the one in figure 32.5.

Fig. 32.5
A workbook with sheet tabs hidden.

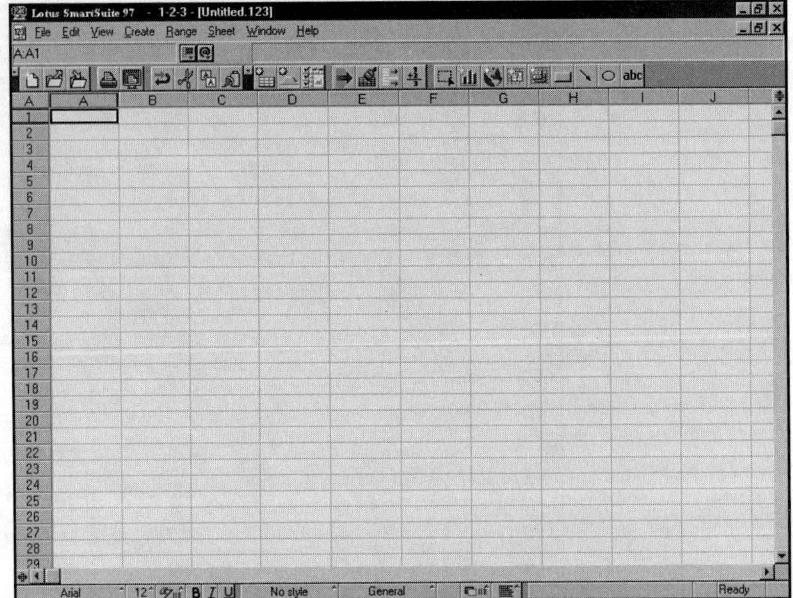

Hiding and Displaying Page Breaks

By default, 1-2-3 displays the markers for both manual and automatic page breaks in workbooks. You can hide these markers using the Workbook Properties dialog box.

Choose the File, Workbook Properties command. On the View tab of the Workbook Properties dialog box, remove the check marks from the Manual Page Breaks and Automatic Page Breaks check boxes and choose OK.

Hiding the Sheet Frame

The worksheet frame contains column letters and row numbers, and is used to identify cell locations. Sometimes, however, you don't need the worksheet frame. For example, you may want to use a workbook in a computerized screen show, where cell locations are not important. Use the Sheet Properties InfoBox to hide the sheet frame.

Click the Sheet Properties SmartIcon and then click the View tab to display the View tab. Remove the check mark that appears in the Sheet Frame check box. 1-2-3 removes the worksheet frame from the edge of the workbook (see fig. 32.6).

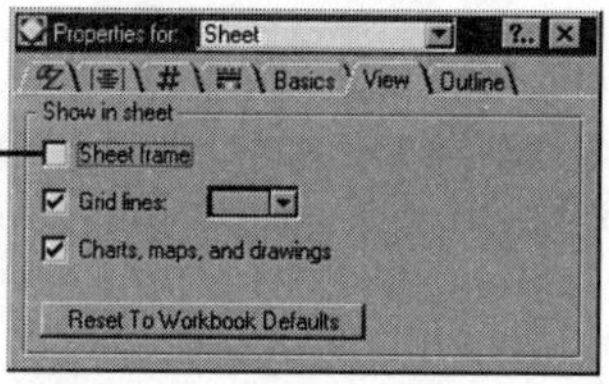

Fig. 32.6
The worksheet frame is hidden in this workbook.

Sheet Frame check box

Hiding and Displaying Formula and Cell Comment Markers

By default, 1-2-3 displays Cell Comment markers but does not display Formula markers. A Cell Comment marker is a mark you see in a cell if a cell comment exists for that particular cell. Formula markers are marks you see in cells that contain formulas. You can hide or display these markers using the Workbook Properties dialog box.

Choose the File, Workbook Properties command. On the View tab of the Workbook Properties dialog box, select or deselect the Formula Markers and Cell Comment Markers check boxes, depending on whether you want to display or hide these markers.

Hiding and Displaying Other Screen Elements

You also can display or hide the following 1-2-3 elements:

- Version names and borders
- Charts, maps, and drawings
- SmartIcons
- Status bar
- Edit line

To display or hide version names and borders, use the Workbook Properties dialog box (choose the File, Workbook Properties command).

If you want to temporarily suppress the display of SmartIcons, the Status bar, or the Edit line, open the View menu and choose the appropriate Hide command. 1-2-3 hides the element you selected and changes its "hide" command to a "show" command—for example, if you choose Hide SmartIcons, 1-2-3 removes the SmartIcons from the screen and changes the command on the View menu to Show SmartIcons. To redisplay any item you hide, reopen the View menu and choose the Show command for the hidden element.

To see as much of a worksheet as possible, turn off the scroll bars, worksheet tabs, worksheet frame, SmartIcons, edit line, and status bar. You then can turn off the grid to make the worksheet display less cluttered. Turning off the display of options also is useful if you need to create on-screen presentations.

Changing the View Preferences Defaults

You can save the settings you enter in the Workbook Properties dialog box as the default settings for every 1-2-3 workbook you create. To do this, click the Make Default for New Workbooks button. This button appears on the View tab of Workbook Properties dialog box. When you click this button, 1-2-3 then records the settings you've entered and applies them to subsequent worksheets you create (except those created using SmartMasters).

Applying Different Colors to the Worksheet Tabs

If you work with multipage worksheets, you may find it useful to color code the worksheet tabs. Not only does this make the worksheet more appealing visually, it can speed up your work. For example, if all your worksheets use red tabs for information about the North sales region, yellow for the South, green for the East, and purple for the West, you can use those visual clues as you work (see fig. 32.7).

If you use Lotus Notes in addition to 1-2-3, you might consider color-coding the tabs in both programs so that they match.

To apply a different color to a worksheet tab, click the worksheet tab whose color you want to change so that it is the current worksheet. Then, click the Sheet Properties InfoBox SmartIcon. On the Basics tab, click the drop-down arrow for Tab Color (see fig. 32.8). From the palette of possible colors that appears, choose the color you want for the worksheet tab.

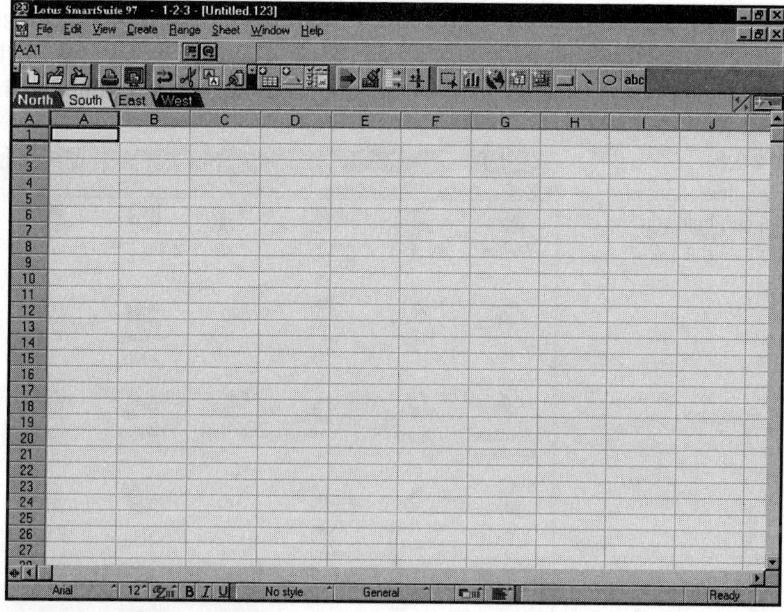

Fig. 32.7
Changing the color of worksheet tabs can give you visual clues to your worksheet's organization.

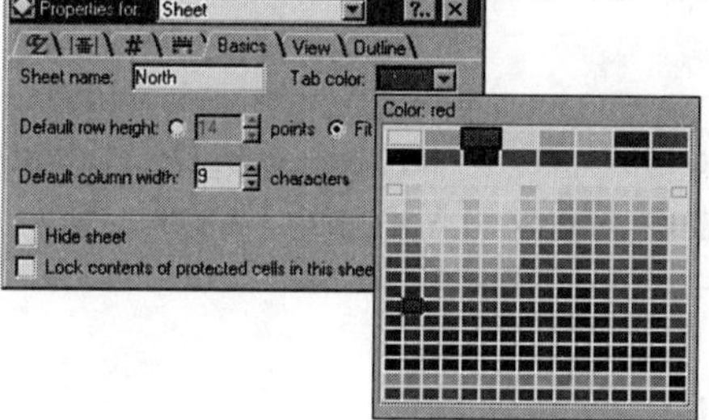

Fig. 32.8
Use the Basics tab of the Sheet Properties InfoBox to change the colors of worksheet tabs.

Customizing 1-2-3 with the Windows Control Panel

Like any product running under Windows, 1-2-3 reflects many of the changes you make in the Windows Control Panel. You can open the Control Panel from the Settings menu that appears after you click the Start button in Windows 95. You can use the Control Panel to add new hardware or software, change Windows color schemes, control the operation of your mouse, set the computer's date and time, configure your printers, and so on.

To view the Control Panel, click the Start button and choose Settings, Control Panel. Figure 32.9 shows a typical version of the Control Panel. Be aware that the elements in the Control Panel vary from computer to computer, depending on the programs installed.

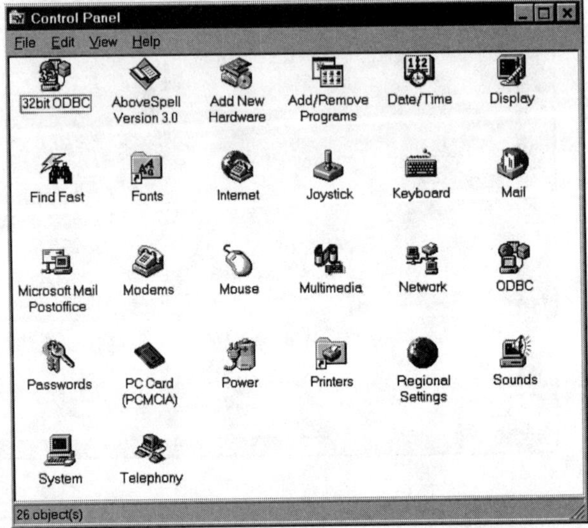

Fig. 32.9
The Windows Control Panel can help you customize the 1-2-3 screen.

The Control Panel contains icons for the different ways in which you can control your system's configuration and the Windows environment. Depending on your system configuration, different icons may appear. If Microsoft Plus is installed on your computer, for example, you'll see the Desktop Themes icon.

Changing Color Schemes

Windows applications have common elements, such as title bars, highlighting, and active and inactive windows. The colors used in these different elements reflect the currently selected Windows color scheme. You can choose a predefined color scheme, modify a predefined color scheme, or create a new color scheme; the screen elements in 1-2-3 will reflect your choice. If you choose a color scheme that specifies green for a highlight, for example, any highlighting in 1-2-3 will be green.

Any color scheme you choose for Windows affects *all* Windows programs, not just 1-2-3.

You switch between color schemes and create your own color schemes by using the Display icon in the Control Panel.

To change to another predefined color scheme, follow these steps:

1. In the Control Panel, double-click the Display icon. The Display Properties dialog box appears. Then, click the Appearance tab (see fig. 32.10).

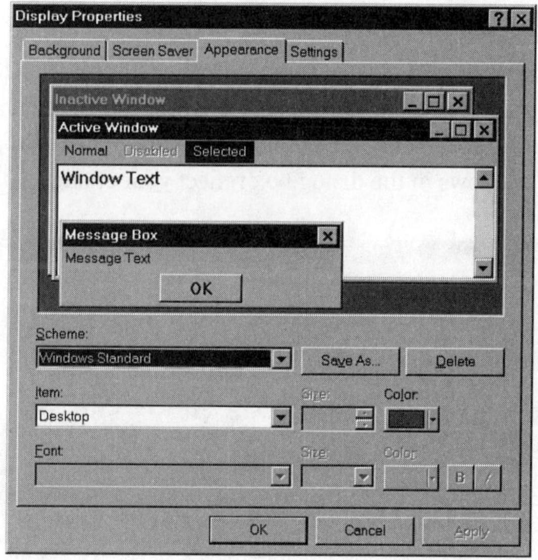

Fig. 32.10
Use the Appearance tab of the Display Properties dialog box to choose a different color scheme.

2. Click the drop-down arrow next to Scheme, and select a color scheme. The sample windows in the dialog box change to reflect your selection.
3. If desired, experiment with different color schemes by pressing the up- and down-arrow keys to select each scheme.

TIP Using a color scheme that includes only solid colors, such as the Windows Default color scheme, can speed screen-refresh time.

4. When you find a color scheme that suits you, choose OK to accept the change.

NOTE If you are using a notebook computer, you might want to choose one of the color schemes labeled "large" or "extra large." These color schemes also enlarge the font size used in dialog boxes, making your screen easier to read.

To modify an existing color scheme or create your own color scheme, follow these steps:

1. Display the Appearance tab of the Display Properties dialog box.
2. Click the Item drop-down arrow to display a list of the screen elements for which you can change color (or click the screen element in the sample display).
3. Select the element whose color you want to change. Windows displays, in the Color box, the current color of the selected element.
4. Open the Color list box. The Color list box expands to display a palette of colors.
5. Select a color or, to customize a color, click the Other button to display the Color dialog box (see fig. 32.11). Select a new color for the element and choose OK. Windows 95 redisplays the Appearance tab of the Display Properties dialog box. The sample windows in the dialog box reflect your change.

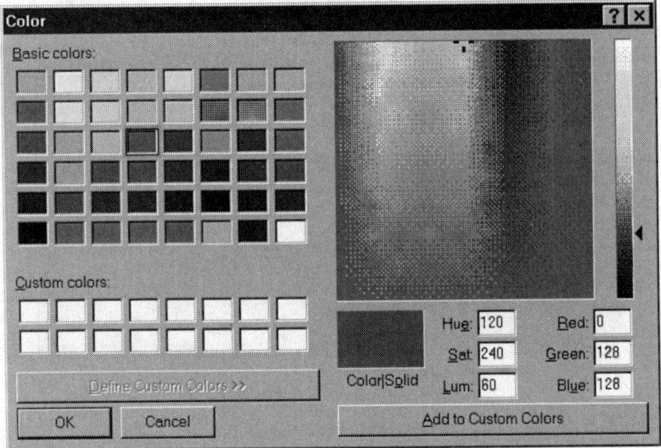

Fig. 32.11
Use the Color dialog box to customize color schemes.

6. Repeat steps 2 through 5 for any screen element you want to change.
7. When you are satisfied with the color scheme, choose OK to use your new color scheme.

NOTE After you change a color scheme, Windows uses the new scheme for every Windows session until you change it again. If you want to save a color scheme so that you can switch back to it after making other changes, click the Save As button on the Appearance tab of the Display Properties dialog box, and supply a name for your scheme.

Modifying the Desktop

When Windows 95 first appears, you see the desktop, which probably contains icons that are shortcuts to start programs. The background of the desktop can appear as a solid color, a pattern, or a picture, commonly known as a wallpaper. You can use, as a wallpaper for your desktop, any picture saved as a bitmap file.

CAUTION

Be aware that using a wallpaper uses computer memory and may make your computer operate slower.

Because you can use any bitmap file as wallpaper, you can create your own wallpaper with Windows Paint or any graphics program that can save a bitmap file. Simply save the image's bitmap file in the Windows folder.

To add a pattern and/or wallpaper, follow these steps:

1. In the Control Panel, double-click the Display icon. The Background tab of the Display Properties dialog box appears (see fig. 32.12).

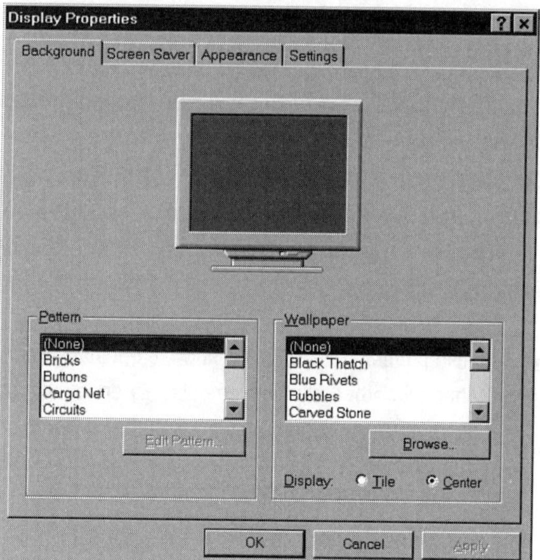

Fig. 32.12
You can use the Background tab of the Display Properties dialog box to select a desktop pattern or wallpaper.

2. To add a pattern, select a pattern from the Pattern list box. You can edit the pattern by clicking the Edit Pattern button and editing the pattern, pixel by pixel, in the Pattern Editor dialog box. Choose Done when you finish editing the pattern to return to the Display Properties dialog box.
3. To add wallpaper, select from the Wallpaper list. Wallpapers are bitmap (BMP) files. The ones you see in the list are stored in the Windows folder. If the wallpaper file is a large graphic, click the Center option button to center the wallpaper on-screen. If the wallpaper file is a small graphic, click the Tile option button to make the graphic repeat until it fills the screen.

If you want to look for BMP files in another location, click the Browse button.

4. Choose OK to accept the changes.

NOTE Any wallpaper that fills the screen—either because it is a large image or because you tiled it—takes precedence over any pattern you may have selected. If you select a pattern and a small wallpaper image, and you center the wallpaper, the wallpaper image appears in the center of the screen, with the pattern in the background around it.

Controlling the Mouse

You can use the Control Panel to control the way the mouse buttons work, the double-click speed, and the rate of motion of the mouse (*tracking speed*). If you are left-handed, swapping the functions of the left and right mouse buttons may help you work more comfortably. Customizing mouse tracking and double-click speeds also can make your work with 1-2-3 and other Windows applications easier. For example, a beginner might like slower tracking and double-click speeds.

Do you tend to lose your mouse pointer in the 1-2-3 window, particularly when you're working with elaborate worksheets, charts, or other graphic elements? Try enabling mouse trails on the Motion tab, or choosing a different pointer scheme (such as the 3D scheme or the large pointers) on the Pointers tab.

To customize the way the mouse works, follow these steps:

1. In the Control Panel, double-click the mouse icon. The Mouse Properties dialog box appears (see fig. 32.13). The dialog box you see might look different depending on the type of mouse and mouse drivers you have installed.

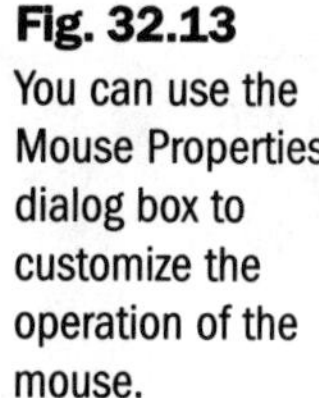

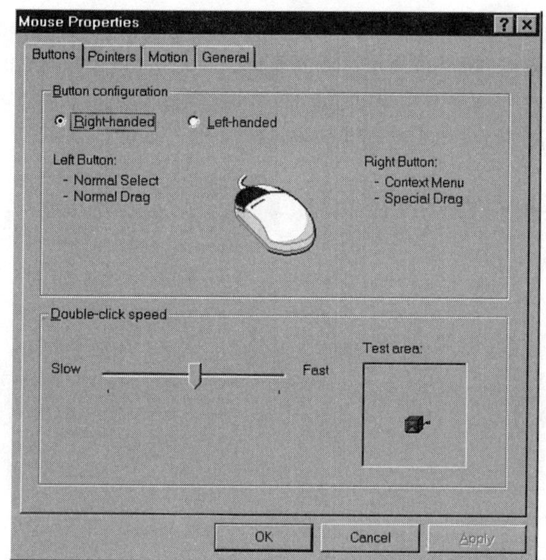

Fig. 32.13
You can use the Mouse Properties dialog box to customize the operation of the mouse.

2. Use the Buttons tab to control whether your mouse operates as a right-handed mouse or a left-handed mouse. Also control the double-click speed from this tab. The faster you set this speed, the quicker you will have to double-click for the double-click to be accepted. You can test the double-click rate by double-clicking the TEST rectangle (a jack-in-the-box appears in the test area when you successfully double-click).
3. If you installed animated pointers when you installed Windows 95, choose to use them from the Pointers tab.

TIP Pointer trails can be particularly helpful on monochrome notebook computers.

4. To control the pointer's motion, use the Motion tab. On this tab, you can adjust the pointer's speed and choose to display pointer trails. The faster you set the pointer's speed, the farther the mouse pointer will travel when you move the mouse. If you choose to show pointer trails, you'll see multiple images of the pointer as it travels across your screen.
5. On the General tab, you can change the actual mouse driver you have installed.

NOTE It may be easier for beginning users to set a slow tracking and double-click speed. However, remember that you become accustomed to the speeds you use. If you start with slow rates, you will have to readjust if you speed the rates up later. It may be better to maintain medium rates rather than make the change. ■

6. Choose OK to accept the changes.

CHAPTER 33

Customizing SmartIcons

by Elaine Marmel

1-2-3 97 provides over 200 SmartIcons, which provide single-click access to 1-2-3 commands and tasks. In addition, 1-2-3 ships with 15 predefined bars, which group together common SmartIcons into a single bar. You aren't limited, however, to the SmartIcons displayed in the standard bars; you can create custom SmartIcons to execute the macros that you create, and you can create your own bars that contain SmartIcons you use regularly. ■

Customizing SmartIcon bars

Although 1-2-3 displays SmartIcon bars appropriate to the task you're performing, you may find you need a SmartIcon that doesn't appear by default. You can customize the SmartIcon bars.

Creating SmartIcons

If you perform a task for which you can't find a SmartIcon—or if you're simply "artistic" and want to use a different picture on a SmartIcon—create your own SmartIcon.

Using SmartIcon Bars

As you work in 1-2-3, you will notice that the SmartIcon bar changes from time to time, depending on your actions. The first portion of the SmartIcon bar is called the Universal Bar, and it always appears on-screen. It contains SmartIcons you might use under any conditions (see figure 33.1).

The rest of the SmartIcons that appear actually depend on what you're doing. For example, when you are working with ranges, the Range bar appears (see fig. 33.1); but when you are working with a chart, the Chart bar appears (see fig. 33.2). Similarly, when you are working with drawn objects in the worksheet, the Draw bar appears (see fig. 33.3).

▶ **See** "Working with Cells and Ranges," **p. 55**

▶ **See** "Manipulating Chart Elements," **p. 322**

▶ **See** "SmartIcon Basics," **p. 30**

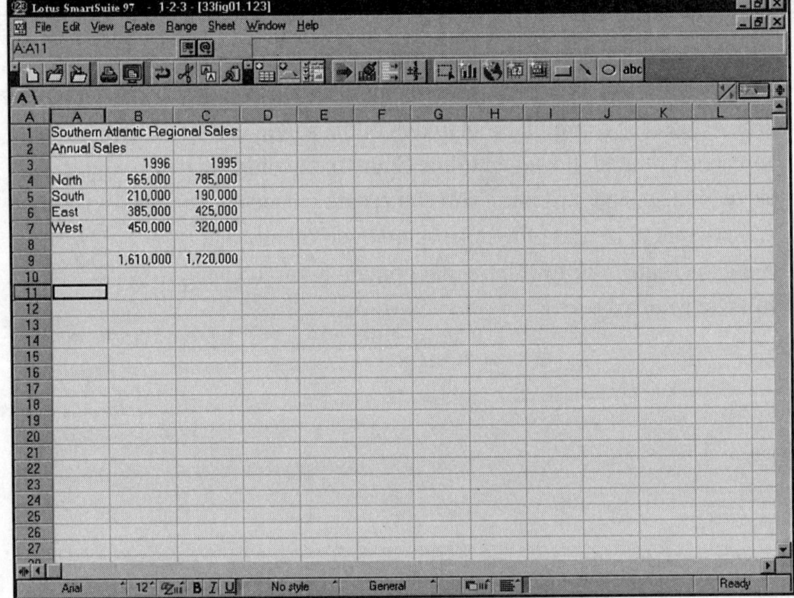

Fig. 33.1
You'll always see the Universal SmartIcon bar, no matter what you're doing. If you're simply working with ranges in a sheet, you'll also see the Range SmartIcon bar.

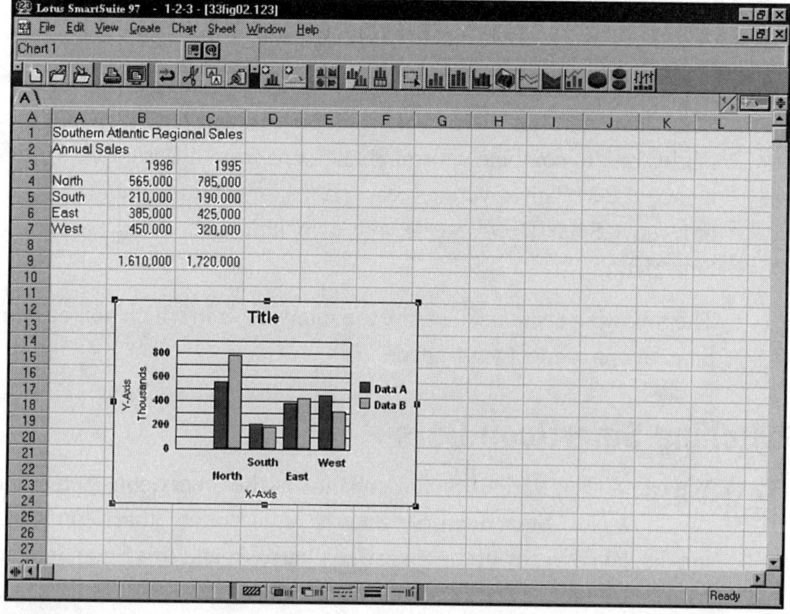

Fig. 33.2
When you select a chart, you'll see the Chart SmartIcon bar, which displays SmartIcons for working with charts.

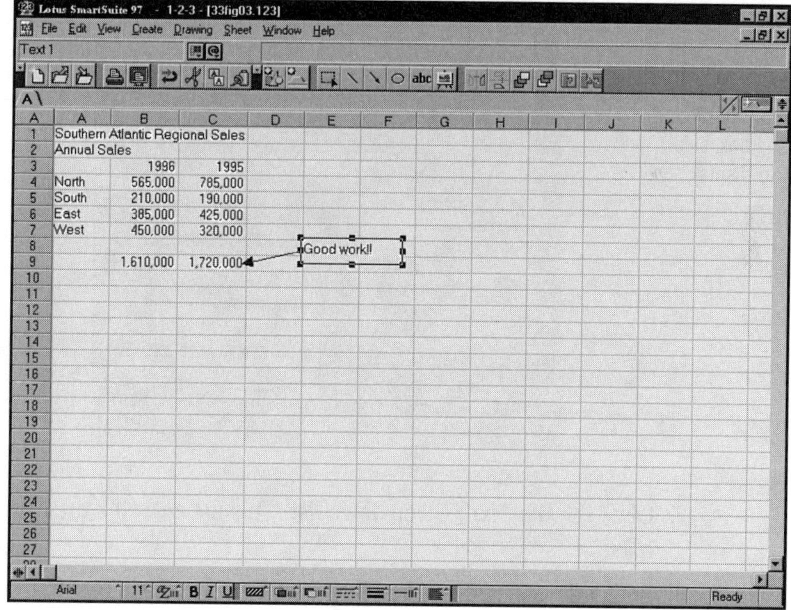

Fig. 33.3
When you select a drawn object, 1-2-3 displays the Draw SmartIcon bar, which you can use to manipulate drawn objects.

Customizing the SmartIcons

Because 1-2-3 97 includes a large collection of SmartIcons, you may find that the SmartIcon you want already exists but isn't displayed in any of the standard bars. Or you might want to combine several SmartIcons from different bars into a single bar for convenience. 1-2-3 97 gives you several options for customizing the SmartIcon bar. You can add or remove SmartIcons, create your own named bars, and even create your own SmartIcons.

The following sections describe the many ways in which you can customize the 1-2-3 97 SmartIcons to meet your needs.

Switching SmartIcon Bars

You can display various SmartIcon bars in the SmartIcons Setup dialog box. You can use the Show Next SmartIcon, Set SmartIcon to switch SmartIcon bars, but this SmartIcon is not displayed in any of the SmartIcon bars. To add this SmartIcon to a bar, refer to "Adding and Removing SmartIcons" later in this chapter. Follow these steps:

1. Choose the File, User Setup, SmartIcons Setup command to access the SmartIcons dialog box (see fig. 33.4).

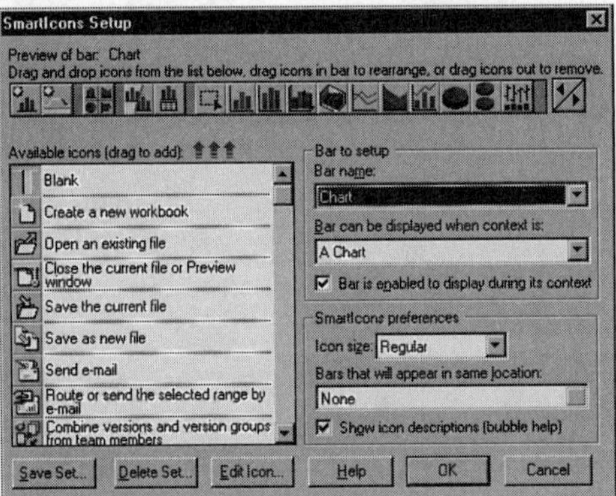

Fig. 33.4
In the SmartIcons dialog box, select the bar to display.

2. Click the Bar Name drop-down list. This list contains the names of all SmartIcon bars.
3. Select the desired bar. You'll see the SmartIcons in that bar in the preview of the bar above the Bar Name drop-down list.
4. Click OK or press Enter.

You can use a shortcut to display the SmartIcons Setup dialog box. At the left edge of each SmartIcon bar, you'll see a control menu button. Click the control menu button, and you'll see a list of commands (see fig. 33.5). Choose the SmartIcons Setup command to display the dialog box.

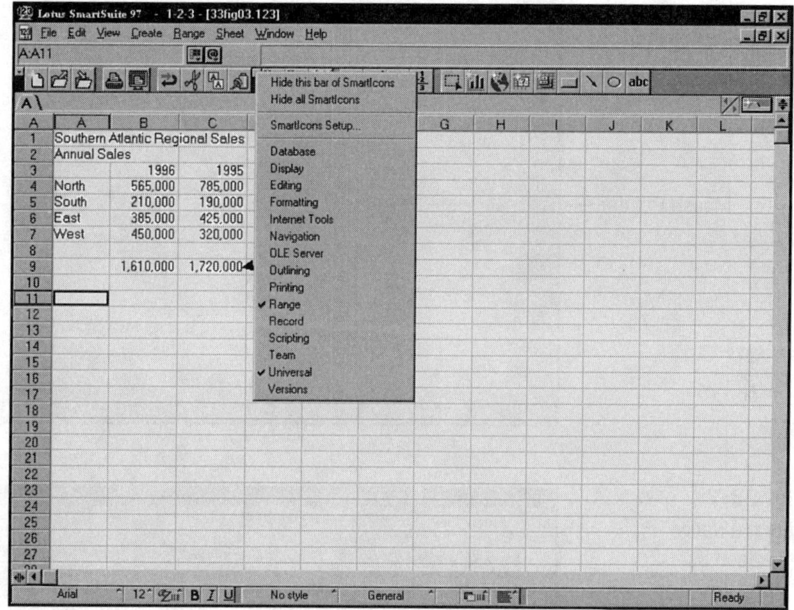

Fig. 33.5
When you click the list box at the left edge of a SmartIcon bar, you see a shortcut menu from which you can display the SmartIcons Setup dialog box.

Changing the Position of a SmartIcon Bar

Initially, the SmartIcon bars are displayed at the top of the Worksheet window. You can move a SmartIcon bar around the screen if you don't like its position. You can position the bar on any side of the screen or make it "float" within the program window.

To move a SmartIcon bar, place the mouse pointer over the area just below the control menu button for that SmartIcon bar. The mouse pointer changes to a hand (see fig. 33.6). Drag the SmartIcon bar to its new location.

If you move the bar out into the center area of the screen, you can change the size and shape of the bar by dragging its edges. Figure 33.7 shows the Range bar resized in the center of the screen. One great advantage of using a floating bar is that you can expand it to accommodate any number of SmartIcons—more than a SmartIcon bar that appears at the edge of the screen. Remember, though, that a larger area filled with SmartIcons leaves less actual working space on the screen.

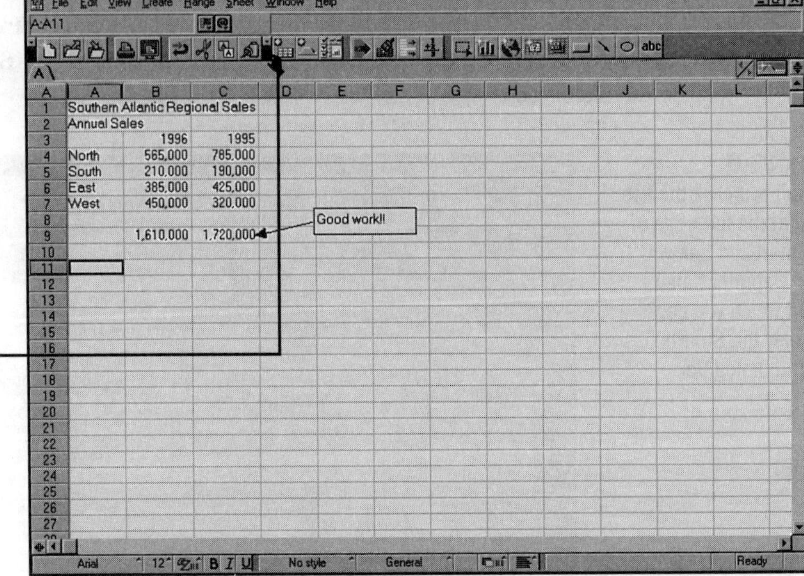

Fig. 33.6
When you place the mouse pointer just below the control menu button of a SmartIcon bar, the pointer changes to a hand, indicating that you can drag the bar to move it.

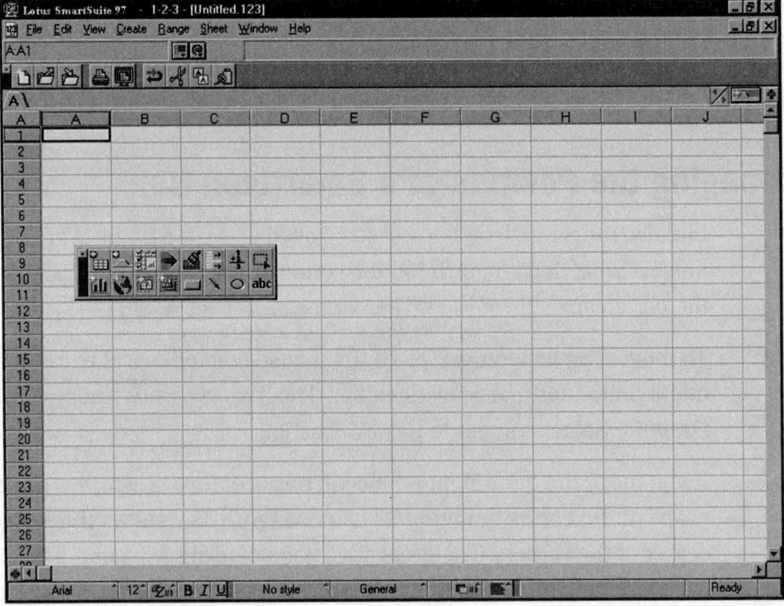

Fig. 33.7
Here the Range SmartIcon bar is floating.

Hiding a SmartIcon Bar

You can "hide" a SmartIcon bar using the menu that appears when you open the SmartIcon list box. Click the SmartIcon bar to remove the check that appears to the left of the SmartIcon bar name.

When you hide a SmartIcon bar, 1-2-3 removes the SmartIcon bar from the screen. You may want to hide the bar when you require maximum screen space for a worksheet. After hiding the bar, you can show it again by opening the menu and choosing the SmartIcon bar.

You can hide all SmartIcon bars using the View, Hide SmartIcons command.

▶ **See** "Hiding and Displaying Other Screen Elements," **p. 755**

Rearranging SmartIcons in a Bar

If you don't like the order of SmartIcons in a bar, you can rearrange them to suit your needs. Rearranging SmartIcons is simple: hold down the Ctrl key and drag the SmartIcon to a new position. Release both the mouse button and the Ctrl key when the SmartIcon appears where you want it. Figure 33.8 shows a SmartIcon being moved.

Our development editor, who often uses other people's equipment, points out that it isn't very nice to move SmartIcons if you share your system with others. She hates having to use somebody else's customized system when she's clicking things and expecting the button to be "right there"—and it isn't.

If you press Ctrl and drag the SmartIcon off the bar, 1-2-3 moves the SmartIcon to the end of the bar.

Adding and Removing SmartIcons

In addition to rearranging the SmartIcons in a SmartIcon bar, you can also add new SmartIcons to a bar or remove SmartIcons that you do not use from a bar.

To add or remove a SmartIcon in a SmartIcon bar, follow these steps:

1. Open the SmartIcons Setup dialog box by choosing File, User Setup, SmartIcons Setup or by clicking the control menu button next to a SmartIcon bar and choosing SmartIcons Setup.

2. Select the SmartIcon bar you want to modify using the Bar Name list box. The SmartIcons in the selected bar appear in the Preview of Bar box.
3. In the Available Icons list box, locate the SmartIcon that you want to add.
4. Drag the SmartIcon up to the bar you selected, positioning the mouse where you want the SmartIcon to appear.
5. Release the mouse button. The SmartIcon appears in the bar where you dropped it.
6. Click OK to save the changes made to the current bar. When you return to the worksheet, the changes you made are reflected in the bar.

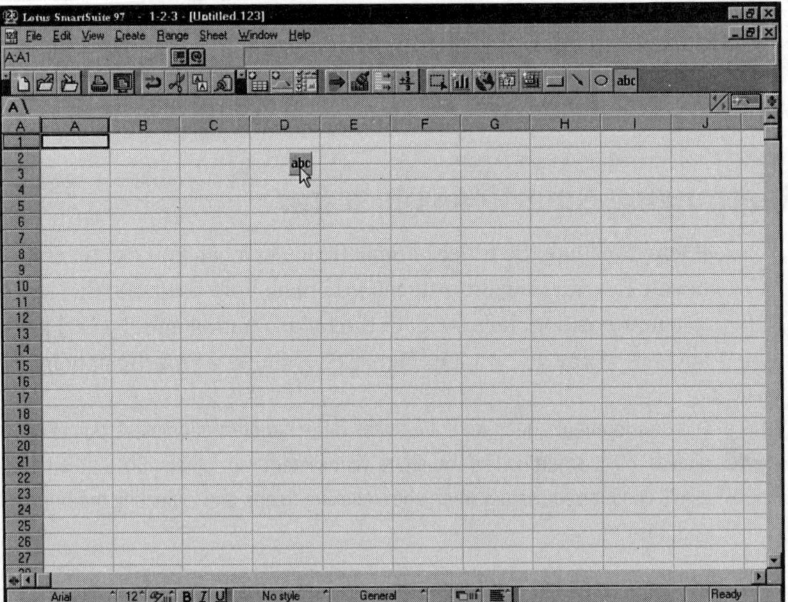

Fig. 33.8
Move a SmartIcon in the current bar by pressing Ctrl and dragging.

If you drop a SmartIcon into a position that already contains a SmartIcon, the new SmartIcon appears next to the current SmartIcon. To remove a SmartIcon from a bar, drag it out of the bar at the top of the dialog box. You can change the order of the SmartIcons by dragging them to new positions on the SmartIcon bar in the SmartIcons Setup dialog box.

You can place as many SmartIcons on a bar as you want. Remember, however, that you might not be able to see all of them if the SmartIcon bar appears at the top, bottom, left, or right edge of the screen. If you can't see all the SmartIcons on a bar, you might want to drag the bar into the center of the screen and resize it (see "Changing the Position of a SmartIcon Bar" earlier in this chapter).

Figure 33.9 shows a SmartIcon being moved onto the Universal bar.

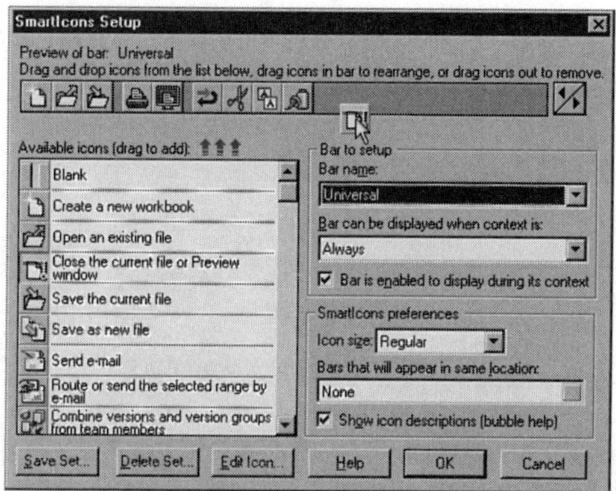

Fig. 33.9
Drag a SmartIcon to add it to the current bar.

Use the Blank SmartIcon (at the top of the Available Icons list box) to separate SmartIcons into groups within a bar. You can use as many blanks as you want.

CAUTION

When you modify an existing SmartIcon bar, the changes you make cannot be undone. If you will be making substantial changes to an existing bar, use the Save Set button to save the bar under a new name. See the next section for more information.

Creating a New SmartIcon Bar

Creating a new SmartIcon bar is a simple variation on the procedure described in the preceding section. In the SmartIcons Setup dialog box, start by selecting a bar that contains some of the SmartIcons you want on the new SmartIcon bar (this is not necessary, but it can make your job easier). Add and remove SmartIcons from that bar as desired until the new SmartIcon bar contains the SmartIcons you want. Then, click the Save Set command button and then Save As New to display the Save As New SmartIcons File dialog box (see fig. 33.10.)

Type a name for the SmartIcon set in the SmartIcons Bar Name text box. Type a new file name for the SmartIcon set in the SmartIcons File Name text box. (Each SmartIcon set is stored on disk under a file name with the extension SMI). Click OK to close the Save as New SmartIcons File dialog box. You return to the SmartIcons Setup dialog box.

Using the Bar Can Be Displayed when Context Is drop-down list, specify when the new SmartIcon bar should appear. Set any SmartIcon preferences you might have (such as Icon size) and click OK to close the SmartIcons Setup dialog box. The new SmartIcon bar will appear when the context on-screen meets the criteria you set in the dialog box.

Fig. 33.10
Enter a name and file name for the new SmartIcon set.

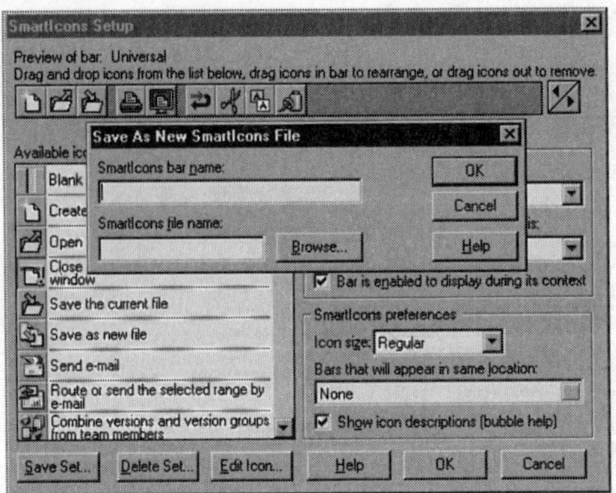

NOTE You can delete SmartIcon bars by using the Delete Set button in the SmartIcons Setup dialog box. This button displays Delete Set dialog box. You can then select as many bars as you want from the Bar(s) of SmartIcons to Delete list box. Choose OK. A Warning box appears asking if you really want to delete the selected sets. Answer Yes or No to return to the SmartIcons Setup dialog box. ■

Changing the Size of SmartIcons

You can display SmartIcons in two sizes: regular and large. By default, 1-2-3 97 displays regular SmartIcons. To display large SmartIcons, follow these steps:

1. Open the SmartIcons Setup dialog box.
2. In the SmartIcons Preferences box, open the Icon Size drop-down list.
3. Choose Large.
4. Choose OK to close the SmartIcons Setup dialog box and return to the worksheet.

NOTE To return to regular size, repeat the preceding steps, but click on Regular in step 3. ■

Figure 33.11 shows the Universal SmartIcons in a large floating bar. Notice that some SmartIcons change when you display them in a larger size; the pictures become more detailed. Large SmartIcons are usually best on super VGA monitors, but can be useful in other situations.

TROUBLESHOOTING

After choosing a SmartIcon, nothing happens. Many of the SmartIcons require that you first select a range or perform some other action before activating the SmartIcon. For example, before you can use the Copy SmartIcon, you must first select the range of cells that you want to copy.

Some of the SmartIcons I added to the bar are not appearing on-screen. What should I do?
If you added more SmartIcons than the bar can display across the top of the screen (or along the side), 1-2-3 truncates the bar. To display all your SmartIcons, drag the SmartIcon bar into the middle of the screen and then drag borders to resize the bar if necessary.

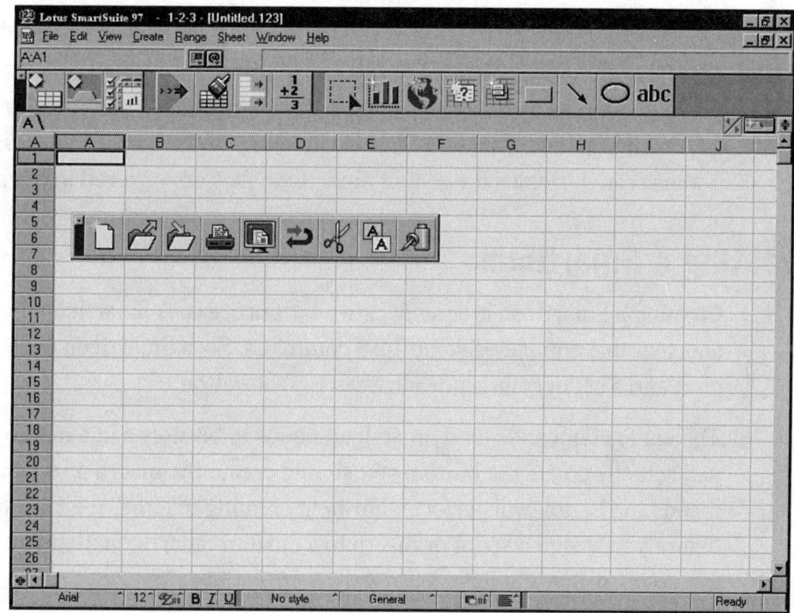

Fig. 33.11
The Universal bar with large SmartIcons.

Creating SmartIcons

Although over 200 SmartIcons are supplied with 1-2-3 97, one of the more interesting features of SmartIcons is the ability to create your own. You can assign to a SmartIcon any 1-2-3 97 task that can be performed by a macro—for example, placing your name and address in a worksheet. Another SmartIcon could perform a more complex task, such as combining data from several files and printing a report that includes the latest sales figures and a chart. The possibilities are endless.

One good use for custom SmartIcons is to automate a worksheet application that you create and distribute to other users in your company. Instead of a standard SmartIcon, such as one that prints a range, your application can have a SmartIcon that prints all the ranges of a standard company report. You can create additional SmartIcons that use other macro commands to automate other tasks.

Understanding Custom SmartIcons

Unlike the standard SmartIcons provided with 1-2-3 97, custom SmartIcons can be modified. You can control their appearance and actions.

Custom SmartIcons are made up of two parts: a Windows bitmap (BMP) file, which contains the image you see on the icon, and the macro actions to be performed when the custom SmartIcon is selected.

When you create a custom SmartIcon, the bitmap file is stored in the \Lotus\123\Icons folder. You can add a custom SmartIcon to any of the bars, regardless of the bar in which it was created. Details for adding SmartIcon files are covered in the next few sections.

Creating a SmartIcon

Creating a SmartIcon is actually a two-part process. A SmartIcon, by its definition, is a shortcut that completes some 1-2-3 command. So, a SmartIcon consists of the button you click and a set of commands attached to that button.

The set of commands for a SmartIcon needs to be stored in a macro or a script. So, before you actually create the button, you should create the macro or script containing the commands the button will perform. For help creating macros, see Chapter 36. Make sure, before you assign a script or macro to a custom SmartIcon, that you test the script or macro to ensure that it runs properly.

▶ **See** "Writing Your First Macros," **p. 814**

To create a custom SmartIcon, you use 1-2-3's icon editor. To create a custom SmartIcon, follow these steps:

1. Open the SmartIcons Setup dialog box.
2. Choose Edit Icon. The Edit SmartIcons dialog box appears (see fig. 33.12). You'll draw your new SmartIcon by clicking in the Picture Editor area. Each click adds a square to the picture.

You can create new icons by using existing icon images as a starting point. Select the image in the Available Icons list box and then use the Picture editor area to change the original.

3. To control the color of the square that appears on-screen, use the color palettes associated with the Mouse button colors:
   - To change the color of the square that appears when you click the left mouse button, use the left mouse button to click on the Left list box. 1-2-3 displays a color palette.

- Change the color of the square that appears when you click the right mouse button by clicking (with the left mouse button) on the Right list box and choosing a color.

You can erase parts of your image by selecting the background color of the icon and drawing over existing colors.

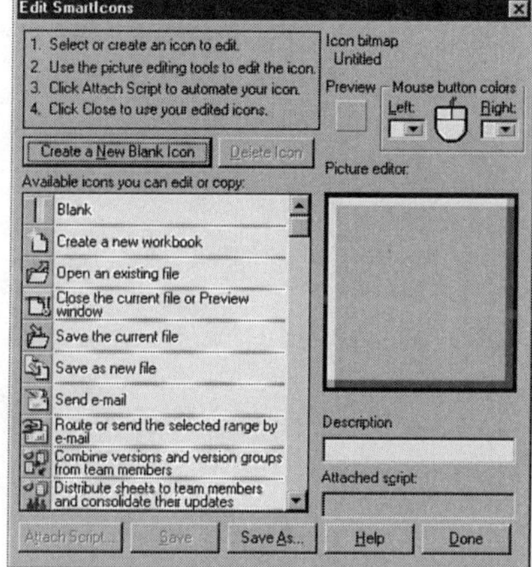

Fig. 33.12
Create an image for the custom SmartIcon in the Edit SmartIcons dialog box.

4. In the Description text box, type a tool tip description for your SmartIcon. These words will appear when you use the mouse pointer to point at your SmartIcon while working in 1-2-3.
5. Click the Save As button to provide a file name for your custom SmartIcon. After you've supplied a file name, click the Save button to redisplay the Edit SmartIcons dialog box.
6. Click the Attach Script button to display the Attach Script dialog box.
7. Select the Script or Macro option button.

   If you select the Script option button: choose in the From drop-down list a file name of an open workbook and then select the script name in the Script Name list box. Or if you choose (External File) in the From drop-down list, type a script file name in the File Name text box. (If needed, click the Browse button to locate the file in the Browse dialog box.)

   If you selected the Macro option button in the Attach Script dialog box, enter macro commands in the text box.

8. Click the Attach button to return to the Edit SmartIcons dialog box.
9. Choose Save to save your SmartIcon, Done to close the Edit SmartIcons dialog box, and OK to close the SmartIcons Setup dialog box.

NOTE Note that the Attach Script button will *not* be available until you have saved your SmartIcon. ■

CHAPTER 34

Working with Templates

by Elaine Marmel

In addition to customizing the 1-2-3 for Windows workspace and SmartIcons palettes, you also can create customized workbook templates. Lotus also provides, along with 1-2-3, a set of workbook templates called *SmartMasters* that you can use to quickly create workbooks. You can use these SmartMasters as is or you can customize them to suit your needs. ■

Working with SmartMasters

1-2-3 enables you to use workbook templates to quickly create new workbooks.

Automatically load workbooks

You may repeatedly use a particular workbook. In that case, have 1-2-3 open it automatically when you start the program.

Working with Workbook Templates

Using *templates* is common practice in most business environments. A template is a workbook that contains predefined settings and data you use routinely in your workbooks. Lotus Corporation calls these templates *SmartMasters*, and they serve as the foundation for workbooks you create. Using SmartMasters, you can quickly set up any type of file in 1-2-3 that you may need—budget worksheets, financial reports, and automated data input forms, just to name a few. Why use SmartMasters? Use SmartMasters to save time—you create the SmartMaster only once but use it many times to create other workbooks.

Lotus Corporation supplies predefined SmartMasters with 1-2-3 that contain data, formulas, macros, scripts, and formatting for common business documents. Because each SmartMaster already contains the data and formulas you need, you can quickly get to work because you don't need to spend time re-creating complicated formulas and workbook formatting. In addition, each of the predefined SmartMasters is automated with 1-2-3 macros and scripts, so you only need to click buttons to perform actions such as printing.

You can use the SmartMasters provided with 1-2-3 exactly as they ship from Lotus Corporation, or you can customize them to suit your needs. If you prefer, you can use them as the foundation to create and design your own SmartMasters. And, of course, you can always create your own SmartMaster from scratch.

When you start 1-2-3, you see a Welcome screen where you can choose to create a new workbook or work on an existing workbook. When you click the Create a New Workbook Using a SmartMaster tab, a series of SmartMasters appears in the list box (see fig. 34.1) on which you can base your new workbook. Similarly, when you click the Create a New Workbook SmartIcon or choose File, New Workbook to create a new workbook, 1-2-3 displays a comparable dialog box that contains the same list of SmartMasters.

To base a new workbook on a SmartMaster, you highlight the name of the SmartMaster you want to use and click OK. When you highlight a SmartMaster, a description of the SmartMaster appears in the Description section of the dialog box. For a complete description of the SmartMasters provided by 1-2-3, refer to table 34.1. If the SmartMaster you want to use doesn't appear in the list, click the More SmartMaster Templates command button. If you want to create a new blank workbook based on default 1-2-3 settings, just select the Create a Blank Workbook command button and click OK.

After you have selected a SmartMaster, 1-2-3 creates a new untitled workbook based on the information and formatting provided by the SmartMaster. All of the predefined SmartMasters that Lotus Corporation ships with 1-2-3 contain information, formatting, and formulas. To use any of these predefined SmartMasters, you simply fill in the input cells with your own data. In each of these predefined SmartMasters, input cells appear shaded.

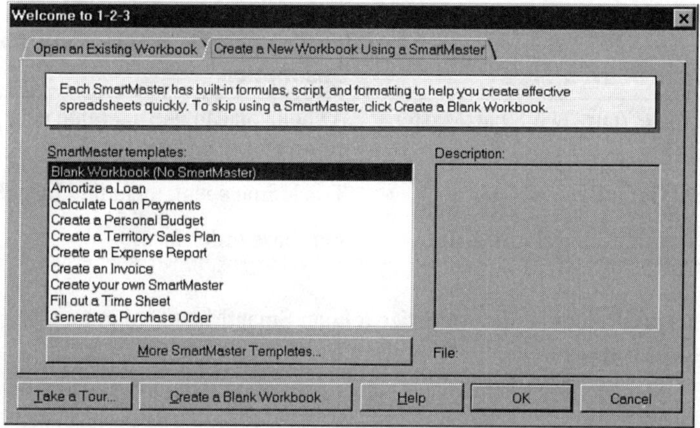

Fig. 34.1
Choose a SmartMaster from the New File dialog box.

> **CAUTION**
>
> Only enter data in the shaded cells. If you enter data in any other cells you may corrupt worksheet formulas.

When you enter data in the shaded cells of a workbook based on a predefined SmartMaster, 1-2-3 recalculates the workbook using the data supplied by you to update formulas that exist in other cells in the workbook. After you have entered the appropriate data in each of the input cells, the workbook is complete and you can then print the workbook.

Table 34.1 1-2-3 SmartMasters

SmartMaster	Description
Blank Workbook	Blank workbook not based on any SmartMaster
Amortize a Loan	Calculate monthly payments and a first year schedule for a loan
Calculate Loan Payments	Supply various combinations of principal interest, and term to calculate monthly loan payments
Create a Personal Budget	Workbook for tracking monthly expenses
Create a Territory Sales Plan	Sales forecast workbook
Create an Expense Report	Workbook for tracking weekly expenses
Create an Invoice	Invoice form

continues

Table 34.1 Continued

SmartMaster	Description
Create Your Own SmartMaster	A shell you can use to create your own SmartMaster completely from scratch
Fill Out a Time Sheet	Track time spent; including billable hours
Generate a Purchase Order	Purchase order form

Let's take a look at the Amortize a Loan SmartMaster to get a sense of how the predefined SmartMasters work.

The Amortize a Loan SmartMaster

Using the Amortize a Loan SmartMaster, you can track your own mortgage payments. In addition, you can use the Amortize a Loan SmartMaster as an analysis tool for calculating the results of different loan amounts, interest rates, and terms. If you are considering refinancing a loan, you can check to see how a lower interest rate could affect your payments. If you simply want to calculate whether or not you have the funds to purchase a home or car, use the Amortize a Loan SmartMaster (see fig. 34.2). To use the Amortize a Loan SmartMaster, choose File, New Workbook, select Loan Amortization from the list of SmartMasters, and click OK.

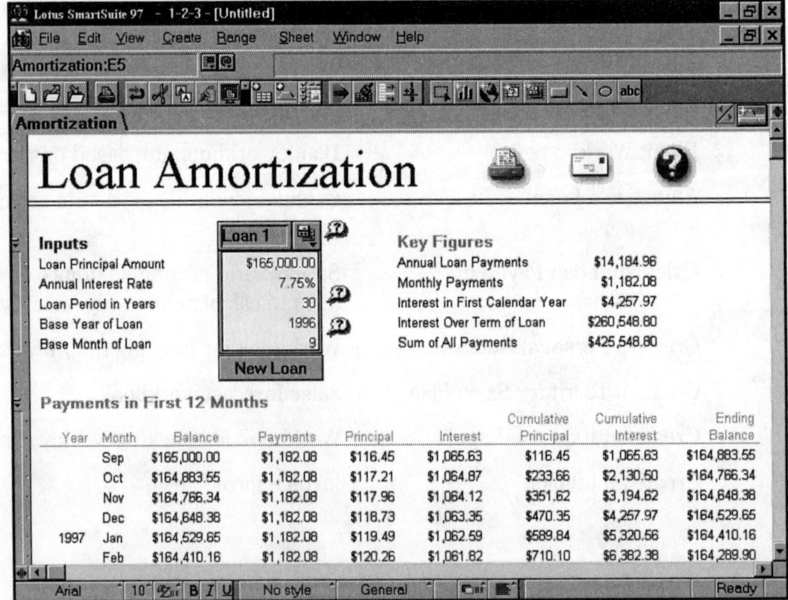

Fig. 34.2
The Amortize a Loan SmartMaster allows you to test the effects of interest rates, loan amounts, and terms.

The inputs required by the Amortize a Loan SmartMaster include the loan principal amount, the annual interest rate, the loan period in years, the base year (the first year) of the loan, and the base month (first month) of the loan.

This SmartMaster takes advantage of the Version Manager feature of 1-2-3 and enables you to perform what-if analyses by saving various combinations of data as separate sets. You can then switch among the various versions to see the end result.

▶ **See** "Understanding Version Manager Basics," **p. 508**

Using 1-2-3's Version Manager, you can test the effects of varying interest rates and loan amounts. Notice the title of the Inputs is Loan 1, the first version. To try your own proposed loan information, click the New Loan button that appears below all the inputs. 1-2-3 clears the contents of the input cells and changes the version name from Loan 1 to Loan 2, indicating you are starting a new scenario.

To make your scenarios more meaningful, change the name of the scenario from Loan 1 to anything you want. For example, you may be testing different interest rates; if so, name the version with its interest rate. To change the name of any version, double-click the version name to edit the name; type the new name for the version, and press Enter.

In the Loan Principal Amount input cell, enter the loan amount, say $100,000. In the Annual Interest Rate input cell, enter the annual rate, say 8%, as a decimal (.08) or with a trailing percent sign (%). In the Loan Period in Years input cell, enter the length of the loan—say 30 years. In the Base Year of Loan input cell, enter the year the loan begins. Last, in the Base Month of Loan input cell, enter the numerical month (for example, June = 6) in which the first payment will be made. As you enter each piece of information, 1-2-3 recalculates the information in the rest of the workbook. You may see ERR in some cells as you enter information; these errors will disappear when you completely enter the loan information. Also, the formulas in the Key Figures area automatically tally the totals.

The Amortize a Loan SmartMaster provides two schedules: The Payments in the First 12 Months of the loan (refer to fig. 34.2) and the Yearly Schedule of Balances and Payments (see fig. 34.3). In addition, each schedule breaks down the payments to show the amount that is paid towards the principal of the loan and the amount that pays interest.

To enter a new set of data for the next scenario, click the New Loan button again and enter new information. Suppose you create several versions and you'd like to return to a version you previously created. No problem, just click the version name list box to display a list of versions (see fig. 34.4). When you switch versions, 1-2-3 redisplays the values in the input cells and recalculates the formulas to reflect the changes in the input cells.

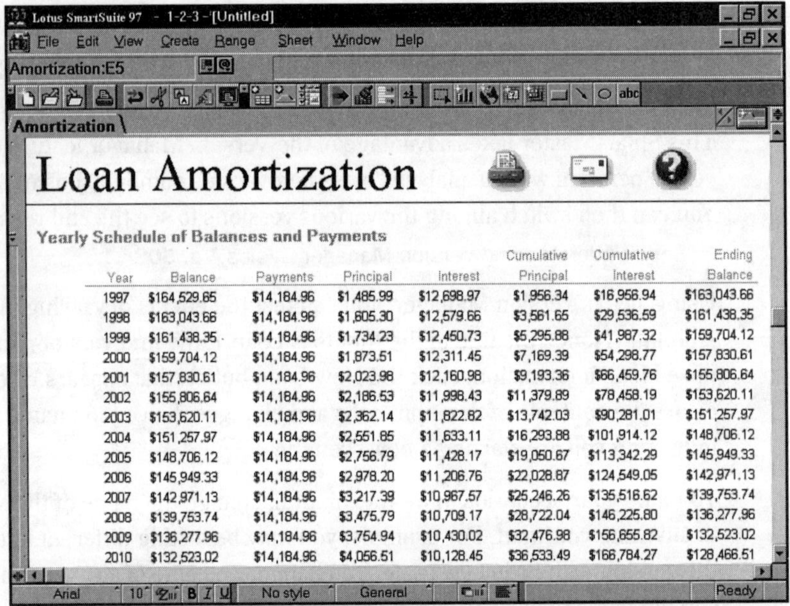

Year	Balance	Payments	Principal	Interest	Cumulative Principal	Cumulative Interest	Ending Balance
1997	$164,529.65	$14,184.96	$1,485.99	$12,698.97	$1,956.34	$16,956.94	$163,043.66
1998	$163,043.66	$14,184.96	$1,605.30	$12,579.66	$3,561.65	$29,536.59	$161,438.35
1999	$161,438.35	$14,184.96	$1,734.23	$12,450.73	$5,295.88	$41,987.32	$159,704.12
2000	$159,704.12	$14,184.96	$1,873.51	$12,311.45	$7,169.39	$54,298.77	$157,830.61
2001	$157,830.61	$14,184.96	$2,023.98	$12,160.98	$9,193.36	$66,459.76	$155,806.64
2002	$155,806.64	$14,184.96	$2,186.53	$11,998.43	$11,379.89	$78,458.19	$153,620.11
2003	$153,620.11	$14,184.96	$2,362.14	$11,822.82	$13,742.03	$90,281.01	$151,257.97
2004	$151,257.97	$14,184.96	$2,551.85	$11,633.11	$16,293.88	$101,914.12	$148,706.12
2005	$148,706.12	$14,184.96	$2,756.79	$11,428.17	$19,050.67	$113,342.29	$145,949.33
2006	$145,949.33	$14,184.96	$2,978.20	$11,206.76	$22,028.87	$124,549.05	$142,971.13
2007	$142,971.13	$14,184.96	$3,217.39	$10,967.57	$25,246.26	$135,516.62	$139,753.74
2008	$139,753.74	$14,184.96	$3,475.79	$10,709.17	$28,722.04	$146,225.80	$136,277.96
2009	$136,277.96	$14,184.96	$3,754.94	$10,430.02	$32,476.98	$156,655.82	$132,523.02
2010	$132,523.02	$14,184.96	$4,056.51	$10,128.45	$36,533.49	$166,784.27	$128,466.51

Fig. 34.3
The payments made over the life of the loan.

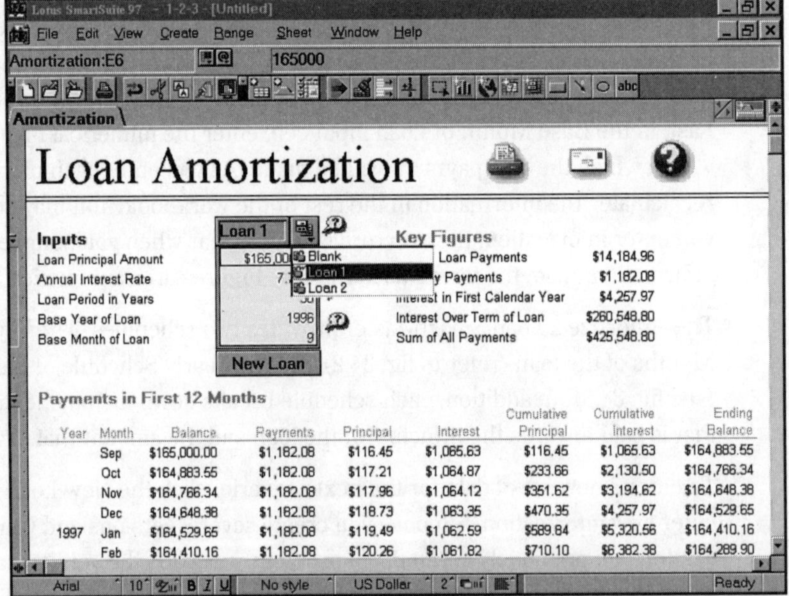

Year	Month	Balance	Payments	Principal	Interest	Cumulative Principal	Cumulative Interest	Ending Balance
	Sep	$165,000.00	$1,182.08	$116.45	$1,065.63	$116.45	$1,065.63	$164,883.55
	Oct	$164,883.55	$1,182.08	$117.21	$1,064.87	$233.66	$2,130.50	$164,766.34
	Nov	$164,766.34	$1,182.08	$117.96	$1,064.12	$351.62	$3,194.62	$164,648.38
	Dec	$164,648.38	$1,182.08	$118.73	$1,063.35	$470.35	$4,257.97	$164,529.65
1997	Jan	$164,529.65	$1,182.08	$119.49	$1,062.59	$589.84	$5,320.56	$164,410.16
	Feb	$164,410.16	$1,182.08	$120.26	$1,061.82	$710.10	$6,382.38	$164,289.90

Fig. 34.4
Use this list box to switch to a version you previously created that you want to view again.

Notice the bubble help buttons that contain question marks. If you click the button, you'll see help that explains how you switch versions and access the Version menu (see fig. 34.5). Click the button a second time to cancel the help box.

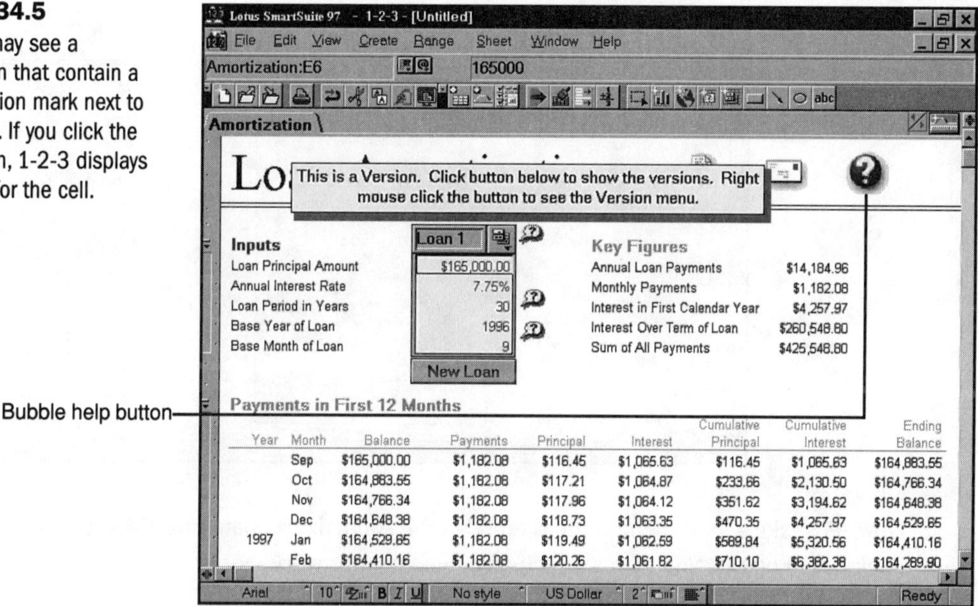

Fig. 34.5
You may see a button that contain a question mark next to a cell. If you click the button, 1-2-3 displays help for the cell.

Suppose you want information about the current version—that is, you want to see the properties of the current version. Click in any input cell for that version. Then, point the mouse at the version list box and press the right mouse button to display the Version menu (see fig. 34.6).

If you want to delete a version, switch to the version to display it. Then, click in any input cell for that version, point the mouse at the version list box, and press the right mouse button to display the Version menu. From the Version menu, choose Delete Current Version.

CAUTION

1-2-3 does *not* display a warning before deleting a version.

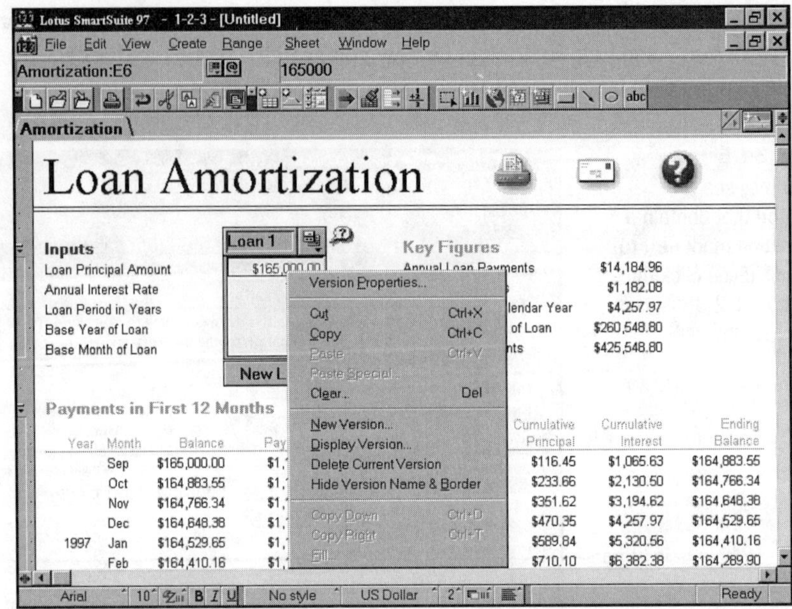

Fig. 34.6
From the Version menu, you can view the properties of the current version.

Now, let's take a look "behind the scenes" of the Amortize a Loan SmartMaster. Any workbook based on this SmartMaster actually contains four worksheets:

- Amortization
- WorkArea
- Strings
- Scripts

You don't actually use these worksheets to enter information; 1-2-3 uses them to set up the workbook and run the macros and scripts that use the information you provide to make calculations.

To see these worksheets, choose Sheet, Unhide. From the Unhide dialog box (see fig. 34.7), unhide each worksheet.

▶ **See** "Hiding Worksheet Data," **p. 399**

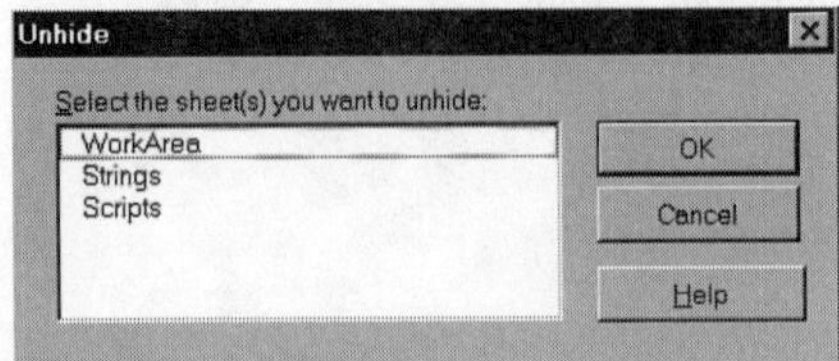

Fig. 34.7
Click to select each worksheet to display.

On the WorkArea sheet (see fig. 34.8), you'll find information about the variables the SmartMaster uses, and you'll find the area where the SmartMaster performs calculations.

On the Strings sheet (see fig. 34.9), you'll find range name and translation information.

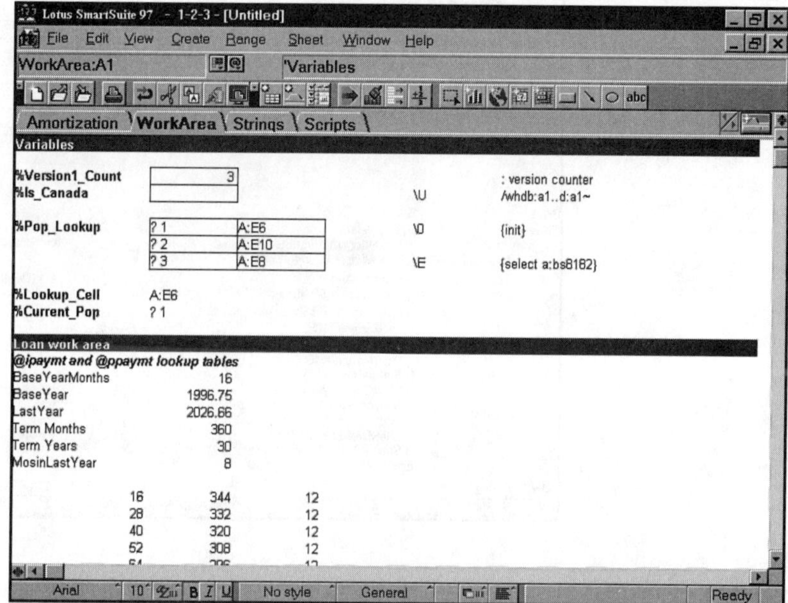

Fig. 34.8 The WorkArea worksheet contains information about the variables the SmartMaster uses.

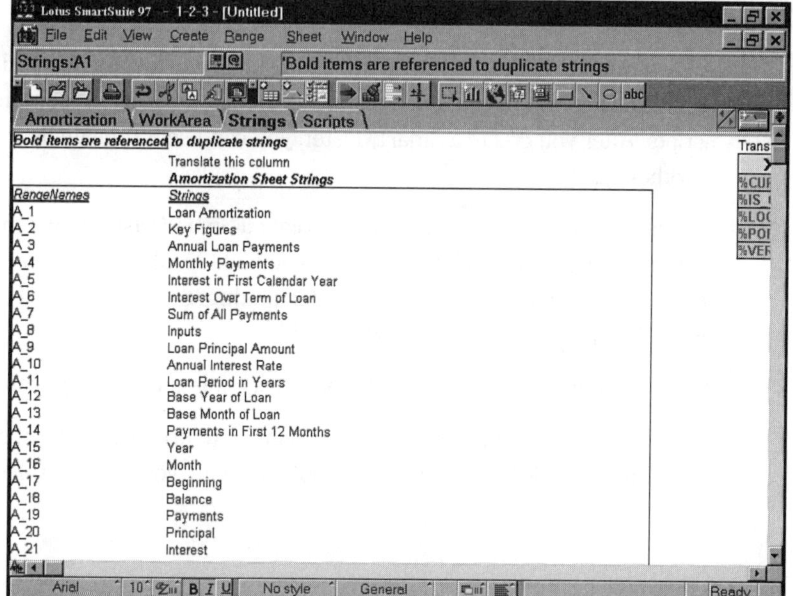

Fig. 34.9 The Strings worksheet contains information about range name and translation information.

On the Scripts sheet (see fig. 34.10), you'll find the scripts used in the SmartMaster.

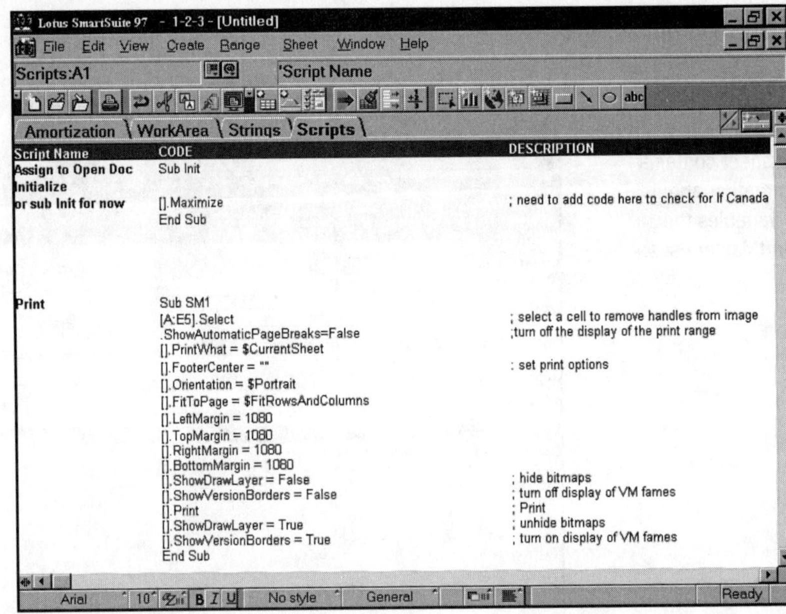

Fig. 34.10 The Scripts worksheet contains the scripts used in the SmartMaster.

TIP If you're having a scripting problem, you can use these scripts as examples to help you solve it.

Creating Your Own SmartMasters

A SmartMaster is nothing more than a workbook that contains predefined data. SmartMasters might contain explanatory labels, formulas, formatting, macros, and scripts. After you create a SmartMaster, you can use it repeatedly to create additional workbooks.

You use the same basic procedure to create a SmartMaster that you use to create any workbook. The main difference is that you include all of the common information, such as text entries, formulas, and worksheet formatting, so that you need to fill in only the appropriate data in order to complete the workbook.

The following list gives you a few tips for creating and working with SmartMasters:

- Use 1-2-3's multiple worksheet capability to organize distinct categories of data. For example, within one workbook, use one worksheet for user input, another worksheet for reports, and a third worksheet to store macro and script commands. This design not only protects macros from harm, but also provides a scheme that helps other users understand the Smartmaster.

▶ **See** "Reorganizing Worksheets," **p. 253**

- Protect cells and worksheet ranges using the Security tab of the Range Properties InfoBox to prevent other users from accidentally changing worksheet data or formulas.

  ▶ **See** "Protecting Workbooks," **p. 278**

- Hide worksheets that contain information—such as macros or data used in calculations—by using the Basics tab of the Sheet Properties InfoBox. This removes the sheet as a visual distraction and prevents users from accidentally changing critical functions in the worksheet.

  ▶ **See** "Managing the Worksheet Display," **p. 389**

- Use the Security tab of the Workbook Properties dialog box to restrict access to the SmartMaster. Doing so maintains the integrity of the SmartMaster and also ensures that standard worksheet data remains the same.

  ▶ **See** "Protecting Workbooks," **p. 278**

- Assign workbook display preferences with the View, Set View Preferences command or File, Workbook Properties, or by clicking the Workbook Properties SmartIcon.

  ▶ **See** "Managing the Worksheet Display," **p. 389**

  ▶ **See** "Customizing the 1-2-3 Screen," **p. 749**

- Define page settings such as margins, headers and footers, and print titles by using the Preview and Page Setup InfoBox. When you define this information within the SmartMaster file, other people who create worksheets based on your SmartMaster need only print the worksheet; they do not have to worry about additional print settings.

  ▶ **See** "Printing Worksheets," **p. 285**

- Use the Range, Name command to assign range names to cells used by formulas or to worksheet ranges that will be manipulated with 1-2-3 commands.

  ▶ **See** "Navigating and Selecting in 1-2-3 for Windows," **p. 45**

- Provide ample notes and documentation explaining the SmartMaster and information on tasks the user may need to perform. You may want to store this explanatory information in a separate worksheet and assign a name such as Help or Notes so that the user can find the information immediately. In addition, you may want to create cell comments to explain the information the SmartMaster is expecting.

Creating a SmartMaster

After you have entered formulas, data, formatting, macros, and scripts, you can save the workbook as a SmartMaster. Before you do this, however, you may want to choose File, Workbook Properties and use the General tab of the Workbook Properties dialog box to supply the SmartMaster with a workbook title and description (see fig. 34.11). When you do, this information is displayed when the SmartMaster is highlighted in the New Workbook dialog box.

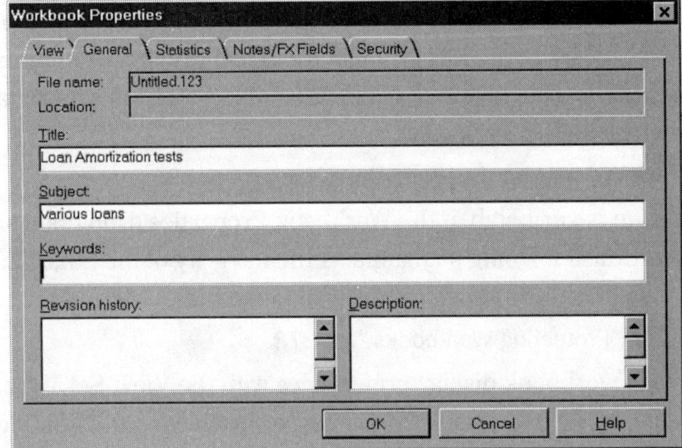

Fig. 34.11
Enter a title and description of the SmartMaster on the General tab of the Workbook Properties dialog box.

To save the workbook as a SmartMaster, display the Save As dialog box (see fig. 34.12). In the File Name text box, enter a name for the SmartMaster. From the Save As Type drop-down list, select Lotus 1-2-3 SmartMaster (12M). In the Save In list box, display the folder containing SmartMasters—typically the \LOTUS\SMASTERS\123 folder. Then, click Save.

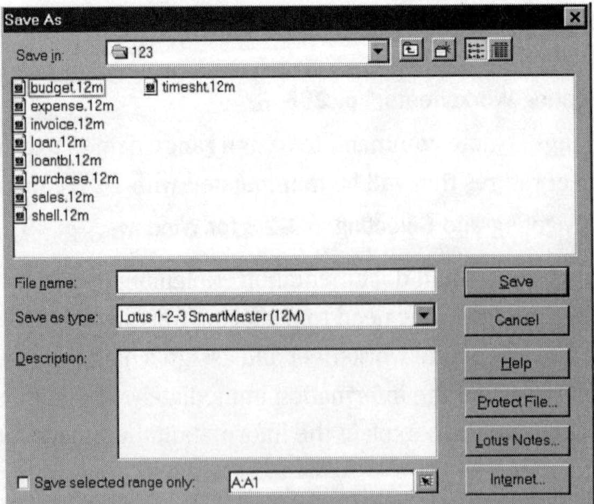

Fig. 34.12
Use the SmartMaster file type when you save a SmartMaster in the Save As dialog box.

Autoloading Workbooks

You can create a workbook that loads automatically when you start 1-2-3. The file can be any 1-2-3 workbook you use on a daily basis. For example, you can create a to-do list workbook and have that file appear automatically every time you start 1-2-3. Or you could create a workbook that contains no data at all, but instead consists of standard workbook settings, such as numeric formats, column widths, and display preferences.

The process of creating an autoloading workbook is really quite simple: Create the workbook. Then, save the file, using any name you want, but make sure you save it to the \LOTUS\123\AUTO folder. The next time you start 1-2-3, the workbook is automatically opened and displayed in the application window. You'll still see the Welcome to 1-2-3 dialog box, but if you click Cancel, you'll see the workbook on-screen.

NOTE As long as you have enough memory on your computer, 1-2-3 will automatically open every file you save in the \lotus\123\auto folder each time you start 1-2-3.

As an alternative, you can have 1-2-3 automatically open a specific file by using the Windows Explorer to create a Windows 95 shortcut for the file. You can then place the shortcut on your Desktop, where you can conveniently use it. Double-clicking the shortcut will tell Windows 95 to load both 1-2-3 and the file for which you created the shortcut. A shortcut for a 1-2-3 file on your Desktop might look like the one in figure 34.13.

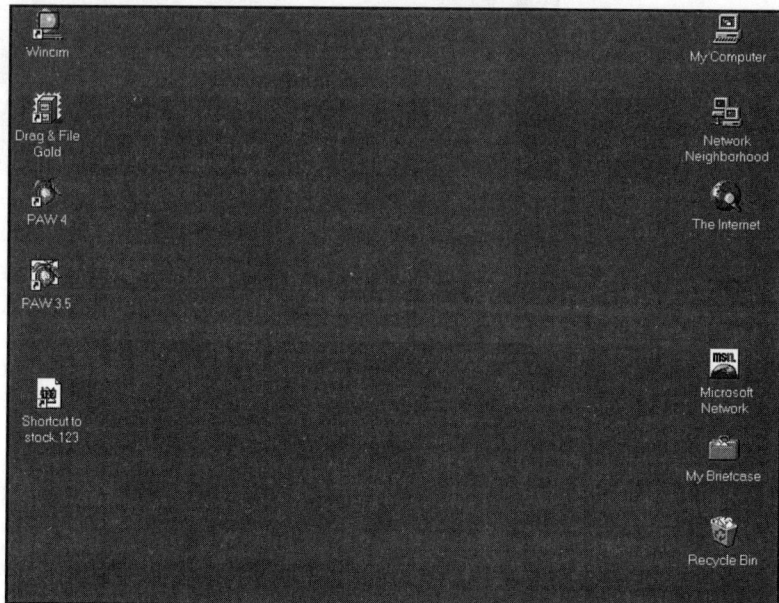

Fig. 34.13
Desktop shortcuts to 1-2-3 files use a 1-2-3 icon.

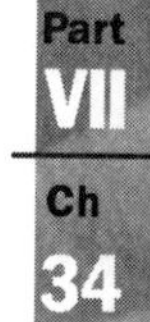

To create a shortcut in the Windows Explorer, follow these steps:

1. From the Programs menu on the Windows 95 Start menu, choose Windows Explorer.
2. Set the size of the Explorer so that it does *not* fill your entire screen.
3. Navigate to the drive and folder containing the file for which you want to create a shortcut. To find 1-2-3 files, look in the Lotus\Work\123 folder.
4. Point the mouse at the file for which you want to create a shortcut and press the right mouse button to display a shortcut menu (see fig. 34.14).

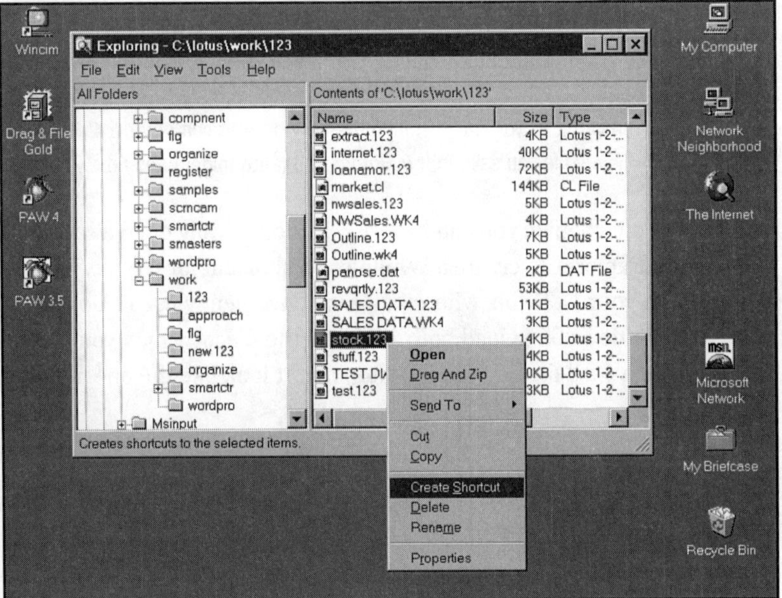

Fig. 34.14
The shortcut menu that appears when you right-click on a file in the Windows Explorer.

5. Choose Create Shortcut. At the bottom of the list of files in the window, Windows 95 creates a file with the same name as your original file, preceded by "Shortcut to."
6. Drag this new file out onto your desktop and close the Windows Explorer.

You can also combine steps 4, 5, and 6 by dragging the file icon onto the desktop using the right mouse button. When you release the right mouse button, choose Create Shortcut Here.

If you want, you can rename the shortcut as in figure 34.13. If the shortcut is not selected, click once on the shortcut to select it. Then, click its name. Windows 95 displays the name completely selected (see fig. 34.15).

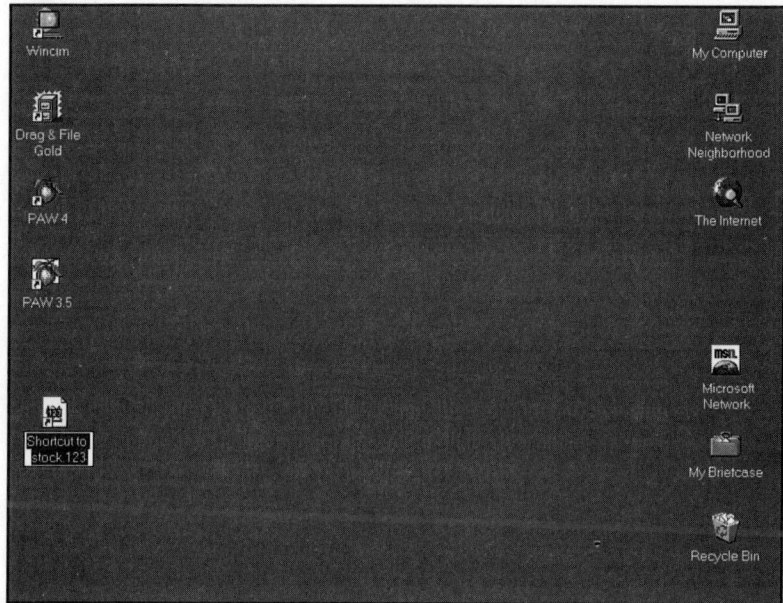

Fig. 34.15
Type over a selected name to rename a shortcut and press Enter.

CAUTION

Although you may click twice, this process is *not* the same as double-clicking. If you double-click the shortcut, you'll launch 1-2-3 and open the file.

CHAPTER 35

Creating Custom Dialog Boxes

by Elaine Marmel

When you write worksheet scripts that you will distribute to other people to use, you often find that your script will require information from the user. And you, as the script writer, need a way to get that information. Typically, any Windows program would display a dialog box, and the user would supply the requested information. Well, that's exactly what you do in 1-2-3—you create custom dialog boxes using the Lotus Dialog Editor. ■

Defining the Lotus Dialog Editor

The Lotus Dialog Editor is a separate program you can install that enables you to create custom dialog boxes.

Upgraders Alert

Creating custom dialog boxes with 1-2-3 97 and the Lotus Dialog Editor, you'll be working somewhat differently than you did in the past.

Use the Lotus Dialog Editor

Learn to create custom dialog boxes that include check boxes, text boxes, and option buttons.

What Is the Lotus Dialog Editor?

The Lotus Dialog Editor is a separate program installed when you install 1-2-3 97, and you use the Lotus Dialog Editor to create *custom dialog boxes.* Custom dialog boxes are the special dialog boxes used in 1-2-3 scripts. Custom dialog boxes contain elements called *controls*, and you use these controls to display messages, to prompt the user for input, or to present an entire series of options in a complex application.

Each control in a custom dialog box is attached to a script, and that script determines exactly what action the control takes. In this chapter, we'll explore creating a custom dialog box, adding and manipulating the visual aspect of a control, and displaying the custom dialog box. To learn more about creating the scripts you need to attach to a control, see "LotusScript" in the on-line help.

A Note to Upgraders

In prior releases of 1-2-3, you could display a custom dialog box from a macro using the macro command {DIALOG}. Starting with this release of 1-2-3, you *cannot* display any new custom dialog boxes that you create using this macro command. Instead, you must display all new custom dialogs that you create using the script Show command.

Be aware, too, that you cannot display any existing (WK4) custom dialog boxes using the script Show command—you must use the {DIALOG} macro command—and you cannot use the Show command to display custom dialog boxes you created in WK4 worksheets. Last, there is no way to upgrade existing custom dialog boxes—you must re-create them, using scripting commands.

Using the Lotus Dialog Editor

Creating a custom dialog box using the Lotus Dialog Editor is a fairly simple process, but one that requires a little planning if you want the dialog box to be useful.

Before you begin creating a custom dialog box, decide what type of output you expect. If the dialog box is intended to select program options, you want to present the user with a predetermined list of choices—perhaps using option buttons, check boxes, or list boxes. On the other hand, if the dialog box is intended to solicit user input, you need to provide text boxes in which the user can type variable information.

You also should decide whether a custom dialog box is really the proper approach to take. Although it may be tempting to create your own variations on standard dialog boxes (such as the Open dialog box), consider whether this approach may confuse, rather than help, your users. Remember, you can use 1-2-3's built-in dialog boxes in your scripts, without having to worry about making sure that they work correctly!

Finally, consider the layout of the objects in custom dialog boxes. You may want to sketch out the dialog box on paper before you begin to create it in the dialog editor. If the objects in the dialog boxes don't line up, the appearance is anything but professional. Consider, too, the order of the objects in the dialog box. If possible, place text boxes and other controls in a logical order so that the user can move easily from one control to the next.

Understanding the Lotus Dialog Editor Window

To start the Lotus Dialog Editor, choose the Edit, Scripts & Macros, Show Dialog Editor command. Figure 35.1 shows the Lotus Dialog Editor program window.

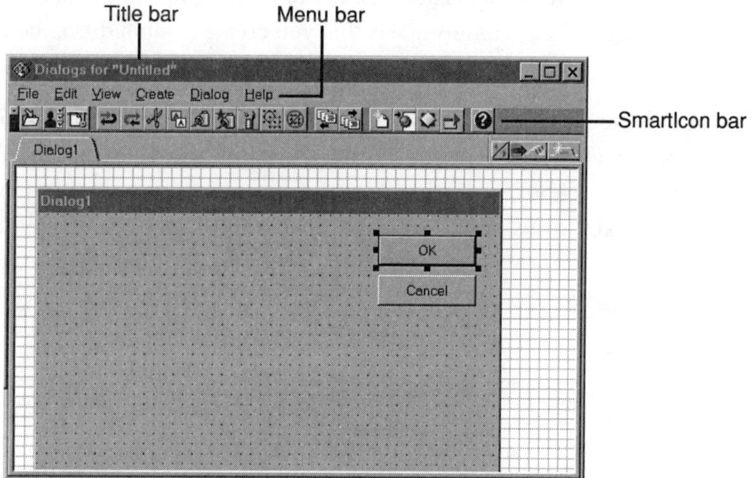

Fig. 35.1
Create custom dialog boxes in the Lotus Dialog Editor window.

You use the Lotus Dialog Editor window to create and edit custom dialog boxes. The Lotus Dialog Editor window looks similar to any Windows program. The menu bar contains six drop-down menus: File, Edit, View, Create, Dialog, and Help:

- Use the File menu commands to save dialog box files and to exit the Lotus Dialog Editor. Also, from the File menu, you can control the SmartIcons that appear on the Dialog Editor SmartIcon palette and the tools that appear on the Dialog Editor Toolbox.
- The Edit menu commands enable you to copy dialog box descriptions to and from 1-2-3; cut, copy, and paste dialog box controls; select and deselect all objects; and delete dialog boxes.

- Using the View menu commands, you can switch between dialog boxes and control whether SmartIcons, the Toolbox, or scripts appear in the Dialog Editor window.
- Using the commands on the Create menu, you can create new dialog boxes and select objects you want to include in a dialog box.
- The Dialog menu offers commands that control the appearance and location of dialog box elements, and from this menu you can test the functioning of your dialog box.
- And, from the Help menu, you can get help about the Dialog Editor and about the various controls.

Understanding Dialog Box Controls

In many ways, custom dialog boxes are similar to the standard dialog boxes displayed in 1-2-3 or other Windows programs. Custom dialog boxes even look like standard dialog boxes. The primary difference is that you create custom dialog boxes to meet your special needs.

The elements in a dialog box are called *controls*. Controls allow users to select program settings and choose options. You can add command buttons, option buttons, check boxes, text boxes, list boxes, preview boxes, combination boxes (text and list, for example), or group boxes to custom dialog boxes. Table 35.1 describes each of these controls.

Table 35.1 Dialog Box Controls

Control	Description
Command button	Executes the choices you set in the dialog box and closes it
Option button	Allows user to select one choice at a time
Check box	Allows user to select multiple choices that are not mutually exclusive
Text box	Allows user to enter up to 32,767 characters
List box	Allows user to pick one item from a list of items. List boxes can be open, or you can let the user open them by clicking a down arrow next to the list box
Combo box	Combines list boxes and text boxes in a single dialog box element
Image	Provides a location for an image to appear
Spin button	Used to increment or decrement a number text box
Progress bar	Shows the user how far along a process is

Control	Description
Slider	Used to increment or decrement non-numeric fields, such as volume
Label	Provides a name or description for a control
Frame	Groups and labels related dialog box elements

NOTE You'll also find HTML controls, which you can include in custom dialog boxes when you intend to publish on the World Wide Web.

The controls you place in a custom dialog box are actually just graphic images—they have no function until you attach a script to them. In this chapter, we'll focus on using Lotus Dialog Editor to create dialog boxes and the controls that appear in them.

As you can see from figure 35.1, the Dialog Editor starts a new dialog box for you, called Dialog1, so you're ready to start adding and arranging dialog box controls.

Adding Dialog Box Objects

The controls you add to a dialog box are actually graphic objects. You can add objects to a dialog box using several different methods. For example, the Create, Control menu shows controls you can add (see fig. 35.2).

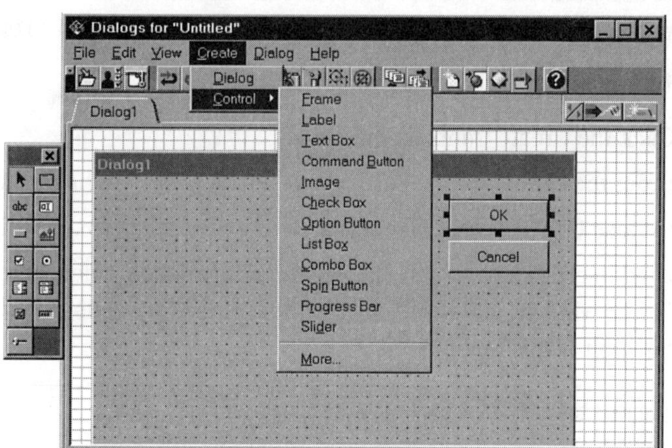

Fig. 35.2
Use the Create, Control menu to add elements to a dialog box.

Or, you can click the Create Control SmartIcon to open a dialog box that lets you select the element you want to add (see fig. 35.3).

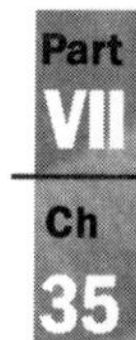

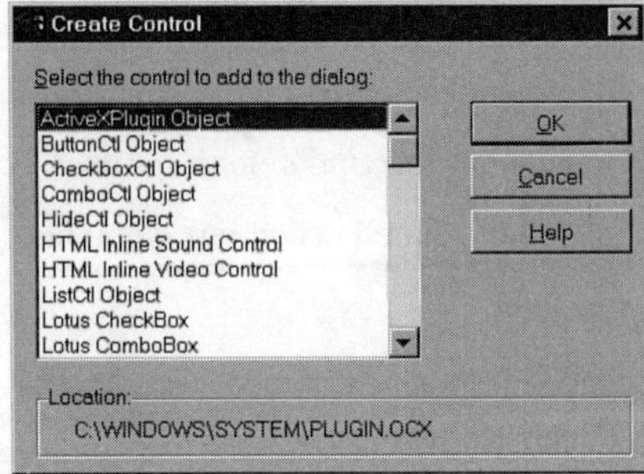

Fig. 35.3
This dialog box appears when you click the Create Control SmartIcon.

Using either of these methods, you click the location where you want to add the object after you select it, and the object appears in a default size. You can change the size by dragging on the handles of the object.

NOTE Some of the controls listed in the Create Control dialog box may not be available for use in your dialog boxes. The Create Control dialog box lists all custom controls installed on your system, including ones which require a license for their use.

If you prefer, you can use the Toolbox to add objects. Using this method, you draw the object to the size you want by dragging. When you first add a control, it appears in the dialog box with a name related to its type, followed by a number that represents how many of this particular type of control already appears in the dialog box. For example, when you add the first text object, the object is initially labeled “Text1”.

To add a text object, follow these steps:

1. Click the Create Control SmartIcon.
2. From the Create Control dialog box that appears, highlight Lotus TextBox.
3. Choose OK. The Text object is added to the dialog box (see fig. 35.4).
4. Double-click the object to display the Script dialog box for the control (see fig. 35.5). In this window, you would supply the script commands that would control the function of this text box.

You can change the size of the control by dragging one of its handles

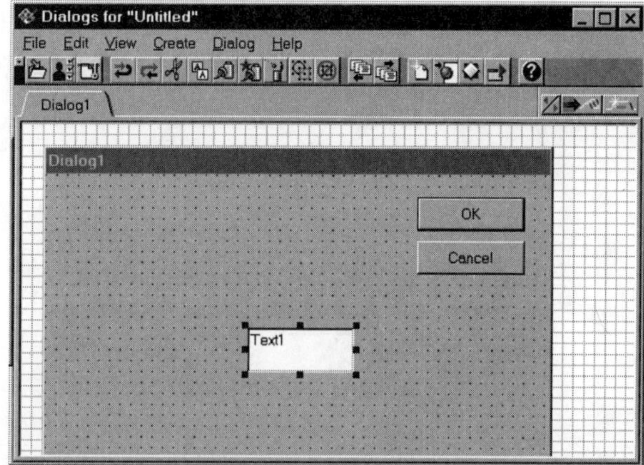

Fig. 35.4
A text box appears in the dialog box.

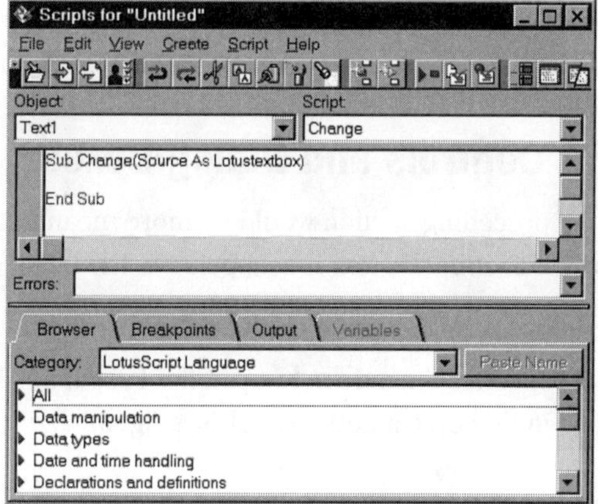

Fig. 35.5
Use the Script dialog box to attach a script to the text object.

A text box is nice, but it would help users if they knew what they were expected to do with it. So, you can add a descriptive label for the text box. This time, let's use the Toolbox:

1. In the Toolbox, click the Lotus Label tool.
2. Move the mouse pointer onto the dialog box area; the mouse pointer changes to a cross hair.
3. Position the intersection of the cross hair where you want the upper-left corner of the label to appear and drag to the lower-right corner of the label. When you release the mouse button, the label control appears selected and its title is Label1 (see fig. 35.6).

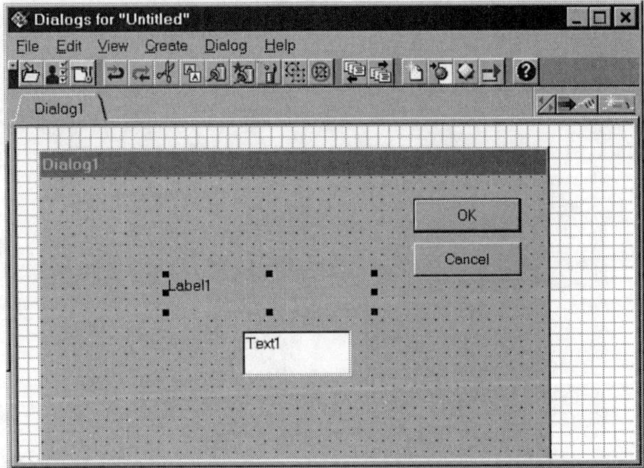

Fig. 35.6
The dialog box after adding a label control.

Using either of the techniques described—the Create Control SmartIcon or the Toolbox—you can add any standard Lotus control to a custom dialog box.

Setting Properties for Controls and Dialog Boxes

The label created in the preceding section would be more meaningful if it didn't say "Label1." Here's how you change the text that appears in the label:

1. Make sure the label control is selected; black handles should appear around it.

2. Click the Show Properties SmartIcon to open the Properties InfoBox for the selected control—in this case a Lotus Label (see fig. 35.7).

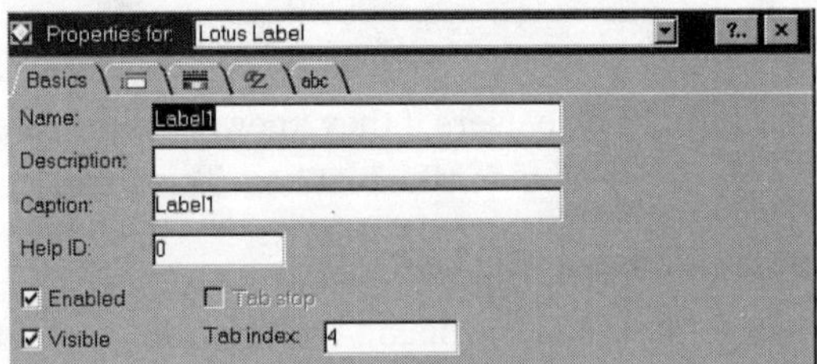

Fig. 35.7
Using the tabs in the Properties InfoBox for a dialog box element, you can control its appearance and location.

3. The Caption text box on the Basics tab controls what the user sees for the label. When you replace the text in the caption box, the Dialog Editor updates the label control in the dialog box (see fig. 35.8).

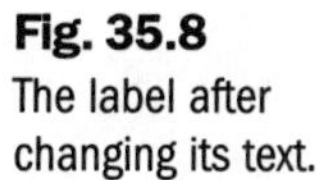

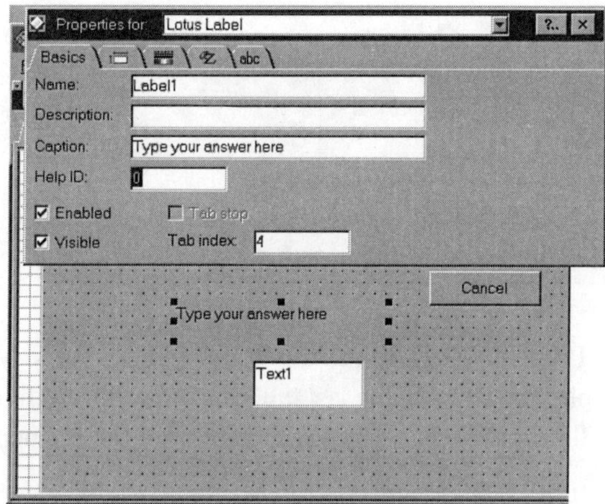

Fig. 35.8
The label after changing its text.

The same technique works for all dialog box controls—change the information the user sees using the Caption text box on the Basics tab for that control.

Before we move on, let's briefly look at the other tabs in a control's Properties InfoBox. From the second tab (see fig. 35.9), you can control numerically the position and size of the element. From the third tab (see fig. 35.10), you can control the appearance, border style, and background color of the element, as well as the mouse pointer's appearance when the control is selected in the dialog box. From the fourth tab (see fig. 35.11), you can control text attributes of the element.

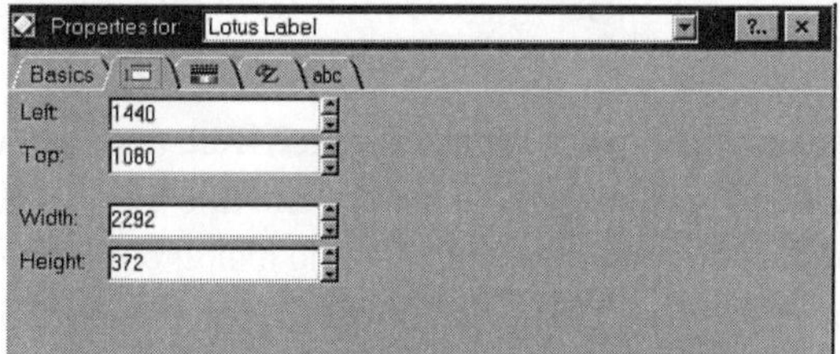

Fig. 35.9
Use this tab to control, numerically, the position and size of the element.

Fig. 35.10
Use this tab to control the appearance of the element and the mouse pointer when the control is selected in the dialog box.

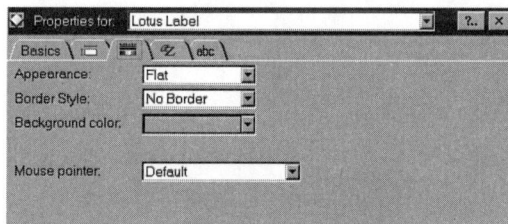

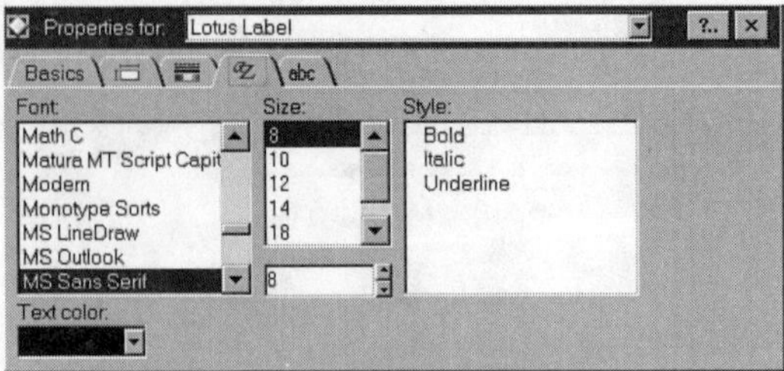

Fig. 35.11
Use this tab to control the font you're using for the element.

The last tab of the Properties InfoBox changes, depending on the type of control. For a text box, for example, you can use the last tab to control the length of the answer the user supplies. For list boxes, you can type the items you want to appear in the list (see fig. 35.12).

Use the Max Length property to control the number of characters in a text box. If you specify 0, you are not limiting the amount of text; therefore, up to 32,767 characters and spaces can be entered.

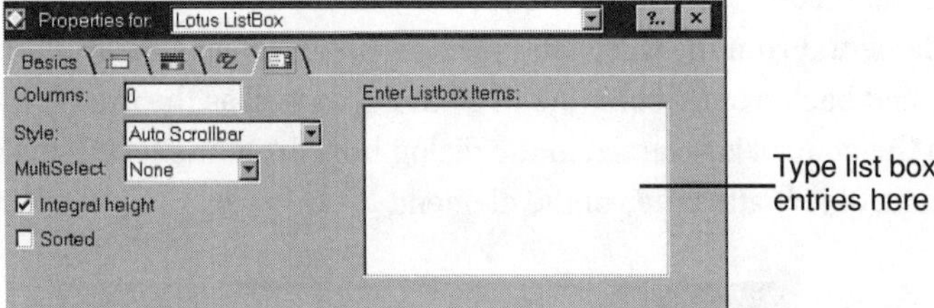

Fig. 35.12
Use this tab to enter list box entries.

But how about the dialog box itself? What's its title? Well, at the moment, it's called "Dialog1"—again, not terribly meaningful. To change the title bar of the dialog box, click anywhere on the dialog box but not on a control in the dialog box. Handles will appear around the perimeter of the dialog box. Click the Show Properties SmartIcon to display the Dialog Properties InfoBox (see fig. 35.13). As you would expect, change the caption to change the dialog box title.

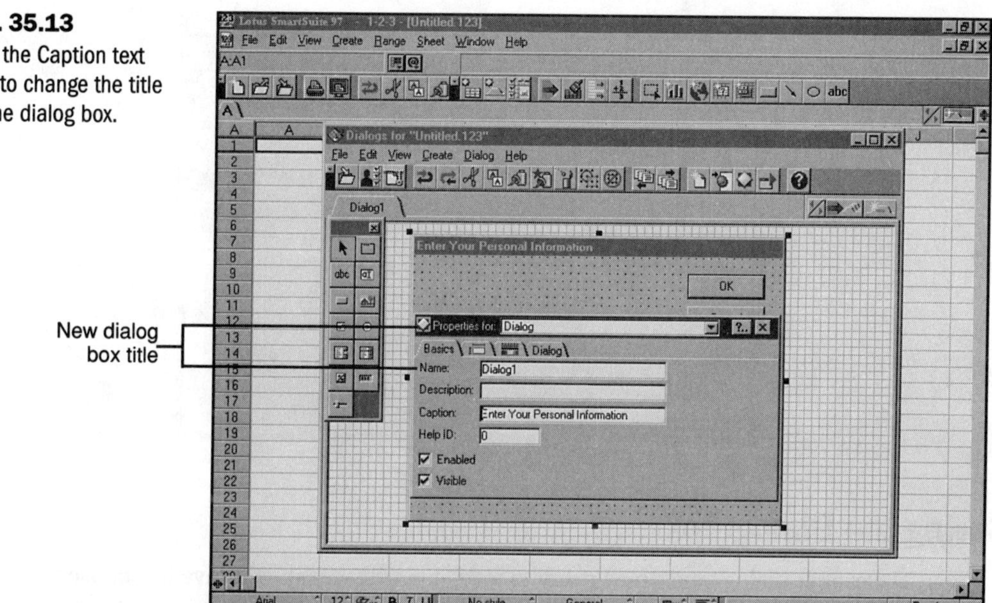

Fig. 35.13
Use the Caption text box to change the title of the dialog box.

NOTE By changing the caption—and therefore the dialog box title—you are *not* changing the name by which 1-2-3 and the Dialog Editor refer to the dialog box. Its name remains Dialog1, and we'll use that name later to display the dialog box in 1-2-3.

Aligning Controls

To make your dialog box look professional, carefully align all dialog box objects. To align controls, start by using the grid that appears in the dialog box. But if you want even more precision, select the controls you want to align and use the commands on the Dialog, Align menu.

To select more than one control simultaneously, click the first control, then hold down the Shift key and click the second control. After two or more controls are selected, the alignment commands become available. Choose Dialog, Align. From the submenu (see fig. 35.14), choose the way in which you want to align the controls.

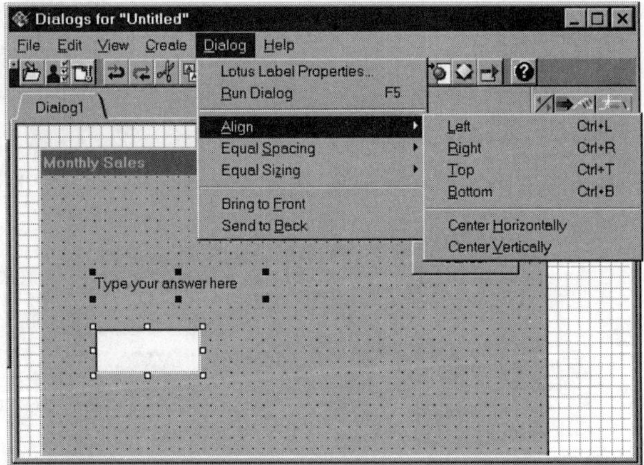

Fig. 35.14
These commands are available only if two or more controls are selected.

Saving the Dialog Box

The sample dialog box is now ready to test—but first you should save it. Choose the File, Save Dialogs command. 1-2-3 displays a dialog box indicating that the workbook in which you are working will be saved (see fig. 35.15). When you choose OK, 1-2-3 displays the Save As dialog box, asking you for a file name for the workbook.

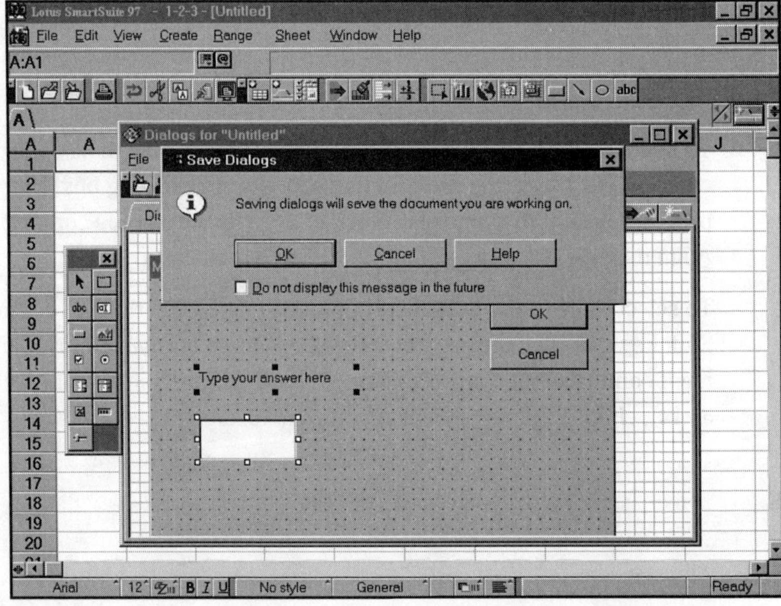

Fig. 35.15
When you save in the Dialog Editor, you actually save the workbook in which you were working when you opened the Dialog Editor.

The file name you use appears in two title bars: your 1-2-3 title bar and the Dialog Editor title bar.

In a few moments, we'll test this dialog box, but first, let's create a new dialog box in the same worksheet. After all, you may need to display more than one dialog box in your script.

Creating a New Dialog Box

As you saw in the beginning of the chapter, when the Dialog Editor opens, it starts a new dialog box for you. But, suppose, for example, that you finish working with the dialog box that appears when you start Dialog Editor, and you still need to create another dialog box. You don't need to exit and reopen the Dialog Editor. Choose the Create, Dialog command. The Dialog Editor displays a new dialog box in the window (see fig. 35.16).

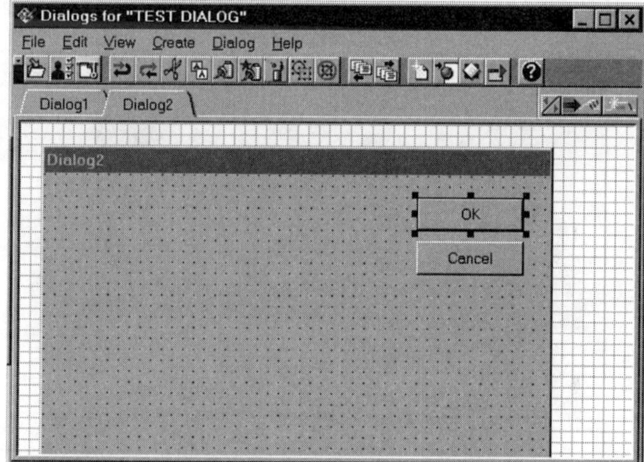

Fig. 35.16
The new dialog box appears on a tab labeled Dialog2 in front of the dialog box you just created.

You add controls to this dialog box and otherwise modify its appearance the same way you did to the first dialog box.

Displaying a Custom Dialog Box

You can test the dialog box from inside the Lotus Dialog Editor, but you also will want to be able to display the dialog after you're back working in 1-2-3. In this section, we'll explore both ways to display a custom dialog box.

Testing a Custom Dialog Box in the Dialog Editor

While we're still working in the Dialog Editor window, let's test the dialog box we created earlier to see what it looks like. And, if you've attached scripts to the controls, you can test the controls to see that they work properly.

To test-run a dialog box, make sure it appears in front in the Dialog Editor window. Then, click the Run Dialog SmartIcon. The Dialog Editor window disappears, and the custom dialog box appears, as shown in figure 35.17.

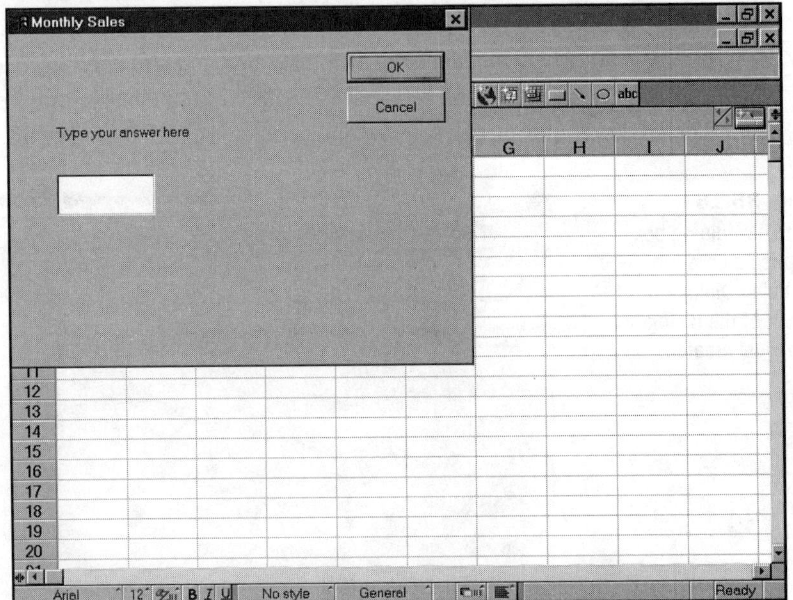

Fig. 35.17
The Dialog Editor displays the custom dialog box.

If you've added scripts to the controls, you can test the controls by selecting them. To return to the Dialog Editor, click the Close button in the dialog box.

Running a Custom Dialog Box from 1-2-3

Okay, you've built the dialog box and now you'd like to use it in a 1-2-3 workbook. Let's attach a script to a button so that when we click the button, the dialog box will appear. Follow these steps:

1. Close the Dialog Editor window by clicking the Close Dialog Editor SmartIcon or choosing File, Close Dialog Editor. You return to the 1-2-3 workbook that contains your custom dialog boxes.

2. Draw a button on the worksheet using the Create a Script Button SmartIcon. When you click the SmartIcon and move the mouse into the worksheet, the pointer changes to a cross hair. Position the cross hair where you want the upper-left corner of the button to appear; then drag down and to the right. When you release, the button appears, named Button 1. In addition, a script window appears.
3. Type the following command into the script window before End Sub (see fig. 35.18):

   Call Dialog1.Show

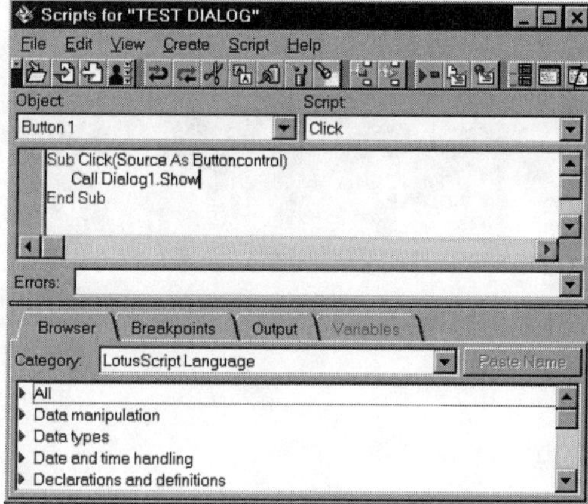

Fig. 35.18
The script window for the button, after you've typed the script.

4. To test that you typed the script correctly, press F2 or click the Check Scripts for this Object SmartIcon.
5. Close the Script Editor by choosing File, Close Script Editor. The Script Editor will automatically save your script.

To use the button to display the custom dialog box, click once anywhere in the worksheet to deselect the button. Then, click the button. The dialog box should appear.

By the way, you may want to change the name of the button. Right-click on the button and choose Drawing Properties from the shortcut menu. The Draw Object InfoBox appears. In the Text box, type the words you want to appear on the button. After you press Tab, 1-2-3 changes the text on the button (see fig. 35.19).

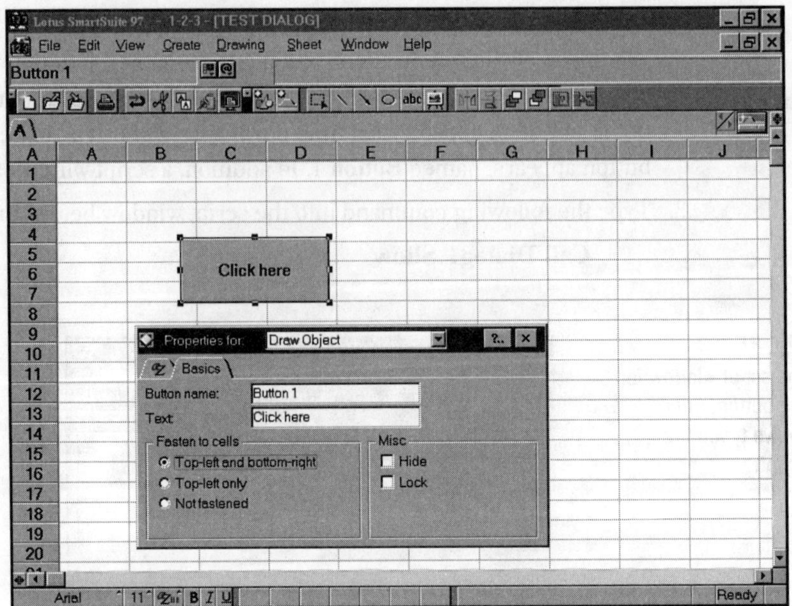

Fig. 35.19
Use the Basics tab of this InfoBox to change the text that appears on the button.

CHAPTER 36

Writing 1-2-3 Macros

by Joyce J. Nielsen

Although the basic worksheet, database, and graphics features of 1-2-3 97 are very powerful, you can greatly enhance their utility by creating and using *macros*. Macros are small programs that automate 1-2-3 procedures. ■

Writing a macro

Learn how to create simple macros in 1-2-3 that automate commonly used tasks and procedures.

Understanding macro guidelines

You can create more effective macros by following these specific guidelines for planning, creating, and documenting a macro.

Protecting macros

If you create macros that others will have access to, you'll want to learn how to protect your macros from unwanted changes.

NOTE 1-2-3 97 includes a new object-oriented programming language, called *LotusScript*, that enables you to automate more complicated 1-2-3 tasks, create custom applications, and use data from other Windows applications. Scripts generally run faster than macros, and provide more flexibility if you need to process large amounts of data.

If you are experienced at writing 1-2-3 macros, you can continue to use the familiar 1-2-3 macro commands and techniques. You can still use existing macro applications created in previous versions of 1-2-3 97 and 1-2-3 for DOS as well. When you use the Record feature in 1-2-3 97, however, your keystrokes and actions are saved as scripts using the new LotusScript language, rather than as macro commands. ■

This chapter covers how to create and use 1-2-3 macros that duplicate the tasks you find yourself performing repeatedly, such as printing worksheets, changing fonts, or entering the same data in several locations.

Defining a Macro

The simplest type of macro is nothing more than a short collection of keystrokes that 1-2-3 enters into the worksheet for you. Because the program stores this keystroke collection as text in a cell, you can treat the text as you would any label. Consider the number of times you save and open workbooks, print reports, and set and reset worksheet formats. In each case, you perform the operation by typing a series of keystrokes—sometimes a rather long series. By running a macro, however, you can reduce any number of keystrokes to a two-keystroke abbreviation.

Consider a simple yet effective macro that enters text. Suppose that your company's name is *Global Computer Products*—an entry that requires quite a few keystrokes. You want to place this name at various points in your worksheets. You can type the entry's many keystrokes every time you want to place the entry in the worksheet, or you can store all the keystrokes in a macro. When you want the company's name to appear in a worksheet, you can use just two keystrokes—the Ctrl key and a designated letter of the alphabet. Such a macro is called a Ctrl+*letter* macro. In a later section, titled "Writing a Macro That Enters Text," you learn how to create such a macro.

You name a Ctrl+*letter* macro by using the backslash key (\) and a single letter of the alphabet, such as \R. DOS versions of 1-2-3 called these macros Alt+*letter* macros, and the Alt key was termed the *macro key*. Windows applications, however, usually reserve the Alt key for invoking the main menu. In 1-2-3 97, therefore, Lotus changed its conventions for invoking macros named by a backslash and a single letter; you now start these macros in 1-2-3 97 by holding the Ctrl key and pressing the respective letter key.

The Ctrl+*letter* method is not the only way to name a macro. You learn about other methods in later sections of this chapter.

Developing Your Own Macros

The steps for creating any macro are basic. Following is an outline of these steps; later sections of this chapter expand on the major steps.

Follow these steps to create a macro:

1. Plan what you want the macro to do.

   Write down all the tasks you want the macro to perform; then arrange those tasks in the order in which they should be completed.

2. Identify the keystrokes or commands the macro should use.

   Keep in mind that macros can be as simple as labels (text) that duplicate the keystrokes you want to replay.

3. Find an area of the worksheet in which you can enter macros.

   When you choose the worksheet area, consider the fact that executed macros read text from cells, starting with the top cell and working down through lower cells. Macros end when they encounter a blank cell, a cell that contains a numeric value, or a command that stops macro execution. Therefore, enter macros as labels in successive cells in the same column.

4. Use the correct syntax to enter the keystrokes and macro commands into a cell or cells.

5. Name the macro.

   You can name a macro in one of three ways:

   - Assign the macro a Ctrl+*letter* name. This type of name consists of a label prefix (such as an apostrophe), and a backslash (\) followed by an alphabetic character (for example, *a*).
   - Choose a descriptive name, such as PRINT_BUDGET, for a macro. Macro names, like other 1-2-3 range names, can contain up to 15 characters.
   - Assign the name \0 (zero) to a macro if you want that macro to run automatically when a workbook is loaded. The General tab of the 1-2-3 Preferences dialog box (choose File, User Setup, 1-2-3 Preferences) enables you to enable and disable the autoexecute feature of macros named \0. The Run File Opened Scripts, Autoexecute Macros check box in this dialog box acts like a toggle switch: When the check box is selected, a macro named \0 executes automatically when a file that contains the macro is opened.

6. Document the macro.

   To facilitate the editing and debugging process, you can document a macro in several ways:

   - Use a descriptive macro name and consistently use range names instead of cell addresses in macros. Addresses entered in the text of a macro are not updated when changes are made to the worksheet. A macro does not work properly with incorrect addresses, which can be caused by moving, inserting, or deleting ranges. Range names in a macro *are* updated when the worksheet changes.
   - Include comments in a separate column to the right of the actual macro within the worksheet.
   - Retain all the paperwork you used to design and construct the macro for later reference.

7. Test and debug the macro.

   Always test and debug your macros for proper operation before giving them to a user. Make certain the macros work correctly before you trust them to process important data.

When your macros become more complex as your expertise increases, continue to use these basic steps to create a macro. Remember that good planning and documentation are important for making macros run smoothly and efficiently.

Writing Your First Macros

The next two sections show you how to write two simple macros. The first macro enters text into a cell. The second macro enters commands specified in the macro.

Writing a Macro That Enters Text

In this section, you learn how to create a macro that enters a company name—*Global Computer Products*—in various locations in worksheets. This simple example introduces the basic concepts required to create macros in 1-2-3. Later, you learn how to use more advanced macro programming commands and techniques to make macros execute faster and more efficiently.

Before you begin creating a macro, plan what you want the macro to do and identify the keystrokes the macro should enter. In the case of the macro that enters a company name in a worksheet, you want the macro to enter the letters, spaces, and punctuation that comprise the company's name. Then, as with any label, you want the macro to complete the entry by performing the equivalent of pressing the Enter key.

You begin building the macro by storing the keystrokes as text in a worksheet cell. After entering the letters that make up the company's name, you enter a tilde (~). In a macro, the tilde (~) represents the Enter key.

Cell B3 in figure 36.1 contains the keystrokes you want 1-2-3 to type:

```
Global Computer Products~
```

The tilde (~) is included at the end of the line. Remember that the tilde represents the press of the Enter key—an important step in ensuring that this macro executes correctly.

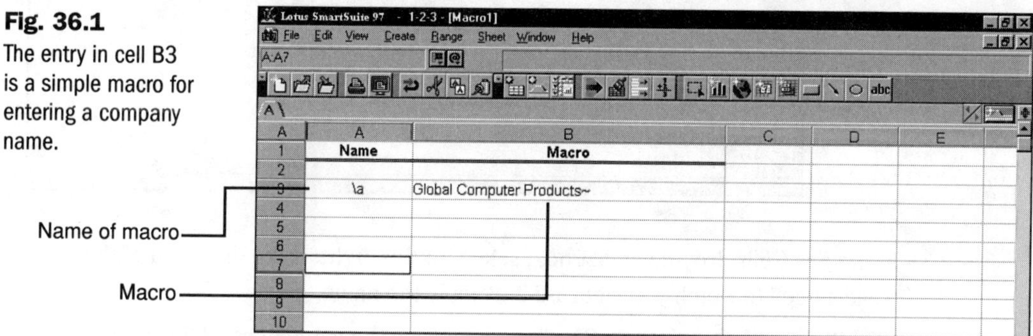

Fig. 36.1
The entry in cell B3 is a simple macro for entering a company name.

The next step in writing the macro is naming this sequence of keystrokes as a macro. This step is optional in 1-2-3 97 because you can use the Run Scripts & Macros dialog box to run macros that have no name. Naming macros, however, has a few advantages, even in 1-2-3 97. First, naming macros gives you a convenient form of self-documentation; second, you can start named macros more quickly.

You can name macros in several ways. This section describes one macro-naming technique; later sections of this chapter describe the others.

▶ **See** "Naming Ranges," **p. 58**

The following procedure is particularly convenient for naming a macro when the name is located to the left of the macro keystrokes, as is the name `\a` shown in figure 36.1. Follow these steps:

1. Select cell A3.
2. Choose Range, Name. The Name dialog box appears (see fig. 36.2).

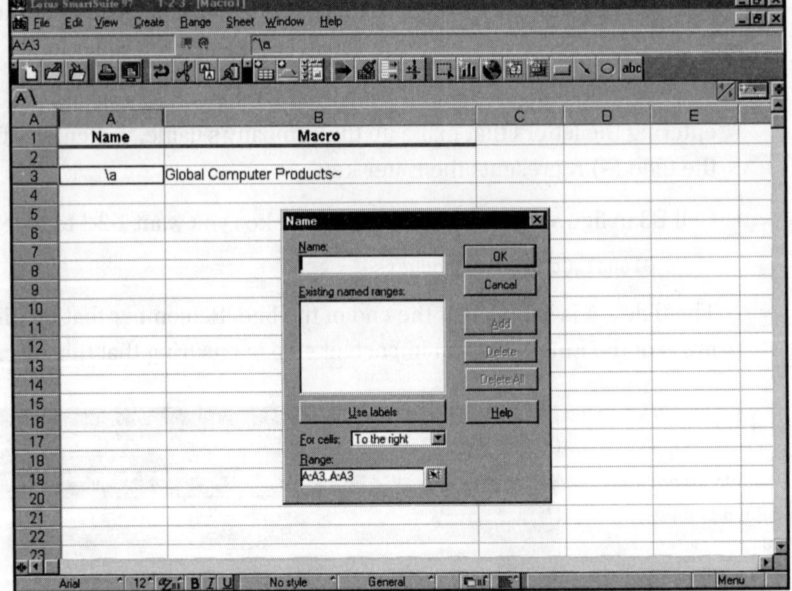

Fig. 36.2
Use the Name dialog box to name a macro.

3. In the For Cells drop-down list box, select To the Right as the direction of the adjacent cell to which you want 1-2-3 to apply the name.
4. Click the Use Labels button. This action assigns the name in cell A3 (`\a`) to cell B3.
5. Choose OK.

By placing the macro's name one cell to the left of the first cell in the macro, you can easily document the macro's name. This technique helps you quickly remember the macro name for later use.

To *execute* (run) this macro, move the cell pointer to the cell in which you want the company name to appear, hold down the Ctrl key, and then press **A**. 1-2-3 enters the sequence of characters identified as the macro \a.

Figure 36.3 shows the result of moving the cell pointer to cell B10 and then running the \a macro. To save this macro for future use, save the file in which the macro is located.

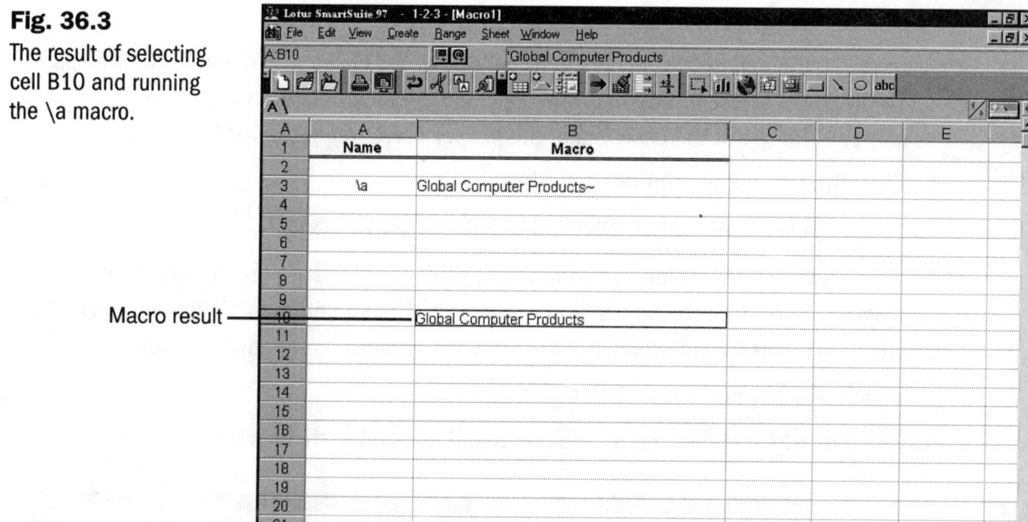

Fig. 36.3
The result of selecting cell B10 and running the \a macro.

Writing a Simple Command Macro

In addition to writing macros that repeat text, you can write macros that enter commands. If you follow the same procedure each time, macro writing should become second nature to you.

1-2-3 command macros, however, do not simply duplicate the keystrokes you use to enter a command. Instead, command macros use a simple ***command language***: a set of terms that replace keystroke representations with easy-to-read words. Macros that use the 1-2-3 command language not only are easier to read, but also function more efficiently than collections of keystrokes; therefore, macros written in this language execute more quickly.

▶ **See** "Online Help," **p. 41**

As described earlier in this chapter, first plan what you want the command macro to do. Then you need to identify each step necessary to complete the task. Suppose that you want to create a simple macro that enters commands, such as the commands for naming a macro (as you did in the preceding section). To perform this task manually, you normally complete the following steps:

1. Select the cell containing the label you want to use as a range name—in this case, cell A3.

2. Choose the Range, Name command.
3. In the Name dialog box, make certain that the For Cells drop-down list box displays To the Right as the direction of the adjacent cell to which you want to apply the name. If this is not the case, make the proper selection in the list box.
4. Click the Use Labels command button.
5. Select OK to confirm your selection and close the dialog box.

These steps tell 1-2-3 to use labels contained in worksheet cells to create range names for those cells to the right of the labels. You can use the macro command language to create a macro that performs this procedure. The equivalent macro command is as follows:

```
{RANGE-NAME-LABEL-CREATE "right"}
```

Cell B5 in figure 36.4 shows the macro command entered in the worksheet.

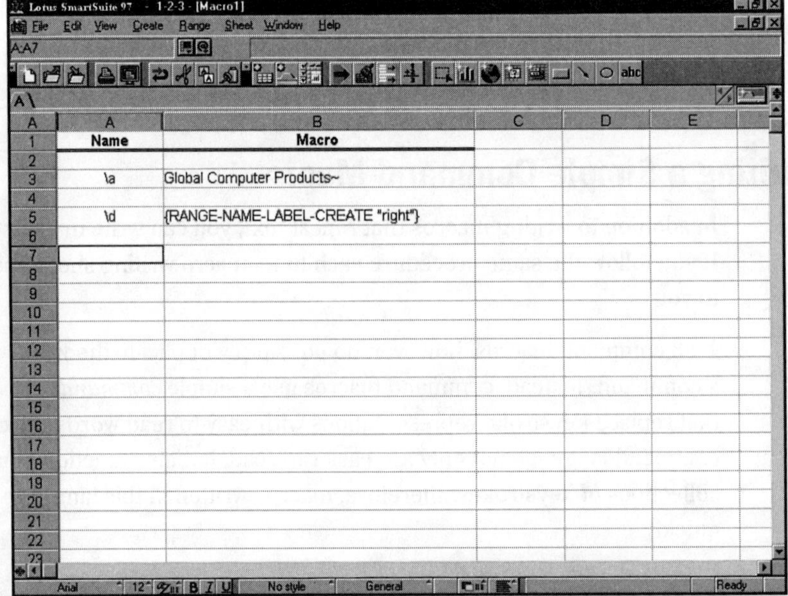

Fig. 36.4
The range-naming macro appears in cell B5.

For the purpose of this example, the intention is to name the macro \d using the label in cell A5. In this case, however, you cannot launch the macro in the typical Ctrl+*letter* fashion, because the name is not yet assigned. You can press Alt+F3 (Run), or choose the Edit, Scripts & Macros, Run command to display the Run Scripts & Macros dialog box and run the macro even before it is named. You also can click the Run or Debug a Script or Macro

SmartIcon to access the Run Scripts & Macros dialog box. Select the Macro option button at the top of the dialog box to view the available options for macros (see fig. 36.5).

The Edit, Scripts & Macros command in 1-2-3 97 replaces the Tools, Macro command from earlier versions of 1-2-3 97.

In figure 36.5, the cell pointer rests in cell A:A5, one cell to the left of the macro's first line. The Range text box displays A:A5 (the current cell-pointer location—and the location of the label you want to use to name the macro). Before you can execute the macro, you must change the Range text box to display the address of the first cell in the macro (in this case, A:B5). Select the Range text box, and either type **A:B5** or click the range selector and select cell A:B5 directly in the worksheet. When you choose Run, the macro in cell A:B5 executes and names itself \d.

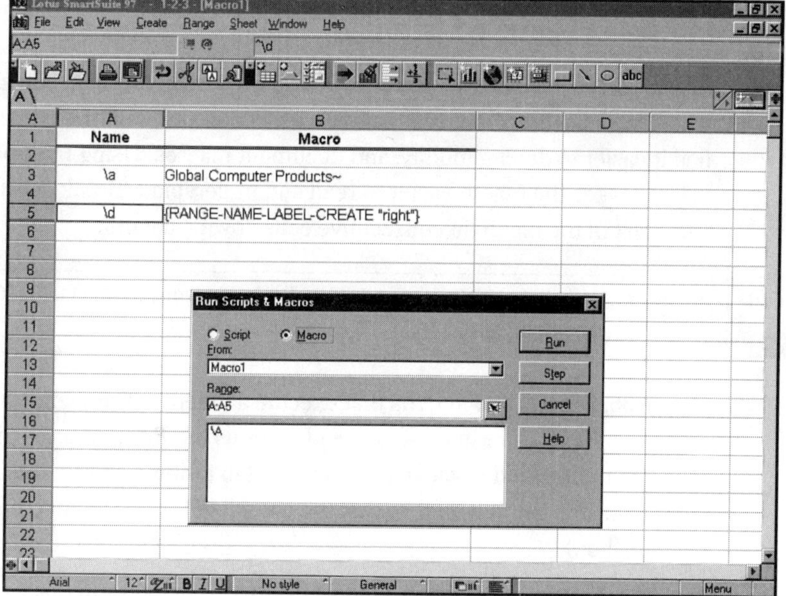

Fig. 36.5
Use the Run Scripts & Macros dialog box (with the Macro option selected) to run an unnamed macro.

After you name the \d macro and assign the name to cell A:B5, you can use this macro to name other macros. Remember to start by positioning the cell pointer one cell to the left of a macro's first cell (that is, in the cell that contains the name you intend to assign to the macro). Then press the keystroke combination Ctrl+D.

Understanding the Guidelines for Creating Macros

In the preceding sections of this chapter, you learned how to write simple macros. You learned the importance of planning the macro and identifying the tasks the macro should perform. The following sections elaborate on the major elements of successful macro creation and execution. These elements include planning the layout of the macro, formatting the macro, naming and running the macro, documenting the macro, and testing and debugging the macro.

Whether your macros simply duplicate keystrokes or use the 1-2-3 command language, macros are easier to create and maintain if you follow the guidelines presented in the following sections.

Planning the Layout of Macros

Although you can enter as many as 512 characters in one cell, you should divide a long macro into smaller, more readable pieces. When you limit the content of each cell, you will find it easier to debug, modify, and document macros. Using multiple cells to store the macro makes the macro easier to read and understand. Break apart a macro by placing each part of the macro in consecutive cells down a column.

An easy way to break a macro into parts is to divide it in terms of small tasks. You can limit each cell to a single task (or a few tasks).

Figure 36.6 shows two macros that execute an identical sequence of keystrokes. The \m macro performs the same sequence of tasks as the Print_Macros macro, but is difficult to read and understand because it is contained in a single cell (in this figure, cell B3 was selected and is being edited so that the complete text of the macro is displayed in the contents box).

Although both macros in figure 36.6 include the same set of macro commands, the Print_Macros macro has several advantages over the \m macro. For example, if you decide to change the range printed by the macro, the Print_Macros macro is much easier to modify. In addition, because the Print_Macros macro fits into a single column, you can easily read the macro commands it contains. Finally, the Print_Macros macro is much easier to document; you can enter comments in the column to the right of the macro commands.

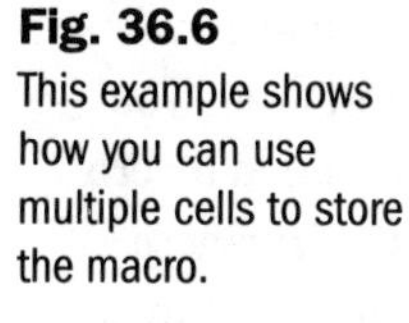

Fig. 36.6
This example shows how you can use multiple cells to store the macro.

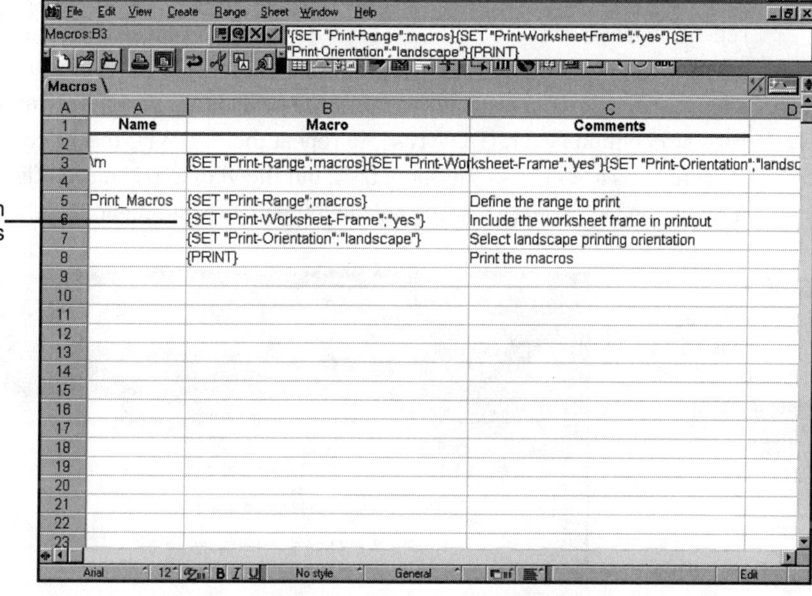
Macros:B3
{SET "Print-Range";macros}{SET "Print-Worksheet-Frame";"yes"}{SET "Print-Orientation";"landscape"}{PRINT}
Macros \
Name
Macro
Comments
\m
{SET "Print-Range";macros}{SET "Print-Worksheet-Frame";"yes"}{SET "Print-Orientation";"landsc
Print_Macros
{SET "Print-Range";macros}
Define the range to print
{SET "Print-Worksheet-Frame";"yes"}
Include the worksheet frame in printout
{SET "Print-Orientation";"landscape"}
Select landscape printing orientation
{PRINT}
Print the macros
Macro stored in multiple cells

The Print_Macros macro works whether you name the macro using just cell B5 or the entire range B5..B8. Remember that the commands execute starting at the upper-left corner cell of the range. After the commands in cell B5 are executed, the macro processor moves down one cell and executes any commands in cell B6. After completing those commands, the processor again moves down one cell. The macro processor continues to move down and execute commands until it encounters one of the following situations:

- An empty cell
- A cell that contains a numeric value, ERR, or NA
- A cell that contains a macro command that explicitly stops a macro

The macros you create will be easier to read and understand later if you logically separate macro commands into separate cells. When you use macro instructions that include braces, such as {SET} and {PRINT}, however, you must keep the entire macro command in the same cell. Splitting the macro command {PRINT} into two cells—`{PR` in one cell, and `INT}` in the cell that follows—doesn't work.

Because macro commands must be labels, the macro processor ignores the label prefix (', ", or ^) in the macro cell when the keystrokes are executed. It doesn't matter which label prefix you use; the macro runs regardless of which alignment you choose.

1-2-3 enables you to repeat certain macro commands by including a *repetition factor*. A repetition factor tells 1-2-3 that you want a command repeated the number of times you specify. The \a and \d macros in figure 36.7 perform the same keystrokes. The \a macro uses four {DOWN} commands to move the cell pointer down four rows. The \d macro uses a repetition factor, {DOWN 4}, to repeat the {DOWN} macro command four times. Both macros accomplish the same task, but the \d macro is more efficient. When you use a repetition factor, leave a space between the macro command and the number.

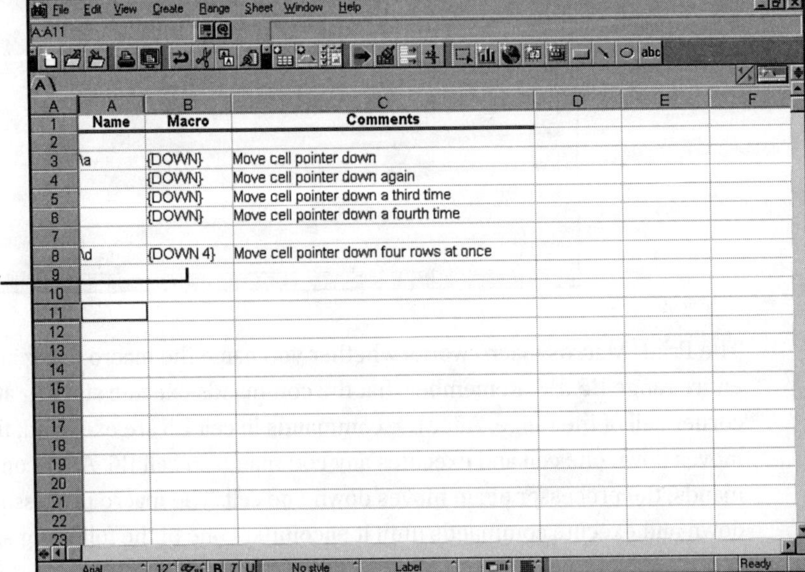

Fig. 36.7 A repetition factor appears in the \d macro in cell B8; this repeats a macro command.

Formatting Macros

Certain formatting features are necessary to ensure the successful operation of 1-2-3 macros. Other conventions simplify the tasks of reading and analyzing macros. These tasks are particularly important when you need to debug or edit a macro by changing or adding an operation. The following sections present certain rules you should follow so that your macros run properly.

Enter Macro Cells as Text or String Formulas When you type a macro in the worksheet, you must enter each cell of the macro as text or as a string formula. Certain keystrokes, such as numbers, cause 1-2-3 to change from Ready mode to Value mode; other keystrokes, such as the slash key (/), change 1-2-3 to Menu mode. Therefore, you must place an apostrophe (') before any of the following characters if that character is to be the first character in a macro cell:

A number from 0 to 9

/ + - @ # $. < (\

The apostrophe (') switches 1-2-3 to Label mode from Ready mode, especially if you are entering a macro that contains a number of lines that 1-2-3 does not recognize as labels. Using an apostrophe before any of the preceding characters and numbers ensures that 1-2-3 does not misinterpret your text entry. If any character *not* in this list is the first keystroke in the cell, 1-2-3 switches to Label mode and prefixes the entry with an apostrophe (') when you press Enter.

Use Correct Syntax for Macro Commands The syntax for 1-2-3 macro commands must be exact. You must place each macro command within one cell; you cannot write a macro command so that the beginning brace is on one line and the closing brace is on another line.

All macro commands are enclosed in curly braces ({ }). The braces tell 1-2-3 where a macro command begins and ends. Some macro commands are a single command enclosed in braces. For example, to quit a macro, you could use the following command, without arguments:

```
{QUIT}
```

Many other macro commands, however, require arguments within the braces. The arguments that follow commands adhere to a syntax similar to that used in 1-2-3's @functions. The following is the general syntax of commands that require arguments:

```
{COMMAND argument1;argument2;...;argumentN}
```

The *command name*, or *keyword* (represented in the example by the word COMMAND), is the part of the command that tells 1-2-3 what action to perform. The *arguments* supply the information 1-2-3 needs to complete the command.

For example, in the following command, BLANK tells 1-2-3 to erase the contents of a cell or range (a range in this example), and the argument A:A1..A:D10 tells the command what cell or range to erase.

```
{BLANK A:A1..A:D10}
```

An argument can consist of numbers, strings, cell addresses, range names, formulas, or functions. Some commands, such as BLANK, only accept one argument. Other commands, such as LET or PUT, require multiple arguments.

The command and the argument are always separated by a space. For most commands, multiple arguments are separated by semicolons (;) with no spaces between the arguments.

To quickly check the syntax for a macro command, type the left brace ({) and the macro command name in the cell. While you are still in Label mode, press F3 to display the Macro Keywords dialog box, which contains a list of macro commands that can be viewed either alphabetically or by command category. Select the name of the command you are looking for; the command syntax and a brief description of the command appear at the bottom of the dialog box. If you choose OK, 1-2-3 enters the command into the cell and highlights any command arguments that you must supply.

Use the Tilde to Represent the Enter Key You use the tilde (~) in a macro to represent the action of pressing the Enter key. Most 1-2-3 macro commands do not require a tilde, but macros that duplicate keystrokes instead of using macro command statements usually do require the tilde.

Use Repetition Factors Use repetition factors in macros whenever possible. For example, instead of typing **{LEFT}** three times, you can type **{LEFT 3}** or **{L 3}**. When you use repetition factors, be sure to place one space between the actual macro command and the number of repetitions.

Naming and Running Macros

You can start macros in several different ways, depending on how the macros are named.

▶ **See** "Naming Ranges," **p. 58**

Consider the following examples:

- Execute a macro named with the backslash (\) and a letter by holding down the Ctrl key and pressing the designated letter. Alternatively, you can use the Run Scripts & Macros dialog box. You invoke this dialog box by pressing Alt+F3 (Run), or by choosing Edit, Scripts & Macros, Run. Select the Macro option button at the top of the dialog box to view the available options for macros.
- Execute a macro with a descriptive name of up to 15 characters by using the Run Scripts & Macros dialog box. Select the Macro option button to view the available options for macros.
- You can launch an *autoexecute macro* (one with the name \0) in two ways. If you selected the Run File Opened Scripts, Autoexecute Macros check box on the General tab of the 1-2-3 Preferences dialog box, such a macro will start when a file

containing the \0 macro is loaded. You also can initiate an autoexecute macro by using the Run Scripts & Macros dialog box.

- Execute any macro, even if it has no name, by using the Run Scripts & Macros dialog box. Select the Macro option button to view the available options for macros. Then, specify the macro's first cell as the address in the Range text box, and choose Run.

Earlier in this chapter, you learned how to name and run a macro with the Ctrl+*letter* combination. In the second method of naming and running macros, you assign a descriptive name to the first cell in the macro and then execute the macro from the Run Scripts & Macros dialog box. In the third method, you create a macro named \0 that executes when you load the file. In the fourth method, you execute *any* macro by using the Run Scripts & Macros dialog box.

When you press Alt+F3, or choose Edit, Scripts & Macros, Run, the Run Scripts & Macros dialog box appears. After selecting the Macro option, you can select a macro from the list of macro names. You also can type the cell address of the macro you want to run; you do not have to specify a range name.

Although you use the \0 name only if you want 1-2-3 to invoke a macro as soon as the file is opened, you can use the Ctrl+*letter* or descriptive name for any other macro. Both types of names have advantages. When you invoke a macro with a Ctrl+*letter* name, you use fewer keystrokes than when you invoke a macro with a descriptive name. The disadvantage of using a Ctrl+*letter* macro name, however, is that you may have difficulty remembering a macro's specific purpose, particularly when you have created many macros. Your chance of selecting the correct macro is greater when you use descriptive names.

The following sections describe all three approaches to creating, naming, and running macros. Figure 36.8 shows three macros that demonstrate the rules and conventions for naming and running macros. Although these macros are intended only to demonstrate the three ways to name and run a macro, each is a fully functioning 1-2-3 command macro. The comments included in column C for each macro explain the function of each line of the macro.

Ctrl+*letter* Macros The \d macro in figure 36.8 demonstrates the Ctrl+*letter* approach to naming a macro. The function of the \d macro is one way to automate the naming of macros. You can use upper- or lowercase characters to name a macro; 1-2-3 does not differentiate between upper- and lowercase letters for range names. Accordingly, \a, \A, and \m are valid names for Ctrl+*letter* macros.

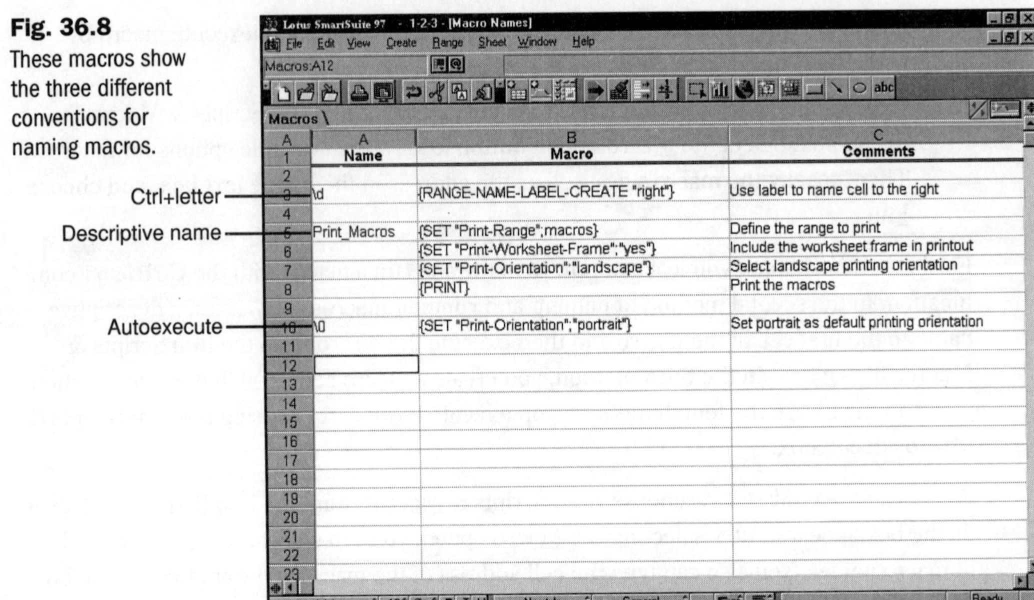

Fig. 36.8
These macros show the three different conventions for naming macros.

1-2-3 assigns keyboard shortcuts to several Ctrl+*letter* combinations (such as Ctrl+B for changing selected text and numbers to boldface). If you use the same Ctrl+*letter* combination to name a macro, the macro executes in place of the keyboard shortcut. To prevent conflicts with keyboard shortcuts, avoid using the letters B, C, E, F, G, H, I, L, N, O, P, R, S, U, V, X, or Z when naming Ctrl+*letter* macros.

To run a macro named with the backslash (\) and a letter, hold the Ctrl key and press the letter key that identifies the macro. For example, to run the first macro in figure 36.8, for example, press Ctrl+D.

Macros with Descriptive Names Because you can use up to 15 characters to name a range in 1-2-3, you can use descriptive names for macros. When naming macros with descriptive names, however, do not use range names that also are macro command names. One way of documenting macros is to give them longer, more descriptive names. Another way is to retain hard copy documentation for macros, including printouts of the macro code. The Print_Macros macro in figure 36.8 automates the preparation of these printouts.

You can use the Run Scripts & Macros dialog box to start macros that have descriptive names. To access this dialog box, press Alt+F3, or choose Edit, Scripts & Macros, Run. Select the Macro option button to view the available options for macros. Figure 36.9 shows how the screen appears after this dialog box is invoked for the sample macros shown in figure 36.8.

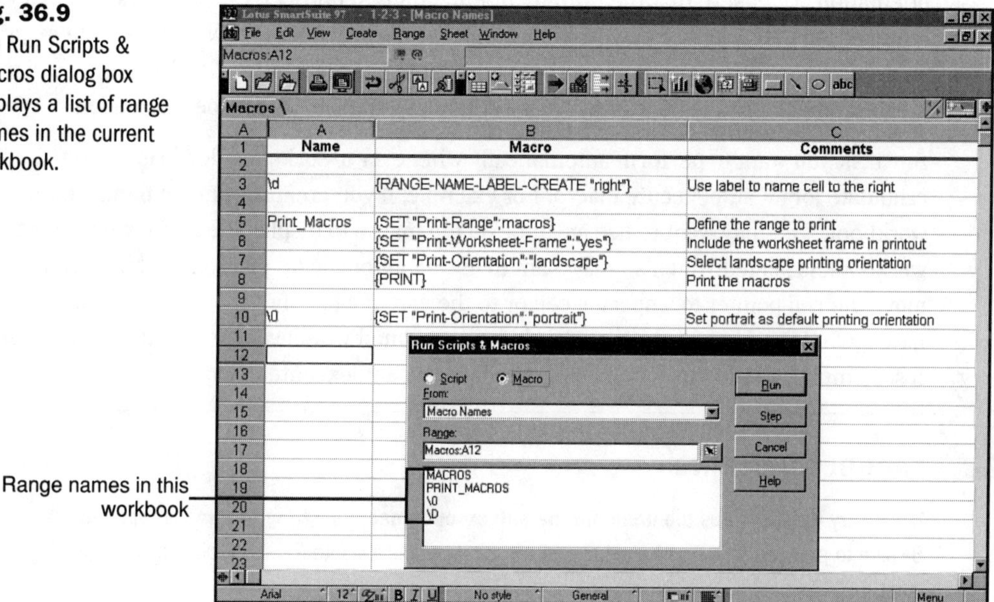

Fig. 36.9 The Run Scripts & Macros dialog box displays a list of range names in the current workbook.

To start a macro from the current workbook, select the range name of the macro you want to run; then choose Run.

When you access the Run Scripts & Macros dialog box and click the Macro option, 1-2-3 displays all the range names in the current workbook, including range names that are not macro names. To run a macro stored in a workbook that is open, but not currently active, select that workbook's name in the From drop-down list box. The Run Scripts & Macros dialog box lists the range names in the selected workbook. Then, in the Range text box, type (or select) the range name of the macro you want to run, and click Run.

You can start a macro in another file without selecting the file; simply precede the macro's name in the Range text box with the name of the file in which it is located. Enclose the file name in double angle brackets (<< >>) and then type the macro name, as in the following example:

```
<<BUDGET.123>>Print_Macro
```

Autoexecute Macros You may want some macros to run automatically when you open the workbooks that contain them. Use \0 to name the macro that you want to run as soon as the workbook loads; such a macro is called an *autoexecute* macro. Each workbook can contain only one autoexecute macro.

Suppose that you print some worksheets in landscape orientation and others in portrait orientation. To ensure that the printing orientation is set properly for a worksheet that requires portrait orientation, you can include in that worksheet the \0 autoexecute macro shown in figure 36.8. By changing the argument from "portrait" to "landscape," you can create a similar autoexecute macro for worksheets that use landscape orientation.

Any task you want to perform automatically whenever a worksheet loads is a good candidate for an autoexecute macro. For example, if you create your own menus for a workbook, you may want to use an autoexecute macro to display the menu whenever the workbook is loaded. You also may want to use an autoexecute macro to automatically move the cell pointer to a specific cell or to the end of a list of entries. In fact, you may have a whole series of tasks that should be performed whenever the workbook is loaded. If so, simply include the correct commands in the autoexecute macro.

TROUBLESHOOTING

When I try to type \0 as the name for the autoexecute macro, a string of zeros is repeated. Be sure to precede the \0 with a label prefix, such as a single quote ('), so that it is entered as a label.

My autoexecute macro will not run when I load a workbook. Make certain that the Run File Opened Scripts, Autoexecute Macros check box is selected in the 1-2-3 Preferences dialog box General tab. Choose File, User Setup, 1-2-3 Preferences to access this dialog box.

Documenting Macros

As with other parts of a 1-2-3 workbook, you need to document the macros you write. You can document macros by using many of the same techniques you use to document workbooks, as follows:

- Use descriptive names as macro names.
- Include comments in the worksheet.
- Save any design notes that you've created on paper.

NOTE In addition to placing macro comments in a worksheet, you can save comments with a file. When you save a file for the first time, or when you choose File, Save As, you see a dialog box that contains a section for comments. Any comments that you save with the file appear when the file name is highlighted in the Open dialog box.

Use Descriptive Names Although a Ctrl+*letter* macro is easy to execute, its name does not describe the macro's purpose. A better naming convention is to use range names as macro names. You can execute such macros by pressing Alt+F3, or choosing Edit, Scripts & Macros, Run.

Include Comments in the Worksheet A description of the macro's function appears to the right of each of the three macros shown in figure 36.8. With these simple macros, you can identify the tasks that the macros perform just by reading the macro code—if you are familiar with the menu structure that the macros reference. The addition of the documentation provides a ready reference.

With longer, more complex macros, you probably will find such internal documentation helpful. Later, when you want to make changes in the macro, you can refer to these internal comments about the macro's purpose and intended action. You may discover that you do not need to comment on each individual macro line, especially when you create simple macros.

Keep External Design Notes Be sure to retain any paperwork you created as part of designing and constructing the macro. In addition to keeping any notes on keystrokes or commands that you incorporated into the macro, you should keep printed copies of all the range names and formulas in each worksheet.

Don't underestimate the value of this type of documentation, it will considerably ease the burden of modifying a macro later. The more people who use a macro, and the more important a macro is, the more critical external documentation becomes.

The most important piece of external documentation—which you should never neglect—is a printout of the macro. Other types of external documentation that may be particularly valuable are notes on who requested a macro, why the macro was requested, who created and tested the macro, the underlying assumptions that determined the overall design, and any diagrams or outlines of macro operations or structure.

If you used reference materials to help develop the macro, consider including a bibliography and page references in the documentation. Any information that you supply in external documentation simplifies any maintenance of, or modifications to, the macro.

Using Step Mode to Test Macros

Macro writers soon recognize that even a well-designed macro program can contain *bugs* (errors that prevent the macro from functioning correctly). Because 1-2-3 executes macro instructions in rapid sequence, you often cannot determine why a macro is failing. This section introduces some methods that help you find and correct errors in macros.

No matter how carefully you construct a macro, it may not run flawlessly the first time. By taking a series of precautions, however, you can minimize your efforts to get macros to work correctly.

Before you create a macro, always invest the time to design the macro carefully. Just as a carpenter never starts construction of a house without blueprints, you should not start construction of a macro without a carefully conceived and well-documented design. Take time to plan the detailed steps a macro is to perform, create good documentation of the macro's purpose and actions, and write descriptions of any range names used in the macro.

Even if you have a good design and thorough documentation, plan to test and debug your macros. Testing enables you to verify that a macro works precisely the way you want. 1-2-3 provides a valuable tool to help you verify a macro's operation and locate macro errors: Step mode. *Step mode* enables you to execute the macro one keystroke at a time. This mode gives you a chance to see, one instruction at a time, exactly what the macro does. When you begin Step mode, a Macro Trace window appears, showing the macro instruction being executed and the cell location of that instruction. Without this tool, macros often execute too rapidly for you to see the problem areas.

To use Step mode to test a macro, follow these steps:

1. Choose Edit, Scripts & Macros, Run. In the Run Scripts & Macros dialog box, select Macro.
2. In the Range text box, specify the range name or the address of the macro you want to test.
3. Choose Step. The Macro Trace window appears in the lower-right corner of the worksheet (see fig. 36.10). Notice that the `Cmd` indicator appears in the status bar as you are running the macro.
4. Choose Step in the Macro Trace window (multiple times, as necessary), to execute each command in the macro, one step at a time. The Macro Trace window highlights the macro instruction being executed and identifies the cell that contains that instruction.

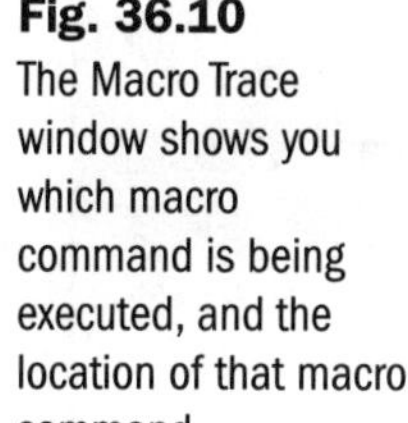

Fig. 36.10
The Macro Trace window shows you which macro command is being executed, and the location of that macro command.

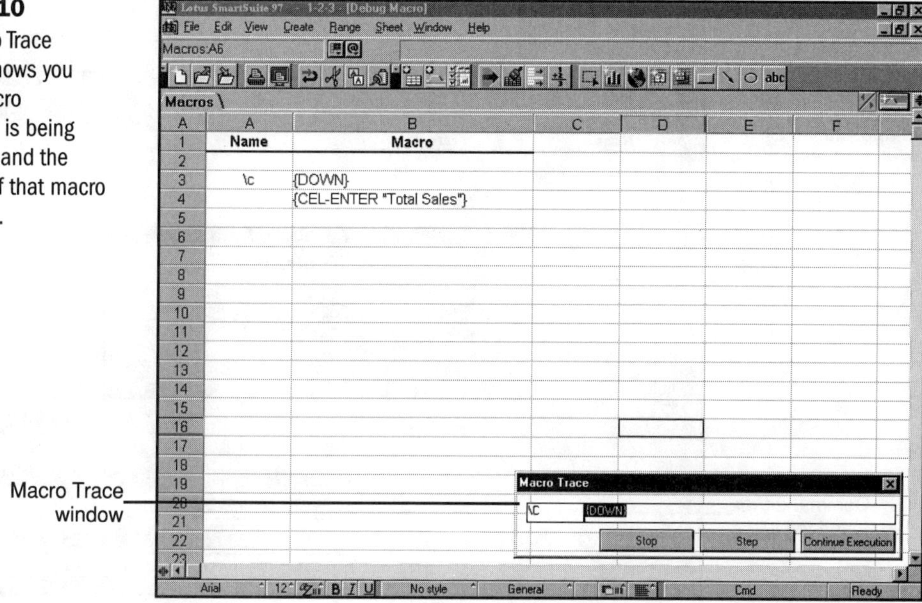

You can click the Stop button in the Trace window to stop running the macro and quit Step mode. Or, you can click the Continue Execution button if you want to execute the rest of the macro without using Step mode.

If 1-2-3 finds an error in the macro, an error message appears and the macro stops. The \c macro in this workbook contains a deliberate spelling error in a macro command in cell A:B4. When Step mode encounters this error, 1-2-3 displays an error message (see fig. 36.11).

5. You cannot edit the macro while it is running, so choose OK to remove the error message and the Trace window from the screen. Edit the macro to correct the error. Then repeat the test procedure (beginning with step 1 of this sequence) in case the macro contains other errors.

NOTE Edit a macro cell as you would any label. Move the cell pointer to the cell containing the label you want to edit (in this case, the macro line), press F2 (Edit) or double-click the cell to go into Edit mode, and then make your changes.

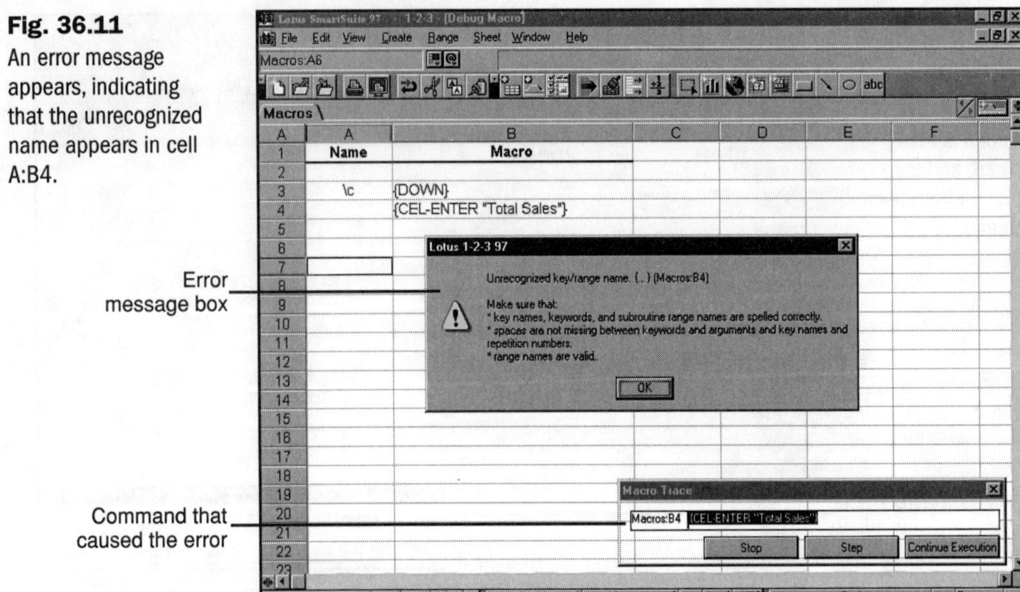

Fig. 36.11 An error message appears, indicating that the unrecognized name appears in cell A:B4.

Protecting Macros

If you create worksheet applications that other people will use, you should secure the macros to prevent their accidental erasure or alteration. Most programs (such as database management systems) separate data and programs into individual files; 1-2-3, however, puts data and programs (macros) in the same files, making access to the macros easy—sometimes too easy.

Even if you place all macros in separate files, the files still are 1-2-3 workbooks; they can be changed by anyone who knows 1-2-3 well enough. You may want to consider saving macros in separate, sealed workbooks. Macros saved in sealed workbooks can be used by anyone who has access to the file, but they can be modified only by someone who knows the correct password to unlock the file.

▶ **See** "Protecting Workbooks," **p. 278**

Most users store macros customized for particular applications in the same files that contain the applications. In these cases, place the macros together outside the area occupied by the main model. Storing the macros together makes it easier to find a macro and also helps prevent accidental overwriting or erasing of part of a macro as you work with the model.

If you store macros in separate worksheets, you can avoid some common problems. Suppose that you want to use 1-2-3 commands to insert or delete columns or rows. When you use these commands—manually or within macros—the macros may become corrupted as rows are inserted or deleted (as can happen if the macros are in the same worksheet as the data being manipulated).

Inserting or deleting columns or rows also can cause problems with the cell addresses used in macros, because changes in cell references that may occur as a result of an insertion or deletion are not reflected in the macros. Accordingly, use range names instead of cell addresses in macros.

Store macros on their own sheet in a workbook. Double-click the sheet tab and type **Macros** to name the sheet.

APPENDIX

Finding Optimal Solutions with the Solver

by Dan Fylstra, President, Frontline Systems, Inc.

The Lotus-developed Solver included with earlier versions of 1-2-3 is no longer supported in 1-2-3 97. But this "cloud" has a silver lining: There's a new and more powerful Solver for 1-2-3 97, developed by Frontline Systems, the same company who developed the Solver in Excel and the Optimizer in Quattro Pro. It solves the same types of problems, provides new capabilities, and offers an upgrade path for users of the earlier Lotus Solver. This appendix shows you where to find the free trial version of the Solver, how to install it, and how to upgrade the trial version to a permanent license. A free trial version of this Solver is being distributed by Lotus on CD-ROM and via the World Wide Web. ■

When to use the Solver

Solver problems can be simple or complex, but most practical problems involve some sort of resource allocation. Examples which will help you recognize such problems in your own work are included here.

How to set up a problem for the Solver

You learn to identify the three essential parts of any Solver problem and how to enter these through the Solver dialog boxes.

How to use Solver options and reports

Learn how to interpret the most important elements of the Solver reports, and when and how to use the most common Solver options.

How to move Solver models between 1-2-3 and Excel

For the first time, Solver models can be moved between 1-2-3 97 and Excel 97, and solved in either program.

How to control the Solver from LotusScript

You can build applications in LotusScript which present a custom user interface while controlling the Solver "behind the scenes."

Installing the Solver

The free trial version of the new Solver which is being distributed by Lotus is a limited use version, good for 100 problem solution attempts (clicks of the Solve button). It is easy to upgrade this trial version to an unlimited-use version: In fact, a "registration wizard" takes you all the way through the process, as illustrated later in the chapter in "Upgrading to a Permanent License."

Obtaining the Solver Trial Version

To install the new Solver, all you need is the file SOLVE123.EXE, which is an installer program or "self-extracting archive." If you received Lotus 1-2-3 97 or SmartSuite 97 on CD-ROM, you should find SOLVE123.EXE in the \EXTRA\123\SOLVER directory.

If you don't have the Lotus CD-ROM, you can download SOLVE123.EXE through the Internet with either a Web browser or an FTP client program. If you're using a Web browser, enter the URL **http://www2.support.lotus.com/ftp/pub/desktop/123/utils/** and click SOLVE123.EXE in the list of available files; or enter the URL **ftp://ftp.-frontsys.com/pub/123** and click SOLVE123.EXE in the list of files there. If you have an FTP client program, connect via anonymous FTP to **www2.support.lotus.com** and use the **cd** and **ls** commands to look for SOLVE123.EXE in the **/pub/desktop/123/utils** directory, or connect to **ftp.frontsys.com** and look in the **/pub/123** directory. Use the **bin** and **get** commands to retrieve the file.

Installing the Solver

To install the Solver, run the program SOLVE123.EXE on your PC. You can choose Run from the Start menu and type the path to this file, or just double-click SOLVE123.EXE in the Windows Explorer. You'll see a Setup dialog box like the one in figure A.1.

This installer finds out everything it needs to know from 1-2-3's entries in the Registry. Just click the Setup button, wait for the files to be unzipped, then click OK at the installation confirmation dialog box. That's all there is to it. The next time you start 1-2-3 and choose Range, Analyze, you'll find a new Solver option on the Analyze submenu, as shown in figure A.2.

A great way to try out the Solver is to open the workbook SOLVSAMP.123, which is installed along with the other Solver files. The next time you run 1-2-3, this workbook appears at the top of your list of recently used workbooks, courtesy of the installer. This workbook contains seven prewritten Solver worksheet models, which are discussed briefly later in this chapter.

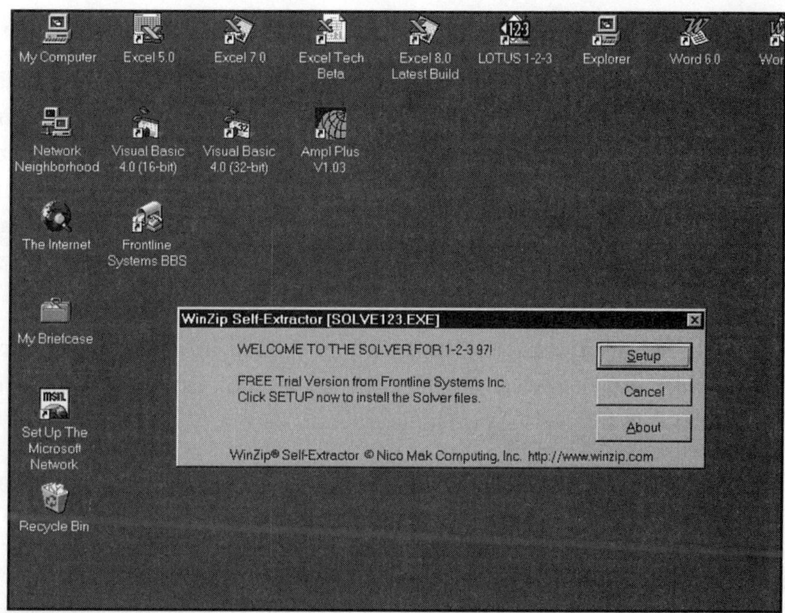

Fig. A.1
Click Setup in this dialog box that was displayed by the SOLVE123.EXE installation program.

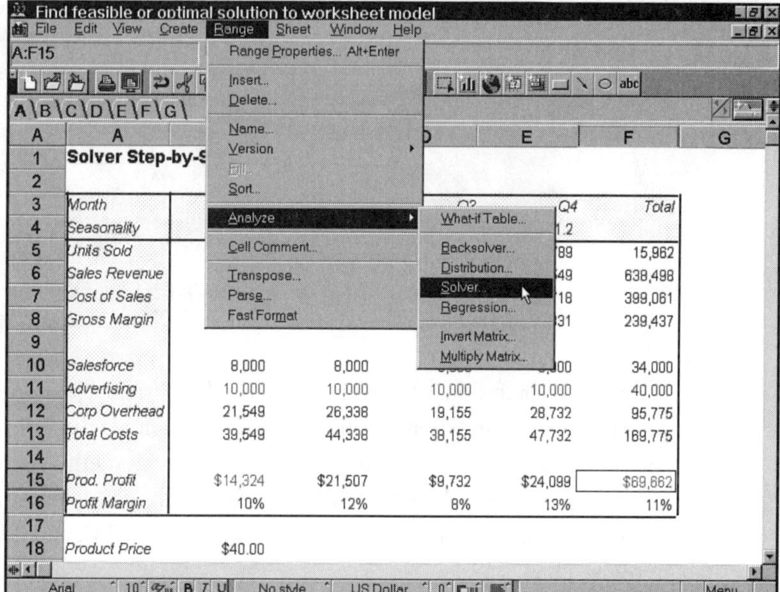

Fig. A.2
A new Solver choice appears on the Range, Analyze submenu.

Upgrading to a Permanent License

The first time you click the Solve button in the Solver Parameters dialog box (after you've set up a problem and are ready to solve it), you'll see a dialog box that reminds you that this is a trial version good for 100 "solves," and invites you to purchase a permanent license. If you click No at this point, the Solver will solve the current problem and subsequent problems, until you are down to 90 "solves," and then will remind you again. This continues until you reach zero remaining "solves," at which point you'll need to register to continue using the Solver.

If you click Yes, the Registration Wizard starts up and takes you through the process, which can be done any time of the day or night, using a series of simple entry screens. The first screen is shown in figure A.3.

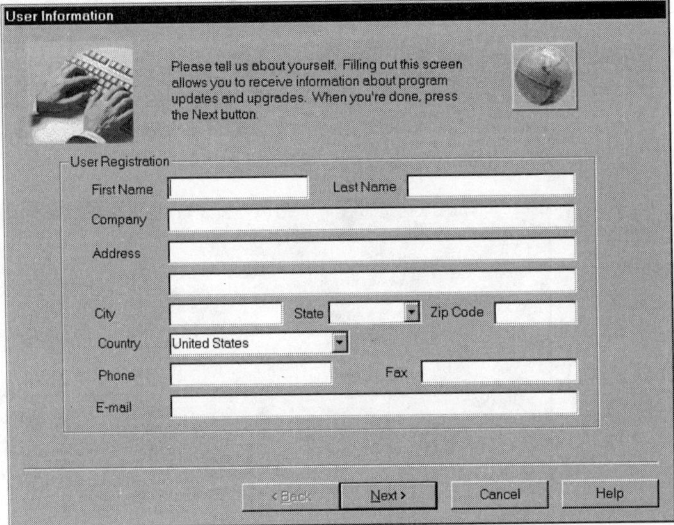

Fig. A.3
You can use the Registration Wizard to obtain a permanent license to use the Solver.

You fill in the registration information, choose the purchase options you want, enter your credit card number, and then complete the transaction via the Internet, a direct modem call, or by phone, fax, or mail. The Internet and modem methods are completely automatic, while the phone, fax, and mail methods require you to enter an unlocking code. Thereafter, the Solver can be used without limit on your PC, and it won't ask you again about registration.

When to Use the Solver

When should you use the Solver? You can learn to recognize opportunities to use the Solver by understanding what the Solver can do, and the types of applications where the Solver's analytical power has proven most useful.

What-If in Reverse

Spreadsheets have always been used for "what-if" analyses: You change the input values, and the spreadsheet recalculates various outputs. But what if you want a certain cell, such as Net Profit, to reach a target such as $100,000? Or what if you'd like to find the maximum Net Profit achievable by changing certain inputs? You may have tried to do this through trial and error, changing the input values and recalculating over and over. What you really want is "what-if" in reverse.

Solver Versus Backsolver

The Solver and Backsolver are designed to find the right input values automatically. The Backsolver, discussed in Chapter 20, "Solving Problems with Backsolver" is the simpler tool: It adjusts one or more inputs to yield a specific value in one cell, such as $100,000 for Net Profit.

The Solver can do everything the Backsolver can do, and much more. Solver can find the maximum or minimum value for a cell, such as Net Profit, that can be achieved by adjusting one or more input cells. And it can simultaneously ensure that one or more other cells, called *constraints*, have specific values or fall within specified ranges.

So the Solver is clearly more powerful (and more complex) than the Backsolver, but what is it good for? As you look at practical Solver applications, you'll find that they usually have in common the idea of allocating scarce resources so as to achieve some goal, such as maximum profit, minimum cost, or best possible quality. The resources may be raw materials, machine time or people time, money, or anything else in limited supply. The constraints in the Solver problem quantify the limits. The Solver finds the best allocation of resources that satisfies the constraints.

Examining the Solver Samples

To see the Solver in action, open the workbook SOLVSAMP.123. This workbook contains seven worksheets. The first one (tab A), titled Solver Step-by-Step Example, is designed to let you set up a Solver model from scratch and try out various features of the Solver dialog boxes. The other worksheets contain predefined Solver models, which you can solve right away: Just click the tab for the worksheet of interest, choose Range, Analyze, Solver, and click the Solve button in the Solver Parameters dialog box.

The following sections describe the other six Solver sample worksheets.

Product Mix

In the worksheet in figure A.4 (tab B), your company is manufacturing three products—TVs, stereos, and speakers—which are assembled from five kinds of parts. The Solver finds the number of products of each type to build from the available parts in inventory which will maximize profits.

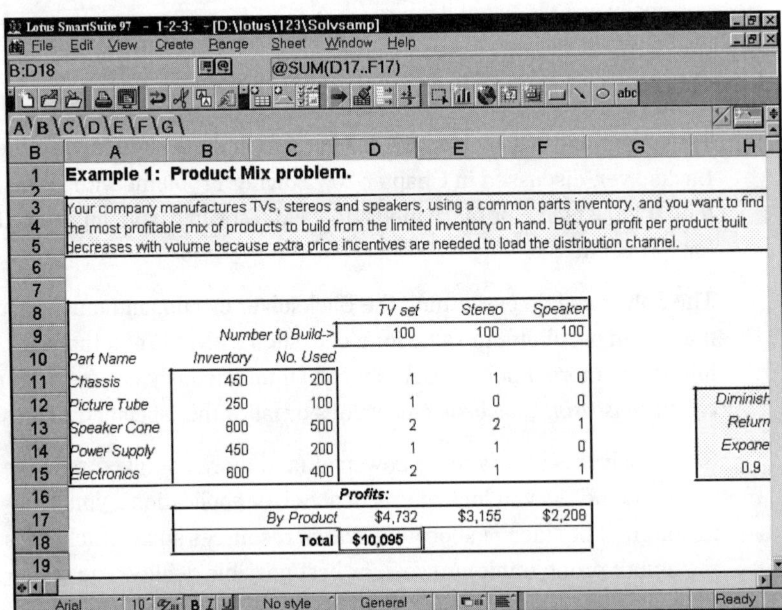

Fig. A.4 Product Mix example worksheet.

The Solver can handle both *linear* and *nonlinear* models. The Product Mix example in figure A.4 can help you appreciate the difference: It has a "Diminishing Returns Exponent" at cell H15, which is used in the calculation of Profits at cells D17 to F17. When this cell contains 1.0, the Product Mix model is linear: The graph of Total Profit is a straight line. (The constraints in this model are simple sums and are always linear.) When this cell contains 0.9 (or any value less than 1.0), the model is nonlinear: The graph of Total Profits slopes off, reflecting diminishing returns from increasing volume. When a model is linear, you can check the Assume Linear Model Box in the Solver Options dialog box, which will give you a faster solution and more information on the Sensitivity Report.

Shipping Routes

The worksheet on tab C illustrates a common situation, known as a *transportation problem*. You have three plants, making products which are shipped to five regional warehouses. Products can be shipped from any plant to any warehouse, but the shipping cost varies with distance. The Solver finds the number of products to ship on each "route" (plant-warehouse pair) to minimize the total shipping cost, while meeting the demand at each warehouse and not exceeding the supply at each plant.

Staff Scheduling

The worksheet on tab D shows how to arrange employees' work schedules so that enough employees are available each day to operate the rides at an amusement park, while minimizing total weekly payroll cost. The key insight is that there are seven possible work schedules, each consisting of five days working and two days off. The Solver finds the number of employees who should work on each schedule. An integer constraint is used to specify that the number of employees on each schedule must be a whole number.

Cash Flow Management

The worksheet on tab E illustrates a period-based model, where the goal is to invest available funds each month in short-term certificates of deposit (CDs), to maximize interest income while ensuring that the company has sufficient cash on hand at all times from maturing CDs. If you imagine a model where you are building products instead of investing money, the Solver could be used to decide how many products to build in each period to, say, minimize total overtime used.

Portfolio Optimization

A Nobel Prize-winning application of the Solver's optimization methods was created by economists Harry Markowitz and William Sharpe, to decide how to allocate funds among stocks in a portfolio so as to earn the maximum return for a given level of risk, or to minimize risk (as measured by the portfolio's variance or standard deviation) for a given rate of return. The result is called an *efficient portfolio*. In the worksheet on tab F, the Solver finds an efficient portfolio using Sharpe's method.

Engineering Design

The worksheet on tab G illustrates a Solver application in science and engineering. For a simple electrical circuit, the Solver finds the value (in ohms) for a resistor which will cause the circuit to dissipate a charge to 1 percent of its initial value within 1/20th of a second from the time a switch is thrown. The resistor's value is an input in a complex calculation, but to the Solver this is a simple one-variable "backsolving" problem (in fact, you also can solve it with 1-2-3's Backsolver).

Allocating Resources with Solver

Note that aside from the Engineering Design problem, all of these examples involved the idea of resource allocation. In the Product Mix model, the resources were the parts held in inventory. In the Transportation Problem, they were products to be shipped. In the Staff Scheduling model, the resources were the employees, and in the Working Capital Management and Portfolio Optimization problems, the resources were available funds. In every case, there were various ways to allocate the resources (quantified by the variables), with different consequences for costs or profits. There were many possible *combinations* of specific resource allocations; the Solver found the combination which minimized or maximized some criterion such as profits or costs. You should look for this pattern in the problems that arise in your own work.

Creating a Solver Model

A Solver model starts with an ordinary 1-2-3 worksheet. You create cells containing numbers, which serve as inputs, and cells containing formulas that will be recalculated. Like most worksheets, your Solver model can be laid out in tabular form, with elements such as products, regions, or time periods determining the columns and rows.

Of all the cells containing numbers, some will be fixed or "given" as far as the Solver is concerned; they are the parameters of your model. Others will be adjusted by the Solver automatically to achieve the optimal solution: These are called *decision variables*, or variable or adjustable cells.

Of all the cells containing formulas, you can choose one that the Solver should maximize or minimize. This is called the *objective* of the Solver problem. Of course, the objective cell formula must depend, directly or indirectly, on the variable cells, or the Solver won't be able to change the value of the objective by adjusting the variable cells. Other formula cells serve as the left or right side of *constraints*.

Constraints are relations such as A1 <= B1, A1 = A2 or A1 >= 0, which impose limits on the values that the specified formula cells may have at the solution. At least one of the formula cells used in a constraint must depend on some of the variable cells; otherwise, the constraint won't participate in determining the optimal solution—it is either satisfied or unsatisfied before the Solver starts. You'll find that constraints usually come in blocks or groups, and the Solver allows you to specify them in one step by writing, for example, A1..A10 <= B1..B10 or A1..E1 >= 0.

The most challenging part of designing a Solver model is identifying the right constraints. Some constraints, like limits on the number of parts in inventory, are easy to identify. Others are more subtle. For example:

- A multiperiod model may require a constraint which specifies that the beginning inventory (or cash on hand, or whatever) in a new period is equal to the ending inventory (or cash on hand) from the previous period.
- A shipping model may require a constraint that specifies that the beginning stock plus the products shipped in must equal the ending stock plus the products shipped out.
- Many models require a constraint which says that "all resources are used." For example, the sum of the allocations of funds to different stocks must equal the total funds in the portfolio.
- A very common constraint, called non-negativity, specifies that variable cells representing some physical quantity, such as parts shipped, cannot be negative. The Solver provides a shortcut for this, through an Assume Non-Negative check box in the Solver Options dialog box.

NOTE Constraints use the same syntax as logical formulas, and the old 1-2-3 Solver used logical formulas (with <=, =, or >= relations) in cells to represent constraints. But the Solver must treat constraints somewhat differently. The constraint is always evaluated within a tolerance (the default, called Precision, is 0.000001). This means that a constraint such as A1 >= 0 would be considered satisfied (or TRUE) even if A1 equaled -0.0000005, whereas a 1-2-3 logical formula such as +A1>=0 in this case would display 0 (or FALSE). The Solver does this because its complex calculations cannot yield perfectly accurate results when the computer stores only a finite number of digits of precision. For the same reason, the Solver doesn't accept constraints such as A1 > 0; this would be indistinguishable from A1 >= 0.

Defining the Solver Problem

After your worksheet model is defined, and you've determined which cells will serve as the objective, variables, and constraints, the task of defining the Solver problem is fairly simple: You select the cells serving these roles in the Solver Parameters dialog box, by either typing cell coordinates or range names, or selecting cell ranges with the mouse.

To begin, choose Range, Analyze, Solver. The Solver Parameters dialog box appears, as shown in figure A.5.

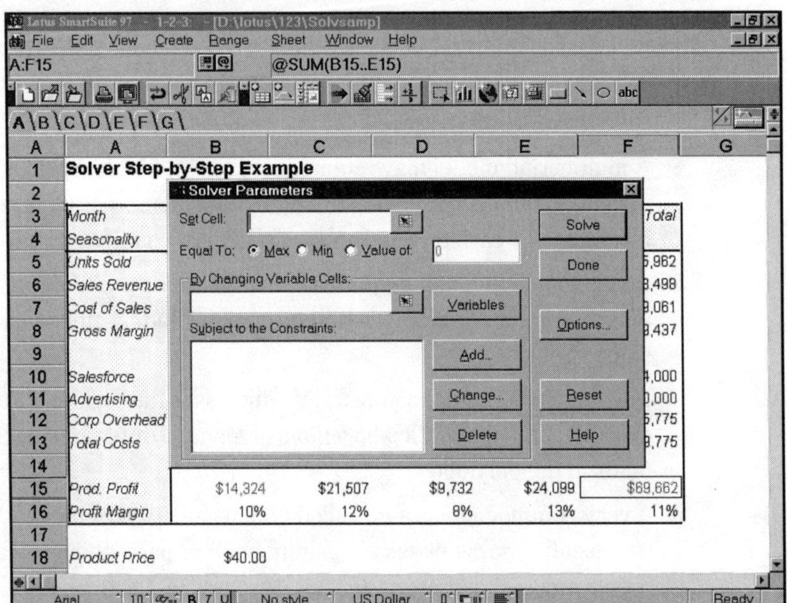

Fig. A.5
In the Solver Parameters dialog box, enter the objective (Set Cell), variable cells, and constraints.

Choosing the Objective

Click in the edit box next to Set Cell, and enter the cell you've chosen as the objective. This must be a single cell. To select the cell with the mouse, click the range selector button just to the right of this edit box. Then select one of the option buttons next to Equal To: Max (the default), Min, or Value Of. If you choose Value Of, type a number into the adjoining text box. (The Value Of choice is intended for compatibility with the Backsolver; you will rarely use this choice with the Solver.)

Selecting the Variables

Click in the edit box just below By Changing Variable Cells, and enter a contiguous range of variable cells. You may type cell coordinates, type a range name, or click the range selector button and select cells with the mouse. If you have more than one contiguous range of variable cells, click the Variables button. The Solver Parameters dialog box changes to look like figure A.6.

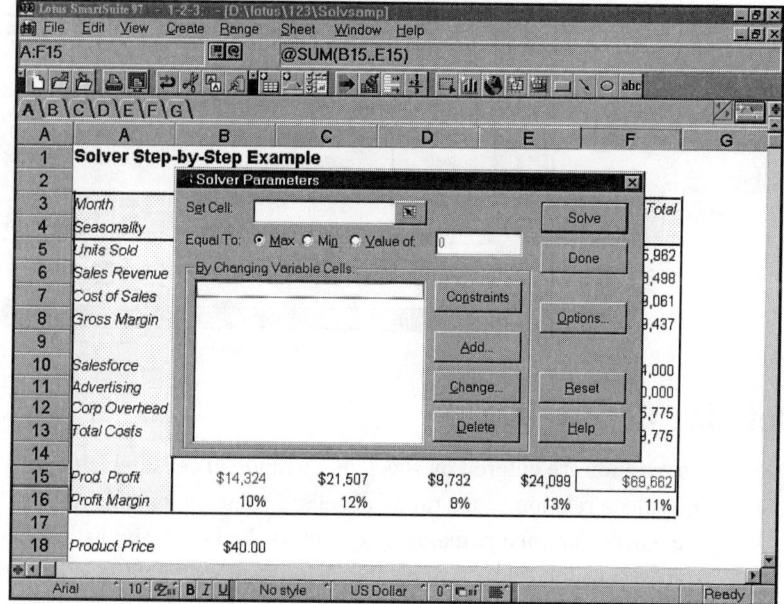

Fig. A.6
When you click the Variables button, the Solver Parameters dialog box changes to display a list of variable cell selections.

You can now use the Add, Change, and Delete buttons to enter, edit or remove additional variable cell ranges. For example, when you click Add, you'll see a dialog box like figure A.7. Type or select a range of variable cells, and click OK.

You will notice that the Variables button in figure A.6 is now labeled Constraints. This button "toggles" the Solver Parameters dialog box between its display of the Constraint list box (when the button allows you to switch to Variables) and display of the Variables list box (when the button lets you switch back to Constraints).

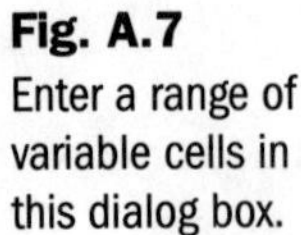

Fig. A.7
Enter a range of variable cells in this dialog box.

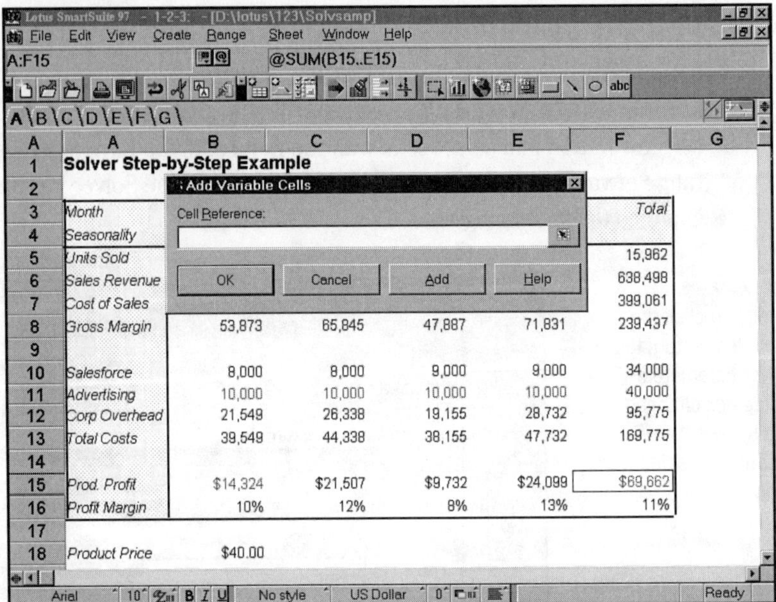

Defining Constraints

Constraints are entered by specifying a range of cells (which may be just one cell) for the left side, a relation, and a range of cells, a constant, or a formula for the right side. When the Solver Parameters dialog box displays the Constraint list box, as it does in figure A.5, you can use the Add, Change, and Delete buttons to enter, edit, or remove blocks of constraints. For example, when you click Add, you'll see a dialog box like figure A.8, where the Relation drop-down list has been opened so you can see the choices.

When this dialog box appears, the edit box labeled Cell Reference is already selected. Type a cell range address or a range name, or use the range selector button to select cells with the mouse. Then select one of the relations <=, =, or >= from the drop-down list in the center of the dialog box. Finally, in the edit box labeled Constraint you may type a constant or a formula, or a cell range address or range name, or you may select a range of cells with the mouse. If this is the only constraint you want to add right now, click OK; if you have more constraints to add, click the Add button.

If you enter a cell range such as A1..A10 on the left side and a single value such as 3 (or a formula which evaluates to a single value) on the right side, you have defined a series of constraints such as A1 >= 3, A2 >= 3, and so on. If you also have a cell range such as B1..B10 on the right side, you've defined a series of constraints such as

A1 >= B1, A2 >= B2, and so on. The number of cells in each range must be the same, but they need not be of the same "shape." For example, one range may be a column while the other range is a row.

To delete a block of constraints, click that block in the Constraints list box to highlight it, then click Delete. To change a block of constraints, highlight the block and click Change. You'll see a Change Constraint dialog box with the same edit boxes and buttons as the Add Constraint dialog box. Just make the changes you want and click OK.

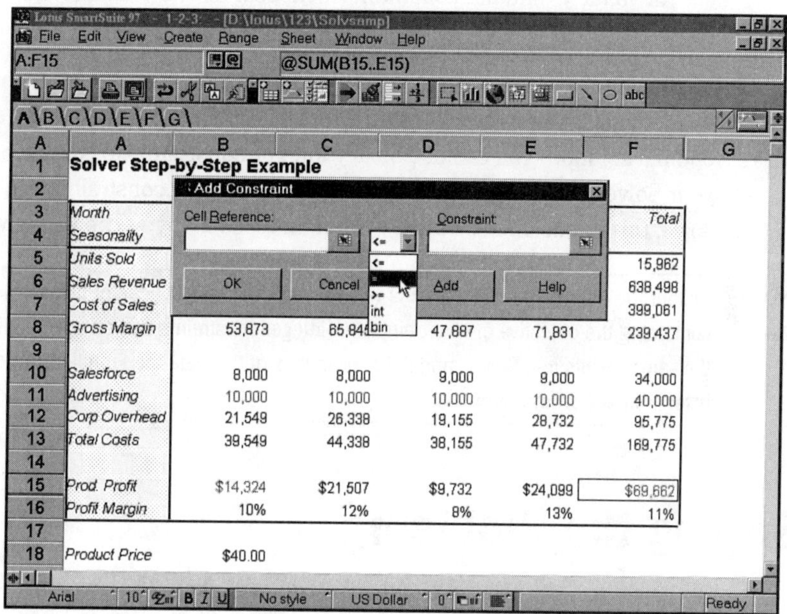

Fig. A.8
You enter a constraint in three parts: left side (Cell Reference), relation, and right side (Constraint).

Loading a Solver Problem from 1-2-3 Release 5

If you have created worksheet models that worked with the Solver in 1-2-3 Release 5, how can you use them in 1-2-3 97? The new and old Solver dialog boxes are different, but they ask for the same information. You can easily select the appropriate objective cell and variable cell ranges on your 1-2-3 Release 5 worksheet.

Constraints are a little different. The earlier Solver used constraints that were logical formulas (containing <=, =, or >=) in one or more cell ranges. A nice feature of the new Solver is that it turns these logical formulas into its own style of constraints. To do this, click Add to display the dialog box shown in figure A.8, then enter the range containing the logical formulas in the left side (Cell Reference) edit box, and click OK. The Solver separates the left and right sides and the relation, and displays them in the Constraint list box.

Using Integer Constraints

Notice that the "relation" drop-down list shown in figure A.8 includes five choices: <=, =, >=, int, and bin. The last two of these can be used to define integer constraints, which require that all or some of the decision variables have *integer* values at the optimal solution. To create an integer constraint, click Add, type or select ***a subset of the variable cells*** in the Cell Reference edit box, and select either int or bin in the drop-down list. Then click OK. You don't have to enter anything in the Constraint edit box; it will be filled with "integer" or "binary" and the constraint will appear as (for example) A1 = integer in the Constraint list box.

The bin choice creates a binary integer constraint. A1 = binary is shorthand for three constraints: A1 = integer, A1 >= 0, and A1 <= 1. This forces A1 to be either 0 or 1 at the optimal solution. You can use binary integer constraints to represent yes/no decisions in your Solver model. Although problems with integer constraints can take a long time to solve, this opens up several new problem types that you can tackle with the Solver.

Neither the old nor the new Solver is very good at handling logical formulas or lookup tables in computing the objective or constraints, but integer constraints can be used instead to achieve the same results in a Solver model. For examples of this, see the Frontline Systems Web site **http://www.frontsys.com**.

Solving the Problem

To have the Solver find the optimal solution—where the objective is maximized or minimized and the constraints are satisfied—click the Solve button. The solution process may take anywhere from a few seconds to minutes or even hours, depending on the complexity of your model and the speed of your computer. The first thing you'll notice is the message `Setting Up Problem...` on the 1-2-3 title bar. This changes to `Trial Solution` followed by an iteration (or trial solution) number and the current value of the objective cell, indicating the Solver's progress.

Trial Solutions

The Solver finds the optimal solution through an *iterative*, or "controlled trial-and-error" process: It plugs trial values into the variable cells, recalculates the worksheet, and observes how the objective and constraint values have changed. Then it determines new values for the variables to try on the next iteration—using sophisticated algorithms that usually bring it closer to the optimal solution, much faster than a random “trial-and-error” search.

If you wish, you can observe the values of the variables and other worksheet cells on each iteration: Select the Show Iteration Results check box in the Solver Options dialog box, shown in figure A.15, before you click Solve. On each trial solution you will see a dialog box like figure A.9. You then click Continue to proceed, or Stop if you want the Solver to stop and return the best solution it has found so far.

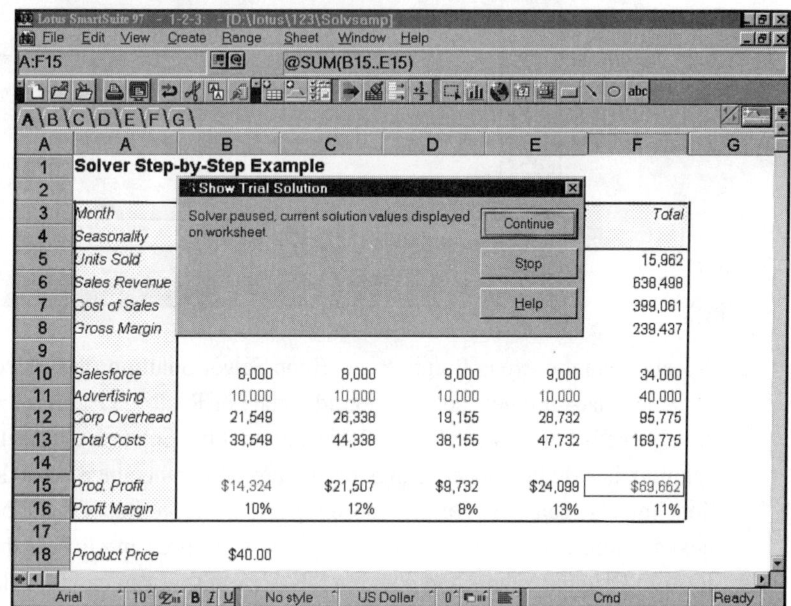

Fig. A.9
When you select the Show Iteration Results option, the Solver pauses on each iteration and displays this dialog box.

Pausing on every iteration slows things down, however, so the Solver provides an alternative. If you press Esc while the Solver is working, it will display the same Show Trial Solution dialog box shown in figure A.9. If you click Continue, the Solver will work at full speed either until it finishes, or you press Esc again.

Using the Solver Results Dialog Box

When the Solver stops—either because it found the optimal solution, encountered an error condition, reached the Max Time or Iterations limit you specified in the Solver Options dialog box shown in figure A.15, or because you interrupted the Solver and clicked Stop as described previously—you'll see a dialog box like the one in figure A.10.

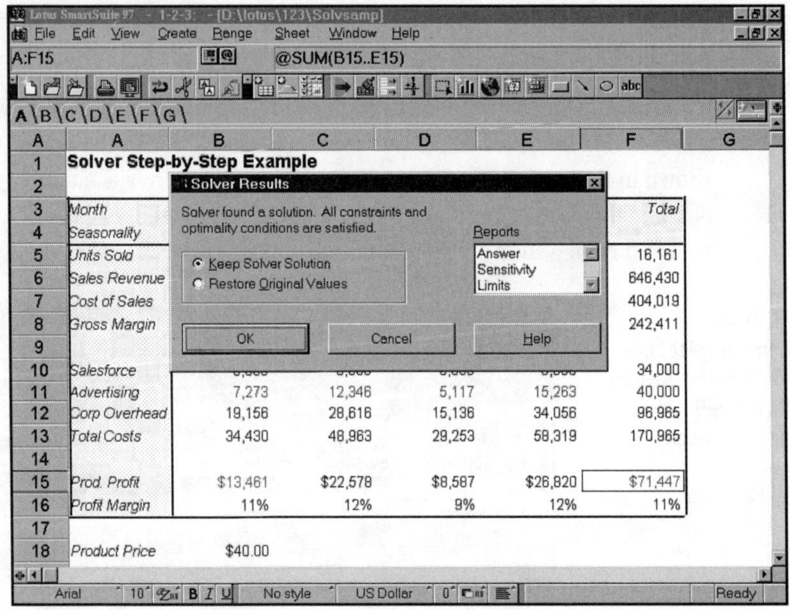

Fig. A.10
The Solver Results dialog box summarizes the outcome of the solution process, and lets you keep or discard the solution and select one or more reports.

Select one of the two option buttons: Keep Solver Solution (the current values of the variable cells—the best solution found so far) or Restore Original Values (the values of variable cells before you clicked Solve). Even if the Solver hasn't yet found the optimal solution, it will often speed things up the next time you solve if you keep the current solution. You also can select one or more reports from the Reports list box as described in the next section. Then click OK. (Clicking Cancel, or pressing Esc, is the same as choosing Restore Original Values and clicking OK, except that you cannot select any reports.)

Producing Reports

If the Solver was able to find a solution, you can select any or all of the three reports shown in the Reports list box of the Solver Results dialog box. (If the Solver encountered an error condition, ran out of time, or was interrupted before it found a solution, the Report list box choices will be grayed and cannot be selected.)

Each report is produced on a new worksheet, which is inserted next to the Solver problem worksheet. Because the reports are worksheets, you can change their formatting, add notes, or create cell formulas that use the report information if you wish. Each report serves a different purpose.

Answer Report

The Answer Report provides basic information about the decision variables, objective, and constraints. It also gives you a quick way to determine which constraints are "binding" or satisfied with equality at the solution, and which constraints have slack. An example Answer Report for the Product Mix example (sheet tab B) in SOLVSAMP.123 is shown in figure A.11.

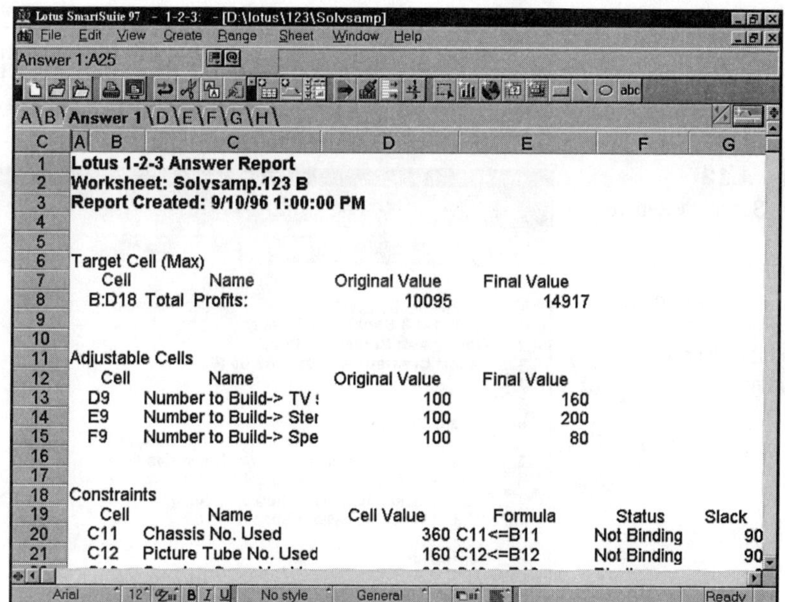

Fig. A.11 The Answer Report contains summary information about the objective, variables, and constraints.

First shown are the objective cell and decision variable cells, with their original values and final values. Next are the constraints, with their final cell values; a formula representing the constraint; a "status" column showing whether the constraint was binding or nonbinding at the solution; and the slack value—the difference between the final value and the lower or upper bound imposed by that constraint. A binding constraint, which is satisfied with equality, always has a slack of zero.

When creating a report, the Solver constructs the entries in the Name column by searching for the first text cell to the left and the first text cell above each variable cell and each constraint (left side) cell. If you lay out your Solver model in tabular form, with text labels in the leftmost column and topmost row, these entries will be the most useful–as in the example shown previously. Also note that the formatting for the Original Value, Final Value, and Cell Value is "inherited" from the formatting of the corresponding cell in the Solver model.

Sensitivity Report

The Sensitivity Report provides information about how the optimal solution would change, if you changed the values in certain parts of your Solver model and re-solved. This can be quite valuable, because it helps you determine whether your solution is "robust" across different parameter values, or highly sensitive to small changes in the parameters. In real-world problems, very few data values are free of "noise" or uncertainty, so it can be helpful to know how sensitive your solution is to these values.

An example Sensitivity Report for the Product Mix example in SOLVSAMP.123, produced by the general-purpose Solver when the Assume Linear Model box is *not* checked, is shown in figure A.12.

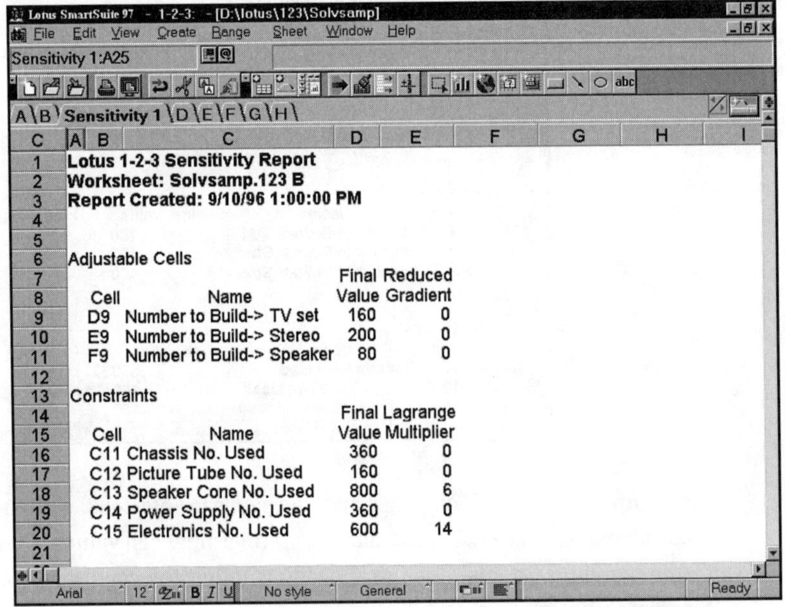

Lotus 1-2-3 Sensitivity Report
Worksheet: Solvsamp.123 B
Report Created: 9/10/96 1:00:00 PM

Adjustable Cells

Cell	Name	Final Value	Reduced Gradient
D9	Number to Build-> TV set	160	0
E9	Number to Build-> Stereo	200	0
F9	Number to Build-> Speaker	80	0

Constraints

Cell	Name	Final Value	Lagrange Multiplier
C11	Chassis No. Used	360	0
C12	Picture Tube No. Used	160	0
C13	Speaker Cone No. Used	800	6
C14	Power Supply No. Used	360	0
C15	Electronics No. Used	600	14

Fig. A.12
The Sensitivity Report tells you how the solution would change if you made small changes in the variables or constraints.

NOTE Constraints which are simple upper and lower bounds on the variables, that you enter in the Constraints list box of the Solver Parameters dialog box, are handled specially (for efficiency reasons) by the Solver, and will not appear in the Constraints section of the Sensitivity report. When an upper or lower bound on a variable is binding at the solution, a nonzero Reduced Cost or Reduced Gradient for that variable will appear in the "Adjustable Cells" section of the report.

So-called "dual values" are the most basic form of sensitivity analysis information. The dual value for a variable is significant only when the variable's value is equal to its upper or lower bound at the optimal solution. Moving the variable's value away from the bound will *worsen* the objective value; conversely, "loosening" the bound will improve the objective. The dual value measures the increase in the objective value per unit increase in the variable's value.

The dual value for a constraint is significant only when the constraint is equal to its bound. Moving the constraint left side value away from the bound will *worsen* the objective value; conversely, "loosening" the bound will improve the objective. The dual value measures the increase in the objective value per unit increase in the constraint's bound. In figure A.12, the dual value for electronics units is 14 (displayed rounded). If you increase the bound on electronics units at cell B15 from 600 to 601 and re-solve, total profit will increase by approximately $14.

NOTE The *dual values* for variables are called *Reduced Costs* in the case of linear problems, and *Reduced Gradients* for nonlinear problems. The dual values for constraints are called *Shadow Prices* for linear problems, and *Lagrange Multipliers* for nonlinear problems. These labels appear at the top of columns in the Sensitivity Report. ■

In linear problems, unlike nonlinear problems, the dual values are *constant* over a range of possible changes in the objective function coefficients and the constraint right sides. The Sensitivity Report for linear models includes this range information. For more information on this topic, click Help in one of the Solver dialog boxes and look up "Interpreting Range Information."

Limits Report

The Limits Report was designed to provide a different kind of "sensitivity analysis" information. It is created by re-running the Solver model with each decision variable in turn as the objective (both maximizing and minimizing), and all other variables held fixed. Hence, it shows a "lower limit" for each variable, which is the smallest value that a variable can take while satisfying the constraints and holding all of the other variables constant, and an "upper limit," which is the largest value the variable can take under these circumstances. An example Limits Report for the Product Mix example is shown in figure A.13.

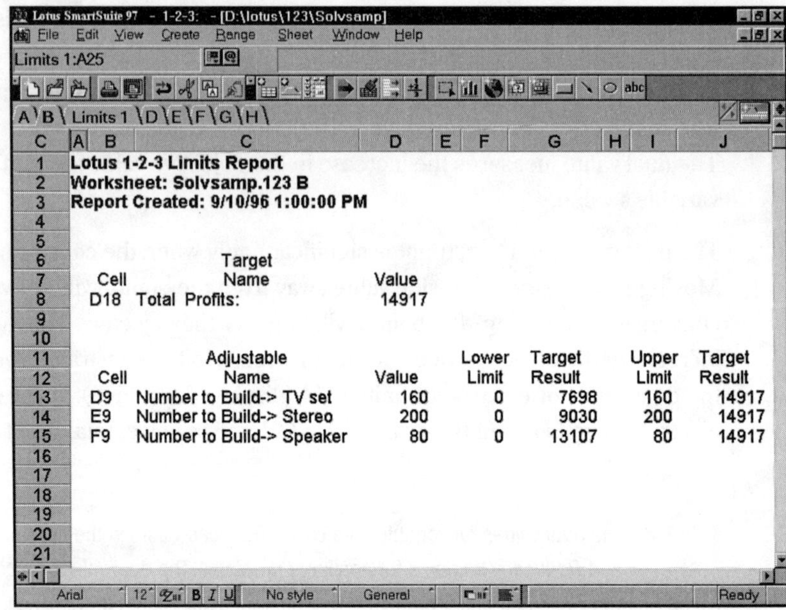

Fig. A.13
The Limits Report shows what happens to the objective if each variable is maximized or minimized while all others are held constant.

Setting Solver Options

When you click the Options button in the Solver Parameters dialog box, the Solver Options dialog box shown in figure A.14 appears.

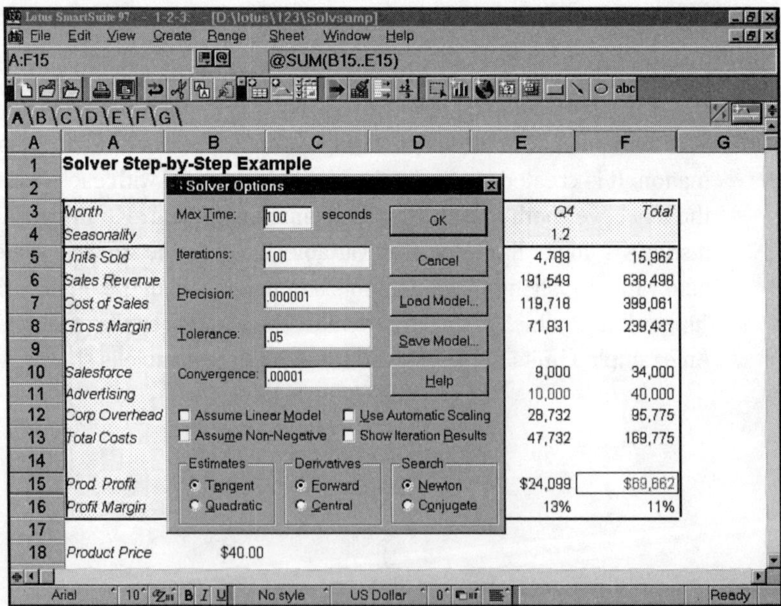

Fig. A.14
The Solver Options dialog box lets you control many aspects of the Solver's operation.

The options you use most frequently determine the limits on solution time or iterations, and solution strategies such as Assume Linear Model, Assume Non-Negative, and Use Automatic Scaling. Some options select numerical tolerances and advanced methods, but these are pre-set to the choices which are applicable to the great majority of problems; you'll rarely need to change these settings.

Max Time and Iterations

The Max Time and Iterations settings determine how much time, or computing effort, the Solver expends on a problem before asking you whether you want to stop. You may have to increase these settings from their default values to solve larger problems. If the maximum time or maximum number of iterations is exceeded, the Solver stops and displays the dialog box in figure A.15. You'll have the option to stop at this point or continue the solution process. If you click Continue, the time and iteration limits are removed, and you will not be prompted again.

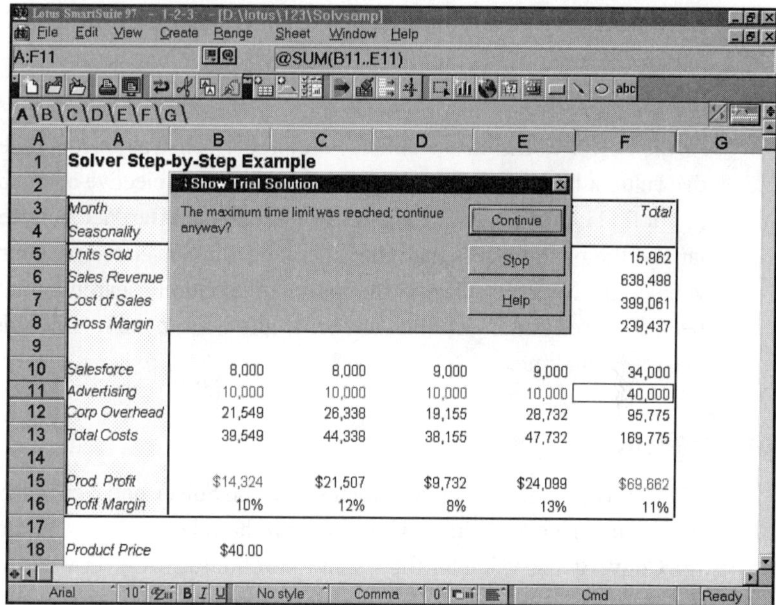

Fig. A.15 The Trial Solution dialog box appears when the maximum time limit or iteration limit is reached.

Precision

This number determines how closely the values of the constraint left sides must match the right sides for the constraint to be satisfied. Remember that a constraint is evaluated within a small tolerance; the Precision value is that tolerance. With the default setting of

0.000001, a calculated left side of –0.0000005 would *satisfy* a constraint such as A1 >= 0.

CAUTION

Use caution in making Precision much smaller than the default, because the finite precision of computer arithmetic virtually ensures that the values calculated by 1-2-3 and the Solver will differ from the expected or "true" values by a small amount. On the other hand, setting the Precision to a much larger value would cause constraints to be satisfied too easily. If your constraints are not being satisfied because the values you are calculating are in units such as millions of dollars, consider checking the Use Automatic Scaling box instead of altering the Precision setting.

Tolerance

Tolerance comes into play only when your Solver problem includes integer constraints. When you solve such a problem, it often happens that the Solver will find a good solution fairly quickly, but will require a great deal of computing time to find (or verify that it has found) the optimal solution. The Tolerance setting may be used to tell the Solver to stop if the best solution it has found so far is "close enough."

As the Solver works on a problem with integer constraints, it updates both the best objective value it has found so far, and a "bound" on the objective of any better solutions that it might find in further searching. If the percentage difference between the best objective so far and the bound is less than the Tolerance, the Solvers stops and reports a solution. If you set the Tolerance to zero, the Solver will continue searching until all possibilities have been explored and the optimal integer solution has been found. This may take a great deal of computing time.

Convergence

The Convergence setting determines how the Solver behaves on nonlinear problems where the objective is improving slowly. If the relative change in the objective is less than the Convergence value for the last five iterations, the Solver will stop and display the message `Solver converged to the current solution`. The default value of 1E-4 (0.0001) is suitable for most problems, but occasionally you may want to reduce this value.

If you get the message `Solver converged to the current solution`, you can change the setting in the Convergence box to a smaller value such as 1E-5 or 1E-6; but you should also consider why it is that the objective function is changing so slowly. Perhaps you can add constraints or use different starting values for the variables, so that the Solver does not get "trapped" in a region of slow improvement.

Assume Linear Model

This check box determines whether the linear Simplex Solver or the nonlinear GRG (Generalized Reduced Gradient) Solver method is used: When it is checked, the problem must be linear and the Simplex method is used; otherwise (and by default) the GRG method is used. The box is labeled Assume Linear Model because the Solver assumes that your model is made up entirely of linear functions for the objective and constraints. However, it does perform simple checks for linearity both before and after solving the problem. If these checks do not indicate that the model is linear, the Solver displays the message `The conditions for Assume Linear Model are not satisfied.`

The default GRG method can solve both linear and nonlinear problems; however, the Simplex method is faster and more accurate on linear problems, and yields more information in the Sensitivity Report. Although both methods are useful, in practice the majority of Solver models are linear.

Assume Non-Negative

When this box is checked, any decision variables without explicit lower bounds (>= constraints) in the Constraints list box will be given a lower bound of zero when the problem is solved. This option has no effect for decision variables which *do* have explicit >= constraints, even if those constraints allow the variables to assume negative values. For example, a constraint A1 >= –3 specifies that A1 can assume values of –3 or higher, even if the Assume Non-Negative box is checked.

Use Automatic Scaling

When this box is checked, the Solver will attempt to scale the values of the objective and constraints internally to minimize the effects of a poorly scaled model. A poorly scaled model is one in which the typical values of the objective and constraint functions differ by several orders of magnitude. A classic example is a financial model with some dollar amounts in millions, and other rate of return figures in percent. Poorly scaled models may cause difficulty in the solution process, again due to the effects of finite precision computer arithmetic.

Poorly scaled models are one of the most common causes of problems in which the Solver appears to stop prematurely without reaching the true optimal solution; it is a good idea to keep this box checked for all of your Solver models.

If your model is nonlinear and you do check the Use Automatic Scaling box, make sure that the initial values for the decision variables are "reasonable," that is, of roughly the same magnitudes that you expect for those variables at the optimal solution. The effectiveness of the Use Automatic Scaling option depends on how well these starting values reflect the values encountered during the solution process.

Show Iteration Results

When this box is checked, a dialog box like the one in figure A.9 will appear on *every* Solver iteration or Trial Solution. This option is most useful when you are having trouble finding an optimal solution, and you want to examine more closely the steps that the Solver is taking towards the solution. Examining the values of the variables on each trial solution may reveal to you that a constraint is missing, or that you need different starting values for the variables.

Estimates, Derivatives, and Search

These are advanced options controlling the operation of the nonlinear GRG (Generalized Reduced Gradient) Solver method. The default settings are appropriate for nearly all problems, but if you are having trouble reaching an optimal solution, you can try the alternate setting for any of these options. (You cannot do any harm by trying the other settings.)

The following general background may give you some insight into these options. On each iteration, the GRG method computes values for the first partial derivatives of the objective and constraints. The Derivatives option is concerned with how these partial derivatives are computed. The Forward choice takes less computing time, but the Central choice can be more accurate, especially if the solution is near the boundaries of one or more constraints.

The GRG method proceeds by first "reducing" the problem to an unconstrained optimization problem, by solving a set of nonlinear equations for certain variables in terms of others. Then a search direction is chosen along which an improvement in the objective function will be sought. The Search option is concerned with how this search direction is determined. The Newton choice uses a Quasi-Newton method, while the Conjugate choice uses a Conjugate Gradient method.

After a search direction is chosen, a one-dimensional "line search" is carried out along that direction, varying a step size in an effort to improve the reduced objective. The initial estimates for values of the variables which are being varied has a significant impact on the effectiveness of the search. The Estimates option is concerned with how these estimates are obtained. The Tangent choice extrapolates from the line tangent to the reduced objective, while the Quadratic choice extrapolates to the minimum (or maximum) of a quadratic fitted to the function at its current point.

Saving and Loading Solver Problems

On each worksheet in a workbook, the Solver problem definition you most recently entered into the Solver Parameters dialog box and the option settings in the Solver Options dialog box are stored automatically and saved with the workbook. When you re-open the workbook and choose Range, Analyze, Solver on any worksheet, the "current" Solver problem appears and you can click Solve immediately.

But at times, you may want to define more than one Solver problem on the same worksheet—with different numerical values, or even different cells playing the roles of objective, variables, and constraints. The Save Model and Load Model buttons allow you to save the Solver problem specifications in a range of cells and reload them later.

CAUTION

The "current" Solver problem definition and option information for each worksheet is actually stored in a hidden sheet named _solverinfo. You can examine this sheet by choosing Sheet, Unhide, but don't try to change its contents–you could easily cause errors in the Solver's handling of the problems on each sheet.

Using Save Model and Load Model

When you click the Save Model button, the Solver asks you for a cell range where it will store the problem specifications, as shown in figure A.16.

Type a cell range or range name, or use the range selector button to select cells with the mouse. The Solver uses one cell for each block of variables, one cell for each block of constraints, and two more cells for the objective and the option settings. But if you just select a single cell, the Solver will automatically extend this range downward for the number of cells needed.

When you click Load Model, a similar dialog box appears. You type or select the cell range containing the problem specifications you want to load. Because the new specifications completely replace the "current" Solver problem settings, you'll be asked to confirm your choice.

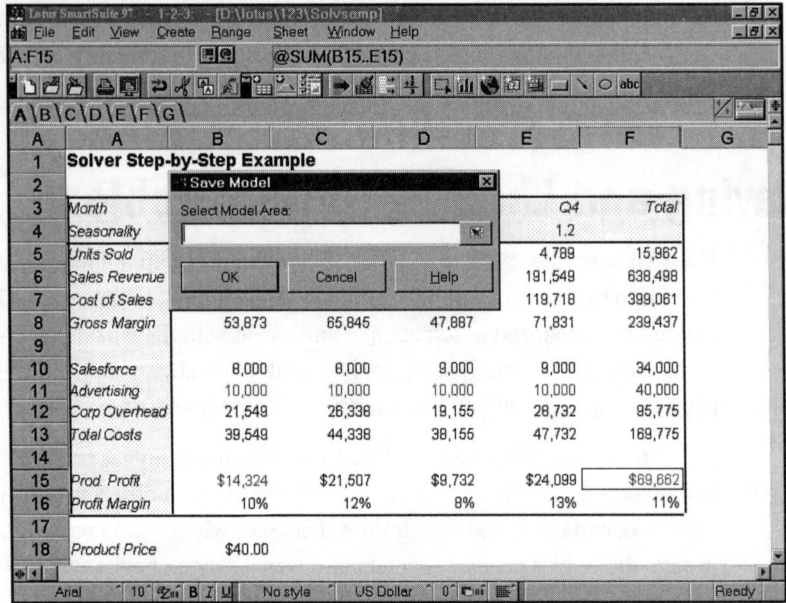

Fig. A.16
In the Save Model dialog box, you specify a range of cells where the Solver problem specifications will be saved.

Transferring Solver Problems Between 1-2-3 and Excel

Previous versions of both 1-2-3 and Excel have featured the capability to load and save worksheets in each other's file formats—but there was no easy way to transfer a Solver problem (with its decision variables, constraints, and objective) from one spreadsheet program to the other. Now there is a way—as long as you have both 1-2-3 97 and Excel 97.

1-2-3 to Excel To transfer a Solver model from 1-2-3 97 to Excel 97, follow these steps:

1. Starting from the Solver Options dialog box in 1-2-3 97, click the Save Model button and save your Solver problem specifications in a cell range.
2. Choose File, Save As and save the workbook with the Solver problem specifications in 1-2-3 Release 5 (WK4) format.
3. Open the saved WK4 file in Excel 97.
4. Choose Tools, Solver to display the Solver Parameters dialog box. Click Options to display the Solver Options dialog box in Excel 97.
5. Click Load Model, and select the cell range containing the problem specifications.

That's all there is to it. You can then click OK in the Solver Options dialog box, and immediately click Solve.

Excel to 1-2-3 You can also transfer Solver problems in the other direction:

1. Choose File, Save As and save your Excel 97 workbook in WK4 format. This step gives a "hint" to the Excel Solver to use a problem specification format that can be read by both Excel and 1-2-3.
2. Starting from the Solver Options dialog box in Excel 97, click the Save Model button to save your Solver problem specifications in a cell range.
3. Choose File, Save to save the WK4 file *with* the Solver problem specifications.
4. Open the saved WK4 file in 1-2-3 97.
5. Choose Range, Analyze, Solver to display the Solver Parameters dialog box. Click Options to display the Solver Options dialog box in 1-2-3 97.
6. Click Load Model, and select the cell range containing the problem specifications.

And that's all there is to it. Once again, you can click OK in the Solver Options dialog box, and immediately click Solve.

Programming the Solver in LotusScript

After you develop a practical Solver model for a specific situation in your business, you may want other, less sophisticated users to run it routinely. If you're worried that these users won't know how to use the Solver dialog boxes, or that they might alter something by mistake, you'll want to develop an application which presents a custom user interface and operates the Solver "behind the scenes." You can easily do this in LotusScript.

Using Solver Functions in LotusScript

There is not room here to illustrate all of the Solver functions that you can call from LotusScript, or teach you about building a custom Solver application. But you can learn about the Solver functions by clicking Help in one of the Solver dialog boxes, and looking up "Solver" in the Index. Chapters 37 through 39 of this book introduce you to programming in LotusScript, and Chapter 35 shows how to create custom dialog box boxes, which you can present to your end user while "hiding" the Solver dialogs.

The Easy Way to Control the Solver

It may be easier than you think to create a custom application using the Solver. Suppose that you have created and tested a Solver model on a worksheet. The "current" Solver problem on a worksheet is available at all times—so all you need to do is call for it to be solved. The following two lines of LotusScript code solve the current problem, keep the final solution, and produce no reports:

```
SolverSolve 0, [dp][dp]
SolverFinish 1, 0
```

The only other code you must have to use the Solver in LotusScript are the following two lines in the (Globals) - (Options) section of your script:

```
Option Public
Use "solver.12a"
```

How to Learn More

Your best resource for learning more about the Solver is Frontline Systems' World Wide Web site, **http://www.frontsys.com**. You'll find many hints and suggestions, references to textbooks which cover the Solver's methods and applications, sample models, and much more information on designing Solver models and programming the Solver in LotusScript and Visual Basic. ●

APPENDIX B

Programming 1-2-3 97 with LotusScript

by Stan Doherty

If you've been waiting years for 1-2-3 to improve its programming features, the wait is over. Furthermore, the combination of a strong programming environment like LotusScript and a strong product like 1-2-3 will make it worth the wait. Best of all, Lotus did not try to force you to learn LotusScript by removing macro support. The new 1-2-3 preserves both the macro and LotusScript programming interfaces, a blend of the old and new.

The LotusScript programming environment

Learn the three major components of the full-featured LotusScript programming environment, a programming language, a set of programming tools, and a library of programmable objects.

Basic concepts for programming in LotusScript

Learn basic concepts about LotusScript programming and the programming environment.

LotusScript programming tools

Learn to use the Integrated Development Environment (IDE) and the Lotus Dialog Editor in developing applications.

1-2-3 objects and classes

Gain some experience working in an object-oriented programming environment.

- *Macro programming.* If you have developed macro applications in previous versions of 1-2-3, you can still run them without modification in 1-2-3 97. You can even write and run new macros that you develop in the same way you did in earlier versions of 1-2-3. As a final treat, 1-2-3 supports macros and scripts calling one another. You can incrementally convert parts of macros into script rather than doing it all at once.
- *LotusScript programming.* LotusScript is an object-oriented version of the BASIC language. It is integrated with several Lotus products: Notes, Approach, Freelance Graphics, and Word Pro. If you have already worked with LotusScript in any of these products, writing your first scripts in 1-2-3 should be easy. LotusScript will also seem familiar if you have developed applications in Microsoft Visual Basic or Visual Basic for Applications because they share the same underlying language: BASIC. You can even convert VBA scripts written for Excel to LotusScript by substituting the 1-2-3 product commands for those in Excel.

This appendix focuses on the transition from macro programming to LotusScript programming in 1-2-3. You may have heard conflicting stories from people who have moved from programming macros to programming scripts in other products. Some say that it's very easy, a no-brainer. Others suggest that learning to write scripts is really challenging, that you need to take some night school courses before you write anything worthwhile. As you'll see, the truth is somewhere in the middle. There are some speed bumps. You do need to learn some things about scripting in 1-2-3, but after that you'll find that your greatest asset in developing 1-2-3 scripts is actually your experience with the product. ■

The LotusScript Programming Environment

LotusScript is a full-featured programming environment that consists of three major components:

- A programming language
- A set of programming tools
- A library of programmable objects (in this case, 1-2-3 objects)

If this sounds very different from your experience with 1-2-3 macros, it shouldn't. Like LotusScript, 1-2-3 macros support a programming language with formal conventions for syntax and program logic. Although you don't use a separate editor to write 1-2-3 macros, there are formal rules for how to enter macros commands in ranges and how to run them. Lastly, all the documents, cells, ranges, charts, and maps that you programmed in previous releases of 1-2-3 (without calling them objects) are back—except now they behave like real objects and work together in powerful new ways. You're closer to developing

LotusScript applications in 1-2-3 than you think. Take a closer look at each of the components in the LotusScript environment.

About the Language

LotusScript is BASIC. Programmers using Visual Basic for Applications or LotusScript have rediscovered the benefits of the BASIC programming language. When these new versions of BASIC run in a graphical environment like Windows, they offer both power and simplicity. Over the years, BASIC has "bulked up," offering many of the advanced features associated with languages like C, Pascal, or Java. Yet it has not abandoned its roots as a relatively easy-to-understand and easy-to-use language.

LotusScript is embedded in Lotus products. There are no icons on your desktop named "LotusScript Editor" or "LotusScript Compiler" because LotusScript requires 1-2-3 or some other Lotus product to run. Although this sounds like a limitation on the surface, you will find that there are several advantages to having the programming environment fully integrated with the product you're programming:

- LotusScript code and dialog boxes are stored with your 1-2-3 documents. You don't need to create or distribute files other than your workbooks.
- LotusScript knows a lot about all your 1-2-3 objects and makes programming them easier with default settings for the commands you enter. For example, the LotusScript command to create a new 1-2-3 document uses several arguments. You won't have to search through the Help system to fill in each of those arguments; LotusScript will create a working document for you using the default settings. LotusScript helps you with the basics until you have time to learn the fancy stuff.
- LotusScript does not require a separate compiler. You can write a script and run it immediately from within 1-2-3. LotusScript checks the syntax of the code you write and provides immediate feedback and context-sensitive Help on potential problems. This saves you a considerable amount of time as you develop your script applications.
- LotusScript is object-oriented. As you write your first script applications in 1-2-3, you probably won't need to know much about object hierarchies, containment, or user-defined classes. But, like owning a car with a good engine, it's good to know that the power will be there when and if you need it. Unlike most other versions of BASIC, LotusScript has been enhanced to understand how real objects work in a product like 1-2-3. Some objects come with 1-2-3, others you can implement as your own classes, and yet others are available from third-party developers. The time you invest in learning about LotusScript and 1-2-3 objects will pay off because you can expand the number of the objects you add to your 1-2-3 script applications.

- 1-2-3 knows LotusScript. 1-2-3 objects have been designed to take advantage of the LotusScript language so all the tasks you perform in 1-2-3 have equivalent LotusScript commands. One of the most useful tools for learning LotusScript in 1-2-3 is the *script recorder*. Like the macro recorder in previous versions of 1-2-3, the script recorder translates your keystrokes and mouse gestures into working code. You can then edit this code to make it work elsewhere in 1-2-3. Using the script recorder, you don't need to know much LotusScript programming to build your first library of scripts.

Basic Concepts for Programming in LotusScript

It would be unrealistic to expect that learning a programming language like LotusScript would require no ramp-up time. There are some basic concepts about LotusScript programming and the programming environment that will get you through the first few days. These are some of those speed bumps. If you don't see them coming or try to ride over them at high speed, you'll have a bumpy ride.

Names, Code, and Comments

Most 1-2-3 macro writers store macro code in three adjacent columns: The left column contains the macro range name, the middle column contains macro code, and the right column stores comments about the code. Even the most organized macro programmers have trouble keeping these columns of information synchronized. Figure B.1 shows how a basic 1-2-3 macro looks in a worksheet.

LotusScript keeps all script information together: the name of the script, the working code, and comments about the code. Figure B.2 shows how the macro in figure B.1 would look when written in LotusScript.

One of the benefits of keeping this information together is that you can export scripts in your 1-2-3 document to text files for review and for editing. Experienced script writers sometimes prefer to write scripts in a programmer's editor, and then import the scripts into 1-2-3 for debugging.

There's also no rule that scripts be long and complicated. The following script is an example of a simple *subroutine* (or *sub*) that does a big job—it creates a 1-2-3 document:

```
Sub MakeNewDoc
    ' The following statement creates a new 1-2-3 document.
    CurrentApplication.NewDocument "MyDocument","","","","",,
End Sub
```

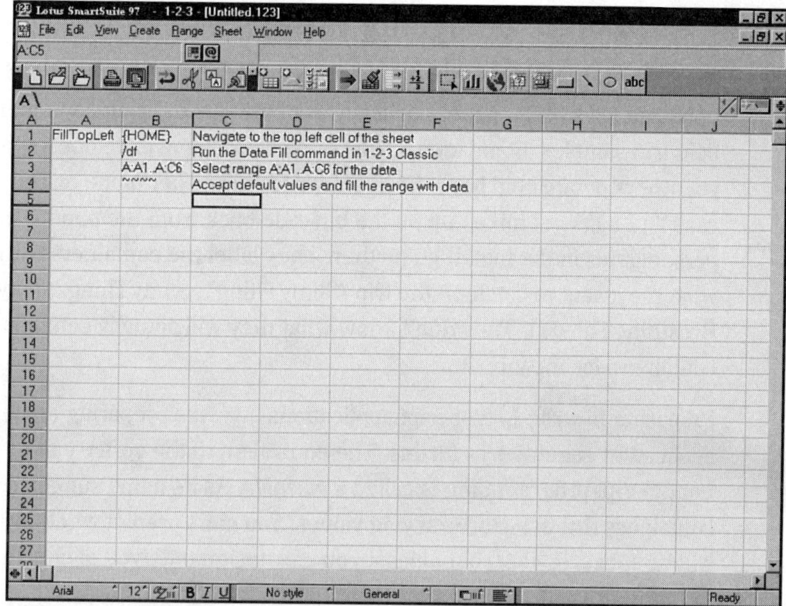

Fig. B.1
1-2-3 macros can be difficult to keep organized.

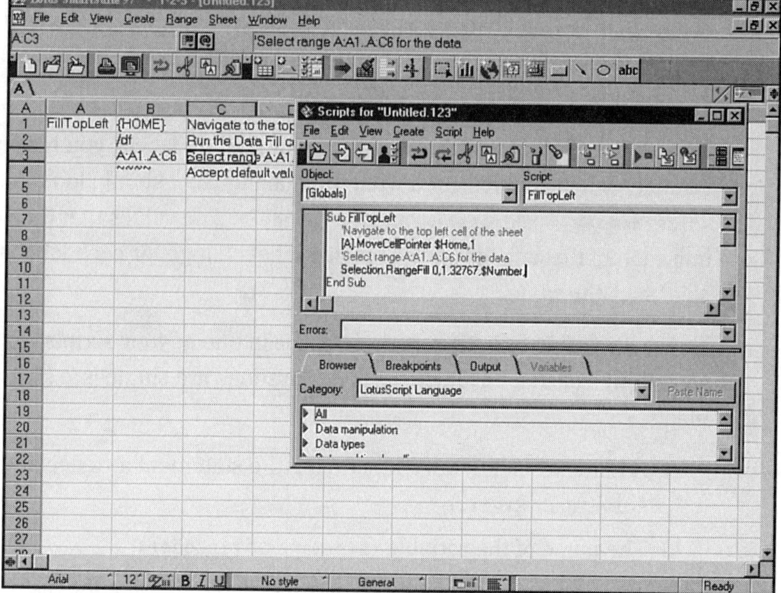

Fig. B.2
When you use LotusScript, your program is much easier to maintain.

Setting the Stage: Designing Variables

If you've ever chaperoned an elementary school field trip, you'll understand how being prepared pays off. Teachers typically ask students to bring containers to school to collect field trip samples. Some kids bring coffee cans, some envelopes, others shoe boxes, and yet others potato chip bags. Each kid writes his or her name on the container in case the cans and bags get mixed up on the bus ride back from the pond. The budding type-A personalities in the bunch go further: They label the containers with names suggesting what they want to catch on the trip (SlimyThing1, SlimyThing2, IckyThing1, and BreathingThing1). They don't know what they will actually catch, but they have the right containers for the job.

Preparing to write LotusScript applications involves preparing containers for the data your application generates as it runs. The equivalent of the coffee can or potato chip bag in LotusScript programming is called a *variable*. As its name suggests, variables are named containers that can store varying values. You can't predict whether the value of a variable will be `1`, `226`, or `10E4`, but at least you can design one type of container that's appropriate for numbers and another that's appropriate for text.

The 1-2-3 macro language does not support variables directly. If you need to track a piece of information that changes as your macro runs, you would typically use a cell or range to capture those values. The value in the cell might change, but its location or name would be constant.

If you have used a word processor to print mailing labels, you have probably created variables when you designed what the mailing label should look like: `<<firstName>>`, `<<lastName>>`, `<<address1>>`, and `<<zipCode>>`. The values that the word processor inserts into each of these fields on the mailing label change for each label, the name of the variable stays the same.

To use a variable like `lastName` or `zipCode` in one of your scripts, you must first define it in something called a *declaration*. All declarations are single-line statements with three elements:

- A LotusScript keyword identifying the statement as a declaration (`Dim`, `Public`, `Private`, or `Static`)
- The name of the variable (`lastName` or `zipCode`)
- The data type or object type of the variable. A value for `lastName` should be a string of text whereas the value for `zipCode` should be a number, an integer. Many 1-2-3 macros go awry when you assume that the value in a cell is one data type, such as a string, and it turns out to be another data type, such as an integer. LotusScript provides greater control over the data in your scripts by preserving consistent data

types. By the way, you can declare variables that will accept *any* data type. This all-purpose data type is called the *variant* because it adapts to the information entered in it.

Here's how these three elements look in a real declaration:

```
Dim lastName as String
Dim zipCode as Integer
```


Because LotusScript supports variables, you can write more powerful and streamlined code to track information in your 1-2-3 scripts. As you get more proficient at writing scripts, you'll find that the time you spend setting up the right variables pays off with more readable and manageable code. The following script illustrates how variables can be used to store values on-the-fly and then to use them in a calculation. Read the comment lines in the script; each comment line begins with an apostrophe.

```
Sub CalculateSimpleInterest
   ' Declare string variables for name of the user,
   ' total amount of the loan, and current interest rate.
   Dim userName as String
   Dim loanAmount as Integer
   Dim interestRate as Long

   ' Display input boxes prompting the user for
   ' values and then assign those values to the appropriate variables.
   ' The answer to the question "What is your name?" is stored
   ' in the variable userName.
   userName = InputBox("What is your name?")
   loanAmount = InputBox("What is the total dollar amount of your loan?")
   interestRate = InputBox("What is the current interest rate?")

   ' Declare a variable named theMessage to store the final
   ' message to the user. LotusScript builds the message piece
   ' by piece and then displays it all together
   Dim theMessage as String
   ' Calculate the simple interest and display
   ' the results in a message box.
   theMessage = "Hi " & userName _           ' Use the value of userName.
      & ", you will pay $" _
      & loanAmount*(interestRate/100) _     ' Multiply two values.
      & " in simple interest."
   ' Display the final message.
   Msgbox theMessage
End Sub
```

If your user responded to the three questions with the values **Bob**, **10000**, and **7**, the final message box would display the results shown in figure B.3.

Variables let you anticipate *how* your script handles information before you know what the particular information *is*.

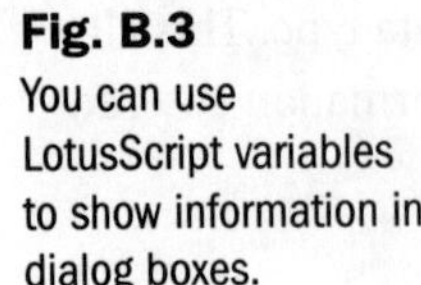

Fig. B.3
You can use LotusScript variables to show information in dialog boxes.

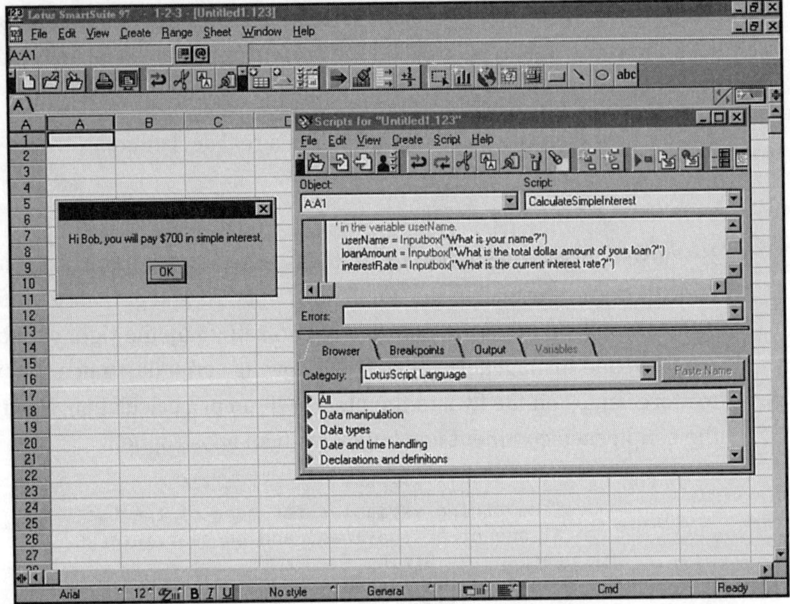

Macro writers will appreciate the fact that this script did all its work in memory and did not rely on any data in your 1-2-3 document. LotusScript lets you do a lot of work behind the scenes so your worksheets don't become cluttered with temporary data. You can spare your users seeing flashing cells and range updates if you use variables to do some of the data crunching in memory, and not in the 1-2-3 sheet. Be a hero or heroine—use variables.

Evaluation and Control Structures

LotusScript simplifies two common tasks in programming: evaluating information as it comes in and determining where the application should go based on the results of that evaluation. A *programming structure* is a wrapper or framework you put around a series of statements. A structure defines how information gets evaluated and what your application should do next.

To build on the previous example, consider how you could add the following `If...Then` structure to evaluate the value of the variable `interestRate`. Here's how it works:

1. When prompted, the user enters a number in the message box.
2. LotusScript reads what the user typed (whatever it is) and stores that value in the variable `interestRate`. In other words, the variable `interestRate` receives what the input box collected from the user.

3. The `If...Then` structure reads the value of `interestRate` and branches one of two ways:

   - If the value of `interestRate` is greater than 10, it displays the first message.
   - If the value if `interestRate` is less than 10, it displays the second message.

```
Dim interestRate as Long
interestRate = InputBox("What is the current interest rate?")
If interestRate  > 10 Then
      Msgbox "Wow, that high interest rate will hurt you!"
   Else
      Msgbox "Well done! You have a low interest rate."
End If
```


Evaluation and control structures can be tricky to learn at first, but they get you out of many programming problems. Some LotusScript structures just make programming easier. The `With...End With` structure, for example, doesn't do fancy evaluation, but it does let you fire a group of related statements at the same object in 1-2-3. You'll see later in "Properties" how the `With...End With` structure can be useful in setting a group of properties for one object.

Access to Windows Tools and Services

LotusScript is more than a generic, one-size-fits-all programming environment. It knows about the applications and system services available in Windows 95 and Windows NT. You can supplement the functions available in 1-2-3 by asking LotusScript to call Windows services. This is analogous to asking your neighbor for a special tool when you don't have one in your garage. Here's a brief example:

```
Sub ShowRacingResults
   ' If you are connected to the World Wide Web
   ' and the file types .HTM or HTML are in the
   ' Windows Registry, the following statement will launch
   ' your default Web browser and display a Web page
   ' containing racing results.
   Dim returnValue As Integer
   returnValue = Shell("http:\\www.track.com\tally.htm", 1)
End Sub
```

At a more advanced level, LotusScript also lets you call Windows API functions that you would normally have to call from a C program. Again, LotusScript provides all the support for you to write really basic scripts or more sophisticated applications.

Event-Driven Scripts

One last speed bump before you look at programming tools and writing scripts. You've probably encountered the term *event-driven* in magazine articles or technical manuals. Here's what it means for programming scripts in 1-2-3.

In a programming environment like Windows, events and the event messages they generate are fundamental. Every time you move the mouse to perform a task or enter text via the keyboard, Windows interprets these actions as an *event*. It sends messages to the operating system: "The mouse moved to coordinates x, y" or " The F1 key was pressed." Objects in 1-2-3 sit quietly in your document until they receive one of these messages. When you move the mouse pointer over a command button in 1-2-3 and click it, Windows tells the button that it has been clicked.

LotusScript lets you determine how an object like a command button responds to an event like a click. You write the code that determines whether the button jumps, spins, or makes coffee in response to the click event. The events an object receives *drive* the behaviors you program for it. Say you create a button on a 1-2-3 sheet named `Button 1` and labeled `Click me for racing results`. When Windows sends the event message "You've been clicked!" to this button, you want the button to respond by running the script in figure B.4.

The button object knows about a variety of events: `Click`, `Selected`, `Deselected`, `NameChange`, and so on. For each of these events, you can write a script defining the behavior of the button when it receives a particular event message.

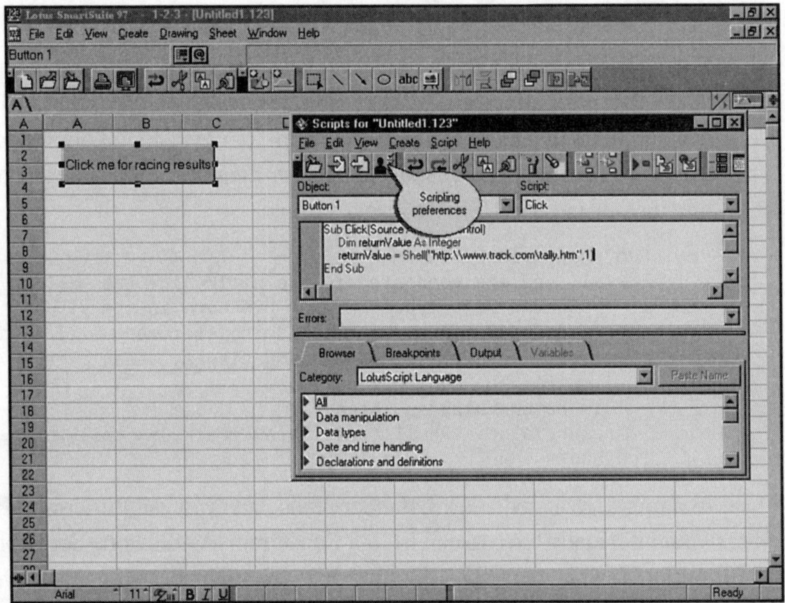

Fig. B.4
Clicking the button runs the associated script.

In order to define an action which occurs when the button is clicked, you need to edit the script named `Click` that is associated with the button object named `Button 1`. All objects and their scripts are unique, so writing code in one event script does not copy information to any other script. In this case, when the user clicks `Button 1`, its Click event script will execute and launch your Web browser.

Events are also relevant to spreadsheet objects. One or more cells are known as *range objects* in 1-2-3 97. The range object can respond to many events: `Cellcontentschange`, `Cellvaluechange`, `Namechange`, `Selected`, and so on. If you're writing a script to help users enter information in a range of cells, you can use events to provide a form of context-sensitive help when the user selects a cell. Here's how it works:

1. The user clicks a cell, let's say A:A1.
2. Cell A:A1 receives the message from Windows "You've been selected!"
3. LotusScript looks at the script called `Selected` for cell A:A1.

```
Sub Selected(Source As Range)
   Msgbox "Enter the total number of dependents in this cell."
End Sub
```

4. LotusScript executes the script, displaying the message box shown in figure B.5.

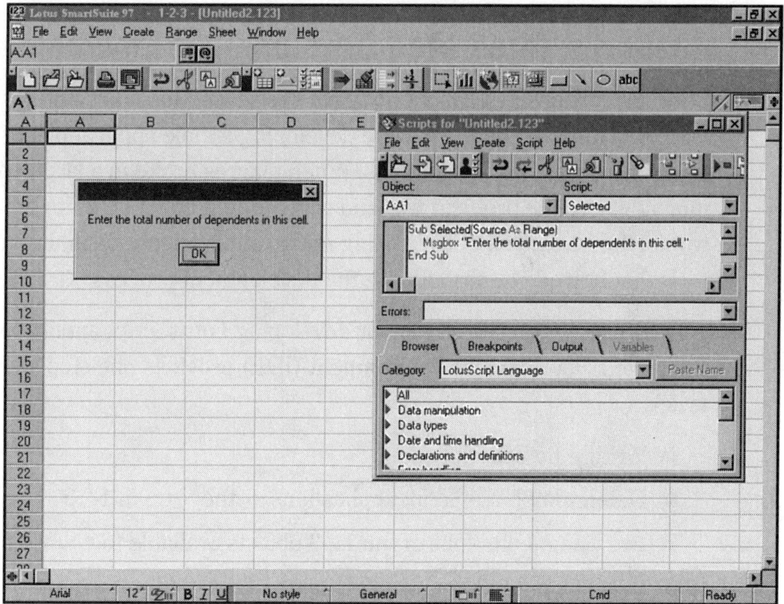

Fig. B.5
You can also create scripts which are attached to cells.

5. The user clicks OK in the message box and enters a value in cell A:A1.

If you're really ambitious, you could write some code for the event `Cellcontentschange` that would evaluate what the user entered as data in the cell.

In effect, you've added a quick-and-dirty form of bubble help to your application. If an object can respond to the event message "You've been selected!", you can add LotusScript statements to its `Selected` event script to make it do interesting things.

LotusScript Programming Tools

The more time you spend developing applications, the more you appreciate quality programming tools. You're going to like working with LotusScript programming tools like the *Integrated Development Environment* (*IDE*) and the *Lotus Dialog Editor* because these tools are both easy to use and powerful. In this section, you look at these tools at a general level: What are they designed to do? What are their parts? How do you launch them? You'll use the IDE and the Dialog Editor in more detail when you develop an application later in this appendix.

The LotusScript Integrated Development Environment (IDE)

Previous versions of 1-2-3 did not have specialized tools for writing, debugging, or running macros. This was fine if you were developing simple applications in 1-2-3, but not for developing more complex applications. When macros broke in a large 1-2-3 application, determining where the problem was and correcting it could be quite time consuming. In other words, the better you got at writing macro applications, the more you felt the absence of tools that helped you throughout the development process.

1-2-3 97 uses a specialized tool for developing LotusScript applications. The LotusScript Integrated Development Environment (IDE) provides one-stop shopping for the following tasks:

- Writing LotusScript code
- Debugging LotusScript applications as they run in 1-2-3
- Browsing definitions of the 1-2-3 objects available to you for programming
- Getting context-sensitive help on the LotusScript language and on 1-2-3 objects

Take a look at the parts of the IDE and how they support each of these tasks.

First, to display the IDE in 1-2-3, do the following:

1. Launch 1-2-3 and open a document.
2. Choose Edit, Scripts & Macros, Show Script Editor from the 1-2-3 main menu.

Whereas some programming environments use multiple windows for each programming tool, the IDE integrates all these tools in one window. This makes programming easier because you can write code in the IDE and see how it runs in 1-2-3 without opening and closing a dozen windows in the process. Figure B.6 shows the principal parts of the IDE window.

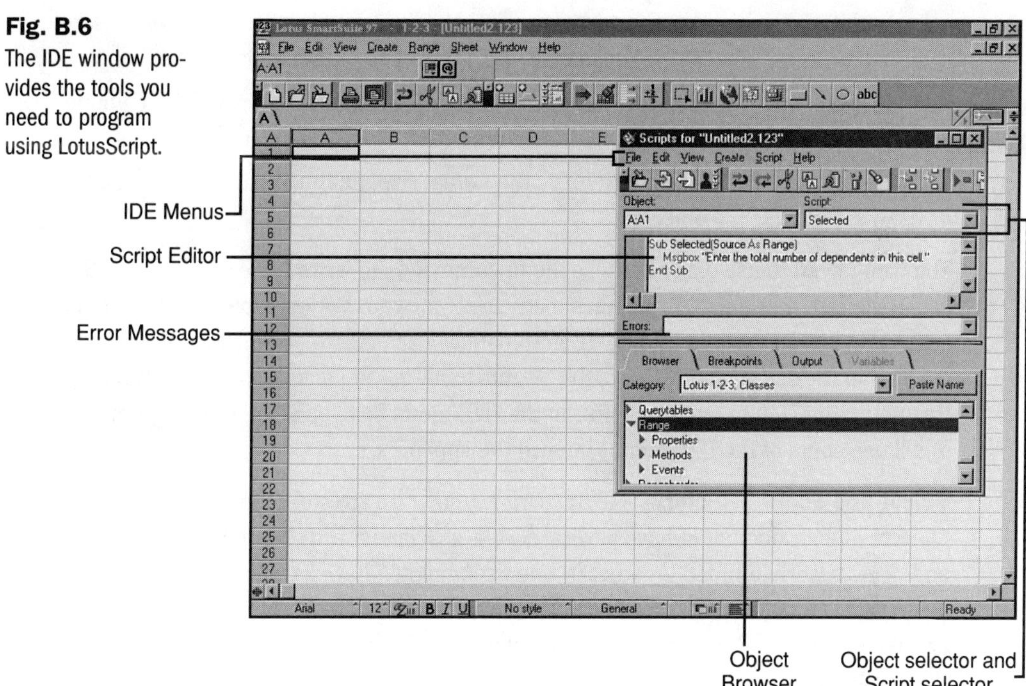

Fig. B.6
The IDE window provides the tools you need to program using LotusScript.

IDE Menus Many of the tasks you perform in the IDE involve menu commands. The following table shows the most common tasks you would perform using the IDE menus.

IDE Menu	Programming Tasks Available on that Menu
File	Save the current document containing scripts, import a text file containing script statements, export one or more scripts in the document to a text file, print one or more scripts, set preferences for the IDE, set preferences for SmartIcons, and close the IDE.

IDE Menu	Programming Tasks Available on that Menu
Edit	Undo the last change, redo the last change, copy selected text to the Clipboard, paste text from the Clipboard, clear selected text, search for text, and replace text.
View	Display the next or previous script in the document, display a specific programming tool (Editor or Debugger) or pane (Browser, Breakpoints, Output, or Variables), and hide or display SmartIcons.
Create	Create a subroutine script and create a Function script.
Script	Run the current script, check scripts for validity, record a script, and set or manage programming breakpoints.
Debug	Step through a script while it is running, stop a script running, and set and manage programming breakpoints.
Help	Display Help for the LotusScript Language, the IDE, and 1-2-3 objects.

You won't need to use many of these menu commands to write basic scripts in 1-2-3 because the IDE automatically handles many tasks for you. For example, if you try to run a script that has an error in it, the IDE automatically selects the script, selects the problematic line in the script, and displays the Script Debugger in place of the Script Editor. At that point, the Debug menu is active in the IDE menu bar, replacing the Script menu. You'll use some of the IDE menus later in the appendix.

Object and Script Selectors All the scripts you write are stored in your 1-2-3 document. Objects in your document have several scripts associated with them. If all these scripts and objects were jumbled together in one listing, you'd have a difficult time finding anything. The Object and Script Selectors are like a file cabinet: objects in your document are like drawers and the scripts associated with each object are like file folders in that drawer. Here's how it works.

When you create a document in 1-2-3, it creates many objects automatically: a document window, one sheet, and lots of cells in that sheet. Figure B.7 shows the default objects you can program in 1-2-3. They appear in the Object drop-down box in the IDE.

NOTE The Object drop-down box lists the 1-2-3 application; the new, untitled document; and a mysterious object called Globals. To continue the metaphor of a filing cabinet, this (Globals) object always appears in your documents as a top cabinet. Unlike the scripts contained in other drawers, scripts in the Globals cabinet can be used by any script contained in any folder elsewhere in the file cabinet. You'll see how scripts for the (Globals) object are used later in the appendix. ■

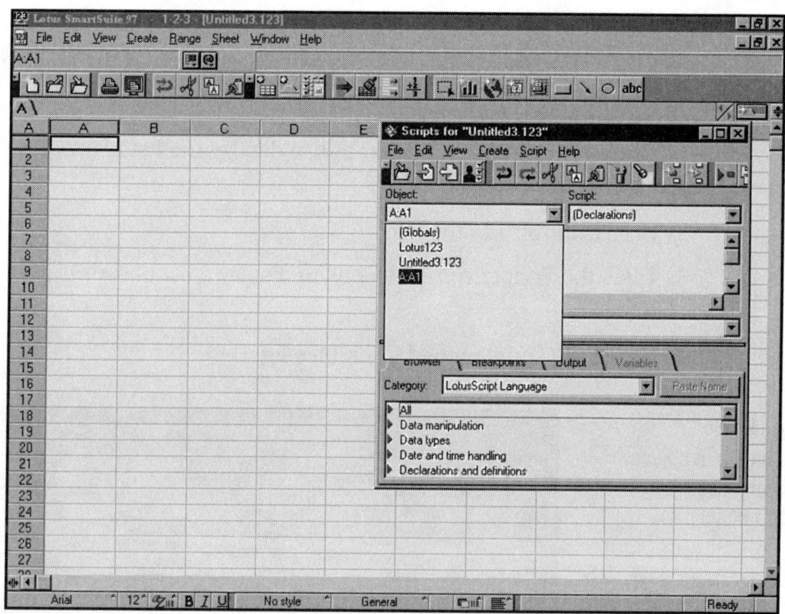

Fig. B.7 1-2-3 automatically creates several objects you can program.

As you add objects to your 1-2-3 document, the Object drop-down box in the IDE adds their names to its list. Figure B.8 shows how the Object drop-down box would appear if you added two buttons and a rectangle to a new document.

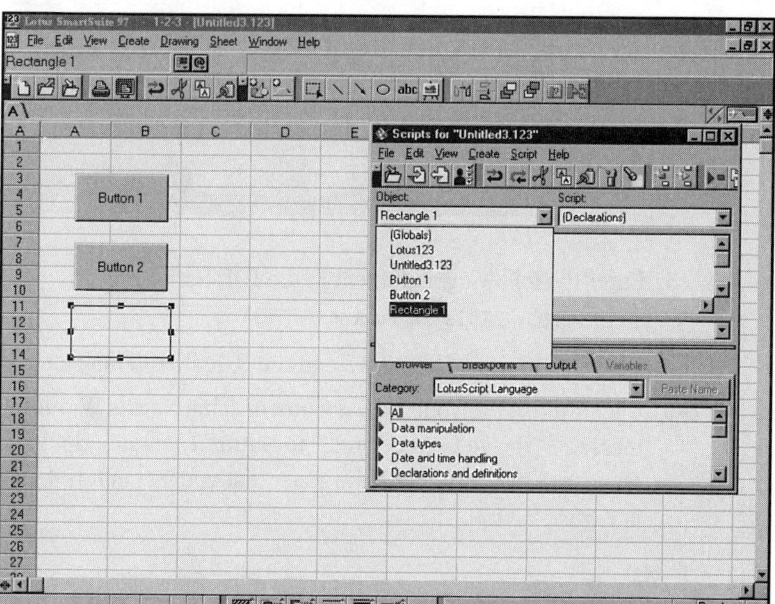

Fig. B.8 When you add objects to the worksheet, they appear on the list of objects you can program.

The contents of the Script drop-down box are determined by the object you select in the Object drop-down box. For example, to write a script for the object named Button 1, do the following:

1. Click the Object drop-down box to display the list of programmable objects in your current document.
2. Select Button 1 in the list.
3. Click the Script drop-down box to display a list of scripts associated with the Button 1 object.
4. Select the script named Click (see fig. B.9).

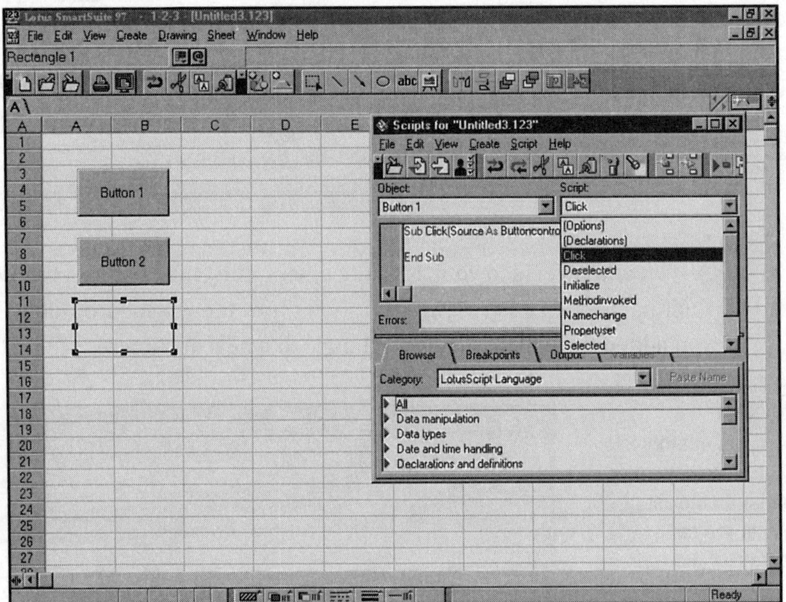

Fig. B.9
Each type of object has an associated group of scripts.

5. Enter the following statement in the IDE Script Editor:

```
Msgbox "This is Button 1."
```

   Figure B.10 shows how 1-2-3 and the IDE should look after you enter this statement.

6. Click Button 1 in your 1-2-3 document. This causes Windows to send the event message "You've been clicked!" to Button 1. LotusScript looks in the script named `Click for Button 1`, sees the statement you just entered, and executes it, as shown in Figure B.11.

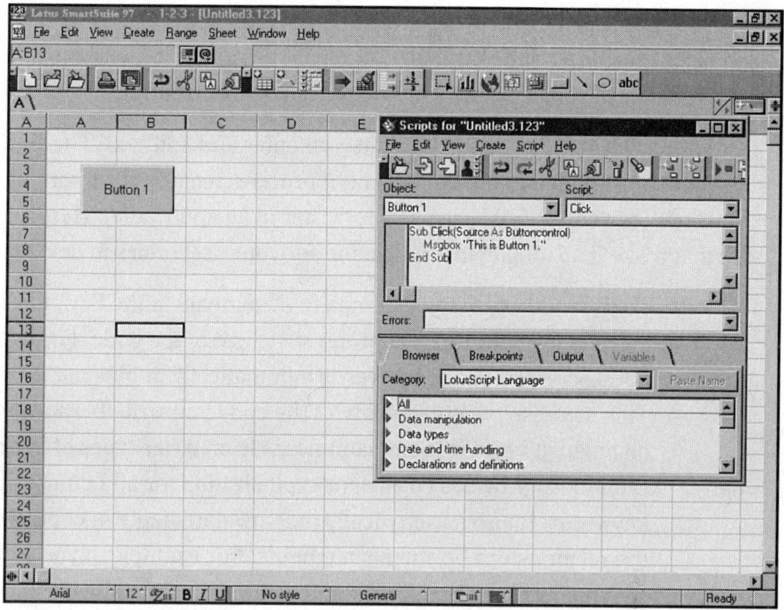

Fig. B.10
Add commands to the Click script to cause an action when the button is clicked.

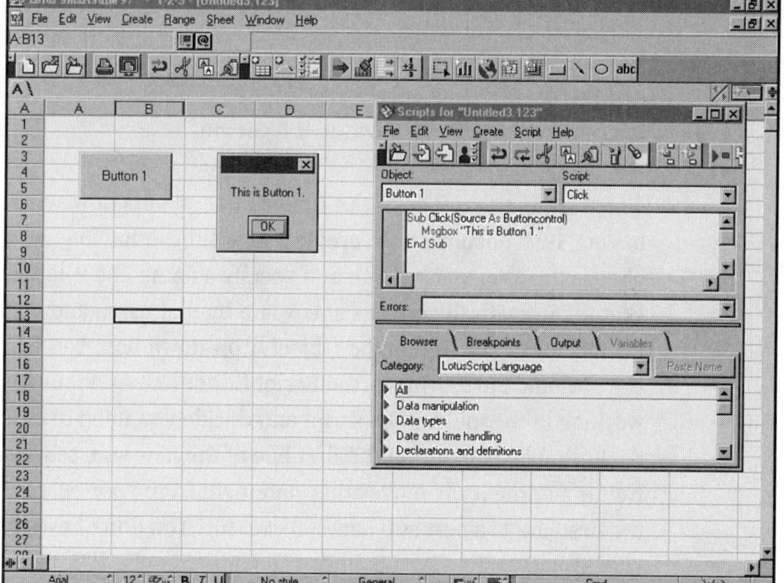

Fig. B.11
Clicking the button displays the message box.

You've just written an event-driven LotusScript application that uses 1-2-3 objects. Consider the Object and Script drop-down boxes as two of your most important tools in navigating to the objects you want to program in LotusScript.

Script Editor Any text editor lets you enter and edit text. The IDE Script Editor adds much more value to the development process because it's aware of how the LotusScript language and 1-2-3 objects work together in an application. Here are some of the features that make it an intelligent companion for your first hours in developing scripts:

- *Code formatting.* As you complete statements in the Script Editor, it reads each line and formats it to accent the structure of the code. For example, it displays LotusScript language keywords automatically in blue and comment lines in green. This increases the readability of the code you write because you can more easily distinguish keywords and comments from other types of information. The Script Editor also provides consistent capitalization for all LotusScript language and 1-2-3 keywords. It also automatically indents statements in control structures to highlight the relationships between statements. For example, if you were to type the following statements in the Script Editor, it would automatically format the keywords and the indentations.

```
Dim value As Integer
value = 10
If value = 10 Then
      Msgbox "The value really is 10."
   Else
      Msgbox "The value is not 10."
End If
```

- *Code management.* The Script Editor understands how scripts should be organized in your 1-2-3 document. To create a new subroutine in your application, you could choose the Create, New Sub and specify a name like `MyNewSub` for it. The Script Editor automatically creates a new sub by that name and adds it to the list of scripts for the object selected in the Object drop-down box. You don't have to tell it to do the obvious. Furthermore, the Script Editor knows about shortcuts. If you're working in the middle of a script and decide you need to create a new sub, you can do so simply by entering the first line of the new sub, `Sub MyNewSub`. The Script Editor automatically moves this statement from your current script and uses it as the first line of a new sub named `MyNewSub`. You don't have to spend a lot of time cutting and pasting scripts in your document—the IDE likes to keep things tidy.
- *Syntax checking.* Another service the Script Editor provides is syntax checking. When you complete a line of text, the Script Editor does some fancy footwork in the background to check whether the statement conforms to all the rules for each of the LotusScript or 1-2-3 keywords you use. If you use the 1-2-3 command `NewDocument`, which requires six arguments, and you enter only five, the Script Editor highlights

the line in red and reports that you have an incorrect number of arguments. You don't have to wait until you run the script to find out there's a syntax problem with the statement.

- *Context-sensitive Help on keywords.* If you hear code warriors around the coffee machine boast that they don't rely on Help very often, don't believe them. To program a product as feature-rich as 1-2-3, programmers go to online Help all the time. The Script Editor is tightly integrated with online Help. To get Help on a LotusScript language or 1-2-3 keyword, place the insert pointer on a keyword and press F1. The Script Editor automatically displays the Help topic associated with that keyword.
- *Breakpoints.* As any script programmer will tell you, you can write hundreds of lines of valid code and still get unexpected results when you run your scripts. The Script Editor helps you figure out where your application takes a wrong turn by enabling you to pause the execution and examine what's happening at specified points. *Breakpoints* are markers you set next to a line of code that function like stop signs. When you run your scripts, the Script Editor turns into the Script Debugger, and pauses execution of your scripts at each line containing a breakpoint so you can see the value of the variables at that point. To set a breakpoint on a line of code you're writing in the Script Editor, click in the margin to the left of the line. The Script Editor displays a breakpoint symbol next to that line (see fig. B.12).

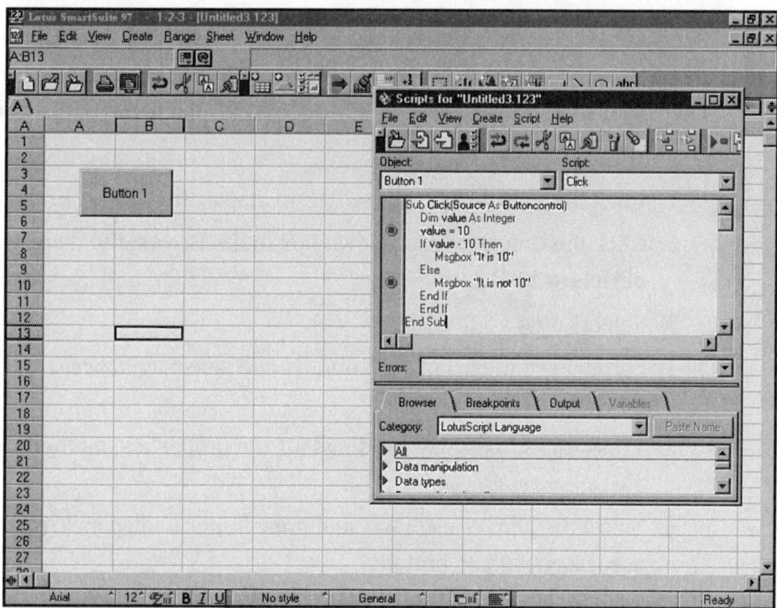

Fig. B.12
Set breakpoints to help you see what is occurring as your script executes.

There are many more features in the Script Editor. Consult online Help for complete documentation of them.

Error Messages The Errors drop-down box displays brief descriptions of each error that the IDE encounters when it checks the syntax of your code or runs the code. To get more information about an error and suggestions for correcting it, click the error message in the Errors drop-down box and press F1.

Object Browser Browsers are tools that connect your computer to information sources. A Web browser connects you to Web pages on the World Wide Web; the IDE Object Browser connects you with definitions of objects. You'll learn the ins and outs of objects in the next section, but for now it's important to understand the purpose of the Object Browser and how it's different from the Object drop-down box.

The Object drop-down box displays lists of *real objects* that exist in your current document. 1-2-3 creates some of these for you, the rest you create as you develop your document. The Object Browser displays a hierarchical list of all *possible objects* in 1-2-3, whether or not they exist in your current document. This sounds like a flashback to some Greek philosophy, but it's actually pretty simple. When you launch the IDE for the first time in 1-2-3, it asks 1-2-3 about all the objects it can create in a workbook: ranges, buttons, query tables, and so on. It then builds a list of all these objects and all the commands these objects understand. Here's an example of how the Object Browser helps you with programming.

Suppose you created a button named Button 1 in a 1-2-3 sheet and you want to write a script to increase its height. To do this, you need to know the name of the property that controls the height of all button objects. To find the name of this property in the Object Browser, do the following:

1. Click the Browser tab in the IDE to display the Object Browser.
2. Click the Category drop-down box in the Browser to display a list of the types of objects in 1-2-3.
3. Select Lotus 1-2-3: Classes.
4. Scroll down the list of 1-2-3 objects and select `Buttoncontrol`, the class name of buttons in 1-2-3.
5. Press Enter to display headings for the properties, methods, and events of `Buttoncontrol`.
6. Select the item `Properties`, and press Enter to display a list of the properties associated with all buttons.

7. Scroll down the list and select the name of the property that looks like it will control the height of buttons. This is an easy one, because button objects have a property named `Height`. The IDE should look like figure B.13.

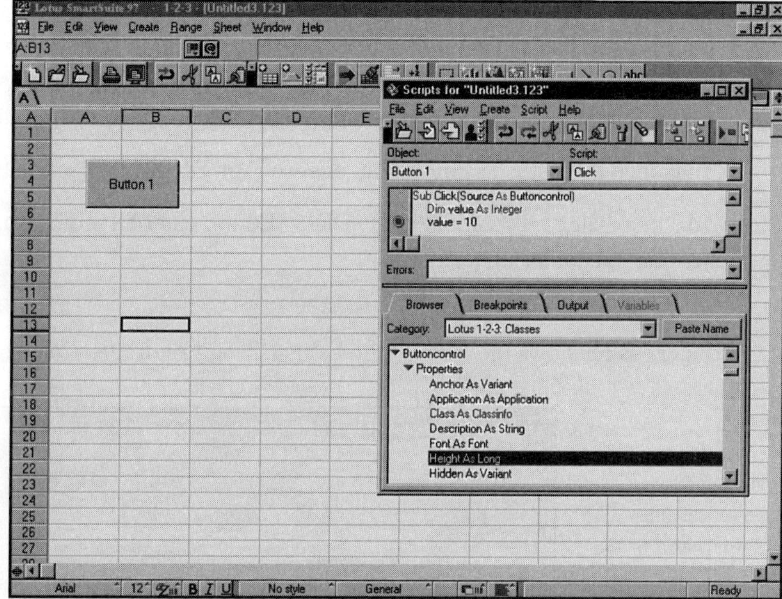

Fig. B.13
Select a property you want to control from the list of properties for the object.

8. (Optional) press F1 to display a Help topic and example on the Height property.
9. Enter the following line in your script to increase the height of the button from its default value:

```
[Button 1].Height = 1200
```

As you work with the Object Browser and learn more about the objects in 1-2-3, you will find that there are many similarities between objects. The Height property, for example, is supported by window objects, drawn objects, and chart objects. If you know how to change the height of any one of these objects, you know how to change it for any of them. The Object Browser provides a view into the structure of objects and the relationships they share.

The Lotus Dialog Editor

If you could develop custom dialog boxes in previous releases of 1-2-3, you should win some kind of prize. Unlike the Lotus Dialog Editor shipping with 1-2-3 97, the old dialog editor was difficult to learn and unforgiving. If you can create drawings in a tool like

Windows Paint, you're ready to design attractive and useful dialog boxes for your script applications.

The Dialog Editor is a layout tool. Use the Dialog Editor to design the appearance of your dialog boxes; use the IDE to write scripts for the controls in each dialog box.

Running the Dialog Editor and Dialog Boxes Running the Dialog Editor and any of the dialog boxes it creates is not mysterious. Unlike the old 1-2-3 dialog editor, you don't need to save information to a range and then play with embedded values in the range.

To launch the Lotus Dialog Editor, choose Edit, Scripts & Macros, Show Dialog Editor.

To run a dialog box created in the Dialog Editor, enter a LotusScript statement in your script in the following format:

```
DialogName.Show 1
```

Figure B.14 shows the parts of the Lotus Dialog Editor after you run it.

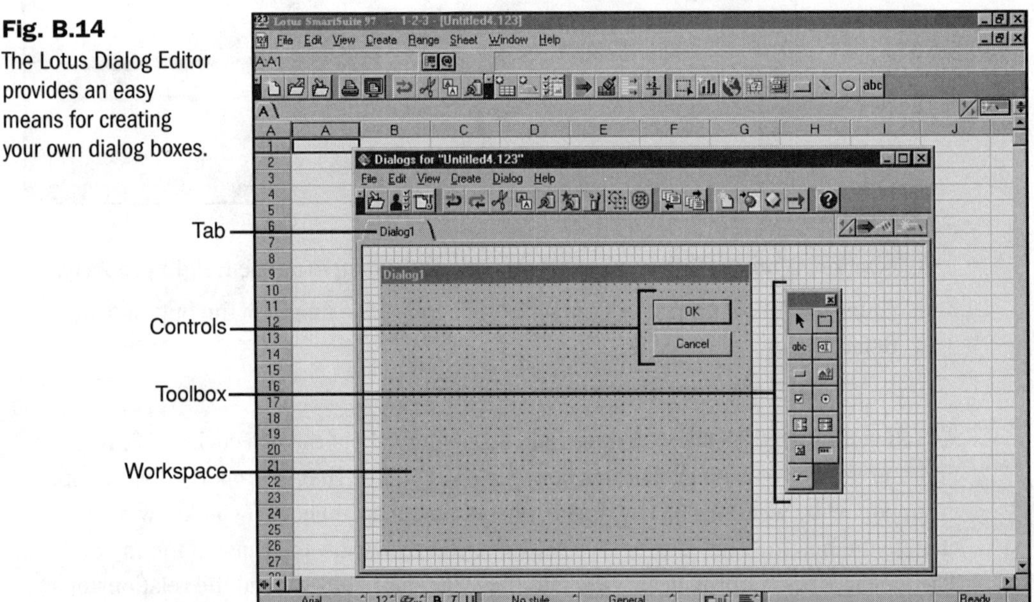

Fig. B.14
The Lotus Dialog Editor provides an easy means for creating your own dialog boxes.

Dialog Menus The menu commands for the Dialog Editor are intuitive, as you can see in the following table.

Dialog Menu	Programming Tasks Available in that Menu
File	Save the current document containing all dialogs, set preferences for the Toolbox, SmartIcons, and Dialog Editor, and close the Dialog Editor.
Edit	Undo the last change, redo the last change, copy the selected text or control to the Clipboard, paste text or a control from the Clipboard, clear selected text or a control , and delete a dialog box.
View	Display the next or previous dialog box in the document, hide or display the Toolbox and SmartIcons, and display scripts in the IDE for controls.
Create	Create a dialog box or control in a dialog box.
Dialog	Set properties for the current dialog box, display the current dialog box, and control the appearance of controls in the current dialog box.
Help	Display Help for the Dialog Editor or for the controls that ship with 1-2-3.

Dialog Tabs You can create many dialog boxes in your document, each one having its own dialog tab. The Dialog Editor creates one dialog box automatically, others you create using the Create, Dialog command. To work on a particular dialog box in the Dialog Editor, click its dialog tab.

Dialog Controls Everything you put in a dialog box is a *control*. By default, the Dialog Editor creates two command button controls with the captions OK and Cancel. You can keep or delete these default controls as you add others to the dialog box. Lotus provides 12 controls with the Dialog Editor; you can add any third-party OCX control you have installed on your system. The controls that ship with Microsoft Visual Basic Version 4 are compatible with the Lotus Dialog Editor.

There are three ways to add controls to a dialog box:

- Double-click one of the control icons in the Toolbox. The Dialog Editor automatically positions the control in the center of your current dialog box. You can then move or resize the new control.
- Click one of the control icons in the Toolbox and draw the outline of the control in the dialog box workspace.
- Choose Create, Control and select a control to add to your dialog box.

Choose Create, Control, More to display a list of all OCX controls installed on your system.

To change the properties of any control, right-click the control and choose Properties from the shortcut menu. If you change the color property of a control to make it green in the Dialog Editor, it will be displayed green when you run the dialog containing the control.

Dialog Workspace The *workspace* is the canvas on which you add controls. To determine the size of the dialog box when it runs, resize the dialog box workspace in the Dialog Editor. To change the color or texture of the dialog when it runs, change those properties in the workspace.

Dialog Toolbox The Toolbox is a palette from which you choose controls for your dialog boxes. Choose File, Toolbox Setup to customize the contents and appearance of control icons in the Toolbox.

You can preview how your dialog boxes will be displayed when they run by choosing Dialog, Run Dialog.

You'll see how to write code for dialog boxes and how to integrate them with the rest of your application later in the appendix.

1-2-3 Objects and Classes

If you haven't worked in an object-oriented programming environment, 1-2-3 97 will be an excellent place to gain some experience. The new version of 1-2-3 doesn't force you to learn new objects *and* a new way of programming them. When you're using the product to do work, you see the same set of objects and the same basic behaviors as previous releases of 1-2-3. At the programming level, almost everything has been rewritten to support objects. This section introduces a few of the basic concepts of object-oriented programming as they affect 1-2-3 97. There's much more going on in the world of 1-2-3 objects than I can cover here, but at least you will have enough under your belt to get going.

The Object-Oriented Programming Model

In previous versions of 1-2-3, data was stored in one place and the commands necessary to do things with the data were stored somewhere else. Here's a very simple example.

Suppose you create a button in a 1-2-3 Release 5 sheet. The button itself is stored as a drawn object. The label displayed in the button is stored as text apart from the button itself. Any commands needed to change the color or size of the button are stored yet somewhere else. To change the background color of this button to red, for example, 1-2-3 needs to do some work at the draw layer, some work with text, some work with the color manager, and more work looking up colors and fill patterns. The button remains passive as all this happens around it.

The same button in 1-2-3 97 has a different structure and a different degree of awareness about what it can and cannot do. All the data related to the button (text, shape, and location) and all the logic necessary to change its appearance are stored in the button object. When you use the 1-2-3 InfoBox to choose a different background color for the button, 1-2-3 sends the button a message like "Make yourself red." The button manages the process of calling other 1-2-3 code to change its background color. In an object-oriented environment, the definition of what an object can and cannot do is critical. The general definition of an object is its class and the particulars about that object is its properties, methods, and events. The following section shows you how this works for the most frequently-used object in 1-2-3 97, the range object.

Properties

The range object has properties that define what data it can contain, how it displays itself, and how it relates to other objects in the 1-2-3 environment. These object properties correspond to the settings in the InfoBox for an object. One way to learn about the properties supported by an object is to call up its InfoBox and examine the various settings displayed in the InfoBox. Each setting in the InfoBox has a corresponding property listed in the IDE Object Browser.

LotusScript code to change the properties of objects takes two forms: one to set properties and another to get the current value of a property.

- To change the value of a property, use the following syntax in your LotusScript code:

  ```
  ObjectName.PropertyName = NewPropertyValue
  ```

- To ask an object for the current value of one of its properties, use the following syntax in your LotusScript code:

  ```
  CurrentPropertyValue = ObjectName.PropertyName
  ```

The following table shows some properties for cell A:B1, a Range object, and what they do.

Range Property	LotusScript Example	Function
ColumnWidth	[A:B1].ColumnWidth = 9	Specifies the width of the column for the range.
Contents	[A:B1].Contents = "1000.42"	Specifies the contents of the cell.
IsSelected	Dim IsItSelected As Variant IsItSelected= [A:B1].IsSelected Msgbox IsItSelected	Provides feedback on whether the range is currently selected (TRUE) or not selected (FALSE).
RowHeight	[A:B1].RowHeight = 16	Specifies the height of the row for the range.
TextWrapped	[A:B1].TextWrapped = True	Specifies whether long labels in cells should wrap.

When you know which properties you want to change for an object, you can set them one by one or all at once. The `With...End With` structure is a convenient way to fire a series of property changes at one object. Instead of specifying the name of the object each time you change its property, you can tell LotusScript to make a group of changes to a particular object. Here's how the `With...End With` structure would look in a script. Note that the period preceding each property statement in the script denotes that it should be applied to the object specified in the first line of the `With` structure.

```
Sub WithSub
    With [A:B1]
        .ColumnWidth = 9
        .RowHeight = 14
        .Font.FontName = "Courier New"
        .TextWrapped = True
    End With
End Sub
```

One of the best ways to learn more about properties for an object is to record scripts in 1-2-3. As you change the properties of objects in 1-2-3, the IDE records the names and current values of those properties in a script. These can serve as templates for more sophisticated scripts that you write.

Methods

Objects also generate and receive actions, which are called *methods*. If properties in LotusScript correspond to settings in object InfoBoxes, methods correspond to 1-2-3 menu commands. When you select a cell, for example, each of the commands in the Edit and Range menus correspond to methods for a range object. To copy the contents of a cell A:B1 to the Clipboard, you can choose Edit, Copy in 1-2-3 or enter the statement `[A:B1].CopyToClipboard` in one of your scripts.

Sometimes a 1-2-3 menu command executes immediately; other times it displays a dialog box prompting you for more information. The information you enter in these 1-2-3 dialog boxes is equivalent to arguments that you must supply to many LotusScript methods. For example, if you select cells A:B1..A:B10 and choose Range, Fill, 1-2-3 displays the dialog box shown in figure B.15.

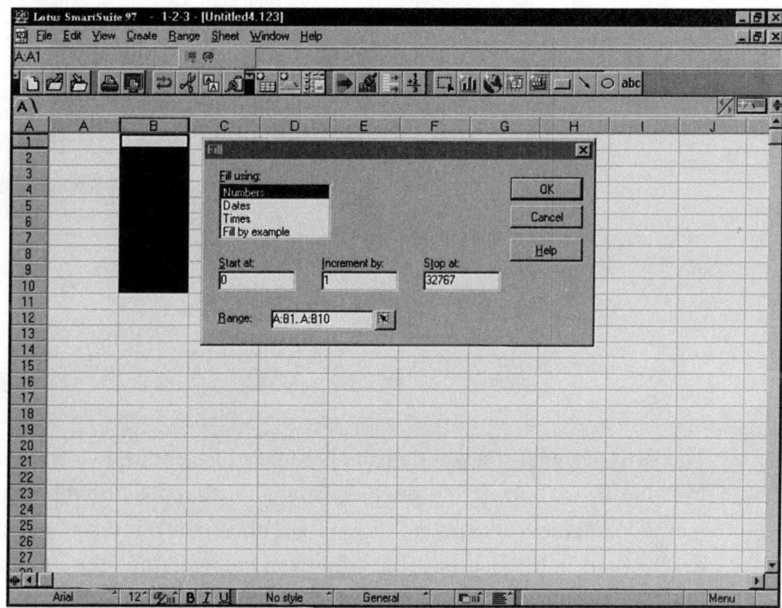

Fig. B.15
The Range, Fill command displays the Fill dialog box so you can enter the necessary information.

Each of the controls in this dialog box specifies information that 1-2-3 needs to fill a range with data. You can accept the default settings that 1-2-3 provides or choose different settings. In either case, 1-2-3 uses these settings when it executes the Range, Fill command. The LotusScript method named `RangeFill` needs the same information. Instead of displaying a dialog box when it runs, the `RangeFill` method requires that you provide the same information that would have been defined in the dialog box. Pieces of information that you must provide to a LotusScript method are called *parameters*. Note the default values in the dialog box for the Range, Fill command: `Numbers`, `0`, `1`, and `32767`. The `RangeFill` method accepts the same four values in the following format:

```
[A:B1..A:B10].RangeFill 0,1,32767,$Number,
```

Each of these values, or parameters, must be separated by a comma. The IDE Object Browser provides information on method parameters in the format shown in figure B.16.

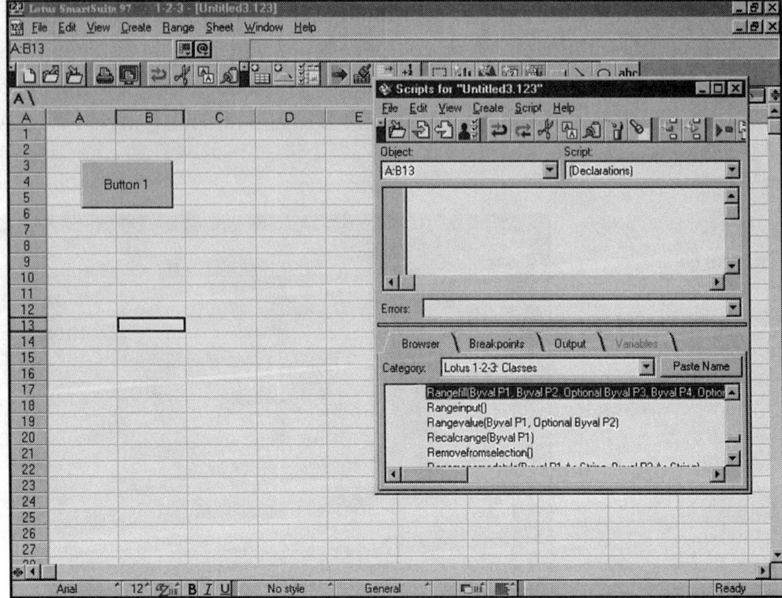

Fig. B.16
The Object Browser shows you how to enter the parameters for a selected method.

The Browser tells you whether the parameter is required or optional, whether it is called by value (`ByVal`) or by reference (`ByRef`), and what position it holds in the complete method statement (`Position1`, `Position2`, and so on). It takes a while to interpret method descriptions in the Browser, but when you get used to it, the Browser turns out to be a great quick reference for entering familiar method statements.

The following table shows some of the most frequently-used methods for the Range object.

Range Methods	**LotusScript Example**	**Function**
`Format`	`[A:B1]. "Scientific", 2`	Applies cell formatting to the range.
`GoTo`	`[A:B1].GoTo`	Selects the object and displays it.
`RangeFill`	`[A:B1..A:B8].RangeFill _ 0,1,32767,$Number,`	Fills cells in a range with a set of values.
`Reshape`	`[A:B1..A:B8].Reshape _ [A:B1..A:B10]`	Expands or contracts the current selection of cells in a range.
`Select`	`[A:B1..A:B8].Select`	Selects the specified cells or ranges.

Events

As users click objects, move them, or enter values in cells, Windows interprets these actions as events and sends event messages to 1-2-3 and its objects. You can't generate an event directly in LotusScript—only users can. If you can anticipate meaningful actions by the users running your application, you can write scripts for the events associated with 1-2-3 objects.

Consider a common example for the Range object, evaluating the contents of a cell after a user has entered a new value in it. Suppose you're writing a 1-2-3 application for users submitting expense reports. Expenditures under $10 can be handled through petty cash, so you want to make sure the amount of the expenditure submitted by the user is $10 or more. Users enter the amount of the expenditure in cell A:A1, so you want to focus on the `CellContentsChange` event for that cell. The cell receives this event when the user types some data in cell A:A1 and presses Enter. Select cell A:A1 in 1-2-3, and then enter the following statements in its `CellContentsChange` event script:

```
If [A:A1].CellValue < 10 Then
  Msgbox "For expenses under $10, use petty cash."
End If
```

If the value in cell A:A1 is less than 10, 1-2-3 displays a message about using petty cash.

Putting it Together: Writing a LotusScript Application

You've worked through a lot of background information about LotusScript, its programming tools, and the 1-2-3 objects that are available to you for scripting. It's time to see how all this stuff works together in building a typical script application in 1-2-3.

The application you're going to build is a simple expense report manager stored in the 1-2-3 document named EXPRPT.123. All the scripts and dialogs you write will be contained in this file.

Designing the Skeleton

Good applications grow from one clear task or process. Here's the essential task that this sample application supports:

1. Display a dialog box that prompts the user for information about an expense to be included in their expense report (see fig. B.17).

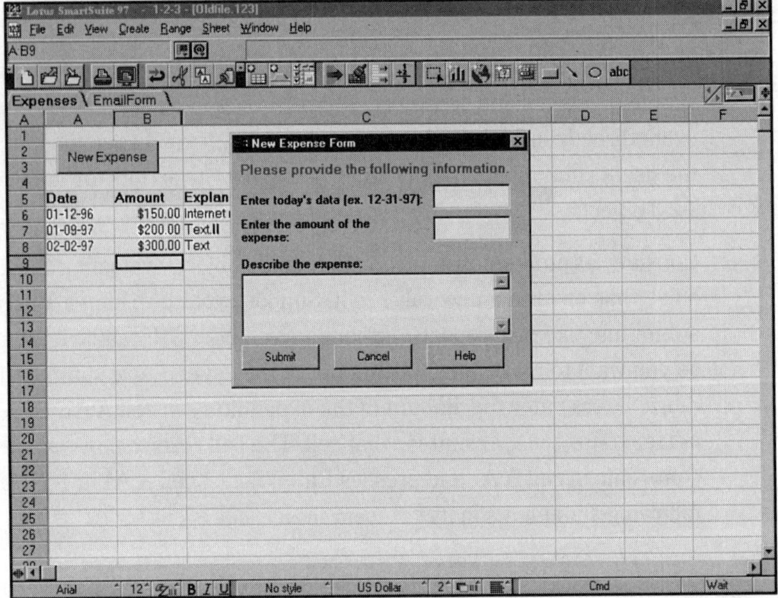

Fig. B.17
Create dialog boxes which clearly show the user what information they need to input.

2. Transfer data that the customer has entered in the dialog to a 1-2-3 table (see fig. B.18). This serves as a local record of expenses that the customer submits.

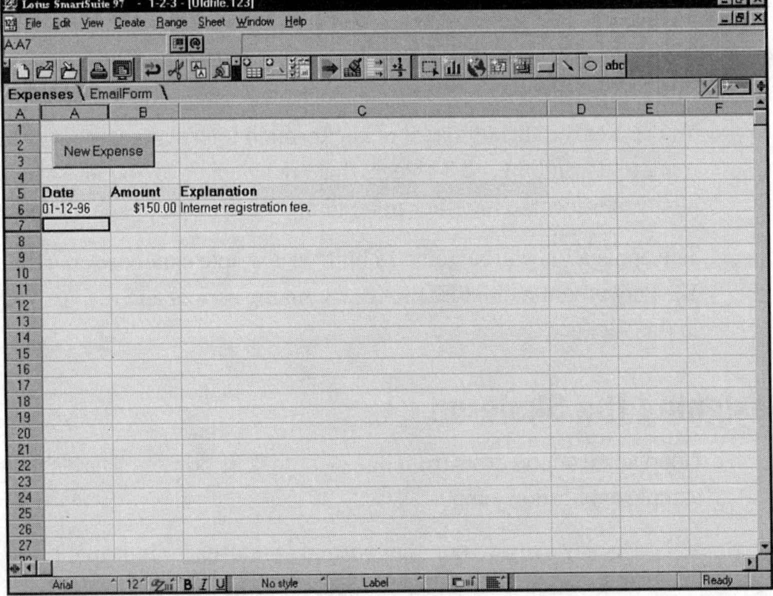

Fig. B.18
Save the user input in a 1-2-3 range.

3. Transfer the same data to a different 1-2-3 range that can be sent to an accounting department as e-mail (see fig. B.19).

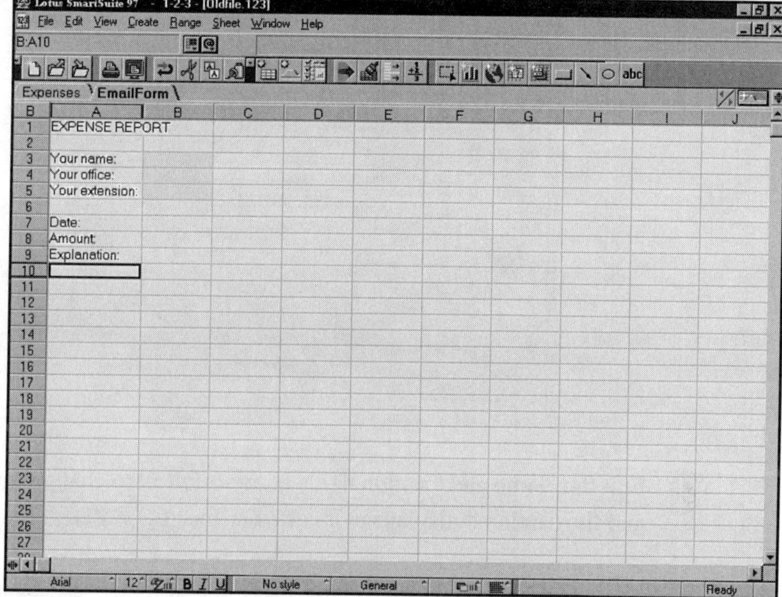

Fig. B.19
If necessary, change the format of the data for other purposes.

Creating Objects

Here's where it gets interesting. To support this task, you need to create some dialog boxes, some dialog box controls, a command button in 1-2-3, and some simple ranges in 1-2-3. Designing dialog boxes represents a challenge, so look at those first.

Designing Dialog Boxes The application uses two dialog boxes initially:

- `dlgInput`. This is the dialog that customers use to enter information about the expense. The customer displays this dialog by pressing the `New Expense` command button. It has several important controls that I will discuss in further detail as we build the dialog box.
- `dlgHelp`. This is a simple dialog that contains some help text. The customer displays this dialog by pressing the Help command button in the `dlgInput` dialog.

To create one of the custom dialog boxes for the application, do the following:

1. Choose Edit, Scripts & Macros, Show Dialog Editor from the 1-2-3 main menu. Note that the Dialog Editor creates a default dialog for you and that it contains two command buttons.

2. Right-click the background of the dialog and choose Properties from the shortcut menu. The InfoBox for the dialog box appears (see fig. B.20).

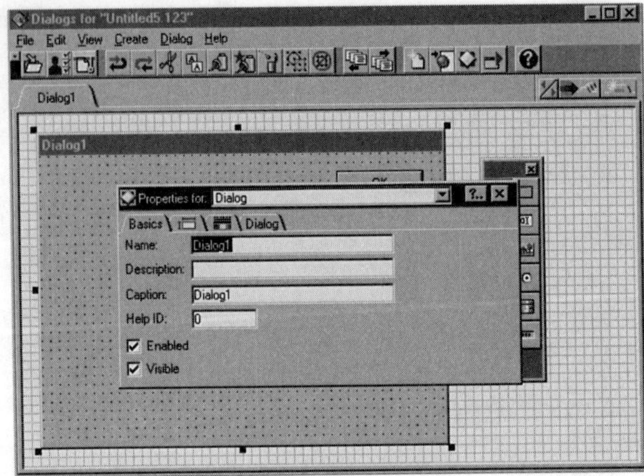

Fig. B.20
The Dialog InfoBox enables you to modify the properties of your dialog box.

3. Edit the Name and Caption fields in the InfoBox to change the name of the dialog and the caption it displays in its title bar (see fig. B.21).

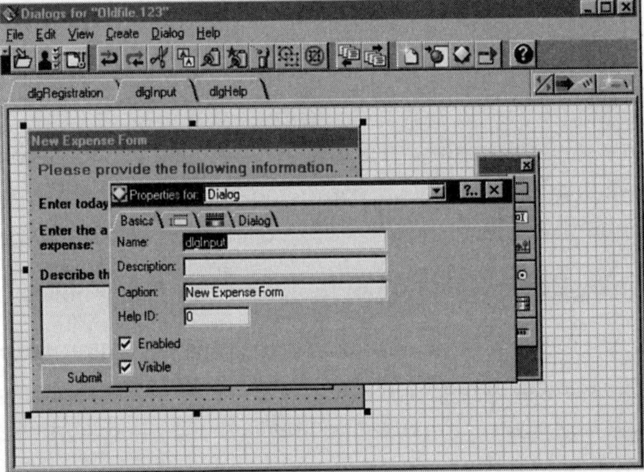

Fig. B.21
Change the name and caption to make it easier to work with your dialog box.

4. Choose File, Toolbox Setup in the Dialog Editor to display a dialog listing all controls installed on your system (see fig. B.22). Use this dialog box to customize the controls you want to add to any of the dialog boxes you create.

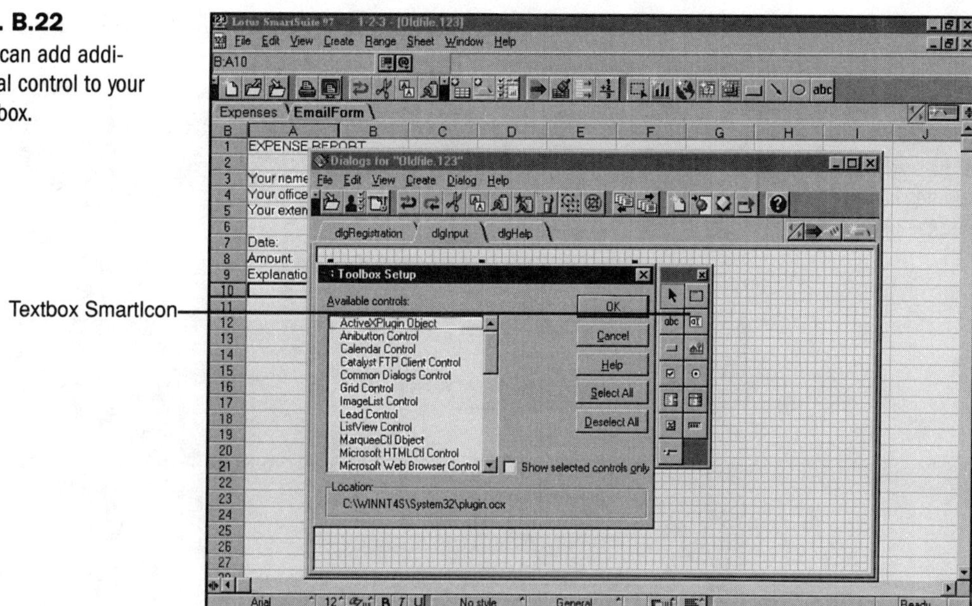

Fig. B.22
You can add additional control to your Toolbox.

5. Click the Lotus Textbox control icon in the Toolbox to select it as the type of control that you want to add to your dialog. Note that the Toolbox provides bubble help on the name of each control when you move the pointer over an icon in the Toolbox.
6. Move the pointer back to the dialog workspace and drag the outline for the textbox control.
7. Right-click the new text box control and choose Properties from the shortcut menu to display the TextBox properties InfoBox (see fig. B.23).
8. Edit the default name of the control in the Name field in the InfoBox to `txtName`. Delete the default value in the Caption field so the control will contain no value when it displays in your dialog.

This is the process by which you add and arrange controls in a dialog box, and use the InfoBox to change their names and properties.

Add controls to this dialog box so that it looks like figure B.24. Change the names of the controls to match the labels. Note that you can develop a naming convention for controls that tells you the type of control you're working with. The prefix `dlg`, for example, is a good shorthand for naming all dialogs. Similarly, `cmd` and `txt` are useful when naming command buttons and text boxes. You will use the name of the dialog box and the names of its controls in your LotusScript code.

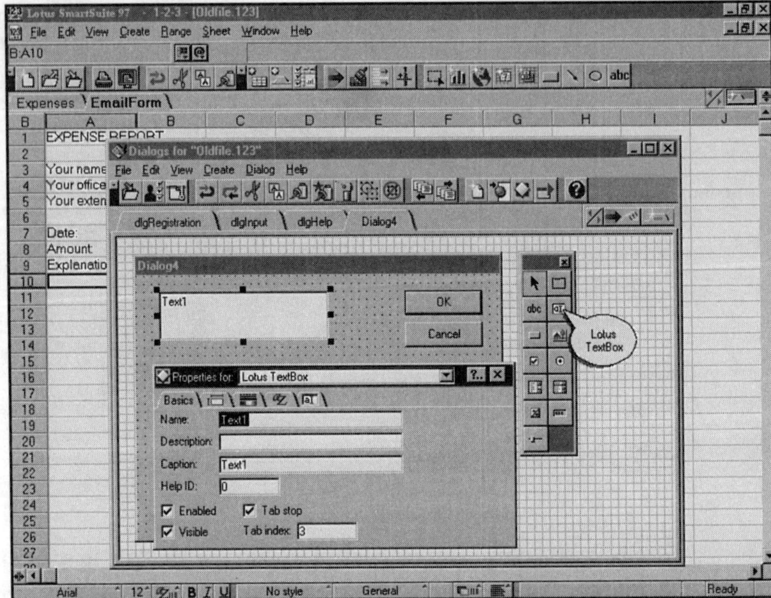

Fig. B.23
Use the TextBox properties InfoBox to adjust the new textbox.

Fig. B.24
Complete the dialog box by adding these controls.

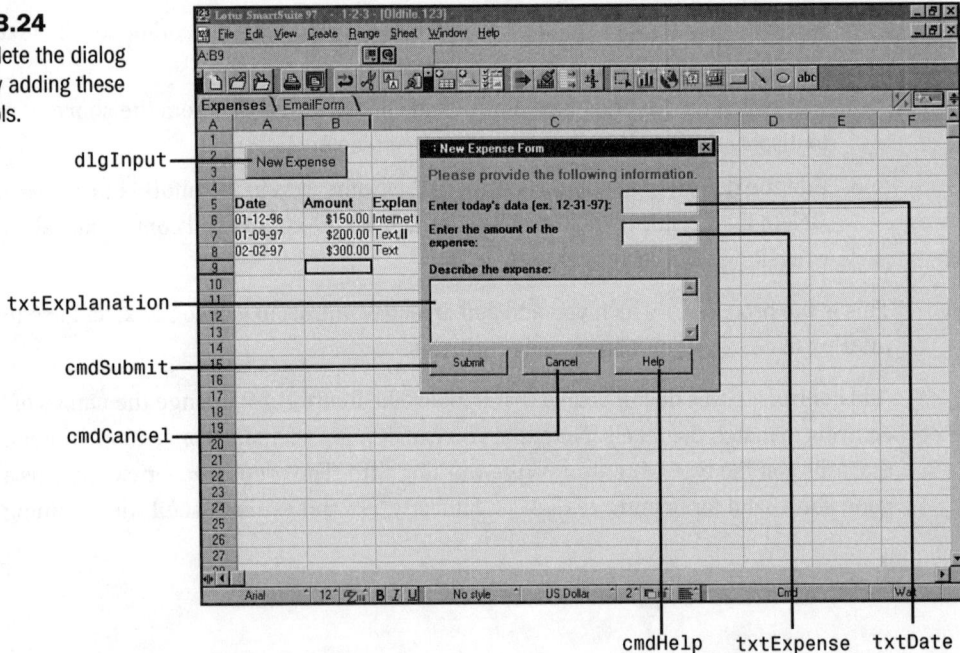

dlgInput
txtExplanation
cmdSubmit
cmdCancel
cmdHelp txtExpense txtDate

Creating and Coding Buttons In this application, the customer creates an expense report by launching the dialog box you just created in the Dialog Editor. To launch the dialog, the customer needs a control button in 1-2-3 that he or she can press to display the dialog and enter data. After the dialog box appears, the user also needs some way to close it. You'll now create a button in 1-2-3 to start the process, add LotusScript code to that button to launch the dialog named `dlgInput`, and add code to the dialog button named `cmdCancel` to cancel data entry and close the dialog.

To create a command button in 1-2-3, do the following:

1. Choose Create, Button from the 1-2-3 main menu.
2. Drag the outline of the button control in your 1-2-3 sheet.
3. Right-click the control and choose Drawing Properties from the shortcut menu to display the InfoBox for that command button.
4. Change the default value in the Name field to `cmdExpenses`.
5. Choose Edit, Scripts & Macros, Show Script Editor to launch the IDE Script Editor. Notice that the new command button is automatically selected in the Object drop-down list and the default event script for that command button, `Click`, is automatically selected in the Script drop-down box.
6. Enter the following statement in the `Click` script:

   ```
   dlgInput.Show 1
   ```

7. Click the Object drop-down list to display a list of objects in the document.
8. Select `dlgInput` from the list, and press Enter to display the names of all the controls you added to the dialog box `dlgInput` (see fig. B.25).
9. Select `cmdCancel` in the list. Notice that the IDE automatically selects the `Click` script for this dialog box control in the Script drop-down box.
10. Enter the following statement in the `Click` script:

    ```
    dlgInput.Close
    ```

You've now created all the objects and underlying code necessary to launch your dialog and to close it after it is displayed. To test this, do the following:

1. Click the New Expense button in 1-2-3 to display the `dlgInput` dialog box.
2. Click the Cancel button in the dialog box to close the dialog.

This is the basic process you use to manage dialogs. You can hook up the `dlgHelp` dialog described earlier in this section by adding the following code to the `Click` script for the `cmdHelp` button in `dlgInput`:

```
dlgHelp.Show 1
```

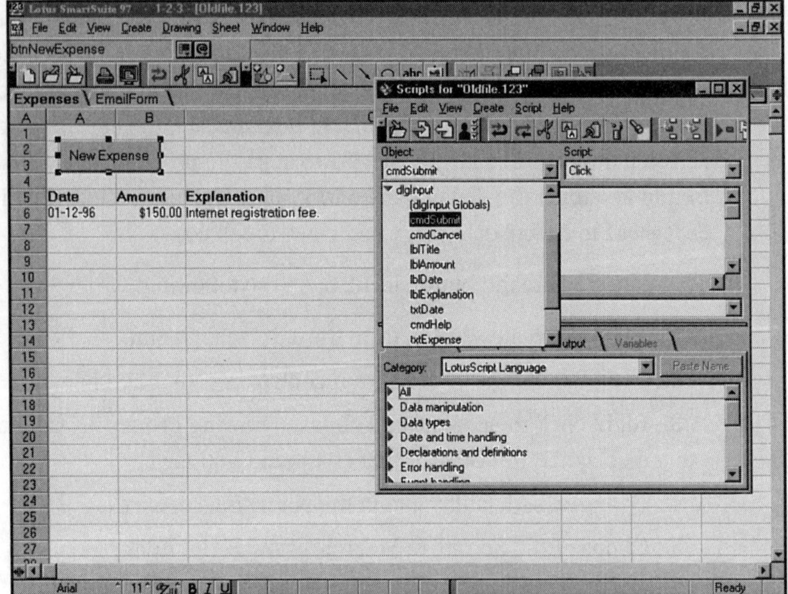

Fig. B.25
Select cmdCancel to edit the control.

Writing Scripts to Process Information Information contained by an object, such as a cell or dialog box control, is a *property* of that object. You can change the contents of a cell (for example, cell B7 in the sheet named Expenses) by changing the value of its Contents property:

```
[Expenses:A7].Contents = "12345"
```

Similarly, you can get the value of a cell by assigning it to a variable.

```
Dim currentValue as String
currentValue = [Expenses:A7].Contents
```

It's like dialing a long distance telephone number. The name of the object is the area code, while the other numbers specify an exchange and particular phone number. In this case, the sheet named Expenses contains the cell A7, which has the property named `Contents`.

The process of extracting data from a dialog box control is identical. When the user enters a value in a dialog box control, that control stores the value the way a cell stores its current value in its `Contents` property. The property that stores values in the text box control is called `Text`. That's a tough one. The following script extracts the current value of the dialog box control `txtName` in the dialog `dlgInput` and assigns it to the variable named `currentValue`:

```
Dim currentValue as String
currentValue = dlgInput.txtName.Text
MsgBox currentValue
```

The dialog box named `dlgInput` contains the control named `txtName` which has the property named `Text`. The variable named `currentValue` is just a temporary container used to extract whatever value happens to be stored in the `Text` property for the control.

The user enters three values into the three text box controls in the dialog box `dlgInput`: `txtDate` (for the current date), `txtExpense` (for the total amount of the expense), and `txtDescription` (for an explanation of the expense). Suppose the user enters the values in `dlgInput` as shown in figure B.26.

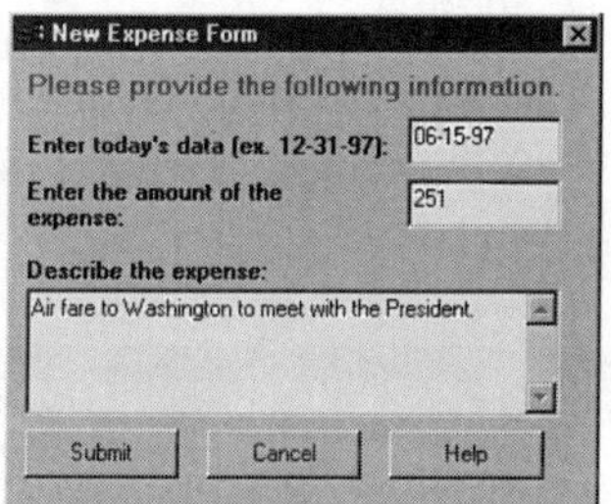

Fig. B.26
The script displays the dialog box so the user can enter the information.

Each text box control stores the appropriate data in its `Text` property: `txtDate (06-15-97)`, `txtExpense (251)`, and `txtDescription (Air fare to Washington to meet with the President)`. To transfer data from these text box controls to cells in 1-2-3, you need to assign the value of the text box `Text` property to the value of the cell's `Contents` property. The following example assigns the value that the user entered in the `txtDate` text box to the cell named Expenses:A7:

```
[Expenses:A7].Contents = dlgInput.txtDate.Text
```

Controls in the dialog box do not process any values, they simply store them until you can write them out to 1-2-3.

Recall that the application performs two tasks with the information a user enters into the dialog box. First, the information gets transferred to a table in the sheet named Expenses. Second, the information gets transferred to a 1-2-3 range in sheet EmailForm for subsequent transmission to the accounting department. Although these tasks use the same data from the dialog box, they're separate tasks that should be handled in separate LotusScript subroutines (called *subs*). Now create two subs to accomplish these tasks:

1. Choose Edit, Scripts & Macros, Show Script Editor to display the IDE Script editor.
2. Select Globals in the Object drop-down list. The two subs you create in Globals can be called by any other subroutine in your document.
3. Choose Create, Sub in the IDE. This first sub will contain code to transfer values from the dialog box to a row in the table in the sheet named Expenses.

4. Name the new sub `Write123Record`.
5. Enter the following code in the sub:

```
[Expenses:A5].Select
[Expenses].MoveCellPointer $EndDown,1
[Expenses].MoveCellPointer $Down,1
Selection.Contents = dlgInput.txtDate.Text
[Expenses].MoveCellPointer $Right,1
Selection.Contents = dlgInput.txtExpense.Text
[Expenses].MoveCellPointer $Right,1
Selection.Contents = dlgInput.txtExplanation.Text
[Expenses].MoveCellPointer $Down,1
```

This code finds the first blank row in the table and fills the three cells in that row with the three values stored in the dialog controls `txtDate`, `txtExpense`, and `txtDescription` (see fig. B.27).

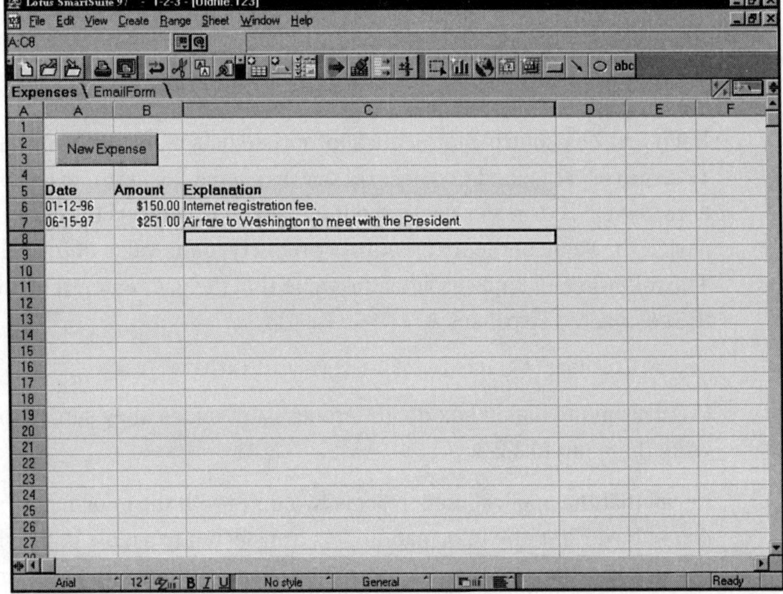

Fig. B.27
The user's input is stored in the worksheet.

6. Create another sub and name it `WriteEmailRecord`. This sub will contain code to transfer values from the dialog box to the range EmailForm:B7..EmailForm:B9.
7. Enter the following code in the sub:

```
[EmailForm:B7].Contents = dlgInput.txtDate.Text
[EmailForm:B8].Contents = dlgInput.txtExpense.Text
[EmailForm:B9].Contents = dlgInput.txtExplanation.Text
```

This code fills the three cells B7, B8, and B9 with the three values stored in the dialog controls (`txtDate`, `txtExpense`, and `txtDescription`), as shown in figure B.28.

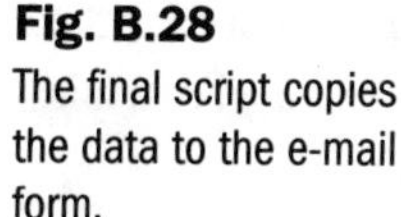

Fig. B.28
The final script copies the data to the e-mail form.

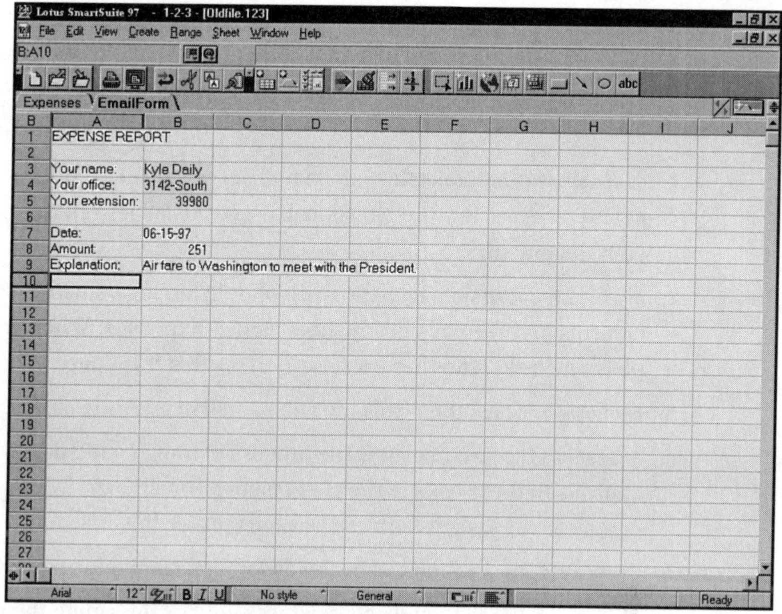

Take inventory for a moment. You have the dialog named `dlgInput` ready for the user to enter values. You have the 1-2-3 command button named `cmdExpense` ready to click to display that dialog. You have two subs ready to process the data that the user enters in the dialog box controls. You need some trigger or event to execute the code in the subs `Write123Record` and `WriteEmailRecord` when the user has completed entering values in the dialog box.

You've actually created a control in the dialog `dlgInput` that can serve as the trigger. When the user has finished entering values in the dialog, he or she can click the `cmdSubmit` command button. To have this command button execute the subs `Write123Record` and `WriteEmailRecord`, do the following:

1. Select `dlgInput` in the Object drop-down box.
2. Press Enter to display a list of the controls in that dialog.
3. Select the control `cmdSubmit`. Note that the IDE automatically selects the event script named `Click` in the Script drop-down box.
4. Enter the following statements in the `Click` script:

```
Call Write123Record
Call WriteEmailRecord
dlgInput.Close
MsgBox "The expense report is ready to mail to accounting."
```

All the objects you have created and all the scripts you have written so far prepare for the execution of this script. A full name for this script would be `cmdSubmit_Click` because it is the `Click` script for the object `cmdSubmit`. Here's what happens when `cmdSubmit_Click` executes:

1. `cmdSubmit_Click` calls the sub named `Write123Record`. Because the sub `Write123Record` is stored in Globals, you can call it from this sub or any other sub in your document.
2. `Write123Record` manages the work of transferring data from three dialog box controls to three cells in the sheet named Expenses. When `Write123Record` completes its task, it notifies `cmdSubmit_Click` that it is done.
3. `cmdSubmit_Click` then calls the sub named `WriteEmailRecord`.
4. `WriteEmailRecord` manages the process of transferring data from three dialog box controls to three cells in the sheet named EmailForm. When `Write123Record` completes its task, it notifies `cmdSubmit_Click` that it is done.
5. `cmdSubmit_Click` then closes the dialog box named `dlgInput`.
6. `cmdSubmit_Click` then displays a message box informing the user that the data is ready to e-mail to accounting. This would be the logical place to call a sub that actually e-mailed the data.

The essential tasks for this application are complete. Your document is now populated with objects, data, and scripts that work together toward the completion of a business task.

Strategies for Further Learning

LotusScript brings a lot to 1-2-3 97. You have just looked at some basic concepts and frequently-used objects in 1-2-3. There's much more to learn about.

Some Advanced Features

Peruse the following features in 1-2-3 97 to take advantage of some of its more powerful programming features:

- *Approach integration.* Scripts to call Lotus Approach and use its advanced database features while working in 1-2-3.
- *Internet publishing.* You can write scripts that read data directly from the Word Wide Web, parse it into 1-2-3 ranges, and save the results of your analysis as HTML tables.

- *Notes integration.* Notes and 1-2-3 97 share the same LotusScript language for programming. You can use LotusScript to embed 1-2-3 objects in Notes or to extract data from Notes into your 1-2-3 documents.
- *Custom classes.* You can use LotusScript to create your own classes in 1-2-3. Like the classes that ship with 1-2-3, these objects can have their own properties and methods.
- *Charts.* You can use LotusScript to program all the new charting features offered by 1-2-3.
- *OLE automation.* You an embed other OLE objects in 1-2-3 and use LotusScript to manage their behavior.

Translating Macros into LotusScript

If you're making the transition from macro programming to LotusScript, try this technique for translating existing macros into LotusScript:

1. Choose Edit, Scripts & Macros, Record Script to start recording actions in LotusScript.
2. Choose Edit, Scripts & Macros, Run.
3. Click the Macro radio button to specify that you want to run a macro (instead of a script).
4. Select the name of a range containing a macro to run, and click Run. Let the macro complete its execution.
5. Choose Edit, Script and Macros, Stop Recording.

For all practical purposes, 1-2-3 has translated your macro into working LotusScript code. As you compare the original macro instructions with the new LotusScript code, you'll see similarities and differences that will support your learning.

Using Examples that Ship with 1-2-3

Lotus provides many sample applications and lots of example code. You can learn a lot about LotusScript simply by using the examples that ship with the product. Here are some places to look:

- If you have purchased 1-2-3 as part of SmartSuite, install the *Developing SmartSuite Applications* online book that ships on the CD version of SmartSuite. This book is invaluable in learning about 1-2-3 and LotusScript, and it includes several 1-2-3 documents that contain working code.

- Search for Frequently Asked Questions in 1-2-3 LotusScript Help. These help topics address common programming tasks in 1-2-3 and provide example code for each task.
- Browse through the reference material in 1-2-3 LotusScript Help. Most help topics for 1-2-3 properties, methods, and events have working examples.

All these resources aside, dive in and start writing your own scripts. ●

APPENDIX C

Upgrader's Guide

The following information is a listing of new features, shortcuts to save time, specific 1-2-3 shortcut keys, and troubleshooting information. You will also find contact numbers for technical support. ■

Guide to New Features

Feature	Description
The Start button	Click the Start button to start a program, get help, find items on your computer, open a document, or change your system settings.
The Windows 95 Desktop	Use drag-and-drop to place programs, shortcuts, accessories, and document icons directly on the desktop, where you can access them with a double-click of the mouse.
My Computer	Double-click My Computer to see a listing of your system's drive and its contents.
Explorer	Replaces File Manager with a complete listing of all drives, folders, and folder contents within your system. You can drag-and-drop to move elements.
Folders	Hold files, applications, and other folders. Folders replace directories and Program Manager groups.
Taskbar	At the bottom of your screen, the Taskbar adds a button for every program you open during your session. Switch to any open program by clicking its button in the Taskbar.
Recycle Bin	Temporarily stores deleted files. They remain in the bin until you empty it (a safeguard against accidental deletions).
Network Neighborhood	If your computer is connected to a network, double-click this desktop icon to see what network resources are available to you.
File Names	Can be up to 255 characters long (as opposed to the eight-character limitation of previous versions).
Shortcut menus	Right-click items to get a special, context-sensitive menu.
Printing subsystem	The Windows 95 32-bit printing subsystem speeds the printing process and gives you more control over your printer's operation.

Feature	Description
Plug and Play	Insert the card for the appropriate Plug and Play hardware in your computer; when you turn on the computer, Windows 95 automatically configures your hardware for you.
System Properties	Enables you to configure your system (accessed through the Control Panel).
Quick View	Right-click a file and choose Quick View to get a preview of the file's contents without opening the associated application.
Microsoft Exchange	Reads and sends e-mail from various systems, such as Microsoft Mail, Internet Mail, or The Microsoft Network. Also sends and receives faxes and other electronic messages.
Dial-Up Networking	Access a corporate network using your modem when on the road.
Internet Connectivity	PPP and TCP/IP are built-in, enabling you to connect to the Internet with no additional software.

Windows 95 Shortcuts

Operation	Shortcut
Start Menu	
Display hidden Start menu	Ctrl+Esc or move pointer to screen edge
Add file/folder to Start menu	Drop file on Start menu
Add/Remove program	Right-click Taskbar, Properties, Start Menu Programs, Add/Remove
Clear documents list	Right-click Taskbar, Properties, Start Menu Programs, Clear
Taskbar	
Hide Taskbar	Right-click Taskbar, Properties, Taskbar Options, Auto Hide
Display hidden Taskbar	Ctrl+Esc or move pointer to screen edge

continues

continued

Operation	Shortcut
Keep on top of other objects	Right-click Taskbar, Properties, Taskbar Options, Always on Top
Show date	Pause pointer over time in Taskbar
Change date/time	Double-click time in Taskbar
Change PCMCIA/Sound	Double-click PCMCIA or sound icon
Application Windows	
Maximize window	Double-click title bar
Tile windows on screen	Right-click Taskbar, Tile Horizontally/Vertically
Cascade windows on screen	Right-click Taskbar, Cascade
Minimize all to Taskbar	Right-click Taskbar, Minimize All Windows
Working with Files	
Open Explorer	Right-click Start, Explore
Find file/folder	Start, Find, Files or Folders, enter search data
Select adjacent files	Click first, Shift+click last
Select nonadjacent files	Click first, Ctrl+click others
Undelete files	Open Recycle Bin, drag file out
Copy file(s) to A:	Right-click file(s), Send To, A:
Open file	Right-click file, Open
Print file	Right-click file, Print
Create a file/folder shortcut	Right-drag to desktop, Create Shortcut Here
Moving or Copying Data	
Create scrap on desktop	Right-drag selections to desktop
Paste scrap into document	Right-drag into document, Move or Create
Copy between applications	Drag selection and drop
Copy to application on Taskbar	Drag to button on Taskbar, pause, drop

1-2-3 97 Shortcut Keys

Moving

To Move...	Do This...
To cell A1 in current sheet	Press Home
To last active cell in sheet	Press End, Home
One screen down/up	Press Page Down/Page Up
One screen right/left	Press Ctrl+→/Ctrl+←
To edge of block	Press End+arrow key
To specific cell reference	Press F5, type reference, choose OK

Selecting

To Select...	Do This...
A range of cells	Press Shift+direction key, or click and drag
Multiple ranges (a collection)	Click and drag first range, Ctrl+click and drag other ranges
An entire row	Click row number
An entire column	Click column letter
All cells in current sheet	Press Ctrl+Shift+Home, or click worksheet letter in frame

Editing

Operation	Shortcut
Undo last action	Ctrl+Z
Clear data and formulas	Del
Cut	Ctrl+X or Shift+Del
Copy	Ctrl+C
Paste	Ctrl+V or Shift+Ins
Activate Edit mode	F2

continues

continued

Formatting

Operation	Shortcut
Bold add/remove	Ctrl+B
Italic add/remove	Ctrl+I
Underline add/remove	Ctrl+U
Remove bold/italic/underline	Ctrl+N
Left-align data	Ctrl+L
Center data	Ctrl+C
Right-align data	Ctrl+R

Miscellaneous

Operation	Shortcut
Run a macro	Ctrl+*letter*
Display Find & Replace dialog box	Ctrl+F
Display Go To dialog box	Ctrl+G
Display Open File dialog box	Ctrl+O
Display Print dialog box	Ctrl+P
Save the current workbook	Ctrl+S

Note: A plus sign (+) in this table indicates that you should hold down the first key while pressing the second key, as in Ctrl+S.

Troubleshooting and Support Information

When you need help or have specific questions, use the following contact information.

Que/Macmillan Computer Publishing

Orders:	1-800-428-5331
Switchboard:	1-800-545-5914 or 1-317-581-3500
CompuServe:	GO **MACMILLAN** or GO **QUEBOOKS**
World Wide Web:	**http://www.quecorp.com**
FTP:	**ftp.mcp.com**

Lotus Technical Support

Customer Service: 1-800-343-5414
(General Info/Products/Upgrades/Returns/Lotus Knowledge Base)

Technical Support: 1-508-988-2500
(Introductory 60 days support for Windows Desktop applications)

900# Support: 1-900-55-LOTUS

Lotus on the Web: **http://www.support.lotus.com**

Lotus FTP Server: **ftp.support.lotus.com**

Note: For information on additional Lotus support options, as well as prices and hours, search on "support" in 1-2-3 Help.

Reseller Phone Numbers

Software Spectrum 1-800-787-1166

Softmart 1-800-328-1319

ASAP 1-800-248-ASAP

Index of Common Problems

Everyday Worksheet Tasks

Working with Charts and Maps

Working with Charts and Maps

If you have this problem...	You'll find help here...
Mixed chart type results in a chart that displays only bars	p. 357
Pie chart won't plot multiple data series	p. 321
Pie slices aren't labeled	p. 321
Title frame does not fit in the chart frame after you enlarged the title frame	p. 321
White space needed on printed page between the worksheet data at the top of the page and a chart at the bottom	p. 307
XY chart ranges appear incorrect when you preselect the range and create an automatic chart	p. 357
Y-axis scale doesn't display dollar signs even though the numbers in the worksheet are formatted for currency	p. 347
Y-axis scale shows single digit numbers with a unit indicator of `Thousands`, but you would prefer to see the actual numbers	p. 347

Optimizing 1-2-3

If you have this problem...	You'll find help here...
Arrow you drew should appear double-headed	p. 409
Choosing File, New, while in Group mode opens a new workbook instead of a new worksheet	p. 423
Clip-art image added to a worksheet does not display data in underlying cells	p. 423
Designer frames added as slide borders appear dark and uninteresting	p. 423
Drawing objects added to a slide move when you insert columns or change column widths	p. 423
Hidden data is too obvious, because of missing letters and numbers in the worksheet frame	p. 389
Polygon you created needs to be redrawn	p. 409
Rectangle added to a worksheet blocks out portion of a chart	p. 409
Screen didn't split when you displayed the Split dialog box and clicked Top-Bottom	p. 389
Screen split resulted in column appearing on the wrong side of the split	p. 389
Slide indents need to be changed as a whole, not individually	p. 423

Managing Worksheets and Databases

Managing Worksheets and Databases

Integrating 1-2-3

Customizing 1-2-3

Index

Symbols

A

B

D

F

G

H

J - K

L

N

P

Q

R

S

T

U

V

W

X

Y

Z